fourth edition

EMERGENCY NURSING

With Certification Preparation & Review

NEDELL E. LANROS, BA, RN, CEN
Emergency Nurse Consultant
Friday Harbor, Washington

JANET M. BARBER, MSN, RN, CEN
Educator and Consultant
Emergency and Critical Care Nursing
Georgetown, Texas

APPLETON & LANGE
Stamford, Connecticut

Copyright © 1997 by Appleton & Lange
A Simon and Schuster Company
Copyright 1988 by Appleton & Lange as *Assessment and Intervention in Emergency Nursing*
Copyright 1983, 1978 by Brady Communications Company, Inc.

97 98 99 00 01 / 10 9 8 7 6 5 4 3 2 1

Prentice Hall International (UK) Limited, *London*
Prentice Hall of Australia Pty. Limited, *Sydney*
Prentice Hall Canada, Inc., *Toronto*
Prentice Hall Hispanoamericana, S.A., *Mexico*
Prentice Hall of India Private Limited, *New Delhi*
Prentice Hall of Japan, Inc., *Tokyo*
Simon and Schuster Asia Pte. Ltd., *Singapore*
Editora Prentice Hall do Brasil Ltda., *Rio de Janeiro*
Prentice Hall, *Upper Saddle River, New Jersey*

Lanros, Nedel E..
    Emergency nursing: with certification preparation and review /
Nedell E. Lanros, Janet Barber. — 4th ed.
        p.   cm.
    Rev. Ed. of: Assessment & intervention in emergency nursing. 3rd
ed. c1988.
    Includes bibliographical references and index.
    ISBN   0-8385-0437-X (pbk. : alk. paper)
    1. Emergency nursing.   2. Emergency nursing—Emaninations,
questions, etc.   I. Barber, Janet Miller.   II. Lanros, Nedell E.,
        Assessment & intervention in emergency nursing.   III. Title.
    [DNLM: 1. Emergency Nursing.   2. Critical Care.   3. Emergency
Service, Hospital—nurses' instruction.   4. Emergency Nursing—
examination questions.   5. Critical Care—examination questions.
WY 154 L293e 1997]
RT120.E2L35   1997
610.73′61—dc21
DNLM/DLC
For Library of Congress   97–456
                                                    CIP

Acquisitions Editor: Lauren A. Keller
Production Editor: Elizabeth C. Ryan
Designer: Mary Skudlarek

0-8385-0437-X

PRINTED IN THE UNITED STATES OF AMERICA

9 780838 504376

Dedication

Thanks, Jack and Don, for your love and patience . . . .
We've finished.

For Skagit Valley Hosp. E.R.

Nedra Lewis-Crawford

Contents

Preface

Since the first edition of this time-honored text was introduced in 1978 there have been many advancements in emergency and trauma nursing practice. *The Core Curriculum for Emergency Nursing* first introduced in 1975 is now in its fourth edition, and the number of nurses who are certified for competence in the practice of emergency nursing (CEN) has reached 25,000. Even the name of the national organization has been changed from the Emergency Department Nurses Association to the Emergency Nurses Association to reflect the broader, new horizons of the specialty. There has been tremendous growth and increasing sophistication within emergency medical services during these past two decades, and nursing has not just been "keeping up," but is often setting the pace for advancements within the discipline. The fourth edition of this text has been written to serve as a practical clinical resource for the contemporary emergency nurse. Sample test questions, previously published separately, are now included at the end of each chapter to assist the reader in preparing for certification.

Part I of the text is devoted to the essentials of assessment and triage. Administrative and management issues in emergency medical services are considered along with the most recent guidelines for conducting the admission processes and initial examination of the ill and injured patient. New standards for infection control are presented with emphasis on emergency department practices designed to prevent, delimit, or control the spread of infectious conditions in the hectic emergency care environment. An update on aeromedical critical care transport and an extensive new section on the administration of conscious sedation have been added. These chapters will provide valuable guidance for today's emergency nurse who is frequently tapped to assist with these procedures.

Part II provides an extensive coverage of life support and resuscitation practices. The latest recommendations for airway and shock management are thoroughly discussed and current standards of practice and the associated procedures are detailed. This section departs from the typical "cook-book" approach of many books, and generous discussions of background theory and rationale are provided for the reader.

Part III is a compilation of individual chapters, each dedicated to a particular body system and its major blunt and penetrating injuries. Special considerations for the child and the elderly trauma patient are also included. For the first time in any emergency nursing textbook medical complications associated with trauma (e.g., rhabdomyolysis, multiple organ systems failure, hypothermia, infections, and coagulopathies) are explored, and strategies for their prevention, detection, and management are presented.

Part IV of the text comprises 14 chapters brimming with vital information for emergency nurses regarding assessment and management of common medical conditions encountered in the emergency department. Each chapter has been rewritten or extensively revised to include the most current pharmacological adjuncts and other interventions.

Part V provides nurses with valuable information that is complementary to their clinical acumen. Legal and forensic aspects of emergency care, disaster planning, and mass casualty responses, as well as contemporary issues and trends in emergency department management, are included.

This fourth edition of *Emergency Nursing* offers a refreshing departure from the usual texts. Although this revision retains the down-to-earth approach that made earlier versions "classics," there are refreshing changes that nurses will surely welcome. This edition is more sophisticated in content, but not esoteric, and planned with the busy emergency nurse in mind. Its design and organization will permit the user to find the right information with dispatch. The inclusion of helpful illustrations and tables, review questions at the end of each chapter, appendices on arterial blood gas interpretation, glossary of abbre-

viations used in the text, organ/tissue donor criteria, and 340 sample test questions to assist the
emergency nurse in preparing for the certification
examination, all add to the book's usefulness as
both a basic textbook and a clinical reference
work. If you had to rely on any one book to pro-

pel your practice into the new millennium, we believe the fourth edition of this text would serve
you well.

Nedell E. Lanros
Janet M. Barber

Acknowledgments

This work originally grew from early efforts in the 1970s to improve emergency nurses' abilities to respond to emergency room crises and the demands of patient care when there were *no* standards or guidelines in place. The Registry for Emergency Nurses Continuing Education Programs (RENCEP) became a pioneering effort in the state of Oregon with loyal determined board members Myra Lee, RN, Barbara Thompson, RN, Alice Sumida, RN, and Sherry Heying, RN; the first edition of this text in 1978 was but one of the outcomes of the RENCEP efforts. After *countless* hours of input and dedicated teaching from emergency physicians and nurses across the state of Oregon, the text grew and changed with each edition. The role and responsibilities of emergency nurses became delineated, national standards for emergency nursing practice were developed, and emergency nurses stepped into their own domain with national certification in place.

The names of the many contributors have been cited along the way in past editions, and deepest thanks continue to be expressed to every one of them for their contributions to rapid and effective emergency department response and quality patient care.

This fourth edition brings together *our* combined efforts in the field of emergency nursing; several colleagues have influenced the content, together with contributors to our earlier publications; our treasured friend Millie Fincke, RN, Peter A. Dillman, PhD, and Mark Eilers, MD have been major influences. Thanks as well to Cynthia Renfro and Lance Frank for many of the illustrations in this current work.

With deep regard, we acknowledge peers, coworkers, students, and mentors who have inspired us and who share our attitudes and views about emergency nursing.

Assessment and Triage

Triage 1

■ EVOLUTION OF TRIAGE
IN EMERGENCY CARE

Major changes in the delivery of health care were made during the early 1970s. Prior to that time, when serious emergencies occurred or illness struck, Americans called their doctors to make house calls. University medical schools staffed "receiving wards" of large municipal hospitals with residents and interns eager to learn; the sick and injured (usually those unable to afford private care) were brought in droves to "ambulance entrances" seeking care. Prehospital care as we know it today was nonexistent; ambulances generally were poorly equipped and more poorly staffed, and the operative philosophy of care was "scoop and run" or "load and go." Receiving wards echoed with the phrase "take a number and wait" unless the trauma was gross enough to capture more immediate attention.

A brief historical perspective is of value here in understanding the evolved role of modern emergency rooms and the nurses and physicians who staff them. Passage of the Emergency Medical Services (EMS) Act of 1971 set many changes in motion as the U.S. Department of Transportation (DOT) funded regional and state EMS councils across all 50 states, each charged with developing new standards for "the emergency care and transportation of the sick and injured." Once organized and funded, the new EMS councils set about developing and providing basic and advanced training and certification for ambulance personnel who were designated as emergency medical technicians (EMTs); the design, procurement, and certification of up-to-date ambulances with state-of-the-art life-support equipment on board; and the acquisition of

communications equipment to facilitate ambulance-to-hospital transmissions with the HEAR System (hospital-emergency-ambulance-radio). The direct outcome was reduction of annual death rates from highway carnage, the primary target when Congress addressed the nationwide need for emergency care, as well as vastly increasing public reliance on existing hospital facilities.

Early standardized EMT training was first based on the trail-blazing text developed by the Committee on Injuries of the American Academy of Orthopedic Surgeons, with input and support of many directly concerned agencies such as the Committee on Trauma of the American College of Surgeons (ACS), the American Heart Association (AHA), the American Medical Association (AMA), the DOT, and others. Every state certified its EMTs on course completion. The "ambulance entrance" soon became a busy doorway to hospitals everywhere; hospital administrators began expanding, equipping, and staffing their facilities, now called emergency rooms (ERs)/emergency departments (EDs). Faced with an increasing number of challenges, emergency-room nurses and physicians immediately realized the need to develop their own standards of care. They founded their own professional organizations, the Emergency Department Nurses Association (EDNA), now the Emergency Nurses Association (ENA), and the American College of Emergency Physicians (ACEP), both of which developed certification boards in their goal of ensuring quality care and setting standards of practice.

Early in the development of EMT, ENA, and ACEP guidelines and protocols for timely and appropriate emergency medical care, it became apparent that an essential component of providing such care was the ability to recognize and evaluate critical situations, or to anticipate potential for development of critical situations. This brought about the use of a triage process to be employed across all three disciplines, both in the prehospital phase of care and on arrival at the emergency facility. The formal triage process rapidly became recognized as a key factor in expediting life-saving interventions and has been employed in one form or another ever since.

TRIAGE DEFINED

Although the history of *triage* is vague in origin, it comes from a French word meaning "choice." Literally, it means "to sort out, choose, or place a priority"; the word has been adapted for our modern usage, but it was originally applied during battlefield sorting procedures in various European wars. Military triage uses a system of sorting the most viable casualties, giving them priority in care, and evacuating them to medical facilities.

Today, in almost direct contrast to battlefield practice, the triage system is applied in emergency care to sort out those patients who are most seriously compromised in their struggle for life. The assigning of obvious priorities has been in practice since patient care began, but formal triage as we employ it today has become a highly refined and detailed methodology with many approaches and formats.

Standard I of ENA's *Standards of Emergency Nursing Practice* states that "emergency nurses shall triage every patient entering the emergency care system and determine priorities of care based on physical and psychosocial needs, as well as factors influencing patient flow through the system." This is based on the rationale that comprehensive triage facilitates the flow of patients through the emergency-care system, ensuring timely evaluation according to the health-care needs of the patients, the spatial and/or temporal needs of the patient and the system, and the administrative needs of the system.

■ PREHOSPITAL TRIAGE

Emergency nurses need to understand and appreciate the judgments that are called for in the field under unique circumstances, as compared to judg-ments made regarding the same patient once inside the ED. In prehospital care, leadership is the key, and the EMT or paramedic in charge at a given scene guides what is being done and decides how and in what order ill or injured people, once stabilized, are to be transported to the nearest qualified medical facility. Judgment must also be made about the proper speed of the ambulance with a particular patient in transport, in view of the fact that excessive speed is rarely necessary as well as highly dangerous to both patient and rescuers. Since prehospital care has translated directly into increased use of hospital emergency facilities, it must be realized that one would be hard put to exist effectively without the other. In providing an essential continuum of care, therefore, the roles of both the EMT and the ED within the system must be understood and regarded.

■ DISASTER DRILLS AND TRIAGE

Disaster drills have become a regular part of EMS preparedness (another component of the EMS system). During these actual exercises, on-scene triage is usually carried out by an assigned medical officer or a team of medical officers. These triage officers respond to actual disaster situations for the purpose of conducting as systematic a triage as possible, dispatching patients to appropriate hospital facilities. In the absence of assigned medical triage officers, the first ambulance EMTs on the scene assume command responsibility.

■ IN-HOSPITAL TRIAGE

Upon arrival at the ED, triage responsibility is usually shifted to the receiving nurse, who reassesses, intervenes as necessary, and assigns a treatment area for further management. In some facilities, however, triage may be carried out by a clerk following written protocols or "clinical algorithms." As a rule, in civilian hospitals, a triage nurse usually has the responsibility and follows formal protocols and guidelines in expediting intervention and further life support and treatment. The triage system employed will generally depend upon the size and capabilities of the hospital, the population area served, and the availability of licensed and adequately trained personnel. Very large hospitals often triage patients directly to their trauma unit, cardiac unit, regular ER, or to clinics; medium-size hospitals do their sorting within the hospital in much the same way routine admissions are categorically assigned. In the small hospital, it is often the nurse who screens (triages) patients for physicians around the clock and assigns them accordingly.

EMERGENCY NURSES ASSOCIATION'S STANDARDS OF PRACTICE

Comprehensive triage, as defined in the ENA's *Standards of Practice,*[1] is performed by an emergency nurse; components of standard I, comprehensive triage, follow the nursing process of assessment, analysis/plan, intervention/collaborative intervention, and evaluation. Each component standard is assigned competence outcome criteria (COC).

A. *Assessment:* Triage assessment shall include rapid, systematic collection of data related to the patient's chief complaint.
   1. Perform symptom analysis of chief complaint on all patients entering the emergency-care system, collecting subjective and objective data.
   2. Evaluate patients in a timely manner according to preset triage priority outcomes.
   3. Reassess patients in waiting area based on triage acuity guidelines and recategorize them as appropriate.
   4. Document triage assessment in succinct, complete fashion.
B. *Analysis/Plan:* Triage assessment shall be analyzed to determine acuity, patient care area, and any appropriate interventions based on triage protocols.
   1. Differentiate severity of patient problems and prioritize care, designating an appropriate acuity level.
   2. Assign patient to appropriate patient care area, based on triage assessment and acuity categorization.
   3. Inform emergency-care team of patient's arrival and communicate pertinent information.

C. *Intervention:* Emergency nurses shall function independently within the parameters established for professional nursing.
   1. Initiate nursing measures according to triage protocols (e.g., ice, splinting).
   2. Facilitate flow of patients through the emergency-care system.
   3. Communicate pertinent information to family/significant others as appropriate.
   4. Mobilize additional resources (e.g., social services, chaplain) as needed for patient or family.
D. *Collaborative Intervention:* Emergency nurses shall function collaboratively to facilitate timely care for patients based on triage protocols.
   1. Initiate diagnostic triage protocols, if indicated (e.g., x-ray).
   2. Initiate treatment triage protocols, if indicated (e.g., antipyretics).
E. *Evaluation:* Quality assurance plan shall be developed and implemented to ensure timely, appropriate triage.
   1. Perform triage within preestablished time frames.
   2. Categorize acuity level consistent with patient evaluation.
   3. Demonstrate complete documentation and consistency with triage protocols per case review.

THE CLINICAL ALGORITHM

The clinical algorithm is a triage tool employed in very large hospitals, many of them government-operated and service-related. Many years ago De-Witt Army Community Hospital (Ft. Belvoir, VA) employed what it called a "logical algorithmic alternative to a nonsystem"; it was discussed in the May–June 1973 issue of JACEP, Journal of the American College of Emergency Physicians. A clinical algorithm is a set of "unambiguous step-by-step instructions for solving a clinical problem." Algorithms are designed to assist in the performance of a specific task.

Medical officers at government hospital EDs devised clinical algorithms for all types of presenting medical and surgical problems; these algorithms permit sorting, designating, and assigning of priorities of problems of an entire walk-in patient population by minimally trained volunteers. These volunteers were given 8 hours of training—three 2-hour classes followed by 2 hours of on-the-job training—and then were ready to follow the series of hard-and-fast rules as laid out in the algorithms, which are really substitutes for crash courses in recognition of serious medical problems (Figs. 1–1 and 1–2). Interestingly, the accuracy of this system is incredibly high, and the system lends itself well to management of great volumes of patients, such as are seen in government-operated medical facilities. There has been an error rate, determined by chart audit, of less than 3 percent in most institutions where it has been employed.

ADVANTAGES OF A NURSE TRIAGE SYSTEM

A formal nurse triage system has many advantages when employed in any hospital of any size. Most ED staffs have concluded that the triage person *should* be a nurse, with responsibility for making rapid decisions based on speedy but accurate assessment of each patient who presents, deciding who needs immediate intervention and where, and who can tolerate a short wait. Some of the advantages include the following:

- Early recognition and assessment of the seriously compromised patient
- Immediate intervention in life-threatening situations
- Expedition of care for the noncritical patient
- Alleviation of fear, anxiety, and tension levels in patients, with marked benefit to the nursing staff as a result
- Employment of the team concept with most effective use of personnel
- More effective follow-through on problems
- Designated responsibility for liaison with families and friends of patients and with the public
- Expedition of preliminary diagnostic studies
- More effective overall management, resulting in smooth patient flow and traffic patterns

■ ESTABLISHING INDIVIDUAL TRIAGE SYSTEMS

CRITERIA

Many triage systems have been developed within individual EDs to meet their specific needs; others may have simply evolved as a result of trial and error. Almost everyone agrees that an efficient triage system should be the hub of the emergency-care wheel, but most must also agree that very few such systems become operational and have adequate personnel education and preparation, effective implementation guidelines, and an ongoing evaluation of outcomes. Currently, there are several well-written manuals for developing a comprehensive triage system adaptable to individual settings. This chapter also presents certain criteria to be considered when setting up an effective nurse triage system. These criteria include the following:

- An *organizational chart.* Triage, by its very definition, should be an orderly process, and an organizational chart defines the functions of physicians, nurses, clerks, and ancillary personnel, placing everyone in the appropriate area of responsibility.
- A *job description* developed with the ED where the nurse is triaging, dependent on hospital policy as well as departmental identities and hospital staffing patterns.
- *Specific courses of action* to be followed by the triage nurse *must* be in writing and should probably be included in the job description. (Triage protocols for assessment and intervention(s) are specific courses of action and should be used as essential triage tools to guide nursing actions.)
- Ongoing *supervision* and *structured critiques* to provide a continuous check on the effectiveness of the system, with periodic reviews of performance, patient flow rates, and patient outcomes.
- *Physician support and participation,* which is an essential component of the successful triage system.
- Established and ongoing channels of *communication,* both inter- and intradepartmental.

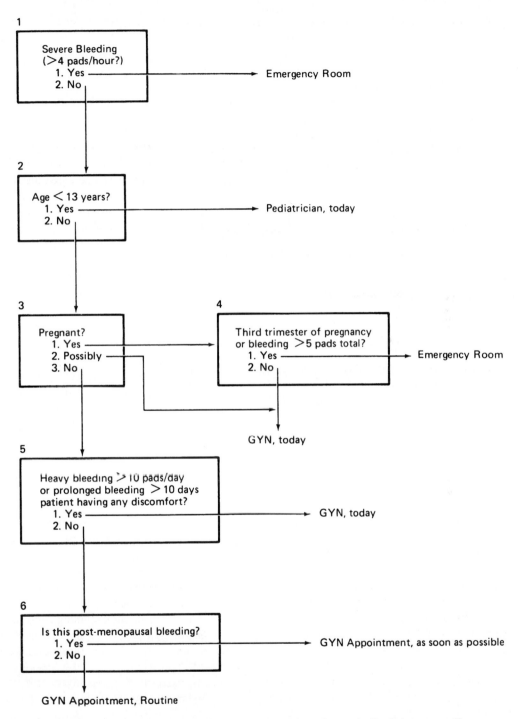

Figure 1–1. Algorithm for vaginal bleeding from DeWitt Army Community Hospital (*from JACEP*[12]).

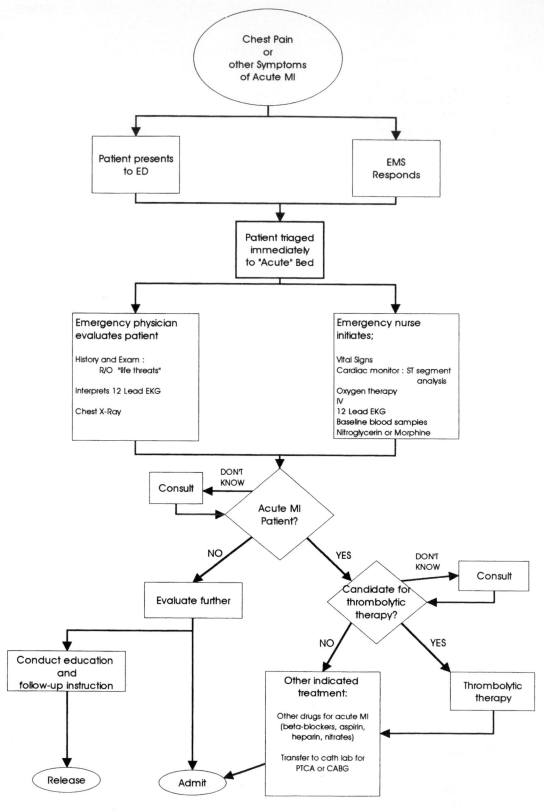

Figure 1–2. Algorithm for use by an emergency medical technician in management of patient with chest pain (*from JACEP*[12]).

- Adequate *orientation* to the responsibilities, policies, and procedures of triaging.
- Enough *qualified and willing* emergency nurses (ENs) within the department to carry out the triage procedures as written.
- A *triage area* that allows patient interviews with privacy. Quiet communication between nurse and patient is essential to establish initial rapport and confidence as assessment is being carried out.

THE TRIAGE NURSE

The triage nurse, then, functions in a pivotal role and becomes the facilitator of patient access to the medical-care system as we know it today, through the ED or outpatient clinic, and must direct patient flow in the most expeditious and appropriate manner, using staff and space as effectively as possible. It is self-evident that the position is demanding and one of extreme importance to both patients and staff, requiring a nurse with very special qualities. Intelligence, the ability to relate to people, a capacity for calm and reasoned judgment in meeting emergencies, and an orientation toward service are essential attributes of the triage nurse. Other obvious qualifications call for someone experienced in ED nursing and skilled in assessment techniques who can tolerate high stress levels while maintaining a working rapport with co-workers, medical staff, families, and the general public.

The skilled triage nurse is able to reassure patients and their families regarding their problems and effectively interpret hospital and departmental policies and procedures when asked. The nurse carrying out triage contributes heavily to improved overall quality of care by maintaining an overview of the entire department, assigning patients to appropriate treatment teams or areas, expediting patient care (when appropriate by initiating preliminary diagnostic studies), and coordinating activities among clerical, nursing, medical, and laboratory services.

THE TRIAGE AREA

Patient access and visibility while still providing privacy, by cubicles or curtains, must be prime considerations. Although one station can serve both ambulatory and litter patients in small facilities, the trend is toward separate triage areas, especially in high-volume settings, in order to maintain distinction in priority and tracking of both groups. This is vital in large departments that absorb clinic overflow and deliver a high percentage of primary care via a fast-track clinic operating as an extension of the ED. Other essential considerations for an adequate triage area include the following:[2]

- Both wheelchair and stretcher storage alcoves, ideally located near the entrance(s) to the ED, as well as dedicated storage space for ambulance exchange equipment;
- A large enough area to permit initial screening of the usual patient flow within 5 to 10 minutes of any patient's arrival;
- Good lighting (at least 1100 lux) and hand-washing facilities;
- Appropriate examination tables, oxygen and suctioning capabilities, and an adjacent soiled utility space are desirable;
- Area design facilitating simultaneous triage of several patients, including physical assessment and orthostatic vital signs, hemorrhage control, airway protection, visual acuity screening, and documentation of a brief medical history.

If laboratory specimens are to be obtained or blood glucose checked in triage, a blood-drawing armchair and equipment are convenient aids. Bathrooms should be immediately adjacent to triage for the collection of voided specimens as well as for patients' convenience when they present with vomiting, diarrhea, or frequent urination.

Careful attention must be paid to maintenance of *infection control measures,* with procedure gloves, disposable surgical masks for infectious respiratory contacts, and ample supplies of disinfectant solutions available at all times, in order to employ universal precautions as they have been prescribed (See Table 3–1).

In these times of increasing violence, hospital security should be within easy access of the ED entry at all times. Many institutions now use metal detectors at their doors, but hostile and violent patients still occasionally make it through the safeguards. Triage nurses should be familiar with techniques of de-escalating violence and hostility and knowledgeable in the indications for and use of restraints; more on that topic is found in Chapters 33 and 34.

DETERMINING PRIORITIES IN TREATMENT

Effective triage and management of ED patients relies directly on categorization of presenting problems. A relatively standard group of three triage categories has been generally accepted by most medical, nursing, and prehospital personnel who function in the decision-making areas of emergency care. By and large, these categories provide reliable guidelines for problem management, although there are certainly exceptions that may crop up and must be dealt with according to priority evaluation. Below are the details of the three major triage categories of *emergency, urgent,* and *nonurgent,* including representative presenting problems:

1. *Emergency:* A condition requiring immediate medical attention. Delay would be harmful to the patient; disorder is acute and potentially threatening to life or function. Highest priority is given to the following:
   - Airway and breathing difficulties
   - Cardiac arrest
   - Cervical spine compromise
   - Chest pain and acute dyspnea and/or cyanosis
   - Open chest or abdominal wounds
   - Seizure states
   - Uncontrolled or suspected severe bleeding
   - Severe head injuries or comatose state
   - Severe medical problems, such as poisoning, overdose, and diabetic complications
   - Severe or impending shock
   - Obvious multiple injuries
   - Excessively high temperature (over 105°F or 40.5°C)
   - Emergency childbirth, complications of pregnancy, hemorrhage, or indications of eclampsia
2. *Urgent:* A condition requiring medical attention within hours; a possible danger exists to the patient if medically unattended.

Second priority is given to these conditions:
   - Chest pain associated with upper respiratory infection
   - Burns
   - Major multiple fractures
   - Dulled or obtunded level of consciousness (LOC)
   - Back injuries with or without spinal cord damage
   - Persistent nausea, vomiting, or diarrhea
   - Severe pain
   - Temperature of 102° to 105°F or 39° to 40.5°C
   - Acute panic states, drug overuse, apparent or suspected poisoning
3. *Nonurgent:* A condition that does not require the resources of an ED or emergency service. Referral for routine medical care may or may not be needed; disorder is nonacute or relatively minor in severity and time is not a critical factor. Conditions of this lesser degree of severity may be candidates for a fast-track clinic or the quick-serve concept.[3] Lowest priority is given to conditions such as the following:
   - Chronic backache
   - Moderate headache
   - Minor fractures or other injuries of a minor nature
   - Obviously mortal wounds where death appears reasonably certain (this is a rarely followed criterion)
   - Obviously dead on arrival

The long delays endured by patients with low-acuity problems have caused many large hospitals to rethink their nonurgent care practices. Long waiting times that cause patients to leave in frustration, the rapid proliferation of freestanding urgent care centers, and the looming threat of health maintenance organizations (HMOs) have fostered the creation of new concepts in care for low-acuity and minor trauma problems. An exciting approach has been the creation of fast-tracks staffed by emergency nurse practitioners (NPs) in several large university hospitals in the East. The goals set were twofold: (1) to relieve congestion in the acute treatment areas and (2) to expedite care of patients with minor emergencies. These providers have been able to maintain their market share as a result of careful thought and planning.[4–6]

TRAUMA VICTIM PRIORITIES

Trauma victims present with some special considerations to which the triage nurse must be alert; a relative urgency *always* exists with the following associated problems:

1. Progressively increasing respiratory difficulty
2. Incipient shock with progression to be anticipated
3. Rising central venous pressure and decreasing pulse pressure
4. Rapidly deteriorating LOC or sudden coma following lucid period
5. Airway or chest wall problems
6. Sudden hypotension with possibility of occult bleeding
7. Penetrating wounds of chest, abdomen, or head

Red Flags

There are many danger signals and circumstances that may contribute heavily to rapid and disastrous deterioration of a traumatized patient. They are referred to variously as red flags, caution indicators, and axioms for management. Regardless of the label, they are signs of, or contributing circumstances to, serious problems and must be recognized by those observing baselines. Any one of these criteria should generally be considered an indication of mandatory admission for further close observation and intervention if necessary, or immediate stabilization and transfer to a level I trauma unit. They include but are not limited to:

- Motor vehicle accidents that occurred at speeds higher than 35 mph (these carry a high probability of ruptured thoracic aorta)
- Forces of deceleration, as in falls or explosions
- Loss of consciousness after accident
- Possible cervical spine trauma in patient with head injury
- Vehement denial by patient of obviously serious injuries, with flighty thought and speech patterns and occasionally inappropriate responses

- Chest or abdominal pain after injury
- Fracture of the first or second rib (associated with high mortality)
- Fracture of the ninth, tenth, or eleventh ribs or more than three ribs
- Possible aspiration
- Possible extensive lung tissue contusions
- Pulse rate over 120 bpm at rest

In the management of trauma victims, the rule of thumb must *always* be to manage as though the most serious problem exists and *be prepared* to cope with it until it is either treated effectively or ruled out. ***Think the worst first*** and when in doubt, ***always upgrade triage.***

ADDITIONAL TRIAGE TOOL: CRITICAL PATHWAYS

Unlike clinical algorithms, critical pathways (CPs) are outcome-based tools that convey the standard of care to be expected for each patient from admission to discharge and follow-up; all are based on the patient's chief complaint and findings on evaluation at triage (e.g., difficulty breathing, radiating abdominal pain, lacerated finger, fever). Variously referred to in different EDs as care maps, care plans, and patient classification systems, CPs are a mechanism by which optimal care goals can be translated into reality with the best patient outcomes achieved in the shortest time and in the most cost-effective manner. They are developed within each ED on the basis of multidisciplinary input, implementation, and ongoing evaluation.

Components of a CP usually include any combination of the following: nursing assessments and interventions (both at triage and follow-up), medications, treatments, laboratory tests, diagnostic procedures, consultations, activities, nutrition, and so forth, on through to discharge planning. CPs for specific clinical situations should be available for the triage nurse for initiating primary documentation when assessing each patient on arrival. Having symptom-based CPs available at the triage desk serves to significantly empower the EN in early triage and treatment.

These pathways should draw from and incorporate, whenever possible and as appropriate, established treatment protocols and standards of care from agencies such as the AHA, ACS Committee on

Trauma, and the Joint Commission on Accreditation of Healthcare Organizations and, of course, state laws governing practice and individual hospital policies. Successful CPs are multidisciplinary and are developed by a team effort among physicians, ENs, therapists, technicians, and all others with direct responsibility for patient care. CPs can help smooth out variations in practice patterns, improve quality of care, and enhance use of resources. Perhaps one of the strongest arguments to be made for their value is their usefulness in preventing oversights in diagnosis and treatment, as well as in deflecting threats of potential litigation. CPs are well worth the time spent on their development, evaluation, and ongoing review.[6-10]

■ INTERHOSPITAL TRANSFER OF PATIENTS

THE CONSOLIDATED OMNIBUS BUDGET RECONCILIATION ACT

The federal legislation known as COBRA (Consolidated Omnibus Budget Reconciliation Act) part of the Social Security Act, was passed by Congress in response to the practice of patient "dumping" by some hospitals (i.e., quickly transferring patients who were uninsured or unable to pay for care). Amendments making the existing COBRA regulations even more restrictive went into effect July 1, 1990, and apply to *any* hospital providing emergency services that has a Medicare provider agreement; this includes specialty facilities such as trauma centers and burn units. Specialty centers are legally obligated to accept all appropriate transfers as long as they have the capacity to treat that patient. Amendments directly affect the responsibility of physicians for examination, treatment, and/or transfer of an individual in a participating hospital, and severe financial penalties are enforced for any violations of the law. ED personnel should have full knowledge of the requirements and amend policies and transfer protocols accordingly. Nurses can also be implicated, as agents of the hospital or physician, in the inappropriate, improper, or improperly documented transfer of patients from one hospital to another. Al-

though true emergencies (multiple trauma, severe head injuries, cardiorespiratory problems, burns, shock, and so forth) account for a relatively small percentage of patients seen in EDs, these patients frequently have so many concurrent injuries or life-threatening problems of such magnitude that transfer to a larger or more sophisticated facility is in the patient's best interest.[11]

Emergency physicians and occasionally nurses find themselves in the position of having to make these determinations. In many areas, they are able to follow established transfer patterns; states that have undergone categorization of their hospitals are able to provide resource references to physicians and hospitals when transfer questions arise.

AMERICAN COLLEGE OF SURGEONS' STANDARDS FOR TRANSFER

Through the 1970s, the only established standards for advanced life support were those of the AHA. Since the early 1980s, guidelines have been developed and disseminated by the ACS, Committee on Trauma for patient management during the initial resuscitative phase of trauma care. Additionally, the Committee on Trauma has prepared a document entitled "Prehospital & Hospital Resource for Optimal Care of the Injured Patient," with a series of relevant appendices. Appendix C of the document deals with interhospital transfer of patients and suggests guidelines,* shown below, to follow for determination of responsibility, accountability, patient management, feedback, and documentation during the transfer process:

1. Arrangements for transfer should be by way of *direct communication* between the referring physician and the receiving physician. The primary responsibility rests with the party who arranges transportation.
2. The *receiving physician is responsible* for arrangements and details of the transfer, including transportation. The referring physician must oversee details of transfer to ensure optimal patient management and should obtain approval for use of local ambulance transport from the receiving physi-

---

*Adapted with permission from the American College of Surgeons, Committee on Trauma: Prehospital & hospital resource for optimal care of the injured patient, with appendices A–J, February 1987.

cian, unless aeromedical transport provided by the receiving hospital is to be employed.

3. The patient must be transported with equipment and trained persons appropriate to his or her life-support needs.

4. The transferring physician should carefully instruct the transfer personnel. Specific instructions on condition and needs during transfer should include but are not limited to:
   - Airway management
   - Fluid volume replacement
   - Any other special procedures indicated

5. A copy of the written record including the problem, treatment given, and status at time of discharge for transfer *must* accompany the patient and should include:
   - Patient identification, address, and next of kin *with* phone numbers
   - History of injury or illness
   - Condition on admission
   - Vital signs from prehospital evaluation, during ED care, and at time of transfer (baseline data)
   - All treatment given, including medications *with* routes of administration
   - Laboratory and x-ray findings, *including copies of films*
   - Fluids given by type and volume
   - Name, address, and phone number of referring physician
   - Name of physician and hospital to which patient is being transferred and name of physician at receiving institution who has been contacted for transfer *(responsible physician)*.

Transfer forms and suggested transfer agreement forms have been developed by the ACS. Further information regarding their use or availability should be obtained by contacting the ACS, 55 East Erie Street, Chicago, IL 60611-2797.

■ REFERENCES

1. ENA. *Standards of Practice.* 2nd ed. St. Louis, Mo: Mosby-Year Book; 1991.
2. Barber JB. Key considerations in emergency and trauma unit design. In Swaim J (ed), Critical Care Unit Design. *Crit Care Nurs Q.* 1991;14(1):71–82.
3. Nollman J, Colbert K. Successful fast tracks: data and advice. *J Emerg Nurs.* 1994;20:483–486.
4. Covington C, Erwin T, Sellers F. Implementation of a nurse practitioner-staffed fast track. *J Emerg Nurs.* 1992;18:124–132.
5. Cardello D, Square H. Implementation of a one-hour fast-track service: one hospital's experience. *J Emerg Nurs.* 1992;18:239–244.
6. Base P. Examples of critical paths for use in the emergency department. *J Emerg Nurs.* 1994;20:174–175.
7. Knudtson D. Practice guidelines: salvation for the emergency department. *J Emerg Nurs.* 1994;20:450.
8. Saul L. Developing critical pathways: A practical guide. *A Cardiac Heartbeat.* 1995;5:1–11.
9. Nelson M. Critical pathways in the emergency department. *J Emerg Nurs.* 1993;19:110–114.
10. Veenema T. The ten most frequently asked questions about case management in the emergency department. *J Emerg Nurs.* 1994;20:289–292.
11. Baier F. Implications of the Consolidated Omnibus Budget Reconciliation "antidumping" legislation for emergency nurses. *J Emerg Nurs.* 1993;19:115–120.
12. *JACEP.* May-June, 1973;185–186.

■ BIBLIOGRAPHY

American College of Surgeons Committee on Trauma. Advanced Trauma Life Support Program. Chicago, Ill: ACS; 1993.

Barber JM, Dillman PA. *Emergency Patient Care.* Reston, Va: Reston Publishing; 1981.

Crummer MB, Carter V. Critical pathways—the pivotal tool. *J Cardiovasc Nurs.* 1993;7:30–37.

Gelfant BB, Lovelace P. The triage nurse. *Ethicon Point of View.* 1987;24:3, 6.

George JE, Quattrone MS, Goldstone M. Triage protocols. *J Emerg Nurs.* 1995;21:65–66.

Holleran RS. *Mosby's Emergency Nursing Review.* St. Louis, Mo: Mosby-Year Book; 1992.

Larson SS. Protocols for Advanced Emergency Management. Bowie, Md: The Brady Company; 1982.

Lumsdom K. Clinical paths: a good defense in malpractice litigation? *Hosp Health Networks.* 1994; 68:58.

McKee NR. A formalized approach to obstetric-synecologic triage. *J Emerg Nurs.* 1993;19:19–27.

Mosby Lifeline: *Pre-Hospital Trauma Life Support Basic and Advanced.* 3rd ed. St. Louis, Mo: Mosby-Year Book; 1994.

Mowad L, Ruhle DC. *Handbook of Emergency Nursing: The Nursing Process Approach.* East Norwalk, Conn: Appleton & Lange; 1988.

Neely KA. Rapid triage, treatment, and transfer of the trauma patient. *Top Emerg Med.* 1987;9.

Nelson MS. A triage-based emergency department patient classification system. *J Emerg Nurs.* 1994;20:511–516.

O'Boyle CM, Davis DK, Russo BA, et al. *Emergency Care: The First 24 Hours.* E. Norwalk, Conn: Appleton & Lange, 1985.

Rowe JA. Triage assessment tool. *J Emerg Nurs.* 1992;18:S40–S44.

Sley LE, Riskin WG. Algorithm: directed triage in an emergency department. *JACEP.* 1976;5:869–875.

Southard P. Legal issues. 3rd ed. In: Sheehy S, ed. *Emergency Nursing Principles and Practice.* St. Louis, Mo: Mosby-Year Book; 1992:23–31.

Thompson JD, Dains JE. *Comprehensive Triage: A Manual for Developing and Implementing a Nursing Care System.* Reston, Va: Reston Publishing; 1982.

VanBoxel A. Improving the triage process. *J Emerg Nurs.* 1995;21:332–334.

■ REVIEW: TRIAGE

1. Define the origin and rationale of the term *triage.*

2. Explain who is in charge at an accident scene. Who is responsible for triaging and transporting multiple victims?

3. Name the four components of the nursing process carried out by the emergency nurse (EN) when following the Emergency Nurses Association (ENA) standards of practice for comprehensive triage. List at least three responsibilities within each.

4. List six advantages of a nurse triage system.

5. List six essential components of a successful nurse triage system.

6. Explain the three categories of determined priorities in treatment/interventions and list at least four examples of each.

7. Describe the potential benefits in patient outcomes when outcome-based tools (e.g., care maps, care plans, critical pathways, patient classification systems) are used in the emergency department (ED).

9. Explain the implications of the COBRA (Consolidated Omnibus Reconciliation Act) legislation on interhospital transfer of patients.

10. Outline the American College of Surgeons (ACS) checkpoints for interhospital patient transfer.

The Emergency Nurse and Flight Transportation

Emergency nurses are frequently involved in the care of patients who arrive at the emergency department (ED) via helicopter or who will be transported to another facility, either by rotor or fixed-wing aircraft. The decision to use aeromedical transportation to a facility or between health-care facilities is based on multiple factors, including equipment accessibility, weather and terrain, urgency of the transport mission, and the potential benefits of aeromedical transportation to the patient and to medical-care providers. Aircraft used in most civilian transports are helicopters or rotor crafts, which do not present the potential hazards that may be imposed by high-altitude flight conditions that may exist with fixed-wing aircraft if cabin pressure is lost during flight. However, it is important that nurses understand both the basic effects of altitude on the body and the potential hazards that changes in altitudes may pose for the traumatized patient.

Aeromedical transportation systems consist of a medically managed transport operation that functions primarily to provide a comprehensive program employing educated emergency medical personnel who have been trained to function in a unique aviation environment. All associated personnel must possess sufficient knowledge to oversee the physiological and psychological factors that may influence the patient's condition. Aeromedical systems are designed to save time while transporting the patient to the medical facility and to provide life-sustaining care, both pre- and intraflight. The neonatal intensive care, team dispatched to stabilize a critically ill newborn in a rural hospital for subsequent transportation to a sophisticated neonatal care center is an excellent example of this concept of on-site stabilization and transfer. Aeromedical transportation is also used to support organ and tissue retrieval and transplantation programs. Through a national network, a donor and recipient are matched, and either the patient is evacuated to the site where the organs or tissues are located or the needed biologic materials are rushed to the awaiting patient by air. At times, the medical transplantation experts are dispatched by aircraft to either the donor or the recipient to ensure a successful linkage. The technology for these transplantation efforts relies heavily on the speed and efficiency of both dedicated and commercial aircraft.

■ ADVANTAGES OF AEROMEDICAL TRANSPORTATION

The usefulness of aircraft in rescuing and transporting the sick and injured has long been recognized in both military and civilian operations. In the early 1900s, the military experimented with fixed-wing aircraft to transport patients from remote areas to distant medical installations. Military aeromedical transportation proved successful and over the years has been refined and expanded into a total system. Since the mid-1970s, the civilian health-care team's ability to sustain life for the critically ill and injured patient has increased exponentially. Unfortunately, emergency medical services (EMS) cannot reach its ultimate effectiveness unless the patient is able to reach the appropriate facility or the community has instituted a plan whereby emergency care can be rendered at the scene. Aeromedical transportation has the capacity to help achieve this goal.

Transporting patients quickly by air from remote sites to the appropriate medical treatment facility has long been recognized as a major advantage. Today, several types of aircraft are used to transport patients. Helicopters can be used for retrieving patients or delivering emergency personnel to sites where other modes of transportation would be unsuitable. Combining the speed, range, flexibility, and versatility of fixed-wing and rotor aircraft, aeromedical transportation makes it possible for patients to receive life-saving or stabilizing care, so that they can be transported to a treatment facility best equipped to handle their particular injury or illness.

An important advantage of aeromedical transportation systems is their usefulness during disasters and mass-casualty scenarios. Patient flow can be regulated to facilities best able to quickly respond to the unique medical needs of the injured or critically ill individual. This permits timely delivery of care and ensures that the resources of various institutions are used appropriately. Such a system enhances cost-effectiveness by limiting the number of hospitals that must be staffed and equipped to deliver a full range of services. Costly specialty services can be pooled at regional centers and outlying hospitals can transport patients to such centers by air. Smaller institutions or those in rural areas can concentrate on basic services aimed at maintaining patients' life processes until they can be transported to a facility providing a higher level of care and treatment. Each community and geographic region should have a plan for efficient aeromedical evacuation of patients who require sophisticated resources of a major medical or dedicated trauma center, and personnel in the ED should be familiar with accessing and using the system's services. It is especially important to have sound medical direction in determining which patients should be aeromedically transported and which ones might be equally well served by land services.

■ LIMITATIONS OF AEROMEDICAL TRANSPORTATION

Fog, snow, low ceilings, freezing precipitation, sand storms, strong or gusting winds, and turbulence may pose hazards for aeromedical transportation. Rescue missions in mountains, over water, and in swamps and other high-risk areas may be especially treacherous for crew members. Even when aeromedical evacuation might be ideal, certain missions may need to be managed by land services or delayed until weather or other conditions might be more favorable (e.g., waiting until daylight).

■ AIRCRAFT TYPES

Aircraft designed for medical use includes both fixed-wing and rotor units (Fig. 2–1). The type of aircraft selected will depend primarily on the type of service needed and the distance the patient is to be transported. Aircraft ordinarily available for emergency and elective transportation include a wide variety of both fixed-wing and rotor models. Fixed-wing aircraft are usually reserved for long-distance transportation in which airport runway facilities or air strips are available. Ground ambulance services must also be available at the dispatch point and end points of the flight. Configurations of the plan must ensure adequate room for the patient and supportive medical equipment and for the crew to carry out its emergency care and monitoring activities. Lighting, ventilation, and temperature must be regulated to ensure both patient and crew comfort. Electrical systems must be capable of supporting all medical equipment without compromising other aircraft operating systems. Either fixed or portable communication equipment is used to maintain contact with medical direction throughout all phases of the flight. The general and specialized medical equipment varies with the unique requirements of the mission and may consist of several types of sophisticated critical-care devices. It is the responsibility of the flight crew to select and evaluate the types of medical systems that may be safely used during unpressurized flights and during flight emergencies in which cabin pressure may change precipitously (see page 19). Space and life-support equipment/accommodations may be a limiting factor for some proposed flights.

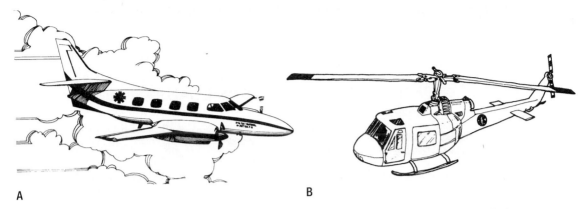

Figure 2–1. A. A fixed-wing aircraft. **B.** A rotor aircraft. (*From Barber JM, Dillman PA.* Emergency Patient Care for the EMT-A. *Reston, Va: Reston Publishing, 1981*)

Helicopters are used in many communities since they are capable of operating from unprepared takeoff and landing areas. Their ability to fly forward, backward, and sideways and to hover and perform completely vertical takeoffs or landings make them ideal for maneuvering into otherwise inaccessible areas and flying into and out of heavily congested locations such as those encountered in most urban centers. Owing to the versatility of today's rotor-wing aircraft, helicopters are the choice of many regionalized systems. However, helicopter use is hazardous in adverse weather situations and should be avoided if air turbulence, severe thunderstorms, heavy rains, or icy conditions prevail.

Some hospitals—and certainly major trauma centers—have designated sites for helicopter takeoffs and landings. These sites must be located in an area where there is minimal obstruction by trees, wires, antennas, or buildings and in which emergency personnel can readily work with the crew and patient upon their arrival. Location immediately adjacent to the trauma center is, of course, most desirable for efficient operations.

■ PATIENT LOADING AND SAFETY

Emergency personnel must be familiar with the procedures and safety precautions involved in loading and unloading patients from the aircraft. The aircraft should not be approached until signaled to do so by the pilot or flight crew member. Helicopters are usually approached from a 45-degree angle from the front of the craft. If the helicopter is on a slope and conditions permit, personnel should approach the aircraft from the downhill side (Fig. 2–2). Under no circumstances should anyone approach the tail of a helicopter. The tail rotor is difficult to see and may be not be noticed in the surrounding noise and flashing lights (Fig. 2–3). Immediately after landing, an individual should be stationed near the rear of the helicopter to warn others to remain clear. Personnel involved in the loading and unloading must keep as low a silhouette as possible and remain clear of the rotor blades at all times. Any bystanders should be kept at a minimum of 100 feet away from the aircraft. Rotor and propellor wash winds in excess of 50 mph can be expected, and the debris they kick up can endanger personnel on the ground. Eye protection should be worn by all personnel who on-load or off-load litters from aircraft (Fig. 2–4). The flight medical crew is in charge of supervising the on-loading and off-loading of patients. Emergency personnel should listen carefully to their directives and follow instructions to ensure that all procedures are accomplished efficiently and safely.

■ SPECIAL CONSIDERATIONS AND COMMON PROBLEMS IN AEROMEDICAL TRANSPORTATION

When transported by aircraft, some patients will experience, in addition to the stresses caused by their underlying medical problems, stresses imposed by fear of flying, changes in altitude and air

Figure 2–2. Approaching a helicopter.

pressures, motion sickness, and other factors; these may complicate nursing care. Preflight preparation that considers these potential problems and their effects on the patient's condition is a shared responsibility of both emergency personnel and the flight crew.

EFFECTS OF ALTITUDE ON OXYGEN SATURATION

As altitude increases, barometric air pressure decreases. This pressure drop translates from about 30 inches of mercury at sea level to about 8 inches at

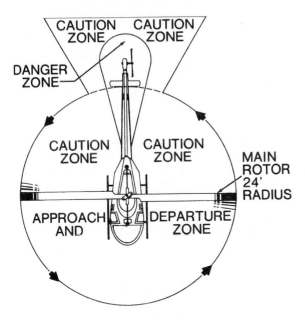

Figure 2–3. Approach and departure zone.

35,000 feet. Even though the atmospheric pressure decreases with altitude, the ratio of gases in the air (i.e., oxygen and nitrogen) remains constant. The amount of oxygen that can be extracted by the blood at the capillary–alveolar membrane is dependent on the pressure exerted by the oxygen. As the partial pressure of oxygen (PO_2) decreases with altitude, hemoglobin saturation (SaO_2) will be impaired.

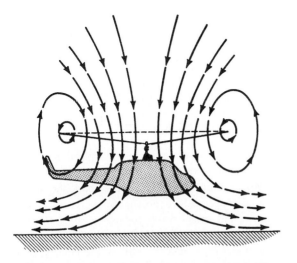

Figure 2–4. Wash winds produced by rotor aircraft. (*From Barber JM, Dillman PA. Emergency Patient Care for the EMT-A. Reston, Va: Reston Publishing, 1981*).

The human body is physiologically adaptable from sea level to about 10,000 ft; this is known as the physiological zone. At sea level, the theoretical normal SaO_2 should be about 100 percent. SaO_2 declines gradually with increasing altitude. At 5000 feet, it will drop to about 95 percent; and 7000 feet, to 90 percent; at 10,000 feet, to 85 percent; and at altitudes in excess of 14,000 feet, it will be about 80 percent. At the 80 percent level, the average, healthy person will begin to display noticeable signs of hypoxia (i.e., headaches, loss of concentration, and tachypnea). Individuals with certain anemias, cardiovascular disease, or pulmonary problems may suffer severe distress. At altitudes that permit the SaO_2 to fall below 90 percent, tissues with a high oxygen requirement (e.g., the retina or brain) may be adversely affected unless supplemental oxygen is provided.

During ascent in a nonpressurized aircraft, the atmospheric pressure drops and various degrees of hypoxia may be experienced. Factors that influence hypoxia include altitude, the rate of pressure change (e.g., rapid ascent or descent), and individual tolerances to oxygen deficiency and stress. The associated hypoxia and hypercapnia associated with a decreased PO_2 even within the physiological zone, may compromise a marginal patient suffering from cardiopulmonary problems, hypovolemia, severe head injury, toxic inhalation, or multiple trauma. Slight atmospheric pressure changes may reduce SaO_2 to an intolerable level for these individuals. A patient with sickle cell anemia will "sickle" at about 4,000 feet and experience considerable distress.

In the physiological deficient zone, between 10,000 and 50,000 feet, there is considerable reduction of atmospheric pressure and insufficient oxygen to sustain normal physiological function. Above 50,000 feet, bodies must be protected by a sealed cabin or a pressure suit, since the environment is extremely hazardous, posing risks for tissue water vaporization as well as oxygen deficiency. Injured patients, of course, would not ordinarily be transported at altitudes within the physiological deficient zone.

BAROTITIS MEDIA

The middle ear is an air-filled space connected to the throat by the eustachian tube. Ordinarily, a slitlike orifice at the throat favors the venting of air outward rather than inward. During aircraft descent, the middle ear cavity air contracts and pressure decreases below the ambient level. Unless air is moved into the middle ear, there is no equalization with ambient pressure. As discrepancies increase between pressures inside and outside the middle ear cavity, pain and trauma may ensue. The inside pressure becomes increasingly negative, creating a partial vacuum, and the eardrum is depressed inward, causing pain, inflammation, and even petechial hemorrhages and tympanic membrane rupture in severe cases (Fig. 2–5). Crew members and other passengers are more likely to experience barotitis media when they have allergies or upper respiratory conditions. Decongestant sprays may be used prophylactically to minimize barotitis media discomfort associated with flight descent. Valsalva maneuvers may be effective for crew members and healthy passengers but should be avoided for cardiac patients and for individuals with hypertension, head injury, aneurysms, or ocular conditions, including glaucoma and trauma. Postoperative maxillofacial, eye, ear, nose, or throat patients should not be permitted to use the Valsalva maneuver to limit discomforts associated with barotrauma. Occasionally, some individuals experience delayed barotitis media after flight (perhaps 2 to 6 hours later) and may require intervention to relieve their discomfort.

MOTION SICKNESS

Turbulence, noise, and vibration can be both annoying and a fatigue factor for anyone flying—even crew members. For the patients being transported, however, such stressors may lead to additional problems that can complicate their medical condition. For example, a patient who has traveled many times by air without experiencing ill effects may experience motion sickness when transported in a recumbent position. Vibration on rotor aircraft is especially problematic, leading readily to nausea and vomiting, which poses a risk of increasing intraocular and intracranial pressures. Prior to flight, patients should be placed on light diets only, with special attention given to ensuring adequate hydration.

DECREASED HUMIDITY

The aircraft cabin is a very dry environment, with extremely low humidity levels during flight. Contact lenses should be removed from patients, and crew members and other passengers must remember to use supplemental moisture drops to prevent corneal irritation from dry contact lenses. Unconscious patients and those with impaired blinking reflexes must wear eye protection, and artificial tears should be used to maintain moisture on the eye surfaces.

AIR EXPANSION WITHIN BODY CAVITIES

As atmospheric pressures decrease with altitude, gas expands according to Boyle's law. (When the temperature remains constant, a volume of gas is inversely proportional to the pressure surrounding it.) At 10,000 feet, a gas bubble increases to 1.5 times its sea-level volume; at 18,000 feet, twice its volume; and at 25,000 feet, three times its volume. In nonpressurized aircraft, flying above 10,000 feet will cause any air trapped inside a body cavity (e.g., the eustachian tubes, sinuses, teeth, the gastrointestinal tract) to expand. For a noninjured passenger, this air expansion may cause minor discomfort or pain; however, for patients with penetrating injuries, such air expansion could be devastating. For example, in an open head injury, air could enter the cranial cavity and expansion could create considerable compression of intracranial blood vessels and brain tissue. In a penetrating injury of the eye, air might enter the intraocular space along the tract of penetration; when the trapped air expands, it is likely to lead to lens extrusion and the loss of vitreous through the penetration. Severe gas problems in the gastrointestinal tract are unlikely unless the flight level exceeds 25,000 feet.

THERMAL STRESSORS

As ill or injured patients are on-loaded and off-loaded from aircraft, they may experience several changes in temperature. Crew members should be prepared to provide a prewarmed aircraft, warm blankets, and warm fluids for use in flight to prevent unnecessary losses of body heat. This is especially vital for neonates, children, the elderly, and for patients with burns or other traumas who have impairments in thermal regulation. Wind, excessive cold or heat, and rain may compound thermal stress as well, and the flight crew and hospital staff

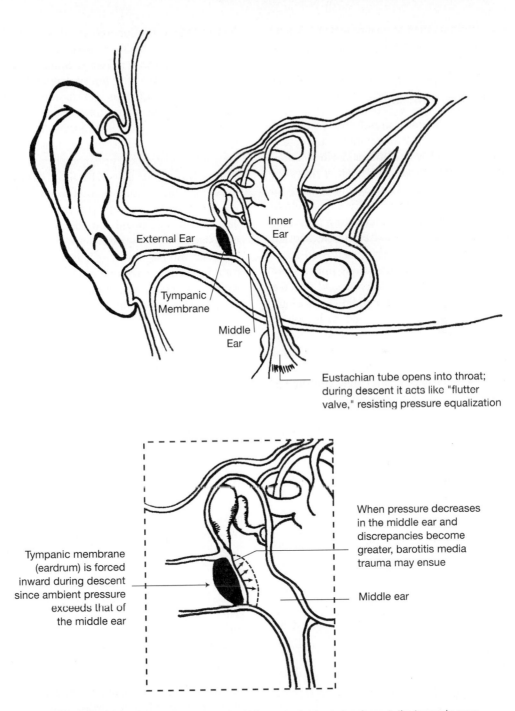

Figure 2–5. Barotitis media. As air within the middle ear contracts during descent, the tympanic membrane is pulled inward. A valsalva maneuver will move air into the middle ear via the eustachian tube and aid in pressure equalization.

must do careful planning to ensure that the patient spends minimal time in inclement conditions.

VIBRATION, NOISE, AND SPACE RESTRICTIONS

The amount of vibration in aircraft may be considerable, especially when helicopters are used. The noise levels may also be intense during certain phases of the flight. It can be difficult at times for the crew to communicate with the patient and with one another, and it may be virtually impossible to reliably accomplish certain monitoring activities such as chest auscultation and electrocardiogram (ECG) monitoring en route. The emergency nurse (EN) must understand the limitations imposed by the cramped space aboard aircraft and by the crew's challenging working conditions. Certain procedures that might be performed with ease in other environments become difficult to accomplish aboard some aircraft. Baseline ECG recordings, fetal heart tones, and other vital signs should be recorded prior to dispatch, and most procedures may need to be delayed until landing, when they can be more easily and safely accomplished. Although some emergency procedures may be required to manage sudden or unexpected in-flight emergencies (e.g., endotracheal intubation, pericardiocentesis, needle thoracostomy), routine procedures should ordinarily be reserved for a more suitable operative environment where more control can be expected.

The patient may be made more comfortable through simple nursing measures that minimize the distress and fatigue associated with vibration and noise. A well-dressed, padded litter is imperative. Limbs should be supported with appropriate immobilizers or props and should be padded to prevent direct contact with stretcher side rails or aircraft surfaces. Earplugs may be employed to reduce environmental noise levels created by vibrations and aircraft operations.

SPECIAL PATIENT CONSIDERATIONS

Neurological Injuries and Postoperative Head/Spinal Cord Patients

As noted previously, both hypoxia and gas expansion within a closed cavity may constitute perils for the neurologically compromised patient. A 4000-feet altitude restriction may be imposed to limit the negative effects that may be associated with reductions in atmospheric pressure. Spinal cord patients in the acute phase after injury may experience respiratory compromise as well as losses of thermal control and vasomotor tone. Hospital personnel and flight nurses must be prepared to provide ventilatory support and to ensure that the patient's body temperature is maintained during the poikilothermic period (see page 98). Since neurologically impaired patients may be both immobile and unable to sense discomfort, special attention needs to be given to alignment, positioning, and support, even during short flights.

The strobe effects produced by lights and rotor blades may precipitate seizures in individuals with a low seizure threshold. Dark glasses and eye shields may be useful to limit photophobia and seizure activity. Certain patients may require sedation.

Pregnant Patients

Pregnant patients, especially after trauma, may deliver at any time, and the flight crew should always be prepared to assist with such emergencies and to manage the neonate.

Cardiovascular Patients

The stresses of flight contribute to a greater myocardial workload and can predispose to dysrhythmias, chest pain, and dyspnea. The diaphragmatic crowding associated with litter positioning may further distress ventilations. All intravenous fluids must be strictly controlled by a mechanical pump to ensure that vibration, motion, and pressure changes do not contribute to precipitant or excessive fluid delivery.

IN-FLIGHT CARE OF TUBES, BAGS, AND DRIPS

Ordinarily, flight nurses prefer that all intravenous fluids be administered using plastic collapsing bags, rather than rigid plastic or glass bottles, which must be vented. Flight nurses should inspect the intravenous solution container, drip set, tubing, and other intravenous accessories to ensure that they pose no special hazards for admitting large amounts of air into the tubing during any rapid descent or decompression emergency that might occur. Most aeromedical flight services have specific criteria for intravenous devices, accessories, and pumps that are considered suitable for use aboard aircraft.

Nasogastric tubes, Salem sump tubes, and other gastrointestinal intubation devices should not be clamped during flight. A latex glove placed over the tubing outlet will collect any escaping air or fluid that might be mobilized by changing gastric or intestinal pressures. If the patient has a colostomy bag, it must be vented with a needle, since considerable gases may accumulate in it while the patient is in the subatmospheric environment.

Nurses must remember that even controlled bleeding sites after injury or surgery may rebleed with the stresses imposed by a higher altitude. All patients should be carefully observed for hemorrhage and developing shock (see Chapter 11).

■ BIBLIOGRAPHY

Lee G. *Flight Nursing: Principles and Practice.* St. Louis, Mo: Mosby-Year Book; 1991.

National Flight Nurses Association Standards Committee (Hepp H, ed.). *Standards of Flight Nursing Practice.* 2nd ed. St. Louis, Mo: Mosby-Year Book; 1995.

USAF School of Aerospace Nursing. Basic flight nursing course curriculum. Brooks AFB, San Antonio, Tex. 1996.

U.S. Department of Transportation. Air medical crew standard curriculum. Washington D.C.: Highway Traffic Safety Administration; 1988.

■ REVIEW: THE EMERGENCY NURSE AND FLIGHT TRANSPORTATION

1. Outline the major advantages, disadvantages, or limitations of aeromedical transportation of emergency patients.

2. Describe the two major types of aircraft used in medical transportation.

3. Explain why helicopters are used for aeromedical transportation in most urban communities.

4. List the recommended safety precautions to be observed when assisting with on-loading or off-loading patients being transported by a rotor aircraft.

5. Explain the effects of altitude on oxygen saturation and identify the types of patients at risk when transported at altitudes exceeding 10,000 feet.

6. Explain the cause of barotitis media, which occurs during aircraft descent. Describe the recommended treatments or interventions to minimize the associated pain and discomfort.

7. List six physiological and psychological stressors encountered during aeromedical flights and describe the nursing measures useful in minimizing the effects of those stressors.

8. Identify the types of patients who cannot be safely transported in aircraft flying at altitudes exceeding 4000 feet.

9. Describe nursing care measures for preparing patients with the following conditions for air transportation:
   a. Elderly woman with spinal cord injury
   b. Woman in third trimester of pregnancy who is experiencing bleeding
   c. Child with 30 to 40 percent of body surface area (BSA) burned
   d. Neonate with respiratory distress
   e. Adult with status epilepticus
   f. Young adult with acute myocardial infarction

10. Identify the special considerations related to equipment/supplies selection (e.g., intravenous accessories, respiratory adjuncts, monitoring instruments) for supporting an aeromedical transportation mission.

Patient Assessment and Vital Signs

3

■ THE NURSING PROCESS AND PATIENT ASSESSMENT

The nursing process begins, whether in the triage area or at the door, with the initial clinical assessment of the patient who presents to the emergency department (ED). Clinical assessment is one of the most important areas of responsibility for emergency nurses (ENs). Since nurses, for the most part, are the first professionals to see patients as they arrive for care, initial nursing assessment frequently exerts a significant influence on the quality of care that follows. Assessment is the systematic collection of data, both objective and subjective, regarding the patient's health-care needs. Objective data is based on the patient's general appearance and physical findings; subjective data is based on the patient's perception of illness, history of illness, and symptoms of illness. A perceptive EN is in a key position to recognize physical manifestations of problems that might otherwise be overlooked in a busy environment. Skilled comprehensive initial assessment is essential to effectively evaluate and triage patients to appropriate areas for treatment; after initial assessment, there must be further evaluation to determine the nursing/working diagnosis and institute the necessary course of action.

Triage areas, as the entry point to emergency care, should provide the requisite space and equipment for adequate assessment, together with the wherewithal to initiate whatever immediate life-support intervention might be needed on the spot.

PATIENT ASSESSMENT AND INFECTION CONTROL IN THE EMERGENCY DEPARTMENT

Of all health-care workers, prehospital and ED personnel are at greatest risk of contracting communicable disease from patients. Every patient brings his or her own personal environment *to* the ED; this presents a vast unknown reservoir of pathogens to the caregivers who wait to attend their needs. In the 1990s, human immunodeficiency virus (HIV), acquired immunodeficiency syndrome (AIDS), hepatitis B virus (HBV), multidrug-resistant tuberculosis (MDR-TB), and an ever-increasing number of sexually transmitted diseases (STDs) are some of the prevalent diseases that have prompted recommendations for more stringent infection-control measures for health-care providers.[1] The ED, therefore, has become a critical area for preventing further transmission of infectious agents such as HBV and HIV; all patients should be presumed to be infectious for HIV and HBV and other blood-borne pathogens. Guidelines for universal precautions (Table 3–1), as outlined by the Centers for Disease Control and Prevention (CDC) should be followed *whenever* there is the chance of being exposed to blood, certain other body fluids (amniotic, pericardial, peritoneal, pleural, synovial, cerebrospinal, semen, vaginal secretions), or any other body fluids contaminated with blood.[1] It remains the EN's individual responsibility to faithfully observe and follow the guidelines for self-protection *and* to prevent further transmission(s); the operative word here is *precaution.* The CDC recommend that each hospi-

TABLE 3–1. UNIVERSAL PRECAUTIONS GUIDELINES

1. All health-care workers (HCWs) should routinely use appropriate barrier precautions to prevent skin and mucous-membrane exposure when contact with blood or other body fluids of any patient is anticipated. Gloves should be worn for touching blood and body fluids, mucous membranes, or nonintact skin of all patients; for handling items or surfaces soiled with blood or body fluids; and for performing venipuncture and other vascular access procedures. Gloves should be changed after contact with each patient. Masks and protective eyewear or face shields should be worn during procedures that are likely to generate droplets of blood or other body fluids to prevent exposure to mucous membranes of the mouth, nose, and eyes. Gowns or aprons should be worn during procedures that are likely to generate splashes of blood or other body fluids.

2. Hands and other skin surfaces should be washed immediately and thoroughly if contaminated with blood or other body fluids. Hands should be washed immediately after gloves are removed.

3. All HCWs should take precautions to prevent injuries caused by needles, scalpels, and other sharp instruments or devices during procedures; when cleaning used instruments; during disposal of used needles; and when handling sharp instruments after procedures. To prevent needlestick injuries, needles should *not* be recapped, purposely bent or broken by hand, removed from disposable syringes, or otherwise manipulated by hand. After they are used, disposable syringes and needles, scalpel blades, and other sharp items should be placed in puncture-resistant containers for disposal; the puncture-resistant containers should be located as close as practical to the use area. Large-bore reusable needles should be placed in puncture-resistant containers for transport to the reprocessing area.

4. Although saliva has not been implicated in human immunodeficiency virus (HIV) transmission, to minimize the need for emergency mouth-to-mouth resuscitation, mouthpieces, resuscitation bags, or other ventilation devices should be available for use in areas in which the need for resuscitation is predictable.

5. HCWs who have exudative lesions or weeping dermatitis should refrain from all direct patient care and from handling patient-care equipment until the condition resolves.

6. Pregnant HCWs are not known to be at greater risk of contracting HIV infection than HCWs who are not pregnant; however, if a HCW develops HIV infection during pregnancy, the infant is at risk of infection resulting from perinatal transmission. Because of this risk, pregnant HCWs should be especially familiar with and strictly adhere to precautions to minimize the risk of HIV transmission.

Centers for Disease Control. Recommendations for prevention of HIV transmissions in health-care settings. MMWR; 36(25):35–125; 1987. (Now called Universal Precautions.)

tal's infection-control committee thoroughly review its entire guidelines and make a decision regarding which of the alternative systems of isolation precautions, beyond universal precautions, to use, having written guidelines quickly available. The triage desk should have a manual at hand for guidance; however, universal precautions in the ED, when carefully followed, are sufficient to protect personnel from the risk of blood-borne pathogens.

In addition to universal precautions, some basic considerations remain as old as nursing itself; they include the following.

Handwashing

Long recognized as *the single most effective means* of preventing the spread of infection, simple handwashing is the most neglected infection-control tool and too often lost in the rush. A research study of handwashing practices in the ED revealed that compliance is low, that nurses wash their hands significantly more often than either staff or resident physicians, but that the average handwashing duration was less than recommended for all groups.[2] For routine patient care, the CDC recommend vigorous, basic soap-and-water handwashing under a stream of water for *at least 10 seconds,* using bar soap, granule soap, soap-filled tissues, or antimicrobial liquid soap. Antimicrobial handwashing agents (any chemical germicide listed with the Environmental Protection Agency [EPA]) are recommended when there are known multiple resistant bacteria present in the environment and before invasive procedures.[1]

Personal Protective Equipment

Routine use of protective barriers in patient care will significantly reduce risk to caregivers. Personal protective equipment (PPE) that will provide the appropriate barriers is required by the Occupational Safety and Health Administration (OSHA) to be available to all health-care workers; gloves, gowns, masks, shoe covers, and protective eyewear are all examples of PPE and should be used to guard against hazards to personal safety. Initial assessment of patients may frequently involve handling soiled clothing, dressings, or body secretions, and the use of disposable procedure gloves, at the very least, cannot be overemphasized as a protective measure. Their use, however, *never* effaces the need for *basic* routine infection control measures such as handwashing between patients and after removing gloves.

Isolation of Contaminated Items

In today's emergency nursing arena, the main concerns are centered around the so-called blood-borne pathogens. OSHA has spelled out standards, requiring compliance in every health-care facility, specifically addressing the availability and use of disposable items and disposal of bloodied and otherwise contaminated linens and care items. All infectious materials require special consideration and handling following OSHA's guidelines. For example, any potentially infectious material must be discarded in closable, leakproof, red or biohazard-labeled bags or containers, and to avoid potentially deadly needle sticks, used needles and syringes are *never* to be recapped or bent but are to be carefully discarded in designated puncture-proof biohazard-labeled containers. Infectious-waste disposal policies, set down by institutions following state and local regulations, must be observed.[3]

Collection of Specimens

Any drawing of blood or obtaining of other specimens at the triage desk or anywhere in the ED should be done following carefully proscribed procedures, using PPE as necessary; specimens should be placed into biohazard-labeled closed containers for transportation to the laboratory.

Housekeeping at the Triage Area

As patients are assessed and processed into the emergency-care system, the triage nurse needs to maintain an ongoing awareness of the constant need to maintain a safe, clean environment. This will help ensure that the ED is not a source of transmission from one patient to another patient or another caregiver. Simple housekeeping practices, such as frequently cleaning surfaces and equipment with a solution of 1 part bleach to 10 parts water (1:10 solution), will support that effort in a cost-effective manner. For surfaces that contact skin *and* have been visibly contaminated with blood or bloody body fluids (e.g., stethoscopes, blood pressure cuffs, splints) an intermediate-level disinfection should be employed. EPA-registered hospital disinfectants that have a label claim for tuberculocidal activity are available; a solution containing at least 500 ppm free available chlorine (approximately ¼ cup of household bleach per gallon of tap water (1:100 solution) is also effective.[1]

APPROACHING ASSESSMENT

Many problems can be and frequently are encountered with the initial patient assessment. The most important component of effective assessment is the nurse who deals with the patient; an EN without empathy will be unable to adequately and accurately assess the patient and establish the initial working rapport that is so vital to allaying apprehension and building trust in the surroundings. Experienced nurses understand that what may appear insignificant to the observer may have marked significance to the one being observed; empathy with objectivity is important here. The nurse is a professional who must demonstrate that distinction by taking what frequently can be unpleasant situations in stride, doing so with patience, understanding, and tact and with the full realization that sick people very often manifest hostility, resentment, and—most frequently—impatience at what is being done (or not done) for them. Often, the challenge in emergency nursing is to receive the hostile patient with a calm, warm, and reassuring manner while proceeding quietly and methodically with observations and easy lines of questioning, exhibiting an interest in the patient's comfort and well-being. When the department is overwhelmed with demands, time constraints often hamper efforts to obtain as complete an initial assessment as one would wish ideally. The interested and perceptive nurse will learn, however, to obtain key information in a limited period of time and couple it with experienced and objective observations.

INITIAL PRIMARY SURVEY

The initial assessment of every patient coming to the ED should be based on a mental checklist of observations addressing the airway, cardiovascular status, and level of consciousness; this rapid primary survey should take no longer than 30 seconds and should identify immediate threats to life. Any necessary intervention(s) will take precedence over further general survey or history-taking, unless they can be carried out simultaneously, which will require a team effort.

Airway

Regardless of what else is happening with the patient, assign priority to the respiratory status. If the patient is unconscious or has known or suspected injuries above the level of the clavicles, the airway must be managed with great caution, using the chin lift or forward jaw thrust. If the patient is conscious, is the breathing free and easy? *If not, initiate steps to clear and maintain the airway and be prepared to support respiration as necessary.* The inability to move air effortlessly tends to translate directly to the level of mental acuity, so it is extremely important to observe and document the patient's respiratory status and any inability to breathe in relaxed fashion, together with the level of mentation. Supplemental high-flow oxygen (O_2) should be used if there are any signs of ventilatory compromise. **Do not** wait until the patient is in respiratory failure. **Do not** withhold oxygen merely to obtain a blood gas on room air. Further assessment and management of airways and respiratory status are discussed in detail in Chapter 10.

Cardiovascular Status

Initial rapid assessment of the cardiovascular status should include the following:

1. Do circulation and perfusion appear adequate? If not, evaluate for cardiopulmonary resuscitation (CPR).
2. Is there profuse bleeding? If so, attempt to control bleeding by direct pressure on arterial pressure points, or as a last resort, tourniquet to prevent exsanguination. Blind clamping of vessels should be avoided.
3. Are there signs of shock or impending shock? If so, initiate shock position (elevate lower extremities) and a large-bore intravenous line immediately.
4. Are there any signs of trauma with the associated possibility of occult bleeding? If so, exercise special care as a precaution against further damage and subsequent bleeding. (Align and immobilize fractures.)

5. Is there chest pain or a "heavy feeling" over the sternal area, a "squeezing feeling in the middle of the chest," uncomfortable dullness in the chest with the feeling radiating up into the jaw or down either arm, or profuse diaphoresis with any of the above? If so, start high-flow nasal O_2 and move immediately to a room equipped for cardiac monitoring and code procedures.

Level of Consciousness

As the initial assessment is conducted, the mental status and level of consciousness (LOC) should be evaluated. Is the patient conscious, responsive, and well oriented as to name, place, and time? If not, detain and question whoever accompanied the patient. Assure that there is adequate oxygenation available; initiate low-flow O_2 by nasal cannula and evaluate further. (Every ED should have written protocols for initiating oxygen administration on an as-needed basis.)

Privacy and Lighting

Two essential elements to an accurate evaluation in this initial assessment are privacy and good light. Without both, the inspection may well fall short of its possible yield; good light is essential to determine abnormalities of color, the state of cleanliness, and the condition of the skin and peripheral circulation. It is hoped, too, that the EN always remains aware of the patient's anxieties and need for privacy, making every effort to provide a position of comfort, a warm blanket, and reassurance while proceeding with the evaluation and checking vital signs. Frequently, it is helpful to imagine yourself as the patient and anticipate the patient's needs accordingly.

THE INITIAL RAPID HEAD-TO-TOE SURVEY OF TRAUMA PATIENTS

Trauma patients should receive immediate assessment on arrival in the ED. A rapid head-to-toe preliminary physical survey affords an initial overview of the patient's condition and indications for life-support interventions. This rapid survey has come to be known in prehospital trauma response and ED trauma care as the "initial 90-second evaluation," and it is essential to rapid assessment and life-saving interventions. It may be done following—or if appropriate, concurrently with—the airway-breathing-circulation–cervical spine (ABCs) checklist of life support, but it should always be done in systematic fashion as follows.

Head

After the evaluation of the ABCs, look at and palpate the skull and posterior ligament of the cervical spine, maintaining immobilization of the cervical spine (if the trauma history is suspicious) until C-spine fracture or displacement has been ruled out by x-ray. Observe for soft-tissue injuries and bone deformities of the scalp and skull.

Ears

Look for cerebrospinal fluid (CSF) or blood. If an otoscope is used, the tympanic membrane should reflect light, move, and not be *blue* (indicating blood behind membrane). Battle sign (bluish discoloration in the mastoid area) usually appears several hours after trauma and is suggestive of basilar skull fracture. Blood or clear fluid draining from the ears *may* be CSF; do *not* stop drainage.

Eyes

Look for gogglelike orbital ecchymosis and swelling around both eyes ("raccoon eyes"), which is indicative of basilar skull or facial fracture; grossly bloody conjunctiva (Pircher sign), indicative of severe abdominal trauma with a surging venacaval injury; or rhinorrhea (CSF-like tears) with higher sugar count than nasal secretions. Carefully palpate facial bones and check for "blowout" fractures of the orbital rim, confirmed if the patient cannot look up; check for contact lenses, PERLA (pupils equal, react to light and accommodation), and extraocular movements (EOMs) by having patient follow your finger with his or her eyes, if conscious and alert.

Mouth

Look for missing teeth and bleeding points or bleeding, edematous tongue, any of which could seriously compromise the airway. With multiple facial fractures, push up on the hard palate to check for an open airway.

Larynx

Injury to the larynx is uncommon, but fracture may occur from steering-wheel impact, wire in-

juries at shoulder height on bikes, or karate chops. Hoarse voice is indicative of such an injury.

Neck Veins

Increased blood volume with jugular vein distension, seen with the patient supine or in semi-Fowler's position, can indicate tension pneumothorax with lateral displacement of the heart, myocardial tamponade, or myocardial contusion (with ST changes on the electrocardiogram [ECG]). Distended neck veins together with systemic hypotension and muffled heart tones comprise Beck's triad, diagnostic of cardiac tamponade.

Chest

Check stability of chest and rib cage with both a sternal press and barrel push against the sides of ribs, toward the center. Feel for subcutaneous emphysema, commonly felt in the neck and subclavicular areas, found concomitantly with pneumothorax and ruptured bronchus (prepare chest tube setup). The diagnostic crunching sound synchronous with the heartbeat heard on auscultation of the precordium is known as Hamman's crunch.

Breath Sounds

Breath sounds should be checked for quality and rate. Are they equal and normal? Are there rales? *Traumatized bronchi secrete more,* and atelectasis will develop if the patient is splinting, or guarding, and not expanding the chest normally.

Abdomen

Again, the patient must be totally undressed and covered with warm blankets. Check breathing patterns; is there a gentle rise and fall of the abdomen, or is the patient splinting? Check for discoloration, marks, wounds, and swelling; *carefully* logroll the patient to examine the back, checking for evidence of retroperitoneal bleeding, exit wounds, and other damage.

Pelvis

Press downward on both of the patient's hips and on the symphysis; even a semiconscious patient will groan if he or she has a broken pubis. Pelvic fracture can cause a great amount of occult bleeding and may easily contribute to severe hypovolemia.

Urinary Meatus

Inspect the urinary meatus for the presence of blood from a sheared urethra, and remember to *document* if is present. *Never* pass a catheter in the presence of frank blood; a urologist should be called.

Rectal Sphincter

Examination of the rectal sphincter is highly useful in pelvic trauma and should always be conducted for the presence of blood at the anus. A flaccid sphincter is highly indicative of spinal cord damage.

Extremities

Check the extremities for pain, deformity, and range of motion (if no deformity is noted) by lightly running both hands downward along both aspects of extremities. Splints in place to align or immobilize fractures should not be removed.

Additional Concerns

If the patient is awake or semiconscious, make every effort as you work to reassure the patient in a positive, calm tone of voice and to explain, as you go, what you are doing. This helps not only reassure the traumatized patient who has just undergone a personal disaster but also serves as a means of evaluating the LOC according to the response received.

If at all possible, the same EN should maintain constant observation of the patient throughout his or her stay in the ED, so that while one obvious injury is being taken care of, a more critical one is not overlooked. Remember that this nurse may have been the one constant in the patient's environment, monitoring the flow of baseline observations, and may well be the first person to notice any significant change in the patient's LOC and general status.

GENERAL ASSESSMENT

In the absence of life-threatening priorities, a general assessment should be carried out in a systematic fashion, with the following specific areas included in the nurse's general survey of the patient.

General State of Consciousness

Do not confuse the LOC with patient apprehension or a language barrier. Be very certain that your patient can *hear* you. Use appropriate questions as necessary to elicit response: "Tell me your name. Where are you? What is the date/time of day/season?"

Restlessness

Is the patient developing hypoxemia and restlessness?

Abnormalities of Color

Is there cyanosis (hypoxia), jaundice (liver or gallbladder involvement), pallor (anemia, lung disease), or redness (elevated temperature, hyperemia)?

Degree of Cooperation

Has the patient been brought to the ED against his or her will? Is the patient overly cooperative, perhaps looking for a disability evaluation or drugs? (However, avoid at all cost the error of making a hasty value judgment with such patients.) Is the patient looking for relief of truly distressing symptoms?

Personal Habits

Observe the state of cleanliness and any apparent deterioration in grooming; look especially for any variation from the apparent norm. For example, note anything such as a well-clothed but poorly groomed man or a woman who has obvious neglected personal hygiene. Observe any clothing unevenly buttoned, donned inside out or in extremely poor repair.

State of Nutrition

Note obesity or intense thinness, which may indicate disease or poor nutrition that could compound presenting problems.

Signs of Chronic Illness

Look for subtle changes such as a dull, waxy appearance to the face and skin, and poor tissue turgor, which may indicate chronic illness.

Body Size and Shape

Note if the patient is grossly larger or smaller than normal. Body size and proportion may be indicative of co-existing disease processes.

Posture

Circulatory disease may cause a struggle for breath when the patient is sitting propped up or is straining forward. Local muscular injuries or pain may cause the patient to take a position that will guard against the pain or reduce its intensity. For example, watch for patients with fractured ribs trying to breathe normally.

Gait

An abnormal gait may be a manifestation of central nervous system (CNS) involvement. Foot drag, shuffle, limp, scissors gait, steppage gait (raising feet unusually high and planting them down), and small-steps gait may be indicative signs of diagnostic value.

Speech

It is important to note how the patient says what he or she says. For example, slurred speech, aphasia, gestures, or nods may indicate vocal cord paralysis or CNS damage.

Odors

Check for the following odors:

- *Sputum:* Foul sputum emanates from a lung abscess or bronchiectasis.
- *Feces:* A particularly foul smell is common in pancreatic insufficiency.
- *Pus:* A nauseatingly sweet odor is a strong indication of a pocket of gas gangrene.
- *Emesis:* The presence of an almond odor may indicate cyanide poisoning.

Skin Lesions

Local skin changes should be noted and described accurately:

- *Papule:* A small, circumscribed, superficial, solid elevation of the skin (less than 0.5 cm in diameter)
- *Tumor:* A morbid enlarged and raised area of skin usually greater than 2.5 cm in diameter
- *Bulla:* A large vesicle usually 2 cm or more in diameter

Local infection or trauma will often change primary lesions, as described above, into scale; exudate of serum, blood, or pus (which dries and forms a scab); ulcers; hyperpigmentation along the margin of the lesion; and signs of excoriation with varying degrees of healing. It is important to note

and *document* the presence of lesions and exudate and to exercise *precautionary techniques* from the outset (especially the use of gloves for any direct contact) to minimize the risk of exposure to and prevent transmission of HIV and HBV.[1]

Edema

Check for the presence and character of edema— localized, generalized, dependent, pitting, bilateral or unilateral. Bilateral, dependent pitting edema is usually cardiogenic; unilateral edema should suggest occlusion of a deep vessel and, rather than pitting, may be "brawny" in nature. The evaluation of pitting edema is subjective, but generally the degree of pitting is graded on a scale of 1+ to 4+ ; 1+ results from light fingertip pressure on the skin and resolves rapidly, while 4+ is a deep depression that disappears slowly, with gradations assigned accordingly.[4]

Summary

Beyond these specific areas of observation, the physical examination will vary with the needs of the patient and the indicated area(s) of assessment. Generally, the review of systems is the responsibility of the physician; however, the nurse would do well to examine and evaluate as a learning tool, comparing findings with those of the physician. If the EN's observations are of a sick but ambulatory patient, a calm, self-assured, helpful manner will help establish an atmosphere of security. If the patient is acutely ill in the ED or the victim of violent trauma, the EN must remain calm and deliberately proceed with observations despite the surrounding confusion. Even acutely ill patients sense the presence of a calm and deliberate person and may frequently respond by relaxing significantly.

■ VITAL SIGNS

Vital signs (VS) are those signs necessary to or pertaining to life and represent essential baseline information in the overall evaluation of any patient; they routinely include temperature, pulse rate, respiratory rate, and blood pressure (BP). It is good practice, however, to include the LOC on all patients to provide complete baseline information on arrival.

Although many nurses find it annoying to obtain complete VS on every patient, there are many good reasons for making this a firm department policy. Not infrequently, the patient is running a low-grade temperature, unaware of a chronic focus of infection; or the patient's blood pressure far exceeds normal bounds and should be further evaluated; or obscure disease processes that would otherwise be missed can be recognized on the basis of VS inconsistent with other findings. It may take just a moment more to obtain complete VS, but the patient deserves a full evaluation.

Frequently, deterioration or marked improvement in the patient's condition may take place during the time spent in the ED, but this cannot be accurately confirmed unless initial baseline data have been obtained and documented on the ED record. Although the triage nurse's assessment will be based on a single set of values, serial vital signs taken and recorded are of major value in providing a clear picture of the clinical trend taking place with the ill or severely injured patient.

Again, remember that where medical audit and the courtroom are concerned, *VS not documented are VS not taken.* Vital signs written on scratch paper in someone's pocket are of no use to the physician, other nurses, or the patient and *must* be written on the chart or flow sheet and made available to other caregivers before the information is somehow irretrievably lost.

RESPIRATIONS

In the acutely ill patient, the *first* VS to monitor is the respiration. If respiration is imperceptible, impaired, or absent, all else must wait until effective respiration has been reestablished.

Assessment of respiration includes rate, depth, and pattern; counting the respirations while still feeling the patient's radial pulse usually requires a nonconversant period and will also decrease the possibility of the patient's consciously trying to control breathing. Respiratory rates should be assessed with an eye to respiratory compromise: cyanosis, restlessness, orthopnea, dyspnea, abnormal breath sounds, and irregularity.

Normally, respiratory rates are affected by age (e.g., normal rates for infants are 30 to 60 breaths per minute; for children, 20 to 30; and for adults, 12 to 20). Exercise, smoking, emotional status, and medications all may exert an effect. Initial observations should include chest movement, noting depth of respiratory inspiration; the equality and degree of chest wall expansion, divulged by palpation; and any paradoxical motion of the chest in trauma patients.

In determining respiratory rate, the number of breaths per minute is counted, again noting character and depth. Respirations may be described as regular, irregular, rapid, slow, shallow, deep, labored, easy, sighing, stertorous (like snoring), or barely perceptible.

The respiratory *pattern* may be highly indicative of the problem at hand. Dyspnea, Kussmaul breathing, orthopnea, or any other deviation from normal, relaxed respiration may be the first index as to the patient's real problem. Alterations in breathing patterns are discussed further in Chapter 9.

TEMPERATURE

The hypothalamus regulates and maintains normal core temperature within 1° of 98.6°F, triggering vasodilation when heat reduction is necessary and vasoconstriction, increased metabolic rate, and shivering when heat production is necessary.

Although obtaining the patient's temperature may be temporarily deferred in some situations, temperature measurement is an essential part of overall assessment. Severe fluctuations in body temperature may seriously compromise the body's ability to maintain equilibrium and can be life-threatening.

In the United States, customary practice has been recording temperature in degrees of Fahrenheit (F), but in recent years many medical-care facilities and schools have converted to degrees Celsius (C). Equivalents are given below with formulas for conversion:

Example: 98.6°F = 37°C

To convert degrees Fahrenheit to degrees Celsius, subtract 32 from the temperature in Fahrenheit, and then multiply by $\frac{5}{9}$:

$$C = F - 32 \times \tfrac{5}{9}$$

To convert degrees Celsius to degrees Fahrenheit, multiply by $\frac{9}{5}$, and then add 32:

$$F = C \times \tfrac{9}{5} + 32$$

Temperature can be accurately measured by means of a glass thermometer or electronic devices. If use of a glass thermometer seems unsafe, or if extreme temperatures, as in hyperpyrexia or hypothermia, must be monitored, a temperature probe with thermocouple or thermistor *should* be available for use. Not all ERs are so fully equipped, however.

Despite 1-minute results noted in the directions for using glass thermometers, a true reading may require as long as 5 to 8 minutes. If using a glass thermometer, always check the thermometer before use to be certain the mercury column is below 98.6°F. (Many of the disposable thermometers in recent use have been shown to be of questionable accuracy; temperatures should be rechecked with a glass thermometer or tympanic membrane thermometer (TMT) whenever the clinical picture disagrees with the reading obtained by a disposable thermometer.) Glass thermometers, when used, require more maintenance and careful sterilization to meet infection control standards.

The TMT, now in wide use, is a battery-operated electronic unit that gathers the infrared energy emitted by the tympanic membrane, digitalizes the signal through its computerized processor, and presents the temperature reading on a liquid crystal display screen in less than 2 seconds. The tympanic membrane shares the blood supply that reaches the hypothalamus, the brain's thermoregulatory control, and assesses the body temperature by measuring the temperature of the blood flowing through it. There is a high degree of accuracy with use of the TMT, it is easy to use and gives fast (1 to 2 seconds) results, and the disposable tip decreases exposure of the nurse to infectious diseases transmitted by rectal or oral mucous-membrane contact.

Diurnal Variation

Normal body core temperature is somewhere slightly above 98°F and may normally rise to 99° to 99.5°F. Temperature is usually the lowest in the morning before one arises and is referred to as the basal temperature. As the day's activity progresses, the temperature will rise; this is called the diurnal variation. Febrile illness tends to produce the greatest temperature elevation in the afternoon and evening, although temperature may drop somewhat in the evening. Ovulation and certain other body functions produce slight but consistent temperature elevations.

Febrile (with fever) range would be an oral or tympanic reading above 98.6°F (some clinicians consider 99.5°F to be the upper limit of normal core body temperature), a rectal temperature above 100.5°F (1° higher than an oral reading), or an axillary temperature of 97.5°F (at least 1° lower than an oral reading). Axillary readings are the least accurate and should be relied upon only if there are *no* other appropriate alternatives to measure body heat.

Increased Heat Production by the Body

Body heat is produced by chemical reactions in metabolism at the cellular level, and a temperature gradient exists between the higher temperature of internal organs (core temperature) and the lower temperature on the skin surface. Causes of increased temperature are either an impaired heat loss or an increased heat production. Impaired heat loss is seen in congestive heart failure, heat stroke (from failure of the temperature-regulating mechanism in the brain), in the face of a climate temperature higher than that of the body, and in the congenital absence of sweat glands when the weather is moderately hot. Some causes of increased heat production include exercise, thyrotoxicosis, systemic infections, localized infection with accumulation of pus, fractured bones, soft-tissue injury from trauma, myocardial infarction, thrombophlebitis, and some hematologic disorders such as leukemia and lymphoma.

Signs of Fever

The following are signs of fever:

- Skin may or may not be warm and flushed. Skin temperature may be normal while internal temperature (core temperature) is elevated.
- Tachycardia is *usually* present (heart rate of 100 bpm or over).
- Chills are a manifestation of thermostatic control operation at a higher level (hypothalamus), with a rapid transition from normal to higher temperature as shivering (from involuntary muscle contractions) produces more heat to raise the temperature.
- Night sweats, with elevated temperature during the night, may be indicative of a

problem, but they are also seen in debilitated patients (tuberculosis, as a prime example) and in healthy children.

Patients with elevated temperatures are more comfortable in a warm room, but excess clothing should be removed to allow the skin to "breathe off" excess body heat. Chilling should be avoided.

PULSE RATE

Pulse rate is the reflection of the force and rate of blood being ejected from the left ventricle during systole. Each beat or pulse wave felt is a reflection of the heart's stroke volume (SV). That SV per heartbeat multiplied by the heart rate (HR) per minute determines cardiac output (CO) per minute:

$$SV \times HR = CO$$

Since an increased heart rate is the body's most effective compensation for a falling cardiac output, a significantly increased pulse rate should be an alerting sign in the face of shock or trauma.

In taking VS, one most frequently palpates the radial artery for heart rate. The presence or absence of a pulse, its rate, and its quality must be determined; any abnormalities are then evaluated and noted. The adult heart rate normally varies between 60 and 80 bpm at rest. Pulse rates below 60 bpm are classified as *bradycardias,* although well-conditioned athletes may exhibit a normal heart rate of 60 bpm or less, even in the face of trauma or stress. Slowing of the pulse or heart rate is also seen in heart block or as the third component of Cushing's triad in the patient with severe head injury. Pulse rates over 100 bpm are classified as *tachycardias,* although apprehension alone may easily reflect in a pulse rate well above the norm.

Patterns and Characteristics

The character of the pulse may be small and barely palpable (thready) or full and bounding. Any deviation from a regular pulse rate of good quality should be documented accordingly, and the physician should be advised. The following are some abnormal pulse patterns that may occasionally be recognized:

- *Water hammer pulse* (Corrigan's pulse) is a jerky pulse with a full expansion followed by a sudden collapse, occurring in aortic regurgitation.
- *Small, late pulse* (almost the opposite of water hammer pulse) is a small, hard pulse that rises and falls slowly. It is also described by the Latin words *parvus et tardus,* meaning "little and late."
- *Thready pulse* is usually so very rapid and fine that it is scarcely perceptible.
- *Pulsus alternans* is the term applied to a variation in the strength of the regular pulse contractions. Every other contraction is weak and is caused by a failing myocardium that responds regularly to the sinus-initiated impulses but does not contract with equal strength to each impulse. Some of the myocardial fibers do not recover rapidly enough after a contraction to respond to the next pulse. The degree of pulsus alternans will vary with the patient's clinical condition and will usually occur if the patient complains of dyspnea; it will be present if there is cardiac enlargement.

Typically, patients are assessed by counting and evaluating a radial pulse, since the site is so easily accessible. However, auscultation of the apical pulse for accuracy in critical or traumatized patients should be a regular practice, and peripheral pulse points other than radial should be assessed as appropriate (e.g., pedal pulses bilaterally in trauma and shock, femoral and carotid arterial points in code situations).

Pedal Pulses

The dorsalis pedis pulse may be obtained on the dorsum of the foot, usually just lateral to the extensor tendon of the great toe, by placing the fingers lightly so as not to obliterate the comparatively fragile pulse (Fig. 3–1). The posterior tibial pulse may be obtained on palpation by curving the fingers posteriorly and slightly below the malleolus of the ankle on the soft tissue (Fig. 3–2). Both of these pedal pulses may be congenitally absent and may be difficult to palpate at best. Absence of the pulses should be documented and evaluated further, especially in situations of hemodynamic instability and pelvic or lower-extremity trauma.

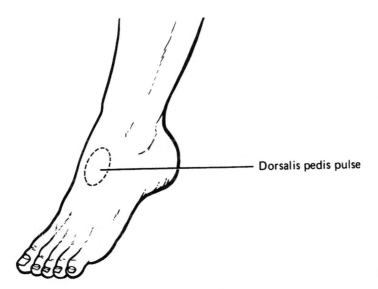

Figure 3–1. Dorsalis pedis pulse.

Evaluation of Peripheral Pulses

Peripheral pulses, whether radial or pedal, should be assessed bilaterally whenever possible, noting the rate, quality, and bilateral equality. Pulses are rated on a scale of 0 to 4+, with 0 meaning absent pulse; 1+, palpable; 2+, normal or average; 3+, full; and 4+, full and bounding (may even occasionally be visible). Temporal, carotid, brachial, radial, femoral, and popliteal pulses should all test 2+ bilaterally. The posterior tibial and dorsalis pedis should test 1+ bilaterally. When distal pulses require frequent checking and evaluation, mark the pulse location with a gentian violet-, or Betadine-tipped applicator, or a skin marking pen.

BLOOD PRESSURE

BP readings reflect (1) the force of ventricular contraction exerted on the aorta during systole and (2) the lowest pressure reached during ventricular diastole. The pulse pressure is the difference between systolic and diastolic pressure and is an important hemodynamic indicator in clinical evaluations.

Normal Ranges of Blood Pressure

Normal BP in adults ranges from 100/60 to 140/90 and represents the pulse pressure of the blood within the systemic arterial system during both

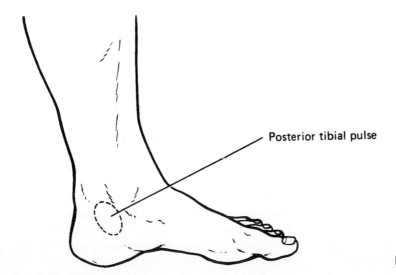

Figure 3–2. Posterior tibial pulse.

systole and diastole. The systolic reading is generally "mercurial" in nature, with rapid fluctuations possible in response to sympathetic nervous system stimulation. A diastolic pressure *consistently* greater than 95 mm Hg, however, is considered borderline hypertensive and merits further evaluation. Normal limits of systolic pressure in children are given in Table 3–2.

Remember that both the emotional and physical status of the patient have an obvious and very direct effect on the BP reading, that BP is very labile (unstable), and that it may vary from moment to moment. Anxiety, anger, pain, frustration, and sudden noises may produce systolic pressure changes of 10 to 14 mm Hg. If possible, let the patient rest a bit before a pressure reading, and if a pressure reading must be double-checked, try to allay the patient's apprehension by explaining that you are trying to get an average reading.

The Sounds of Korotkoff

A properly taken and accurately recorded BP provides one of the most important areas of baseline information about an acutely ill patient. The taking of a BP consists of listening for the onset and disappearance of arterial sounds, known as the sounds of Korotkoff, below the cuff. These sounds change in intensity and character during the procedure, and the changes provide important information. The sounds heard over an artery below a BP cuff, which is being deflated, consist of a tapping sound and a murmur. On the basis of the character of the tapping sound and the presence or absence of the murmur, the sounds have been divided into five phases[5]:

- *First phase:* The onset of the tapping sound, which gradually increases in pitch and intensity
- *Second phase:* A murmur that follows the tap
- *Third phase:* The tapping sound alone, which is loud and high-pitched
- *Fourth phase:* The tap suddenly becomes lower pitched and less intense (muffled)
- *Fifth phase:* The disappearance of sound

The first spurt of blood that gets through the artery beneath the cuff and distends the wall of the artery reflects the systolic pressure, which is read in millimeters of mercury on the manometer by a needle indicator on the aneroid manometer. The beginning of the fourth phase, or muffling, should be the event related to the occurrence of diastolic pressure. The fifth phase, silence, is closer to the true diastolic pressure, but determination of both of these phases depends greatly on technique, level of noise in the room, and ability to recognize the changes. Also, in some persons there may be no fourth or fifth phase, and this may have special significance; therefore, it is recommended that the onset of both the fourth and fifth phases be recorded as accurately as possible.

Technique

The technique used in monitoring BP can influence the quality of the sounds heard; it is important to understand the mechanism by which the sounds are produced. The tapping sound is produced by the sudden distension of the walls of the collapsed artery as the peak of the pulse wave exceeds the cuff pressure and the blood suddenly enters the collapsed artery. The murmur is produced by the flow of blood from the narrowed artery underneath the cuff into the wider artery distal to the cuff. During a BP determination, the forearm and hand are cut off from the general circulation by the inflated cuff. With the low pressure in the forearm, the tap is louder and the murmur longer and louder.

While the cuff is being inflated, the venous return is cut off first. If inflation is slow, blood is trapped in the forearm with each beat; therefore, rapid inflation of the cuff will decrease the amount of blood in the forearm and louder sounds will be obtained. A second procedure for decreasing the amount of blood in the forearm is to raise the arm and forearm for several seconds so that the venous blood drains out. The cuff is then inflated while the arm is elevated. A third technique is to instruct the patient to open and close the fist rapidly 8 to 10

TABLE 3–2. NORMAL LIMITS OF SYSTOLIC PRESSURE IN CHILDREN

Age	Normal Systolic Pressure
Birth to 3 months	60–80 mm
3 months to 1 year	80–100 mm
1–12 years	Add 2 mm for every year +100

times after the cuff is inflated above the systolic level. (A pressure 20 to 30 mm higher than needed to block the radial pulse should be obtained.) This produces an increase in the blood-holding capacity of the vessels in the forearm and lowers the BP in the forearm.

During inflation, *do not stop* between systolic and diastolic pressure readings and then reinflate to take another systolic reading; this permits the forearm to fill with blood, affecting the intensity and changes in the sounds.

Application of the cuff is important for an accurate result. A fully deflated cuff is applied evenly and snugly around the arm, with the lower edge 1 to 2 in. above the antecubital space, centered over the artery, anteriorly and medially over the arm. If the cuff is not over the artery, the reading will be too high; if the cuff is too loose, it reduces the effective width, reflected in too high a reading. The stethoscope is placed over the brachial artery below the cuff, avoiding too much pressure, which could compress the artery and produce a false murmur.

Cuff Size

Cuff width is important, because the pressure of the cuff is best transmitted to the tissues at the center of the cuff and fades off toward the edge. Cuff sizes are as follows:

- *Adult cuff:* This is 12 cm wide × 23 cm long (or 5 × 9 in.). This cuff must be used on neither obese persons, because it may give a high reading, nor on children, because it may give a low reading. Special wider, longer cuffs are required for larger-than-average sized arms.
- *Children's cuff:* A narrow cuff is necessary: a 5-cm (2-in.)-wide cuff for children under 5 years of age, a 7-cm (2.75-in.)-wide cuff for those 5 to 8 years old; a 9.5-cm (3.5-in.)-wide cuff for those 8 to 14 years old, and a standard (adult) cuff for those 14 years and over.

Torn cuffs, torn cuff stitching, and improper cuff sizes can all contribute to significant measurement errors. Faulty or incorrect equipment should be taken out of service.

Manometers

Mercury manometers should be checked at intervals to be sure that with no pressure applied, the mercury meniscus (the arc of the crescent-shaped structure appearing at the surface of the mercury column) is at the zero mark. Aneroid manometers (dial and indicator needle) should be handled with care in order to maintain their ability to give accurate readings; frequent dropping and jarring can affect their calibration significantly. If in doubt about an initial reading, recheck BP with another instrument. All personnel should be carefully instructed on the correct care of manometers in order to prolong their accuracy.

Auscultatory Gap

An auscultatory gap is the absence of the second phase (murmur), which results in a silent period between the first and third phases. This occurs when the cuff is inflated above the third phase but *not* above the first phase (Fig. 3–3). The pulse pressure (the difference between the systolic and diastolic pressures; usually about one third of the systolic pressure) is low as a result. When this is noted, the procedure should be repeated with the cuff inflated to 200 mm Hg or to 300 mm above the disappearance of the radial pulse. An auscultatory gap is likely to occur if inflation is slow (which also gives a false reading).

Warning Signs for Impending Shock

A *decrease* in the intensity of the tap and murmur in a patient who had good sounds previously is a possible indication of a diminishing cardiac output. This, coupled with a *narrowing pulse pressure,* is an ominous sign of a lowering cardiac output due to cardiac failure, shock (hypovolemic), or pulmonary embolus. As one of the body's most immediate compensatory mechanisms, tachycardia occurs rapidly, and when coupled with these other clinical findings, it should be recognized as an *early* warning sign of hypovolemia even before hypotension becomes fully apparent in the patient who is a candidate for shock.

Orthostatic Vital Signs

With a narrowing pulse pressure, tachycardia, and the possibility of significant fluid loss, postural (orthostatic) VS are an effective evaluation tool.

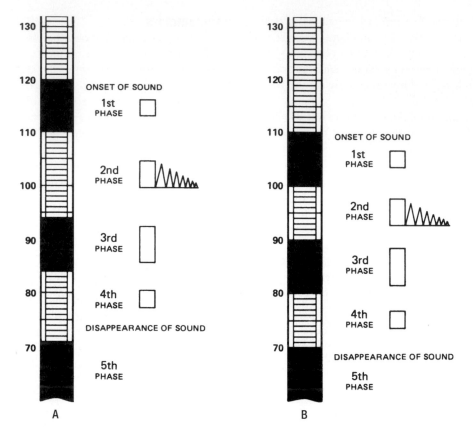

Figure 3–3. Five phases of sound in obtaining blood pressure. **A.** Normal blood pressure. The nature of the tap and murmur in the five phases is illustrated. The height of the tap indicates its intensity. The murmur is illustrated by a series of spikes whose height indicates intensity and length indicates duration. **B.** The blood pressure in this patient would be recorded as 100 (beginning of first phase)/70 (beginning of the fifth phase) (*from Ravin*[5]).

When in doubt, orthostatics should be taken; frequently, they can lead to early recognition of the volume-depleted patient.

If postural variations in BP and pulse rate are indicated and can be obtained without jeopardy to the patient, they should be checked and recorded. Obtain a BP reading and pulse rate with the patient supine and *record;* with minimal delay, sit the patient up and repeat the BP and pulse rate measurements and *record.* A decrease of 20 mm Hg or more in systolic or diastolic pressure or an increase in pulse rate of 20 bpm or more is considered positive, and if significant changes are elicited during the second phase of evaluation, do not jeopardize the patient's hemodynamic status further by standing the patient up for a third evaluation (Fig. 3–4).

LEVEL OF CONSCIOUSNESS

When the LOC is being evaluated, it is best to take a comprehensive overall look and determine whether the patient is alert, drowsy, lethargic, or unresponsive—and *document.* Determine whether the patient is oriented to time and place, and if so, whether he or she is confused in other areas. If the patient appears alert and oriented, this too should be noted, and any behavioral deviation from this norm should be recorded in brief but descriptive terms as an important component of the nursing assessment.

If there is any witnessed deterioration in the LOC, the Glasgow Coma Scale (GCS) should be used to assess pupil state, eye opening, and verbal and motor responses (Table 3–3).

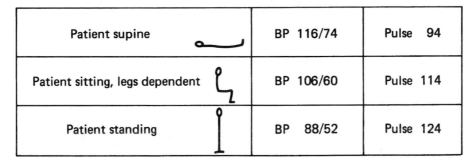

Patient supine	BP 116/74	Pulse 94
Patient sitting, legs dependent	BP 106/60	Pulse 114
Patient standing	BP 88/52	Pulse 124

Figure 3–4. Orthostatic vital signs. An example of recording significant changes in pulse and blood pressure that may occur with postural variations in the volume-depleted patient.

■ EVALUATION OF PAIN

Pain is a sensation of hurting or strong discomfort in some part of the body caused by injury, disease, or functional disorder; it is a basically unpleasant sensation and is both a sensory and perceptual experience. Pain, to one extent or another, is the reason most patients seek medical help, and many look to the nurse for pain relief. ENs *must* be concerned with the careful and objective evaluation of pain and the most effective means of alleviating that pain whenever possible.

The quality and intensity of pain are influenced by a history of pain in childhood, the meaning of pain to that person, and the state of mind as related to the degree of anxiety and the degree of pain. One characteristic of pain is that it enforces increased preoccupation with the body—an important concept of which the EN should be aware. The healthy person generally takes pain-free existence for granted as a way of life. Conversely, when illness strikes and pain becomes a constant companion, that person's body becomes the center of his or her attention.

In evaluating the patient with severe abdominal pain, it is necessary to recognize pain patterns: with irritation of the peritoneum, the patient will lie *very* still; with colic, the patient won't hold still; and with pelvic inflammatory disease (PID), a woman will exhibit a bent posture to protect the

TABLE 3–3. GLASGOW COMA SCALE

Eyes:	Open	Spontaneously	4
		To verbal command	3
		To pain	2
	No response		1
Best motor response:	To verbal command	Obeys	6
	To painful stimulus[a]	Localizes pain	5
		Flexion—withdrawal	4
		Flexion—abnormal (decorticate rigidity)	3
		Extension (decerebrate rigidity)	2
	No response		1
Best verbal response[b]		Oriented and converses	5
		Disoriented and converses	4
		Inappropriate words	3
		Incomprehensible sounds	2
	No response		1
Total			3–15

[a]Apply knuckles to sternum; observe arms.
[b]Arouse patient with painful stimulus if necessary.

irritated peritoneum as she moves. There are several situations recognizable as catastrophic when they cause an immediate stop in voluntary physical activity; ruptured ectopic pregnancy, perforated peptic ulcer, pancreatitis, and ruptured abdominal aneurysm are significant examples.

BASIC NURSING GUIDELINES

Pain is a subjective experience; there are no means of obtaining "blood levels" for pain, nor is there a "thermometer" to gauge pain intensity. ENs must accept the description of pain as the patient gives it; pain is real to the person experiencing it and requires evaluation in the context of other presenting signs and symptoms.

Frequently, a significant degree of pain relief may be obtained through use of such basic nursing measures as positioning the patient comfortably, using supporting bolsters and pillows, applying heat or cold (hypothermia is frequently used to control intractable pain), and even by listening attentively to the patient and demonstrating an interest in the problem. Any nursing measures available that will help the patient to relax and that will reduce anxiety and the sense of helplessness will aid in pain reduction. Continual assessment of the patient's pain experience is important, noting any changes in character, location, or intensity, as well as the modalities of treatment to which the pain responds. EDs are well known for their inadequate treatment of severe pain; when analgesia is ordered, it should be given *as ordered* and without equivocation by the nurse, unless, of course, the nurse has reason to question the safety of the drug or the dosage ordered.

Pain control and conscious sedation are discussed in detail in Chapter 7; detailed pain assessment is discussed in Chapter 5 as part of the nursing history.

PAIN PATTERNS IN ASSESSMENT

A key to effective pain assessment is careful observation of the patient both in motion *and* at rest; emerging pain patterns in injury tend to manifest somewhat differently than those resulting from disease processes.

Knowledge of activity patterns peculiar to inflammatory, colic, and catastrophic disease processes is an essential tool in nursing assessment. Generally, the patterns are as follows:

- *Acute inflammatory:* The patient moves *very* little and *very* carefully, as in peritoneal irritation and PID, tends to lie *very* still, and if required to walk, does so with a bent-over shuffle, protecting the extremely tender visceral and parietal peritoneum.
- *Colic:* A spasm of hollow organ muscular walls generates severe episodic pain and usually results in extreme restlessness and tossing; the patient has difficulty lying quietly.
- *Catastrophic:* All voluntary activity stops with any sudden onset of continuous, severe pain; there is a silent, boardlike abdomen, extreme apprehension, and perhaps hemoconcentration with incipient shock.

STRUCTURAL PAIN PATTERNS OF ORGANS

Additional generalized pain patterns for specific organs are important to understand. Remember that both solid and hollow organs lie in the upper abdominal cavity, while organs lying in the lower abdomen are *all* hollow, except the ovaries. Although the following is perhaps a simplistic description, remember in your assessments that solid organs have steady, constant pain, while hollow organs have colicky pain. Some patterns that should be watched for include the following:

- *Bowel (stomach and small bowel):* Crampy, sharp pain, with 2- to 3-minute repeat cycles; large bowel is slow and pain-free in most cases.
- *Capsulated organs (liver, kidney, ovary):* Sharp, steady pain *without* relation to body functions.
- *Muscle-walled cavities (uterus, bladder, gallbladder):* Sharp, cramping pain related to function.
- *Arteries:* Severe, steady pain with very sharp accentuations.
- *Blood in abdominal cavity:* Dull awareness, then sharp, steady pain.
- *Myocardium:* All pain is referred; dull, heavy ache is usual and worsens with activity.

• *Paired organs:* Usually unilateral pain, but may be bilateral.
• *Referred pain:* Almost *never* referred across the midline.

ORGAN-SYSTEM PAIN PATTERNS

Lactic Acidosis

Lactic acidosis can occur in the diabetes mellitus patient on phenformin. There is a sudden onset of sharp, steady, diffuse pain; palpation shows rebound tenderness with absent or hypoactive bowel sounds.

Appendicitis and Terminal Ileitis

In appendicitis and terminal ileitis, there may be diffuse, dull pain in the umbilical area followed later with sharp, crampy right lower quadrant (RLQ) pain.

Acute Myocardial Infarction

Acute myocardial infarction may be indicated by heavy, dull pain, frequently vaguely localized to the epigastrium or left upper quadrant (LUQ).

Lower-Lobe Pneumonitis

Pneumonitis in the lower lung lobe can produce steady, full to sharp pain in the LUQ, frequently accentuated on deep inspiration.

Acute Cholecystitis

Acute cholecystitis generally causes a diffuse, dull, slow onset of epigastric pain that develops into sharp right upper quadrant (RUQ) pain on palpation. There may be RUQ rebound tenderness, usually pain in the right scapular area (referred pain, steady and severe, known as a Kehr sign).

Rupturing Aortic Aneurysm

A rupturing aortic aneurysm may produce sudden, sharp lower-quadrant pain, testicular pain (referred), palpation tenderness in the area of maximum pain, and hypoactive or absent bowel sounds.

Ectopic Tubal Pregnancy Rupture

When an ectopic tubal pregnancy ruptures, there is a rather sudden, sharp, steady pain in the lower quadrant (lateralized); usually, bowel sounds are normal or hypoactive. There is deep palpation tenderness over the area of maximum tenderness and pain at the base of the neck and scapular area (again, referred pain, from diaphragmatic irritation due to free blood in the abdomen).

Ileal or Jejunal Obstruction

Ileal or jejunal obstruction may cause sudden and diffuse dull to sharp pain in the umbilical area, then crampy (colicky) sharp pains every 2 to 3 minutes; between cramps, pain is still present but dull and steady.

Renoureteral Lithiasis

Renoureteral lithiasis may produce sudden and severe sharp, colicky lumbar (costovertebral angle) pain, moving around the flanks toward the inguinal area; steady testicular pain is usually present in male patients.

ANXIETY

The severity of pain is affected by distraction and is increased with anxiety. Anxiety is frequently associated with three states of mind that threaten the self-image: a sense of helplessness (which accompanies the patient into the hospital environment and is most prevalent in men), a sense of isolation (time spent in intensive care or critical care units), and insecurity (accentuated sharply when the patient's lifestyle is in jeopardy and the prognosis is uncertain). For the EN to effectively allay a patient's anxiety, he or she must be aware that the patient is indeed anxious. Then the patient is helped to recognize that anxiety, to gain an insight into the anxiety, and to cope with whatever threat he or she is facing, *one step at a time.* The patient's knowledge of pain should be assessed, because anxiety increases with ignorance. The attitudes of others toward the patient should be assessed, because loss of control by family and friends will increase the patient's anxiety. The family especially should be reassured in this regard.

PAIN MANAGEMENT

A great deal can be accomplished toward allaying anxiety by establishing rapport with the patient by the following methods:

• Using touch and eye contact
• Calling the patient by his or her first name (after requesting permission to do so)

- Allowing the patient to participate in arranging his or her own comfort
- Not bargaining with the patient; give medication *as ordered*
- Reassuring the patient about the doctor's availability
- Reassuring the patient that his or her responses are appropriate (reinforcement)
- Teaching how to treat pain other than with medication
- Providing sensory input in the form of distractions
- Promoting rest and relaxation

NURSING GUIDELINES FOR GIVING ANALGESICS

Employ a positive attitude in giving medications: "You will [not *may be*] be more comfortable." Medicate in the anticipatory stage; stay ahead of pain. Again, if medication is ordered, give it as ordered and do not moralize. Emphasize the value of nonnarcotic medications for analgesia (e.g., antibiotics) when possible: "This will help the infection and the pain will improve." Explain when medication is ordered for problems other than pain, but assure the patient that it, too, will help. Analgesics that are administered orally should *not* be given on a full stomach (unless otherwise ordered), as this interferes with absorption. Keep medications on schedule as ordered. Use other pain-relief methods and reinforce those behaviors that will reduce pain; preparing the patient for painful procedures and telling the patient when the procedure is terminated is an effective means of reducing apprehension. Further discussion of obtaining a concise and factual pain history is found in Chapter 5.

■ REFERENCES

1. Centers for Infectious Diseases. *CDC Guideline for Isolation Precautions in Hospitals.* August 1983;9–11.
2. Meengs MR, Giles BK, Chisholm CD, et al. Handwashing frequency in an emergency department. *J Emerg Nurs.* 1994;20:183–188.
3. Dobbing EA. Preventing transference of bloodborne pathogens in the workplace. *Point of View* 1994;Jan.:8–12.
4. Sana JM, Judge RD. Physical Appraisal Methods in Nursing Practice. Boston, Ma: Little, Brown; 1975.
5. Ravin A. *The Clinical Significance of the Sounds of Korotkoff.* West Point, Pa: Merck Sharp & Dohme; 1970.

■ BIBLIOGRAPHY

Assessing Vital Functions Accurately. Horsham, Pa: Nursing 77 Books; 1977.

Bates B, ed. *A Guide to Physical Examination.* 5th ed. Philadelphia, Pa: JB Lippincott; 1991.

Centers for Disease Control. Guidelines for prevention of transmission of human immunodeficiency virus and hepatitis B virus to health care and public safety workers. *MMWR Morb Mortal Wkly Rep* 1989;38: 1–35. Abstract.

Cirolia B. Understanding edema. *Nursing 96.* Feb. 1996: 66–70.

Emergency Nurses Association. *Emergency Nursing Core Curriculum.* 4th ed. Philadelphia, Pa: WB Saunders; 1994.

Fincke MK, Lanros NE, eds. *Emergency Nursing: A Comprehensive Review.* Rockville, Md: Aspen Publishers; 1985.

Gardner SS. Skills in rapid field assessment. *Top Emerg Med.* 1987;9:12–23.

Harrahill M. Glasgow Coma Scale: a quick review. *J Emerg Nurs.* 1996;22:81–83.

Jarvis CM. Vital signs. *Nursing 76,* April 1976;31–37.

Larson LL. *Protocols for Advanced Emergency Management.* Bowie, Md: Brady Company; 1982.

McVan B. Assessment of odors. *Nursing 77.* Apr. 1977; 46–49.

Mize J, Kozial-McLain J, Lowenstein SR. The forgotten vital sign: temperature patterns and associations in 642 trauma patients at an urban level I trauma center. *J Emerg Nurs.* 1993;19:306–312.

O'Boyle CM, Davis DK, Russo BA et al. *Emergency Care: The First 24 Hours.* E. Norwalk, Conn: Appleton & Lange; 1985.

OSHA. Occupational exposure to bloodborne pathogens. *OSHA.* 1992;3127:1.

OSHA. Personal protective equipment cuts risk. In: *Bloodborne Facts Sheet.* OSHA Publications.

OSHA. Bloodborne pathogens and acute care facilities. *OSHA.* 1992;3128:7.

Pugliese G. Universal precautions: now they're the law. *RN* 1992;September:63.

Ravin A. *The Clinical Significance of the Sounds of Korotkoff.* West Point, Pa: Merck Sharp & Dohme; 1970.

Roach B. Assessment of color changes in dark skin. *Nursing 77.* January 1977;48–51.

Simoneau JK. Physical assessment. In: Sheehy SB, ed. *Emergency Nursing Principles and Practice.* 3rd ed. St. Louis, Mo.: CV Mosby Year Book; 1992.

■ REVIEW: PATIENT ASSESSMENT AND VITAL SIGNS

1. Explain the rationale for and importance of observing universal precautions in all phases of prehospital and emergency department (ED) patient care.

2. Describe the correct procedure for simple but effective handwashing.

3. Describe the OSHA (Occupational Safety and Health Administration) guidelines for managing bloodied and otherwise contaminated items of potentially infectious waste.

4. Identify the three key components of the initial nursing assessment (primary survey).

5. Describe the first intervention an emergency nurse (EN) should consider if a patient being triaged exhibits respiratory difficulty and signs of ventilatory compromise.

6. Describe the first interventions an EN should initiate immediately if a patient presents with chest pain or a "heavy feeling" over the sternal area.

7. Identify two essential environmental elements of an accurate initial patient evaluation.

8. Describe the head-to-toe checkpoints of an initial 90-second evaluation.

9. Explain the implications of Battle sign or "raccoon eyes" following head trauma.

10. Contrast the pain pattern differences of solid organ and of hollow organ systems.

Adjuncts to Physical Assessment

4

Since clinical laboratory and radiological procedures play such a significant role in emergency department (ED) case diagnosis and management, emergency nurses (ENs) are expected to demonstrate proficiency in obtaining laboratory specimens and expediting radiological procedures as ordered. Frequently, ED policy dictates that the triage nurse or charge nurse may initiate certain appropriate diagnostic laboratory tests and request x-ray views as an adjunct to initial physical assessment. These should be anticipated and/or requisitioned as soon as possible to expedite treatment and enhance case outcomes. This chapter discusses the generally employed adjuncts to physical assessment provided by the clinical laboratory and the radiology department, together with some appropriate guidelines for nursing participation.

■ CLINICAL LABORATORY

Whether the physician or the EN initiates orders for laboratory and radiological procedures, the EN should be comfortable with the procedures and techniques involved as well as understand routine evaluations. Needless error, loss of valuable time, and unnecessary cost can be averted initially if the EN takes care to accurately, legibly, and completely fill out the laboratory request with the patient's name, location, and specific test(s). Specimens must be transported *without delay* to the laboratory—or stored properly if there is to be a delay. Table 4–1 correlates some clinical findings with the laboratory tests indicated, and may be of value as a partial guideline during initial assessment. Since laboratory analysis is performed on both venous and arterial blood and the techniques and equipment for each vary, they are discussed separately.

VENOUS DRAWS AND STICKS

Venous blood is obtained by *phlebotomy*, the ancient term for incising a vein and withdrawing blood. Venous, or deoxygenated, blood provides baseline information for treatment as well as diagnostic confirmation and may be collected by capillary tubes, evacuated blood collection system (EBCS), or by syringe and transferred to a tube with the correct additive.

Tubes and Needles

The EBCS system is the most widely used and allows collection of several specimens with one successful venipuncture. Once the vein is accessed, a preselected vacuum tube with the correct additive is advanced into the sleeve and onto the collection needle, where it fills. Vacuum tubes come in a variety of sizes and color coding to indicate their additives and designated use; appropriate needles are also coded, by color and by number, with the smaller number indicating a larger gauge and, conversely, the higher number indicating a finer gauge. The largest needle suitable to the vein selected should be used in order to avoid traumatizing blood cells.

Tube Top	Additive	Purpose
Red 5-cc	None	For serum samples; most chemistries, serology, type and crossmatch (T&C)
Red & black 10-cc	None, but contains silicone gel	Gel separates cell from serum; serum pours off easily after centrifuging

TABLE 4–1. SOME SPECIFIC CLINICAL MANIFESTATIONS AND THE APPROPRIATE LABORATORY EVALUATION TO BE REQUISITIONED

Clinical Presentation	Emergency Room Laboratory Test Usually Employed
Acute hypovolemic shock	Hematocrit (packed cell volume [PCV])
Hemorrhagic state	Prothrombin time (PT)
	Partial thromboplastin time (PTT)
	Fibrinogen
Possible myocardial infarction	Cardiac enzymes: lactate dehydrogenase (LDH), serum glutamic oxaloacetic transaminase (SGOT), creatine kinase–MB (CK-MB)
Shock state	Lactic acid (serum lactate)
Chronic anemia	Hemoglobin (Hgb)
Diabetes	Blood glucose
Intoxication, mentation changes	Alcohol/ethanol (ETOH)—for medical purposes
	P_{CO_2}, pH, arterial P_{O_2}
	Barbiturate level
	Bromide level
	Magnesium (Mg) level
	Salicylate level
Smooth-muscle damage (heart)	CK-MB
Tetany	Calcium (Ca^{2+}) level
Electrolyte imbalance	CO_2 (HCO_3)
	Chloride level
	Potassium (K^+) level—cardiac dysrhythmias
	Sodium (Na^+) level
Renal dysfunction	Blood urea nitrogen (BUN)
Pancreatitis	Amylase

(*Adapted from U.S. Department of Health, Education, and Welfare.*[10])

Tube Top	Additive	Purpose
Gray 3-cc	Sodium fluouride and potassium oxylate	For blood glucose and blood alcohol determinations
Lavender 3-cc	EDTA	An anticoagulant that preserves cells for hematology
Blue 3-cc	Sodium citrate	Prevents clotting for coagulation studies

Venous Access

Venous specimens are most often obtained from a vein in the antecubital fossa of the arm. Since the number of accessible veins per patient is limited, the EN should take great care with the technique used and observe the following points:

1. Identify the patient and be *certain* that you have the right person. If the patient cannot respond to voice inquiry, check for an armband or with a family member.

2. After explaining the procedure to the patient, position the draw site, double-check your equipment, including the supply of adequate tubes and needles, and *put on procedure gloves.*

3. Apply the tourniquet 2 to 3 in. above the puncture site. To avoid hemoconcentration, do not leave it in place for more than 2 minutes. Release and refasten.

4. After cleansing the site in circular fashion with a 70 percent alcohol pledget, allow the skin to dry briefly and then insert a needle at a 20- to 30-degree angle while "anchoring" the vein with your thumb below the puncture site, preventing skin stretch as the needle enters.

5. Remember to *gently* roll or agitate the tube once filled in order to mix the additive; too-vigorous agitation may cause hemolysis of blood cells, and another specimen will be required.

6. If you are unable to access a vein, *do not* attempt more than two punctures. Notify the appropriate person when a specimen has not been obtained.
7. If syringe and needle are used to obtain blood specimens, the blood should be rapidly transferred to the appropriate color-coded tube: remove the needle from the syringe and the stopper from tube; *gently* inject blood from the syringe into the tube, allowing it to flow down the tube sides to prevent hemolysis; and replace the stopper(s), apply the correct labels, and transport the specimen(s) to the laboratory. Hemolysis of blood and loss of the specimens are particularly serious in the very aged or the very young, as blood vessels are small, fragile, and of limited accessibility.

Capillary Sticks

Occasionally, when blood must be obtained from infants and small children, or for blood glucose evaluation in diabetics, the lancet/capillary tube method is used. Skin must be cleansed with 70 percent alcohol and allowed to dry, then punctured with a *shallow* lancet that will not penetrate underlying structures. The first drop of fluid should be wiped away since it contains tissue serum. The capillary tube is touched at a sharp angle to the blood drop until it is filled; the process is repeated until the correct number of filled capillary tubes have been obtained. The tubes are then placed in their container, labeled, and transported to the laboratory without delay, with *capillary specimens* specified on the laboratory slip, since capillary specimens are more fragile and will deteriorate sooner. In multipatient situations, the use of plastic capillary tubes is recommended to reduce the risk of injury from breakage.[5]

Blood Glucose Monitors

The use of hand-held blood glucose monitors (BGMs), which use a blood drop obtained by capillary stick, has increased substantially in recent years. The BGM has become a standard evaluation tool in many triage areas, easily and economically employed for initial assessment of the diabetic patient.[1] Some authors have reported BGMs to be highly accurate[2,3] when compared to conventional laboratory blood glucose evaluations and have es-

timated the cost of their use to be 3 percent of the conventional laboratory cost.[4]

Spinning Hematocrits

Some EDs dedicate a small on-the-spot laboratory space for immediate determination of hematocrits; frequently, ENs carry out the procedure, as follows:

1. A capillary stick is done to fill a special capillary tube of glass, plastic, or glass-lined Kevlar.
2. A special clay preparation is used to plug the end of the capillary tube.
3. The capillary tube containing the anticoagulated blood is placed in a flat metal tray, held with a plate on top, and spun in a centrifuge for 5 minutes.
4. After the tube is removed from the centrifuge, the height of the red blood cell (RBC) column is measured and compared with the height of the original whole blood column; the percentage of RBC mass to original blood volume is the hematocrit, and it is determined by holding the tube against a hematocrit reader scale calibrated from 100 percent to 0 percent. Normal hematocrits are usually about three times the hemoglobin value; normal adult values are 40 percent to 54 percent for males and 37 percent to 47 percent for females.

ARTERIAL BLOOD GASES

Arterial blood gases (ABGs) are a reflection of the normal and abnormal blood gas values; they should be considered a look at the entire body and are clinically essential information when patients are hypoxic, hypoxemic, hypercapnic, or hypercarbic. ABG values and interpretations are given in Appendix A.

Arteriopuncture is the means by which arterial blood is obtained for analysis of blood gases; venous specimens cannot be used for evaluation of alveolar function since venous blood has been deoxygenated. The exception to this consideration is in infants, when the capillary stick using heparinized capillary tubes is sometimes employed. Selection of the puncture site will most likely depend on the clinical situation and the rapidity with which the sample must be obtained, as well as the circulatory status of the patient. The three readily available sites are the radial, brachial, and femoral arteries; the latter is most frequently selected in trauma code situations when peripheral pulses may be compromised. The femoral artery is not only accessible but is frequently peripheral to the central areas of activity. When using the brachial or radial artery, it is best to hyperextend the arm or wrist to facilitate palpation, locating the artery and bracketing the puncture site with your fingertips.

Arterial puncture must be done with great care to avoid radial artery spasm: arteriospasm of the pierced vessel can result in oxygen deprivation to distal tissues, with severe damage.

The Allen Test

If the radial artery is the chosen site, it is *essential* to first check the patency of the ulnar artery, ensuring circulation to the hand in case of radial arteriospasm. This is done by means of the Allen test, and the patient's record should reflect documentation of a patent ulnar artery. The Allen test is accomplished by elevating the patient's hand and arm while encircling the wrist, with your thumb depressing the ulnar artery and your fingers depressing the radial artery. Instruct the patient to open and close the hand several times, which will cause the palm to blanch from occlusion of the blood supply. Release pressure over the ulnar artery and observe closely; a patent ulnar artery will allow the hand to flush with arterial blood and restore color.

Important Procedural Points

When performing arteriopuncture, use the following procedure:

1. Explain the procedure to the patient if the situation permits.
2. The patient's temperature, respiratory rate, and the amount of oxygen being received (room air, 10 L/min, or whatever) must be noted on the laboratory slip, since these measurements are taken into consideration when the sample is evaluated. (There is a lag time of 15 to 20 minutes when oxygen (O_2) is started or d.c.'d before arterial blood reflects the change.)
3. The syringe must be heparinized by withdrawing a sufficient amount of heparin (1000 USP units/mL) into the syringe to wet the plunger completely and prevent

blood from clotting. The syringe must be held in an upright position and all excess heparin and air bubbles must be expelled.
4. Proper skin preparation with a germicide is essential. Using sterile technique, bracket the area of maximum pulsation in the artery with the fingertips of your free hand as the needle is inserted into the artery, bevel upward, at a right angle or slightly acute angle to the artery. As the needle enters the artery, the pulsating flow of blood will easily fill the syringe, after which the needle is withdrawn.
5. Firm direct pressure must be maintained on the puncture site for at least a *full* 5 minutes to prevent the formation of a hematoma, and if the patient is on an anticoagulant medication, direct pressure must be applied over the puncture site for *15 minutes,* after which a firm pressure dressing must be in place for 3 to 4 hours.
6. Immediately occlude the needle by sticking the end into the rubber plug; this prevents room air from mixing with the specimen. Place it in the container of ice, labeled with the patient's name and the time drawn. Be certain that the accompanying laboratory requisition reflects the patient's temperature, respiratory rate, and the oxygen percentage being administered. If the patient is on room air, indicate room air.
7. The specimen, placed in the basin of ice and properly labeled, must be taken to the laboratory without delay. ABG determinations should be made immediately since gas tensions and pH can change rapidly.
8. Following puncture, the site must be reinspected frequently, and other assessments of the patient must be made. Hematoma, arterial thrombosis, arterial spasm, and ulnar nerve puncture are complications following this procedure, so the patient requires careful observation.

Arterial Puncture Kit

A sampling for blood gas analysis is obtained by assembling the following, or using a prepared kit:

- 2-mL syringe with 25-gauge needle for site infiltration if necessary

- 1 percent lidocaine (optional to have on hand)
- 10-mL syringe with 19- or 20-gauge needle for adults and a 22- or 25-gauge needle for children
- Sodium heparin (1000 U/mL)
- Rubber stopper or cap to seal air from the needle
- Sterile sponges and skin germicide
- Small basin or bag for ice
- Tape for label
- Sterile procedure gloves

Some basic guidelines and methods for interpretation of ABGs are given in Appendix A.

Pulse Oximetry as an Alternative to Arterial Blood Gases

Pulse oximeters are now used widely in EDs as adjuncts to ABGs for monitoring oxygen saturation and detecting hypoxemia. Pulse oximeters are electronic devices that calibrate and transpose the transmission of light through oxygenated tissues into the percentage of arterial saturation. This is achieved via light-emitting diodes housed in a sensor attached to an earlobe or fingertip. Pulse oximetry has come to be recognized primarily as a useful *trending* device, with the general recommendation that critical and poorly perfusing patients be first evaluated with an arterial sample for the baseline. Some pulse oximeters have shown a margin of error up to 5 percent;[6] when the oximeter registers 98 percent to 100 percent, there is little cause for concern because even if a 5 percent error *does* exist, the saturation is probably acceptable. If, however, the reading is 95 percent to 98 percent, a 5 percent deficit could be of significance in a compromised patient. As on ongoing tool for monitoring oxygen saturation, pulse oximetry is a beneficial ED adjunct any time sedatives, narcotics, or muscle relaxants are given, or for any ED patient who has been placed on a ventilator. Accuracy of readings, however, can be affected by various things, such as hypothermia, vasoconstriction, hypovolemia, improper probe positioning, patient movement causing motion artifacts, darker skin pigmentation, and the presence of red fingernail polish when the probe is used on a fingertip.[6,7]

COLLECTING AND STORING URINE SPECIMENS

Urinalysis (UA) is routinely performed on patient admission and frequently is a key diagnostic factor in the ED. While it has long been thought that anything less than a "clean-catch urine" was a disservice to the patient, some researchers have demonstrated that there is "no difference in the rate of bacterial contamination between the specimens obtained by the clean-catch method and those obtained by the non–clean-catch method" *and* that the cost of the non–clean-catch is less than half that of the clean-catch.[7] It is preferable, of course, to use a technique minimizing the chance of bacterial contamination; this can be done by instructing the patient how to collect a midstream catch and providing the patient with a sterile specimen cup and plastic gloves. Urine specimens should go immediately to the laboratory for analysis, but if there is a delay, they should be refrigerated in a utility room refrigerator until they can be delivered.

Both urine color and odor should be noted and documented if other than within normal limits. Ordinarily, fresh normal urine has little odor and the appearance is clear and of a straw color. If a strong odor is present (e.g., an ammonia odor, indicating fermentation within the bladder, or a foul smell, indicating infection) or if the color is other than within normal limits, a note should be made in the assessment record. Although perception of color is highly subjective, general observations can be made. Colorless urine denotes dilute urine with a low specific gravity; yellow with milky sediment may indicate either phosphate precipitation in early-morning specimens or pus in the urine and infection; orange indicates concentrated urine or alkaline urine and dark orange indicates bile or the presence of dye from pyridium or "azo" drugs; red indicates gross blood and hemoglobin breakdown; burgundy may indicate cathartic laxatives (e.g., cascara, rhubarb); blue or blue-green indicates dyes and specific medications. Again, any characteristics other than normal should be well documented.

MISCELLANEOUS TESTS

Chemical Reagents

Hemastix, Dextrostix, Ketostix, and Guaiac tests are all examples of chemical reagent products that allow noninvasive evaluation and provide immediate feedback for the presence or absence of blood, sugar, ketone bodies, and occult blood in body fluids and stool specimens. All testing strips and slides are disposable after use and should be discarded into biohazard-labeled containers. These assessment adjuncts are extremely helpful in spot-checking patients, when indicated, for glycosuria, hematuria, ketonuria, elevated blood glucose, and occult blood in the stool prior to requisitioning clinical laboratory studies for further confirmation and quantitation.

When using any of the chemical reagents, it is extremely important to read the directions carefully as the manufacturer provides them, to keep containers tightly capped after removing a test strip or unit, and to be certain the product is being used before the expiration date shown on the label.

Slides and Potassium Hydroxide Preparations

In some settings, ENs are expected to collect and prepare slide materials, such as potassium hydroxide (KOH) slides for diagnosis of *Candida albicans* overgrowth (moniliasis or candidiasis), often seen in predisposing conditions (e.g., pregnancy, diabetes mellitus, chronic corticosteroid use, antibacterial therapy, acquired immunodeficiency syndrome [AIDS], and chronic debility). Light scrapings from a lesion, stained with a 10 percent solution of KOH, will reveal budding yeast forms. Saline and Gram stains are also used.

Other slide preparations, such as gram stains, require special procedures and solutions; if the ED has a small laboratory area, ENs may wish to learn techniques of preparing specimens for microscopic examination. For example, a simple saline slide preparation is used for confirmation of *Trichomonas,* commonly seen in vaginal discharge.

CULTURE TECHNIQUES: OBTAINING AND STORING

ENs are frequently called upon to obtain cultures from draining wounds, eyes, sore throats, and so forth. Widely available culture tube kits (Culturettes) allow swab cultures to be taken as appropriate and replaced in the tube and provide selective media that allow growth of pathogens while inhibiting growth of the "normal flora"; the media are provided by crushing an internal pulvule within the tube. All cultures should be incubated at

$37°C$ ($98.6°F$). Stool specimens to be examined for ova and parasites must also be stored at body temperature in covered specimen containers until they are transported to the laboratory. Urine cultures are generally made from specimens obtained by catheter or clean midstream second voidings caught in a sterile container. The specimen should either be cultured immediately or refrigerated if culturing must be delayed. Again, universal precautions must be observed in any contact with any body fluid or exudate.

■ BASIC RADIOLOGY IN THE EMERGENCY DEPARTMENT

IMAGING TECHNIQUES

Although newer options for imaging techniques have become available to physicians in recent years, and despite the hazard of cumulative ionizing radiation, x-rays are still holding their own in the emergency-care setting because of their ease, speed, reasonable cost, and availability. Although the basic guidelines of preparing the patient and requisitioning the appropriate x-ray studies are the focus of this section, a brief overview of the other imagery modalities is presented.

Nuclear Studies

Nuclear studies (radionuclide imaging) represent the next oldest imaging technique after x-ray studies. Nuclear studies are relatively more expensive and involve administration of specific radioisotope materials, after which nuclear scans of bones and organs can be done. Scanning with radionuclides yields valuable physiological metabolic information that cannot be obtained with any other imaging modality. An example would be the heart perfusion scans done both before and after treatment with streptokinase for a blocked coronary artery.[8]

Computed Tomography

Computed tomography (CT) followed nuclear studies in development and has become quite popular. A modified x-ray technique, CT scanning involves radiation exposure, is three-dimensional, and shows all densities—air, bone, and everything in between—as opposed to x-rays, which are two-dimensional and give only spatial and contrast resolution. CT is best used on normal-weight to heavy patients and is preferred for evaluating brain pathology above the tentorium and for searching out occult tumors and metastases.[8,9] The newest development in CT scanning is dynamic CT, which produces 30 images per second. It is valuable, for instance, in the diagnosis of acute myocardial infarction, because of its ability to show hypokinesis of the left ventricle and the reactive hyperemia. Dynamic CT is so new that very few units are available for use.[9]

Ultrasound

Ultrasound (sonography) is the least expensive of the newer imaging modalities. It produces images with high-frequency sound waves rather than ionization radiography. No contrast media are required; units are portable to the ED, operating room, and intensive care unit, and the procedure is rapid and safe. It is especially valuable in investigating specific spots and masses and for guidance during percutaneous procedures such as abscess drainage, aspiration, and biopsy. Fetal assessment, cardiac information, and gallstone evaluation are among other frequent uses. Best visual results are obtained with thin patients because the ultrasound beam has less tissue to penetrate.[8]

Positron Emission Tomography

Positron emission tomography (PET) is the newest development in nuclear medicine; in the late 1980s, there were only about 12 machines in the United States. Isotopes produced in a cyclotron are used to make glucose radioactive, with a very short half-life of 2.5 minutes. Injected into the patient, glucose isotopes decay and emit positive electrons, or positrons, which are detected and made visible through tomography. Two basic purposes of PET are (1) to determine the amount of blood flow to specific body tissues, especially the brain and heart; and (2) to show how adequately those tissues use blood (metabolic rate). This is the only imaging technique that can diagnose Alzheimer's disease at this time.[9]

Monoclonal Antibody Scanning

Monoclonal antibody scanning is a powerful new nuclear technique with the unique ability to track down metastases anywhere in the body and sometimes destroy them. This technique has been proven to be effective in locating metastatic dis-

ease when CT scanning has failed and should be used increasingly in the future for that purpose.[9]

Magnetic Resonance Imaging

Magnetic resonance imaging (MRI) is relatively new and revolutionary; its imaging ability is a complex technique based on generation of a static magnetic field. The patient is placed inside a long cylindrical tunnel, much like a CT scanning unit, that contains a powerful magnet. The static magnetic field that is created lines up all the atoms in the body having an odd atomic number. Because hydrogen is the human body's most abundant atom, has the atomic number 1, and emits the strongest signal (and since 70 percent of the body is water), the major body mass is encompassed. When the magnetic-field atoms are excited, like atoms of the body respond, realign with the magnetic field, and resonate; a radio signal is returned that can be picked up externally. The radio signal, in turn, is processed by computer to show the status and abundance of hydrogen atoms in the patient's body, as well as to provide chemical analysis of the inside of the body. Cross-sectional images on multiple planes in extraordinarily fine detail are provided.[8,9]

MRI has the advantage of zero exposure to ionizing radiation, but it is over 30 percent more expensive than CT scanning. The procedure is time consuming (45 to 90 minutes), and there may be problems with patient claustrophobia. MRI cannot be used with life-support paraphernalia in place, cardiac pacemakers, or metal clips on intracranial aneurysms. It will not image calcium, is better than CT for intracranial and intraspinal lesions, and is the preferred modality for brain studies.[8]

Digital Radiology

Digital radiology is a state-of-the-art capability that converts x-ray images into electronic images displayed on a viewing screen, replacing the x-ray film in many studies with video images. As a spinoff of this, digital angiography is rapidly replacing invasive catheter techniques in screening for cerebrovascular diseases and has greatly simplified vascular diagnostic procedures.

Magnification Radiography

Magnification radiography is the most recent development in conventional x-ray capabilities. The

Japanese have developed an x-ray tube capable of magnification that allows use of a 0.09-mm-diameter focal spot with about the magnification of the low-power microscope. Valuable applications of such magnification include study of anatomic detail in newborn hearts and lungs and of bones and joints, with the purpose of clearly identifying small cortical interruptions (invisible on a standard x-ray).[9]

Color Radiography

Even color radiography is now a practical possibility with the recent development of a device that converts the gray scale into color at minimal cost. Colored perfusion scans, color digital angiography, and color CT will all become available to diagnosticians.[9]

X-Rays

Standard x-rays remain the basic imaging modality used routinely in emergency medical care, even in the face of their known cumulative ionizing radiation and two-dimensional limitations. X-rays are the modality ENs work with closely on a daily basis.

USING DIAGNOSTIC X-RAYS

Familiarity with some of the very basic concepts of radiology and departmental procedures as they relate to the ED is helpful to ENs in understanding (1) why certain x-rays are requisitioned with specific views; (2) which x-rays the nurse should be able to requisition to expedite management of single-extremity trauma when the physician is tied up with more severe problems; (3) how the patient should be prepared and transported to the radiology department, as well as which patients should remain in the ED and have portable films done; (4) why the requisition itself is extremely important, as it relates not only to the diagnostic interpretation but to the medical record as well; and (5) how to apply some very basic radiological concepts and guidelines in a gross examination of an x-ray film as it relates to the patient and the available medical history.

PREPARING THE PATIENT

In many hospitals, the intramural relationship between the radiology department and the ED is too often laced with misunderstandings, petty criticisms, loss of valuable time for patient care, and, too frequently, unnecessary films. A constructive working rapport between the two departments is essential if the patient is to receive the best possible care and if members of both departments are to work at their most effective levels.

Radiology technologists should be able to receive properly prepared patients, disrobed to the extent that the area being filmed will be totally unencumbered by clothing or metal parts (including jewelry, safety pins in garments, and bra snaps and hooks) and stripped clean of mud, broken glass, and other impediments to filming. Every trauma victim (usually the most heavily soiled) should be totally disrobed in any event for a thorough examination in the ED before being sent on to radiology dressed in a patient gown and covered with clean, warm blankets. Stretcher patients should go to radiology on their stretchers, wheelchair patients should go in wheelchairs, and the rare walking patient should be accompanied. *Never* allow a patient to wander off to radiology and assume he or she will get there. Department policy should state that *all* patients are accompanied to the radiology waiting area. Neither patients with any significant head trauma nor any acutely ill or unstable patient should be allowed to wait in the hall unattended. As a general rule, it is wise to request portable films in the ED with *any* seriously compromised patient (if portable equipment and a technician are available), since the x-ray rooms are rarely equipped or staffed to handle a real crisis situation.

One further consideration involves the patient's valuables. Purses and wallets containing credit cards and money should never be left behind unattended in the ED but should go with the patient or to a waiting family member. This will avoid *many* problems.

LOGICAL REQUISITIONING

Most x-ray requisition slips request a considerable amount of information, and there is a good reason for all of it. Therefore, it is important to make a consistent effort to be thorough and accurate. The requisition is necessary not only for the sake of complete medical and fiscal records but also for evaluation of the problem and for making the decision as to which examination should be employed so that the radiologist may render an accurate interpretation.

The patient's name (including middle initial) *must* be spelled correctly and written legibly, with hospital numbers, the patient's age, and name of physician included. Some forms ask whether the patient has had previous films taken in that department. In the space usually provided for the reason the film is being ordered, the problem may be stated as follows:

1. Chief medical complaint of the patient (e.g., swelling, unexplained pain, limited range of motion, hemoptysis)
2. To rule out (R/O) a fracture, foreign body, renal stone, pneumothorax, dissecting aortic aneurysm, cervical spine fracture, and so on.

The purpose is to provide the technician with a brief indication of the reason for films. If, for instance, the chief complaint is pain in the abdomen, pain duration should be noted, as should the side on which there is pain and whether the patient is febrile (and if so, the temperature). Chronic pain without injury indicates quite a different sort of evaluation than pain following injury. If the film is to be a "recheck," note the time elapsed since the first film(s) and whether a procedure (such as thoracentesis, remanipulation of a fracture, or passage of catheter) has been done since the last examination.

ENs should not be concerned with x-ray views but rather the area to be examined. They are—and should be—expected to use correct terminology in these requisitions to avoid confusion, error (costly to the patient), delay, and personal criticism. There is a strong economic consideration to be kept in mind, so specific areas must be defined and filmed only as needed diagnostically. Remember, too, that the patient should not be exposed to any more radiation than absolutely necessary.

Specific nomenclature should be used with hands and feet: thumb, index finger, middle finger, ring finger, fifth finger, great toe, second toe, third toe, fourth toe, fifth toe. The foot and ankle areas should be indicated specifically: ankle, tarsal area, toes, os calcis (heel), and so on. In other words, the actual area desired to be x-rayed should be specified with the correct anatomic terms as indicated by the physician, and this will then be interpreted

by the x-ray technician into the most meaningful views of the indicated area, minimizing radiation exposure and expense to the patient.

BASIC PRINCIPLES OF RADIOLOGY

Radiology is defined as the science of radiant energy and radiant substances, especially that branch of medical science dealing with the use of radiant energy in the diagnosis and treatment of disease. *Roentgenology* is defined as the branch of radiology that deals with the diagnostic and therapeutic use of roentgen rays, producing roentgenograms, or x-rays. The roentgen (pronounced rĕnt´-gĕn) was named for Wilhelm Konrad Roentgen (a German physicist, 1845–1923), who discovered roentgen rays in 1895 and was awarded the Nobel prize in physics for 1901. The roentgen is the recognized international unit of x or y radiation. It is abbreviated as R. The principle of using roentgenograms (x-rays) to visualize diagnostic evidence is based on the fact that dense materials such as bone are radiopaque and will not permit the passage of radiant energy (x-rays), with the representative areas appearing light or white on the exposed film, whereas other materials such as air are radiolucent and permit the passage of radiant energy while offering some resistance to it (depending on density), with representative areas appearing dark on the exposed film. The basic roentgen densities are shown in Table 4–2.

Views typically taken are PA (posterior to anterior or posteroanterior), AP (anterior to posterior, or anteroposterior), lateral (sagittal), and oblique (angled). Decubitus films are films taken while the patient is lying down with the x-ray beam horizontal and are designated as right lateral decubitus when the patient is lying on the right side and left lateral decubitus when the patient is lying on the left side.

TABLE 4–2. BASIC ROENTGEN DENSITIES

Element or agent	Roentgen density
Gas, air	Dark
Fat	Intermediate (dark)
Water, organs, blood	Intermediate (light)
Bone, contrast media	Whitish (lighter) or gray scale
Metal (barium, lead),	Solid white

It should be remembered that in x-ray films, the farther away the part, the larger it shows on film; therefore, angulations and displacements farther from the film will tend to be exaggerated.

In looking at a film, it is important to think about it three-dimensionally, since the x-ray is a composite "shadowgram" and represents the added densities of many layers of tissue. There are five densities to be aware of when looking at films: gas, fat, water, calcium (bone), and metal (lead and barium); cartilage does not show on x-ray unless calcified. The viewer is required to think in layers when looking at any given x-ray film, remembering that (1) calcium is the prime example of metal density *normally* found in the body and that (2) water density viewed in *anatomic* contact with another water density will obliterate the existing interface. An example of the latter is pneumonia; water density of the pneumonia in anatomic contact with the water density of the heart border obliterates that border.

GENERAL GUIDELINES FOR FILMS OF SPECIFIC AREAS

Some generalities regarding the basics of radiology are included here, but it should be borne in mind that procedures and standard views for specific examinations may vary somewhat, as does terminology, from hospital to hospital, and the EN should be familiar with those used in the specific hospital or practice area.

Skull Series

The skull series, when ordered, usually includes a PA view, lateral (both sides) view, and Towne view (an oblique view from the anterior hairline caudally for visualization of the basal skull area). This makes four views in all; a Waters view (for visualization of orbital structures) is sometimes indicated in addition if an orbital fracture is suspected. However, if facial bone or orbital fracture is suspected, order x-rays of the specific area (e.g., orbital or facial bones), and the technician will determine which views will be required.

Skull films are not an immediate priority if taken just to see fractures. Emergency requisitioning of a skull film is justified when it is unclear as to whether the patient's condition is deteriorating or when a patient who was apparently stable begins to develop lateralizing neurological signs. The rationale in ordering these films is to determine if the patient has a calcified pineal gland. The position of a normally calcified pineal gland on a skull film can confirm without a doubt the presence of an intracranial hematoma, if the pineal gland has been displaced from its normal midline position more than 1 cm. (The pineal gland calcifies in 75 percent to 80 percent of people at about 15 years of age.)

Again, remember that the busy radiology department is unable to closely monitor a patient with a head injury who is lying unattended in the waiting area. If the nurse assigned to that patient does not stay in attendance, a lethargic patient may rapidly become comatose before returning from radiology without anyone's being aware of the deterioration. *Never* leave a seriously ill patient unattended in the radiology department.

Facial Fractures

Specific films are taken in most radiology departments and generally do not include mandible and nasal bone views. Most facial fractures are diagnosed by observation and palpation (light ballottement), with follow-up confirmation by film:

- Facial bones require multiple zygoma views.
- Mandible examination requires an exaggerated Towne view, specifically for evaluation of the manibular condyles. Right and left oblique views are taken of the mandible; over 90 percent of fractures reveal medial displacement of the fractured superior segment of the condyle.
- Temporomandibular joint examination may require CT.
- Nasal bones require a specific examination; they are not adequately checked in routine facial bone or mandible examination.

Epiglottitis

When acute epiglottitis is suspected, a lateral view of the neck should be taken, using a soft-tissue technique for confirmation of epiglottis with soft-tissue swelling. Airway management equipment must be close at hand in case of sudden airway obstruction during the procedure.

Spinal Films

Patients requiring examination of the cervical spine should have the head immobilized in whatever fashion is required if they have been victims of severe trauma. If the patient is comatose, it is probably safe to use sandbags, with 3-in. tape across the forehead to the sides of the stretcher or backboard; but if the patient is conscious, whether cooperative or not, it is essential for someone to assume the responsibility of applying and maintaining head traction until x-ray films have ruled out a fracture. This may entail use of portable x-rays in the ED even before the patient is moved off the ambulance stretcher, or it may mean accompanying the patient to the x-ray room and staying throughout the filming procedure. With the seriously injured patient or the real candidate for permanent damage, *never* assume someone else will stay with the patient. Be certain. Again, when possible, order portable films in the ED. The patient who walks in complaining of a whiplash injury may be more comfortable in a cervical collar until evaluated but does not require the rigorous regimen that has just been described. Let common sense be the guide. Be aware of the following points:

- Three films are taken of the cervical spine (anterior, odontoid, and lateral). Lateral flexion and extension views may be indicated, but these should not be obtained unless a radiologist is in attendance.
- Always be certain that *all seven* cervical vertebrae are fully visualized. This is of critical importance not only to the patient's well-being and to optimum case outcome, but also to the hospital's risk management.
- The odontoid process may be congenitally absent or very small. Fracture of the odontoid is a high-risk injury and may not heal. The odontoid process is hooked to C-2, upon which C-1 swivels.
- Films of the thoracic spine must visualize *all 12* thoracic vertebrae.
- Films of the lumbar spine must visualize *all five* lumbar vertebrae and usually will include T1-1 and T1-2, where unsuspected fractures are often seen.
- When a film of the spinal column is traced, there should be midline alignment of *all facets,* with clear interspaces.

- Suspected hip fractures require special handling until ruled out. These may be subtle and impacted (at times difficult to diagnose) or grossly deformed.

Chest

Anatomic structures of the chest (see Fig. 4–1) are recognized on an x-ray film by their differences in density, as discussed earlier. The normal chest x-ray film shows them as water density of the heart, muscles, and blood; the metal (calcium) density of the ribs; the gas (air) density of the lungs; and streaks of fat density around the muscles. The fifth density, that of heavy metal and contrast media, is not present in the normal chest film. The normal cardiac silhouette falls within the range of less than half the distance across the chest area. Lateral films of the chest are routinely taken on the left because this does not enlarge the cardiac silhouette and provides a standardization for follow-up comparison. Normally, the chest contains air, arteries and veins, the heart, and the ribs. There should be the following (which are but a few of the many things looked for in the normal chest film):

- Sharp symmetrical angles at the diaphragm (fluid blunts the angle)
- Symmetry of the diaphragm, with a little more bulge on the left side
- Midline trachea with clavicular heads in the center
- Costophrenic gutter on the lateral view

Pneumothorax will show a blacker line around one lung, most prominent at the top, and density (more whiteness) within the lung area may indicate pneumonia, tumor, embolus, or other conditions.

The chest x-ray in trauma is an important part of diagnosis for injuries but is not the most essential step. *After* initial resuscitation or stabilization, the x-ray film should be used to assess the status of the heart, lungs, and mediastinum.

Abdomen

To repeat, it is important to be certain all clothing has been removed, as well as jewelry that might obscure the film. This should be done in the ED, since the x-ray technician is entitled to assume it has been done. For abdominal films requiring contrast media, preparation is not always necessary,

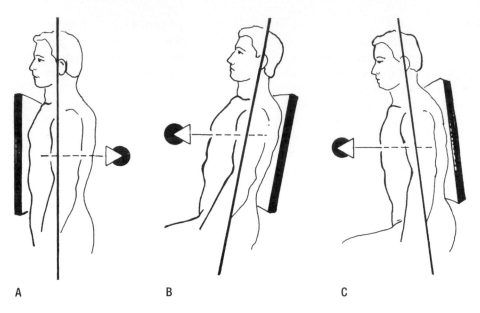

A   B   C

Figure 4–1. Positioning for portable AP chest film in the emergency department. **A.** Normal position for posteroanterior (PA) chest film. **B.** Most common position for portable anteroposterior (AP) chest film. **C.** True erect position for AP film (optimum). (*Adapted from Cardona VD, et. al.* Trauma Nursing, *2nd ed. Philadelphia, Pa: WB Saunders; 1994.*)

depending on what the physician wants to know. ENs should know the following:

- An intravenous pyelogram (IVP) can be done without preparation for stones and renal trauma.
- Upper gastrointestinal (GI) studies are not usually done on an ED basis, but plain films can be made for perforated ulcers. If there has been massive bleeding, an upper GI series will be helpful after the stomach has been cleared of blood by 8 to 12 hours of suction.
- The colon needs adequate preparation for visualization of polyps, diverticulitis, and so on, but emergency films of intussusception, massive internal bleeding, or obstruction can be done without preparation. A massive rectal bleed is frequently from the upper GI tract (stomach); therefore, a barium enema is not the first examination needed. A massive rectal bleed often occurs from the right side of the colon and should be suspected unless the patient is also vomiting blood.

- The old "flat plate" of the abdomen is obsolete.
- Ordering a kidney, ureter, and bladder (KUB) film will net the same results as ordering an abdominal film.
- Abdominal films for foreign bodies (such as intrauterine devices [IUDs] or bullets), kidney stones, pregnancy, gallstones, and so on all require *one* AP view.
- Abdominal series, surgical abdominal series, or surgical series all mean that three or four views will be taken; one supine (lying with face upward) abdominal AP, one upright abdominal AP, and one chest PA. A lateral decubitus view may also be taken, especially if the patient cannot be upright. This is a highly useful diagnostic series when, for instance, a right lower lobe (RLL) pneumonia presents as abdominal pain.
- On acute abdominal films there are two common conditions to consider: (1) perforation of the bowel with free air (this air shows between the diaphragm and liver);

and (2) obstruction, most often of small bowel (the small bowel loops will be dilated and there will be air-fluid levels on the upright and lateral decubitus views). Detection of free air and air-fluid levels requires horizontal x-ray beam films upright, lateral decubitus, or both. Free air in the abdomen or chest is a *bad* sign.
- When sending a pregnant (or possibly pregnant) female patient to x-ray, specify on the requisition that the abdomen be shielded, unless of course the studies are to be abdominal in nature.

Extremities

When the extremities are to be x-rayed, be aware of the following:

- Air splints or cardboard splints are suitable for immobilization of an injured extremity prior to x-ray examination.
- Again, all clothing and jewelry *must* be removed to prepare for x-ray examination, so that such things as rings and watches do not occlude findings.
- It is generally considered good practice to film the joint nearest to a suspected fracture.
- Foot and ankle films should always include PA, lateral, and oblique views. In most departments, this is a routine practice, but if not, the oblique view should be requisitioned for only the part involved.

■ SUMMARY

The basic concept to remember is that after evaluating the patient, the EN should order specific examinations or examination by area(s) as required, and x-ray personnel will obtain the specific views that will enable the radiologist to make the roentgenologic diagnosis. If, owing to unusual circumstances, additional information is thought to be necessary, consultation with the radiologist is indicated. Most radiologists and x-ray technicians will be more than willing to assist ED personnel in obtaining the best care for their patients.

■ REFERENCES

1. DeGroote NE, Pieper B. Blood glucose monitoring at triage. *J Emerg Nurs.* 1993;19:131.
2. Clarke W, Cox D, Gonder-Frederick L, et al. Evaluating clinical accuracy of systems for self-monitoring of blood glucose. *Diabetes Care.* 1987;10: 95–99.
3. North D, Steiner J, Woodhouse K, Maddy J. Home monitors of blood glucose: comparison of precision and accuracy. *Diabetes Care.* 1987;10:360–366.
4. Vitanza A, Giacola G, West K. Evaluation of a new glucose reflectance meter for use in the neonatal ICU. *J Perinatol.* 1988;8:435.
5. Emergency Care Research Institute. Blood glucose monitoring in the emergency department. *J Emerg Nurs.* 1994;20:31.
6. When to double-check pulse oximetry readings. *Emerg Med.* 1995; Jan.:76–77.
7. Emergency Care Research Institute. ED technology and equipment. *J Emerg Nurs.* 1992;18:533–534.
8. Rodibaugh D. Choosing an imaging technique. *Emerg Med.* 1987;19:26–64.
9. Viamonte M Jr. New images of imaging. *Emerg Med.* 1985;17:23–55.
10. U.S. Department of Health, Education, and Welfare. *A Training Program for Hospital Emergency Room Personnel.* Rockville, Md: USDHEW; 1972.

■ BIBLIOGRAPHY

Bates B, ed. *A Guide to Physical Assessment.* 5th ed. Philadelphia, Pa: JB Lippincott; 1991.

Cardonna VD, ed. *Trauma Reference Manual: Maryland Institute for EMSS.* Bowie, Md: Brady Company; 1985.

Corbett JV. *Laboratory Tests & Diagnostic Procedures.* 4th ed. Stamford, Conn: Appleton & Lange; 1995.

Emergency Nurses Association. *Emergency Nursing Core Curriculum.* 4th ed. Philadelphia, Pa: WB Saunders; 1994.

Engberg S. Arterial blood gases. In: Fincke MK, Lanros NE, eds. *Emergency Nursing: A Comprehensive Review.* Rockville, Md: Aspen Publishers; 1986.

Felson M, Weinstein A, Spitz H. *Principles of Chest Radiology: A Programmed Text.* Philadelphia, Pa: WB Saunders; 1965.

Harris JH, Harris WH. *The Radiology of Emergency Medicine.* 2nd ed. Baltimore, Md: Williams & Wilkins; 1981.

Kee JL. *Laboratory & Diagnostic Tests with Nursing Implications.* Stamford, Conn: Appleton & Lange; 1995.

Knezevich-Brown BA. *Trauma Nursing Principles and Practice.* E. Norwalk, Conn: Appleton & Lange; 1986.

Lillis CA. *Brady's Introduction to Medical Terminology.* 3rd ed. E. Norwalk, Conn: Appleton & Lange; 1992.

Mahon CR, Manuselis G. *Textbook of Diagnostic Microbiology.* Philadelphia, Pa: WB Saunders; 1995.

Squires F. *Fundamentals of Roentgenology.* Cambridge, Ma: Harvard University Press; 1964.

Treseler KM. *Clinical Laboratory and Diagnostic Tests: Significance and Nursing Implications.* 3rd ed. Stamford, Conn: Appleton & Lange; 1995.

Wasserman MR, Keller EL. Fever, white blood cell count, and culture and sensitivity: their value in the evaluation of the emergency patient. *Top Emerg Med.* 1989;10:81–88.

Weist PW, Roth PB. *Fundamentals of Emergency Radiology.* Philadelphia, Pa: WB Saunders; 1996.

■ REVIEW: ADJUNCTS TO PHYSICAL ASSESSMENT

1. Explain the importance of performing the Allen test prior to radial artery puncture.

2. Describe the clinical value and use of pulse oximetry.

3. Describe the optimal method of collecting and storing urine specimens in the emergency department (ED).

4. Explain the rationale for observing universal precautions when obtaining specimens of blood or body fluids in the ED.

5. Identify at least six imaging techniques currently available to most hospital EDs.

6. Explain the importance of attending a head-injured patient waiting to be x-rayed.

7. Identify the mineral that is a prime example of metal density in x-rays of the body.

8. Explain the clinical indications for x-rays of the skull.

9. Describe the number of cervical vertebrae that *must* be visualized when cervical spine films are ordered.

10. Describe the proper positioning for portable upright chest films in the ED.

Nursing History and the Interview

The purpose of this chapter is to help the emergency nurse (EN) understand the importance of formulating a concise and accurately documented working history derived from the primary patient interview and nursing assessment and to offer guidelines for specific areas of focused and appropriate inquiry.

■ THE NURSING HISTORY

The nursing history is a distillation of all the observations and measurements that the nurse has made and gathered; it is a further step in the critical nursing process of assessment. Physicians point out repeatedly that a good working history on the patient is probably 85 percent responsible for the formulation of the diagnosis. The first nurse who receives the patient is in the best position to begin that formulation by eliciting a short, meaningful, working history based on a rapid primary assessment *before* the physician is available to begin the medical assessment. This can prove to be a very valuable asset in expediting treatment. The diagnostic process begins when the nurse first sees the patient.

BARRIERS TO FULL INFORMATION

ENs have sought and gained expanded roles in patient care through the development of primary assessment and intervention skills, thus enhancing early case management capabilities. Nursing histories have taken on new importance and meaning and are being accorded greater credence as long-standing barriers fade and physicians begin to support nursing's expanded role. Although ENs as a

group continue to gain new skills and responsibilities, many individual ENs will also continue to face discouraging practice conditions that for the most part are beyond their ability to control. Staffing problems, patient overloads, negative hospital policies, patient language difficulties, inadequate triage areas, and chronic fatigue all qualify as barriers to effective and competent primary assessment and history taking. All things change, however, and while working toward change for the better, ENs should continue to apply their assessment skills to every patient possible and recognize the barriers as they present and persist and be ready to work through them.

APPROACHING THE INTERVIEW

At the onset, the EN must be mindful that when a patient presents at the ED or brings in a family member, he or she is concerned about a problem. Even though perhaps 80 percent of patients seen in the ED are not *true* medical emergencies but fall somewhere into the less-urgent and nonurgent categories, each patient considers his or her problem important enough to come in for help.

Patients look to the EN for fast responses and efficient care. The EN is called upon to respond accordingly, receiving the patient in the same way that he or she would wish to be treated and giving the level of care that the EN would expect for him- or herself. Although it may present a challenge at times, the Golden Rule has an important application here.

The fact that the patient has come to the ED for help provides a major advantage in obtaining pertinent history. The patient's fear of the truth may, however, become a major drawback in ob-

taining full information: the patient may be highly anxious about what *really* may be wrong. The fastest way to dispel that anxiety is to demonstrate warm interest with a smile (no matter how difficult that may be sometimes in chaotic or stressed situations); to employ a polite, empathic, and positive manner; and to begin the interview with confidence.

SOME GUIDELINES FOR THE FOCUSED INTERVIEW

The initial interview is considered to be focused because it concentrates on rapidly defining the nature of the problem from the patient's point of view. The purpose of this focused interview is to maximize accuracy in determining the patient's real reason for coming to the ED while facilitating effective communication and reducing irrelevancies. The interview should be focused but not rigid; some important guidelines for conducting an effective and productive interview are discussed here.

Nurse–Patient Interaction

There are several aspects involved in interacting with the patient:

- Introduce yourself and smile. The exact wording of your greeting is not important, but it should convey your sincerity in wanting to know what you can do for the patient. Although the patient may not respond initially with the *real* chief complaint, he or she will certainly be assured that the nurse is present to assist.
- Greet the person by name and do not be afraid to use first names.
- Establish and maintain eye contact with the patient throughout the interview, if at all possible.
- It is important to establish physical contact with the patient for several reasons. The good old "laying on of hands" often provides the EN with a direct evaluation of the warmth and texture of the skin as well as of the patient's response to touch. A great deal of reassurance can be given in many instances by a simple touch, reinforcing the fact that someone is there to be concerned and offer help.

Enhancing Communication

To ensure good communication, use the following guidelines:

1. Use open-ended questions; never lose sight of the initial or chief complaint. Begin your questioning with *what,* allowing the patient to express his perception of whatever is happening, how it began, when it began, and how long it has been going on. Imagine yourself in the patient's place and experience the symptoms and events as they are related.
2. Focus on the *when, where, and how* components of information and avoid the *why;* the interview is bound to start off on a negative note if the patient is made to feel guilty with a series of "why" questions that may trigger flashbacks to learned childhood attitudes of disapproval and perhaps even blame.
3. Remember that most patients do not possess what can be referred to as an organized knowledge of diseases and that symptoms may be described in an unconnected and disorganized manner as they come to mind. Again, an ability to see the problems from the patient's point of view can make your questions more meaningful.
4. Make sure you use terms that can be understood but at the same time will not sound as though you are talking down to the patient; avoid using medical terminology that may easily confuse and lead to misinterpretation of your meaning.
5. Listen *closely* to responses to questions regarding family history, past illnesses, and surgical history and *document carefully.*
6. Give nonverbal reinforcing cues by facial expression and body posture, exhibiting a sympathetic attitude and encouraging the patient to continue talking, although in the interests of obtaining prompt treatment, do not allow aimless rambling.
7. Paraphrasing the meaning of what the patient has said or stating your perception of what has been said to you clarifies and confirms information, allows meanings to

be corrected as necessary, and summarizes the problem. Your understanding of the story will convey assurance that something will be done; this in itself has positive effects.

8. Be silent when it is appropriate, allowing the patient to ventilate verbally; you can then sort out and paraphrase the pertinent information to verify your documentation.

Interviewer's Attitude

The EN's attitudes can color the interview findings. Avoid this by taking the following steps:

1. Know your own hang-ups and avoid being judgmental at all costs. The patient may well have reservations about some of your questions if your attitude seems hostile or judicial; this will surely result in negative answers, closing up the patient's responses, and impeding the free flow of information.

2. Be careful not to jump to conclusions that may lead to a trap and jeopardize patient welfare.

3. Try to use your knowledge of human motivations and respect your patients as individuals, treating each one as you would wish to be treated.

Again, document carefully and as concisely as possible the essentials of what the patient has communicated to you, both verbally and visually. Remember to *use your eyes* while interviewing your patient and be as observant as possible when the patient is responding to questions. In fact, use all your senses and your experience to formulate your best assessment of nursing management and intervention priorities.

Be willing to concede that very often the patient's own statement is a highly reliable index to his or her actual condition; it is not unreasonable to consider that the patient knows more about his own body than you or the physician can know as strangers on first encounter.

Always try to explain what will be happening next after you have obtained your information. Realize and remember that anxiety and apprehension walk in side by side with the patient and that you will be in the best position to calm and reassure by explaining what is going to happen next and why.

THE NURSING HISTORY FORMAT

Basic Content

The nursing history must be both concise and accurate and should include, at the very least, full patient identification (e.g., age, race or color, gender, mode of admission, chief complaint (cc) or "complains of" (c/o)) and the general mental status of the patient on admission. The chief complaint should always be written in quotes in the patient's own words. It is vitally important to record any allergies and current medications.

Vital signs (VS), the first clinical baseline information documented, must be accurate and should include specific descriptors where possible: for example, blood pressure (BP) should indicate right or left arm; temperature should indicate oral, tympanic, rectal, or axillary; pulse should be noted as regular or irregular and its quality should be described; and respirations should be described as easy or difficult. VS, although not written as part of the nurse's narrative, must be considered an integral part of the history and a *prime* responsibility in documentation. ENs should never forget that VS not documented are vital signs not taken if and when a medical audit or a courtroom encounter ensues.

Objectivity and Discretion

The most difficult aspect of documentation for the EN is probably the ability to condense or crystallize initial impressions and observations of the patient into written form. The EN must record impressions objectively, realizing that the history will become part of the permanent medical record of that patient; *discretion* is therefore strongly advised in the use of descriptions that may be construed later as derogatory. A strong example is a written statement that a patient is "drunk" or "smells of alcohol." That same patient could just as easily be described as "staggering" or "uncoordinated" with "slurred speech." This will corroborate the physician's notation (which is the physician's prerogative) indicating that the patient has "ETOH (ethyl alcohol) on breath" and will tell the story well enough if it ever becomes a courtroom matter, which it all too often does. A conscious effort to avoid being swayed by subjective findings and opinions must be maintained and every effort must be made to document only the objective findings in concise, accurate, and meaningful fashion, avoiding value judgments at all costs.

Documentation

Developed from the problem-oriented system of patient-care documentation, the SOAP format is widely used for gathering and recording patient data in concise fashion. It is easily used and understood and provides a standardized format from which all care providers can benefit.

SOAP is the acronym for the following format:

S   *Subjective* information (i.e., statements made by the patient *in the patient's own words* (chief complaint, onset, duration, relation to pain—with descriptors)

O   *Objective* information (i.e., that which you have observed, such as level of consciousness [LOC], VS, physical assessment findings)

A   *Assess/analyze* the presenting problem(s) and formulate a nursing diagnosis

P   *Plan* for management priorities and immediate intervention(s)

Many EDs use patient forms that provide a very small box or just a few lines for nursing documentation, although there has been a trend toward adding a separate sheet for nursing admission notes and ongoing assessment. Whatever your department uses, be certain to document *clearly and legibly* as you create the patient's database, initiating what will become a key part of that patient's permanent medical record.

■ KEY POINTS IN TAKING A HISTORY

PAIN

Pain is a universally experienced symptom that leads to a preoccupation with the body, although some patients with serious or even fatal disease may not necessarily experience pain. When pain is a symptom, the EN should use a gentle, methodical questioning technique to determine the following features of the pain:

- *Location:* Have the patient point with one finger to where pain is worst at the moment
- *Chronology:* The sequence of development of symptoms from onset
- *Severity:* This is usually expressed in terms of the effect of pain on pertinent functions and its degree when at its worst. Since eval-

uating severity is a subjective matter, ask the patient to rate his or her pain on a scale of 1 to 10, and document.

- *Aggravating or precipitating factors:* Activity or time relationships
- *Alleviating or soothing factors:* Position, medication, and so forth; if medication, what?
- *Association with other symptoms or bodily functions*
- *Radiation to other organs or locations:* Have the patient point again to the area(s) of radiation
- *Course:* Is the pain getting better or worse?
- *Recurrence:* Has this patient had this pain before, and if so, was the patient seen? By whom? What was diagnosed?

Further discussion of pain assessment and management can be found in Chapter 7; however, for purposes of pain descriptors and their documentation, Figure 5–1 provides an idea for standardizing pain documentation on an ED form or nursing assessment/flow sheet.

VITAL SIGNS

Complete VS, including LOC, allergies, and immunizations, as well as all regular medications, should be recorded for *all* patients. Note skin color and diaphoresis, if present, and record in the chart

---

Pain documentation.

What time did your pain start? _____

Are you having pain at this time?   Y ____   N ____

Where? _____

Description? _____

Duration? _____

Any pain med aboard?   Y ____   N ____

If so, what?/when taken? _____

Level of pain: 1   2   3   4   5   6   7   8   9   10

Figure 5–1.

as "skin appears . . ." or "patient appears . . ." In addition, for all patients with abdominal pain or significant trauma, record time of last meal, fluid ingestion, or both.

THE CRITICALLY INJURED PATIENT

Information to be obtained for the critically ill patient includes the following:

- What position was the patient in when injury occurred?
- Where does the patient hurt *now?*
- Has the patient ever had or does the patient now have any other serious illnesses or injuries?
- Is the patient on drugs or medication of any kind, especially insulin, digitalis, or anticoagulants?
- Does the patient have a bleeding tendency? (All you have to ask is "Are you a bleeder?" The patient who is a bleeder knows it and will tell you.)
- Does the patient have any allergies, especially to antibiotics, that are likely to be used before or during an operation?
- When and how much was the last meal or fluid intake?

MOTOR VEHICLE ACCIDENTS

With motor vehicle accidents (MVAs), there are frequently additional bits and pieces of information relative to the accident that have significant value in diagnosis; law-enforcement personnel can usually supply much of the information if the victim cannot recall it. Whenever possible, obtain accident information from the police *and* from the patient; the patient's degree of response and recall may confirm, for instance, his or her level of consciousness immediately after trauma. Use the following list as a guide in eliciting information:

- When recording VS, always include PERLA (pupils [are] equal, react to light, and accommodate) and LOC.
- When (date and time) and where did the accident happen?
- How many vehicles were involved?
- What speed was the vehicle traveling? (Aortic tears occur on deceleration.)
- Was the patient driving or a passenger?

- Were restraints in place (lap/chest/airbags)?
- Was the patient thrown from the vehicle?
- Was there unrestrained cargo?
- What are the injuries and locations? (For example, the driver's head and sternum hit the windshield, dash, or steering column; the passenger's knees and head hit the dash, causing femoral fractures and head and facial injuries.)
- Were the police at the scene? Have they been contacted?

ACUTE-ON-CHRONIC MEDICAL PROBLEMS

For chronic conditions complicated by acute problems, also ascertain the following:

- Name of physician
- Length of illness, age at onset, family history of illness
- Medications currently taken

NEAR DROWNING

For victims of near drownings, ask for the following information:

- Saltwater or freshwater accident?
- Time of accident
- How long submerged
- Water quality (brackish water aspiration predisposes to secondary infection.)
- Water temperature (Extremely cold temperature holds a better survival prognosis.)
- Resuscitation on scene: aspiration? vomitus?
- Accident details: associated injuries (fractures, intra-abdominal trauma, child abuse with forced submersion)

ORTHOPEDIC INJURIES (SPRAINS, STRAINS, PAINS OF UNKNOWN ORIGIN, POSSIBLE FRACTURES)

For orthopedic injuries, obtain the following:

- Location of injury and pain
- Where injury occurred (work, home, school)
- Time of injury
- Treatment since injury
- Location of injury; for ribs, ask if pain is worse on coughing or deep breathing; for

foot or leg, ask if there is more pain on motion or weight bearing; for arm or fingers, ask if there is pain on extension or flexion; verify whether range of motion (ROM) and sensory perception are intact

ILLNESSES

All illnesses should be investigated as to any sudden, recent weight loss or gain; careful documentation is important.

Upper Respiratory Tract Infection

For apparent upper respiratory tract infections (URTIs), find out the following:

- Any symptoms of sore throat, painful ears, cough, or nasal drainage?
- Temperature? Has the patient had any aspirin within the last 3 to 4 hours, and if so, how much?
- How long has the patient had symptoms?
- Has there been any previous treatment for the illness, and if so, when and what?

Nausea and Vomiting or Diarrhea

In the case of nausea and vomiting (N & V) or diarrhea, ascertain the following:

- Full VS and temperature
- Details of symptoms:
    How long (days and hours)?
    How many times in 24 hours?
    Any related pain or injury?
- Any treatment given, including acetylsalicylic acid (ASA)?
- Any blood (bright or dark) noted in vomitus or stools?
- Any changes in appetite or diet in the past 2 to 3 days?
- Amount of liquid being retained? What kind?

Urinary Tract Infection

A urinary tract infection (UTI) requires recording of full VS and temperature. Also, ask the following:

- Location of pain (lower abdomen, flank pain, or both)?
- Urinary frequency, urgency, burning? Scant urine?
- Any blood in urine?

- Any chills or fever?
- Duration of problem in days and hours?
- History of any similar episodes?
- History of previous antibiotic therapy?

Always obtain a clean-catch urine specimen if UTI is suspected, unless a catheterized specimen is ordered. In this situation, anything less than a clean-catch urinalysis is a disservice to the patient.

LACERATIONS

If there are lacerations, note the following:

- Location on body? If on head, note unconsciousness at any time as well as present LOC.
- When and where was the person at the time (work, school, home), and what was he or she doing?
- What caused the laceration(s) (glass, metal, knife)?
- How long ago did the laceration(s) occur?
- Type of bleeding (oozing versus spurting, if observable)?
- Is the ROM or sensory perception affected? Document.
- Date of last tetanus booster and known allergies? Document.

BURNS

For burn patients, take BP if possible and temperature, pulse, and respirations (TPR). Then:

- Note the area of body burned and approximate the percentage of burn.
- Note the type of burn (water, grease, chemical, thermal, electrical).
- Ask how, when, where burn occurred (work, school, home).
- Ask how long ago it occurred.
- Document the date of the last tetanus booster and known allergies.

POISONINGS AND OVERDOSES

For poisonings and overdoses, take full VS and record LOC. Then:

- Note the type and amount of material ingested if known (e.g., dosage per tablet); if unknown, note this.

- Note time of ingestion.
- Note any known reason for ingestion.
- Note any symptoms: coma, nausea and vomiting, burns in the mouth, odor, coughing, shortness of breath, burns in throat.

VAGINAL BLEEDING

With vaginal bleeding, *always* position a clean pad on the patient immediately so that the amount of bleeding can be accurately established while you proceed to obtain the history and full VS. The safest practice is to always assume the patient is pregnant until proven otherwise; then:

- Ascertain the date of last menstrual period (LMP).
- Ask if the patient is pregnant (gravida? para?). What was the date of last birth?
- Ask if the patient is using oral contraceptives or an intrauterine device (IUD)
- Ask if there is any pain. Note type and severity, location (bilateral, unilateral, vaginal), and duration (steady, intermittent, radiating).
- Note and document the severity, duration, and nature of bleeding (e.g., dark clots, heavy bright flow).
- Note the color of the skin (pale, blanched, flushed).
- Note the quality and rate of the radial pulse.

■ LABORATORY DIAGNOSTIC PROCEDURES

After completing the overview of the patient and the initial general assessment, anticipate or requisition appropriate laboratory tests as discussed pre-viously to expedite treatment (presuming that the hospital and ED policies allow the triage or charge nurse to do so).

■ BIBLIOGRAPHY

Bates B, ed. *A Guide to Physical Examination.* 5th ed. Philadelphia, Pa: JB Lippincott; 1991.

Bello TA. The Latino patient in the emergency department. *J Emerg Nurs.* 1980;6:13–16.

Buckingham W, Sparberg M, Brandfonbrener M. *A Primer of Clinical Diagnosis.* 2nd ed. New York, NY: Harper & Row; 1979.

Cahill SB, Balkus M, eds. *Intervention in Emergency Nursing: The First 60 Minutes.* Rockville, Md: Aspen Publishers; 1986.

Cullen HA. Words to the wise. *J Emerg Nurs.* 1993;19:171–172.

Daniels JH. Believing the patient: the lost art of emergency nursing. *J Emerg Nurs.* 1993;19:2.

DeGowin E, DeGowin R. *Bedside Diagnostic Examination: A Comprehensive Pocket Textbook.* New York, NY: Macmillan; 1981.

Dorland's Illustrated Medical Dictionary. 26th ed. Philadelphia, Pa: WB Saunders; 1985.

Eggland ET. How to take a meaningful nursing history. *Nursing 77.* July 1977;22–30.

Emergency Nurses Association. *Emergency Nursing Core Curriculum.* 4th ed. Philadelphia, Pa: WB Saunders; 1994.

Gardner SS. Skills in rapid field assessment. *Top Emerg Med.* 1987;9:12–13.

Knezevich-Brown BA. *Trauma Nursing: Principles and Practices.* E. Norwalk, Conn: Appleton & Lange; 1986.

Larson LL. *Protocols for Advanced Emergency Management.* Bowie, Md: Brady Company; 1982.

Navarro MR, LaCourt G. Helpful hints for use with deaf patients. *J Emerg Nurs.* 1980;6:26–28.

■ REVIEW: NURSING HISTORY AND THE INTERVIEW

1. Identify six barriers to effective and competent primary assessment and history taking.

2. List the points of information basic to a concise and meaningful nursing history.

3. Identify the components of a successful nurse–patient relationship.

4. List at least eight questions to be asked regarding the patient's pain.

5. List at least six points of information that should be clarified and documented regarding the critically injured patient.

6. Explain the rationale for determining when the critically injured patient last ate or drank and how much.

7. List some specific questions appropriate to the following situations:
   a. Near drowning
   b. Upper respiratory tract infections (URTIs)
   c. Nausea, vomiting, or diarrhea
   d. Urinary tract infections (UTIs)
   e. Lacerations
   f. Poisonings or overdoses
   g. Vaginal bleeding

8. Identify the one assumption that should be made until proven wrong when a female of childbearing age presents with vaginal bleeding.

Altered States of Consciousness

Assessment and Management

6

The purpose of this chapter is to assist the emergency nurse (EN) in understanding the multiple causes of an altered state of consciousness and the associated neurological assessments that are accomplished in the emergency department (ED). Rationale and components of the neurological examination are discussed in terms of identification of impairments of the brain, spinal cord, and the peripheral nervous systems, stressing nursing care and protection of the neurologically injured patient.

■ LEVEL OF CONSCIOUSNESS

The level of consciousness (LOC) is the most important observation in the initial evaluation of the neurologically impaired patient. It involves distinct observations of the state of arousal and the content of consciousness.

STATE OF AROUSAL

The assessment of the state of arousal requires an evaluation of the reticular-activating system (RAS), a network of ascending neuronal pathways that originate in the brainstem and send impulses to the thalamus and thus "arouse" or effect higher functions. The RAS is the regulatory control center for the sleep–wake cycle, and when stimulated, it assists in focusing the individual's attention to a specific task. If a patient is unarousable or unresponsive to *any* stimuli, this person is described as comatose. Remember that drugs, alcohol, and hypoxia are common factors that alter the state of arousal as well as the content of consciousness.

The initial stimulus for arousing a patient should be a verbal one (e.g., a voice command, such as "Open your eyes"). If there is no response, tactile stimuli, such as patting the cheek or arm, may be applied. This, combined with statements ("Wake up" or "Can you hear me?") may elicit a response. The final step in evoking arousal is the application of painful stimuli. Acceptable ones include sternal compression (*not* knuckle-rubbing, which can create abrasions on the delicate skin at this site when repeated frequently), a trapezius pinch, or the application of nail-bed pressure, calf pressure, or supraorbital pressure applied at the nerve notch near the nasal margin. Nipple pinching and pubic hair pulling are to be avoided, even if one suspects that an individual is "faking" unresponsiveness. Describe what the patient does in response to a painful stimulus (e.g., "pulls away" or "withdraws the limb"). Note any asymmetry, such as moving only one extremity when withdrawing from pain. Once unconsciousness is established and documented, make sure that multiple emergency personnel do not unnecessarily repeat pain-provoking maneuvers that may eventually result in abrasions and contusions, suggesting patient battering. There are several variations in the state of arousal. For example, a patient may be easily arousable but tend to lag back into sleep quite readily or may arouse with difficulty but be able to maintain an awake state for an extended period of time. The EN should determine if the patient is arousable or not and if so, how long the patient remains awake before returning to sleep. Words such as *lethargic, stuporous,* or *obtunded* should be avoided, since their definitions are ambiguous.

Only objective descriptions of the state of arousal should be reported or recorded in the medical record.

CONTENT OF CONSCIOUSNESS

The content of consciousness can be determined only in the arousable or responsive patient. Of course, the longer the patient can remain awake and focused, the easier it will be to assess the content of the patient's verbalizations. The most ideal state is "alert and oriented ×3" (i.e., to person, place, and time). Variations may manifest in confusion, disorientation, nonsense, or inappropriate responses.

The combination of state of arousal and content of consciousness provides vital information about brain functioning, ranging from the brainstem to the cerebral cortex. Serial observations of these two neurological evaluations provide vital clues to improvements or deterioration in central neurological functions, especially when combined with pupillary signs and motor function tests.

■ EYE SIGNS

When the brain and cranial nerves are functioning normally, the pupils should be round, regular, equal, and reactive (i.e., constrict to light). Alterations in pupillary size and reactivity may indicate dysfunction of the diencephalon, midbrain, and pons. Since these structures are anatomically adjacent to the RAS, eye assessment may provide valuable clues to developing brainstem lesions that contribute to coma.

Both parasympathetic and sympathetic nerves are intricately involved in pupillary responses, and each type has distinct pathways of innervation. Understanding these networks and their interfaces is useful in deciphering the results of pupillary assessments. Parasympathetic fibers arise in the midbrain along with the oculomotor nerve (CN III) at a site proximal to the tentorial notch, an outlet in the meningeal fold that accommodates the brainstem (i.e., the falx tentorium). The CN III fibers and parasympathetic fibers connect directly to the eye from this site. Parasympathetic fibers are responsible for pupillary constriction (i.e., miosis). Sympathetic fibers originate in the hypothalamus

and traverse the brainstem and both lower cervical and upper thoracic spinal cord segments as preganglionic fibers before synapsing and ascending as postganglionic fibers en route to the orbit. Sympathetic fibers effect contraction of the pupillodilator muscles of the iris, causing dilation (i.e., mydriasis). When either of these systems becomes impaired, the expression of the other is unopposed, and thus it becomes dominant. Parasympathetic dysfunction results in 8- to 9-mm pupils (i.e., widely dilated); sympathetic dysfunction results in 1.5- to 2.5-mm pupils (i.e., pinpoint). Midsize pupils, 4 to 5 mm, which are fixed or react only sluggishly, indicate abnormalities in both parasympathetic and sympathetic function.[1]

Pupil abnormalities and their underlying pathophysiologies are summarized in Table 6–1.

PUPILS

The EN should note the size, shape, and quality of pupils before assessing reactivity. Prior eye surgery, an eye prosthesis, or a congenital irregularity in pupil size or shape may affect baseline findings. Since many drugs also affect pupil size, it is useful to elicit a history of recent drug use. Pupillary size is best recorded in millimeters, but in the ED, it is customary to document merely "constricted," "dilated," or "normal."

The direct light reflex should be assessed by noting the pupillary response to a penlight introduced from the sides. Cover the eye that is not being tested. Note first the response of the ipsilateral pupil. Repeat the maneuver with both eyes uncovered and note the response of the contralateral pupil. When one eye is stimulated, the consensual light reflex will induce the identical response in the opposite eye.

EXTRAOCULAR MOVEMENT

If the patient can follow commands, check extraocular movement (EOM), which may reveal damage to the third, fourth, and sixth cranial nerves. CN III controls medial eye movement; CN IV and CN VI permit downward lateral gaze and horizontal lateral gaze, respectively. Test EOMs by instructing the patient to follow your finger without moving his or her head. Cranial nerve lesions are revealed by dysfunction of ipsilateral pupils except for the rare contra coup injury. Since

TABLE 6–1. LOCALIZATION OF BRAIN LESIONS IN A COMATOSE PATIENT

Anatomic Level	Mental Status	Pupillary Size and Position	Oculomotor	Motor Responses	Respiratory and Circulatory
Diencephalon	Drowsy	Small (1–2 mm)	Normal	Abnormalities of flexion	Cheyne–Stokes
Midbrain	Coma	Fixed in midposition	Dysconjugate	Abnormalities of extension	Hyperventilation
Pons	Coma	1 mm in primary pontine injury; fixed and 4–5 mm with prior midbrain injury	Complete paralysis	Abnormalities of extension	Hyperventilation
Medulla	Variable	Variable	Variable	Flaccid	Apnea, circulatory collapse

(*From Bongard and Sue.*[3])

CN III and CN VI have especially long courses through the intracranial vault, abnormalities in the patient's gaze may be an early sign of intracranial pressure.

Documentation of pupils that are equal and reacting to light is usually noted by writing or checking *PERL* (pupils [are] equal and react to light) in the medical record. PERLA is a variation that indicates that the patient's accommodation is also normal. *Accommodation* is the ability to follow an object (e.g., finger) that is held up and moved from a distant to a near point; the eyes can be seen to converge and the pupils to constrict slightly.

ABNORMAL EYE MOVEMENTS

Eye movements are controlled by three cranial nerves: III (oculomotor), IV (trochlear), and VI (abducens). If a patient has a depressed LOC and cannot voluntarily cooperate with an ocular assessment, assuming that the brainstem is intact, eye movements may be random but should be conjugate and cover the normal range of gaze. Changes in the ocular motor system may occur with several types of neurological injury. This system, which is responsible for eye movements, resides between CN VI in the pons and CN III in the midbrain. Adjacent to CN VI is a gaze control center called the pontine paramedian reticular formation (PPRF). Prior to moving an eye laterally (a CN VI function), there is rapid neural firing in the PPRF. The contralateral eye deviates medially via fibers that travel from the PPRF, cross in the pons, and move medially to the contralateral CN III nucleus in the medial longitudinal fasciculus. (Fig. 6–1). This system can be tested by the doll's eye reflex.

Reflex eye movements include both the oculocephalic and oculovestibular reflexes. The involved cranial nerves are VIII (acoustic), III, and VI. Abnormalities in reflex eye movement signal brainstem dysfunction. They *should not* be tested in a conscious patient, however.

Doll's Eye Reflex

The doll's eye reflex test is an assessment of the oculocephalic reflex. The patient's head is positioned with a 30-degree neck extension and horizontally rotated (with the eyes open) from a midline position. Normally, the eyes should first move in the opposite direction and then rest in a few seconds at midline position. In a patient with an impaired reflex, the eyes will move in the same direction with the head (remaining midline) as though they were merely artistic renderings on an antique doll's face. The response to rotation should be tested in both left and right horizontal planes. Vertical head movements may also be assessed. Normally, the eyes will remain for a few seconds in the direction opposite of head movement. If they move with the head, they are considered abnormal (Fig. 6–2).

Cold Calorics

The cold caloric stimulation test is designed to assess the oculovestibular reflex, which may persist even after the loss of the oculocephalic reflex. Ensure that the patient is unresponsive, that cervical spine injury has been ruled out, and that there are

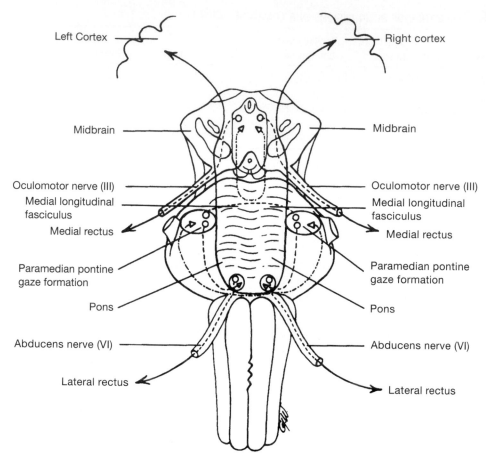

Figure 6–1. Anatomic representation of the reciprocal connections with the pontine paramedian reticular formation (PPRF) horizontal gaze center. (*From Bongard and Sue.*[3])

intact tympanic membranes *before* performing this test. With the patient in a 30-degree upright position, ice water (about 10 mL will usually be adequate for a response) is introduced slowly into the ear canal using moderate pressure. After 1 or 2 minutes (a time period that permits heat transfer), responses may be evaluated. During unconsciousness, the fast component of nystagmus is lost, allowing the slow component to carry both eyes tonically toward the test ear for a few minutes (i.e., horizontal nystagmus), assuming that the brainstem is intact between the vestibular nuclei and the extraocular muscles. If the patient is not unconscious (e.g., faking a coma or is unconscious from psychogenic causes), violent nystagmus, intense nausea, and even vomiting will result. These reactions mark intact functioning of vestibular mecha-

nisms. Both ears should be assessed in the unconscious patient, but the examiner should wait at least 5 minutes before testing the opposite ear. The caloric stimulation test is often used to differentiate a metabolic coma from one of a neurological origin, since the response to caloric stimulation is ordinarily preserved in metabolic coma states. In brain death, responses are absent.

■ MOTOR ASSESSMENT

Motor strength, pathological reflex activity, and abnormal posturing may be tested to determine the extent of neurological injury. The responses will depend upon the patient's LOC and may be affected by muscle and limb trauma as well as by le-

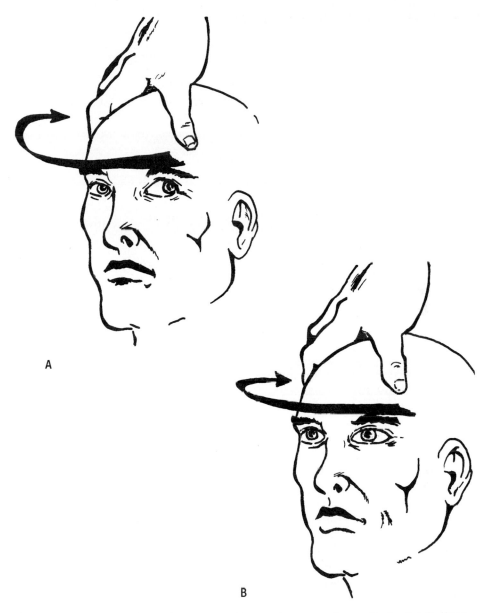

Figure 6–2. Doll's eye maneuver. **A.** Normal. Head is rotated, eyes move in opposite direction. **B.** Abnormal. As head is rotated, eyes remain in midline.

sions of the brain and spinal cord. In a responsive patient, facial weakness can be noted while accomplishing the mini–cranial nerve test. Ask the patient to show his or her teeth, wrinkle his or her forehead, open his or her eyes widely and shut them tightly, extend his or her tongue, and open and close his or her mouth against resistance. In addition to providing a brief assessment of cranial nerve functioning, this sequence may quickly provide important information about motor strength. In the unconscious patient, the cranial nerve testing procedure is modified (Table 6–2). It is extremely important to serially assess and document changes from initial baseline information about motor responses since they may signal significant neurological changes.

TABLE 6–2. CRANIAL NERVE TESTING IN COMATOSE PATIENT

Cranial Nerve(s)	System/Area Controlled	Test
I	Olfactory	Not tested
II	Optic	Pupillary reflex: direct and consensual
III	Oculomotor	Pupillary reflex: direct and consensual and spontaneous or induced medial, superior, or downward eye movements
IV and VI	Abducens Trochlear	Eye movements: spontaneous or oculocephalic reflexes (i.e., doll's eyes)
V	Trigeminal	Corneal reflex, jaw reflex, supraorbital compression
VII	Facial	Observe facial movement while checking corneal reflexes or upon application of supraorbital pressure
VIII	Acoustic	Oculocephalic reflex and cold water calorics
IX and X	Vagus Glossopharyngeal	Gag, cough, and carotid sinus reflex
XI	Spinal accessory	Spontaneous or induced elevation of shoulders
XII	Hypoglossal	Tongue movement against examiner's finger

EXTREMITY STRENGTH AND TONE

If the patient is responsive, test his or her grip by having the patient hold just two of your fingers and pull the fingers out against resistance to test for strength. Have the patient close his or her eyes and extend his or her arms. Observe for downward drift of one arm in 30 to 60 seconds (an indication of weakness). Test arms and hands bilaterally. A gegenhalten response (i.e., counterholding or involuntary resistance to passive movement) may be noted in certain cerebral cortical disorders and is thought to be an early motor indication of rostral-caudal deterioration. It may be revealed during passive motion of extremities, the head, or the trunk. Note general tone and evidence of flaccidity in all extremities.

REFLEXES

Babinski Reflex

The Babinski reflex, an important one, is elicited by stroking the sole of the foot firmly upward, starting at the lateral aspect of the heel and curving medially toward the big toe. A Babinski reflex should be elicited with the least painful stimulus. A normal or negative Babinski reflex is demonstrated when the great toe flexes downward and the other toes flex down or stay in normal position. A positive Babinski, indicating an organic lesion of the pyramidal tract, is marked by dorsiflexion of the great toe upon stimulus.

Brudzinski Reflex

The Brudzinski reflex involves flexing the patient's neck forward. Pain and involuntary flexion of the hips and knees is considered a positive sign for meningeal irritation.

POSTURAL REFLEXES

In patients with an altered state of consciousness, motor function can be assessed by application of painful stimuli and observing whether the responses are appropriate. In an individual with an intact nervous system, pain will evoke a facial grimace, moaning, or purposeful movement in an attempt to push away or withdraw from the stimulus. If sensory pathways or corticospinal tracts are disrupted, the results will include flexor and extensor spasms, abnormal posturing, or flaccidity. Flaccidity is a grave sign, indicating central motor system impairment or extensive damage to the PPRF or denervation of the periphery. Abnormal posturing may be initially noted upon the application of a noxious stimulus, but it may occur spontaneously later. Serial assessments are required to evaluate the extent of injury and its progression, since abnormal posturing changes dynamically in the acute period of neurological injury.

Decorticate Posturing

Decorticate posturing involves abnormal flexion of the arm, wrist, and fingers, with adduction of the upper extremities and extension, internal rotation, and plantar flexion of the lower extremity (Fig. 6–3). Decorticate posturing is indicative of hemispheric involvement or lesions in the basal ganglia or diencephalon that interrupt activity of the corticospinal tracts.

Decerebrate Posturing

Decerebrate posturing indicates a descending lesion of the brain stem. It is characterized by extended, adducted, and hyperpronated arms and rigid leg extension with plantar flexion (see Fig. 6–3.) Opisthotonus may also be noted in severe cases and is marked by an arched body position caused by tetanic spasm. Decerebrate posturing is a hallmark of rostral-caudal deterioration and may signal brain herniation.

■ GLASGOW COMA SCALE

The Glasgow Coma Scale (GCS) is a widely used tool for quickly assessing the patient's neurological state and predicting case outcome. Three factors are scored: eye opening, best verbal response, and best motor response. The maximum score for the GCS is 15. A score of 13 to 15 is considered a mild injury with an excellent prognosis; a score of 9 to 12 indicates a moderate injury. A score of 8 or below indicates coma and a grave prognosis (Table 6–3). This scale is a useful adjunct to neurological examination, but it has several limitations for use in the traumatized patient. For example, maxillofacial trauma may limit eye opening or speech, the presence of an endotracheal tube would prevent any verbal response, and limb fracture could limit motor responses. The efficacy of the GCS is also limited in patients who speak a foreign language or are deaf or under the influence of alcohol. Use of neuromuscular-blocking agents obviously alters utility of the GSC as well. There are several adaptations of this scale and other similar tools have been developed, but the GCS is the dominant one used by prehospital care and ED personnel. Chapter 18 contains the modified GCS for use in neonates and children.

■ DIFFERENTIATION OF COMA STATES: NEUROLOGICAL VERSUS METABOLIC

Blood flow or cerebral metabolism is decreased in all conditions leading to coma. Oxygen levels below 2 L/100 g of brain tissue per minute are incompatible with an alert, oriented state of consciousness. Glucose and other substrates must also be continually supplied in order to maintain synaptic interactions. Oxygen deprivation, endocrine disorders, and a wide range of liver, kidney, and lung pathologies can induce changes in LOC.

There are times when a patient arrives in the ED with some alteration in the level of consciousness and the underlying cause cannot be determined promptly. When assessing patients, the EN should identify factors in the history—especially sequential deterioration of functioning—that would suggest a metabolic basis for the coma. In addition, tremors, asterixis (i.e., liver flap), and multifocal myoclonus point to an extraneurological basis. Also, one must recall that lower brainstem reflexes seldom give clues to the cause of coma, because only the deepest intoxicants (e.g., chemical toxins and harmful biologic substrates) abolish cough, swallowing, and breathing reflexes. Pupillary responses tend to be resistant to metabolic insults to the brain, and thus the presence of a light reflex may be the singular most valuable clue in detecting a metabolic coma.[2]

Other clues to a metabolic coma may include cardiac dysrhythmias, muscle weakness, tetany, flaccidity, and hyperactive deep tendon reflexes due to a decreasing level of ionized calcium, which accompanies an increase in pH. Kussmaul (deep, rapid) respirations tend to reflect the severe acidosis commonly associated with a metabolic abnormality. Arterial blood gases (ABGs) may also be useful in detecting metabolic origins for an altered LOC. If there is no clear cause for the patient's coma, liver and thyroid function tests should be done in addition to ABGs. Serum sodium, glucose, urea nitrogen, creatinine, and a toxicology screen are considered imperative for detecting the precise underlying pathophysiology that gives rise to the altered state of consciousness.[3]

Infection, especially in the elderly patient, may be the primary etiology for coma. Urinalysis and chest radiography should be performed early to detect the most likely sources of sepsis in the older individual.

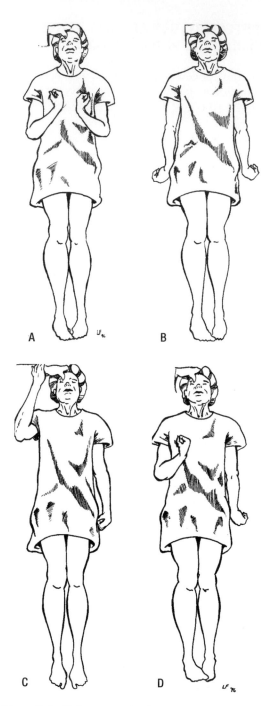

Figure 6–3. Postures seen in the severely brain damaged patient. **A.** Bilateral decortication is marked by abnormal flexion; note that the legs are extended and internally rotated. **B.** Bilateral decerebration is characterized by extension; wrists are externally rotated, legs extended, and feet rotated internally. **C.** Lateralized response; right side is purposeful. Left side is decorticate. **D.** Right side is decorticate; left side is decerebrate.

Since some metabolic causes of coma (e.g., hypoglycemia, hyponatremia, hypoxia) can be quickly reversed, vital signs (VS) should be assessed promptly upon the patient's arrival. Supplemental oxygen and ventilatory support are among initial measures to be implemented. If the gag reflex is not present, endotracheal intubation is an appropriate intervention to prevent aspiration.

■ NURSING CARE OF THE PATIENT WITH AN ALTERED STATE OF CONSCIOUSNESS

Nursing diagnoses include:

- Ineffective breathing pattern related to altered ventilatory mechanics
- Ineffective airway clearance related to paralysis of intercostals and abdominal muscles
- Decreased cardiac output related to neurogenic shock
- Altered urinary elimination related to loss of voluntary control and compromised reflexes
- Impaired skin integrity related to immobility and sensory loss

The EN should recognize that neurologically injured patients have limitations in protecting themselves while they are cared for in the ED. Remember that such a patient is unable to change positions or move away from items that could create pressure or injury. Ensure that the stretcher surfaces are free of wrinkles and debris (e.g., discarded needle caps, intravenous tube sheaths, dentures) that might create skin problems. Provide blankets for a sense of warmth and security. Adjust the patient's position, when feasible, to relieve pressure and prevent stasis. Ensure that limbs are supported and free from impingements from medical equipment, side rails, or monitoring devices. The eyes must be protected, too, if the blink reflex is impaired; artificial tears may be used to keep surfaces moist during prolonged ED stays. Protective eye shields are indicated if there is a lot of activity near the head of the bed, since the sleeves of lab coats, gowns, and gloves may contribute to corneal abrasions. Patients with an impaired LOC may not be able to detect that their bladder is distended or to convey a need to

TABLE 6–3. GLASGOW COMA SCALE: ASSESSMENT OF AROUSABILITY[a]

Category	Response	Score
Eyes open	Spontaneously—eyes open spontaneously	4
	To speech—eyes open to verbal command	3
	To pain—eyes open to painful stimuli	2
	None—no eye opening to any stimulus	1
Best verbal response	Oriented—converses appropriately; knows person, time, date, place	5
	Confused—converses inappropriately; answers to questions inaccurate; uses language appropriately	4
	Inappropriate words—no sustained conversation; speech random, disorganized, and inappropriate	3
	Incomprehensible—mumbles, moans, but does not use recognizable words	2
	None—no verbal sounds even to painful stimuli	1
Best motor response	Obeys commands—performs simple tasks when asked to do so	6
	Localizes pain—appropriate attempt to locate and remove painful stimulus	5
	Flexion withdrawal—flexes arm appropriately to withdraw from source of painful stimulus	4
	Abnormal flexion—flexes arm at elbow, pronates, and makes a fist in response to painful stimulus; decorticate posturing (see Fig. 6–3)	3
	Abnormal extension—extends arm at elbow and adducts with internal rotation in response to painful stimulus; decerebrate posturing (see Fig. 6–3)	2
	None—no response to painful stimulus, flaccid	1

[a] Maximum score, 15; minimum score, 3.

void. Placement of a Foley catheter should be an early step in the nursing care.

Pain is probably perceived, at least in some way, by patients with an altered LOC, but they may be unable to correctly interpret noxious stimuli and to request medications. That pain medication and sedation should be withheld because drugs may interfere with neurological assessment is an archaic but tenaciously held belief of some emergency personnel. It is well documented that judicious use of selected analgesics and sedatives is in fact highly desirable and may limit adverse effects of pain and agitation on brain activity, intracranial pressure, respiratory efficacy, and VS.[4]

Even though neurologically impaired patients may seem unresponsive, the EN should consistently relate to and interact with them as though they *were* responding. Explain your actions and reassure these patients that you are there to care and support them. When a patient with an impaired LOC must be transported outside the department for tests and procedures, ensure that caregivers who will be involved actually understand and appreciate the patient's limitations and are sensitive to the fact that the patient may be feeling, hearing, and comprehending all that is going on in the environment even though unable to react because of devastating neurological injuries.

■ REFERENCES

1. Ruppert SD, Kernicki JG, Dolan JT: *Dolan's Critical Care Nursing.* 2nd ed. Philadelphia, Pa: FA Davis; 1996:538.
2. Plum F, Posner J. *The Diagnosis of Stupor and Coma.* 2nd ed. Philadelphia, Pa: FA Davis; 1982:46.
3. Bongard FS, Sue DY. *Current Critical Care: Diagnosis and Treatment.* E. Norwalk, Conn: Appleton & Lange; 1994:525.
4. Crippen DW: Brain failure and critical care medicine. *Crit Care Nurse Q.* 1994;16:80–95.

■ BIBLIOGRAPHY

Bongard FS, Sue DY. *Current Critical Care Diagnosis and Treatment,* E. Norwalk, Conn: Appleton & Lange; 1994:522–554.

Braithwaite CE, Collin EM, Stein SC, Sherman C. Initial management of head injury: pitfalls and complications. *Trauma Q.* 1991;8:22–33.

Garcia-Perez FA, O'Malley KF. Errors and complications in the initial assessment and resuscitation of the trauma patient. *Trauma Q.* 1991;8:1–21.

Gutierrez G. Cellular energy metabolism during hypoxia. *Crit Care Med.* 1991;19:619–626.

Harad FT, Kerstein MD. Inadequacy of bedside clinical indicators in identifying significant intracranial injury in trauma patients. *J Trauma.* 1992;32:359–363.

McIntosh TK, Morgan AS. New trends in neurodiagnostics and therapeutics. *Trauma Q.* 1992;8:58–73.

Rosenwasser RH, Young WF. Critical care management of head injury. *Trauma Q.* 1992;8:30–57.

Ruppert SD, Kernicki JG, Dolan JT. *Dolan's Critical Care Nursing.* 2nd ed. Philadelphia, Pa: FA Davis; 1996:501–595.

Urden LD, Davie JK, Thelan LA. *Essentials of Critical Care Nursing.* St. Louis, Mo: Mosby-Year Book; 1992:295–322.

Weist PW, Roth PB. *Fundamentals of Emergency Radiology.* Philadelphia, Pa: WB Saunders; 1996.

■ REVIEW: ALTERED STATES OF CONSCIOUSNESS

1. Describe the two essential components to be evaluated in determining the level of consciousness (LOC) and explain what component of neurological functioning is tested in determining state of arousal and content of consciousness.

2. Explain significant abnormalities of pupillary size and reactivity in terms of neurological impairment.

3. Explain the unique value of oculovestibular assessments in unconscious patients.

4. Outline the procedure and nursing responsibilities related to the dolls's eye reflex and icewater calorics.

5. List the recommended steps in performing an evaluation of motor functioning.

6. Describe the features of both decorticate and decerebrate posturing and explain the implications of each aberration.

7. Explain the special value of using the Glasgow Coma Scale (GCS) in initial assessment of a head trauma patient.

8. List four factors useful in differentiating a neurologically induced coma from a metabolically induced coma.

9. State five nursing diagnoses pertinent to a patient with an altered state of consciousness.

10. Cite at least three nursing considerations for protecting the neurologically impaired patient during the emergency department (ED) treatment phase.

Pain Control and Conscious Sedation

7

Control of pain and agitation is vital for minimizing intracranial pressure and the many negative side effects of the unrelenting stress patients experience in the emergency department (ED) after trauma. Although powerful endorphins are liberated during this acute phase and they do provide some analgesic benefits, other adjuncts are often required to augment these naturally occurring substances.

The emergency nurse (EN) must have extensive knowledge of pain and how it can be managed during acute illness and immediately after trauma without compromising patient assessments. It has been widely accepted for many years that analgesia and sedation are reserved for special patient scenarios, such as acute myocardial infarction, renal calculi, and immediately preoperatively; meanwhile, countless patients suffering other types of distress are denied medications, even when they are obviously in need of analgesia or sedation. Common reasons given for withholding such medications are that they may interfere with assessments (e.g., narcotics alter pupil size and may drop blood pressure) and that benzodiazepines may impair memory consolidation and make the individual "more confused." Some physicians believe that if patients are "too comfortable," they may fail to respond to abdominal tenderness, referred pain, and visceral irritation, and this phenomenon may make it more difficult to detect underlying pathology. Emergency personnel should appreciate that carefully selected and monitored analgesia and sedation are actually beneficial for both patients and staff and that their judicious use can do much to facilitate assessment, monitoring, and interventions. Furthermore, if an assessment requires a patient state unaltered by analgesia and sedation, re-

versal agents (e.g., Narcan or Romazicon) may be employed to "cancel" drug effects temporarily to accommodate the examinations. The EN should recall that intramuscular medications have limited application in major trauma owing to the reduced blood flow to the periphery in shock states that may accompany the injury. Many supposedly non-nursing measures (e.g., verbal reassurance and explanations of procedures) are also helpful to relieve the patient's distress. Any analgesia or sedation given in the prehospital environment or in the ED must be carefully documented for anesthesia, critical-care personnel, and others who may provide continuing care.

This chapter is designed to assist the EN in understanding and appropriately managing pain during acute illness and after trauma, which includes the administration of conscious sedation to facilitate diagnostic and therapeutic interventions.

■ PAIN MANAGEMENT IN THE EMERGENCY DEPARTMENT

Pain is a highly subjective experience for the patient and is affected by a wide range of factors, including not only the underlying condition of the individual but also a series of social and cultural variables as well. The EN is often required to give analgesia and sedation without the benefit of information about patients' health-care history or their usual responses to pain and anxiety.

COMPONENTS OF PAIN

The components of pain are perception (the awareness of pain in response to impulses in terms of intensity, frequency, and duration) and reaction (the psychological and physiological responses to painful stimuli). Reaction to pain is of three types: (1) autonomic, (2) somatic (skeletal muscle), and (3) psychological. These three responses, collectively, are called the pain reaction (Fig. 7–1).

PURPOSE OF PAIN

Pain is a mechanism for self-protection because it warns the organism of internal or external threats and continues to warn because there is no sensory adaptation to pain stimuli. The pain reaction serves to prepare the organism for coping with threats; it enhances alertness and perception and readies the body for increased muscular activity. Basically, pain reactions evoke the fight-or-flight response; verbalization of the pain experience serves to communicate the suffering and need for help.

VARIABLES IN PAIN PERCEPTION

Some sociological studies done on the generalities of pain by Zborowski[1] in the 1960s concluded that people differ markedly in their experience of pain, their complaints about symptoms, and their response to the same treatments. It was found that (1) there are strong cultural differences in attitudes towards pain, (2) age has an influence on the acceptance of pain, and (3) sensory restrictions decrease the tolerance for pain.

PAIN THEORIES

The theory of specificity and the gate control theory are two of the leading theories regarding perception of pain; they are discussed here to help promote an understanding of pain as a reality in patient assessment and nursing management.

The Theory of Specificity

The theory of specificity is the traditional theory regarding pain and was developed as early as 1644. This theory asserts that pain has both an immediate and a delayed response. The immediate response is analogous to a bell-ringing mechanism; the theory is also known as the bell ringing theory of pain, as when someone pulls a rope at the bottom of a bell tower and rings the bell on top. This describes the spinal cord's reflex arc, the immediate response in which the stimulus is carried by afferent (sensory) neurons to the spinal cord and returned through efferent (motor) neurons to cause muscle contraction.

The specificity theory also addresses a delayed response to pain in which the stimulus from receptors is sent along afferent neuronal paths to the spinal cord, the brainstem, the thalamus (where initial perception occurs), the cerebral cortex (where interpretation of the painful stimuli occurs), the hypothalamus, and then back down the brainstem and through the efferent neurons to the skeletal muscle. This delayed response is autonomic, skeletal, and psychological.

The Gate Control Theory

The gate control theory of pain, developed in 1965 by Melzack and Wall[2] has broadened our view of clinical pain and its treatment. This theory challenges the older specificity theory; the latter does not account for social, psychological, and cultural influences upon pain.

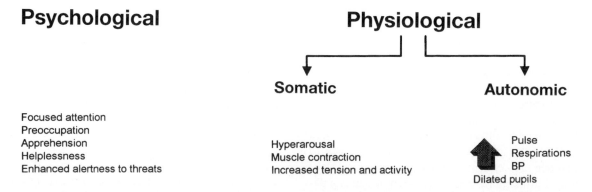

Figure 7–1. The pain reaction—psychological and physiological responses.

The gate control theory suggests there are spinal cord mechanisms that influence the amount of sensory input transmitted from peripheral nerves. The amount of input received at any one time is dictated by the ratio of activity between large and small peripheral nerve fibers. Small fibers (A–delta and C) conduct pain; large fibers (A–beta) conduct other sensations (e.g., touch and pressure). According to the gate control theory, stimulating the large fibers can overload the system and, at the first spinal synapse, inhibit the activity of the smaller pain-conducting fibers. Thus, innocuous sensations carried by the large fibers trigger the brain to "close the gate" against the pain sensations transmitted by the A–delta and C fibers. The important clinical implication of this theory is the possibility that pain may be relieved or inhibited by stimulating the large nerve fibers; both acupuncture analgesia and transcutaneous nerve stimulators (TNSs), which are used widely in relief of chronic pain, are examples of the applications of the gate control theory.

The Role of Endorphins

In 1975, researchers identified a small polypeptide that attached to opiate receptors in the body and called it enkephalin (Greek for "in the head") since it was isolated in pigs' brains; not only did it produce analgesia when injected into animals, but the analgesia was reversed with administration of naloxone (Narcan).

Eventually all similar substances isolated in the brain were renamed endorphin (combining *endogenous* and *morphine*), and the term is now used generically to include all the opiatelike peptides. Research on endorphins is active and ongoing. Many important conclusions have been reached, including beliefs that endorphins:

- Are found in high levels in people with less pain than expected from injury
- May account for pain relief associated with placebo administration
- Are probably depleted by continuing demand in patients with chronic pain
- Sometimes cause euphoria in athletes who stress their bodies beyond the pain level
- May contribute to reduction of anxiety, which is known to increase the perception of pain.[3]

■ CONSCIOUS SEDATION

ENs must be thoroughly familiar with the administration and monitoring of conscious sedation since it is often used as an adjunct for procedures (e.g. chest tube insertion, endoscopy, cardioversion, orthopedic reductions, suturing, incision and drainage of wounds). The trend toward the accomplishment of simple diagnostic and surgical procedures in the ED and without the use of general anesthesia requires that nurses fully understand conscious sedation procedures. Although each facility and department may have slightly different guidelines for conscious sedation, this chapter focuses on basic concepts and principles that are important in any setting to ensure both patient safety and pharmacological efficacy of the agents used.

Conscious sedation is the administration of general, spinal, or other major regional anesthesia or sedation, with or without analgesia, for which there is a reasonable expectation that, in the manner used, the sedation or analgesia will result in the loss of protective reflexes for a significant percentage of a group of patients.[4] Dependent upon the dosage titration and the individual's response to the agents employed, the range of sedation that results can vary from light sedation to general anesthesia, in which the patient loses all protective reflexes and must be mechanically ventilated. Since there are obvious risks associated with conscious sedation, regulatory groups, including the Joint Commission on Accreditation of Healthcare Organizations (JCAHO), and specialty nursing organizations have published guidelines for the role of nurses in the administration and monitoring of conscious sedation. Most emphasize the importance of careful indoctrination of staff prior to implementing conscious sedation procedures. This should, of course, include any medicolegal implications, based on the state's nurse practice act, as well as the nurse's job description and associated institutional policies. The acquisition and validation of education and skills pertinent to the administration and monitoring of conscious sedation is imperative. This includes extensive information about the drugs that might be used as well as the care and safeguarding of the patient before, during, and after procedures. All environments within the EDs where conscious sedation might be administered must have emergency resuscitation equipment, including airway and ventilatory adjuncts, the capabilities to deliver 100 percent oxygen, suctioning, emergency medications, and a defibrillator. Of course, these items should be immediately at hand and there should be expert emergency support personnel to assist in event of a crisis.[5,6]

PATIENT SELECTION

Children, adolescents, and developmentally disabled persons may not be suitable candidates for conscious sedation since their possible psychological instability may pose a safety hazard during the procedure. Furthermore, physiologically immature children often experience unpredictable responses to drugs owing to impaired capabilities to metabolize, use, and eliminate their active components. Any patient's emotional state, ability to communicate and to understand informed consent, and perceptions about the procedure and conscious sedation are vital factors to be considered. Certain individuals may have liver or renal impairment that could alter the actions and side effects of the drugs, or they could be taking other medications that might interact with those used to provide conscious sedation. Patients with dysrhythmias, cardiovascular disease, seizures, an unstable medical condition, those affected by substance abuse (including drugs, alcohol, and tobacco), the obese, the elderly, pregnant patients, or any individual having allergies or sensitivities to opioids, benzodiazepines, or components of propofol (i.e., eggs, soybean oil) pose special risks.

Conscious sedation is designed to permit diagnostic procedures, minor surgery, and selected therapies to be accomplished without the use of general anesthesia. Drugs are administered in dosages that are expected to alter the mood of the patient, elevate the pain threshold, and produce partial amnesia of the events involved, while permitting the patient to retain the ability to control the airway and to respond to directives and various stimulation. The goal of most sedation in the ED is light sedation, preserving the patient's response to verbal stimuli and certain protective mechanisms (e.g., gag reflex). Safe administration of conscious sedation can be assured only by precise titration of carefully selected agents. Nurses must understand the pharmacokinetics of each drug or drugs used in combination and be prepared to deliver, titrate, and

monitor them, without direct medical supervision in some instances. Some forms of regional anesthesia may also fall under the guidelines for conscious sedation since their effects may modify patients' reflexes and interfere with their abilities to breathe or to independently protect their airway.

Dangers that accompany conscious sedation include acute airway obstruction, respiratory depression, seizures, and cardiac arrest. These crises can occur during induction, maintenance, or reversal of conscious sedation.

NURSING DIAGNOSES FOR PATIENTS RECEIVING CONSCIOUS SEDATION

- Risk of injury related to altered state of consciousness
- Ineffective breathing pattern related to respiratory depression
- Ineffective airway clearance related to compromised cough
- Rise for seizures related to cerebral hypoxia
- Alterations in sensory/perceptual processes related to sedation

CONSIDERATIONS PRIOR TO ADMINISTRATION OF CONSCIOUS SEDATION

Nurses who participate in the administration or monitoring of conscious sedation must have specific indoctrination, education, and skills in regard to the procedures involved and must possess a thorough understanding of the actions, side effects, and pharmacokinetics of the agents used. Knowledge and skills in drug titration within a prescribed dosage range are imperative to ensure that the desired pharmacological effects are achieved with minimum amounts of the agent delivered.

Policies should be written, annually reviewed, and readily available in the ED for reference. These policies should address patient selection, monitoring responsibilities, medication that may be administered by nurses, required documentation, postprocedure care, and relevant discharge responsibilities. Emergency physicians, anesthesia personnel, ENs, administrators, risk managers or legal consultants, and clinical pharmacists should collaborate in the development, implementation, and evaluation of policies or procedures associated with conscious sedation.

Nurses who are not certified as registered nurse anesthetists must obtain and maintain documentation of appropriate education and training for participation in conscious sedation regimens. Each health-care facility must ensure nurses participate in a credentialing process and provide regular documentation in all aspects of conscious sedation, including administering and monitoring of the drug used, management of associated crises, and how and when to summon others to manage a developing crisis. Most facilities require advanced cardiac life support (ACLS) course completion or its equivalent, which includes airway management, arrhythmia recognition, and resuscitation procedures for respiratory and cardiac arrest. A program for competency verification must be in place for ENs (Fig. 7–2). Any competency verification program must include knowledge of the medications used for conscious sedation.[7]

DRUGS USED IN CONSCIOUS SEDATION

The major drug groups used in conscious sedation include narcotics, benzodiazepines, intravenous anesthetic agents and central nervous system (CNS) depressants. The choice of an agent, or drugs used in combination, are dependent upon the patient's age, health history, current condition, anticipated length of procedure, and ease and safety of administration.[8,9]

Narcotics

Narcotics include those agents that relieve pain and provide sedation by attaching to opioid receptor sites in the brain or spinal cord. A chief action is their ability to diminish end organ responses to catecholamines. They produce vasodilation of splanchnic beds through release of histamine and by direct effects on neural mediators. These actions may create hypotension and reduce preload and right heart filling pressures. Occasionally the histamine release can also incite bronchospasm, inducing asthma in susceptible individuals. Opiates depress pontine and medullary centers, which regulate minute ventilation, thus decreasing respiratory rate and volume and reducing responsiveness to the carbon dioxide component of the respiratory drive. For example, a morphine dose of 0.15

mg/kg will increase partial pressure of carbon dioxide (PCO_2) by 3 mm Hg, even in healthy, non-injured people. These potential impacts on ventilations must be considered when an agent is selected. Opiates also readily accumulate in the aged and in persons with renal or liver disease, since they are dependent on these organ systems for metabolism and elimination. Other commonly observed effects of narcotics include euphoria, depression, pruritis, and depression of the immune system.

Morphine and fentanyl are frequently used in conscious sedation. Although most ENs are well versed in the administration and monitoring of morphine, only a few have some, if any, experience with fentanyl.

Fentanyl (Sublimaze) is a synthetic opioid that is 700 times more lipophilic than morphine, thus allowing it to pass readily into the brain. It is 200 times more potent than morphine, and thus is dosed in micrograms. It acts rapidly, in 1 to 2 minutes and has a 40 to 60-minute duration of effect with a 100 µg dose. This is equivalent to 10 mg of morphine or 75 mg of Demerol. Fentanyl must be used carefully with benzodiazepines, droperidol (Inapsine), and nitrous oxide, since these combinations can create cardiac depression and a significant decrease in blood pressure. There is little associated respiratory depression and minimal histamine release; however, the EN must remember that respiratory effects of fentanyl persist longer than the analgesic effects. It is therefore a very useful agent for short-term pain control or conscious sedation for procedures. The dosage for conscious sedation usually ranges from 2 to 20 µg/kg per hour IV. Larger doses may cause apnea.

The EN may occasionally be requested to administer meperidine (Demerol) for conscious sedation. This agent should be reserved for young adults who have no impairments of the cardiovascular, renal, or central nervous systems. It can be highly toxic to the elderly, owing to the presence of normeperidine, a metabolic by-product of meperidine that results from biotransformation. The initial dose in any patient should not exceed 10 mg given by slow IV push. The dose may be repeated if the procedure is prolonged. The onset of action is prompt, and effects may persist for up to 4 hours.

Hydromorphone (Dilaudid), 1 to 2 mg slow IV push over 2 to 3 minutes, is another alternative

Competency Verification Record: Conscious Sedation/Analgesia
Directive: JCAHO Accreditation Manual for Hospitals
Date of Checklist Creation: March 1995
Target Group: All Emergency Nurses
Name _____

I. Cognitive
Objective(s)
  1. Define conscious sedation and its purposes.
  2. Identify the differences between conscious sedation, deep sedation, and general anesthesia.
  3. Identify staff qualifications for administration of conscious sedation.
  4. Describe preprocedure, intraprocedure, and postprocedure assessment and monitoring.
  5. Demonstrate knowledge of pharmacological agents used for conscious sedation.
  6. Anticipate and recognize potential complications of IV conscious sedation in relation to the type of medication administered.
  7. Demonstrate skills in airway management, cardiopulmonary resuscitation, dysrhythmia recognition, and treatments.
Teaching Methodology
  a. Read local policies on conscious sedation/analgesia.
  b. Read Gahart BL. Intravenous medications. 12th ed. St. Louis: Mosby-Year Book, 1995.
  c. Read the following: Guidelines for the elective use of conscious sedation, deep sedation and general anesthesia pediatric patients. Pediatrics 1985;76:317–21.
  d. Gagnon L. President's message: administration of intravenous conscious sedation in the emergency department. J Emerg Nurs 1991;17:123.
  e. Neff JA. Patient care guideline: conscious sedation. J Emerg Med 1992;18:170–2.
Method of Evaluation/Standard: Closed-book written test/90%.
Frequency of Reverification: Annual
Reverification Requirements: Retest.
Written test passed on _____ with a score of equal to or greater than minimal passing score of 90%. Member's test score is maintained in _____ for record purposes. Member is proficient in the cognitive phase of conscious sedation.

Signature of Preceptor

II. Performance
Objective(s)
  1. Uses hospital guidelines to prepare patient for conscious sedation.
  2. Ensures consent form has been signed.
  3. Obtains baseline vital signs to include pulse oximetry, last oral intake, weight, and allergies.
  4. Initiates a patent intravenous access.
  5. Obtains all drugs to be used and their antagonists before start of procedure.
  6. Has all equipment for resuscitation available and operational, including oxygen.
  7. Maintains all flow sheets according to documentation policies.
  8. Never leaves the patient unattended.
  9. Communicates effectively with providers, other nurses, and family on the patient's condition.
  10. Initiates appropriate treatments in response to complications; notifies physician.
Teaching Methodology
  Demonstration, supervised practice, and record review.
  NOTE: Stop procedure and correct deficiencies if nurse is failing to meet standards.
Method of Evaluation/Standard
  Based on the following criteria:
  1. (1) Procedure for nurses with prior ED/conscious sedation experience.
  2. (2) Procedures for nurses with other experience.
  3. (4) Procedures for new nurses.
  4. (1) Procedure under supervision for reverification.
Frequency of Reverification: Annual
Reverification Requirements: Same as initial requirements.
Performance Checklist: Critical Behaviors
Part I: Preprocedure Assessment
  A. Prepare the patient for conscious sedation:
    1. Check for allergies.
    2. Ensure informed consent is done.

(continued)

Figure 7–2. Competency verification for conscious sedation/analgesia. JCAHO, Joint Commission on Accreditation of Healthcare Organizations. (*Courtesy 89th Medical Group, Andrews Air Force Base, Maryland.*)

   3. Establish last oral intake.
   4. Obtain weight.
   5. Initial vital signs to include pulse oximetry.
   6. Establish level of consciousness.

 B. Assemble equipment/supplies:
   1. Automatic BP monitor (manual cuff)
   2. Patient IV site/emergency drugs.
   3. Oxygen 2 L nasal cannula.
   4. Functioning suction apparatus.
   5. Cardiac monitor with electrodes.
   6. Bag-mask-valve device with appropriate site masks.
   7. Airway adjuncts.
   8. Defribrillator.

 C. Obtain medications and antagonists:
   1. Verify correct medication dosages with physician's orders.
   2. Check expiration dates on all medication.
   3. Demonstrate knowledge of medication: dosages, route of administration, dilution if needed, expected actions, and contraindications.
   4. Communicate effectively with physicians, nurses, and other members of the care team.

Part II: Intraprocedure Assessment/Notes
   1. Position patient to maintain patent airway.
   2. Monitor vital signs and record every 5 minutes to include pulse oximetry.
   3. Document medication dosage, route, and patient's response to medication.
   4. Constantly monitor patient's level of consciousness, respiratory status, and response to procedure.
   5. Notify physician if any changes occur.

Part III: Postprocedure Assessment
   1. Monitor vital signs and record every 15 minutes, monitor respiratory effort, level of consciousness, and pulse oximetry.
   2. Assess and document patient's Aldrete* score every 30 minutes.
   3. Document patient's response to sedation.
   4. Remain with the patient at all times.
   5. Monitor patient for a minimum of 30 minutes.

Part IV: Discharge Data
   1. Recommend discharge when Aldrete score reaches 10 (after 30 to 60 minutes)
   2. Document patient's condition at discharge.
   3. Document patient's disposition (with whom, where).
   4. Ensure follow-up appointment is given to patient/escort.
   5. Ensure a written instruction sheet is given to and reviewed with the patient or accompanying responsible adult.
   6. Document time of discharge.
   7. Complete all documentation.
Checklist completed on _____ with a score of Satisfactory. Member is proficient in the performance phase of conscious sedation.

Signature of Preceptor

Figure 7–2. Continued. (*Aldrete scoring tool consists of 5 components: 1) activity, 2) respirations, 3) circulation, 4) consciousness, and 5) color.)

opiate. The onset of action is within 10 to 15 minutes, necessitating its administration well ahead of the start of a procedure. The duration of effect is 2 to 3 hours.

Benzodiazepines

Unlike the narcotics, benzodiazepines have no analgesic properties, and their use for conscious sedation must always include the concurrent administration of an analgesic. Patients receiving benzodiazepines have little perception of discomfort, owing to the action of the drug on the limbic system via γ aminobutyric acid (GABA), a neuroinhibitory transmitter. Effects include amnesia, hypnosis, and skeletal muscle relaxation. Since they are dependent upon the liver for biotransformation and are excreted via the kidneys, drug action may be prolonged in diseases of these organs, or if shock or congestive heart failure is present. Respiratory depression can occur in patients with pulmonary disease, due to the relaxation of respiratory-related muscles as well as from central depression of the ventilatory drive. Smaller doses should be used for the elderly and for patients with hepatic or cardiovascular disease.

Midazolam (Versed), 0.5 to 2.5 mg slow IV push, has several important characteristics that make it ideal for conscious sedation. The onset of action is within 1 to 3 minutes, with a duration of 1 to 4 hours. Although Versed is short-acting and respiratory depression is infrequently experienced, it is recommended that it be diluted in at least 5 mL of saline to promote slower absorption. *Do not deliver this drug by rapid bolus!* Administer over 2 minutes, waiting 2 to 3 minutes prior to repeating a dose. Up to 5 mg may be required for effect. The dosage should be reduced by one third if a narcotic premedication has been given. If the patient is over 60 years of age, a lower dose is also recommended. There is a distinct risk of underventilation in the chronically ill or elderly patient, even when Versed is given slowly, in small increments. Antereograde amnesia persists for 20 to 40 minutes after dose.

Diazepam (Valium), 0.1 mg/kg (usually 10 to 30 mg), may be given at a rate not exceeding 5 mg/min. (Valium may be diluted with saline prior to administration.) Any bolus doses should be given slowly. Onset of action is swift, with a 1 to 3-hour effect. A large vein must be selected, and if Valium is given via intravenous tubing, it should be introduced very close to the tube insertion site.

Lorazepam (Ativan) is diluted 1:1 before administration. The dose is 0.05 mg/kg, up to 4 mg. Although the onset of action is within 1 to 5 minutes, it is recommended that this drug be given 15 to 20 minutes prior to the procedure to ensure the maximum amnesiac effect. Slow administration is a must, with frequent aspiration checks to ensure venous patency. If the patient will be receiving a narcotic concurrently, the usual opiate dose should be reduced by one third. Although it is an unlikely coadministered drug, scopolamine is never used concurrently with Ativan since CNS and cardiovascular side effects are unpredictable and may be counterproductive or disastrous. *Do not use* Ativan for perioral or pharyngeal procedures, during pregnancy, or for any patients with alcoholism or hepatic or renal disease. Use in children under 18 or in adults over 50 is also discouraged. The drug must be stored in the refrigerator and protected from light to ensure its quality.

Special Considerations for Benzodiazepine Use

After administration of any benzodiazepine (i.e., a muscle-relaxing drug), safety considerations need to be addressed in an ambulatory setting since patients may be weak and unsteady after administration.

The reversal agent for benzodiazepines is flumazenil (Romazicon), given as follows: 0.2 mg over 30 seconds, followed by 0.3 mg over the next 30 seconds and 0.5 mg within 60 seconds. The agent must be used with caution for seizure patients since it lowers the seizure threshold. Seizures should always be anticipated during delivery of Romazicon. Although the reversal agent may assist in combating respiratory depression, it should not be used as a substitute for mechanical ventilatory assistance if the patient is breathing ineffectively. Assist at once with a bag-valve-mask unit and supply supplemental oxygen.

Propofol

Propofol (Diprivan) is an intravenous sedative hypnotic that originally was used for induction and maintenance of anesthesia; later, it was employed during monitored anesthesia care, and now is used in many settings for conscious sedation. Effects of propofol range from antianxiety to sedation and even full anesthesia, so dosage must be carefully calculated, and precise titration is required throughout a procedure to ensure desired effects. Action onset is prompt, within seconds of drug delivery, and effects may be maintained easily by dosage adjustments. This agent may produce several cardiovascular responses, owing to its effect on systemic vascular resistance. It must be cautiously employed if patients have hypovolemia, impending heart failure, or coronary artery disease. It decreases cerebral blood flow and thus requirements for oxygen. It is thought that the use of propofol may be quite beneficial as a sedative agent if the patient has any intracranial vascular pressure elevation. When propofol administration is terminated, patients emerge from the sedation smoothly and their consciousness level reverts promptly to the preprocedure state.

Propofol cannot be used for patients allergic to soybean oil or egg lecithin, since the drug vehicle is Intralipid. It is not recommended for use in pregnant patients or nursing mothers and those individuals with hyperlipidemia.

Propofol can be administered through either a peripheral or central line, but extreme care must be used to avoid any contamination of the intravenous route since this drug does not contain any preservatives and would serve as an excellent nutrient media for microorganisms. Other precautions include avoiding rapid infusion at the onset of delivery, since hypotension, bradycardia, and apnea have been reported in such instances. Hetastarch may be used if the blood pressure drops precipitously. Arrhythmias (especially bradycardia), seizures, apnea, and anaphylaxis have also been reported, so all life-support equipment should be at the bedside on standby.

Propofol sedation is usually initiated with 5 μg/kg and the dose is incrementally increased until the desired level of sedation is achieved.

Although other intravenous anesthetic agents (e.g., ketamine [Ketalar], etomidate [Amidate]) may be given by anesthesia personnel for achieving conscious sedation, nurses in most settings are not permitted to administer these agents.

Central Nervous System Depressants

Barbiturates (e.g., methohexital [Brevital], pentobarbital [Nembutal]) are rarely used for conscious sedation, owing to their cardiovascular side effects, such as dysrhythmia production. Chloral hydrate, a sedative/hypnotic agent, may be employed for brief pediatric procedures. The "pediatric cocktail" combinations (usually meperidine, thorazine, and phenergan) are not advised for conscious sedation, owing to their prolonged respiratory depressant effects.[10] Although hydroxyzine (Vistaril) and promethazine (Phenergan) may be used as adjuncts to conscious sedation (increasing sedation and decreasing the likelihood of nausea and vomiting), these agents do not produce sufficient sedation to be used alone.

PATIENT PREPARATION FOR CONSCIOUS SEDATION

Conscious sedation should be administered only in a setting in which the patient can be monitored and in which full resuscitation support is immediately available. Although all EDs possess the required resources for life-support efforts, staffing and other departmental nursing responsibilities limit achievement of the most ideal conditions for drug administration and patient monitoring. These factors must be considered fully prior to initiating conscious sedation.[11]

Be certain that informed consent has been obtained and that all documentation has been accomplished prior to giving any medications. The EN should also ensure that patients have someone to transport them home if discharged from the ED after a procedure, since the drugs used for conscious sedation impair abilities to drive. Most institutions require baseline blood work and perhaps an electrocardiogram (ECG) prior to using conscious sedation. Ideally, the patient should have been NPO (nothing by mouth) for several hours (i.e., about 4), but in the emergency setting, it is sometimes difficult to ascertain when the last food or beverage was consumed. Baseline vital signs (VS), height, weight, and allergy/sensitivity history should be documented. Medications such as antihypertensives, antidysrhythmics, diuretics, anticonvulsants, insulin, oral hypoglycemics, and antihistamines can pose special risks when administering conscious sedation. Assess the upper airway and ensure that the patient can open the mouth wide and hyperextend the neck to facilitate emergency intubation if it were to become necessary at any point. Certain dentures and oral appliances may need to be removed, and the EN should discuss any concerns with the physician prior to initiating conscious sedation. It is vital to establish intravenous access and ensure patency. An armboard is essential for maintaining unimpeded flow throughout the procedure. If the patient is hypovolemic, this should be corrected before administering conscious sedation. Cardiac and pulse oximetry monitors should be in use, and baseline recordings should be reviewed to detect any abnormalities. Supplemental oxygen is delivered before and during the procedure, since blood oxygen desaturation can occur precipitously while opioids and sedatives are being delivered. Any measures that will help to put the patient at ease are useful because a comfortable and relaxed individual is likely to require less medication than one who is anxious. Assure patients that they will be not be unconscious and tell them that they may experience unpleasant sensations during the procedure and that they will be expected to let the staff know

DEPARTMENT OF EMERGENCY MEDICINE; CONSCIOUS SEDATION DOCUMENTATION

I. PRE-PROCEDURE ASSESSMENT   Diagnosis: _____ Allergies: _____

Last PO Intake: _____ Weight: _____ Procedure: _____

Provider: _____

Informed Consent Obtained ___Yes/No___

Equipment: Patient IV _____ Oxygen _____ Cardiac Monitor _____ B/P Monitor _____ Airway Adjuncts: _____

Defibrillator: _____ Pulse Ox: _____ Suction Apparatus _____ Ambu Bag _____ Antagonist/Emergency Drugs _____

A. LOC: Awake and Oriented _____ , Confused _____ , Drowsy _____ , Lethargic _____ , Unconscious _____

B. Skin: Warm _____ , Cool _____ , Dry _____ , Moist _____ , Color _____

C. IV Site: _____ IV Solution: _____

D. Emotional Status: Calm _____ , Apprehensive _____ , Restless _____ , Crying _____ , Assessed by: _____

E. Vital Signs: Temp _____ , Pulse _____ , Resp _____ , B/P _____/_____ , Pulse OX _____

II. INTRO-PROCEDURE ASSESSMENT/NOTES

Sedation Start: _____ Procedure Start: _____
A. Positioning: Supine ____ , Prone ____ , Lateral ____ , Left ____ , Right ___
B. LOC: Awake and Oriented _____ , Confused _____ , Drowsy _____ ,
    Lethargic _____ , Unconscious _____
C. Emotional Status: Calm _____ , Apprehensive _____ , Restless _____ ,
    Crying _____ , Assessed by: _____
D. Nurses Notes: _____
_____
_____
Sedation End: _____ Procedure End: _____

III. POST-PROCEDURE ASSESSMENT/MONITORING

Ancillary Nurse Notes ___Yes / No___
A. LOC: Awake and Oriented _____ , Confused _____ , Drowsy _____ ,
    Lethargic _____ , Unconscious _____
B. Skin: Warm _____ , Cool _____ , Dry _____ , Moist _____ , Color _____
C. IV Intake: _____ Output: Urine _____ , Emesis _____
D. Resp Status: Breathing Unassisted _____ , Ventilated _____ ,
    Oxygen per Cannula _____ L/min, Mast _____ L/min
E. Movement: Moving U/L Extremities _____ , Not Moving, Location _____
F. Emotional Status: Calm _____ , Apprehensive _____ , Restless _____ ,
    Crying _____ , Assessed by: _____

	TIME						TIME				
Medication											**Response**
Dose											
Route											
B/P											
Pulse											
Resp											
Pulse Ox											
Aldrete Score											

Modified Aldrete Scoring

	SCORE		SCORE
I. Activity:		IV. Consciousness	
Able to move 4 extremities............. 2		Fully alert and able to	
Able to move 2 extremities............. 1		answer questions.... 2	
Not able to control any extremities........ 0		Arousable............. 1	
II. Respiration:		Failure to elicit response.. 0	
Able to breathe deeply and cough........ 2		V. Color	
Limited respiratory effort (dyspnea)....... 1		Normal Pink........... 2	
No spontaneous respiratory effort........ 0		Pale, dusky, blotchy...... 1	
III. Circulation:		Frank cyanosis......... 0	
B/P +/− 20% pre-sedation level.......... 2			
B/P +/− 20–50% pre-sedation level........ 1			
B/P +/− 50% pre-sedation level.......... 0			

Patient Name: _____
SSN: _____
Date: _____ Log #: _____

IV. DISCHARGE   Condition at release:

Alert/Reactive	Y / N
Aldrete Score	

Discharge to care of: _____

Admit to hopsital: _____

Post Procedure Instructions to: Patient _____ Escort _____

Follow-up appt/date/time: _____

Time Released: _____

Nurses Notes: _____
_____
_____
_____
_____
_____

Figure 7–3. Conscious sedation documentation form. (*Adapted from material of the Joint Commission on Accreditation of Healthcare Organizations, Oakbrook Terrace, Ill., with permission. Form Courtesy of 89th Medical Group, Andrews Air Force Base, Maryland.*)

if more pain control is needed. A prearranged way to signal discomfort is useful for both the patient and staff, and this should be confirmed and reinforced verbally throughout the procedure (e.g., "raise your hand or arm or 'make a face' if you need more medication to be comfortable"). It is also important to explain that memories about the procedure may be minimal since medications commonly used for conscious sedation create varying degrees of amnesia. At the onset on conscious sedation, take a few moments to be certain that the patient is comfortable on the stretcher or examination table. Side rails, safety belts, and extremity supports should be used as necessary to ensure that skin and bony prominences are well protected; make sure there are no items that might impede circulation or contribute to nerve compression (e.g., armboard, side rail, restraints).

OBSERVATIONS DURING THE PROCEDURE

Minimum monitoring parameters throughout the procedure include cardiac rate and rhythm, respiratory rate by auscultation and observation, arterial oxygen saturation by pulse oximetry, blood pressure by manual or automatic cuff, and the patient's level of consciousness. The intervals for documentation of monitoring parameters are determined by the drugs used and the age of the patient and may vary. Children and the elderly must be watched especially closely, owing to their unpredictable responses.[12] The EN should note any evidence of pain, such as tearing, muscle rigidity, facial grimaces, groaning, agitation, or changes in heart and respiratory rates, either increases or decreases. Hypotension or hypertension, blurred vision, nausea, euphoria, and dizziness may also indicate adverse drug actions. Respiratory or cardiac arrest or the onset of seizure activity requires immediate cessation of conscious sedation drugs and the prompt initiation of resuscitative measures.

ENs participating in administration or maintenance of conscious sedation should have no other responsibilities that would remove them from the patient's side, even for a moment, during the sedation period. Conscious sedation should not be initiated before the physician is available to start the procedure.

DOCUMENTATION

There are many forms appropriate for the documentation of conscious sedation. If your hospital does not already have an approved form, you may wish to develop one for use in the ED (Fig. 7–3).

RECOVERY AND DISCHARGE PROCEDURES

Discharge criteria commonly include stable VS, airway patency and satisfactory ventilation of the lungs; mobility; intact protective reflexes; absence of protracted nausea or vomiting; ability to take oral fluids and to urinate; preprocedure sensorimotor abilities (e.g., able to dress, walk, and communicate); satisfactory postprocedure results of checks of wounds, surgical dressings, tubes, and orifices, and other relevant findings pertinent to risks of bleeding or other postoperative complications. Ordinarily patients must be observed and monitored for 1 to 3 hours after a procedure, with regular documentation of LOC, airway patency, VS, and ventilatory efficacy. ENs who are monitoring the recovery of patients from conscious sedation should not be distracted from this responsibility by other ED duties. It is imperative to provide constant vigilance and to be immediately able to respond to a developing crisis.[13] When it is determined that the patient can be discharged, a responsible adult must accompany the individual and provide transportation. Written discharge instructions should include warnings about operating machinery, driving, alcohol consumption, and the potential for delayed drug effects. Remember that some amnesia occurs as a result of conscious sedation, so verbal instructions must be duplicated in writing and verbalized by an attending adult.

■ REFERENCES

1. Zborowski M. People in Pain. San Francisco, Calif: Jossey-Bass; 1969.
2. Mclzack R, Wall PD. Pain mechanisms: A new theory. *Science.* 1965;150:971.
3. Fincke MK, Lanros NE. *Emergency Nursing: A Comprehensive Review.* Rockville, Md: Aspen; 1985.
4. Joint Commission for Accreditation of Healthcare Organizations. *Accreditation Manual for Hospitals.* Chicago, Ill: JCAHO; 1996.

5. Position statement on the role of the RN in the management of patients receiving IV conscious sedation for short-term therapeutic, diagnostic or surgical procedures. *AORN J.* 1992;55:207–208.

6. Association of Operating Room Nurses. Proposed recommended practice: monitoring the patient receiving IV conscious sedation. *AORN J.* 1992;56:316–324.

7. Nelson MS, Walter VE, Watkins LM. Competency verification for conscious sedation. *J Emerg Nurs.* 1996;22:116–119.

8. Barber JM. *Sedatives, Analgesics and Neuromuscular-Blocking Agents.* Lewisville, Tex: Barbara Clark Mims Associates; 1995.

9. Crippen DW. Brain failure in critical care medicine. *Crit Care Nurs Q.* 1994;16:80–95.

10. Feliciano DV, Moore EE, Mattox KL. *Trauma.* 3rd ed. Stamford, Conn: Appleton & Lange; 1995:893.

11. Snyder J. How we do it: monitoring patients who receive conscious sedation in the emergency department. *J Emerg Nurs.* 1993;19:2:147–149.

12. Woodin LM. Resting easy: how to care for patients receiving IV sedation. *Nurs 96.* 1996;33–40.

13. Somerson SG, Husted CW, Sicilia MR. Insights into conscious sedation. *AJN.* 1995;95:26–32.

■ BIBLIOGRAPHY

Aitkenhead AR, Willatts SM, Collins CH et al. Comparison of propofol and midazolam for sedation in critically ill patients. *Lancet.* 1989;2:704–708.

American Association of Nurse Anesthetists. Qualified providers of conscious sedation. Park Ridge, Ill: AANA; 1991:2.2.

American Society of Post Anesthesia Nurses. Standards of post anesthesia nursing practice, 12991. Richmond, Va: ASPAN; 1991:26–29.

Association of Operating Room Nurses. Proposed recommended practice: monitoring the patient receiving IV conscious sedation. *AORN J.* Aug 1992;56:316–324.

Armstrong DK, Crisp CB. Pharmacoeconomic issues of sedation, analgesia, and neuromuscular blockade in critical care. *Sci Pract Acute Med.* 1994;2:85–93.

Barber JM. *Sedatives, Analgesics and Neuromuscular-blocking agents.* Lewisville, Tex: Barbara Clark Mims Associates; 1995.

Cardona VD, Hurn PD, Bastnagel Mason PJ, et al. *Trauma Nursing.* 2nd ed. Philadelphia, Pa: WB Saunders, 1994.

Chernow B, ed. *The Pharmacologic Approach to the Critically Ill Patient.* 3rd ed. Baltimore, Md: Williams & Wilkins; 1994.

Crippen DW. Brain failure in critical care medicine. *Crit Care Nurs Q.* 1994;16:80–85.

Emergency Nurses Association. ENA position statement on conscious sedation: emergency nurses practice (rev. Sept. 1994). Chicago, Ill: ENA; 1992.

Freeman JW, Hoptkinson R. Therapeutic progress in intensive care sedation and analgesia: part II. Drug selection. *J Clin Pharm Ther.* 1988;13:41–51.

Greenlee KK. Pain and analgesia: considerations for the elderly in critical care. *Clin Issues Crit Care Nurs.* 1991;2:720–728.

Murphy EK. Monitoring IV conscious sedation: the legal scope of practice. *AORN J.* 1993;57:512–514.

Neff J. Patient care guidelines: conscious sedation. *J Emerg Med.* 1992;18:170–172.

Nelson MS, Walter VE, Watkins LM. Competency verification for conscious sedation. *J Emerg Nurs.* 1996;22:116–119.

Position statement on the role of the RN in the management of patients receiving IV conscious sedation for short-term therapeutic, diagnostic or surgical procedures. *AORN J.* 1992;55:207–208.

Snyder J. How we do it: monitoring patients who receive conscious sedation in the emergency department. *J Emerg Nurs.* 1993;19:147–149.

Somerson SG, Husted CW, Sicilia MR. Insights into conscious sedation. *AJN.* 1995;95(6):26–32.

Watson DS, James DS. Intravenous conscious sedation: implications of monitoring patients receiving local anesthesia. *AORN J.* 1990;51:1512–1522.

Willen JS. Giving fentanyl for patients outside the OR. *AJN.* 1994;94:24–29.

Woodin LM. Resting easy: how to care for patients receiving IV sedation. *Nurs 96.* 1996;33–40.

Ziehm SR. Intravenous haloperidol for tranquilization in critical care patients: a review and critique. *Clin Issues Crit Care Nurs.* 1991;2:729–740.

■ REVIEW: PAIN CONTROL AND CONSCIOUS SEDATION

1. Explain how pain and anxiety can negatively affect physiological processes and interfere with assessment and interventions in the acute phase of illness or after trauma.

2. Describe the role of endorphins in modulating the pain patients experience in the post-trauma period.

3. Differentiate between the characteristics of acute inflammatory pain and colic.

4. Describe pain patterns for:
   a. Gastrointestinal (GI) tract
   b. Capsulated organs (e.g., liver, kidneys, ovaries)
   c. Muscle-walled cavities (e.g., uterus, bladder, gallbladder)
   d. Intra-abdominal bleeding

5. Outline nursing approaches that are useful in allaying fears and anxieties typically accompanying pain.

6. Define *conscious sedation.*

7. Explain the rationale for the steps associated with patient and environmental preparation prior to induction of conscious sedation.

8. Cite actions, administration guidelines, monitoring parameters, and adverse side effects for narcotics, benzodiazepines, and other agents commonly used for conscious sedation.

9. List five standards of practice that have been established to ensure the safe administration of conscious sedation.

10. Outline the discharge criteria for patients who have received conscious sedation in the emergency department (ED).

Spinal Cord Assessment

8

Approximately 10,000 new cervical and thoracic spinal injuries are reported annually within the United States.[1] They result from vehicular trauma, diving, and other sports-related mishaps, firearms injuries, and falls. Since the highest number occur among children and young adults, lifelong effects are often catastrophic. The individual disabilities pose multiple physical and psychosocial challenges for the victims and often constitute an enormous financial burden for the family and the health-care system.

The main tracts in the spinal cord are as follows:

- Dorsal spinothalamic tract (through the spine to the thalamus), which mediates position, deep pressure or touch, and vibration
- Lateral spinothalamic tract, which mediates pain and temperature
- Ventral spinothalamic tract, which mediates light touch
- Lateral corticospinal tract (80 percent of all motor fibers run through this tract)
- Ventral corticospinal tract (the remaining 20 percent of motor fibers run through this tract)

The vertebral spine is divided into five sections: 7 cervical, 12 thoracic, 5 lumbar, 5 sacral, and 4 coccygeal. Both the sacral and coccygeal vertebrae segments are fused, each segment functioning as a singular bone. The front part of each vertebra is a round, solid bone. The posterior part is an arch open toward the inside. This series of arches forms a tunnel that runs the length of the spine and creates the encasement for the spinal cord. (Fig. 8–1). Vertebrae are separated from one another by cartilaginous disks, which act as cushions between the bones. The disks permit some motion, such as turning the head, bending the trunk forward or backward, and leaning it to either side, but they also restrict motion of the vertebrae to prevent spinal cord injury. If there is any force that fractures, compresses, or displaces one or more of the bony segments, the cord can be easily damaged (Fig. 8–2). There are 31 pairs of spinal nerves, one pair for each segment of the spinal cord: 8 cervical, 12 thoracic, 5 lumbar, 5 sacral, and 1 coccygeal. Each spinal nerve has a dorsal (posterior) root and a ventral (anterior) root, carrying sensory and motor fibers. The main supply of blood to the cord is provided by the vertebral artery and a network of small spinal arteries.

■ MECHANISMS OF INJURY

The primary mechanical forces of spinal cord injury include hyperextension-hyperflexion (e.g., an acceleration force from a rear-end collision), hyperflexion-hyperextension (e.g., deceleration force from high-impact vehicular crash or diving injuries), compression (e.g., fall from heights with landing on the feet), and rotation of the vertebral column (e.g., side forces or multiple trauma forces). The spinal cord may be injured in four major ways: contusion, concussion, compression, and transsection.

CONTUSION

Contusion occurs when the vertebrae or ligaments are injured, permitting instability in the vertebral column and impairment of circulation, which induces ischemia. Although the cord's blood supply is modest at best, an associated deficiency of collateral circulation may lead to tissue necrosis.

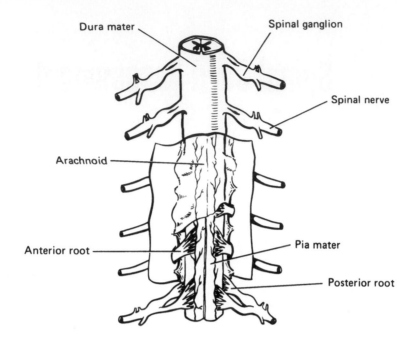

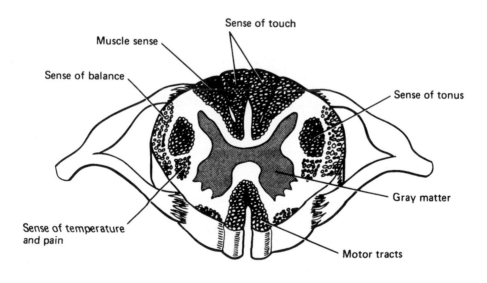

cross section

Figure 8–1. Spinal cord.

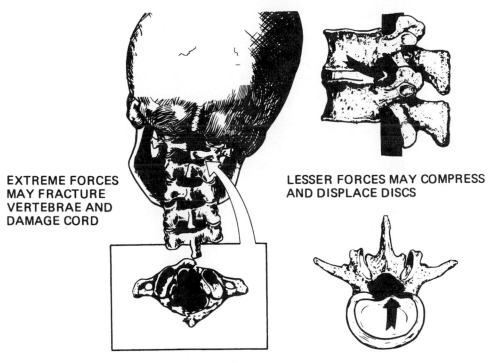

EXTREME FORCES
MAY FRACTURE
VERTEBRAE AND
DAMAGE CORD

LESSER FORCES MAY COMPRESS
AND DISPLACE DISCS

Figure 8–2. Spinal cord trauma.

Spinal cord contusions are characterized by local edema, microscopic hemorrhages, and degenerative changes in the cord.

CONCUSSION

Concussion is a short-term interruption of function *without* residual loss of function.

COMPRESSION

Compression occurs when the cord is trapped or impinged by injured bony fragments (which may be either malaligned or fractured) and the associated edema at the site of injury. If the cord's circulation is affected, ischemia may result. Early recognition of spinal cord compression ensures that surgical decompression can be accomplished prior to irreversible cord damage.

TRANSSECTION

Transsection of the spinal cord may be either a complete injury with loss of all function below the level of injury, or incomplete, with sparing of selected activity. The latter injury is sometimes re-

ferred to as a partial section or laceration. The outcomes of functioning for the patient will directly relate to the level of injury (Table 8–1).

■ PARTIAL CORD INJURY SYNDROMES

Sacral sparing may occur with certain spinal cord injuries. A peripheral rim of tissue supplied by radicular arteries may carry sensation from the lower sacral segments. The individual may have saddle area sensation in the presence of what would be, in most cases, complete paralysis and loss of sensation below the level of the lesion. Partial cord injury syndromes can be described as follows.[2]

ACUTE ANTERIOR CERVICAL CORD SYNDROME

Acute anterior cervical cord syndrome is usually associated with cervical flexion injuries, resulting in complete loss of motor function, pain, and temperature perception, with preservation of proprioception and perception of vibration and light touch below

TABLE 8–1. SPINAL CORD INJURIES

Level Affected	Outcome Potential
C-1 to C-3	No arm motor function; absent respiratory muscle contractions; patient can support neck if C3 is spared
C-4	If C4 is functional, only initial ventilatory support required; may self-ventilate with muscle strengthening; quadriplegic
C-5	Deltoids, biceps, brachialis muscles functional; can shrug shoulders, flex elbows, and pronate forearm; phrenic nerve usually spared, but intercostal functioning impaired
C-6	Wrist extension intact
C-7	Upper-extremity motion preserved with intact triceps, extensor digitorum and flexor carpi ulnaris innervation (i.e., elbow, finger, and wrist extension); however, poor grasp due to weak finger flexors
C-8	Most hand muscles innervated with acceptable function
T1-3	Intact neck, shoulder, arm, and hand strength; loss of muscle functioning above nipple line, throughout trunk, and lower extremities
T4-10	More chest and trunk muscle functioning; paraplegic
T11-L2	Bladder control, erection, and seminal emission affected; voluntary bladder and bowel control lost; reflex control and emptying possible
L3-S4	Improved leg functioning

the level of the injury. It can occur as a result of direct trauma to the anterior aspect of the cord or to the anterior spinal artery, which supplies blood to the anterior two thirds of the cord. Surgical decompression is required to restore normal functioning.

CENTRAL CERVICAL SPINAL CORD SYNDROME

Central cervical spinal cord syndrome is due to a hyperextension injury, usually in an older individual with cervical spondylosis or stenosis. There are more pronounced sensorimotor deficits in the upper extremities (centrally located within the cord) than lower ones, and the distal parts are characteristically more involved. (Lumbar leg and sacral tracts are located in the periphery of the cord and may be spared). Upper-extremity weakness is a distinguishing feature of the central cord syndrome and is caused by hemorrhagic necrosis of the gray matter of the cervical cord. Bladder function may be affected in varying degrees as well. Since there is no bony involvement, the treatment may be directed toward reducing edema by administration of steroids.

BROWN–SÉQUARD SYNDROME

Brown–Séquard syndrome occurs with hemisection of the cord, often from penetrating trauma such as stab wounds or gunshots. The resultant injury consists of ipsilateral paralysis and loss of dorsal column function (i.e., vibration, proprioception, discriminatory touch) immediately below the level of injury. There is associated contralateral loss of pain and temperature perception one or two levels below the injury. (Spinothalamic tracts decussate [cross to the opposite side of the cord] within one to two levels of their entry.)

POSTERIOR SPINAL CORD SYNDROME

Posterior spinal cord syndrome is due to an impairment of the posterior columns of the cord, resulting in loss of vibration, proprioception, and touch sensations below the level of the injury.

■ VERTEBRAL INJURIES

ATLANTO-OCCIPITAL DISLOCATION

Atlanto-occipital dislocation is often seen in children owing to their immature craniovertebral articulations. Such dislocations can be fatal because of their devastating impact on the brainstem, cervical cord, nerve roots, or the vertebral artery. Cervical traction should not be used in these cases since it will further aggravate the injury. Special care should be taken to ensure that cervical spine films in these cases are accomplished without traction (see page 92).

JEFFERSON FRACTURE

The Jefferson fracture of the atlas is a burst fracture of the atlas ring resulting from an axial force. This injury may be asymptomatic. An open mouth x-ray that demonstrates displacement is required for diagnosis. A halo vest device (see Fig. 8–4) or a hard cervical collar is employed for immobilization during healing.

AXIS FRACTURES

A simple fracture (type 1) of the odontoid tip is managed by a cervical collar, but if the fracture is through the odontoid base (type 2), there may be a high incidence of nonunion without surgical fusion. Occasionally a halo immobilization device may be used for those fractures with minimal displacement. Odontoid screws may also be employed for fixation. In a type 3 fracture, which involves the base with some extension into the vertebral body, only a halo vest is needed to ensure fusion. Hangman fractures (bilateral fractures of C-2 pedicles with anterior displacement of C-2 onto C-3 are common hyperextension injuries. They may occur when a victim hits the windshield in an automobile accident. These fractures are characteristically unstable and require immediate traction followed by immobilization in a halo vest. Isolated laminal or spinous process fractures usually are managed with a hard cervical collar. If there is a combined atlas and axis fracture, it is treated according to the axis fracture features.[1]

FACET DISLOCATIONS

Facet dislocations involve two adjacent vertebrae and occur when the superior vertebra slides forward over the superior articular facet of the lower one. Lateral cervical films demonstrate anterior subluxation, with the anteroposterior (AP) views indicating alignment of the spinous processes. Skeletal traction is used promptly to reduce the fracture, but operative intervention is often required. A unilateral facet dislocation results from simultaneous flexion and rotation trauma and may be followed by a syndrome of chronic pain due to nerve root injury. Surgery may eventually be required to relieve the symptoms.

WEDGE COMPRESSION FRACTURES

Wedge compression fractures result from hyperflexion, causing compression of a vertebra against an adjacent one. Treatment varies, based upon the fracture characteristics, and may include use of a hard cervical collar or early operative fusion or closed realignment with skeletal traction, followed by halo vest application.

FLEXION TEARDROP FRACTURES

Flexion teardrop fractures are caused by hyperflexion with an associated intervertebral disk injury. This type of fracture may be accompanied by catastrophic neurological injury. Emergency management includes traction realignment, followed by surgical arthrodesis or use of a halo vest immobilization device.

■ EMERGENCY MANAGEMENT AND STABILIZATION OF SPINE INJURY PATIENTS

When spinal trauma is sustained, several systemic changes may occur, depending on the extent of damage. The first signs and symptoms may include such sensory changes as tingling and numbness, followed by weakness or total paralysis distal to the level of injury. Since the greatest flexion and extension ability is found between C-4 and C-5, and C-5 and C-6, these are the areas where most cervical injuries are seen.

All injured patients are initially assumed to have spinal cord injury. Most will arrive on a backboard with a cervical collar in place; however, some of these immobilization aids still permit considerable flexion, extension, and rotational movement of the neck. The airway must be managed with great caution in the unconscious patient or when there are known or suspected injuries above the level of the clavicles. The initial airway maneuver to be used is the chin lift or forward jaw thrust. An oropharyngeal or nasopharyngeal airway may be used, but neither results in secure isolation of the trachea from the oral cavity. Cervical protection may only be disregarded in two instances: (1) if radiological evidence has ruled out cervical spine injury or (2) if there is an airway emergency that cannot be managed with cervical protection in place. Endotracheal intubation should not be delayed if life-threatening circumstances exist—even if the cervical spine integrity has not been verified. About 80 percent of spinal cord injuries associated with fractures occur at the time of the original impact. Rather than a rigid laryngoscope and blade, a flexible fiberoptic bronchoscope may be employed for endotracheal tube placement. Blind nasotracheal intubation is another alternative but requires a spontaneously breathing patient. If the accident victim is wearing a helmet, it should be left in place until cervical spine integrity has been assured. Only personnel skilled in helmet removal should be involved in the procedure.

A nasogastric tube should be placed early to manage the abdominal distension that occurs as a result of gastric atony and the resultant paralytic ileus. If vomiting occurs, logroll the patient, maintaining alignment.

Initial cervical spine films should be obtained without traction since subluxation can occur in patients with fractures or ligamentous injuries. If there is no evidence of pain or injury after the initial films, traction can be used with minimal risk.

Respiratory failure is apparent with complete cervical lesions at C-4 and above, owing to loss of innervation to the diapraghm, intercostals, and abdominal muscles. This condition is sometimes referred to as respiratory quadriplegia or pentaplegia. Since the diaphragm has its nerve roots at this level, patients experience acute respiratory insufficiency or respiratory arrest. Common respiratory indicators of compromise include hypoventilation with reduced tidal volume and vital capacity, ineffective or absent cough, and retention of secretions. Supplemental oxygen (100 percent) should be used if there are any signs of ventilatory compromise. Do not wait for deterioration in respiratory efficacy before taking action. Never withhold oxygen in such instances merely to obtain an arterial blood gas sample on room air.

In order to identify an injury level of the spinal cord, several reflexes can be tested:

C-5 and C-6	Biceps jerk, radial reflex, or radialis periosteal reflex
C-7 and C-8	Triceps jerk, flexor finger jerk, and Hoffmann's reflex
L2, L3, L4	Knee jerk and adductor reflex; cremasteric reflex
L5	Posterior tibial reflex
S-1 and S-2	Ankle jerk
T-6 and T-12	Cutaneous abdominal reflexes

In addition to these maneuvers, loss of sensation over a specific dermatome region will help to identify the level of injury. (Fig. 8–3).

Although most spinal cord injury occurs at the time of the injury, secondary damage can occur from moving the patient with an unstable vertebral column. Throughout the early post-trauma period, emergency personnel employ several measures to ensure that the injury is not extended or complicated. Prompt application of a cervical collar and use of backboards and special extrication devices are among standard precautions. When spinal cord injury has been detected, a halo brace may be used to ensure reduction and alignment. This permits removal of the cervical collar, facilitating observations of the neck area for distended neck veins, ecchymosis over the laryngeal zone, and subcutaneous emphysema, which suggest serious life-threatening complications. The halo immobilization brace also ensures stability of the upper spine until surgical intervention may be accomplished (Fig. 8–4). Insertion of Gardner–Wells or Crutchfield tongs is reserved for the operating room (OR).

The EN should anticipate prompt surgical intervention if any of the following are noted:

- Progressive neurological defect
- Bony fragments present in the spinal cord on radiological studies
- Locked facets, preventing reduction of the fracture
- Suspected blockage to cerebrospinal fluid (CSF) flow

■ DIAGNOSTIC ASSESSMENTS

A cervical spine series with lateral, AP, and odontoid (open-mouth) views should be obtained promptly. (The odontoid view is essential if an axis [C-2] or Jefferson fracture [C-1] is suspected.) Clues to injury are prevertebral soft tissue swelling, malalignment of anterior and posterior aspects of vertebral bodies, angulation of the bony

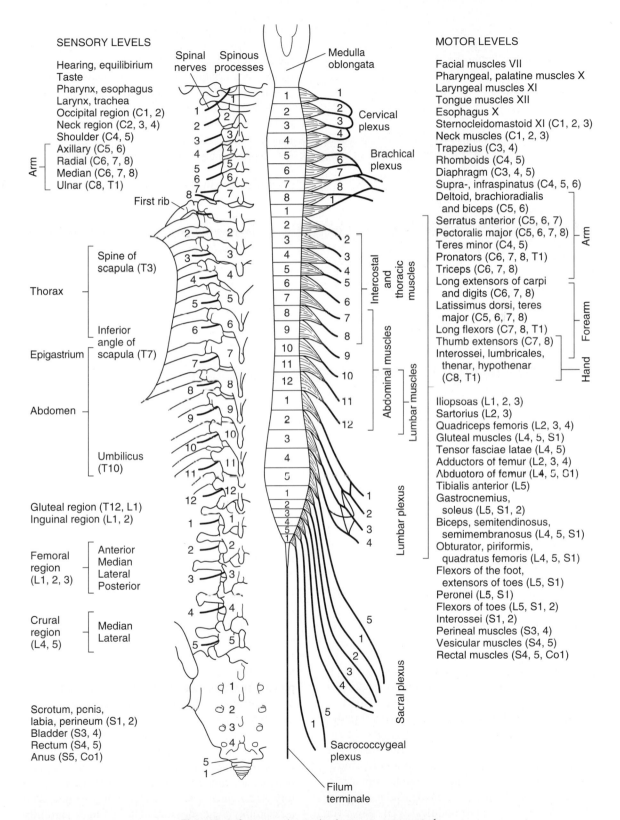

Figure 8–3. Sensory and motor levels (*from Bongard and Sue*[1]).

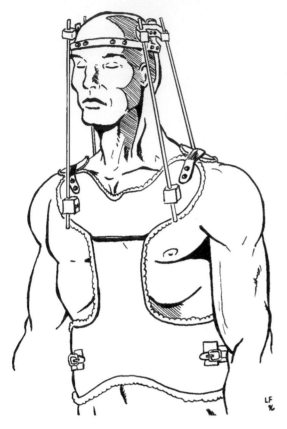

Figure 8–4. Halo immobilization device.

spinal canal, and fractures.[1] Dynamic flexion and extension cervical films may be obtained in awake and cooperative patients to identify instability due to ligamentous injury.

A computed tomography (CT) study of the spine in which bony structures are readily visualized is the second step in evaluating a fracture or subluxation. A magnetic resonance image (MRI) is usually reserved for patients with positive findings and no radiological evidence of bony abnormalities. The MRI demonstrates cord and soft-tissue structures with great clarity and can identify intra-axial contusion and cord compression from a herniated disk or hematoma. MRI studies do not demonstrate bony abnormalities well, however (Figs. 8–5 and 8–6).

Most spinal cord injuries involve the cervical region, which is highly mobile and poorly protected from many forces of injury. The cervical spinal cord contains lower motor neurons as well as long motor and sensory fibers that can be readily injured, creating problems ranging from minor neurological impairments to cardiorespiratory arrest.

Appropriate nursing diagnoses related to spinal cord injury would include the following:

- Ineffective breathing pattern related to altered ventilatory mechanics
- Ineffective airway clearance related to paralysis of intercostals and abdominal muscles
- Decreased cardiac output related to neurogenic shock
- Altered urinary elimination related to loss of voluntary control and compromised reflexes
- Impaired skin integrity related to immobility and sensory loss

■ SPINAL SHOCK

The normal activity of the spinal cord is dependent upon continual tonic discharges from higher centers, and with injury, such impulses abruptly cease, creating spinal shock as a result of altered hemodynamics. This condition may occur early after injury and last for days or even months. There may be complete suppression of all reflex activity below the level of injury. With blood pooling in the venous capacitance vessels, owing to a loss of tone, cardiac output declines. Bradycardia is experienced, owing to unopposed parasympathetic stimulation of the heart. Blood flow at the site of injury may be further impaired as a result of released histamines, catecholamines, and endorphins. Enzymes that are liberated at the injury site also contribute to local ischemia and edema formation, which can create compressive forces capable of extending cord injury. High cord injuries (e.g., C-5) may threaten the airway by affecting phrenic nerve function at C-3 or C-4. High cord–injured patients are at considerable risk for sudden respiratory arrest, and these individuals may be intubated as a prophylactic measure. The EN must carefully monitor the vital signs (VS), respiratory excur-

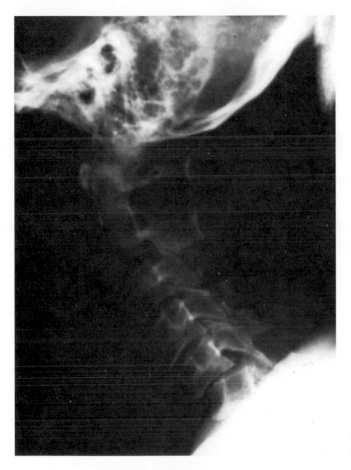

Figure 8–5. X-ray of cervical spine, which demonstrates dislocation of C-6–7.

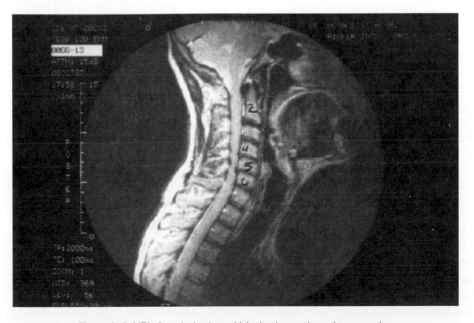

Figure 8–6. MRI of cervical spine, which clearly reveals cord compression.

sions, level of consciousness (LOC), and other neurological signs that could mark deterioration.[3]

Major nursing problems during the acute phase after a major spinal cord injury include those associated with cardiac, respiratory, and thermal stability.

Cardiovascular problems may include hypotension and bradycardia resulting from the loss of sympathetic outflow and vasovagal responses due to parasympathetic activity unopposed by the sympathetic nervous system. Other dysrhythmias also may be noted, especially during the early period of instability after injury. Their treatment will be dependent upon the existence of other injuries and their impact upon the patient; treatment may include fluid administration and vasopressors for the altered cardiac output, atropine and occasionally temporary transvenous pacing for the bradycardia, and other usually prescribed drugs for abnormal cardiac rhythms that might be present owing to cardiac output changes or the effects of ischemia on the myocardium. Poikilothermic patients will need to be protected from temperature extremes since they have no ability to maintain their thermal stability within the emergency environment.

In recent years, new pharmacological modalities have been used to improve outcome of spinal cord injuries by early reduction of edema, enhancement of circulation to the affected area, and stimulation of cellular mechanisms that favor cord repair. Agents used have included steroids, opiate antagonists (e.g., Naloxone), and calcium channel blockers, among others. GM_1 (monosialotetrahexosylganglioside) a glycolipid found naturally in the central nervous system (CNS) has shown promise as an enhancer of the recovery of damaged neurons by stimulating axonal sprouting.[4]

Respiration may be seriously affected by damage to the phrenic nerve, which arises from C-3, C-4 (at the shoulder level), and C-5. If there is an ascending cervical lesion secondary to extending edema, respirations may be impaired. The vital capacity of an individual can be reduced by as much as one fourth to one half of normal. Respiratory efficiency, both rate and pattern, must be monitored carefully.

Circulation may be seriously compromised without innervation of the autonomic nervous system secondary to the cord trauma, and hypotension may develop rapidly. The patient's legs should be elevated, and atropine may be indicated to combat ensuing bradycardia.

Since the autonomic nervous system innervates smooth muscle and all the viscera, a problem with gastric dilation and paralytic ileus must be anticipated. A nasogastric tube should be placed as soon as possible to decompress the stomach and to eliminate the hazard of vomiting and aspiration. A Foley catheter should also be inserted to ensure bladder decompression, since sensations associated with the voiding urge may be altered or obliterated.

The efforts of ENs are directed toward minimizing spinal cord damage from the original injury and ensuring that partial injuries are not converted to complete, permanent ones as a result of poor immobilization or careless patient management. Early assessments are aimed at detecting the injured cord in order to effect the earliest and most aggressive surgical decompression.

When the EN is assessing a patient who has potential for spinal cord injury, the following observations should prompt concern and alert the staff to observe all precautions to prevent further damage:

- Flaccid and areflexive lower extremities
- Atonic rectal sphincter
- Diaphragmatic respirations
- Forearms flexed over the chest with hands half closed; arms spontaneously return to this position after straightening them (characteristic of a C-6–level injury)
- Pain above nipple line (but not below) that elicits a grimace (characteristic of a C-6–level injury)
- Hypotension without other signs of shock; slow pulse
- Priapism

■ REFERENCES

1. Bongard FS, Sue DY. *Current Critical Care: Diagnosis and Treatment.* E. Norwalk, Conn: Appleton & Lange; 1994.
2. Hickey R, Sloan TB, Albin MS. Acute spinal cord trauma. In Ayres SM, Grenvik A, Holbrook PR, Shoemaker WC (eds.). *Textbook of Critical Care.* 3rd ed. Philadelphia, Pa: WB Saunders; 1995, p. 1457.
3. Doberstein C, Rodts GE Jr., McBride DQ. Neurosurgical Critical Care. In Cardona VD, Hurn PD,

Bastnagel Mason PJ et al. *Trauma Nursing.* 2nd ed. Philadelphia, Pa: WB Saunders; 1994, p. 539.

4. Geisler FH, Dorsey FC, Coleman WP. Recovery of motor function after spinal cord injury: a randomized placebo-controlled trial with GM-I ganglioside. *N Engl J Med.* 1991; 324:1829.

■ BIBLIOGRAPHY

Ayres SM, Grenvik A, Holbrook PR, Shoemaker WC. *Textbook of Critical Care.* 3rd ed. Philadelphia, Pa: WB Saunders; 1995.

Barie PS, Shires GT. *Surgical Intensive Care.* Boston, Ma: Little, Brown; 1993.

Cardona VD, Hurn PD, Bastnagel Mason PJ et al. *Trauma Nursing.* 2nd ed. Philadelphia, Pa: WB Saunders; 1994.

Clochesy JM, Breu C, Cardin S, et al. *Critical Care Nursing.* Philadelphia, Pa: WB Saunders; 1993.

Grenvik A, Ayres SM, Holbrook PR, Shoemaker WB. *Pocket Companion to Textbook of Critical Care.* Philadelphia, Pa: WB Saunders; 1996.

Levine RL, Fromm RE Jr. *Critical Care Monitoring from Pre-Hospital to the ICU.* St. Louis, Mo: Mosby-Year Book; 1995.

Maull KI, Rodriguez A, Wiles CE. *Complications in Trauma and Critical Care.* Philadelphia, Pa: WB Saunders; 1996.

Phippen ML, Wells MP. *Perioperative Nursing Practice.* Philadelphia, Pa: WB Saunders; 1994.

Ruppert SD, Kernicki JG, Dolan JT. *Dolan's Critical Care Nursing.* 2nd ed. Philadelphia, Pa: FA Davis, 1996.

Urden LD, Davie JK, Thelan LA. *Essentials of Critical Care Nursing.* St. Louis, Mo: Mosby-Year Book; 1992.

Weist PW, Roth PB. *Fundamental of Emergency Radiology.* Philadelphia, Pa: WB Saunders; 1996.

■ REVIEW: SPINAL CORD ASSESSMENT

1. Describe four mechanical forces that can result in spinal cord injury.

2. Describe the outcome potential for complete spinal cord injuries at:
   a. C-4 or above
   b. C-7
   c. T-4 to T-10
   d. T-11 to L-2

3. Describe the characteristics of:
   a. Acute anterior cervical cord syndrome
   b. Central cervical spinal cord syndrome
   c. Brown–Séquard syndrome
   d. Posterior spinal cord syndrome

4. Identify the vertebral injury that contraindicates any use of traction.

5. Explain the general principles for managing unstable fractures of the vertebral axis.

6. Name two major instances in which cervical precautions may be disregarded in the emergency department (ED).

7. Explain the mechanism underlying respiratory quadriplegia or pentaplegia.

8. Indicate which deep tendon reflexes are helpful in identifying a specific level of a spinal cord injury.

9. Identify the nursing precautions that must be exercised in order to prevent secondary injury of a patient with spinal cord trauma.

10. List the four spinal cord injuries that mandate immediate surgical intervention.

11. Describe the added benefits of a computed tomography (CT) scan and a magnetic resonance image (MRI) when compared to basic radiological studies of the vertebral column.

12. List four nursing diagnoses pertinent to acute spinal cord injury.

13. Outline major signs and symptoms of spinal shock.

14. Describe the recommended nursing and medical interventions to minimize effects of spinal shock on vital functions (e.g., respirations, ventilation, hemodynamics).

15. Identify observations that should alert the emergency nurse (EN) to suspect spinal cord injury when dealing with any trauma patient.

Chest Assessment 9

■ INDICATIONS FOR CHEST ASSESSMENT

A nursing examination of the chest, including the lungs and the heart, should be conducted on patients who present with problems related to the cardiorespiratory system. The indications for and techniques of both respiratory and cardiac assessment are presented in this chapter.

INITIAL NURSING MANAGEMENT

Remembering that the first step in assessment is observation, look at the patient's facial expression, skin color, posture, chest movements or lack of them, and quality of respiratory activity.

IMPORTANCE OF RESPIRATORY STATUS

Any patient presenting with respiratory difficulties requires an immediate assessment of his or her respiratory status, with appropriate intervention. While dyspnea or shortness of breath may herald the onset of cardiac crises, they may also be primarily respiratory in origin and while appearing to be of lesser acuity, may in fact be building to respiratory collapse with all the complications that can rapidly ensue. Remember that the body has no oxygen stores; it requires ongoing and adequate respiratory activity and air exchange to survive, and the brain and vital centers will be irretrievably damaged if oxygen deprivation exceeds 4 minutes. Patients who present with any signs of respiratory distress require immediate evaluation and appropriate nursing intervention with rapid administration of high-flow oxygen, which may, if nothing else, deflect a developing respiratory crisis while the reasons for the patient's breathing difficulty are determined.

NURSING EXAMINATION

Emergency nurses (ENs) who have the opportunity should take the initiative and pursue development of their own skills in chest assessment; this valuable capability, however, can be acquired only through practice. Patients generally appreciate the interest and attention shown during the initial assessment, and even though the examination is apt to be repeated by the physician, a competent initial evaluation of the chest by the EN is an appropriate procedure that can contribute important information toward effective nursing management. Respiratory compromise, for whatever reason, deprives the patient of essential oxygenation and cannot always wait for the attending physician; the competent EN will be able to expedite effective and appropriate interventions.

■ ASSESSING CHEST SOUNDS

MECHANICS OF RESPIRATION

Breathing is controlled by a series of respiratory centers in the nervous system. One center is in the medulla, located at the top of the spinal cord. Breathing action can be triggered by the centers when there is an increase in the amount of carbon dioxide in the blood or when there is a drop in the oxygen level of the blood. Conversely, forced breathing (hyperventilation) depletes carbon dioxide levels in the blood and results in failure to trigger the respiratory center; temporary interruption of the breathing pattern occurs for a moment.

The lungs are living bellows, encased by the rib cage, diaphragm, and intercostal muscles (Fig. 9–1). Each lung is enclosed in a double-membrane

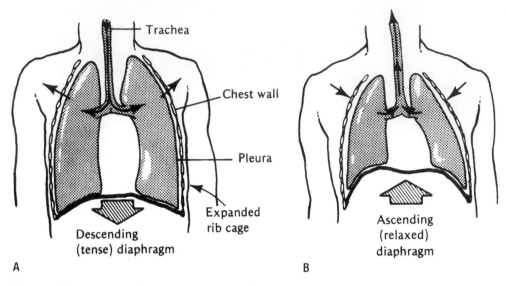

Figure 9–1. The mechanics of respiration and motion of respiratory structures on **(A)** inhalation and **(B)** exhalation. *(From Barber JM, Dillman PA.* Emergency Patient Care for the EMT-A. *Reston, VA: Reston Publishing, 1981.)*

sac called the pleural sac. The sac is airtight and contains a lubricating fluid; the pleural layers keep the lung surface from rubbing against the chest wall. The pleural lining that covers the lungs is called visceral pleura, and that which lines the chest wall is called the parietal pleura. A negative pressure of −4 to −6 mm Hg exists between the pleura during expiration.

The right lung has three lobes: the upper, middle, and lower; the left lung has two lobes: the upper and lower. A small tonguelike structure projects from the lower portion of the upper lobe of the left lung called the lingula. All lobes of the lungs have separate bronchi.

There are 12 pairs of ribs, with the top 10 pairs attached by strips of cartilage to the sternum and the bottom 2 pairs, called floating ribs, attached to only the spinal column. The first seven pairs of ribs are attached directly to the sternum by cartilaginous joints and work like a bucket handle, moving up and down with the intercostal and diaphragmatic action. The primary moving force of the human bellows in respiratory activity is the diaphragm, a dome-shaped sheet of muscle fibers and tendons separating the organs in the chest from the organs in the abdomen. The diaphragm is attached to the sternum anteriorly, to the spinal column posteriorly, and to the lower ribs bilaterally. When the muscle fibers of the diaphragm

contract, the sheet of tissue is drawn downward, creating a partial vacuum in the chest cavity and causing air to flow into the trachea, bronchi, and alveoli. Expiration occurs when the diaphragm muscles relax, closing the "bellows" and forcing the air out again.

During expiration, the diaphragm rises up to the level of the fifth intercostal space at the midaxillary line, an important landmark in trauma. The diaphragm receives its innervation from the phrenic nerve, which originates at the level of C-4 and C-5 and runs down along the esophagus and near the heart.

The intercostal muscles between the ribs also participate in the breathing action. In forced breathing, abdominal muscles assist in expiration, and the neck muscles assist in inspiration by pulling upward and outward on the first rib and the sternum. This has a chain-reaction effect on the other ribs, increasing the capacity of the chest. This is referred to as the use of accessory muscles and is seen in varying degrees of respiratory distress.

TIDAL VOLUMES AND VITAL CAPACITIES OF THE LUNGS

Spirometry is the measurement of breathing capacity of the lungs or the lung volume. Tidal volume (VT) is the amount of air exchanged in easy breathing and is approximately 500 mL per respiration in the normal adult at rest.

Vital capacity (VC) is the maximum amount of air a person can exhale after maximal inhalation. Normally, the VC is 3000 to 6000 mL, with 5000 mL being the norm for a 70-kg man. Normal lungs should exhale 80 percent of the VC in 1 second when being tested; this is referred to as the forced expiratory volume in 1 second (FEV_1).

Functional residual capacity (FRC) is the volume of air or gas that remains in the lungs at the end of normal expiration; residual volume (RV) is the volume of air or gas remaining in the lungs after maximal expiration. Remember that once the lung is inflated at birth, there will *always* be a reservoir of gas present.

RESPIRATORY PATTERNS

Nursing assessment of the chest and respiratory activity should begin with an evaluation of the rate and quality of respirations that are observed with the patient at rest and in a position of comfort, with or without oxygen being administered. Variations in both rate and quality of respiration may exist in normal as well as in compromised respiratory function, so knowledge of both clinical presentations is essential to effective nursing assessment.

Normal Variations and Rates

The normal adult respiratory rate at rest is between 12 and 20 breaths per minute. Children have a slightly higher rate, infants may have rates as high as 40 per minute, and neonates may take as many as 60 breaths per minute.

Tachypnea, or excessive rapidity of respiration, occurs in many normal situations. During exercise, people breathe more rapidly and therefore become tachypneic. Patients who are anxious, apprehensive, febrile, anemic, obese, or who have heart or lung disease are often tachypneic. Adult patients are considered to be tachypneic when their respiratory rates exceed 20 breaths per minute.

Bradypnea, on the other hand, is an abnormal slowness in breathing and is usually a sign of some abnormality such as brain disorder, drug or alcohol overdose, or some metabolic imbalance. Adult patients may be considered bradypneic when their respiratory rates are less than 10 breaths per minute.

Hyperpnea (rapid, deep respirations) and hypopnea (slow, shallow respirations) may be associated with normal sleep patterns or with clinical abnormalities of respiration.

Abnormal Breathing Patterns

Recognition of abnormal breathing patterns is frequently very helpful in early awareness of underlying disease. Three of the more common abnormal breathing patterns seen are Cheyne–Stokes respiration, Biot's respiration, and Kussmaul respiration:

- Cheyne–Stokes (Chān´–stōks) respiration, named for John Cheyne, a Scottish physician (1777–1838), and William Stokes, an Irish physician (1804–1878), is breathing characterized by rhythmic waxing and waning of the depth of respiration, gradually becoming deeper and faster, then shallow and slow, with regularly occurring periods of apnea lasting up to 20 seconds. Cheyne–Stokes respirations are seen especially in coma resulting from damage to the nervous centers, occasionally in sleeping children, and in terminal stages of congestive heart failure and uremia.
- Biot's (Bē-ōz´) respiration, named for Camille Biot, a French physician of the nineteenth century, is breathing characterized by irregular periods of apnea, alternating with periods in which four or five breaths of identical depth are taken. This condition is usually associated with patients who have increased intracranial pressure.
- Kussmaul respiration, also known as "air hunger," is a distressing dyspnea occurring with paroxysms at a rate usually greater than 20 per minute. This respiratory pattern usually indicates a metabolic abnormality and is seen frequently in diabetic acidosis as well as renal failure.

EXAMINATION OF THE CHEST

The chest examination should begin with the posterior chest and proceed to the anterior chest, comparing one side of the chest to the other as the examination advances, from top to bottom. Four skills are necessary for examining the chest: inspection, palpation, percussion, and auscultation. Inspection and palpation, or examining by touch, are techniques commonly used by nurses, but percussion and auscultation (by means of a stethoscope) are newer to the nursing profession generally.

Inspection

Inspection of the chest and lungs begins with some questions to be answered through observation:

1. What is the patient's attitude lying in bed? Is the patient calm and at ease or apprehensive and restless, lethargic, dyspneic? What do your eyes tell you?
2. What is the quality of the patient's respiration?
3. What is the patient's color?
4. Does the chest move symmetrically with respiration?
5. What muscles are used during respiration (diaphragm, accessory muscles, intercostals)?
6. Is the skin dry or moist?
7. Do the respirations appear labored?
8. Is the trachea midline?
9. Is an abnormal pattern of respiration present?

Palpation

The chest and neck should be palpated for the position of the trachea and any evidence of tenderness in the muscles of the chest wall and the chondrocostal (the ribs and costal cartilage) areas. The vibrations caused by resonance of voice sounds, which can be felt by placing the hands on the chest wall, are called fremitus. This examination is conducted on both posterior chest walls while the patient (in a sitting position, if at all possible) repeats "ninety-nine" in as low a voice as possible, because a large number of vibrations are generated and transmitted through the chest in this manner. Sound is conducted best through solid matter, which acts as a bridge, then through water, and least through air. If consolidation is present in the lungs from such causes as pneumonia, accumulated secretions, or masses, you should feel fremitus over the affected area. Conversely, fremitus will be absent or barely noticeable in the presence of pneumothorax, emphysema, and pleural effusion.

Percussion

Percussion is accomplished by laying the middle finger against the chest and tapping it with the middle finger of the other hand. There is no normal percussion note as such. It will vary from person to person and even from place to place on the same individual. Five sounds can be heard when the chest is percussed:

- *Tympany:* Tympany is heard over air-filled areas and has a high-pitched musical or drumlike quality of long duration. It is typically heard over hollow air-filled organs like the bubble of the stomach.
- *Hyperresonance:* This sound is percussed between the head of the humerus and the base of the neck and is an exaggerated resonance with a low pitch.
- *Resonance:* Heard over areas of normal fremitus, resonance is the prolongation and intensification of sound produced by the transmission of its vibrations to a cavity, as elicited by percussion, with a moderately low pitch.
- *Dullness:* This sound is heard at the diaphragm and over the heart; it has a muffled quality and a moderately high pitch.
- *Flatness:* Flatness is the sound heard over large bone areas, with a high pitch and a soft thud.

Auscultation

Auscultation is defined as the act of listening for sounds within the body, chiefly for ascertaining the condition of the lungs and other organs. Direct auscultation is performed without the stethoscope, with the naked ear. More commonly, "mediate" auscultation is performed, with the aid of the stethoscope interposed between the ears and the part being examined.

The Stethoscope. Most stethoscopes in use today are binaural (both ears). The chestpiece may be either the bell type, the diaphragm, or a combination of both (Sprague type). The bell chestpiece (Ford model) is a hollow cone and transmits all sounds; it is of particular value when listening for low-pitched sounds, to the apices of the lungs, between ribs on thin patients, or in other less accessible areas. It is necessary to use the bell to hear mitral stenosis and fetal hearts. The diaphragmatic chestpiece (Bowle's model) is a flat, shallow cup covered with a diaphragm made of Bakelite or celluloid. This diaphragm filters out low-pitched sounds so that high-pitched sounds can be heard more clearly. Because most chest sounds are high-pitched, the diaphragmatic chestpiece is usually used in auscultating the chest for breath sounds and the heart for such sounds as regurgitant aortic murmurs.

Damaged stethoscope diaphragms must be replaced with the proper material (*not* x-ray film), or the acoustic quality of the instrument will be impaired. The soft rubber or plastic tubing should be thick-walled and its outside diameter should not be smaller than the caliber of the connecting tubes. Optimally, the tubing should not exceed 30 cm (about 12 in.). Shorter tubing is inconvenient, and long tubing is thought to compromise the quality of the sound transmitted. It is also important that the earpieces fit the listener's ears comfortably without pressure and discomfort, forming an airtight seal to promote transmission of sound without extraneous noises, which is the only function of the stethoscope, because it does *not* amplify sound.

When the stethoscope is used, the bell type should touch the surface of the skin lightly but firmly enough to form an air seal on the surface; the diaphragm type should be held firmly on the skin so that external sound is filtered out. Extraneous noises are a common distraction in the use of a stethoscope; for example, your breath on the tubing or rubbing hair with the chestpiece may produce sounds like rales, and movements of muscles or tendons may sound like friction rubs. Proper interpretation takes a good deal of practice. It should be added that stethoscopes require examination and service periodically to be certain that tubing diaphragms are intact and that the pieces are clean and free of ear wax, lint, and other debris (or insects).

Positioning the Patient. The proper positioning of the patient for auscultation is as follows:

1. Place the patient in a relaxed sitting position with shoulders drooping forward slightly to reduce the bulk of the back muscles.
2. Instruct the patient to turn his or her face to the side and breathe a little more deeply than normal to increase the intensity of sounds and to breathe through the mouth, not the nose.
3. Inhalation should be active and exhalation should be passive. Do not let the patient force expiration. Often, it is easier to demonstrate than to explain, thereby avoiding induced hyperventilation.
4. Start at the apices of the lungs and work downward, comparing both sides as you move down the chest wall posteriorly and then anteriorly.

NORMAL BREATH SOUNDS

All normal breath sounds consist of the vesicular sound, the bronchial sound, or a combination of both. There are four components of each breath sound to be evaluated on both inspiration and expiration: pitch, amplitude, quality, and duration.

Vesicular

The vesicular element is the sound produced by air entering the alveoli directly under the stethoscope and is thought to result as the alveoli distend and separate on inspiration. Vesicular breath sounds are breezy sounds, resulting from the air passage directly under the stethoscope. Although the actual time consumed for expiration is slightly longer than that of inspiration (approximately a 6:5 ratio), the audible range reverses, and the inspiratory phase becomes 3:1 over the expiratory phase, with no pause heard between the phases (Fig. 9–2A). Vesicular breath sounds are harsher in children because of their thinner chest walls and more elastic lungs.

Bronchial

Bronchial breath sounds (also called tubular) are harsher sounding than vesicular sounds and are usually heard only over the manubrium (body) of the sternum in normal patients. They are loud and high-pitched, with a short pause between phases; the expiratory phase is 1.5 times longer than the inspiratory phase (Fig. 9–2B).

Bronchovesicular

In the normal lung, bronchovesicular breath sounds are heard where the trachea and bronchi are closest to the chest wall, above the sternum and between the scapulas. Characteristically, these

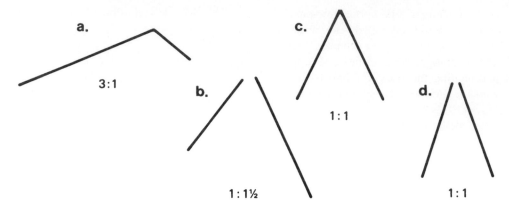

Figure 9–2. The four breath sounds that may be auscultated: **A.** vesicular breath sound; **B.** bronchial breath sound; **C.** bronchovesicular breath sound; **D.** tracheal breath sound (glottic hiss).

breath sounds have an almost equal inspiratory and expiratory phase, with no pause heard between phases, and a medium to high pitch with a muffled blowing sound (Fig. 9–2C).

Tracheal

Tracheal breath sounds are heard only over the trachea as very high-pitched, loud, harsh tubular sounds. This is the purest form of the glottic hiss (Fig. 9–2D), having a short phase between inspiratory and expiratory phases.

ADVENTITIOUS SOUNDS

Occasionally, extra sounds, or adventitious sounds, are heard that are not normally heard in the chest and are superimposed on the breath sounds. Most commonly, these originate from the lungs or airways and are termed rales (pronounced "rahls"). Generally, there are considered to be five types of rales, the first of which is called musical and is composed of continuous sounds, as opposed to the four other types, which are essentially showers of discrete (or separate) individual sounds.

Musical Rales

Musical rales are both sibilant and sonorous. Sibilant rales are high-pitched hissing sounds similar to that produced by suddenly separating two oiled surfaces. They are produced by the presence of a viscid secretion in the bronchial tubes or by thickening of the walls of the tubes, as heard in asthma and bronchitis. (The sound is also referred to as a wheeze. Sonorous rales are fine, moist sounds resembling

the cooing of a dove and are produced by the passage of air through mucus in the capillary-bronchial tubes. They are heard in capillary bronchitis and asthma and are sometimes called a snore.

Crepitant Rales

Crepitant rales are very fine rales resembling the sound produced by rubbing a lock of hair between the fingers or by particles of salt thrown on a fire. This rale is heard at the end of inspiration and is also referred to as a fine, moist rale.

Subcrepitant Rales

Subcrepitant rales are heard in conditions associated with liquid in the small tubes and airways. They are also called crackling or medium, moist rales; are not nearly as high-pitched; and are composed of many discrete sounds that are usually present at the end of inspiration. Fluid from alveoli emptying into smaller airways can cause crepitant rales to become subcrepitant, as in pneumonia and pulmonary edema.

Bubbling Rales

Bubbling rales are moist and finer than a subcrepitant rale and are heard in bronchitis, the resolving state of exudative pneumonia, and over smaller cavities. They have a bubbling quality in sound and are produced when air passes through fluid.

Gurgling Rales

Very coarse rales resembling the sound of large bubbles bursting are called gurgling rales. In pulmonary edema, they are heard over large cavities that contain fluid, and they can be heard without a stethoscope. When present in the trachea, they are referred to as the death rattle and are very low-pitched, loud, wet-sounding, discrete rales.

NONPULMONIC ADVENTITIOUS BREATH SOUNDS

Other chest sounds to be considered on auscultation are the nonpulmonic adventitious sounds. These are extra sounds in the chest that are *not* pulmonic in origin.

Pleural Friction Rub

The pleural friction rub is apt to be loud, grating, and intermittent and is produced by inflamed and roughened pleural surfaces rubbing together. Its pitch is similar to that of a crepitant rale but is more intense and of a different quality. Its grating or scraping quality is more commonly heard during inspiration and may disappear after the first few respiratory efforts when the pleural surfaces have become better lubricated. The sound produced when hair is moved under the diaphragm of the stethoscope can be confused with a pleural friction rub. To avoid this confusion, eliminate the possibility by wetting the chest hair and pressing the diaphragm firmly against the chest wall.

Subcutaneous Emphysema Sounds

Resembling crepitant rales or a pleural friction rub, the sounds of subcutaneous emphysema are not related to the respiratory cycle and should not be confused with any other sounds. Subcutaneous emphysema is produced by very small air pockets under the skin that are moved back and forth by the pressure of the diaphragm of the stethoscope on the skin. These air pockets under the skin may be the result of rupture of the trachea, bronchus, or esophagus; pneumothorax; mediastinal trauma; or elective neck surgery. Subcutaneous emphysema is a highly significant finding and is a harbinger of greater problems.

Bone Crepitus

Bone crepitus may be heard when the chest is auscultated following trauma. It is a grating sound related to the respiratory cycle and is produced when two ends of a fractured rib rub together. It may or may not be heard without a stethoscope.

SUMMARY

Remember to position the patient properly when preparing to evaluate chest sounds and to use a binaural stethoscope of good quality when auscultating the chest. A quality stethoscope is a most worthwhile investment for the EN and should be carried at all times on duty. Experience is still the best teacher, and the most beneficial way to learn to recognize and evaluate chest sounds is to listen to every chest, if it is appropriate to the needs of the patient and time permits.

■ THE CARDIAC EXAMINATION

Before discussing the proper and most productive ways for a nurse examiner to evaluate heart sounds and cardiac status, the necessity for immediate interventions when a patient presents with complaints of sudden onset chest pain must be stressed. All patients with a potential for cardiac rhythm disturbances *must* be monitored for arrhythmia detection. Shock, hemorrhage, myocardial infarction, neurological trauma, septicemia, or any other process that results in hypoxemia, disturbances in arterial blood gas (ABG) values or acid–base balance, or alteration in serum electrolyte levels predisposes to the development of dysrhythmias and necessitates cardiac monitoring.

EMERGENCY INTERVENTIONS

Initially, when a patient presents complaining of chest pain or severe pressure, pain radiating from the chest, shortness of breath, fainting spells, or any other signs of poor cardiac output, *assume the worst* and move quickly to initiate the necessary steps for intervention and management; chest assessment becomes secondary in the emergency situation. Take the patient immediately to a bed in the area equipped to handle "codes," and after removing at least the top half of clothing to expose the chest and precordial area, proceed as follows:

1. Administer oxygen at a rate of at least 6 L/min (30 percent to 40 percent) oxygen delivery by means of nasal prongs until further evaluation.
2. Apply cardiac monitor leads in lead II configuration and assess for arrhythmias requiring immediate intervention.

3. Get an intravenous line in fast (the antecubital vein is easiest and fastest in emergencies, although it is bothersome later). If it is the responsibility of the emergency department (ED) to draw blood for the lab, a 20-mL syringe of blood should be drawn at this time and injected into the appropriate Vacu-tubes. Run D_5W TKO (to keep open) with a pediatric microdrip set.

4. Position the patient comfortably (Fowler's or semi-Fowler's position), call for a stat-electrocardiogram (ECG), and continue closely monitoring vital signs (VS) and clinical status as they relate to the monitor tracing.

EXAMINATION GUIDELINES

The examination should be conducted with the patient properly and comfortably positioned in a semi-Fowler's position, because the heart is assessed chiefly by examination through the anterior chest wall, with most of the anterior cardiac surface represented by the right ventricle. The left ventricle, lying to the left and behind the right ventricle, makes up only a small portion of the anterior cardiac surface; it forms the left border of the heart and produces the apical impulse, which is usually referred to as the point of maximum impulse (PMI). The PMI may not always be apical, however, depending on the existing pathology.

When assessing heart sounds, always stand to the patient's right and proceed with the examination using a quality stethoscope of the binaural type, employing both the bell and the diaphragm in the auscultation of the heart. Again, experience is the best teacher, and the EN wishing to develop skills in this area must take advantage of every available opportunity to listen to heart sounds and develop an "ear."

EXAMINATION COMPONENTS

Assessment of cardiac status by examination of the chest wall includes inspection, palpation, percussion, and auscultation, combined with the continued observation of blood pressure.

Inspection and Palpation

The overall inspection of the patient begins with the head and goes all the way to the feet in order to check for visual evidence of effective circulation by the heart. Inspection is, in reality, carried out simultaneously with palpation, which is defined in *Dorland's Medical Dictionary* as "the act of feeling with the hand; the application of the fingers with light pressure to the surface of the body for the purpose of determining the consistence of the parts beneath in physical diagnosis." In other words, it is necessary to look and to feel.

Head and Neck. Inspection begins with the head and neck, noting color of skin, lips, ears, nose, and mucous membranes, and looking for distension of superficial vessels or cyanosis of any parts, the respiratory status, and the general appearance and behavior of the patient. With the bed in a semi-Fowler's position, the neck should be checked for distension of the jugular veins and any obvious pulsation. Visible distension of the jugular veins while the patient is lying at a 45-degree angle is an indication of an elevated central venous pressure (CVP). The carotid pulse should be lightly palpated for rate and quality, bilaterally, evaluating one side at a time.

Extremities. The extremities should be inspected for color and temperature. Cold skin, pallor, or cyanosis of an extremity may well be an indication of impaired circulation from cardiovascular disease or may be an indication of impending or incipient shock. Occluded arterial circulation will result in a reduction in pulses (or a decreased intensity) and possibly an entirely obliterated pulse, so that no palpable pulse can be obtained. Bruits may be heard; these are audible manifestations of turbulence in vessels from drastic changes in the caliber of the vessel wall. Atrophy of muscles from chronic occluded circulation is manifested by thin, shiny skin and thickened fingernails. Elevation of an occluded extremity will cause it to turn pale; placing it in a dependent position will precipitate rubor (redness or flushing).

Look for cold, mottled extremities. Look at the color of the skin on the legs; a brawny induration of the tibia and the malleolus develops from long-term congestion of venous return in the circulation. The presence of congestion in the venous circulation must *always* be evaluated, and the EN must always be observant for any signs of dependent peripheral edema of the ankles, sacrum, or scrotum.

Peripheral Pulses. Pedal pulses should be checked; the dorsalis pedis pulse may be obtained on the dorsum of the foot, usually just lateral to the extensor tendon of the great toe, placing fingers lightly so as not to obliterate the comparatively fragile pulse. The posterior tibial pulse may be obtained on palpation by curving the fingers posteriorly and slightly below the malleolus of the ankle on the soft tissue. Both of these pedal pulses may be congenitally absent and, at best, may be difficult to palpate. Peripheral pulses, whether radial or pedal, should be assessed bilaterally, noting the rate, quality, and bilateral equality. Pulses are rated on a scale of 0 to 4+, with 0 meaning absent pulse; 1+, palpable; 2+, normal or average; 3+, full; and 4+, full and bounding (may even occasionally be visible). Temporal, carotid, brachial, radial, femoral, and popliteal pulses should all test 2+ bilaterally. The posterior tibial and dorsalis pedis should test 1+ bilaterally. When distal pulses require frequent checking and evaluation, it is helpful to mark the pulse, once located, with a gentian violet-, or Betadine-tipped applicator, or a skin marker.

Locating the Point of Maximum Impulse. Following inspection and the accompanying palpation of head, neck, and extremities, the anterior chest wall should be palpated over the precordial area for the PMI, observing for precordial "lift," rocking motion, and so on. The PMI is usually located in the left fifth intercostal space, within the midclavicular line (MCL), and will normally be felt as a single impulse (Fig. 9–3). A double or paradoxical impulse that waxes and wanes with respirations may be indicative of myocardial disease, which could lead to congestive heart failure.

The PMI may be palpated by placing the right hand horizontally against the lower part of the sternum, with the heel of the hand over the sternum and the fingers extending leftward to the region of the apex in the midclavicular line, feeling for:

- Apical impulse (PMI), normal or exaggerated
- Thrust against the chest wall
- Rocking motion within the chest wall
- Systolic or diastolic thrills (*Thrill* is defined in *Dorland's Medical Dictionary* as a "sensation of vibration felt by the examiner on palpation of the body, as over an incompetent heart valve.")

Percussion

Percussion techniques are the same as those used in percussing the lungs and will help determine heart size. Normally, the left cardiac border (LCB) is near the PMI, usually at or within the MCL. Place the patient recumbent in the semi-Fowler's position and stand on the patient's right; begin percussing the left anterior axillary line at the fifth intercostal space, moving to the fourth intercostal space if necessary, percussing toward the sternum until you hear dullness. The point of dullness indicates the left border of cardiac dullness (LBCD). Normally, this is usually 10 to 12 cm from the midsternal line and most always within the MCL. If the LBCD is greater than 12 cm from midsternum and is outside the MCL, the heart may be considered enlarged, except in a highly trained athlete.

Auscultation for Heart Sounds

When the stethoscope is used, one sound should be listened to at a time. Each heart valve sound (Fig. 9–3) is reflected to a specific area of the chest wall.

Valve Sounds and Auscultatory Areas. The aortic sound is best heard in the second right intercostal space (ICS); the pulmonic sound, in the second left ICS; and the tricuspid sound, at the fifth right ICS near the sternum or at midline below it. The mitral valve sound, or apical sound, will be heard in the fifth left ICS near the MCL. This will approximate the PMI. It should be noted that sounds related to the movement of heart valves and the flow of blood across them are heard best *not* over the anatomic locations, but in the auscultatory areas bearing their names.

The sounds of S_1, the first heart sound, and S_2, the second heart sound, differ according to location. S_1 is louder at the apex (if one pictures the heart as an upside-down pyramid) and S_2 is louder at the base (or actually at the top). Begin a systematic assessment by listening at the top of the aortic and pulmonic valves, moving to the apex over the tricuspid and mitral valves. You may start the other way around, but the important thing is to be

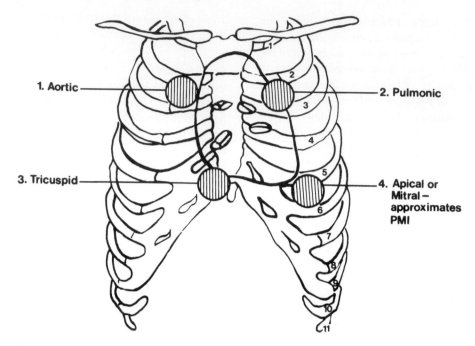

1. Aortic
2. Pulmonic
3. Tricuspid
4. Apical or Mitral — approximates PMI

Figure 9–3. Location of the point of maximum impulse (PMI) and suggested sequence for auscultating aortic, pulmonic, tricuspid, and apical or mitral valve sounds.

consistent and systematic in order to train your ear. Listen for these four values:

1. Gross timing
2. Degree of intensity at the PMI
3. Pitch and quality
4. Fine timing

S_1 is thought to be the closure of both the mitral and tricuspid valves (atrioventricular) just before the ventricular systole. The closures occur almost simultaneously; however, the left-sided events in the heart occur slightly before the right-sided events. Thus, the mitral valve closes slightly before the tricuspid, and because of the difference in timing, the first sound can actually be split into mitral (M_1) and tricuspid (T_1). The vibrations generated by the mitral valve closure are of higher intensity and frequency than those generated by tricuspid closure, and this mitral component is heard over much of the precordium and is the main component of the heart sound at the apex. The S_1 sound, then, is the *lub* of *lub-dub*. The second sound, S_2, is the closing of both semilunar valves (the aortic and pulmonic) just before diastole. Near the end of systole, the rate of ejection slows as the ventricular and arterial pressure begin to diminish. Ventricular pressure drops rapidly at the onset of ventricular relaxation. Blood in the base of the aorta and in the base of the pulmonary artery rushes back toward the ventricular chambers, but this movement is abruptly stopped by the closure of the aortic and pulmonic valves. The momentum of the moving blood overstretches the valve cusps, and the recoil initiates oscillations in both the atrial and ventricular cavities. S_2 is the *dub* of *lub-dub*.

For further definitive information on the study of heart sounds, including S_3 and S_4, the student is referred to Bates' *A Guide to Physical Assessment* and to the American Heart Association's publications on heart examination.

Murmurs. If you hear what you think are murmurs, try to evaluate and record their location, gross timing, intensity (PMI), pitch, quality, and the fine timing. Murmurs are graded 1 through 6. *Dorland's Medical Dictionary* defines *murmur* as "an auscultatory sound, benign or pathologic, particularly a periodic sound of short duration of cardiac or vascular origin." The intensity grades for evaluating murmurs are:

- *Grade 1:* Extremely faint, elusive, and difficult to hear in all positions
- *Grade 2:* Quiet but immediately obvious to the ear when the stethoscope is placed on the chest
- *Grade 3:* Moderately loud with *no* associated thrill
- *Grade 4:* Loud and *may* have an associated thrill
- *Grade 5:* Very loud and may even be heard with the stethoscope partly off the chest; *may* have an associated thrill
- *Grade 6:* Loud enough to be heard without the stethoscope and has an associated thrill

The pitch of a heart murmur may be high, medium, or very low, and the quality may be that of "blowing," "rumbling," "harshness," or periodically harmonious sound. Remember that high-pitched sounds or relatively high-pitched sounds, such as the first two heart sounds and the murmurs of aortic and mitral regurgitation, can be heard with the diaphragm of the stethoscope. The bell is best used for hearing low-pitched sounds, such as the S_3 and S_4 and the diastolic murmur of mitral stenosis. The bell of the stethoscope should *just* make contact with the skin, forming an air seal.

Murmurs are categorized either as systolic or diastolic; therefore, consider both. When the heart is in systole, adventitious sounds may be created by:

- Aortic stenosis
- Pulmonary stenosis
- Mitral regurgitation
- Tricuspid regurgitation

Systolic Ejection Murmur. This murmur occurs predominantly in midsystole when ejection volume and velocity of blood flow are at their maximum. It is heard in aortic or pulmonary stenosis, is of a medium pitch, and can be heard when there is an increased stroke volume, as with anemia and pregnancy.

Diastolic Murmur. This murmur occurs during diastole—that is, after the second heart sound. Heard at the apex, it is a sign of mitral obstruction; heard at the base of the heart, it is due to aortic regurgitation or, more rarely, to pulmonary regurgitation with a backflow into the ventricles. A murmur caused by tricuspid or mitral stenosis is best auscultated by using the bell of the stethoscope at the apex of the

heart. Regurgitation during diastole, whether pulmonic or aortic, will cause a backflow into the ventricles and a high-pitched murmur heard at the left sternal border. This murmur is best heard with the diaphragm of the stethoscope.

Palpitation

Palpitation is a frequently heard complaint, and though its cause may be trivial, it can seriously frighten the patient, requiring a determination of cause and a satisfactory explanation. The term is applied to the symptom in which the patient is conscious of his heart action, whether fast, slow, regular, or irregular. The sensation is often described as "pounding," "fluttering," "flopping," "skipping a beat," "jumping," or "turning over." The frequency, rate, and intensity depend on the underlying cause. Some causes of palpitations are exertion, high cardiac output at rest (anxiety, hypertension, thyrotoxicosis, flutter, or paroxysmal tachycardia), cor pulmonale, pressure on the heart (mediastinal tumor or tympanites), and stimulus of drugs (e.g., tobacco, tea, coffee, alcohol, epinephrine). Causes for persistent complaints of palpitations require further evaluation.

■ SUMMARY

A nursing examination of the chest, including the lungs and the heart, should be conducted on patients who present with problems related to the cardiorespiratory system, including the following:

- History of angina
- Palpitations
- Intermittent claudication
- Edema
- Paroxysmal nocturnal dyspnea (PND)
- Orthopnea
- Other history of heart disease, including high blood pressure

Remember to position the patient properly when preparing to evaluate heart and lung sounds and to use a binaural stethoscope when auscultating. A quality stethoscope is a most worthwhile investment for the EN and should be carried at all times on duty. Experience is still the best teacher: the most beneficial way to learn to recognize and evaluate chest sounds is to listen to every chest, if it is appropriate to the needs of the patient and time permits.

■ BIBLIOGRAPHY

Assessing Vital Functions Accurately. Horsham, Pa: Nursing 77 Books; 1977.

Bates B, ed. *A Guide to Physical Examination.* 5th ed. Philadelphia, Pa: JB Lippincott; 1991.

Boyce BA. *Nursing Practice: Respiratory Care Terminology.* Part 1. New York, NY: American Lung Association; 1976.

Cahill SB, Balskus M. *Intervention in Emergency Nursing: The First 60 Minutes.* Rockville, Md: Aspen Publishers; 1986.

DeGowin E, DeGowin R. *Bedside Diagnostic Examination: A Comprehensive Pocket Textbook.* 5th ed. New York, NY: Macmillan; 1987.

Delaney MT. Examining the chest, part I: the lungs. *Nursing.* 1975;75:12–14.

Druger G. *The Chest: Its Signs and Sounds.* Los Angeles, Calif: Humetrics; 1973.

Emergency Nurses Association. *Emergency Nursing Core Curriculum.* 4th ed. Philadelphia, Pa: WB Saunders; 1994.

Jarvis CM. Perfecting physical assessment, part 2. *Nursing 77.* June 1977; 38–45.

Kidd PS, Wagner KD. *High Acuity Nursing.* 2nd ed. Stamford, Conn: Appleton & Lange; 1996.

O'Boyle CM, Davis DK, Russo BA et al. *Emergency Care: The First 24 Hours.* E. Norwalk, Conn: Appleton & Lange, 1986.

Stiesmeyer JK. A four-step approach to pulmonary assessment. *AJN.* August 1993; 22–31.

Thibodeau GA, Patton KT. *Anatomy and Physiology.* 2nd ed. St. Louis, Mo: CV Mosby; 1993.

Timmons, J. Breath sounds. *J Emerg Nurs.* 1980; 16–18.

Wilkins RL, Dexter JR. *Respiratory Disease, Principles of Patient Care.* Philadelphia, Pa: FA Davis; 1993.

■ REVIEW: CHEST ASSESSMENT

1. Identify the important preliminary step to evaluating the chest.

2. Explain why oxygen deprivation in the brain cannot be allowed to continue for longer than 4 minutes.

3. Explain the effect of carbon dioxide on the respiratory center in the brain.

4. Define *tachypnea* and *bradypnea.*

5. Describe the characteristics of Kussmaul respiration and Cheyne–Stokes respirations.

6. Identify the four skills employed in the chest assessment.

7. Identify the four breath sounds heard on auscultation.

8. List the five sounds heard when the chest is percussed and their characteristics.

9. Describe the proper patient positioning for auscultation and percussion.

10. Explain the reason subcutaneous emphysema should not be confused with any other adventitious chest sounds.

11. Explain the rationale for assuming the worst and acting accordingly when a patient presents with chest pain, severe chest pressure, pain radiating from the chest, shortness of breath, or *any* signs of poor cardiac output.

12. Identify the first and most important intervention for such patients.

13. Define the term *point of maximum impulse* and identify the location of this point.

14. List the component parts of a cardiac examination.

15. Identify the two main heart sounds, what they represent, and where they are heard the best.

Life Support and Resuscitation

Airway Management 10

■ AIRWAY, AIRWAY, AIRWAY

When emergency patient assessment and interventions are underway, absolute priority must *always* be assigned to ensuring and maintaining a patent airway with adequate ventilation and oxygen administration if appropriate. Maintaining the patient's "lifeline," a clear airway and adequate air exchange, is paramount no matter what else is involved. For this reason, this following chapter contains what may well be some of the most important information in this book because it deals directly with the responsibility of the emergency nurse (EN) to effectively provide oxygen, the essence of life, to the compromised patient.

It is now universally recognized that when clinical death (the cessation of cardiac and respiratory function) occurs, there is an incredibly short period of *only 4 minutes* before biologic death (death of the brain cells) occurs (Fig. 10–1). After this length of time, there will have been irreversible brain damage from anoxia to the brain cells, even though the cardiovascular function of the patient may have been effectively restored. Prolonged oxygen deprivation can manifest itself in varying degrees, from a permanently dull mentality following an otherwise apparently successful resuscitation to a condition termed functional death, defined as the total and permanent destruction of the central nervous system [CNS], with vital functions sustained by artificial means. A frequently quoted description of this sort of tragedy is attributed to John Scott Haldane (1860–1936), a physician and physiologist born and educated in Edinburgh, Scotland, who pioneered in the field of anesthesia and respiratory studies. His major work, from 1905 to 1911, involved the physiology of res-

piration; he is chiefly noted for his elucidation of the process of gas exchange during respiration, from which evolved his now classic remark: "Anoxia not only stops the machine but wrecks the machinery."

The development of respiratory therapy as a highly skilled specialty area of patient care has been an extremely significant factor in the overall quality of care delivered in emergency departments (EDs) and acute-care areas of hospitals. ENs have grown to appreciate the knowledge and skill of respiratory therapists (RTs) and the convenience of calling for airway management assistance in cardiac arrests and trauma codes, but the inevitable occurs as too many nurses grow comfortable with the assumption that someone else will take airway responsibility.

While airway neglect is never intentional, it can and does happen unless airway management remains the top priority in emergency nursing assessment and intervention. It is basic and essential for every EN to acquire and maintain both the knowledge and skills required for safe and effective airway management and the foresight required to *anticipate* airway problems. Four minutes is a very short time, but 4 minutes without oxygen means a lifetime for the anoxic patient; alert, accountable, and skilled emergency nursing can, and frequently does, make the critical difference.

■ RESPIRATION

Respiration is the interchange of gases between an organism and the medium in which it lives. The main functions of the human respiratory system (Fig. 10–2) are the exchange of oxygen and carbon

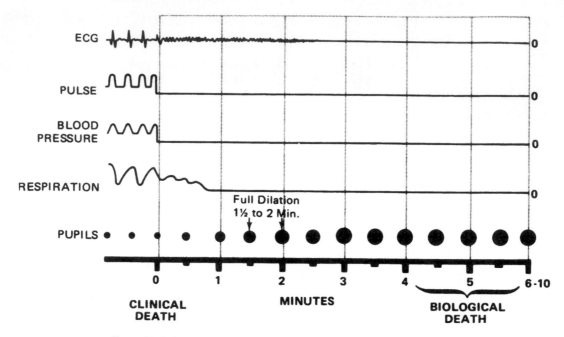

Figure 10–1. Sequence of events from clinical to biologic death in cardiac arrest.

dioxide, as air moves in and out of the lungs, with diffusion or the passive movement of gas across the alveolar capillary membrane (external respiration) and the circulation of oxygen through the bloodstream to the cells, returning carbon dioxide to the alveoli (internal respiration).

THE RESPIRATORY TRACT

The Nose

External respiration begins and ends with the nose. The nose has been compared to an air-conditioning unit because it controls the temperature and humidity of the air entering the lungs and filters foreign particles from the air. The interior of the nose is divided by a wall of cartilage and bone called the septum. Near the middle of the nasal cavity and on both sides of the septum are a series of scroll-like bones called the conchae, or turbinates. The purpose of the turbinates is to increase the amount of tissue surface within the nose so that incoming air will have a greater opportunity to be "conditioned" before it continues on its way to the lungs. The surfaces of the turbinates, like the rest of the interior walls of the nose, are covered with mucous membranes that continuously secrete a fluid called mucus, which drains slowly into the throat. The mucus gives up heat and moisture to incoming air, serves as a trap for bacte-

ria and dust in the air, and also helps dilute any irritating substances. In addition to the mucus, the membrane is coated with cilia, or hairlike filaments, that wave back and forth a dozen times per second. The millions of cilia lining the nasal cavity help the mucus clean the incoming air. When we breathe through the mouth, we lose the protective benefits of the cilia and mucus.

The Pharynx

The incoming air that has been filtered, warmed, and moistened in its trip through the nasal cavity next passes into the pharynx. The pharynx is one of the more complicated parts of the body because it serves as a passageway for both food and air. The incoming air travels through the nasal cavity, into the pharynx, and through the larynx, or voice box, by crossing over the path used by food on its way to the stomach.

Similarly, food crosses over the route of air on its way from the nose to the larynx. But when food is swallowed, a flap of cartilage called the epiglottis folds over the opening of the larynx. The base of the tongue pushes down the epiglottis as the food is moved back into the throat during the swallowing action. At the same time, the larynx moves up to help seal the opening. This action can be observed

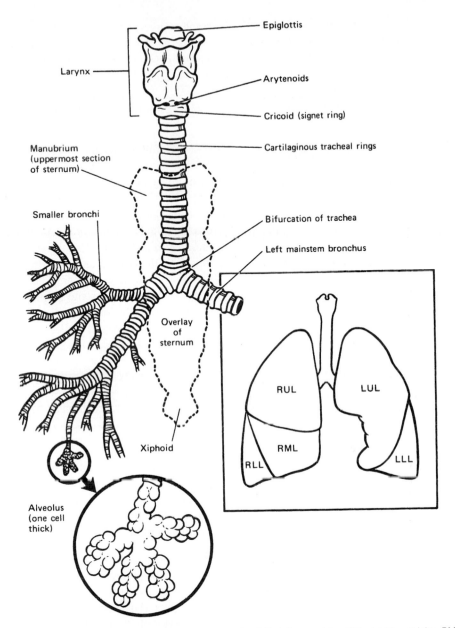

Figure 10–2. The respiratory tract. LLL, left lower lobe; LUL, left upper lobe; RLL, right lower lobe; RML, right middle lobe; RUL, right upper lobe.

by watching a person's Adam's apple, part of the larynx, move up at the start of swallowing. (The Adam's apple is actually the upper part of the thyroid cartilage, below which lies the cricoid cartilage; the cricothyroid membrane separates the two.)

The Tonsils

On each side of the pharynx, behind the mouth cavity, are tonsils. Tonsil tissue is also located at the base of the tongue, and it may appear at the back and sides of the pharynx as adenoids. Tonsils usually are more prominent in children than adults. Their purpose is to guard the body against infections that may enter through the mouth or nose.

The Larynx

The larynx, also called the voice box, is at the top of the column that finally takes the air into the lungs, the trachea. Two folds of membrane, the vocal cords, are attached to the front of the larynx wall and are held (posteriorly) by a pair of tiny cartilages (the aretynoids). The cartilages are attached to muscles that contract and relax to move the vocal cords toward or away from the center of the larynx.

The Trachea

Inferior to the larynx is the trachea, which continues down the neck and into the chest. A series of C-shaped rings of cartilage hold open the trachea. Lack of rigidity of the trachea permits us to bend the neck. The path of the esophagus, which carries food to the stomach, runs immediately posterior to the trachea. At the point behind the middle of the sternum, where the aorta arches away from the heart, the trachea divides into two branches, the right and the left bronchi (also referred to as the right and left mainstem bronchi). The point at which the trachea divides is called the carina.

The Bronchi and Alveoli

Each bronchus divides and subdivides many times into smaller cartilage-ringed branches that reach deep into the right and left lungs. The tiniest bronchi, almost too small to be seen without a microscope, have cartilage rings in their walls. However, as the tubes become still smaller, they have little or no cartilage; instead, they have muscle cells in their walls. Bronchi of this size are called bronchioles. Finally, the bronchiole ends in a tiny air sac called an alveolus. The lungs contain nearly 1 billion of these microscopic, balloonlike alveoli. The alveoli, with their air-filled spaces, make the lungs appear somewhat like large sponges. Each alveolus has a thin membrane wall, one cell thick; networks of blood capillaries surround the alveoli. When air is breathed into the lungs, the molecules of oxygen gas pass through the thin membrane walls of the alveoli and through the capillary walls, attaching to the hemoglobin on red blood cells and turning the oxygenated blood a bright red.

■ HAZARDS OF AIRWAY MANAGEMENT

Three major hazards of airway management are (1) airway trauma with soft-tissue injury and swelling, (2) introduction of infection into the res-

piratory tract, and (3) aspiration of foreign matter or gastric contents. Aspiration is by far the greatest hazard encountered in attempts to adequately manage the patient's airway.

DELAYED GASTRIC EMPTYING TIME

Patients with empty stomachs rarely vomit and aspirate; a full stomach can create problems in an emergency situation. Gastric emptying time after an ordinary meal is probably 3.5 to 4 hours; gastric emptying slows or may cease altogether with the onset of pain, trauma, or an emotional crisis or the onset of labor in the pregnant woman. Furthermore, administration of analgesic drugs following injury or the use of amnesic drugs during labor will also prolong gastric emptying time. Accordingly, accident victims and women in labor, when brought to the hospital as emergencies, are most likely to have delayed gastric emptying and are therefore predisposed to vomiting and the risk of aspiration. A good rule of thumb is to assume that if the patient has eaten within 4 hours of injury, the stomach will not be empty for up to 10 hours following injury, and possibly longer.

ASPIRATION

Aspiration is defined as the act of inhaling. Several types of aspiration syndromes may be seen in the ED and are probably due either to a diminished gag reflex with a full stomach or to poor dentition. Their causes could be classified as follows:

- Toxic or chemical fluid (aspiration of acids, hydrocarbons, alcohol, or mineral oil)
- Bacterial pathogens, both aerobic and anaerobic (poor dentition)
- Inert substances (such as steak); this type of aspiration is also known as a "café coronary"

Caution Index

The aspiration of gastric contents during emergency resuscitation procedures is associated with a very high mortality rate; signs of aspiration should be included in the caution index following resuscitation, and are as follows:

- Dyspnea within several hours of aspiration
- Bronchospasms with wheezing

- X-ray films showing white, fluffy changes in the lung fields
- Frothy sputum without purulence
- Hypotension
- Lungs filling with fluid and demonstrating reduced compliance in volume–pressure relationship.

Prevention of aspiration is the real key. If the patient is conscious risks are minimal since the patient's gag and cough reflexes are intact. If the patient is semiconscious or restrained, as on a backboard, have suction on standby, be ready to place the patient in a Trendelenburg position, and turn the patient's head to the side to mechanically remove vomitus using a *rigid* tonsil suction tip (Yankauer type), tongue blade, fingers, or whatever is available.

INAPPROPRIATE USE OF AIRWAYS AND TUBES

The inappropriate use—meaning unnecessary use—of oropharyngeal airways can cause vomiting and laryngospasm by triggering the gag reflex in a conscious or semiconscious person. The same is true, of course, with attempts at endotracheal (ET) intubation during active resuscitation of a semiconscious person. As the patient's state changes from unconscious to semiconscious during resuscitation as a direct result of the improved oxygen supply, gagging and vomiting frequently occur if there is a tube or airway in place; aspiration of vomitus during resuscitation is all too common as a result.

ENs should always be able to anticipate which patients are candidates for vomiting and aspiration and be ready to immediately position and suction to prevent any problem. Remember that it is best to *undertreat* when insertion of an airway is possibly indicated until the real need for the use of one is determined.

■ ESTABLISHING A PATENT AIRWAY

Establishing and maintaining a patent airway is *always* of the highest priority. The best method depends on the cause and degree of obstruction, along with the patient's relative condition. The treatment must be related directly to the degree of the problem; this usually requires rapid evaluation and prompt intervention. The goal is to accomplish improvement of gas exchange at the cellular level with a reversal of signs and symptoms resulting from inadequate pulmonary ventilation. It is necessary to be able to recognize when the exchange of air is adequate and when improvement is seen. Recognition of adequate exchange can be tricky, but if the signs of anoxia begin to reverse, exchange is then adequate.

AIRWAY MANEUVERS AND ADJUNCTS

Head-Tilt/Chin-Lift Maneuver

American Heart Association (AHA) standards for cardiopulmonary resuscitation (CPR) and emergency cardiac care (ECC)[1] currently endorse the head-tilt/chin-lift maneuver as being more effective in opening the airway than the previously recommended head-tilt/neck-lift and as having less risk in case of possible existing unrecognized cervical spine injury.

Initially, the mouth and pharynx must be cleared of all blood, mucus, vomitus, foreign bodies, and frequently dentures, by reaching with fingers, gauze wipes, or rigid suction tip. The tongue is the most common cause of airway obstruction. This problem can be easily managed with the simple head-tilt/chin-lift maneuver; frequently, this is the only requirement for breathing to resume spontaneously (Fig. 10–3).

To perform the head tilt, first place the patient in a supine position. Place one hand on the patient's forehead and apply firm, backward pressure with your palm to tilt the head back. To complete the head-tilt/chin-lift maneuver, place the fingers of your other hand under the bony part of the lower jaw near the chin and lift to bring the chin forward and the teeth almost together, thus supporting the jaw and helping to tilt the head back.[1] Bringing the chin forward lifts the tongue away from the back of the throat. Anatomic obstruction of the airway caused by the tongue's dropping against the back of the throat is thereby relieved. The head must be maintained in this position at all times with an unconscious patient (Fig. 10–4). If the patient has loose dentures, the head-tilt/chin-lift maintains their position and makes a mouth-to-mouth seal easier. The standards for CPR recommend removal of dentures if they cannot be managed in place.

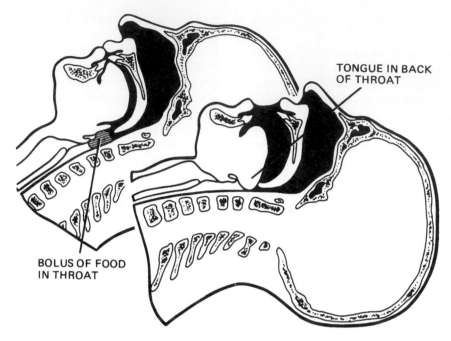

TONGUE IN BACK OF THROAT

BOLUS OF FOOD IN THROAT

Figure 10–3. Two major causes of airway obstruction.

Figure 10–4. Head-tilt/chin-lift. (*From* Textbook of Advanced Cardiac Life Support. *Copyright American Heart Association, 1994. Used with Permission.*)

Jaw-Thrust Maneuver

Although the head-tilt/chin-lift is considered the recommended technique for opening the airway, the jaw-thrust maneuver is considered the next best option. Forward displacement of the mandible is accomplished by kneeling at the patient's head, grasping the angles of the patient's lower jaw and lifting with both hands, one on each side, while tilting the head backward. The jaw-thrust technique without head-tilt, performed from a position at the top of the patient's head, is the safest first approach to opening the airway of the patient with suspected neck injury, according to AHA standards; the jaw-thrust can usually be accomplished without extending the neck. With known head injury and suspected cervical spine injury, the head should be carefully supported without tilting it backward or turning it from side to side. If jaw-thrust alone is unsuccessful, the head should be tilted backward very slightly.[1] If cervical spine injury has been ruled out and if the respirations persist in sounding somewhat obstructed, sometimes turning the patient's head to one side or the other can make an appreciable difference. If both of these maneuvers fail to provide an open airway, the EN must assume there is an upper airway obstruction.

With upper airway obstruction, the patient will probably be making strong inspiratory efforts; a cursory look at the neck will reveal contraction of the cervical muscles with retraction at the suprasternal notch and the supraclavicular fossae, coincident with each attempt at inspiration. The intercostal spaces and epigastrium will also retract on inspiration. The patient's color may be cyanotic or ashen gray by this point.

Heimlich Maneuver/Abdominal Thrust

The simple first-aid technique employed to free airways obstructed by a bolus of food or by drowning is known as the "Heimlich maneuver." It was developed by Henry J. Heimlich, M.D., a Cincinnati, Ohio, surgeon, and president of the Heimlich Institute. The rescuer stands behind the victim and wraps his or her arms around the victim's waist. The rescuer makes a fist and places it against the victim's abdomen above the navel and below the xiphoid process. The fist is then grasped with the other hand and pressed forcefully into the victim's abdomen with a quick upward thrust. The *quick* thrust is important, for if the movement is slow, it will be ineffective. If the victim is lying face up, the rescuer kneels astride him or her and, facing the victim's head, places one hand on top of the other, the heel of the lower hand against the victim's abdomen slightly above the navel and below the xiphoid process in the midline. The rescuer then presses forcefully into the abdomen with the same quick upward thrust, repeating if necessary. This maneuver is not used on infants or pregnant women; for these victims, the chest thrust is used. The fist is placed over the sternum for a pregnant woman; an infant is placed over the rescuer's hand and forearm.

A significant consideration in either abdominal or chest thrust is the possibility of damage to internal organs, such as rupture or laceration of abdominal or thoracic viscera. The rescuer's hands should never be placed on the xiphoid process of the sternum or on the lower margins of the rib cage. Hands should be placed below this area for the abdominal thrust and above this area for the chest thrust, as in positioning for CPR. Use of the abdominal thrust instead of the chest thrust in the older age group might prevent the fracture of brittle ribs; regurgitation may occur as a result of abdominal thrust and should be anticipated.

The 1992 National Conference on Standards and Guidelines for CPR and ECC produced the following general recommendations[2]:

1. Use the Heimlich maneuver (or subdiaphragmatic abdominal thrusts) for foreign-body airway obstruction removal in the adult. Use of only this method, which is at least as effective and as safe as any other single method, will simplify training programs and should result in better skills retention. Because of data suggesting that, as a single method, back blows may not be as effective as the Heimlich maneuver in adults, and in an effort to simplify training, the Heimlich maneuver is the only method recommended at this time.

2. As supported in the past by the conference, use of the chest thrust in markedly obese persons and in women in the ad-

vanced stages of pregnancy, where there is no room between the enlarging uterus and the rib cage in which to perform the thrusts, is not advised.

3. Under no circumstances should students practice subdiaphragmatic abdominal thrusts on each other during CPR training.

4. Use devices for relieving foreign-body airway obstruction only if you are properly trained in their use and application. The two types of conventional forceps that are acceptable at present, in the hands of trained personnel, are the Kelly clamp and the Magill forceps; both should be used only with a light source for direct visualization of the foreign body.

5. Teach and encourage the general public to use the "distress signal of choking," which is clutching the neck between the thumb and index finger.

Following removal of a foreign body from an unconscious victim, artificial ventilation or CPR may be required. If so, this should be performed according to the standards for CPR and ECC and the training programs of the AHA, the American National Red Cross, and other agencies that provide basic life-support training.

Mouth-to-Mouth Resuscitation

Rescue breathing using the mouth-to-mouth or mouth-to-mask (preferred) technique requires that the rescuer inflate the patient's lungs adequately with each breath. The rescuer should take a breath after each ventilation, and each individual ventilation should be of sufficient volume to make the chest rise. An excess of air volume and fast inspiratory flow rates are likely to cause pharyngeal pressures that exceed esophageal opening pressures, allowing air to enter the stomach and resulting in gastric distension. Gastric distension invites regurgitation during resuscitation procedures, and aspiration, followed by death, is likely to result.[3]

Recommendations from the 1992 Conference on Standards for CPR and ECC on the ventilation rate for rescue breathing are as follows:

1. The "four quick" initial ventilations formerly recommended in one-rescuer CPR have been changed to *two initial breaths of 1 to 1½ seconds each.*

2. The "staircase effect" has been eliminated. By giving the ventilations with a slower inspiratory flow rate and by avoiding trapping air in the lungs between breaths, the possibility of exceeding the esophageal opening pressure will be less.[4]

Details of the current AHA standards should be carefully studied by ENs for additional updated content.

If mouth-to-mouth resuscitation is necessary, supplemental oxygen should be used as soon as it becomes available. Rescue breathing (exhaled air ventilation) will deliver about 16 percent oxygen to the patient; ideally, this will produce an alveolar oxygen tension of about 80 mm Hg. However, because of the low cardiac output associated with external cardiac compression and the presence of intrapulmonary shunting and ventilation–perfusion abnormalities, marked discrepancies will occur between the alveolar and arterial oxygen tension, and hypoxemia may ensue. Hypoxemia leads to anaerobic metabolism and metabolic acidosis, which frequently impair the beneficial effects of chemical and electrical therapy in a "code" situation when resuscitation and advanced life-support procedures are being carried out.

For this reason, at the 1992 AHA conference on CPR, it was recommended that 100 percent inspired oxygen (FiO_2 = 1.0) be supplemented as soon as possible with the use of bag-valve-mask (BVM) or bag-valve-tube systems to enhance myocardial and cerebral oxygenation, essentials for successful resuscitation.[5]

An effective alternative to mouth-to-mouth resuscitation is the use of a pocket mask (Fig. 10–5), a clear-domed collapsible mask with an inflated cushion and an optional oxygen port. When the mask is held in place and properly seated over the patient's mouth and nose, it is possible to deliver an inspired oxygen content of more than 50 percent with oxygen attached at a flow rate of 10 L/min. The pocket mask allows both hands to position the patient's head and maintain an open airway, protects the operator from direct contact and contamination from the patient's nose and mouth, and provides a clear dome to observe for regurgitation during resuscitation. Personnel with less expertise in airway management are able to achieve better lung ventilation with the pocket mask. In

Figure 10–5. The pocket mask. The mask is applied to the face and held firmly by placing the thumbs on sides of mask. The index, middle, and ring fingers grasp the lower jaw just in front of the earlobes, and the jaw is pulled forcefully upward. The victim's mouth should remain open under the mask; the operator then blows in through the opening of the mask.

pediatric resuscitation efforts, the mask may be used, even on infants, if applied to the face upside down, with the narrower nose portion covering the patient's chin and the wider section covering the child or infant's mouth and nose.

Airways

Oropharyngeal airways should be used whenever a BVM system or automatic breathing device with a mask is used, but only by a properly trained person. Airways should be used only on deeply unconscious persons. If introduced into a conscious or stuporous person, an airway may promote vomiting or laryngospasm. Care is required in the placement of the airway because incorrect insertion can displace the tongue back into the pharynx and itself produce airway obstruction. Oropharyngeal airways should be available in infant, child, and adult sizes in every ED. An oropharyngeal airway should be held between the thumb and first and second fingers and inserted into the patient's mouth with the tip of the airway curving and pointing toward the roof of the mouth. As the airway is carefully advanced, it should be rotated 180 degrees and dropped into place at the base of the tongue (Fig. 10 6).

Nasopharyngeal airways also may be used for adults; however, as with all adjunctive equipment, explicit training and practice must be required for their use. A nasal tube is first lubricated with a water-soluble lubricant, the nares are lifted, and the tube is inserted along the floor of the nose with gentle, steady pressure. The left nostril is most generally employed because it is thought to be larger than the right one in most people. S-tubes are an extension of the oropharyngeal airway; they are available in numerous styles. S-tubes range from simple tubes with mouthpieces and bite blocks to more elaborate devices with valves. Despite being available in many different designs, they share certain limitations. Specifically, S-tubes:

- Do not provide as effective an airway seal as mouth-to-mouth or mouth-to-mask ventilation

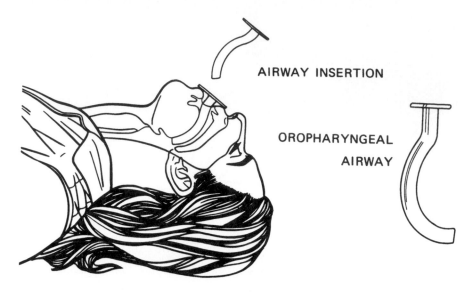

AIRWAY INSERTION

OROPHARYNGEAL AIRWAY

Figure 10–6. Placement of oropharyngeal airway with 180-degree rotation.

- Do not reduce potential transmission of infection
- Require training for safe and effective use
- Induce vomiting if used improperly
- Require the single rescuer to move to the victim's head and reposition the S-tube to inflate the lungs between chest compressions and CPR.

S-tubes do offer useful features, such as (1) overcoming aesthetic problems of direct mouth-to-mouth contact, (2) assisting and maintaining a patent airway, and (3) keeping the mouth open. However, it is generally found that direct mouth-to-mouth or mouth-to-mask ventilation provides more effective artificial ventilation.

Endotracheal Intubation

The AHA standards for advanced life support (ALS) (Part III) recognize ET intubation as one of the quickest and easiest ways to ensure a protected airway, when simpler airway adjuncts have been ineffective. ET intubation will isolate the airway, keep it patent, prevent aspiration, and ensure delivery of a high concentration of oxygen to the lungs (Fig. 10–7). The 1992 AHA conference and the 1994 AHA textbook, *Advanced Cardiac Life Sup-*

port, both recommend that because of the difficulties, delays, and complications involved in properly placing an ET tube, the use of such tubes should be restricted to medical personnel and professional allied-health personnel who are highly trained and either use ET intubation frequently or are retrained frequently in this technique. The indications for ET intubation include:

- Cardiac arrest
- Respiratory arrest
- Inability of the rescuer to ventilate the unconscious patient with conventional methods
- Inability of the patient to protect his or her own airway (coma, areflexia)
- Prolonged artificial ventilation

Once an ET tube has been passed, placement must be confirmed simultaneously with delivery of the first manual breaths. Auscultation of both lungs' apices and bases with breath sounds present should be documented. If the chest fails to rise and fall with ventilations, the tube must be immediately withdrawn and proper placement must be reattempted after the patient has been well oxygenated. The standards for ALS recommend venti-

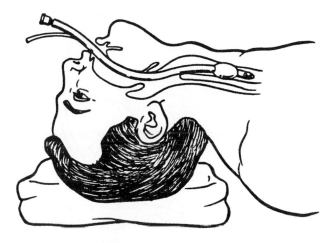

Figure 10–7. Positioning the head for endotracheal intubation.

lating with a tidal volume of 10 to 15 mL/min, with slightly more for very large patients and slightly less for those with fragile intrathoracic airways, and a respiratory rate during resuscitation of 10 to 12 breaths per minute. Each breath should be delivered over 2 seconds.[6]

Devices to confirm placement of the ET tube, measuring end-tidal carbon dioxide concentrations, have been developed and are widely used in both prehospital and in-hospital settings. These detectors are of various designs, but all attach to the end of the ET tube and confirm proper tube placement, with electronic readouts or color changes indicating the amount of carbon dioxide being exhaled. Their use as an adjunct to assessment of ET tube placement is encouraged by the ALS standards.[7]

Another method being employed has been syringe aspiration of air, easily done after correct placement of the ET tube in the trachea but meeting resistance if esophageal intubation has occurred. This technique has the advantage of being fast, inexpensive, and reliable, using a 60-mL syringe connected to a straight ventilator-circuit adapter and fastened to the ET tube.[8]

Sellick's maneuver: Sellick's maneuver involves a second rescuer applying slight pressure with the thumb and index finger of one hand, anterolaterally and directed posteriorly, to the cricoid cartilage during intubation, compressing the walls of the esophagus and protecting against regurgitation and aspiration of gastric contents.

Blind intubation–nasal route without hyperextension of the neck: An emergency procedure available for the patient who has sustained a neck injury and cannot have the neck hyperextended is the so-called blind intubation procedure in which the patient is effectively intubated without direct visualization of the vocal cords. An ET tube is carefully inserted into the nostril for a distance equivalent to that from the tip of the nose to the tragus of the ear. Insertion of the tube for that distance places the tip of the tube right above the epiglottis; *when the patient breathes,* the tube is advanced into place. Listening to the end of the tube, the EN confirms, by audible movement of air, that the tube has entered the trachea. It is said that most of the time, this route is relatively simple to use because of the curve of the tube. This route may be indicated in severely compromised patients with neck injuries, but remember that it can be accomplished only in a patient who is breathing.

Blind intubation—oral route: Place the bite block to prevent being bitten, hyperextend the head, locate the larynx with the index finger of the nondominant hand, and pull the epiglottis forward (Fig. 10–8). Pass the ET tube by using the placed index finger as a guide with the curvature of the tube, pointing the tip anteriorly, and slowly advancing the tube past the aretynoids into the trachea; the balloon is then inflated after proper placement is confirmed.

ET intubation tray inventory: The ET intubation tray should contain the following items:

1. Straight blade (Miller) or curved blade (MacIntosh), laryngoscope with a bright

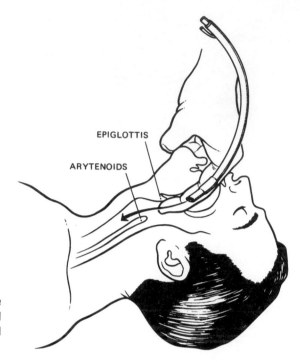

EPIGLOTTIS

ARYTENOIDS

Figure 10–8. Blind intubation. Hyperextend the neck and pull the epiglottis toward you with the index finger. Insert the tracheal catheter, using the top surface of the inserted finger as a guide, and slowly advance the tube past the arytenoids into the trachea.

light and fresh batteries. Adult sizes— numbers 2, 3, and 4—as well as pediatric sizes should be on hand.

2. An assortment of endotracheal tubes with intact cuffs; average adult sizes are 32, 34, 36, and 38 Fr, or 7, 7.5, 8, 8.5, and 9 mm. Pediatric sizes should also be on hand. (Many experienced anesthesia personnel say that one can "guesstimate" the adequate size of an ET tube according to the size of the patient's little finger. A pediatric hospital study determined, however, that when used for children, this method generally resulted in choosing a tube larger than necessary; the study suggested instead matching the tube size to the width of the fifth fingernail.[9]

3. Wire guides, or stylets, should be available but should *never* be used *except by* a physician or anesthesia personnel.

4. One 10 mL syringe for cuff inflation.

5. A selection of adapters for connection of the tube to the respirator or bag unit.

6. Contoured forceps (Magill or Rovenstein).

7. Spray for topical anesthesia (for the conscious, alert patient).

8. Water-soluble lubricant (for use with cuffed tubes).

9. 0.5-in. adhesive tape, tincture of benzoin, and applicators.

10. Tongue depressors.

Other items at hand should be: oxygen, suction, and resuscitation equipment, including a manual resuscitation bag; a pillow, folded towel, sandbag, or other under-shoulders support; and a stethoscope to check tube placement.

A primary responsibility of *all* ENs is to check the status of the intubation tray at the beginning of *each* and every shift. Rechargeable handles should be plugged into wall outlets for charge, and batteries should be replaced in other handles if the light is dimming. The full supply of tubes should be checked, as should the presence of a syringe for endotracheal tube cuff inflation, McGill forceps, and water-soluble lubricant. Any EN who has had a dead battery or light on the laryngoscope during a "code" procedure knows the importance of checking at the beginning of each shift to be certain that there is a dependable light source on the laryngoscope, should the equipment be needed.

Guidelines for ET intubation are summarized in Table 10–1.

Rapid-Sequence Intubation

Rapid-sequence intubation (RSI) is a technique employed to provide a secured airway in serious trauma patients and in those with altered levels of consciousness and potential airway compromise. On the premise that all trauma patients have full stomachs and are candidates for aspiration, RSI provides a controlled method for preventing further life-threatening complications; apneic patients are, however, intubated immediately regardless. The RSI technique involves a controlled and systematic approach in which four basic areas are addressed:

1. Necessary intubation equipment on hand and in readiness, including full capability for oxygen administration and suction
2. Preoxygenation with 100 percent oxygen for 3 to 5 minutes

3. Intravenous administration of a neuromuscular blocking agent and a short-acting induction adjunct (e.g., succinylcholine and thiopental, respectively); the induction agent may be omitted if the patient is already unconscious.
4. ET intubation while Sellick's maneuver is performed by an assistant. Cricoid pressure must be maintained until the cuff is inflated.

The RSI requires skill and teamwork, and once the sequence begins, it must be carried out within 3 minutes to avoid further oxygen deprivation. Ideally, cervical spine x-rays should be obtained prior to the procedure, but in any event, intubation must be carried out while a third person provides in-line traction, which may be achieved by pulling the patient's hair in a direct line with the cervical spine.[10,11]

Alternative Invasive Airways

Recently, several devices have come into use for blind intubation in situations in which ET intuba-

---

TABLE 10–1. GUIDELINES FOR ENDOTRACHEAL INTUBATION

Indications for intubation	Helpful hints during procedure
Inadequate ventilation	Remember to reassure even an apparently comatose patient
Gastric lavage in drug-overdosed patients to prevent aspiration	Assemble *all* equipment in advance and check the cuff of the tube for leaks
Airway to be maintained during tracheostomy	Check working condition of laryngoscope light
Ventilation requiring assistance during resuscitation	Position the patient's head carefully
Acute severe pulmonary edema	Protect patient's teeth
	Never persist in intubation attempt *any longer than you can hold your own breath*, without reoxygenating the patient
Possible contraindications to intubation	*Always* listen to breath sounds and the apices of both lungs after intubation
Any question of unstable cervical spine fracture	Secure the tube in proper position with 0.5-in. adhesive or an elastic holding device, being careful to avoid any pressure on the nares
Presence of foreign bodies in upper airway	Recognize excessive coughing as a possible sign of irritation to tracheal carina (the point at which the trachea bifurcates into right and left mainstem bronchus, approximately 2 in. below the suprasternal notch)
Previous long-term or repeated tracheal intubations	
Laryngeal edema, usually accompanied by acute laryngitis	
Mandibular fractures	
Common errors of intubation	
Intubating inappropriately in emergency situations when an oropharyngeal airway and bag or mask unit are adequate	
Wasting time	
Failing to see tracheal opening	
Passing tube too far into right mainstem bronchus with resulting collapse of left lung	
Choosing too small a tube	

Modified from American College of Physicians.[15]

tion is not permitted and airways require extended protection and ventilation. These devices include the esophageal obturator airway (EOA), the esophageal gastric tube airway (EGTA), the pharyngotracheal lumen (PTL) airway, and the combination esophagotracheal tube (esophagotracheal Combitube, or ETC). The basic principle of all is occlusion of the esophagus to prevent vomitus and aspiration, together with delivery of oxygen through the vocal cords into the trachea and lungs, but *all* require training, practice, and demonstrated proficiency in their use.

EOA and EGTA: The EOAs are used in the management of cardiac arrest and cases of extensive facial trauma. They appear to be useful airway adjuncts but have become controversial since cases of esophageal trauma have been documented with their use. Further, when compared to efficacy of ET tubes, ventilation and oxygen delivery had been inferior.

The airway consists of a 15-in. cuffed tube (similar to an ET tube) mounted through a face mask and modified with a soft plastic obturator blocking the distal orifice, with multiple openings in the upper one third of the tube at the level of the pharynx. With the mask in place on the tube, the tube is passed down the back of the throat into the esophagus (Fig. 10–9). The mask is then tightly seated on the face and the 30-mL cuff of the tube is inflated, using a one-way valve system. When mouth-to-tube or BVM ventilation is performed, the air is discharged through the pharyngeal openings in the tube and passes down the

trachea, owing to esophageal blockage. Theoretically, this will prevent gastric distension and regurgitation during resuscitation. As an additional feature to protect the airway, the EGTA has a patent tube permitting suction of gastric contents should regurgitation occur. EOAs should be inserted only in patients who are not breathing or who are deeply unconscious.

The potential advantages of the EOA are that no visualization is required for introduction and that it can be placed more easily and quickly than an ET tube without hyperextension of the head and neck. In a large series of cardiac arrest cases, successful use of the airway was documented without injury to the esophagus when used by professional allied-health personnel who had been trained in its use on intubation mannequins and unconscious patients. However, the potential for damage to the esophagus is *always* present unless use of the airway is restricted to adequately trained individuals. Removal of the esophageal airway, like removal of an ET tube, frequently is followed by immediate regurgitation. To cope with this, the airway should *not* be removed until the patient is becoming conscious and is breathing *or* has a return of reflexes. When it is to be removed, the patient should be turned onto his or her side and adequate suction should be available and ready. A standard cuffed ET tube should be introduced into the trachea *prior* to removal of the esophageal airway if necessary. Remember that a patient coming into the ED with a *yellow-, white-,* or *red-tipped* intubation tube in place probably has an EOA. The 30-mL

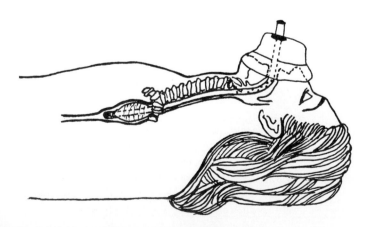

Figure 10–9. Correct positioning of the Esophageal Obturator Airway (EOA), with inflated cuff lying below the carina at the bifurcation of the right and left mainstem bronchi and with the face mask firmly seated.

balloon cuff must be deflated fully before any attempts at extubation are made in order to avoid trauma to the soft tissue of the esophagus.

PTL and ETC: Both of these devices are double-lumen tubes, structurally and functionally similar, and shorter than EOAs. Both are inserted without visualization of the vocal cords. Location assessment is made and the patient is then ventilated through the appropriate ports. The ETC has a self-adjusting and self-positioning posterior pharyngeal balloon and allows for both oxygen delivery and immediate suctioning of gastric contents.

Cricothyroidotomy

In desperate situations of complete or near complete upper airway obstruction secondary to injuries of the face, mandible, throat, or entrapped foreign bodies in the larynx, any measure short of an emergency cricothyroidotomy may prove fatal. In these situations (if none of the previously described measures can be used), the cricothyroid membrane must be opened at once, using any relatively sharp instrument, a penknife, scissors, or even a nail file (Fig. 10–10).

The cricothyroid membrane can be identified by feeling for the transverse indentation, which is located about 0.5 in. (1.5 cm) below the Adam's apple. This area is relatively avascular, and serious bleeding does not occur. The instrument should be inserted transversely to obtain a sufficient opening.

Once the trachea has been entered, a piece of rigid tube, if available, should be inserted into the airway to keep the edges of the aperture apart; a small tracheostomy tube or infant airway will work very well.

The insertion of intravenous needles in the cricothyroid membrane has been recommended, but even those of large bore will improve the airway very little unless either two 14-gauge or one 10-gauge, 3-in. angiocatheter is placed. The needle is directed at a 45-degree angle caudally, aspirating as it is advanced; aspiration of air signifies entry into the tracheal lumen.

Percutaneous Translaryngeal Oxygen Jet Insufflation

Percutaneous translaryngeal oxygen jet insufflation (PTOJI) consists of intermittent high-pressure oxygen insufflation into the larynx via a small bore (14- or 16-gauge) catheter-outside-needle inserted percutaneously. This is a technique for oxygenation and ventilation, increasingly employed for selected cases in intrahospital resuscitation and anesthesia. In contrast to cricothyroidotomy, PTOJI requires compressed oxygen and special equipment, consisting of tubings, connectors, stopcocks, and flexible cannulas.

PTOJI can be an alternative when tracheal intubation is not possible, if the necessary equipment is immediately available. Cricothyroidotomy can be accomplished with pocket-size equipment and permits an adequate airway through the cannula for exhalation of air. In addition to requiring special equipment, PTOJI also depends upon the victim's upper airway, above the point of its insertion in the larynx, for exhalation. Therefore, in using PTOJI, inability to exhale must be watched, and if the lungs do not deflate, cricothyroidotomy should be performed.

A caveat in the current AHA standards specifically directs that *all* alternative invasive devices require considerable training for their safe and appropriate use and should be employed only by specially trained and experienced medical professionals. Even with adequate training serious complications may occur, and the ET tube remains the optimal adjunct to protect the airway and maintain adequate ventilation during resuscitation.[12]

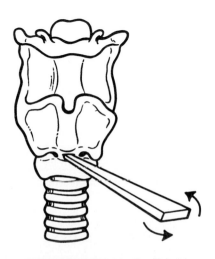

Figure 10–10. The cricothyroidotomy.

Tracheostomy

A tracheostomy procedure may be lifesaving in chest-injured patients. However, in an acute emergency, tracheostomy is far inferior to ET intubation. In the first place, it will take 10 to 15 minutes, as compared to the few seconds required to insert an ET tube. Furthermore, a hastily done tracheostomy with inadequate assistance, poor lighting, and improper instruments in a patient who is rapidly expiring often leads to troublesome bleeding, which may significantly increase the airway difficulty.

Tracheostomy, therefore, should ordinarily be deferred until it can be carried out carefully under suitable conditions, preferably in the operating room, and as an *elective* procedure. The ET tube should not be withdrawn until the tracheostomy has been completed.

OXYGEN ADMINISTRATION

Oxygen is listed as a drug in the national formulary and requires a doctor's order for administration; therefore, EDs should have written protocols for oxygen delivery. Because there are no body stores of oxygen, oxygen-enriched air must be continuously provided to compromised patients, regardless of the cause of their problems. However, it must be remembered that some patients with chronic obstructive pulmonary disease and chronic respiratory failure depend on hypoxemia to stimulate the respiratory drive. When they present with acute-on-chronic respiratory failure, they need oxygen, but only enough to restore their small alveolar partial pressure of oxygen (PAO_2) to what is normal for them, which is probably a PAO_2 of about 50 mm Hg. In other words, they need continuous controlled oxygen therapy. In emergency situations, the vast majority of patients with any form (or suspicion) of respiratory failure should be given continuous high concentrations of oxygen; when administration is prolonged, the concentration is adjusted to give a normal PAO_2. Oxygen toxicity does not occur with low-flow methods of delivery (nasal prongs) or with concentrations below 50 percent even after prolonged administration. The effect of oxygen therapy in a chronic lung patient should be monitored with arterial blood gases (ABGs). Oxygen administered by nasal cannula or mask for a short term (30 minutes to 1 hour) should not require humidification unless the patient is asthmatic or emphysemic, or unless the relative humidity of the air itself is very, very low and the patient's status is compromised.

When humidifier bottles are used for oxygen administration, they must be changed after each patient use. Disposable humidifier bottles should be removed from the flow meter when they are no longer in use and disposed of. Reusable humidifier bottles should be removed from the flow meter, emptied, cleansed, and replaced in dry condition. Water-filled bottles hanging at room temperature for any considerable length of time have been found to be prolific sources of *Pseudomonas* growth and represent a severe health hazard to the next patient receiving humidified oxygen from that source. Oxygen may be administered in the emergency setting by nasal catheter, nasal cannula, face mask without reservoir bag, and face mask with reservoir or rebreathing bag.

A comparison of oxygen concentrations available to the patient with various delivery systems is presented in Table 10–2; it is interesting to note that both the nasal catheter and the nasal cannula can produce relatively high percentages of oxygen at a low flow, while the face mask with the reservoir or rebreathing bag produces the highest percentage of oxygen at a high flow rate.

TABLE 10–2. DELIVERY RATES FOR LOW-FLOW OXYGEN[a] DEVICES

Oxygen Flow (L/min)	Nasal Cannula %	Oropharyngeal Catheter (%)	Simple Mask (%)	Nonrebreathing Mask (%)
2	25	28		
4	36	36	28–40	
6	44	≥44	40–50	60
8–10	60–70	60–70	>60	≥99

[a] Variables affecting the percentage of oxygen delivered are (1) the capacity of the available anatomic oxygen reservoir (e.g., the nose, nasopharynx, and oropharynx), (2) the liter flow per minute, and (3) the patient's ventilatory pattern. Normal ventilatory pattern is assumed with the rates given here.

ESSENTIAL SUPPORTIVE EQUIPMENT

Bag-Valve-Mask Units

When BVM units are used, they usually provide less ventilatory volume than mouth-to-mouth or mouth-to-mask ventilation because of the difficulty in providing a leakproof seal to the face while maintaining an open airway. Extensive, specialized training and demonstrated continuing proficiency are required with the bag BVM device (Fig. 10–11).

Positioning: The rescuer must assume a position at the top of the patient's head and must then maintain the head in extension, keep the lower jaw elevated, and secure an optimum mask fit with one hand while using the other hand to squeeze the bag. Attempts have been made to achieve effective ventilation with these devices by using two rescuers, one to hold the mask and one to squeeze the bag, but this is an awkward procedure. However, some BVM units have extension tubing from the bag to the mask, which allows the bag to be placed between the arm and the chest wall while holding the mask in place with both hands and forming the seal as the bag is squeezed between the arm and the body.

When an ET tube or EOA is used, the rescuer may assume a position at the patient's side. When a mask is used, the rescuer should *always* be positioned at the top of the patient's head and *not* at the side, maintaining a leakproof seal between the mask and the face to achieve maximum ventilation; again, this is a technique that requires a great deal of skill and ongoing practice.

High-flow oxygen delivery: When the intent is to deliver 100 percent oxygen via the BVM unit, care should be taken to ensure that oxygen flow rate is set at 15 L/min and that both hands are used to compress the reservoir bag, allowing a longer refill time between compressions.[5,13]

BVM criteria: An adequate BVM unit should fulfill these criteria:

- Self-refilling design, but without sponge rubber inside because of the difficulty in cleaning, disinfecting, eliminating ethylene oxide, and fragmentation
- Nonjam valve system at 15 L/min oxygen inlet flow
- A transparent, plastic face mask with an air-filled or contoured resilient cuff
- No pop-off valve, even on pediatric models
- Standard 15- and 22-mm fittings/adaptors
- A system for delivery of high concentrations of oxygen through an ancillary oxygen inlet at the back of the bag or by means of an oxygen reservoir
- A true nonbreathing valve
- Satisfactory design for practice on mannequins

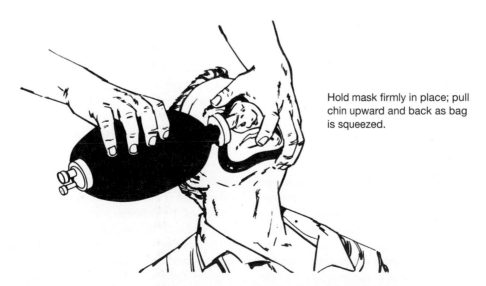

Hold mask firmly in place; pull chin upward and back as bag is squeezed.

Figure 10–11. Bag-valve-mask resuscitation. The appropriate compression–ventilation ratio must be maintained, with an adequate tidal volume delivered (10 to 15 mL/kg) each time the bag is squeezed.

- Satisfactory performance under all common environmental conditions and extremes of temperature
- Availability in adult and pediatric sizes

Suction

Suction, whether portable or installed, is *the most essential adjunct* to airway management and must be available for airway maintenance emergencies. The portable unit should provide vacuum and flow adequate for pharyngeal suction. It should be fitted with large-bore, nonkinking suction tubing and semirigid pharyngeal suction tips (Yankauer or "tonsil" type). There should be multiple sterile suction catheters of various sizes for suctioning with ET or tracheostomy tubes, a nonbreakable collection receptacle, and a supply of water for rinsing tubes and catheters.

The installed suction unit should be powerful enough to provide an airflow of over 30 L/min at the end of the delivery tube (powerful enough to immediately evacuate material the thickness of catsup) and a vacuum of over 300 mm Hg when the tube is clamped. The amount of suction should be controllable for use on children and intubated patients.

There should be an additional set of rigid pharyngeal suction tips (tonsil suction tips) and sterile, curved tracheal suction catheters of various sizes. For tracheal suction, a Y- or T-piece or a lateral opening should be between the suction tube and the suction source for on-off control. The suction yoke, collection bottle, water for rinsing, and suction tubes should be readily accessible to the attendant at the head of the litter. The tube should reach the airway of the patient regardless of his or her position. Suction apparatus must be designed for easy cleaning and decontamination.

Suction readiness: An excellent fail-safe procedure to follow when anticipating the arrival of a patient who may suddenly require immediate vigorous suctioning is to have the suction equipment assembled, turned on, and clamped off with an instrument or by wedging a fold of tubing into an intravenous pole receptacle on the stretcher. This seemingly small item of preparedness can save precious seconds of time when a desperately compromised patient vomits and is in danger of aspiration.

Bronchial suctioning: If the patient requires suctioning beyond the oropharyngeal area or through an ET tube, sterile suction catheters must be used with sterile gloves if possible. The one-hand sterile technique is generally most workable; the catheter tip should be handled with a sterile glove as it is advanced down the airway. Catheters used for suctioning bronchial secretions should be soft plastic or latex with a whistle tip and should be discarded after each use. The diameter of the catheter is important, since it displaces the passage of air or oxygen in the airway. Usually a 14 Fr catheter is adequate for adults and a 10 Fr, for children.

The catheter should have a Y connection or a thumb port so that the tube can be passed into the bronchus without extracting the oxygen supply and then slowly withdrawn as the suction is applied and as the catheter is gently rotated.

The same rule applies here as for ET intubation: never occlude the patient's airway with a tube any longer than you can hold your own breath, and never suction a patient for more than 10 seconds at a time, maximum, allowing several minutes between suctioning efforts so that the patient does not become even more hypoxic.

PHARMACOLOGICAL ADJUNCTS TO VENTILATION

When attempting to establish and protect the airway in patients who are semiconscious and have some degree of muscle control or in those who may be combative, health-care personnel are selectively using succinylcholine (Anectine) in both prehospital (under medical control) and ED settings. Long used in surgical settings with prolonged anesthesia, succinylcholine is a valuable adjunct for easing intubation, with minimal soft-tissue trauma.

Succinylcholine is a skeletal muscle relaxant given intravenously, usually in doses between 0.3 and 1.1 mg/kg. It produces neuromuscular block with flaccid paralysis in about 1 minute; maximum block lasts 2 minutes. One study indicated that of a group of 40 patients who were over 12 years of age and not in cardiac or respiratory arrest, 39 (97.5 percent) were successfully intubated following intravenous administration of 1.5 mg/kg of succinylcholine.[14] The flaccid paralysis following administration is selective, initially involving, consecutively, the levator muscles of the face, the glottis, and the intercostals, diaphragm, and all other skeletal muscles. Respiratory support, therefore, must be *uninterrupted;* further delay in oxygen delivery and ventilation carries the risk of permanent damage to the patient.

■ SUMMARY

As patient assessment is underway by emergency-care providers, absolute priority must be assigned to ensuring and maintaining a patent airway and adequate ventilation, with oxygen administered as appropriate.

Airway distress in a patient is usually quite obvious, but the EN should evaluate every patient closely by looking and listening. Evaluate the pattern (rapid or slow), the quality (shallow or deep), and the sound (quiet, raspy, crowing, gurgling) of respiration; skin color (pale, cyanotic, ashen); and facial expression (relaxed, anxious, frantic); and check for use of accessory muscles.

Some guidelines for competent and effective airway management are as follows:

1. The airway is *always* the first concern.
2. Proper positioning of the head will be the major factor in clearing most airways, remembering that the tongue is the most common form of airway obstruction.
3. Never use an airway on a responsive or semiresponsive patient if a gag reflex is present.
4. Be careful to avoid soft-tissue damage when inserting and removing oropharyngeal or nasopharyngeal airways.
5. Have the suction on and ready for all extubations.
6. Have rigid tonsil suction tips and large-bore tubing available at all times on the suction apparatus.
7. Always check the laryngoscope at the beginning of every shift. Never assume that someone on the last shift has done it.
8. Keep only water-soluble lubrication on the endotracheal tray.
9. Always auscultate the apices and bases of both lungs after intubation, regardless of the type of tube placed, to be certain that breath sounds are present bilaterally.
10. Never persist in the intubation attempt any longer than you can hold your own breath without reoxygenating the patient.

Maintaining the "lifeline"—a clear airway and respiratory function—is paramount no matter what else is involved. Be absolutely certain that your patient's airway and respiratory functions are competently managed by a qualified person, whether yourself or someone else.

■ REFERENCES

1. Standards and guidelines for cardiopulmonary resuscitation (CPR) and emergency cardiac care (ECC). *JAMA.* 1992;268:2186.
2. Standards and guidelines for cardiopulmonary resuscitation (CPR) and emergency cardiac care (ECC). *JAMA.* 1992;268:2194.
3. Standards and guidelines for cardiopulmonary resuscitation (CPR) and emergency cardiac care (ECC). *JAMA.* 1992;268:2187.
4. Standards and guidelines for cardiopulmonary resuscitation (CPR) and emergency cardiac care (ECC). *JAMA.* 1992;268:2187.
5. Standards and guidelines for cardiopulmonary resuscitation (CPR) and emergency cardiac care (ECC). *JAMA.* 1992;268:2199.
6. Standards and guidelines for cardiopulmonary resuscitation (CPR) and emergency cardiac care (ECC). *JAMA.* 1992;268:2202.
7. Standards and guidelines for cardiopulmonary resuscitation (CPR) and emergency cardiac care (ECC). *JAMA.* 1992;268:2202.
8. Verifying endotracheal tube position in the ED. *Emerg Med.* December 1994:47.
9. Quick sizing for pediatric intubation. *Emerg Med.* November 1993:52.
10. Powell L, Holt P. Rapid sequence induction in the emergency department. *J Emerg Nurs.* 1995;21:305–309.
11. Bjornson K. Anesthesia in the trauma patient. *Top Emerg Med.* 1987;9:43–51.
12. Standards and guidelines for cardiopulmonary resuscitation (CPR) and emergency cardiac care (ECC). *JAMA.* 1992;268:2203.
13. Corley M, Ledwidge MK, Glass C, et al. The myth of 100% oxygen delivery through manual resuscitation bags. *J Emerg Nurs.* 1993;19:48.
14. Krisanda TJ, Eitel DR, Cooley MP, et al: Prehospital use of succinylcholine (Anectine) as a pharmacological adjunct to emergency intubation in a suburban ALS system. *J Emerg Nurs.* 1994;20:16.

15. American College of Physicians Medical Skills Library, ROCOM. *Endotracheal Intubation.* Philadelphia, Pa: American College of Physicians; 1972.

■ BIBLIOGRAPHY

American College of Physicians Medical Skills Library, ROCOM. *Endotracheal Intubation.* Philadelphia, Pa: American College of Physicians; 1972.

American College of Surgeons Committee on Trauma. Advanced Trauma Life Support Program. Chicago, Ill: American College of Surgeons; 1993.

American Heart Association. *Textbook of Advanced Cardiac Support,* Chap. 2, Dallas, Tex, 1994.

Barrett AS. A guide to airway management. *Emerg Med Services.* 1984;13.

Bates B, ed. *A Guide to Physical Assessment.* 5th ed. Philadelphia, Pa: JB Lippincott; 1991.

Benumof J. *Airway Management: Principles and Practice.* St. Louis, Mo: CV Mosby; 1995.

Boyce B. *Nursing Practice: Respiratory Care Terminology.* New York, NY: American Lung Association; 1976.

Cardona VD, ed. *Trauma Reference Manual, Maryland Institute for EMSS.* Bowie, Md: Brady Company; 1985.

Cummins RO, ed. *Textbook of Advanced Cardiac Life Support.* Dallas, Tex: American Heart Association; 1994.

Emergency Nurses Association. *Emergency Nursing Core Curriculum.* 4th ed. Philadelphia, Pa: WB Saunders; 1994.

Emergency Nurses Association. *Trauma Nursing Core Course.* 4th ed. Chicago, Ill: Emergency Nurses Association; 1995.

Fincke MK, Lanros NE, eds. *Emergency Nursing: A Comprehensive Review.* Rockville, Md: Aspen Publishers; 1986.

Fuchs P. Getting the best out of oxygen delivery systems. *Nursing 80.* Dec. 1980; 10:34–43.

Grigsby J, Rottman S. Prehospital airway management: esophageal obturator airway or endotracheal intubation? Controversies in emergency medicine. *Top Emerg Med.* 1981;3:25–29.

Hayden RA. What keeps oxygenation on track? *AJN.* December 1992;32–41.

Intubation in a hurry. *Emerg Med.* 1981;13:10.

Jacquette G. To reduce hazards of tracheal suctioning. *Nursing 71.* 1971; 2362–2364.

Kacmarek RM. The art of artificial airways. *Emerg Med.* 1984;16:17.

Kidd PS, Wagner KD. *High Acuity Nursing.* 2nd ed. E. Norwalk, Conn: Appleton & Lange; 1992.

Kirilloff L, Maszkiewicz R. Guide to respiratory care in critically ill adults. *AJN.* 1979;79:2005–2012.

Knezevich-Brown BA. *Trauma Nursing Principles and Practice.* E. Norwalk, Conn: Appleton & Lange; 1986.

Kyes FN. Dynamics of ventilation. In: Fincke MK, Lanros NE, eds. *Emergency Nursing: A Comprehensive Review.* Rockville, Md: Aspen Publishers; 1986.

Mateer JR. Avoiding hypoxemia during intubation. *Emerg Med.* December 1993; 41.

Matthews PJ. Safely delivering a breath of fresh air. *Nursing 95.* May 1995;66–69.

Moody A. Oxygen therapy. *J Emerg Nurs.* 1979;5: 15–20.

Myers EM, Iko BO. The management of acute laryngeal trauma. *Trauma.* 1987;27.

Naclerio A. *Chest Trauma.* Summit, NJ: Ciba Pharmaceutical; 1970.

O'Boyle CM, Davis DK, Russo BA, et al. *Emergency Care: The First 24 Hours.* E. Norwalk, Conn: Appleton & Lange; 1985.

Perro K, Goetze C, Monaghan J. Making every minute count with an esophageal gastric tube airway. *Nursing 80.* August 1980;10:61–65.

Pierson DJ. Comparing oxygenation monitors. *Crit Care Alert.* 1994;2:1–8.

Promisloff RA. When, why, and how to administer oxygen safely. *Nursing 80.* Oct. 1980;10:54–56.

Roberts R, Lange DA, Robin AP, Barrett J. Chest trauma: emergency diagnosis and management of airway problems and intrathoracic injuries. *Top Emerg Med.* 1987;9:53–70.

Standards for cardiopulmonary resuscitation (CPR) and emergency cardiac care (ECC). *JAMA.* 1992;268: 2171–2302.

Stein JM. Difficult adult intubation. *Emerg Med.* 1985; 17:3.

Stringer LW. *Emergency Treatment of Acute Respiratory Diseases.* 3rd ed. Bowie, Md: Brady Company; 1982.

Sweetwood H. *Nursing in the Intensive Respiratory Care Unit.* 2nd ed. New York, NY: Springer; 1979.

Thompson SW. How to use the Heimlich maneuver on choking infants and children. *Pediatr Nurs.* Jan/Feb 1983;13–14.

Whitten CE. Endotracheal anatomy. *Emerg Med.* April 30, 1989;171–173.

Whitten CE. Difficult intubations: tricks to remember. *Emerg Med.* Jan 15, 1990;85–102.

Wilkins RL, Dexter JR. *Respiratory Disease, Principles of Patient Care.* Philadelphia, Pa: FA Davis, 1993.

Wright SW. Intubation when the C-spine may be injured. *Emerg Med.* Sept 15, 1992;73.

■ REVIEW: AIRWAY MANAGEMENT

1. Define the terms *clinical death, biologic death,* and *functional death.*

2. Define *respiration.*

3. Identify the anatomy of the respiratory tract.

4. List the three major hazards of airway management in the emergency department (ED).

5. Explain the hazards incurred after trauma with delayed gastric emptying time and the rule of thumb that should govern preventive management.

6. List at least five signs of aspiration.

7. Identify the most common cause of airway obstruction.

8. Describe the proper method of performing the head-tilt/chin-lift maneuver in airway clearance.

9. Describe the Heimlich maneuver and identify two clinical indications for its use.

10. Explain the rationale for and list four advantages of the use of the pocket mask.

11. Identify the indications and advantages of endotracheal (ET) intubation.

12. Describe Sellick's maneuver.

13. Identify the four basic components of rapid-sequence intubation.

14. Identify the criteria for an adequate bag-mask unit.

15. List four criteria for providing effective suction capability.

16. List at least eight airway management guidelines for the emergency nurse (EN).

Shock States and Fluid Resuscitation

11

Shock in the emergency department (ED) may result from several problems that accompany trauma, and the emergency nurse (EN) must understand basic principles about recognizing and management of shock states.

■ PATHOPHYSIOLOGY OF SHOCK

Shock may be categorized in several ways, but is invariably defined as a condition in which the cells are unable to obtain and use oxygen, from either low blood flow or unevenly distributed blood flow.[1] The initiating events may be hypovolemia, cardiac pump failure, or collapse of the peripheral resistance, but all eventually lead to multiple organ failure. The pathophysiology involves changes in blood flow dynamics and impaired oxygen transportation patterns, culminating in tissue hypoxia, organ dysfunction or failure, and ultimately death of the patient.

The clinical detection of shock has been historically based on associated findings such as pallor, clammy skin, thready pulse, unstable blood pressure, and altered mental status. These characteristics of shock can be linked to the multiple neurohormonal compensations, cascades of biochemical mediators, and inflammatory responses that accompany the underlying problem that triggered the syndrome. Each precipitating event has a unique pathophysiological sequence; therefore, clinical treatment approaches vary considerably. Any plan for managing shock must go beyond merely correcting hemodynamic values reflected in blood pressure, heart rate, and urinary output and must be directed instead to the overall circulatory dynamics that can affect tissue perfusion.[1]

COMPENSATION IN SHOCK STATES

There are three primary components essential to ensuring circulation: blood volume, the pumping force of the heart, and peripheral resistance. When any one of these factors is significantly impaired, shock will result, since the needs of cells will not be met.

Blood volume must be sufficient to "prime the cardiac pump" and to reach even the most distant vascular beds. Furthermore, blood must contain oxygen and the substrates required to meet the needs of cells throughout the body. Deficits in the overall vascular volume may occur from hemorrhage, "third-spacing," or from any excessive fluid loss from diarrhea, vomiting, wound drainage, rapid respirations, or poorly controlled diuresis. When fluid is lost initially from the circulatory network, a series of adjustments occur promptly to maintain balance. These are dependent on several neural and hormonal responses.

When the body experiences a crisis (e.g., a drop in blood pressure), the sympathetic nervous system responds, and contractility and heart rate are boosted to augment cardiac output and to increase the venous tone of the periphery. Arterial tone is also increased at this time to maintain a satisfactory perfusion pressure. Antidiuretic hormone (ADH) is released from the posterior pituitary, aiding in renal conservation of blood volume. At the point when renal perfusion becomes perilously low, renin, a precursor to angiotensin I, is released. Angiotensin-converting enzyme (ACE) mediates the transformation of angiotensin I to angiotensin II within the vascular epithelium of the heart, lungs, kidneys, brain, and adrenals. Not only is angiotensin II a powerful vasoconstrictor, but it triggers the release of aldosterone by the adrenals, which stimulates the kidneys to retain water and sodium. During this compensatory phase, adrenocorticotropic hormone (ACTH) is released, causing the adrenal glands to release cortisol as well. One of the special actions of cortisol is to sensitize arteriolar smooth muscle to the effects of catecholamines. When epinephrine and norepinephrine are released, there is increased myocardial contractility, the heart rate is boosted to augment cardiac output, and peripheral tone is improved. The contraction of the vascular bed assists in shunting more blood into the central circulation in an attempt to improve cardiac preload. Although vital organs can function during hypotensive states, if blood pressure (BP) falls below 50 mm Hg, dysfunction and damage will rapidly ensue as a result of inadequate cellular perfusion. It is imperative to promptly take measures to correct underlying shock mechanisms. Organs rapidly insulted include the heart, lungs, liver, and the intestines.

The heart is affected swiftly when coronary blood flow decreases, leading to myocardial ischemia. Oxygen demand and consumption, however, rise in response to the surge of catecholamines and the increased workload demands. If vasoconstriction is intense, afterload increases, and pumping abnormalities and dysrhythmias follow.

Impairments at the capillary–alveolar membrane arise from multiple factors that relate to complement activation (C3a and C5a). Not only do aggregated granulocytes obstruct the pulmonary capillaries, they release enzymes and oxygen radicals that impair lung tissue. Eventually, the integrity of the alveolar–capillary interface is lost, gas exchange is compromised, and pulmonary vascular resistance increases to a level that negatively affects right heart performance.

The liver suffers insults from inadequate perfusion early in shock states, and thus it becomes relatively weak in its ability to control clotting factors and handle the escalating production of toxins that accompanies the progression of shock. Furthermore, at this point, the intestinal wall has become more permeable, permitting bacteria and toxins to migrate into circulation.

There are many other known and unknown organ and humoral factors in shock, but researchers agree that the key to survival is prompt control of the underlying cause (e.g., hemorrhage) and restoration of volume with appropriate fluids, which can raise the cardiac index, oxygen delivery, and oxygen use to supranormal values.[1]

Although oxygen saturation may be normal in severely traumatized patients, supplemental oxygen is recommended until all injuries have been fully appreciated, since even a small increase in the availability of dissolved oxygen may assist in salvaging vital organs. A snug mask or nasal cannula is appropriate for the nonintubated patient.

■ NURSING MANAGEMENT OF SHOCK

PRESENTATION

Nursing diagnoses for shock states include:

- Altered cardiac output due to decreased venous return
- Altered tissue perfusion related to reduced circulating volume and myocardial depression
- Fluid volume deficit related to hemorrhage, fluid shifts, and vasodilation
- Potential for impaired gas exchange related to hypovolemia, altered alveolar–capillary membrane permeability, and compensatory tachypnea or hyperventilation

During the period of compensation in shock states, hypotension may not be apparent, but other evidence of effects from massive amounts of circulating catecholamines are observed. These include tachycardia; rapid, shallow breathing; cold, clammy extremities; agitation and restlessness; and a decrease in urine output. Even before the patient has an obvious fall in BP in the supine position, it may be evident when the patient is raised to a sitting position. Ordinarily, when a patient assumes an upright position, gravity fills vessels in the lower extremities from capacitance vessels that promptly constrict, effecting little or no appreciable change in BP. A volume-depleted patient has already maximized vasoconstrictor capabilities in the initial phase of volume loss and therefore cannot compensate for postural changes. After the patient is returned to a supine position, the BP declines markedly and does not return to normal for several minutes. When postural changes create a decrease of 20 mm Hg or more in the systolic or diastolic readings or increase the heart rate by 20 bpm or more, the patient is considered to have hypovolemia. In a noncritical patient who has sustained major trauma, comparisons can be made among three BP and pulse variables (i.e., lying, sitting, and standing). The EN must be aware that patients may become weak or dizzy or experience syncope during such postural changes, so care must be taken to ensure their safety while checking orthostatic vital signs. Orthostatic hypotension may occur with blood losses of 10 to 20 percent.[2] The following is the recommended procedure for obtaining orthostatic vital signs:

1. Record the BP and pulse rate with the patient lying down.
2. Assist the patient to a Fowler's position; wait only 1 or 2 minutes and retake the BP and pulse. (Note: Even weak compensatory mechanisms and marginal fluid volume may equilibrate with BP and pulse rates if given several minutes to do so. Waiting longer than 2 minutes may give false reassurance of normal intravascular volume.) If the test result is positive at this time (e.g., significant drop in BP or significant increase in pulse rate), omit step 3.
3. Assist the patient to stand and record the BP and pulse after waiting no longer than 1 minute, once again looking for significant changes.

OTHER OBSERVATIONS

Skin
Skin, especially in the periphery, will be cool, moist, and pale as a result of intense vasoconstriction mediated by catecholamines. Mottling and cyanosis may be evident in severe shock states.

Capillary Refill
Capillary refill is a good indicator of fluid volume status. In healthy individuals with normal intravascular fluid volume, it is brisk, less than 2 seconds. If there is sluggish capillary refill when large muscles are blanched, shock should be suspected. Nail beds may also be used to assess capillary refill, but their circulatory status may be affected early by other problems such as peripheral vascular disease

or low body temperature. Such factors must be considered when assessing this indicator of shock.

Jugular Veins
The jugular veins may be flat in hypovolemic shock as well as in other conditions that affect right heart filling (e.g., pericardial tamponade, tension pneumothorax). They are best evaluated by placing the patient in a 30-degree upright position. A normal right atrial pressure will distend the neck veins about 4 cm above the manubrium.[3] The internal jugular is the best indictor of central venous pressure (CVP), since the presence of venous valves in the external jugular may produce misleading results.[4]

Central Venous Pressure
CVP readings may be low, high, or normal in shock states, so serial readings are required to determine the patient's response to fluid administration. A low CVP (< 5 cm H_2O) suggests hypovolemia; elevations above 10 cm H_2O point to the right heart's inability to handle venous return. Underlying pathology includes tension pneumothorax, pericardial tamponade, congestive heart failure, and pulmonary edema.

MONITORING PATIENT STATUS

Oximetry and capnography are used along with other clinical indices to evaluate respiratory status. CVP monitoring may be useful in patients with a high potential for pulmonary edema (e.g., the elderly, those with cardiovascular disease). However, vital signs and other indicators of improvement are used in the majority of patients to determine the response to fluid administration. Placement of a central venous catheter in a flat vessel is associated with the several complications of extravasation and thus is reserved for selected patients. Insertion of a pulmonary artery catheter is typically delayed until the individual reaches the surgical suite or the intensive care unit.

Electrocardiographic monitoring must be done throughout the acute shock phase to detect any irregularities of cardiac rate and rhythm and to see early indications of compromise, such as dysrhythmias, which result from hypoxia and the effects of chemical mediators. Continuous noninvasive BP readings and urinary output monitoring will also assist in evaluating the hemodynamic status of the patient.

LABORATORY TESTS

The hematocrit may remain near normal in early shock states, owing to compensatory mechanisms. If the hematocrit is drawn prior to the shift of interstitial fluid into the vascular system, it will be normal. If the patient has lost circulating volume over an extended period of the time, the recognition of shock is delayed, or if crystalloid fluid replacement has been initiated, hematocrit values will be low. Fluid loss from nonsanguineous sources (e.g., emesis, stool, wounds) often results in a high hematocrit. High lactic acid levels, a decreased serum bicarbonate, and a slight increase in the white blood cell (WBC) count may also accompany certain shock states.[3]

■ SHOCK CLASSIFICATIONS AND CURRENT THERAPIES

HYPOVOLEMIC SHOCK

Hypovolemic shock is caused by an inadequate circulatory volume. Hemorrhage is the principal cause, but it can also result from "third-spacing," which depletes intravascular volume. The American College of Surgeons Committee on Trauma has developed a classification of traumatic shock that relates clinical presentation to the amount of blood lost from the circulating volume. (Table 11–1).

The EN must appreciate that blood loss may be concealed in body cavities, in closed fracture sites, and other body tissues, and may not be obvious upon initial assessment of the patient. In these instances, a high index of suspicion should be maintained, and ongoing clinical observations, as well as diagnostic testing, will be required to identify the factors contributing to shock.

Oxygenation

Hypovolemic shock is characterized by tachycardia, hypotension, cool (possibly cyanotic or mottled) extremities, collapsed neck veins, oliguria or anuria, and altered mental state. There is ordinarily prompt improvement in the clinical condition when volume has been restored. Initial concerns with shock resuscitation are addressed concurrently with the primary survey (i.e., airway and breathing). Remember that all seriously injured trauma patients should be given supplemental oxygen throughout the resuscitation period, since there may yet be undetected or hidden organ damage that poses a threat to cellular oxygenation. A diminished oxygen-carrying capacity secondary to major injuries and blood loss is a vital consideration in all major trauma cases. If the patient is not intubated, nasal prongs or a mask should be used for supplemental oxygen delivery. Oxygenation should be monitored by oximetry and serial arterial blood gases (ABGs) as well as ongoing clinical observations. Gastric distension may interfere with effective ventilation, and vomiting may have devastating consequences if aspiration occurs. However, placement of a gastric tube must be done

TABLE 11–1. CLASSES AND CLINICAL SIGNS OF HEMORRHAGIC SHOCK

	Class I	Class II	Class III	Class IV
Blood loss (mL)	Up to 750	750–1500	1500–2000	≥ 2000
% blood volume	Up to 15%	15%–30%	30%–40%	≥ 40%
Heart rate (bpm)	< 100	100–120	120–140	> 140
Blood pressure	Normal	Normal	Decreased	Severe hypotension
Pulse pressure	Normal or increased	Decreased	Decreased	Decreased
Respirations (per minute)	14–20	20–30	30–40	>35 (shallow)
Urine output (mL)	> 30	20–30	5–15	< 5
Capillary blanch	Normal	Slight delay	Defined delay	No filling noted
Skin	Pink, cool	Cold, pale	Cold, moist	Cold, cyanotic, mottled

Adapted from Sommers.[9]

with great caution if there is known or suspected facial or cranial trauma (see Chapter 13.)

Intravenous Therapy Delivery

At least two 14- to 16-gauge intravenous lines should be placed for patients with major trauma. Anatomic locations where there are penetrating injuries, however, should be avoided. Do not place lines in lower extremities in abdominal trauma when the vena cava or portal circulation may be compromised, since the infused volume may pool in the abdomen, never reaching the central circulation to augment cardiac output. Placement of central intravenous lines should be deferred until the patient is stabilized, since taking the time to place them will delay other resuscitative measures and, in some cases, actually confound efforts (e.g., a hastily installed subclavian line which creates a pneumothorax). It is thought that central veins collapse as early as peripheral ones; thus, central lines may hold few advantages over peripheral lines.

It is useful to start one line with blood tubing so that a "change-out" is not required when blood and blood product administration is initiated. An anesthesia extension tube is desirable, too, since it facilitates tubing changes, drug delivery, and other procedures dependent upon the intravenous access site.

REPLACEMENT OF EXTRACELLULAR VOLUME: FLUID SELECTION AND ADMINISTRATION

Crystalloids Versus Colloids

Both crystalloids and colloids have been used to replenish intravascular volume, and some controversy still exists regarding the use of these products. Crystalloids are favored by most authorities, owing to their capability to restore volume promptly while improving microcirculation by reducing the viscosity of blood. They are also hypoallergenic and cost-effective. However, crystalloids have a transient effect on volume, owing to their lack of oncotic properties. Those who advocate initial or early use of colloids believe that they minimize edema-associated complications, since they are quite effective in restoring oncotic pressure, even when given in limited quantities.

Survival of vital organs, especially the brain, is the driving force for resuscitation efforts. Crys-

talloids, such as Ringer's lactate and normal saline, are considered the agents of choice in mild or moderate shock states. These balanced-salt solutions partially correct metabolic acidosis by replenishing sodium chloride and water lost externally or into the cell. Crystalloids decrease blood viscosity and improve microvascular circulation. Ringer's lactate has remained the fluid of choice in most emergency centers because it is isotonic and its electrolyte composition mimics that of plasma. Concerns about lactic acidosis may be set aside in most cases, since the added lactate in this intravenous solution is readily converted to bicarbonate in the liver. Patients who received large quantities of normal saline in a short time period during the initial resuscitation (e.g., 4 to 6 units in the first hour) may develop a hyperchloremic metabolic acidosis, requiring renal efficiency for excreting the significant chloride load.[3]

There is some evidence that hypertonic saline tends to improve hemodynamics.[5] It tends to expand plasma volume by osmotic—not hydrostatic—forces. It may also mediate a vagal pulmonary reflex, which causes arterial dilation with constriction of venous capacitance vessels, and exert a direct inotropic effect on myocardial contractility.[6]

Small volumes of hypertonic saline or hypertonic saline combined with Dextran are currently being used in research settings as a mode of fluid resuscitation for the trauma patient. Both 3 percent and 7.5 percent concentrations have been used as a means to osmotically extract water from the intracellular compartment to supplement intravascular volume. Some positive outcomes that have been noted stem from the fact that less volume is required (about one sixth as much as crystalloids) to boost BP and augment cardiac output, so there is less edema and greater urinary output with less salt retention. Other positive outcomes noted are a lower incidence of ileus, improved heart rate and contractility, and improved splenic and hepatic perfusion. Disadvantages noted (primarily with high-dose therapy) are decreased peripheral resistance, kaliuresis, hypernatremia, hyperchloremic metabolic acidosis, and hyperosmolality leading to seizures and coma. Bleeding may also be aggravated, because hypertonic saline decreases adenosine diphosphate (ADP)-mediated platelet aggregation.[3] Furthermore, some studies have demonstrated that its powerful vasodilating properties may increase blood loss via open vessels after trauma. Its use is considered experimental.

At the onset of initial fluid administration procedures, blood should be drawn for type and cross-match, hemoglobin, hematocrit, electrolytes, toxicology, blood urea nitrogen (BUN), WBC count, and blood sugar. A lactate level and coagulation studies may also be obtained for a baseline.

Judging the effectiveness of initial fluid replacement in shock is based on clinical observations, such as improvement in vital signs and resumption of urinary flow to at least 1 mL/min. The EN should also observe the overall status of the patient, using the baselines obtained upon admission to the ED. If the fluid resuscitation does not improve the patient's condition, prompt operative intervention is required to control the source of hemorrhage.

Crystalloid Fluid Challenge Procedure

An initial crystalloid fluid challenge is designed to determine the BP response to a volume load. A 400-mL bolus is administered over a 3- to 5-minute period, and then BP and pulse rate are assessed to detect a desired response. If an increase in BP occurs, a second bolus of 200 mL is given, and once again the vital signs (BP and pulse rate) are assessed. Additional 200-mL boluses are delivered over a 5-minute period until the BP stabilizes and no further improvements are noted. The maximum volume infused during this fluid challenge is ordinarily 1500 to 2000 mL. At this point, the patient should be readied for the administration of blood and blood products as well as for immediate operative intervention.

The initial fluid challenge should be administered by macrodrip or pressure bags, and more than one intravenous site may be required to achieve this rapid rate of infusion. Most ordinary intravenous pump systems cannot deliver fluids at this accelerated rate. There are high-capacity pumps and fluid warmers, especially designed for surgery and trauma, which may be useful.

Volumes of crystalloids that exceed 2 or 3 L, even if delivered promptly, may be counterproductive in instances in which the bleeding remains uncontrolled. Excessive crystalloid resuscitation may elevate BP to a supranormal level, thus increasing bleeding from any uncontrolled sources and per-

mitting a greater intracavity blood accumulation. Either of these circumstances is associated with a higher mortality. High-volume fluid resuscitation, which raises pulse pressure, also alters hemostasis, making any clot formation less stable, thus effecting a longer duration of hemorrhage as well as a higher incidence of rebleeding.[7]

Colloids in Shock Resuscitation

Colloids are used after the initial fluid resuscitation to sustain intravascular volume. (Without colloids, only about 20 percent of the crystalloid will remain in circulation within 2 hours). Colloids include hetastarch, Dextran, albumin, and modified gelatin compounds. Although colloids are more expensive than crystalloids, they can replete circulatory volume at rates of up to four to five times their own volume (e.g., 500 mL of 25 percent albumin can effect a 2000-mL or greater increase in the circulating volume).

Hetastarch (hydroxyethyl starch [HES]) is a useful artificial colloid that exerts an effect for 3 to 24 hours. Although it is inexpensive, it tends to decrease the platelet count, prolonging the partial thromboplastin time (PTT), owing to its anti-factor VIII effect. It is cleared slowly from circulation: 46 percent is eliminated by the kidneys within 2 days and 64 percent, within 8 days. Some can be detected in circulation 42 days after infusion.[3]

Dextran, a polysaccharide, is available in two molecular weights. The Dextran 40 solution, with lower-molecular-weight molecules, is filtered by the kidney, producing diuresis. Therefore, Dextran 70 is preferred for fluid resuscitation and has a half-life of several days. Although the risk is small, use of Dextran has been associated with renal failure, anaphylaxis, and coagulopathies. Any blood samples for type and cross-match must be obtained *before* administering this agent, since it tends to interfere with the laboratory processes involved in cross-matching.

Albumin use is controversial. It has been associated with hypertension problems after resuscitation, increases in intravascular volume at the expense of the interstitium, low levels of circulating immunoglobulins, and curtailed albumin synthesis. Administration of 25 percent albumin has advantages over use of crystalloids in regard to albumin's ability to improve cardiac index, mean arterial pressure, stroke work, and wedge pressure. However, the effects on cardiac and pulmonary function are not fully appreciated. There are data to suggest that albumin may contribute to decreased pulmonary function and myocardial depression. The cost of albumin is quite high in comparison to crystalloids and some of the other colloids, but it has a long serum half-life, with only 10 percent leaving the vascular network by 2 hours after delivery.[3]

Blood and Blood Products in Volume Replacement

Whole blood and one or more of several blood components may be used during the acute resuscitation period for hypovolemic shock unless the patient is of a religion that disallows it (e.g. Jehovah's Witness). It should be noted, however, that the administration of these is ordinarily reserved for patients in whom administration of colloids has already been accomplished.

Oxygen transportation and consumption may be seriously impaired unless red blood cells (RBCs) are replaced promptly. For blood loss of less than 30 percent, blood is the colloid of choice to improve oxygen-carrying power. Although a risk of hepatitis C and acquired immunodeficiency syndrome (AIDS) transmission is invariably associated with blood transfusion, new screening procedures have reduced it to a minimum. In massive transfusion, when the total blood volume is replaced in under 6 hours, thrombocytopenia and hypocalcemia are more likely. Hyperkalemia is of little concern unless there is renal insufficiency. Other concerns with massive transfusion therapy include pulmonary complications from fluid overload and microaggregation in the pulmonary bed, which can contribute to acute respiratory distress syndrome (ARDS). Perfluorocarbon emulsions and stroma-free hemoglobin are blood substitutes that have oxygen-carrying capacity; currently unavailable in the U.S., they may be used in the future as a substitute for whole blood or its products.

Low-titer type O-negative RBCs can be given if needed until type-specific blood can be obtained, but extensive use may lead to cross-matching problems. Plasma is seldom used in acute hemorrhagic states, since it has virtually no hemoglobin and its effects are quite transient. A wide range of plasma substitutes, however (e.g., Dextran, hetastarch) are used, since their colloidal properties are valued, and side effects are minimal.

There are a number of blood substitutes currently under investigation that have desirable properties and show promise for resuscitation when other blood is not readily available. These agents are not approved for clinical use at this time.

Autotransfusion

Autotransfusion is a system that permits patients to receive their own blood after it is collected from a body cavity (usually the chest). One system collects the shed RBCs and washes them to remove debris and contaminants before returning them to the patient by transfusion. Less sophisticated systems merely collect and filter the cells prior to returning them. A cell-saving team, usually personnel from the operating room (OR), are ordinarily responsible for assisting with this procedure in the ED.

Although blood from the abdomen may be also recovered, concern for contamination is obviously higher than for blood salvaged from the chest. The transfusion of autologous blood eliminates concerns about transmission of blood-borne disease (e.g., AIDS or hepatitis) and antigenic reactions. The autotransfused blood does not require warming, and it maintains 2,3-diphosphoglycerate (2,3-DPG) and platelet counts required for normal oxygen delivery.

Mechanical Aids to Volume Restoration

Position: The use of a head-down (Trendelenburg) position is not beneficial in shock states other than those of neurogenic origin. Elevation of the legs, however, may ensure that large pools of venous blood are returned to central circulation.

Pneumatic antishock garments (PASGs): These resuscitation aids are used for fewer purposes now than in the last few decades of trauma resuscitation. There is a new emphasis on the definitive control of bleeding instead of compensating for it. Studies and case reports indicate that bleeding may actually worsen with aggressive resuscitative efforts that are aimed at raising the BP. The venous fill in the upper extremities is augmented, increasing the systemic vascular resistance (SVR), cardiac preload and output, and elevation of the BP. The rise in mean arterial pressure (MAP) is a result of increased SVR, which may mimic aggressive fluid administration, with the attendant problems of actually increasing the potential for blood loss. When a PASG is inflated, any pooled venous blood returns to central circulation. This initial autotransfused volume may contain high lactate levels, aggravating cellular dynamics even more.

The PASG abdominal compartment may tamponade pelvic fractures and control intra-abdominal hemorrhage, but negative effects include:

• Decreased abdominal/lung–chest compliance, creating an increased work of breathing
• Elevation of the diaphragm, which can decrease tidal volume, increase MAP, and decrease venous return from the head, resulting in an increase in intracranial pressure (ICP)
• Increased pulmonary vascular pressure, which may exacerbate pulmonary edema

The PASG has been blamed for compartment syndrome development, limb loss, low cardiac output due to increased systemic pressure, and impairment of venous return through the inferior vena cava when the abdominal portion is fully inflated. Its principal use is for the stabilization of pelvic and long-bone fractures.

Emergency Department Thoracotomy

In cases in which there is massive trauma and the patient cannot be transported promptly to the OR, a thoracotomy may be done in the ED to clamp the thoracic aorta as an attempt to control exsanguinating hemorrhage. The procedure redistributes the remainder of the circulating volume to vital organs, such as the heart and brain. The procedure obviously is not without peril, since occlusion of a major vessel can create considerable ischemic damage in the organs affected by circulatory deprivation. Eventually, unclamping is also associated with several hemodynamic and metabolic problems. Thoracotomy may also be used to manage cardiac arrest associated with massive trauma. Massive blood loss, effects of profound hypoxia, the administration of cold fluids, and the use of cardiac stimulants during shock can precipitate cardiac arrest. The EN should be prepared to retrieve the necessary trays and the associated resuscitation equipment that might be required (e.g., internal defibrillator paddles) and to assist with the procedure (see Chapter 14).

Pharmacological Adjuncts to Limit Shock-Related Complications

In shock states, there is activation of the humoral systems (complement, coagulation, fibrinolysis, kallikrein-kinin), which creates havoc in hemorrhagic states. Complement-split products (C5A) are chemotactic and can stimulate polymorphonuclear neutrophil (PMN) oxidative metabolism and degranulation. Activation of the clotting cascade via tissue thromboplastin releases thrombin, thus stimulating platelet aggregation. Platelet aggregation primes PMNs, and their activation stimulates the release of platelet-activating factor (PAF) and other mediators. PAF is largely responsible for propagating shock states. The biologic active form of tumor necrosing factor (TNF), a cytokine, mediates an entire spectrum of inflammatory and metabolic effects (e.g., capillary leak causing necessity for increased intravenous fluids to maintain cardiac filling pressures and BP). Endothelial cell damage occurs via an oxygen radical–dependent mechanism, linking PMN oxidant activity to microvascular injury. Cellular changes, release of chemical mediators, propagation of oxygen-free radicals, and other events have stimulated research on novel drugs that may alter effects of humoral activation and its deleterious results. Among these are ibuprofen, oxygen-derived free-radical scavengers, calcium channel blockers, and a host of others. An opioid antagonist (e.g., Narcan) may be useful to increase norepinephrine activity and the responsiveness of the heart and blood vessels to catecholamines, thus improving regional blood flow. Considerable research must be done, however, to fully appreciate the clinical values and limitations of these agents to treat shock.

Recombinant human erythropoietin (rHuEPO) accelerates erythropoiesis and accelerates a return to a baseline hematocrit. The agent may alleviate the need for blood transfusions for some patients.

The use of vasopressors, diuretics, sodium bicarbonate, and naloxone are rarely indicated in the initial phases of resuscitation from shock syndromes. Early acidosis and low BP will be reversed, in most cases, after volume repletion. Steroids, digitalis, and narcotics may be indicated for some patients with clinical shock syndromes.

Rewarming Strategies

Hypothermia is associated with an increased mortality from shock, especially if it persists for longer than 2 hours. A low temperature contributes to clotting abnormalities equivalent to serious clotting factor deficiencies from other causes. Temperatures of 35°, 33°, and 31°C prolong PTT to the same extent as a reduction of factor IX levels to 39, 16, 2.5 percent, respectively.[8] Transfusion requirements are greater for hypothermic patients who have tissue edema due to capillary leak syndrome, and adenosine triphosphate (ATP) synthesis is reduced and myocardial depression occurs. Physiological results of hypothermia in trauma differ significantly from hypothermia that is systematically induced using controlled methods during anesthesia. ENs must appreciate that there is no value in permitting a trauma patient to remain cool in the ED and that any activities that can contribute to a lower core temperature should be minimized.

Hypothermic trauma patients have increases in heart rate, stroke volume, oxygen delivery, and oxygen extraction as the hematocrit falls. In a noninjured hypothermic patient, the gradual lowering of core temperature is accompanied by a decrease in heart rate, myocardial contractility, oxygen delivery, hepatic function, and adrenal output. Essentially, there is a "sympathetic switch-off," and compensatory activities are placed on standby. Of course—and fortunately so—the sympathetic nervous system remains active after trauma, thus altering the usual benefits of a state of "suspended animation" from hypothermia that is induced during anesthesia to accommodate certain surgical procedures. The bottom line is clear for the EN: keep the patient warm during the resuscitation period in the ED.

All resuscitation fluids, especially after the initial fluid challenge, should be warmed, since the addition of large quantities to replenish the intravascular network may significantly reduce the core temperature and thus contribute to dysrhythmias and even cardiac arrest.

DISTRIBUTIVE SHOCK STATES

Distributive shock is caused by a failure of arteriolar tone induced by sepsis and perhaps by other conditions that alter sources of vasoactive mediators. Theoretically, volume is normal in distributive shock, but it fails in its *distribution* to certain body cells. Neurogenic shock, septic shock, and anaphylaxis are commonly associated with maldistribution of blood flow.

Neurogenic Shock

Neurogenic shock occurs when there is direct injury to the medullary vasomotor center or when the spinal cord is traumatized, resulting in sympathetic interruption to all areas below the level of the lesion. This creates bradycardia, hypotension, and decreased systemic vascular resistance and does not permit the patient to compensate for hypovolemia.

Septic Shock

Septic shock occurs most often as an accompaniment to infectious states, but it can occur after trauma if transportation to the hospital and initiation of definitive therapy are delayed. The mechanisms for septic shock include multiple reactions to endotoxins, which are released by microorganisms. Recent research has implicated several protein mediators that are believed to be proximal causes of septic shock, and shown that macrophages are the principal mediators of endotoxic shock. The mechanisms that such cells use to produce shock and death are subjects of contemporary investigations.[1]

When a patient presents to the ED with a history and signs or symptoms commonly associated with septic shock, the EN must suspect and detect sepsis. In order to do so, the EN must be familiar with the hemodynamic and metabolic abnormalities associated with septic shock.

The major hemodynamic features of septic shock are an elevated cardiac output (primarily in response to tachycardia), decreased systemic vascular resistance, and hypotension. In the progression of sepsis, both right and left ventricular ejection fractions decline along with left ventricular stroke work. Fluid administration to increase preload has a minimal effect on these factors. Concurrently, pulmonary hypertension develops, contributing to dysfunction of the right ventricle. There are both changes in the pattern of blood flow and ventilation perfusion mismatching in response to escalating metabolic demands. However, systemic oxygen consumption decreases steadily, leading to multiple organ failure. The sequence of organ failure varies but usually is initiated by pulmonary crisis, followed shortly by hepatic and renal failure. Early attempts to improve hypoxia by increasing concentrations of inspired oxygen are not effective. The toll taken by pulmonary hypertension, increased extravascular lung water, decreased pulmonary compliance, respiratory muscle fatigue, and depressed diaphragmatic contractility render respiratory support nearly futile. Liver and renal failure are predictable soon after pulmonary failure. In addition to the problems caused by the mechanisms triggered by the presence of endotoxins, parenchymal damage is compounded by the use of antibiotics required to treat underlying causes of sepsis.

The septic syndrome (Table 11–2) appears before the shock state with its hemodynamic crisis.

Septic shock is associated with a mean blood pressure of less than 60 mm Hg (systolic pressure < 90 mm Hg) or a decrease in systolic blood pressure of more than 40 mm Hg from baseline in a patient with evidence of an infection.[3] Temperature abnormalities (either fever or hypothermia), rapid pulse and respirations, and obtundation are common. The skin may remain warm if there is no hypovolemia; hence, septic shock is sometimes termed warm shock. Laboratory findings include leukocytosis with a "shift to the left" (i.e., increase in immature neutrophils indicating active phagocytosis.), coagulopathies, and hyperglycemia (probably from counterregulatory hormone effects), which may precede a dramatic drop in blood sugar when the patient is terminal. ABGs reveal hypoxemia and metabolic acidosis.

TABLE 11–2. DIAGNOSTIC CRITERIA OF THE SEPTIC SYNDROME

Clinical evidence of an infection site
Hypothermia (< 96°F) or fever (> 101°F)
Tachycardia (> 90 bpm)
Tachypnea (> 20 bpm)
Inadequate organ perfusion or dysfunction as evidenced by *one* of the following:
    Poor or altered cerebral function
    Hypoxemia (P_{AO_2} <75 mm Hg)
    Elevated plasma lactate
    Oliguria (urine output < 30 mL/h or < 0.5 mL/kg body weight per hour)

From Bongard and Sue.[3]

Although ENs may be requested to obtain blood cultures to identify the offending microorganism and determine its sensitivities to pharmacological agents, treatment is usually begun promptly with a potent, broad-spectrum agent.

Supportive therapy includes crystalloid administration, pulmonary support, dopamine or dobutamine, and other vasoactive agents warranted by the patient's condition. Steroids are not used in sepsis unless there is associated adrenal insufficiency.[3] Advanced drug therapy (e.g., immunotherapy using monoclonal antibodies) is reserved for the intensive care unit environment where invasive cardiopulmonary monitoring and other management strategies are feasible.

Anaphylactic Shock

Anaphylactic shock occurs in response to an antigen-antibody reaction. Vasoactive mediators create vasodilation and increased capillary permeability, with ensuing hypotension, laryngeal edema, bronchoconstriction, urticaria, and other symptoms of anaphylaxis. In addition to elimination of any obvious source of the allergic reaction, epinephrine, antihistamines, steroids, and bronchodilators may be used to treat the condition. Advanced life-support measures may be required in the most severe cases (see Chapter 25).

Cardiogenic Shock

Cardiogenic shock, or pump failure, occurs in any condition in which the heart can no longer serve as an effective pumping mechanism. Causes of this condition include myocardial infarction, cardiomyopathy, mitral or aortic insufficiency, pericardial tamponade, and ruptures involving the heart (e.g., septum, wall, papillary muscle). Since the management of this type of shock may vary considerably from the standard protocols already discussed, the EN must be alert to its potential by suspecting it. Cardiogenic shock is discussed in Chapter 23.

■ REFERENCES

1. Shoemaker WC. Diagnosis and treatment of the shock syndromes. In: Ayres SM, Grenvik A, Holbrook PR, Shoemaker WC, eds. *Textbook of Critical Care.* 3rd ed. Philadelphia, Pa: WB Saunders; 1995:85.

2. Mullins RJ. Management of shock. In: Feliciano DV, Moore EE, Mattox KL. *Trauma,* 3rd ed. Stamford, Conn: Appleton & Lange; 1994.

3. Bongard FS, Shock and resuscitation. In: Bongard FS, Sue DY, eds. *Current Critical Care Diagnosis and Treatment.* E. Norwalk, Conn: Appleton & Lange, 1994:14.

4. Clochesy, JM, Breu C, Cardin S, et al. *Critical Care Nursing.* Philadelphia, Pa: WB Saunders; 1993.

5. Krausz MM, Landau EH, Klin B, Gross D. Hypertonic saline treatment of uncontrolled hemorrhagic shock at different periods of bleeding. *Arch Surg.* 1992;127:93–96.

6. Krausz M, et al. "Scoop and run" or stabilize hemorrhagic shock with normal saline or small-volume hypertonic saline? *J Trauma.* 1992;33:6–10.

7. Stern SA, et al. Effect of blood pressure on hemorrhage volume and survival in a near-fatal hemorrhage model incorporating a vascular injury. *Ann Emerg Med.* 1993;22:155–163.

8. Gentilello LM, et al. Continuous arteriovenous rewarming: rapid reversal of hypothermia in critically ill patients. *J Trauma.* 1992;32:316–326.

9. Somers MS. Fluid resuscitation following multiple trauma. *Crit Care Nurse.* 1990;10:74–81.

■ BIBLIOGRAPHY

Ayres SM, Grenvik A, Holbrook PR, Shoemaker WC, eds. *Textbooks of Critical Care.* 3rd ed. Philadelphia, Pa: WB Saunders; 1995.

Barie PS, Shires GT, eds. *Surgical Intensive Care.* Boston, Ma: Little, Brown; 1993.

Cardona VD, Hurn PD, Bastnagel Mason PJ, et al. *Trauma Nursing.* 2nd ed. Philadelphia, Pa: WB Saunders, 1994.

Chernow B, ed. *The Pharmacologic Approach to the Critically Ill Patient.* 3rd ed. Baltimore, Md: Williams & Wilkins; 1994.

Edmundowicz, SA, Zuckerman, GR, eds. *Manual of Medical Therapeutics.* 26th ed. Boston, Ma: Little, Brown; 1989.

Grenvik A, Ayres SM, Holbrook PR, Shoemaker WB, eds. *Pocket Companion to Textbook of Critical Care.* Philadelphia, Pa: WB Saunders; 1996.

Levine RL, Fromm RE Jr, eds. *Critical Care Monitoring from Pre-Hospital to the ICU.* St. Louis, Mo: Mosby-Year Book; 1995.

Marelli TR. Use of a hemoglobin substitute in the anemic Jehovah's Witness patient. *Crit Care Nurse.* Feb. 1994; 31–38.

Maull KI, Rodriguez A, Wiles CE, eds. *Complications in Trauma and Critical Care.* Philadelphia, Pa: WB Saunders; 1996.

Phippen ML, Wells MP, eds. *Perioperative Nursing Practice.* Philadelphia, Pa: WB Saunders; 1994.

Ruppert SD, Kernicki JG, Dolan JT, eds. *Dolan's Critical Care Nursing.* 2nd ed. Philadelphia, Pa: FA Davis; 1996.

Urden LD, Davie JK, Thelan LA, eds. *Essentials of Critical Care Nursing.* St. Louis, Mo: Mosby-Year Book; 1992.

Wilkins RL, Dexter JR, eds. *Respiratory Disease, Principles of Patient Care.* Philadelphia, Pa: FA Davis; 1993.

■ REVIEW: SHOCK STATES AND FLUID RESUSCITATION

1. Define *shock* in terms of the two major precipitating pathological events.

2. Differentiate the various types of shock by their distinguishing signs and symptoms.

3. Explain the hemodynamic, neurological, and endocrine mechanisms that contribute to compensation in shock states.

4. Relate compensatory mechanisms in shock states to nursing observations and interventions.

5. Describe the procedure for assessment and interpretation of orthostatic vital signs (VS).

6. State the protocols for fluid resuscitation and pharmacological adjuncts useful in the initial management of hypovolemia associated with major trauma.

7. Explain the rationale for use of crystalloids or colloids in shock management.

8. State the procedure for administering a crystalloid fluid challenge.

9. Outline the guidelines for using whole blood or the several blood components during shock states.

10. Define *autotransfusion* and explain its value in treating hypovolemic shock.

11. Identify the indications for emergency department (ED) thoracotomy and describe the role of the emergency nurse (EN) in this emergency procedure.

12. Correlate the consequences of hypothermia with hemodynamic and metabolic impairments that are inherent in shock states.

13. Explain three methods of rewarming that are valuable for minimizing cellular dysfunction in shock states.

14. Cite three major causes for the development of distributive shock states.

15. List clinical signs and symptoms that characterize septic shock.

16. Describe special modifications of shock therapy for patients who do not wish to receive blood or blood products.

Trauma

Major Trauma 12

Trauma is a multisystem problem and its optimum management requires the application of every advancement of medical science and nursing intervention. Since the 1970s, major strides have been made in controlling both morbidity and mortality associated with trauma; however, staggering statistics continue to mount for loss of life, permanent disability, and financial burdens for society in general and health-care providers in particular.

One of the major issues in trauma is the role of the public in its prevention. Even though there are many new technologies that can assist in both the prevention and the minimization of the devastating and costly effects of accidents, there are those who live in denial, defying the odds and refusing to use child seats, adult auto restraint systems, motorcycle and bicycle helmets, and other safety gear that have demonstrated their efficacy. Furthermore, crimes of violence continue to mount, creating tremendous threats to people of every age and social class.

TRAUMA STATISTICS

Statistically, trauma is recognized as the leading cause of death in the first four decades of life and the third major cause of death for all ages. In 1990, trauma created 9 million disabling injuries; 340,000 of these resulted in permanent impairment.[1] Trauma deaths in the United States exceed 140,000/y; an additional 70 million people suffer nonfatal injuries. Severe trauma and death rates from motor vehicle accidents (MVAs) have been reduced substantially with creation of public awareness, the use of safety devices, and the advent of effective emergency medical services (EMS) with their rapid response to accident scenes. Homicides, predominantly from gunshot wounds (GSW) to young men, have overtaken crash rates; in many states, homicide has become a major cause of death among black males between 15 and 19 years of age.[2–4] The direct and indirect cost to society for all of this contemporary carnage has been estimated to exceed $80 billion/y or $228 million/d.[5]

EMERGENCY MEDICAL SERVICES SYSTEMS AND TRAUMA CENTERS

In 1973, the U.S. Department of Health and Human Services began to fund EMS regions across the country for development of EMS systems, providing training and certification for ambulance personnel together with updated ambulances, life-support equipment, and radio linkage to tie it all together for notification and response. Grants were written, monies were disbursed, and systems were built with state-of-the-art capabilities for immediate response, basic/advanced life support, and transportation to the nearest medical facility for anyone calling for help by dialing 911, the universal access number. Seven critical patient care areas were targeted for development: major trauma, acute cardiac conditions, burns, spinal cord injuries, poisonings, high-risk neonatal situations, and behavioral emergencies.

Emergency Room Updating

By the mid-1970s, all the prehospital response capabilities were falling into place, with services delivering the desperately needed interventions and, indeed, improving steadily. By contrast, hospital emergency rooms (ERs) by and large lagged behind, sticking with the old ways, in which physicians had to be called for each patient who arrived; very few ERs were physician-staffed, with perhaps interns or residents in the larger hospitals and university medical facilities. Few, if any, ER nurses had the security of in-place policies, procedures, and protocols for immediate assessment and interventions. Hospital administrators soon realized the need for expanding, updating, and marketing their facilities. Staffing ERs so that they had 24-hour physician coverage became standard; ER nurses began developing their own body of knowledge addressing the wide and ever-changing array of challenges coming through their doors in increasing numbers. Before long, both the American College of Emergency Physicians (ACEP) and the Emergency Nurses Association (ENA)—originally known as the Emergency Department Nurses Association (EDNA)—had developed their own standards of practice, ongoing education programs, and appropriate certification/designation for their respective bodies of clinical knowledge and expertise.

Despite all this progress toward improving care of the sick and injured, development of a truly standard national EMS system has been slower than one would hope, owing to inadequate funding, public apathy in certain areas, and multiple, highly complex political issues. The United States has come a very long way in its capability to salvage victims of trauma and sudden illness—the catastrophes we cannot always anticipate—but much remains to be accomplished. Many states and localities have successfully developed optimal resources for trauma care, including sophisticated prehospital care systems and trauma centers staffed with trauma specialists. While schools of nursing have been slow in making curricular changes that incorporate emergency and trauma content, graduates have continued to migrate to organizations and agencies that offer programs to increase their knowledge and skills in this rapidly developing specialty. The emergence of more graduate programs, opportunities for certification and clinical specialization, and multidisciplinary endeavors to improve the quality of trauma care have ensured a cadre of dedicated personnel to care for multiply injured patients.

Designated Trauma Centers

By the late 1970s, several task forces had developed a plan to categorize hospitals as trauma facilities, based primarily on the resources that hospitals were willing to commit for receiving and treating trauma victims, together with their geographic location, population density, availability of resources and personnel, and their ability to withstand the fiscal demands of expanding and equipping for heavy trauma loads. Categorization involves determining three levels of capability, identified as follows: (1) level I, location in a metropolitan area and having 500 or more beds, presence of a solid fiscal commitment, and availability of personnel resources to meet demands (24-hour availability of staff specialists, such as trauma surgeon, anesthesiologist, neurosurgeon); (2) level II, usually a large institution but one that could not provide around-the-clock specialist coverage, whether based on actual availability or fiscal constraints; and (3) level III, smaller hospitals located in communities having neither a level I nor level II facility but with a strong commitment to trauma care, observing strict treatment protocols and transfer agreements to the next larger facility when appropriate. All else falls into the level IV category with the hope that committed efforts are made to sustain victims of trauma with available resources, rapidly transferring to appropriate facilities.

Trauma Registries: Purpose and Methodology

Since the early 1970s, trauma registries have been maintained regionally for the purpose of evaluating trauma care, from the time of injury through hospital discharge or death. Trauma registries are able to provide a regional perspective by combining data for all trauma patients, including those treated in trauma hospitals, those treated in non-designated hospitals, and those declared dead on the scene. High-risk injuries are identified with the help of trauma scoring scales used to give quantitative values to organ and systems injuries; some scoring systems are useful in predicting prognosis or outcome. Data from trauma registers are highly dependent upon the use of objective scoring tools to:

- Study injury control and epidemiology
- Focus education and medical research
- Improve patient care
- Aid in quality assurance
- Evaluate resource use

- Control costs
- Identify problems in access or availability of care
- Establish standards for management of specific injuries
- Predict consequences of various injuries

Data collection for trauma registry purposes requires ongoing dedicated staff time for contemporaneous as well as retrospective entry and evaluation. Four types of data sets are typically found in use; limited data sets facilitate EMS system evaluation and are taken from law enforcement, prehospital care, and emergency department (ED) records; minimum data sets that additionally include demography, epidemiology, intervention, severity, and outcome comprise the most widely used methodology. Extended data sets are used primarily for research, and special data sets address issues of specific concern, such as spinal cord and burn injuries.[6]

EMERGENCY NURSES ON THE TRAUMA TEAM

ENs function as key members of the trauma team. Once the ABCs (airway, breathing, circulation, cervical spine) have been addressed, initial assessment has been done, and life-support interventions are underway, the skills of further assessment must be employed rapidly; time is of the essence with the critically injured patient. Full evaluation of massive trauma and the extent of the injury remain the physician's responsibility, but the skilled EN should be capable of an accurate and rapid assessment in conjunction with or in the absence of the physician.

Since ENs are frequently the first ED personnel to see and evaluate trauma patients, skillful initial nursing assessment with appropriate immediate interventions can significantly affect outcomes. One physician in a busy department cannot always be available instantly, but competent knowledgeable nursing response can fill that gap. As a clinician once remarked, "we see what we look for; we recognize what we know;" ENs can prepare themselves for that challenge.

It is unfortunate that many legal actions are brought on behalf of dead, brain-damaged, or permanently paralyzed trauma patients against hospitals, physicians, and ENs who failed to recognize

dangers and intervene effectively. The public expects competent care in hospital EDs; it is our responsibility to ensure it, and as committed and qualified ENs, we can provide that competency.

■ CONCEPTS FOR EXPEDITING TRAUMA CARE

Advanced trauma life support (ATLS), trauma protocols, and critical pathways (CPs) are becoming integral components in trauma care.

ADVANCED TRAUMA LIFE SUPPORT AND THE GOLDEN HOUR

Disaster has been described as a sudden and massive disproportion between the hostile elements of any kind and the survival resources that can be brought into action in the shortest possible time. This definition certainly applies to the individual with massive injuries and multiorgan trauma who is brought to the ED in critical condition. The survival resources that can be brought into action in the shortest possible time are the skilled ED personnel ready to meet the trauma challenge, coupled with, at the very least, a basic minimum of life-support equipment and the patient's remaining vital reserves.

Improved outcomes for trauma patients are directly related to adequate early resuscitation based on rapid primary assessment with airway control, aggressive management of shock, and appropriate definitive care. Skilled and timely intervention in the *first hour* after trauma has been shown to significantly decrease morbidity and mortality in severely traumatized patients; this first hour has been termed the "golden hour" by traumatologists.

Surgeons who pioneered the ATLS program at the University of Nebraska did so believing that trauma is a surgical disease, best treated by surgeons following established and agreed-upon standards of intervention and care. In 1979, the American College of Surgeons (ACS) Committee on Trauma adopted ATLS as the national standard of care for trauma victims. Central to ATLS is the concept of the golden hour, emphasizing the critical importance of early recognition and intervention for trauma victims. Following the now nationally accepted ATLS guidelines, emergency teams of physicians, nurses, and paramedics must be capable of life-support interventions in the shortest possible time frames as they proceed with evaluation, stabilization, and appropriate care. Elapsed time between accident and definitive intervention has become recognized as the enemy in trauma; the use of stabilizing interventions within the first golden hour after injury is key to increasing victims' chances for return to normal function.

Accordingly, trauma resuscitation in the 1990s has modified its methods; field care is being limited to the basics and emergency medical technicians (EMTs) are encouraged to "scoop and run" (but not like the old days) rather than "stay and stabilize" if transportation time is less than 30 minutes. Procedures that may delay loading and transportation have been curtailed, especially if there is evidence of noncompressible bleeding sites or life-threatening injuries that cannot be stabilized in the field.

ED interventions are being limited to the factors required for stabilization (e.g., ABCs); tests and procedures are directed at making critical decisions (e.g., surgery or transport to a higher-level facility). Nursing activities that have been traditionally accomplished in the ED may at some future time be continued in the operating suite; it is entirely possible that eventually roles of ENs could include perioperative care.

TRAUMA PROTOCOLS

In order to carry out effective and timely trauma care, there needs to be a clearly defined action plan for the team of qualified responders; specific roles for each member of the team must be spelled out. Individual responsibilities are clearly outlined and preassigned; each participant is accountable for his or her assigned area. Established protocols clearly serve as the framework within which trauma interventions are effectively carried out as a team effort, and collegial relationships between physicians and nurses are valued; teamwork, discipline, and communication are requisites. Periodic review of protocols must be an ongoing responsibility of the trauma team, updating as necessary and modifying as appropriate when situations warrant.

In reality, trauma centers and well-equipped, fully staffed hospitals with trauma teams and protocols in place are not found in every locality across the United States. When serious trauma occurs in areas that are less than optimally prepared

to fully and definitively care for a seriously injured person, those facilities should have protocols in place that provide for immediate stabilization and transfer to the closest facility capable of providing the required definitive care. The ATLS provider manual contains transfer guidelines in Appendix C that define responsibilities for transfer and list preparation steps to be followed prior to transfer and management steps to be followed during transportation.

As discussed in an earlier chapter, the 1990 COBRA (Consolidated Omnibus Reconciliation Act) amendments are in force for the definitive management of traumatized patients, requiring all hospitals with a Medicare provider agreement, which includes trauma centers, burn units, and neonatal centers, to accept all appropriate patient transfers (those who require the care provided by such centers) as long as the center has the capacity to treat if the transferring hospital cannot. When a physician determines that a patient requires more sophisticated care and that the benefits of transfer outweigh the risks, *neither* hospital can delay transfer while determining the patient's financial status. The patient must (1) be informed of the hospital's obligations to transfer, under federal law, (2) be informed of the risks versus benefits of transfer, and (3) sign a written request for transfer. In lieu of a patient's written request for transfer, the transferring physician must sign a certificate confirming the need for transfer, stating that benefits outweigh the risk, and complete the original medical record to accompany the patient. Additionally, if an on-call specialist has refused to see the patient or has failed to appear within a reasonable time to stabilize the patient, his or her name and address must be included with the transfer documents.

CRITICAL PATHWAYS FOR TRAUMA VICTIMS

CPs, or patient-care guidelines, are multidisciplinary in character and provide a means of delivering an assured continuity of nursing care while minimizing variations, lowering costs by eliminating unnecessary procedures or tests, and reducing malpractice liability by following standards of care. Typically, a CP is an abbreviated, one-page version of a care plan for a given category of patient, identifying key actions/events and a time frame within which they must occur.[7–9]

CPs for the trauma patient should be simple and straightforward printed approaches to delivery of recognized emergency interventions for specific areas of trauma; their very nature will provide ENs with a significant degree of autonomy in patient care, functioning much like standing orders.

■ THE NURSING PROCESS IN ADVANCED TRAUMA LIFE SUPPORT

ENs who function in trauma-care settings find themselves involved concurrently with two processes: one follows the basic systematic approach to patient assessment and interventions that is called ATLS, and the second follows the systematic strategy of patient management that we call nursing process (NP). ENs perform both simultaneously without necessarily realizing it; the actuality is that both processes are closely associated, whatever term is applied. ATLS is a medical format, while NP is the nursing format; both processes share the same goal of meeting physiological needs for life support and restoration to an optimum quality of life after trauma.

Nursing Process	ATLS
Assessment	Primary survey
Subjective/ objective data	ABCs of resuscitation
Life support	Life support
Planning	Further resuscitation
Nursing diagnosis	Secondary survey: in-depth, head-to-toe
Nusing interventions	
Implementation of	Definitive care
nursing care plan	In-depth management
Evaluation	Stabilization/transfer

Assessment is ongoing in the nursing process, with needs prioritized as they are determined, but whether one follows the NP model or the ATLS model, life-threatening or physical needs take priority. ENs need to be comfortably aware of how the two processes are intertwined; they are equally valuable and necessary for meeting the challenges the multitrauma patient presents.[10]

NURSING ASSESSMENT IN TRAUMA

Readiness is very important. Experience dictates that anticipatory responses can be made with a high degree of certainty based on reports of pre-hospital responders when trauma is involved. Prior to the patient's arrival at the ED, advance radio contact with ambulance personnel makes known much of the vital patient information. The mechanism of trauma, patterns of injuries sustained with apparent major injuries, and the vital signs reported are extremely valuable preparatory data for ED personnel in advance of the patient's arrival. This information additionally cues personnel for preparation and allows specific allocation of duties by the trauma team leader, all of which facilitates a staff in readiness—initial setups in place (e.g., oxygen and suction in readiness (kinked off and tucked under mattress) and personnel on standby (e.g., x-ray, specialists).

Mechanisms of Trauma/Patterns of Injury

Think through the mechanism and circumstances of injury, and logic will help you anticipate probable as well as possible findings; there is a high predictability in identifying injuries based on that information. A thorough understanding of the mechanical forces that caused injury will be valuable in assessing victims and attempting to predict the nature and extent of organ/tissue damage. In motor vehicle trauma, for example, answers to several key points are essential to assessment: Was the injured party wearing a seatbelt? Was the car hit from the front, the side, or the back? Did the car hit a heavy, fixed structure sustaining deceleration forces?

There are many efforts being undertaken to understand the mechanical forces of trauma so that they can be controlled during accidents. The motor vehicle industry has been very active in multiple efforts to make cars safer to operate and to enable passengers to survive, even after heavy-impact trauma. Highway engineers, manufacturers of safety gear, and insurance companies are among others who are working to better understand the anatomy of trauma and to develop ways to minimize its costly and devastating effects.

Blunt trauma: Trauma experts emphasize that in major vehicular crashes there are basically three collisions that occur on deceleration, creating blunt trauma injury (Fig. 12–1):

1. The vehicle collides with an object.
2. The victim collides with the inside of the vehicle.

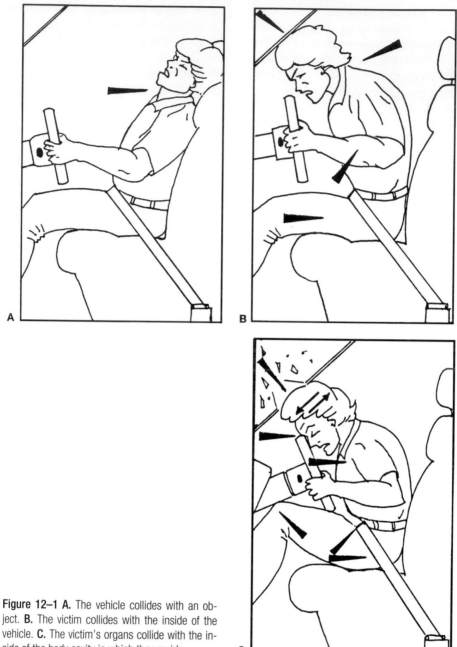

Figure 12–1 A. The vehicle collides with an object. **B.** The victim collides with the inside of the vehicle. **C.** The victim's organs collide with the inside of the body cavity in which they reside.

3. The victim's organs collide with the inside of the body cavity in which they reside.

Despite implementation of airbags as safety devices in automobiles, researchers are finding that even among drivers protected by the bags, serious internal injuries may be present in some severe crashes but not externally apparent. Serious internal injuries are often survivable if detected and treated in time but can be fatal if not detected and treated appropriately and promptly. Any visible deformity of the steering wheel should be regarded as an indicator of potentially serious internal injury to the driver.[11] Blast injuries are another cause of significant morbidity and mortality, with possible extensive pulmonary contusions, and should not be minimized.

Penetrating trauma: In penetrating trauma, the injured area is more precise and the traumatized tissue follows a rather predictable course because the penetrating object tears, cuts, rips, shreds, or forces organs and/or tissues out of its path. Patterns of injury vary with high- and low-velocity penetration; penetrating wounds will require surgical intervention, as will open fractures, once the patient is stabilized. Pedestrians struck down can often be anticipated to have open tibia-fibula fractures, head injuries, and probably injuries in between (e.g., wrists, forearms, hips).

Falls: Both blunt and penetrating trauma should be anticipated when falls from high places occur. Forces of deceleration account for blunt damage, while soft tissue is at risk of penetration by anything protruding on the landing surface. Victims of falls from a great height can be anticipated to have serious injuries to the torso, spinal column, and extremities.

Trauma in the Elderly

All injuries in the elderly are potentially life-threatening, despite trauma injury scores. The elderly are prone to multisystem organ failure (MSOF) and sepsis and require a higher index of suspicion for rapid deterioration potential:

- The very elderly who regularly take cardiac medications or those with pacemakers will not be able to mount a typical compensatory tachycardia during hypovolemia; thus, heart rate is an unreliable indicator of low volume. Their limited physiological reserves severely affect heart and lung dynamics; oxygenation and hemodynamics are prone to failure.
- Intracranial trauma can be mistaken for senility; existing brain atrophy facilitates easy progression of bleeding without obvious signs and symptoms.
- Although perception of pain is thought to be diminished in the elderly, control of pain must be handled cautiously to avoid respiratory compromise—but pain *must* be controlled.
- Diagnosis of abdominal injury may be complicated owing to previous surgeries/pathologies.

- Caution must be exercised with contrast studies; the elderly are more prone to renal failure.

GATHERING THE DATABASE

As the patient is being admitted, transferred from the stretcher, and undressed preparatory to initial assessment (beyond immediate airway requirements), there is a brief opportunity to begin obtaining all the information possible for the database. The ambulance crew is present with firsthand observations of the scene; occasionally, family members or the patient's physician, who has been called in advance, will be on hand. Essential areas of information for the database are outlined below; answers to all of these points, as appropriate, will trigger reasonable indices of suspicion and strongly guide decisions based on knowledge of the mechanism of trauma and patterns of injury. Most importantly, document the information clearly, concisely, and completely. The baseline data you record will follow the patient through hospitalization—and beyond, perhaps—and becomes the basis for both medical and nursing diagnoses.

The Mechanisms of Trauma

A. *MVA:* Remember that blunt injury occurs with the impact and shearing forces of deceleration (Fig. 12–1).
  1. Type of vehicle, driver or passenger, speed on impact?
  2. Circumstances on impact: stationary, moving, remained in vehicle, thrown from vehicle?
  3. Direction of forces: head-on, rear-end, broadside, on quarter, or what?
  4. Use of shoulder harness, lap belt?
  5. Airbag deployed?
  6. Steering wheel bent?
  7. Suspect:
    a. Possible soft-tissue trauma on lower abdomen or retroperitoneal injury with lap belts;
    b. Steering-wheel trauma with possible facial bone damage and airway compromise, damage to sternal area, fractured ribs, and possible cardiac contusion or tamponade;
    c. Facial trauma and airway compromise; right front seat passenger may

have been thrown into or through the windshield. Lacerated knees in motor vehicle trauma are commonly associated with a fractured femur, as well as high-velocity impact fractures to the femoral head.

    d. Compound injuries when victims are thrown from a moving vehicle.

B. *Motorcycle Injuries:*

    1. Speed on impact? Wearing helmet? Thrown from vehicle?

    2. Anticipate head injuries with concomitant facial lacerations, neck and cervical spine injury, and fractured femurs.

C. *Penetrating Injuries:* These include impalements, GSWs, and wounds from knives, icepicks, screwdrivers, and glass shards.

    1. Penetrating object and force of penetration?

    2. Estimated angle of entry and depth of penetration?

    3. Special points:

        a. In GSWs, always look for entrance *and* exit wounds. Complete removal of patient's clothing and a head-to-toe check are essential.

        b. For knife wounds, remember that if a man wields the blade, the thrust will probably be upward, while a woman tends to stab with arm raised and at a downward angle. A knife wound found at the costal margin, delivered by a male assailant, will probably be confined to the chest and lungs. If the assailant is female, suspect downward penetration of both lung and abdominal cavity.

        c. Any penetrating object should be left in place and stabilized until surgical removal is accomplished; the object may be tamponading a slashed artery.

D. *Falls:* This is the "pile driver" constellation of injuries from high falls and severe deceleration.

    1. Cause of fall (syncope, slipped, jumped)?

    2. Distance of fall?

    3. Surface of landing (water, hard or soft ground, cement, lawn)?

    4. Position on landing (on feet, on head, supine, prone)?

    5. Suspect:

        a. Compression fractures of the spine from forward flexion, fractures of the heels, knees, and hips;

        b. Deceleration injuries to the liver (subcapsular hematoma) and spleen and lacerations of the aorta just distal to the left subclavian artery (the last point of attachment).

E. *Blunt Abdominal Trauma:*

    1. Major problems are encountered in the ED with this type of trauma, commonly presenting with evidence of contusions of the lower chest wall, guarding of the abdominal wall, and localized tenderness.

    2. Be alert for fractures of the lower third of the chest accompanied by pain in the shoulder or for absence of peristalsis together with nausea, vomiting, and distension of the abdomen.

    3. Blood in the vomitus, stool, or urine is significant and frequently indicates intraperitoneal injury (abdominal trauma patterns are discussed more fully in Chapter 15).

    4. Victims of major blunt trauma may have multiple areas of injury that will need accurate assessment and treatment.

F. *Head and Neck Injury:* Such injuries occur from both primary and secondary causes.

    1. Primary causes encompass the damage caused from the original mechanical insult (e.g., scalp injuries, skull fractures, contusions, perforating injuries of the cranial vault, lacerations, diffuse axonal injury, and cranial nerve damage that occurs during basilar fracturing). If head trauma is evident, hyperventilate with 100 percent oxygen to prevent increased intracranial pressure from developing.

    2. Secondary injuries include insults that follow head trauma, such as hypoxia, hypotension, infection, seizures, hematomas, intracranial hypertension, and herniation. Most secondary injury can be prevented, or at least managed to minimize its effect, if ENs are alert to its potential and aggressively manage the patient throughout the post-trauma period. (Head, neck, and maxillofacial trauma are covered in Chapter 13).

3. For initial assessment purposes, the neck should be divided into three anatomic regions for evaluation of traumatic insult:

   a. Zone 1 extends from the level of the cricoid cartilage to the level of the clavicle. It includes the proximal carotids, the subclavian vessels, and other major vessels in the chest, upper mediastinum, esophagus, trachea, and thoracic duct.

   b. Zone II extends from the area above the clavicle to the mandibular angle. Injuries in this region are the easiest to assess and manage.

   c. Zone III extends from the mandibular angle to the base of the skull.

   The presence of a penetrating injury or hematoma in any of these zones warrants scrutiny. It is imperative that the neck and upper chest are explored in detail since expanding hematomas, infections, airway compromise, and asphyxia can result. Astute observations from ENs who care for the trauma patient must include ongoing observations of the ABCs.

G. *Additional Critical Information for Documentation:*
   1. Any known drugs/alcohol aboard now?
   2. Any allergies?
   3. Any medical problems?
   4. Time and amount of last food or fluid ingestion?
   5. Alcoholic withdrawal or delirium tremens (DTs)?
   6. Date of last tetanus booster?
   7. Is patient a bleeder, or does patient take anticoagulants?

PRIMARY SURVEY INTERVENTIONS

The purpose of the primary survey is to identify immediate threats to life after physical trauma. Obviously, this should be accomplished in a rapid manner. Since resuscitation is being accomplished concurrently with the primary survey, a team effort is vital. Once the primary survey is complete and immediate threats have been taken care of, a systematic secondary survey follows with definitive measures. Initial assessment is covered in an earlier chapter, but some additional important points specific to trauma are discussed here.

Make it a practice to talk calmly and reassuringly to the patient as you conduct the survey, realizing that you may be able to exert a calming effect by talking him or her through the catastrophe that has befallen. Patients' anxiety and apprehension can be diminished if they can anticipate what is going to happen next and why.

Points to Assess

A. *Airway and Cervical Spine:*
   1. The airway must be managed with great caution in the unconscious patient or when there are known or suspected injuries above the level of the clavicles. The larynx is considered the landmark that divides the concerns of airway and breathing.
   2. The initial airway maneuver used is the chin lift or forward jaw thrust. An oropharyngeal or nasopharyngeal airway may be employed, but they do not effect isolation of the trachea from the mouth.
   3. Although semirigid cervical collars are twice as effective in stabilization of the neck than the soft type, they are only 50 percent effective in preventing flexion, extension, and rotational movement.
   4. Cervical protection may only be disregarded in two instances: if radiological evidence has ruled out cervical injury *or* if there is an airway emergency that cannot be managed with cervical protection in place.
   5. Helmets should be left in place until there is a clearance of the cervical spine. Only personnel skilled in helmet removal techniques should be involved in the procedure.
   6. Endotracheal intubation (ET) should not be delayed if life-threatening circumstances exist, even when the cervical spine has not been cleared. About 80 percent of spinal cord injuries associated with fractures occur at the time of the original impact.
   7. Initial cervical spine films should be obtained without traction, since subluxation can occur in patients with fractures or ligamentous injuries. If there is no evi-

dence of pain or injury after these initial films, traction can be used with minimal risk.

8. Supplemental oxygen (100 percent) should be used if there are any signs of ventilatory compromise. *Do not* wait until the patient is in respiratory failure. *Do not* withhold oxygen merely to obtain a blood gas on room air. Although oxygen saturation may be normal in severely traumatized patients, supplemental oxygen is recommended until all injuries have been fully evaluated, since even a small increase in the availability of dissolved oxygen may assist in salvaging vital organs. A snug mask or nasal cannula with high-flow oxygen is appropriate for the nonintubated patient.

9. Oxygenation should be monitored by oximetry and serial arterial blood gases (ABGs) as well as clinical observations.

10. Gastric distention may interfere with effective ventilation, and vomiting may be devastating; placement of a gastric tube, however, must be done with great caution if there is known or suspected facial or cranial trauma.

B. *Breathing:* The three immediate threats to ventilation are:
   1. Tension pneumothorax
   2. Flail chest
   3. Open pneumothorax. A massive hemothorax occasionally can compromise ventilation as well as circulation. (All three threats to ventilation are discussed in detail in Chapter 14.)

C. *Circulation:*
   1. Initial assessment of circulation should be accomplished by noting the skin, pulse rate and quality, mental status, and capillary refill. The pulse pressure and urine output are also helpful indices.
   2. Rules of thumb for initial vital signs are:
      a. A pulse of over 120 bpm indicates hypovolemia;
      b. If the radial pulse is palpable, the blood pressure (BP) is 80 mm Hg or greater;
      c. If the femoral pulse is palpable, the BP is 70 mm Hg or greater;
      d. If the carotid pulse is palpable, the BP is 60 mm Hg or greater;
      e. Altered mental status associated with cerebral hypotension is not apparent unless the BP is less than 60 mm Hg, owing to compensatory mechanisms.

3. Brisk arterial bleeding is best controlled with direct digital pressure. Control is inferior with the application of bulky dressings, elastic wraps, and air splints. Blind clamping of vessels should be avoided.

4. Fluid resuscitation is handled as follows:
   a. At least two 14- to 16-gauge intravenous lines should be placed for patients with major trauma;
   b. Avoid anatomic locations where there are penetrating injuries and avoid lower extremities in abdominal trauma when the vena cava or portal circulation may be compromised;
   c. Central lines should not be installed until stabilization of the patient has been achieved, since they may compound resuscitation problems (central veins collapse as early as peripheral ones);
   d. Start one line with blood tubing to avoid a "change-out" for blood or blood product administration. Anesthesia extension tubing is a desirable adjunct;
   e. Survival of vital organs, especially the brain, is the driving force for resuscitation efforts. The initial fluid of choice is Ringer's lactate, administered at a rate of 1000 mL every 35 minutes until the circulatory system has been truly challenged. There is no evidence that use of this fluid aggravates lactic acidosis. Response to this fluid challenge dictates the need for blood products administration;
   f. Normal saline should be reserved as an adjunct for blood administration, since using it in large quantities can result in a hyperchloremic crisis;
   g. During this fluid challenge, blood should be drawn for type and crossmatch, hemoglobin, hematocrit, electrolytes, toxicology, blood urea nitro-

gen (BUN), white blood cell (WBC) count, and blood sugar. A lactate level and coagulation studies may also be obtained as a baseline.

D. *Mechanical Aids to Volume Restoration:*
1. The use of a head-down (Trendelenburg) position is not beneficial in shock states other than those of neurogenic origin. Elevation of the legs, however, may ensure that large pools of venous blood will be returned to central circulation.
2. The pneumatic antishock garment (PASG) has been blamed for compartment syndrome development, limb loss, low cardiac output due to increased systemic pressure, and impairment of venous return through the inferior vena cava when the abdominal portion is fully inflated. Its principal use is for the stabilization of pelvic and long-bone fractures.

E. *Neurological Examination:*
1. The brief assessment of the neurological system should be accomplished after stabilization of the ABCs has been ensured. The initial examination should include:
   a. Size and reactivity of pupils
   b. Motor and sensory responsiveness
   c. Level of consciousness (LOC)
2. The ATLS mnemonic *AVPU* is useful in assessing the level of consciousness:
   • A = alert
   • V = responds to vocal stimuli
   • P = responds to painful stimuli
   • U = unresponsive
3. Use of the Glasgow Coma Scale (GCS) should be reserved until the secondary survey.

F. *Words of Caution:*
1. Patients have backs as well as fronts. When the patient is completely disrobed, logroll him or her and thoroughly palpate/inspect the posterior surfaces for life-threatening wounds.
2. Once the primary survey is complete, cover the patient to ensure modesty and to prevent unnecessary heat loss, which compromises oxygen and glucose stores.
3. *Watch what you say,* even with patients who appear unresponsive. All too often, a patient who appears unconscious regains consciousness and has entirely too much recall about what was said in the room. It is good practice to talk directly to the unconscious patient as though he or she is indeed conscious; this may even allay some anxiety for a listener who cannot respond.
4. By its very nature, trauma is a bloody business. Before being locked into the intervention process, anticipate the risk of exposure and gown/glove yourself as appropriate; observe universal precautions as you continue with systematic assessment and interventions. The barriers available are for your protection in a very high risk arena.

OTHER NURSING RESPONSIBILITIES AND CONSIDERATIONS

Trauma Drugs

Vasopressors, naloxone, sodium bicarbonate, and diuretics are not usually appropriate during this early period of resuscitation. Early acidosis and low BP will be reversed, in most cases, after volume repletion. ENs are, however, expected to maintain a current knowledge of the drugs employed in management of trauma cases; the general groups are listed here:

• Oxygen
• Cardiac drugs
• Immunizations
• Antibiotics (legitimately administered prophylactically) for facial injury, skull fracture, open fractures, penetrating wounds, and peritoneal wounds)
• Analgesics and sedatives
• Steroids specifically for sepsis, aspiration, and head trauma
• Intravenous solutions
• Blood products

Patient Monitoring

Specific parameters must be monitored (with serial documentation) in most trauma management and should include (but are not limited to):

• Cardiac rhythm strips
• Continuous invasive or noninvasive BP
• Pulse oximetry
• Urine output
• Serial laboratory parameters

Laboratory Tests

Initial laboratory tests should basically include the following on stat requisitions:

- Hemoglobin (Hgb) and hematocrit (Hct) (for baseline) to estimate effects of massive blood loss or hemoconcentration associated with shock.
- Typing and cross-matching of blood; typing can be done with a "hold" on the cross-match if there is a question of need (less expensive for the patient)
- The complete blood cell (CBC) count; used primarily as a baseline and of little value in the immediate situation
- Serum amylase; may be of help but may also be confusing in the presence of head injury, when the amylase may be elevated as a result of salivary gland trauma (a significantly elevated amylase without concurrent salivary gland involvement would probably be highly indicative of pancreatic trauma)
- Blood sugar and, if indicated, a toxicology screen for barbiturates, salicylates, alcohol, and abused drugs
- ABGs for partial pressure of carbon dioxide (PCO_2), partial pressure of alveolar oxygen (PAO_2), and pH
- Electrocardiogram
- Intravenous pyelogram and cystogram (defines kidneys, ureters, and bladder and verifies the presence of two kidneys in case of anticipated surgery on a damaged kidney)
- Urinalysis as soon as possible for presence of red blood cells (RBCs)

TRAUMA SCORING

Once initial/primary assessment is completed and interventions are established, the severity of trauma can be assessed. High-risk injuries can be identified with the help of trauma scoring scales, which are used to give quantitative values to organ and systems injuries. Some scoring systems are useful in predicting prognosis or outcome, and data from trauma registers are highly dependent upon their use.

Examples of the most widely used trauma scoring tools are the GCS, the Maryland Trauma System (MTS) Score, the Injury Severity Score (ISS), and the combined ISS–GCS, known as the Trauma Score (TS).

Glasgow Coma Scale

The GCS is a neurological evaluation tool that has remained the most universally used; simplicity and interobserver reliability make it a valuable tool for all disciplines and a relatively practical way of monitoring changes in the level of consciousness. The GCS assigns a number—a quantitative value—to three components: eye opening, verbal response, and motor response. The total score is the sum of the three components, ranging from 3 (flaccid and unresponsive) to 15 (grossly neurologically intact).

The rating is inaccurate if the patient is under the influence of alcohol or drugs; the important aspect, however, is evaluating changes in the LOC. Additionally, determination of the patient's orientation to person, time, and place, if obtainable, is helpful in establishing the LOC and mental acuity.

Beyond the initial team assessment using the GCS, a neurological flow sheet may be employed in the ED to document a more thorough and ongoing nursing assessment for baseline comparisons.

Maryland Trauma System Score

The MTS Score combines data sets from admission profile (first 24 hours after admission) and hospital course (diagnostics, operative procedures, anatomic complications, infectious complications, and systems failures). The tool is still being studied, but it may prove more accurate than the TS or ISS.

Injury Severity Scale

The ISS assigns values of 1 to 5 for all injuries. The most critical injury in six major body regions (head and neck, face, chest, abdominal or pelvic contents, extremities or pelvic girdle, and external) are considered. ISS is most useful in blunt trauma, is based on subjective selection and definition of criteria, and incorporates no physiologic component except brain dysfunction.

Trauma Score

The TS (Table 12–1), a numerical grading system for estimating the severity of injury, is composed of the GCS (reduced to approximately one third total value) and four measurements of cardiopulmonary function (CPF): respiratory rate, respira-

TABLE 12–1. TRAUMA SCORE[a]

Paramater	Value/Response Obtained	Score
Respiratory Rate		
	10–24/min	4
	24–35/min	3
	≥36/min	2
	1–9/min	1
	None	0
Respiratory expansion		
	Normal	1
	Retractive	0
Systolic blood pressure		
	≥90 mm Hg	4
	70–89 mm Hg	3
	50–69 mm Hg	2
	0–49 mm Hg	1
	No pulse	0
Capillary refill		
	Normal	2
	Delayed	1
	None	0
Glasgow Coma Scale		
Eye opening		
	Spontaneous	4
	To voice	3
	To pain	2
	None	1
Verbal response		
	Oriented	5
	Confused	4
	Inappropriate words	3
	Incomprehensible words	2
	None	1
Motor response		
	Obeys command	6
	Localizes pain	5
	Withdraw (pain)	4
	Flexion (pain)	3
	Extension (pain)	2
	None	1
Total trauma score		1–16

[a] The Trauma Score is a numerical grading system for estimating the severity of injury. The score is composed of the Glasgow Coma Scale (reduced to approximately one third total value) and measurements of cardiopulmonary function. Each parameter is given a number (high for normal and low for impaired function). Severity of injury is estimated by summing the numbers. The lowest score is 1, and the highest score is 16.
From *Journal of Trauma* 1989: *Trauma Score and Revised Trauma Score,* with permission.

tory effort, systolic blood pressure, and capillary refill. Each parameter is given a number (high for normal and low for impaired function). Severity of injury is estimated by summing the numbers of the GCS and CPF; the lowest score is 1 and the highest score is 16. The TS is considered the most comprehensive for prediction of long-range outcomes and is most widely used in trauma treatment settings.

NURSING DIAGNOSIS

When formulating nursing diagnoses for victims of trauma, be certain you have gathered the necessary baseline of information. Typically in traumatized patients, the ABCs are addressed as priority diagnoses, ensuring that interventions are focused and effective. Consider your patient's clinical status, identify all the actual or potential problems that might be encountered (you might even list what can be identified and then pursue it further in the taxonomy), and select the nursing diagnosis that most closely aligns with your patient's problems.

It should be self-evident that nursing diagnoses related to trauma victims directly relate to areas of oxygenation and circulation (e.g., airway clearance, aspiration, breathing patterns, cardiac output, gas exchange, tissue perfusion), areas of nutrition (e.g., fluid volume—deficit, deficit potential, or excess), and areas of safety or security (e.g., anxiety, fear, hypothermia, high risk of injury, high risk of infection, knowledge deficit, pain, impaired or high risk of impairment of skin integrity, and impaired tissue integrity).

Remember that nursing diagnosis is a clinical judgment about the individual's response to actual or potential health problems and life processes. Nursing diagnoses provide the basis for selection of nursing interventions to achieve outcomes for which the nurse is accountable; representative nursing diagnoses are included in other chapters in this book as appropriate.

■ TISSUE AND ORGAN DONATION

If a trauma patient cannot be successfully resuscitated, ENs should be prepared to preserve organs for donation. Detailed protocols for this procedure should be available in the trauma resuscitation area for immediate reference, since many organs become useless for donation if they have not been properly maintained throughout the resuscitation period. Appendix C defines specific criteria for organ and tissue length of viability.

ENs have always played an important role in initiating and facilitating organ donation and in supporting and caring for donor family members or significant others. Organ procurement agencies now exist in every state; federal and state governments have enacted "required request" laws that mandate identification and referral of potential donors, and nurse coordinators facilitate the process once initiated. Donor numbers have increased significantly in very recent years because of the renewed efforts nationwide to identify and facilitate the donor process by education and financial support.

The United Network for Organ Sharing (UNOS), the national umbrella agency for tissue and organ procurement and assignment, readily assures those concerned that once permission is given for organ harvest, any further life-support expense incurred is billed to the recipient, the insurer, or Medicare if it covers the particular transplantation. This knowledge will frequently assuage overwhelming financial concerns of grieving families. Further, it behooves care providers to effect timely intervention on behalf of families and potential recipients. All agencies responsible for procurement and assignment of donor tissues agree that each donor should be evaluated on an individual basis.

TISSUE DONOR CRITERIA

Any patient who dies can be considered for tissue donation. The approximate age ranges of patients whose tissues would be suitable for donation is as follows:

- Bone: 16 to 65 years
- Eyes: birth to 75 years for transplantation; any age for research
- Skin: donor must be over 5 feet tall and weigh more than 100 lb.

ORGAN DONOR CRITERIA

Organ donor criteria are as follows:

- Approximate donor age range birth to 65 years
- No cancer (except first-degree brain tumor)

or acquired immunodeficiency syndrome (AIDS)
- Brain death imminent or declared

BRAIN DEATH CRITERIA

Brain death criteria are as follows:

- Known cause of condition
- No hypothermia present (temperature > 32.2° C or 90° F)
- No drug intoxication or significant metabolic disturbances
- No gag, cough, or corneal reflex
- No response to painful stimuli
- Pupils fixed and dilated
- No spontaneous respirations or movements according to apnea test:
   Preoxygenate for 10 minutes at a pH of more than 7.3
   Disconnect ventilator; give oxygen at 8 to 12 L/min by tracheal cannula
   Observe for spontaneous respirations
   If possible, after 10 minutes, draw ABGs; PCO_2 should be over 60 mm Hg for accurate test
   Reconnect the ventilator; the patient is apneic if PCO_2 is over 60 mm Hg and there is no respiratory movement
   If hypotension and/or arrhythmias develop, immediately reconnect the ventilator; consider other confirmatory tests

■ EQUIPPING FOR TRAUMA

Trauma resuscitation can and most often does become a cluttered affair. The time spent in the ED for seriously injured trauma victims and the subsequent clutter can be substantially reduced if the trauma bays/rooms are fully equipped and in readiness. Most EDs, depending on their size and patient flow, have standardized their equipment and incorporated protocols for responding staff. The time saved by this readiness can save lives, frayed tempers, and postcrisis interventions. Furthermore, it can be cost-effective.

TRAUMA TUBES

Abundant supplies of trauma tubes are critical in effective trauma response. Standard to every patient bay should be intravenous tubings, blood transfusion tubings, oxygen administration catheters/cannulas, and both rigid and bronchial suction tips. Additional trauma tubes that must be employed are discussed here in order of priority; ENs are expected to be proficient in their setup and use.

Endotracheal Tube

The ET tube is available in French sizes (tube circumference in millimeters) and millimeter sizes (inside diameter of tube); in case of confusion, use the tube closest in size to the patient's little finger (or to the nail of the little finger, for a child). Always check for a patent cuff and a universal adapter to fit the bag unit for ventilating the patient once the tube is placed. If necessary, use mouth to tube (16 percent O_2 is better than *no* O_2). If a rigid stylet is used to place the tube, it must never be used without a clamp or a bend at the adaptor and must be positioned 1 cm back from the tip of the ET tube. Again, the intubation tray must be checked regularly for completeness, including a working light on the laryngoscope and water-soluble lubricant.

Nasogastric Tube

Most seriously injured persons should have a nasogastric (NG) tube placed as soon as possible. These patients are likely to be on oxygen or forced positive-pressure breathing that will inflate the stomach, hindering heart and breathing action. The NG tube avoids the problem of acute gastric dilation as well as unmanageable emesis, bearing in mind that the shock of trauma increases likelihood of stomach contents remaining from time of last ingestion. Put the NG tube down early.

NG intubation is a simple, frequently employed procedure in the ED for the following purposes:

- Decompressing the stomach contents (air, food, and so on)
- Diluting and lavaging of ingested poisons
- Removing blood in cases of gastrointestinal (GI) hemorrhage and accommodating lavage

The equipment required is minimal:

- NG tube, usually a Levin, Ewald, or Salem sump tube in various sizes. The Levin and sump tubes are used in sizes 12 to 18 Fr,

while the Ewald is used in 32, 34, and 36 mm sizes for rapid lavage of gastric contents.
- Water-soluble lubricant, a towel, emesis basin, a glass of water with a straw, and 0.5 in. adhesive tape.
- Stethoscope and syringe

It is important to have the patient understand the procedure, and he or she should be instructed to mouth-breathe and swallow as the tube is passed. Have the patient sit upright with neck flexed and a towel across the chest. Dentures should be removed. Decide on a signal (such as raising a finger) to indicate "wait a minute" because of gagging or discomfort. The tube should be chilled on an ice bed to make it rigid for passage. Some plastic tubing may need to be dipped into warm water if too stiff. Mark the distance the tube is to be passed by measuring the distance on the tube from the patient's earlobe to the bridge of the nose plus the distance from there to below the xiphoid process. Mark this spot on the tube with a piece of adhesive tape (which will usually fall between the second and third circular markings at the nares when the tube is in place). Lubricate the tip of the tube for about 6 to 8 in., lift the patient's head, and insert the tube into the nostril, gently passing it along the floor of the nose until it reaches the pharynx, at which time the patient may gag. Let the patient rest a moment, and then, with the patient holding the head in a normal position, have the patient take several sips of water, advancing the tube while he or she swallows. Do not use force.

If there are signs of distress, such as gasping, coughing, or cyanosis, immediately pull the tube back to the nasopharynx and try again. To check the position of the tube when it is in the stomach:

1. Aspirate the contents of the stomach with a 50-mL irrigating syringe with adapter.
2. Place the end of the tube in a glass of water to check for air bubbles.
3. Place a stethoscope over the epigastrium and inject 20 to 30 mL of air into the NG tube.

The only sure way to confirm the presence of the tube in the stomach is by x-ray unless you are obtaining a satisfactory return of stomach contents. Adjust the tubing to proper position and tape into place using a skin "tackifier" and hypoallergenic tape; be certain *not* to obstruct the patient's vision or cause any pressure against the nasal septum.

Central Venous Pressure Lines

In the past, there has been disagreement regarding the early use of central venous pressure (CVP) lines in the traumatized patient; the ACS's ATLS course advocates early use of CVP lines to monitor the candidate for shock, in order to manage an effective fluid challenge and evaluate adequacy of volume replacement. As the ATLS standards point out, the CVP line is *not* a primary intravenous resuscitation route and is initiated on an elective basis rather than an emergency one.

When CVP lines are used, the preferable sites are the jugular vein, the left antecubital (with a long-line CVP), or the subclavian; ideally, the puncture should not be made on the injured side if chest trauma is present. Respiratory fluctuations must be present. Initiation of subclavian lines is a high-risk procedure with complications, which include infection, vascular injury, embolization, thrombosis, and frequently pneumothorax. Strict surgical asepsis should be the rule when preparing the site and placing the catheter, in the hope of minimizing unnecessary complications.

Nursing participation in placement of CVP lines includes appropriate positioning of the patient (slight Trendelenburg), aseptic preparation of insertion site, and ongoing monitoring of the CVP readings. Readings are taken with the patient supine and the manometer zero at the level of the right atrium. The normal range is 4 to 10 cm H_2O. Readings over 10 cm H_2O may indicate right heart failure, tamponade, fluid overload, pulmonary edema, tension pneumothorax, or hemothorax. Readings below 4 cm H_2O may indicate shock, dehydration, or hypovolemia.

Intra-arterial Blood Pressure Catheter

In the hypotensive traumatized patient, direct intra-arterial BP measurement is obtained by means of a 20-gauge catheter in a radial artery, which provides continuous pressure tracings as well as access to samples for serial ABG measurements. This procedure is usually deferred until the patient is in the operating room or the intensive care unit.

Foley Catheter

Foley catheters are indicated in all multisystem injuries except when there is a straddle injury or blood evident in the urethral meatus. An indwelling catheter with urimeter collection bag is essential to monitor intake and output and kidney perfusion. A minimum output is 0.5 mL/kg of body weight per hour, or 30 to 35 mL/h for a 150-lb. (70-kg) person. Placement of a Foley catheter also allows for total evacuation of all urine and gross observation of urine for blood. Be cautioned that when the catheter does not readily enter the bladder or when blood is evident at the meatus, a urethrogram should be done immediately to determine the status of the urethra before proceeding further and a urologist should be called.

The Tieman Foley catheter is recommended by many urologists for catheterizations of male patients because the configuration of the tip reduces trauma to the prostatic urethra and facilitates passage of the catheter.

Chest Tubes

Chest tubes are positioned posteriorly (midaxillary line at the fourth or fifth intercostal space) to drain fluid, and anteriorly (midclavicular line at the second intercostal space) to release air, with areas prepared accordingly (see Chapter 14).

Diagnostic Peritoneal Lavage

The technique employed in diagnostic peritoneal lavage (DPL) is similar to that of inserting a peritoneal dialysis tube with multiple holes. The lavage takes 20 to 25 minutes at best and carries a 96 percent chance of indicating significant injury if the results are positive. The procedure is indicated in trauma victims with altered consciousness, central nervous system (CNS) injuries, spinal cord injuries, negative abdominal tap (if done), shock, and multiple trauma. It is contraindicated with obvious penetration of the abdomen, known probable adhesions, dilated bowel, pregnancy beyond the second trimester, and massive abdominal distention (see Chapter 15).

TAILORING FOR TRAUMA

Universal Trays for Invasive Lines

With a sharp eye on the economy of both physical energies and funds, many ED staffs have worked out special equipment and tray setups using a universal tray concept. Basic sterile setups for use with invasive monitoring procedures are assembled; depending on the need, appropriate individual tubes and lines are dropped in surgical fashion from peel-packs onto the sterile field once the setup is opened or transferred to the tray with dry sterile transfer forceps. Waste, confusion, and duplication can be avoided using this type of system; significant economies are realized and passed along to the patient.

Trauma Carts

Necessity has become the mother of invention and adaptation in responding to trauma resuscitation. Spatial constraints of shelves and working surface in trauma bays have resulted in the evolution of trauma carts, specifically equipped for full-scale resuscitations. Multiple labeled bins containing tubes, collection containers, tubings, needles, solutions, dressings, restraints, and universal precautions gear (e.g., gowns, gloves, goggles, masks) are housed on supply carts about 4 feet high with an open workspace on top for assembling equipment for surgical procedures. The result, of course, is rapid mobile response to the patient anywhere in the ED with minimization of footwork, confusion, and time loss.[12-14]

■ NURSING MANAGEMENT REVIEW

Some final thoughts in reviewing the management of the multiple trauma victim include the following:

A. Areas of observation that should alert the EN:
1. Hypotension is always a sign of hypoxia, and if there is frank shock without heavy blood loss or the possibility of significant occult bleeding, suspect spinal cord injury, transsection, and so on.
2. Cyanosis is a sign to check the airway again and be sure that the patient is ventilating adequately and getting a high enough concentration of oxygen; remember that cyanosis is a late manifestation of hypoxia and must be anticipated and avoided.
3. Patient anxiety and tachycardia should cause the EN to suspect blood loss and incipient shock.
4. Delirium is an excellent indication of decreased cerebral blood flow and incipient shock.

5. Skin changes, such as cool, clammy skin, piloerection, and mottled extremities, are caused by the release of epinephrine in the shock state. Check the lower legs for warmth and color.
6. Distended neck veins with the patient in a 45-degree position indicate the likelihood of severe chest damage, tension pneumothorax, cardiac tamponade, or congestive heart failure (CHF).
7. Flat neck veins (low CVP) accompany clammy, pale skin with major bleeding somewhere.
8. Urine output is the major monitor of visceral blood flow (the window of the viscera), and low output indicates the probable need for fluid. (A good level is 30 mL/h.)

B. Learn to anticipate the needs of the patient *and* the physician. Time is of the essence.

C. Call for extra help when you really need it and make certain you have a "runner" for stat laboratory work, to make the necessary phone calls, and to go ahead to hold the elevator for the critical patient who is being transferred from the ED to the intensive care unit (ICU) or the OR.

D. Provide portable oxygen and a suction unit during transfer.

E. Before transferring the patient out of the ED, be very sure that you have ruled out or know the patient's status regarding:
1. Hypoxia
2. Cervical spine fracture
3. Aortic tear
4. Pneumothorax
5. Hemothorax
6. Hemoperitoneum
7. Esophageal or bronchial trauma

F. Documentation is extremely important. Again, clear, concise flow sheet documentation remains an important nursing responsibility with traumatized patients and trauma codes. Most EDs have devised their own flow sheet formats; some have become extremely comprehensive. Vital signs (VS), LOC, flow rates, medications, drainage amounts, and sequential interventions *must* be charted. Not only does good documentation pass along the information accurately to the next shift, the ICU, the OR, or the hospital to which the patient is transferred, it presents a medicolegal record of that patient's presence and clinical status as well as care given (or not given). If serial VS are not charted, for instance, a court of law would assume they were not taken; "not documented means not done," so protect your EN practice and your hospital with careful, legible, and concise recording.

■ SUMMARY

The management philosophy for traumatized patients is grounded in rules that have been validated by trauma surgeons as fail-safe guidelines for that golden hour; ENs recognize them as rules that guide their effective interventions when trauma patients present:

1. Think the worst first. (Anticipate and stay ahead of developing crises.)
2. Don't panic. (Focus on the needed task and work with speed and accuracy.)
3. Use a systematic approach to evaluate and treat the multiply injured patient.
4. Look beyond the obvious.
5. Be aggressive with your management.

ENs should qualify themselves to participate fully in the trauma team response, secure in their knowledge of what constitutes appropriate and timely interventions; nursing pursuit of competency in current trauma management protocols will facilitate the surgical life-support team's abilities in affecting positive outcomes and restoring victims of trauma to the hoped-for return to normal lives. Always remember that time is of the essence.

■ REFERENCES

1. National Safety Council, 1991.
2. Adolescent homicide—Fulton County, Georgia, 1988–1992. *Morb Mortal Wkly Rept.* 1994;728–730.
3. Homicide of persons aged < 18 years—Fulton County, Georgia, 1988–1992. *Morb Mortal Wkly Rept.* 1994;43(14):254–261.
4. The MMWR file: Gunshot wounds overtake motor vehicle crashes. *J Emerg Nurs.* 1992;18:417.
5. Trauma: combatting a major killer. Trauma nursing core course. Emergency Nurses Association; Chicago, Ill. 1991.
6. Mayer TA, Keaton BF. Data sets. *Trauma Q.* 1989;5:19.
7. Base P. Examples of critical paths for use in the emergency department. *J Emerg Nurs.* 1994;20:174–175.
8. Nelson MS. Critical pathways in the emergency department. *J Emerg Nurs.* 1993;19:110–114.
9. Saul L. Developing critical pathways: a practical guide. *Heartbeat.* 1995;5:1–4.
10. Dubois M, Griffin S. Nursing practice and ATLS: point of view. *Ethicon.* 1994;31(2):3–5.
11. Lombardo LV, Randon SD. New patterns of injury in drivers protected by air bags. *Etcetera.* January 1994; p.4.
12. Matthews K. Streamlining trauma care in one level I trauma center emergency department. *J Emerg Nurs.* 1995;21:319–323.
13. Mattice C. Mobile trauma carts: they go where the patient goes. *J Emerg Nurs.* 1992;18:529–531.
14. Nayduch D, Sullivan SL. The problems of intrahospital transfer of patients with trauma and one solution: the "trauma transfer backpack." *J Emerg Nurs.* 1992;18:383–389.

■ BIBLIOGRAPHY

American College of Surgeons Committee on Trauma. Advanced Trauma Life Support program. Chicago, Ill: ACS; 1993.

Barber J. *Controversies and Special Problems in Trauma Management.* Lewisville, Tex; Janet Barber and Barbara Clark Mims Associates; 1993.

Barber J. *Day 1—Trauma in the Adult.* Lewisville, Tex; Janet Barber and Barbara Clark Mims Associates; 1992.

Barber JM, Dillman PA. *Emergency Patient Care.* Reston, Va; Reston Publishing; 1981.

Baxt WG. A trauma triage rule that works. *Emerg Med.* March 1993;73.

Cahill SB, Balskus M. *Intervention in Emergency Nursing: The First 60 Minutes.* Rockville, Md: Aspen Publishers; 1986.

Cardona VD, ed. *Trauma Reference Manual, Maryland Institute for EMSS.* Bowie, Md: Brady Company; 1985.

Cardona VD, Hurn PD, Bastnagel Mason PJ, et al. *Trauma Nursing.* 2nd ed. Philadelphia, Pa: WB Saunders; 1994.

Champion HR, Sacco WJ. Measurement of injury severity and its practical application. *Trauma Q.* 1984;1:25–36.

Champion HR, Sacco WJ, Copes WS, et al. A revision of the trauma score. *J. Trauma.* 1989;29:623–629.

Current issues in trauma. *Trauma Q.* 1985;1(3).

Emergency Nurses Association. *Emergency Nursing Core Curriculum.* 4th ed. Philadelphia, Pa: WB Saunders; 1994.

Emergency Nurses Association. *Trauma Nursing Core Course.* 4th ed. Chicago, Ill: ENA; 1995.

Fincke MK, Lanros NE, eds. *Emergency Nursing: A Comprehensive Review.* Rockville, Md; Aspen Publishers; 1986.

Hoyt DB, Shackford SR, McGill T, et al. The impact of in-house surgeons and operating room resuscitation on outcomes of traumatic injuries. *Arch Surg.* 1989;124:906–910.

Kidd PS, Wagner KD. *High Acuity Nursing.* 2nd ed. Stamford, Conn: Appleton & Lange; 1996.

Knezevich-Brown BA: Trauma Nursing Principles and Practice. E. Norwalk, Conn: Appleton & Lange; 1986.

Laskowski-Jones L. Will trauma centers become extinct? A review of factors affecting trauma center financial viability. *J Emerg Nurs.* 1993;19:121–126.

Lee, G. *Flight Nursing: Principles and Practice.* St. Louis, Mo: Mosby-Year Book; 1991.

Lindsay, KK. Assisting professionals in approaching families for donation. *Crit Care Nurs Q.* 1995;17: 1–7.

Lockhart C, Mattox K, Philley C. A review of autotransfusion. *J Emerg Nurs.* 1979;5:338–342.

McSwain NE, Kerstein MD. *Evaluation and Management of Trauma.* E. Norwalk, Conn: Appleton & Lange; 1987.

Meislin HW, ed. *Priorities in Multiple Trauma (TEM).* Rockville, Md; Aspen Publishers; 1980.

Multisystem trauma. *Trauma Q.* 1984;1(1).

O'Boyle CM, Davis DK, Russo BA, et al. *Emergency Care: The First 24 Hours.* E. Norwalk, Conn: Appleton & Lange; 1985.

Paul BK, Savino JA. General monitoring techniques in the trauma patient. *Trauma Q.* 1987;3(3).

Penetrating trauma. *Trauma Q.* August 1985;1(4).

Phippen ML, Wells, MP. *Perioperative Nursing Practice.* Philadelphia, Pa: WB Saunders; 1996.

Ramzy AI. Trauma Management. *Top Emerg Med.* 1987;9:33–42.

Shaffer MA, Walraven G. Trauma assessment and scoring. *Trauma Q.* 1986;3(1).

Smith SL. *Tissue and Organ Transplantation: Implications for Professional Nursing Practice.* St. Louis, Mo: CV Mosby; 1990.

Southard P. Trauma economics: suggestions for decreasing the cost of trauma care. *J Emerg Nurs.* 1993;19:262–263.

Southard P. The community obligations of a trauma center. *J. Emerg Nurs.* 1994;20:334–335.

Southard P. Trauma quality management: closing the loop. *J Emerg Nurs.* 1993;19:362–363.

White KM, DiMaio VJM. Gunshot wounds: medicolegal responsibilities of the ED nurse. *J Emerg Nurs.* 1979;5:29–35.

Younger SJ, Landefeld CS, Coulton CJ, et al. "Brain death" and organ retrieval: a cross-sectional survey of knowledge and concepts among health professionals. *JAMA.* 1989;261:2, 205–220.

■ **REVIEW: MAJOR TRAUMA**

1. Describe the four categories of hospital capabilities in the care of trauma victims and the designation of trauma center levels.

2. Explain the rationale of the *golden hour* concept in trauma care.

3. Describe three benefits of using critical pathways, or patient care guidelines, in responding to the needs of trauma victims.

4. Explain the terms used in the medical approach in advanced trauma life support (ATLS) and compare them with the steps of the nursing process.

5. Explain the three basic collision events that occur in deceleration injuries manifesting as blunt trauma.

6. Cite at least four important considerations to be kept in mind when assessing trauma in the elderly.

7. Explain the importance of gathering and documenting a complete database on victims of trauma.

8. List at least six general drug groups employed in the early management of trauma.

9. Identify three important types of tissue that are currently sought in donor programs.

10. Cite the three primary criteria for organ donor selection.

Head, Neck, and Maxillofacial Injuries

13

Head injury continues to be a chief cause of both morbidity and mortality from trauma. Although the use of restraint systems in automobiles, including lap/shoulder belts and airbags, is widespread, the emergency nurse (EN) will continue to care for large numbers of patients with injuries to the head, neck, and facial structures. Firearms, recreational mishaps, and human assaults are among the other major causes of these potentially life-threatening injuries.

Failure of emergency personnel to suspect, identify, and aggressively manage head, neck, and maxillofacial injuries can result in increased morbidity and mortality for up to a half million patients each year in the United States alone.

■ MECHANICS OF INJURY

A thorough understanding of the mechanical forces involved in the accident is of great value to the nurse who is doing the assessment and attempting to predict the nature and possible extent of organ and tissue damage that might be present.

BLUNT INJURY

Blunt injuries that can affect the head, neck, and face include abrasions, bruises, contusions, lacerations, and fractures. Although surface trauma can suggest underlying tissue damage, the most serious injuries are those that impact the skull with sufficient force to impair or destroy vital brain centers or to directly interfere with upper airway efficacy.

These include cerebral contusions, lacerations, and fractures of the bony structures of the cranium, face, and cervical spine.

Blunt trauma of the head usually involves two separate events, each with their own potential for injury. First, the individual collides with an object, and then the organs collide with the inside of the body cavity in which they reside.

PENETRATING TRAUMA

In penetrating trauma, the injured area usually can be quickly detected and related adjacent tissue trauma can be reasonably determined. When penetrating forces hit the body, skin, blood vessels, and bone may be destroyed anywhere along the path of the object. Resultant problems include interruptions in blood supply, displacement of vital tissue, and destruction of skin and bone, which ordinarily protect the body's organs. Of course, whenever there is a penetrating wound, the object involved may carry or disperse foreign substances (e.g., hair, clothing fibers, microorganisms, other environmental contaminants) along its path.

■ HEAD INJURIES

The major focus in assessment and management of head injury is protecting the brain. Although the brain represents only about 2 percent of the body's weight, it is responsible for 20 percent of the resting oxygen consumption and demands 15 percent of the cardiac output to meet its metabolic requirements. The brain has an exceptionally high metabolic demand—49 mL/min of oxygen and 60 mg/min of glucose. It is easy to appreciate that early efforts after injury are aimed at the maintenance of oxygen and nutrients required for the brain's functions. Hypoglycemia can promptly result in impaired neuronal activity, seizures, coma, and death.[1] If the brain's cells are not working properly, other body systems also are soon negatively affected and a vicious circle of organ dysfunction follows in several body systems. Early resuscitation of the brain frequently will include not only aggressive oxygen administration but the correction of hypoglycemia by administration of 50 mL of 50 percent dextrose, along with 100 mg of thiamine to prevent Wernicke's encephalopathy (see Chapter 20).

PATHOPHYSIOLOGY OF MAJOR BRAIN INJURY

Head injuries occur from both primary and secondary causes. Primary causes encompass the damage caused from the original mechanical insult. They include, for example, scalp injuries, skull fractures, contusions, perforating injuries of the cranial vault, lacerations, diffuse axonal injury, and cranial nerve damage, which occurs during basilar fracturing. Secondary injuries include insults that follow head trauma, such as hypoxia, hypotension, infection, seizures, hematomas, intracranial hypertension, and herniation. Most secondary injury can be prevented or at least managed to minimize its effect if ENs are alert to its potential and aggressively manage the patient throughout the post-trauma period.

Intracranial Hemodynamics and Metabolism

Cerebral blood flow (CBF) requires a cerebral perfusion pressure (CPP) of about 80 mm Hg, with 60 mm Hg being the lower limit of normal.[1] CPP is the difference between mean arterial pressure (MAP) and the intracranial pressure (ICP). A change in CPP can be effected by either arterial pressure or changes in the ICP (e.g., systemic hypotension or intracranial hypertension). A system of autoregulation normally maintains a constant blood flow despite some variations in CPP. Autoregulatory control seems persistent within a range of MAPs of 50 to 150 mm Hg. However, when the limits of autoregulation are exceeded, CBF can fall or rise along with pressure changes. If the CBF rises, creating serious intracranial hypertension, the blood–brain barrier breaks down and focal cerebral edema occurs. Hypoxemia can also create cerebral vasodilation, increased CBF and volume, and intracranial hypertension. Increases in partial arterial carbon dioxide pressure (P_{ACO_2}) from 40 to 80 mm Hg doubles CBF, while P_{ACO_2} levels of 20 mm Hg cut CBF in half.

Compensatory Mechanisms

The Monro–Kellie hypothesis states that a change in the volume of brain, cerebral blood volume or cerebrospinal fluid (CSF) must be accompanied by a reciprocal change in one or both of the other components to avoid an increase in ICP. For example, if the brain volume increases as a result of a blood–brain barrier failure, the ICP will rise unless there is a concurrent fall in either the cerebral blood volume or the CSF volume. Normally compensation is accomplished by several inherent mechanisms in order to protect the delicate brain. However, in the face of devastating trauma, compensatory mechanisms may fail, and the brain tissue will be compressed. The limits of early adjustments (i.e., decreased blood flow to the head, increased CPP) are soon exceeded, giving rise to the loss of autoregulation. Passive dilation, venous congestion, and further increases in ICP and decreases in CPP follow, leading to cellular hypoxia and brain death. The EN must ensure that early attention is given to maximizing the factors of CPP that can be controlled externally. Administration of oxygen, a head-up position (30 degrees), good alignment of the head to ensure that venous outflow is unrestricted, and correction of systemic hypotension are vital in the early care of the head-injured patient. Therapies to treat elevations in ICP include measures to decrease one of the components (e.g., hyperventilation, diuretics, and hyperosmolar agents [Lasix, urea, mannitol, or Plasmamate]) and CSF drainage or surgery. Glucocorticoids (e.g., Decadron) may be used to stabilize the vascular membrane. Barbiturates, which decrease the cerebral metabolic rate of oxygen and reduce both cerebral edema and ICP, also are used.

INITIAL ASSESSMENTS

Some patients may arrive in the emergency department (ED) with a major complaint of head injury, but many others will have a history of major trauma in which there is potential for head injury. In either case, the EN must be able to perform a systematic neurological examination and to note signs of rostral-caudal deterioration or the development of increasing intracranial pressure (see pages 178 and 183). Any conditions that might interfere with interpreting neurological status (e.g., alcohol, drugs, chronic illness) must be taken into consideration.

A history of the patient's condition should be obtained from family members, prehospital personnel, or others who might be able to provide useful information. It is important to establish whether there has been a deterioration in the level of consciousness (LOC). A patient who was responsive at the accident scene but is now experiencing a lower LOC may have a serious brain injury such as a contusion. An unconscious patient at the scene who becomes responsive and then deteriorates also represents cause for great concern. A "lucid interval" between the initial injury and later declines in consciousness indicates serious brain deterioration.

Data about prior medical conditions, drug and alcohol consumption, and mechanics of any accident will undoubtedly prove valuable. Since use of alcohol or recreational drugs is associated with 40 to 50 percent of head injuries, this information is vital. The Glasgow Coma Scale (GCS) score should be calculated, and pupillary responses should be evaluated. Be certain to inspect for contact lenses at this point, and remove them if they are noted. Any cranial nerve III palsy or traumatic iridoplegia (i.e., nonreactive pupil) should prompt rapid intervention. If there is associated hypotension, crystalloids are used aggressively to maintain the CPP.

AIRWAY MANAGEMENT AND SPINAL CORD PROTECTION

Patients with head, neck, or facial injuries are also suspect for cervical spine injuries, so cervical spine precautions (see Chapter 8) must be maintained throughout the early assessment period until the extent of injury can be ascertained. The airway must be managed without hyperextension. The jaw-thrust and chin-lift maneuvers are recommended means of establishing the airway, and respirations may need to be assisted early with a bag-valve-mask unit, since any oxygen deficit contributes to cerebral edema. The brain is capable of storing a very short supply of oxygen (i.e., about 10 seconds), so metabolic demands of vital tissue suffer promptly in the event of poor ventilation and perfusion. The seriously head-injured patient should be ventilated with supplemental oxygen (10 to 12 L/min) at a rate of 24 breaths per minute. If the patient is unconscious, baseline arterial blood gases (ABGs) should be obtained and endotracheal (ET) intubation promptly accomplished. Care should be taken to ensure that the tape or other device used to secure the ET tube does not cross or compress the jugular areas, which might restrict venous outflow from the head. Sedation and narcotic analgesics may be used in the intubated patient to control noxious stimulation, which can increase ICP. Neuromuscular-blocking agents also may be employed to prevent increases in venous pressure associated with the Valsalva effects that accompany ventilatory support.

Hypercarbia is a potent cerebral vasodilator. Controlled hyperventilation should be maintained in anyone with suspected high ICP. The end goals are to maintain the partial pressure of oxygen (PO_2) at over 70 mm Hg and the $PACO_2$ between 25 and 30 mm Hg, which causes arteriolar vasoconstriction, thus reducing cerebral blood volume. The $PACO_2$ should not be lowered further, however, since extreme vasoconstriction can result in either ischemia or cerebral infarction.[2] The upper level of pH should be 7.50 to 7.55. Since neurogenic pulmonary edema can be induced by fluid shifts to low-pressure circulatory networks such as the pulmonary beds during massive sympathetic stimulation after injury, respiratory status must be closely monitored.

The threats of vomiting and aspiration are always present after trauma. Early nasogastric (NG) intubation and decompression are vital for preventing these sequelae, which further aggravate intracranial pressure. If there is facial trauma that might disrupt the bony confines of the upper airway (e.g., nasal, orbital, or maxillary-mandibular fractures), great caution must be used to prevent the possibility of further iatrogenic brain injury from NG tube insertion, which can be introduced into the cranial vault via a fracture of the cribriform plate. If there is any leakage of CSF fluid from the nose (rhinorrhea) or from the ear (otorrhea, or hemotympanum), there is a likelihood of a fracture of the basal or frontal skull, permitting a direct communication from the upper airway structures to the brain. Such outflow of CSF should not be restricted in any way. Occasionally a patient may complain of a "salty taste" in the mouth or throat, suggesting CSF fluid leakage. The EN may wish to confirm the nature of any clear fluid by performing the "target sign." Fluid on a gauze pad will separate out, leaving a bluish border and a center aggregation of red blood cells (RBCs). Although CSF fluid will test positive for sugar, a Dextrostix test will be unreliable. An oxidation-reduction reaction is required to test for CSF; this can be accomplished with Test-Tape. Suctioning should be avoided, since it raises ICP and may be a conduit for the introduction of microorganisms into the brain via the penetrated meninges. ICP monitoring is a useful technique for tracking and modulating elevation in ICP in the intensive care setting, but is not ordinarily available in the ED.

VITAL SIGNS

Vital signs (VS) should be regularly recorded, since they may provide clues to developing shock as well as ICP elevations. Monitors should be promptly placed for oximetric measurements, electrocardiogram (ECG), and blood pressure (BP) readings, and for constant temperature assessment.

Blood Pressure

BP and pulse ordinarily are stable in the early period after head injury, but when CPP becomes threatened, from any cause, pressor receptors in the vasomotor center of the medulla are stimulated to raise the BP. Elevations in BP and widening pulse pressures are reflections of ischemic processes affecting the medulla, of increased ICP, or of a myocardial cause, in some cases. Low BP is not typical in neurological injury until death is imminent.

Pulse

Pulse is usually slow and bounding in association with major head injury. If bradycardia is present, it suggests pressure on the brainstem, a mass in the posterior fossa, or a spinal cord injury in which ascending sympathetic pathways have been interrupted. In severe cases of increased ICP, it is slow and full, often at a rate of 40 to 50 bpm. The presence of tachycardia suggests hypotension deserving volume resuscitation. A rapid, thready, irregular pulse may accompany the terminal decompensation of increased ICP. Dysrhythmias occur in patients with blood in the CSF and in association with certain brain insults, such as those involving the posterior fossa.

Temperature

Temperature may be useful in the overall assessment of coma, since patients with certain metabolic problems may have either elevations or declines from normal that are mediated by the hypothalamus. Ruptures of a ventricular aneurysm and certain infections of the central nervous system (CNS) are accompanied by temperature elevations. However, in acute head injury, temperature may fluctuate considerably, and either hypothermia or hyperthermia may be experienced. A rectal probe is normally employed for continuous monitoring.

Respiration

Respiratory rate and pattern may be very helpful in assessment of the head-injured patient (see Fig. 13–1).

Cheyne–Stokes respirations are characterized by increases and decreases in the depth of excursions, followed by a period of apnea. The pattern is triggered by heightened sensitivity of the medulla to carbon dioxide. The apneic phase is related to decreased stimulation from the cerebral hemispheres. Cheyne–Stokes respirations are associated with bleeding into the basal ganglia, conditions that exert pressure on the medullary respiratory center, a bilateral hemispheric lesion in the cerebrum, or a dysfunction of the cerebellum, midbrain, and upper pons. Hypertensive encephalopathy can also give rise to this phenomenon.

Central neurogenic hyperventilation is sustained hyperventilation at a rate of 40 to 50 breaths

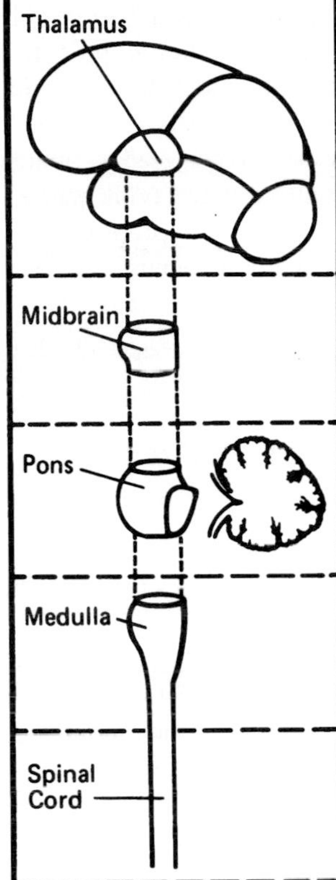

CNS Level Affected	Respiratory Pattern	LOC	Pupils	Posture	Doll's Eye
Thalamus	① ～～～ or ② ～￦～	Stupor Semi-Coma	Small Reactive	Decorticate	—
Midbrain	③ ∿∿∿∿ or	Coma	Mid-position Nonreact	Decerebrate	+
Pons	④ ∿∿∿ or	Coma	"	Flaccid	+
Medulla	⑤ ～∿～	Coma	"	Flaccid	+
Spinal Cord	① Normal respiration ② Cheyne-Stokes with decreased response to pain and decreased corneal reflexes				
	③ Neurogenic Hyperventilation Not responsive to O_2 and "patterned"				
	④ Biot's respiration with regular periods of hyperventilation and irregular periods of apnea				
	⑤ "Apneustic" respiration with ataxic, gasping, shallow pattern				

Figure 13–1. Clinical signs in the neurologically damaged patient.

per minute; it may be due to pons infarction or to the impinging of any lesion on the pons (e.g., cerebellar hematoma). It may also accompany hypothalamic-midbrain lesions and some of the metabolic causes of unconsciousness, such as diabetic ketoacidosis, lactic acidosis from any cause, or uremia. In order for confirmation of this respiratory pattern, the patient must have a PaO_2 greater than 70 mm Hg for at least 24 hours.

Apneustic breathing (e.g., deep inspiratory gasps followed by a 2- to 3-second pause) signifies structural damage to the respiratory control center in the middle to lower pons, usually suggesting imminent death.

Cluster breathing is an irregular respiratory pattern with irregular intervals of apnea. It is associated with lesions of the lower pons or the upper medulla.

Ataxic breathing is similar to Cheyne–Stokes respirations except that the apneic spells are irregular. Ataxic breathing points to medullary damage or increased pressure within the posterior fossa. Cerebellar or pontine hemorrhage and severe meningitis also give rise to ataxic respirations.

OTHER MONITORING PARAMETERS

Reflexes and motor systems should also be serially evaluated (see Chapter 6). As the motor assessments continue, both sides should be tested and compared. Abnormal posturing should be noted, and the EN must determine whether such posturing is exaggerated by stimulation.

Signs of increasing ICP should also be noted throughout the ED stay. These include:

- Headache
- Projectile vomiting
- Eyes deviating to the side of the lesion
- Change in motor tone or strength
- Seizures
- Increases in BP and decreases in pulse pressure
- Respiratory changes
- Tachycardia
- Abnormal posturing (i.e., decerebrate or decorticate)

OTHER PROBLEMS ASSOCIATED WITH HEAD INJURY

Seizure

Seizure activity is not uncommon in severe head injury. Seizure precautions and care should be according to the guidelines outlined in Chapter 20. Anticonvulsant therapy (e.g., phenytoin) is aimed at preventing seizures that accelerate cerebral blood flow and raise ICP.

Carotid–Cavernous Sinus Fistula

Note any eye pulsations that could suggest carotid–cavernous sinus fistula, a trauma-related condition in which the damaged carotid artery

bleeds into the sinus. Certain traumatic injuries, such as basilar skull fracture, can give rise to this problem. The cavernous sinus communicates with ophthalmic veins, and a fistula permits blood to enter the network under arterial pressure.[3] The danger in this condition is that the "steal" of blood diverted by the fistula creates ischemia to vital tissue within the eye, which can lead to blindness. A bruit may be present over the orbit, and a downward displacement of the eye (proptosis) often ensues. A carotid–cavernous sinus fistula can be demonstrated by carotid angiography and treated by balloon occlusion, usually accomplished in the radiology department (Fig. 13–2).

HEAD INJURY CLASSIFICATION

Scalp Wounds

The scalp should be searched for wounds or gross evidence of skull fracture. Any impaled object or foreign body should be left in place and covered with a sterile dressing, taking care not to place any pressure upon the wound. Lacerations of the scalp tend to bleed profusely and should be managed by the application of direct pressure. Failure to control bleeding can result in shock. Since some lacerations are not easy to detect, search the scalp carefully with a gloved hand, parting the hair to facilitate inspection. Palpate the skull and note any indentations or obvious bone fragments. Do not put any pressure on unstable skull bone or brain tissue if a fracture is apparent, since brain tissue and its surrounding blood vessels could be injured further. Any open fracture should be loosely covered with a sterile dressing.

The hair around scalp lacerations should be shaved and the wound cleansed, debrided, and thoroughly inspected before closure. Owing to the scalp's mobility upon the impact of mechanical forces, fractures may not be directly under the obvious defect (Fig. 13–3).

Skull Fractures

Linear fractures: About 80 percent of skull fractures are linear, half of which involve the temporal or parietal bones. These fractures seldom require any treatment. However, if the fracture line extends into the orbit or the paranasal sinuses, or if a fracture crosses the middle meningeal artery or the superior sagittal sinus, there is risk of major bleed-

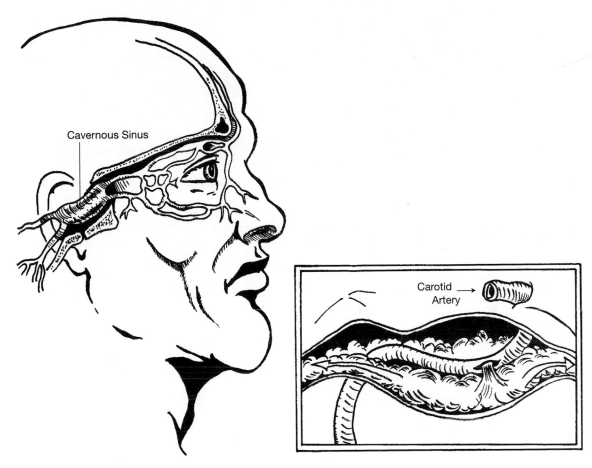

Figure 13–2. Carotid-cavernous fistula. Carotid artery empties into venous sinus (inset) and permits blood to enter the ophthalmic veins. (*Adapted from Hartshorn.*[3])

ing. A fracture of the occiput can damage the occipital artery or the transverse sinus, resulting in epidural hematoma.

Depressed fractures: These fractures can be either simple or compound, and the patient often has signs and symptoms of focal, rather than diffuse, brain injury. In addition to tissue destruction from the impact (e.g., torn dura or brain laceration), further insults to the brain may result from impaled bone or other debris, which gives rise to infection complications.

Basilar fractures: Basal skull fractures are identified primarily by clinical findings that point directly to the injury. Look for ecchymosis over the mastoid bone (Battle's sign) or under the eyes. In middle fossa basilar skull fractures, blood leaks into tissue spaces in these regions, creating a bruised appearance. Otorrhea and rhinorrhea occur from dural tears of the meninges, which permit CSF leakage. If the tympanic membrane is not torn, blood and CSF will remain behind it and can be noted on otoscopic examination, which will reveal a bluish discoloration of the eardrum. Palsies of cranial nerves I, VII, and VIII are associated. Patients may be admitted for observation if the basilar skull fracture is an isolated event, but admission is often preferred for observation and perhaps the administration of prophylactic antibiotics to minimize the threat of meningitis. Most fracture sites close within 7 to 10 days without surgery.

Concussion

Concussion is a transient loss of consciousness in which no structural damage to the brain occurs. The concussion "knocks out" neural transmissions to the reticular activating system as the brain is set

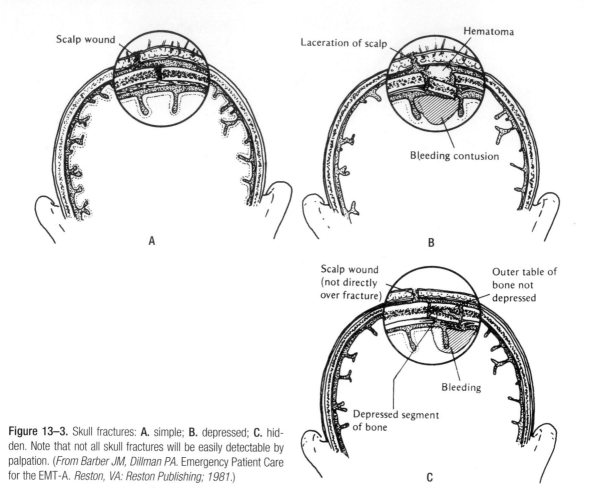

Figure 13–3. Skull fractures: **A.** simple; **B.** depressed; **C.** hidden. Note that not all skull fractures will be easily detectable by palpation. (*From Barber JM, Dillman PA.* Emergency Patient Care for the EMT-A. *Reston, VA: Reston Publishing; 1981.*)

in motion, twisting the brainstem and interrupting electrical energy transmissions. Immediate unconsciousness after head injury is due to concussion, not contusion. Patients may report a period of amnesia ranging from a few seconds to several minutes. Longer periods of unconsciousness tend to represent the more serious injuries. The EN should determine what the patient remembers just prior to the trauma and the first things he or she recalls after trauma so that the extent of the transient period of unconsciousness can be properly estimated. Although memory loss, headaches, tinnitus, and irritability may persist after injury, the brain tissue remains intact, but subtle structural changes have obviously occurred. Since hematomas may coexist with concussion, any later declines in the level of consciousness heralds deterioration.

Contusions

Contusions are heterogeneous hemorrhages that affect the brain parenchyma, and resultant neurological dysfunction is dependent upon the areas affected. Contusions that jeopardize the blood–brain barrier may extend rapidly and cause widespread intracranial tissue destruction, with associated elevations in ICP, secondary to bleeding and edema. Escalating pressures within the calvaria will displace tissue downward, posing the risk of herniation of the falx tentorium.

Brain tissue can be directly affected under the site of impact, but injury can also occur on the opposite side of the cranial cavity, contre coup, as the brain rebounds from the mechanical forces and bridging veins are torn and other structures are contused or lacerated from the resultant impact

(Fig. 13–4). Patients with concussions or contusions remain stable or improve. If not, acute hemorrhage or hematomas must be considered.

Hematomas

Intracranial hematomas: These are often associated with head injury and may be epidural, subdural, or intracerebral. As blood collects in this confined space, it displaces brain tissue, elevates ICP, and lowers the LOC. Deterioration of the LOC tends to progress more rapidly with arterial bleeding than venous bleeding. If the brainstem is involved, the reticular activating system will be dysfunctional, leading to coma, respiratory compromise, and abnormal posturing.

Occasionally when arterial injury occurs, there may be a rapidly developing hemorrhagic condition that is life-threatening, owing to compression of brain tissue. This type of injury should be expected if there is a loss of consciousness followed by an interval of consciousness, and then later, a deterioration of the LOC. This characteristic sequence of coma, consciousness, and deterioration (i.e., lucid interval) demands prompt attention, especially when there are concurrent findings such as spontaneously dilated and fixed pupil(s), slow pulse, rising BP, narrowing pulse pressure, and respiratory compromise. Hematomas within the cranial vault may occur in any of the meningeal spaces.

Epidural hematomas: These frequently involve the middle meningeal artery, resulting in brisk bleeding. The incidence of these hematomas is low, but they occur usually in younger patients. These injuries are associated with the lucid interval. Surgical intervention is required to arrest the deterioration in the LOC and prevent tentorial herniation.

Subdural hematomas: These arise primarily from the tearing of bridging veins that drain from the cortex to the superior sagittal sinus. (Arterial bleeds rarely account for subdural hematomas). The extension of bleeds associated with subdural hematomas is limited only by the tentorium and falx barriers, so they may be quite extensive (Fig. 13–5). They occur commonly and are associated with a poor prognosis. Patients who take anticoag-

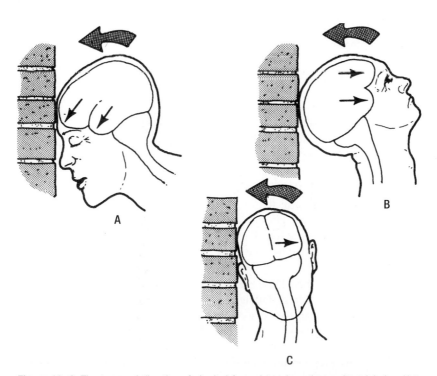

Figure 13–4. The type and direction of physical force determines the resultant injuries. Note that bleeding injury may occur on the side opposite impact. (**B** and **C**). (*From Barber JM, Dillman PA.* Emergency Patient Care for the EMT-A. *Reston, VA: Reston Publishing; 1981.*)

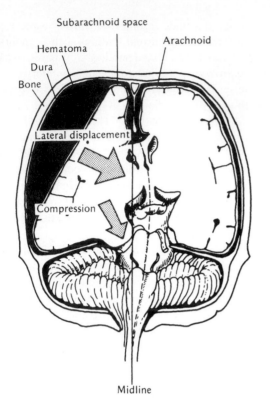

Figure 13–5. Subdural hematoma. Note the displacement and compression of brain tissue. (*From Barber JM, Dillman PA. Emergency Patient Care for the EMT-A. Reston, VA: Reston Publishing; 1981.*)

ulants or who have blood dyscrasias may experience this without trauma. These hematomas may be either acute or chronic. In the slowly developing or chronic subdural, the patient may experience confusion and a decreasing LOC without injury that can be recalled. At best, there may be a history of a fall or blow to the head that occurred several days or weeks prior to ED presentation. It is thought that a resolving clot may become osmotically active, thus creating the phenomenon of an enlarging mass. Hematomas in elderly individuals and those who abuse alcohol may go unnoticed, since these patients may experience ongoing stumbling, falling, confusion, and disorientation. Although the hemorrhage is usually the result of slower, venous bleeding, it may extend widely since there are no dural attachment barriers to limit its progression. Craniotomy is the treatment for these lesions, but even early intervention carries a guarded prognosis.

Hemorrhage

Subarachoid hemorrhage usually is preceded by trauma. Even though it may not cause significant neurological damage, hydrocephalus and cerebral vasospasm may follow as delayed complications, and these conditions may lead to impairment. Classic symptoms include headache, nuchal rigidity, and photophobia.

Diffuse Axonal Injury

Diffuse axonal injury is the shearing of brain tissue with disruption of the neuronal axon projections within the white matter. Although it is a microscopic injury and not detectable on computed tomography (CT) scans, neuronal damage may be devastating. However, associated hemorrhagic lesions, such as hemorrhages in the corpus callosum or brainstem, may be noted.

DIAGNOSTIC STUDIES

Computed Tomography Scans and Magnetic Resonance Imaging

CT scans are superior to conventional skull films in the evaluation of head injuries because they can delineate parenchymal contusion, locate epidural and subdural hematomas, demonstrate cerebral edema and hydrocephalus, and pinpoint areas of cerebral infarction. Magnetic resonance imaging (MRI) scans may take considerable time and are not available in some centers that perform the initial evaluation of head injuries. However, they may be useful during the later course of head injury management as an aid in monitoring ICP.

Cerebral Angiography

Cerebral angiography may be employed in the assessment of vascular disorders associated with trauma, but is used less often since CT scanning with contrast is widely available.

Transcranial Doppler Ultrasonography

Transcranial Doppler ultrasound may be used to confirm vasospasm or absent blood flow in the basal cerebral arteries. It is a useful tool in confirming brain death.

HEAD INJURY DISPOSITION

The disposition of a patient with a head injury will depend upon several factors, including the patient's condition, the capabilities of the facility in which the emergency care is being provided, and reliability of family or other support for monitoring the neurological status in the event that the patient is discharged.

Patients with severe head injury must be cared for in a facility designated as a major trauma center, and transfers to other facilities, either by air or ground, should be set into motion promptly. Unless the facility has the capabilities for neurosurgical intervention and neurological intensive care, procedures such as CT scans should be accomplished after transfer since they may create inordinate delays. Patients are usually transported promptly to a regional trauma center if they have a deteriorating LOC, a depressed skull fracture or penetrating injury of the CNS, post-traumatic seizures, or local or lateralizing syndromes or if they are victims of multiple trauma with head injuries. Preschool children with skull fractures are also high-risk patients requiring specialized care.

Admissions for observation are imperative for concussed patients who are not yet fully oriented, for children, and for some individuals with basilar skull fractures in which the risk of meningitis may be significant. Individuals with head injuries associated with alcohol or drug ingestion are admitted until effects of these substances can be distinguished from neurological findings. Patients with a history of concussion who are now responsive and improving, as well as those with scalp wounds not associated with brain injury, may usually be discharged safely if there is a responsible adult who can follow instructions on "take-home" instruction sheets for the head-injured patient.

Urgent Interventions for the Head-Injured Patient Awaiting Disposition

Emergency surgery may be indicated for cerebral contusion, intracranial hematomas, and for removal of certain foreign bodies. If there is an urgent need to lower ICP, emergency ventricular drainage may be required. Prior to surgery, often in the ED, osmotic agents and diuretics may be employed. Serum osmolarity should be monitored and maintained between 305 and 310 mOsm/L throughout the administration of such agents, since hyperosmolarity and renal dysfunction may be side effects of the therapy.[4]

Mannitol is the drug of choice because of its rapid ability to effect diuresis. Mannitol creates an osmotic gradient between the blood and brain tissue, drawing fluid from the cerebral extracellular spaces into the bloodstream. Dosages are usually started at 0.25 to 0.5 g/kg of body weight, with the dose repeated in 10 to 15 minutes if there is no response.[4] Any crystals that form in mannitol during its shelf life must be dissolved prior to administration. Ordinarily, this can be accomplished by warming the container under a flow of hot water while agitating it. The EN should ensure that the infusion site is patent, since extravasation can cause necrosis. *Do not give mannitol by direct injection.* An in-line filter and an infusion pump are recommended to accomplish administration. During the course of mannitol therapy, there is some risk of circulatory overload, so the EN should be alert for early signs such as tachycardia and basilar rales. A Foley catheter must be in place as an adjunct to monitoring the diuresis.[5]

Nursing diagnoses for head injury include the following:

- Altered thought processes related to cerebral ischemia and hypoxia
- Impaired gas exchange related to neurogenic pulmonary edema
- Ineffective breathing pattern related to altered ventilatory mechanics
- Ineffective airway clearance related to compromised protective reflexes
- Risk for injury related to altered state of consciousness and neurological defects
- Anxiety related to decreased cerebral oxygenation
- Altered sensory/perceptual functioning due to neurological defects
- Risk of infection due to interruption in integrity of skin barrier

■ MAXILLOFACIAL TRAUMA

Maxillofacial trauma may create airway problems, shock from profuse bleeding, intracranial injury, and even damage to the cervical spine. As the EN assesses a patient with obvious or suspected trauma to the face, initial attention should be given to the airway, with all cervical spine precautions being observed.

The oral cavity should be assessed regularly for blood, secretions, CSF drainage, and foreign objects such as teeth that have been displaced. Suction the airway as necessary unless there is evidence of CSF leakage. In the latter case, avoid any suctioning, since there may be a direct communication from the nose or mouth to the base of the brain. Airway devices and supplemental oxygen, as well as assisted ventilation, may be required to maintain oxygenation. The patient should be positioned with considerations for concurrent injuries to the head, neck, chest, abdomen, and the status of the VS. If feasible, the mouth should be dependent to permit the gravity drainage of blood and saliva from the mouth.

BLUNT TRAUMA

The EN should appreciate the fact that facial fractures may not be obvious. Careful inspection and palpation are required to discover certain injuries. Bleeding, loss of teeth, or malocclusion; increased salivation; or the inability to talk, swallow, or open and close the mouth suggest facial trauma. CSF leaks from the nose or ears, the presence of a blow-out fracture, or asymmetry of facial structures are other clues to such injuries. A neurological evaluation, including assessments of the LOC, is in order to detect the presence of a serious coexisting intracranial injury. Special attention should be given to victims of assault, vehicular crashes, and sporting accidents, because significant forces may have produced the injury.

Nasal Fractures

Nasal fractures involve both bone and cartilage. The deformity is usually easily observed, and there is crepitation and mobility on palpation. Edema ensues rapidly. It is estimated that about 75 lb. of force is required for fractures of the nasal bone structure. Epistaxis usually accompanies these fractures. Treatment of nondisplaced nasal fractures, without septal hematoma or other injuries, is generally conservative. Local application of ice and administration of analgesics may be all that is required. Displaced nasal fractures are ideally treated before edema becomes significant. Closed reduction is performed using local anesthesia (5 to 10 percent cocaine hydrochloride topically to the nasal mucosa and 1 to 2 percent lidocaine hydrochloride with epinephrine 1:200,000 infiltrated around the nasal spine). If there is no other head injury, sedation may be used. After the reduction has been accomplished, either by open or closed method, the fracture should be immobilized with anterior nasal packing. Prior to packing, a 5 to 8 Fr suction catheter may be placed along the floor of the nostril to equalize pressure in the nasopharynx and to help alleviate the "fullness" in the ears often felt by patients with nasal packing. Packing should be layered, not "stuffed" into the cavity, to facilitate removal. An external plaster splint may also be used. The packing and splint remain in place for 7 to 14 days. Oral decongestants may be used during this time to relieve the associated rhinorrhea.

Open nasal fractures require debridement and repair in the operating room (OR).

Septal Hematoma

A septal hematoma may develop, dissecting the mucosa off the septal cartilage and robbing the blood supply. If the hematoma becomes infected, the septum will necrose in 24 hours or less, yielding cartilage destruction and deformity. This hematoma must be drained, and the nose must be packed with antibiotic ointment and gauze packing. These patients must be instructed not to blow the nose because of the danger of transmitting infection to the brain or eyes. Patients presenting with any history of nasal trauma should be carefully examined for the presence of a septal hematoma.

Naso-orbital Fractures

Naso-orbital fractures usually result from severe blows to the nose. Such fractures may be comminuted and difficult to repair. CSF rhinorrhea is common, and localizing neurological signs may be present because of the posterior and superior projections of the nasal bones through the cribriform plate and penetration of the frontal lobes (Fig. 13–6). In addition to brain injury, there may be

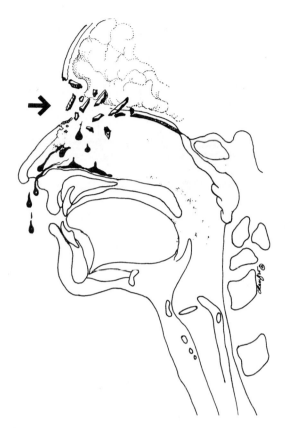

Figure 13–6. Naso-orbital fracture. Note the potential for perforating injuries to the frontal lobe of the brain.

damage to the underlying lacrimal apparatus, noted by lack of tears being produced on the affected side and persistent rhinorrhea, not associated with CSF leakage. Concern for developing meningitis is paramount, and antibiotics are prescribed early in these cases.

Zygomatic Fractures

The zygomatic region is involved in one of four maxillofacial fractures, but the zygoma itself is rarely fractured. Usually its attachment points (maxilla, frontal and temporal bones) are disrupted, and when all three are involved, it results in the "tripod fracture" or a LeFort III fracture. When the zygoma is displaced, disruption of the lateral orbital wall and the orbital floor occurs, resulting in a blow-out fracture.

Blow-Out Fractures

A blow-out fracture is a fracture of the floor of the bony eye orbit due to blunt trauma involving large objects in most cases (e.g., baseballs, fist). When the eye receives the blow, the intraorbital pressure is increased and the relatively weak lower portion of the orbital wall gives way into the adjacent maxillary sinus cavity. The inferior rectus muscle often becomes entrapped in the fracture site, resulting in restricted eye movement and diplopia. Diplopia is created by dysconjugate eye motions. Visual acuity and eye mobility must be assessed and recorded. The patient with a blow-out fracture should have bilateral eye patches placed promptly when the injury is discovered (Fig. 13–7).

Mandibular Fractures and Dislocations

Fractures of the mandible result from trauma. Dislocations may be associated with trauma, but they may occur during laughing, yawning, or even chewing. An anterior dislocation causes great pain, since the mandibular condyle cannot return to its articular surface, causing the internal and external pterygoids and masseter muscles to spasm, thus "locking" the jaw in place. These dislocations may be unilateral or bilateral. There may be swelling in front of the ear due to displacement of the head of the condyle. Bilateral dislocations prevent the patient from closing the anterior teeth, creating an open-mouth appearance. Palpation over the condylar heads usually reveals a lateral projection. Dislocations of the mandible ordinarily can be reduced by manual manipulation. Benzodiazepine sedation may be required to accomplish the procedure.

LeFort Fractures

The LeFort classification of facial fractures (Fig. 13–8) is based upon the lines of weakness in the facial architecture.

LeFort I fractures result from a blow directed to the area below the nose. This causes a horizontal fracture through the body of the maxilla, which separates from the base of the skull above the palate and below the zygomatic attachment.

Examination may reveal elongation of the patient's face, ecchymosis, and edema of the gums. Malocclusion of the teeth may be seen; that is, the anterior teeth remain open when the articular surfaces of the posterior teeth are closed. The maxilla becomes "free-floating" and is mobile on palpation. Epistaxis may also be present and can range from minor to severe.

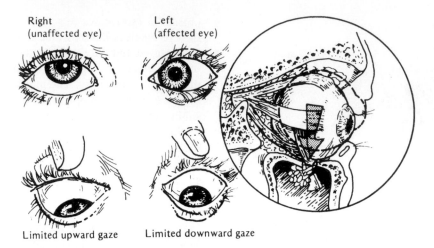

Right (unaffected eye)   Left (affected eye)

Limited upward gaze   Limited downward gaze

Figure 13–7. Blow-out fracture. Fracture of orbital floor creates limited upward and downward gaze of the affected (left) eye. Inset shows anatomic defect characterizing the injury. Dotted line represents normal position of eyeball. (*From Barber JM, Dillman PA.* Emergency Patient Care for the EMT-A. *Reston, VA: Reston Publishing; 1981.*)

LeFort II fractures are subzygomatic fractures with a pyramidal configuration, located in the central maxillofacial region. These fractures involve both infraorbital rims and the nasal bones. Fracture lines extend through the maxillary sinuses and across the bridge of the nose. Injuries to the lacrimal apparatus and canaliculi should be suspected. Physical examination reveals the patient's entire midfacial region to be swollen. Subconjunctival hemorrhage is usually present, and once again, minor to severe epistaxis may exist. One should also look for and be suspicious of CSF leakage, which is common in this type of fracture. Palpation of the facial architecture reveals mobility of the maxilla and the nose. Malocclusion may be noted.

LeFort III fractures are also known as craniofacial disjunctions. The face is fractured through the frontozygomatic suture line across the orbits, through the base of the nose, and through the nasoethmoid complex. The force of impact drives the face along the base of the skull at a 45-degree angle, giving it a characteristic flattened or "dish face" appearance. Physical examination reveals periorbital ecchymosis and edema, probably CSF rhinorrhea and/or epistaxis, and an "open" bite anteriorly. Palpation of the facial architecture reveals mobility of the teeth and zygomas.

Panfacial fractures are a combination of facial fractures, usually severely comminuted, that result from high-velocity impact, such as that generated by motor vehicle accidents (MVAs). Patients with

these fractures may not present with acute airway problems; however, they should be watched carefully. Pharyngeal hemorrhage and edema are common; crepitus may be noted over the face on palpation, and serious deformity is present.

Most patients with midfacial fractures have little pain; therefore, palpation and movement of the various facial structures can be performed without much discomfort. Exsanguinating epistaxis is uncommon but can occur. Surgical intervention may be necessary to stop persistent hemorrhage if conventional methods such as packing fail.

All LeFort fractures are difficult to diagnose by x-ray alone; CT scanning may be of some benefit. A Waters view may be beneficial for assessing LeFort II and III fractures. However, as in most facial trauma, one must rely heavily on clinical findings.

MANAGEMENT OF FACIAL TRAUMA

Treatment of LeFort and panfacial fractures is usually delayed for 3 to 7 days, until soft-tissue edema subsides. Acute situations are those requiring airway establishment and hemorrhage control, those associated with ophthalmologic emergencies (e.g., penetrating global injuries), and any skull fractures with communications to the cranial cavity.

If CSF leakage exists and cervical spine injury is ruled out, the patient's head should be elevated 40 to 60 degrees, allowing soft tissue above that area of

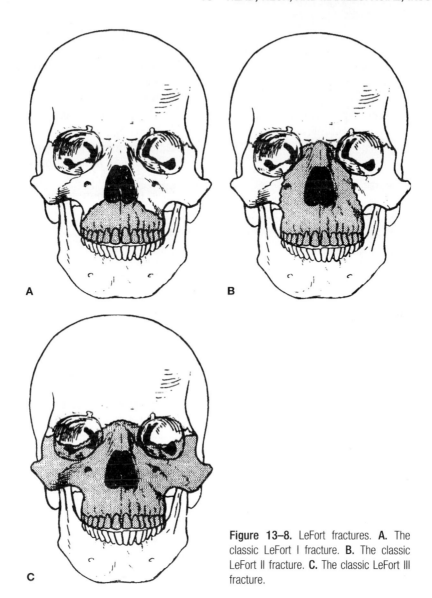

Figure 13–8. LeFort fractures. **A.** The classic LeFort I fracture. **B.** The classic LeFort II fracture. **C.** The classic LeFort III fracture.

leakage to assist in a tamponading process and limiting further CSF loss. In addition to monitoring and protecting the airway, the EN may administer prophylactic antibiotics and assist in repair of soft-tissue wounds associated with the fractures.

SOFT-TISSUE INJURIES OF THE FACE AND NECK

Soft-tissue wounds (e.g., from blast injuries) are seen in increasing numbers as violence escalates in our society. Early care is directed toward establishing a patent airway and providing ventilatory support. Often, surgical airways are required because the nose, frontal facial features, and other ar-

chitectural landmarks are destroyed or obscured by the trauma. Cervical spine precautions should be observed, since bony disruption is common when there is massive soft-tissue destruction. The great vessels of the neck, too, should be scrutinized for injury, and arteriography may be indicated to rule out occult defects. Anteroposterior (AP) and lateral skull films are often accomplished, primarily to assist in locating foreign projectiles.

Epistaxis

Epistaxis usually results from an anterior nasal septum hemorrhage. Epistaxis also occurs from the lateral aspect of the nose; this type of bleed is profuse. Patients with epistaxis should be kept sitting upright and leaning slightly forward to let the blood drip from the nose, thus discouraging swallowing it. Direct pressure should be placed over the nares (by pinching the nostrils) for a period of at least 5 minutes to control anterior bleeds.

Essential equipment: The basic equipment necessary for the management of epistaxis includes the following items:

- Headlamp of a quality that will allow two free hands to work
- Tray containing:
    Nasal speculums, one short and one long
    Frazier suction tip (small metal angulated tip with suction port)
    Bayonet forceps
    Petroleum jelly (Vaseline) gauze (0.5 × 36 in.) packs, applicators, cottonballs, sterile cotton pledgets
    Sterile medicine cup or basin
    Silver nitrate sticks (must be held *firmly* over most bleeding points for 3 to 5 minutes; 2 minutes is adequate over a very small vein)
    Topical Adrenalin (1:1000)
    Topical Xylocaine (4 percent)
- Back-up tray containing:
    Assortment of sterile ENT instruments— pharyngeal mirrors, assorted speculums, forceps, suction tips
    Selection of posterior packs
    Electrocautery tips
- Electrocautery unit

Initial management:

1. Three essentials that must be ready and in working order for the physician are a good light source, nasal speculum, and adequate suction with the proper tip.
2. *Always* have a cover gown ready for the physician as well as mask, gloves, and protective eyewear for all personnel working with the epistaxis patient.
3. If the patient is bleeding heavily, send blood to the laboratory for hemoglobin, hematocrit (Hct), and blood-typing. Hold for cross-match.
4. Caution must be used when administering analgesics or sedatives; keep a close watch on the BP.

5. Use of topical cocaine (4 or 10 percent) may precipitate an adverse reaction, so always have resuscitation equipment close by and benzodiazepines (e.g., Ativan) at hand for reversal of seizures.
6. Clots *must* be removed before treating bleeding sites.
7. A posterior bleeding point is *trouble* and requires a posterior pack to exert pressure. A Foley catheter with 10 to 15 mL water in the balloon, tension as needed, and secure anchoring is effective, or string packs can be placed. *Never* tie strings *around* the septum, but tie separately on a dental roll placed *between* the nares to avoid pressure.
8. Antibiotic ointment should be used on nasal packing to avoid infection and complications as well as an overpowering stench on removal.
9. Always *document* the number of packs and the types placed in the nose.
10. Remember that probably 20 percent of patients with bilateral posterior nasal packs and a history of cardiorespiratory disease will be significantly morbid with precipitating heart attacks from the progressive anoxia. Be alert for increased CO_2 and decreased O_2 levels (dry mouth, confusion, tachycardia, restlessness, and even belligerence).

Epistaxis telephone instructions: When patients call the ED about nosebleeds, the following instructions may be very helpful and fall within a sensible range of telephone advice:

1. Blow nose gently to remove clots.
2. Hold pressure by pinching the nose as far back on the nostril as possible for a *full 5 minutes* by the clock.
3. Remove pressure.
4. If bleeding starts again, repeat steps 1, 2, and 3.

Probably 50 percent of nosebleed patients can avoid coming to the ED if this procedure is used. Instruct the nosebleed patient in this manner on discharge, should the bleeding start again.

Nasal packing technique: An anterior nasal pack should be placed from the top to the bottom and left in place *no more than 1 to 2 days.* The pack must not be started on the floor of the nose, for it will obscure vision. The physician places a finger on the tip of the nose to anchor the speculum, and with a bayonet forceps, takes one strip of petroleum jelly (Vaseline) gauze with *antibiotic ointment applied* and places one loop to the back of the nostril. The speculum is used *under* the packing to lift and pack it into place. The strip gauze is placed with bayonet, packing to the top of the space until it is filled. Finally, the end of the packing is taped at the external nares.

Posterior packing should be removed in 3 to 5 days. Usually, the posterior pack is placed and then followed with an anterior pack, but both must be covered with antibiotic ointment to minimize sinusitis from occlusion of the nasopharynx.

Carefully monitor these patients for *hypoxia* and *signs of restlessness or confusion.* Oxygen administration may be required.

Penetrating Trauma

Facial trauma may involve lacerations to the cheek, which is richly supplied with blood. Pressure may need to be applied on both internal and external surfaces by a compression dressing to successfully control bleeding. Foreign bodies may require removal if they contribute to hemorrhage or make it difficult to retard bleeding. This is the only site from which an impaled object can be removed without fear of additional structural damage.

Parotid duct injuries are of special concern. Wounds of the lateral portion of the face are not uncommon and may result in severance of the parotid duct and the body of the gland. Such injuries must be identified and treated early to prevent complications such as sialocele, extraoral salivary fistula, and cyst formation (Fig. 13–9).

Facial nerve injuries may be associated with deep lacerations of the parotid gland. This nerve emerges from the stylomastoid foramen, then

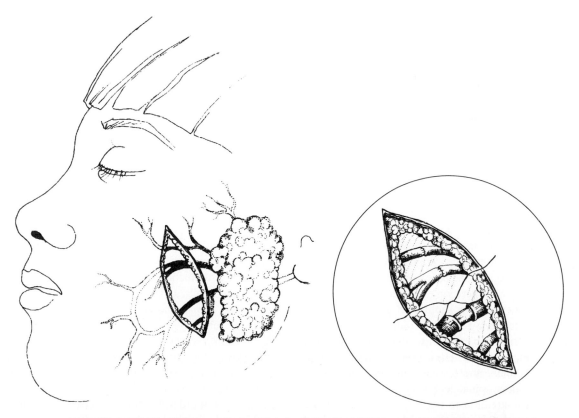

Figure 13–9. Facial injuries may sever parotid ducts. Parotid duct injuries must be promptly identified and repaired to prevent salivary fistula or cyst formation (see inset).

curves forward and laterally before branching into the posterior auricular, posterior digastic, and the stylohyoid portions. It then enters the parotid gland and divides into the temporofacial and cervicofacial branches. These divisions divide within the gland, producing five or more nerve segments. As soon as the patient's condition permits, repairs should be accomplished to ensure the best functional return of the facial nerve and its branches (see Fig. 13–9). Unfortunately in some facial trauma, other more life-threatening injuries and impaired LOC may retard attention to the parotid duct and facial nerve.

Associated Dental Injuries

Displaced teeth is a common problem associated with facial trauma. The tooth (or teeth) should be saved for reimplantation by placement in a saline solution or milk. If the victim is alert and has no breathing or swallowing problems, the tooth may be placed back into the socket, under the tongue, or between the gingivae and buccal jaw lining for preservation. There is some evidence that the chance for successful reimplantation is heightened by keeping the tooth warm and in a neutral, moist environment.

■ NECK TRAUMA

The neck is divided into three anatomic regions for the study of traumatic insult to its structures (Fig. 13–10). Zone I extends from the level of the cricoid cartilage to the level of the clavicle. It includes the proximal carotids, the subclavian vessels, and other major vessels in the chest, upper mediastinum, esophagus, trachea, and thoracic duct. Zone II extends from the area above the clavicles to the mandibular angle. Injuries in this region are the easiest to assess and manage. Zone III extends from the mandibular angle to the base of the skull.

Shortly after verifying the integrity of the cervical spine, attention should be given to assessment of the neck for either blunt or penetrating trauma. Penetrating wounds may involve great vessels, the larynx, trachea, thoracic duct, thyroid, salivary glands, and nerves (phrenic, glossopharyngeal, vagus, spinal accessory, and hypoglossal). After early attention to the ABCs, all penetrating neck wounds deserve careful exploration and study. Any hematoma formation in zones I, II, or III warrants scrutiny. It is imperative that the neck

and upper chest are explored in detail, since expanding hematomas, infections, airway compromise, and asphyxia can result. Astute observations from ENs who care for the trauma patient must include attention to neck wounds and their potential for affecting oxygenation and circulation.

OROPHARYNGEAL HEMATOMA

A serious threat to the upper airway is a hematoma that develops at the base of the tongue or in adjacent structures within the oropharynx. Since the glossal muscle, highly vascular, is confined in a semiclosed compartment, any hematoma expansion can promptly obstruct airflow. This problem may be accompanied by other indices of oral and facial injuries (e.g., lacerations, broken or missing teeth, fractures, dislocations). The individual may be unable to extend the tongue or to speak. This serious threat may be manifest in the unconscious patient by a large, protruding tongue, resulting from glossal edema or hematoma expansion. Prompt surgical decompression is required. Occasionally when this cannot be accomplished, a surgical airway may be indicated. Neck or oral trauma gives rise to this serious problem, and the EN should ensure that a thorough inspection of the mouth and throat is done upon the patient's arrival.

LARYNGEAL OR TRACHEAL FRACTURES

Occasionally, trauma results in a fractured larynx. A direct blow to the neck by a fist, a steering wheel, or baseball can injure this structure, producing edema, subcutaneous emphysema, hemorrhage, and airway obstruction. Such severe neck injuries may be accompanied by cervical spine trauma, too, so careful immobilization is imperative. Signs and symptoms of laryngeal fracture may be easily overlooked during the basic examination, since other traumatic injuries may be more obvious. However, the EN should observe and palpate the neck for edema and be cognizant of subjective complaints. Hoarseness or aphonia, swelling, crepitation of neck tissues, drooling, and airway obstruction with respiratory stridor suggest laryngeal injury. A surgical airway is usually required to ensure ventilation, so prompt medical consultation is in order. Suction the airway as required and provide supplemental oxygenation. Avoid positive-pressure ventilation, since it may exaggerate or extend subcutaneous emphysema.

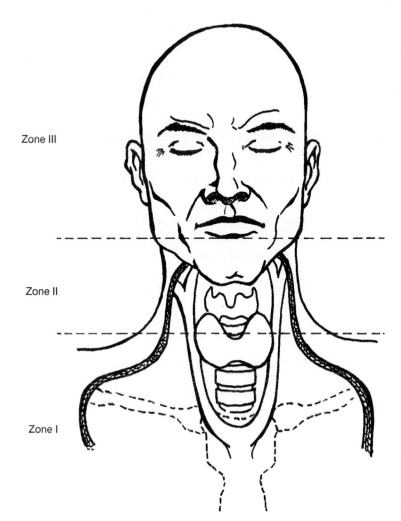

Zone III

Zone II

Zone I

Figure 13–10. Anatomic regions of the neck. (*Adapted from Feliciano DV, Moore EM, Mattox KL.* Trauma, *3rd ed. Stamford Conn: Appleton & Lange, 1996.*)

VASCULAR INJURIES

Injuries to major blood vessels in the neck can create fatal hemorrhage or air embolism. The injury may be missed, since its signs and symptoms are frequently attributed to head injury. Sometimes only bruises or abrasions will be apparent on the skin, and the presence of a cervical collar may obscure these wounds.

Bleeding from penetrating wounds of the neck (zone II) should be controlled by digital pressure, not by a large pressure dressing. A vascular injury in zone I will require prompt thoracotomy for control. Two large intravenous lines (prefer-

ably, one of these should be a central access) should be established. A lower-extremity line is recommended for suspected innominate vein or superior vena cava injuries. Chest tubes may be placed early, before pressure-assisted ventilations are initiated, to prevent tension pneumothorax. The patient should be transported to the OR for extended explorations and definitive surgical care once hemodynamic stabilization is assured.

Since many penetrating vascular injuries may be missed in the early post-trauma period, they may be noted hours or days later, resulting in complications ranging from mere paresthesias to carotid artery occlusion and death.

ESOPHAGEAL PERFORATION

A wound that permits a leaking of corrosive digestive juices, food, or bacteria into the paraesophageal spaces can produce devastating complications. In some cases, when the perforation extends into the pleural cavity, mediastinitis and bacterial infection occur. The presence of an esophageal perforation should be suspected in major trauma of the neck and chest. Upright chest films may demonstrate mediastinal emphysema, pleural effusion, and pneumothorax; cervical films may show displacement of the trachea, a widening of the superior mediastinum, and the presence of air in the tissue spaces. Gastrographin swallows can be used to localize the perforation if the patient's overall condition permits such studies.

IMPLICATIONS FOR EMERGENCY NURSES

The care of patients with maxillofacial and neck trauma is highly challenging, since these injuries are frequently difficult to detect. However, during the initial period in which the patient is in the ED, attention to airway, ventilation, and cerebral functioning are vital because they provide clues to the nature and progression of injuries. Appropriate nursing diagnoses include:

- Ineffective breathing pattern related to altered ventilatory mechanics
- Ineffective airway clearance related to mechanical obstruction
- Impaired gas exchange related to upper airway edema
- Risk for injury related to altered state of consciousness and neurological defects
- Anxiety related to decreased cerebral oxygenation
- Alteration in self-concept related to changes in body image associated with physical appearance
- Risk of infection due to interruption in integrity of skin barrier

■ REFERENCES

1. Nikas DL. Critical aspects of head trauma. *Crit Care Nurse Q.* 1987;10:19–44.

2. Doberstein C, Rodts GE, McBride DQ. Neurosurgical critical care. In: Bongard FS, Sue DY, eds. *Current Critical Care Diagnosis and Treatment.* E. Norwalk, Conn: Appleton & Lange; 1994: 539.

3. Hartshorn JC. Carotid–cavernous fistula. *Focus Crit Care.* 1983;10:32–35.

4. Mitchell PH. Closed head injuries. In: Cardona VD, Hurn PC, Bastnagel Mason PJ, et al., eds. *Trauma Nursing.* 2nd ed. Philadelphia, Pa: WB Saunders; 1994: 383.

5. Moreau D (ed). *Nursing 96 Drug Handbook.* Springhouse, Pa: Springhouse Corporation; 1996.

■ BIBLIOGRAPHY

Ayres SM, Grenvik A, Holbrook PR, Shoemaker WC, eds. *Textbook of Critical Care.* 3rd ed. Philadelphia, Pa: WB Saunders; 1995.

Bongard FS, Sue DY, eds. *Current Critical Care Diagnosis and Treatment.* E. Norwalk, Conn: Appleton & Lange; 1994.

Cardona VD, Hurn PD, Bastnagel Mason PJ, et al., eds. *Trauma Nursing.* 2nd ed. Philadelphia, Pa: WB Saunders; 1994.

Chernow B, ed. *The Pharmacologic Approach to the Critically Ill Patient.* 3rd ed. Baltimore, Md: Williams & Wilkins; 1994.

Clouchesy JC, et al., eds. *Critical Care Nursing.* Philadelphia, Pa: WB Saunders; 1993.

Grenvik A, Ayres SM, Holbrook PR, Shoemaker WB, eds. *Pocket Companion to Textbook of Critical Care.* Philadelphia, Pa: WB Saunders; 1996.

Levine RL, Fromm RE Jr, *Critical Care Monitoring from Pre-Hospital to the ICU.* St. Louis, Mo: Mosby-Year Book; 1995.

Maull KI, Rodriguez A, Wiles CE. *Complications in Trauma and Critical Care.* Philadelphia, Pa: WB Saunders; 1996.

Moore EE, Eiseman B, Van Way CW III. *Critical Decisions in Trauma.* St. Louis, Mo: CV Mosby; 1984.

Phippen ML, Wells MP. *Perioperative Nursing Practice.* Philadelphia, Pa: WB Saunders; 1994.

Physicians' Desk Reference. 50th ed. Montvale, NJ: Medical Economics; 1996.

Ruppert SD, Kernicki JG, Dolan JT, eds. *Dolan's Critical Care Nursing.* 2nd ed. Philadelphia, Pa: FA Davis; 1996.

Urden LD, Davie JK, Thelan LA, eds. *Essentials of Critical Care Nursing.* St. Louis, Mo: Mosby-Year Book; 1992.

Weist PW, Roth PB, eds. *Fundamentals of Emergency Radiology.* Philadelphia, Pa: WB Saunders; 1996.

■ REVIEW: HEAD, NECK, AND MAXILLOFACIAL TRAUMA

1. Compare and contrast the nature and extent of head, neck, and maxillofacial injuries associated with blunt versus penetrating forces of trauma.

2. Explain the Monro–Kellie hypothesis as it relates to assessment and management of acute head injury.

3. Define the ideal physiological environment for brain tissue in terms of blood gas requirements and metabolic support.

4. Relate changes in vital signs (VS) that provide clues to intracranial pressure (ICP) elevations and brain injury.

5. List eight signs of increasing ICP.

6. Describe the one major threat inherent in a developing carotid–cavernous sinus fistula.

7. Outline the guidelines for managing scalp wounds associated with head injury.

8. Describe three major types of skull fractures.

9. Differentiate between concussion and contusion in terms of clinical identification and management.

10. Describe the major types of intracranial hematomas and hemorrhages in terms of their etiology, signs and symptoms, and clinical management.

11. Identify the recommended diagnostic study for evaluation of acute head injuries and explain why it is preferred in most clinical settings.

12. State the criteria for determining the disposition of patients with acute head injury.

13. List six nursing diagnoses pertinent to acute head injury.

14. Identify the primary considerations in assessment and stabilization of maxillofacial injuries.

15. Describe the management approaches for nasal fractures and septal hematomas.

16. Define *blowout fracture* and describe how it is identified and managed.

17. Describe how a mandibular dislocation is revealed during clinical assessment and the usual therapy that is indicated.

18. Define the various types of Le Fort fractures and describe the special risks associated with panfacial fractures.

19. Explain the clinical management of epistaxis and describe the special roles and responsibilities of the emergency nurse (EN).

20. Describe the steps recommended for preservation of displaced teeth.

21. Identify the most vulnerable zone for life-threatening neck trauma and explain why.

22. Name five signs or symptoms that suggest laryngeal fracture.

23. Identify the special dangers associated with esophageal perforation.

24. List six nursing diagnoses pertinent to head, neck, and maxillofacial trauma.

Chest Trauma 14

An important concept in considering chest trauma is recognizing that there are often other associated injuries and certainly, at a minimum, the involvement of other organ systems—skin, musculoskeletal, cardiovascular, and respiratory. Severe blunt trauma to the chest is one situation in which rapid and correct diagnosis within minutes of arrival can make the difference between survival and death.

IMMEDIATE NURSING ACTION

It is essential to the patient's optimum chances for positive outcomes that emergency department (ED) personnel guarantee an established airway immediately with administration of high-flow oxygen by nonrebreathing mask, evaluate rapidly and accurately, alert the physician, obtain vital signs (VS), initiate two large-bore intravenous lines, and prepare the patient for further examination and procedures. These patients must be carefully monitored to detect early signs of deterioration, with frequent auscultation of the chest and abdomen, continual assessment of level of consciousness (LOC), and serial blood gas analysis. Alterations in arterial blood gases (ABGs) *always* precede the onset of clinical changes of respiratory distress. Reliance on visual observations alone often delays therapy, and any patient who becomes confused, restless, or violent should have an immediate ABG determination as a first step in the evaluation of these symptoms. Again, do not wait until the patient has obvious difficulty breathing to initiate high-flow oxygen.

PREVENTING ASPIRATION

Aspiration is a common cause of severe respiratory distress and death. Victims of motor vehicle accidents (MVAs) vomit and aspirate frequently because they have had a large meal or fluid intake several hours prior to the trauma. Aspiration of acidic gastric juices in the bronchial tree and lungs causes chemical pneumonitis, which seriously increases edema and respiratory insufficiency and rapidly leads to abscess formation and empyema. Particles of food in the bronchial tree can cause obstruction of some of the ventilatory units, and absorption atelectasis results. Close nursing observation and rapid intervention with appropriate positioning and adequate suctioning can reduce the occurrence of aspiration.

STATISTICS ON CHEST TRAUMA MORBIDITY AND MORTALITY

Chest injuries are responsible for approximately one quarter of all trauma-related deaths each year and are a major factor in another 50 percent. About two thirds of these deaths occur *after* the patient reaches the hospital, meaning either that the care providers failed to recognize the extent of injury in time or that fatal complications set in after admission.[1] An estimated 80 percent of blunt chest trauma is related to MVAs and sudden deceleration; of all injuries to the chest, 40 percent have associated skeletal injuries, 37 percent have associated neurological injuries, and 9 percent involve the liver and spleen.[2]

RED FLAGS

Indices for caution in significant chest trauma, with its attendant risk of occult deterioration and need for intensive care unit (ICU) admission or transfer to the next level trauma facility, include:

- Deceleration trauma occurring at speeds greater than 35 mph, contributing to high risk of ruptured thoracic aorta;
- Fracture of the first rib, associated with subclavian and aortic trauma;
- Fractures of the ninth, tenth, and eleventh ribs, or more than three ribs, associated with extensive pulmonary contusions, parenchymal tears, and damage to adjacent organs;
- Possible aspiration, leading to atelectasis or chemical pneumonitis;
- Pulmonary contusions, leading to potential for perfusion failure.

■ RESPIRATORY SUPPORT IN CHEST TRAUMA

Patients with maxillofacial, head, and chest injuries require special ventilatory strategies. Other patients with multiple injuries and complicated resuscitations (e.g., the elderly, patients with chronic illness, or anyone who has undergone massive fluid administration or suffered blast injury or inhalation of toxic gases) also may need respiratory support.

ANATOMIC AND PHYSIOLOGICAL VARIABLES IN ASSESSING RESPIRATIONS

The condition of the diaphragm will provide valuable clues to injury and the ventilatory compromise that follows (Fig. 14–1). The right dome, or hemidiaphragm, is displaced upward by the liver and is ordinarily superior to the left one. On full inspiration, the diaphragm lies at the sixth to eighth rib anteriorly and the tenth to eleventh rib posteriorly. On full expiration, the diaphragm rises to the fourth to fifth rib anteriorly and the tenth thoracic vertebrae posteriorly; therefore, any perforating chest injury below the fifth rib may turn out to affect the abdomen as well. It is also important to be aware that a large, flexible chest can accommodate fluid/air entrapment up to as much as 4000 mL, while a small, inflexible chest may accommodate only about 1000 mL.

INITIAL ASSESSMENT GUIDELINES

During initial, progressive, assessments of pulmonary efficiency, there should be a systematic check of the following points:

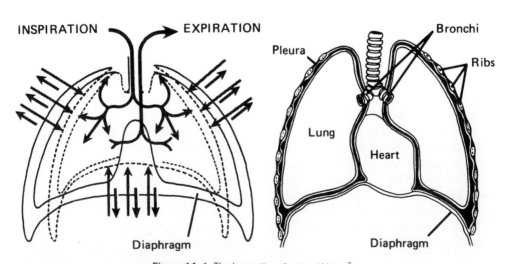

Figure 14–1. The lungs (*from Grant and Murray*[7]).

1. Observe ventilatory excursions, noting any paradoxical motion.
2. Palpate the trachea for position shifts away from the midline.
3. Palpate both carotids, count the pulse, and auscultate for bruits.
4. Assess the neck veins for flatness/distension with the patient at a 45-degree angle in bed.
5. Note crepitus in the neck or over the thorax and observe for hematomas.
6. Palpate the chest wall for unstable thoracic cage segments and note any guarded breathing.
7. Percuss the chest for dullness or hyperresonance, which indicates blood or air accumulations.

CHEST X-RAY EVALUATION

The x-ray film of greatest value in chest evaluation in most instances is the true upright film (patient sitting up at 90 degrees with the chest tilted forward), providing the best opportunity to identify blood or fluid in the pleural cavity. Additionally, cardiac/aortic borders are less distorted with this view (see page 56). The film should be scrutinized for specific indications of injury, such as rib fractures, pneumothorax, pulmonary contusions (infiltrates or opacities on the film), aortic rupture (with widening of the superior mediastinum and blurring or obliteration of the aortic knob, displacement of the trachea to the left, and displacement of the left mainstem bronchus), or evidence of increasing atelectasis, (as in tracheobronchial injuries).

■ PENETRATING AND BLUNT CHEST TRAUMA

Chest trauma significant enough to compromise the normally functioning lungs is categorized as either penetrating or blunt. Penetrating injuries, those that interrupt the chest wall and violate the intrathoracic organs, include stab and bullet wounds, shrapnel, and violent trauma with associated rib fractures. Blunt or nonpenetrating injuries, those that do not interrupt the chest wall, include steering-wheel injuries, deceleration injuries, falls from heights, crush injuries, blast injuries (high positive-pressure waves), and trauma associated with the forces of shearing and torsion.

PENETRATING CHEST TRAUMA

Etiology

Integrity of the chest wall, negative pleural pressures, and bacterial barriers are all lost when the chest wall is penetrated. Serious life-threatening outcomes of chest wall penetration include open pneumothorax, tension pneumothorax, and hemothorax; all require rapid and accurate assessment with appropriate ventilatory interventions and represent major respiratory emergencies.

Hemothorax: This is the presence of free blood in the pleural cavity that occurs when penetrating injury lacerates the highly vascular pulmonary beds and/or great vessels (Fig. 14–2). It is usually defined as the accumulation of 1500 to 2000 mL of blood within the pleural space and requires immediate and aggressive intervention.

Open pneumothorax: This is commonly referred to as a sucking chest wound because of the characteristic sound of air moving through the chest wall. An open pneumothorax (Fig. 14–3) is the most likely outcome of penetrating chest trauma. Some small wounds may self-seal, but larger defects in the chest wall can lead to difficulties as outside air passes directly through the defect into the pleural space and out again.

Tension pneumothorax: Tissue flaps in small penetrating wounds may act as one-way valves, trapping and increasing air volume in the pleural cavity and causing a tension pneumothorax to develop (Fig. 14–4). A chest wall defect approximately two thirds the diameter of the trachea is capable of turning an open pneumothorax into a tension pneumothorax unless the defect is effectively sealed.[2] The mediastinal shift resulting from a tension pneumothorax compresses the great vessels, esophagus, and opposite lung and requires swift action to reverse a very real life-threatening situation.

Nursing Assessment/Diagnoses

The mechanism of injury, combined with clinical signs and symptoms, should guide the nursing assessment with anticipation of further problems. Look for:

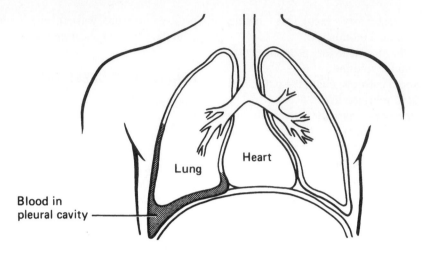

Figure 14–2. Hemothorax.

- History of the accident
- Respiratory distress with shortness of breath, dyspnea, chest pain
- Presence of a wound site or soft-tissue injury
- Sucking sound on inspiration, decreased or absent breath sounds, or hyperresonance on the affected side (with percussion)
- Signs of shock (pulse greater than 120 bpm, diaphoresis, pallor, apprehension)
- Signs of tension pneumothorax (deviated trachea, distended neck veins, cyanosis, and increasing respiratory distress)

Nursing diagnoses appropriate to penetrating chest trauma would include:

- Impaired gas exchange related to disruption of chest wall
- Ineffective breathing pattern related to disruption of chest wall
- Decreased cardiac output related to decreased venous return
- Potential for fluid volume deficit
- Injury (potential for cervical spine damage)
- Pain related to dyspnea and lung collapse

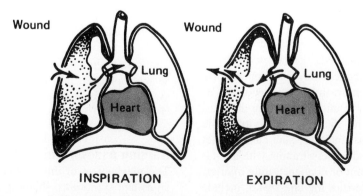

Figure 14–3. Open pneumothorax (*from Grant and Murray*[7]).

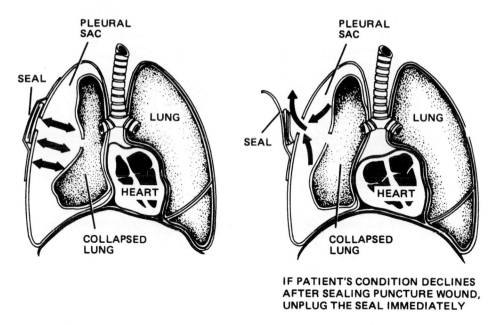

Figure 14–4. Tension pneumothorax (*from Grant and Murray*[7]).

- Nursing problem (potential for infection)
- Anxiety related to dyspnea

Nursing Interventions

The essential points of priority consideration in a patient with penetrating chest trauma are:

A. *Management of the Airway:* Use immediate high-flow supplemental oxygenation by nonrebreathing mask and prevent aspiration. Again, always carefully evaluate for cervical spine damage before attempts are made at hyperextending the head for airway positioning or intubation.

B. *Management of Bleeding and Shock:* This must be a consideration if hemothorax is present. The lung beds are a reservoir of blood, with 900 mL readily available to the systemic circulation. Following trauma, the chest can accommodate 3 to 5 L blood; *one* hemi-thorax can hold as much as 3 L. The approximate amount of blood needed to show on x-ray films of the chest in an upright position is 500 mL; as much as 1 L can be occult on x-ray films in the supine patient.

1. Massive volume replacement with large-bore intravenous lines and crystalloid infusion. Blood should be typed and cross-matched; if the hemothorax is massive, 8 units of blood should be readied for administration. The oxygen-carrying capacity of the blood will be diminished if large volumes of crystalloid solution are used without additional blood being given. This is a situation calling for auto-transfusion, with the patient's own blood from the chest cavity drained into citrated vacuum transfusion bottles, filtered, and returned intravenously to the patient, reducing the risk of blood–borne infection.

2. Placement of a chest tube through the third, fourth, or fifth intercostal space in the midaxillary line with attachment to a water seal drainage unit (Fig. 14–5). Occasionally, bleeding points may tamponade and stop. However, careful monitoring of the amount of blood being lost is essential, and it is generally believed that 6 hours of bleeding at 200 mL/h or 12

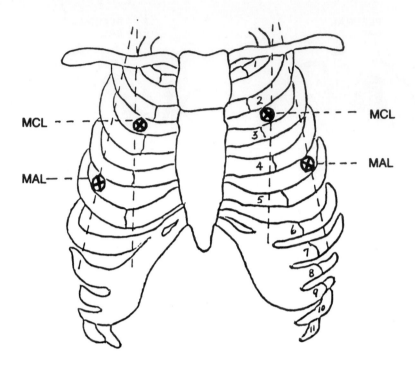

Figure 14–5. Chest needle and tube placement sites. *Needle*—2nd Intercostal Midclavicular Line—(MCL); *Tube*—4th or 5th Intercostal Midaxillary Line—(MAL).

hours of bleeding at 100 mL/h is an indication for operative intervention.

C. *Emergency Management of Open Pneumothorax With a Sucking Chest Wound:*
1. Seal the wound with petroleum jelly (Vaseline), gauze, or plastic (Saran) wrap; it is essential to stabilize the mediastinum and prevent shock caused by the side-to-side shift, distortion of the great vessels, and collapse of the remaining lungs, with decreased venous return and decreased cardiac output. The seal should be released periodically to prevent development of a tension pneumothorax, with the patient under continual close observation. An occlusive dressing, taped securely on three sides, will also provide a flutter-type valve effect.[3]
2. Place a chest tube or large-gauge needle (number 10-gauge angiocatheter) at the second or third intercostal space in the midclavicular line with an attached flutter valve (Heimlich valve) (Fig. 14–6).

D. *Evaluation for the Possibility of Other Organ Injury:* The dome of the diaphragm is found normally at the fifth intercostal space with exhalation; any injury below the fifth rib, therefore, should be considered abdominal as well as thoracic because the liver, spleen, kidneys, and upper bowel content also lie within the rib cage. Operative repair of injured intra-abdominal organs will be achieved through a thoracotomy (an incision through the chest wall) for upper abdominal viscera, maintaining ventilation by endotracheal (ET) intubation and positive-pressure ventilation.

E. *Continued Close Observation of the Patient:* This should be supplemented with chest x-rays taken every 4 hours for at least two series. The films should be inspiratory as well as expiratory.

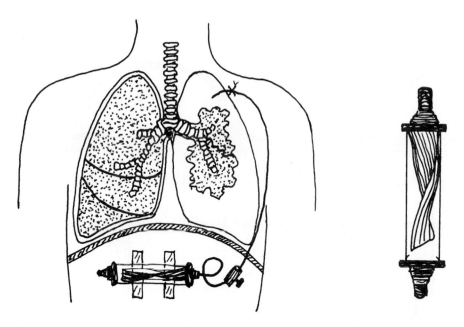

Figure 14–6. Diagrammatic representation of a chest tube inserted and stitched into place at the second or third intercostal space, midclavicular line, and attached to a one-way stopcock and Heimlich one-way flutter valve for evacuation of a left pneumothorax. The Heimlich valve (right), a rigid clear plastic device containing a flat rubber "sleeve," permits one-way evacuation of air and fluid from the thoracic cavity and may be taped or strapped to the chest or abdomen, permitting ambulation when clinically indicated.

F. *Serial ABGs* and pulse oximetry.

G. *Anticipation of Infection from the Open Pathway:* Empyema is commonly a late development in penetration by foreign body. Although antibiotics should not be used indiscriminately, they should be given to treat specific anticipated infections; tetanus toxoid should *always* be given with contaminated wounds.

BLUNT CHEST TRAUMA

Etiology

Blunt chest trauma from direct impact, deceleration, or blast injuries can and does result in extreme shearing forces within the delicate tissues of lung parenchyma, supporting structures, and vascular beds. Whether bony injury is sustained or not, pulmonary contusions and lung lacerations occur in 30 to 75 percent of blunt trauma; the mortality from pulmonary contusions is between 14 and 40 percent.[4]

Blunt chest trauma causes the mechanical force of injury to be distributed over a wide area. When deceleration occurs, there is compression, twisting, and shearing of relatively delicate tissues, causing contusion and subsequently serious pulmonary compromise. Early data gathered at Detroit General Hospital on 2000 trauma victims indicated that shock alone carried a mortality of 7.3 percent, while shock complicated by respiratory failure secondary to chest trauma accounted for a mortality of 73.1 percent—a 10-fold increase.[5]

Pulmonary contusion: Blending almost imperceptibly with adult respiratory distress syndrome (ARDS) is the most common potential lethal chest injury seen in this country—pulmonary contusion. It is listed *potentially* lethal because the resulting respiratory failure develops over a period of time rather than instantaneously. The definitive management of pulmonary contusion develops with time and requires close ongoing clinical monitoring.[3]

Damage to the lung parenchyma, with edema and hemorrhage but without pulmonary laceration,

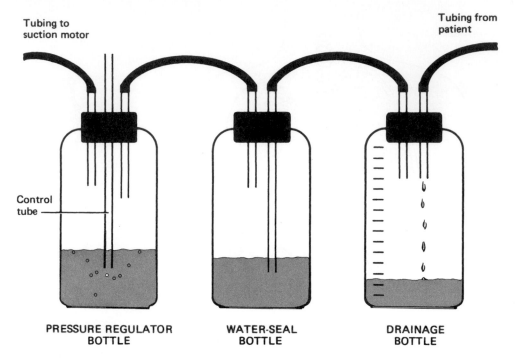

Figure 14–7. The three-bottle seal. The most commonly employed type of drainage system is the three-bottle system, a sterile procedure. It creates negative pressure, or vacuum, when attached to a low-pressure pump. This restores negative intrapleural pressure following interruption of integrity of lung surface or chest wall.

results progressively in impaired gas exchange and eventually in respiratory failure. Onset may be from 1 to 6 hours; careful nursing observation and monitoring, with a high index of suspicion, will facilitate early recognition, intervention, and respiratory support. Management is discussed further under "Lung Trauma and Pulmonary Contusions" later in this chapter.

Hemopneumothorax: Although rare, hemopneumothorax is the presence of both air and blood in the pleural space. It is an often-missed complication of blunt chest trauma secondary to torn parenchyma and vessels or to lung lacerations from the ends of fractured ribs driven inward by impact. Respiratory distress, and perhaps hemoptysis in varying degrees, will be present. This condition is usually discovered when shock is associated with the absence of breath sounds or dullness on percussion on one side of the chest.

Nursing Interventions

Management of closed-chest trauma is much like that in penetrating trauma. Airway maintenance is primary, respiratory support is provided with high-flow supplemental oxygen by nonrebreathing mask, chest decompression is accomplished with rapid needle thoracotomy, and shock is addressed with initiation of large-bore intravenous lines and rapid crystalloid infusion. *Then* chest tubes are inserted, usually midaxillary at the nipple level (fourth intercostal space), and connected to three-bottle water seal drainage, as is done with penetrating chest trauma and hemothorax (Fig. 14–7).

Comorbidity

The bony thoracic cage and the very delicate tissues it houses cannot be injured singly. Forces that injure rib cage structures also contuse tissue both covering the surface and lying beneath; skin, bone, pleura, vascular beds, and lung tissue itself are all involved to one degree or another. In blunt chest trauma, there are always injury combinations, such as:

- Thoracic cage injury with fractures of clavicle, ribs, sternum, and ruptured diaphragm
- Pleural injury with resulting hemothorax or pneumothorax
- Lung injury with contusion or bruising and damage without actual laceration or tearing of tissue (interstitial and intra-alveolar hemorrhage and edema are present)
- Actual lacerations of lungs
- Damage to main trachea and bronchi
- Damage to esophagus
- Damage to heart and pericardium, aortic arch, and major branches of the aorta
- Ruptured diaphragm

Chest-injured patients must be triaged according to whether the injuries (1) interfere with vital physiological functions (10 to 15 percent of chest trauma cases), so that there is no time to waste (these patients must go immediately to the operating room [OR]); (2) are severe but offer no immediate threat to life and afford stable VS (allowing time for x-ray films and evaluation); or (3) produce occult damage (aorta, spleen, liver, tamponade, and so on) and require extremely close bedside monitoring.

Fractured ribs: Fracture of the upper five ribs is an indication of serious trauma with high probability for life-threatening pulmonary injury; ribs 4 through 10 are the most often fractured. Fracture of the first three ribs is especially serious, since they have protection of the scapula and shoulder girdle; fracture of the well-protected first rib has an associated mortality of approximately 40 percent because of frequently associated lacerations of the left subclavian artery and vein.[6] Approximately 90 percent of first-rib fractures are also associated with esophageal and tracheal rupture, as well as significant aortic trauma, and require very close nursing observation. Hepatic injuries occur in 10 percent of right lower rib injuries, and splenic injuries in 20 percent of left lower rib injuries.[6]

Isolated rib fractures are usually benign; the patient is seldom admitted unless three or more ribs are fractured; exceptions are the elderly, chronic obstructive pulmonary disease (COPD) patients, or the chronically ill who have decreased vital capacity (VC) and the inability to clear secretions.

With rib fractures, there is pain and secondary dyspnea. Bruising may be visible, and crackling of ribs may be audible, as may subcutaneous emphysema. Appropriate nursing diagnoses in fractured ribs would include:

- Ineffective breathing pattern
- Alteration in levels of pain/comfort
- Knowledge deficit: discharge instructions for deep breathing

Nursing interventions are as follows:

1. Control pain to allow adequate ventilation and prevent atelectasis. It is important to realize that secretions are increased in traumatized lungs; as one physician puts it, "The lung is dumb. It always responds to trauma by weeping [interstitial edema]." Strapping the chest can seriously compromise ventilation and should be avoided. Local block of the intercostal nerves should be accomplished with bupivacaine hydrochloride (Marcaine); appropriate oral analgesia should be given as needed, and the patient should be encouraged to deep-breathe.

   The intercostal block is done as far back toward the vertebrae as possible to anesthetize most of the nerve and generally should be placed about one hand's width from the vertebral column. Three intercostal blocks should be accomplished for one injured rib (that rib plus the rib above and the rib below), because an overlap of the nerve supply exists from rib to rib; the appropriate area must be prepared accordingly. Bupivacaine (Marcaine) with epinephrine will provide pain relief for a minimum of 8 to 10 hours.

2. Administer analgesia as ordered.

3. Place the patient in a position of comfort, using pillow bolsters for support.

4. Take care of secretions with adequate tracheobronchial suctioning or by encourag-

ing coughing. The patient should be made to cough every 15 minutes, depending upon the amount of secretions, while given manual support or hugging a pillow bolster to support the chest and help decrease pain. If the patient is unconscious, secretions must be cleared by orotracheal or nasotracheal suction.

Flail chest: This occurs as a result of multiple rib fractures, with each rib fractured at two points, disrupting the continuity of the chest wall and creating a "flail" segment (Fig. 14–8) and paradoxical respirations. The flail segment "moves in" on inspiration, and there is cross-ventilation, with air moving from the lung on the affected side to the unaffected lung. The patient is usually cyanotic, tachypneic, and in pain. Pulmonary contusion is almost always associated; myocardial contusion or hemopneumothorax is also possible.

Appropriate nursing diagnoses for flail chest would include:

- Impaired gas exchange
- Ineffective breathing pattern
- Alteration in levels of pain/comfort
- Anxiety

Immediate stabilization is required for adequate ventilation and oxygen administration. Intubation and positive-pressure ventilation is the most effective therapy; oxygen concentration should be that required to produce a minimal alveolar partial pressure of oxygen (PaO_2) of 80 mm Hg, decreasing as rapidly as feasible to 40 percent oxygen. Analgesia and careful attention to the airway are essential, as is careful control over administration of crystalloid intravenous solutions to prevent overhydration. Before placing the patient on a ventilator, place chest tubes if surgical emphysema or pneumothorax is present, to prevent tension pneumothorax. In these patients, remember that hypoxia is the most common cause of combativeness. Additional nursing measures include:

- Continuous monitoring
- Positioning on injured side
- Splinting of flail segment with opposing pressure bolster
- Continuous checking of perfusion (capillary blanch test)

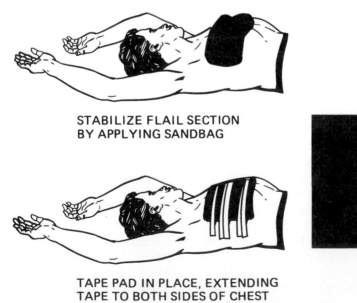

STABILIZE FLAIL SECTION
BY APPLYING SANDBAG

TAPE PAD IN PLACE, EXTENDING
TAPE TO BOTH SIDES OF CHEST

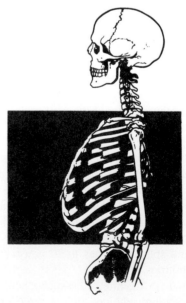

Figure 14–8. Flail chest (*from Grant and Murray*[7]).

Fractured sternum: Sternal fracture is difficult to demonstrate on x-ray films; a lateral view will best show a fracture. There is a high mortality from associated injuries, and a fractured sternum may herald subsequent severe developments, again signaling the need for extremely close monitoring. There is increased chance of severe pulmonary contusions and ventricular ruptures.

Ruptured diaphragm: Crushing chest injuries and deceleration trauma occasionally cause rupture of the diaphragm. The common mechanism is a compressing force on the abdomen, such as that from a steering wheel or a high-riding seatbelt being driven into the abdomen. After a relatively asymptomatic period, the stomach or bowel may become distended; ARDS and pain may develop, the latter of which is usually referred to the shoulder. Abdominal contents herniated into the chest may cause lung and mediastinal compression with decreased venous return.

Nursing diagnoses for a ruptured diaphragm would include:

- Ineffective airway clearance related to increased intrathoracic pressure
- Impaired gas exchange related to decreased ventilation
- Decreased cardiac output related to compression of abdominal contents
- Pain related to injury and increased intrathoracic pressure

Nursing interventions are as follows:

1. Respiratory support with oxygen administration and ABGs
2. Insertion of nasogastric (NG) tube to decompress the distended stomach
3. Positioning and suctioning
4. Chest decompression, if indicated
5. Prompt surgical intervention

Ruptured esophagus: A sudden increase of intraluminal pressure may cause rupture of the esophagus in traumatic pneumothorax and should be suspected if mediastinal emphysema is present. This requires *immediate* surgical intervention and will frequently cause sepsis in the mediastinum. This is an extremely serious complication. Cough, hemoptysis, dyspnea, dysphagia, and sudden pain occur.

Rupture of the trachea or bronchi: Caused by the shearing force of severe blunt trauma, this type of trauma is usually transverse, about 2 cm above the bifurcation of the trachea (carina), or one main bronchus may tear about 2 cm below the carina. It is diagnosed by bronchoscopy or bronchography. Treatment is *immediate* surgery and repair.

Lung Trauma and Pulmonary Contusions

Usually, lung injury accompanies chest trauma and is manifested in many ways; it may occur with or without rib fractures or damage to other structures. Infiltrates or opacities on chest film with progressive hypoxemia are hallmarks, with the severity usually worsening during the initial 24 to 48 hours after trauma. Pulmonary contusion is important because it may be initially asymptomatic (with no fracture of the bony cage in 50 percent of cases) and then may abruptly lead to severe respiratory distress. A developing problem should be anticipated if there is tachypnea, tachycardia, a decrease in PAO_2, or a decrease in partial pressure of carbon dioxide (PCO_2) followed by a later rise.

Nursing diagnoses: Appropriate nursing diagnoses in lung trauma would include:

- Impaired gas exchange related to extravasation of blood into lung tissue
- Potential fluid volume deficit
- Pain related to injury and chest movement with breathing
- Anxiety related to dyspnea

Nursing interventions: Cornerstones of management are ET intubation with volume ventilator, diuretics to reduce septal edema of the lungs, and strict control of fluid intake and output (I and O). Along with the septal edema, there may be hemorrhage, some hemoptysis, and in severe cases, intra-alveolar hemorrhage from rupture of pulmonary capillaries. When properly managed, pulmonary contusions will usually resolve in 3 to 10 days. Steroids were once used to reduce edema associated with pulmonary contusions, but their effectiveness has not been supported and their use is no longer advocated.[1] Chest tube insertion may be indicated if there is laceration of the lung tissue with loss of surface continuity and leakage of air and blood, causing pneumothorax, hemothorax, or both.

Damage to the Heart, Pericardium, and Aortic Arch

Injuries to the heart, pericardium, and aortic arch require massive amounts of blood replacement, so start blood type and cross-match immediately.

Myocardial contusion: The most common cause of myocardial contusion is injury by a steering wheel, caused by sudden deceleration in MVAs. A history of this injury found on assessment should evoke a high index of suspicion and continued close nursing observation. The injury may vary from simple contusion, with or without the electrocardiogram (ECG) signs of infarction, to rupture of the atria or complete ventricular rupture; ventricular ruptures are the most common heart laceration in blunt thoracic injuries to seat belt wearers. In unbelted victims, the right ventricular wall, owing to its proximity to the sternum, is the most injured site, being especially vulnerable to direct blows from the steering wheel. Direction of the impact does not appear to affect distribution of heart injuries, but the impacting object invariably does.

In a frontal crash, the steering wheel is the impacted object; in a lateral crash, the car interior is the impacted object. The overwhelming number of heart injuries occur when the victim's vehicle hits a larger, heavier one. (Although it is frequently debated whether seat belts contribute to injury in some cases rather than prevent it, seat belt use does eliminate ejection from the vehicle, a major cause of fatality).

The symptoms of myocardial contusion are retrosternal pain, anginal in character and refractory to nitroglycerin but frequently responsive to oxygen, tachycardia, conduction disturbances, and perhaps ECG alterations, depending on the location and extent of the trauma. Treatment requires following up with serial ECG and enzyme studies. Acute hemopericardium producing tamponade requires immediate aspiration of the pericardial sac.

Pericardial tamponade: Massive deceleration trauma, extensive lacerations, or large-caliber gunshot wounds (GSWs) to the heart, which are quickly fatal as a result of sudden and voluminous blood loss, can all cause pericardial tamponade. Small wounds, however, as from an ice pick or a small-caliber bullet, rarely cause immediate death but require emergency intervention.

Because the pericardium is inelastic, the patient may suddenly go into shock or die if the volume of blood trapped in the pericardial sac reaches 150 to 200 mL. The signs of cardiac tamponade, known as Beck's triad, include muffled heart sounds, distended neck veins, and a falling blood pressure (BP).

Appropriate nursing diagnoses in cardiac trauma would include:

- Actual fluid volume deficit
- Alteration in cardiopulmonary or peripheral tissue perfusion
- Decreased cardiac output related to decreased circulating volume
- Dysrhythmias
- Hypovolemic shock

Immediate aspiration of the pericardial sac as a mandatory first-aid measure is required. Aspiration of as little as 15 to 20 mL can save an apparently dying patient or at least buy time. The pericardial tap is done with a large-gauge (16 to 18), short-bevel 4-in. needle attached to a 50-mL syringe, with the needle inserted about 3 cm to the patient's left of the xiphoid process (Larrey's point) and aimed toward the left posterior shoulder. The usual depth of insertion should be about 4 cm (1.5 in.). The patient should be continually monitored by oscilloscope during the procedure with a V-lead attached to the needle hub with an alligator clip so that penetration of the myocardium or improvement in the cardiac function can be immediately ascertained. (Concerns over possible electrical hazard to the patient have made this technique somewhat controversial.) Bleeding is apt to recur, and the patient must be very closely observed for further deterioration, in which case thoracotomy for repair of the injury is immediately indicated. A three-way stopcock should be attached to the needle after aspiration of blood so that repeated aspirations can be done if signs of tamponade persist.

Ruptured aorta: Deceleration impact injury is too frequently a cause of ruptured aorta. The most common rupture site, in over half of all thoracic aortic tears, is distal to the left subclavian artery, the last point of attachment on the descending thoracic aorta. This injury accounts for nearly one sixth of early deaths from MVAs when associated injuries have detracted from early recognition and a chance at survival. An ascending aortic rupture frequently occurs in conjunction with cardiac rupture and may occur without skeletal fractures; deceleration and high pressure may be the sole mechanisms of this devastating injury.

Aortic injuries must be suspected and aggressively managed, since 80 to 90 percent of victims with thoracic injuries of the aorta will die within the first hour after trauma. The 10 to 20 percent of remaining victims develop a "pseudoaneurysm" which temporarily creates some stabilization. Early surgical intervention can salvage these patients.

The symptoms of aortic rupture are upper limb hypertension, absent or delayed femoral pulse, left hemothorax, and reduction in urine output. In full-thickness tears of the aorta, death from exsanguination will result immediately; if the tear is partial, the patient may survive for a period of time, allowing surgical intervention.

■ SUMMARY OF NURSING MANAGEMENT GUIDELINES IN CHEST TRAUMA

Chest trauma should be managed according to the following guidelines:

1. A well-cleared airway is always essential in chest trauma. Use suction, an oropharyngeal airway, intubation, or as a last resort, cricothyroidotomy or tracheostomy. Again, always listen to the apices of both lungs following intubation to be certain the tube has not slipped into the right mainstem bronchus, causing nonexpansion or collapse of the left lung, and confirm with an end-tidal carbon dioxide detector.
2. Draw an ABG sample before oxygen administration, if possible, for a baseline.
3. Oxygen should be given in carefully metered doses to meet the specific need of the patient. It should be heated to body temperature and fully humidified to 100 percent relative humidity at 37°C (98.6°F).
4. Start at least one large-bore intravenous line with Ringer's lactate.
5. Apply ECG monitor leads.
6. Anyone with a chest injury will have some degree of respiratory distress. With labored respiration, the accessory muscles

are used, opening up the inferior constrictors and thus opening up the esophagus and creating a high negative pressure that allows air to be sucked down into the stomach. This almost invariably causes acute gastric dilation, and passage of a NG tube is important at the outset to prevent this. *Remember that all tubes and catheters inserted in the patient must be clearly radiopaque.*

7. Careful monitoring of intake and output is essential.
8. Anticipate the need for a volume ventilator in the following situations:
   A PCO_2 greater than 60 mm Hg
   A PAO_2 less than 60 mm Hg on an oxygen mask
   Flail chest with associated injuries
   CNS depression
   Generalized peritonitis (especially subdiaphragmatic
   Previous severe pulmonary disease
   Severe prolonged shock
   Severe smoke inhalation
9. Know the equipment, including the thoracotomy tray, chest tube setup, and water seal chest drainage equipment available. The Pleur-E-vac (Deknatel), Thoraklex (Davol), Aqua-Seal (Argyle), and Water-Seal Chest Drain (Atrium Medical), *disposable* units are used in hospitals in place of the older three-bottle setup (see Fig. 14–7). A four-bottle system manufactured by the Sherwood Laboratories is also used in some hospitals.

■ REFERENCES

1. Laskowski-Jones L. Meeting the challenge of chest trauma. *AJN*. September 1993;23–30.
2. Roberts R, Lange DA, Robin AP, Barrett J. Chest trauma: emergency diagnosis and management of airway problems and intrathoracic injuries. *Top Emerg Med*. 1987;9:53–70.
3. American College of Surgeons Committee on Trauma. *Advanced Trauma Life Support (ATLS) Manual*. Chicago, Ill: ACS; 1988.
4. Cardona VD, ed. Trauma injuries. In: *Trauma Reference Manual, MIEMSS*. Bowie, Md: Brady Company; 1985:40–45.

5. Webb R. *A Protocol for Managing the Pulmonary Complications: No. of Patients in Shock.* Kalamazoo, Mich: Upjohn; 1975.
6. Smelcer MG. Respiratory emergencies. In: Emergency Nurses Association. *Emergency Nursing Core Curriculum.* 4th ed. Philadelphia, Pa: WB Saunders; 1994:500–515.
7. Grant H, Murray R. *Emergency Care.* 2nd ed. Bowie, Md: Brady Company; 1978.

■ BIBLIOGRAPHY

American College of Surgeons Committee on Trauma. Advanced Trauma Life Support program. Chicago, Ill: ACS; 1993.

Barber J. *Critical Care Pharmacology: Sedatives, Analgesics, and Ventilatory Adjuncts.* Lewisville, Tex: Janet Barber and Barbara Clark Mims Associates; 1994.

Bartlett R. Myocardial contusion: using the index of suspicion for assessing blunt chest trauma. *Dim Crit Care Nurs.* 1991;10:133–139.

Bates B, ed. *A Guide to Physical Assessment.* 5th ed. Philadelphia, Pa: JB Lippincott; 1991.

Baumann M, Sahn SA. Tension pneumothorax: diagnostic and therapeutic pitfalls. *Crit Care Med.* 1993;21:177–178.

Bayley EW, Turcke SA. *A Comprehensive Curriculum for Trauma Nursing.* Boston, Ma: Jones and Bartlett; 1992.

Cardona VD, Hurn PD, Bastnagel Mason PJ, et al. *Trauma Nursing: From Resuscitation Through Rehabilitation.* 2nd ed. Philadelphia, Pa: WB Saunders; 1994.

Champion HR, Sacco WJ, Carnazzo AJ, et al. A revision of the trauma score. *J Trauma.* 1989;29:623–629.

Connolly JP. Hemodynamic measurements during a tension pneumothorax. *Crit Care Med.* 1993;21:294–298.

Emergency Nurses Association. *Emergency Nursing Core Curriculum.* 4th ed. Philadelphia, Pa: WB Saunders; 1994.

Emergency Nurses Association. *Trauma Nursing Core Course.* 4th ed. Chicago, Ill: ENA; 1995.

Fackler M. Wound ballistics: a review of common misconceptions. *JAMA.* 1988;259:2730–2736.

Fackler M, Bellamy R, Malinowski J. The wound profile: illustration of the missile-tissue interaction. *J Trauma.* 1988;28(suppl):S21–S29.

Fincke MK, Lanros NE, eds. *Emergency Nursing: A Comprehensive Review.* Rockville, Md: Aspen Publishers; 1986.

Hoyt DB, Shackford SR, McGill T, et al. The impact of in-house surgeons and operating room resuscitation on outcome of traumatic injuries. *Arch Surg.* 1989;124:906–910.

Jacobs LM, Hsieh JW. A clinical review of autotransfusion and its role in trauma. *JAMA.* 1984;251:3282–3287.

Kidd PS, Wagner KD. *High Acuity Nursing.* 2nd ed. Stamford, Conn: Appleton & Lange; 1996.

Lance E, Sweetwood H. Chest trauma when minutes count. *Nursing 78.* Jan. 1978;28–33.

Lee G. *Flight Nursing: Principles and Practice.* St. Louis, Mo: Mosby-Year Book; 1991.

Maull KI, Rodriguez A, Wiles CE. *Complications in Trauma and Critical Care.* Philadelphia, Pa: WB Saunders; 1996.

Murdock MA, Roberson ML. Reported use of autotransfusion systems in initial resuscitation areas by one hundred thirty-six United States hospitals. *J Emerg Nurs.* 1993;19:486–490.

Naclerio EA. Chest trauma. *Clin Symp.* 1970;22:86–109.

Naclerio EA. *Wounds of the Heart and Great Vessels in Thoracic Injuries.* New York, NY: Grune & Stratton; 1971.

Nursing 96 Drug Handbook. Springhouse, Pa: Springhouse Corporation; 1996.

Phippen ML, Wells MP. *Perioperative Nursing Practice.* Philadelphia, Pa: WB Saunders; 1994.

Pons PT, Honigman B, Moore EE, et al. Prehospital advanced trauma life support for critical penetrating wounds to the thorax and abdomen. *J Trauma.* 1985;25:828–832.

Ramponi DR, Somerville P. Chest trauma. In: Fincke MK, Lanros NE, eds. *Emergency Nursing: A Comprehensive Review.* Rockville, Md: Aspen Publishers; 1986.

Roberts R, Lange DA, Robin AP, Barrett J. Chest trauma: emergency diagnosis and management of airway problems and intrathoracic injuries. *Top Emerg Med.* 1987;9:53–70.

Ruth-Sahd L. Pulmonary contusion: the hidden danger in blunt chest trauma. *Clin Issues Crit Care Nurs.* 1991;11:46–57.

Smith RN, Fallentione J, Kessel S. Underwater chest drainage: bringing the facts to the surface. *Nursing 95.* Feb. 1995;60–63.

Webb R. *A Protocol for Managing the Pulmonary Complications of Patients in Shock.* Kalamazoo, Mich: Upjohn; 1975.

White KM, DiMaio VJM. Gunshot wounds: medicolegal responsibilities of the ED nurse. *J Emerg Nurs.* 1979;5:29–35.

Wilkins RL, Dexter JR. *Respiratory Disease: Principles of Patient Care.* Philadelphia, Pa: FA Davis; 1993.

■ **REVIEW: CHEST TRAUMA**

1. Categorize the types of chest trauma and describe the priorities of management.

2. Describe the points of immediate nursing actions necessary to ensure optimum outcomes for victims of chest trauma.

3. Identify one of the most common causes of severe respiratory distress and death following vehicular trauma.

4. List at least four red flags related to vehicular trauma that should alert the emergency nurse (EN) to the potential for significant chest trauma.

5. Describe the steps of a systematic initial assessment of pulmonary efficiency following chest trauma.

6. Define and give examples of penetrating injuries of the chest wall and blunt or nonpenetrating injuries to the chest wall.

7. Define and describe the implications of an open pneumothorax.

8. Explain the mechanism by which an open pneumothorax can convert to a tension pneumothorax and describe the simple intervention that can be effected.

9. Describe the effect of a mediastinal shift and explain the importance of rapid recognition and intervention.

10. Outline six nursing diagnoses appropriate to penetrating chest trauma.

11. Describe placement of a chest tube for emergency management of hemothorax.

12. Describe placement of a tube or large-bore needle for decompression or evacuation of a pneumothorax.

13. Describe the lung pathology that can develop following blunt chest trauma.

14. Identify at least six states of comorbidity that may be seen as a result of blunt chest trauma.

15. Identify the implications of fractures occurring in the first five ribs.

16. Define flail chest and outline the important nursing interventions.

17. List the signs of a developing problem when there has been lung trauma and probable pulmonary contusions.

18. Describe the mechanisms involved in pericardial tamponade and define *Beck's triad*.

19. List four nursing diagnoses appropriate to cardiac trauma.

20. List at least eight nursing management guidelines for caring for the patient with severe chest trauma.

Abdominal and Genitourinary Trauma

15

The mechanics of blunt and penetrating injuries of the abdomen and genitourinary organs are relatively straightforward and are considered in this chapter together with their assessment and nursing interventions. Blunt injuries are created by high- or low-energy deceleration trauma; gunshot wounds (GSWs) and stab wounds represent the typical penetrating injury. In blunt abdominal trauma (BAT), solid-organ injury is created by the deceleration and compression forces that fracture the capsule and parenchyma of noncompressible organs, such as the liver, spleen, and kidneys. Hollow organs, which occupy the most space in the abdomen and pelvis, are often victims of penetrating abdominal trauma (PAT).

■ ABDOMINAL TRAUMA

The initial overall evaluation of abdominal trauma depends upon, among other things, the examiner's knowledge of abdominal anatomy and topography and of the organ systems and their specific characteristics.

TOPOGRAPHY

The human torso is a single anatomic unit composed of thoracic and abdominal and pelvic viscera arbitrarily separated by the diaphragm. During expiration, the diaphragm may ascend as high as the fourth intercostal space (at the nipple line), causing the upper abdominal organs to be vulnerable to lower chest injuries; penetrating injuries between the nipple and lower costal margin, therefore, may be either thoracic or abdominal in nature, depending on whether the victim was inhaling or exhaling at time of injury.

While terms *epigastrium, suprapubic area,* and *flank area* are sometimes useful as descriptors, the abdomen is divided for clinical purposes into four quadrants by an imaginary longitudinal and a vertical line through the umbilicus. The patient's right upper quadrant (RUQ), left upper quadrant (LUQ), left lower quadrant (LLQ), and right lower quadrant (RLQ), and the solid organs lying within the rib cage should be visualized in the mind's eye (Figs. 15–1 and 15–2) and are described below.

- The RUQ contains the hepatic flexure of the colon, the pylorus, duodenum, head of the pancreas, a portion of the right kidney, portions of the ascending and transverse colon, the gallbladder, and the lower edge of the liver. The bulk of the normal liver lies with the right rib cage, topped by the diaphragm.
- The LUQ contains the stomach, left lobe of the liver, spleen, body of the pancreas, a portion of the left kidney, portions of the transverse and descending colon, and the splenic flexure of the colon. These organs are normally not felt; nor is the normal spleen, which lies within the left rib cage, topped by the diaphragm.
- The LLQ contains the sigmoid of the descending colon (often felt when filled with stool), the left salpinx and ovary in females, the left spermatic cord in males, the female uterus if enlarged, the lower pole of the left kidney, the left ureter, and the bladder if distended.

211

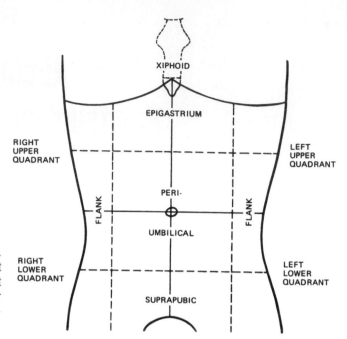

Figure 15–1. Topographical anatomy of the abdomen. The abdomen may be divided into quadrants (i.e., right upper quadrant [RUQ], left upper quadrant [LUQ], right lower quadrant [RLQ], and left lower quadrant [LLQ], or specified areas (i.e., epigastrium, flanks, and suprapubic regions. (*Adapted from Buckingham, et al.[6]*).

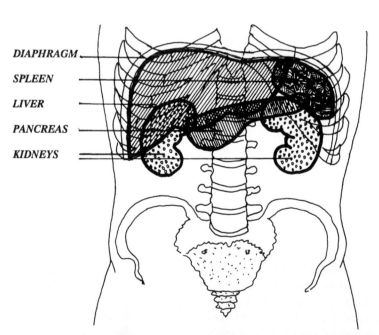

Figure 15–2. The solid abdominal organs, housed to a great extent within the protection of the rib cage (*adapted from Grant and Murray[7]*).

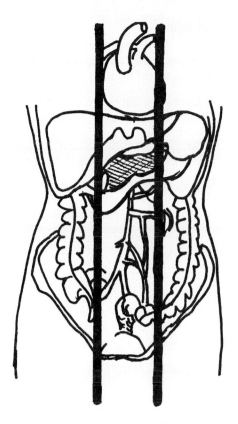

Figure 15–3. Vertical zones of the abdomen.

and the lower half, the ureter. The existence of ecchymosis in the flanks signals a profound retroperitoneal bleed, which may originate from a torn aorta or other major vessel. Absence of one or both femoral pulses, even in the shock state, may be a valuable clue as to which artery is damaged.

If one were to divide the chest and abdominal cavities into three vertical zones, the midzone would be associated with the highest mortality, since it contains the heart and great vessels (see Fig. 15–3). Using a transverse division of the torso into thirds (Fig. 15–4), it can be said that the lower zones usually require operative intervention, while the uppermost one can often be managed nonoperatively. These conceptual divisions are helpful in making rough determinations about potential for major complications. Of course, the major vulnerabilities in the lower thorax and abdomen involve the presence of (1) capsular organs, which hemorrhage profusely; (2) great vessels, which can create exsanguination; and (3) hollow organs, which, if penetrated, can introduce life-threatening organisms and toxins into the surrounding cavity.

- The RLQ contains the cecum, appendix, a portion of the ascending colon, the right salpinx and ovary in females, the right spermatic cord in males, the female uterus if enlarged, the lower pole of the right kidney, the right ureter, and the bladder if distended.
- The epigastrium lies below the xiphoid, two thirds of the way to the umbilicus, midline in the upper abdomen, and contains the duodenum, transverse colon, pylorus of the stomach, and descending abdominal aorta. Except for the aorta, these organs are not detectable in the normal person.
- The suprapubic region normally contains intestine but may contain an enlarged bladder, ovary, or uterus.
- The flanks are the lateral portions of the abdomen. The upper half contains the kidney,

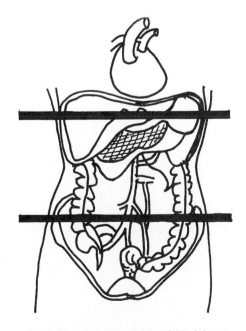

Figure 15–4. Transverse zones of the abdomen.

MECHANISMS OF INJURY IN BLUNT ABDOMINAL TRAUMA

Falls from heights, blast injuries, and domestic violence (often unreported), among other things, result in blunt trauma (Fig. 15–5), but the major cause today of blunt trauma in our society is motor vehicle accidents (MVAs). As discussed in Chapter 12, injury occurs as the result of three collisions: (1) the vehicle collides with an object, (2) the victim collides with the inside of the vehicle, and then (3) the victim's organs collide with the inside of the body cavity in which they reside.

Forces of Injury

Compression, deceleration, and shear forces are the result of accidents, causing blunt injury to organs and structures of the body as follows:

- Compressive forces are crushing in nature and disrupt the parenchyma of the organ involved; injury occurs to organs that are highly vascular and relatively incompressible (e.g., the liver, spleen, and pancreas).
- Forces of deceleration, typically resulting from high-speed impact, injure organs by causing tearing. For example, when the

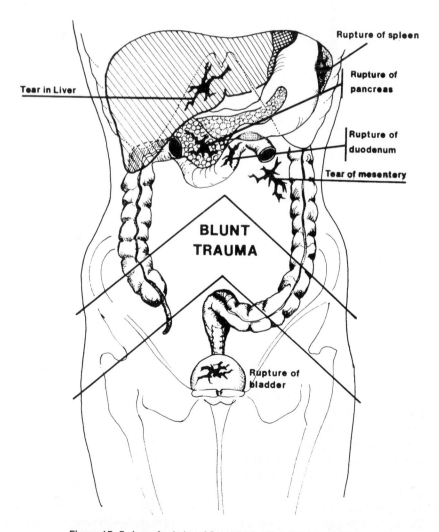

Figure 15–5. Areas for *Index of Suspicion* in blunt abdominal trauma.

blood-filled aorta continues to travel after the victim's body has decelerated against the inside of the vehicle, it tears at fixed points of attachment (e.g., aortic root, left subclavian artery).

- Shear forces are those that oppose each other on a given plane; an example of the effects of these forces is extensive degloving of the scrotum or an extremity.

Victims of blunt trauma present assessment difficulties, especially when other more visible injuries are associated. Head, chest, maxillofacial, and musculoskeletal injuries tend to overshadow the less obvious and frequently occult signs of blunt trauma; a high index of suspicion must be maintained, for instance, with lower rib fractures and potential seat belt injuries or bruises anywhere on the abdomen or flank.

Restraint Syndromes

While the increased use of auto seat belts in recent years has reduced MVA mortality rates by decreasing the numbers of accident victims being thrown from their vehicles, another constellation of injuries is commonly seen with use of improperly placed lap belts. On rapid deceleration, the body jackknifes over a high-riding secured lap belt and adjacent organs sustain the forces of impact, most commonly the hollow viscus organs (full bladders are prime candidates), great vessels, solid organs of the abdomen, and the lumbar spine. Severe compression and shearing forces are transferred to these adjacent organs and significant damage is sustained. Occult injury must *always* be suspected until ruled out when rapid deceleration and lap belts are involved in trauma. Too often, injuries go unrecognized until life-threatening consequences, such as hemorrhage or sepsis, manifest.

Three-point restraints have been mandatory for front-seat and passenger positions since 1968 and remain the most effective design for reducing both the frequency and severity of injuries sustained by occupants in a MVA.[1] Injuries to the neck, chest, and abdomen are frequently sustained on rapid deceleration as those areas collide with the cross-torso shoulder strap, and when the shoulder strap alone is employed, the body may slide under as it travels forward, resulting in cervical

spine injury, tracheal fractures, vascular injury, and partial if not complete decapitation.

MECHANISMS OF INJURY IN PENETRATING ABDOMINAL TRAUMA

Assessment and intervention after penetrating injury is considered more straightforward than after blunt injury; entry and exit wounds often afford important answers to trajectory and path of damage sustained. As discussed in Chapter 12, traumatized tissue follows the rather predictable course of the penetrating object as it tears, rips, cuts, shreds, or forces organs and/or tissues out of its path. Patterns of injury will vary with high- and low-velocity penetration.

Because of their size and anterior location, the liver, small bowel, colon, and stomach are most commonly injured in PAT; damage to the great vessels carries rapid deterioration and high mortality rates. Violence committed against victims by others with sharp instruments and high-velocity missiles, farm and industrial accidents, and propeller trauma among fishermen and boaters all account for much of the PAT seen.

Stab and Missile Wounds

Stab wounds are caused by low-velocity penetration of an organ or viscera by the wounding agent. Immediate and long-term consequences are related to the organ injured, spillage of enteric contents, laceration of vasculature, or foreign bodies retained in the wound tract or injured tissue. In general, the wounding potential of a knife is more predictable and lesser in magnitude than that of a missile because of the defined wound tract and the lower kinetic energy.[2]

Missile wounds carry a greater potential for significant injury because of their higher velocity, the amount of kinetic energy imparted to the tissues, and the motion characteristics as the missile travels through tissue and bone, destroying structures in its path. Entry and exit wounds provide some information but do not reveal damage between the two points, making surgical exploration mandatory in all cases.

Penetration of the Diaphragm

The arbitrary boundaries of the diaphragm make it an important landmark in assessing penetrating wounds, determining whether the injury is thoracic or abdominal. Stab wounds inflicting injury on the diaphragm may be sustained over a wide area, extending from the nipple line to the costal margins; stabs to the flanks or lateral chest wall may involve the diaphragm, creating perforations. A simple thoracostomy tube will not reduce such injuries, so patients who do not improve after this procedure should be suspect for diaphragmatic penetration.

By contrast, diaphragmatic injury from blunt trauma is not as easy to detect, since there may be few obvious clues. Even a ruptured diaphragm may be associated with only abrasion from a seat belt. A chest film is often the tool that helps emergency personnel find this serious injury, one of the most difficult to diagnose in trauma management. It should be noted, however, that the film may not highlight some penetrating injuries; about 50 percent of the time, even in the presence of perforation of the diaphragm, the film may be read as "within normal limits." The path of the knife or missile must be explored since it is more likely to suggest injury to the diaphragm.

When ordering films during the secondary survey period, emergency nurses (ENs) should be aware that some hemidiaphramatic injuries will require both an inspiratory and expiratory view to demonstrate their extent and severity.

If a nasogastric (NG) tube is ordered with a diaphragmatic injury, it may be difficult to introduce because the esophagogastric junction may be distorted from gastric herniation. Force, of course, should not be employed, and only low suction should be used. If the stomach cannot be entered, swallowed air will be evacuated from the distal esophagus. If there is respiratory embarrassment, endotracheal (ET) intubation is imperative. Bag or mask ventilation will create gastric and intestinal distension and compromise cardiopulmonary efficiency.

Peritoneal Penetration

Local exploration of stab wounds is a well-established means of determining whether the peritoneum has been penetrated. If the end of the tract cannot be visualized, mandatory exploratory laparotomy is usually indicated, although some centers perform diagnostic peritoneal lavage (DPL) first to determine the need for surgery. Stab wounds are usually left open to heal by granulation if the end of the wound tract can be visualized and the patient is hemodynamically stable.

Criteria for Surgical Exploration

In PAT, then, both the inability to fully visualize the end of a stab wound tract and abdominal penetration by GSW mandate exploratory laparotomy. Additionally, knife impalement, hypotension, peritoneal signs, free air in the abdomen, evisceration, gross blood in the NG tube, hematuria, and blood in the rectum all dictate mandatory exploration. Rapid preparation for surgery must be made, with consents signed, blood typed and cross-matched, and diagnostic reports (e.g., laboratory results, imaging reports) made available.

EXAMINING THE ABDOMEN

Inspection, Auscultation, Palpation

The abdomen should be examined by visual inspection, auscultation, and palpation.

Visual inspection, done from the patient's right side, requires careful observation both from above and from the side with the light falling obliquely across the abdomen, so that minor changes in elevation will produce shadows and be more readily observed. Abdominal scars should be noted because the presence of scars may yield considerable useful information about the patient's medical history, as well as indicate a potential for old adhesions.

Auscultation for bowel sounds should be carried out before palpating, since palpating increases bowel sounds.

Palpation is considered the most important step in the examination of the abdomen, and although this is traditionally the area of the physician, the EN—by observation, trial, and practice—can develop skills in the techniques of light, moderate, and deep bimanual palpation. Enlarged solid organs and distended hollow organs, as well as associated tenderness, may all be detected by this technique.

Descriptive Terms Used

Some terms commonly used to describe reactions elicited by palpation are described here so that accurate documentation can be made of findings:

- *Guarding:* Voluntary or involuntary tension (reflex contraction) of the abdominal muscles over an area of tenderness.
- *Rigidity:* An extreme form of guarding, with the entire abdominal musculature

tense and stiff. The term *boardlike rigidity* is sometimes used to indicate extreme stiffness of the abdominal muscles, and a silent abdomen (with loss of bowel sounds as a result of a paralytic ileus) will often accompany this degree of rigidity.

- *Rebound tenderness:* Indicates irritability of the parietal peritoneum, generally produced by peritonitis or irritation of the peritoneum adjacent to an inflamed organ.
- *Referred or reflected pain:* Pain present in an area separate from the site of examination. This may have definite localizing value.

Nursing Assessment and Intervention

Nursing assessment and intervention for PAT is as follows:

1. Observe and note:
   Breathing pattern
   Degree of distension
   Penetrating or blunt injury; logroll the patient and examine the back
   Bruises and scars
   Hematuria (full bladder on impact)
   X-ray bindings.
2. Palpate for guarding, rigidity, rebound tenderness, and referred pain.
3. Listen—auscultate bowel sounds. This is the best screening for abdominal injury. If the bowel is silent, be suspicious.
4. Perform/assist with:
   Rectal examination for frank blood or flaccid sphincter
   Pelvic examination if indicated in a female patient
   Special examinations and procedures (abdominal paracentesis, peritoneal lavage, and stab wound injection).
5. Observe—abdominal trauma victims should be observed carefully with a high index of suspicion for occult damage and bleeding. The early administration of fluids after trauma may dictate survival.

As indicated before, blunt abdominal injuries pose the major problems in the emergency department (ED), and they must always be suspected in every multisystem injury. The prime examples are a ruptured spleen or other ruptured viscus. Perforating injuries to the abdomen or any obvious opening in the abdominal wall should be covered with sterile gauze soaked with normal saline solution; bowel protruding through such a wound should not be replaced.

CLINICAL FINDINGS WITH SPECIFIC INJURIES

Solid Organs

Hepatic injury: With advent of improved diagnostic computed tomography (CT) scanning, it has been recognized that the liver is more frequently injured in abdominal trauma than the spleen, a confirmation of previous thought. Liver injuries are more likely to occur in PAT (30 percent) than in BAT (20 percent); despite improved resuscitative approaches, the overall mortality is still quite high (10 percent). PAT has a mortality rate of 5 percent, and BAT, particularly complex injury, has a mortality rate of 25 percent.[3]

The clinical features of injury to the liver are localized pain in the RUQ with radiation to the shoulder, absence of bowel sounds, and shock. Fifty percent of these patients will exhibit signs of hypotension and 70 percent will have associated injuries. Since the liver is a solid, fixed organ, lacerations of the liver are quite common in deceleration injuries.

Splenic injury: The spleen is probably the most frequently injured organ in BAT; injury to the spleen is often associated with fractures of the lower left rib cage. The degree of splenic disruption depends on patient age, preexisting disease, and mechanism of injury. With severe deceleration, the spleen can be totally avulsed from the retroperitoneal and hilar vessels; rib fractures resulting from blunt compression can penetrate the parenchyma of the spleen. Prompt splenectomy in all cases has been replaced by efforts for splenic salvage when feasible.[4]

Manifestations of splenic injury include signs of blood loss, abdominal pain localized to the LUQ, and pain radiating to the left scapula or shoulder when the patient is lying flat (Kehr's sign).

Pancreatic injury: Pancreatic injury is usually the result of severe upper abdominal trauma and is often associated with trauma to other organs such as the stomach, duodenum, and liver. Occasionally, injury to the pancreas may be accompanied by damage to the major blood vessels, including the portal vein and the vena cava. Damage to the pancreas is manifested by abdominal tenderness, an elevated white blood cell (WBC) count, and elevated serum amylase, with the diagnosis strongly supported by a history of an impaling force.

Hollow Organs

Gastric and intestinal injuries: Both penetrating and blunt forces contribute to gastric and intestinal injuries. Stomach and intestinal rupture from BAT is rare, but direct blows to the abdomen can cause lacerations, shearing force injuries, and even bursting under certain circumstances. Full-thickness injury to any portion of the stomach or gut results in bacterial contamination of the peritoneal cavity and introduces the risk of subsequent septic complications. A bloody gastric aspirate, signs and/or symptoms of chemical peritonitis (i.e., severe epigastric pain), and developing shock and sepsis are indicative of serious gastrointestinal (GI) trauma. The history of the accident will provide valuable insight into the potential for such injuries.

Duodenal injuries: Pancreatic and duodenal injuries are rare, owing to the protected location of these structures deep within the abdomen. Only heavy penetrating trauma or massive forces are likely to injure these structures. Since these injuries are seen in the patient with serious, multiple trauma, they carry a high morbidity and mortality. The indication for suspecting duodenal *and* pancreatic injuries is a history of massive upper abdominal trauma with hemorrhage and peritonitis.

DIAGNOSTIC AND RESUSCITATIVE PROCEDURES

Diagnostic Peritoneal Lavage

DPL is used extensively in trauma management because it is considered more diagnostically reliable than physical examination in both BAT and PAT. The technique employed is similar to that of inserting a peritoneal dialysis tube with multiple holes. The lavage takes 20 to 25 minutes at best and carries a 96 percent chance of indicating significant injury if the results are positive. The procedure is indicated with altered consciousness, central nervous system (CNS) injuries, spinal-cord injury, shock, and multiple trauma. It is *contraindicated* with obvious penetration of the abdomen, adhesions, dilated bowel, pregnancy beyond the second trimester, and massive abdominal distension.

The generally accepted procedure for peritoneal lavage is as follows:

1. After it is certain that the patient's bladder has been emptied, the abdomen should be prepared, draped, and anesthetized in the low midline, one third of the distance from the umbilicus to the pubic symphysis, using 1 percent lidocaine with epinephrine (to minimize bleeding and subsequent blood contamination from skin and subcutaneous tissues).

2. The skin and subcutaneous tissues are then incised vertically to the fascia; the fascia and peritoneum are incised and a peritoneal dialysis catheter is inserted and advanced, directed toward the left or right pelvis. If the aspirant reveals no gross blood, Ringer's lactate, 10 mL/kg body weight, is instilled into the peritoneum.

3. Gentle agitation of the abdomen distributes the fluid throughout the cavity and increases the mixing with blood, if present; the infused fluid should be allowed to remain 5 to 10 minutes before attempting to obtain return flow. Some proponents advise lowering the bottle and waiting for the return flow, whereas others advocate disconnecting the tubing and allowing the return flow to follow capillary action. An obviously bloody return will, of course, dictate the need for abdominal exploration, but in any case, the color of the return is significant. As little as 75 or 100 mL blood within the peritoneal cavity will tint the fluid to a salmon or straw color, which would be interpreted as a weakly positive result. Gross blood (if you cannot read newsprint through the tubing) is strongly positive, but regardless of the findings visually, the fluid should be examined for WBCs, bacteria, bile, and fecal content. An elevated fluid amylase suggests possible pancreatic injury (although the pancreas is retroperitoneal) or perforation of the duodenum or the upper small bowel.

Occult Blood Losses

Estimating blood loss is important in patient assessment. Most of the time, the losses are underestimated. The normal blood volume in the average adult is about 6000 mL (12 units), and the body can safely compensate for up to a 10 percent blood loss (600 mL) without progressing into a shock state. The body can lose the first pint without any change at all in the pulse rate or blood pressure (BP). In trauma, however, a pulse rate of 120 bpm is by definition a 2-pint loss, and if BP is also falling, it represents a 3-pint deficit.[5]

Severe fractures of the pelvis can result in occult blood losses of up to 3000 mL (6 units), which will migrate into the retroperitoneal area as well as throughout the pelvic areas. Another site of severe blood loss to remember in the multiply traumatized victim is femur fracture, which can result in occult blood loss of as much as 2000 mL (4 units) or a fracture of the tibia, with a loss of 1000 mL (2 units). Concomitant orthopedic trauma can significantly potentiate hemodynamic instability.

Volume Replacement

In trauma, blood should be drawn immediately for type and cross-match. In the interim, crystalloid fluids must be administered to restore circulating volume as indicated. For initial replacement, the general choice of fluid in trauma resuscitation is Ringer's lactate, because it closely mimics the extracellular fluid. The lactate is metabolized into carbon dioxide and water, providing 80 to 100 mL free water, thereby providing water in addition to the resuscitation fluid.

OTHER ASSOCIATED PROBLEMS

Fat Embolus

Fat embolus is seen in crush injuries and long-bone fractures, but the mechanism is obscure because symptoms have not been reproduced by the intentional injection of fat globules into the bloodstream. It is believed, however, that the incidence is probably reduced by early fixation of fractures to prevent manipulation. Stabilization of long-bone fractures will also minimize blood loss tremendously by allowing the fascia lata (muscle sheath) to tense and create a tamponade effect around the bone and bleeding points in the femur and hip. Again, remember that the upper thigh (cylindrical form) can accommodate 1 to 2 L blood with resulting shock. Fat embolus can lead to interstitial pneumonitis and is a more frequently rec-

ognized threat to the victim of multiple trauma than it was formerly, although it generally occurs 24 to 72 hours after trauma. Symptoms of fat embolism include sudden onset of cyanosis, disorientation, delirium, and other signs of hypoxia. High-flow oxygen should be started immediately.

Crush Injuries

Crush injuries with massive tissue damage causing fat embolus, disseminated intravascular coagulation (DIC), and destruction of tissue with the release of potassium into the bloodstream, can cause extreme problems. This type of trauma is frequently seen with MVAs, industrial accidents, beatings, and any trauma resulting in massive cellular damage, although probably fewer than 20 percent of abdominal crush injuries will produce marks on the skin, making recognition difficult. Decrease in the intracellular potassium with a rise in the serum potassium level can cause irreversible kidney injury, and the serum potassium level will continue to rise if kidney function is inadequate.

Treatment involves initial resuscitation, management of shock, and exploration for abdominal injuries. The EN should monitor carefully for signs of impending hypovolemic shock, pain, signs of peritonitis, fever, guarding, abdominal distension, and rebound tenderness (measure the abdominal girth and record with vital signs [VS]). Diagnosis is confirmed by x-ray films for air in the peritoneum and by signs of pancreatic or splenic injury. Hematuria requires an intravenous pyelogram (IVP) and kidney, ureters, and bladder (KUB) x-rays. Kidney rupture is a frequent occurrence with a ruptured renal artery and tamponade or rupture of the capsule.

Disseminated Intravascular Coagulation

DIC (also known as consumption coagulopathy or defibrination syndrome) is an intermediary mechanism of disease following shock, trauma with anaerobic metabolism, burns, septicemia, snake bite, metastatic carcinoma, malaria, heat stroke, obstetric trauma, and intravascular hemolysis. Although DIC is rarely seen as a primary presentation in the ED, ENs should be familiar with its manifestations because it becomes rapidly fatal unless early intervention is undertaken.

The mechanism is that of normal clotting starting in an abnormal manner in small vascular areas; there is a rapid fibrin formation, and then the liver lags in fibrinogen production to maintain the clot mechanism. Paradoxical bleeding and clotting occur simultaneously, plasmin is activated, and the consumptive clotting factors are used up.

Diagnosis is made following severe trauma from an unexplained drop in BP, followed by petechiae, ecchymosis, bleeding from at least three points at once (hemoptysis, epistaxis, hematuria, GI bleeding), local ooze at an injection site, and coma. Laboratory reports will show the platelets and prothrombin time (PT) down, partial thromboplastin time (PTT) increased, fibrinogen levels down, and a hemolytic anemia present, with erythrocytes fragmented on a smear. Treatment involves early intervention with anticipation of rapid shock, oxygen administration, maintenance of BP, vigorous treatment of infection or bleeding, and administration of heparin (2500 to 5000 units subcutaneously every 8 to 12 hours). This relieves the consumable factors and stops thrombin formation, breaking the paradoxical cycle. Administration of fresh blood components may also be indicated.

DIAGNOSTIC IMAGING

Plain Radiographic Films

Indicated in hemodynamically stable patients only, abdominal plain films include a supine and upright and a posteroanterior (PA) upright chest view. If upright films cannot be obtained, a left lateral decubitus view should be substituted. Plain films can identify vertebral, rib, and pelvic fractures; free air in the peritoneum; hemoperitoneum with opacification in the paracolic gutters; and hepatic and splenic trauma.

Contrast Studies

Upper GI series in hemodynamically stable patients are done for suspected gastric, duodenal, and rectal perforations, as well as for obstructions such as duodenal intramural hematomas when perforation has been ruled out.

Aortography

With suspected aortic or mesenteric vascular injury in the rare stable patient, aortography is employed to locate the lesion.

Nuclear Scans

When diagnosis of the liver or spleen is equivocal, the liver-spleen scan is helpful in detecting parenchymal defects, capsular irregularities, and enlargements.

Computed Tomography Scans

CT of the abdomen has an advantage over DPL in being noninvasive and allowing direct visualization of both solid and hollow abdominal viscera. Injuries to the retroperitoneal structures may also be identified. While CT is an extremely useful adjunct, it must be reserved for hemodynamically stable patients who can be transported to the scanner unit, since CT scanners are not found in every trauma resuscitation room.

Ultrasound

Ultrasound has value in assessment of traumatic abdominal aortic aneurysms, determination of fetal viability and age in pregnancy trauma, and detection of abnormalities in size and parenchyma of solid viscera. It is not routinely employed in trauma otherwise.

Laparoscopy

While laparoscopy can define the location and magnitude of intra-abdominal injuries in stable patients, it has several contraindications, is expensive, requires special expertise, and has some severe risks associated with its use in traumatized patients.

LABORATORY DATA

Hematology

Hematocrit (Hct), or packed cell volume (PCV), is an indicator of hemodynamic status. A rule of thumb is that the normal Hct-to-hemoglobin value falls into a ratio of 3:1; for example, if the hemoglobin (Hgb) is 14, the hematocrit should be close to 42.

A decrease in Hct indicates dilution in the red blood cell (RBC) mass. Plasma refill rate in humans is proportional to the degree of hemorrhagic shock. A 10 to 20 percent loss results in the movement of 40 to 90 mL/h fluid from the interstitial space into the intravascular space; 30 to 40 hours are needed for completion of this process. Patients with blood loss of 40 percent or more have refill rates as high as 1500 mL in the first 90 minutes following injury;

therefore, even without exogenous crystalloid transfusions, significant dilution with decreases in Hct can occur over a short period of time.

An increase in Hct, with greater concentration of RBCs, may indicate significant third-spacing of fluids (interstitial space) if there is no hemorrhage present.

An increase in the WBC count to 20,000/mm³ with a moderate left shift occurs frequently within several hours of injury and persists for several days, owing to the tissue damage, acute hemorrhage, and peritoneal irritation.

Electrolytes

Decreased potassium levels (hypokalemia) will result from persistent vomiting secondary to peritonitis or rapid crystalloid replacement without additional potassium. Blood urea nitrogen (BUN) will increase with significant third-spacing of fluids and an intravascular volume loss. Bicarbonate will be decreased, owing to hypotension, leading to inadequate tissue perfusion and lactate production (e.g., metabolic acidosis).

Blood Chemistry

Increased amylase may or may not be an indication of severe pancreatic damage. Blunt pancreatic trauma is known to elevate the amylase, although amylase may remain normal in the presence of injury. Various toxins such as alcohol and narcotics, hypotension creating pancreatic ischemia, a variety of other diseases, and trauma to the salivary glands, can account for increased amylase, so in trauma it is the *trend* of persistently elevated or rising values that warrants surgical investigation.

Urinalysis

While hematuria is a finding in genitourinary (GU) trauma, it may well be associated with abdominal trauma as well. Frank blood at the meatus is generally—although not always—an indication for operative intervention.

NURSING DIAGNOSES

Appropriate nursing diagnoses for abdominal trauma and injury would include:

- Fluid volume deficit related to hemorrhage
- Pain related to blunt or penetrating abdominal injury and hemorrhage into abdominal cavity
- Potential for infection in penetrating trauma, with peritoneal contamination
- Anxiety related to procedures and unknown outcomes

■ GENITOURINARY TRAUMA

Trauma to the kidneys, ureters, bladder, and urethra must always be considered a possibility in any patient presenting with chest, back, or abdominal trauma. Blunt trauma, from direct impact blows or deceleration forces, and penetrating trauma, from foreign objects or bone fragments, can and do account for significant GU injury and bleeding as well as extravasation of urine, but these injuries are easily overlooked in the presence of more obvious traumas. The occult nature of most major GU trauma requires a high index of suspicion when conducting the initial assessment; signs of shock with no other obvious explanation may be due to hemorrhage in the renal capsule, which may or may not eventually tamponade.

REVIEW OF THE URINARY TRACT

The normal urinary tract is composed of two kidneys, two ureters, one urinary bladder, and the urethra (Fig. 15–6). The kidneys are large, bean-shaped organs capped by the adrenal glands and located in the thoracolumbar region in the space behind the abdominal cavity (retroperitoneal). The right kidney lies just anterior to the twelfth rib and the left kidney lies just anterior to the eleventh and twelfth ribs. The right kidney is slightly lower because of downward displacement by the posterior edge of the liver. The two ureters convey urine from the kidneys to the urinary bladder, where it is collected and voided through the urethra.

Kidneys

The kidneys function to control extracellular fluids (volume of water, concentration of electrolytes, osmolarity, and concentration of hydrogen ions), to produce erythropoietin necessary for RBC maturation, and to indirectly control BP by a hormonal mechanism called the renin-angiotensin system. The kidneys are the site for excretion of the wastes of metabolism and derive their rich blood supply from the renal arteries, which are branches of the abdominal aorta. Occlusion of the aorta, whether

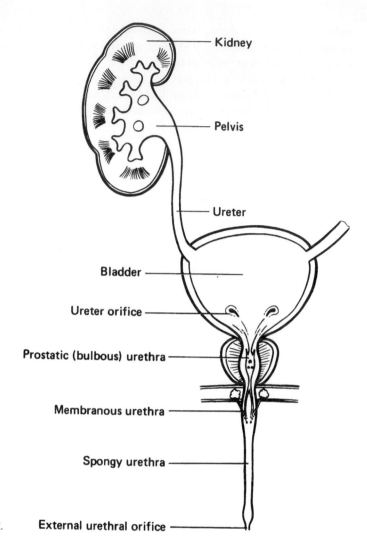

Figure 15–6. Outline of structures of the urinary tract.

due to thrombi, emboli, or obstruction secondary to trauma located above the origin of the renal arteries, may deprive the kidneys of adequate blood flow and predispose to renal failure. The kidneys are each encapsulated by a membrane tough enough to tamponade a considerable amount of bleeding as long as that capsule remains intact.

With each heartbeat, approximately one fourth of the blood pumped by the heart circulates through the kidneys for filtration, eliminating all the excess water that is not lost through the GI tract, lungs, or skin. The kidneys filter approximately 170 L blood per day and resorb all but 1.7 L waste water, excreted as urine. Normally, urine output in a healthy adult should be approximately 1 mL/kg/per hour.

Ureters

The ureters begin at the lower end of the renal pelvis and normally lie behind the lower pole of the kidney; the average length of the adult ureter is about 10 in, depending somewhat on the height of the individual. The ureteric orifices of the bladder vary considerably in size, shape, and appearance. The internal urinary meatus and the two ureteric orifices form the three angles of the trigone of the bladder. Urine passes from the pelvis of the kidney, down the ureter, and into the bladder by means of a series of peristaltic waves.

Urinary Bladder

The urinary bladder is a hollow, muscular organ lying in the anterior part of the pelvis, behind and somewhat above the symphysis pubis. The bladder is chiefly muscular, with a complete mucous lining, and when the normal bladder is relaxed, the mucous coat is quite smooth. When it contracts, the muscle fibers bundle up all over the organ, except on the trigone, which remains perfectly smooth. Blood is supplied to the bladder by two main vessels, the superior vesicle and the inferior vesicle arteries, one each of which lies on either side, as does the nerve supply that comes from the pelvic plexus. The bladder is frequently torn in association with fractures of the pelvis or by BAT, allowing urine to leak into the abdominal cavity.

Urethra

The female urethra is about 2 to 3 cm long and is not liable to injury by the same forms of trauma as in males. An accurate knowledge of the anatomy of the male urethra is important in appreciating the different types of injury, especially of the closed variety. The male urethra is approximately 20 cm (8 in.) long in the average adult and is divided into three parts: (1) the posterior or prostatic urethra, lying above the GU diaphragm (membrane) and therefore inside the pelvis; (2) the membranous urethra, which is very short and transverses the diaphragm obliquely; and (3) the anterior part, sometimes referred to as the spongy urethra, which reaches from just below the inferior layer of the GU diaphragm to the external meatus.

VISUALIZATION OF THE GENITOURINARY TRACT

Injuries of the GU tract are simple in nature, generally speaking, and comparatively easy to deal with because all parts of the GU tract can be visualized without the general surgery involved in opening the abdomen and visualizing traumatized organs. Radiologic visualization of the GU tract is accomplished by:

- *IVP:* Requires injection of radiopaque substances, provides a view of the collecting system, and is nontraumatizing
- *Cystogram:* Requires injection of radiopaque substances and provides a view of the bladder

- *Retrograde pyelogram:* Involves cystoscopy and catheterization of the ureters to visualize the tract
- *Cystoscopy:* Provides visualization of the bladder wall, prostate, and anterior urethra (vaginoscopy with cystoscope in young females is done for visualization of a foreign body or infection)
- *Renal angiogram:* Involves threading a catheter up the femoral artery to the aorta and selectively introducing dye for visualizing kidney vascularity (1 to 2 percent morbidity)

Contrast studies for visualization of the GU tract, which will involve intravenous administration of radiopaque substances, require an additional informed consent signed by the patient, in case of untoward reaction to the injected dyes.

RENAL INJURIES

Renal injuries are rarely found singly, and 80 percent have associated chest or intraperitoneal injuries caused by direct force crushing against adjacent body structures of the spine, ribs, and abdominal flank areas (Fig. 15–7) as well as by indirect injury from falls and violent muscular action. Some general considerations of renal injuries would include the fact that the kidneys lie in a protected position, so that serious injuries are relatively uncommon, although minor trauma can produce severe renal injury, especially in diseased kidneys, which are more prone to injury. Definitive diagnosis of renal injuries must be made by a urologist; the initial diagnosis is usually made in the ED. Some of the key factors affecting decisions and the management of renal trauma are the following:

- Unilateral renal agenesis is present in 1 out of every 500 people, and 10 to 14 percent of all people are born with *some* anomaly of the GU tract. It is therefore mandatory to assess renal function or the presence or condition of the contralateral kidney.
- One third of patients with renal trauma may have major visceral injuries, one half may have skeletal injuries, and one third may have no other serious injuries.
- Severe hemorrhage usually causes a tamponade effect, which occurs within Gerota's

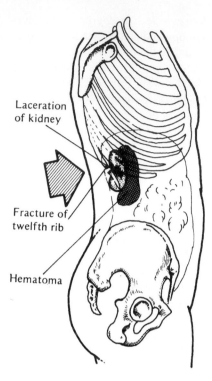

Laceration of kidney

Fracture of twelfth rib

Hematoma

Figure 15–7. Abdominal flank injuries.

fascia (the capsule surrounding the kidney) after 800 to 1200 mL of bleeding.
- Retroperitoneal bleeding, secondary to trauma, is almost impossible to stop immediately, and many surgeons believe that administration of up to 20 units of blood is allowable before surgical intervention for a nephrectomy is mandated.
- Urinary extravasations *must* be drained within a few days unless they are of minor degree and are transitory.

Signs and Symptoms

The signs and symptoms of severe renal trauma include flank pain, tenderness, possible hematuria, rigidity, fever, leukocytosis, paralytic ileus, and shock.

Nursing Interventions

Intervention comprises clinical assessment, fluid resuscitation, and laboratory evaluation, including urinalysis, Hgb and Hct, renal function, urine cul-

ture and sensitivity (C&S) tests, and x-ray studies as ordered. The retrograde pyelogram is 90 percent diagnostic, but be wary of large doses of intravenous contrast media in situations favoring heart failure or volume overload, shock, or dehydration. These hypertonic radiopaque solutions may increase serum osmolality by 30 percent. Insertion of a Foley catheter with careful ongoing monitoring of output for both volume and presence of blood are key nursing responsibilities.

URETERAL INJURIES

Ureteral injuries from penetrating or crushing trauma are rarely seen. These injuries may usually be repaired at operation, so a retrograde pyelogram is required for diagnosis and early definitive treatment is surgery. Hematuria may be absent.

BLADDER INJURIES

Bladder injuries, like lung injuries, may be classified as penetrating and nonpenetrating (or blunt), with the mechanism of injury being a fractured pelvis, trauma to the abdomen, or deceleration injury from a seat belt (whether or not the victim has a full bladder at the time). The symptoms may include shock, pain, hematuria, and the inability to void as desired. However, remember that even with a ruptured bladder, hypotonic or isotonic urine may cause little pain initially in the peritoneal cavity and may remain asymptomatic for a period of time.

URETHRAL TRAUMA

Urethral injuries are classified as intrapelvic (above the GU membrane) and extrapelvic (below the GU membrane). Both are discussed here.

Intrapelvic Urethral Injuries

Intrapelvic GU injuries (above the GU membrane) involve the same tract in the male and female, except for the prostate in the male (Fig. 15–8).

It is less likely for the urethra to be torn off the GU diaphragm in females, but urethral fistulas are common. Persistent watery drainage from the vagina after a surgical procedure usually indicates a urethrovaginal (vesicovaginal) fistula below the GU diaphragm, and the patient will have uriniferous discharge from the urethra and vagina on voiding. Other intrapelvic GU problems for women in-

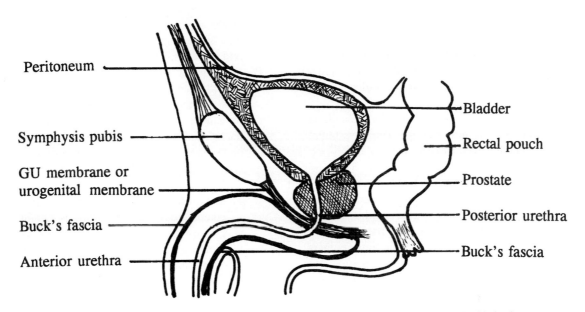

Figure 15–8. Schematic saggital diagram of the genitourinary or urogenital membrane and Buck's fascia in the male genital structure.

clude cystocele (a prolapse of the bladder into the vagina, with stress incontinence) and occasionally the presence of foreign bodies in the urethra and bladder that present removal problems.

In the male, avulsion of the prostate (commonly seen with a fractured pelvis) may be found in conjunction with a severed and free-floating bladder neck. The bladder neck will constrict, the bladder will distend with urine, and the patient will be unable to void; there may or may not be blood from the meatus. The patient has pelvic tenderness and, although generally not in shock, must be watched closely, with VS carefully monitored. A KUB film will show a lot of haze in the pelvis. Treatment is extremely conservative, with as little surgical dissection as possible; too much dissection or instrumentation may threaten later sexual potency in the male.

EXTRAPELVIC URETHRAL INJURIES

Most urethral injuries occur below the GU membrane, and some of the more commonly seen injuries are:

- *Straddle injury:* (the most classic type seen) crushes the bulbous or prostatic urethra between the inferior border of the pubic arch and the object on which the pa-

tient falls, causing partial or complete tear of the urethra.

The signs and symptoms include pain and the inability to void or a "stuttering" stream when voiding. The patient may void once, but extravasation of urine from the damaged urethra will cause sphincter spasm, preventing further urination. Blood may be seen at the external meatus, with extravasation of blood locally.

Retrograde urethrography and pelvic x-ray films are indicated, although the pelvis is not usually fractured. The patient should be catheterized in emergency situations; meticulous aseptic technique is required. If the catheter cannot be passed for any reason, either a suprapubic cystotomy or perineal exploration is indicated. (Fractured pelvis is associated with about 20 percent of injuries of the urinary tract.)

- *Perforated posterior urethra:* from instrumentation (iatrogenic), meaning physician-caused, although it could be caused by anyone caring for the patient)
- *Crush injuries of the penis with protracted outcomes*
- *Penetrating injuries with fairly obvious damage*

- *Periurethral abscess:* seen generally in older diabetic men
- *Injury within Buck's fascia:* the envelope of deep fascia surrounding the penile structure; this injury manifests with blood in the voided urine
- *Injury outside Buck's fascia:* seen as blood extravasated into the perineum, scrotum, and up the abdominal wall

Evaluation of Bleeding Sources

All of the urinary tract is extraperitoneal, an important concept to remember. Kidneys and ureters lie behind the posterior parietal peritoneum, and the bladder lies in the anterior part of the pelvis under the parietal peritoneum. The GU membrane (GU diaphragm, urogenital diaphragm) runs from the urethra, down along the perineum to the anus, and back to the coccyx to hook onto the sacrum, forming a complete envelope around the pelvic bone. Any extravasation of blood within the pelvic floor, therefore, will not be evident externally, owing to the barrier effect of the GU membrane, nor will any bleeding external to the pelvis be allowed to enter the pelvis. If bleeding occurs in the urethra, blood will be evident at the meatus, but if diluted blood is passed in the urine, look for a problem in the bladder or higher up the GU tract, in the ureters and kidneys. If hematuria is present, be certain to ask the patient *where* in the urine stream the blood occurs. This information will likely give a general indication of the bleeding source. If blood is present throughout the stream, it is mixed in the bladder; if blood is present at the beginning of the stream, there is a bleeding point somewhere down the urethra.

TRAUMA TO MALE GENITALIA

Emergencies involving the external male genitalia are not uncommon and must be managed carefully and rapidly to avoid damaging consequences. Some of the more commonly seen problems with some general guidelines for emergency intervention are as follows:

A. For wounds of the penis, preserve the tissue, divert the urine if necessary, and control bleeding with sutures and pressure. Detached penile skin should be wrapped in sterile 4 × 4s moistened with Ringer's lactate, sealed in a zipper-locked plastic bag, and placed in an iced solution.

B. Wounds of the penile skin and scrotum should be cleansed and debrided once surface anesthesia is achieved. Cover with sterile Ringer's or normal saline solution (NSS) packs and prepare for the OR. Specific emergencies involving the scrotum and its contents include:

1. Scrotal tears, which are commonly seen in farming communities that use power takeoff equipment. Clothing is caught in the equipment, and the skin of the scrotum is avulsed, or degloved, as a result. Treatment is accomplished with skin grafts; emergency treatment is to cover the wounded scrotum with sterile Ringer's or saline packs and prepare the patient for rapid admission to the OR.

2. Scrotal hematomas, which are seen after delivery in newborns, in straddle injuries, and sometimes following vasectomies. There is no treatment other than to watch for infection and treat for comfort. These hematomas are *not* drained, because of the high risk of infection, unless there is a break in the skin.

C. Strangulation of the penis is managed by removing the constricting agent, diverting the urine, and preserving the maximal viable length surgically.

D. Priapism (sustained painful erection of the cavernous bodies of the penis) requires sedation, ice packs, and analgesia as necessary (after 12 to 24 hours). The etiology must be determined if possible (penile cancer, blood diseases, psychological situations, and spinal cord trauma).

E. Minor trauma to the testes requires support and cold packs. Testicular mobility mitigates against injury in that it diminishes or lessens the chance of testicular trauma from entrapment.

1. Marked hematoma and swelling of the scrotum requires surgical exploration to drain, and lacerations must be ruled out or repaired.

2. Remember that torsions can occur as a result of trauma.

3. All penetrating scrotal wounds must be explored, debrided, and drained.

4. Remember that "traumatic" epididymitis is rare and that tumor of the testes often presents after relatively minor trauma.

F. Hematuria is significant as an indication of a stone or injury, rather than torsion or epididymitis. In trauma, *blood at the meatus requires a urethrogram before a Foley catheter is passed, and then by a urologist or emergency physician only.*

G. When evaluating a scrotal mass or swelling, remember that fluid in the scrotum will transilluminate when a flashlight is held behind it; a solid mass will not. The presence of fluid indicates less likelihood of an emergency situation and is also less likely to be painful.

H. Torsion of the spermatic cord is surprisingly common. It is most likely to be found in teenagers who present with abrupt onset of testicular pain, tenderness, vomiting, and often a history of previous episodes. Pathological and clinical studies indicate that *6 to 10 hours* is the critical time period; to avoid the problem of delayed surgery, males with the appropriate clinical picture should be assumed to have spermatic cord torsion and treated *immediately;* the physician must be notified without delay.

APPROPRIATE NURSING DIAGNOSES

Appropriate nursing diagnoses for GU trauma include:

- Fluid volume deficit related to blood loss
- Pain related to intra-abdominal bleeding
- Anxiety related to discomfort, procedures, surgery, prognosis, loss of function, and alteration of body image

NURSING INTERVENTIONS

Intervention comprises ongoing clinical assessment, fluid resuscitation, and monitoring for potential bleeding. Serial VS, Hgb, and Hct are essential to establish the trend based on original baseline data. Beyond that, ongoing assessment of renal function and support of the patient with GU trauma requires:

- Hourly intake and output monitoring unless specifically stated otherwise
- Daily serum BUN and creatinine, and urine creatinine
- Ongoing assessment for development of a flank mass, gently measuring abdominal girth
- Scrupulous technique in caring for lines (e.g., arterial lines, intravenous lines, Foley catheter)
- Pain management with analgesia as appropriate, ice packs, and scrotal support if indicated
- Psychological and emotional support for anxieties related to loss of function and alteration of body image

■ SUMMARY

Again, the management philosophy for traumatized patients is grounded in rules that have been validated by trauma surgeons as fail-safe guidelines for that golden hour; ENs recognize them as rules that guide their effective interventions when trauma patients present:

- Remember that time is the essence.
- Think the worst first. (Anticipate and stay ahead of developing crises.)
- Use a systematic approach to evaluate and treat the traumatized patient.
- Look beyond the obvious.
- Be aggressive in your management.

Become comfortable with your facility's trauma protocols and participate as an effective member of the trauma team. Victims of abdominal and GU trauma are at high risk for so many pitfalls and oversights in care, but rapid and competent emergency nursing assessment and intervention can and does make a significant difference in patient outcomes.

■ REFERENCES

1. Feliciano DV. Surgery for liver trauma. *Surg Clin North Am.* 1989;69:273–284.
2. Frankel P. Trauma notebook injuries associated with safety-belt use. *J Emerg Nurs.* 1992;18:546–547.

3. Morgan AS. Solid visceral injuries: diaphragm, liver, spleen and kidneys. *Top Emerg Med.* 1993;15:22–38.

4. Plaistur BR, Jacobs LM. Management of penetrating abdominal trauma. *Top Emerg Med.* 1993;15:51–67.

5. Freeark RJ. Excerpts from a talk. *Emerg Med.* October 1973;5:29.

6. Buckingham WB, Sparberg M, Brandfonbrener M. Examination of the abdomen. In: *A Primer of Clinical Diagnosis.* New York, NY: Harper & Row; 1971:172–210.

7. Grant H, Murray R. *Emergency Care.* 2nd ed. Bowie, Md: Brady Company; 1978.

■ BIBLIOGRAPHY

American College of Surgeons Committee on Trauma. Advanced Trauma Life Support program. Chicago, Ill: ACS; 1993.

Amroch D, Schiavon G, Carmignola G, et al. Isolated blunt liver trauma: is nonoperative treatment justified? *J Pedtr Surg.* 1992;27:466–468.

Bates B, ed. *A Guide to Physical Assessment.* 5th ed. Philadelphia, Pa: JB Lippincott, 1991.

Cardona VA, Hurn PD, Bastnagel-Mason PJ, et al. *Trauma Nursing: From Resuscitation Through Rehabilitation.* 2nd ed. Philadelphia, Pa: WB Saunders; 1994.

Champion HR, Sacco WJ, Copes WS, et al. A revision of the trauma score. *J Trauma.* 1989;29:623–629.

Corriere JN Jr, Sandler CM. Management of the ruptured bladder: seven years of experience with 111 cases. *J Trauma.* 1986;26:830–833.

Daffner RH, Deeb ZL, Lupetin AR, Rothfus WE. Patterns of high-speed impact injuries in motor vehicle occupants. *J Trauma.* 1988;28:498–501.

Demaria EJ. Management of patients with indeterminate diagnostic peritoneal lavage results following blunt trauma. *J Trauma.* 1991;31:1627–1631.

Emergency Nurses Association. *Emergency Nursing Core Curriculum.* 4th ed. Philadelphia, Pa: WB Saunders; 1994.

Emergency Nurses Association. *Trauma Nursing Core Course.* 4th ed. Chicago, Ill: ENA; 1995.

Fackler M, Bellamy R, Malinowski J. The wound profile: illustration of the missile-tissue reaction. *J Trauma.* 1988;28(suppl):S21–S29.

Fontanarosa PB. Genitourinary emergencies. *Top Emerg Med.* 1991;13(1).

Frankel P. Injuries associated with safety-belt use. *J Emerg Nurs.* 1992;18:545–546.

Hammond JC, Canal DF, Broadie TA. Nonoperative management of adult blunt hepatic trauma in a municipal trauma center. *Am Surg.* 1992;5:551–558.

Harrahill M. Open pelvic fracture: the lethal injury. *J Emerg Nurs.* 1994;20:243–245.

Hoyt DB, Shackford SR, McGill T, et al. The impact of in-house surgeons and operating room resuscitation on outcome of traumatic injuries. *Arch Surg.* 1989;124:906–910.

Karkal SS. Overcoming pitfalls in penetrating abdominal trauma. *Emerg Med Rep.* 1990;11:53–62.

Kidd P. Genitourinary trauma patients. *Top Emerg Med.* 1987;9:71–87.

Kidd PS, Wagner KD. *High Acuity Nursing.* 2nd ed. Stamford, Conn: Appleton & Lange; 1996.

Lee G. *Flight Nursing: Principles and Practice.* St. Louis, Mo: Mosby-Year Book; 1991.

Maull KI, Rodriguez A, Wiles CE. *Complications in Trauma and Critical Care.* Philadelphia, Pa: WB Saunders; 1996.

Morgan AS, Lane-Reticker A. Blunt and penetrating abdominal trauma, part 1. *Top Emerg Med.* 1993;15(1).

Morgan AS, Pepe JL. Blunt and penetrating abdominal trauma, Part 2. *Top Emerg Med.* 1993;15(2).

Nursing 96 Drug Handbook. Springhouse, Pa: Springhouse Corporation; 1996.

Phippen ML, Wells MP. *Perioperative Nursing Practice.* Philadelphia, Pa: WB Saunders; 1994.

Pons PT, Honigman B, Moore EE, et al. Prehospital advanced trauma life support for critical penetrating wounds to the thorax and abdomen. *J Trauma.* 1985;25:828–832.

Wisner DH, Blaisdell FW. Visceral injuries. *Arch Surg.* 1992;127:687–693.

Zhi-Yong S, Yuan-Lin D, Xiao-Hong W. Bacterial translocation and multiple system organ failure in bowel ischemia and reperfusion. *J Trauma.* 1992;32:148–153.

■ REVIEW: ABDOMINAL AND GENITOURINARY TRAUMA

1. Identify the abdominal quadrants and the organs located within each.

2. Describe the three forces of injury that occur in blunt trauma to the abdomen.

3. Identify the abdominal organs most commonly injured in penetrating trauma and explain the reason.

4. Describe the implications of a stab wound at the midaxillary line between the fourth and fifth rib.

5. List at least six examples of penetrating abdominal trauma that mandate exploratory laparotomy.

6. Identify and describe the three steps in abdominal examination.

7. Define the following terms used to describe reactions elicited by abdominal palpation:
   a. *Guarding*
   b. *Rigidity*
   c. *Rebound tenderness*
   d. *Referred* or *reflected pain*

8. List at least five visual observations that the emergency nurse (EN) should include in the initial assessment of abdominal trauma.

9. Explain the diagnostic implications of Kehr sign.

10. Describe the rationale and procedural steps involved with diagnostic peritoneal lavage.

11. Define the normal blood volume for the average adult and explain the degree of the compensatory mechanism before a shock state ensues.

12. Explain the implications of a heart rate of 120 beats per minute (bpm) following significant abdominal trauma.

13. Describe three serious outcomes that are possible following massive tissue damage after crush injury.

14. List six diagnostic imaging techniques employed in management of abdominal trauma.

15. Identify the important laboratory value that indicates hemodynamic status following trauma and the rule of thumb as it normally relates to hemoglobin (Hgb).

16. List four nursing diagnoses that would be appropriate for serious abdominal injury.

17. Define the normal per-hour urine output for the average healthy adult.

18. List five methods of visualizing the genitourinary (GU) tract and explain the rationale for obtaining an additional informed consent for contrast studies.

19. Identify at least four key considerations in the definitive management of renal trauma.

20. Explain the ways in which a bleeding source in the GU tract can be evaluated.

21. Cite the precaution *always to be taken* before a catheter is passed when there is blood at the male meatus following trauma.

22. List at least four rules in trauma when performing initial assessments that contribute to optimal outcomes for the victim.

Musculoskeletal Trauma 16

By and large, orthopedic injuries are rather straightforward in their involvement unless associated with other organ systems following trauma. Trauma to the axial skeleton is rarely considered an emergency situation but frequently does require attention on an urgent basis. The two very real orthopedic emergencies do exist, however, and they are (1) fractures or dislocations of the elbow or knee, since these are not only exquisitely painful but can easily cause permanent damage to nerves and vessels distal to the injury if not attended to immediately, and (2) closed compartment syndrome in extremities.

A predisposition to fractures does exist in some people. Skeletal bones are strong because of the presence of several factors; the absence of these factors predisposes to fractures with very little trauma as a causative agent. However, bone that is stressed over a long period of time—for instance, the os calcis (heel) in gymnasts—develops a denser deposit of calcium to withstand the repeated impacts sustained on landing without resultant fracture. Nutritional factors, such as the amount of protein ingested (to supply the protein collagen fibers) as well as adequate amounts of calcium and vitamin D in the diet, are important to building strong bones. Hormonal levels of estrogens play a part in offsetting osteoporosis, which is commonly seen in the pathological fractures of elderly women whose estrogen levels have significantly diminished.

BONES AND JOINTS

The human skeleton is composed of some 206 bones and serves 5 major functions: support, locomotion, protection for major organs, formation of specific blood cells, and storage and exchange of calcium and phosphate. Humans have an axial skeleton (head, neck, and trunk) and an appendicular skeleton (bones of the extremities, with bones classified according to their shape (i.e., long, short, flat, irregular).[1]

Long bones have a length greater than their width and include the clavicle, humerus, radius, ulna, femur, tibia, and fibula. They also include the metacarpals, metatarsals, and phalanges. Short bones are almost equal in their dimensions and include the bones of hands (carpals) and feet (tarsals). Flat bones include the ribs, sternum, scapula, and some bones of the skull.

Irregular bones are differently shaped bones that include the vertebrae, pelvic bones, and some bones of the skull.

Joints are the articulating surface where two or more bones meet, allowing for body motion with minimum friction. They are named for the two bones that articulate, or meet, with each other. Movable joints are termed synovial joints because of the thick gel-like synovial fluid that provides lubrication, generated by a vascular synovial membrane filling the joint cavity. Other joints, such as skull bones and the symphysis pubis, allow little or no motion and are termed fused joints. Synovial joints allow for range of motion (ROM) that is determined by the influence of muscles, ligaments, and shapes of the articulating bone. Four major types of joints are described:

- *Ball and socket joint (spheroidal):* The shoulder joint is an example. The head of the humerus (the ball) fits into a depression of the scapula (the socket). Because of this articulation, the arm has the capability of extension, flexion, adduction, abduction, and circumduction; so does the hip joint.

- *Hinge joint (ginglymus):* As the name implies, this joint acts only as a hinge; finger and knee joints are examples, as they allow for only extension and flexion.
- *Pivot joint (trochoid):* This joint allows bones to pivot on one another. Movement of the radius on the ulna is an example; the joint allows the forearm to go into supination and pronation, aided by the distal radius and ulnar joint.
- *Saddle joint (sellar):* By their conformation, bones of this joint act as saddles; joints of the wrist (radiocarpal) and hand (carpometacarpal) are examples, allowing for flexion, extension, abduction, adduction, and circumduction. The thumb, which is a carpometacarpal joint, is the most important, as it permits opposition as well.

Range of Motion

If the ROM of a joint goes beyond its maximum allowable limits, several different types of injuries may occur:

- Stretched or torn ligaments (sprain)
- Stretched or torn muscles (strain)
- Avulsion fractures
- Dislocations (displacement may be anterior, posterior, medial, or lateral)

Following orthopedic injury, ROM is an important parameter to assess and document.

Assessing Neural Status

Neural damage is frequently sustained in significant orthopedic trauma. When assessing ROM, motor assessment can be accomplished almost simultaneously by asking the patient to perform specific motor functions, except in the case of open fractures. (Table 16–1 identifies bones, neural structures at risk of injury, and specific deficiencies in motor function that identify neural damage.

DEFINITIONS: FRACTURES AND DISLOCATIONS

A fracture is defined as the disruption in the continuity of bone—a break in the surface either across its cortex or through its articular surface—and can range from a simple crack to complete disruption of the bony architecture. Forces strong enough to break bones may also injure muscles, blood vessels, and other surrounding soft tissue. A dislocation is defined as the displacement of any part, more especially of a bone—also called luxation (or subluxation, referring to partial dislocation)—usually creating an obvious and significant deformity. Although not as numerous in types as fractures, dislocations can be incredibly more painful than fractures because of the disruption of tendons, nerves, and vessels traversing the jointed areas.

■ FRACTURES IN GENERAL

CLOSED VERSUS OPEN FRACTURES

Fractures are most generally classified as closed and open (Fig. 16–1), although they used to be identified as simple and compound. The current

TABLE 16–1. MOTOR ASSESSMENT WITH NEURAL DAMAGE

Bone	Nerve	Motor Assessment
Depressed clavicle fracture or anterior shoulder dislocation	Brachial plexus	Cannot raise the shoulder; cannot externally rotate arm; cannot supinate forearm or hand
Middle and distal third of humerus	Radial	Cannot extend wrist or fingers—"wrist drop"; cannot extend thumb
Distal humerus, proximal and distal radius and ulna	Median	Cannot flex wrist—"monkey hand"
Medial epicondyle of humerus	Ulnar	Pain deficit on ulnar aspect of little finger
Proximal lateral fibula, dislocated knee	Peroneal	Cannot dorsiflex or evert the ankle
Ischial fractures or posterior hip dislocation	Sciatic	Cannot flex the leg at the knee joint; cannot extend the hip joint
Tibial fracture	Tibial	Cannot plantar-flex ankle or flex the toes

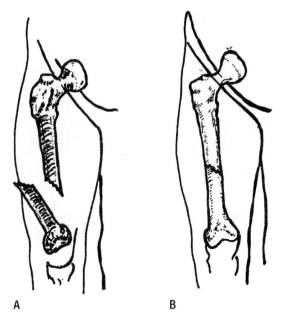

Figure 16–1. Open versus closed fractures. **A.** Open fracture. **B.** Closed fracture.

terminology assigns synonymity to *closed* and *simple* and to *open* and *compound.* In other words, if the skin is unbroken, the fracture is closed (or simple), regardless of how many bones are in how many pieces; conversely, a fracture is open (or compound) if the skin is broken, even though the fracture may be single and minor in nature. An open (compound) fracture is considered to be more serious because of the risk of infection. An equally serious threat exists, however, in closed fractures because of the potential for development of compartment syndrome. Both situations challenge nursing awareness and assessment skills.

CLASSIFICATION OF FRACTURES

Fractures are classified according to the direction of the fracture line (Fig. 16–2). Classifications include:

- *Greenstick fracture:* one in which one side of the bone is broken, the other being bent;

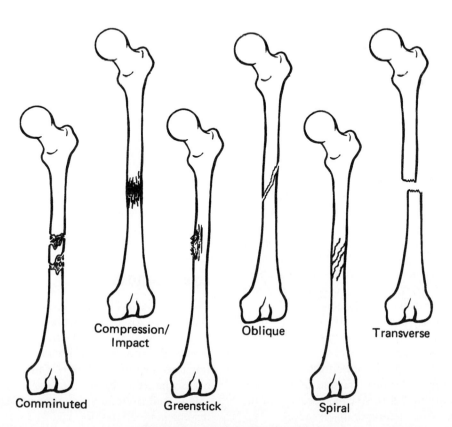

Figure 16–2. Classifications of fractures.

called also hickory-stick or willow fracture (this type of fracture occurs only in children and young adolescents)

- *Transverse fracture:* one at right angles to the axis of the bone
- *Oblique fracture:* a bone broken in a diagonal line (45-degree angle)
- *Spiral fracture:* one in which the bone has been twisted apart; also called torsion fracture
- *Comminuted fracture:* one in which the bone is splintered into multiple pieces or crushed
- *Compression fracture:* caused by compression, commonly with vertebral bodies, and usually due to diving accidents, falls from heights, or acceleration-deceleration
- *Impacted fracture:* a fracture in which the bone fragments are embedded in the substance of one another
- *Avulsion fracture:* an indirect fracture caused by avulsion or the pull of a ligament at the point of attachment
- *Colles fracture:* fracture of the lower end of the radius in which the lower fragment is displaced posteriorly (if the lower fragment is displaced anteriorly, it is a reverse Colles or Smith's fracture)
- *Direct fracture:* fracture at the point of injury
- *Dislocation fracture:* fracture of a bone near an articulation with concomitant dislocation of that joint
- *Double fracture:* fracture of a bone in two places (also called segmental fracture)
- *Epiphyseal fracture:* fracture at the point of union of an epiphysis with the shaft of a bone
- *Fatigue fracture:* attributed to the strain of prolonged walking or exercise (march or stress fracture usually seen in foot and tibia)
- *Indirect fracture:* one occurring at a site distant from the site of injury
- *Pathologic fracture:* one occurring from mild injury due to preexisting bone involvement with tumor, cyst, infection, absence of estrogens, and so forth
- *Silver-fork fracture:* fracture of the lower ends of the radius; so called because of the shape of the deformity that it causes

FRACTURE HISTORY AND MECHANISM OF INJURY

Fractures present in a variety of ways, but if the patient provides a history of trauma followed by sudden pain, tenderness, swelling, and discoloration, as well as any degree of deformity and grating (or crepitus) caused by broken bone ends rubbing together, the injured part should be considered a fracture site and treated as such until ruled out by x-ray films.

Knowing the mechanism of injury is important in determining the extent of tissue and bone damaged sustained; when any force exceeds bone strength, musculoskeletal injuries occur accordingly. Factors that may cause fractures include:

- *Direct trauma:* the injury occurs at the point of impact (e.g., a broken leg caused from the bumper of a car)
- *Indirect trauma:* the injury occurs away from the point of impact (e.g., a fractured forearm occurring when the hand is used to shield the fall)
- *Disease process:* an illness causes the bone to weaken or decay so that a slight bump may be all that is necessary to cause a fracture (e.g., cancer, rickets)
- *Compression force:* a force flattens or presses one bone into another (e.g., a patient who jumps from a high place may incur a compression fracture of his or her vertebrae); also common in acceleration-deceleration injuries
- *Muscle contraction:* injury or illness causes the muscle to contract so violently that the bone fractures (e.g., electric shock, seizures, tetany)

COMPLICATIONS

Occult blood loss leading to shock or compartment syndrome, closed compartment syndrome in and of itself, and risk of infection and chronic osteomyelitis are the significant threats of major fractures. Deformity, loss of function due to neurovascular damage, and even loss of a limb can result as well from failure to properly assess and intervene in timely fashion.

Occult Blood Loss

Because bones are living tissue, they are richly supplied with blood vessels and nerves; neurovascular structures lie deep in the limb, close to the skeleton for protection. Long bones are supplied with a nutrient artery that pierces compact bone at the shaft and divides lengthwise into two major branches that supply the marrow and compact bone. Arteries that supply the joints pierce the compact bone and supply the spongy (soft) bone and ends of the bone. It is extremely important for growth purposes that this blood supply not be disturbed; fractures to these areas are dangerous to normal bone growth.

Fractures of the long bones are apt to produce a steady, slow occult bleed (Table 16–2) that, in time, may account for loss of as much as 1 unit in the lower leg and 2 units in the thigh. These patients must be closely watched for incipient shock, with the long-bone fracture immobilized for comfort and to allow the fascia lata to function as a splinting mechanism. Ongoing assessment of distal pulses, sensory perception, and limb circumference are essential nursing responsibilities.

TABLE 16–2. AVERAGE BLOOD LOSS WITH FRACTURES

Bone	Blood Loss (mL)
Pelvis (generally)	1000–2000
Posterior pelvis	1000–3000
Ribs	125 per rib
Femoral shaft	500–1000
Distal femur	500–800
Humerus	150–350
Distal humerus	250–500
Radius and ulna	250–500
Tibia and fibula	250–600

Acute Compartment Syndrome

Acute compartment syndrome (ACS) is a serious development frequently seen in closed fractures as well as secondary to circumferential third-degree burns, severe dislocations, tight dressings and casts, and vascular lesions (Fig. 16–3). After reestablishment of arterial continuity in an injured part, bleeding, muscle edema, or reactive vasodilation can cause compartment compression, resulting in ischemic damage and *permanent* contrac-

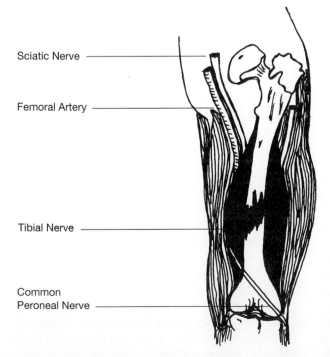

Sciatic Nerve

Femoral Artery

Tibial Nerve

Common
Peroneal Nerve

Figure 16–3. Diagrammatic representation of the acute compartment syndrome seen in a closed femur fracture; bleeding from the fracture site is trapped in the closed fascial compartments, severely compressing major blood vessels and nerves and seriously compromising distal structures.

tures. Tissues distal to the compromised area suffer greatly and results can be disastrous.

Thirty-eight of the body's 46 compartments—areas or chambers of muscles, blood vessels, and nerves tightly bound by inelastic fasciae—are in the arms and legs. Each upper arm contains three compartments, each forearm contains two, and each hand contains four. Each thigh has two compartments; the calves and feet each contain four.[2-4] Anything seriously impeding normal blood flow and causing increasing intercompartmental pressure will lead to ACS unless timely intervention occurs.

The five P's of vascular occlusion in ACS (pain, pulselessness, pallor, paresthesia, and paralysis) provide excellent assessment guidelines.[5] With closed fractures, pain (intense, persistent, and refractory to serious analgesia) is a heralding factor in the closed compartment syndrome, particularly on passive motion or stretching of the extremity, and should alert the nurse to problems. The patient, however, must be conscious in order to confirm three of the P's—pain, paresthesia, and paralysis. Maintaining a high index of suspicion is the best way to stay ahead of ACS, and *immediate* orthopedic consultation is indicated if developing ACS is suspected; proximal and distal pulses may or may not be present, but pressure may have been rising even with peripheral pulses present. Severe prolonged tamponading of distal circulation and neural innervation has resulted too many times in amputation of the ischemic parts. Intervention with surgical decompression (fasciotomy) within less than 4 hours is *essential* for optimum results.[3]

While history and physical assessment of injuries can usually help make the diagnosis of ACS in classic cases, tissue pressure measurement is required much of the time for confirmation. Techniques employed for monitoring tissue pressure measurements are (1) the needle injection technique known as Whitesides technique and (2) the infusion technique using a transducer monitoring system with various slit catheters, wicks, and needles. The latter method can be used for continuous monitoring and is considerably more accurate than the needle injection method. Pressure up to 10 mm Hg is considered normal; pressure above 30 to 40 mm Hg should be carefully monitored for trends and clinical symptoms.[3,5]

Nursing intervention: Distal pulses, skin temperature and color, motor function, sensory perception, and circumference measurements must all be carefully monitored and documented. Release any constriction, position the extremity for comfort at or below heart level, administer analgesia as ordered, and prepare for fasciotomy if necessary. The patient will require calm explanations and support.

Nursing diagnoses: Appropriate nursing diagnoses in ACS would include:

- Altered tissue perfusion related to increased intercompartmental pressure
- Pain related to increasing ischemia
- Potential impaired skin integrity related to decreased blood supply
- Potential for further injury: loss of limb, paralysis
- Anxiety related to pain and unknown prognosis

Fat Embolus Syndrome

Long-bone fractures and crush injuries have been associated with fat embolus syndrome, or adult respiratory distress syndrome (ARDS), an insidious interstitial pneumonitis that develops in victims of multiple trauma. The mechanism is obscure, because symptoms have not been produced by the intentional injection of fat globules into the bloodstream; the condition occurs 24 to 72 hours following trauma. It is thought that the incidence of fat embolus can be reduced by early fixation of long-bone fractures to prevent further manipulation. Stabilization of long-bone fractures also minimizes further blood loss by allowing the muscle sheath (fascia lata) to tense and create a tamponade effect around bleeding points. Remember that the upper thigh (cylindrical form) can accommodate 1 to 2 L of blood; this results in shock.

Symptoms of fat embolism include a sudden onset of cyanosis, tachycardia, tachypnea, disorientation, delirium, and other signs of hypoxia; petechiae often develop, especially in the axillae. The immediate nursing intervention is administration of high-flow oxygen; if the respiratory defect is not treated aggressively, death may ensue.[6]

Managing Open Fractures

Wound assessment is important in open fractures, specifically assessment of whether it is a full- or partial-thickness wound. By definition, a partial-thickness wound over a fracture is a closed fracture. If an open fracture is suspected, motor activity should *not* be tested; the limb should be moved as little as possible, checking pulses frequently. Bony fragments protruding through the skin are obviously indications that the fracture is angulated, contaminated, and no doubt compromising the local nerve supply and circulation. These require immediate attention (e.g., realignment under controlled circumstances, care to the wound to prevent further contamination and risk of long-term infection of the bone itself, and restoration of integrity of vessels and nerves supplying areas distal to the fracture site, to the degree possible). Depending on severity, fractures may or may not involve either loss of use or at least a guarded motion in adjacent joints. Until medical evaluation has been completed, optimal management at the very least requires covering the open fracture site with moist, sterile normal saline solution (NSS) or Ringer's lactate solution dressings to prevent further contamination.

The best method of preventing wound infection following open fracture is a protective interim dressing and immediate (as soon as possible) surgical debridement with *cleansing, cleansing, cleansing.* The degree and severity of soft-tissue injury significantly influences the risk of infection and the recovery of satisfactory function, but protection from further contamination, once in the emergency department (ED), is a serious nursing responsibility. Use of scrupulous wound care technique with the open fracture contributes heavily to optimizing chances for positive outcomes.

Traumatic Amputation

Advances in clinical microsurgery have made extremity replantation an option in some instances of traumatic amputation. Successful revascularization, the restoration of blood flow to an attached but unperfused extremity or digit, and replantation, the microsurgical reattachment of a severed extremity or digit, depend on (1) the extent of crush injury to the circulatory base, (2) the length of the ischemic interval, and (3) consideration of appropriate priority relative to the patient's other injuries in the hierarchy of trauma care. Indications and guidelines for nursing responsibilities are discussed in Chapter 17.

■ UPPER-EXTREMITY FRACTURES

SKELETAL BONES OF THE UPPER EXTREMITIES

Skeletal members of the upper extremities include the clavicle, scapula, humerus, radius, ulna, carpal, metacarpals, and phalanges. Injuries to each are discussed here with their signs and symptoms, complications, and stabilization.

Clavicle

Fractures to the clavicle (Fig. 16–4A) usually occur between the inner two thirds and outer one third of its length. Clavicle fractures are common

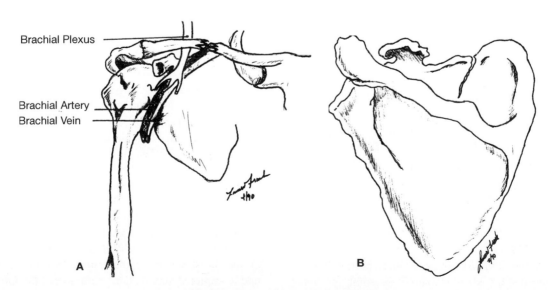

Brachial Plexus

Brachial Artery
Brachial Vein

A

B

Figure 16–4. A. Clavicular fracture. **B.** Scapular fracture.

in children and occur frequently in contact sports and falls onto an outstretched arm.

Signs and symptoms: Because of the clavicle's close proximity to the humerus, the patient with a fractured clavicle will usually have his or her arm close to his or her side and not move it. There is point tenderness over the injured area upon palpation and there may be deformity. Both clavicles should be lightly palpated and the contour of both shoulders compared from the front *and* back.

Complications: If the fracture occurs in the inner two thirds of the clavicle, be alert to the possibility of a pneumothorax. Listen for breath sounds. The top of the lung can extend above the first anterior rib during inspiration, so the lung apex lies close to the clavicle. The subclavian artery and vein, as well as the brachial plexus, lie inferior to the clavicle and could be injured. Check the circulatory and neural status of the arm on the injured shoulder side.

Stabilization: The fractured clavicle is stabilized by the sling and swath, or a "figure-eight" splint is applied with the patient's shoulders back and squared; quality of distal pulses should be checked carefully. If there is any reason to believe that pulmonary status has been compromised from the injury, insist the patient remain in a wheelchair or on a gurney elevated to 45 degrees with the arm on the injured side immobilized.

Scapula

A fractured scapula (Fig. 16–4B) is an uncommon injury because the bone is embedded in muscle. However, severe direct trauma could cause scapular fracture.

Signs and symptoms: Scapular fractures can be indicated by bruising, swelling, point tenderness, and pain upon shoulder movement.

Complications: Since posterior ribs two through seven lie under the scapula, they could be fractured from serious trauma and puncture the underlying lung. The possibility of pneumothorax must be ruled out; auscultate lung fields—front and back.

Stabilization: The injured shoulder should be immobilized by applying a sling and swath.

Humerus

The humerus is divided into three portions to describe fracture sites: proximal, midshaft, or supra-

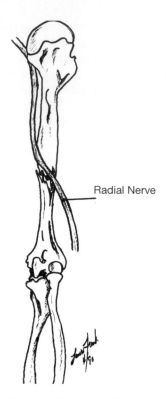

Radial Nerve

Figure 16–5. Upper arm (humeral shaft) fracture with potential involvement of radial nerve.

condylar. The supracondylar or distal portion of the humerus is discussed in elbow fractures.

Signs and symptoms: Be alert for swelling, crepitus, deformity, pain, point tenderness, and inability to move the arm.

Complications: The radial nerve passes around the midshaft portion of the humerus and may be injured in a midshaft fracture (Fig. 16–5). The radial nerve allows for dorsiflexion of the wrist and elevation of the thumb; if the radial nerve is disrupted, the wrist hangs limply in a flex position known as a "wrist drop." Radial nerve integrity can be tested by asking the patient to extend the thumb in a "hitchhiker sign" position.

Stabilization: The humerus is splinted using any conventional rigid splint. The medial side of the humerus should rest closely to the side of the chest wall and a rigid splint should be applied to the lateral side of the upper arm. The splint should immobilize the shoulder joint above and the elbow joint below the fracture. With a roller bandage securing the splint, place the injured arm in a sling and complete stabilization with a swath. Other splinting techniques can be used, depending on concurrent injuries, but the joint above and below the injured site should be immobilized.

Elbow

The elbow (Figs. 16–5 and 16–6) is the most anatomically complicated joint in the upper extremity. It consists of the distal end of the humerus and proximal ends of the radius and ulna, all articulating together to make the elbow joint. These are serious fractures and are common in children but uncommon in adults. Direct and indirect trauma (e.g., shielding against a fall with an outstretched hand) are the usual causes.

Signs and symptoms: Swelling occurs rapidly. Deformity, pain, and inability to move the arm and forearm are characteristic.

Complications: Rapid swelling can occur as bone fragments press against the brachial artery and median nerve. An absent radial pulse in the presence of a supracondylar fracture may produce a condition that cripples the hand and forearm, known as Volkmann's ischemic contracture. This condition is due to an absence of blood or oxygen supply to muscle tissue and must be corrected within *4 to 8 hours* or muscles in the forearm and hand will shrink and harden, leaving the patient with a stiff forearm and a clawlike hand deformity.

Figure 16–6. Forearm (radius or ulna) fracture.

Stabilization: A supracondylar fracture can be stabilized by using any type of rigid splint. If the arm is bent at the elbow, a sling and swath may be added. If the fracture is angulated, splint the arm in the position found. The splint should immobilize the shoulder joint and the wrist joint so no movement of the arm or forearm is allowed. Remember to assess the radial artery and neural status before and after splinting—and document.

Proximal Radius and Ulnar Fractures

Proximal radius and ulnar fractures (see Fig. 16–6) are common in adults. Indirect trauma, such as shielding against a fall with an outstretched hand, is usually the cause.

Signs and symptoms: Inability to move the arm and forearm, pain, rapid swelling, deformity, and crepitus are usually present.

Complications: Because of the close proximity of the brachial artery in this area, it could be occluded, predisposing to a Volkmann's contracture.

Stabilization: As with a supracondylar fracture, splint according to presentation and monitor the neurovascular status.

Forearm Fractures

Any force strong enough to break one bone in the forearm (see Fig. 16–6) usually breaks the other because of the close relationship of the radius and ulna. Direct or indirect trauma is usually the cause, and again, shielding against a fall with an outstretched hand is a common mechanism of injury in the adult. Greenstick fractures are common at this location in children.

Signs and symptoms: Crepitus, deformity, point tenderness, swelling, and inability to move the injured area are common occurrences in the presence of these fractures.

Complications: Neurovascular compromise and Volkmann's contracture may occur.

Stabilization: Stabilize with a rigid or inflatable splint, immobilizing the elbow and wrist joints.

Distal Radius and Ulnar Fractures

Fractures of the distal radius and ulna (see Fig. 16–7A) are common in the middle and later decades of life. Again, the most common cause is shielding against a fall with an outstretched arm and hand; fracture of the elbow or shoulder may accompany this injury.

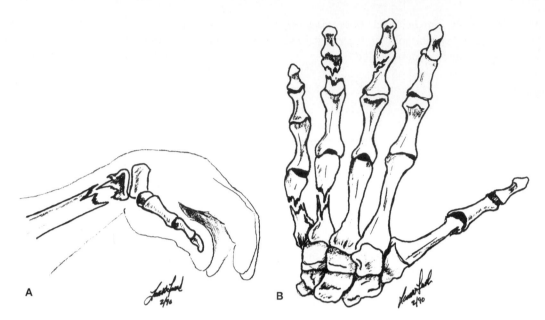

Figure 16–7. A. Wrist (distal radius, distal ulna, carpal bone) fracture. **B.** Hand (carpals and metacarpals) fracture or finger (phalanges) fracture.

Signs and Symptoms: Swelling, inability to move the wrist and hand, crepitus, pain, and deformity may be present. Deformity is classic and is known as Colles fracture or silver-fork deformity (because the angle of the fracture in association with the forearm and hand looks like a dinner fork). The opposite angle fracture at this site is known as Smith's fracture.

Complications: There are usually no complications with these fractures.

Stabilization: These fractures should be stabilized with rigid splints that immobilize the elbow and wrist joints. Monitor neurovascular status and document.

Carpal, Metacarpal, and Phalangeal Fractures

Fractures of the small bones of the hand (Fig. 16–7B) are frequently seen in the ED as a result of participation in contact sports and of a variety of industrial accidents. Complications are rare; stabilization involves immobilizing the hand in the anatomic position. Fingers can be immobilized by splinting one against the other or splinting the whole hand in the position of function. Fingertips must always be visible, or at least accessible, for confirmation of neurovascular status.

■ SPINAL COLUMN AND PELVIC GIRDLE FRACTURES

The vertebral, or spinal, column constitutes the longitudinal axis of the skeleton and serves two purposes: to support the head and upper part of the body and to provide rigid protection for the spinal cord, which carries motor and sensory impulses between the brain and all other parts of the body. The pelvic girdle is constructed of three bones: the ilium, ischium, and pubic ramus.

Vertebral Fractures

Thirty-three vertebrae are stacked in a column (Fig. 16–8) that is divided into five parts and forms a protective arch for the spinal cord as it descends from the brain housed in the cranial vault to the coccyx:

- The first seven vertebrae form the cervical spine (C-1 to C-7), or neck. The skull sits atop the uppermost of these vertebrae, C-1, which swivels atop the odontoid process of C-2.
- The next 12 vertebrae form the thoracic spine (T-1 to T-12), or upper back; 12 pairs of ribs that make up the thorax are joined to these vertebrae at the costovertebral angles.

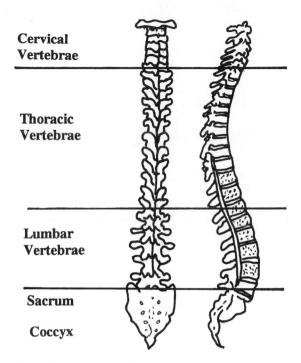

Figure 16–8. Anatomy of the vertebral column that constitutes the longitudinal axis of the skeleton.

Cervical Vertebrae

Thoracic Vertebrae

Lumbar Vertebrae

Sacrum

Coccyx

- The next five vertebrae form the lumbar spine (L-1 to L-5), or lower back.
- The next five vertebrae are fused together into a rigid sacral spine that forms the posterior part of the pelvis.
- The last four vertebrae form the coccygeal spine, or coccyx, also referred to as the "tailbone."

The vertebral column as a whole articulates with the head, ribs, and pelvic girdle; individual vertebrae articulate with each other in joints between their bodies and between their articular processes. The seven cervical vertebrae constitute the skeletal framework of the neck, with eight pairs of sensorimotor spinal nerves exiting from the spinal cord through the small holes in the sides of the vertebrae called foramina. C-1 through C-7 and T-1 are the vertebrae most at risk for fracture and displacement in trauma, with resulting damage to the delicate spinal cord that runs through them, risking paralysis of motor activity below the level of injury. The thoracic spine is relatively stable, with support provided by the ribs and sternum.

Signs and symptoms: Pain may or may not be present. There may also be numbness or tingling of extremities, paralysis, respiratory difficulty and diaphragmatic breathing, weakness, incontinence, signs of spinal shock (e.g., hypotension from vasodilation and venous pooling), and bradycardia from sympathetic block. There may be no objective findings and no neurological compromise if the cervical fracture is nondisplaced.

Complications: Possible complications include potentially severe injuries, with respiratory paralysis, quadriplegia, and/or paraplegia of varying degrees.

Stablization: The cervical spine should be immobilized immediately in any suspected cervical spine trauma. Maintain immobilization until cervical spine injury has been ruled out, with radiographic confirmation of all seven cervical vertebrae and T-1.

Pelvic Girdle Fractures

Fractures of the pelvic girdle (Fig. 16–9) may involve the pubis, ilium, or ischium bones. The ilium is considered the posterior portion of the pelvis. The ischium and pubis are considered the anterior pelvis. Fractures to the pelvic bones occur frequently in direct trauma (e.g., automobile and motorcycle accidents, crushing injuries, and falls). They are more common in the adult and elderly patient.

Signs and symptoms: Pain, inability to move the legs, muscle spasms in the lumbar spine, crepitus, point tenderness, and ecchymosis are common findings. When assessing trauma patients, the iliac crests and pubic rim should always be lightly compressed to elicit a pain response if ruling out pelvic fracture.

Complications: Fractures to the posterior pelvis (ilium) may also injure large blood vessels, nerves (sciatic), and viscera that lie close to the bone. Sixty to 70 percent of these patients will require blood transfusions averaging 7 or 8 units of blood. Anterior pelvic fractures (ischium and pubis) are usually not accompanied by damage to large blood vessels and nerves but they may injure the urethra, bladder, and other viscera that lie in close proximity to these bones. Hypovolemic shock is common with pelvic fractures; refer to Table 16–2 for occult blood loss values.

Stabilization: Patients with these fractures should be placed on a long padded spine board; a

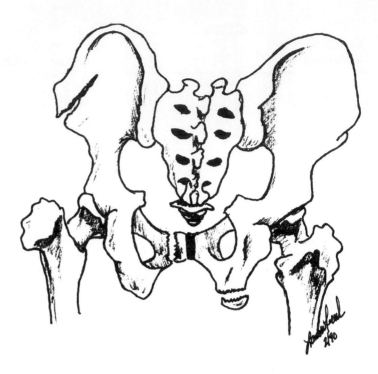

Figure 16–9. Pelvic fractures.

pillow may be placed under the knees to reduce muscle spasm and provide comfort. If signs and symptoms of shock begin to develop, a pneumatic antishock garment (PASG) should be applied and inflated to 30 to 40 mm Hg to stabilize the fracture. If the patient's blood pressure (BP) is not stabilized, inflate the trousers to 50 to 70 mm Hg and check the circulatory and neural status every 5 minutes.

Nursing intervention for closed pelvic fractures: Closed pelvic and femoral trochanteric fractures especially require close assessment for occult bleeding and volume replacement; PASG and large-bore intravenous administration of Ringer's lactate may be indicated. Elevate or support affected parts with position of comfort; monitor distal pulses, skin temperature, and sensorimotor function. Cleanse, irrigate, and debride any soft-tissue injury as appropriate; administer tetanus toxoid and antibiotics as ordered. Explain procedures and give reassurance as care progresses.

Nursing diagnoses for closed pelvic fractures: Appropriate nursing diagnoses would include:

- Fluid volume deficit, actual or potential
- Alteration in tissue perfusion
- High risk for altered urinary elimination
- Pain secondary to disruption of bone cortex
- Impaired skin integrity
- Impaired physical mobility
- Anxiety

■ LOWER-EXTREMITY FRACTURES

SKELETAL BONES OF THE LOWER EXTREMITIES

Skeletal bones comprising the lower extremities include the hip bones (since they articulate with the femur), femur, patella, tibia, fibula, tarsus, os calcis, metatarsal bones, and phalanges. Injuries to each of these is discussed here.

Hip Fractures

The hip is defined as the proximal end of the femur from just below the greater trochanter to the head of the femur, and the iliac acetabulum of the pelvic girdle. Hip fractures (Fig. 16–10) are defined by x-ray and can be of five types:

- *Subcapital:* base of the femoral head
- *Transcervical:* through the neck of the femur
- *Basal:* base of the neck of the femur
- *Intertrochanteric:* through the trochanter
- *Subtrochanteric:* just below the trochanter

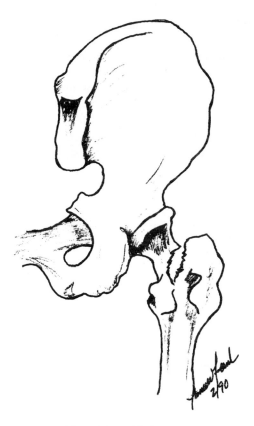

Figure 16–10. Hip fracture.

Hip fractures are very common in the elderly patient because of falls and in the young adult because of trauma (e.g., motor vehicle accidents [MVAs] or falls from high places).

Signs and symptoms: Classically, there will be shortening of the injured leg, with external rotation of the hip and leg. Pain with associated muscle spasm and inability to move the leg are also usually present.

Complications: Hypovolemic shock is common; its presence depends on the extent of injury.

Stabilization: Hip fractures are difficult to distinguish from pelvic fractures. If only a hip fracture exists, the patient should be placed in a traction splint; if a fractured pelvis coexists with the injured hip, a padded long spine board should be used. Again, place pillows under the flexed knees for comfort during confinement to the board. If signs and symptoms of shock appear, a PASG should be applied and inflated to stabilize the BP; a traction splint may be placed over the PASG if indicated.

Femur Fractures

The femur is the longest, largest, and heaviest bone in the body; therefore, injuries to this bone (Fig. 16–11) can be serious. Femur fractures are common in both children and adults, usually occurring as the result of direct trauma.

Signs and symptoms: Severe pain, deformity, angulation, muscle spasms, crepitus, inability to move the leg, and shortening of the leg are all common findings.

Complications: Hypovolemic shock is very common. This patient may lose as much as 1 to 2 L blood; open fractures are also common.

Stabilization: The fractured femur should be placed in a traction splint whenever possible; a PASG should also be used if indicated. Vital signs (VS) must be checked every 5 minutes. Trauma severe enough to fracture the femur may have produced other injuries, so a high index of suspicion should be maintained.

Knee Fractures

The knee joint consists of the distal femur (supracondylar area) and the proximal tibia, which artic-

Figure 16–11. Femoral fracture.

ulate with one another, and the patella. Fractures to the knee (Figs. 16–11 and 16–12) are common in both children and adults and usually occur from direct trauma (e.g., auto and motorcycle accidents, pedestrian–auto accidents [bumper fracture]). Like the elbow in the upper extremity, the knee is the most anatomically complicated joint in the lower extremity.

Signs and symptoms: Pain, deformity, angulation, rapid swelling, crepitus, and inability to move the injured leg are common signs.

Complications: The popliteal artery or peroneal nerve may be damaged. If the popliteal artery has been disrupted, the patient will not have distal pulses; if the peroneal nerve is damaged, the patient will not be able to dorsiflex or evert the ankle, and sensation over the lateral surface of the foot will be lost. These neurovascular structures must be checked and the findings documented.

Stabilization: The injured knee should be stabilized *in the position it is found,* using rigid splints, with the entire leg immobilized if possible.

Figure 16–12. Tibial and/or fibular fracture.

Fractures to the Patella

The patella is a small triangular sesamoid bone. Direct trauma is usually the cause of injury (e.g., the knee hits the dashboard of the car). The patella is held in place by the quadricips femoris tendon and the bone helps protect the joint. The quadriceps femoris is the large bulky thigh muscle that extends the leg.

Signs and symptoms: Swelling, deformity, pain, and point tenderness are all common. Classically, the patient will not be able to raise the leg with the knee extended.

Complications: There are usually no complications; however, forces strong enough to injure the patella may also injure the knee, pelvis, femur, and lower leg. The entire extremity should be assessed for possible injury.

Stabilization: Splint the injured area above and below the knee joint to completely immobilize the leg; make certain to monitor distal neurovascular status and document.

Lower-Leg Fractures

The lower leg includes the tibia and fibula, running parallel to one another. As in the forearm, a force strong enough to break one bone usually breaks the other. Common in both children and adults, lower-leg fractures (see Fig. 16–12) occur frequently from direct and indirect trauma and from twisting forces (e.g., in ski injuries).

Signs and symptoms: Pain, deformity, angulation, swelling, crepitus, and inability to move the leg are common findings.

Complications: Because the tibia (shinbone) lies so close to the skin surface, fractures of the tibia are often open. Soft-tissue damage often accompanies these fractures, because of angulation. Fibula fractures are rarely a problem because the fibula is buried deep in muscle.

Stabilization: If the tibia is severely angulated, it should be straightened and put into a traction splint. Air splints work equally well for short-term application; make certain to monitor distal neurovascular status and document.

Ankle Fractures

The ankle consists of the distal portion of the tibia and fibula and tarsal bones (talus), which articulate with one another. The ankle is one of the most frequently injured areas of the skeletal system, because of the repeated stress put on it. Running, jumping, and twisting injuries, as well as direct and indirect trauma, are the usual causes of ankle fractures, (Fig. 16–13A) which are common in all age groups.

Signs and symptoms: Rapid swelling, pain, point tenderness, and inability to move the foot are common findings.

Complications: As in all joint fractures, neurovascular impairment can occur.

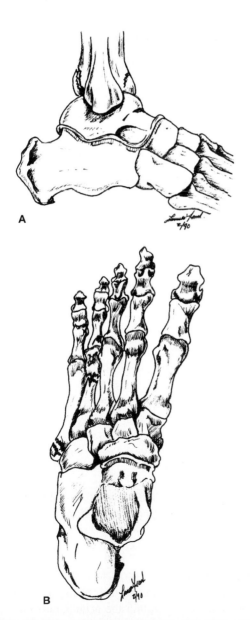

Figure 16–13. A. Ankle fracture. **B.** Foot (metatarsal) fracture.

Stabilization: A pillow splint is ideal for this fracture; air or board splints may be used equally as well. Check continually for distal pulses and neural status.

Foot Fractures

Fractures to the heel bone (os calcis), metatarsal bones, and phalanges (Fig. 16–13B) are all due to direct trauma. Compression fractures to the lumbosacral spine are often associated with a fractured os calcis, owing to the compression force of a sudden stop. With fractures of the feet, pain, swelling, point tenderness, ecchymosis, and inability to bear weight on the foot are all seen. Fractures of the second and third metatarsal bones are usually associated with constant weight bearing after prolonged walking, hiking, or marching and are called stress fractures or fatigue fractures. Pillow splints usually provide the greatest comfort.

■ HEALING PHASES OF BONE

The process of bone healing is very similar physiologically to soft-tissue healing; there is a lag phase of about 5 to 7 days that peaks at about the fourth day. During this time, the phagocytes clean away the dead cells of bone and tissue so that the actual healing can take place with vascularization of the clot formation, which then modifies and forms bone matrix. The average healing time is 6 to 16 weeks, depending, of course, on the extent of the bone injury. Formation of callus, an unorganized meshwork of woven bone developed on the pattern of the original fibrin clot following fracture of the bone, will be ultimately replaced by hard cortical bone about 1 year later.

Many orthopedic physicians prefer to allow up to 1 week after a fracture before attempting to set and cast a fracture, since this delay will allow soft-tissue swelling to reduce and the lag phase to complete. Frequently, emergency nurses (ENs) are required to apply a nonabsorbent cotton compression wrap (sometimes called a Manchu wrap) or some type of rigid padded appliance with Velcro or buckle closures, specifically designed to immobilize that injured part, which should be worn by the patient until swelling has subsided and the physician is ready to reduce the fracture. It should be noted that Manchu cotton compression splints can stay in place for *many* days—even 1 or 2 weeks—without causing skin problems, whereas air splints can macerate the skin after several hours.

■ DISLOCATIONS, SPRAINS, AND STRAINS

CLASSIFICATIONS OF DISLOCATIONS

Loss of motion is particularly diagnostic of a dislocation, which causes disruption of the joint surfaces and loss of continuity. Trauma severe enough to cause fracture-dislocation may also have caused spinal cord trauma; this should serve as a red flag in patient assessment.

Dislocations are commonly referred to in the following terms:

- *Complete dislocation:* completely separates the articulating surfaces of a joint, tearing the ligaments
- *Compound dislocation:* occurs when the joint communicates with the external air
- *Habitual dislocation:* often recurs after replacement
- *Incomplete dislocation:* a subluxation; a slight displacement
- *Pathological dislocation:* results from paralysis, synovitis, infection, or other disease
- *Simple displacement:* the joint is not penetrated by a wound.

The most common complaints with a dislocation are severe pain and inability to move the joint involved, as well as obvious deformity.

MOST COMMON SITES OF DISLOCATION

Elbows, fingers, hips, ankles, jaws, and less commonly, the wrist or knee, can all dislocate, but shoulder dislocation is seen most frequently.

Acromioclavicular Dislocation

As the most frequent site of dislocation, the shoulder joint (Fig. 16–14) may be disrupted anteriorly, posteriorly, and very rarely, inferiorly, but 95 percent of shoulder dislocations are anterior and subcoracoid. The first time a shoulder dislocates, it should be splinted and immobilized for 6 weeks; the second occurrence should indicate the need for

Figure 16–14. Acromioclavicular dislocation.

surgical correction, since the problem tends to become chronic if not addressed.

Pain is extremely severe in all three types of shoulder dislocations, and the patient should be supported and transported in the most comfortable position, which is usually sitting up with the arm and shoulder supported in whatever way is the least painful.

Elbow Dislocation

Dislocations of the elbow (Fig. 16–15) are usually caused by a fall that "jams" the elbow, causing a deformity that is very apparent and exquisitely painful. These injuries should always be splinted and immobilized *in the position as found* and should be seen immediately by a physician for evaluation and reduction before damage is done to the nerves and vessels. Any numbness or paralysis distal to the dislocation is an indication of pressure on the nerves, while loss of pulse or coldness of the distal part indicates pressure on the arterial vessels, which requires *immediate* medical intervention.

Hip Dislocation

The hip joint, formed by the head (ball) of the femur articulating within the acetabulum (socket) of the ilium, can be dislocated (Fig. 16–16) anteri-

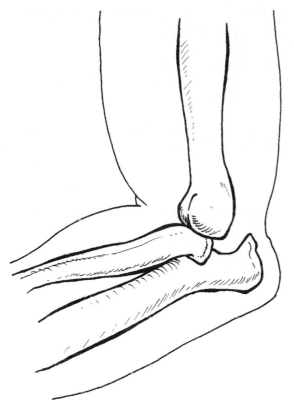

Figure 16–15. Elbow dislocation.

orly or posteriorly. Anterior dislocation is quite rare; posterior dislocation is more common and usually occurs when the knee hits the dashboard of a car or the extended leg is stopped on impact by the floorboard of the vehicle. The posterior dislocation is more common because when the hip is flexed (sitting position), the protective ligaments are more relaxed. Hip dislocation not only is painful and extremely awkward to manage but can severely compromise the sciatic nerve that innervates all the muscles below the knee. Distal neurovascular status must be carefully monitored.

SPRAINS

Sprains occur when ligaments are torn by force beyond the ROM of the joint involved. The damage to the ligament varies in severity, and the more serious injuries to ligaments may well resemble a fracture or dislocation, because sprains all manifest with pain, swelling, discoloration, and impairment of motion. Sprains do not manifest with deformity, however, and in this way are differentiated from dislocations, but x-rays are required to rule out fracture. The two most commonly seen areas of sprain are the ankle and knee, and both

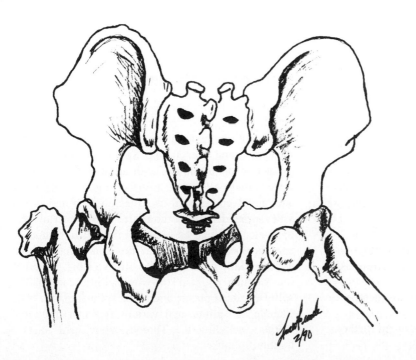

Figure 16–16. Hip dislocation.

should be immobilized for comfort until seen by a physician for further evaluation.

STRAINS

A strain is injury to muscle from overextension or overexertion and may cause intense pain, some swelling, and difficult movement. Strains are most frequently seen in the muscles of the back and arms and are rarely truly serious.

NURSING INTERVENTIONS

Injured parts in sprains and strains are kept elevated to prevent circulatory congestion and splinted for support and comfort. Initially, sprains and strains are treated much the same; the mnemonic *RICE* is helpful as a teaching device for the patient:

- R = rest
- I = ice
- C = compression
- E = elevation

Standard measures are rest, ice packs, or cold compresses for the first 24 to 36 hours (followed by warm packs or soaks to facilitate healing and circulation); soft, rolled wrapping of the part for support and comfort; and elevation to offset congestion and stasis. The patient should be carefully instructed on correct procedures for removing, rerolling, and rewrapping the elastic bandage to provide support but avoid pressure spots and circulatory compromise. Use of canes, crutches, and walkers should all be carefully explained and demonstrated.

NURSING DIAGNOSES

Appropriate nursing diagnoses for dislocations, sprains, and strains would include:

- Potential alteration in neurovascular function related to dislocation, nerve injury, or vascular injury or swelling
- Pain related to swelling and dislocation
- Potential for impairment of skin integrity
- Impaired physical mobility related to dislocation and pain
- Knowledge deficit related to therapeutic regimen
- Anxiety related to pain, treatment methods, and lifestyle implications

■ SPLINTING TECHNIQUES FOR FRACTURES AND DISLOCATIONS

ENs should be knowledgeable and skilled in the application of stabilization devices in the ED. Emergency medical technicians (EMTs) and ambulance personnel across the country are taught to deal with fractures and dislocations in a manner that will *do no harm.* They are taught that most fractures, except open fractures with massive bleeding, do not require speed in either treatment or transportation and that in fact, these patients should be treated and transported slowly and deliberately, with the realization that the manner in which initial care is given determines in many instances whether there is a favorable case outcome.

EMTs are taught that no matter how short the distance to the hospital, all injuries to bones and joints must be splinted as if they were known fractures until proved otherwise because the patient may not be treated immediately upon arrival in the ED. The exception is dislocation, which should never be straightened because movement of the displaced bones may damage nerves and vessels that have already been displaced. These are splinted *as they are found.* Jewelry should always be removed from an injured part before a splint is applied; splints should always *immobilize the joint above and the joint below* when fractures are involved.

TYPES OF SPLINTS AND APPLICATIONS

ENs should be familiar with the various types of splints employed in the prehospital phase of care and should understand the rationale involved with the application of each type. Splints are applied for protection of the injury, with an attempt to minimize damage and prevent further trauma to the tissues involved, as well as to lessen pain and provide some degree of comfort. Any material or appliance that can be used to immobilize traumatized bones and tendons qualifies as a splint. Many commercially made varieties are available, including wooden splints, soft-wire splints, cardboard splints, padded plastic and metal splints, plastic inflatable air splints, and various types of traction splints, including the Thomas, Hare, and Sager traction splints.

Rigid Splints

Rigid splints are effective only if they are long enough to allow the entire fractured bone to be immobilized, are padded sufficiently, and are secured firmly to an uninjured part.

Air Splints

The effectiveness of air splints is limited to fractures of the lower leg and forearm. When they are applied in cold weather, they must be carefully monitored because air in the splint will expand as it warms and may exert potentially dangerous pressure. An air splint should be inflated only by mouth and only to the point at which an indentation in the splint can be made easily with the thumb. Distal toes and fingers must be carefully monitored for perfusion, just as circulation is checked with a new cast, and the air splint should be deflated periodically or removed as soon as possible to prevent maceration of tissues under the moist pressure. One of the distinct advantages of the air splint is that it immobilizes as it also tamponades the bleeding site while still allowing visual access to the injury. Remember that when air transportation is used for an injured patient, caution must be taken to decrease air volume within splints at flight altitude and to closely reassess the neurovascular status regularly; the same cautions apply to PSAGs when used in pelvic fractures. Minimum inflation should be used prior to achieving flight altitude; the zipper type is not made with pop-off capabilities.

Traction Splints

Traction splints are applied not to reduce the fracture but to align it and immobilize the bone ends to prevent further damage during movement and transportation to the hospital. If the circulation, color, and sensation of the distal parts are within normal limits on the patient's arrival at the ED, the splint should be left in place until definitive treatment takes place. For this reason, hospitals and ambulance companies should have interchangeable rotating equipment that can be left with one patient while a replacement is obtained for the next time of need.

REVIEW OF GUIDELINES FOR SPLINTING INJURIES

With upper extremity injuries, the following guidelines apply:

- A fractured humerus should be immobilized with a short splint and bound to the body with a sling-and-swath arrangement.
- Injured elbows are to be immobilized in the position in which found, and the patient should be transported without delay to the nearest medical facility.
- Angulated fractures of the forearm are to be straightened carefully with manual traction before splinting, and pillow bolsters may provide comfort.
- Injured hands are to be splinted in position of function, whereas injured fingers can be splinted with a padded tongue blade.

With hip and lower extremity injuries, the following guidelines apply:

- Fractured or dislocated hips should be immobilized with a long board splint or by simply padding between the legs, tying both legs together, and placing the patient on a long backboard for transport. Dislocated hips manifest with marked deformity at the joint with some flexion and inward rotation of the leg. Once transferred to bed in the ED, the patient will be more comfortable with the leg on the injured side slightly flexed and supported with pillow bolsters.
- Severe angulation of the femur must be corrected by steady traction after the femur has been placed into neutral alignment, using traction splinting, a well-padded board splint, and a full backboard, or again, tying the legs together with adequate padding between the thighs, knees, and ankles.
- Knee fractures or dislocations must be immobilized *in the position found* with a well-padded splint or possibly a pillow molded around and tied much like a Manchu cotton compression dressing.
- Lower-leg fractures should be placed in neutral alignment and immobilized with air splints, pillow bolsters, or traction splints.
- Foot and ankle injuries can be immobilized with a pillow splint molded around the injured foot, with pins and cravats securing it in place. There is also an air-splint boot available; it is effective, but the injury must be watched carefully for circulatory shutdown.

■ THE CAST ROOM

In cast application, although the basic equipment and rationale still apply, many physicians have their own personal preferences for casting materials. ENs should be comfortable with and proficient in the casting process, being knowledgeable in the application of all materials in stock and in the use of the basic tools.

Several types of instruments are usually necessary, including cast knives, cutters, and saws needed for removing old casts. Bandage scissors are necessary for removing bandages under the cast, and a heavy pair of shears should be available for cutting heavy felt padding. Sheet wadding or a thin nonabsorbent cotton web covered with starch to hold it together is commonly used for padding. Piano felt, cut in suitable sizes, is used to provide additional protection against pressure on bony prominences, and sponge rubber padding is also occasionally used. Materials for reinforcing the cast at stress points will include aluminum strips, yucca board, and even plywood, with additions of walking heels and wedges for leg casts. Tubular stockinette in assorted widths is used for the cast lining.

HANDLING CASTING MATERIALS

Assisting in cast application can be a very enjoyable and satisfactory experience if the materials are properly handled. When handling plaster, gloves and gowns should be on hand for physician and assistant, and a deep bucket of water that is between 95°F and 105°F is essential. Water cooler than this will delay the setting of the plaster.

Some of the newer forms of plaster casting set in a matter of minutes, while some of the older ones take up to 24 hours, depending on the extent of the cast. They should all be handled in the same manner, however; submerge the roll of plaster on edge until the bubbling ceases, lift it vertically from the water, and hold it horizontally with the ends secured in the palms. Water is expelled by very gently compressing the roll in a short twist, no more than it takes to supinate the right hand a single time, keeping the left hand in pronation. The roll should not drip when handed over but also must not be wrung so dry that the physician will have difficulty in incorporating it into the cast. The end of the plaster roll is unrolled 2 to 4 in. before

handing it to the physician, and only one roll should be submerged at a time. When casting is completed, care should be taken to pour the plaster residue that has settled in the bottom of the bucket down only sinks that have special plaster traps and not down plumbing with a standard trap. The faucet should be wide open to assist in washing the plaster down rapidly. A very good practice in lieu of pouring residue down sinks is to line the plaster bucket with a plastic bag, and after plaster residue has settled, the water is poured off and the plastic bag with residue is lifted out and deposited in the waste container. This method will minimize plumbing problems and speed clean-up time.

Fiberglass casting products, on the other hand, are widely used and have advantages over plaster casting in that they can be applied and cured in a matter of minutes with use of ultraviolet light. Additionally, there is no plaster clean-up involved. The material is waterproof and facilitates bathing around injured parts without damaging cast structure and integrity.

When assisting with application of a fiberglass casting material, open the package and unroll the fiberglass material and hand it to the physician in the same fashion that plaster is handed. Specialized splints can also be fashioned in a short time for immobilization and support of injured extremities and are sturdy, protective, and waterproof.

DISCHARGE INSTRUCTIONS AFTER CAST APPLICATION

Patients leaving the department with *any* sort of orthopedic appliance that might possibly affect or hinder circulation must be instructed carefully regarding danger signals and proper care of the wounded part. The patient should be instructed to:

1. Keep the injured part elevated (at least 6 in. above heart level) for the next 48 hours.
2. Check for pink, warm-feeling fingers and toes continually. If fingers or toes become dusky or even pale, if there is numbness and severe tingling, and if the extremity becomes cold, the physician should be notified immediately.
3. Realize that pain should begin to subside and that the physician will prescribe med-

ication as he or she determines the need. *Persistent, severe pain unresponsive to medication should be reported to the physician without delay.*

4. Release tensor bandages and adjustable splints and reapply if circulation is compromised or pain is too severe from the compression.

■ INSTRUCTING PATIENTS IN THE USE OF CRUTCHES

When assisting a patient in learning to use crutches, first make very certain that the crutches are properly fitted, have stable hand grips adjusted to permit 30-degree elbow flexion, and have rubber tips with good traction ability. Allow for a two-finger–width space between the anterior axillary fold and the armpiece when the patient is standing erect with the crutches at the side so that weight will be born on the hands, *not* on the axillae. Weight borne on the axillae can damage the brachial nerve and produce "crutch paralysis."

Determining crutch length is most accurately done as follows:

1. Stand the patient against the wall with his or her feet slightly away from the wall. The patient should be wearing flat, firm walking shoes (or shoe).
2. Measure and mark (with chalk) 2 in. out to the side from the toe of the shoe.
3. Then measure 6 in. straight ahead from the first mark and mark this point.
4. Measure from 2 in. below the axilla to the second mark. This will give an approximate crutch length that is more accurate than the old method of subtracting 16 in. from the patient's height and adjusting the crutches accordingly.

The three-point gait is usually indicated when weight cannot be borne on an injured leg or foot. This is a fairly rapid gait but requires strength and balance. If crutches are to be used safely, the patient's arms must be strong enough to support his or her entire body weight.

The crutch–foot sequence (Fig. 16–17) is as follows:

1. With weight borne on the hands, both crutches and the injured lower extremity are moved forward simultaneously.
2. Then the stronger (uninjured) lower extremity is brought forward.

When resting, the patient should stand with the two crutches and feet making a triangle to support the torso and relieve some of the stress on the stronger leg (Figure 16–18).

When going up and down stairs, the patient should move as follows:

1. *To go up stairs:* Advance the stronger uninjured leg first to the next step; then advance the crutches and the injured leg/foot.
2. *To go down stairs:* Place feet forward as far as possible on the top step; advance the crutches to the lower step. The weaker leg is advanced first with crutches for support, then the stronger one follows. The stronger leg shares the work of raising and lowering the body weight with the patient's arms. Remember: stronger legs go up stairs first and down stairs last.

■ REVIEW OF GENERAL MANAGEMENT GUIDELINES

Any patient arriving in the ED with fracture or dislocation of the knee, elbow, or a pulseless extremity must be considered a real emergency, as should the patient with a fracture of the femur. The person with a fractured femur may be having significant occult blood loss and requires rapid evaluation and ongoing monitoring for increasing swelling of the injured part and changing VS. If a traction splint has been applied, this should be left in place until completion of assessment, which includes evaluation of distal pulses, sensory perception, and motor power of the toes and circumferential measurement of the injured part.

A. Always immediately assess the whole patient and document findings. Be sure the airway is open, checking level of consciousness (LOC), ROM, deformities, open wounds, and so on.
B. Always assume the possibility of cervical injury in an unconscious patient with head

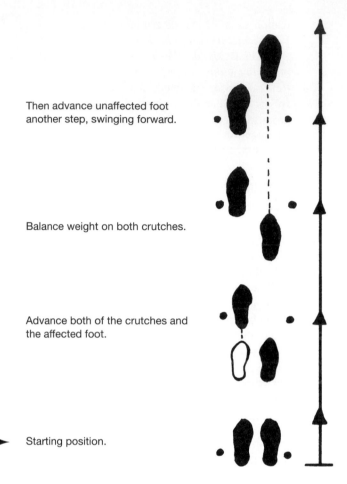

Then advance unaffected foot another step, swinging forward.

Balance weight on both crutches.

Advance both of the crutches and the affected foot.

Figure 16–17. Crutch walking sequence for the three-point gait. Both crutches and the weaker (affected) lower extremity are moved forward simultaneously; then the stronger (unaffected) lower leg is moved forward.

Starting position.

injury after trauma. Be prepared to manage airway and vomitus without endangering the cervical spine.

C. Deformities should be noted, and an assessment of circulation is essential. A pulseless extremity is a grave emergency.

D. If the patient is severely injured, start a flow sheet for vital signs and initiate an intravenous line. A large-bore catheter or needle should be inserted into an appropriate vein, particularly one in the upper extremity or an opposite uninjured limb, to draw blood for complete blood count (CBC), type and cross-match, and to start volume replacement with Ringer's lactate. Remember the potential for occult bleeding in long-bone and pelvic fractures.

E. *After* the patient has been stabilized and the limb completely immobilized, the appropriate x-rays may be requisitioned and obtained.

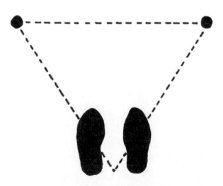

Figure 16–18. Tripod crutch position. A good tripod position must be constantly maintained, with both crutches held fairly widespread out front while both feet are held together in the back. This position provides a safe resting stance, with weight borne on the hands and unaffected leg.

F. Always supervise transfer of the patient to the appropriate stretcher, gurney, or x-ray table, maintaining traction and supporting the injured part.

G. Lacerations may be washed and covered with moist, sterile dressings of NSS.

H. Refrain from cutting off clothes unless necessary, but *do not* refrain from getting them off.

I. Be alert for associated injuries and common combinations, such as the following:
1. A patient falling from a great height with obvious fracture of the calcaneus may also have a compression fracture of the spine.
2. A patient with injuries to the spine or pelvis may develop a paralytic ileus.
3. Commonly associated injuries are:
   a. Kidney injuries with blows to the spine
   b. Spleen or liver injuries combined with rib fractures
   c. Genitourinary injuries combined with pelvic fractures
   d. Injury to a joint adjacent to an obvious fracture
   e. Fractured patella from an MVA combined with a fractured or dislocated hip or femur

J. When ordering x-rays (*most* radiology departments observe these points):
1. Have joint above or below the fracture included in the films.
2. Always have at least two planes filmed.
3. Knees require anteroposterior (AP), lateral, *and* a patellar or "sunrise" view.
4. Ankles require AP, lateral, and oblique, rolling leg inward 10 to 15 degrees for visual alignment.
5. Wrist injuries in young adults should routinely include the navicular view, since fractures of the fossa navicularis do not displace.

K. If general anesthesia is anticipated for an immediate reduction, enforce NPO (nothing by mouth) and be certain to document the time of last ingestion, height, and weight; obtain operative consent.

L. Remember that elevation and cold packs to injured areas can minimize congestion of the returning venous circulation.

M. As a general rule, pain from musculoskeletal injuries can be controlled within reason by proper immobilization, elevation of the injured part, and application of cold packs. If the patient continues to be in great discomfort, the whole problem should be reevaluated for complications requiring immediate attention (entrapment of a nerve, improper splinting of a joint or fracture, or developing compartment syndrome). Usually, the main problem is anxiety and not pain, but be certain.

N. When applying splints:
1. Be certain injuries are splinted with adequate padding over pressure points; when splinting the wrist or forearm, the hand should be maintained in a functional position with fingers bolstered around a bandage roll and visible so temperature and neurovascular status can be monitored.
2. *Carefully check extremity pulses* with deformity injuries. If a pulse is not obtainable, assess the capillary refill time (normally 2 seconds) by compressing and then quickly releasing pressure on the nail bed. Extremities must be closely monitored to assure adequate blood supply.
3. Before applying any splint that will exert pressure (air, Manchu, or plaster reinforcements), carefully assess and document the absence or presence of normal motor and sensory status, to avoid having someone later contend that the splint caused sensorimotor problems.

O. Fracture of the clavicle (collar bone) is one of the most common fractures seen, with pain, deformity, and the tendency to support the arm on the injured side. A "figure-eight" splint is applied with the patient's shoulders back and squared, checking carefully for quality of distal pulses.

P. Pelvic fractures may not be obvious until full evaluation is done and the pelvic girdle has been stressed by pressure over the symphysis. The patient will complain of pain in the groin without much deformity, if any. Remember that pelvic fractures can account for occult bleeding of up to 6 units (3 L).

■ REFERENCES

1. Barber JM, Dillman PA. *Emergency Patient Care for the EMT-A.* Reston, Va: Reston Publishing; 1981:345.
2. Gambron R. Taking the pressure out of compartment syndrome. *AJN.* August 1988;1076–1080.
3. Mubarak SJ, Hargens AR, Karkal SS (eds). Compartment syndromes and Volkmann's contracture. *Emergency Medicine Reports.* 1988;9:185–192.
4. Lavin RJ. The high-pressure demands of compartment syndrome. *RN.* February 1989;22–25.
5. Emergency Nurses Association: *Emergency Nursing Core Curriculum.* 4th ed. Philadelphia, Pa: WB Saunders; 1994:432.
6. Heckman JD. Fractures: emergency care and complications. *Clin Symp.* 1991;(43)3.

■ BIBLIOGRAPHY

American Academy of Orthopaedic Surgeons. *Emergency Care and Transportation of the Sick and Injured.* 5th ed. Park Ridge, Ill: AAOS; 1992.

American College of Surgeons Committee on Trauma. *Advanced Trauma Life Support Manual.* Chicago, Ill: ACS; 1993.

Barber JM, Dillman PA. *Emergency Patient Care for the EMT-A.* Reston, Va: Reston Publishing; 1981.

Cahill SB, Balskus M. *Intervention in Emergency Nursing: The First 60 Minutes.* Rockville, Md: Aspen Publishers; 1986.

Cardona VD, ed. *Trauma Reference Manual, Maryland Institute for EMSS.* Bowie, Md: Brady Company; 1985.

Chipman C, ed. Orthopaedic emergencies. *Top Emerg Med.* 1981;2(4).

Committee on Injuries, American Academy of Orthopaedic Surgeons: *Emergency Care and Transportation of the Sick and Injured.* 4th ed. Chicago, Ill: AAOS; 1986.

Dykes PC. Minding the five p's of neurovascular assessment. *AJN.* 1993:38–39.

Emergency Nursing Association. *Emergency Nursing Core Curriculum.* 4th ed. Philadelphia, Pa: WB Saunders; 1994.

Emergency Nurses Association. *Trauma Nursing Core Course.* 4th ed. Chicago, Ill: ENA; 1995.

Feliciano DV, Moore EE, Mattox KL. *Trauma.* 3rd ed. Stamford, Conn: Appleton & Lange; 1995:733–818.

Foss J. Orthopedic injuries. In: Fincke MK, Lanros NE: *Emergency Nursing: A Comprehensive Review.* Rockville, Md: Aspen Publishers; 1986.

Grant H, Murray R. *Emergency Care.* 4th ed. Englewood Cliffs, NJ: Prentice-Hall; 1986.

Harrahill M. Upper extremity nerve assessment: a quick review. *J Emerg Nurs.* 1995;21(4):360–362.

Heckman JD. Fractures: emergency care and complications. *Clin Symp.* 1991;43(3).

Hodge D, Gregg J, Christofersen M, Wong J. Trauma to elbows, knees, and ankles. *Pediatr Emerg Care.* 1991;7(3):188–194.

Knezevich-Brown BA. *Trauma Nursing Principles and Practice.* E. Norwalk, Conn: Appleton & Lange; 1986.

Lee G. *Flight Nursing: Principles and Practice.* St. Louis, Mo: Mosby-Year Book; 1991.

Maull KI, Rodriguez A, Wiles CE. *Complications in Trauma and Critical Care.* Philadelphia, Pa: WB Saunders; 1996.

McSwain NE, Butman AM, Caukin B, et al. (eds). *Pre-Hospital Trauma Life Support Basic and Advanced.* 3rd ed. St. Louis, Mo: Mosby Lifeline; 1994.

Mubarak SJ. Coping with the diagnostic complexities of the compartment syndrome. *Emerg Med Rep.* 1988;9: 185–192.

O'Boyle CM, Davis DK, Russo BA, et al. *Emergency Care: The First 24 Hours.* E. Norwalk, Conn: Appleton & Lange; 1985.

Phippen ML, Wells MP. *Perioperative Nursing Practice.* Philadelphia, Pa: WB Saunders; 1994.

Rodi M. *Emergency Orthopedics, Emergency Care: Assessment and Intervention.* 2nd ed. St. Louis, Mo: CV Mosby; 1978.

Rourke K. The evaluation and treatment of acute ankle sprains. *J Emerg Nurs.* 1994;20:528–539.

Sandzen SC Jr. Crush injuries of the upper extremity. *Am Fam Physician.* Sept 1990;721–733.

Schneider FR. *Orthopaedics in Emergency Care.* St. Louis, Mo: CV Mosby; 1978.

Sonzogni JJ, Gross ML. Hip and pelvic injuries in the young: fractures and special disorders. *Emerg Med.* June 1993;19–37.

Sonzogni JJ, Gross ML. Hip and pelvic injuries in the young: biomechanics and soft-tissue insults. *Emerg Med.* May 1993;74–94.

Thompson DA. When a 'wing' breaks, keep looking. *Emerg Med.* August 1992;110–112.

Weeks PM. *Acute Bone and Joint Injuries of the Hand and Wrist: A Clinical Guide to Management.* St. Louis, Mo: CV Mosby; 1981.

■ REVIEW: MUSCULOSKELETAL TRAUMA

1. Describe the types of bones comprising the human skeleton and the five major functions they serve.

2. Explain the difference between synovial joints and fused joints and give two examples of each.

3. Describe the rationale for documentation of range of motion (ROM) and neural status following trauma.

4. Explain the categories of fractures and their classifications.

5. Describe initial nursing assessment and management of a forearm injury that is followed by sudden pain, tenderness, slight swelling, and a slight deformity.

6. List five factors that may contribute to bone fractures and identify three significant threats that can result from bone fractures.

7. Describe the mechanisms involved in acute compartment syndrome and identify the five P's of vascular occlusion.

8. Explain the critical time factor for intervention in acute compartment syndrome and identify end results if the pressure is not relieved in time.

9. Explain the importance of assessing and monitoring distal pulses when fractures or dislocations are present.

10. List at least four appropriate nursing diagnoses for acute compartment syndrome.

11. Describe the appropriate nursing management of an open fracture.

12. Describe the best method of preventing wound infection following open fracture.

13. Describe the way in which traumatically amputated tissue should be handled and preserved.

14. Identify the most anatomically complicated joint in the upper extremity and describe the management of associated fractures/dislocations.

15. Describe the serious complications that may occur following fractures to the posterior pelvis and describe stabilization techniques.

16. List at least six appropriate nursing diagnoses for closed pelvic fractures.

17. Identify the amount of blood loss possible in a fractured femur and describe the initial management for femoral fracture.

18. Describe evaluation of neural status following fractures to the knee and outline the appropriate stabilization procedure.

19. List the important points of patient instruction for those leaving the emergency department (ED) with *any* sort of orthopedic appliance that might possibly affect or hinder circulation.

20. Describe the way in which crutch length should be determined for a patient and the crutch–foot sequence for using the three-point gait.

Surface Trauma 17

The human skin, or integumentum, is made up of a complex combination of epithelial and connective tissues; it forms a tough, pliable, and remarkably adaptable protective covering for the body, performing many diverse functions as its largest organ. With its density, texture, and color genetically determined, the skin covers between 1.6 and 1.9 m^2 on the average adult human. Since the skin is the organism's only barrier between itself and the environment, it is probably inevitable that injury of one degree or another will occur to the skin during a lifetime of even normal daily activity; the marvel is the skin's resiliency and ability to heal itself, given a fair chance.

An inordinate number of patients seeking care in emergency- and primary-care facilities present with surface trauma, either as an isolated incident or in association with other traumatic injuries. Nurses attending these patients are routinely called upon, within their expanded role, to establish the working database; intervene as necessary; and assess, cleanse, infiltrate, and dress most wounds. In recent years, a significant number of nurses who have received special instruction and clinical supervision in wound closure have been given the opportunity to function in that expanded capacity when appropriate.

This chapter addresses the most frequently seen types of surface trauma and discusses their management in detail. The premise is that a thorough understanding of the elements of wound assessment and management will result in optimum wound care, whether or not the reader ever actually undertakes any suturing, which has heretofore been primarily the physician's domain. In years past, many nurses sutured wounds, either under direct supervision, in emergency situations, or during late hours when the physician was unavailable and they were instructed to do so. The primary purpose of this chapter is to present a body of directly applicable information that will help emergency nurses (ENs) contribute to optimum outcomes for their patients.

The goal in caring for surface trauma is to restore function of the injured part while achieving the best cosmetic result; the intent is to accomplish both without doing further harm.

■ ANATOMY AND PHYSIOLOGY OF THE SKIN

Skin (Fig. 17–1) is composed of two layers: the epidermis ("the skin upon") and the dermis; subcutaneous tissue layers lie immediately under the dermis. As the largest organ of the body, skin performs multiple complex functions for the organism it covers.

The skin's primary function is to protect deeper tissues and structures from injury, drying, and bacterial invasion. Other functions include maintenance of body temperature, excretion of water and some organic salts, absorption of water and a very few chemical agents, and sensory awareness (touch, pain, temperature, and pressure). Skin is never static, undergoing constant change, renewal, and adaptation to meet the body's needs. Consider the difference in skin appearance in various body sites; it is smooth and soft in some regions but rough and furrowed in others. Thick, coarse hair grows in areas such as the eyebrows, axillas, and pubis, but only downy

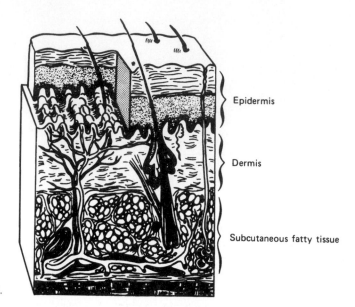

Figure 17–1. Anatomy of the skin.

Epidermis

Dermis

Subcutaneous fatty tissue

fuzz is visible on the forehead. Skin appearance varies with age and race, as well as from place to place on the same individual's body. Wide variations in thickness exist; the skin of the eyelid is almost paper-thin, for instance, whereas the soles of the feet are perhaps 10 to 20 times thicker.

Although providing a pleasing physical and cosmetic appearance is not considered an essential function of the skin in terms of survival, it is most certainly an important consideration in the emotional well-being of most human beings; a *great* deal of attention is given to this aspect of wound management by those who have suffered damage to their appearance. Cosmetic results are extremely important to most healthy individuals. Physicians and ENs have a serious obligation, therefore, to all patients to provide wound care with integrity and accountability, remembering that patients will "wear" the results of that care for the rest of their lives.

To appreciate what causes poor cosmetic results and scarring of repaired areas in skin trauma, it is necessary to understand the structure and functions of epidermis, dermis, and underlying subcutaneous tissue.

EPIDERMIS

Epithelial tissues of the epidermis appear microscopically to have several layers but no blood supply. The several top layers of epidermis are dead, working to the surface from the living cells of the deeper germinative layer of epidermis, which lies adjacent to the dermis and derives nourishment from interstitial fluid provided by the dermis. This deep layer is also where melanin (pigment) is produced; melanin provides skin color and shading and causes freckles.

The epidermis has two characteristics of particular significance in wound management; (1) it has no tensile strength and (2) it has the ability to regenerate as long as germinative cells remain at the wound site. The epidermis will, as healing progresses, regenerate and eventually cover the dermal layer below. Where epidermal tissue has been completely destroyed over broad areas, as is often the case in extensive burns, skin grafts are necessary to replace the destroyed germinative layer of the wounded area.

The epidermis is like tissue paper over most areas of the body except for the soles of the feet and palms of the hands, where it thickens as necessary to afford protection to underlying tissues. Anyone who has suffered a severe sunburn will remember peeling away large areas of thin, dead, translucent skin; that skin was actually layers of epidermis lifted off the dermal base by blistering. It is important to remember that since epidermis has no tensile strength, it will not hold sutures; sutures must *always* be placed well through the dermal layer.

DERMIS

The dermis (corium), or true skin, is by comparison more complex. It has two layers, one of which (the papillary layer) contains capillaries that bring blood into close proximity with the germinating layers of the epidermis. The deeper layer (the reticular layer) is a dense mass of elastic, connective tissue fibers containing sensory receptors, nerves, vascular structures, fat, hair follicles, and sebaceous glands.

The two dermal characteristics of significance in wound management are that (1) the dermis does not regenerate and (2) it has tensile strength. Wounds involving lost dermal tissue result in scarring unless wound revision is undertaken before closure; acne pits and chickenpox scars are excellent examples of dermal loss with reepithelization of the excavated surface plane and permanent scarring as a result.

Causes of Scarring

As already discussed, loss of dermal surface is a frequent cause of visible surface defect. Another is uneven approximation of wound edges, with one surface healing higher than the other from overriding edges; the "scar" effect is accentuated by light and shadows. A wound with matched planes will not generally be visible, even if it is wide, so long as it is flat, flexible, and does not have an overly reddish cast once the maturation phase has completed and hyperemia has faded. With loss of dermis, a deep scar will stand out permanently, no matter how narrow.

The most common cause of scarring is poor approximation of wound edges and loose stitches, allowing the migration of collagen fibers and fibroblasts from subcutaneous tissues up through the wound sinus to the surface, where they are deposited as scar tissue (Fig. 17–2). For scarring to occur, there must be an opening in the dermis through which these scar-forming substances can reach the surface for deposit. There is nothing in skin itself that scars; there is only the migration of substances up from the subcutaneous layer to the surface through poorly approximated wound edges. Understanding the reason for well-placed sutures and closely approximated wound edges is essential to achieving good cosmetic results in wound repair.

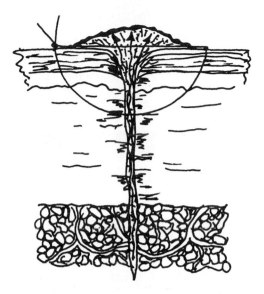

Figure 17–2. Migration of fibroblasts to the surface causes scarring; this is the result of a poorly placed (too shallow) and loosely tied suture.

Sutures left in tissues longer than necessary tend to create a wicklike effect, allowing fibroblasts and collagen fibers to also migrate upward and deposit small "buttons" of scar tissue at puncture sites. This is sometimes seen, for instance, on the abdomen of a patient who had a long midline incision with silk suture closure placed many years ago, when sutures were left in place for 10 to 12 days after surgery. The wick action of the old silk sutures created a great many scars; today's silk suture has been engineered to eliminate wick action but is seldom used now for cutaneous closure. To minimize any chance of scar-forming deposits from wick action, plastic surgeons generally remove sutures as soon as primary healing is underway, sometimes as early as 12 to 24 hours after wound closure. The wound, however, is always sturdily reinforced with skin strips and tape before suture removal.

■ PATHOPHYSIOLOGY OF SURFACE TRAUMA

Soft-tissue injury, exclusive of thermal injury, is generally categorized as being one of four groups or types; contusions, abrasions, lacerations (including avulsions and amputations), and puncture wounds (Fig. 17–3).

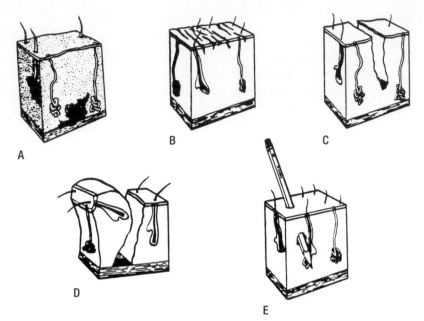

Figure 17–3. Types of soft-tissue injuries: **A.** contusion, **B.** abrasion, **C.** laceration, **D.** avulsion, **E.** puncture wound.

PARTIAL- VERSUS FULL-THICKNESS WOUNDS

Within the four injury categories, surface injuries are further defined as partial-thickness or full-thickness wounds. When the dermis remains intact, the injury is called a partial-thickness injury. A wound that extends through the dermis and exposes subcutaneous tissues or structures is termed a full-thickness injury and requires closure with appropriate suture material. Partial-thickness injuries, on the other hand, may be treated more easily, since there is less chance of scarring and infection with the dermal barrier intact against collagen fiber migration and bacterial invasion. After inspection and cleansing, these wounds are frequently closed with skin strips and/or tape using the "butterfly" method of bridging wound edges, followed with an appropriate dressing and routine follow-up care.

CONTUSIONS

A contusion (see Fig. 17–3A) is usually a closed, nonpenetrating localized injury of subcutaneous tissue caused by blunt force that results in tears of the small blood vessels, extravasation of red blood cells (RBCs) into interstitial spaces, and discoloration. Contusion implies bruising. Frequently, the skin splits open from impact; this is called "impact lacerations" or "linear lacerations." These

wounds technically are lacerations but have contused edges and to heal uneventfully, require surgical revision before the wound can be closed. Any nonviable tissue must be removed.

Hematoma Formation

A frequent problem occurring in tandem with severe contusion is hematoma formation. Venous beds may continue to ooze significantly if the shearing/crushing force of impact was great enough, causing blood to pool and "pocket." This pooled blood may be resorbed in time, but hematoma formation bears close watching to be certain that no problem is developing. Hematomas distort wound edges and hamper optimum healing if allowed to persist; hematomas are dangerous because they support bacterial growth, which may lead to serious wound complications and can also evolve into a compartment syndrome.

Time Patterns in Resolution

As RBCs escape venous walls into the surrounding interstitial spaces, lyse, and slowly resolve, they cause visible color changes. Understanding these color patterns as they relate to the passage of time (Fig. 17–4) is valuable in assessing the age of wounds; this is frequently pertinent medicolegal information, so ENs should document any patterns or colors observed when assessing such injuries. A

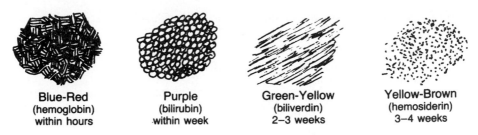

| Blue-Red (hemoglobin) within hours | Purple (bilirubin) within week | Green-Yellow (biliverdin) 2–3 weeks | Yellow-Brown (hemosiderin) 3–4 weeks |

Figure 17–4. Time patterns in resolution of bruises and discoloration. Rate of resolution and fade depends on (1) size of bruise, (2) age of patient, and (3) efficiency of local circulation.

case in point is the knowledgeable assessment of injuries in possible child-abuse situations.

A bruise is initially blue-red, changing to purple, then green-yellow, and finally to brown before it slowly disappears. The color change is due to the local conversion of hemoglobin released from the ruptured RBCs to bilirubin (red bile), then to biliverdin (green bile), which in turn is converted to golden-yellow hemosiderin. Broadly speaking, the swollen, blue-red discoloration of the area becomes evident within 1 hour or so of injury, with the discoloration gradually phasing and finally disappearing within 2 to 4 weeks. Many factors affect the rate of change, including the size of the contusion and the patient's age, circulatory condition, and nutritional status.[1]

ABRASIONS

An abrasion (e.g., friction burn, pavement skid) is a painful wound involving the epidermis and upper layers of the dermis (see Fig. 17–3B). It is a forceful loss of skin surface from scraping on a harder surface. The mechanism of injury often contributes imbedded foreign material that requires careful and scrupulous removal; otherwise, the epidermis regenerates, covers the defect, and seals in the discoloration. The result is a permanent tattoo.

LACERATIONS

A laceration (see Fig. 17–3C) is a wound resulting from tearing or incisional forces against the skin and may involve crush injuries, avulsions, and amputations as well. In the wound sense, a laceration is really any traumatic opening of the skin, as opposed to a surgical incision, and of course involvement may range from superficial to deep structures. Lacerations may affect subcutaneous tissues,

fascial planes, tendons, nerves, muscles, and large blood vessels.

An avulsion (see Fig. 17–3D) is tissue torn away from its circulatory base. Complexity of management in lacerations is compounded by depth and numbers of underlying structures involved. Painstaking measures must be taken to assess damage accurately and manage it appropriately. Specific management approaches for lacerations, avulsions, and amputations follow later in this chapter.

PUNCTURE WOUNDS

In a puncture wound (see Fig. 17–3E) a foreign object, usually pointed or sharp, penetrates the skin and in some instances remains imbedded in the tissue. Such injuries are most commonly incurred by stepping on nails, pins, or staples; by accidental or intentional stabbing with sharp, pointed objects; and by animal or human bites. Puncture wounds are frequently the direct result of vehicular trauma, with victims being impaled by flying glass and metal, being thrown from vehicles (bicycles, motorcycles, automobiles), and an assortment of bizarre incidents. Inherent in all puncture wounds, however, is the threat of occult damage to underlying structures and a high risk of wound infection. These injuries require careful and accurate confirmation of the patient's tetanus immunization status and other specific management considerations that are detailed later.

■ PHASES OF HEALING

Wound healing takes place in three phases. Understanding these phases and their implications contributes significantly to the EN's ability to achieve optimum management of wounds and to intelligently instruct patients in their own wound care. A great deal of unnecessary anxiety can be avoided if accurate information about the wound is shared with the persons most concerned. Optimum outcomes are achieved in both the healing process and patient satisfaction if patients are helped to understand the phases their wound will undergo.

LAG PHASE

The lag phase is the autolytic, or catabolic, stage, when the injured tissues and dead cells are being torn down and cleared away by the phagocytic action of white blood cells (WBCs). Edema, swelling, and perhaps inflammation are present in proportion to the amount of tissue damage involved; the phase usually lasts from 5 to 7 days. This is a weak period for the wound, as the fibrin network is being formed to bridge the defect, capillaries are beginning to proliferate, and granulation tissue is developing to provide a physiological barrier against bacterial invasion of already-compromised tissues. The wound seals during this period as the sutured edges unite, but it remains unstable. This consideration plays a significant role in determining when sutures should be removed and how suture lines can best be reinforced until the wound has gained strength.

ANABOLIC PHASE

The anabolic, or building-up, phase of healing follows next, with all dead tissue cleared away and the basic bridgework of healing in place and secure. An increasing migration of fibroblasts and collagen fibers occurs; capillary bed proliferation increases, bringing greater blood flow to the area (which accounts for the *normal* erythema of wound edges); and the wound itself steadily gathers tensile strength. Scar tissue within the wound gradually forms as the wound heals from below, with upward migration of collagen and fibroblasts. Epithelial cells regenerate and, so to speak, gradually resurface the defect itself as the subsurface healing progresses.

This anabolic phase usually lasts from 2 to 3 weeks, depending on the depth and location of the wound. It is generally safe, therefore, to remove sutures in 7 to 10 days, reinforcing the wound

carefully with skin strips prior to suture removal. This technique is discussed later in the chapter.

MATURATION PHASE

During the maturation phase, which may last from 2 or 3 months to 2 years, more collagen is laid down, with other interlaced fibers already in place; the wound is further strengthened. Surface scarring gradually matures as redness fades and suture lines flatten and become thinner. Hoped-for cosmetic effects often cannot be fully realized until a full 2 years have elapsed.

Patients should leave the emergency facility with a clear understanding of the stages their wounds will undergo and what they may correctly anticipate under normal circumstances.

■ INTENTION IN WOUND HEALING

There are three approaches in facilitating wound healing; each approach is employed for specific reasons. Primary intention, secondary intention (granulation), and tertiary (delayed) intention are used to achieve optimal results in the face of each individual set of wound circumstances.

PRIMARY INTENTION

Sometimes referred to as first or primary closure, the primary-intention method is the desirable way of closing wounds and is possible in most wounds that are clean, incision-type lacerations or that have been adequately cleansed and satisfactorily revised to meet the criteria for this approach.

Underlying structures are reapproximated and sutured with care to make certain that no dead spaces exist for "pooling" of serum and the formation of hematomas, as well as to ensure they will support the surface closure that follows. Opposing wound edges are then carefully and precisely approximated in hopes of restoring function to as near normal as possible.

Criteria for wounds that should undergo primary closure include:

- A "clean" wound
- Minimal damage to edges and surrounding tissues (or capability of being adequately revised to same)

- Minimal superficial or deep-tissue loss
- Absence of infection or of high risk of infection
- A time lapse of less than 6 hours from injury

A time lapse of more than 6 to 8 hours usually contraindicates primary closure by anyone other than perhaps a plastic surgeon with special expertise in evaluating and managing high-risk potentials in older wounds. This concern stems from the "golden period" concept; that is, bacteria have an advantageous lead time to become established in wounds that remain contaminated and uncleansed for a significant period. If the wound is in a highly vascular area and the degree of contamination appears small, however, the time may be extended to as long as 12 hours. This risky sort of determination requires a physician's judgment. ENs should *never* attempt actual wound closure under these circumstances but should instead pursue a careful assessment of the damage, control of bleeding, and thorough cleansing and preparation as appropriate. When contamination is heavy and there is any question about the vascular supply, it is generally wise simply to cleanse thoroughly and use delayed closure as the method of choice.

SECONDARY INTENTION

Most commonly referred to as "granulation," secondary intention is the method of intentionally delaying closure, allowing the wound to heal from the inside out, closing itself as best it can. These wounds usually involve either a loss of tissue significant enough that wound edges cannot be approximated accurately or gross contamination that makes primary closure an extremely high-risk procedure. The resulting scar formation and subsequent contraction of the scar lead to greater deformity. Loss of function in the area involved often requires later surgical release of contractions and plastic surgery revision of the wound.

Wounds that are usually allowed to close by secondary intention include gunshot wounds (GSWs), gaping deep-tissue avulsions, full-thickness burns, associated extensive crush injuries, and wounds where infection is established.

TERTIARY INTENTION

Tertiary intention is a delayed closure employed for a specific time to combat infection or gross contamination. Essentially the wound remains open, although it may be pulled together loosely to allow free wound access and drainage. During this time, the wound is continually cleansed and debrided as a minimal amount of granulation tissue is allowed to form. Wound revision with surgical closure is performed as soon as possible, but this delayed closure may also result in greater scar formation. All things considered, tertiary intention is generally far more acceptable cosmetically than allowing the wound simply to heal by secondary intention with its resulting unsightly granulated scar.

Wounds requiring this type of management may include puncture wounds, animal and human bites, surrounding cellulitis, and "barnyard" contamination with the threat of anaerobic pathogens, and abscesses.

■ NURSING MANAGEMENT OF SOFT-TISSUE INJURIES

Before specific considerations in each of the soft-tissue categories are discussed, the four basic considerations in the initial management of all wounds are reviewed here:

- *Bleeding must be controlled by the most appropriate means.* Direct pressure, with elevation and immobilization of the part if possible, is usually the most effective method. Ice-pack application may help slow venous oozing. *Direct pressure* means exactly that; never expect stacks of 4 × 4's wrapped on tightly with a roller bandage to do what direct pressure with the palm of the hand can do. More than a few patients have nearly "bled out" because someone relied on this assumption. Strong, direct pressure *must* be held over a spurting, pulsating, bleeding site; the patient may become severely volume-depleted in a surprisingly short time otherwise. Tourniquets are absolutely contraindicated unless exsanguination will result without their use. A great deal of damage has been done by the injudicious application of tourniquets; direct pressure would often have done the job without jeopardizing tissue and structures distal to the bleeding site.

- *Preserve the injured vessels as well as possible.* A common misconception is that one will "bleed to death" or exsanguinate if arteries are severed. Arterial walls are muscular and, when completely severed, they constrict and retract; this appears to be the body's way of preserving the blood supply. Bleeding in this situation is less significant than we tend to expect and, as a rule, responds to simple, direct pressure.
- *Lacerated* arteries, however, can be the source of massive blood loss because the injured arterial wall is *not* able to constrict itself and conserve blood loss. These bleeding points really challenge the EN and demand application of direct pressure until appropriate surgical steps can be taken.
- Until rather recently it was thought that spurting arteries should be clamped while waiting for the physician to arrive and intervene. Now we realize that clamping injured arteries with anything less than a vascular clamp contributes little to preserving the valuable arterial wall for anastomosis. Do not waste time and energy trying to "retrieve" and clamp spurting arteries.
- If bleeding is unresponsive to direct pressure over the wound, or if vascular damage is really extensive, the next recourse is using the major arterial pressure points to control the threat of exsanguination.
- *Prevent further contamination and trauma to the wound.* Protect tissues by handling them gently during inspection and cleansing them thoroughly during preparation. Minimize tissue trauma by maintaining a moist, sterile environment and prevent dryness by covering the wound with sterile normal saline solution (NSS) sponges.
- *Areas being cleansed for surgical repair should be shaved as little as possible.* It is now recognized that shaving increases desquamation of the epithelium, compounding contamination of the area being prepped. *Never* shave eyebrows. They do not always grow back fully, and their loss

may result in costly legal action and damages. They also serve as useful landmarks during apposition of wound edges in repair.

CONTUSIONS

The subsurface damage in contusions may extend to varying depths and is usually accompanied by swelling and pain. Small bruises require no special emergency attention; in more severe soft-tissue injuries, swelling and extravasation beneath the skin can often be reduced by applying firm padding and a soft roller bandage to exert pressure. Early application of cold packs minimizes venous ooze and may contribute to the patient's comfort. As the contusion begins to heal, application of warm compresses may augment comfort levels, as well as accelerate the healing process.

As a general rule, hematomas require evacuation so that resolution can proceed normally and without the threat of a wound-complicating breakdown and infection.

ABRASIONS

Not only are extensive abrasions extremely painful, but they also pose nursing management problems that are frequently time consuming and tedious to resolve. Abrasions must be carefully and thoroughly cleansed; appropriate anesthesia must be provided before cleansing is begun.

The best topical agent to use for anesthesia is aqueous 4 percent lidocaine (Xylocaine), which is available in pour-top bottles of various sizes. Sterile 4 × 4s soaked in this solution should be laid over abraded areas and allowed to remain in place for at least 10 minutes. Since the lidocaine is absorbed systemically, care must be taken not to exceed normal dose limits of 20 mL 1 percent solution in adults, and 3 mg/kg in children. A 2.5 percent lidocaine/2.5 percent prilocaine creme is available that provides topical anesthesia within 1 to 2 hours. Once administration limits have been met using these agents and anesthesia is still required, the next alternative may be the application of ice packs to achieve comparable, short-term anesthesia.

Following this, the wound area should be irrigated copiously with warm, sterile NSS until it is cleansed as well as possible. Any remaining imbedded foreign matter must be removed to prevent possible tattooing. A sterile needlepoint or a #11 scalpal blade works well; a light "flipping" motion should be used to remove small specks. A soft plastic surgical scrub sponge or sterile applicator may have to be used to cleanse the surface area lightly, followed again by copious irrigation with warm, sterile NSS.

Denuded nerve ends in the dermis account for the wound's extreme sensitivity. Comfort is provided by covering the wound and preventing air contact as soon as possible. Some physicians advocate the use of antibacterial ointment prior to dressing; others prefer using a thin application of sterile Vaseline and no dressing. In any event, the primary layer of the dressing, if used, should be a fine mesh that allows weeping serum to pass through without adhering. (Dressings are discussed later in the chapter, with particular attention to materials recommended for the primary layer.) A snugly applied top layer adds to the patient's comfort, acting as a pressure dressing.

Pseudomonas infection is a relatively common occurrence with abrasions, as it is with burns. The patient should be advised and instructed carefully on regular dressing changes and signs of infection to watch for and report rapidly.

LACERATIONS

Although lacerations are thought of as incisional injuries, we must realize that lacerations take many forms. Technically, a laceration is any break in the skin. It follows that with lacerations, the risk of injury to underlying tissues is always a major concern. For this reason especially, lacerations of all types and from all causes must be carefully assessed for occult damage. Subcutaneous tissues, fascial planes, tendons, nerves, muscles, and larger blood vessels all become potential injury sites once the skin has been pierced or torn.

More often than not, the mechanism of injury suggests the probable type and extent of damage. A sharp blow, such as slamming a door on a finger, may result in a splitting laceration of the soft tissue with an underlying fracture—an open fracture. A slice into the skin done with a kitchen knife or on a broken glass rim submerged in the sink is frequently associated with at least a nicked tendon sheath. Deep lacerations caused by barbed wire should be considered to carry a high risk for barn-

yard organisms and should be treated accordingly. Lacerations from metal stripping and flashing account for many significant hand and forearm lacerations of arteries and tendon sheaths. Lacerations are *always* suspect for underlying occult injury until proved otherwise; careful inspection, evaluation, and scrupulous wound preparation are essential nursing responsibilities in the ED.

AVULSIONS

In an avulsion, tissue is torn away from its supportive circulatory base; avulsions require special management considerations. Frequently, tissue lifted as a "flap" may not even be of full thickness. In this instance, the wound should be thoroughly irrigated and cleansed as appropriate; the flap should then be laid back in place as well as possible after debridement and secured with sterile adhesive skin strips.

Necrotic areas around the perimeter may develop, but the major portion of central tissue frequently heals back into place. When a large chunk of tissue has been torn away from its circulatory base and is hanging by a thin strip of skin, sever the tissue and treat it as you would an amputated part. Salvageability of avulsed tissue depends on careful handling.

Wound site cleansing and thorough inspection may require topical anesthesia, as with abrasions, and hemostasis may have to be achieved with pressure, Gel-foam, or topical thrombin.

Large degloved areas of skin may sometimes be replanted successfully on their original sites. Care providers should be instructed, when possible, to handle tissue by rolling it up so that subcutaneous tissue and fat are inside and protected from being dried out while en route to the ED from home, factory, or field. The area from which tissue has been avulsed should be protected with moist, sterile (if possible), NSS-soaked gauze pads, with bleeding controlled in the appropriate manner.

AMPUTATIONS AND REPLANTATION

During trauma resuscitation, the EN may face the need to preserve anatomic parts for replantation or donation. Guidelines for the procedures should be immediately available to personnel in the trauma resuscitation areas. Replantation is a microsurgical procedure in which severed parts can be reattached to their circulatory and neural base. There are no absolute rules that govern the procedure, so every single patient must be individually considered; certain guidelines are widely accepted, however.

Indications and Contraindications

Table 17–1 lists replantation indications and contraindications. All thumb amputations should be considered for replantation since the thumb is a vital component of the useful hand. When multiple digits are amputated, they may be reattached singly or in groups to achieve a functional grip. Other indications for attempts at replantation include amputations in children; clean amputations at the wrist, forearm, or palm; or individual digits amputated distal to the superficialis insertion. Contraindications to replantation are massive associated injuries, medical problems that prohibit surgery, crush injuries, avulsion injuries, and individual digit amputations that involve the proximal interphalangeal or metacarpophalangeal joints.

Nursing Interventions

When a patient with a traumatic amputation presents, ENs should:

1. Assess the patient for associated skeletal, neurological, or visceral injuries;
2. Establish intravenous access with a large-bore (14- to 16-gauge) catheter using Ringer's lactate solution to "keep open";
3. Irrigate the wound with Ringer's lactate to remove dirt. (Ringer's lactate is preferred over NSS because fewer histological changes in small blood vessels are produced.) Do not debride. Do not use hydrogen peroxide or povidone iodine since they are toxic to freshly wounded tissue;
4. Cover the hand or extremity wound with sponges moistened with Ringer's lactate;
5. Control hemorrhage without interfering with blood flow to healthy tissue; *do not* use clamps to control bleeding vessels;
6. Instruct the patient to remain NPO (nothing by mouth) and to abstain from smoking or chewing tobacco;
7. Administer broad-spectrum antibiotics and tetanus toxoid (if indicated);
8. Give 600 mg aspirin by suppository (if not contraindicated) for antiagglutinant effects on platelets, thus preventing thrombosis in reanastomosed vessels;
9. Medicate for pain but *do not* use any local digital nerve blocks;
10. Maintain the extremity in an elevated position above heart level.

Care for the Injured Extremity

Handle an injured extremity as follows:

1. Do not use clamps; use pressure to control bleeding. If a tourniquet is required to control bleeding in a partially amputated limb, release it every 10 to 15 minutes and permit the wound to bleed for at least 5 minutes to wash out anaerobic metabolites;
2. Apply splints to maintain patient comfort.

Care for the Amputated Part

Handle an amputated part as follows:

1. Wrap the part in a slightly moistened (not wet) gauze and place in a sterile, dry container or plastic "zipper-lock" bag (container *must* be waterproof). Allowing the part to "soak" will macerate the tissues,

TABLE 17–1. REPLANTATION INDICATIONS AND CONTRAINDICATIONS

Indications	Absolute Contraindications	Relative Contraindications
Age <55 y	Associated life-threatening injuries	Active psychiatric diagnosis
Thumb amputation	Severe avulsion or crush injury of tissue base	Single-digit amputation
Multiple digit amputations	Segmental amputations	Warm ischemia > 12 hours
Hand amputation	Debilitating systemic illness	
Forearm amputation	Prior significant injury to extremity	
Pediatric amputation	Extreme contamination	

(Adapted from Sood R, et al.[15])

deform microstructures, and render re-plantation an impossibility.

2. Place the container in an ice chest and cover with ice and water; (Do not "pack" in ice).

3. Label the container with the time of injury and of onset of cold ischemia, defined as the period of time during which the part is kept very cold to reduce the tissue's oxygen consumption without blood supply. Parts kept in a state of cold ischemia will survive up to 10 hours, as opposed to those kept in warm ischemia; parts kept at room or body temperature have a survival time of only 6 hours.

4. Cool the part to 39.2°F or 4°C—do not freeze or use dry ice;

5. Keep the amputated part *with the patient* throughout any transportation process to prevent accidental separation or loss.

Note: Even badly damaged tissue or parts should be preserved in the manner above; they may be useful in the replantation procedure.

PUNCTURE WOUNDS

Puncture wounds, of course, involve dermal layer penetration to varying degrees; very frequently, imbedded foreign bodies are present, compounding the problem considerably. Damage to underlying structures and the high risk of infection are the two salient concerns. If wound depth and organ or structure involvement appear to be significant, the patient may be a candidate for the operating room (OR). Puncture wounds are particularly prone to tetanus, and the immunization status of these pa-tients must be clarified and updated as necessary; extensively contaminated puncture wounds usually will additionally require prophylactic antibiotics.

Prophylaxis Against Tetanus

After assessing the extent of the puncture wound and immunization status, follow the current guidelines of the American College of Surgeons (ACS) for protection against tetanus. ACS recommendations are based on the condition of the wound and the patient's immunization history. Table 17–2 outlines some of the clinical features of wounds that are prone to develop tetanus. A wound with any one of these clinical features is a tetanus-prone wound. A summary guide to tetanus prophylaxis of the wounded patient appears in Table 17–3. History of tetanus immunization should be verified from medical records so that appropriate tetanus prophylaxis can be accomplished. The table refers to Td (tetanus and diphtheria toxoids adsorbed for adult use) for active immunization and TIG (human tetanus immune globulin) administered to provide passive immunization. In extensively contaminated wounds, prophylactic antibiotics are frequently prescribed as well.

Animal and Human Bites

Again, with such penetrating wounds of the soft tissue, primary concerns are the high risk of infection and functional damage to underlying structures. Four major factors are important to consider in assessing wound infection risk:

- Source of bite: dog, cat, or human
- Site of injury (vascularity, underlying structures)

TABLE 17–2. WOUND CLASSIFICATION: TETANUS-PRONE VERSUS NON–TETANUS-PRONE

Clinical Features	Tetanus-Prone Wounds	Non–Tetanus-Prone Wounds
Age of wound	> 6 hours	≤ 6 hours
Configuration	Stellate wound, avulsion, abrasion	Linear wound
Depth	> 1 cm	≤ 1 cm
Mechanism of injury	Missile, crush, burn, frostbite	Sharp surface (e.g., knife, glass)
Signs of infection	Present	Absent
Devitalized tissue	Present	Absent
Contaminants (e.g., dirt, feces, soil, saliva)	Present	Absent
Denervated and/or ischemic tissue	Present	Absent

(*From the American College of Surgeons, Committee on Trauma.*[16])

TABLE 17–3. TETANUS IMMUNIZATION SCHEDULE

History of Absorbed Tetanus Toxoid (Doses)	Tetanus-Prone Wounds		Non–Tetanus-Prone Wounds	
	Td[a]	TIG	Td[a]	TIG
Unknown or fewer than 3	Yes	No	Yes	Yes
3 or more[b]	No[d]	No	No[c]	No

[a] For children less than 7 years old: DTP (DT, if pertussis vaccine is contraindicated) is preferable to tetanus toxoid alone. For persons 7 years old and older, Td is preferable to tetanus toxoid alone.
[b] If only three doses of fluid toxoid have been received, a fourth dose of toxoid, preferably an adsorbed toxoid, should be given.
[c] Yes, if more than 10 years since last dose.
[d] Yes, if more than five years since last dose. (More frequent boosters are not needed and can accentuate side effects.)
DTP, diphtheria-tetanus-pertussis; Td, tetanus and diphtheria toxoids adsorbed (for adult use); TIG, tetanus immune globulin (human). Td and TIG should be administered with different syringes at different sites.
(*From the American College of Surgeons, Committee on Trauma.*[16])

- Type of resulting wound (depth, degree of damage)
- Time interval between wound infliction and treatment

Dog bites are far the most common type of mammalian bite, with German shepherds implicated in a large and perhaps disproportionate number of reported cases. Of the estimated 1000 dog bites treated daily in the United States, children suffer the greatest incidence. Most bites occur to children under the age of 14 during the summer months while they are lightly dressed and playing outdoors; the dog is usually their own or a neighbor's pet rather than a stray.[2]

It has been determined that German shepherds, Dobermans, and a few other large breeds can bite with a force of about 400 lb/in². Wounds subjected to these intense pressures require careful evaluation for crush injuries, with appropriate and meticulous wound debridement and revision. Satisfactory outcomes are doomed otherwise, and deep scarring and disfigurement will result. Children are especially prone to severe injury from dog bite; reports have included skull perforations, septicemia, and even death.

Dog-bite wounds, as compared to cat-bite and human-bite wounds, when properly cleansed and cared for, rarely seem to become infected for reasons that are not clear to the medical profession. In contradiction to human saliva, the saliva of the dog usually contains less than 100,000 bacteria per milliliter of saliva. Experimental data have confirmed this for dogs that eat meal. Meat-eating dogs, however, have been shown to have *more* than 100,000 bacteria per milliliter of saliva; a

dog-bite wound from a meat-eating dog, therefore, is considered essentially the same as a human-bite wound for risk of infection.[3]

Cat-bite wounds are more likely to become infected than wounds inflicted by either dog or human bites. Cats have long, sharp teeth; they frequently inflict their wounds on avascular areas of the hands and are more likely to harbor *Pasteurella multocida* in their mouths than are dogs. These organisms predispose the wound to a 40 to 50 percent higher likelihood that infection will develop within 24 hours. Deep tendon and bone may be involved; since these structures are difficult to inspect, irrigate, and debride adequately, systemic infection may develop from these comparatively trivial-looking injuries.

Human-bite wounds contrary to common belief, do not always become infected. Although the literature estimates only a 20 to 30 percent infection rate, we often underestimate the severity of injury to underlying structures, especially when the hand is involved with closed-fist injuries, referred to in some EDs as "knuckle sandwiches." A good rule to follow is that any laceration over the knuckles must be suspected of being a human bite even though the history may be somewhat vague or misleading. Typically, these injuries present in the late hours on weekends after tavern parking lot "discussions," have not been cleansed immediately, and frequently present only after infection and discomfort have set in. Injuries near the metacarpophalangeal joints should be suspect for joint involvement, because on examination the laceration may appear retracted proximally from its original location over the metacarpophalangeal joint when the fist was closed.[4] The most common infecting organisms are β-hemolytic streptococci and *Staphylococcus aureus;* oral anaerobes may also be involved.

With all contaminated bite wounds, whatever the animal involved, the four most important management steps are:

1. Immobilization and elevation
2. Extensive irrigation
3. Adequate exploration
4. Debridement as necessary

As a rule, wounds that may cause disfigurement, except for hand wounds, are considered for primary closure after thorough cleansing. Antibiotics, usually penicillin or tetracycline, are employed prophylactically if the wound is considered to hold a very high risk, although the use of prophylactic antibiotics remains very controversial in the medical community. Bite-wound infection within 24 hours is probably due to *P. multocida;* infection that develops after 24 hours is probably caused by streptococci or or staphylococci, or perhaps both. Tetanus protection is *always* routinely administered.

These are difficult wounds to cleanse; pathogens and particles of debris have been deposited into deep, often inaccessible tissues, and are trapped there as an eschar forms over the top of the puncture site. Irrigation with NSS *under pressure* is necessary in order to effectively cleanse these wounds; this can be easily achieved using stock equipment. A standard bulb syringe generates pressures of only 0.05 psi; however, a 35-mL syringe fitted with a 19-gauge needle, with full force on the plunger, will generate the necessary pressure of 7 psi or more.[5] An irrigation with 250 mL sterile NSS is usually sufficient for each small wound to be cleansed, if delivered at a right angle to the wound.[6]

Prophylaxis Against Rabies

The greatest risk of rabies stems from being bitten by a wild animal. Because such bites account for only 1 percent of animal bites reported annually, the risk is small. Offenders include bats, foxes, coyotes, skunks, bobcats, and raccoons (but not rodents or rabbits); rabies should be suspected if the bite was unprovoked, since rabies is known to cause a change in temperament and behavior.

The Centers for Disease Control and Prevention (CDC) in Atlanta, Georgia, recommend that all bites and wounds suspected of rabies contamination be immediately cleansed thoroughly with soap and water, irrigated copiously, and washed with 70 percent isopropyl alcohol or (preferably) one of the quaternary ammonium compounds (aqueous Zephiran 1:1000), both of which are rabicidal (Table 17–4). The current *Rabies Postexposure Prophylaxis Guide* is available from the CDC on request.

TABLE 17–4. PROPHYLAXIS AGAINST RABIES

Animal Species	Condition of Animal at Time of Attack	Treatment of Exposed Person
Household pets: dogs and cats (5% of all cases)	Healthy and available for 10 days of observation	None unless animal develops rabies; at first sign of rabies in animal, treat patient with RIG and HDCV; symptomatic animal should be killed and tested as soon as possible.
	Rabid or suspect unknown (escaped)	RIG and HDCV; consult public health officials—if treatment indicated, give RIG and HDCV
Wild animals: skunks, raccoons, bats, foxes, coyotes, bobcats, other carnivores (90% of all cases)	Regard as rabid unless proved negative by laboratory tests; if available, animal should be killed and tested ASAP.	RIG and HDCV
Other animals: livestock, rodents, lagomorphs (e.g., rabbits, hares) (5% of all cases)	Consider individually. Local and state public health officials should be consulted on the need for prophylaxis; bites by the following almost never call for antirabies prophylaxis: squirrels, hamsters, guinea pigs, gerbils, chipmunks, rats, mice and other rodents, rabbits, and hares.	

HDVC, human diploid cell vaccine; RIG, rabies immune globulin.
(*Adapted from* MMWR.[17])

EMBEDDED FOREIGN BODIES

Wounds from embedded foreign bodies present their own set of inherent problems. Unless the patient can clearly describe the circumstances and is certain what the foreign body was, as well as its angle of entry, management of the wound can be time consuming, risky, and tedious. If an embedded foreign body is a certainty, exploration is required, in either ED or the OR.

Surgical exploration for an embedded foreign body involves committing a room and personnel for as long as retrieval takes, which is frequently a significant period. For this reason, in-depth wound exploration should be carried out in the OR under controlled circumstances, with appropriate anesthesia readily available. Tying up an ED room for this procedure is a foolish practice and unfair to the wounded patient, to other patients waiting to be seen, and to personnel trying to be accountable to everyone involved.

Soft-tissue radiographs are helpful in locating metal or glass objects; wood splinters are more difficult to visualize. Left in the tissues, they commonly cause a rapidly fulminating infection, since woods with a high acid content (especially redwood, hemlock, and cedar) set up severe local tissue reactions. These are urgent situations and must be remedied without delay; many fingers, hands, and forearms have been lost to pieces of wood left embedded in soft tissue. Embedded wood splinters should not be soaked. Soaking may allow the wood to absorb liquid and break apart as removal is attempted. For this reason, it is best to cleanse the area appropriately and allow it to remain dry for investigation and further treatment.

If a splinter has lodged under the nail bed, a V-shaped wedge may have to be cut in the nail in order to grasp and remove the culprit; application of appropriate topical medication and a clean, dry dressing should follow. Better visualization of the splinter's shape and size may be achieved by painting the site with povidone-iodine surgical solution. Allow the splinter to absorb the color, cleanse again with alcohol or saline solution, and proceed.

Deeply embedded foreign bodies must be left in place until a surgeon is ready to remove the object and repair any damage that may have been done. Frequently, such an object has lacerated underlying vascular structures; leaving it in place may result in a life-saving tamponade, while removing it prematurely may have a disastrous outcome.

Foreign bodies that have penetrated superficially can usually be removed by applying steady, careful traction. Once recovered, the object if small enough should be attached to the patient's chart with cellophane tape as part of the permanent medical record or photodocumented. In time, it may have medicolegal value.

Deep-tissue foreign-body wounds can be quite painful. Exploration for and removal of the offending body require that appropriate anesthesia be considered. If a finger is involved, digital block may be the choice rather than infiltration of the area itself.

Embedded fishhooks require a special removal technique. Embedded barbs should be pushed on through the tissue and forced to the surface, the shaft of the hook cut with wire cutters (which should be standard department equipment), and the remaining shaft rotated out of the tissue bed.

Patients with puncture wounds should be instructed to use warm soaks at least three times a day (preferably four) in either plain water or Epsom salts, to watch closely for signs of infection, and to use analgesia as appropriate. *Any* signs of infection should be reported and an immediate reevaluation of wound status should be made. Wound sites should remain covered with an adhesive bandage or appropriate dressing for several days to prevent bacterial recontamination of the entry site. This is especially important for puncture wounds on the plantar surface of the foot.

Dressings applied to bite or puncture wounds should be snug and comfortably secured but *must not* interfere with free circulation to the injured part.

■ BASIC WOUND MANAGEMENT AND PREPARATION

ESTABLISHING THE DATABASE

The nursing history, in as concise a form and with as many pertinent details as possible, is essential to knowledgeable evaluation and management of surface trauma. Patients or their "historian" must be questioned carefully for details because specific wound-care decisions will be based on available information.

Key areas of information that comprise the essential database include:

- Type of injury (blunt versus sharp versus both)
- Mechanism of injury (what, how)
- Environment of injury (clean versus dirty)
- Elapsed time since injury
- Known allergies
- Tetanus immunization status
- Age (affects rate of collagen deposits)
- Circulatory status
- Preexisting diseases (e.g., diabetes, renal disease)
- Currently taken medications (aspirin, anticoagulants, steroids)

All these factors combine to affect the way in which, and the speed with which, wounds heal. All must be taken into account before the wound can be competently assessed and managed.

PSYCHOLOGICAL PREPARATION OF THE PATIENT

Wound pain, fear of disfigurement, fear of further pain, and fear of what seems the strange environment of an ED all contribute to high levels of patient anxiety. The EN can intervene quietly and effectively with calm explanations of what has been decided and what will be happening next and—when possible—assurances of positive outcomes. So much anxiety can be dispelled with simple explanations and a quiet but warm and reassuring manner.

Frightened children can be very challenging to treat, but as a rule, they respond to warmth and reassurance. Never promise "it won't hurt," because it probably will, to some extent. Giving children permission to cry sometimes gives them the control they need over a frightening situation—they often will not make a squeak then. The question of allowing parents to remain in the room requires making a judgment call on a case-by-case basis. While there is strong support for allowing parents to remain with the children for psychological support during wound repair, some children respond more calmly with the parents absent. Each situation is unique, but the merits of parental presence should be weighed carefully, evaluating each parent's "stability."

During wound preparation and repair, try to use the best psychological approach for the particular patient, combining your skills with thoughtful use of language. Avoid references to *stitches, needles, cutting, shots,* and such other things that, while routine terminology in the ED, strike fear and intimidation in the heart of most patients, adult and child alike.

INITIAL INSPECTION

Concerns in Hand and Forearm Injuries

The CDC have estimated that almost 30 percent of occupational injuries seen in EDs annually are finger injuries. These figures are underestimates because not all injuries are included in the reporting system. Finger and hand injuries involve many small and complex structures operating together within relatively confined spaces. These underlying structures are more prone to injury because of their close proximity to the surface, requiring careful evaluation of possible damage distal to the wound. Nurses should develop detailed assessment skills in evaluating these wounds and documenting findings concisely before wound repair begins.

Assessing Range of Motion and Sensory Perception

Injured fingers should be tested for full range of motion (ROM) and sensory perception. Nerve injury results in paresthesias distal to the point of injury; tendon injury manifests as pain when the injured digit is stressed in apposition. Numbness and paresthesias may be determined by gentle pricks with a sterile needle or brushing a cotton applicator across the fingertip. Always compare fingers on both sides of the injury, as well as the same finger on the other hand. If findings are negative, "full ROM, sensory perception appears intact" should be documented.

Wrist and forearm injuries require evaluation for damage to the radial, median, and ulnar nerves as follows:

- *Radial nerve:*
  - Motor: The patient should be able to hyperextend thumb and wrist against resistance.

- Sensory: Looking away, with the hand extended out flat, the patient should be able to feel a cotton applicator tip lightly drawn across the surface of the area between base of index finger and thumb pad.
- *Median nerve:*
  - Motor: The patient should be able to lift the thumb off the palm of the hand, touch the little finger in opposition, and flex the wrist.
  - Sensory: Test for sensation on both anterior and posterior aspects and distal tip of the index finger as the patient looks away and extends the hand out flat.
- *Ulnar nerve:*
  - Motor: The patient should be able to place the hand on a flat surface, spread the fingers, and move the middle finger from side to side.
  - Sensory: Test for sensation on both anterior and posterior aspects of distal joint of little finger as the patient looks away and extends the hand out flat.

GENERAL CONSIDERATIONS

Competent and detailed assessment of wounds expedites care in the ED, reduces patient anxiety, and assists the physician in further evaluation and repair. Speedier referral to specialists for definitive care results as well, augmenting optimum outcomes.

Nursing inspection and management of surface trauma should follow set guidelines. All tissue should be handled gently, with sterile gloves and instruments, and should be systematically checked. Vascular supply (always check distal pulses, comparing side to side), involvement of underlying structures (nicked tendons, bone fractures, severed nerves), presence of foreign bodies, and other considerations should all be taken into account in the overall assessment, concisely documented, and called to the physician's attention.

ENs who do wound closures must be *certain* that the initial inspection is thorough and accurate and that closure is appropriate to their skill level. If any doubt exists after initial inspection, the EN should defer to the physician unless extenuating circumstances exist.

WOUND PREPARATION

Preparing the wound is a nursing function and a fairly straightforward procedure. Thorough cleansing and debridement make the difference between a clean, healthy wound and an infected one with a delayed course of healing. Study after study has borne out the theory: the key to optimum healing is a thoroughly cleansed wound. The method employed to ensure this is the mechanical action of a sterile cleansing solution: irrigate, irrigate, irrigate.

Skin Cleansing

Regardless of the cleansing agent used, the surgical scrub should be performed according to the time-honored protocols of strict surgical technique. Again, minimal shaving of the skin is encouraged, and eyebrows must never be shaved. Surgical scrub solutions available in the ED are usually chosen by the hospital purchasing agent. If a choice exists, several cleansing agents have proved to be relatively nontoxic to the tissues; one of them should be stocked and used for optimum results.

Both Hibiclens and povidone-iodine (Betadine) preparations are effective as skin cleansers, but both are known to be toxic to tissue and blood cells and should not be used *in* the wound itself. While both have been commonly used for many years for wound management, the povidone-iodine preparations and Hibiclens are now considered to adversely effect fibroblast functions, retarding epithelialization and decreasing wound tensile strength.[6,7]

Pluronic F-68 (Shur-Clens), a nonionic surfactant, has been shown in extensive studies to provide effective and nontoxic cleansing of both skin and the wound itself, although no antibacterial properties are claimed for it. Once opened, however, the aliquot bottle of solution must be used or discarded; it is poured directly into and onto the wound.

Poloxamer 188, also a member of a family of surfactants, has been used in thousands of wound treatments without discernible toxic effects and with no significant damage to the wound's resistance to infection, to healing ability, or to the cellular components of blood. It causes no pain on contact with the injured tissues.[6]

Chlorhexidine gluconate (CHG) has been shown to effectively reduce flora after a 15-second wash (its speed of germ-killing is classified as intermediate), but it remains chemically active on the skin for at least 6 hours. The antiseptic combination of the rapid effect of alcohol, used as a hand rinse, and the persistence of CHG (0.5 percent CHG) would seem to be desirable.[8]

For use *other than* direct preparation of open wounds, of all the topical antimicrobial agents available for use in the ED, a 70 to 92 percent concentration of isopropyl alcohol remains the most efficient. In one study, after a soap-and-water wash failed to effectively reduce counts of artificially applied bacteria when the organisms were rubbed onto the skin surface, the application of 70 percent alcohol to contaminated hands resulted in a 99.7 percent reduction in bacteria counts. Alcohols applied to the skin are among the safest known antiseptics.[8] Infection-control concerns would suggest that using alcohol preparations for department housekeeping and wipedowns of equipment and working surfaces would provide a fast, effective, and economical means of reducing the incidence of nosocomial infections in highly contaminated areas. Although alcohols are tuberculocidal, fungicidal, and virucidal, they do, however, *lack* sporacidal properties.[18]

Wound Irrigation

Again, keep bactericidal detergents out of the wound, scrubbing only from wound edges outward to the perimeter and observing strict surgical protocol. The scrub should take at least several minutes, perhaps longer, depending on the size of the area. The skin is then flushed with sterile water or saline and the wound itself copiously irrigated with a Toomey or control syringe with a 18- or 19-gauge needle to create an effective "hydraulic action." If the wound is really extensive, hang irrigant bottles of NSS with screw-on irrigant tubing; narrow the tubing tip with a hemostat, and raise the hanger until a forceful stream of irrigant can be directed into the wound crevasses.

The key to proper wound cleansing is mechanical action, and if foreign material is present, it must be scrubbed out with a surgical scrub sponge and then reirrigated. Wounds must also be debrided of loose and torn tissue before closure. A guide for adequate irrigation of wounds is the Kirz rule: Irrigate with 50 mL NSS per inch of wound per hour of wound age. This will be sufficient in most open gaping wounds, but use more irrigant when flushing dirty, ragged, older wounds and less with clean little kitchen knife–type cuts. In small wounds, a 5-mL syringe with a 20-gauge needle works well to force an irrigating jet into the wound and cleanse effectively. If the patient cannot tolerate the irrigation and cleansing, anesthetize the wound first, and then cleanse.

When irrigation is complete, the prepared and washed area should be painted with the approved appropriate surgical solution and covered lightly with sterile towels or sponges if closure is going to be delayed.

Surgical Technique

During close wound handling, ENs should observe surgical protocols; a short preliminary hand scrub, sterile surgical gloves, surgical face mask, and a cover gown are required to provide protection to both patient and caregiver. The CDC have pointed out that 30 to 40 percent of normal people may shed coagulase-positive *S. aureus* in their nasal secretions; using a face mask during wound repair procedures may afford significant protection to the wound.

Anesthesia

In recent years, several topical anesthetic agents have come into more frequent use. Topical aqueous 4 percent lidocaine is used widely for managing deep abrasions. The key to using topical lidocaine, as with all local anesthesia, is to allow time for absorption and effectiveness.

Topical 4 percent cocaine solution, previously used to control epistaxis, is now used by some physicians for wound anesthesia with good results. A sterile sponge soaked in the solution is laid in the wound and along wound edges.

EMLA cream (lidocaine 2.5 percent and prilocaine 2.5 percent) provides effective topical anesthesia if applied and covered with an occlusive dressing for at least one hour (preferably two) to achieve maximal dermal analgesia.

Many practitioners have come to prefer the topical application of TAC (tetracaine 25 mg/5 mL, adrenaline 1:2000, cocaine 590 mg/5 mL) to lidocaine injection for children; this combination has shown anesthetic efficacy in small wounds, comparable to that of lidocaine in older patients. Use of TAC on fingers, toes, penis, nose, and ears and with elderly people should be avoided, however, for fear of vascular compromise in end arterioles; both adrenaline and cocaine are potent vasoconstrictors. Mucosal surfaces should also be avoided because of more rapid absorption of the substance there.[9] If TAC anesthesia is less than adequate, intradermal lidocaine—*not* more vasoconstrictors—should be administered next.

Anesthesia infiltration should be accomplished following several very clear guidelines:

- Minimize discomfort with the use of a 27- to 30-gauge needle; inject *slowly* through wound margins, *not* through skin surface. The tissue is already compromised; why add another insult?
- Double-check allergies. If your patient is "allergic" to dental Novocain, do not take any chances, even though lidocaine and Novocain (procaine) are different "-caines." Use alternative anesthesia. Several alternatives are:
    Topical agents as already discussed
    Diphenhydramine hydrochloride (Benadryl) 50 mg diluted in 2 to 3 mL sterile water or NSS and infiltrated
    Infiltration of sterile NSS
    Packing with ice for 10 to 15 minutes
    Nitrous oxide (Nitronox) inhalant, available in some EDs and physicians' offices
- Give the infiltrate time to take effect before starting wound repair
- Know the dose limits of lidocaine:
    Adults: 4 mg/kg without epinephrine; 7 mg/kg with epinephrine
    Children: 3 mg/kg
- Be alert to the side effects of lidocaine, which may include:
    Shivering, tremors, euphoria, convulsions
    Respiratory depression and arrest
    Cardiac arrest and vascular collapse
- In the event of serious side effects from lidocaine, administer high-flow oxygen immediately and have lorazepan (Ativan) or diazepam (Valium), ready for IV administration in case convulsions begin; stay calm, but be ready for airway management.
- Bupivacaine (Marcaine) is four times as potent as lidocaine (0.25 percent bupivacaine = 1% lidocaine; 0.50 percent bupivacaine = 2 percent lidocaine). Bupivacaine appears to have a protracted analgesic effect, helping to reduce narcotic doses postoperatively; used in intercostal blocks for fractured ribs, one injection frequently provides analgesia for days.
- Restrict the use of epinephrine to highly vascular areas, such as the scalp; *never* use it on fingers, toes, penis, nose, or ears, and *never* with elderly people.

Once adequate anesthesia is accomplished, the wound should be given one last careful inspection for foreign bodies (dirt, clots, wood bits, hair particles, grass); reevaluate for damaged structures (e.g., tendons, nerves, and blood vessels). If necessary, flush the wound again and repaint with approved surgical wound preparation. The wound is then ready to be draped and covered until closure.

WOUND CLOSURE TECHNIQUES

With primary closure of wounds, the choices are twofold, depending on several factors. Wounds may be managed by using either noninvasive or surgically invasive techniques. Surgical skin strips may be applied to "butterfly" wound edges together in opposition; the alternative is to sew the wound edges together with suture material appropriate to the wound's requirements.

Skin Strips

The noninvasive technique using adhesive strips has many advantages that should be considered if the wound qualifies for their use. Adhesive strips can be used only on small, superficial wounds without wound edge tension, or partial-thickness lacerations. There are several advantages: (1) no anesthesia is required; (2) less tissue trauma and scarring are involved; (3) the infection rate is lower because the surface is not penetrated; and (4) less time is required for application and removal. Dollar considerations are not taken into account here.

Disadvantages of skin strips are that (1) there is a greater potential for wound edge inversion (discussed later), (2) the strips have less strength than sutures, and (3) maintaining effective adherence is sometimes difficult.

Skin strips have a special value in reinforcing healing wound margins during the anabolic phase.

They should always be placed between stitches along the suture line *before* sutures are removed. This "insurance" buys extra time for the healing process and minimizes the danger of suture line separation and scarring.

In preparation for the application of skin strips:

1. Wound edges should be gently cleansed with cotton applicators and peroxide to remove dried necrotic matter, rolling the applicator toward the wound margin. *Never* exert pressure away from the wound margin. Recleanse with alcohol along the wound margin.
2. Skin areas vertical to the wound margin, where strips will be laid, should be cleansed with alcohol or acetone to remove any skin oils that may have accumulated. The areas are then dried by rolling a sterile cotton applicator over the surfaces.
3. A "tackifier" (spirit gum, tr. of benzoin, Mastisol) should be applied to the clean, dry skin where strips will be laid, except for the wound margin itself; allow the skin to air dry for at least 1 minute.
4. Using thumb forceps, the strips are peeled backward off of the card, always removing in an oblique direction in order to prevent curling.

Strips are applied with the thumb forceps, laying down one side of the strip first, gently pulling the opposite side of the wound very slightly toward it, and laying the balance of the strip over the wound margins and down the other side. This exerts a gentle reinforcing tension on the area. Strips applied in this manner generally have the best adherence. Instruct the patient to keep them clean and dry and to watch for signs of infection. Usual time to removal is about 1 week; some strips are left in place until they come off by themselves.

Choice of Suture

Two general types of suture materials are available for wound closure. Research and development in suture manufacturing have made many new materials available, including absorbable synthetic sutures, which cause less toxic reaction in tissues than those of animal origin (gut from sheep or cattle).

Absorbable sutures: ED use of absorbable sutures is generally limited to closing dead spaces and lacerated galea (the tough, fibrous layer between the skull and cutaneous scalp). As always, it becomes a matter of preference, but many practitioners now favor absorbable synthetic sutures (Dexon, Vicryl) over surgical gut. The synthetics "self-destruct" gradually (degradation by hydrolysis) after a period of several weeks and have a lower incidence of infection. Surgical gut, both plain and chromic, is absorbed through inflammatory reaction with tissues. Plain gut is absorbed in 7 to 10 days; chromic gut is absorbed in 21 or more days with less inflammation. Dexon 4–0 or Vicryl 4–0 is the suture of choice for galea, the integrity of which must be maintained to protect the skull from physical forces and 3–0 or 4–0, the choice for subcutaneous closure.

Nonabsorbable sutures: The old standby sutures of cotton, silk, and stainless steel are used very seldom in minor wound closures. Modern synthetics, such as nylon, polyester, and polypropylene monofilaments, provide excellent tensile strength, minimize the wick factor that contributes to scar formation, and cause less tissue reaction and local infection. Most practitioners seem to prefer nylon or polypropylene suture; the latter tends to relax and require fewer "throws" on the knot. Most wounds can easily be managed with 5–0 sutures, 6–0 is used on the face and for most plastic surgery closures, again, to minimize scarring.

If areas under increased tension (lacerations over large muscle bodies) are being sutured, use a 4–0 suture with greater tensile strength (4–0 suture is rated as having a breaking point of 8 lb).[10]

Suturing the Wound

General guidelines: Although there are many methods of placing sutures, the same fundamental principles apply to the basic handling of wound edges and closure:

- Absolute hemostasis must be obtained. Dead spaces should be eliminated and bleeding should be controlled by elevation, pressure, and ice packs. It may be necessary to clamp and tie arterial bleeders, using fine-gauge, absorbable suture.
- Precise approximation of skin edges is essential. Use existing anatomic landmarks

(eyebrows, skin creases, linear skin folds) as the starting point to begin approximation unless the wound requires only a simple, straightforward closure. The "halving principle" may be helpful. Mentally divide the wound into halves, placing the first suture at the halfway point; the point of entry for the next suture is then halfway between the previous suture and the end of the wound on both sides, and so on until the wound is approximated.[11]

- Wound edges must be perpendicular (squared off) for precise approximation; edges may need to be revised carefully with iris scissors, #15 blade, or bladebreaker tool. Revision of wound edges requires a skill necessitating a good deal of practice; defer to someone who has the skill. An exception to revision is in hairy areas, where the wound should be parallel to the hair follicles.
- Be certain that *all* crushed tissue has been excised along wound edges. As a guide for excision, paint peroxide, then aqueous benzalkonium (Zephiran), along wound edges; this produces a white patch wherever dead tissue remains.
- Test wound alignment and skin tension; undermine tissue gently if necessary to approximate edges without tension. Tissues should approximate easily (Fig. 17–5).
- Tissue must be handled gently. When using a grasping tool to manage skin edges, use

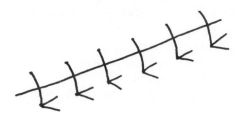

Figure 17–6. Even placement of sutures. Evenly placed sutures perpendicular to the wound will prevent diagonal pull and distortion of wound line.

only one side of a mouse-tooth forceps or a skin hook as a lifting tool. Do not add another insult to the wound.
- Tissues should not be strangulated by the tied-down suture; no single ligature should include a large tissue mass. Take only a small bite with each suture.
- Finer sutures should be used whenever possible; sutures should be placed into the tissues as gently as possible.

Placement of suture: The general practice is to place sutures as far from wound margins as the dermal flap is thick, with an equal distance between stitches along the wound line. Skin edges should always be slightly *everted* in apposition. To avoid diagonal distortion of the suture line, the entry/exit points of suture in the skin must be squared to and equidistant from the wound line (Fig. 17–6).

Although a continuous "running" suture is most efficient in terms of time, using interrupted sutures is the most accurate method of approximating wound edges. When closing superficial wounds, if a stitch is unevenly placed or distorts the wound edge, remove it and place another stitch. In other words, "if in doubt, take it out."[12]

A suture placed so it is angling away from wound edges is bottle shaped and produces a closing with everted edges. A suture placed with its width greater than its depth will invert the wound edges and healing will be retarded, leaving a deep, defined scar. A suture placed with depth greater than its width will evert the wound edges and heal properly (Fig. 17–7).

The Kirz square rule for suturing: Suturing skills can be practiced in workshops on pigs' feet

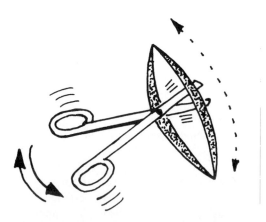

Figure 17–5. Undermining wound edges with blunt tips of Metzenbaum scissors.

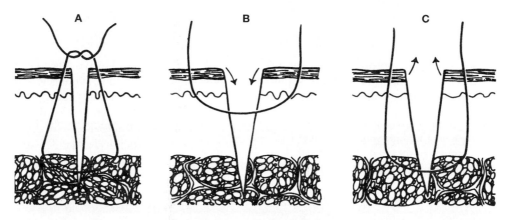

Figure 17–7. Suture placement. **A.** A suture placed angling away from wound edges is bottle shaped and produces a closing with everted edges. **B.** A suture placed with its width greater than its depth will invert the wound edges. **C.** A suture placed with depth greater than its width will evert the wound edges and facilitate a precise approximation.

or on rolled surgical towel bolsters in the ED with unused, discarded suture and a needle holder. ENs who are serious about developing their suturing capabilities are wise to learn suture handling, stitch placement, knot tying, and alternative suture techniques. When repairing actual wounds you will be much less anxious if you have had enough practice. The technical hand–eye skills required for fine wound closure are relatively simple to acquire. By following systematic guidelines and developing a degree of dexterity, one can learn to close simple wounds properly, but *not* without some concerted effort and a good deal of practice. The techniques can ultimately become second nature.

The Kirz square rule for suturing, developed by Howard Kirz, M.D., while teaching suture workshops for nurses in the Pacific Northwest, is as follows:

1. Hold the needle *squarely* in the needle-holder, between the middle and proximal one third of the needle (Fig. 17–8A).
2. Hold the needle *squarely* (perpendicular to the skin), and after piercing the tissue with the needle by using firm, steady pressure downward rotate the wrist (Fig. 17–8B).
3. Use the *square* stitch method to accomplish eversion of wound edges (placing

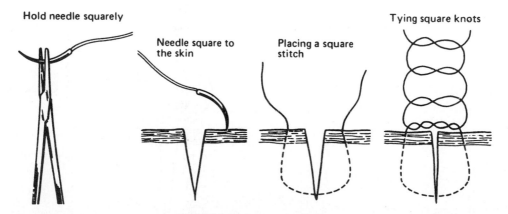

Figure 17–8. The Kirz square rule.

the stitch deeper than it is wide, with a squared or "bottle bottom" configuration) (Fig. 17–8C).

4. Tie *square* knots—"throw" a *minimum* of two full square knots, cutting the suture ends about 1 cm in length from the knot (Fig. 17–8D).

Square knots are tied passing "right over left" and "left over right," as shown in Figure 17–9. The first loop of knot is wound several times in order to provide a "lock knot" to hold tension on wound edges. When closing wound edges, these square knots are accomplished with the use of a needle-holder or forceps.

The instrument tie: The instrument tie should be practiced as shown in Figure 17–10, tying square knots on suture evenly placed into towel bolsters, oranges, pig's feet, or whatever, until ease and proficiency are achieved.

Kirz has simplified the instrument tie technique as well, on the proven theory that as long as the needle-holder is placed on top of the long end of the suture and the suture is wrapped and tied ("thrown"), one cannot tie anything but a square knot:

1. Place the suture through wound edges (or orange, towel, bolster, pig's foot), one side at a time, testing for approximation of edges, and pull through until 2 to 3 in. suture remain on the short end (see Fig. 17–10A).

2. Remember to always place needle-holder on top of the long end of the suture. With the needle-holder in your right hand (your thumb and ring finger in the handles as your index finger rests over the instrument hinge for stability, and the instrument held over the long end of suture), form a loose double loop around the point of the instrument; this is a "double throw" (see Fig. 17–10B).

3. Reach over and pick up the free end ("bitter" end) with the instrument and pull it through the double loop, laying the knot flat by crossing your left hand over your right and laying out the long end of suture to your right (see Fig. 17–10C).

4. Lock the first half of this square knot by pulling the short end of the suture (which is still in the needle-holder) back to the right in the same direction as the long end of the suture (as in Fig. 17–10D). This is referred to as the lock knot because it locks down or "kinks" the tension of the suture while the second throw is being accomplished; it is critical to precise approximation.

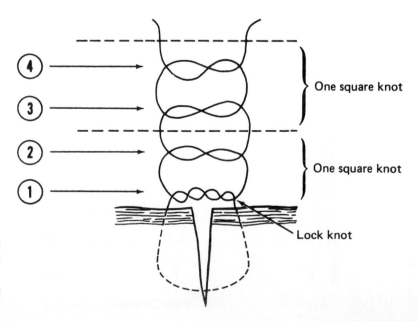

Figure 17–9. Tying a surgical square knot. Use "double throw" lock knot on first loop only. Follow this with a minimum of three more single throws for two full square knots.

One square knot

One square knot

Lock knot

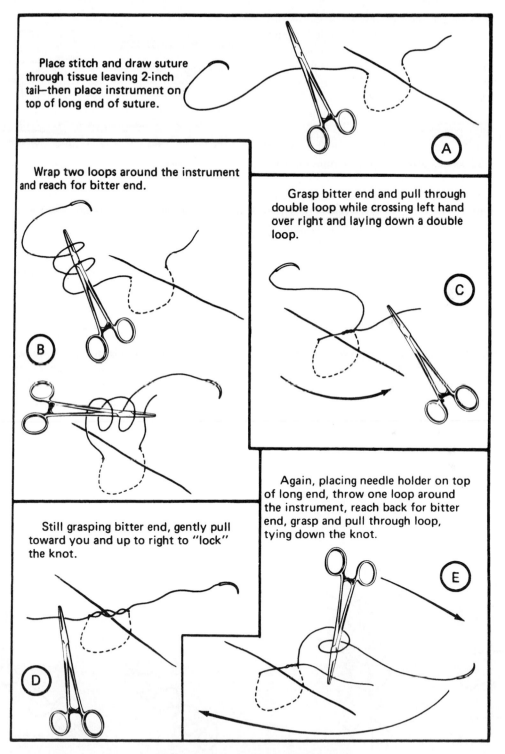

Place stitch and draw suture through tissue leaving 2-inch tail—then place instrument on top of long end of suture.

A

Wrap two loops around the instrument and reach for bitter end.

B

Grasp bitter end and pull through double loop while crossing left hand over right and laying down a double loop.

C

Still grasping bitter end, gently pull toward you and up to right to "lock" the knot.

D

Again, placing needle holder on top of long end, throw one loop around the instrument, reach back for bitter end, grasp and pull through loop, tying down the knot.

E

Figure 17–10. The Kirz method instrument tie.

5. Now tie the second "throw" of the square knot by placing the needle-holder again on top of the long end of the suture (now to your right) and make one loop around the instrument (see Fig. 17–10E).

6. Lay the knot flat by pulling on the strands in opposite directions; this completes one full square knot.

7. Repeat the square knot (two throws) at least once, always tying a minimum of two complete square knots regardless of the type of suture used. Some may require more if they are "wiry," but two is the minimum. Any fewer puts the wound in jeopardy. Remember: a suture is no stronger than its knot.

Interrupted sutures: Interrupted sutures are placed in such a way that each stitch is separate and tied independently of other stitches (Fig. 17–11A). Beyond being simple, single interrupted sutures effectively bolster wound edges, can alter the angle of pull, and provide optimum approximation of edges with the least amount of suture material. Referred to as the figure eight mattress, it is the favorite of many surgeons (Figure 17–11B).

A regular mattress stitch is simply another version of the interrupted stitch. It is made by taking a second bite with the needle either vertical or horizontal to the wound edge. Vertical mattress stitches are used to reinforce and bolster wounds;

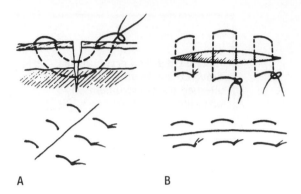

Figure 17–12. Interrupted sutures: **A.** vertical mattress; **B.** horizontal mattress.

they work well on both thick and thin skin and achieve good eversion of edges. Horizontal mattress stitches achieve good eversion but must be applied loosely (Fig. 17–12).

Continuous sutures: Continuous sutures employ a single strand of suture material, with stitches following one after the other without interruption. The suture is secured at each end. Stitching is accomplished more quickly, but control of approximation is lessened (Fig. 17–13).

The simple running stitch (see Fig. 17–13A) is suitable for linear wounds; it makes for a fast closure but tends to invert wound edges. The subcuticular stitch (see Fig. 17–13B) achieves good results and has the advantage of leaving no marks.

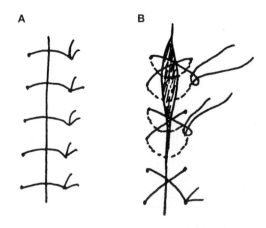

Figure 17–11. Interrupted sutures. The two basic interrupted sutures: **A.** single interrupted, and **B.** figure-eight mattress stitch.

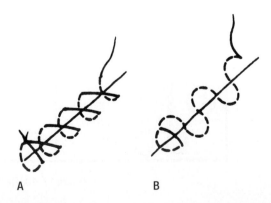

Figure 17–13. Continuous sutures. **A.** simple running suture; **B.** subcuticular running stitch.

DRESSINGS

Wound dressings are sterile when applied; bandages are used to hold dressings in place. Dressings are easily taken for granted until one meets the challenge of suiting a wound and engineering a dressing that must meet many demands. The greatest challenge of all seems to be keeping the dressing in place for the time required. Dressings should be considered in terms of what they are expected to provide: wound protection, antisepsis, pressure, immobilization, absorption, support, comfort, packing, and last but not least, information. Keeping specific wound needs in mind, a dressing can be applied that will fill requirements if a simple three-layer concept is employed (Fig. 17–14).

Layer 1 is the contact layer. Every wound has some amount of exudate. The skin contact layer, therefore, must be (1) nonabsorbent and hydrophilic to permit passage of exudate to the second (absorbent) layer without wetting the contact layer itself; (2) soft and pliable for conformity to surface continuity, eliminating dead space between wound margins and dressing; and (3) of sufficiently fine mesh to prevent granulation tissue from penetrating. Good examples of appropriate contact layer materials are Adaptic, Owens gauze, Vaseline petrolatum gauze, Aquaflow gauze, and Xeroform gauze; these should be impregnated with 3 percent bismuth to mildly deodorize a potentially odorous wound.

Layer 2 is the absorbent layer, tailored to wound size and needs. Sterile 4 × 4s, fluffs, and ABD pads can be used to exert pressure, protect, and provide information on the character and amount of wound drainage.

Layer 3 is simply the outer wrap; it binds dressings in place. It should conform to overall contours and be stretchable (to accommodate swelling and ease of movement) unless the area is to be splinted or immobilized. The advent of clinging/stretching bandages (Kling, Kerlix, Koban, Ace, Tensor, and the like) and stretchable tape (Elastoplast) has provided many easy options for binding dressings in place. When applying Tubegauze, be certain to avoid causing a tourniquet effect at the base of fingers. Instruct the patient to check circulation and sensation regularly and to maintain the finger in neutral alignment (never straight).

There are alternatives to the three-layer dressing that meet the needs of simpler wounds. Several are frequently used for facial and scalp wounds:

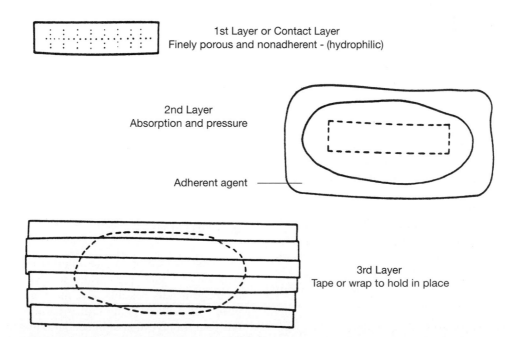

Figure 17–14. Three-layer dressing method. The dressing should be tailored to the needs of the wound and the comfort of the patient.

- Spray dressings
- Collodion (requires ether or acetone for removal)
- Thin mesh gauze and paper tape (beige, preferably) with thin, cleansed and "tackified" with tincture of benzoin, Mastisol, or other agent
- Simple application of short skin strips

The semiocclusive polyurethane film dressings (e.g., OpSite, Tegaderm) are used in many EDs, but it has been reported that wounds covered with some of these products had higher bacterial counts (Gram-negative predominated) than those left open to the air.[13]

ENs often instruct patients to keep healing wounds clean and dry. Significant personal difficulties are encountered by patients so often that physicians who have taken time to examine this issue have determined that most sutured wounds are sealed with a coagulum within hours of being sutured, and that gentle washing is reasonable within 48 hours of repair. A controlled study of patients with sutured head and neck wounds found that washing wounds 8 hours after closure did not appear to alter the healing process or the incidence of infection.[14]

■ SUTURE REMOVAL AND DISCHARGE INSTRUCTIONS

As patients are discharged with instruction sheets for wound care, they should be advised when to return for suture removal. They should then be given printed instructions to keep the wound elevated if possible, to keep it clean and dry (for the appropriate time period, depending on location, extent of wound, and vascularity), and to watch it for signs of infection (redness, pain, swelling, purulent drainage). After reviewing the instructions with the patients, ask them to repeat the instructions; this gives you a chance to make certain they understand. A date for their return should be written in a very visible place on the instruction sheet so that sutures will be removed in timely fashion. Suture removal is generally scheduled after wound repair as follows:

- *Facial sutures:* 3 to 5 days to minimize scarring; skin strips are applied before suture removal

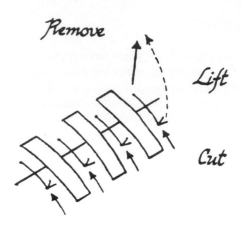

Figure 17–15. Suture removal. After thoroughly cleansing sutures and wound line, apply surgical skin strips. When strips are in place, grasp suture knot with forceps, gently lift knot, cut suture at skin level *beneath* knot as arrows indicate, then lift and remove in upward direction (pulling cut end through wound tract), avoiding tension on suture line as stitches are removed.

- *Scalp sutures:* 5 to 7 days (also head and neck)
- *Trunk, arm, dorsum of hand:* 7 to 10 days
- *Legs:* 7 to 14 days
- *Palms and soles of feet:* 7 to 14 days

Suture removal should be performed after wound edges and sutures are cleansed and dried with hydrogen peroxide, alcohol, and sterile, dry applicators. Again, skin strips should be in place, according to the procedure described earlier, before suture removal begins. Two important concepts must be recognized in the process of removal: (1) sutures must be removed gently and carefully, always pulling *toward* the wound line to prevent stressing wound margins; (2) the risk of infection must be minimized by pulling as little suture through the wound from the surface as possible (Fig. 17–15).

■ SUMMARY

The goal in care of surface injuries is to restore function of injured parts while achieving the best cosmetic results possible; the intent is to accomplish both without doing further harm. Implicit in this goal is prevention of infection so that uneventful and speedy healing can occur. Two key nursing responsibilities in achieving these goals are (1) maintenance of surgical integrity and (2) thorough mechanical cleansing and preparation of the wound, using copious amounts of irrigant. A well-prepared wound supports meticulous hemostasis and precise approximation, the essentials for uneventful healing and minimal scarring.

■ REFERENCES

1. O'Halloran RL. *Aging Contusions.* Portland, Ore: Oregon State Medical Examiners Office, 1980.
2. Jacobs R. Summer summary of bite care: 1. The first crucial steps. *Modern Medicine.* 1982; 127–135.
3. Robson MC. Disturbances of wound healing. *Ann Emerg Med.* 1988;17:1274–1277.
4. Talan DA. Management of serious wound infections. *Top Emerg Med.* 1989;10:33–41.
5. Rodeheaver GT, Pettry D, Thacker JG, et al. Wound cleansing by high pressure irrigation. *Surg Gynecol Obstet* 1975;141:357.
6. Edlich RF, Rodeheaver GT, Morgan RF, et al. Principles of emergency wound management. *Ann Emerg Med.* 1988;17:1284–1302.
7. Gogia PP. The biology of wound healing. *Ostomy Wound Management.* 1992;38:19.
8. Larson E. Guidelines for use of topical antimicrobial agents. *Am J Infect Control.* 1988;16:253–263.
9. Bukata WR. Wound management. Presented at the American College of Emergency Physicians' Scientific Assembly; September 1983; Dallas, Tex.
10. Zeccardi JE, Sevin EG. Wound care. *Point of View.* 1983;20:1.
11. Stuzin JA, Engrav LH, Buehler PK. Emergency treatment of facial lacerations. *Postgrad Med.* 1982;71:81–94.
12. Kirz H. Square rule for suturing. Presented at the American College of Emergency Physicians' Scientific Assembly; September 1974; Seattle, Wash.
13. Mertz PM, Eaglesten WH. The effect of a semiocclusive dressing on the microbial population in superficial wounds. *Arch Surg.* 1984;119:287.
14. Goldberg HM. Effect of washing closed head and neck wounds on wound healing and infection. *Am J Surg.* 1981;141:358.
15. Sood R, Bentz ML, Shestak KC, Browne EZ. Extremity replantation. *Surg Clin North Am.* 1991;71:312.
16. American College of Surgeons, Committee on Trauma. Prophylaxis against tetanus in wound management. Chicago, Ill: ACS; 1987.
17. *MMWR Morb Mortal Wkly Rep.* August 28, 1987; 36(suppl):BS.
18. Rutala WA. APIC guidelines for selection and use of disinfectants. Am J Infect Cont. August 1996;24 (4):313–342.

■ BIBLIOGRAPHY

Alkan M, Gefen Z, Golcman L. Wound infection after simple suture at the emergency ward. *Infect Control.* 1984;5:562–564.

American Academy of Orthopaedic Surgeons, Committee on Injuries. *Emergency Care and Transportation of the Sick and Injured.* 4th ed. Chicago, Ill: AAOS: 1986.

Barber JM, Dillman PA. *Emergency Patient Care.* Reston, Va: Reston Publishing, 1981.

Berk WA. Demystifying treatment of simple lacerations. *Emerg Med.* Feb. 1993;26–39.

Boriskin MI. Primary care management of wounds. *Nurse Pract.* 1994;19:38–58.

Cain HD. *Flint's Emergency Treatment and Management.* 7th ed. Philadelphia, Pa: WB Saunders; 1985.

Callaham ML. When an animal bites. *Emerg Med.* Aug. 1991;105 113.

Cardona VD, Hurn DD, Bastnagel-Mason, PJ, et al., eds. *Trauma Nursing: From Resuscitation Through Rehabilitation.* 2nd ed. Philadelphia, Pa: WB Saunders; 1994.

Carson JP, Minard G. Trauma assessment suture treatment record. *J Emerg Nurs.* 1994;20:225–227.

Clostridia when it's clean. *Emerg Med.* 1976;8(5).

Cosabb W, Smith JW. *Plastic Surgery.* Boston, Mass: Little, Brown; 1973.

Doezema D. No increase in wound infection with TAC. *Emerg Med.* 1991;23(2):56–57.

Doyle DJ. A closer look at local anesthetics. *Emerg Med.* April 1991;147–152.

Dushoff I. About face. *Emerg Med.* 1973:5(1).

Dushoff I. A stitch in time. *Emerg Med.* 1973:5(1).

Edlich RF, Rodeheaver GT, Morgan RF, et al. Principles of emergency wound management. *Ann Emerg Med.* 1988;17(12):1284–1302.

Emergency Nurses Association. *Emergency Nursing Core Curriculum.* 4th ed. Philadelphia, Pa: WB Saunders; 1994.

Emergency Nurses Association. *Trauma Nursing Core Course,* 4th ed. Chicago, Ill: ENA; 1995.

Ernst AA, et al. Lidocaine versus diphenhydramine for anesthesia in the repair of minor lacerations. *J Trauma.* 1993;34:354.

Fackler M. Wound ballistics: a review of common misconceptions. *JAMA.* 1988;259:2730–2736.

Fackler M, Bellamy R, Malinowski J. The wound profile: illustration of the missile-tissue interaction. *J Trauma* 1988;28(suppl):S21–S29.

Fincke MK, Lanros NE, eds. *Emergency Nursing: A Comprehensive Review.* Rockville, Md: Aspen Publishers; 1986.

Foley JJ. TAC (tetracaine, adrenaline, cocaine): a controversial topical anesthetic for suture of skin lacerations. *J Emerg Nurs.* 1994;20:221–222.

Frank IC. Avulsed scalp replantation. *J Emerg Nurs.* 1979;5(4):8–11.

Gogia PP. The biology of wound healing. *Ostomy Wound Management* 1992;38:12–22.

Guyton AC. *Textbook of Medical Physiology.* 7th ed. Philadelphia, Pa: WB Saunders; 1986.

Hass J. Emergency management of soft tissue injuries. *J Emerg Nurs.* 1980;6(5):20–25.

Heller MB. Management of bites. *Res Staff Physician.* Feb 1982:75–84.

Hunt TK. Physiology of wound healing. *Ann Emerg Med.* 1988;17:1265–1273.

Lanros NE. Surface trauma and wound management. *Traum Q.* 1987;3:34–63.

Larson E. Guideline for use of topical antimicrobial agents. *Am J Infect Control.* 1988;16:253–263.

Myers MB. Sutures and wound healing. *AJN* 1971;71(9).

Noe JM, Kalish S. *Wound Care.* Greenwich, Conn: Cheeseborough-Ponds; 1975.

Norris MKG, House MA. *Organ and Tissue Transplantation: Nursing Care From Procurement Through Rehabilitation.* Philadelphia, Pa: FA Davis; 1991.

Pryor GJ, Kilpatrick WR, Opp DR. Local anesthesia in minor lacerations: topical TAC vs lidocaine infiltration. *Ann Emerg Med.* 1980;9(11):568–571.

Reagan L. Care of simple wounds. In: *Physicians in Hospital Emergency Departments.* Rockville, Md: U.S. Department of Health, Education, and Welfare; 1971.

Roberts N. Hand injuries. *J Emerg Nurs.* 1980;6(6): 8–13.

Robson MC. Disturbances of wound healing. *Ann Emerg Med.* 1988;17(12):1274–1278.

Rodeheaver G, Bellamy W, Kody M, et al. Bactericidal activity and toxicity of iodine-containing solutions in wounds. *Arch Surg.* 1982;117:181–185.

Smeltzer SC, Bare BG, eds. *Brunner and Suddarth's Textbook of Medical-Surgical Nursing.* 7th ed. Philadelphia, Pa: JB Lippincott; 1992.

Steele MT. Which wounds contain glass? *Emerg Med.* April 1993;65.

Stevenson T, et al. Cleansing the traumatic wound by high pressure syringe irrigation. *JACEP.* 1976;5(1).

Talan DA. Management of serious wound infections. *Top Emerg Med.* 1989;10(4):33–41.

Thompson RV. *Primary Repair of Soft Tissue Injuries.* Melbourne, Australia; University Press; 1969.

Tindall JP, et al. *Pasteurella multocida* infections following animal injuries, especially cat bites. *Arch Dermatol.* 1972:105.

Trott AT. Dealing with the dirty wound. *Emerg Med.* July 1994;16–26.

Trott, AT. Digital anesthesia: metacarpal vs. digital block. *Emerg Med.* Dec 1994;55.

Trott AT. *Wounds and Lacerations: Emergency Care and Closure.* St. Louis, Mo: Mosby-Year Book; 1991.

Wenzel RP. Hand disinfection—easier said than done. *Emerg Med.* Feb. 1993;117.

When the dog bites. *Emerg Med.* 1981;15(9):62–71.

Willey T. Use a decision tree to choose wound dressings. *AJN.* Feb. 1992;43–46.

Zimmer B. Animal and human bites. *J Emerg Nurs.* 1979;5(8).

Zukin D, Simon R. *Emergency Wound Care: Principles and Practices.* Rockville, Md: Aspen Publishers; 1987.

■ REVIEW: SURFACE TRAUMA

1. Identify and describe the three layers of the skin.

2. Define open and closed soft-tissue injuries and give examples of each.

3. Explain the time patterns in resolution of soft-tissue contusions and the rationale for careful nursing assessment and documentation.

4. Define the following terms:
   a. *Full-thickness wound*
   b. *Partial-thickness wound*
   c. *Hematoma*
   d. *Laceration*
   e. *Avulsion*
   f. *Puncture wound*

5. Describe the three phases of healing.

6. Identify four key criteria for wounds that should have primary closure.

7. Define the *golden period* in wound management and the factors that may alter the guidelines.

8. Outline four major considerations for the emergency nurse (EN) in primary wound management.

9. Describe the way in which direct pressure is effectively applied to a bleeding wound.

10. Explain the reason venous bleeding and arterial bleeding carry different outcome implica-tions and require different management approaches.

11. Describe the appropriate nursing disposition of an extensively abraded area and cite normal dose limits of lidocaine for both adults and children.

12. Describe the preliminary considerations of wound evaluation.

13. Describe the proper method of cleansing and preparing a wound for repair and closure.

14. Explain the formula for wound irrigation.

15. List at least six guidelines to follow for infiltrating the wound with local anesthesia.

16. Explain the Kirz square rule for wound repair.

17. Identify the types of sutures commonly employed in wound closure and the rationale for each.

18. List the situations in which the EN should *never* close the wound.

19. Describe the three-layer concept of dressing a wound. Explain the rationale as well as the function of a dressing.

20. Identify the two essentials for uneventful healing and minimal scarring in wound repair.

Special Considerations in Trauma　18
Pediatric and Geriatric Patients

This chapter provides vital information on the assessment and management of injured children and elderly people, with an emphasis on the unique anatomic and physiological characteristics that influence the primary survey and secondary assessments of injury. Current guidelines for life support and trauma resuscitation are presented in detail.

■ PEDIATRIC TRAUMA

Trauma is the leading cause of death in children after the first year of life. Half of this trauma is due to motor vehicle accidents (MVAs). Other major causes include drowning, burns, child abuse, and home accidents. It is estimated that there are about 15,000 deaths annually, with over 2 million children sustaining permanent, crippling injuries each year. The peak range for accidents is 4 to 12 years of age, with the highest frequency occurring at age 8. As might be expected, boys tend to have more accidents than girls. For example, 80 percent of all childhood injury involves blunt trauma to boys. One of every 12 children will be hospitalized for trauma in the first year of life. Falls are the major causes of injury to children between 1 and 6 years of age. During adolescence, sports accidents and MVAs account for the greatest incidence of injury. The annual cost of pediatric trauma exceeds $15 billion.[1] The morbidity and mortality from pediatric trauma can be significantly reduced by trauma-care systems that include a pediatric trauma center, referral hospitals, and a network of prehospital care providers skilled in management of the injured child.

EQUIPMENT FOR THE PEDIATRIC TRAUMA PATIENT

All emergency departments (EDs) should possess equipment and supplies in a full range of sizes to handle victims from infancy to adulthood (Table 18–1). In addition, monitoring devices for electrocardiograms (ECG), apnea, oxygen saturation, blood pressure (BP), and temperature are essential. Calculators and computers that permit caregivers to accurately compute pediatric drug doses or fluid requirements will prove most useful, too, and can minimize potential for error when staff members must work quickly under stressful conditions. Overhead warming units, blanket warmers, thermal blankets or pads, and fluid warmers are imperative for the care of the infant or small child who is critically ill or injured, since compromises in core temperature can significantly affect case outcomes. A table scale or stretcher capable of weighing the patient should be at hand when accurate weights must be obtained. A heated crib or incubator is useful for newborns or small infants, permitting treatment to continue without compromising thermal stability. A decontamination area and an isolation room with negative air flow are also desirable in a center serving the pediatric population.

APPROACHES TO THE INJURED CHILD

Emergency nurses (ENs) who ordinarily do not work with children may find it challenging to deal with an injured pediatric patient. Although it is helpful to have an understanding of childhood development and socialization at various ages, there

TABLE 18–1. ENDOTRACHEAL TUBE/SUCTION CATHETER SIZE

Age	Endotracheal Tube (Internal Diameter in mm)	Suction Catheter
Newborn	3.0	6
1–6 mo	3.5	8
6–12 mo	4.0	8
1–2 y	4.5	8
3–4 y	5.0	10
5–6 y	5.5	10
7–8 y	6.0[a]	10
9–10 y	6.5	10
12 y	7.0	10
14 y	7.5	12
Adult female	8.0	12
Adult male	9.5–10.0	14

[a] Uncuffed polyvinyl chloride clear endotracheal tubes through size 6.0, then cuffed tubes.

are some general considerations useful in dealing with all pediatric patients and their families.

The child and the parents (or surrogate caregivers) must be treated as a unit. ENs must accept and respect their values, beliefs, and defense mechanisms and use these as a starting point for establishing rapport. Although challenging behaviors may be presented by both the child and the accompanying adults, remember that they are each exhibiting the best behaviors that they are capable of in a difficult situation.

Separation of the child from parents creates a basis for unnecessary fear and distrust and often for suspicions of malfeasance. Parents and their children intuitively resist separation; there is invariably some parental guilt associated with injury, and bad feelings tend to be compounded through separation. If possible, parents should be permitted to remain with the young child and to lend support in any way possible. Avoid asking parents to participate in care, though, since the child needs them exclusively as a support. When they are removed from this role (e.g., to help restrain the child or to monitor the intravenous drip), they become just more people doing something *to*—not *for*—the child. They must be permitted to give their undivided attention to the young patient, function solely as a loving, nurturing advocate. Asking the parent to take some responsibility for care is often

a temptation when the EN is very busy with other responsibilities, but to do so is unfair to both the parent and the child.

If separation is deemed necessary or appropriate, the EN should ensure that parents are fully informed about what will be happening to the child during their absence. Periodic updates from staff can do much to make the waiting time less anxiety provoking for parents who may feel guilty, helpless, and somewhat out of control. However, if the parents choose to leave the treatment area, respect this decision, because if they are forced to remain despite their inability to cope, their fear may be counterproductive and upsetting to the already stressed child.

Children who are injured or ill tend to exhibit disorganized behavior. If they are calm and unresponsive, a shock state must be suspected. Some reactions may be quite difficult for the staff to manage; kicking, screaming, biting, and fighting are typical. These protests often make technical care procedures challenging, but such normal defenses should not be taken away from the child. They serve to release anxiety and tension and help the youngster to gain some control over feelings of utter powerlessness. When feasible, permit children to sit up during examination or treatment. In this position, they tend to be less resistant than when forced to lie on their backs. Restraints should be a last resort; when they are used, however, the staff should continue to enlist cooperation from the child and thus resist making a show of force, since this will only make matters worse. Furthermore, it will result in the child's feeling like a vulnerable victim among big, unfriendly nurses and doctors who do things that hurt. Several types of physical restraints may be used to facilitate procedures (Fig. 18–1).

When the EN remains calm and appears to be organized and in control of the situation, both the patient and attending adults will be reassured. Convey to the child that it is okay to cry, even if the parents tell the child that big boys/girls do not cry. Reassurance should be provided when using large equipment (e.g., a portable x-ray unit) and during unfamiliar procedures. One helpful rule is to use the smallest tool possible and apply the smallest possible patches on wounds, minimize the use of overwhelming tools and techniques. When practical, explain and demonstrate, but if there is

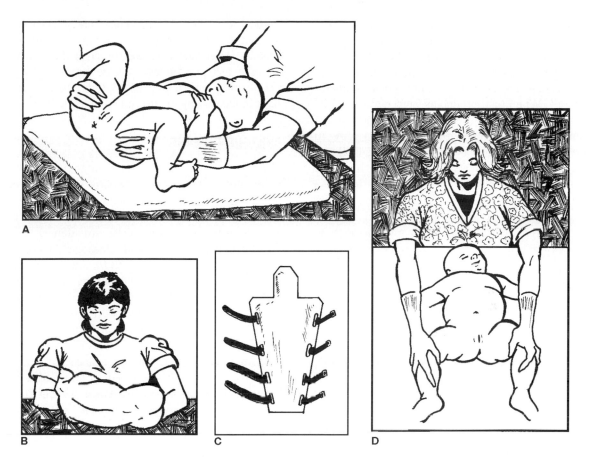

Figure 18–1. Pediatric restraints used for emergency department procedures. **A.** Thigh flexion-abduction (perineal and rectal examinations and procedures). **B.** Knee-neck flexion (lumbar puncture). **C.** Pediatric restraint board. **D.** Frog position (femoral venipuncture).

not time for "play therapy," maintain constant human contact—an effort that requires more thoughtfulness than time. Whenever the opportunity arises, compliment a child and the parents on their positive actions or behaviors. This reinforces desirable responses and improved cooperation throughout the ED stay.

During examinations or procedures that require cooperation, use positive statements to enlist the child's assistance. Say exactly what he or she can do to help you and why it is important. Avoid threatening, intimidating commands such as "Don't move or it will hurt worse." When feasible, give children time to muster their courage and provide step-by-step explanations for those old enough to understand. Talking yourself and the child through a difficult procedure often has long-term positive effects on how the young patient

feels about health-care personnel. Trust that is learned in crises can be invaluable in subsequent encounters. Rapid, rough, and careless work conveys anger and indicates to everyone present that the matter is "out of control." Such behavior is detrimental and does not build the mutual confidence that is essential to maintain during a frightening time.

When painful parts must be inspected or manipulated, this should be done only after routine examinations are completed. Once the "hurt" is addressed and the child tenses and reacts, it is most difficult to regain the composure necessary to accomplish the remainder of assessments. For instance, it is difficult to hear heart and breath sounds if the child is sobbing or crying.

Visual contact should be ongoing throughout the encounter. If the child is able to verbalize, ask questions and develop friendly interactions. Using first names and animated dialogue are important tactics to ease the child's crisis in the ED.

It is commonplace for accidents and illness to be associated with painful examinations and therapeutics. When pain-producing procedures must be accomplished, approach the child with honesty. If something will hurt, say so. If the hurt is going to be "quick" and then over, explain this. Children can often tolerate adversity if they know it will be fleeting. Avoid asking young patients to make choices. Forcing children to choose may actually exaggerate anxiety and do little to convince them that emergency care is a participative, democratic process. Being able to choose whether to get a "shot" in the left arm or the right arm is of little consequence compared to the fear of the anticipated pain.

Protect the child's modesty, exposing only those body parts that need to be to uncovered for the examination or treatment. Remove underclothing only when necessary. In addition to protecting the child from the embarrassment of exposure, draping and covering ensures optimum maintenance of body heat, a vital factor for the ill or injured child, who is already metabolically compromised.

Depending on the child's age, examination may be impaired if communication is limited. Older school-age children may minimize or exaggerate signs and symptoms of injury. In accidents in which the child is injured because of carelessness in play or while engaged in forbidden activities, the injury may be "played down" because of fear of punishment for getting hurt during a prohibited activity. In instances such as these, children need reassurance from their parents that they are okay even though they were injured while being disobedient. ENs and physicians must be sensitive to these human issues because in their zeal to gather exact details about the accident, they may make the child feel "trapped," "on trial," and guilty. A brief explanation about the detailed questioning may help both the child and parents to understand that the purpose of gathering information is to assist with the diagnosing of injury, not to establish a basis for punishment of behavior that led to the injury. Some children, although only a few, feign severe injury to escape a school examination or other unpleasant event. Feigned problems and overstatements may be discovered quickly by the medical team, but certain "actors" are so convincing that they prove most troublesome to both parents and clinicians who are trying to distinguish between fact and fantasy. Astute history taking, examination, and review of records are the first steps in identifying the juvenile malingerer.

CHILDHOOD FEARS

Children tend to fear the same things as adults; death, mutilation, loss of body parts, pain, and loss of control. If the EN can remain calm and authoritative, thus seeming in control, the initial step is taken to maintain order in a crisis situation.

Reactions to injury and subsequent medical care are influenced by the child's developmental age; previous experiences with injury, separation, and hospitalization; the seriousness of the injury; and the quality of available support systems.

The infant (birth to 3 months) can seemingly tolerate mild pain with distraction only. Older infants may demonstrate both resistance and uncooperativeness. In this age group, a knowledge of what to expect increases resistance, so ED staff should avoid displaying equipment before performing procedures.

The toddler expresses mainly separation anxiety through protests and acts of despair. Detachment and denial occur when the child suffers repeated bouts of illness or injury without receiving proper parental or staff support. The display of physical resistance is basically a reaction to a loss of autonomy. At this critical developmental stage, intrusive examinations into bodily orifices threaten body boundaries and must be avoided when possible. Toddlers are familiar enough with their bodies that they can usually localize pain. Their expressions of discomfort are genuine, and they rarely fake or exaggerate.

Preschoolers suffer fears stemming from loss of control, physical restrictions, and enforced dependency. They tend to view injury as a punishment for misdeeds. Fears of bodily intrusions and loss of body integrity are paramount; these are so crucial that at times, preschoolers are even aggressive and assaultive to caregivers.

Schoolchildren and adolescents have a greater understanding, of course, both of their bodies and of the consequences of illness and injury. They fear an altered body image and loss of identity from injured or missing body parts. Separation from family and peers becomes a major focus of their anxiety when they are confronted with illness, injury, and hospitalization. Death, an ultimate separation, is a real preoccupation of the school-age child with major emergency medical problems. Honest, straightforward statements are appreciated by this age group. Such "one adult to another" interactions evoke their trust in hospital personnel, and they sense added control over their circumstances when they are genuinely involved in and informed about their care.

ENs will find their tasks more rewarding when working with pediatric patients if they apply these simple principles that stem from developmental theory and real experiences.

ASSESSMENT PARAMETERS AND NORMS

The Pediatric Trauma Score (PTS) is a tool for the triage of patients to the appropriate level of facility. It has been designed specifically for the types and patterns of injury seen in childhood. About 25 percent of injured children with moderate or severe injuries will require specialized trauma care, but the majority of children can be appropriately cared for outside the highly specialized, sophisticated pediatric trauma center. The PTS is a simple way to calculate trauma and has exhibited a high correlation of findings between examiners, both physicians and paramedics. A seriously ill child with high-risk injuries can be promptly distinguished from the less seriously ill child without life-threatening injuries. Table 18–2 is one example of a pediatric scoring tool.

VITAL SIGNS

Initial assessment of vital signs (VS) should include weight, respirations, pulse, BP, and temperature (see also page 457). VS must be measured

TABLE 18–3. VITAL SIGNS IN CHILDREN: RESPIRATION RATE

Age	Range (breaths per minute)
Birth	35–60
1 mo–1 y	26–34
2 y	20–30
2–6 y	20–30
6–10 y	18–26
10–18 y	15–24

using appropriate techniques, or erroneous results may be generated. This is truly one area of assessment in which *poor data* are indeed worse than *no data;* a physician with poor data is using false or misleading VS recordings as a basis for important clinical decisions, such as whether to obtain blood cultures or to perform a spinal tap. Common errors in pediatric VS evolve from carelessness in technique, such as not leaving a thermometer in place for the prescribed period of time; improperly positioning the thermometer in the mouth, ear, or rectum; or using faulty electronic equipment or an improperly sized BP cuff. The skilled and experienced EN should periodically validate that technical staff are obtaining accurate VS. Pulse rates, respiratory rates, and BP are difficult to obtain from a child who is crying hysterically. Waiting for the child to calm down somewhat is preferable to pressing on and eliciting false readings. Letting the child use a pacifier or permitting the child to sit in the parent's lap or to be held may quiet the young patient enough to enable the EN to hear heart or breath sounds or to record the BP. VS should represent at-rest states. If they do not, this fact should be noted clearly on the chart for the physician to take into consideration. Tables 18–3

TABLE 18–2. PEDIATRIC TRAUMA SCORE (PTS)[a]

Component	+ 2	+ 1	−1
Size	> 20 kg	10–20 kg	< 20 kg
Airway	Normal	Maintainable	Unmaintainable
Systolic blood pressure	> 90 mm Hg	50–90 mm Hg	< 50 mm Hg
Central nervous system	Awake	Obtunded	> Comatose/decerebrate
Skeletal fractures	None	Closed	Open/multiple
Cutaneous injuries	None	Minor	Major/penetrating

[a] PTS > 8 = 0% mortality; PTS ≤ 0 = 100% mortality; PTS ≤ 8: Child should be transported to highest level trauma facility.

TABLE 18–4. VITAL SIGNS IN CHILDREN: AVERAGE PULSE RATES AT REST

Age	Lower limits of normal		Average		Upper limits of normal	
Newborn	70		120		170	
1–11 mo	80		120		160	
2 y	80		110		130	
4 y	80		100		120	
6 y	75		100		115	
8 y	70		90		110	
10 y	70		90		110	
	Girl	Boy	Girl	Boy	Girl	Boy
12 y	70	65	90	85	110	105
14 y	65	60	85	80	105	100
16 y	60	55	80	75	100	95
18 y	55	50	75	70	95	90

through 18–5 provide average ranges for pediatric vital signs.

Weight

Body weight of the child is essential information for selecting supplies and equipment and determining fluid therapy or medication requirements. If you do not have a scale, ask the child (if old enough) or the parents for a recent weight. They often can readily provide this information. There

are also methods for estimating a child's weight using a commercial tape measure or a table of estimated weights (Table 18–6). It is helpful to have the weight in kilograms because fluid therapy and medications are calculated according to weight in kilograms. It is also recommended that ENs precalculate doses for advanced cardiac life support (ACLS) agents and other emergency drugs using a standard computer program or calculator and that they ensure that this information is available at the bedside for all care providers. Many EDs routinely create printouts of emergency drug doses, based on weight, promptly after the child's arrival.

Respirations

The respiratory rate should be counted by observing abdominal excursions in infants and thoracic excursions in the older child. Respirations should be counted for a full minute because variations are likely over shorter time intervals. Note whether there is a struggle in breathing or if the respirations seem to be an exhausting process for the youngster. The appearance of restlessness, cyanosis, retractions and/or nasal flaring indicate respiratory compromise.

Healthy newborns are nose-breathers and do not tolerate mouth-breathing well. The usual respiratory rate is rapid (35 to 60 breaths per minute),

TABLE 18–5. VITAL SIGNS IN CHILDREN: NORMAL BLOOD PRESSURE VALUES AT VARIOUS AGES

Age (years)	Mean Systolic	Range in 95% of Normal Children	Mean Diastolic	Range in 95% of Normal Children
$\frac{1}{2}$–1	90	±25	61	±19
1–2	96	±27	65	±27
2–3	95	±24	61	±24
3–4	99	±23	65	±19
4–5	99	±21	65	±15
5	94	±14	55	±9
6	100	±15	56	±8
7	102	±15	56	±8
8	105	±16	57	±9
9	107	±16	57	±9
10	109	±16	58	±10
11	111	±17	59	±10
12	113	±18	59	±10
13	115	±19	60	±10
14	118	±19	61	±10
15	121	±19	61	±10

TABLE 18–6. PEDIATRIC WEIGHT ESTIMATES

Age	Kilograms	Pounds
Newborn	3–5	6–11
1 y	10	22
3 y	15	33
5 y	20	44
8 y	25	55
10 y	30	66
15 y	50	110

and excursions are shallow. Considerable motion of the diaphragm is noted. It is not unusual for newborns to exhibit irregular rhythms or patterns of breathing owing to immaturity and instability of their respiratory mechanisms. As an infant proceeds through the first year of life, the chest wall muscles develop and grow stronger. Thus, their role in the respiratory process is greater, and the diaphragm plays a less significant (at least less visible) part in air exchange.

Remember that tachypnea is a normal reaction to stress in children. If there is not a tachypneic response, suspect head or spinal cord injury, or look for abdominal distension, which can thwart normal breathing.

Preschoolers (2- to 5-year-olds) and schoolage youngsters breathe at an approximate rate of 20 to 25 breaths per minute. The rate does not change appreciably until adolescence, when it stabilizes at 12 to 20 breaths per minute, the rate characteristic for the average adult.

Breath sounds should be assessed by the use of a stethoscope to detect any sounds of obstruction. Grunting, stridor, wheezing, rales, and rhonchi may be noted. While listening for breath sounds, one can also record the apical pulse rate. There is limited value in attempting to listen for bilateral breath sounds, since any breath sound is generally heard throughout the entire chest in the young child. X-rays are required to confirm individual lung activity.

Pulse Rate

The child's pulse rate is normally more rapid than the adult's. It rises sharply when the child is crying or otherwise distressed. Fever as well as shock will increase the pulse rate. Bradycardia characteristically is associated with increased intracranial pressure (ICP), hypoxia, hypoglycemia, and hypothermia. Pulses are usually obtained at the brachial, carotid, or femoral sites in the child, depending upon the age, and when feasible, should be assessed simultaneously with the apical pulse. When possible, count the apical pulse rate, but do not bypass the palpation of peripheral pulses, which provides valuable clues to circulatory status. The brachial pulse site is recommended for infants; the femoral, carotid, and temporal sites in older children. The apical area in the schoolage child is at the fifth intercostal space in the midclavicular line; in younger children, it is higher and more medial.

Blood Pressure

BP is a significant factor in cardiovascular assessment after injury, but surprisingly, it is often not recorded, because the child is crying or resisting. At times, BPs are not assessed because an appropriately sized pediatric cuff is not available. The width of the cuff should encase approximately one half to two thirds of the upper arm or thigh, and as in the adult, the arm should be supported at the level of the heart while the recording is obtained. In children, the diastolic reading is most accurate if the muffling point is used rather than the complete disappearance of sound. If a pediatric cuff is not available, an adult cuff can be used on the thigh for some children. The BP may be difficult to obtain, and unless the cuff is the right size, wrong data may be obtained. The normal BP, according to the approximation rule, is $80 + 2 \times$ the age in years (systolic); the diastolic is two thirds the systolic. Age-specific charts should be readily available for reference. In a child younger than 1 year of age, the systolic pressure in a thigh is approximately equal to the arm reading. In older children, it may yield a 10 to 40 mm Hg higher reading. Diastolic pressures usually do not vary. Children younger than 1 year usually have inaudible BPs unless an electronic stethoscope or Doppler are used to amplify sounds. Such devices should always be at hand in the ED. Note that tachycardia, by itself, is not a reliable indicator of a shock state.

Temperature

A baseline temperature reading is crucial in the injured child. Remember that some children may have been ill and febrile prior to injury or may have been thermally stressed, which could alter the course of resuscitation and management. Satisfactory readings can be obtained with an ear probe, and this newer technique is quicker in an emergency and does not aggravate an already stressed child. Occasionally, when the ear canal is obstructed with cerumen or a foreign body, or following severe head injury when cerebrospinal fluid (CSF) or blood is draining from the ear, a rectal or axillary reading may be the best approach. Oral readings are sometimes appropriate, too, if there is no facial trauma that would affect the safety or efficacy of this method. Skin probes are not recommended for use in the traumatized child, because they rely primarily on non-compromised circulation for accuracy.

Electrocardiogram

An electrocardiogram may be indicated for children with chest trauma and a suspected cardiac contusion. Several important considerations must be taken into account when obtaining an ECG.

Lead placement and ECG recording are not easy unless the child is able to hold very still. Some authorities recommend using various distractions, such as a moving flashlight or an entertaining face, to gain the child's attention while the electrodes are being placed and the tracing obtained. Whatever technique works for the EN and the child should be used to obtain good lead placement; otherwise, results will be equivocal (Fig. 18–2).

Electrodes should not be permitted to touch one another even though they may be placed very close together. Electrode paste that "connects" leads may result in the same complex's being recorded across the precordium. Apply paste sparingly and confine it to the electrode spot only.

Standardization should appear on every lead. Since the cardiac voltage is high in children, the ECG may be recorded at one-half standard. If so, the physician must be alerted to multiply the wave voltage by 2 to achieve an accurate assessment. The waves and intervals are also variable for children (Fig. 18–3). U waves are most common among children. Right-sided precordial leads (e.g., V_1, V_{3R}, V_{4R}) may be used to define right ventricular forces. At least one to two positions should be used.

The pediatric ECG must be interpreted with the following facts in mind:

- Since the right ventricular region is predominantly active in prenatal life, the right ventricle is electrically dominant.
- There may be a low R/S ratio until the child is 4 or 5 years old, when the R/S approximate. From that age on, the right waves gradually decrease until the adult pattern is reached (small R, deep S wave pattern in right chest leads).
- The ST segment may be displaced for 1 or 2 mm in children for standard leads and up to 4 mm in the right precordial leads.
- Electrical axis readings are variable (Fig. 18–4).

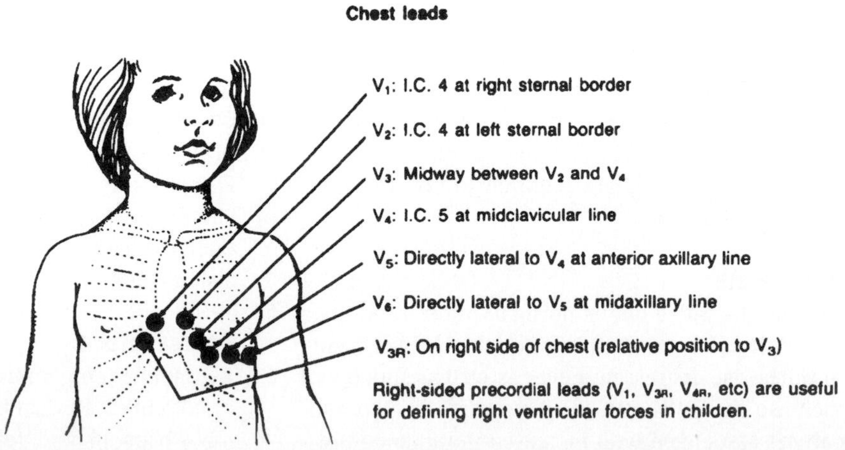

Chest leads

V_1: I.C. 4 at right sternal border

V_2: I.C. 4 at left sternal border

V_3: Midway between V_2 and V_4

V_4: I.C. 5 at midclavicular line

V_5: Directly lateral to V_4 at anterior axillary line

V_6: Directly lateral to V_5 at midaxillary line

V_{3R}: On right side of chest (relative position to V_3)

Right-sided precordial leads (V_1, V_{3R}, V_{4R}, etc) are useful for defining right ventricular forces in children.

Figure 18–2. Proper lead placement for pediatric ECG.

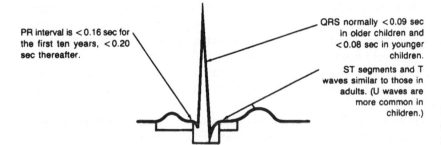

PR interval is <0.16 sec for the first ten years, <0.20 sec thereafter.

QRS normally <0.09 sec in older children and <0.08 sec in younger children.

ST segments and T waves similar to those in adults. (U waves are more common in children.)

Figure 18–3. Normal electrocardiogram waves and intervals for the pediatric patient.

RESUSCITATION AND STABILIZATION IN TRAUMA

Upon receiving notification that a seriously injured child is en route to the ED, the staff should immediately ready all supplies and equipment for pediatric resuscitation. If an estimate of the child's age and weight can be obtained in advance, these data will be invaluable in assisting in the selection and collection of equipment and supplies. (If the family is present, ask the parents what the child weighs; they often know.) If the child can respond, he or she may also be able to provide an approximate number that can be used to estimate sizes of equipment, drugs doses, and so on. Body surface area can be estimated if other factors such as age, general build, and developmental stage, are known. When exact weights are not known, any feasible data should be put into play to predict reasonable fluid and pharmacological therapy and to facilitate resuscitation preparation before the child's arrival.

Among critical items are airway adjuncts, intravenous lines (both central and peripheral), and an electronic stethoscope or Doppler. A warming hood is also recommended for the very young or multiply traumatized child with impending or in actual shock. A tape measure is desirable for measuring abdominal girth, head circumference, and large muscle mass circumferences. It should be on hand, as should a skin-marking pencil for annotating landmarks used in subsequent assessments. Blood tubes should be readied for complete blood count (CBC), type, and cross-match; amylase and glucose levels, baseline clotting studies; and electrolytes. Two heparinized syringes prepared for arterial blood gas (ABG) sampling must be immediately available, along with all crash-cart items needed to support a full-scale resuscitation. Remember—it is always better to overprepare than to underprepare. Chest, abdominal, tracheostomy, and venesection trays should be out and ready for prompt setup. Having the pediatric blades for the laryngoscope and suctioning at hand can avoid much fumbling upon the child's arrival. Table 18–1 indicates the needed sizes of endotracheal (ET) tubes and suction catheters for individuals of all ages. Other things can be accomplished in advance include summoning specialists; alerting x-ray personnel and placing cassettes on the gurney; prewarming the gurney to prevent the loss of body heat during resuscitation (when clothes are removed and the body is poorly protected); having oxygen, suctioning, and oximetry probes in a ready-to-go status; and any other action deemed prudent based on field reports.

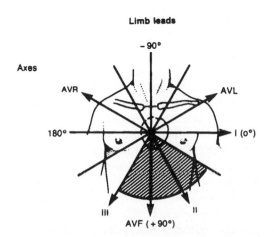

Figure 18–4. Electrical axis readings in pediatric electrocardiagrams. Note that axes are between + 30° and + 120° (shaded area) in young children.

Establishing a plan to deal with the family, such as calling the chaplain, should also be done in advance so that no member of the resuscitation team is "lost" to perform duties that could be accomplished by other hospital team members. It is also worth noting that a stethoscope and BP cuff (suitable for the child's age and weight) should be secured before they are needed, along with several tourniquets and pairs of gloves for physicians and house staff who will want to act without a second's delay.

Shock in a young child becomes evident only after a loss of 15 to 20 percent of the blood volume. Minimal perfusion pressure, regardless of age, is 40 to 45 mm Hg. A child who is calm or unresponsive after trauma is probably in shock. Other signs are a weak cry, nonresponsiveness to stimulation, pallor, cyanosis, poor capillary filling, shallow respirations, and reduced body temperature revealed by cool extremities. Tachycardia is not a reliable indicator of shock. In the neonate, a prolonged shock state (e.g., following extended transportation by land or air) may be accompanied by a waxy, tallowlike hardening and discoloration of the skin called *sclerema neonatorum*. This rare condition is obvious to the experienced practitioner. Shock in children, like adults, must be managed promptly and aggressively by experts, just after the ABCs (airway, breathing, circulation, cervical spine) of basic life support are ensured.

Infants and young children lose body heat readily in a trauma room when they remain exposed for examination and procedures. The skin should be kept dry and any fluids on the surface areas from wound care or other routines should be dried promptly to prevent evaporative cooling. Use an overhead radiant warmer and blankets and minimize contact with cold surfaces (x-ray cassettes, radiological tables, and instruments). Hypothermia contributes to metabolic acidosis, declines in cardiac output, ventricular dysrhythmias, and apnea. All fluids, of course, should be warmed prior to intravenous delivery, irrigation, or use on the body surfaces.

INITIAL RESUSCITATION

Airway

Trauma in children frequently results in compromise of structures that support ventilation. Phrenic nerve injury, flail chest, and pulmonary contusions are examples of conditions that mandate prompt recognition and employment of mechanical ventilation. With major chest injury, the mediastinum shifts readily and compresses the ipsilateral and contralateral lungs, thus inducing respiratory failure. Aspiration is also common in the injured pediatric patient. It is imperative that ENs who work with this population have knowledge and skills to support ventilation after trauma.

First and foremost, it must be recognized that a child's tongue is larger proportionately than an adult's, that the airways are smaller and softer in structural stability, and that there are special implications in establishing a patent airway. The angle formed by the posterior pharynx and the larynx is different from that in adults; hyperextending a child's head during intubation, as would be done with an adult, will obscure the cords and compress the airway. Instead, for effective ventilation, the head should be placed in the "sniffing" position with the neck flexed forward, the head extended on the neck, and the jaw held forward with the chin lift. If airway obstruction is present and ET intubation is indicated, an uncuffed tube is used, taking great care not to pass it too far down into the right mainstream bronchus. Tube size determination is best made by pairing the tube size with the width of the child's little fingernail (see page 128). Correct placement is determined by visually determining equal bilateral chest expansion during ventilating. If intubation is not possible or if cervical spine injury precludes positioning the head adequately, a needle cricothyroidotomy is considered an invaluable technique; use a #10 or #14 angiocatheter and attach oxygen.

A child's breathing is dependent upon a patent airway. Breathing is assessed to determine the work of breathing, the respiratory rate, and the mechanics. For example, abdominal excursions are normal in infants, but chest excursions are normal for older children. A rule of thumb for arriving at an approximate normal respiratory rate is to subtract the age of the child (in years) from 40. Look for retractions, flaring, and paradoxical motion that signal obstruction. Listen for breath sounds that indicate air movement. Severe pulmonary damage can be evident without fractures of the rib cage. Pulse oximetry should also be employed as a noninvasive mode for assessing respiratory efficiency and oxygenation.

Infants are obligatory nose-breathers because their large tongues and small mandibles limit the potential for mouth-breathing except during crying. The infant's and young child's epiglottis assumes a 45-degree angle from the anterior pharyngeal wall, whereas in the adult, it lies parallel to the base of the tongue. The infant's larynx is high in the neck and vocal cords are concave. Oropharyngeal airways or ET intubation may be necessary to bypass nasal obstructions after trauma. Bear in mind that infants ventilate primarily by using their diaphragm, and the efficiency of the diaphragm may require the decompression of the stomach by using a 10 Fr (or larger) tube to accomplish. If a nasogastric (NG) tube is required for stomach decompression, care should be taken to ensure that it does not jeopardize nasal breathing. The resting position of the NG tube should be confirmed by x-ray. It is not sufficient to merely listen, because any sounds are readily transmitted throughout the chest and thus their point of origin cannot be definitely determined. Infants develop retractions early and increase their respiratory rate to compensate for any decreased lung volume. This will significantly impair tidal volume. Any distension resulting from ileus or other trauma-related causes will promptly elevate the diaphragm and further interfere with pulmonary activity. If spinal trauma has been ruled out, children who are breathing spontaneously should be placed in a semi-Fowler position to minimize diaphragmatic compression.

The jaw-thrust maneuver is recommended for ensuring an open airway. Of course if there is potential for cervical spine injury, in-line traction must be maintained until the cervical spine has been cleared. The cervical spine is properly immobilized in neutral position when the ear aligns to the shoulder. In small children, a towel may be placed under the shoulders to prevent the large occiput from causing flexion of the cervical spine. Elevation of the backboard is necessary to achieve cervical spine neutrality in children younger than 8 years.[2] A cervical collar provides poor immobilization since most pediatric cervical spine injuries are high in the cervical spine. Up to 50 percent of children with cervical spine injuries have normal findings on x-rays. Computed tomography (CT) and magnetic resonance imaging (MRI) scans are preferred.

Supplemental oxygen should be provided, even if the child's color is adequate and there are no apparent breathing difficulties. Cyanosis is a late indicator of hypoxia in children. Do not use an oxygen mask if it agitates the child and increases the work of breathing. A hood or cone or a nasal cannula might be better choices. Provide positive-pressure ventilation using a bag-valve-mask unit if there is apnea, gasping, or cyanosis. Bagging a child can be a challenge without a properly fitting mask. Improvising (e.g., turning the adult mask upside down, employing mouth-to-mouth breathing, or using a rescuer device with nasal prongs) may be a workable alternative to a properly fitting mask in an emergency. Remember to gauge volume delivered by chest motion. The small airways produce high resistance and thus underventilation is common. Oxygen should be delivered during assisted ventilation at about 40 percent concentration to guard against secondary respiratory distress syndrome (RDS) in the very young child. If feasible, the oxygen should be humidified to relieve the excessive loss of water and drying that occur in the respiratory tract with nonhumidified oxygen delivery. Oral airways pose risks for both vomiting and aspiration and should be avoided. When the PCO_2 (partial pressure of carbon dioxide in the blood) exceeds 35 mm Hg, a mechanical ventilator should be considered.

If respiratory arrest occurs, hyperventilation with 100 percent oxygen is imperative to reverse respiratory acidosis, decrease ICP, and increase cerebral vasoconstriction, thus improving reflow to nonperfused areas and restoring the brain's autoregulation of blood flow dynamics.

Suction should be minimized if there is coexisting head trauma, since it tends to aggravate further a rising ICP. The PCO_2 should be maintained between 20 and 25 mm Hg. Head elevation to 30 degrees is thought to improve venous drainage during arrest states. Diuretics, steroids, and barbiturates should be used as indicated to aid in brain resuscitation.

Small airways exert a high resistance to airflow, so ventilation of children can be hard work. Evaluate effectiveness by looking and listening. Pop-off valves are no longer used, because they may actually produce hypoventilation.

It is important to remember that the airway is never considered secure until the threat of vomiting and aspiration is minimized by gastric decompression.

Endotracheal Intubation

ENs should be skilled in assisting with ET intubation of children. Selection of proper tubes, properly positioning the child, and having all equipment at hand are important responsibilities. ET intubation is usually achieved easily in children because their larynx and mandible are quite flexible. Extension should never be forced, however.

Although there are many tables or references that prescribe the recommended size of ET tube for a child of a certain age, many clinicians still rely on the "rule of the little finger." The width of the child's little fingernail approximates the appropriate size of the ET tube. Tubes of up to size 6.0 are uncuffed to avoid edema, ulceration, and stenosis, which are prevalent owing to their anatomic variances at the region of the larynx.

The child should be positioned to ensure proper airway alignment for tube placement. The tongue is large and exposure of the glottis is often difficult. The larynx and glottis are more cephalad, and the child's large occiput creates neck flexion and slight head extension. The short trachea in infants (5 to 7 cm from the vocal cords to the carina) may result in accidental bronchial intubation. The tube needs to be advanced only 2 to 3 cm below the cords. Blind nasotracheal intubation is not effective in young children.

A surgical cricothyroidotomy is discouraged in the young child because it contributes to subglottic tracheal stenosis. A large-bore (14 to 18-gauge) needle should be inserted into the cricothyroid membrane instead.

Oral intubation aggravates increased ICP secondary to hypoxia, hypercapnia, or gagging. Use of a paralyzing agent and a sedative for this procedure is advised. Lidocaine, 1 mg/kg, may depress ICP waves and decrease gagging.

Circulation

Children have a large per-unit (80 mg/kg) intravascular volume, so relatively small losses (i.e., 200 to 300 mL) can represent up to 20 percent of the circulating blood volume. After the child's weight has been obtained (or estimated), the EN should calculate the child's approximate circulatory volume. Blood lost during hemorrhage and that required for laboratory testing should be carefully documented to ensure that fluid replacement remains on target.

In initial evaluation, any obvious hemorrhage must be controlled by digital pressure or other direct means. Two intravenous lines should be started at once. Even if one line has been established in the field by emergency medical technicians (EMTs), the second one should be established promptly for obvious serious trauma to ensure access for crystalloid fluid delivery. The lower extremities should be avoided, since they have limited efficacy in abdominal trauma, which is common in children.

Sites for intravenous fluid administration vary, depending on the age of the child and the nature of the injuries. In the neonate, an umbilical vessel can be used. The scalp, hand, and foot are appropriate choices for the child through the first year of life; use a 22 or 23-gauge device for cannulation. After age 2, the scalp is seldom a good option, but the hand and foot continue to be useful. The antecubital site is an appropriate choice after age 5 or 6. The saphenous vein is a tempting target, but it is not a good option in cases of abdominal injury or if there is serious hemorrhage in the lower extremities, since inferior vena cava blood flow may be drastically impaired. Always restrain the extremity prior to the procedure—for the child's and the staff's safety. When high flow rates are needed (i.e., > 1.5mL/kg per minute), catheter introducer sheaths are ideally suited, owing to their short length and large internal diameter. They may be placed in either a central or large peripheral site. However, since peripheral placement will result in lower flow delivery rates, owing to higher vein resistance, the central sites are preferred. A large-capacity micropore filter (40 μm) has been shown to be of substantial benefit for maintaining a normal platelet count and for reducing transfusion-related complications such as febrile reactions. A pressure infusion pump is required to assist in overcoming the resistance that is inherent within the intravenous circuit, and ideally, this pump should be capable of an output temperature of 37°C to prevent hypothermia in children. Countercurrent heat-exchange fluid pumps are more efficient for the warming process and are preferred over immersion or dry wall warmers, especially for children who are transfused with multiple units of fluid and blood at a rate exceeding 150 mL/min.[3]

Although venesection is not highly desirable in children, it may be required when other access sites are unattainable. Children under 4 years of age are candidates for an external jugular cutdown

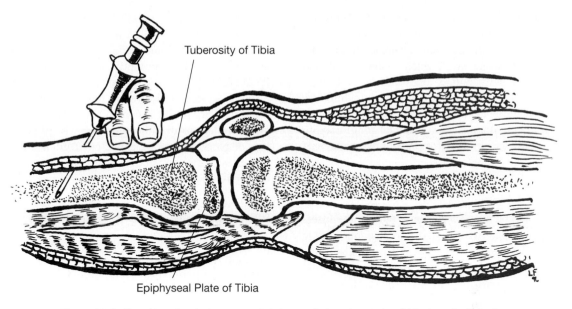

Tuberosity of Tibia

Epiphyseal Plate of Tibia

Figure 18–5. Site of insertion for intraosseus inferior needle into the anterior tibial tuberosity. Note that the needle is angled away from the epiphyseal plate.

if a central line is deemed important for fluid delivery or central venous pressure (CVP) measurement, since the subclavian vein is small and the top of the lung is relatively high, contributing to the potential for iatrogenic pneumothorax. The superior vena cava catheter (passed via the right subclavian or jugular) is a good choice for replacing volume quickly, too.

Intraosseus Infusions

Intraosseus infusions are useful in children under 6 years of age when attempts to gain other circulatory access have failed. Sites include the distal femur, tibia, sternum, clavicle, and humerus (Figs. 18–5 and 18–6). The preferred site for insertion is the anterior medial aspect of the tibia, one third of a finger width below the proximal tibial tuberosity. An alternate site would be the distal third of the femur, midline, three finger breadths proximal to the external condyle. (Use an 18- to 20-gauge spinal needle for children up to 18 months of age; use a 13- to 16-gauge bone-marrow needle for older children.)

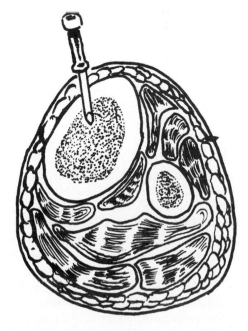

Figure 18–6. Site for placement of an intraosseous needle.

Among fluid and drugs that can be administered by the intraosseous route are saline, glucose, blood, sodium bicarbonate, atropine, dopamine, epinephrine, diazepam, selected antibiotics, phenytoin, and succinylcholine.

Complications of intraosseous infusions are rare but include cellulitis, osteomyelitis, extravasation, and hematoma. The EN should avoid making multiple sticks in a bone to prevent the leakage of fluid or drugs into soft tissue.

Procedure

1. Drape the area selected; prepare the insertion site with alcohol and povidone-iodine solution and air-dry. When time permits, use local anesthesia. Examine the needle and confirm a landmark appropriate to expected penetration.
2. Insert the needle perpendicular to the bone, or 60 degrees inferiorly with the bevel directed upward. Ensure that the needle is being directed away from the growth plate. Use pressure and a rotary motion until decreased resistance is felt. A "pop" will be detected as the needle penetrates the medullary cavity. Aspirate marrow or blood to verify entry. If unable to aspirate and the needle feels firmly embedded, flush the needle with saline. If there is no resistance or evidence of infiltration, attach the prepared intravenous solution and proceed with drug administration as indicated.
3. Immobilize the administration needle and the extremity. Continue to observe the site for infiltration.

SHOCK

Children in shock are characteristically quiet and their extremities are pale and cool. Other indicators of shock are a decrease in the level of consciousness (LOC) and low urine output. The BP may be normal in compensatory shock states with blood losses of up to 20 to 25 percent. Infants have a fixed stroke volume; their bodies can increase cardiac output only by increasing the heart rate. Their bodies' ability to concentrate urine is also poor, so urine osmolality may not be a reliable indicator of dehydration.

Remember that a child in hypovolemic shock state has lost between 25 and 50 percent of the total blood volume and therefore should be typed and cross-matched promptly for blood equalling 25 to 50 mL/kg of the total body weight. Capillary refill is a good indicator of tissue perfusion. A brisk capillary refill (2 seconds) is normal. A sluggish capillary refill indicates shock. A 10 percent loss of blood volume is expected if the heart rate increases by 20 bpm; and a 20 percent blood loss if it increases by 30 bpm.

PROTOCOLS FOR FLUID RESUSCITATION

A child has a large percentage (about 50 percent) of total fluid volume in highly unstable extracellular compartments. Hypovolemia can occur quickly, with devastating consequences. The fluid resuscitation of a hypovolemic child is based on a formula that replaces volume per kilogram of body weight. A child's total blood volume is approximately 70 to 80 mL/kg. The initial bolus of fluid is ordinarily a crystalloid (Ringer's lactate or normal saline solution [NSS]) and is administered over 5 to 10 minutes. The volume infused is 20 mL/kg of body weight. The desired effects of the initial bolus are decreased heart rate, improved skin coloring, increased BP, improved capillary refill, improved extremity warmth, increased urinary output, and a clearing of the sensorium. If these do not seem evident, the same bolus dosage should be repeated. At this point, monitor the child carefully. If there is not a rapid improvement, immediate preparations should be made for blood or blood component therapy and perhaps for surgical intervention. Note that after the second bolus, half of the total circulating blood volume has been replaced. Crystalloid replacement is based on a 3-to-1 rule; that is, for every unit of lost circulating volume, three are replaced. If the estimated blood loss is equal to or less than 20 mL/kg, Ringer's lactate will suffice. If the blood loss is greater than 40 mL/kg, resuscitation must advance to a second phase involving the administration of whole blood to sustain the hematocrit (Hct).

After the initial use of crystalloids, the second phase of resuscitation for hypovolemia is the administration of type-specific or type O, Rh-negative blood (20 mL/kg) or packed red blood cells (RBCs) (10 mL/kg). Request blood that is less than 5 days old. Fresher blood has a lower potassium level and 2,3-diphosphoglycerate (2,3-DPG) is greater, thus optimizing the delivery of oxygen to the child's vulnerable tissues. Whole blood or packed RBCs should be infused over a 2 to 3-hour period and is expected to raise the hemoglobin by 3 g/dL. Fresh frozen plasma is acceptable for replacing coagulation factors, but it should not be used as a volume expander.

When the child is stabilized in the shock state, maintenance fluids are infused. Dextrose 5 percent with one quarter NSS is the crystalloid of choice. Potassium chloride (2 mEq/100mL) is added. Very small infants may experience depletion of liver glycogen and thus develop hypoglycemia. They should receive 10 percent dextrose in 0.2 percent NSS. The serum glucose must be monitored carefully.

All resuscitation fluids for the child should be warmed, because hypothermic stress can be readily induced during shock states. The result of such stress is exhaustion of catecholamines and muscle shivering, which aggravates acidosis. Hypothermia may be refractory to shock therapy, may induce bleeding disorders, and cause the child to have experienced prolonged effects from anesthetic agents. Remember that children possess a very poor thermal regulatory system during their early years because they have a high ratio of body surface to mass. Furthermore, the small glycogen stores in the liver, an accelerated metabolism and caloric expenditure, and thin skin compounded by the lack of subcutaneous tissue all contribute to their plight as their bodies attempt to maintain normothermia.

ENs should keep the child covered, especially the head, which accounts for considerable heat loss. Cellophane wrap can be employed during resuscitation to prevent conductive heat loss while permitting visual access to skin surfaces. The resuscitation room should be maintained at 75° to 80°F and a warming hood or heating blanket should be used. Any irrigating fluids must also be warmed. Environmental stealers of heat (cold equipment, wet clothes, and drafts from fans or ventilation systems) must be noted and eliminated.

TRAUMA EVALUATION: ANATOMIC AND PHYSIOLOGICAL VARIABLES AND THEIR IMPLICATIONS FOR ASSESSMENT AND MANAGEMENT

When the EN examines injured children, it is important to be mindful of the anatomic and physiological variables that influence their responses to major trauma.

Injury Evaluation

An accurate account of the accident scenario and the mechanics of impact will be invaluable in the assessment of pediatric injuries. Important factors are knowledge of a blunt versus penetrating injury, of the presence of soft-tissue damage, and of whether a limb, neck, or joint was forced beyond the normal range of motion (ROM). Forces of acceleration and deceleration produce varying sequelae, and lateral impacts to the body produce unique injuries as well. All injuries are dependent upon the generation of gravitational forces. The weight of the victim at the time of impact is a product of body weight and gravitational forces.

Extensive crushing injuries, straddle injuries, and trauma from explosions all have highly predictable consequences. For example, genitourinary trauma is an almost certain result of a fractured pelvis or a straddle injury. A fracture of the first or second rib is associated with high morbidity and mortality owing to vascular and soft-tissue damage within the chest of these patients.

The condition of a vehicle after an accident may be a valuable clue. If it is "totaled," suspect major injury, even if there are no apparent wounds. If bicycle spokes were noted to be bent after an accident, a bike fork compression injury should be predicted. The use of restraints, car seats and protective head gear will usually influence the injury morbidity significantly, too. It is often overlooked but important to determine whether other occupants of a motor vehicle were properly restrained. Often, restrained passengers are severely injured when nonrestrained passengers are thrown against them. Loose objects in a car can also be missiles that contribute to major injury. Handbags, cartons of soda, umbrellas, books, or bowling balls can do serious damage to a youngster's head.

Compression injuries of the spine are associated with falls from considerable heights or with impact injuries, in which the victim is hurled against a fixed object with great force (e.g., a skiing accident in which someone hits a tree or a diving accident in which the diver strikes his or her head against the bottom of the pool).

ENs should always scrutinize anatomic areas immediately above, below, or adjacent to obvious areas of injury. For example, blunt trauma above the clavicles is often associated with cervical spine injury; pelvic trauma is likely to occur along with a fractured femur. Be cautious and do not permit obvious nonlife-threatening injuries to detract from the search for occult ones. For example, a major burn may be so horrifying and attention-consuming that one overlooks internal injuries from the associated explosion or fails to notice airway compromise from smoke inhalation.

General Physical Characteristics of the Child

Body proportions are variable throughout childhood, but in the early years, there is dominance of the head and upper extremities. Children's large heads and small legs make them head-first flying missiles when they are hit in a MVA unless they are properly restrained. They have a high metabolic turnover and limited glycogen stores; thus, nutrient or hydration deficiencies can result in extremely heavy demands on oxygenation and circulatory efficiency and in prompt development of hypoglycemia. Since small children have a relatively high body surface area, body heat can be lost readily during hypermetabolic states and stresses associated with injury. Their immature organ systems do not permit maximum compensation in shock states; for example, their liver glycogen stores are minimal, their kidneys cannot concentrate urine efficiently, and their cardiovascular responses to catecholamines are labile. Also, their immune systems are slow and incomplete. All severely traumatized children, therefore, must be managed with these vulnerabilities in mind.

Head and Neck

Again, childhood trauma is the leading cause of death in children after the first year of life, and head injury is the chief cause of this trauma-related death. One fourth of all head injuries are potentially life-threatening. They frequently occur in re-

lation to other injuries and often are the result of child abuse.

The head of the young child is quite large and heavy in proportion to the rest of the body. Muscular support of the neck is poor, permitting the neck to snap sharply in flexion or hyperextension upon impact. This vulnerability, coupled with the unprotected, poorly myelinated, and vascular cord, is likely to produce marked bleeding and edema, as well.

The bones and tissues that protect the head and neck are thinner, softer, and more pliable. The cranial vault has a rich blood supply to support its growth, so skull fractures heal within 3 to 6 months in infants and toddlers, but healing takes up to 1 year in the older child because the bone is becoming increasingly ossified. Suture lines are not fused completely until the child is about 4 years of age. There is a 3-mm gap at 2 years of age and a 2-mm gap at 3 years. Sutures open easily with edema or bleeding until the child is 4 or 5 years old, and even in adolescence, they may open under considerable ICP. Some authorities suspect that intracranial contents can force relaxation of suture lines up to the age of 15. In general, the young child can tolerate significant increases in edema and ICP without vital brain tissue becoming compressed. A child's head can sustain major trauma, resulting in a cerebral contusion without skull fracture, owing to the factors that contribute to resiliency of the head. Children's conditions tend to deteriorate more quickly after major head injury than do those of adults; however, they also recover remarkably, even after prolonged periods of unconsciousness.

The growing skull and intracranial contents are richly supplied with a vascular network to support growth. The scalp bleeds profusely after injury, which can actually contribute to a shock state. Meningeal tissue is fragile, but the dura adheres closely to the skull in early childhood, discouraging epidural hematoma. The dura, especially at the foramen, is a common site for bleeding. The fragile bridging veins are responsible for subdural hematomas, however. The middle meningeal artery is not embedded until age 2, so it is less vulnerable until then since it is unfixed, merely sliding away from direct force. Children have a high percentage of blood in their heads, but isolated head injury rarely results in shock after the first year of life, because there is insufficient intracranial space for containing the blood loss necessary to produce a shock state. If shock and head injury coexist, look for other injuries.

Because of a high intracranial vascularity, cerebral edema can develop quite promptly after head injury. In young children, however, signs and symptoms may appear in a delayed fashion because intracranial contents can expand freely (because of suture line release); thus, compression of vital brain tissue may be obscured. It is important, therefore, always to measure head circumference through early adolescence in accident victims, since this information can be useful in the early discovery of cerebral edema and resultant head expansion. Pupillary and ocular changes result from infratentorial cerebral edema. Weak ocular muscles may make it difficult to assess conjugate eye motion, however.

Anterior facial bones resist injury better than adult bones do. Cavitation and bone weakening, which result as sinuses develop, do not occur until the early school years. The young child's facial bones are quite solid, so direct trauma to eye orbits, the maxima, and frontal bones must be severe to produce fractures. If there are facial fractures, look for subcutaneous emphysema at the mediastinal area, which can occur with severe facial trauma. Since facial bones are highly resistant to trauma during early childhood, the identification of facial fractures suggests major impact, such as from a deceleration MVA or from a severe blow incurred through intentional abuse.

Head Injury Assessment. The initial assessment of head injury involves obtaining a history of the trauma to ascertain the physical forces and circumstances involved. It is vital to know whether there was any loss of consciousness at the time to determine the length of the lucid interval. VS, LOC, presence or absence of reflexes (both deep tendon and oculovestibular), and assessment of the cranial nerves must be recorded. The modified Glasgow Coma Scale (GCS) may be used for preverbal children (Table 18–7.) Severe head injury (GCS score of between 3 and 8) is less frequently encountered in children; when it is, the mortality is significantly lower than among adults. The motor score component of the GCS is the most predictive of outcome in children.[4]

The head should be inspected, with special attention to scalp bleeding, which can be quite severe. "Ping pong" fractures without epidural injury are common findings in the very young child, and they can often be "popped" back into place without sequelae. Nasal and auditory canals should

TABLE 18–7. MODIFIED GLASGOW COMA SCALE FOR CHILDREN

Category	Response		Score
	Child	*Infant*	
Eyes	Opens eyes spontaneously	Opens eyes spontaneously	4
	Opens eyes to speech	Opens eyes to speech	3
	Opens eyes to pain	Opens eyes to pain	2
	No response	No response	1
Motor	Obeys commands	Spontaneous movements	6
	Localizes	Withdraws to touch	5
	Withdraws	Withdraws to pain	4
	Flexion	Flexion (decorticate)	3
	Extension	Extension (decerebrate)	2
	No response	No response	1
Verbal	Oriented	Coos and babbles	5
	Confused	Irritable cry	4
	Inappropriate words	Cries to pain	3
	Incomprehensible words	Moans to pain	2
	No response	No response	1
Total score			3–15

be scrutinized for blood and CSF drainage. Eyes must be inspected for movement, pupillary size and responses, and visual acuity. The mouth must be examined for malocclusion, buccal lacerations, missing teeth, or tongue lacerations that could threaten the airway through bleeding and glossal edema. The neck should be inspected for tracheal deviation, vein distension, and ecchymosis. Palpation for subcutaneous emphysema, bony abnormalities, and tenderness should also be done during the quick, initial examination to detect any immediate threats to life, such as a fractured trachea or larynx.

The pineal gland, classically used to mark the intracranial midpoint, does not calcify until adolescence and is not a valuable radiological marker of shifting intracranial structures. As noted earlier, however, cervical spine films are not to be overlooked. Any skull films should always be coupled with a lateral study of the cervical spine. Fractures of vertebral bodies are not common, but subluxation or dislocation has a high enough incidence that real suspicion should prevail. Cervicomedullary spinal cord injury (e.g., from neck hyperextension in football and diving accidents) can produce devastating results. There is a classic area of poor circulation at C-2, and central cord destruction and hemorrhage, accompanied by a peripheral zone of cord edema, can occur without any clinical evidence of blockage on the Queckenstedt–Stookey test. When in doubt about the status of the cervical spine, do not force the neck into extension in attempts to secure the airway. Alternate approaches to establish the airway must be used.

Examination of the head-injured child may or may not include radiological studies. Skull films have questionable value. The cross-table cervical spine film is the best to detect air in the cranial vault and to assess for air/fluid in the sphenoid sinuses, which indicates basilar or compound fracture of the skull. Tangential views will reveal double densities associated with depressed skull fractures. Skull films often identify bone fragments and foreign objects and reveal fractures that cross the path of the middle meningeal artery or dural venous sinuses. They are also useful in detecting fractures entering the foramen magnum, which are high-risk, owing to the vascularity there. The absence of fractures does not rule out serious intracranial bleeds, however. Skull fractures are generally not considered serious, but they may be associated with soft-tissue damage. CT scans are used for most acute injuries because the patient can be easily monitored during the short procedure. MRI scanning is used for study of the posterior fossa, the spinal cord, and certain lesions, but it is costly and patient monitoring may be compromised during the lengthy procedure.

Depressed or stellate fractures should cause suspicion of child abuse. The child may present with a delayed complication of a leptomeningeal cyst, usually at the lambdoidal suture, up to 6 months after injury. A portion of the arachnoid protrudes through a dural tear and is trapped. Pulsations of CSF enlarge the fracture and increase associated damage. Surgery is required. "Pingpong" fractures occur in infants and are benign depressions that often resolve spontaneously. Surgical intervention is avoided because of the high risk of dural laceration and cerebral injury.

Basilar skull fractures may be serious. Signs and symptoms are the same as in the adult, (i.e., Battle's sign, hemotympanum, periorbital ecchymosis, otorrhea and rhinorrhea, and palsy of cranial nerves). The child may be admitted for 48 to 72 hours of observation and a course of antibiotics. Most basilar skull fractures will close in 7 to 10 days without surgery.

Minor Head Injuries. Minor head injuries include scalp hematoma, lacerations, and concussion. Cephalhematomas should not be aspirated. Bleeding from most lacerations can be easily identified and controlled, but selected lacerations of the scalp may bleed profusely, even producing shock. Transient changes in neurological function may be generalized or focal and include seizures, vomiting, and possibly headache. The pediatric concussion syndrome, characterized by pallor, diaphoresis, lethargy, and even unresponsiveness, usually is short-lived but has been associated with post-traumatic epilepsy.[4] Children with ventricular shunts, congenital malformations of the brain, or blood dyscrasias deserve a thorough investigation in the event of even a trivial head injury, since intracranial complications could be devastating.

Head Injuries with Intracranial Bleeding. Signs and symptoms of intracranial bleeding depend upon the area of the brain involved, (i.e., cerebral cortex, motor areas, or brainstem). Epidural bleeds are usually arterial, with temporal and frontal lobes accounting for most. The middle meningeal artery is the major vessel involved. Seventy-five percent are associated with skull fracture, often the temporal portion of the petrous bone. This type of injury is seldom seen in a child less than 2 years old because this artery is not entrapped in the bone until then. The mortality of epidural hematomas is high (20 percent), despite aggressive therapy. Tachycardia is more common than Cushing's triad. Signs and symptoms of elevated ICP are not dramatic. Young children may be unable to accurately report them, and the changes are more subtle than those in adults, owing to the expandable cranium. Subdural hematomas are usually venous, owing to the rupture of bridging veins. About 25 percent occur in association with skull fracture. They may present within hours of being produced by cerebral or brainstem contusion. Half of the mortality is due to associated injuries. Decreasing LOC, contralateral hemiparesis, and ipsilateral pupillary dilation are indications of a subdural. Treatment is surgical. Subacute subdurals are less common in children than in adults; chronic subdurals are rare in children except those with blood dyscrasias or repeated battering injuries. Occasionally, a clot will retract and the resultant osmotic pull will effect an enlarging mass with structural downward displacement of intracranial contents Signs and symptoms of possible herniation include ipsilateral cranial nerve III palsy, contralateral limb weakness, alteration in LOC and coma, decorticate and decerebrate posturing, respiratory irregularities, and cardiopulmonary arrest.

Management of Major Head and Spinal Cord Injury.
Ventilatory support is the vital concern after head injury. Maintenance of alveolar partial pressure of carbon dioxide ($PaCO_2$) between 20 and 25 mm Hg and of an upper-level pH of 7.50 to 7.55 are guidelines. A common complication is neurogenic pulmonary edema, which can be induced by fluid shifts to low-pressure circulatory networks (i.e., pulmonary) during massive sympathetic stimulation after injury. The ICP must be carefully monitored and controlled by the use of diuretics, cautious fluid volume delivery, and mechanical control of ICP by a bolt in some instances. Other aspects of care include seizure prophylaxis, temperature regulation, prevention of infection, and support of vital functions during the acute states of the major head injury.

Acute spinal cord injury with documented neurological deficits may be initially treated with Solu-Medrol (30 mg/kg, mixed in 50 mL NSS and administered via piggyback over 15 minutes). This loading dose is followed by 5.4 mg/kg per hour for the next 23 hours in an attempt to retard tissue destruction associated with the injury and to improve regional blood flow at the area.[5]

Chest
A child's thorax is pliable and resists fracture. However, damage to soft tissue (e.g., heart, lungs, mediastinum) may be increased because fracturing does not occur (and thus the force of injury is not absorbed) and the resultant energy is transmitted to underlying soft tissue, especially the lung parenchyma. Furthermore, the small respiratory passages are prone to develop respiratory insufficiency after contusion, requiring mechanical ventilatory support. The mediastinum has not yet fibrosed and become fixed, thus permitting wide swings of the viscera. Mediastinal flexibility also permits significant derangement of cardiovascular mechanics.

The heart lies high in the chest and is vulnerable to chest impact injuries. The heart wall is thin and the pericardial sac is quite small. Contusions and lacerations are not uncommon after blunt trauma and may result in the child's rapid demise from cardiac tamponade.

The sternum is soft and easily penetrated by small objects such as BBs (shot pellets), staples, glass fragments, or needles.

Chest Injuries.
Although abdominal injuries are more common than thoracic ones, thoracic injuries now exceed abdominal injuries as a cause of death in children, second only to head injuries. Data from the National Pediatric Trauma Registry indicate that major thoracic injuries (excluding lung contusion) carry a mortality rate of more than 50 percent.[6]

The chest (front and back) should be searched for wounds or ecchymosis. Breath excursions, breathing rate, and rhythm should be noted. Ideally, heart and breath sound auscultation should be accomplished prior to any percussion for signs of dullness or hyperresonance. While making these assessments, note any retractions, paradoxical respirations, nasal flaring, tachypnea, dyspnea, distended neck veins, or tracheal deviation that may be indicative of pneumothorax or cardiac tamponade. The stability of the chest cage should be checked and any masses, subcutaneous emphysema (especially mediastinal), or areas of tenderness should be noted. Scrutinize the sternum, which is easily penetrated by the smallest foreign body or projectile. Look for lacerations, abrasions, and contusions, which signal potential intrathoracic organ injury such as pulmonary or cardiac contusions. Even when aided by creatine kinase (CK) isoenzymes, ECGs, and echocardiography, the physician may find it difficult to detect cardiac contusions, however.[7] The child should be promptly placed on constant ECG monitoring to ensure that any cardiac compromise is identified. ST segment elevation and inverted T waves, however, are late and ominous symptoms. Initial and serial chest films must be obtained to detect life-threatening disasters in the thorax, since surgical risk is significantly increased once cardiac output has been seriously compromised. Flail chest, ruptured diaphragm, penetrating trauma (except as a result of fractured ribs or clavicle), and aortic rupture are rare injuries in children. Sixty percent of chest trauma in children has associated pulmonary contusions.

Aspiration is common. There may be extensive soft-tissue injury without any fractures of the bony thorax, owing to its plasticity. Tracheal deviation and neck vein distension are *not* useful indicators of pneumothoraces. The mediastinum is very mobile, with easy dislocation of the heart, angulation of great vessels, and compression of the lungs and trachea. Mortality from chest injuries is quite high in the preschool age group owing to the limited respiratory reserve and high oxygen demand in these children. Hypoxemia and hypotension are the principal concerns in chest-injured children.

A tension pneumothorax in a child may be decompressed with a large-bore needle at the fourth or fifth intercostal space in the midaxillary line. The evacuation should be followed by a tube placement at the same site. If a child requires a chest tube for a simple pneumothorax, it is placed either at the axilla behind the head of the pectoralis major muscles in the second or third intercostal space, or at the anterior second or third intercostal space in the midclavicular line. Continuous suction at 20 to 40 cm H_2O is adequate to evacuate fluid or air from the chest. X-rays are obtained immediately after tube placement to ensure tube efficacy. If a hemothorax is present, the EN should be alert to excessive bleeding, because chest-tube blood loss can accumulate quickly. A child may lose up to 30 to 40 percent of circulating volume into one pleural space. More than 10 mL/kg per hour of blood loss warrants prompt operative intervention.

Abdomen

The child's abdominal wall is thin and the rectus abdominis muscle provides poor protection in younger children for the large organs. The paucity of intra-abdominal fat "padding" leaves the organs, such as the highly vascular kidneys, loosely attached and vulnerable to shearing forces. High-impact injuries thrust the abdominal contents against the bony spine, creating both lacerations and contusions. The freely mobile abdominal organs rebound after impact, tearing vessels and traumatizing viscera. The relatively large, highly vascular liver lies exposed below the rib margin, as does the spleen. Both of these organs are easy targets for injury in either blunt and penetrating trauma. The stomach, when distended with food, is vulnerable to compression forces and at risk of rupture in trauma.

Abdominal Assessment. Abdominal evaluation of children is complicated since they are often unable to communicate verbally about their symptoms or to respond meaningfully to the usual abdominal examination. When examining the child after trauma, inspect the anterior abdomen for signs of injury; logroll the child and look for contusions, abrasions, or evidence of retroperitoneal bleeding or hematoma, which may be reflected by discoloration of the lumbar spine (Grey–Turner sign). The bleeding in this region is slow, so repeat the assessment several times during the first hours after admission. Measure the girth of the abdominal wall at the level of the umbilicus. Landmarks for measuring must be documented to facilitate subsequent measurements, usually with a skin-marking pen. An increase in abdominal girth is one indicator of abdominal distension that accompanies bleeding or rupture of an abdominal viscus. Note if the abdomen is distended or concave and whether the conscious child tends to flex the lower extremities in an attempt to alleviate pain. Look for muscle spasms, note old surgical scars, and document wounds, hematoma formation, or ecchymosis. The abdomen should be palpated for subcutaneous emphysema, tenderness, and pelvic bone stability. Percuss for fixed dullness, too.

The flank should be examined for bulging that would indicate the potential for renal trauma. A ruptured spleen has the classic findings of Kehr's signs (left shoulder pain), increased pain on inspiration, and abdominal wall bruising. The white blood cell (WBC) count rises promptly. Syncope, shock, abdominal distension (even with a NG tube in place) and ileus are concomitant findings. Since the spleen produces immunoglobulins and tuftsin, splenectomy is avoided and a repair is done instead. Some splenic bleeding will stop spontaneously, but delayed splenic rupture is a threat for at least 1 week after injury. Often, this condition is asymptomatic, other than expansion of the splenic site. The second most vulnerable organ, after the spleen, is the liver. A ruptured liver is associated with avulsion of the hepatic veins from the inferior vena cava, as well as from bruising of the parenchyma. Many children with liver and spleen trauma will not be surgically managed initially but will be observed for deterioration. Surgical intervention is deferred unless the child develops a hemodynamic compromise, increased peritoneal signs, or requires transfusion of more than 30 to 50 percent of his estimated blood volume.[8] Pancreatic injury requires prompt debridement and drainage to prevent devastating intra-abdominal complications from enzymatic tissue destruction.

Bowel sounds are labile in children, so their absence is of little value in abdominal assessment. In acute abdominal injury they may be absent, hyperactive, or hypoactive. Several minutes (5 to 8) may be required to elicit bowel sounds or to be relatively certain that they are absent. Remember, it is not uncommon after trauma for there to be a paralytic ileus, but the presence of normal bowel sounds would be indeed reassuring. Abdominal bruits are grave findings because they reflect large vessel injury.

Children under 6 years of age are highly dependent upon the diaphragm for breathing, and any abdominal discomfort may compromise ventilation. As might be expected, 90 percent or more of the serious abdominal injuries in children are due to blunt, sometimes trivial trauma to the abdomen. The child often is noted to have considerable gastric distension from bagging, aerophagia, or a reflex ileus, interfering with both assessment and management. A CT scan of the abdomen and peritoneal lavage are among common diagnostic modes.

Peritoneal lavage is indicated only when the patient has concurrent neurological injury, is obtunded, requires general anesthesia, or is hemodynamically unstable with fractures of the chest, pelvis, or lumbar spine. It is not routinely undertaken early after trauma, because it is highly irritating to the abdomen and may confound other clinical assessments. The lavage is accomplished only after the bladder and stomach are decompressed, to avoid their injury. The peritoneal lavage involves the infusion of Ringer's lactate (10 mL/kg, up to 1000 mL) over 10 minutes. A strongly positive lavage in hemodynamically stable children no longer mandates immediate exploratory surgery. A negative lavage result may accompany retroperitoneal injuries, including those to the duodenum and pancreas; results are positive in most cases of pelvic fracture.

Ultrasound, however, has been shown to be superior to peritoneal lavage for detecting intraperitoneal organ injuries with or without concomitant free fluid, as well as retroperitoneal and intrathoracic injuries.[9] A CT scan is indicated for a declining Hct or unsuccessful fluid resuscitation, if the child has concurrent neurological injuries or multiple injuries, more than one detectable bleeding site or hematuria. It is most useful when used with contrast media.

Urinalysis is vital in the evaluation of any child who has a trauma history in which abdominal injury is a potential complication. Asymptomatic microscopic hematuria alone is sufficient reason to pursue an abdominal CT scan.[10] The EN should ensure that a urine specimen is obtained promptly.

Surgical exploration may follow the in-depth clinical examination and the analyses of laboratory blood study results (i.e., CBC, type and crossmatch, prothrombin [PT] and partial thromboplastin time [PTT], amylase, ABG), especially in penetrating injuries when the extent of trauma is difficult to appreciate. An elevated amylase or a very high WBC count could point to a ruptured spleen or other abdominal catastrophe. Changes in results of serial studies, however, can be most valuable in pointing to trends that contribute to diagnosis. The EN should recall that the Hct is slow to change, even in major blood loss states, so this indicator is not wholly reliable early after trauma. Free air on the x-ray is an immediate signal of ruptured viscus and the need for prompt surgical intervention.

If there are peritoneal signs and bloody drainage from the NG tube, stomach injuries are suspected. Pneumoperitoneum is noted on x-ray. Duodenal injuries are rare, but when they do occur, they are usually the product of blunt trauma. They may present as "delayed injuries," 24 hours to 7 days after trauma, especially if they involve the retroperitoneal duodenum. Small-intestine trauma is likely to involve the ligament of Treitz or the ileocecal valve. The intestine may be transsected across the bony spine upon severe impact. Since an ileus develops early after intestinal trauma, there may be minimal or no free intraperitoneal air. If rectal injuries are noted, they are usually the product of child abuse, deviant sexual behavior, or occasionally straddle injuries.

Genitourinary Trauma. Significant trauma to the abdomen or lower extremities should motivate emergency personnel to consider thoroughly the possibility of genitourinary injury. Genitourinary injuries in children may include bladder rupture, renal contusion, or urethral injuries, primarily from blunt trauma.

Inspect the meatus for blood and the scrotum and perineum for wounds or ecchymosis. A fractured pelvis relates closely to bladder-urethral trauma; thus, a thorough assessment is vital before assuming the absence of urethral or other related trauma. If a child with a pelvic fracture or intra-abdominal injury is unable to void and is experiencing significant lower abdominal pain, a ruptured bladder should be suspected. A renal contusion is often not accompanied by hematuria. Tenderness and pain in the flank might suggest such injury, but a CT scan, renal scan, or intravenous pyelogram is required to confirm it. If there is a history of a straddle injury or if blood is noted on the mea-

tus or appears on underclothing (sometimes along with urine), urethral transsection may have occurred. Urethral injuries tend to produce an intense urge to void. Do not permit voluntary voiding, because urine could extravasate into the peritoneal cavity, creating an additional problem for the trauma team to manage. Prompt urologic consultation is in order in such instances. A suprapubic bladder tap is the procedure recommended for relieving a highly distended bladder that interferes with therapy or is intolerable to the patient.

SUPRAPUBIC BLADDER TAP. To perform a suprapubic bladder tap, ascertain that the infant or child has not recently voided and palpate the bladder. If the bladder cannot be palpated, no attempt should be made to proceed with the procedure. Once bladder distension is confirmed, the child should be placed in a supine position and restrained if needed. After the skin has been prepared with an antiseptic solution, the superior border is once again palpated, and the needle (1.5-in., 23-gauge) is introduced into the midline of the border. The needle is held perpendicular upon entry. The physician will pull back slightly on the plunger while carefully advancing the needle, directing it slightly downward until urine is obtained. If no urine is obtained, a gloved finger may be introduced into the rectum to push up on the bladder while the aspirating needle is guided to the urine pool. A small dressing is usually placed over the site of entry.

A rectal examination noting prostate position, sphincter tone, and any presence of gross blood may assist in identification of perforations of the colon or rectum. Loss of rectal tone is also an indicator of spinal trauma; thus, a rectal examination is a useful adjunct to assessing the unconscious child. The child with abdominal injuries should not be catheterized if a urethral injury is thought to exist, because doing so may convert a minor injury into a major one.

Musculoskeletal System

Bones of infants and children are soft, pliable, and richly supplied with blood. They are easily injured from falls and twisting motions, because bone growth is faster than gains in muscle or ligament strength. However, the relative strength of ligaments is greater. The epiphyseal growth plate is more prone to injury than long-bone shafts, and epiphyses of long bones do not fuse completely until about 16 years of age in females and 28 years of age in males.

Two thirds of all significant childhood injuries involve the musculoskeletal system (e.g., fractures, dislocations, sprains and associated soft-tissue damage).

Assessment of Traumatized Extremities. In cases for which the mechanism of trauma is unknown, the EN should recall that 25 percent of fractures in children under 3 years of age are due to child abuse. When assessing musculoskeletal trauma, consider that all fractures may result in significant blood loss and circulatory support must be ensured early. Neurosensory and extremity pulse checks should be done initially and frequently throughout the emergency period. The initial detection of an arterial pulse does not confirm the absence of vessel injury, since collateral circulation may be pulsatile, giving false reassurance. Girth measurements of injured limbs may be useful in detecting significant hidden blood loss. Skin temperature and color are also valuable indices of any circulatory impairment. Note any loss of sensation, tenderness, deformities, loss of muscle strength, abnormal posturing, spasticity, hemiplegia, or altered extremity function. Do not palpate crepitations, because this is unnecessarily painful to the child.

Compartment syndrome may occur with displaced fractures of the tibia and even nondisplaced fractures of the proximal third of the tibia; vulnerability extends for up to 24 hours after injury. The leg compartments of children are sensitive to increased pressure, and assessment must rely on the presence of increased pain at rest, accompanied by pain on passive stretch when attempting to detect compartment syndrome. Distal pulses may persist, owing to collateral filling, so their presence may be confusing. Sensory changes should be elicited, because they may be reasonable clues to the development of compartment syndrome.

X-rays of at least two projections (posteroanterior [PA] and lateral) with a study of the joints above and below the fracture are required. In a growing child, comparative studies of the opposite extremity are imperative. Condylar and supracondylar fractures of the elbow carry a high risk of peripheral nerve injury, malunion, and residual deformity; they deserve expert orthopedic management. Volkmann's ischemia of the volar compartment of the forearm is a serious risk that must be addressed (Fig. 18–7). (See also page 239.)

The types of injuries that produce torn ligaments or dislocations in adults tend to produce epiphyseal plate fractures in the child. In young children, torus and greenstick fractures are common (Fig.18–8); epiphyseal fractures are seen in older children until fusion of the bone plate occurs during adolescence. The junction of the physis and metaphysis is the most structurally weak area. The separation between calcified and uncalcified layers of the plate (the weakest part) is usually responsible for growth-plate injuries. Every fracture that involves the epiphyseal growth plate is of great importance; a poor repair can result in retarded bone growth and asymmetry of limbs. Injury to the epiphyseal plate is a major complication of pediatric gunshot wounds (GSWs), and long-term follow-up care is required to ensure that this problem has not been overlooked.[11]

Epiphyseal Injuries. The Salter–Harris classification is used to describe various types of epiphyseal injuries (Fig. 18–9). Type I is caused by a shearing or avulsion force that separates the epiphysis from the metaphysis; injury may not be visible on x-ray but may be identified by the presence of tenderness over the growth plate rather than the ligaments. Type II involves a separation of the epiphysis from the metaphysis, accompanied by an avulsion of a portion of the metaphysis; it is the most common type. Type III epiphyseal injuries are intra-articular and are most often at the lateral condyle of the distal humerus; splitting forces cause the fracture to extend through the growth plate into the metaphysis. Type III fractures have a variable prognosis; angular deformities may easily develop. Type IV injuries are intra-articular and extend from the joint surface through the epiphysis and across the epiphyseal plate and include a portion of the metaphysis. Type V injuries are caused by an axial compression that results in a crushing of the epiphyseal plate. Although they are rare (usually of the knee or ankle), they carry a high probability of complications despite expert treatment.

Stabilization for Transportation

When the pediatric trauma patient cannot be cared for adequately in the facility to which he or she was initially brought and requires transport for further treatment, the trauma team should ensure that the airway is secure, that oxygen is being delivered with humidity, and that cervical spine stabilization has been achieved if indicated. A NG tube should be in place to prevent gastric dilation and a pneumatic antishock garment (PSAG) should be in place, even if it need not be inflated upon dispatch. The immediate readiness of a PSAG may save a life if sudden cardiovascular collapse occurs during transportation. For security, two stable intravenous lines must be in place and functioning, even if only at a keep-open rate. A Foley catheter should be anchored and regularly monitored for transportation lasting more than 20 to 30 minutes. One last consideration is the child's warmth and comfort: blankets, kind and skillful attendants, and parents should accompany the traumatized child when feasible.

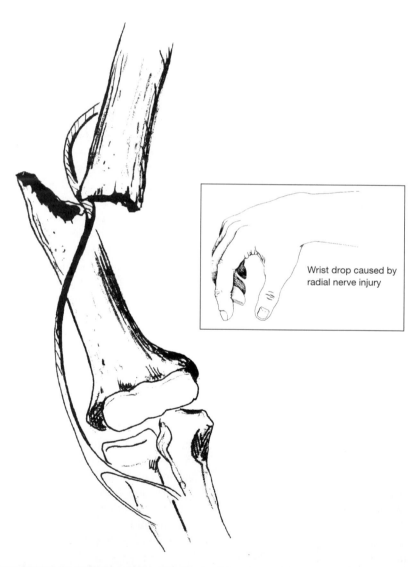

Wrist drop caused by radial nerve injury

Figure 18–7. A. Humeral shaft fracture. Radial nerve injury due to entrapment may lead to wrist drop (see inset).

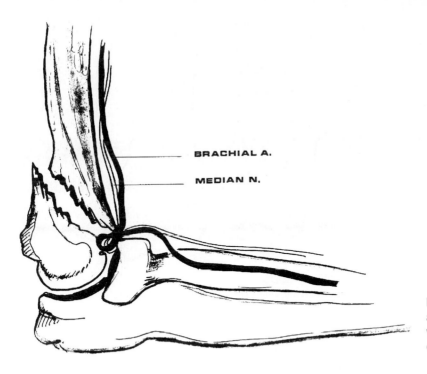

BRACHIAL A.

MEDIAN N.

Figure 18–7. B. Vascular entrapment associated with fractured humerus, which can lead to Volkman's ischemia of the forearm.

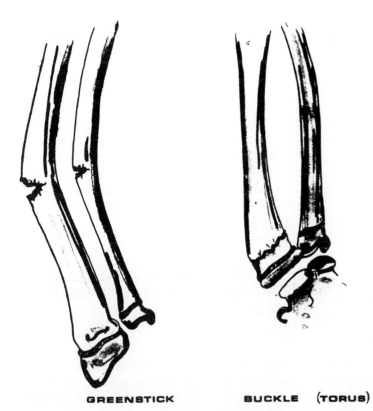

GREENSTICK   **BUCKLE   (TORUS)**   **Figure 18–8.** Common fractures in children.

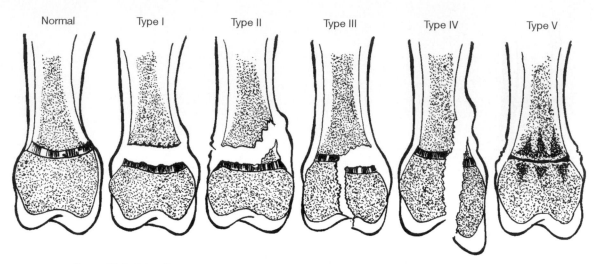

Figure 18–9. Salter–Harris classification of epiphyseal fractures.
Type I: shearing or avulsion forces separate the epiphysis from the metaphysis; may not be seen on X-ray; characterized by tenderness over growth plate rather than ligaments.
Type II: epiphysis is separated from metaphysis with avulsion of portion of metaphysis; is most common type.
Type III: splitting forces cause fracture that extends through growth plate into metaphysis; angular deformities may develop from this intra-articular injury, especially at lateral condyle of distal humerus.
Type IV: Intra-articular injury that extends from joint surface through epiphysis and across epiphyseal plate; includes portion of metaphysis.
Type V: Injury from axial compression which crushes epiphyseal plate; often involves knee or ankle; risk of serious complications despite appropriate treatment.

■ GERIATRIC TRAUMA

There is an increasing number of older citizens in the United States, and thus the incidence of trauma among this population group is steadily expanding, too. In the twenty-first century, about 20 percent of the U.S. population will be over 65 years of age. However, the EN must recognize the wide variations of the aging process and appreciate that many older patients are vital, contributing individuals who deserve to be treated aggressively after trauma, in order that they might have the greatest potential to return to their usual patterns of living.

According to findings of the National Safety Council, injuries from falls, burns, and MVAs comprise 65 percent of deaths of older patients. Deaths and injuries from automobile crashes is expected to increase as more people over 65 years of age continue to drive.[12] Accidents are in part due to the older individual's changes in functional status and the special senses (i.e., hearing, vision,

touch). Medication use and alcohol abuse may be involved in some trauma scenarios, too.

Present findings from trauma data bases do not provide sufficient information regarding how trauma care should be modified for the elderly or how they respond uniquely to injury.[12] Until more research has been translated into clinical standards of practice, ENs must rely on general concepts and principles to guide their management of geriatric trauma.

ANATOMIC AND PHYSIOLOGICAL CHANGES IN AGING: IMPLICATIONS FOR ASSESSMENT AND MANAGEMENT

There are many important changes in body structure and function that accompany aging (Table 18–8). Those that affect the cardiovascular responses, however, are perhaps the most important ones relating to trauma assessment and management.

TABLE 18–8. SUMMARY OF ANATOMIC AND PHYSIOLOGICAL CHANGES OF THE AGING PROCESS

Sensory: Deterioration of cochlear duct; atrophy of organ of Corti and hearing impairment; loss of vision due to changes in elasticity of lens and alteration in pupil size; onset of degenerative diseases such as glaucoma and cataracts; loss of acuity for taste, smell, and other sensations

Cardiovascular system: Stiffened arterial walls; loss of ventricular compliance; cardiac reserve, stroke volume, and cardiac output are diminished by 30–40%; heart rate is less responsive to catecholamines; increased peripheral resistance; impaired arterial flow due to calcification and fibrosis of arteries; decreased oxygenation of vital organs

Respiratory tract: Decreased cough strength, slowed mucus transportation; oropharyngeal dysphagia; reduced ciliary activity; decline in muscle mass; stiffened thoracic cage; loss and rearrangement of collagen; enlargement of bronchi, bronchioles, and alveoli; loss of cilia; increased number of mucous glands; thoracic muscle atrophy; increase in residual lung volume; reduced vital capacity; impaired alveolar–capillary perfusion

Integument: Hair follicles decrease in size and number, graying of the hair and accelerated growth of hair in ears, nose, and eyebrows; brittle, ridged, and slow-growing nails; fragile, dry skin due to loss of sebaceous activity and dehydration; prominent veins

Musculoskeletal systems: Loss of skeletal muscle mass, lean muscle mass, and subcutaneous fat; loss of bone density; degenerative arthritis

Gastrointestinal system: Decreased gastric juices; slowed peristalsis; decreased sense of taste and smell; loss of teeth may create problems in chewing; changes in pharyngeal and esophageal motility may lead to choking; decreased absorption of nutrients

Central nervous system: Impaired cognition due to neuronal loss, decrease of dendrites, and alteration in neurotransmitter synthesis

Urinary tract: Decreased bladder capacity and sphincter tone; prostatic hypertrophy; loss of bladder tone; decline in functioning nephrons; loss of visceral reflexes, which impairs control of voiding; urination frequency and urgency is common owing to bladder changes; incontinence may occur owing to loss of sphincter control or cognitive impairments

Immune system: Atrophy of thymus gland (responsible for maturation of T lymphocytes); labile febrile response and absence of diaphoresis, even with infection

Genitalia and breasts: Subcutaneous tissue loss leads to sagging and drooping of breasts and external genitalia; vagina shortens and loses elasticity; pH of vagina becomes more alkaline, permitting increased bacterial growth; pelvic muscles weaken; pubic hair growth declines; male sexual organs atrophy

Heart

As individuals age, the heart rate, stroke volume, and ejection fractions and cardiac output remain unchanged from those of younger adults at rest, but with exercise, several vulnerabilities appear. The elderly have limitations in rate acceleration, but they can increase stroke volume during exercise. However, the ejection fraction and cardiac output are less responsive, and typically, any increases are quite limited. There is a marked increase in early diastolic left ventricular filling and an increase in late diastolic left ventricular filling. A noticeable decline in ventricular compliance is also common. Initial measurements of BP and heart rate may be misleading because of compensatory changes or prior pathology (e.g., hypertension or the presence of a pacemaker). ECG monitoring should be promptly begun, with frequent observation to note any adverse trends. Since rhythm disturbances may be triggered by hypoxemia or cardiac trauma, these should be thoroughly considered before assuming that they are chronic for the patient. All elderly patients should have a "rule-out" for acute myocardial infarction as a trauma cofactor. Fluid resuscitation should be promptly initiated to correct volume deficits. Although the patient should be closely observed for signs and symptoms of fluid overload, withholding of fluid is equally perilous in the presence of low perfusion due to hypovolemia. Prompt placement of a Swan–Ganz catheter to monitor responses to fluid therapy, to obtain cardiac output measurements, and to plot ventricular function curves is indicated. Inotropic support may be required for patients whose bodies fail to adequately respond to fluid replacement.[12]

Lungs

Pulmonary changes reflect an overall deterioration as the individual ages, and the mechanisms for cough and mucociliary clearance become less efficient. There is also a significant reduction (50 percent) in ventilatory responsiveness to hypoxia and in responsiveness to CO_2, (40 percent). Changes in position (e.g., moving from supine to upright) are accompanied by a 6 to 10-mm Hg reduction in arterial partial pressure of oxygen (PAO_2); however, arterial pH or PCO_2 are not seemingly affected. ABGs should be obtained early and frequently to note any deleterious trends.

Intubation is indicated with an Injury Severity Score (ISS) of more than 25 or if there is a flail chest or preexisting pulmonary disease, because the elderly patient typically has a limited pulmonary reserve. Local anesthesia for control of pain associated with blunt chest trauma seems to increase success with mechanical ventilation.[12] Turning, humidification, and strict asepsis in airway management should be maintained, because the elderly have limited ability to handle secretions. Even in the ED, coughing should be encouraged while the patient is in an upright position.

Pulmonary infection is responsible for 80 percent of deaths in the aged, so prolonged mechanical ventilation carries a poor prognosis. Mechanical support should be initiated early, but discontinued as promptly as feasible, based on the patient's respiratory status.

Kidneys

There is a steady decline in creatinine clearance that accompanies the aging process, and there is an appreciable loss of functional renal mass. The renal weight decreases by about 30 percent and the renal blood flow is reduced by 50 percent between young adulthood and the eighth decade of life. The change in renal blood flow occurs gradually, about 10 percent per decade.[5] A urinary catheter should be inserted to monitor output, even though it may pose an additional risk of infection. Owing to changes in renal efficiency, the output may remain high, even when there is hypovolemia, so urine output may not be a dependable index of fluid deficits or shock.

Neurological and Musculoskeletal Systems

The older patient is likely to have some vision, hearing, and other sensory losses, and often manifests some related changes in mental status or responsiveness. Since older individuals may not respond well given multiple stressors, cognitive abilities may be poor immediately upon arrival at the ED. Later assessments may yield more reliable data. Motor movement, strength, and mobility may also be impaired. Osteoarthritis and other chronic conditions may significantly affect ROMs. Ecchymosis should be noted and evaluated in terms of concurrent medications (e.g., anticoagulants) and the usual capillary fragility that accompanies aging.

INFECTIONS AND USE OF ANTIBIOTICS IN THE AGING

Infections pose a real hazard to the older patient because the elderly have both a higher morbidity and mortality with any infection. Furthermore, there are pharmacological problems in setting drug dosages, owing to the physiological changes of aging. Adverse reactions, side effects, and renal failure are not atypically associated with the use of antibiotics with the geriatric patient. ENs must appreciate that older patients do not necessarily have fever, diaphoresis, and other symptoms normally linked to the onset of infection. Older patients may present with anorexia, fatigue, weakness, or changes in functional or mental capacity; delirium is not uncommonly associated. The basal body temperature of older adults is 1 to 2 degrees lower than younger adults, and thus they may have a severe infection without a characteristic elevation of 2.4 degrees above the "normal" 98.6°F reading. After trauma, infection can pose a life-threatening situation for the elderly because its onset may go unnoticed.

Sepsis, kidney infections, pneumonia, endocarditis, meningitis, or shingles may complicate the course of trauma recovery from the primary injuries.

Bioavailability of antibiotics may be affected by marginal hepatic function; drug extraction is decreased and side effects may occur, even with a reduced dosage. The absorption of oral drugs may be influenced by alterations in intestinal pH, decreased gastric emptying time, and altered pH of the gastric or small bowel lumens. The times for peak plasma concentrations are also changed, so "peak and trough" monitoring may reflect longer response times. The decrease in the total body water content, increase in total body fat, and decrease in lean body mass that occur in old age also affect drug distribution of medications that are water-soluble. Half-life is extended for lipid-soluble agents owing to the wider distribution in body fat. Plasma protein binding is affected by decreased serum albumin and decreased plasma protein binding; changes occur in the ratio of free to bound drug, and at least a 30 percent reduction in plasma clearance should be anticipated. Metabolism and excretion of drugs may also be impaired. Toxicities from antibiotics and other drugs are likely to occur earlier in the course of therapy, and at lower doses. Since hepatic efficiency is affected by decreases in liver size, blood flow, and microsomal enzymatic oxidation in cells, the processes involved in extracting drugs from circulation and in converting lipid-soluble drugs to water-soluble metabolites are impaired. Drug effects are extended, and overdoses and toxicities are not uncommon, even within usual dosing parameters. Renal excretion of drugs may be decreased by almost 50 percent in older patients. Since pharmacological therapy is a major adjunct in treating trauma victims, ENs must be aware of the many vulnerabilities of the aged individual when administering and monitoring drugs.

HUMAN SUPPORT AND PAIN CONTROL

ENs should communicate with the patient by voice, touch, and eye contact throughout the stay in the EDs. Hypothermic stress may be considerable for the older patient, who is likely to have impaired thermal regulation and peripheral vascular compromises. Thermal blankets, warmed fluids, and heated humidification are in order to prevent unnecessary heat loss.

Pain control is imperative for several reasons, but ensuring maximum respiratory effort without mechanical ventilation ranks at the top of the list. If the patient's injuries mandate ventilator support, both sedation and analgesia should be considered. These types of medications should not be withheld merely to avert concerns of hypotension, respiratory depression, or changes in responsiveness.

Delirium in the hospitalized elderly can be due to many causes, but poorly controlled pain is among the chief precursors.[13]

ELDER ABUSE

It is estimated that 1 to 2 million of our older citizens are abused or neglected in domestic settings. Self-neglect accounts for a substantial number of these cases, perhaps about 40 percent.[14] Forms of abuse or neglect include physical abuse, psychological abuse (e.g., infliction of mental anguish by threat, intimidation, humiliation), financial exploitation (e.g., unauthorized use of elderly person's resources), caregiver neglect, and self-neglect. Although many of these abusive acts occur in nursing homes and other institutions, family members who care for older individuals may be responsible for a significant number of such incidents. The reports from the U.S. House of Representatives Select Committee on Aging reveals that two-thirds of elder abuse perpetrators are family members, most often an adult child or spouse.[14] Although the criminal justice system has provisions for preventing abuse and protecting victims, it is perceived that older patients are reluctant to report abuse since they are dependent on others for shelter and care. Emergency nurses and physicians are often among the first to detect signs and symptoms of elder abuse.

Abusing Family Members or Caregivers

Stress and lack of knowledge often contribute to caregiver stress. As older patients become more dependent, toileting, transfers, ambulation, eating, elimination and other activities of daily living become real chores, especially when the caregiver has limited skills in such matters. Other types of abusers are those who enjoy power over others, and who use the vulnerability of the elderly for their selfish pleasure. Alcohol and drug abusers and those with mental health problems may be unable to tolerate frustration; they may engage in harmful behaviors when emotionally unstable or out-of-control as a result of substance abuse. It is not uncommon for these individuals to excuse their behaviors based on their personal social problems or circumstances, e.g. unemployment, financial stressors, or an unhappy marriage.

Risk Factors and Indications of Abuse and Neglect

Older individuals who are vulnerable to abuse include those who are physically and mentally impaired and those who exhibit behavioral problems such as confusion, wandering, and inappropriate social skills (e.g. removing dentures during a family meal or failing to flush the toilet after use). Small problems tend to accumulate and caregivers who do not cope well with stressors may begin to "strike back." Although burns, welts, bruises, cuts, and fractures are obvious signs of injury, they do not necessarily indicate abuse; the older individuals frequently have accidents that could result in such trauma. Care must be taken to note injuries that are inconsistent with the reported cause, a prolonged interval between the accident and the visit to the emergency department, and evidence of sexual assault, such as bruises on thighs, genitalia, or breasts. Special attention should be given to evaluation of mental status, noting any obtundation from overdosing of sedatives or other drugs. Then assessing compliance with therapy for any chronic condition, ensure that the patient has a current prescription and that medications are being administered regularly as prescribed. The failure to obtain prescriptions or to give needed medications constitutes neglect and may point to the need for further study of the domestic situation.

Physical Neglect

Physical neglect may be revealed by poor hygiene, dehydration and malnutrition, dirty or inadequate clothing, decubiti or non-treated wounds, fecal impaction, broken glasses or dentures, and overgrown nails. Failure to respond to serious illness by prompt medical intervention is also an indicator of neglect. When you feel concern about the adequacy of the domestic environment ensure that follow-up is accomplished by a home care nursing referral or social service visit to permit a thorough evaluation of the living conditions within a home or other facility. Emergency personnel should ensure that the patient's weight is recorded and that comparisons are made with earlier data. Significant weight loss or excessive fluid retention are clues that nutrition may be inadequate or that medications may not be administered as needed. Note also whether the elder patients seem intimidated by the caregivers, reluctant to speak on their own behalf, obviously withdrawn, or severely depressed.

Tips on Interviewing

Most victims of abuse are afraid and ashamed. Nurses must maintain eye contact when interviewing these individuals and convey empathic concern. If evidence of abuse is noted or if the patient reports being abused, professional staff must avoid showing anger, disbelief, outrage or horror, although these are legitimate reactions. Remember that caring and concern are more appropriate than sympathy. Disclosure of abuse may take more time than is readily available to emergency personnel since a trusting relationship takes time to establish. Emergency nurses must appreciate that even "poor care" within a family home may be more desirable to an older individual than placement into a nursing home.

Ensure that you do not "jump to conclusions." Remember that abuse and neglect can occur in any family or economic situation, and that it is a product of unique individual cultures, lifestyles, and coping strategies. Use open and frank lines of questioning, such as:

"I note that you have a lot of mosquito bites. Do you have screens on the windows in your room?"

"I notice that you are not wearing any underwear or socks. Do you need help to dress yourself?"

"Your diabetes is severely 'out of control' today. Has someone been home to help you with your insulin and to prepare your meals?"

"You seem very frightened by your daughter-in-law. Has she ever hurt you or threatened to hurt you?"

"There seems to be a lot of tension in your home. Does anyone you live with have problems with drugs or alcohol?"

"I notice you have bruises on both inner thighs. Has anyone forced you to do something that you did not want to do?"

"Do you ever do things that cause family members to yell at you?"

"Do you ever feel that you need help and family members have refused to help you?"

Careful listening to the patient is certain to provide valuable clues to potential abuse that warrants further investigation. When exploring living conditions at home, attempt to determine whether the patient has thought about alternate living arrangements. "If you weren't living with your son, where else could you go that you might be more comfortable?" Fear of institutional placement ranks among the most common reasons for failing to report abuse. Be certain to discuss the various alternatives for care and protection and arrange for social service follow-up if the situation merits immediate attention. Abused or neglected elderly patients may require a short-term admission stay to allow you to pursue suspected abuse and neglect and to arrange for safer living conditions.

Legal Aspects

All states require reporting of suspected elder abuse and neglect and have adult protective programs for in-home supportive services and legal assistance. Unfortunately, however, few states have sufficient resources to investigate and follow problem homes and institutions. Many cases are unrecognized; even more sadly, nurses and physicians feel overwhelmed or powerless in detecting and reporting the many potentially adverse living conditions that impact the health and welfare of the elderly. The criminal justice system does enable victims to press criminal charges against abusers, and domestic violence provisions do permit court protection orders compelling the abusers to leave the home. Remember, however, that the elderly may prefer the "known" to the "unknown" living space, even when the known space entails the negatives of physical and psychological abuse or out-right neglect.

■ NURSING DIAGNOSES

Appropriate nursing diagnoses for the severely traumatized child or elderly patient would include:

- Ineffective breathing pattern related to altered ventilatory mechanics
- Ineffective airway clearance related to mechanical obstruction
- Risk of injury related to altered state of consciousness and neurological defects
- Alteration in cardiac output due to hemorrhagic shock, tension pneumothorax, or cardiac injury

- Fluid volume deficit—actual or potential—related to blood loss
- Risk of infection due to interruption in integrity of skin barrier
- Pain related to tissue, nerve, or vessel disruption from penetrating, blunt, or extremity trauma
- Alteration in tissue perfusion related to hypovolemia impaired blood supply or vascular compromise from fractures

■ REFERENCES

1. Barber JS. *Trauma Update: Pediatric Trauma.* Lewisville, Tex: Barbara Clark Mims Associates; 1994.
2. Treloar DJ, Nypaver M. Neutral cervical spine positioning. In: *Proceedings of the Fourth National Conference of Pediatric Trauma.* Boston, Ma: Kiwanis Pediatric Trauma Institute; 1992:127.
3. Presson RG. Techniques for rapid infusion. In: *Proceedings of the Fourth National Conference of Pediatric Trauma.* Boston, Ma: Kiwanis Pediatric Trauma Institute; 1992:21–25.
4. Luerssen TG. Head injuries in children. In: *Proceedings of the Fourth National Conference of Pediatric Trauma.* Boston, Ma: Kiwanis Pediatric Trauma Institute; 1992:27–33.
5. Apostol NC, Norman D. Care of the elderly patient. In: Bongard FS, Sue DY eds. *Current Critical Care Diagnosis and Treatment.* E. Norwalk, Conn: Appleton & Lange; 1994:360.
6. Cooper A, Barlow B, DiScala C, String D. Mortality and thoracoabdominal injury: the pediatric perspective. In: *Proceedings of the Fourth National Conference of Pediatric Trauma.* Boston, Ma: Kiwanis Pediatric Trauma Institute; 1992:97.
7. Stephanopoulos DE, Mainwaring R, Peterson B. Pediatric cardiac contusions: an eight-year retrospective review. In: *Proceedings of the Fourth National Conference of Pediatric Trauma.* Boston, Ma: Kiwanis Pediatric Trauma Institute; 1992:95.
8. Lebet Ruth M. Abdominal and genitourinary trauma in children. *Crit Care Nurs Clin North Am.* 1991;3:433–444.
9. Akgur FM, Arzu K, Kovanlikaya I, Aktug T. Initial evaluation of children sustaining blunt abdominal trauma: ultrasonography vs. diagnostic peritoneal lavage. In: *Proceedings of the Fourth National Conference of Pediatric Trauma.* Boston, Ma: Kiwanis Pediatric Trauma Institute: 1992: 80.

10. Hakim LS, Velcek F, Macchia RJ, Glassberg KI. Hematuria as an indicator of abdominal injury after blunt trauma in children. In: *Proceedings of the Fourth National Conference of Pediatric Trauma.* Boston, Ma: Kiwanis Pediatric Trauma Institute; 1992:122.

11. Villarreal D, Arnold TC. Pediatric extremity gunshot wounds. In: *Proceedings of the Fourth National Conference of Pediatric Trauma.* Boston, Ma: Kiwanis Pediatric Trauma Institute; 1992:99.

12. Cardona VD, Hurn PD, Bastnagel Mason PJ, et al. *Trauma Nursing: From Resuscitation Through Rehabilitation.* 2nd ed. Philadelphia, Pa: WB Saunders; 1994.

13. Crippen DW. Brain failure in critical care medicine. *Crit Care Nurs Q.* 1994;16:80–95.

14. American Association of Retired Persons. *Fact Sheet on Elder Abuse and Neglect:* 1993.

■ BIBLIOGRAPHY

Ayres SM, Grenvik A, Holbrook PR, Shoemaker WC. *Textbook of Critical Care.* 3rd ed. Philadelphia, Pa: WB Saunders; 1995.

Campbell LS, Campbell JD. Musculoskeletal trauma in children. *Crit Care Clin North Am.* 1991;3:445–456.

Cardona VD, Hurn PD, Bastnagel Mason PJ, et al. *Trauma Nursing: From Resuscitation Through Rehabilitation.* 2nd ed. Philadelphia, Pa: WB Saunders; 1994.

Clochesy JM, Breu C, Cardin S, et al. *Critical Care Nursing.* Philadelphia, Pa: WB Saunders; 1993.

Dandrinos-Smith S. The epidemiology of pediatric trauma, *Crit Care Clin North Am.* 1992;3:387–390.

Day S, McCloskey K, Orr R, et al. Pediatric interhospital critical care transport: consensus of a national leadership conference. *Pediatrics.* 1991;88:696–704.

Greenberg EM. Violence and the older adult: The role of the acute care practitioner. *Crit Care Nurs Q.* 1996; 19:76–84.

Kelley SJ, *Pediatric Emergency Nursing.* E. Norwalk, Conn: Appleton & Lange; 1988.

Lebet RM, Abdominal and genitourinary trauma in children. *Crit Care Clin North Am.* 1991;3:433–444.

Levine RL, Fromm RE Jr. *Critical Care Monitoring from Pre-Hospital to the ICU.* St. Louis, Mo: Mosby-Year Book; 1995.

Maull KI, Rodriguez A, Wiles CE. *Complications in Trauma and Critical Care.* Philadelphia, Pa: WB Saunders; 1996.

Moloney-Harmon PA. Initial assessment and stabilization of the critically injured child. *Crit Care Clin North Am.* 1991;3:399–410.

O'Brien R. Starting intravenous lines in children. *J Emerg Nurs.* 1991;17:225–230.

Phippen ML, Wells MP. *Perioperative Nursing Practice.* Philadelphia, Pa: WB Saunders; 1994.

Physicians' Desk Reference. 50th ed. Montvale, NJ; Medical Economics; 1996.

Ruppert SD, Kernicki JG, Dolan JT. *Dolan's Critical Care Nursing,* 2nd ed. Philadelphia, Pa: FA Davis; 1996.

Smith MF. Renal trauma, adult and pediatric considerations. *Crit Care Clin North Am.* 1990;2:67–77.

Stamatos CA, Sorensen PA, Tefler KM. Meeting the challenge of the older trauma patient. *AJN.* May 1996;96:40–48.

Thompson SW. *Emergency Care of Children.* Boston, Ma: Jones and Bartlett; 1990.

Tecklenburg FW. Minor head trauma in the pediatric patient. *Pediat Emerg Care.* 1991;7:40–47.

Weist PW, Roth PB. *Fundamentals of Emergency Radiology.* Philadelphia, Pa: WB Saunders; 1996.

Wilkins RL, Dexter JR. *Respiratory Disease: Principles of Patient Care.* Philadelphia, Pa: FA Davis; 1993.

Winn DG, Agran PF, Castillo DN. Pedestrian injuries to children younger than 5 years of age. *Pediatrics* 1991;88:696–704.

■ REVIEW: SPECIAL CONSIDERATIONS IN TRAUMA

1. Describe recommended nursing approaches unique to the following:
   a. Neonates
   b. Toddlers
   c. School-age children
   d. Adolescents

2. Identify the five childhood fears that must be taken into consideration when caring for the ill or injured child.

3. Explain assessment techniques for children and interpretation of pediatric vital signs (VS).

4. Describe the modifications that are imperative to accurately record and evaluate the pediatric electrocardiogram (ECG).

5. List unique equipment required for the resuscitation of the pediatric trauma patient.

6. Describe the special approaches to assessment and management of the infant's and child's airway and circulation after trauma.

7. Outline the procedure for intraosseous infusions.

8. Identify the clinical indicators that would suggest a child is in shock.

9. Outline the protocols for pediatric fluid resuscitation in hypovolemic shock.

10. List anatomic and physiological variables that affect the assessment and management of pediatric trauma.

11. List the modifications for assessment and management of the following pediatric conditions:
    a. Head and spinal cord injuries
    b. Chest and abdominal injuries
    c. Genitourinary (GU) trauma
    d. Skeletal fractures

12. Describe the implications and importance of the Salter–Harris classification when assessing and managing pediatric epiphyseal injuries.

13. Describe the anatomic and physiological changes of aging and relate them to assessment and management of trauma.

14. Explain the special precautions in assessment of geriatric infections and the use of antibiotics.

15. List four clues that suggest elder abuse.

Medical Complications of Trauma 19

There are many complications that can accompany major trauma. Since they are major reasons why patients suffer unnecessary morbidity or mortality, it is vital that all emergency nurses (ENs) fully appreciate the sequelae of major trauma and understand how to detect and manage these actual or potential problems.

■ RHABDOMYOLYSIS

Rhabdomyolysis results from a large amount of muscle necrosis occurring because of delivery of intracellular contents into the extracellular space. Crush injuries and ischemia from any cause can precipitate myoglobin-induced acute renal failure. Rhabdomyolysis also results from status epilepticus, delirium tremens, air embolism, strenuous exercise (e.g., running a marathon), drug overdose, and carbon monoxide poisoning. Certain burns, especially those associated with electrical injury, also tend to favor the development of rhabdomyolysis. The significant electrolyte imbalances (i.e., hypomagnesemia, hypokalemia, and hypophosphatemia) associated with alcoholism and acute intoxication have also been implicated in the etiology of this condition. When there is volume depletion or hypotension associated with any underlying condition, the risks for myoglobin-induced renal failure are high. There are multiple other causes for rhabdomyolysis and hemolysis, noted in Table 19–1.

The acute state of rhabdomyolysis is marked with hyperkalemia, hyperuricemia, hyperphosphatemia, and hypocalcemia. The creatinine level is typically elevated out of proportion to the blood urea nitrogen (BUN) concentration. The urine appears darkly pigmented (i.e., reddish brown) and contains coarsely granular casts and tubular cell casts.[1] When urine dipstick test results are positive for heme in the absence of red blood cells (RBCs), this is considered a hallmark for diagnosis. A 3 + or 4 + heme reaction with minimal hematuria (3 to 5 RBC/hpf) is equally suggestive of myoglobin-induced renal failure. An elevated creatine kinase (CK), as high as 200,000 U/L,[2] and the release into circulation of other muscle enzymes (i.e., aspartate aminotransferase [AST] lactate dehydrogenase [LDH] and aldolase [specific for muscle damage]) assist in confirming the diagnosis.[3] Rhabdomyolysis can lead to compartment syndrome, so the EN should watch for pain, swelling, and tenderness over involved muscle masses. The role of imaging studies, such as computed tomography (CT), ultrasound, or intravenous pyelography (IVP), is limited to finding associated renal injury.

The emergency team must ensure that any high-risk patient promptly receives fluids and other therapies (mannitol and furosemide) to maintain high renal output (at least 200 to 300 mL/h). This, along with alkalinization of the urine with fluid volume, is thought to be an appropriate course of action, even though research to support these therapies is scant. The multiple electrolyte imbalances must also be managed. Early use of dialysis may be required for the treatment of hyperkalemia. If oliguric renal failure is evident, mannitol and sodium bicarbonate, used for alkalinization, may be counterproductive, resulting in pulmonary edema.[3] In addition to restoring fluid volume and initiating diuresis, the EN must monitor cardiopulmonary functions because both the underlying condition and the therapies can contribute to arrhythmias and heart and pulmonary failure.

TABLE 19–1. CAUSES OF PIGMENT NEPHROPATHY: HEMOLYSIS AND RHABDOMYOLYSIS

Rhabdomyolysis
   Physical trauma: crush injury, heat stress, electrocution, exercise, hypothermia, malignant hyperthermia
   Anoxic injury: arterial occlusion, seizures, tetanus, compartment syndrome
   Metabolic: hypokalemia, hypophosphatemia, diabetic ketoacidosis, myxedema, carnitine deficiency, hereditary muscle enzyme deficiency
   Infections: influenza-like viral infections, gas gangrene, pyomyositis
   Inflammation: polymyositis, dermatomyositis
   Poisons and toxins: ethanol, amphetamine, cocaine, snake and spider venom
Hemolysis
   Transfusion reactions
   Drug toxicities: quinine sulfate, hydralazine
   Poisons and toxins: benzene, aniline, fava beans, snake and spider venom
   Mechanical trauma: valvular prothesis, extracorporeal circulation, march hemoglobinuria
   Enzyme deficiencies: glucose-6-phosphate dehydrogenase deficiency
   Osmotic stress: intoxication with hypotonic fluids: drowning, transuretheral prostatectomy, incorrect priming of extracorporeal circulation
   Infections: malaria
   Autoimmune: drugs, systemic lupus erythematosus

(From Bongard and Sue.[3])

■ FAT EMBOLUS

Fat embolism syndrome may be due to mobilization of fat globules in association with injury, or it may result from alterations in the metabolism of fat. Some clinicians believe that changes in lipid mobilization, which is mediated by trauma-related stress and the subsequent release of catecholamines, may contribute to the condition. The clotting cascade is thought to be activated by fat and tissue thromboplastin that is released into circulation, and this may account for some clinical findings.

Fat embolism appears in about 2 percent of patients with a long-bone fracture and in up to 10 percent of those with the multiple fractures that accompany major pelvic injuries.[4] When hypovolemia has been prolonged, the condition seems more likely to develop. The syndrome of fat embolization primarily involves the lodging of emboli in the pulmonary vessels, but emboli may also affect the brain, kidneys, and other organs.

The presence of fat emboli is marked by hypoxemia, pulmonary infiltrates, and other findings noted shortly after injury, usually within 24 to 72 hours. These phenomena are thought to occur in response to fat's entering the pulmonary capillaries via the great veins. Occasionally, the presentation will be dramatic, with a sudden onset of cyanosis, disorientation, delirium, and hypoxia. In addition to pulmonary embarrassment, the patient may have changes in mental status and level of consciousness (LOC). Petechiae may be evident in the conjunctivas and are also frequently noted on the chest wall. These diverse indicators of fat embolization reflect the mobilization of fat and the associated coagulopathy that accompany major bone injury.

The role of emergency personnel is primarily to prevent fat embolism by ensuring prompt stabilization of fractures. Handling and moving the patient who has fractures should be minimized because such care will limit extravasation of blood and limit release of fatty substances from the soft tissue or bone into the bloodstream. Fluid resuscitation should be aggressive in major orthopedic trauma, and in the event that fat embolism syndrome is already apparent, ventilatory support is vital.

■ DISSEMINATED INTRAVASCULAR COAGULATION

Disseminated intravascular coagulation (DIC) is a condition triggered by excess thrombin in system circulation. Underlying conditions include sepsis, malignancy, leukemia, and major trauma. First, the disease or injury permits the thrombogenic process to be generalized throughout the circulatory networks, and this is soon to be followed by a systemic thrombolysis in an effort to effect clot dissolution. Eventually, there is a depletion or consumption of clotting factors; hence, this condition is sometimes referred to as consumptive coagulopathy.

ENs should be able to identify patients at risk for this condition. These include obstetric crises, sepsis, cancer, anaphylaxis, and overdose of anticoagulants. Any trauma or vascular injury that produces shock can also result in DIC.

In the emergency department (ED), the patient will experience a drop in blood pressure (BP), followed by the appearance of petechiae, ecchymosis, and bleeding from multiple body sites. Platelets, fibrinogen, and prothrombin (PT) levels will be decreased, and the partial thromboplastin time (PTT) will be markedly increased. In anticipation of rapidly developing shock, two infusion sites should be established for the administration of clotting factors, heparin (to inhibit formation of new clots *only*, by inactivation of thrombin), and vitamin K. Heparin therapy must precede the administration of blood products to prevent consumption of components in the DIC process. Platelets, fresh-frozen plasma, cryoprecipitate, and packed cells may be employed. The patient should be promptly transferred to an intensive care setting for advanced therapy and continuous monitoring.

■ MULTISYSTEM ORGAN FAILURE

After major trauma, there is a hypermetabolic process that can become pathological, leading to organ failure throughout the body. This syndrome of multisystem organ failure (MSOF) is thought to be in response to the dramatic increases in metabolic rates after trauma. The prolonged presence of necrotic tissue, unrepaired fractures, and inadequately debrided wounds is thought to be a contributory factor. Since MSOF is responsible for about 90 percent of surgical deaths in critical care units, the EN must understand precursors to this devastating complication.

The high demand for glucose in trauma states is usually met by a rapid conversion of glycogen, but this mechanism is short-lived. With fat needing to be mobilized for energy, there is an excess of free fatty acids, which alters the metabolism of trace elements, vitamins, and minerals, quickly resulting in serious deficiencies. Sodium and water retention ensue, there is lymphopenia, and the levels of norepinephrine and ADH (antidiuretic hormone) rise sharply. Eventually, protein is used to meet the needs for energy as well as to support wound healing and immunologic activities, leading to a negative nitrogen balance. This hypermetabolic phase peaks over 3 to 4 days and is charac-

terized by variations in oxygen consumption and a wide range of metabolic abberations. In the presence of endotoxins and shock, these can be devastating. There is a transition period leading to MSOF in which there is an increased tissue oxygen demand, an onset of pulmonary failure, and finally alteration of tissue oxygen extraction, which leads to organ failure. Although ENs are not likely to witness these several phases of the overall hypermetabolic response to trauma, they can ensure that the factors that induce them are kept at a minimum.

Prompt oxygen supplementation and ventilatory support are imperative any time a patient is seriously injured, to prevent unnecessary accumulation of an oxygen debt. Fluid resuscitation should be aggressive. Wounds must be scrupulously cleansed and carefully debrided, and care should be taken to limit any sources of inflammation or infection. Surgery should be accomplished as soon as possible to remove sources of sepsis, such as open or unstabilized fractures, hematoma collections, or necrotic tissue. Prompt administration of antibiotics is usually required, with initial doses being delivered during the first minutes after arrival at the ED. The role of drugs (ibuprofen, oxygen-derived free radical scavengers, calcium channel blockers, opioid antagonists, and γ-interferon) is uncertain, but the EN may administer one or more agents from these groups in order to prevent or retard the progression of MSOF.

■ THERMAL STRESS

The most common thermal stress problem after trauma is cold stress. In addition to ambient cold-weather conditions, air-conditioning in the ED may contribute to heat loss. When the injured patient arrives, all clothes are typically removed promptly to facilitate basic assessments and accommodate certain resuscitative interventions such as intravenous line placements or insertions of tubes. Although children and older individuals may be most affected by these thermal stressors, healthy adults are also placed at risk. Since hypothermia is associated with increased mortality, it should be prevented when possible and promptly managed if it is manifested. Hypothermia produces clotting abnormalities equivalent to any other serious clotting factor deficiencies. Furthermore, transfusion requirements are greater for hypothermic patients who have tissue edema due to capillary leak syndrome. Since adenosine triphosphate (ATP) synthesis is reduced, myocardial depression occurs, too.

In hypothermia, the patient has decreases in heart rate, myocardial contractility, oxygen delivery, hepatic function, and adrenal output. Concurrently, there is an impairment in the oxygen–hemoglobin dissociation curve and considerable fluid loss due to dysfunctions of tubular resorption. Conventional rewarming causes fluid shifts and changes in vascular tone, reduces BP and venous return, and compromises cardiac output, owing to vasodilation of the periphery. As more blood moves to the skin and other superficial body zones, there is a concurrent rise in the metabolic demands in this peripheral tissue, shunting blood away from the core, where it is obviously needed most. Merely rewarming a very cold patient by application of external heat sources and by preventing further heat loss by use of blankets and other strategies is not enough because the cold, acidotic peripheral blood will be shunted to the core, further stressing organ systems. Core rewarming, which improves circulation to the vital organs, is preferred because it will stimulate organs to generate heat as their metabolic condition improves. This, of course, discourages coagulopathy and counteracts myocardial depression. There are several methods used to accomplish core rewarming, including continuous arteriovenous rewarming, dialysis, use of body compartment lavages with warmed fluids, and circulatory bypass (see Chapter 11). The EN should take all measures that can prevent heat loss during the resuscitation period and be prepared to assist in various forms of rewarming.

■ COMPARTMENT SYNDROME

Acute compartment syndrome (ACS) is precipitated from increased pressure within a confined anatomic space. There are 46 places in the body where muscle, nerve, and blood vessels are located within inelastic spaces composed of skin, epimysium (fibrous sheath around muscle), fascia, and bone. Although 8 are located in the trunk region, the remaining 38 are located in extremities, and these are likely sites for ACS. The dorsal and volar aspects of the forearm and the four compartments of the lower leg are most commonly involved in ACS, but thighs and buttocks may also be involved.

Pressure builds when bleeding and edema continues within the confined space or if external pressures impinge on the area from devices such as pneumatic antishock garments (PSAGs), air splints, casts, or dressings, thus decreasing the compartment's size. ACS can also be seen without orthopedic injury; forced marches or other strenuous exercise have been associated with its pathophysiology. The EN should understand that a fascial defect is not essential for its development.

Excessive pressure within a compartment first affects the venous ends of the capillary beds, but eventually arterioles are compressed. If shock coexists, less pressure is required to compromise blood flow within the compartment.

ACS is suspected in patients who have pain out of proportion to the injury, especially when accompanied by a compartment noted to be quite tense upon palpation. Passive stretching of the involved muscles evokes severe pain. Paresthesia, anesthesia, paresis, or paralysis may be noted. Pulses, however, are intact, thus distinguishing this problem from acute arterial occlusion. The two-point discrimination test can be most helpful in detecting ACS because small nerve fibers are highly susceptible to any ischemia. If the patient can cooperate with serial assessments, this subjective data can be considered, along with other information, in developing a clinical management plan for the problem. The EN should bear in mind that in patients who are unconscious, intoxicated, or otherwise unable to provide feedback, ACS may be missed, especially if they have other injuries which are immediately life-threatening.

Compartment pressure may be measured. Normally it is less than 5 to 10 mm Hg. Usually, surgical decompression is done if it rises to 30 to 40 mm Hg.[3] The pressure can be assessed using a needle manometer, which is hooked via a T-connector to a saline-filled syringe with an 18-gauge needle inserted into the suspect compartment. Pressure is applied to the syringe until the saline overcomes the inherent pressure and flows into the compartment. The pressure at which this occurs is the tissue pressure. Doppler ultrasound can also be used to detect changes in blood flow. Several other more sophisticated techniques for measuring compartment pressure may be used in the intensive care setting, where more technical monitoring capabilities exist.

Fasciotomy is the usual treatment for ACS. It is desirable to accomplish this in the operating room (OR), but under extreme circumstances, it can be done in the ED under local anesthesia. Hypertonic mannitol may be used to reduce associated swelling and to act as a scavenger of oxygen-free radicals. It may also be beneficial to decrease the incidence of reperfusion injury, which can occur with ACS.[5]

■ INFECTIONS

There are multiple infection opportunities for the trauma patient, and these can be minimized by ENs if they use excellent technique. ED patients are especially vulnerable early after injury because of the multiple stressors that affect several body systems. The immune system, of course, is of utmost importance to consider.

Ordinarily, the healthy host has considerable protection against the invasion of microorganisms. The intact skin, normal flora, and a healthy immune system all serve as modes of protection. However, after trauma, there are multiple invasions of the barriers, induced not only by injury wounds, but also by tubes, lines, and incisions, which are a necessary part of patient care.

Procedures in the prehospital environs and ED may be accomplished hastily as life "hangs in the balance," and thus there are more than a few opportunities for breaches in aseptic technique, which may be apparent through the development of a local or systemic infection process.

Factors that have been demonstrated to impair the immune system are shock, thermal stressors, pain, advanced age, medications that alter lymphocyte function (e.g., steroids, dopamine), and poor nutrition.[6] Surgery and the use of anesthesia also induce a state of transient immune depression characterized by lymphopenia and reduced phagocytosis.[7] Some of these vulnerabilities cannot be changed by caregivers. However, ENs have a grave responsibility to minimize risks to patients by ensuring that their carelessness does not add to patient morbidity.

ENs should regularly assess their environment to detect factors that could serve as sources of infection. Note items of equipment that may not be disinfected between patients (e.g., infusion pumps, electrocardiogram [ECG] leads, suction cannister brackets, x-ray cassettes, stethoscopes, BP cuffs, and stretcher side rails). Ensure that housekeeping personnel and nursing staff exert maximum efforts to correct deficiencies in cleaning and that the engineering department staff change filters in the air-handling system on a regular basis. Handwashing should be done often, using approved antimicrobial agents. Gloves do not replace the need for handwashing.

When the patient arrives, remove as much street clothing and debris as possible from the treatment area. Remove blood and other body fluids from the wound promptly, because they are excellent media for containing and propagating microorganisms. Close doors to minimize airflow that can carry contaminating particulate matter into the room. Use appropriate skin preparation techniques when placing intravenous lines; take the few extra seconds to defat the skin with alcohol and permit the betadine to dry before making a skin puncture, for example. Maximum barrier techniques, including use of gowns, masks, gloves, and sterile drapes, must of course be used for installation of central lines. Keep patients warm and treat pain early. Manage any evidence of hypoxia and shock aggressively, taking corrective measures before serious deterioration occurs. When the patient has open wounds, query the physician promptly regarding which antibiotics will be used so that their administration can be initiated early in the course of resuscitation before the immune function becomes more impaired. Most EDs have specific protocols for selecting and administering antibiotics in major trauma cases. Remember, however, that antibiotics are not a substitute for asepsis.

■ NURSING DIAGNOSES

Nursing diagnoses appropriate to the medical complications of trauma are:

- Alterations in fluid volume due to impaired renal functioning
- Electrolyte imbalances related to impaired renal functioning
- Impaired gas exchange due to altered pulmonary blood flow and disruption of the capillary–alveolar membrane

- Risk of altered body temperature due to loss of skin integrity and environmental heat losses
- Alteration in pulmonary and peripheral tissue perfusion due to microcirculatory obstruction
- Risk of sepsis-related loss of skin integrity

■ REFERENCE

1. Ayers SM, Grenvik A, Holbrook PR, Shoemaker WC. *Textbook of Critical Care.* 3rd ed. Philadelphia, Pa: WB Saunders; 1995, p.1036.
2. Harper J. Rhabdomyolysis and myoglobinuric renal failure. *Crit Care Nurse.* 1990; 10: 32–36.
3. Bongard FS, Sue DY. *Current Critical Care Diagnosis and Treatment.* E. Norwalk, Conn: Appleton & Lange; 1994.
4. Hurst JM. Fat embolism syndrome. In: Kempczinski RF, ed. *Common Problems in Trauma.* Chicago, Ill: Year Book Medical Publishers; 1987: 373–379.
5. Barie PS, Shires GT. *Surgical Intensive Care.* Boston, Ma: Little, Brown; 1993, p. 531.
6. Barber J. *Life-Threatening Infections in the Critically Ill: Pathophysiology, Antibiotics and Clinical Management.* Lewisville, Tex: Barbara Clark Mims Associates; 1996.

■ BIBLIOGRAPHY

Benumof J. *Airway Management: Principles and Practice.* St. Louis, Mo: CV Mosby; 1995.

Cardona VD, Hurn PD, Bastnagel Mason PJ, et al. *Trauma Nursing.* 2nd ed. Philadelphia, Pa: WB Saunders; 1994.

Grenvik A, Ayes SM, Holbrook PR, Shoemaker WB. *Pocket Companion to Textbook of Critical Care.* Philadelphia, Pa: WB Saunders; 1996.

Levine RL, Fromm RE Jr. *Critical Care Monitoring from Pre-Hospital to the ICU.* St. Louis, Mo: Mosby-Year Book; 1995.

Maull KI, Rodriguez A, Wiles CE. *Complications in Trauma and Critical Care.* Philadelphia, Pa: WB Saunders; 1996.

Moreau D, ed. *Nursing 96 Drug Handbook.* Springhouse, Pa: Springhouse Corporation; 1996.

Phippen ML, Wells MP. *Perioperative Nursing Practice.* Philadelphia, Pa: WB Saunders; 1994.

Ruppert SD, Kernicki JG, Dolan JT. *Dolan's Critical Care Nursing.* 2nd ed. Philadelphia, Pa: FA Davis; 1996.

7. Clochesy JM, Breu C, Cardin S, et al. *Critical Care Nursing.* Philadelphia, Pa: WB Saunders; 1993, 1097.

■ REVIEW: MEDICAL COMPLICATIONS OF TRAUMA

1. Define *rhabdomyolysis, compartment syndrome,* and *fat emboli* as they relate to the traumatized patient.

2. State two management strategies that can minimize the threat of rhabdomyolysis.

3. List three signs and symptoms that suggest the presence of fat emboli.

4. Cite precursors to disseminating intravascular coagulation.

5. Describe the usual progression of multisystem organ failure (MSOF) after trauma.

6. Explain three methods of minimizing thermal stress in the trauma patient.

7. Enumerate four ways that emergency nurses (ENs) can limit the threat of infectious complications after trauma.

8. List six nursing diagnoses pertinent to medical complications of trauma.

Medical Emergencies

Headaches, Seizures, and Encephalopathies

20

There are many conditions that can present to the emergency department (ED) with the manifestations of headache, seizures, or encephalopathies. The goal is to treat the crisis while attempting to pinpoint the underlying condition responsible for the patient's signs and symptoms.

■ HEADACHE

CAUSES

There are many causes of headache; it is among the chief problems for which ambulatory patients seek relief in an ED. The emergency nurse (EN) should assess the headache in terms of time of onset and duration, precipitating events (if known), site and quality of pain, and associated symptoms and factors that influence the severity of pain, such as position or bright lights or other visual stimuli. The individual patient history, with special reference to the pattern of the headache, is the best determinant of the form of management within the ED.

Among the more serious problems that cause headache are meningitis, brain tumors or other space-occupying lesions, temporal arteritis, and hypertensive crisis. Although most patients are primarily seeking relief for their pain, the ED physician must rule out life-threatening pathology before ordering analgesics. In some instances, neurological consultation, imaging studies, and other diagnostic tests will be required.

DIFFERENTIAL FEATURES

Vascular headaches (e.g., tension, cluster, migraine) are related by common pain pathways that involve serotonin, prostaglandins, and other substances that serve as biochemical messengers.[1]

Tension Headache

The patient with a tension headache ordinarily complains of a bandlike tightness around the head that becomes progressively worse throughout the day. Pain may be prominent in the posterior, cervical, or temporal regions, where muscle spasm is most pronounced and palpable (Fig. 20–1A). The pain is aggravated by neck motion or strains induced by certain postures. All diagnostic parameters are normal, and oral analgesics (e.g., aspirin, acetaminophen) usually afford relief. Massage, local heat, and other therapies that promote relaxation may be helpful.

Cluster Headache

Cluster headaches are severe and last 1 to 2 hours. They begin on one side of the face and involve the eye, temporal region, and often the neck (Fig 20–1B). There is a characteristic flushing on the involved side due to vasodilation. A watery nasal discharge, tearing, and ipsilateral pupil constriction may be also associated. An examination of the conjunctiva reveals congestion. Cluster headaches have been associated with alcoholism, and the condition is more likely to occur in males.

Hypertensive Headaches

The headache associated with hypertension is ordinarily throbbing (Fig. 20–1C). Most patients will have, of course, a distinctly elevated blood pressure (BP). Pain is usually worse over the vertex and occipital regions but promptly dissipates with relief of the hypertension (see pages 382–383).

Migraine

Migraine tendency is largely familial (about 65 percent of patients with migraines report a parent with migraine). The ratio of females to males with migraine is about 7:1. Coffee, chocolate, nuts, and foods containing tyramine, monosodium glutamate (MSG), or nitrates are often implicated. The EN should determine whether suspect items were ingested prior to the onset of the headache. Alcohol and stress are also related to the genesis of migraine attacks in some patients.

The migraine episode is induced by cerebral vasospasm so severe that some patients experience neurological deficits during this phase, placing them on notice for an impending attack. The site of onset may vary with each episode but frequently involves the ocular region (Fig 20–1D). (If the site never varies, a lesion, rather than migraine, should be suspected.) When the vasospasm ceases, vessels dilate and become congested. It is this dilation phase that is responsible for the intense pain that eventually prompts the patient to seek emergency treatment.

When such patients arrive at the ED, they are in such severe pain that they are barely able to tolerate the initial triage and registration processes. They will usually express the desire to lie down in a darkened room, owing to the photophobia and pain. Usually, patients will describe the pain as throbbing; at times, they will describe an aura of zigzag light flashes or other visual images, and peripheral vision may be impaired. Nausea occurs commonly with migraine; the patient may experience some relief upon vomiting. The EN should assist the patient as quickly as possible to a darkened room where the patient can lie down to await

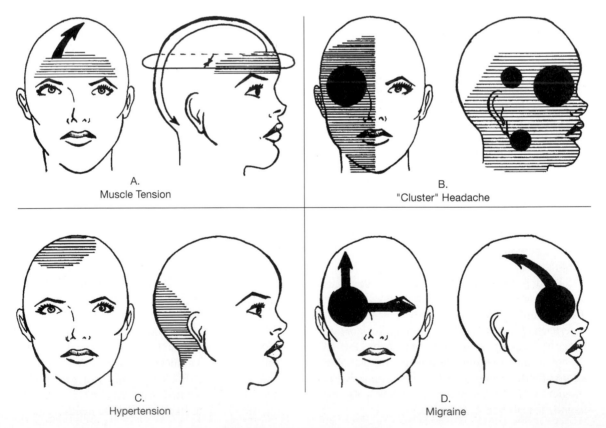

A.
Muscle Tension

B.
"Cluster" Headache

C.
Hypertension

D.
Migraine

Figure 20–1. Headache pain patterns

further questioning and evaluation. Patients with migraine should not be asked to remain in the waiting room.

All study results and vital signs (VS) are normal with migraine, and the patient's medical record will be most helpful in making decisions regarding case management in the ED. Since drug-seeking behaviors must always be considered, the physician must take this into account when prescribing therapy.

Treatment should be directed toward averting the headache if the patient is still in the vasospastic phase; if in the dilation phase, analgesics, antiemetics and other symptomatic therapies are indicated. ENs should elicit a complete history of medications taken prior to or upon recognition of a migraine attack to avoid inducing iatrogenic reactions.

Antiemetics: Prochlorperazine (Compazine), metoclopramide (Reglan), or hydroxyzine (Vistaril) may be used, but the EN should remember that these agents can cause several side effects, including dystonias and akasthisias, which may complicate the patient's emergency management. These drugs are usually ordered for parenteral administration; their order may be accompanied by an order for diphenhydramine (Benadryl) to relieve any extrapyramidal side effects that could be induced.

Analgesics: Mild analgesics may be effective very early in the course of migraine, but by the time the patient is prompted to visit the hospital ED, other agents are in order to relieve the pain. Agents containing ergotamine, caffeine, and other drugs may be used to effect vasoconstriction and some pain relief early in the episode. Ergotamine, if given before the vasodilation phase, may be useful for some patients because it tends to induce vasoconstriction. However, its side effects may compound existing nausea, headache pain, and other discomforts. Ketorolac (Toradol) is a useful analgesic for many patients. Most narcotics, however, are not regularly used for a patient with recurring migraine, because they do not alter the pathophysiological events and could create drug dependency.

Sumatriptan (Imitrex) is a relatively new agent for migraine; it has actions similar to those of dihydroergotamine, an ergot compound similar to ergotamine. When given subcutaneously in a 6-mg dose, it provides some relief within 10 to 20 minutes, and relief is nearly complete within 1 or 2 hours for most patients. Repeat doses are not recommended, even if relief is not complete.[1] The EN should understand that most patients will have some local warmth and tingling at the injection site and that some redness may appear. Some patients report a chest tightness, and almost half experience headache recurrence within 24 hours. This latter problem can be minimized with brief dexamethasone treatment, which may be provided by oral or intravenous administration.

Sumatriptan is available for patients to use at home, and many report they no longer require ED visits, because they can manage their migraine episode via this self-administered medication, available in prepackaged syringes or vials. It is not suitable for individuals with ischemic heart disease or hypertension. Great caution must be taken if the drug is used during pregnancy. If patients are prescribed "at home" sumatriptan, they must be cautioned regarding potential side effects, such as persistent chest pain, wheezing, and allergic reactions, and should be instructed to seek immediate medical attention if these or similar phenomena occur.

Other Headaches

Headaches due to acute meningitis are generalized and radiate to the neck. Fever, emesis, and signs of meningeal irritation are prominent features. The patient should be assessed for prior conditions of the upper respiratory tract, such as a sore throat or a cold. Anyone who presents with a variable, intermittent headache that is localized and worsened by activities that increase intracranial pressure (ICP), such as bending, coughing, or straining, should be suspected of having a space-occupying lesion such as a brain tumor. Conditions such as brain tumors are likely to be associated with changes in mental status and neurological deficits.

There is a wide range of other headaches that may be due to chronic conditions (e.g., postconcussion syndrome) or may be of psychogenic origin. Again, a careful history of headache onset, progression, and characteristics will be instrumental in planning for further medical assessment. Headache pain due to eye, ear, and sinus conditions is localized around the involved areas, and a thorough EENT (eyes, ears, nose, and throat) examination is usually all that is required to pinpoint the cause.

■ SEIZURES

Seizure disorders represent a dysfunction of the brain that can result from a wide variety of causes, including infection, alcohol withdrawal, fever, trauma, metabolic disturbances, and interference with the blood supply to this vital organ. A seizure can be defined as a sudden change in sensation, behavior, muscle activity, or level of consciousness (LOC). The EN should consider any seizure activity as a clue to an underlying condition of the central nervous system (CNS).

Some individuals who have repeated seizures or frequent bouts of seizure activity are warned by an aura, which is a highly individualized sensory experience including visual, auditory, gustatory, olfactory, or other sensations triggered by the involved area of the brain. In some cases, the aura may include automatic speech (e.g., nonsense phrases that are repeated) and neurological phenomena, depending on the area of brain dysfunction. This information is quite important to elicit, since it may provide valuable clues to the underlying brain pathology or to an associated metabolic disturbance.

Epilepsy is a condition in which the patient has recurrent episodes of seizure activity but there is no defined or known causative problem. Epilepsy ordinarily has its onset between early childhood and young adulthood. It involves seizures of several types but does not affect any physical or mental processes, and the individuals can continue normal lifestyles in most instances if they comply with a regimen of anticonvulsant medications. The regular use of these agents controls seizures by raising the threshold for their onset. Among the most common drugs are phenobarbital (Luminal), carbamazepine (Tegretol), ethosuximide (Zarontin), ethotoin (Peganone), felbamate (Felbatol), mephenytoin (Mesantoin), mephobarbital (Mebaral), trimethadione (Tridione), phenytoin sodium (Dilantin), primidone (Mysoline), lorazepam (Ativan), and diazepam (Valium). The EN should suspect seizures as one cause of unconsciousness if a patient is found to have such drugs in a pocket or handbag. Many patients with chronic seizures carry wallet cards or wear a Medic-Alert tag, and these should be noted.

Even if patients take their medications regularly, it is possible for seizures to occur as a result of unusual stress on the body. Fatigue, fever, infections, pregnancy, constipation, and menstrual periods may be factors that contribute to a lowering of the threshold for seizures. A careful history from the patient, the family, or friends may be useful in identifying these underlying causes of stress.

TYPES

Neonatal Seizures

The newborn may have seizures that are easily missed because signs of them are unique, owing to the immaturity of the CNS. The only clues that the tiny infant is seizing may be unusual posturing, rigidity, or apnea. Tremors, loss of muscle tone, spasmodic crying, facial twitching, chewing movements, or apparent shivering may also be indicators of neonatal seizures. If such patterns are recognized, the EN must summon medical assistance at once, because this condition can be life-threatening. Supplemental oxygen should be administered promptly and intravenous access should be gained for the administration of emergency drugs (see pages 468–469).

Febrile Seizures

Young children (between 6 months and 6 years of age) may have a seizure in response to fever, owing to the brain's inability to adapt to a sudden increase in temperature. These seizures typically accompany upper respiratory tract infections (URTIs). Treatment is aimed at the underlying cause of the fever (see page 469).

Petit Mal Seizures

Certain patients have petit mal seizures, which are essentially momentary lapses of consciousness. A blank stare or a transient "unawareness" or "dropping out" may be the only evidence of seizure activity. Petit mal seizures are seldom the primary reason for the ED visit, but occasionally, during the brief period of "blackout," the patient may be injured. Therefore, any history of such activity should be elicited, because the anticonvulsant drug therapy may need to be adjusted to prevent further attacks. Noncompliance may occur, especially in adolescents, so the EN should take the opportunity to stress the regular use of prescribed agents.

Jacksonian Seizures

Jacksonian seizures are marked by hyperactivity of certain muscle groups. There may be involvement of an arm or a leg, usually progressing to adjacent areas on the same side of the body. There is no loss of consciousness. This type of seizure activity may progress to a generalized or grand mal seizure.

Psychomotor Seizures

Psychic phenomena are experienced without recall in psychomotor seizure. Motor behavior may involve purposeless activity, such as hand wringing or picking at clothes. Emotions that occur at the same time may reflect anger, fear, rage, or frustration. Speech may be nonsensical or rambling.

Grand Mal Seizures

The grand mal seizure or convulsion is the type of seizure that usually presents to the ED. Since the seizure itself is short-lived, by the time that the patient reaches the ED, he or she is in a postictal state and thus the history given by the family member or bystander becomes most important. The EN should note clues to seizure activity, including injury to the tongue, soiled clothing from incontinence, and limb trauma that might have occurred during tonic-clonic motions. Ordinarily, the patient will seem confused or sleepy. It is highly likely that the patient may seize again during the ED visit, and if this occurs, immediate steps must be taken to protect the patient from injury and to ensure that the airway and ventilation are protected during the event. Suction should be at hand, and a plastic bite-stick or oropharyngeal airway may be used between the teeth. Large, padded tongue blades are to be discouraged because they are likely to obstruct the airway and may traumatize the perioral structures or cause gagging during insertion. The cyanosis that may accompany major seizure activity is in most cases due to a temporary "paralysis" of the diaphragm and chest muscles and does not indicate an obstructed airway. This transient interruption in ventilatory excursions is not of serious concern in a single seizure, but it can result in considerable hypoxia if seizures are recurrent within a short period of time. During a seizure, secretions collect in the oropharynx and should be suctioned to clear the airway. It is usually futile to attempt to oxygenate the patient during the seizure, owing to impairments of ventilatory motions, but immediately after the seizure, supplemental oxygen should be given by a bag-valve-mask unit in an attempt to raise the threshold for further seizure activity.

The patient should not be stimulated during the postictal state but should be allowed to rest because movement, talking, and other activity may evoke further convulsive activity. If an intravenous line is not already established and the patient has suffered more than one or two seizures, a line should be established promptly (normal saline solution [NSS] is recommended) for the administration of anticonvulsant medications.

In addition to taking vital signs, the EN may obtain blood and urine for analyses. A complete blood count (CBC), blood sugar test, anticonvulsant drug level test, toxicology screen, liver function studies, and electrolyte levels are ordinarily requested. A dextrose-strip analysis should be done at once. Requests for further studies will depend on findings of the expanded history and physical examination and may include an electroencephalogram (EEG), computed tomography (CT) scan, and lumbar puncture.

Status Epilepticus

If a grand mal seizure occurs successively without an interim period of consciousness, a condition called status epilepticus exists. Status epilepticus is a grave disorder due to the brain hypoxia and acidosis that result from these repeated seizures. Respiratory arrest, hypertension, hyperthermia (due to massive hypermetabolism), and elevated ICP accompany these major seizures. Status epilepticus is a dire emergency requiring intensive emergency intervention. Airway maintenance and supplemental oxygen are key factors in patient protection. These successive seizures may recur until anticonvulsant drugs are administered in large doses, the airway is well established, and high levels of oxygen are again reaching the brain. During status epilepticus, VS should be carefully monitored and supplemental oxygen should be administered; prepare for emergency intubation. As soon as feasible, an arterial blood gas (ABG) sample should be obtained as a baseline and to guide further therapy. The patient should be placed on a cardiac monitor and an oxymetric probe should be placed to aid in assessing ventilatory efficiency. Dextrose 50 percent (50 mL) and 100 mg thiamine are given to treat underlying metabolic aberrations that might be associated with the seizures.

Drugs to control status seizures include lorazepam (Ativan), diazepam (Valium), phenytoin (Dilantin), and phenobarbital (Luminal). Lorazepam is considered the drug of choice for interrupting status seizures because it has no deleterious metabolites and protects the patient from further seizures for between 4 to 14 hours, as opposed to diazepam's limited 20 minutes. It is typically administered intravenously at a rate of 2 to 4 mg/min, and the dose is repeated at 5-minute intervals if the seizure activity continues. (Lorazepam must be diluted 1:1 because it is quite viscous.) The maximum dose is ordinarily 10 mg. Diazepam may also be used in 2 to 4 mg increments, up to a maximum dose of 40 mg, but recurring seizures are very likely, because its duration of action is short. Midazolam (Versed) is used if the seizures are refractory to the other benzodiazepine agents.[2] While the initial doses of lorazepam or diazepam are being administered, the EN should be preparing the Dilantin drip. This agent must be given in NSS in a dose of 10–20 mg/kg. The rate of administration should not exceed 50 mg/min. A loading dose of phenobarbital (10 to 20 mg/kg) is given, too, at a rate of 0.2 to 0.4 mg/kg per minute, followed by an infusion of 0.25 to 2.0 mg/kg per hour. Although paraldehyde (by nasogastric [NG] or rectal tube or deep intramuscular injection only) and general anesthesia may be required in the most severe cases when the patient does not respond to other drugs, the administration of these agents is not recommended within the ED. Since status epilepticus carries a high morbidity and high mortality, even with aggressive therapy, these patients should be transferred to an intensive-care setting as early as possible for invasive monitoring and the in-depth study required for further interventions. Rhabdomyolysis, hyperthermia, and cerebral edema are among the most serious sequelae.

■ ENCEPHALOPATHIES

HYPERTENSIVE ENCEPHALOPATHY

Hypertensive encephalopathy was once thought to occur as a result of cerebral blood vessel spasm. It is now postulated that it is due to marked cerebral vasodilation and disruption of the blood–brain barrier.[3] The patient presents to the ED with headache, restlessness, confusion, projectile vomiting, visual disturbances, seizures, and focal neurological changes. The patient may complain of chest pain or heaviness. In some instances, there may be accompanying behavioral changes that may resemble psychosis. The triage nurse may be alerted by a family member that the patient is acting strangely, that he or she is "out of control" or "seeing things." The BP is elevated, although sometimes rather modestly (e.g., 150/100 mm Hg). However, in most patients, the pressure is very high (e.g., 250/150 mm Hg). Papilledema, with retinal hemorrhages and exudates, is typically observed, and urinalysis may reveal hematuria and proteinuria.

The patient may be unaware of having hypertension, or preexisting hypertension may be out of control owing to lack of compliance with therapy or other causes. Since the presenting signs and symptoms may be similar to those for stroke, drug overdose (i.e., amphetamines and cocaine), uremia, vasculitis, and space-occupying lesions in the cranium, these are among the conditions considered for differential diagnosis.

In hypertensive encephalopathy, the patient's symptoms improve dramatically, usually within hours, when the BP is reduced (see page 383).

WERNICKE'S ENCEPHALOPATHY

Wernicke's encephalopathy (characterized by inflammatory hemorrhagic lesions of the brain), is a rare but easily treated cause of coma. The patient most likely to present with this condition is a malnourished alcoholic. The administration of glucose, without thiamine, can also precipitate this condition, which is marked by eye muscle paralysis, diplopia, nystagmus, ataxia, and mental deterioration.

HEPATIC ENCEPHALOPATHY

Hepatic encephalopathy results from severe liver disease in which there is an inadequate degradation of metabolic toxins by the liver, and when these accumulate, they interfere with brain function. These toxins include ammonia, fatty acids, and methionine. Treatment requires admission, and therapies to reduce ammonia levels are initiated. Severity of hepatic encephalopathy may range from subtle alterations in mental processes to coma with decerebrate posturing.

The EN must be aware that a large range of problems can produce alterations in mental status and behavior, and the underlying problem may be metabolic or vascular in origin. Therefore, in addition to conducting basic neurological assessments, the EN should look for chronic medical conditions such as alcoholism and hypertension, which can give rise to encephalopathy.

■ NURSING DIAGNOSES

Nursing diagnoses related to headaches, seizures, and encephalopathies include:

- Alteration in comfort due to pain
- Ineffective breathing pattern related to altered ventilatory mechanics
- Ineffective airway clearance related to inability to handle secretions
- Risk of injury related to altered state of consciousness and neurological defects
- Anxiety related to decreased cerebral oxygenation
- Impaired communication related to seizure activity and altered state of consciousness

■ REFERENCES

1. Foley JJ. Pharmacologic treatment of acute migraine and related headaches in the emergency department. *J Emerg Nurs.* 1993;19:225–230.
2. Ayers SM, Grenvik A, Holbrook PR, Shoemaker WC. *Textbook of Critical Care.* 3rd ed. Philadelphia, Pa: WB Saunders; 1995.
3. American Heart Association. *American Heart Association's Hypertension Primer.* Dallas, Tex: AHA; 1993.

■ BIBLIOGRAPHY

Bongard FS, Sue DY. *Current Critical Care Diagnosis and Treatment.* E. Norwalk, Conn: Appleton & Lange; 1994.

Chernow B, ed. *The Pharmacologic Approach to the Critically Ill Patient.* 3rd ed. Baltimore, Md: Williams & Wilkins; 1994.

Grenvik A, Ayers SM, Holbrook PR, Shoemaker WB. *Pocket Companion to Textbook of Critical Care.* Philadelphia, Pa: WB Saunders; 1996.

Levine RL, Fromm RE Jr. *Critical Care Monitoring from Pre-Hospital to the ICU.* St. Louis, Mo: Mosby-Year Book; 1995.

Moreau D, ed. *Nursing 96 Drug Handbook.* Springhouse, Pa: Springhouse Corporation; 1996.

Physicians' Desk Reference. 50th ed. Montvale, NJ: Medical Economics; 1996.

Ruppert SD, Kernicki JG, Dolan JT. *Dolan's Critical Care Nursing.* 2nd ed. Philadelphia, Pa: FA Davis; 1996.

■ REVIEW: HEADACHES, SEIZURES, AND ENCEPHALOPATHIES

1. Describe the characteristic pain patterns associated with these headaches:
   a. Tension
   b. Cluster
   c. Hypertensive
   d. Migraine

2. Outline the nursing management of a patient with a migraine headache, including use of sumatriptan and other agents.

3. Describe the way in which symptoms of a headache associated with meningeal irritation differ from other types of headache.

4. Describe the classic signs of a neonatal seizure and identify the two vital, immediate nursing interventions.

5. Explain why status epilepticus is a life-threatening condition, outline the requirements for clinical monitoring, and identify three drugs given initially during this crisis.

6. Explain the reason lorazepam is the drug of choice for controlling seizures and list three guidelines for safe administration of this agent.

7. List three types of encephalopathies and identify the one that can be induced by administration of 50 percent glucose without thiamine.

8. Name two medical conditions that are precursors to encephalopathies and identify clues that would be characteristically observed by the triage nurse.

Eye, Ear, Nose, and Throat Emergencies

This chapter is designed to expand emergency nursing capabilities in the recognition and management of EENT (eyes, ears, nose, and throat) problems as they present in the emergency department (ED). A brief anatomic review of the eye, ear, and nose is provided, together with standard terminology relating to the eye. Nursing interventions and appropriate diagnoses are addressed, and guidelines covering a broad spectrum of practical management techniques are included.

■ THE EYE

ANATOMY

The eye is a sensory organ that functions to provide vision. The structures of the eye are the globe or eyeball and its contents, the bony orbit (socket), muscles and tendons, conjunctiva, eyelids, tear ducts and glands, the optic nerves, and that portion of the occipital lobe of the brain that is concerned with vision (Fig. 21–1). Terminology relating to the eye is presented in Table 21–1.

CLASSIFICATION OF INJURIES

Eye injuries can be classified as superficial, penetrating or perforating, or nontraumatic medical emergencies. Regardless of the classification, it is essential to use common sense as your guide to treatment. Any patient seen in the ED with trauma to the facial region is a candidate for some degree of damage to one or both eyes, and a thorough check is required.

MANAGEMENT GUIDELINES

All patients with eye problems should be questioned for a complete history of injury or cause, as well as observed for the presence of an ocular prosthesis (glass eye). Pupil size and shape are important to note; constricted or pinpoint pupils may indicate use of narcotics while, dilated pupils accompany barbiturate intoxication. In functional disorders as well, the pupils are characteristically dilated, equal, and reactive. There is an occasional person with a condition known as anisocoria, the congenital inequality of pupil diameter. Any deviance from normal reactive pupils should be noted in the nursing history, regardless of cause.

Testing Visual Acuity

Visual acuity (VA) should be checked with the patient wearing glasses or contact lenses, if they are normally worn. The Snellen eye chart should be used to check both eyes and the findings recorded. Recording is done as OD (oculus dexter or right eye) 20/? and OS (oculus sinister or left eye) 20/?. Every ED should be equipped with a standard size wall-mounted Snellen eye chart and a smaller version, to be used for patients who must remain on a stretcher. The small Snellen chart is used while holding it 14 in. from the eyes (Fig. 21–2).

The Eye Tray

An eye tray should be available in every ED and should contain a minimum of the following items:

- Small Snellen eye chart
- Ophthalmoscope

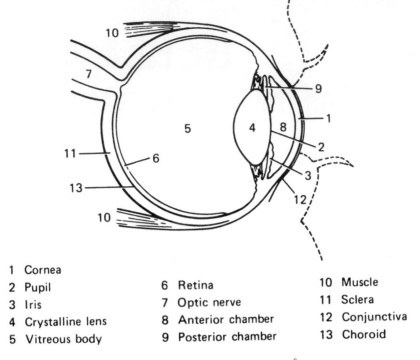

1 Cornea	6 Retina	10 Muscle
2 Pupil	7 Optic nerve	11 Sclera
3 Iris	8 Anterior chamber	12 Conjunctiva
4 Crystalline lens	9 Posterior chamber	13 Choroid
5 Vitreous body		

Figure 21–1. The eye (*from Ethicon, Inc.*[6])

- Flashlight or penlight
- Pair of magnifying eye loupes
- Cobalt-blue diffuse light or Wood's lamp for visualizing fluorescein stains
- Small suction bulb for removing hard contact lenses, and disposable lens storage cases
- Sterile irrigating solutions (ophthalmic isotonic buffered solution)
- Fluorescein strips (solution will support *Pseudomonas* growth)
- Clean 4 × 4 gauze pads
- Sterile applicators
- Sterile eye pads
- Clear tape (1-in width)
- Assorted medications in single (unit-) dose-dispensing packages:
    Topical anesthesia such as proparacaine HCl solution (Ophthaine) (must be kept under refrigeration)
    Antibiotics (ophthalmic ointments and solutions)
    Cycloplegics (for paralysis of accommodation)
    Mydriatics (for dilating the pupil)
    Miotics (for constricting the pupil)
- A sterile lid retractor

Administering Medications

If the patient is in too much pain to be examined adequately, wait until topical anesthesia has been administered and then check for the visual acuity bilaterally. Opthalmic ointments should always be applied by everting the lower eyelid and spreading the ointment from the inner to the outer canthus of the conjunctival sac; drops are applied in the same manner, dropping medication into the conjunctival sac. Errors frequently occur during this procedure, so the following procedure is given as a guideline:

1. Have patient lie on his or her back.
2. Carefully inspect for contact lenses. Always ask the patient if he or she wears them. Lenses can be identified by shining a beam of light from the side.
3. Remove contact lenses if necessary.
   Hard lenses are removed with a small suction bulb and placed in a container.

TABLE 21–1. TERMINOLOGY RELATING TO THE EYE AND ITS FUNCTION

Term	Purpose, Function
Anterior chamber	Frontal space in eyeball, bounded by cornea, iris, and lens
Aqueous humor	Watery, transparent fluid found in anterior and posterior chambers of eye; helps maintain conical shape in front globe and assists in focusing light rays on retina
Bony orbit	Rounded socket in cranium in which eyeball is partially sunk
Conjunctiva	Mucous membrane that lines eyelids and covers anterior surface of globe except for cornea
Cornea	Transparent frontal layer of eyeball
Crystalline lens	That part of eye just behind anterior chamber which, in addition to the cornea, refracts light rays and focuses them on the retina
Extraocular	Adjective meaning *outside* the globe of the eye
Globe	Eyeball
Intraocular	Adjective meaning *inside* the globe of the eye
Iris	Colored membrane of eye separating the anterior and posterior chambers; contracts and dilates to regulate entrance of light rays
Lacrimal ducts and glands	System of ducts and glands that secretes and conducts tears
Occipital lobe	Posterior section of brain where mental images are formed of what is seen
Optic nerve	Second cranial nerve with special sense of sight
Posterior chamber	Space between iris and lens that is filled with aqueous humor
Pupil	Opening at center of iris
Retina	The "seeing" membrane lining inside of posterior eye, where images are focused by lens and cornea, then transmitted to brain by optic nerve
Sclera	White outer coat of eye that extends from optic nerve to cornea
Sensory receptors	Rods and cones in retinal layer that are stimulated by light rays to conduct nerve impulses to brain by optic nerve
Vitreous humor	Transparent substance having consistency of raw egg white that fills posterior cavity of eyeball; also called hyaloid.

Soft lenses are removed by sliding downward on eyeball and "pinching" the lens gently between thumb and forefinger. Note: Soft lenses must be placed in normal saline solution (NSS) or special soft-lens disinfecting solution only. Any other solution containing buffers can irrevocably damage soft lenses.

Place lenses in a container with appropriate solution and label R (right) and L (left).

4. Gently pull lower lid of the eye downward, instruct the patient to look up, and place two drops of the anesthetic solution in the pouch of the lid.

5. Instruct the patient to close the eyes and try to relax. Explain that the topical agent may sting for a few seconds, causing the eyes to water heavily. Have cleansing tissue handy.

6. Clearly write the medication, number of drops; R, L, or OU (oculus uterque—each eye); and time administered on paper tape, and apply this to the patient's forehead upside down so that the next person on the scene will notice the message, read it, and not repeat administration of the medication.

7. Record the same information immediately on the ED chart.

8. Have the eye tray on a stand at the head of the table in readiness for the examination. Remember that depth perception and reflex responses are seriously affected if the eyes have been dilated or anesthetized for examination and that any patient who has had anesthesia instilled should have that eye patched after treatment, until the effects of anesthesia wear off. This precaution will protect the

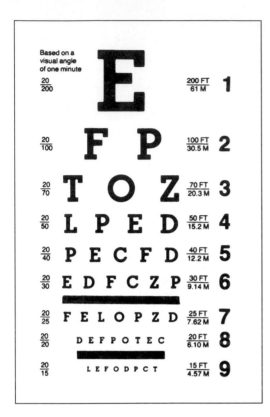

Figure 21–2. The Snellen eye chart for evaluation of vision. Someone standing 20 feet away who can read line 8 has 20/20 vision.

eye from foreign-body invasion or further trauma.

Patching Eyes

When patching an eye, the important thing is to use enough pressure to keep the lid from moving across the corneal surface, as well as to exclude light and keep the eye at total rest. Use as many patches as necessary to fill the orbital depth, bringing the height of the patch to above the frontal ridge; in some patients with deep-set eyes, it may be necessary to fold one eye patch in half to build up a base and then proceed with other layers. The patch should then be firmly taped, with clear and highly adhesive 1-in. tape high on the forehead and down across to the cheek, as many times as necessary to anchor the patch and exclude light.

■ EYE INJURIES AND EMERGENCIES

SUPERFICIAL INJURIES

Superficial injuries are the most commonly seen eye problems in the ED and include corneal abrasions (scraping injuries that denude skin or membrane), trauma caused by foreign bodies, chemical burns, and heat and flash burns.

Corneal Abrasions

Corneal abrasions are common and present with copious tearing, spasms of the eyelid, and squinting. A complete history is extremely important, and VA must be checked—for immediate management and for medicolegal implications that may arise. Topical anesthesia will usually be required before VA can be assessed. The abrasion is defined by the use of fluorescein strips and a few drops of NSS or ophthalmic irrigating solution, which will show the denuded surface epithelium under cobalt-blue diffuse light.

Nursing Intervention. An antibiotic ophthalmic ointment of choice (usually neomycin or a sulfa preparation) is applied, and the eye is patched and kept at rest for 24 hours, following which it should be seen again for follow-up examination by an ophthalmologist.

Foreign Bodies

Foreign bodies are probably the most common ocular injury, although most are relatively simple in nature. The history is *extremely* important because if the eye has been penetrated by an oxidizing metal (e.g., ferrous metals, copper, leaded glass), problems can develop later with scarring that may cause blindness of the afflicted eye. These patients should be referred to an ophthalmologist directly from the ED.

The VA is checked, the eye is anesthetized, and then it is examined. The presence of a small puncture wound and point of entry would indicate the necessity to rule out perforation of the orb, and leakage of humor or blood would be indicative. The lid must be everted for a thorough examination to determine whether the foreign body is embedded in the lid and riding over the cornea with every blink of the eye.

Eversion of the upper lid (Figure 21–3) is ac-

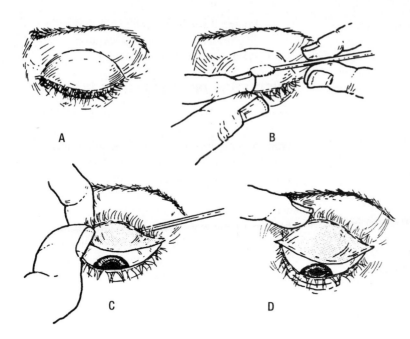

A

B

C

D

Figure 21–3. Steps in everting eyelid. **A.** Patient looks downward. **B.** Upper lid is pulled downward by grasping eyelashes with fingers. **C.** Eyelid is pulled outward and rolled upward over a small rod (applicator stick or wood match, for example). **D.** Everted lid facilitates removal of foreign body using *moistened* cotton applicator; lid is returned to normal position by having patient look up. (*From Barber,[7] p. 295*.)

complished by having the patient look downward toward the feet as the lashes of the upper lid are grasped to exert downward and outward pull away from the eye; gentle, direct pressure is applied against the lid (at about the "fold" line) with an applicator stick as the lid everts back over the stick. Having the patient look up will readily flip the lid back to its normal position.

Nursing Intervention. If a foreign body is successfully removed, apply antibiotic ointment or drops and patch. The patient should be seen by an ophthalmologist in 24 hours. If, however, the object is *not* successfully removed, the patient should go to the x-ray department, with full instructions to the technician for special views if indicated, and an ophthalmologist should be called.

Displaced Contact Lenses

Excessive tearing and rubbing the eyes can cause contact lenses to shift position and be displaced into the cul-de-sac between orb and lid, usually the upper lid. Lens recovery is accomplished by eversion of the lid and removal by either cotton-tipped applicator or a gentle stream of sterile NSS. A lens displaced for a long period may have dried and adhered to the conjunctiva; if it does not move readily with an applicator, irrigate gently until it *does*

move. An opthalmologist should be called if the lens persists in adhering. If a trauma patient has only one contact lens visible on examination, check the other eye carefully by retracting both lids and inspecting with a strong light source.

Chemical Burns

Chemicals spilled or splattered into the eye are *always* a serious consideration in management, and immediate dilution of the chemical may be the single most important factor in determining the outcome. Additionally, severity of a chemical burn to the eye is determined by the type and concentration of the offending chemical, the duration of contact, and whether it is a liquid or powdered substance. As a rule, alkalis are more dangerous than acids because they can rapidly penetrate the anterior chamber of the eye; acids, on the other hand, combine with tissue proteins and are unable to penetrate the barrier. *Any* suspicion of involvement with a damaging chemical requires immediate and extensive irrigation, initially using the most readily available source of clean water at the scene. Once the patient is in the ED, continuous irrigation should be maintained, using sterile water, NSS, or Ringer's lactate; minimal irrigation time for acid and alkali burns ranges from 20 minutes to between 2 and 4 hours.[1,2] Depending on the exposure severity, acids are more easily irrigated away from tissues and require less time to wash away. Alkalis (e.g., potassium hydroxide, ammonia, ammonium chloride, and many cleaning substances), once on the tissues, continue to burn and require longer irrigation time to ensure complete removal and damage control.

Nursing Interventions. The Morgan lens and similar irrigation devices are scleral lenses with irrigation ports attached that cover the entire orb and permit efficient, continuous irrigation of the eye. They are extremely effective in removing caustic materials and free personnel for other tasks as the lavage is underway. Topical anesthesia is immediately provided to the eye; the irrigant is set up much like an intravenous line and is attached to a Morgan lens–type device, or perhaps simply hand-held intravenous tubing if the more sophisticated device is not available. A Morgan lens is placed with the patient looking down as the upper eyelid is retracted; the lens edge is placed under the lid. With the patient looking up, the lower lid is retracted in the same way and the lens edge is inserted downward. With the patient's head turned to the affected side, a folded towel under the patient's face can collect irrigant as the solution runs, or perhaps an irrigation tray, with a catch-bucket on the floor below, can be used. Continuous topical anesthesia may be required for patient comfort as irrigation diminishes the amount of the anesthetic agent; remain alert to the patient's comfort level. These patients must be referred to an ophthalmologist for immediate evaluation and treatment.

Heat and Flash Burns

Heat and flash burns from welder's arcs, ultraviolet light (sunlamps), and flash heat are fairly common in the ED. A history is taken, VA is checked before or after the eyes have been anesthetized, and antibiotic drops or ointment are applied. Both eyes should be patched for 24 hours to provide complete rest for the corneal insult.

Nursing Diagnoses

Appropriate nursing diagnoses for superficial eye injuries include:

- Pain related to injury
- Potential for infection related to injury
- Potential for self-care deficit related to visual impairment

- Potential for injury related to corneal scarring or change in depth perception
- Anxiety related to prognosis

PENETRATING OR PERFORATING INJURIES

Penetrating or perforating injuries caused by blunt trauma or foreign bodies (e.g., sticks, glass, rocks, metal) require essentially the same initial management as those caused by simple foreign body presence. The history of penetration, including the time of the accident and the mechanism of injury, type of pain, and VA, is important. If the anterior chamber of the eye is bloody (hyphema), an ophthalmologist should be called. This is a very serious sign and an emergency condition. A ruptured globe (ocular rupture) may involve retinal detachment (diagnosed by poor vision), a soft orb, and severe pain. In examining this eye, touch only *once* if the eye is soft, or touch lightly and gently with two fingertips over the lid.

Nursing Intervention. Once global penetration is confirmed, an ophthalmologist should be called immediately. The patient should be kept flat and at rest, the eye should be protected with a *loose* eye shield, and reassurance should be provided.

Nursing Diagnoses. Appropriate nursing diagnoses for penetrating or perforating injuries would include:

- Pain related to injury
- Potential for infection related to injury
- Potential for self-care deficit related to visual impairment
- Potential for injury related to change in depth perception
- Anxiety related to prognosis
- Knowledge deficit relative to prevention of injury

NONTRAUMATIC MEDICAL EMERGENCIES

Nontraumatic acute eye problems include glaucoma, iritis, and keratoconjunctivitis.

Acute Glaucoma

Acute glaucoma can precipitate blindness in hours. The pupil is dilated and fixed, the eye is red and *hard* (press lightly), and there is very severe pain. Intraocular pressure, when tested with a tonometer, will exceed 20 mm Hg. This requires prompt attention, and an ophthalmologist should be called for an order for pilocarpine and diuretics; surgical intervention may be required (i.e., iridectomy), thus preventing recurrence.

Central Retinal Artery Occlusion

Considered a true ocular emergency, central retinal artery occlusion by a thrombus or embolus is generally seen in older patients with a history that predisposes to an occlusion. There is a sudden and painless unilateral loss of vision; the affected eye is dilated, nonreactive, and perceives light only. Nursing intervention is limited to offering comfort and support, having the patient breathe into a paper bag to increase carbon dioxide for vasodilation of retinal arterioles, and explaining procedures as well as possible to alleviate anxieties. An ophthalmologist must be summoned immediately.

Nursing Diagnoses. Appropriate nursing diagnoses would include:

- Altered tissue perfusion to the optic nerve related to vascular blockage
- Anxiety related to sudden loss of vision
- Knowledge deficit related to causative factors
- Potential for injury due to decreased visual capacity

Acute Iritis

Acute iritis may be of bacterial, viral, or autoimmune disease (lupus) origin. Diagnosis is made because of the presence of a red iris (limbic flush), where the sclera meets iris, and a small pupil. Treatment is the use of a cycloplegic agent, pain medication, and dark glasses for the relief of severe photophobia.

Keratoconjunctivitis

Keratoconjunctivitis is a general inflammation of the outer coating of the eye that may be caused by virus *or* bacteria; diagnosis is made because of the presence of pus in the eye, conjunctivitis, ocular discharge, redness, swelling, and so on. Treatment depends on the causative agent, so cultures should be taken for bacterial presence and sensitivity as a baseline before any medication is administered:

- "Pink eye" (i.e., conjunctivitis) is generally thought to be a viral infection but is really

bacterial in origin and responds to sulfa drugs. It is highly contagious among children; those in the acute phase should be kept out of school. Hands should be very carefully washed after examination.
- Herpes simplex is viral and responds to idoxuridine (Stoxil); steroids *must* be avoided.
- "Gooey" eyes with purulent exudate are usually bacterial infections, and antibiotics are indicated (neomycin or sulfa).

Nursing diagnoses: Appropriate nursing diagnoses would include:

- Pain related to the inflammatory process
- Knowledge deficit related to the infection process
- Anxiety related to discomfort and prognosis

GENERAL NURSING GUIDELINES

General nursing interventions and guidelines for dealing with all eye emergencies include the following:

1. Learn to anticipate and manage contact lens removal and storage. Always check for contact lenses before instilling medications; remove lenses as discussed earlier, making certain they are properly labeled and placed with the patient's belongings.
2. Always check the eyes for injury after any head or facial trauma has been sustained.
3. Suspect a detached retina if the patient complains of loss of vision with *or* without a history of trauma, fuzzy vision (also present with an elevated blood sugar), and a halo effect around lights.
4. When administering any eye medication, *never* put cortisone, steroids, or any medication containing steroids into an inflamed eye. Herpetic ulcerations will "go crazy" with steroids applied; some fungal infections will do the same.
5. When eyes require irrigation, always retract the lids *after* anesthetizing the surfaces. A bent paper clip, wiped with alcohol and air-dried, makes a good retractor if all else fails or no retractor is available.
6. Remember, generally, if an eye injury is of any real significance, *both* eyes should be patched to keep the injured eye *completely* at rest.

7. For lid lacerations, cover both eyes with sterile NSS dressings until treatment by the ophthalmologist, with no manipulation in the interim.

8. Remember that eye injuries generally repair well if infection is controlled, so careful technique is important.

9. Acquaint yourself with the use and care of eye examination equipment, such as the slit lamp, the tonometer (for testing intraocular pressure in glaucoma), and the eye tray contents.

■ COMMON EAR PROBLEMS

ANATOMY OF THE EAR

Ear problems are not frequently seen on an urgent or emergency basis, but it is appropriate here to review the anatomy of the ear before further discussion. Figs. 21–4 and 21–5 depict the ear anatomy most often involved in ED care.

The most common ear emergency encountered, perhaps, is that of a partial or complete amputation of the outer ear from trauma, management of which consists of placing a moist dressing over the site and preserving any amputated tissue according to replantation guidelines outlined in Chapter 17.

Blood or fluid draining from the ear should be considered in light of relation to potential head injury. However, it may also be due to infection or local trauma. Diving injuries, a concussive slap over the ear, or sudden altitude changes can result in rupture of the tympanic membrane simply because of the sudden, severe pressure change. Tympanic rupture will be accompanied with complaints of pain, dizziness, ringing in the ear, and possibly hearing impairment.

Nursing intervention involves making the patient as comfortable as possible and placing the injured side down with a dressing on the ear to collect drainage (informational) and to protect from further trauma or contamination, reducing as much as possible the threat of spreading infection.

MANAGEMENT GUIDELINES

Some of the more commonly seen less-urgent ear problems follow, together with their management guidelines.

Hematoma

Hematoma of the helix may occasionally be seen. Unless intervention takes place rapidly, it will dissect the perichondrium off the cartilage, causing rapid necrosis and disfiguration of the external ear structure. Treatment is incision and drainage,

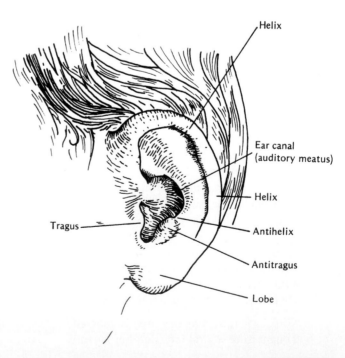

Figure 21–4. Structures of the external ear that can be the object of soft-tissue trauma (*from Barber,*[7] *p. 229*).

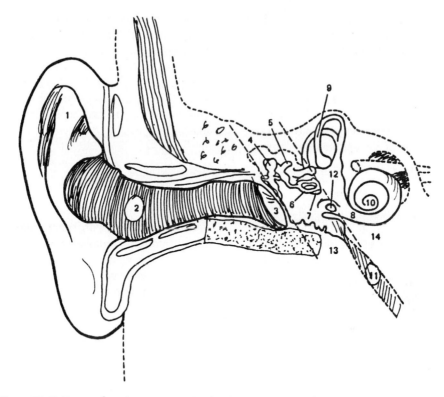

Figure 21–5. The ear. Sound waves, transmitted to the hair cells of the inner ear, stimulate the cells by displacement or distortion to send impulses to the brain so that humans may hear. **1.** External ear (pinna); **2.** external auditory canal; **3.** tympanic membrane (eardrum); **4.** malleus; **5.** incus; **6.** stapes; **7.** oval window; **8.** vestibule; **9.** semicircular canals; **10.** cochlea; **11.** eustachian tube; **12.** round window; **13.** middle ear; **14.** inner ear. (*From* Point of View. *Ethicon, Inc.*[6]).

packing with moist cotton, and application of a mastoid pressure dressing. Careful instructions to the patient for follow-up care are important.

Wax or Foreign Body

Anything lodged against or very close to the tympanic membrane can be painful. Wax is frequently irrigated out with warm saline and a control syringe, although there is a school of thought that supports wax removal by blunt curette only. A significant number of practitioners believe that cerumen protects the external auditory canal from infection, and some have documented its antimicrobial activity.[3,4]

Vegetable foreign bodies (e.g., beans, corn, peanuts) lodged in the external ear canal, a fairly frequent occurrence with small children, should never be irrigated with warm water because of the possibility of causing the material to swell and creating a greatly complicated removal process.

Swimmer's Ear (Acute Otitis Externa)

Water trapped in ears after swimming may be relieved with a mixture of 4 parts 70 percent isopropyl alcohol and 1 part vinegar poured into the ear and "swished" around. This weak acetic acid solution will break the surface tension, allowing the ear to drain freely, thus minimizing the potential for infection due to entrapped organisms.

Acute Otitis Media

Frequently seen in children with persistent upper respiratory tract infections (URTIs), acute otitis media can be extremely painful for the patient. Usual treatment involves administration of decongestants to open the eustachian tubes and of antibiotics; sometimes myringotomy is performed to relieve the pressure and clean out the accumulated "gunk" in the middle ear. Rupture of the tympanic membrane (eardrum) can result in damaged hearing; a clean incisional myringotomy will heal without damage to the membrane, thereby avoiding further risk of hearing loss.

Chronic Otitis Media

Untreated otitis media advances to a chronic condition, frequently with spontaneous perforation and drainage. Culture and sensitivity should be done prior to administration of any antibiotics; otherwise, treatment is much the same as for acute otitis media.

Labyrinthitis (Menière's Disease)

Whether toxic, drug-induced, viral, or of unknown etiology, labyrinthitis is a dysfunction of the labyrinth that usually presents with unsteady gait, dizziness, nausea, and occasional head pain; nystagmus, deafness, or hearing loss in conjunction with "head noises" (tinnitus) may also accompany the other symptoms. Labyrinthitis is generally treated with mild sedatives, analgesia, antivertigo agents, and a low-sodium diet. Patient teaching and careful management should include an awareness that resolution of labyrinthitis is often a slow process and that patience is a necessity.

■ COMMON NASAL PROBLEMS

ANATOMY OF THE NOSE

The nose (Fig. 21–6) is the beginning of the respiratory tract, the passageway for air traveling into the airways on inspiration. The mucous membranes lining the nose and its turbinates filter, warm, and moisten (humidify) the incoming air to facilitate gaseous exchange in the alveoli. The vascular nasal septum receives its blood supply from a rich capillary network and is vulnerable to bleeding from many causes, such as trauma, URTIs, nose-picking, allergies, and the presence of foreign bodies. The two most commonly seen nasal problems are epistaxis and those caused by foreign bodies. Both can be management challenges.

MANAGEMENT GUIDELINES

Foreign Bodies

The presence of foreign bodies in the nose is frequently a problem with small children and occasionally presents removal problems. Occlusion of the nasal passage by foreign bodies for a period of time can precipitate severe local swelling and infection. Pain and foul-smelling, purulent, unilateral nasal discharge in a small child should alert one to the probability of a lodged foreign object.

If the small child is unable to blow his or her nose to dislodge the foreign body, it may be necessary to use topical anesthesia so that the item can be retrieved by a small surgical instrument or suction; the child should be seen by the physician without delay. Antibiotics may be required for certain cases.

Epistaxis

Probably the most common nasal emergency is epistaxis that either is refractory to simple treatment or was not initially treated properly before the patient arrived at the ED. Most nosebleeds (80 to 90 percent) are bleeding points from the anterior nasal septum, known as Little's or Kiesselbach's

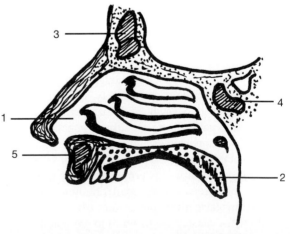

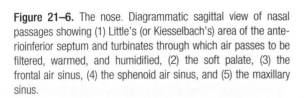

Figure 21–6. The nose. Diagrammatic sagittal view of nasal passages showing (1) Little's (or Kiesselbach's) area of the anterioinferior septum and turbinates through which air passes to be filtered, warmed, and humidified, (2) the soft palate, (3) the frontal air sinus, (4) the sphenoid air sinus, and (5) the maxillary sinus.

area; the area is richly supplied with capillaries. Many also occur from the lateral side of the nose and may bleed profusely. A posterior bleeding point is *trouble* and usually requires a posterior pack to exert sufficient pressure for tamponade.

General Management. Patients with epistaxis should be kept sitting in an upright position and leaning slightly forward to let the blood drip out of the nose rather than being swallowed. Reassurance is needed, and special attention must be paid to the cardiovascular status; careful monitoring of the blood pressure (BP), especially in elderly patients with coexisting hypertension, is essential. Hypotension, on the other hand, may develop insidiously owing to a lack of oxygen if the nostril has been packed for a period of time.

Nasal Packing Technique. When nasal packing is necessary, the posterior pack (if needed) is usually placed first, then the anterior pack. Both *must* be covered with antibiotic ointment prior to placement to minimize the risk of infection and sinusitis from occlusion of the nasopharynx, as well as to minimize overpowering odors on removal.

When placing the posterior pack, use a Foley catheter passed through the nares, with 10 to 15 mL water in the balloon and tension as needed, and anchor it securely; alternatively, place string packs in the posterior nasopharynx. When string ties are employed, *never* tie strings *around* the septum; tie them separately on a dental roll placed *between* the nares to avoid pressure on the nasal septum. The number and types of packs placed and the time of placement must be carefully documented in the patient's record. Posterior packs should be removed in 3 to 5 days.

An anterior nasal pack should be placed from the top to the bottom and left in place *no more than 1 to 2 days*. Do not start the pack on the floor of the nose, for it will obscure your vision. Place a finger on the tip of the nose to anchor the speculum and, with a bayonet forceps, take one strip of petroleum jelly (Vaseline) gauze—with antibiotic ointment applied—and place one loop to the back of the nostril. Use the speculum *under* the gauze to lift and pack it into place and keep feeding the material with a bayonet forceps, packing to the top of the space until it is filled. Tape the end of the packing at the external nares.

Nursing Intervention. The emergency nurse (EN) should be aware of risk factors; probably 20 percent of patients with bilateral posterior nasal packs and a history of cardiorespiratory disease may be significantly affected by progressive anoxia, which can precipitate heart attack. Be alert for increased carbon dioxide and decreased oxygen levels (manifested as confusion, tachycardia, restlessness, and even belligerence); administer high-flow oxygen by mask until directed otherwise.

Nursing Diagnoses. Appropriate nursing diagnoses for epistaxis would include:

- Actual or potential fluid volume deficit related to blood loss
- Anxiety related to hemorrhage and uncertainty of treatment
- Knowledge deficit related to cause of bleeding

Epistaxis Telephone Instructions. When patients call the ED about nosebleeds, the following instructions may be very helpful and fall within a sensible range of telephone advice:

1. Blow the nose gently to remove clots.
2. Apply pressure by pinching the nose as far back on the nostril as possible for a *full 5 minutes* by the clock.
3. Remove pressure.
4. If bleeding starts again, repeat steps 1, 2, and 3.

Most ENT (ear, nose, and throat) physicians will agree that probably 50 percent of patients with epistaxis can avoid going to the ED if this procedure is used. Instruct the patient with a nosebleed in this manner before discharge, so that the instructions can be followed at home should the bleeding start again.

ESSENTIAL EQUIPMENT FOR NASAL EMERGENCIES

The basic equipment necessary for the management of nasal emergencies includes the following items:

- Headlamp of a quality that will allow two free hands to work (Goode-Lite or Storz-Lampert are two good examples)

- Tray containing:
     Nasal speculums, one short and one long
     Frazier suction tip (small metal angulated tip with suction port)
     Bayonet forceps
     Petroleum jelly (Vaseline) gauze (0.5 × 36 in.) packs, applicators, cotton balls, sterile cotton pledgets
     Sterile medicine cup or basin
     Silver nitrate sticks (must be held firmly over bleeding point for 3 to 5 minutes; 2 minutes is adequate over a very small vein)
     Topical epinephrine
     Topical Xylocaine 4 percent
- Back-up tray containing:
     Assortment of sterile ENT instruments—pharyngeal mirrors, assorted speculums, forceps, suction tips
     Selection of posterior packs
     Electrocautery tips
- Electrocautery unit

■ COMMON THROAT PROBLEMS

THRUSH

Seen increasingly in EDs, oral candidiasis or thrush (also called oral moniliasisis), is a contagious infection caused by the yeast *Candida albicans,* with a variable incubation period. Thrush is common in newborn nursery settings, where the yeast has been spread from mother to child during the birth process and the infant's immune system is not yet fully activated. White, slightly raised patches, resembling milk curds, cover the membranes of the palate, tongue, gum, tonsils, and oropharynx and may extend into the respiratory and gastrointestinal tract, in severe cases. Denuding the white patches leaves painful bleeding surfaces on the membrane. Systemic factors predisposing to candidiasis are general debilitation (especially in the elderly), long-term antibiotic therapy, chemotherapy, diabetes mellitus, high-dose adrenal corticosteroids, and certain immune deficiencies such as acquired immunodeficiency syndrome (AIDS). Oral candidiasis persisting in children over 6 months of age, for a period of over 2 months, is considered one criterion for diagnosis

of human immunodeficiency virus (HIV) infection, and they should be evaluated further for other concurrent conditions.[5]

Oral clotrimazole lozenges and nystatin oral suspension are both effective for treatment of oral thrush, and should be given in addition to treatment aimed at ameliorating the underlying/predisposing cause of flourishing yeast. The EN should be aware of the contagious aspect of thrush and use scrupulous technique when caring for patients who have it; use concurrent disinfection or dispose of all contaminated objects.

PHARYNGITIS AND PHARYNGEAL ABSCESS

The sore throat tends to be relegated to a "garden-variety" category and frequently gets very little attention in the ED. The patient with an acute pharyngeal infection, however, is in great distress and pain, and may be having systemic reactions. The alert EN should examine the throat, palpate the cervical and sublingual glands, and possibly obtain a throat culture while preparing the patient for examination by the physician. Septic sore throat and pharyngeal abscess from acute streptococcal infection, diphtheria, Vincent's angina, infectious mononucleosis, and even pharyngeal gonorrhea are being seen more frequently. These patients are in real distress and need careful evaluation and immediate comprehensive management. Staphylococci, pneumococci, and *Haemophilus influenzae* are also causative agents; chronic pharyngitis and abscess formation can result from repeated irritation and recurrent infections.

Nursing Interventions

Analgesia and perhaps topical anesthesia, together with warm saline throat irrigation, may be provided as ordered.

Nursing Diagnoses

Appropriate nursing diagnoses include:

- Pain related to infection and the inflammatory process
- Infection related to bacterial invasion of tissues
- Knowledge deficit related to self-care

EPIGLOTTITIS

Very recently, a surprising increase has been noted in the numbers of epiglottitis cases seen in adults; one theory proposes a diminished resistance to the *H. influenzae* organism after generations of widespread ampicillin usage. These patients present with the classic symptoms of difficulty in swallowing, toxic appearance with high temperature, and a tendency to hold the head forward and very still; there is usually a history of a URTI several days prior. The typically swollen and "cherry red" epiglottis can readily cause a total airway obstruction if manipulated during an examination. Therefore, it is *essential* to have emergency airway management equipment on hand and in readiness before beginning any examination. If a lateral neck film for soft-tissue swelling is indicated, it should be done in the ED or with airway management personnel and equipment accompanying the patient to x-ray (see also pages 464–465).

PERITONSILLAR ABSCESS

What used to be called "quinsy" is a peritonsillar abscess that can result in a very sick and febrile patient. Following a bout of acute tonsillitis, peritonsillar tissue can become infected, with streptococcal abscess formation and pus evident on the tonsils. Sore throat, extreme pain on swallowing, muffled voice, fever, and even airway compromise are the signs and symptoms.

Nursing Interventions

Appropriate nursing interventions include:

- Close monitoring of vital signs (VS) and respiratory status
- Administration of oxygen if respiratory distress is present
- Initiation of intravenous lines for fluids and antibiotics as ordered
- Administration of medications as ordered
- Provision of warm saline gargle if tolerated
- Provision of an ice collar for comfort and pain relief

Nursing Diagnoses

Appropriate nursing diagnoses include:

- Potential ineffective airway clearance related to edematous tissue
- Pain related to infection and inability to swallow
- Infection related to unresolved tonsillitis

■ SUMMARY

The critically important acute senses of sight, sound, balance, and smell are all involved when dealing with EENT emergencies. Both trauma and infection can present potentially serious consequences if they are not handled knowledgeably and without delay.

A comfortable working knowledge of EENT procedures and the equipment necessary to have on hand for assessment and management is essential for ENs. If nothing else, further harm can be prevented while waiting for physicians to assume management and begin definitive care.

■ REFERENCES

1. Pfister RR. Chemical corneal burns. In: Olson RJ, ed. *Common Corneal Problems*. Boston, Ma: Little, Brown;1984:157–168.
2. Lubeck D, Greene JS. Corneal injuries. *Emerg Med Clin North Am*. 1988;6:73–94.
3. Chai TJ, Chai TC. Bactericidal activity of cerumen. *Antimicrob Agents Chemother*. 1980;18:638–641.
4. Stone M, Fulghum RS. Bacterial activity of wet cerumen. *Ann Otol Rhinol Laryngol*. 1984;93:183–186.
5. MMWR. 1994 revised classification system for human immune virus infections in children less than 13 years of age. *MMWR*. Sept. 30, 1994;43 (RR-12):6.
6. *Point of View*. Somerville, NJ: Ethicon, Inc. 1976.
7. Barber JM, Dillman PA. *Emergency Patient Care*. Reston, Va: Reston Publishing Co.; 1981.

■ BIBLIOGRAPHY

Anderson D, Cosgriff J. Epistaxis. *J Emerg Nurs*. 1976;2.
Barrett AS. Maxillofacial trauma. In: Fincke MK, Lanros NE, eds. *Emergency Nursing: A Comprehensive Review*. Rockville, Md: Aspen Publishers; 1986:196–212.
Boyd-Monk H. Examining the external eye, part 1. *Nursing 80*. May 1980;10(5).

Boyd-Monk H. Examining the external eye, part 2. *Nursing 80.* June 1980;10(6).

Cahill SB, Balskus M. *Intervention in Emergency Nursing: The First 60 Minutes.* Rockville, Md: Aspen Publishers; 1986.

Domine LM. Ear, nose and throat: infections and trauma. In: Fincke MK, Lanros NE, eds. *Emergency Nursing: A Comprehensive Review.* Rockville, Md: Aspen Publishers; 1986:351–366.

Eade GG. Emergency care of severe facial injuries. *Clin Plast Surg.* 1975;2:73.

Emergency Nurses Association. *Emergency Nursing Core Curriculum.* 4th ed. Philadelphia, Pa: WB Saunders; 1994.

Ingram NM. Trauma to the ear, nose, face, and neck. *J Emerg Nurs.* 1980;6(4):8–12.

Kelly CA. Ocular trauma. *J Emerg Nurs.* 1978;4(2): 23–28.

Kidd PS, Wagner KD. *High Acuity Nursing.* 2nd ed. Stamford, Conn: Appleton & Lange; 1996.

Knezevich-Brown BA. *Trauma Nursing Principles and Practice.* Stamford, Conn: Appleton & Lange; 1986.

Kremen RM. Eye emergencies. In: Fincke MK, Lanros NE, eds. *Emergency Nursing: A Comprehensive Review.* Rockville, Md: Aspen Publishers; 1986.

Lee B, Hansen E, Poppell M. Facial fractures take a special kind of nursing care. *Nursing 80.* Aug. 1980;10(8):42–46.

Marlowe FI. Otolaryngolic emergencies. In: Tintinalli JE, et al., eds. *Emergency Medicine: A Comprehensive Study Guide.* 2nd ed. New York, NY: McGraw-Hill;1988.

O'Boyle CM, Davis DK, Russo BA, et al. *Emergency Care: The First 24 Hours.* E. Norwalk, Conn: Appleton & Lange; 1985.

Stair T, ed. EENT and mouth emergencies. *Top Emerg Med.* 1984;6(3).

Turbiak TW. Ear trauma. *Emerg Med Clin North Am.* 1978;5:243.

Weimert TA. Common ENT emergencies part 1: the acute ear. *Emerg Med.* April 1992;134–148.

Weimert TA. Common ENT emergencies part 2: the acute nose and throat. *Emerg Med.* April 1992;26–46.

Weimert TA. Early diagnosis of acute laryngeal injuries. *Injury.* 1979;12:154.

■ REVIEW: EYE, EAR, NOSE, AND THROAT EMERGENCIES

1. Describe the recognition and treatment for various types of eye injuries, including foreign bodies, chemical burns, superficial injuries, penetrating and perforating injuries, and nontraumatic medical emergencies.

2. Describe the use of the Snellen eye chart in checking visual acuity.

3. Describe the way in which visual acuity is recorded in the patient record.

4. Explain the correct procedure for administering eye medication.

5. Describe the Morgan lens, its placement, and the rationale for its use.

6. Identify two true ocular emergencies, their signs/symptoms, and the indicated interventions.

7. Describe the correct method for effectively applying eye patches.

8. Identify the nasal area most frequently seen as the site of epistaxis.

9. Outline the management guidelines, treatment, and dangers of epistaxis.

10. List the equipment necessary for adequate management of epistaxis.

11. Identify the most common ear problems seen in the emergency department (ED) and the general management for each.

12. Describe the classic appearance of acute epiglottitis and the precautions to be taken *before* examination.

13. Describe the presenting appearance of a patient with peritonsillar abscess and outline appropriate nursing interventions.

Pulmonary and Respiratory Emergencies

22

This chapter provides an overview of the disease states that can lead to and culminate in respiratory failure. Basic concepts of ventilation and perfusion and factors affecting tissue oxygenation are presented and discussed. For each of the clinical situations, nursing assessment, appropriate nursing diagnoses, guidelines for nursing intervention, and drug hazards to be considered are all fully described.

■ BASIC CONCEPTS

Respiratory failure is due to hypoxemia, hypercapnia, or a combination of both. The normal partial pressure of arterial oxygen (PaO_2) for a given patient depends on patient age, the altitude of the environment, and the fraction of oxygen in the inspired air. Generally, a PaO_2 of 80 to 90 mm Hg is considered normal breathing on room air. Respiratory failure occurs when the lungs fail to provide adequate oxygenation or ventilation for the blood. Oxygenation failure exists when the PaO_2 is less than 60 mm Hg, even though there is an increase in the fraction of inspired gas (FIO_2) to 0.50 or higher. Ventilatory failure denotes inadequate ventilation between the lungs and the atmosphere, resulting in the elevation of CO_2 in the blood to a level greater than 45 mm Hg, with a partial pressure of carbon dioxide ($PaCO_2$) greater than 50 mm Hg.[1] Because the lungs are a simple, symmetrical unit dealing with the exchange of blood and gases and the airway is the means of conducting atmospheric gases into those lungs, it follows that respi-

ratory failure is a disease state caused by either (1) impaired ventilation (transportation of atmospheric gases to the alveoli) or (2) impaired diffusion and gas exchange at the alveolar or cellular level.

The degree of alveolar ventilation for clinical purposes is reflected by the level of a $PaCO_2$. Some basic significant factors to remember are:

- A normal $PaCO_2$ indicates effectiveness of alveolar ventilation;
- An increased $PaCO_2$ means hypoventilation is occurring;
- A decreased $PaCO_2$ means hyperventilation is occurring.

There are other factors that affect tissue oxygenation that must be taken into consideration, including cardiac output, the hemoglobin (Hgb) concentration of the blood, pH, and temperature.

■ NURSING ASSESSMENT AND INTERVENTION

A careful nursing assessment of the patient's respiratory pattern is apt to pick up early signs of respiratory failure even before arterial blood gases (ABGs) are obtained and evaluated. Readily observable signs include labored respirations with use of accessory muscles (scalene, sternocleidomastoid, intercostals), a pulse rate at rest of over 120 bpm (without evidence of trauma or occult bleeding), a respiratory rate of over 30 breaths per minute and irregularity in respiratory pattern. The patient with impending respiratory failure will not be inclined to talk; rather, stern apprehension will be characteristic. Irritability, confusion, and even belligerence can be cardinal signs of hypoxia.

Immediate nursing intervention begins with giving quiet, gentle reassurance, placing the patient in a semi-Fowler's or Fowler's position for comfort, using pillow props under both of the patient's arms; and administering oxygen appropriate for the respiratory condition. Do not delay the administration of oxygen in order to obtain ABG samples on room air. An intravenous line should be promptly established in anticipation that drug therapy may be indicated.

The causes of impaired ventilation can be categorized as acute airway obstruction, chronic airway obstruction, and restrictive defects.

■ ACUTE AIRWAY OBSTRUCTION

Acute obstruction of the airway (by the tongue, decreased swallowing reflexes, epiglottitis, croup, laryngeal edema, or foreign bodies) is commonly seen in children, and assessment for respiratory embarrassment must be conducted early and carefully.

The acutely ill child in a toxic state from severe respiratory infection such as croup or epiglottitis may progressively and quietly hypoventilate from the degree of soft-tissue obstruction as well as fatigue and may be in serious and too often irreversible straits unless carefully and continually monitored for rate and quality of respirations. An infant exhibiting grunting respirations and flaring nostrils, using accessory muscles of respiration and having a bulging abdomen on expiration, is in serious respiratory trouble.

FOREIGN BODIES

The healthy child suffering an airway obstruction from the aspiration of a common foreign body, such as beans, toys, peanuts, or any other item small enough to find its way into the trachea or bronchi, will probably have noisy respirations (though not necessarily) and will be anxious and probably coughing, depending on where the foreign body lodges. Sometimes these children can be all but asymptomatic, and the diagnosis is confirmed only by auscultation and x-ray. A foreign

body lodged deeply and causing serious obstruction may result in heavy coughing, retching, struggling, laryngospasm, and even bronchospasm. By this point, the child will be extremely cyanotic; foreign bodies can be a serious management problem and rarely allow for wasted time or movement.

Nursing Intervention

Treatment varies with the diagnosis. Frequently, the Heimlich maneuver is considered an effective means of dealing with upper airway obstruction. In small children, however, the maneuver requires modification by holding the child over either your arm or hand and delivering a sharp blow between the shoulder blades in order to "pop" the object out of position by the forceful expulsion of a sudden gust of air from the lungs. Bronchoscopy in the operating room (OR) is sometimes necessary; on rare occasions, pneumonotomy is required.

Many times, unknown foreign-body aspirations occur in small children; signs of bronchial irritation, with occasional mild hacking, may be present. Presence of a foreign body can be confirmed with chest x-rays, both inspiratory and expiratory. Small aspirated objects often lodge in the right mainstem bronchus and cause air to flow into the right lung more slowly than the left; the mediastinum will shift away from the foreign body on expiration. Once location of the object is known, appropriate postural drainage can be initiated for gravitational assistance; the child lies on the side opposite the obstructed lung. Cupped-hand percussion over the upper scapula on the involved side may assist significantly, as the child is quietly encouraged, if possible, to breathe very gently and to cough frequently once the object is dislodged. This conservative approach will often obviate the need for bronchoscopy or even pneumonotomy in the OR.

CROUP

Croup (laryngotracheobronchitis) is an upper airway infection usually seen in small children between the ages of 6 months and 4 years. This viral infection causes inflammation and edema in the subglottic area with a characteristic "seal bark" type of cough (see Chapter 29).

Epiglottitis

Epiglottitis is a life-threatening problem that is generally confined to children between the ages of

3 and 7 years, but it can also occur in adults. It fulminates rapidly and must always be considered an eventuality in patients presenting with high temperatures; a toxic, anxious appearance; and respiratory difficulty. Sudden obstruction of the adult airway due to epiglottitis is just as acute a problem, and greater attention is now being focused on prompt recognition and management of adult epiglottitis in the emergency department (ED). The increasing rate of incidence in recent years is thought to be due to a diminished resistance to the *Hemophilus influenzae* organism after a generation of widespread ampicillin use. It can also be caused by *Staphylococcus, Streptococcus,* and occasionally parainfluenza virus, all more commonly isolated from the blood than from the epiglottis.

The picture is classic: sudden onset, progressive difficulty in swallowing, toxic appearance and high temperature, and a tendency to hold the head forward and very still, all coupled with the usual history of upper respiratory tract infection (URTI) several days prior. As edema progresses, breathing becomes stridorous and difficult, the patient favors an upright posture, and the voice is muffled. Since the individual cannot swallow secretions, drooling is evident. In severe cases, there may even be cyanosis or sternal retractions.

The typically swollen and "cherry red" epiglottis can readily cause a total airway obstruction if manipulated during an examination. For that reason, many ED physicians rely on a lateral neck film to show measurable soft-tissue swelling in patients whose condition engenders a high index of suspicion for epiglottitis before they put any instruments into the patient's throat. Emergency airway management equipment should be located near the patient at all times, in readiness for airway obstruction. X-rays should be taken in the ED for maximum patient safety; if this is not possible, airway management personnel and equipment must accompany the patient to the x-ray department.

See Chapter 29 for a complete discussion of epiglottitis in children.

■ SMOKE INHALATION INJURIES

When a burn victim has associated inhalation injury, the morbidity and mortality data are greatly increased. Firefighters and industrial workers exposed to products of combustion in closed spaces, along with thermal injuries, account for many of the inhalation injuries seen by emergency personnel. The upper airway is always at risk of inhalation injury from toxic fumes, superheated gases, and irritating substances, both dry and moist. Facial burns, singed nasal hair, and carbonaceous deposits in the airway and sputum are hallmarks of inhalation injury, but the absence of these does not rule out inhalation injury. Factors such as blistering, edema, accumulation of thick saliva, and glottic closure can lead to partial or complete airway obstruction. The emergency nurse (EN) should recognize that stridor, hoarseness, difficulty speaking, and chest retractions point to upper airway injury. Laryngospasm and sloughing of tissue may be present with severe exposures. Since vascular leakage is likely due to the associated high-volume fluid resuscitation of burns, the condition will progressively worsen as the resuscitation progresses.

The lower airway becomes involved when exposure to high concentrations of toxic fumes or irritating substances is prolonged. Tracheobronchitis, bronchospasm, bronchorrhea, and pulmonary edema can occur if irritation has extended deep into the tracheobronchial structures. Bronchial blood flow will intensify, and the edema in the airways and alveolar tissue may be aggravated. Other problems include surfactant dysfunction, increased lung water, decreased lung compliance, increased airway resistance, and increased pulmonary vascular resistance leading to V/Q (ventilation–perfusion) mismatching and an increase in physiological dead space, which decreases the PaO_2, increases the alveolar-to-arterial oxygen pressure $[P(A-a)O_2]$, and increases the necessary minute ventilation to normalize the $PaCO_2$. The central nervous system (CNS) and myocardium respond to reductions in oxygen transportation and its use at the cellular level; oxygen cannot exit readily from the Hgb, and the oxyhemoglobin dissociation curve shifts to the left. The anemia and hypoxia persist despite favorable plasma PaO_2. Cerebral edema occurs from hypotension and the impaired oxygen transportation. In some cases, there is cell death due to the presence of certain toxins.[2]

If the patient arrives in an unconscious state, there is a high likelihood of carbon monoxide and hydrogen cyanide poisoning. The EN must be able to promptly recognize the classic indices of these two life-threatening inhalation-related poisonings.

CARBON MONOXIDE

Carbon monoxide (CO) poisoning occurs when individuals breathe the products of incomplete carbon combustion. Examples of where such fumes may be present are any area where there is automobile exhaust and confined areas where gas-flame heating units and charcoal grills are used. Since CO has a 200-fold greater affinity for Hgb than oxygen, it will preferentially bind, thus limiting oxygen availability. Furthermore, recent studies indicate that CO may also bind to myoglobin and cytochrome oxidase, thus interfering with intracellular respiration.[3] CO is readily taken up by a fetus because the fetal Hgb has even more affinity for CO than that of the typical child or adult,[4] so pregnant patients and their unborn are at significant risk even in the presence of low levels of exposure.

Treatment must be based on presenting signs and symptoms and the presence of CO in the blood. The patient with CO poisoning cannot be properly evaluated with a pulse oximeter, because oxyhemoglobin and carboxyhemoglobin (COHB) have similar light absorption spectra. The documented pulse oximetry reading will be falsely elevated in CO poisoning.[2] ABGs are also unreliable because the P_{O_2} is a measurement of the partial pressure of oxygen in millimeters of mercury (mm Hg), *not* of the oxygen saturation of hemoglobin.[3] Carboxyhemoglobin spectrophotometry is the standard measurement for CO poisoning. CO breath analyzers have also been shown to be reliable.[2]

The clinical manifestations of CO poisoning are obscure until the blood level of CO reaches 20 to 40 percent. Up to that point, only exercise-induced angina (in susceptible individuals), and mild headache occur. However, at higher blood levels, these symptoms worsen and vomiting, muscular weakness, visual disturbances, dizziness, and impaired judgment are noted. Tachypnea, tachycardia, seizures, syncope, and irregular breathing follow when levels reach 40 to 60 percent. Above 60 percent, shock, coma, apnea, and death occur. *The classic "cherry-red skin" sign of CO poisoning is an unreliable determinant of this life-threatening condition.*

Patients with indices of CO inhalation require oxygen administration at 100 percent flow rates. The half-life of carboxyhemoglobin is 3 to 5 hours in room air; on oxygen, it is 30 to 80 minutes. Moderate acidosis is not aggressively treated because hydrogen ions shift the Hgb dissociation curve to the right, thus improving oxygen delivery to tissues. Hyperbaric therapy is often used in severe cases, but there are no controlled studies that confirm its superiority to regular modes of oxygen therapy. Considerations for its use include coma, cardiovascular involvement, pregnancy, and carboxyhemoglobin levels of over 40 percent.[3]

CYANIDE POISONING

Cyanide is extensively used in industrial and agricultural applications and is released into the air by the burning of wool, silk, nylon, and polyurethanes. It occurs naturally in some plants and in fruit pits. Hydrogen cyanide gas is used in suicide and in legal executions (capital punishment) and has been associated with mass executions (e.g., the Nazi extermination camps of World War II, the 1978 Jonestown, Guyana, massacre). Since cyanide can be inhaled, injected, ingested, or absorbed through intact skin and mucous membranes, it is of great concern in the face of chemical warfare and terrorist tactics. Some drugs (e.g., sodium nitroprusside) also contain cyanide that is liberated during metabolism. Cyanide binds to the ferric ion and interrupts electron transportation, which results in the cessation of pyruvate metabolization in the Krebs cycle. Metabolic acidosis follows.

Signs and symptoms in the patient with cyanide poisoning are nonspecific and include anxiety, agitation, flushing, tachycardia, tachypnea, and dizziness, followed quickly by seizures, metabolic acidosis, coma, and death. The odor of bitter almonds is classically associated with cyanide poisoning, but only about 65 percent of all health care professionals can detect this smell.[3]

Treatment includes ventilatory support with supplemental oxygen and prompt use of amyl nitrite, sodium nitrite, and sodium thiosulfate, contained in the "cyanide kit" that ought to be *readily available in the ED*. If it must be obtained from the hospital pharmacy (as might be the case during the night or on weekends), delays could be devastating.

Emergency personnel should wear protective clothes when dealing with suspected cyanide poisoning cases since skin, vomitus, and other body fluids can contain the agent.

HYDROGEN SULFIDE

Hydrogen sulfide is also a cellular asphyxiant, and although carboxyhemoglobin from CO inhalation and cyanide are classic examples, hydrogen sulfide can also produce rapid morbidity and death, depending on the concentration and duration of exposure. Like cyanide, hydrogen sulfide produces cytotoxic anoxia by binding with ferric iron in cytochrome oxidase. It is a natural product in nature, generated by putrefaction of sewage and animal waste, and it has a characteristic rotten-egg odor. A high concentration of hydrogen sulfide accumulating in a small, closed space can be rapidly deadly. There are multiple incidents involving attempts to fix clogged toilet drains by removing the toilet and pouring acid down the open hole onto raw sewage in the trap, resulting in the unwitting inhalation of the deadly hydrogen sulfide fumes that bubble up. Too frequently, the unsuspecting rescuer is also a victim of the fumes.

Presenting signs and symptoms include several ocular phenomena, such as blepharospasm, pain, conjunctival injection, and blurred, iridescent vision. Confusion, dyspnea, stupor, cyanosis, coma, and respiratory arrest are seen in severe cases.[4]

Both hydrogen sulfide and cyanide have the same mechanism of action, and both respond to almost the same treatment. The immediate administration of the amyl nitrite and sodium nitrite contained in the Lilly cyanide kit (Eli Lilly Co, Indianapolis) will rapidly reverse the profound metabolic acidosis of the cytotoxic anoxia caused by hydrogen sulfide. (Sodium thiosulfate should not be administered, however.[4]) Beyond reversal of the metabolic acidosis, careful monitoring and oxygen administration are indicated.

◼ PNEUMONIA

Pneumonia, an acute inflammatory process within the lung parenchyma, is the fifth leading cause of death in the United States. The patient with pneumonia usually comes to the ED with serious respiratory problems and can present a real challenge to nursing assessment and intervention, since pneumonia is largely an opportunistic disease and most frequently strikes the person already at high risk with other disease processes. It is recognized that the severity of the pneumonia is directly related to preexisting (usually noninfectious) diseases.

BACTERIAL

Bacterial pneumonias frequently follow an URTI, and patients present with fever and a productive cough with yellow, green, or rusty sputum. Occasionally, they will have fever and shaking chills. Sharp, pleuritic pain and dyspnea are hallmarks. *Pneumococcus* accounts for about 75 percent of these infections.[5]

Streptococcus (group A β-hemolytic) pneumonia is seen in about 5 percent of the bacterial pneumonias. Chest pain, cough with purulent sputum, tachycardia, tachypnea, and fever are all signs and have usually been preceded by a viral infection or pharyngitis.

S. aureus causes extreme illness and should always be considered in high-risk patients with respiratory distress (immunosuppressed, postinfluenza, elderly, narcotic abusers). A cough of mixed blood and pus produces a thick creamy sputum. Bacteremia and vascular collapse are frequent; the overall mortality rate may range from 15 to 50 percent, with a high rate of serious complications such as empyema, lung abscesses, pericarditis, and glomerulonephritis.

H. influenzae is highly virulent, causes acute suppurative inflammation of lung tissue, and is associated with extrapulmonary complications, including meningitis and endocarditis. Infected sputum droplets with upper respiratory colonization is thought to be the most likely pathogenesis; this pneumonia tends to follow viral infections, frequently affecting patients with chronic obstructive pulmonary disease (COPD) and alcoholism.

Klebsiella, Pseudomonas aeruginosa, and *Escherichia coli* are organisms causing the most frequently seen gram-negative pneumonias in middle-aged and older patients, predominantly men, and are associated with alcoholism, diabetes, and cancer. These pneumonias are frequently hospital-acquired; preexisting lung disease will contribute to respiratory failure. Thick, tenacious sputum, sometimes grossly bloody, may pose a problem in airway maintenance.

Mycoplasma pneumonia (one of the atypical pneumonias) is common in young adults, causing severe myalgias and arthralgias, a persistent cough, and occasionally an associated rash whose eruptions are central livid areas surrounded by a pale pink zone.

Legionella pneumophilia pneumonia, known as Legionnaire's disease, is a more severe primary atypical pneumonia with abrupt onset and a short prodrome. Patients almost always display confusion; early symptoms are nonspecific with chills, fever, dry cough, and malaise. Abdominal pain, diarrhea, and hematuria associated with tubular necrosis are often present.

Confirmation of bacterial pneumonia is based on clinical assessment that includes pulmonary consolidation findings on chest films, the presence of leukocytosis, and a sputum culture and Gram stain that demonstrate the organism. If the patient is unable to produce a suitable specimen by expectoration, chest physical therapy or tracheal stimulation with a heated nebulizer may be used to induce sputum. Use of a mucus trap is considered ideal because it minimizes the risk of oropharyngeal organism contamination. The choice of an initial antibiotic is dependent upon the suspected organism and the patient's underlying condition. ED management will include supplemental oxygenation, hydration, and completion of diagnostic tests.

VIRAL

Viral pneumonias are caused primarily by inhalation of infected sputum droplets. Viral pneumonias demonstrate a wide spectrum of involvement, which in severe cases resembles the adult respiratory distress syndrome (ARDS), with mechanical changes in small airways and alveolar collapse. Most common causative agents are the influenza and parainfluenza groups, varicella-zoster virus group, and cytomegalovirus. Following a typical influenza infection, pneumonia develops 12 to 36 hours after the onset of fever, myalgias, and headache. Dyspnea, chest pain, and cyanosis rapidly develop; together with hypoxia in the presence of a "viral illness," these are considered ominous signs. Sputum production is characteristically scant in viral pneumonias, and findings on pulmonary examination may be unremarkable.

PROTOZOAN

Pneumocystis carinii pneumonia will be seen in greater numbers in EDs as the number of patients with acquired immunodeficiency syndrome (AIDS) rapidly increases.[6] This opportunistic protozoan infection will result in severe respiratory problems for the AIDS patient, with fever, cough, shortness of breath, and a white, foamy sputum. The $P(A-a)O_2$ may be less than 40 mm Hg. Findings on chest films often are normal. Diarrhea is present in 3 of 4 patients with *P. carinii*.[7] It is often the precipitating factor for hospital admission and accounts for a significant mortality rate, owing to hypoxia and sepsis. Mechanical ventilation is ordinarily required to treat this pneumonia, and vasopressors may be used in some cases to treat the associated hypotension.

ASPIRATION

Pneumonia (frequently iatrogenic) can result from aspiration of organisms present in the mouth and hypopharynx, blood, water, or vomitus. Severity and extent of the pneumonia will depend on a combination of three factors: (1) the pH of the aspirated stomach contents, (2) the presence in the aspirate of particulate matter that plugs the bronchi, and (3) the overgrowth of a mixture of aerobic and anaerobic bacteria drawn from the mouth during the process of aspiration. Signs and symptoms of aspiration include vomitus in the oropharynx, cyanosis, wheezing, coughing, hypoxemia, pulmonary edema, and hypotension. Findings on early chest films may be normal. Steroids and antibiotics are no longer routinely used prophylactically; such therapies are reserved for secondary pneumonias. Interventions may include oxygen therapy, mechanical ventilation, and bronchoscopy to remove large particles from the airway.

NURSING ASSESSMENTS

A carefully directed history is important in initial assessment of the patient with pneumonia, since so many underlying factors, such as prior debilitating illness and poor living conditions, contribute to the severity of the illness. The EN should question medical history, present medical status, and medications (especially antibiotics and steroids). A smoking history is crucial and should be recorded as "number of pack years" (multiply the number of packs smoked per day by the number of years the patient has smoked); elapsed years since quitting smoking should also be noted. Alcohol consumption, occupation, recent travel, and family history should all be covered by specific questions, depending on the symptoms. The history should include duration of symptoms and whether the onset was sudden or gradual. Was the onset preceded by an URTI? Is the cough productive? Is there sputum, and what are its characteristics (i.e., color, presence of blood, amount)? Has there been fever, chills, shortness of breath, or weight loss preceding this presentation? Advanced age, debilitation, COPD, alcoholism, and immunosuppression are all significant risk factors to be considered in the management of pneumonia.

Respiratory distress is usually evident with these patients; nursing steps include provision of quiet reassurance, administration of supplemental oxygen for significant or even suspected hypoxia ($PO_2 < 60$ mm Hg), and initiation of an intravenous line for fluid replacement if needed. Antipyretics may be ordered for significant temperature elevation; antibiotics are frequently administered but should be withheld until blood or sputum specimens have been obtained.

■ CHRONIC AIRWAY OBSTRUCTION

Emphysema, chronic bronchitis, and chronic asthma all produce chronic airway obstruction. Although the etiologies differ, the essential clinical approach to relief for these patients is similar as it relates to airway management and the use of oxygen and ventilatory support.

EMPHYSEMA

Emphysema is frequently referred to as COPD or chronic obstructive lung disease (COLD). It is a generalized obstructive condition of the lungs that produces varying degrees of dyspnea and disability owing to hyperinflation of the lungs with a loss of elasticity in the alveoli. The alveoli remain overdis-

tended with air that cannot be expelled, and this can produce acute respiratory embarrassment on exertion; the patient is apprehensive and short of breath and may exhibit tachycardia and even cyanosis.

For these patients, breathing is generally characterized by the use of the accessory muscles of respiration, by a characteristic forward-leaning position, and by prolonged expiration through pursed lips, with occasional audible wheezes and rales. ABGs generally show a lowered pH with hypoxemia and hypercapnia.

CHRONIC BRONCHITIS

Chronic bronchitis is another disease that is referred to as COPD and is the long-standing disease of the tracheobronchial tree. It is frequently associated with emphysema. Bronchitis is characterized by chronic inflammation and atrophic changes in the mucous membranes and deeper bronchial structures. It is also frequently associated with pulmonary fibrosis and other COPD and is not a reversible airway obstruction, because degenerative changes have taken place. The resulting bronchial rigidity often restricts normal ventilation and becomes a factor in the patient's ventilatory insufficiency and a prominent cause of dyspnea. There is usually a chronic cough with expectoration, becoming more troublesome during the winter months. Chronic bronchitis is characteristically afebrile, and the physical signs are few, other than those of COPD. When the need for oxygen is indicated, it should be administered at a low-flow rate of 2 to 3 L/min.

ASTHMA

A reversible obstructive airway disease, asthma is a disease of unknown etiology until proved otherwise and is characterized by spasm and increased secretion of the bronchial tree. Asthma can be intrinsic (no evidence of allergen) or extrinsic (associated with an allergen). Some factors responsible for precipitating asthmatic attacks are cold air, strong odors, infections (especially viral), and emotional factors (after asthma is an established entity). The acute asthmatic attack exhibits characteristic signs of labored respiration, particularly in the expiratory phase, frequently associated with audible wheezing. On auscultation, the expiratory phase, and occasionally the inspiratory phase, is accompanied by rales and wheezes, with the typically prolonged expiratory phase. Unless there is an URTI present as well, the vital signs (VS), white blood cell (WBC) count, and chest x-ray findings will all be within normal limits. If the asthma is of the allergic type, there may be an eosinophilia present in the differential count. The patient may be severely dyspneic, apprehensive, and even diaphoretic without exhibiting central cyanosis initially, but cyanosis will develop shortly unless the obstruction is eased and finally reversed. Most patients with recognized asthma have their own medication regimen and know what works best for them; they rarely present to the ED unless their problem is complicated by an URTI or their asthma has not responded effectively to their medications. When this occurs, alveolar collapse may develop secondary to dehydration following prolonged labored respiration, with formation of mucus plugs in the small airways, unless the patient is managed properly and without delay.

Severe attacks that must be managed promptly are marked with:

- Use of accessory muscles at rest
- Parodoxical pulse
- Peak flow of less 100 L/min
- Both inspiratory and expiratory wheezing or *no wheezing (indicating no movement of air)*
- Deterioration in sensorium
- Inability or unwillingness to talk

Emergency Interventions

The patient must be triaged promptly and placed on a stretcher, and supplemental oxygen should be immediately given. An intravenous line should be initiated for emergency drug therapy and a cardiac monitor and pulse oximeter should be placed to evaluate the patient's overall condition and to provide information that will serve as a guide for further clinical management.

An overbed table is useful to permit the patient to lean forward and brace his or her hands or elbows to assist in creating a mechanical advantage for the accessory muscles to assist breathing. A chest x-ray is promptly obtained to detect underlying conditions (e.g., pneumonia, atelectasis, pneumothorax) and to identify the characteristic hyperinflation of lungs associated with asthma.

Peak flow meter use: An initial peak flow reading should be obtained as a guide to therapy if the patient can perform the forced expiratory test. In some severe and advanced cases, use of the peak flow meter in the initial period within the ED is not practical, owing to the patient's severe respiratory distress. When instructing patients in the use of the peak flow meter, tell them to take as deep a breath as possible and, with lips closed tightly around the mouthpiece, to blow as hard and fast as possible (i.e., a "hard puff"). Two or more trials may be required to ensure a meaningful reading. When using a hand-held unit, ensure that the patient's fingers are not obstructing the marker and that it returns to baseline after every trial. A peak flow of < 100 L/min indicates severe obstruction.[1]

The initial therapy should be directed toward improving oxygenation and bronchodilation and decreasing airway inflammation. The early use of inhaled β-agonist bronchodilators is imperative. Although the metered-dose inhaler may be used for patient self-administration, these agents may also be delivered in the ED by an aerosol, using a small-volume nebulizer. Since metered-dose inhalers are frequently used by the patient at home, the EN should ensure that the patient understands the proper use of these devices. Instructions should include the following important points:

1. Shake the canister for 30 seconds to mix the drug and the propellant.
2. Clear the nose and throat before using the unit.
3. Hold the canister away from the mouth before using it and inhale through the nose and exhale gently through the mouth.
4. While holding the unit about 1.5 in. from the open mouth, inhale through the mouth while delivering the drug (these two actions must be simultaneous). (The open-mouth approach allows twice as much drug to reach the respiratory tract than the closed-mouth approach).[8]
5. Close the mouth and hold the breath for a count of 10 and then exhale through pursed lips.
6. Wait 2 to 5 minutes before delivering the second or third doses of the drug (Fig. 22–1).

Figure 22–1. How to use a metered-dose inhaler. Patients should be instructed to 1) hold the canister about 1½ inches from the mouth, 2) inhale and simultaneously depress the canister to deliver the medication, and 3) close mouth and hold breath for a count of 10 before exhaling through pursed lips.

Updrafts or aerosolized medications: These may be given by the EN or respiratory therapist. Ordinarily, the medications are diluted in normal saline solution (NSS)—usually 1:5—and given intermittently or continuously to the patient in a unit driven by compressed air or oxygen, from a wall outlet. It is imperative to observe the patient carefully to ensure that the medication is being delivered into the airways and not onto the patient's face. In the case of severe obstruction to airflow, this sometimes occurs. Occasionally, subcutaneous or intravenous delivery of epinephrine or other agents may be required until the airways are less obstructed. The EN must observe the patient carefully throughout the procedure, monitoring heart rate and other VS, because these drugs have significant impacts on the cardiovascular system.

Meanwhile, a theophylline level is drawn, and intravenous theophylline may be given if the attack is severe. Steroids are often added to the treatment plan in the acute phase to control inflammatory reactions within the airway. Occasionally, inhaled atropine may be indicated when β-agonist bronchodilators are not effective. Sedatives should not be given, because they may predispose to ventilatory failure. Inhaled corticosteroids, Mucomyst, cromolyn sodium, and dense aerosols may heighten bronchospasm because they can irritate the airway; they are not typically used in the emergency setting.[9] Hydration, by oral or intravenous routes, is imperative to enhance the expectoration of secretions. If the $PaCO_2$ continues to rise, if the peak flow falls, or abdominal paradox is present, intubation and mechanical ventilation are in order. Confirmation of respiratory failure is hypoxemia, despite high FIO_2, respiratory acidemia (pH < 7.25), and central cyanosis. Without mechanical ventilation, pulse and respiratory effort will fail and cardiopulmonary arrest is inevitable. *Status asthmaticus* is the term used to describe the state of bronchial asthma when standard treatment fails and the attack is prolonged.

NURSING INTERVENTION

It is important to remember that a patient with chronic respiratory obstruction may be severely hypoxemic without necessarily being cyanotic and will require humidified *low-flow* oxygen at 2 to 3 L/min to prevent depression of the respiratory drive. CO narcosis can be induced by lack of respiratory drive and is noted by a flushed face, flaccidity or twitching of the extremities, mental confusion, and hypotension. If the patient cannot ventilate sufficiently to supply baseline needs, assisted breathing by a bag-valve-mask unit or mechanical ventilator may be required.

■ IMPAIRED DIFFUSION AND GAS EXCHANGE

Knowledge of alveolar oxygen tension (PAO_2) is fundamental to adequate clinical appraisal of ventilatory status and the recognition of impaired diffusion and gas exchange. For any given PAO_2, there is a corresponding expected PaO_2 that is only slightly lower than the alveolar level in normal subjects. The difference between the PAO_2 and the PaO_2 is called the A–a gradient and is normally about 30 mm Hg at high PO_2 and 10 mm Hg at low PO_2. If the $P(A–a)O_2$ is substantially larger, the presence of an intrapulmonary process that interferes with gas exchange, such as shunt, diffusion disturbance, or a V/Q imbalance, is indicated.

By contrast, failure to find an increased $P(A–a)O_2$ in the presence of hypercapnia indicates hypoventilation caused by extrapulmonary factors, such as narcosis, muscle weakness, or paralysis. The patient is hypoxemic while breathing room air, but this results only from the hypoventilation.

PULMONARY EDEMA

Pulmonary edema is usually of cardiac origin, with acute left ventricular failure, but it may be of noncardiogenic origin, with damage to pulmonary capillary tensions from chemical irritation of fumes, smoke, radiation, nitrogen oxides, particulate matter, or heroin overdose. Whatever the cause, there is an increased permeability of the alveolar–capillary membrane, with seepage of plasma from the capillaries of the lung bed into the alveoli. This directly results in a compromised gas exchange with varying degrees of hypoxemia; later, hypercapnia develops, with dyspnea; tachycardia; apprehension; hemoptysis (there may be copious, frothy, blood-tinged sputum); distended neck veins; tender liver; cool, sweaty extremities;

cyanosis; orthopnea; paroxysmal nocturnal dyspnea (PND); and loud, gurgling rales.

Significant reduction or loss of surfactant production capability from inhalation of toxic substances will gradually result in ARDS; 12 to 24 hours after the inhalation incident, the patient may develop dyspnea, cough, and then edema with rales, wheezes, and rhonchi throughout the lung fields. There is high morbidity and significant mortality associated with the severe V/Q mismatches that result.

Nursing Intervention

The patient with noncardiogenic pulmonary edema caused by an alveolar irritant requires only two things: (1) as much oxygen as possible—preferably 100 percent, by nonrebreathing mask—along with whatever ventilatory support is necessary, and (2) positive end-expiratory pressure (PEEP). The aim is to provide a mechanism for keeping the gradually collapsing alveoli and small bronchioles open in the hope that the patient's lungs will shortly recover the ability to make surfactant. The only emergency drugs appropriate for prehospital administration are steroids, and then only if the patient has a very long haul ahead before reaching a facility that can provide definitive care. See pages 380–382 for interventions for cardiogenic pulmonary edema.

The patient with pulmonary edema will be extremely apprehensive and anxious, so the EN should stay close by and have a confident, reinforcing attitude to help alleviate the anxiety as much as possible.

NEAR DROWNING

Drowning can occur from trauma (e.g., accidents that create unconsciousness or paralysis), exhaustion, or hypothermia, or from the effects of drugs and alcohol. Suicide attempts, heart attacks, seizures, and hyperventilation are also associated with drowning. It should also be recognized that many good swimmers hyperventilate to blow off carbon dioxide and enrich their body with oxygen so they can stay under the water a long time; since the presence of carbon dioxide is the normal stimulus for breathing but has been blown off by hyperventilating, the breathing drive is lowered. The swimmer becomes hypoxic and finally loses consciousness.

When a person in water realizes that he or she cannot make it to safety, a struggle begins to stay afloat and to breathe, and panic ensues. At this point, as the victim bobs up and down, water may be swallowed and aspirated into the lungs. Water may also be inhaled into the trachea, creating laryngospasm. Hypoxia and unconsciousness follow. On occasion, the laryngospasm prevents further entry of air and water into the lungs and the stomach, thus limiting the massive pulmonary injury that is related to large amounts of water entering the lungs.

The term *near drowning* refers to those individuals who have been successfully resuscitated and survive at least 24 hours. It should be recalled that many of these individuals, despite aggressive on-scene and ED care, will succumb to renal failure, sepsis, ARDS, or brain death. Drowning involves a neurological impairment from hypoxia and ischemia, a pulmonary insult, hemodynamic and electrolyte aberrations, and on occasion, sequelae from associated trauma such as cervical spine or head injury. This discussion focuses on the management of the pulmonary aspect of drowning.

Emergency Management

The outcomes of drowning may be predicted by the Glasgow Coma Scale (see Table 3–1). Victims of near drowning with an initial GCS score of 4 or less have an 80 percent chance of dying or suffering permanent neurological sequelae. Patients with a GCS score of 6 or better have a very low risk of permanent neurological sequelae or death.[10]

Even if the patient arrives awake and alert, all victims of near drowning are admitted for observation and prophylactic therapy to prevent complications associated with the pulmonary and neurological insults. Despite their apparent good condition, oxygen should be given while x-rays are obtained and blood study results are being evaluated. Threats that may become evident during the initial hours after injury are hypoxemia, increases in intracranial pressure (ICP), and toxicity from alcohol or drugs associated with the event.

Upon the victim's arrival at the ED, basic and advanced life-support measures will still be in progress in many cases. The unresponsive patient should be promptly intubated and baseline ABGs should be drawn. In past decades, there has been considerable discussion about the differences between managing fresh- and salt-water drownings; however, although there may be slight variations in physiological response at the pulmonary level, empirical treatment is the same. Intrapulmonary shunting often exceeds 70 percent of the cardiac output, so PEEP is used to improve V/Q ratios.[10] Some patients can tolerate continuous positive airway pressure (CPAP). Bronchospasm is treated with administration of an aerosolized bronchodilating agent. Steroids and prophylactic antibiotic therapies are no longer routinely used in these cases.

Hypothermia that accompanies near drowning should be managed both on scene and later in the ED (see Chapter 19).

PULMONARY EMBOLUS

Pulmonary embolus (obliterative pulmonary vascular disease) can be caused by thromboembolism of blood, fat, bone marrow, or amniotic fluid in the pulmonary artery. Patients who have acute pulmonary edema due to pulmonary thromboemboli will usually have some predisposing causes that can be identified. Thrombosis of the leg veins, use of oral contraceptives, long-bone fractures, and prolonged immobilization (frequently following trauma) are most often the cause. The patient presenting with respiratory distress, pleuritic pain, and blood-tinged sputum of sudden onset should be regarded with a high degree of suspicion and treated as possibly having a pulmonary embolus until proven otherwise. The patient will probably be extremely apprehensive and exhibit a sense of impending doom, pallor, cyanosis, and engorged neck veins.

HYPERVENTILATION SYNDROME

Occasionally, individuals "hyperventilate" when they are extremely anxious or otherwise emotionally upset. Increased alveolar ventilation results in a reduced P_{CO_2}. A rapid fall in the P_{CO_2} induces alkalosis, which in turn reduces the concentration of free ionized calcium, causing the characteristic neurological findings of carpopedal spasm and paresthesias. Other characteristic signs and symptoms include dizziness, faintness, numbness and tingling of the hands and feet and around the mouth, and even chest pain. The patient perceives considerable air hunger. VS ordinarily reveal both tachycardia and tachypnea, but the BP will be normal.

The EN should listen carefully to the chest to check for overall air movement and determine if there are any abnormal breath sounds that could indicate respiratory causes for the hyperventilation, some of which are life-threatening. They include metabolic acidosis, salicylate overdose, sepsis, and hypoxia caused by pneumothorax, pneumonia, and pulmonary embolus. Determine if the patient has used any drugs or inhaled any substances that could give rise to an abnormal breathing episode, too.

Having the patient breathe his or her own expired air will be useful in returning blood gases to normal. The EN must recognize that the patient is frightened and will need much support at this time. Encouraging the patient to gradually extend exhalation time while reducing inhalation time is a helpful coaching technique. Silently counting each second for exhalation and inhalation during this maneuver will often distract the patient enough to interrupt the hyperventilation syndrome. ENs must realize the patient's extreme anxiety and be sensitive to the need for understanding and support. Before the patient is discharged, the EN should offer the patient suggestions for coping with such attacks in the future.

■ NURSING DIAGNOSES

Nursing diagnoses related to pulmonary and respiratory emergencies include:

- Ineffective airway clearance related to mechanical obstruction
- Impaired gas exchange related to upper airway edema
- Anxiety related to decreased cerebral oxygenation
- Risk of infection due to interruption in integrity of skin and mucous membrane barriers
- Alteration in oxygenation due to V/Q mismatching

■ REFERENCES

1. Wilkins RL, Dexter JR. Introduction to respiratory failure. In: Wilkins RL, Dexter JR. *Respiratory Disease: Principles of Patient Care.* Philadelphia, Pa: FA Davis; 1993:1–13.
2. Hicks GL. Smoke inhalation and burns. In: Wilkins RL, Dexter JR. *Respiratory Disease: Principles of Patient Care.* Philadelphia, Pa: FA Davis; 1993:129–150.
3. Clancy C, Litovitz TL. Poisoning. In Ayers SM, Grenvik A, Holbrook PR, Shoemaker WC. *Textbook of Critical Care.* 3rd ed. Philadelphia, Pa: WB Saunders; 1995:1186–1210.
4. Jenkins JL, Loscalzo J. *Manual of Emergency Medicine: Diagnosis and Treatment.* 2nd ed. Boston, Ma: Little, Brown; 1990:450.
5. Jenkins JL, Loscalzo J. *Manual of Emergency Medicine: Diagnosis and Treatment.* 2nd ed. Boston, Ma: Little, Brown; 1990:77.
6. Masur H. Pneumonia in the immunosuppressed patient. In: Ayres SM, Grenvik A, Holbrook PR, Shoemaker WC. *Textbook of Critical Care.* 3rd ed. Philadelphia, Pa: WB Saunders; 1995:1269–1278.
7. Ayres SM. Infection with HIV, AIDS, and the intensive care unit. In: Ayres SM, Grenvik A, Holbrook PR, Shoemaker WC. *Textbook of Critical Care.* 3rd ed. Philadelphia, Pa: WB Saunders; 1995:1279–1283.
8. Lindell KO. How to use a metered-dose inhaler. *AJN.* March 1990;35–36.
9. Williams RL, Dexter JR. Asthma. In: Wilkins RL, Dexter JR. *Respiratory Disease: Principles of Patient Care.* Philadelphia, Pa: FA Davis; 1993:15–27.
10. Goodwin SR, Boysen PE, Modell JH. Near drowning—adults and children. In: Ayres SM, Grenvik A, Holbrook PR, Shoemaker WC. *Textbook of Critical Care.* 3rd ed. Philadelphia, Pa: WB Saunders; 1995:65–74.

■ BIBLIOGRAPHY

Barie PS, Shires GT. *Surgical Intensive Care.* Boston, Ma: Little, Brown; 1993.

Benumof J. *Airway Management: Principles and Practice.* St. Louis, Mo: CV Mosby; 1995.

Bongard FS, Sue DY. *Current Critical Care Diagnosis and Treatment.* E. Norwalk, Conn: Appleton & Lange; 1994.

Chernow B, ed. *The Pharmacologic Approach to the Critically Ill Patient.* 3rd ed. Baltimore, Md: Williams & Wilkins; 1994.

Dean J, Kaufman N. Prognostic indicators in pediatric near-drowning: The Glasgow Coma Scale. *Crit Care Med.* 1981;9:536.

Grenvik A, Ayres SM, Holbrook PR, Shoemaker WB. *Pocket Companion to Textbook of Critical Care.* Philadelphia, Pa: WB Saunders; 1996.

Jacobsen W, et al. Correlation of spontaneous respiration and neurologic damage in near-drowning. *Crit Care Med.* 1983;11:487.

Mahon CR, Manuselis G Jr. *Textbook of Diagnostic Microbiology.* Philadelphia, Pa: WB Saunders; 1995.

Physicians' Desk Reference. 50th ed. Montvale, NJ: Medical Economics; 1996.

Ruppert SD, Kernicki JG, Dolan JT. *Dolan's Critical Care Nursing.* 2nd ed. Philadelphia, Pa: FA Davis; 1996.

■ REVIEW: PULMONARY AND RESPIRATORY EMERGENCIES

1. List the three causes of impaired ventilation and identify clinical indications and blood gas values that mark pulmonary failure.

2. Differentiate between croup and epiglottitis in terms of presenting signs and symptoms.

3. Describe the characteristics of a smoke inhalation injury as it affects airway tissues and the pathophysiological changes that occur in the upper and lower airways.

4. Identify the mechanism of cellular toxicity in carbon monoxide inhalation and explain why arterial blood gases (ABGs) or pulse oximetry assessments are of little value in these cases; outline treatment.

5. Name presenting signs and symptoms of hydrogen sulfide exposure and describe the treatment protocol.

6. Compare and contrast clinical findings of bacterial, viral, and protozoan pneumonia and identify the recommended factors to be addressed in the nursing assessment.

7. Explain how nursing assessments and management of emphysema and chronic bronchitis differ from those for patients with pneumonia.

8. Explain the progression of an acute asthmatic crisis that evolves into status asthmaticus and list the six indications of a severe attack; identify the recommended steps in management of these patients.

9. Describe the correct procedure for using a metered-dose inhaler and how to instruct/demonstrate the proper technique to patients.

10. Outline the treatment of noncardiogenic pulmonary edema.

11. Cite the series of events that occur in a near drowning episode; identify both the assessment tool that is useful in predicting the outcome for the patient and the recommended emergency interventions.

12. List the three classic signs and symptoms suggesting an acute pulmonary embolus.

13. Explain the events associated with the hyperventilation syndrome and identify the four classic findings that alert the triage nurse to the problem.

14. Identify the ABG value most beneficial for confirmation of the hyperventilation syndrome and the nursing measures that may be helpful in management.

15. List four nursing diagnoses that relate to pulmonary and respiratory emergencies.

Cardiovascular Emergencies 23

Patients with cardiac-related emergencies are among the most challenging for the emergency nurse (EN). Problems that affect the cardiovascular system can be an immediate threat to life; thus, interventions are often initiated while further clinical evaluations are in progress. This chapter discusses the EN's role in the assessment and management of chest pain, arrhythmias, hypertension crises, and other major conditions affecting the heart and great vessels.

■ CHEST PAIN

Chest pain is a common presenting complaint in the emergency department (ED), so ENs must be prepared to promptly triage these patients and provide basic supportive care while definitive assessments are pending.

The majority of individuals who experience chest pain develop considerable anxiety that they could be having a "heart attack." The patients' fears often distort their ability to specifically describe the exact nature of their complaint. Some patients may exaggerate their symptoms to ensure that their concerns are taken seriously; others minimize theirs because acknowledging the possibility that they are experiencing a life-threatening cardiac problem is too anxiety provoking.

INITIAL CONSIDERATIONS

When a patient presents to the ED with a complaint of chest pain, one must assume a life-threatening problem. This dictates foregoing registration formalities and promptly moving the patient to a treatment area. The EN should exhibit calm, reas-

suring mannerisms and explain the rationale for the care being provided. The patient should be placed at rest in a semi-Fowler's position and oxygen administration should be initiated at once at 4 to 6 L/min by nasal cannula. (If the individual has a history or evidence of chronic obstructive lung disease [COLD], 2 L/min is appropriate for early conservative therapy.) Masks may be used for flow rates higher than 4 L/min, but they are usually poorly tolerated because the patient often senses a "smothering-like" shortness of breath that seems to be aggravated by the presence of the mask.

Vital signs (VS) that should be assessed include apical-radial pulses, respirations, and blood pressure (BP). Cardiac monitoring should be established for dysrhythmia recognition. A lead II or MCL_1 lead placement is the recommended configuration for detecting both atrial and ventricular dysrhythmias (see page 370).

A well-secured peripheral intravenous line of D_5W set at a keep-open rate should be promptly established using a cannulation device capable of supporting a resuscitation effort. A 16 to 18-gauge angiocatheter is a suitable choice for this initial line.

As soon as the above tasks have been addressed, a 12-lead electrocardiogram (ECG) (see page 372) should be recorded and laboratory blood samples should be obtained as indicated by the abbreviated history and early clinical indices.

IMMEDIATE LIFE THREATS

The immediate threats to life should be considered after the initial stabilization of vital functions. Life threats are those disorders that demand emergency identification and specific, aggressive intervention; those commonly encountered in the ED are unstable (crescendo) angina, pneumothorax, pulmonary embolus, aortic dissection, and pericarditis/pericardial tamponade. Early attention to these disorders should be an integral part of initial assessment of patients presenting with chest pain.

Unstable (Crescendo) Angina

A common precursor of an acute myocardial infarction is an abrupt change in the anginal symptoms of a patient. Increases in the severity, duration, or frequency of attacks; a decreasing exertional tolerance; or an increase in anginal pain at rest should cause ENs to view the pain with concern. Crescendo angina is thought to be an immediate step between angina pectoris and acute myocardial infarction.

Pneumothorax

A significant pneumothorax can give rise to a sudden pleuritic chest pain that is aggravated by respiratory excursions. A developing tension pneumothorax also contributes to "mediastinal shift" and thus a compression of the heart and great vessels. As venous return is impeded to the right atrium, the neck veins become distended. The patient's condition quickly deteriorates, owing to decreased ventilation and a dramatic reduction in cardiac output. Decompression of the pneumothorax by needle thoracostomy or the placement of chest tubes is mandatory to restore vital respiratory functions (see Chapter 14).

Pulmonary Embolus

When a major portion of the pulmonary vasculature is blocked by an embolism, cardiac function is compromised. If a large pulmonary embolus obstructs a major pulmonary artery, sudden death may occur. Because pulmonary emboli result from a free-flowing thrombus, usually from a venous system source, patients who have a history of prolonged bed rest, thrombophlebitis, or sedentary posture for extended intervals (e.g., long-distance travelers) and pregnant women are at risk of developing pulmonary emboli. The pain of pulmonary embolus is of sudden onset and without apparent cause. It is usually worsened by deep breathing and is associated with severe dyspnea. It is unaffected by rest or nitroglycerin. Rales, blood-stained sputum, tachycardia, cyanosis, hypotension, and syncope may also be noted, especially with extensive embolic processes.

Aortic Dissection

Aortic dissection is a tearing process between the intimal and medial layers of the aorta with consequent leakage of blood into the potential space that is created. The dissection may occlude major vessels that branch off the aorta to supply the heart, brain, kidneys, or mesentery, or it can produce death from cardiac tamponade or exsanguination. The pain of dissection is characterized by a tearing sensation that originates in the retrosternal area and may radiate to the neck, back, or legs. Its onset is sudden and it is unrelenting and excruciating (see page 383).

Pericarditis/Pericardial Tamponade

Pericarditis manifests itself as sharp, stabbing, pleuritic-like left anterior chest pain. The patient may experience some relief by changing posture (i.e., sitting up or leaning forward). A history of viral illness may be associated with the presentation. The auscultatory findings of a three-component friction rub may be fleeting. Instructing the patient to lean forward or to kneel on the hands and knees may accentuate the friction rub. The life threat of pericarditis is manifested by myocarditis and/or pericardial tamponade.

Myocarditis may present with signs and symptoms similar to those of pericarditis. Associated life threats are the resultant cardiac dysrhythmias and/or myocardial (pump) failure. Monitoring cardiac activity will permit early life-saving intervention.

Pericardial tamponade is marked by muffled heart tones, distended jugular veins, and hypotension. This three-part complex of symptoms is sometimes referred to as Beck's triad. As the fluid pressure within the pericardial sac increases, cardiac filling is compromised and thus cardiac output is reduced. This may progress until profound hypotension results in death. A clinician who recognizes cardiac tamponade and uses pericardiocentesis to remove just a few milliliters of blood may save the patient's life (see Chapter 4). Continuing attention must be paid to reaccumulation of fluid within the pericardium because this condition can lead to a delayed demise of the victim.

HISTORY

Having assessed the vital functions and attended to the immediate threats to life, the clinician can pursue more complete information about the patient's chest pain. Because numerous disease processes may present as chest pain, any of the intrathoracic or intra-abdominal organs may be involved in the pathological process. It is helpful to understand the pathophysiology of chest pain and why so many variations in presentation may occur.

Intrathoracic and intra-abdominal organs share closely associated or interconnecting neuronal circuits with surface sensory pathways throughout the region. These associations arise from a common embryonic developmental relationship. As the embryonic precursors of the major visceral organs grow, differentiate, and specialize in function, they also migrate to their final adult locations. The neuronal circuits maintain their embryonic surface association as they migrate into their final configuration for extrauterine life. In addition, cardiovascular, gastrointestinal (GI), respiratory, and other organs may share common or closely associated neuronal pathways in the extrauterine form. Thus, ischemic myocardial pain may manifest itself by pain radiating down the left arm because associated embryonic cells were associated with the surface sensory pathways that developed within the arm. When the myocardial cells are stressed, the related and neuronally interwoven pathways of the myocardium and arm are stimulated. This stimulation results in left arm pain associated with a radiation of myocardial pain. Any other organ in the region with neuronal association will manifest similar responses to pathology, hence the potential confusion in teasing apart the historical and physical findings of myocardial or other intrathoracic/intra-abdominal diseases from the other possibilities.

Specifically, the myocardium is perfused by the coronary arteries. Delivery and maximal extraction of the nutrients by the myocardium are achieved in a single passage of blood. As can be surmised, as the demand for nutrients increases, so must the flow of blood through the coronary arteries. When pathology (most commonly atherosclerosis) prevents increased flow, metabolic toxins and other physiological poisons accumulate. These substances stimulate nerve endings, which causes the body to perceive pain. Pain pathways are tra-

versed through a multiplicity of interconnections, both of embryonic and commonly associated origins. This explains the sometimes obtuse manifestations.

Chest pain evaluation is heavily dependent on the patient's description of pain and the historical data that can be elicited. Although there are variable approaches to data collection, the following factors should be incorporated into the process. Patients should be encouraged to describe the pain in their own words. The history taker must guard against putting words into the patient's mouth. For example, one should say, "Describe your pain. Does it go anywhere? What brings it on? What makes it better? What makes it worse?" Providing opportunities for the patient to compose his or her own response will produce much more meaningful data than asking questions that call for merely a yes or no response. Patients who are frightened will answer yes to almost any question in such circumstances, which often leads to false conclusions. It is easy to appreciate how one could elicit a classic, although perhaps inaccurate, history by asking, "Is the pain viselike? Does it radiate down your left arm? Does it make you short of breath? Is it stabbing?" The use of the mnemonic PQRST is a helpful reminder of one method for organizing the history.

Provoking Factors
Determine what brings on the pain or what causes it to subside. It is vital to know if the patient can engage in any behaviors, such as eating, sitting up, taking nitroglycerin, or resting, that bring relief.

Quality
Ask the patient to describe the pain, using his or her own expressions. Remember to avoid using leading questions. It is sometimes helpful to ask patients to compare the present pain to other pain they have experienced.

Region and Radiation
Ask where the pain is located and if it travels anywhere. Sometimes it is helpful for the patient to trace the pathway of radiating pain.

Severity
The patient's description of the severity of pain is, of course, subjective. Some clinicians suggest that

the patient compare the present pain to the worst pain he or she has ever experienced in the past, on a scale of 1 to 10, in order to obtain some appreciation of severity. Observe for objective signs that may indicate extensive sympathetic stimulation commonly associated with severe pain, such as diaphoresis, tachycardia, pallor, cool skin, and widely dilated pupils.

Timing

Determine when the pain started. Was its onset gradual or abrupt? Has it been constant or intermittent? These temporal characteristics add much to the historical database.

Other Considerations

Finally, all other aspects of a patient's health should be considered with the historical factors and the findings on physical examination. Allergies, medications taken regularly, past medical and surgical history, and the presence of chronic illnesses must be noted. It is commonly known, for example, that diabetics tend to have "silent" myocardial infarctions with little or no pain or an atypical pain presentation, probably due to regional neuropathy. Such considerations should be ever present in the mind of the EN during history taking and physical assessment.

PHYSICAL EXAMINATION

A physical assessment should be conducted in an effort to determine the clinical status of the patient as well as to search for diagnostic clues.

Heart

Inspect the chest for signs of trauma and note any visible cardiac activity, such as heaves. Palpate the chest for tenderness, lifts, heaves, or thrills. Auscultate for rate, rhythm, extra sounds, heart sounds, or murmurs. A new murmur of papillary muscle dysfunction should alert the EN to an ischemic process. An S_3 gallop suggests a noncompliant diseased left ventricle. A crunching sound suggests a pneumopericardium.

Lungs

Observation of respiration will often help the EN detect evidence of respiratory distress. The use of

accessory muscles is valuable information that suggests distress. Auscultate the chest for wheezing, rales, or rubs. Wheezing and/or rales of bronchospasm/pulmonary edema provide supportive data for assessment and diagnosis. Rubs of infarction of the lung are also a valuable clue to underlying problems.

Neck

Jugular veins must be evaluated. Observe the external jugular at or near the sternocleidomastoid muscle. Their distension, pulsation at a given angle, and rate of refilling after emptying provide information about the heart's ability to handle the preload volume from the venous system. Neck veins that are distended 3 cm about the base of the neck when the patient is elevated 30 degrees suggest the left atria's inability to handle the flow presented to it. The triad of distended neck veins, hypotension, and muffled heart sounds is a classic presentation for pericardial tamponade.

Skin and Other Systems

A systematic, rapid overview of the patient's condition should also incorporate assessments of the skin and other systems. Valuable clues may be elicited that may assist the EN in determining the nature and extent of the patient's general problem. Cool, clammy skin, for example, suggests a sympathetic stimulation and may hint that there is a severely compromised cardiovascular system that is struggling hard to compensate for the existing pathology.

ADJUNCTIVE LABORATORY DATA

Chest X-Ray

Radiographic study of the thoracic region provides information about the lungs, great vessels, heart, diaphragm, pericardium, and rib cage. It is, of course, a fundamental study in the evaluation of chest pain.

Arterial Blood Gases

Arterial gas tension levels, or arterial blood gases (ABGs) provide critical data on cardiovascular and pulmonary physiology. Physical examination fails to reveal the subtleties of pulmonary gas exchange, and cyanosis is a late, severe sign that cannot be relied upon.

Differential Blood Pressures

BPs in arms and legs should be compared to assess the possibility of dissection. As the dissection progresses, differential pressure may be identified as circulatory compromise (see page 384).

Cardiac Enzymes

Cardiac enzymes are a critical component of advanced coronary care diagnosis that should be initiated in the ED. Catalytic enzymes normally stay inside the cell, but certain cellular damage can cause them to leak into the bloodstream. Although there are enzymes present in nearly all cells, the brain, myocardium, skeletal muscle, kidneys, and red blood cells (RBCs) have unique enzymes. Although baseline cardiac enzyme levels are obtained in the ED, results are usually not available for interpretation until the patient is admitted to the intensive care unit (ICU). Remember that there are several reasons, including unstable angina, muscle trauma (repeated needle sticks, bruising, cardiopulmonary resuscitation), pericarditis, and a hemolyzed blood specimen, for false-positive serum enzyme test results.[1]

Creatine Kinase. Creatine kinase (CK) is found in the skeletal muscle and brain, as well as in the myocardium, and if the myocardium is damaged (i.e., by infarction), the CK from the myocardial cells will be present in the bloodstream. This specific enzyme, a marker for the myocardium, is referred to as CK-MB. Designators for similar phenomena involving the brain and skeletal muscle are CK-BB and CK-MM, respectively.

In normal, healthy patients, the CK in the circulation is CK-MM, leaked from skeletal muscle from normal physiological activities. If larger amounts of CK-MB are noted within 4 to 8 hours after a cardiac event (e.g., chest pain or infarction), this denotes myocardial tissue damage. Results from the traditional CK-MB assay require up to 2 hours for completion and therefore may not be helpful to physicians in the ED. (A reliable diagnosis from CK-MB levels cannot be made until 8 to 12 hours after onset of symptoms.)

Ordinarily, CK-MB levels peak in 12 to 24 hours and return to normal in about 3 days after infarction. The normal CK level is 5 to 75 mU/mL. It may increase with cardioversion, trauma, or invasive procedures. Since the CK-MB levels may not increase for several hours after myocardial infarction (MI), a normal level does *not* rule out myocardial damage. Monitoring the rise and noting the peak elevation is one method of estimating the size of an infarction.

Newer testing methods using monoclonal antibodies are capable of greater sensitivity and specificity and can produce results within 30 minutes.

Measuring levels of the subforms of CK-MB, MB_1 in the plasma and MB_2 in the tissues, is also useful in the detection of myocardial damage. In healthy individuals, both are present in equal amounts; if the myocardium is damaged, there is an increase in the MB_2 fraction. The ratio of these two enzyme fractions may be identified in the first hour after symptoms; peak levels are noted in 4 to 8 hours.

Serum Glutamic Oxaloacetic Transaminase and Lactate Dehydrogenase. Serum glutamic oxaloacetic transaminase (SGOT) and lactate dehydrogenase (LDH) levels take longer to be elevated and usually are within normal range in the ED. Once elevated, levels may remain so for 5 days or longer. LDH also has isoenzymes that can be measured—LDH_1 and LDH_2. Normally, the level of LDH_1 is lower than that of isoenzyme LDH_2. However, after a myocardial infarction, these levels reverse, with the level of LDH_1 exceeding that of LDH_2. This is a useful diagnostic finding when an individual with a suspected MI presents several days after the onset of symptoms.

Myoglobin. Myoglobin is a heme protein found in myocardial and skeletal muscle. Early elevations of this substance are noted after the onset of MI symptoms. Although it is ordinarily present in muscles, it is nonspecific for acute MI but is an excellent test to *exclude* MI. It is a valuable marker of reinfarction, too, especially after successful reperfusion therapy (see pages 375–379).

Troponin. Troponin is a contractile protein with subforms highly specific for cardiac muscle. With use of a monoclonal antibody technique, a rise that persists for several days can be detected after MI. Unlike many other enzymes, this particular one is never detectable in healthy persons; their serum levels of troponin are unaffected by injury. Troponin subforms assays have been noted to be most useful as a rapid test for acute MI.

ELECTROCARDIOGRAPHIC MONITORING AND THE TWELVE-LEAD ELECTROCARDIOGRAM

ECG changes are a crucial element in the diagnosis of acute myocardial damage. Both bedside monitoring and obtaining the 12-lead ECG are important responsibilities of the EN. If there is at least a 1-mm ST segment elevation or a Q wave in two contiguous leads, a 70 percent chance of an acute MI is present. Half of all chest pain patients, however, will have a nondiagnostic ECG.[1]

Today's ECG technology permits several choices for lead placement to facilitate diagnosis and to monitor the patient's clinical course. During the ED phase of cardiac care, however, sparse information about the patient's overall medical history, and in particular the cardiac status, may limit the database that nurses ordinarily use to select among the various lead placement options. There are certain configurations that are especially useful in the ED and can be used even when technological support is limited. They yield the most information during an acute episode of chest pain, dysrhythmia, or pacemaker malfunction.

Electrodes are placed primarily to detect electrical changes associated with ischemic changes of the myocardium. Oxygen deprivation can be noted by an inverted ST segment. After tissue injury has occurred, current flows during systole from healthy to injured tissue and creates the characteristic ST segment elevation. To identify ischemia, ST segment analysis may be accomplished (see page 371). The occurrence of either increases in duration and depth of Q waves or new Q waves suggests potential myocardial cell death.

Lead 2

The use of lead II (Fig. 23–1) is a standard placement for initial monitoring because it produces a prominent P wave and a tall upright R wave, which are essential elements for study when endeavoring to detect atrial dysrhythmias such as atrial flutter. Lead II is also used for ST segment monitoring and for atrioventricular (AV) heart block detection in patients with inferior wall infarctions. Lead II is *not recommended* for distinguishing supraventricular tachycardia with bundle branch block or aberration from ventricular tachycardia.[2] Both leads I and II can be used to determine axis deviation pending the use of a 12-lead ECG.

MCL₁

MCL_1 is preferred for most bedside continuous monitoring. It is especially helpful when emergency personnel are diagnosing electrical changes associated with an acute MI. For example, an emerging bundle branch block produces a significant pattern change in the QRS complex on MCL_1. During an anteroseptal infarction, a new bundle branch block suggests myocardial instability that may progress to complete heart block or ventricular asystole. This lead is also helpful in distinguishing ventricular tachycardia from supraventricular tachycardia with aberrancy or preexisting bundle branch block.[2]

When a three-wire monitor is used, the MCL_1 lead configuration is accomplished by selecting lead I and placing electrodes as follows: LA+ at the fourth intercostal space at the right sternal border, RA− at the left shoulder, and the LL ground at the fifth intercostal space, along the midaxillary line (Fig. 23–2). Precise placement of the chest lead is especially important to ensure the accuracy of MCL_1 monitoring.

Right Ventricular Leads

Right ventricular leads are precordial placements used to detect right ventricular pathology. A right ventricular infarction often is associated with a left ventricular inferior wall infarction and the management of right and left hemodynamics of the infarction varies. Because the standard 12-lead ECG records left ventricular activity, it is inadequate for diagnosing right ventricular problems. It is essential, therefore, that ENs are aware of the value of monitoring using right ventricular leads. Leads V_4,

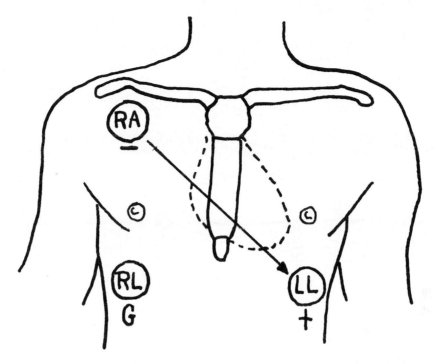

Figure 23–1. Standard Lead II electrode placement. The negative lead is placed below the right clavicle; the positive lead is placed below the left pectoral muscle, with the ground usually positioned below the right pectoral muscle.

V_5, and V_6 are merely moved to the right side of the chest and should be denoted on the strip as V_{4R}, V_{5R}, and V_{6R}. Important changes in right-sided leads are transient, so they should be recorded soon after the patient's arrival at the ED and whenever chest pain or other indices of ischemia or infarction are noted (Fig. 23–3).

ST Segment Monitoring

Because changes in the ST segment baseline are important indicators of the oxygenation and the efficacy of the myocardium, many newer monitoring systems are equipped to focus specifically on this important parameter. The initial response to ischemia is ST segment depression; a change of 1 mm is significant. If the ischemia is prolonged, myocardial injury will create the characteristic ST

elevation. There are several problems other than ischemia that can affect the ST segment, including unstable angina, early repolarization, bundle branch block, ventricular hypertrophy, electrolyte abnormalities, pacemakers, and certain drugs such as digoxin and antiarrhythmics.[2]

ENs should use ST segment monitoring for patients with chest pain or other indicators of infarction, in unstable angina, when a 12-lead ECG cannot be promptly obtained, and when monitoring reperfusion or reocclusion associated with administration of thrombolytic agents. The characteristic signs of acute MI can be readily appreciated in serial tracings.

Alarms should be set for 1 mm above and 1 mm below the patient's baseline and 60 to 80 ms from the junction of the QRS complex and the ST

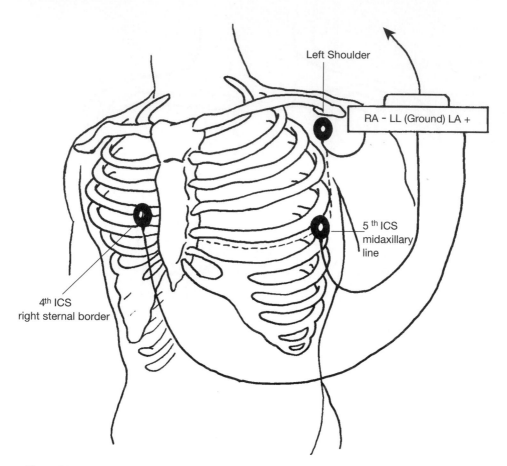

Figure 23–2. Lead placement for MCL₁ using a three lead-wire monitor. **1.** Select Lead 1 on the monitor. **2.** Place LA (+) lead wire on the 4th ICS at the R sternal border. **3.** Place RA (-) lead wire on the L shoulder. **4.** Place ground lead wire (G) on the 5th ICS L midaxillary line.

segment (i.e., the J point) (Fig. 23–4). Ischemia is confirmed by a sustained elevation (60 seconds) that displaces the ST by at least 1 mm over the ischemic zone (preferably in more than one lead).

Twelve-Lead Electrocardiogram

The value of the 12-lead ECG is in that it records the electrical activity of the heart from 12 different views, each of which provides a unique picture of the heart's electrical impulses. Six are limb leads and six are precordial leads. Leads I, II, and III use two electrodes each and are called bipolar; the remaining three limb leads are considered unipolar because each uses only one electrode at a time to record electrical activity. These leads are designated as aVR, aVL, and aVF for the right arm, and left leg, respectively. The *a* means that the leads are augmented and that the electrical activity is electronically enlarged; the *V* designates unipolarity. The positive lead is the limb electrode (i.e., the right arm is positive in a VR, the left arm is positive in aVL, and the left leg is positive in aVF.) The six chest leads are unipolar and are labeled V_1, V_2, V_3, V_4, V_5, and V_6. They are placed on the chest (Fig. 23–5) as follows:

- V_1: fourth intercostal space, right sternal border
- V_2: fourth intercostal space, left sternal border

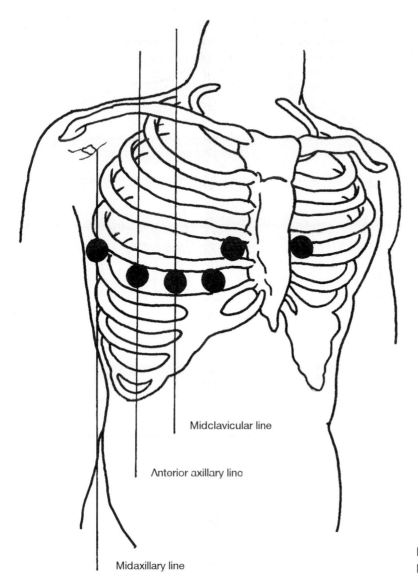

Midclavicular line

Anterior axillary line

Midaxillary line

Figure 23–3. Right-sided chest lead placement.

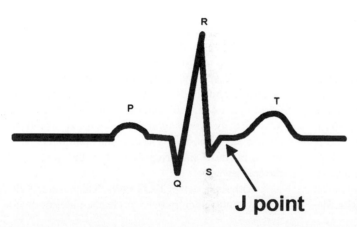

J point

Figure 23–4. The J point is the junction between the QRS complex and the ST segment. The J point is the baseline for determining ST elevations or depressions.

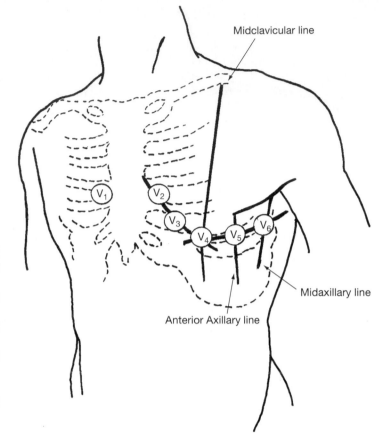

Figure 23–5. Chest lead placement for 12-lead electrocardiogram. The six chest electrode sites are as follows:

V_1: Fourth intercostal space, right sternal border

V_2: Fourth intercostal space, left sternal border

V_3: Fifth intercostal space, midway between V_2 and V_4

V_4: Fifth intercostal space, midclavicular line

V_5: Fifth intercostal space, anterior axillary line

V_6: Fifth intercostal space, midaxillary line

- V_3: fifth intercostal space, midway between V_2 and V_4
- V_4: fifth intercostal space, midclavicular line
- V_5: fifth intercostal space, anterior axillary line
- V_6: fifth intercostal space, midaxillary line

The placement of precordial leads should be precise in order to derive a valid picture of ventricular function. Leads V_1 and V_2 represent the right ventricle and right atrium; leads V_3 through V_6 represent the left ventricle. The six precordial leads will increase the amplitude of the R wave and decrease the amplitude of the S wave. Because each lead reveals activity in a unique section of the heart, exact areas of damage or dysfunction can be detected.

The EN should understand the important aspects of monitoring and obtaining the 12-lead ECG. Before attaching electrodes at any site, the skin should be thoroughly cleansed with an alcohol wipe and excess hair clipped, if necessary. Make sure that when placing electrodes on women with pendulous breasts that the breast tissue is elevated to ensure location and proper placement of the electrode on the chest wall rather than on breast tissue. Make sure that no leads are in direct contact with another. (This may be a problem in patients with small frames and in children). Although conducting media (i.e., paste or gel) may be required, it should be used sparingly. Excessive amounts may ooze from the intended electrode and inadvertently make a connection to an adjacent one, thus distorting the ECG readings. Watches that may generate electrical impulses should be removed. The patient should be kept warm because shivering can affect the quality of the tracings.

Although newer ECG units "standardize" the tracing automatically between leads, older or more basic units may not; therefore the EN must ensure that this is accomplished because this permits the ECG evaluator to compare waveforms against a standard isoelectric measurement. Because fluorescent lights and other electrical equipment in the room may hamper tracings by production of an artifact, they may need to be turned off during the ECG.

When the ECG is completed, the electrodes should be removed promptly and the skin should be cleansed of conductive media because residua can alter chest wall impedance for subsequent defibrillation, if required. The leads and wires should be wiped with an approved disinfectant and allowed to air-dry before use on another patient.

THERAPY DURING ACUTE CHEST PAIN

The intravenous route must be used for drug administration associated with chest pain and other cardiac emergencies because intramuscular tissue circulatory status may be compromised. Medication delivered intramuscularly that is not rapidly absorbed may pool in the muscle and be precipitously absorbed into circulation when adequate peripheral perfusion is reestablished. Furthermore, intramuscular injections affect enzyme levels, important in the diagnosis of myocardial insult.

Pain Management

Relief of pain caused by MI is a vital therapeutic objective. Morphine sulfate, the usual drug of choice, is given at a rate of 2 to 5 mg as an intravenous push over 1 or 2 minutes. Dosages may be repeated every 5 minutes as indicated by persisting pain. Stable or adequate VS indicate that it is safe to repeat dosages. BP must be closely observed because hypotension can occur in response to morphine. Although the patient is receiving supplemental oxygen, the EN should ensure that there are efficient ventilatory excursions, because respiratory functions can also be depressed by narcotics. A bag-valve unit for positive-pressure assistance must be immediately available at the bedside. Rapid, pure narcotic reversal may be achieved by using naloxone (0.4 to 0.8 mg).

Both sublingual and intravenous nitroglycerin may be used to relax vascular smooth muscle. In addition to dilating the larger coronary arteries, they increase coronary collateral blood flow and decrease left ventricular workload and wall tension by inhibiting venous return, which decreases ventricular volume and wall stress.[3] Sublingual nitroglycerin has little effect on systemic vascular resistance and is the drug of choice for an episode of angina. One tablet (0.3 to 0.4 mg) may be repeated twice at 5-minute intervals. Ordinarily, patients with a history of cardiac problems begin their use of nitroglycerin before coming to the hospital, so the EN should establish a record of previous use. Although patients may have taken nitroglycerin from their own prescription supply, it may be necessary to order additional tablets from the ED's source because the quality of patient's drug may have deteriorated, rendering the tablets ineffective.

Intravenous nitroglycerin is used for individuals with ischemic heart disease and evidence of congestive failure because it lowers systemic arterial resistance and increases venous capacitance. Because of its potent anti-ischemic effects, it is often used in the ED. It must be used judiciously in acute myocardial infarction cases, however, because it may compromise coronary artery perfusion even more by its resultant hypotension.

Nitroglycerin may be administered by bolus or infusion. A 50-μg bolus is followed by a continuous infusion at a rate of 10 to 20 μg/min. The infusion may be titrated upward by 5 to 10 μg/min every 5 to 10 minutes until the relief of chest pain or the desired hemodynamic response is achieved. Most patients' conditions respond to dosage rates of 50 to 200 μg/min.[3] Both hypotension and bradycardia can result from intravenous nitroglycerin. Elevation of the legs and fluid administration are used for hypotension; atropine is indicated for the bradycardia. Headache, syncope, and nausea may also accompany use of nitroglycerin. There are numerous hemodynamic responses that must be monitored continuously in order to ensure patient safety. In certain hospitals, the use of intravenous nitroglycerin may be confined to the ICU, where invasive monitoring capabilities are extant.

Thrombolytics

The efficacy of thrombolytics in the treatment of early MI is well documented. Major clinical trials with these agents demonstrated that both short- and long-term benefits could be derived from administration of thrombolytics if the treatment is initiated promptly after clotting, within 30 to 60 minutes of an acute event (e.g., chest pain or ECG changes) suggesting coronary occlusion. The GUSTO (Global Utilization of SK and t-PA for Occluded Coronary Arteries) studies further noted that survival rates could be improved with an accelerated dosing schedule for the recombinant form of tissue plasminogen activator (rTPA). Angiographic studies done as part of the GUSTO trials revealed that rapid and complete restoration of blood flow through the infarcted artery could reduce postinfarction left ventricular performance problems and improve survival.[4] This report discussed two complications of prolonged ventricular dysfunction: myocardial stunning (hypocontractile state due to excess calcium release from sarcoplasmic reticulum damaged by oxygen-derived free radicals or thrombolysis) and myocardial hibernation (persistent contractile dysfunction associated with a decline in coronary flow that is reversed with reperfusion). Because many patients experience their symptoms at home and exhaust part of this time reaching the ED, the hospital staff must ensure that there are no in-hospital delays that would impede the prompt delivery of a thrombolytic agent. A 50 percent reduction in mortality can be realized with use of prompt thrombolytic therapy.[5]

Thrombogenesis and the onset of necrosis usually occur during the first 6 hours after the onset of symptoms associated with an acute myocardial infarction. If thrombolytic agents are not given within the critical period of thrombogenesis, 85 to 100 percent of these patients develop some necrosis of the myocardium. About 15 percent of the myocardium at risk dies for every 30 minutes of occlusion.[6] Some value may be derived from later administration of these agents, too, because marginal tissue surrounding the infarct may be salvaged by opening of the major vessels, which have the capability to feed collateral circulation. The aim of thrombolytic therapy is to accelerate the body's own fibrinolytic processes, because they ordinarily take several days to effect clot lysis. The principal action of thrombolytic drugs is to convert plasminogen to plasmin, which lyses clots (Fig. 23–6).

There are three major drugs used for thrombolysis: streptokinase, Eminase, and Activase or Alteplase, commonly referred to as TPA because of its chemical composition.

Streptokinase. Streptokinase links to plasminogen in the circulatory network and forms a complex that breaks down plasminogen into plasmin; plas-

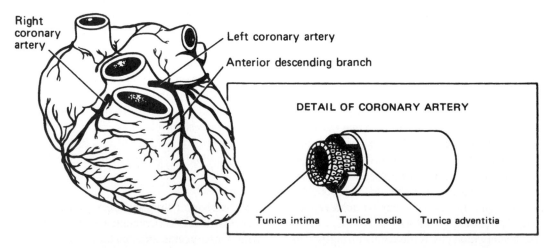

Figure 23–6. When a major coronary artery is occluded, 15 percent of the associated myocardium dies every 30 minutes. Early use of thrombolytics often opens collateral circuits, which salvages injured and ischemic tissue adjacent to the infarction.

min breaks down the fibrin in clots, creating lysis and relieving occlusion. Plasmin also breaks down circulating fibrinogen, a coagulation factor required for hemostasis, thus activating fibrinolysis throughout the body. During this phase, fibrin split products are created, inducing a state of generalized anticoagulation that can last 12 to 24 hours.

Streptokinase is antigenic; patients can have an allergic response to the agent with rash, fever, tachycardia, hypotension, urticaria, and bronchospasm. It is given with great caution to patients with previous exposure to β-hemolytic streptococci or to those who have received streptokinase within the past 6 months to 1 year. Although steroids and Benadryl are sometimes given to reduce allergic reaction potential, some authorities believe that steroids may negatively affect the healing of the myocardium and that allergic responses are relatively rare, so routine pretreatment is not advised.[7] It is usually not considered the drug of choice for anyone who has received it previously and therefore would have antibodies capable of destroying it, thus limiting its effectiveness. Although rTPA (i.e., Activase or Alteplase) given in an accelerated dosage seems to work most rapidly and efficiently in early clot lysis; the rates of patency achieved by streptokinase are equal to it (i.e., TPA) at the 3-hour post-dose interval. Authorities believe, however, that the "catch-up" occurs too late to be of value in early improvement of ventricular functioning or mortality reduction.[7]

The initial dosage is 1.5 million U mixed in 100 mL of D_5W, delivered over 60 minutes. Heparin may be initiated to maintain the partial thromboplastin time (PTT) at 1.5 to two times control. It may be started before streptokinase, administered concurrently, or started immediately after streptokinase; the GUSTO studies illustrated that the effect of early administration of intravenous heparin is not necessary for reduction in mortality or reinfarction and has a minor effect on patency, reocclusion, and left ventricular performance. Furthermore, the study noted that intravenous heparin had no specific advantages over subcutaneous heparin as an adjunct to streptokinase administration. The half-line of streptokinase is 30 minutes in plasma, so great care is exercised to ensure that reocclusion does not occur after the administration is complete. Streptokinase administration may be repeated during the first 24 hours if results are not evident with the initial dose.

Eminase. Eminase is basically a time-released form of streptokinase; it is not a totally distinct drug. The molecule of this agent remains inactive until it reaches the plasma, where it breaks down gradually into a streptokinase–plasminogen complex. The plasminogen splits into plasmin, which breaks down fibrin clots and circulating fibrinogen. The half-life is 90 to 120 minutes, but the allergenic properties of streptokinase are inherent in its use. The dosage is 30 U via IV bolus over 2 to 5 minutes. Heparin therapy can be delayed for up to 8 hours after drug delivery because of the extended half-life, which discourages reocclusion. Heparin is not required to maintain patency or to improve clinical outcome, however. It has been used successfully in prehospital care because of the simplicity of its one-time bolus dosing.

When mixing Eminase, reconstitute the drug with 5 mL sterile water. The stream must be directed against the side of the vial. The drug should be gently rolled to facilitate mixing, never shaken. Once reconstituted, it must be administered within 30 minutes.

Recombinant Tissue Plasminogen Activator.

Recombinant Tissue Plasminogen Activator (rTPA, Activase, Alteplase) is considered the optimum thrombolytic for most patients, even though it is more expensive. Although it carries the highest risk of any thrombolytic agent for producing intracranial bleeds, it is still the preferred agent for most patients. Its actions are clot-specific (i.e., the enzyme is fibrin-specific in converting plasminogen to plasmin). The 100-mg dosage is administered over 90 minutes in most settings as follows:

1. An initial bolus of 15 mg
2. Within the first 30 minutes following the initial bolus, an additional 50 mg is infused
3. In the following hour, the remaining 35 mg is given

This standard dosing is weight-adjusted (1 mg/kg) for individuals who weigh less than 65 kg to reduce bleeding potential.

This drug must be mixed with sterile water, *not bacteriostatic water,* using an 18-gauge needle to aim the stream against the drug; the agent must be allowed to stand several minutes before administration to permit large bubbles and foam to dissipate. Excessive agitation should be avoided. The agent may be further diluted with an equal volume of normal saline (NS) or D_5W to yield a concentration of 0.5 mg/mL. After reconstitution, the drug remains stable for 8 hours.

Heparin must be given concurrently or immediately following the administration of rTPA to accelerate lysis and to maintain coronary patency. The heparin may be continued for 3 to 7 days.[8] If no heparin is administered with, or after administration of rTPA, coronary patency is reduced by 30 percent during the first 24 hours.[7]

Other Considerations. Coumadin, dipyridamole (Persantine), ticlopidine (Ticlid), aspirin, and other antiplatelet agents are employed to prevent secondary occlusive vascular disease. They may be used alone or in combination with other agents. Studies indicate that aspirin in small doses (75 to 100 mg) may be the best therapy to prevent reocclusion; treatment is started with higher doses (200 to 300 mg) until the full antiplatelet effect is realized, and then lower doses are used to limit side effects.

The risks and complications of thrombolytic therapy include active bleeding (especially intracranial), allergic reactions (to streptokinase or Eminase) hypotension, reocclusion, and dysrhythmias.

Nursing Care Considerations

The EN should identify suitable candidates for thrombolytics, which include those patients with chest pain of less than 6 hours' duration, those with ST segment elevation of 0.1 mV in two leads, and in evolving MIs in patients with a new bundle branch block.

Baseline blood work may include a complete blood cell (CBC) count, clotting studies, blood urea nitrogen (BUN) and creatinine, serum electrolytes, and cardiac enzymes.

During therapy, the EN must continue to provide care for the evolving infarction (i.e., oxygen administration, pain management, and continuous ECG and hemodynamic monitoring). It is important to observe for bleeding at any puncture site, (e.g., the Foley catheter, nasogastric (NG) tube,

endotracheal (ET) tube). Allergic and other untoward responses should be promptly detected and may include neurological changes associated with intracranial bleeding.

All blood samples must be obtained from lines, with the first 6 to 10 mL discarded; all drainage, excretions, and emesis must be tested for occult blood. Meanwhile, the EN must observe for signs of reperfusion, which include:

- Resolution of chest pain
- Resolution of ST segment elevation (may take up to 24 hours in some cases)
- Onset of reperfusion arrhythmias (e.g., ventricular tachycardia, sinus bradycardia, accelerated idioventricular rhythm)

Cardiac enzymes may be unreliable for monitoring reperfusion. Early CK-MB elevations and peaking are due to a wash-out effect (i.e., when blood returns to the previously unperfused myocardial tissue.) Recall that this enzyme marker usually peaks 24 to 36 hours after onset of symptoms. Since this and other enzymes are so dramatically altered by thrombolytics, they are considered unreliable for estimating the extent of the infarction. Nuclear imaging techniques are usually required for valid assessment of tissue injury.

Minor bleeding, such as oozing from punctures or epistaxis, may be treated with direct compression. In the event of major bleeding (e.g., intracranial or GI hemorrhage), the thrombolytic agents are stopped and stat blood work is obtained. However, do not wait for results to begin treatment. Protamine sulfate (50 mg IV over 1 to 3 minutes) reverses the effects of heparin. Packed RBCs may be employed if the patient is hypotensive or the hematocrit (Hct) is less than 25 percent. Cryoprecipitate (10 U IV) should be given for low fibrinogen levels. Occasionally, patients may experience fever, which can be managed by aspirin or acetaminophen. Hypotension, unassociated with anaphylaxis, may be a transient response to the agent and rarely calls for its discontinuation. Slowing the drug and administering fluids may be all that is required. Rigors that are created from the plasminogen breakdown ordinarily can be controlled with low-dose meperidine (Demerol) (25 mg IV).

Reperfusion arrhythmias are to be expected and ordinarily are not treated unless there is hemodynamic compromise. Transient ventricular tachycardia is common and usually tolerated for up to 10 minutes before intervention is mandated. Idioventricular rhythms are not treated if the heart rate is less than 120 beats per minutes (bpm) and there is no hypotension.

Third-degree AV block is common with reperfusion of an inferior MI; it is usually of short duration. However, if it is persistent, treatment with atropine, fluids, and a pacing unit may be required.

The Bezold–Jarish reflex (i.e., profound bradycardia with hypotension) can occur during precipitant reperfusion of the right coronary artery. This vessel has an abundance of vagal afferent fibers and when blood flow is restored, increased parasympathetic activity slows the heart rate and induces hypotension. Treatment includes atropine, fluids, and a temporary pacing unit. Vasopressors may be used in selected cases.

CLASSIFICATIONS OF MYOCARDIAL SITE

Inferior Wall Infarction

Inferior wall infarction is associated with occlusion of the right coronary artery or, in some cases, a dominant left circumflex artery. Because the right coronary artery supplies the AV node and the bundle of His in most patients as well as the sinus node in over half of all individuals, conduction defects are commonly associated. Results of this infarction are sinus bradycardia, sinus arrest, escape beats, AV block, and atrial dysrhythmias. Nausea, vomiting, tracheal burning, bronchospasm, and syncope may occur, too, as a result of intense vagal stimulation. Bradycardia or progressive AV block are treated with drugs, temporary pacing, or both. Thrombolytic therapy is indicated in patients with precordial ST depression associated with acute inferior MI.

Q-Wave Versus Non–Q-Wave Infarction

A complete occlusion of a thrombotic coronary artery results in transmural myocardial necrosis and a Q-wave on the ECG. Patients who have sufficient collateral circulation or quick reperfusion will experience a subendocardial or non–Q-wave infarction, which is smaller and seems to preserve left ventricular function. Non–Q-wave infarctions must be aggressively managed to prevent reinfarction, however.

Right Ventricular Infarction

The proximal segment of the right coronary artery can produce an infarction of the right ventricle in combination with infarction of the left ventricle. One third to one half of patients with an inferior wall MI have right ventricular involvement because the right coronary artery supplies both the right ventricle and the inferior wall of the left ventricle. Because the therapy for right-sided infarction is different than for left-sided infarction, early recognition is imperative and must incorporate right-sided precordial leads (see page 373). Symptoms of right ventricular infarction are those of inadequate left ventricular filling (i.e., elevated systemic venous pressure, decreased cardiac output, and little or no pulmonary congestion). Volume expansion is the key therapeutic tactic. Drugs to achieve diuresis or to reduce preload are inappropriate because they further contribute to the deficit in right ventricular filling pressures. Dobutamine is often used to improve the cardiac index and ejection fractions of both the right and left ventricle. Pacing may be required, too, because the heart may be impaired from preexisting nodal ischemia. Close observation is required because these patients are at increased risk of ventricular fibrillation.

Lateral Wall Infarction

The circumflex artery and left anterior descending artery is responsible for the lateral wall infarction. Q waves may be seen in V_5 and V_6. Typically, infarction in the lateral wall is not as likely to create serious hemodynamic compromises as other types, and clinical signs and symptoms are ordinarily not dramatic. Treatment is directed toward limiting extension and pain relief.

Posterior Wall Infarction

This infarction can follow occlusion of the right coronary artery or a branch of the circumflex artery and may accompany infarction of the inferior wall. The ECG diagnosis is complicated because the typical precordial leads cannot directly reflect the damage. ECG changes are described as reciprocal changes over the opposite wall, V_1 to V_4 (i.e., "mirror images" of typical infarction changes). Abnormal Q waves will be absent and tall R waves are dominant. ST segments will be depressed, and ischemia will be indicated by peaked T waves, not inverted ones. Bradycardia, conduction defects, and various degrees of heart block may be noted. Drugs with positive inotropic and chronotropic effects (e.g., isoproterenol [Isuprel] or atropine) ensure the maintenance of impulse formation and conduction until ventricular pacing is restored.

Anterior Wall Infarction

The main left coronary artery supplies the anterior two thirds of the ventricular septum as well as all or part of the right and left bundle branches. This type of infarction is associated with extensive myocardial damage and seriously impairs the functional efficacy of the left ventricle. Cardiogenic shock, arrhythmias, and conduction defects all contribute to a guarded prognosis.

Cardiogenic Shock. Cardiogenic shock carries a mortality rate of up to 80 percent. Complete heart block and ventricular standstill occur when both fascicles of the left and right bundles are blocked. ENs must stand ready to assist with emergency pacing because heart block may occur precipitously. The patient in cardiogenic shock should be promptly transferred to the ICU for advanced therapies, which may include intra-aortic balloon pumping, insertion of invasive monitoring lines, use of multiple antiarrhythmic and inotropic agents, and adjunctive ventilatory support. Vasodilator therapy (e.g., nitroprusside) is administered to reduce preload and afterload (see page 382).

Angiotensin-Converting Enzyme Inhibitor Therapy. During the process of acute myocardial infarction, the physician may choose to begin angiotensin-converting enzyme (ACE) inhibitor therapy to treat ejection fractions that are lower than 40 percent or if the patient is in impending heart failure. After an acute MI, many neurohumoral events begin to occur; these continue for several days and greatly alter contractility, preload, and afterload. Drugs of this type assist in dilating coronary arteries as well as systemic arteries and arterioles. In addition, they reduce preload by increasing venous capacitance. Early use is thought to aid in preventing heart failure associated with acute MI. Intravenous enalaprilat (Vasotec) may be initiated in the ED by bolus or infusion. The EN must understand that the BP can dramatically decline with the delivery of the initial bolus and should be prepared to manage hypotensive episodes promptly.

RESUSCITATION

In the event that the patient with chest pain suffers a cardiopulmonary arrest, the EN must be able to promptly institute basic life support and prepare for additional measures as outlined by the American Heart Association's *Textbook of Advanced Cardiac Life Support.* In addition to performing chest compressions or managing the airway, the EN has several other important roles to fulfill as the resuscitation continues, such as giving drugs, assisting with defibrillation and pacing, monitoring and documenting activities, and giving human support to significant others.

CONGESTIVE HEART FAILURE

There are several precipitating events for congestive heart failure, but MI is the most common cause of decreased contractility and decreased left ventricular compliance. Symptoms range from some minor pulmonary congestion to cardiogenic shock, depending upon the extent of myocardial damage, either acute or chronic. Cardiogenic shock occurs when more than 40 percent of the left ventricle is involved, but it can also occur if the right ventricle is involved or if there are certain mechanical defects, such as papillary muscle infarction or ventricular septal rupture. Prolonged bradyarrhythmias from advanced blocks and sustained tachyarrhythmias may also produce heart output failure. Heart failure is classified into four categories, commonly referred to as the Killip Classifications, according to severity[8] (Table 23–1).

EMERGENCY MANAGEMENT OF ACUTE PULMONARY EDEMA

Acute pulmonary edema is usually of cardiac origin with acute left ventricular failure, but it may be of noncardiogenic origin with damage to pulmonary capillary tensions from chemical irritation

TABLE 23–1. KILLIP'S CLASSIFICATIONS OF HEART FAILURE

Class	Description
I	Little evidence of pulmonary congestion (no rales or third heart sound) or hypoperfusion
II	Pulmonary congestion without hypoperfusion; presence of S_3 gallop and mild or moderate pulmonary congestion in the lower half of the lung fields
III	Hypoperfusion without pulmonary congestion; acute pulmonary edema and hemodynamic impairment
IV	Hypoperfusion and pulmonary congestion; shock syndrome (i.e., blood pressure < 90 mm Hg, oliguria, mental obtundation)

of fumes, smoke, or particulate matter. Whatever the cause, there is an increased permeability of the alveolar–capillary membrane with seepage of plasma from the capillaries of the lung bed into the alveoli. This directly results in a compromised gas exchange with varying degrees of hypoxemia; later, hypercapnia develops, with dyspnea, tachycardia, apprehension, and hemoptysis. Other indices are frothy, blood-tinged sputum; distended neck veins; clammy extremities; cyanosis; severe orthopnea; and rales.

The patient with acute pulmonary edema must have prompt support of vital functions, including oxygen administration and establishment of an intravenous access point. The patient should be placed in a Fowler's position to facilitate breathing. When respiratory distress is severe, or if there are signs of acidosis and BP failure, early intubation is imperative. The ECG, BP, and pulse oximetry must be carefully monitored throughout the ED stay. As soon as feasible, a 12-lead ECG should be obtained, and blood should be drawn for a CBC count, electrolytes, and ABGs. A portable chest x-ray should also be promptly requisitioned while the physician decides on the pharmacological management of the patient.

Pharmacological Therapy in Ventricular Failure

Understanding the neurohormonal responses in heart failure is vital to ensuring that short-term improvements in hemodynamics do not incite pathological responses that will negatively affect the patient on a long-term basis. Traditional management of congestive heart failure is based on stroke volume manipulation (i.e., contractility, preload, afterload), primarily for symptoms control. Inotropes are used to enhance cardiac contractility and output; diuretics, nitroglycerin, and fluid titration are used to decrease preload; vasodilators and ACE-inhibitors are used to decrease afterload; and β-blockers are sometimes given to offset negative effects of prolonged sympathetic stimulation.

Inotropes. Digitalis reduces plasma renin, aldosterone, and norepinephrine levels and tends to inhibit sympathetic activity prior to exerting its hemodynamic effects. Digitalis may be used alone or with ACE-inhibitors (see page 380). Catecholamines function as inotropic agents, too, because of their effects on neurohumoral responses to myocardial dysfunction. The agents may be selected for either β_1 effects (i.e., increasing heart rate, AV conduction, and force of contraction) or β_2 effects (i.e., relaxing the bronchial and vascular smooth muscles). Dopamine is known for its dopaminergic effects, which cause vasodilation of the renal and mesenteric blood vessels. In ventricular failure, it is used for both inotropic and vasopressor effects. In low doses (1 to 3 µg/kg per minute), it functions to increase renal and mesenteric blood flow; when low doses are given with dobutamine (Dobutrex), both cardiac output and renal perfusion are improved. Moderate-dose therapy (5 to 10 µg/kg per minute) is ideal when only an inotropic effect is desired. In high doses (> 10 µg/kg per minute), dopamine will also stimulate α-receptors, creating an inotropic/vasopressor effect. Dopamine responses, however, are highly dependent on releasable stores of norepinephrine.[5] Dobutamine is a β_1-agonist that decreases aortic impedance and systemic vascular resistance. It is also a potent inotrope and vasodilator. It can increase cardiac output by 20 to 55 percent without an increase in heart rate. It has negligible effects on BP if the patient is well hydrated. The EN should expect a fall in BP, however, if the patient is hypovolemic because of the considerable peripheral vasodilation that dobutamine may induce. The usual dose for low cardiac output states is 2.5 µg/kg per minute, titrated upward as needed. It may be combined with an agent to reduce afterload (i.e., a vasodilator) to avoid myocardial ischemia while increasing the cardiac output. Epinephrine and norepinephrine (Levophed) are *not* used for cardiac failure: epinephrine may cause serious rhythm disturbances (occasionally, it may be employed to replenish catecholamines during prolonged dopamine therapy), and norepinephrine has strong alpha effects that would be detrimental to the efficacy of the left ventricular function during failure. Isoproterenol (Isuprel) is a pure β-agonist that is seldom used in failure because it can incite rhythm disturbances. It has both inotropic and chronotropic effects and consistently elevates cardiac output by increasing the rate, not stroke volume. Phosphodiesterase inhibitors such as amrinone and milrinone (Inocor and Primacor, respectively) produce increased contractility and vasodilation, which yields enhanced cardiac emptying and improves output. These may be given with dobutamine to potentiate the inherent inotropic effect. Both agents must be mixed with saline because glucose-containing solutions reduce the potency of the agent. If the patient is also receiving furosemide (Lasix), it cannot be given into the same line, because it will precipitate in the presence of either agent. Loading doses are usually about 0.75 mg/kg over 3 to 5 minutes, followed by a second equal bolus 30 minutes later if required. The bolus should be given in divided infusions of 1 to 1.5 mg/kg over several minutes with close monitoring of the BP. Rapid administration may result in hypotension. Subsequent bolus doses are given every 10 minutes, followed by an infusion of 5 to 10 μg/kg per minute. The effects of infusion therapy do not peak until 7 or more hours have elapsed; with bolus augmentation, effects will peak within several minutes.[7]

Vasodilator Therapy. The goal of using vasodilators is to decrease afterload. These agents are used only for patients with a normal or elevated BP, however. Decreases in systemic arterial pressures may affect baroreceptors in the carotid sinus and the aortic arch; this will stimulate even more the already overactive neurohumoral system, leading to additional vasoconstriction. Variables manipulated by vasodilators include arterial compliance, arteriolar resistance, and venous capacitance. Nitroglycerin, 10 to 100 μg/min IV, along with diuretics works well to relieve pulmonary congestion. Use of nitroglycerin requires hemodynamic monitoring; its use in the ED is constrained. Nurses who prepare and titrate this agent must be aware of its idiosyncrasies and be able to closely monitor the patient's hemodynamic status during its use. Nitroprusside (Nipride) decreases preload and afterload and improves the failing cardiac output owing to its potent vasodilatory actions, too. Its use is paramount when hypertension accompanies the failure (see page 383).

Diuretics. The goals of diuretic therapy include relieving peripheral edema and pulmonary congestion, reducing preload, and normalizing cardiac filling pressures.[9] Furosemide (0.5 to 1 mg/kg IV) is the initial drug of choice to increase venous capacitance; it should not be used, however, if the BP is below normal and there is evidence of hypoperfusion. The diuresis associated with furosemide usually does not occur until the pulmonary edema is resolved.[3] The EN must realize that patients in various stages of heart failure need continuous BP monitoring because BP may change rapidly during acute episodes when other hemodynamic variables are being manipulated by drug therapy. Intravenous nitroglycerin is also useful in reducing preload because of its vasodilator effects. It may also be given for its effects on capacitance and to reduce ventricular filling pressures.

Other Agents. Morphine (2 to 5 mg) is useful for increasing venous capacitance as well as for decreasing the anxiety associated with severe ventricular failure and acute pulmonary edema. It is usually one of the initial drugs given if the patient is *not* hypotensive.

If the underlying cause can be promptly identified, treatment is directed toward it when the condition is reversible (e.g., thrombolytics or [PTCA] percutaneous transluminal coronary angioplasty for acute MI). Surgery may be performed for aortic or mitral regurgitation, cardiac rupture, or a ventricular septal defect if facilities and resources are promptly available.

HYPERTENSIVE EMERGENCIES

There are numerous conditions that can precipitate hypertensive emergencies or crises. These include acute MI, unstable angina, acute left ventricular failure, dissecting aortic aneurysm, and numerous neurological and renal disorders. Abrupt interruption of long-term antihypertensive therapy can also result in the patient's arriving at the ED with a dangerously high BP. It may be precipitated by many conditions, but the pathophysiology invariably encompasses an abrupt rise in vasoconstrictor substances.

Hypertensive Urgencies

Hypertensive urgency is defined by a diastolic BP greater than 130 mm Hg, *without evidence of end organ involvement* such as chest pain or encephalopathy (see page 334). This may occur from rapid withdrawal of antihypertensives, burns, or other conditions that change vascular reactivity. Oral antihypertensives are used to treat the condition, but great care is taken to reduce the mean arterial pressure cautiously to ensure that it does not fall below limits for autoregulation of the cerebral blood flow. Low doses of oral agents are used to avoid sudden drops in BP that could precipitate stroke or acute MI. Nifedipine (Procardia), Clonidine (Catapres), and Captopril (Capoten) are common agents used initially. Intravenous agents are reserved for nonresponsive cases.

Hypertensive Crisis

Hypertensive crisis is defined as elevation of diastolic BP to 130 mm Hg, with evidence of cardiovascular compromise (e.g., chest pain or heart failure), encephalopathy, intracerebral bleeding, or dissecting aneurysm. In these cases, the goal is to lower the mean arterial BP by 25 percent or to decrease the diastolic BP to 100 to 110 mm Hg over several minutes to hours. The BP should not be precipitously lowered because it could fall below the lower limits of autoregulation, resulting in impaired cerebral perfusion; ischemia or stroke could result. The management of hypertensive crisis should be accomplished in an ICU, where invasive monitoring devices are available that allow close monitoring of BP during the titration of drugs. In cases of dissecting aneurysm, the systolic BP should be lowered to 100 to 120 mm Hg or to a mean arterial pressure (MAP) of below 80 mm Hg as quickly as possible, preferably without compromising the central nervous system (CNS) or cardiac and renal perfusion. In the case of dissecting aneurysm, the goal is limiting the dissection process. In cases of intracranial infarction or hemorrhage, antihypertensive therapy is ordinarily withheld unless the diastolic BP exceeds 130 mm Hg. Although the lowered BP would prevent increased bleeding and ischemia, it might also contribute to cerebral hypoperfusion.

Drugs used in the treatment of hypertensive crisis include nitroprusside, nitroglycerin, and an array of other antihypertensives reserved for unique clinical circumstances (e.g., eclampsia, overdose of street drugs). Nitroprusside is the initial drug of choice for most patients because it has a rapid onset and short duration of action that permits minute-to-minute control of the BP. It may be combined with a β-blocker in aortic dissection. (The negative inotropic effect of β-blockers is vital to decreasing shearing forces caused by the reflex adrenergic stimulation of nitroprusside.) In acute MI or unstable angina, the use of intravenous nitrates reduces systemic vascular resistance while improving coronary perfusion. Labetalol (Normodyne) and calcium channel blockers may also be used to reduce the BP and to improve myocardial oxygenation. In these cases, nitroprusside may cause a "steal" from ischemic areas because of a more generalized vasodilation. Hydralazine (Apresoline) and diazoxide (Hyperstat) are not often used, because they increase heart rate and increase myocardial oxygen demand.

DISSECTING ANEURYSMS

In a dissecting aortic aneurysm, blood flows into the medial layer of the aortic wall and weakens the vessel. It also partially or completely occludes the origin of arteries that arise in its pathway. If it occurs in the ascending aorta, it can involve the aortic valve, leading to aortic regurgitation. Weakening of the aortic wall as a result of the dissection can lead to rupture. The location of the resultant bleeding can be the pericardial sac, the mediastinum, the pleural cavity, or the abdomen, depending on the site of rupture. Hypertension is the usual cause of a dissecting aneurysm, but other conditions can also be responsible for this life-threatening vascular defect. These include pregnancy, congenital aortic stenosis, coarctation of the aorta, or injury induced by surgery from cannulation or other intraoperative manipulations.

Dissections are divided into three types:

- Type I: Involves the ascending aorta, the arch, and the descending aorta
- Type II: Is confined to the ascending aorta
- Type III: Is confined to the descending aorta

Another classification scheme separates dissections into two classes: type A, which involves the ascending aorta, and type B, which involves the descending aorta.

The aortic aneurysm is often chronic, and the aventitial layers of the vessel remain intact. In other cases, there is a temporary tamponade by the adventitia or aorta and mediastinal pleura, and the crisis is contained for 24 to 48 hours, permitting emergency surgical intervention. However, with the transsection of all layers of the aorta, death results promptly from the rupture.

Emergency Presentation

The patient usually presents with chest or abdominal pain. The pain is characterized by abrupt onset, reaching its maximum intensity almost immediately. It is generally severe and is classically described as tearing or lacerating. As the dissection progresses, the location of the pain can shift. Associated clinical manifestations are variable, depending on the location and extent of dissection and the structures involved. Occlusion of the vessels supplying the brain can result in neurological manifestation. If there is pressure around the aortic arch from a hematoma, the patient may experience hoarseness. Occlusion of the renal arteries can be suggested by associated oliguria, hematuria, or anuria. Occlusion of vessels supplying the GI structures can lead to epigastric pain, vomiting, hematemesis, or melena. Arterial blood supply to one or more extremities can be partially or completely interrupted, and pulses may be imperceptible or BPs varied from one leg to the other. Involvement of the aortic valve can result in acute aortic regur-

gitation and manifestations of left ventricular failure. Involvement of a sinus of Valsalva can cause coronary artery occlusion and an acute MI. Rupture to the pericardial sac can precipitate the onset of pericardial tamponade. The EN must understand that the structures involved create the signs and symptoms; thus, clinical presentations may vary considerably. Although a true upright chest film can reveal great vessel disruption (i.e., a widened mediastinum), a supine or semierect chest film distorts the mediastinum and makes it appear widened, even when there is no actual dissecting process.

Clinical Management

The BP is lowered using intravenous antihypertensive agents (see page 383). β-blockers (e.g., propranolol [Inderal]) are used to depress the left ventricular contractility and the steepness of its ejection curve that contribute to the propagation of the dissecting process. When the pain is controlled as a result of BP reduction, a diagnostic aortogram is usually done, and surgery is scheduled to correct certain defects after the BP is well stabilized. Patients with dissecting aneurysms are not held for prolonged periods in the ED but are promptly transferred to the ICU for the invasive monitoring that is required with intravenous antihypertensive therapy.

DIGITALIS TOXICITY

The initial presentation of digitalis toxicity usually includes GI complaints, such as nausea, vomiting, anorexia, and perhaps diarrhea. The patient usually indicates that these complaints emerged over 1 or 2 days and were soon followed by confusion, lethargy, and other CNS manifestations. Visual disturbances are also common and include inability to perceive green and red or seeing yellow or green halos around objects. When the patient appears in the ED, he or she may have bradycardia or heart block; syncopal episodes are also often reported. Alternative atrial rhythm disturbances include sinus tachycardia, atrial fibrillation, paroxysmal atrial tachycardia (PAT) with block, AV nodal tachycardia with AV disassociation, and ectopy. Ventricular rhythm indices of digitalis toxicity include bigeminy, trigeminy, ectopy, and tachycardia.[10]

Although the serum digitalis level is useful, the normal therapeutic range (0.8 to 2.0 ng/mL) is quite narrow, and patients may have signs and symptoms of toxicity before the serum level indicates toxicity.[10]

■ CARDIAC DYSRHYTHMIAS

ANTIARRHYTHMIC THERAPY FOR PAROXYSMAL SUPRAVENTRICULAR TACHYCARDIA

Atrioventricular Nodal Reentrant Tachycardia or Paroxysmal Atrial Tachycardia

The genesis of the rhythm disturbance paroxysmal supraventricular tachycardia (PSVT) is within the AV node and perhaps an associated small rim of perinodal atrial tissue. It may involve a slow pathway or a fast pathway. In the first type, AV nodal reentrant tachycardia (AVNRT), there is a block in the fast pathway that will not permit a premature beat to be conducted down the fast pathway, so it is consequently shifted to the slow anterograde conduction route. The beat conducts back up the fast pathway (retrograde limb of the circuit), initiating the tachycardia.[11] Because the retrograde conduction via the fast tract is equaled by the anterograde conduction time through the His–Purkinje system, depolarization of the atria occurs concurrently with depolarization of the ventricles, and P waves are lost in the QRS segment. The resultant tachycardia is characterized by a long P-R interval and a short RP′ interval, where P′ is the retrograde-conducted P wave. In the other type (i.e., fast pathway), the retrograde limb of the circuit conducts slowly, resulting in an atypical fast-slow or long RP tachycardia. There is a visible P wave before each narrow QRS segment.

Atrioventricular Reciprocating Tachycardia

AV reciprocating tachycardia (AVRT) involves the AV node and an extranodal bypass tract. There are two types of AVRT: orthodromic (AV anterograde conduction and retrograde accessory conduction), which is characterized by a narrow QRS segment, and antidromic (AV retrograde conduction with anterograde accessory pathway conduction). In antidromic tachycardia, the QRS segment is wide; this rhythm can be confused with a prelethal ventricular arrhythmia.

Both AVNRT and AVRT are normally regular tachycardias with rates of 120 to 300 bpm. They have a sudden onset and cessation and tend to occur mostly in young adults who do not have known structural heart disease. The P waves within the ST segment are in a 1:1 relationship with the QRS segment. A special type of AVRT is known as the Lown–Ganong–Levine syndrome and is characterized only by a short P-R interval.

Wolff–Parkinson–White Syndrome

Wolff–Parkinson–White (WPW) syndrome is an accessory-pathway conduction tachycardia. In this syndrome, there is a direct connection of working myocardial fibers between the atrium and ventricles that carry electrical impulses outside the normal conduction system. They may travel down the AV node and return by a retrograde, accessory pathway *or* may initially proceed down the accessory pathway and then travel retrograde up the AV node. When an extranodal path conducts in an anterograde direction, it causes preexcitation of the ventricles. Hallmarks are a short P-R interval (0.12 seconds); because there is no delay at the AV node and a fusion of normal and abnormal depolarization occurs, the resultant QRS segment is wide. A delta wave may be present; it is indicated on the ECG by a slurring of the initial QRS deflection. The QRS segment of a left-sided bypass tract is characterized by an upright QRS complex in lead V_1; in a right-sided bypass tract, the QRS complex in this lead will be negative.

DRUG THERAPY FOR RHYTHM DISTURBANCES

Note: The American Heart Association's *Textbook of Advanced Cardiac Life Support* should be used for its algorithms for management of cardiac emergencies, including cardiac arrest. The material in this chapter is designed to augment that resource, not to replace it.

Adenosine

Adenosine (Adenocard) is the initial drug of choice for most supraventricular tachycardias. It is the most widely used agent for the termination of PSVT. It is a physiological antiarrhythmic that stimulates production of cyclic adenosine monophosphate (cAMP) and the adenosine receptors A_1 and A_2. This drug slows conduction time through the AV node, thus interrupting AVRTs. Adenosine is used as a first-line drug for PSVT, Wolff–Parkinson–White syndrome, and AVNRT. It is not effective for atrial flutter, atrial fibrillation, or ventricular tachycardia (VT), but in most cases it will not create additional problems if it is administered. Adenosine is also used for wide-complex tachycardia that is unresponsive to lidocaine and to differentiate wide-complex tachycardia from supraventricular tachycardia (SVT). Because the drug has a high sensitivity and specificity, it is used in diagnostics to determine mechanisms of other arrhythmias (e.g., adenosine may reduce ventricular response in atrial flutter, revealing increased numbers of flutter waves, thus making it easier to diagnose the rhythm in patients with 2:1 conduction and flutter waves hidden within the QRS segment). The test does present some risk: it has been known to generate a life-threatening rapid ventricular response (e.g., Torsades de pointes) in some patients.

Adenosine has a short half-life (0.6 to 1.5 seconds) and must be given by rapid intravenous bolus, followed immediately by a 20-mL saline flush. The duration of action is 1 to 2 minutes. Adenosine must be placed in the port most proximal to the vein or directly into the hub of an intravenous catheter. If the drug is given into an extremity, elevation of the extremity and milking of the limb toward the heart may assist in delivery of the drug to central circulation before expiration of its half-life.[12] Adenosine is contraindicated for patients with a history of chronic obstructive pulmonary disease (COPD), sick sinus syndrome, and second- or third-degree heart block without pacer protection.

Dosage and Administration. A dose of 6 mg is given by IV push over 1 to 2 seconds. A repeat bolus of 12 mg over 1 to 2 seconds may be administered 2 minutes after the first dose. The 12-mg bolus may be repeated if necessary; but ordinarily, the maximum amount delivered is not to exceed 30 mg. It may also be given via a central venous catheter in 3-mg pulse doses, but this method has not been well studied.[8] A new alternative dosing method is the administration of 1 to 3 mg initially, followed by a 2.5 to 3.0-mg dose until a maximum dose of 20 mg is reached.[7] Remember the onset of action for adenosine is immediate and it has a plasma half-life of less than 10 seconds; plasma clearance is less than 50 seconds.

When being given adenosine, the patient may feel short of breath and experience flushing, chest pressure or headache, nausea, lightheadedness, syncope, or dizziness; warn the patient that these reactions may be quite unpleasant, but reassure them that they are transient. Although serious adverse effects are not common, they may include AV conduction defects. Asystole may last up to 15 seconds in some cases, but this converts spontaneously to normal sinus rhythm. In some cases, a persistent tachycardia may resume. It is vital that the EN understand that if wide complex tachycardias do not respond to adenosine, the ECG should be reassessed to rule out ventricular tachycardia.

Diltiazem

Diltiazem (injectable Cardizem) is a calcium channel–blocking drug that acts by inhibiting calcium influx during membrane depolarization of cardiac and smooth muscle. It slows conduction time and prolongs refractoriness in the AV node, thus slowing the ventricular response during atrial flutter or fibrillation with a rapid ventricular response. It converts PSVT to normal sinus rhythm (NSR) by interruption of the reentrant pathway. BP can fall promptly because of the drug's effects on vascular smooth muscle. Diltiazem should *not be used if the patient has an accessory pathway,* because the drug could stimulate a rapid ventricular response. It is also not used for patients with sick sinus syndrome if they do not have a ventricular pacemaker in place or for patients with second- or third-degree AV blocks, hypotension, or acute MI with associated pulmonary congestion.

Dosage and Administration. The usual dosage of diltiazem is 0.25 mg/kg injected over 2 minutes. A repeat bolus may be administered (0.35 mg/kg) over 2 minutes. Other boluses may be given, but transition to another antidysrhythmic should take place within 3 hours after bolus of the initial dose. A short-term infusion (10 to 15 mg/h) may also be initiated, but when possible, this should be accomplished within the ICU, where invasive monitoring is readily available.

Adverse effects from diltiazem include hypotension, itching and burning at the injection site, flushing, headache, and dysrhythmias, often associated with chest pain or syncope. Nausea, vomiting, dizziness, paresthesias, dry mouth, dyspnea, and edema have also been noted.

When giving diltiazem, all emergency equipment including a defibrillator and pacer, must be at hand. If hypotension occurs, the drug should be discontinued at once and fluids given as tolerated. Shock position may also be employed to augment circulating volume.

Esmolol

Esmolol (Brevibloc) is a β-blocking agent with a rapid onset and short duration of action. It decreases heart rate, prolongs sinoatrial node recovery time, and prolongs AV conduction. Because it is also an antihypertensive agent, it decreases systolic BP, left and right ventricular ejection fractions, and the cardiac index. Esmolol inhibits β_1-receptors in cardiac muscle and, at high doses, inhibits β_2 receptors in bronchial and vascular musculature. It is used to control the ventricular rate in patients with atrial flutter and fibrillation with a rapid ventricular response. It rarely causes conversion to normal sinus rhythm. It is *not* used for patients with hypotension, depressed myocardial contractility, bronchospastic disease, or heart block greater than first degree.

Dosage and Administration. The EN should add 5 g of esmolol to 500 mL of fluid to achieve a dilution of 10 mg/mL. The loading dose of 500 μg/kg/per minute is infused over 1 minute and followed with 50 μg/kg/per minute over 4 minutes and titrated for effects. If the patient's tachycardia does not respond, the loading dose can be readministered and followed with an escalated dose by infusion. At this point, the patient should be prepared for transfer to the ICU for advanced monitoring of hemodynamics. Throughout the ED stay,

the EN should observe for AV block, bradycardia, and hypotension.

EMERGENCY MANAGEMENT OF PAROXYSMAL SUPRAVENTRICULAR TACHYCARDIA WHEN UNDERLYING MECHANISMS ARE UNKNOWN

If the patient with PSVT is experiencing an unstable hemodynamic status, cardioversion should be done promptly. Sedation should be provided, usually with a benzodiazepine agent such as diazepam (Valium) or midazolam (Versed), and in some cases, a narcotic analgesic may be added to make the patient more comfortable. The sequence for synchronized cardioversion begins with 100 J and is escalated if the rhythm persists. If the patient is stable in the ED, vagal maneuvers may be tried first. Drug therapy should begin in most cases with adenosine, followed by procainamide (Pronestyl). Other agents, such as sodium channel blockers, potassium channel blockers, and miscellaneous agents, may be employed. The EN should recognize that patients with PSVT are usually anxious, short of breath, and uncomfortable. During all patient encounters, the EN should provide reassurance and an explanation of all therapies.

BRADYARRHYTHMIAS AND BLOCKS

When patients present with chest pain, shortness of breath, or decreased level of consciousness (LOC), a slow heart rate might be suspected, especially if the BP is low and there are signs of pulmonary congestion or evidence of an acute MI. The EN should promptly take steps to ensure an airway, ventilation, and circulation. Supplemental oxygen must be provided without delay and an intravenous route must be established. Monitoring devices should include a pulse oximeter, automatic BP cuff, and an ECG monitor while the patient's initial history is obtained and an examination is conducted. A 12-lead ECG and a portable chest film should also be obtained in this early phase of care.

The drug of choice for bradycardia is atropine, 0.5 to 1.0 mg, repeated at 5-minute intervals as necessary up to a total of 0.04 mg/kg. In the meantime, preparations should be made for transcutaneous pacing, using analgesia and sedation as necessary. If the patient has a denervated heart (transplanted), it will not respond to atropine, and pacing must be done initially, along with a catecholamine infusion in most cases. Dopamine (5 to 10 µg/kg/per minute) or epinephrine (2 to 10 µg/min) are the agents that are ordinarily administered after atropine. In the meantime, preparations should be made for insertion of a transvenous pacer.[8]

VENTRICULAR RHYTHM DISTURBANCES

Pulseless ventricular tachycardia and ventricular fibrillation rapidly lead to hemodynamic decompensation and death without immediate emergency action. Cardiopulmonary resuscitation and the delivery of advanced life support drugs are vital—they must be accomplished swiftly to minimize morbidity and mortality. Ventilatory support and chest compressions are continued while the defibrillator is being readied. If the patient has an implanted defibrillator, this should in no way deter the emergency team from performing its usual interventions, including external defibrillation. When a patient has such a device, even if it fires, attending personnel are not in danger. When placing paddles, a standard apex-sternum positioning is used to avoid directly shocking the generator, which could damage or turn off the unit (Fig. 23–7).

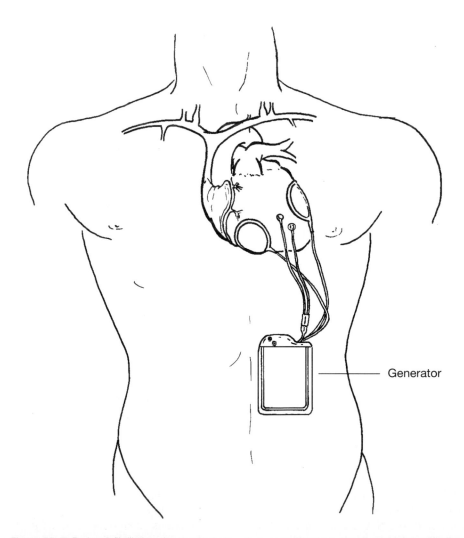

Generator

Figure 23–7. During defibrillation, the standard apex-sternum positioning is used to avoid damaging the generator of the implanted defibrillator.

■ NURSING DIAGNOSES

Appropriate nursing diagnoses for cardiac emergencies include:

- Alteration in tissue perfusion related to coronary artery occlusion or ventricular dysfunction
- Alteration in cardiac output related to arrhythmias, left ventricular dysfunction, hypovolemia, or right ventricular infarction
- Impaired gas exchange due to increased pulmonary capillary pressure
- Alteration in comfort: pain related to myocardial ischemia or pericarditis
- Anxiety related to pain and prognosis

■ REFERENCES

1. Apple S. Advanced strategies for diagnosing acute myocardial infarction. *Heartbeat, A Cardiac Newsletter.* 6:1, 1995. Available from: Adverceutics, Inc., 5565 Sterrett Place, Columbia, Md.
2. Thomason TR, Riegel B, Carlso B, Gocka I. Monitoring electrocardiographic changes: results of a national survey. *J Cardiovasc Nurs.* 1995;9:1–9.
3. American Heart Association. *Textbook of Advanced Cardiac Life Support.* 2nd ed. Dallas, Tex: AHA; 1987:115–127.
4. GUSTO angiograph investigation report: the effects of tissue plasminogen activator, streptokinase or both on coronary-artery patency, ventricular function, and survival after acute myocardial infarction. *N Engl J Med.* 1993;329:1615–1622.
5. Barber JS. *Critical Care Pharmacology.* Lewisville, Tex; Barbara Clark Mims Associates; 1995.
6. Ayres SM, Grenvik A, Holbrook PR, Shoemaker WC. *Textbook of Critical Care.* 3rd ed. Philadelphia, Pa: WB Saunders; 1995:475–481.
7. Chernow B, ed. *The Pharmacologic Approach to the Critically Ill Patient.* 3rd ed. Baltimore, Md: Williams & Wilkins; 1994:347–364.
8. Freed M, Grines C. *Essentials of Cardiovascular Medicine.* Birmingham, Mich: Physicians' Press; 1994:196–215.
9. Wright JM. Pharmacologic management of congestive heart failure. *Crit Care Nurse.* 1995;18:32–44.
10. Cooke DM. Shielding your patient from digitalis toxicity. *Nursing 92.* 1992;22:44–47.
11. Shapiro S, Brundge B. Cardiac problems in critical care. In: Bongard FS, Sue DY. *Current Critical Care Diagnosis & Treatment.* E. Norwalk, Conn: Appleton & Lange; 1994:427–453.
12. Conover MB. Diagnosis and management of arrhythmias associated with Wolff–Parkinson–White syndrome. *Crit Care Nurse.* 1994:4:30–39.

■ BIBLIOGRAPHY

Bongard FS, Sue DY. *Current Critical Care Diagnosis and Treatment.* E. Norwalk, Conn: Appleton & Lange; 1994.

Clochesy JM, Breu C, Cardin S, et al. *Critical Care Nursing.* Philadelphia, Pa: WB Saunders; 1993.

English ME. Advanced concepts in heart failure. *Crit Care Nurse Q.* 1995;18:1.

Ide B. Bedside electrocardiographic assessment. *J Cardiovasc Nurs.* 1995;9:10–23.

Levine RL, Fromm RE Jr. *Critical Care Monitoring from Pre-Hospital to the ICU.* St. Louis, Mo: Mosby-Year Book; 1995.

Moreau D, ed. *Nursing 96 Drug Handbook.* Springhouse, Pa: Springhouse Corporation; 1996.

Physician's Desk Reference. 50th ed. Montvale, NJ: Medical Economics; 1996.

Ruppert SD, Kernicki JG, Dolan JT. *Dolan's Critical Care Nursing.* 2nd ed. Philadelphia, Pa: FA Davis; 1996.

Urden LD, Davie JK, Thelan LA. *Essentials of Critical Care Nursing.* St. Louis, Mo: Mosby-Year Book; 1992.

Vasca PL. Ischemic heart disease. *Adv Pract Acute Crit Care.* 1995;6:3.

Weist PW, Roth PB. *Fundamentals of Emergency Radiology.* Philadelphia, Pa: WB Saunders; 1996.

Wilkins RL, Dexter JR. *Respiratory Disease Principles of Patient Care.* Philadelphia, Pa: FA Davis; 1993.

■ REVIEW: CARDIOVASCULAR EMERGENCIES

1. Identify the six immediate threats to life that may present to the emergency department (ED) as chest pain.

2. Explain the PQRST method of evaluating chest pain and cite the additional data that should be elicited from the patient to supplement this anecdotal information.

3. Identify the four organs or systems addressed in physical assessment of chest pain and cite findings in each that would suggest a cardiac origin for the pain.

4. Identify the adjunctive laboratory data required to establish a diagnosis of myocardial origin.

5. Describe the significance of isoenzymes in the study of myocardial infarction and identify extraneous noncardiac factors that might contribute to alterations in enzyme levels.

6. Describe recommended electrocardiogram (ECG) electrode placement for:
   a. Monitoring the ST segment
   b. Determining axis deviation
   c. Tracking the progression of a new bundle branch block
   d. Distinguishing supraventricular tachycardia with aberrancy from ventricular tachycardia (VT)
   e. Identifying right ventricular pathology

7. Explain the procedure for obtaining a 12-lead ECG, including precise placement of leads, and identify the extraneous factors that can interfere with obtaining a useful tracing.

8. Outline the therapy for acute chest pain, including medications to relieve the acute pain, and describe the parameters for using oral and intravenous nitroglycerin, including special precautions that must be observed.

9. List the standard criteria used to select suitable candidates for administration of thrombolytics.

10. Compare and contrast the three major thrombolytic drugs in terms of their actions, side effects, and administration guidelines, including clinical indices used to evaluate their efficacy.

11. Describe the characteristics of:
    a. Inferior wall infarction
    b. Right ventricular infarction
    c. Lateral wall infarction
    d. Posterior wall infarction
    e. Anterior wall infarction

12. Describe the significant features of a Q-wave and a non–Q-wave infarction.

13. Define *cardiogenic shock* and outline its immediate management within the emergency department (ED).

14. Explain Killip's classifications of heart failure.

15. Justify the use of angiotensin-enzyme inhibitor therapy for acute myocardial infarction (MI).

16. State the rationale for using the following agents in heart failure:
    a. Morphine
    b. Inotropes
    c. Vasodilators
    d. Diuretics

17. Differentiate between a hypertensive urgency and a hypertensive crisis, citing the drugs recommended for treating each type.

18. Describe the presentation of a dissecting aortic aneurysm and its ED management.

19. Describe the signs and symptoms of acute digitalis toxicity and the ECG findings that are classically associated with this condition.

20. Explain the significance of reentry circuits as they relate to supraventricular tachycardias.

21. Distinguish between the characteristics of atrioventricular (AV) nodal reentrant tachycardia and AV reciprocating tachycardia.

22. Define *orthodromic* and *antidromic tachycardias* in terms of their ECG complexes.

23. Identify the major danger in treating Wolff–Parkinson–White tachycardia with a calcium channel blocking agent such as verapamil.

24. Outline the nursing guidelines for the administration of adenosine in the treatment of supraventricular tachycardia.

25. List the recommended sequence of interventions for the emergency management of paroxysmal supraventricular tachycardia (PSVT) when the underlying mechanisms are unknown.

26. Identify the three major therapies that are indicated in the treatment of bradyarrhythmias and blocks.

27. Describe the paddle placement recommended for defibrillation of a patient with an implanted defibrillator.

Hematological Emergencies

24

This chapter focuses on the functions and components of blood, blood types, and the mechanisms of coagulation and addresses the major blood dyscrasias—those most commonly confronted in emergency-care populations—as they relate to tissue perfusion and support of vital functions. While massive bleeding and severe blood loss provide the most dramatic of real hematologic emergencies, many other less obvious blood-related emergencies are presented daily, many never recognized as the threat they may be. A working awareness of blood's components, types, and coagulation characteristics, together with commonly seen blood dyscrasias, is an important and valuable asset for emergency nurses (ENs). Anemias, bleeding disorders, and leukemias are discussed here, together with guidelines for administration of special factors in the emergency department (ED).

■ BLOOD AND ITS COMPONENTS

FUNCTIONS

As blood is carried to the tissues, it maintains an internal environment that is normal for the cells of the body. Blood picks up oxygen from the lungs, carries it to the tissues, and carries carbon dioxide back to the lungs for elimination; blood absorbs digested food materials from the digestive tract, carries it to the tissues for energy and cell building, and carries waste products of cellular metabolism to the kidneys and other excretory glands for elimination; blood helps coordinate the activities of various organs with each other as it transports hormones, the body's chemical regulators; blood

functions in the regulation of body temperature and facilitates the body's ability to fight infection and disease. Of all the functions of blood, however, the most urgent is oxygen supply at the cellular level.

COMPONENTS

Under normal conditions, blood is composed of a straw-colored fluid called plasma in which are suspended red blood cells (RBCs), white blood cells (WBCs), and the platelets. Plasma, the fluid fraction, makes up approximately 55 percent of whole blood, and the formed elements make up approximately 45 percent.

Blood Plasma

Water is the most abundant single element of blood, comprising about 91 to 92 percent of plasma, and its principal function is to act as a solvent and suspending medium for the various materials found in blood. Normal blood volume represents, on average, about five L, or 7 percent of body weight (Table 24–1). In addition to water, plasma is 7 to 7.5 percent proteins; three basic groups of protein have been designated; albumin (55 percent of total plasma proteins), globulin (44.8 percent of total), and fibrinogen (about 0.20 percent of total plasma proteins).

Plasma proteins serve many functions, the most important being maintenance of the proper osmotic pressure between circulating blood and the tissue spaces, facilitating the exchange of materials across cellular membranes by osmotic and hydrostatic pressure. Any alteration of the normal osmotic/hydrostatic pressure, either a decrease in

TABLE 24–1. NORMAL BLOOD VOLUME—APPROXIMATE VALUES FOR BLOOD VOLUME IN ADULTS

Age	Approximate Blood Volume (% of Body Weight)	Range of Approximate Blood Volume (mL)
Women (60-kg person)		
20–40 y	7.0	4200 ± 400
40–60 y	6.5	3900 ± 350
> 60 y	6.0	3600 ± 300
Men (70-kg person)		
20–40 y	8.0	5600 ± 500
40–60 y	7.5	5250 ± 450
> 60 y	7.0	4900 ± 400

plasma proteins or an increase in venous pressure, results in accumulation of fluid in tissue spaces (i.e., edema). Other functions of plasma proteins are:

- Assisting in regulation of the blood pH
- Contributing to viscosity of the blood
- Participation, through fibrinogen, in the clotting mechanism
- Forming antibodies from globulins to act against organisms, their toxic products, and other chemical substances
- Transporting lipids, including fat-soluble vitamins and steroid hormones
- Functioning as a food source for the body in protein starvation

Other substances to be found in plasma include nonprotein nitrogen compounds, such as urea, amino acids, creatinine, and uric acid; the inorganic salts, sodium, potassium, calcium, and magnesium; and blood sugars and lipids.

Blood Cells

The so-called formed elements of the blood that represent 45 percent of the blood volume include RBCs, or erythrocytes, WBCs, or leukocytes, and blood platelets, or thrombocytes (an older term).

Red Blood Cells, or Erythrocytes. In embryos, RBCs are formed in the liver and spleen; in adults, they are formed in the bone marrow, under normal conditions. Erythrocytes are disk-shaped elements having a biconcave contour that gives the advantage of equal and rapid diffusion of oxygen to its interior and a relatively large surface area for the absorption of gases. The cell membrane consists mostly of protein and lipid material; the interior protoplasmic mass is called the stroma and is made up of the same materials found in the membrane. The oxygen-carrying red pigment, hemoglobin, is bound up in the stroma substance and makes up about 33 percent of the cell volume; the remainder of the cell is about 65 percent water and 2 percent protein.

The average number of RBCs is usually given as $5,000,000/mm^3$ of blood for males and $4,500,000/mm^3$ for females. Normal values may be somewhat higher; 6,000,000 is not unusual for a large, healthy man. The RBC count may also vary about $1,000,000/mm^3$ per day; the high point of bone marrow delivery is in the morning and afternoon.

RBC counts are increased (erythrocytosis) by exercise, emotional states, after ingestion of a full meal, some diseases, and higher altitudes; for each 1000-foot rise of elevation, the lowering of barometric pressure increases the RBC count approximately $50,000$ cells$/mm^3$ within 24 to 48 hours.

RBC counts are decreased (erythrocytopenia) by the final months of pregnancy, an increase in barometric pressure, and after severe hemorrhage and blood loss.

White Blood Cells, or Leukocytes. WBCs are formed in both the lymph glands and the bone marrow and are divided into two basic types: granulocytes, which possess granules in their cytoplasm, and agranulocytes, which are free of granules in their cytoplasm. Granulocytes are formed in the bone marrow, and on the basis of their staining, they are divided into three types: neutrophils (60 to 65 percent of WBCs; they take a neutral stain), eosinophils (about 4 percent of WBCs; they take an acid stain), and basophils (those that stain with basic stain but are not found in any significant numbers in adults).

Agranulocytes are divided into three types: large lymphocytes, small lymphocytes, and monocytes. Lymphocytes are formed in the lymph glands and spleen; monocytes are formed in bone marrow.

Both neutrophils (granulocytes) and lymphocytes (agranulocytes) are actively motile and capable of diapedesis: they can traverse vascular walls, leaving the blood vessels at will to migrate to areas of the body being invaded by bacteria or foreign particulate matter. As phagocytes, they surround, engulf, and ultimately digest such particles; neutrophils ingest bacteria and small particles, while monocytes ingest larger particles such as worn-out RBCs and other cells. The normal WBC count varies from 5000 to 10,000/mm^3 of blood. An increase above 10,000 is referred to as leukocytosis, and a decrease below 5000 is called leukopenia. Leukocytosis is seen in most acute infections and can result physiologically from severe muscular activity, digestion of a meal, emotion, massage, dehydration, and certain drugs. A decrease, or leukopenia, occurs in diseases such as typhoid fever, measles, influenza, dengue fever, malaria, many of the anemias, malnutrition, metal poisonings, and alcohol or morphine poisoning.

Blood Platelets or Thrombocytes. Platelets are largely formed in the bone marrow; a few are formed in the spleen. In circulating blood, platelets are small, colorless bodies that usually appear as irregular spindles or oval disks. The normal count is 150,000 to 350,000/mm^3 and their average life span is about 10 days. Platelets initiate the critical processes of blood clotting and hemostasis; although interrelated, the two are separate and distinct functions. *Hemostasis* refers to the stoppage of blood flow and may occur as an end result of any one of several body defense mechanisms, while *clotting* refers to the adherence of platelets to the damaged lining of a vessel, forming a hemostatic platelet plug within 1 to 5 seconds after injury to a vessel wall. If injury is extensive, the blood clotting mechanism is activated to assist in further hemostasis.

Thrombocytopenia, or a decrease in platelets, results in a defective clotting mechanism in the face of injury or perhaps the slightest tissue trauma. For the most part, platelet deficiencies will manifest by nosebleeds, menorrhagia, gastrointestinal (GI) bleeds, disproportionate bleeding from a cut or scratch, superficial ecchymoses formed around venipuncture sites, and petechial patches or purpura (hemorrhages into skin, mucous membranes, or other tissues that do not blanch or disappear under spot pressure).

Causes of platelet deficiencies fall into four categories: (1) decreased production (e.g., bone marrow suppression caused by chemotherapeutic agents, alcohol toxicity effect on bone marrow, folate or vitamin B$_{12}$ deficiency, or by other drugs, toxins, or infections); (2) pooling and splenic sequestration (from disorders that produce marked splenic enlargement); (3) increased destruction caused by diseases creating antiplatelet antibodies (e.g., lymphoma and leukemia, collagen vascular disease, and particularly systemic lupus erythematosus [SLE], by drugs causing immune thrombocytopenia (e.g., quinine and quinidine, digitoxin, sulfonamides, phenytoin, aspirin) by disseminated intravascular coagulation or thrombotic thrombocytopenic purpura; and (4) dilution because of massive transfusion. In rare cases, immune thrombocytopenia can be a belated transfusion reaction.[1]

TYPES

The term *blood type* refers to the type of antigens present on RBC membranes. An antigen is a substance capable of stimulating formation of other substances called antibodies that can combine with the antigen, for example, to agglutinate or clump it. Antigens A, B, and Rh are the most important blood antigens as far as transfusions and newborn survival are concerned, although other less important antigens exist.

Every person's blood belongs to one of the four universally recognized AB blood groups, named according to the antigens present on RBC membranes:

- *Type A:* Antigen A on RBCs
- *Type B:* Antigen B on RBCs
- *Type AB:* Both antigen A and antigen B on RBCs
- *Type O:* Neither antigen A nor antigen B on RBCs

Type O blood is referred to as universal donor blood, which implies that it can safely be given to any recipient. This is not true, however, because the recipient's plasma may contain agglutinins other than anti-A and anti-B antibodies; therefore, if at all possible, the recipient's *and* donor's blood should be cross-matched, even if the donor's is type O, mixed and observed for agglutination of the donor's RBCs.

Universal recipient (type AB) blood contains neither anti-A nor anti-B antibodies, so it cannot agglutinate type A or type B donor RBCs. Again, other agglutinins may be present in the so-called universal recipient blood and can clump unidentified antigens (agglutinogens) in the donor's blood; cross-matching should be done before use for safety.

In addition, every person's blood is either Rh positive or Rh negative. The term *Rh* was taken from the Rhesus monkey, in which the Rh factor was first identified. The term *Rh-positive blood* means that Rh antigen is present in the RBCs. *Rh-negative blood,* on the other hand, is blood whose RBCs have no Rh antigen present on them. Normally, blood does *not* contain anti-Rh antibodies; these appear only in the blood of an Rh-negative person *after* Rh-positive RBCs have entered the bloodstream (i.e., by transfusion or by the carrying of an Rh-positive fetus).

COAGULATION

Unlike platelet abnormalities, blood coagulation disorders, or coagulopathies, tend to cause bleeding into the soft tissues. Nosebleeds, menorrhagia, and GI bleeds are rare, but hematomas and hemarthroses are commonly seen.

The mechanism by which blood clots is a highly complicated process and one that is still incompletely understood. Plasma proteins carry 13 special factors (numbered I through XIII) that have a special interrelationship in the clotting mechanism. A "coagulation cascade," involving sequential interaction of coagulation factors, occurs, with generation of fibrin and clot formation. The intrinsic pathway, composed of factors XIII, IX, XI, and XII and monitored by partial thromboplastin time (PTT), interacts and operates with the extrinsic pathway, composed of factor VII and tissue factors, to combine with factors V and X to form prothrombin, then thrombin, and then fibrinogen-activated fibrin. While this mechanism is extremely complex, the coagulation of blood may be characterized as the formation of a fibrin clot that can be represented as occurring in three stages, described below.

First Phase—Formation of Thromboplastic Activity. Initiation of blood clotting is believed to begin with injury to the blood vessel, which provides a contact surface and a site for accumulation of the platelets and formation of thromboplastin. Special factors called into play are factor IV (calcium), factor VIII (antihemophilic globulin), factor IX (plasma thromboplastin component), factor X (Stuart–Prower factor), factor XI (PTA, or plasma thromboplastin antecedent), and factor XII (Hageman).

Second Phase—Conversion of Prothrombin to Thrombin. In the actual coagulation of the blood, the plasma thromboplastin is capable of converting prothrombin to thrombin directly. It is believed that an accessory mechanism exists with the release of tissue thromboplastin; conversion of PT to thrombin under this type of thromboplastin requires the additional presence of factors V, VII, and VIII.

Third Phase—Factor I (Fibrinogen) is Converted to Fibrin. Thrombin formed in the second phase enzymatically converts fibrinogen to fibrin. This conversion is believed to be accelerated by calcium. The molecules of fibrin then mesh to form a fibrinous filamentous network generally recognized as a fibrin clot. RBCs and platelets adhering to the fibrin clot give its characteristic external appearance.

Two other events occur after actual formation of a clot. The first is clot retraction, the consolidation or tightening of the fibrin clot, expressing clear yellow fluid, or serum, produced by removal of fibrinogen from plasma during the clotting process. The second event is the eventual lysis or dissolution of a fibrin clot by fibrinolysis, triggered by an enzyme called plasminogen.

SCREENING TESTS FOR BLEEDING PATIENTS

The platelet count, prothrombin time (PT), and partial thromboplastin time (PTT) are considered the three primary screening tests for bleeding patients.

Platelet Count

Platelet count is a straightforward, direct count, usually done electronically; normal count is 150,000 to 350,000 platelets/mm^3 of blood.

Prothrombin Time

Tissue thromboplastin (whole brain extract) is added to plasma and the time required for clotting is measured; normal range is 11 to 13 seconds. The PT tests the integrity of the extrinsic pathway, a more rapid interaction in the clotting sequence.

Partial Thromboplastin Time

The intrinsic pathway in the production of thrombin for the clotting sequence, activated by the contact of blood with a foreign surface, is measurable by the PTT. An "incomplete" thromboplastin is substituted for whole brain extract, an activator is added, and the time is measured. The normal PTT ranges from 25 to 40 seconds, depending on the technique employed. When a factor in the intrinsic or the common portion of the pathway is less than 25 percent, the PTT becomes prolonged.

A specific factor assay can be done by mixing the patient's plasma with plasma from a congenitally deficient individual with zero factor activity; the clotting time of the mixture allows determination of the amount of coagulation factor in the patient's plasma. Normal activity is defined by use of pooled plasma from a large number of healthy persons.

■ BLOOD DYSCRASIAS

ANEMIAS

By definition, patients with anemia have a significant reduction in RBC mass and a corresponding decrease in the oxygen-carrying capacity of the blood; anemia is said to be the symptom, not the disease. With the exception of acute hemorrhage, anemia is accompanied by a decrease in the concentration of RBCs or hemoglobin (Hgb) in a sample of peripheral blood. Anemias can be caused by many things, from a straightforward massive blood loss to hemolysis, both inherited and acquired. The congenital hemolytic anemias are the sickle cell diseases; acquired hemolytic anemias include transfusion reactions, infections, acute drug reactions, poisonings, venoms, thermal injury, physical injury, liver disease, immune responses, uremia, and bone marrow depression.

Primary Blood Loss Anemia

Primary blood loss anemia may be caused by either acute hemorrhage or chronic blood loss over a long period of time.

Acute hemorrhage generally presents clinical signs and symptoms secondary to hypovolemia and hypoxia. The patient will have weakness, fatigue, light-headedness, stupor, or coma, depending on the severity of blood loss. Hypotension and tachycardia will be in proportion to the degree of hemorrhage; therefore, postural signs are useful in the initial evaluation of blood loss. Peripheral blood may not show a significant decrease in packed cell volume (hematocrit [Hct]) or Hgb, if the blood loss has been acute and recent, since the RBC mass and plasma volume are decreased in parallel.

Intervention. As appropriate, determine the source of blood loss and stop the bleeding. Initial treatment for an acute hemorrhagic blood loss can then proceed, following resuscitation protocols:

1. Administer high-flow oxygen;
2. Initiate large-bore intravenous line(s) for immediate restoration of an adequate circulating volume, using Ringer's lactate; whole blood, colloids, or blood products may be administered if the bleeding is prolonged or cannot be controlled by prompt surgical intervention;
3. Install a central venous pressure (CVP) line to monitor the hemodynamic response to volume replacement;
4. Insert a nasogastric (NG) tube if GI bleeding is suspected;
5. Insert a Foley catheter to monitor urine output;
6. Monitor EKG, oxygen saturation, and other vital signs;
7. Obtain an emergency coagulation profile if hemorrhage is present in skin, mucous membranes, or urine.

Nursing Diagnoses. Appropriate nursing diagnoses include the following:

- Impaired gas exchange related to decreased tissue perfusion
- Fluid volume deficit related to hemorrhage
- Decreased cardiac output related to altered preload or afterload
- Altered tissue perfusion related to fluid volume deficit and decreased cardiac output
- Anxiety related to shock state
- Potential for cardiogenic shock related to altered coronary artery perfusion

Chronic Blood Loss Anemia

Chronic blood loss, however, manifests itself much like iron-deficiency anemias, and there may be little or no anemia at all. The slow blood loss over time is usually due to lesions in the GI tract or the uterus; an often overlooked part of evaluation in anemia is testing stool for occult blood. Emergency treatment of chronic blood loss is rarely necessary; emergency blood transfusion is indicated only for *serious* symptoms attributable to a low Hgb level. Transfusion, if necessary, should be done with packed RBCs, since blood volume is usually normal in chronic anemias and circulatory overload must be avoided.

Pernicious Anemia

Pernicious anemia is a deficiency resulting from failure of the stomach to secrete amounts of intrinsic factor (gastric juices) sufficient to ensure intestinal absorption of ingested vitamin B_{12}. Pernicious anemia is characterized by megaloblastic anemia, the complete absence or marked diminution in amount of gastric juice, and neurological damage; megaloblasts are large, nucleated, oval, and slightly irregular, abnormal RBCs, also seen in folic acid deficiency.[3] The disease is thought to have a hereditary basis, although the congenital and adult forms do not appear to be related genetically.

The onset is generally insidious; at least two of the diagnostic triad of symptoms are encountered (e.g., weakness, sore tongue, numbness and tingling in the extremities). Other complaints are anorexia, weight loss, diarrhea, and various other GI symptoms. The degree of tongue soreness varies greatly and involvement may be complete or patchy. The patient may exhibit pallor, slight or marked yellowish skin color with faint icterus of the sclera, a rather wasted appearance, tachycardia, and neural manifestations.

Interventions. Adequate amounts of vitamin B_{12} are given, which is followed by a reticulocyte response (immature RBCs) that reaches its peak 5 to 8 days after the start of therapy. The patient may feel better within 48 hours, experiencing increased appetite, a sense of well-being, and disappearance of tongue symptoms. The extent of neural involvement, however, changes slowly.

Iron-Deficiency Anemias

Iron deficiency is considered to be the most common form of anemia worldwide. Iron is one of the three prime constituents required to make Hgb; Hgb accounts for about 95 percent of the dry weight of RBCs and is the magnet that attaches oxygen to RBCs for transportation. Factors that probably contribute most heavily to iron-deficiency anemias are (1) insufficient iron in the diet; (2) impaired absorption; (3) increased requirements, and (4) loss of blood. Chronic blood loss, (e.g., menstrual loss in women over time and GI bleeding in men) is the most common factor.

Interventions. Appropriate interventions are as follows:

1. Administration of iron is the first step, with careful evaluation of the preparation to be given; iron taken orally may have some side effects, such as nausea, abdominal cramps, and diarrhea. When iron doses are small at first and increased gradually, fewer GI side effects develop.
2. Parenteral administration of iron is rarely required; iron dextran can be given intramuscularly or diluted and given by direct infusion.
3. Transfusion of blood is rarely needed.

Nursing Diagnoses. Nursing diagnoses for the nonacute anemias would include:

- Potential for activity intolerance related to weakness

- Fatigue related to imbalance between oxygen supply and demand
- Knowledge deficit related to need for ongoing dietary and physiological needs

HEMOGLOBINOPATHIES

Three most commonly seen hemoglobinopathies are sickle cell anemia (SS), sickle cell trait (SA), and β-thalassemia.

Sickle Cell Anemia

SS is the most common genetic hemoglobinopathy seen. It is an inherited genetic disorder affecting primarily black people; about 0.15 percent of black children in the United States have the disease.[3] The incidence is lower among adults because those with SS have a decreased life expectancy.

Under deoxygenation, the RBCs containing Hgb S change from a biconcave disk to an elongated cresent-shaped or "sickle"-shaped cell. Sickled cells become rigid, clog the microcirculation, obstruct blood flow and tissue oxygenation, cause severe localized pain, and precipitate further sickling. Approximately 20 percent of the sickled cells are irreversibly sickled, leading to a severe hemolytic anemia. Cumulative organ damage from infarcts, recurrent infections, and painful crises take a heavy toll with the disease.

Sickle Cell Trait

About 8 percent of black Americans carry the SA. Individuals with sickle trait have about 35 percent Hgb S and 60 percent Hgb A; their RBCs require a much lower oxygen tension for sickling than SS and therefore may develop sickle cell crises *only* if they become severely hypoxic. The sickling process is the same as with SS; however, people with SA have minimal clinical problems and their overall life expectancy is about that of individuals with Hgb A.

Sickle-β-Thalassemia

Sickle-β-thalassemia is commonly encountered in those from Mediterranean countries as well as those from central Africa, but it tends to be milder in blacks. There is a congenital hemolytic anemia of variable severity, with splenomegaly in about

70 percent of cases. Microcirculatory clogging occurs, but painful crises are less frequent and less severe. Splenic sequestration of RBCs sometimes leads to splenectomy.

Interventions for the Hemoglobinopathies

Management is primarily supportive and conservative. Because of increased risk of infection, appropriate antibiotics should be given early; increased requirement for folic acid to treat the anemia requires daily oral administration; adequate analgesia for the painful crises must be made available, adequate hydration must be maintained, and low-flow oxygen provided to reverse hypoxia and sickling.

Nursing Diagnoses

Nursing diagnoses for the hemoglobinopathies would include:

- Altered perfusion of vital organs related to microcirculation obstruction
- Acute pain related to sickling and oxygen deprivation to tissues
- Potential fluid volume deficit related to inadequate oral intake
- High risk of infection related to compromised tissues
- Knowledge deficit related to avoiding high altitudes and unpressurized airplanes

COAGULOPATHIES OR BLEEDING DISORDERS

Bleeding disorders that can present in the ED include the hemophilias, type A and type B, von Willebrand's disease, and DIC.

Hemophilia Type A

Hemophilia type A is a well-known hereditary disease in which a sex-linked characteristic is transmitted by females but in which hemorrhagic difficulties occur almost exclusively in males; severity is consistent from generation to generation. Hemophilia A is recognized as the most common clotting factor deficiency; if a patient tells you he is bleeding, he probably is. Hemophiliacs produce plenty of factor VIII (the antihemophiliac globulin essential in the first phase of clotting), so their antigen levels are normal, but the antigen has low activity because the factor VIII they produce is defective. Although they can bleed anywhere, the most common sites are the joints, deep muscles, urinary tract, and intracranial region (rare, but the major cause of death in hemophiliacs at all ages).[1] Repeated bleeding into the joints, most commonly knees, elbows, and ankles, is the major cause of morbidity in hemophilia; repeated bleeds lead to synovitis, further bleeding, and eventually crippling arthritis.

A prolonged PTT is indicative of the factor VIII activity level in hemophilia. Activity levels are rated (normal, any activity above 5 percent; moderate, activity of 2 to 5 percent; severe, activity of less than 1 or 2 percent, with frequent episodes of spontaneous bleeding). Bleeding after trauma or surgery must be a serious concern because the onset of post-trauma bleeding may often be delayed anywhere from 8 hours to several days.

Interventions. Treatment for bleeding episodes is factor VIII therapy, with administration of cryoprecipitate, preferred over commercial factor VIII because of the commercial preparation's higher risk for hepatitis B virus (HBV) and human immunodeficiency virus (HIV) transmission. Dosage of cryoprecipitate is calculated in units per kg of body weight for the determined percent of factor VIII activity.

Hemophilia Type B

Hemophilia type B, or Christmas disease, named for the patient in whom it was first described, is a deficiency of factor IX, which is essential for the formation of intrinsic blood thromboplastin. Although it is only one fifth as common as type A hemophilia, the same type of symptoms appear in both type A and type B, and with equal degrees of deficiency. Diagnosis is made by factor IX assay if the factor VIII assay results are within normal limits.

Intervention. Treatment is administration of human blood concentrate with elevated concentrations of the deficient factor IX.

von Willebrand's Disease

A prolonged bleeding time, a decreased level of factor VIII antigen, and abnormal platelet aggregation together are diagnostic of von Willebrand's disease, another inherited coagulopathy. The disease is usually milder; mucosal and cutaneous

bleeding are common, but bleeding into the joints and deep muscles is rare.

Intervention. Cryoprecipitate is given to supply factor VIII and to stimulate a progressive increase in the patient's own antihemophilic factor. Plasma is also given.

Nursing Diagnoses

Appropriate nursing diagnoses for the hemophilia group of coagulopathies include:

- Potential or actual fluid volume deficit related to bleeding
- Potential for altered tissue perfusion
- Potential for organ injury related to prolonged bleeding
- Knowledge deficit related to therapeutic regimen

Disseminated Intravascular Coagulopathy

DIC is an acquired disorder in which coagulation proceeds abnormally within the vascular tree and microcirculation; it can cause a severe hemorrhagic tendency by depleting essential hemostatic elements. DIC may occur after massive blood transfusions, abruptio placentae, or extensive trauma; in reaction to venoms; in children with massive septicemia typified by massive meningococcal invasion; and in response to other severe assaults to the clotting mechanism. The term *disseminated* means that this condition involves all aspects of the coagulation system, from platelets to fibrin, not necessarily that it occurs throughout the body. The fine balance between coagulants and their inhibitors is lost; platelets and coagulation factors—particularly fibrinogen and factors V, VII, and VIII—are consumed so rapidly that replacement processes are unable to maintain normal levels.[4]

An acute generalized hemorrhagic state may set in with sudden, severe hypotension followed by multiple organ thrombi, appearance of fibrin degradation products, destruction of RBCs as they are squeezed through fibrin deposits during circulation, and finally, local tissue necrosis. Death can result from acute renal failure, liver necrosis with hepatic failure, acute pancreatitis, bowel necrosis, or extensive lung or brain infarcts.

The degree of catastrophe seems to be directly related to the degree of shock; without some form of anticoagulant and replacement of the depleted clotting elements, shock becomes rapidly irreversible and death ensues.

Interventions. The underlying disease must be identified and treated immediately, but the most important first step is to *reestablish and maintain the blood pressure* (BP) to reverse the process of consumption.

1. Administer high-flow oxygen.
2. Establish large-bore intravenous access for fluid administration.
3. Maintain adequate fluid volume to prevent renal tubular obstruction from RBC destruction, to maintain BP, and to reverse shock.
4. Replace blood volume; administer whole blood or sedimented RBC transfusions (to resolve the anemia as well as the consumptive coagulopathy), platelet concentrate, and/or clotting factors as appropriate.[4]
5. Insert a Foley catheter to monitor urinary output.
6. Closely monitor VS.
7. Limit the number of skin punctures.

Nursing Diagnoses. Appropriate nursing diagnoses for DIC would include:

- Fluid volume deficit related to pooling of peripheral circulation
- Altered tissue perfusion related to microemboli and deficit in circulating RBCs
- Potential for further injury related to subcutaneous hemorrhagic state
- Anxiety related to disease process and fear of death

LEUKEMIAS

Leukemia is defined as an acute or chronic, progressive, malignant disease of blood-forming organs, classified according to the dominant cell type and severity of the disease. Of unknown etiology, it is characterized by unrestrained growth of leukocytes and their precursors in the tissues.

Acute Leukemia

In acute leukemia, most of the clinical abnormalities are due to failure of the bone marrow to function adequately. Anemias, infections accompanied by high fever, bleeding as a result of decreased platelet formation, and fatigue are symptoms. Infiltrating WBCs disrupt functions of organs such as the spleen and liver, the lymphatic system, and the central nervous system (CNS). Bone pain, pallor, purpura, and hepatosplenomegaly are seen; the WBC count is usually between 10,000 and 50,000/mm^3 but may also be depressed. A concomitant anemia or thrombocytopenia is frequently present.

Interventions. The presence of fever or bleeding is considered medically urgent; fever is usually bacterial initially and it may be appropriate to obtain cultures of blood, urine, and sputum and begin broad-spectrum antibiotics. Thrombocytopenia is treated with platelet transfusions; chemotherapy is initiated promptly once the diagnosis of leukemia is established.

Chronic Leukemias

Chronic leukemias have an insidious onset and progress over a period of years, not months. Generalized adenopathy, splenomegaly, an extremely elevated WBC, fatigue, malaise, and low-grade fever are frequent presenting manifestations. Generally, these leukemias do not present as emergency disorders unless infection or bleeding complicate the status. Chemotherapy is the treatment of choice.

Nursing Diagnoses for Leukemias

Appropriate nursing diagnoses for leukemias would include:

- Pain related to infiltration of tissue by expanding bone marrow
- Potential for infection, hemorrhage, and anemia
- Anxiety related to prognosis and feelings of helplessness
- Knowledge deficit related to diagnostic and therapeutic procedures

■ ADMINISTRATION OF BLOOD COMPONENTS

Specific separated blood components can be administered from a single donation of blood. Components can often be concentrated to higher levels than those found in whole blood, eliminating volume overload in the patient. Each component can be maintained under optimal conditions for preservation of its particular activity; maximized therapeutic benefits can be gained without transfusion-associated risks.

GUIDELINES

When handling blood or any of its components in the ED, there are some guidelines that must be followed to ensure maximum safety and positive outcomes for the blood recipient (Table 24–2). When handling components, one basic tenet holds for all: they should be infused as soon as possible once they leave the blood bank. This is particularly important for platelet concentrate, which should be infused immediately.

TABLE 24–2. SUMMARY CHART ON ADMINISTRATION OF BLOOD COMPONENTS

Component	Major Indications	Action	Special Precautions	Rate of Infusion
Whole blood	Symptomatic anemia with large volume deficit	Restoration of oxygen-carrying capacity, restoration of blood volume	Must be ABO identical Labile coagulation factors deteriorate within 24 hours after collection	For massive loss, fast as patient can tolerate
Red blood cells (RBCs)	Symptomatic anemia	Restoration of oxygen-carrying capacity	Must be ABO compatible	As patient can tolerate but less than 4 hours
Red blood cells (RBCs), leukocytes removed	Symptomatic anemia, febrile reactions from leukocyte antibodies	Restoration of oxygen-carrying capacity	Must be ABO compatible	As patient can tolerate but less than 4 hours
Fresh frozen plasma (FFP)	Deficit of labile and stable plasma coagulation factors and thrombocytopenia	Source of labile and stable plasma factors	Should be ABO compatible	Less than 4 hours
Cryoprecipitated anti-hemophilia factor (AHF)	Hemophilia A, von Willebrand's disease, hypofibrinogenemia, Factor XIII deficiency	Provides Factor VIII, fibrinogen, von Willebrand factor, Factor XIII	Frequent repeat doses may be necessary	Less than 4 hours
Platelets (pheresis)	Bleeding from thrombocytopenia or platelet-function abnormality	Improves hemostasis	Should not use some microaggregate filters (check manufacturer's instruction)	Less than 4 hours
Granulocytes (pheresis)	Neutropenia with infection	Provides granulocytes	Must be ABO compatible, do not use depth-type microaggregate filters	One unit over 2–4 hour period; observe closely for reactions

From Carico CJ, Mileski WJ, Kaplan HS: Transfusion, Autotransfusion, and Blood Substitutes. In: Feliciano DV, Moore EE, Mattox KL: Trauma, 3rd ed. Stamford, Conn, Appleton & Lange, 1996, with permission.

Additional rules and guidelines are as follows:

- Under no circumstances should any blood product be put in an unmonitored refrigerator in patient-care areas.
- The infusion rate of products other than platelets is determined by the clinical situation, but no blood product should hang for more than 4 hours at room temperature.
- *All* blood components require an in-line filter; the standard blood product infusion set has a pore size of 170 μm.
- *Only* physiologic saline (0.9 percent) should be added to blood products, because:
  Calcium-containing solutions can cause clotting;
  Low–ionic-strength solutions such as D_5W damage the cell membrane and lead to hemolysis;

Drugs are *never* added to blood; additives may cause clotting, hemolysis, or other untoward reactions.

Cell-containing blood components are living fluids and must not be pumped through small-gauge needles or heated above 37°C. (98.6°F)—hemolysis, a shortened survival time, or both can result.[5]

SPECIFICS FOR INDIVIDUAL COMPONENTS AND SPECIAL FACTORS

Some specifics regarding individual components and their administration are as follows:

- *Whole blood:* Usually restricted to patients with an acute loss of more than 15 percent of their total blood volume.
- *Packed RBCs:* Indicated when a patient needs oxygen-carrying capacity but does not require volume restoration, or for anemia that cannot be corrected with iron or other therapy. RBCs needed for oxygen-transporting purposes should not have been sitting for more than 7 days.
- *Platelet concentrate:* Given when diffuse bleeding in the face of a restored blood volume suggests thrombocytopenia. Platelets have a shelf life of 5 days and must be stored at 20° to 24°C. Do *not* use a microaggregate filter during administra-

tion; *use a platelet filter obtained at time of pickup from the blood bank* or a standard blood administration set; again, platelets must be infused immediately after pickup.
- *Fresh-frozen plasma:* Indicated when coagulopathy results from deficient clotting factors as a result of liver dysfunction, congenital absence of factor, or transfusion of factor-deficient blood products. It is contraindicated for any condition that is responsive to a specific concentrate.
- *Cryoprecipitate:* Useful in treating factor VIII deficiency (e.g., hemophilia A, von Willebrand's disease); also helpful in hypofibrinogenemia. It contains factor VIII and fibrinogen in a relatively higher concentration than fresh-frozen plasma, allowing a smaller volume to be given, and it carries a smaller HBV risk than purified factor VIII concentrates made from pooled plasma. Use of cryoprecipitate entails consideration of several other points: it contains a number of other proteins in addition to factor VIII that can cause itching, hives, and fever, and some practitioners will pretreat with diphenhydramine, 25 to 50 mg IV; it has to be thawed, and once thawed, it has to be given within 4 hours; it can be infused with a platelet concentration infusion set rather than a regular blood filter. Platelet infusion sets have their own filter and permit a slow intravenous push.
- *Factor IX concentrate (human):* useful in treating factor IX deficiency (i.e., hemophilia B, Christmas disease). Dried, it has elevated concentrations of factor IX; depending on the manufacturer, it may have varying amounts of concentrated factor II (prothrombin) and factors VII, X and XI.

CAVEATS

When administering *any* blood product, be very certain to check details as thoroughly and carefully as you would when administering medication. Mistakes are made in both patient and blood sample identification, in judging the time necessary for cross-matching and release of appropriate blood or blood components, and finally to administration in the correct fashion with the proper equipment for the specific blood component. Watch carefully for clerical errors that can happen so easily in busy EDs. Remember that selection of a particular unit of blood for a given patient is a decision made with finality; there is simply no way to recover the wrong unit of blood once it has been infused into a recipient.

■ REFERENCES

1. Hamilton GC: Hemostasis out of order. *Emerg Med.* 1995;17(19):83–112.
2. Ellman L. Hematologic emergencies. In: Wilkins FN, Dineen JJ, Moncine AC, Fitzgerald CP, eds. *MGH Textbook of Emergency Medicine.* Baltimore, Md: Williams & Wilkins; 1978:275.
3. Dressler DK. Hematologic physiology. In: Clochesy JM, Breu C, Cardin S, et al. *Critical Care Nursing.* Philadephia, PA.: WB Saunders; 1993: 1048.
4. Ayres SM. Diagnosis and management of bleeding disorders. In: Ayres SM, Grenvik A, Holbrook PR, Shoemaker WC. *Textbook of Critical Care,* 3rd ed. Philadelphia, Pa.: WB Saunders; 1995:1324–1334.
5. Collins ML, Kafer ER. Lab rounds: using blood components: I. *Emerg Med.* 1985;17(11):131–142.

■ BIBLIOGRAPHY

Brusch JL. Targeting the cause of unexplained fever. *Emerg Med.* Mar. 1989;108–119.

Burns ER. When to suspect a bleeding disorder. *Emerg Med.* June 1990;67–73.

Bush MT, Roy N. Hemophilia emergencies. *J Emerg Nurs.* 1995;21:531–540.

Collins ML, Kafer ER. Lab rounds; using blood components: I. *Emerg Med.* 1985;17(11):131–141.

Gawlikowski J. White cells at war. *AJN.* 1992;3:45–51.

Griffin JP. *Hematology and Immunology: Concepts for Nursing.* E. Norwalk, Conn: Appleton and Lange; 1986.

Guyton AC. *Textbook of Medical Physiology.* 8th ed. Philadelphia, Pa: WB Saunders; 1990.

Hackett PH, Hornbein TF. Disorders of high altitude. In: Murray FJ, Nadel JA, eds. *Textbook of Respiratory Medicine.* Philadelphia, Pa: WB Saunders; 1988.

Hackett PH, Roach RC. Medical therapy of altitude illness. *Ann Emerg Med.* 1987;16:980.

Hamilton GC. Hemostasis out of order. *Emerg Med.* 1985;17(19):83–112.

Junqueira C, Carneiro J, Kelley RO. *Basic Histology.* 8th ed. Stamford, Conn: Appleton & Lange; 1995.

Kjeldsberg C, et al. Practical Diagnosis of Hematologic Disorders. Chicago, Ill: ASCP Press; 1989.

Klein HG. When is transfusion the best option? *Emerg Med.* April 1992;59–66.

McMillen MA. The use of blood and blood products in surgical and critically ill patients. In: Cerra FB, ed. *Manual of Critical Care.* St. Louis, Mo: CV Mosby; 1987.

Sheldon GF, Lim RC Jr, Blaisdell FW. Fresh whole blood: *less* than the sum of its parts. *J Trauma.* 15:670.

Wallerstein RO Jr. Best tests for bleeding disorders. *Emerg Med.* April 1989;145–161.

Wheby MS. Sizing up the seriousness of anemia. *Emerg Med.* Aug. 1989; 179–192.

Zond JR. Autologous transfusion for elective surgery. *Emerg Med.* Oct. 1992;73–77.

■ REVIEW: HEMATOLOGIC EMERGENCIES

1. List the four primary functions of blood and identify the most important one.

2. Identify the components of blood, the volume percent they normally represent, and the functions of each.

3. Describe the means by which blood is typed and identify the three most important antigens.

4. Define the term *universal recipient.*

5. Identify the three primary screening tests for bleeding patients and describe their implications.

6. Define *anemia.* Identify at least five types; give the appropriate interventions for hemoglobinopathies.

7. Define the major coagulopathies, or bleeding disorders, seen in the emergency department (ED) and outline the general management of each.

8. Explain the etiology of disseminated intravascular coagulopathy (DIC) and outline the most important steps in intervention.

9. Identify the one basic tenet that holds for administration of *all* blood products. Outline specific considerations for administration of:
   a. Whole blood
   b. Packed red blood cells (RBCs)
   c. Platelet concentrate
   d. Fresh-frozen plasma
   e. Cryoprecipitate
   f. Factor IX concentrate (human)

10. List at least four critical areas to be double-checked when administering blood products in order to avoid potentially disastrous situations.

Allergies and Immune Responses   25

Emergency personnel frequently encounter allergic responses and immune-related problems, and assessments and interventions require an understanding of the basic pathophysiology of such conditions, which may range from mild, aggravating symptoms such as watery eyes, rash, and pruritis to life-threatening anaphylaxis. It is helpful for the emergency nurse (EN) to understand the basic mechanisms involved in immune responses as well as antigenic reactions such as anaphylaxis.

A potent mechanism of the immune system is the reaction initiated by immunoglobulin E (IgE)-dependent stimulation of tissue mast cells and their basophil counterparts. When antigens bind to IgE molecules preattached to the surface of such cells, mediators are promptly released that cause vascular permeability, vasodilation, bronchial and visceral smooth-muscle contraction, and inflammation at the local site.[1] This phenomenon is responsible for the hypersensitivity that begins quite promptly, and in the most extreme form (i.e., anaphylaxis) can result in cardiovascular collapse. Atopic (i.e., allergic) individuals are prone to the development of reactions in the face of mast cell-derived or basophil-derived mediators. About 20 percent of individuals have some type of allergy and may manifest signs and symptoms in several different ways, including hives, hay fever, asthma, and skin edema. Immediate hypersensitive reactions tend to be related to late-phase reactions, a host defense mechanism that is not yet fully understood (Fig. 25–1).

■ TYPES OF ANTIGENS

The substances that can trigger allergic responses include antibiotics, foreign proteins (e.g., latex, insulin, equine serum, venom, pollen, whole blood and immunoglobins), endogenous hormones, drugs such as aspirin or other non-steroidal agents, and a large number of other commonly used medications including local anesthetic agents, egg-based vaccines, steroids, and acetaminophen. Opiates, radiopaque contrast dyes, and dextran have been associated with allergic reactions secondary to direct mast cell and basophil degranulation and the release of histamine. Although physical factors such as exercise may create an anaphylactic-like response, the mechanisms are unclear, but cases have been known to be related to certain provocative foods consumed prior to exercise.[2]

■ SIGNS AND SYMPTOMS OF AN ALLERGIC REACTION

The earlier the patient experiences manifestations of an allergic reaction, the more severe it is likely to be. Antigens that are injected into the body will evoke a more immediate reaction than something that is ingested or inhaled. The reactions within the various body systems or target organs will be dependent upon the mediators and invariably involve characteristic signs and symptoms.

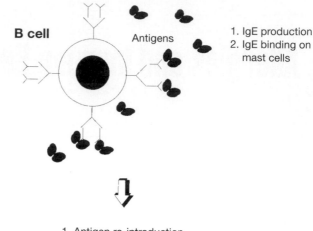

B cell   Antigens

1. IgE production
2. IgE binding on mast cells

1. Antigen re-introduction
2. Cross-linking of bound IgE

1. Mast cell activation
2. Release of histamine and other mediators

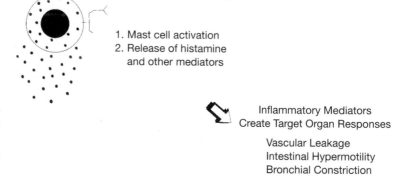

Inflammatory Mediators
Create Target Organ Responses

Vascular Leakage
Intestinal Hypermotility
Bronchial Constriction

Figure 25–1. Type I immune response. Contact with antigens leads to IgE synthesis by B cells. Secreted IgE binds to mast cells. Upon later exposure to the antigen, hypersensitivity is triggered by cross-linkage of the IgE molecules.

Respiratory and cardiovascular reactions are among the first to be noted in patients and include rhinitis, laryngeal edema, wheezing, brochospasm, dysrhythmias, and circulatory collapse. The patient may complain of sneezing, hoarseness, tightness in the throat, hypersalivation, shortness of breath, lightheadedness or syncope, or chest pain or palpitations. Upon examination, there may be discernible supraglottic and glottic edema, electrocardiogram (EKG) changes, cyanosis and shock. Such dramatic indices of a severe allergic reaction calls for prompt and aggressive resuscitative measures.

Skin reactions include urticaria and angiodema. Pruritus, tingling and a warm sensation, flushing, hives, swelling, and rash may be evident. Angioedema may be noted around the eyes or mouth. The eyes frequently exhibit conjunctivitis with itching, tearing, and redness.

Gastrointestinal symptoms, including dysphagia, nausea, vomiting, and intestinal cramping, are present in some patients. Some will have central nervous system (CNS) indications of allergies, including headache, confusion, sense of impending doom, anxiety, and in rare instances, seizures and coma. Fibrinolysis and disseminating intravascular coagulation, with evidence of bruising and bleeding, may be noted. Female patients may experience vaginal bleeding or pelvic discomfort, and both men and women may be incontinent.

■ EMERGENCY MANAGEMENT

Some patients who have experienced severe allergic reactions in the past may possess an anaphylaxis or "bee sting" kit that they may use prior to coming to the hospital. Most of these contain 50 mg diphenhydramine (Benadryl), either tablet or prefilled syringe, and 0.3 mL epinephrine (1:1000) for injection. Metered dose inhalers with aerosolized epinephrine may be used for counteracting laryngeal edema, bronchoconstriction, and other restrictions of the upper airway. Both basic life support and advanced cardiac life support measures may be required to sustain the patient prior to reaching the hospital emergency department (ED). Local measures (tourniquets, ice, dependent positioning) may be used to help contain antigenic stimuli in an extremity. A local infiltration of epinephrine or antivenin may be used as well, proximal to the site of bites or stings.

Once the patient has reached a primary treatment facility, additional parenteral epinephrine and Benadryl may be ordered and oxygen is started promptly. An intravenous route is established and the patient is attached to monitors capable of continuous recordings of heart rate, blood pressure (BP), and oxygenation. Fluid replenishment and the shock position should be employed to relieve the shock inherent in severe anaphylaxis. In severe anaphylaxis, (laryngeal edema, respiratory failure, or shock), drugs are given intravenously. Epinephrine (1 mL of 1:10,000 over 5 minutes) and 50–100 mg of Benadryl (given over 3 minutes) are typical intravenous drug doses in life-threatening instances. These agents either inhibit the release of chemical mediators or reverse the effects of these substances on target tissue.[2]

Epinephrine has several α-agonist effects, including improved peripheral resistance, reduction of vascular permeability, and elevation of BP. β-agonist effects include bronchodilation and both inotropic and chronotropic cardiac stimulation, thus alleviating bronchospasm and enhancing cardiac output. Great care should be taken in monitoring to ensure that the increased oxygen consumption and changes in myocardial contractility do not contribute to dysrhythmias, hypertension, or infarction. Although such complications are more likely in older or debilitated patients, they can also occur in younger, otherwise healthy patients, especially with the use of intravenous epinephrine. Benadryl is used for its antihistamine effects.

Naloxone, vasopressors, antidysrhythmics, cardioversion, and other resuscitative therapies may be indicated to treat cardiovascular crises. If there is evidence of an ingested antigen, activated charcoal, cimetidine, and glucagon may also be indicated.

Severe laryngeal edema requires aggressive measures, including intubation or a surgical airway. Heliox (80 percent helium and 20 percent oxygen) may be useful to ensure upper airway integrity by improving laminar flow of gases and thus reducing respiratory work. Racemic epinephrine may be given by inhalation (0.5 mL of 2.25 percent in 2.5 mL of normal saline [NS]). Steroids, such as methylprednisolone (Solu-medrol 125–250 mg) may be given to aid in coping with the laryngeal edema. Aminophylline, both a loading and maintenance dose may be helpful when used with other agents to manage bronchospasm that is resistant to other therapies.

■ PREVENTION OF ANAPHYLAXIS

Emergency personnel should ensure that all measures are taken to identify the antigen responsible for triggering anaphylaxis. Patients should be made aware of these and similar culprits and minimize the possibility of future contact. Referral for follow-up care is imperative. Anaphylaxis kits should be prescribed for self-administration in the event that the antigen is encountered again. ENs should bear in mind that if the antigen is unknown, reexposure can occur inadvertently, so the patient needs to be prepared to promptly administer the agents, because attack severity tends to increase with succeeding exposures to the responsible antigen. All patients should be encouraged to wear a medical identification bracelet. Education of patients and family is of vital importance. They should be taught to recognize impending allergic reactions and the techniques of administering epinephrine.

Health-care professionals should be instructed to ask about allergies before administering any drugs. Whenever a drug is given, especially parenterally, the patient should be under observation for 30 minutes after receiving it before leaving the health-care facility. Oral administration is safer than parenteral and should be used when possible. ENs should be aware of the biochemical cross-reactivity of drugs (e.g., penicillin and cephalosporins); if a drug allergy is part of a patient's history, the physician should be notified so a substitute agent may be used.

If it is critical to a patient's health that an offending drug be administered, appropriate consultation can provide alternate therapy or a pretreatment protocol of corticosteroids. In short, all reasonable avenues should be explored to try to prevent the occurrence of any potentially fatal anaphylactic reactions.

The EN must be able to identify who is at risk, know the presenting clinical symptoms, be aware of what agents trigger anaphylactic reactions, and know what immunologic and cellular events may occur that can result in death. Acute anaphylaxis is a rare condition, but when it does occur, all personnel must be prepared to respond aggressively to combat the rapidly developing shock state (see Chapter 11).

◼ ANGIOEDEMA AND URTICARIA

Although the underlying mechanisms for angioedema and urticaria are similar to those of anaphylaxis, they are often triggered by physical forces such as exercise, infections, tumors, and collagen diseases. Angioedema is associated with the administration of certain drugs (e.g. angiotensin-converting enzyme (ACE)–inhibitors (see page 380). Hereditary angioedema results from an autosomal-dominant inherited deficiency or functional abnormality of C1 esterase inhibitor. In the latter form, the antecedent events may be emotional upsets, sudden temperature changes, infections, and trauma. Episodes begin in childhood and may last 2 or more days.[3]

The characteristic presentation of angioedema is a nonpruritic subcutaneous swelling of skin or mucous membranes. There may be associated urticarial lesions. Hoarseness, stridor, dyspnea, and even death can be associated with the condition. Gastrointestinal discomfort, including cramping abdominal pain, nausea, and diarrhea, may occur.

Laboratory tests for angioedema should include a complete blood cell (CBC) count, erythrocyte sedimentation rate (ESR), and urinalysis, followed later by a skin biopsy. Treatment includes those measures indicated in anaphylaxis, plus the addition of C1 inhibitors and fresh-frozen plasma in some cases to inhibit complement activation (Table 25–1).

◼ THE IMMUNOCOMPROMISED PATIENT IN THE EMERGENCY DEPARTMENT

There are a number of conditions that can impair the patient's immune system, including acquired immunodeficiency syndrome (AIDS), malnutrition, widespread cancer, blood dyscrasias, infections, iatrogenic immunosuppression from drug therapy (including chemotherapy), and splenectomy. These patients share a common vulnerability in the ED, and ENs must take steps to minimize additional risks for such individuals. When possible, these patients should be identified in triage and placed promptly in an area where they are not in direct contact with patients with communicable diseases. They should not be permitted to remain in the waiting room with febrile children, coughing adults, or other types of patients who could easily transmit infectious microorganisms.

All personnel who care for the immunocompromised should understand their special needs for protection. Procedures should be done only when necessary, with care taken not to make unnecessary venipunctures or to place tubes unless absolutely essential. For even minor injuries, antibiotics may be required since these patients have perilously inadequate immune functions that do not provide them the ordinary protection in trauma and illness.

Any immunocompromised patients who have even a slight fever or signs of inflammation should be handled as if septic, because their bodies are not able to mount an adequate immune response. Even minor problems can develop into major ones within hours for these vulnerable patients. In addition to isolating these patients, ENs may find it advisable to wear masks to protect such patients from their upper respiratory flora, which may contain easily transmitted nosocomial microorganisms that do not ordinarily pose a significant risk to most patients but could be near lethal for these immunocompromised hosts.

The triage EN may not always know precisely who is immunocompromised but should as-

TABLE 25–1. TREATMENT OF SERIOUS ALLERGIC DISORDERS: ANAPHYLAXIS AND ANGIOEDEMA

Treatment	Indications	Dosages	Goals	Complications
Airway or Cutaneous Reaction				
Initial therapy				
Epinephrine	Bronchospasm, laryngeal edema, urticaria, angioedema	0.3–0.5 mL of 1:1000 dilution (0.3–0.5 mg) SC every 10–20 minutes	Maintain airway patency, reduce fluid extravasation and pruritus	Arrhythmias, hypertension, nervousness, tremor
Oxygen	Hypoxemia	40–100%	Maintain $P_{O_2} > 60$ mm Hg	None
Metaproterenol or other β_2-agonist	Bronchospasm	0.3 mL (5% solution) in 2.5 mL of saline inhaled through nebulizer	Maintain airway patency	Same as for epinephrine
Secondary therapy				
Antihistamines	Urticaria	25–50 mg of hydroxyzine or diphenhydramine IM or orally	Reduce pruritus, antagonize H_1 effects of histamine	Drowsiness, dry mouth, urinary retention
		300 mg of cimetidine IV or PO every 6 hours	Antagonize H_2 effects of histamine	
Corticosteroids	Bronchospasm	250 mg of hydrocortisone or 50 mg of methylprednisolone IV every 6 hours for two to four doses	Block or reduce prolonged late-phase reactions	Hyperglycemia, fluid retention, hypokalemia
Aminophylline	Bronchospasm	Loading dose, if necessary, 6 mg/kg IV over 30 minutes; 0.3–0.6 mg/kg per hour IV as maintenance	Maintain airway patency	Arrhythmias, nausea, vomiting, seizures
Cardiovascular Reactions				
Initial therapy				
Epinephrine	Hypotension	1 mL of 1:1000 dilution in 500 mL of D_5W IV at a rate of 0.5–5 µg/min	Maintain systolic blood pressure > 80–100 mm Hg	Arrhythmias, hypertension, nervous tremor
Intravenous fluids (normal saline, albumin)	Hypotension	1 L every 20–30 minutes as needed	Maintain systolic blood pressure > 80–100 mm Hg	Pulmonary edema, electrolyte disturbances
Secondary therapy				
Antihistamines	Hypotension	25–50 mg of hydroxyzine or diphenhydramine IM or PO every 6–8 hours as needed	Antagonize H_1 effects of histamine on myocardium and peripheral vasculature	Drowsiness, dry mouth, urinary retention
Norepinephrine	Hypotension	4 mg in 1 L of D_5W IV at a rate of 2–12 µg/min	Maintain systolic blood pressure > 80–100 mm Hg	Arrhythmias, hypertension, nervousness, tremor
Glucagon	Refractory hypotension	1 mg in 250 mL of D_5W IV at a rate of 5–15 µg/min	Increase heart rate and cardiac output	Nausea

(continued)

TABLE 25–1. TREATMENT OF SERIOUS ALLERGIC DISORDERS: ANAPHYLAXIS AND ANGIOEDEMA (Continued)

Treatment	Indications	Dosages	Goals	Complications
Angioedema				
Initial therapy				
Epinephrine	Bronchospasm, laryngeal edema, urticaria, angioedema	0.3–0.5 mL of 1:1000 dilution (0.3–0.5 mg) SC every 10–20 minutes	Maintain airway patency, reduce fluid extravasation and pruritus	Arrhythmias, hypertension, nervousness, tremor
Oxygen	Hypoxemia	40–100%	Maintain $Po_2 > 60$ mm Hg	None
C1 inhibitor	Hereditary angioedema	Mix in D_5W. Give IV over 10–45 minutes	Inhibit complement activation	None
Fresh-frozen plasma	Hereditary angioedema or preoperatively	2 units IV	Inhibit complement activation	None
Maintenance therapy				
Danazol or stanazolol	Prevent recurrence of hereditary angioedema	Danazol: 200 mg PO three times daily; stanazolol: 2–4 mg PO once daily	Increase concentration of C1 esterase inhibitor and C4	Virilization; contraindicated in children and pregnant women

IM, intramuscularly; IV, intravenously; PO, orally; SC, subcutaneously (*from Bongard and Sue*[3]).

sume that if the patient looks unusually debilitated or reports a history of blood disease, repeated infections, AIDS, organ or tissue transplantation, or long-term use of steroids or chemotherapy, he or she may be immunocompromised. These are important clues to potential immunodeficiency and should stimulate prompt, aggressive responses from all personnel coming into contact with these patients.

NURSING DIAGNOSES

Appropriate nursing diagnoses for the immunocompromised patient include the following:

- Impaired gas exchange resulting from airway edema
- Ineffective breathing pattern secondary to airway obstruction
- Altered tissue perfusion resulting from cardiovascular collapse
- Impairment of skin integrity related to atopy
- Anxiety related to acute allergic reaction
- Potential for infection secondary to immunocompetence

■ REFERENCES

1. Abbas AK, Lichtman AH, Pober JS. *Cellular and Molecular Immunology.* 2nd ed. Philadelphia, Pa: WB Saunders; 1994:279.
2. Rosen P, Barkin R, et al. *Emergency Medicine: Concepts and Clinical Practice.* 3rd ed. St. Louis, Mo: Mosby-Year Book; 1992:1042–1065.
3. Bongard FS, Sue DY. *Current Critical Care Diagnosis and Treatment.* E. Norwalk, Conn: Appleton & Lange; 1994:618–635.

■ BIBLIOGRAPHY

Ayres SM, Grenvik A, Holbrook PR, Shoemaker WC. *Textbook of Critical Care.* 3rd ed. Philadelphia, Pa: WB Saunders; 1995.

Benumof J. *Airway Management: Principles and Practice.* St. Louis, Mo: CV Mosby; 1995.

Chernow B, ed. *The Pharmacologic Approach to the Critically Ill Patient.* 3rd ed. Baltimore, Md: Williams & Wilkins; 1994.

Grenvik A, Ayres SM, Holbrook PR, Shoemaker WB. *Pocket Companion to Textbook of Critical Care.* Philadelphia, Pa: WB Saunders; 1996.

Levine RL, Fromm RE Jr. *Critical Care Monitoring from Pre-Hospital to the ICU.* St. Louis, Mo: Mosby-Year Book; 1995.

Maull KI, Rodriguez A, Wiles CE. *Complications in Trauma and Critical Care.* Philadelphia, Pa: WB Saunders; 1996.

Moreau D, ed. *Nursing 96 Drug Handbook.* Springhouse, Pa: Springhouse Corporation; 1996.

Phippen ML, Wells MP. *Perioperative Nursing Practice.* Philadelphia, Pa: WB Saunders; 1994.

Physicians' Desk Reference. 50th ed. Montvale, NJ: Medical Economics; 1996.

Ruppert SD, Kernicki JG, Dolan JT. *Dolan's Critical Care Nursing.* 2nd ed. Philadelphia, Pa: FA Davis; 1996.

Urden LD, Davie JK, Thelan LA. *Essentials of Critical Care Nursing.* St. Louis, Mo: Mosby-Year Book; 1992.

Wilkins RL, Dexter JR. *Respiratory Disease Principles of Patient Care,* Philadelphia, Pa: FA Davis; 1993.

■ REVIEW: ALLERGIES AND IMMUNE RESPONSES

1. List six common antigens that incite an allergic reaction.

2. Describe the respiratory and cardiovascular manifestations associated with severe allergic reactions.

3. Outline the emergency management of anaphylaxis and identify the three drugs considered vital in these cases.

4. Explain the underlying mechanisms for angioedema and urticaria and the laboratory tests indicated.

5. Describe the special precautions that should be observed when an immunocompromised patient presents to the emergency department (ED).

6. Cite four nursing diagnoses related to allergic reactions and immune responses.

Abdominal and Gastrointestinal Emergencies

26

The patient with an upper gastrointestinal (GI) or abdominal complaint is one of the frequent presentations in the emergency department (ED). Since the underlying problem can be potentially life-threatening, the emergency nurse (EN) must be able to perform a thorough evaluation to rule out potentially serious disease before instituting symptomatic treatment. This chapter deals primarily with disease processes rather than trauma of abdominal organs; a working knowledge of abdominal contents and their anatomic locations in the assessment of a patient with abdominal distress is essential.

■ ASSESSMENT

The abdomen is divided into four quadrants topographically as well as into areas above, below, and lateral to the umbilicus (e.g., epigastrium, suprapubic area, and flanks). The EN should know what structures underlie the topography and what signs and symptoms are associated with abnormalities of the organs in that particular part of the abdomen (Fig. 26–1). In addition, ENs should be alert to changes in body motion, abdominal contour, and patient behavior that suggest abdominal pathology. Skill in abdominal palpation is essential. The patient's relaxed, nontender areas can provide a useful baseline for the identification of tender and guarded areas. The indirect finger-tapped-to-finger percussion is an important technique to elicit so-called rebound tenderness and give a tonal quality to the abdomen (i.e., a dull sound for solid organs and fluids and tympany for air-filled organs). Aus-

cultation of the bowel may reveal hypoactive, normal, hyperactive, or abnormal sounds. *Borborygmi* are audible bowel sounds heard without the use of a stethoscope.

During bowel assessment, the patient should be lying down and relaxed as much as possible. Observe the general appearance of the abdomen and determine if it is flat, distended, scaphoid or depressed, or rounded. If there are scars or signs of trauma, these should be explored further when recording the history. If the patient draws up the legs, places hands over a painful area, or guards a particular site during the examination, this should be noted. Determine if the patient has had any recent changes in bowel habits, bladder function, or menses. The presence of nausea, vomiting, cramping, or other discomfort is recorded, along with details regarding the factors that provoke the symptoms and specifics of quality, intensity, duration, and association with any pain.

PAIN PATTERNS

Abdominal disease can be categorized into three general groups, although the signs and symptoms overlap. If the pain pattern description is complete, there is a high likelihood of placing the problem into the correct category and determining the optimum management regimen.

Visceral pain can be caused by problems in the hollow organs, such as the gut, gallbladder, or urinary bladder, as well as in the capsules of solid organs, including the liver and kidneys. It is one of the earliest symptoms but is often poorly localized

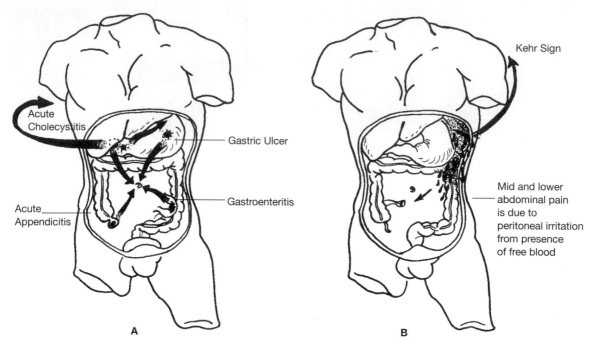

Figure 26–1. A. Pain patterns associated with abdominal conditions. **B.** Ruptured spleen produces neck and proximal shoulder pain (Kehr sign).

and difficult for the patient to describe in specific terms. Nausea, vomiting, pallor, and diaphoresis accompany visceral pain. If the pain arises from the liver, gallbladder, stomach, or duodenum, it is felt in the epigastrium. Periumbilical or midabdominal pain can be caused by problems in the small intestine, appendix, or cecum. Discomfort associated with the colon, kidneys, bladder, and uterus is localized in the epigastrium.

Somatic pain is characteristically sharp and more localized and is often the result of chemical or bacterial inflammation. Guarding and tenderness are present and may be helpful indicators for determining the organ or structures involved.

Referred pain patterns are often helpful in detection of the underlying problem. Pain on the side of the neck and proximal shoulder (Kehr sign) is associated with diaphragmatic irritation, such as a ruptured spleen. Groin pain is indicative of ureteral colic; periumbilical pain reflects appendicitis and small-bowel obstruction in some patients. Back or subscapular pain may suggest referral from pancreatitis or cholecystitis, respectively.

A thorough, detailed history is extremely important for the evaluation of abdominal and GI complaints. In addition, certain signs that can be elicited during the physical examination may be useful in pinpointing the problem. The obturator sign reflects an inflamed organ. The patient is positioned with the thighs flexed and the leg is rotated internally and externally; an inflamed obturator muscle will cause pain (e.g., appendicitis). Murphy sign denotes cholecystitis. The examiner places a hand firmly over the right quadrant and the patient is instructed to take a deep breath. As the gallbladder is compressed against the hand by the descending diaphragm, there will be inhibition of inspiration from the pain. Rovsing sign is characterized by pain in the right lower quadrant during palpation of the opposite side of the abdomen; it is indicative of appendicitis. The iliopsoas sign is elicited by having the patient flex the thigh against the examiner's resistance; pain indicates inflamed or irritated organs in the area.

In female patients, a pelvic examination is crucial for a full assessment of the abdomen. Both male and female patients should have a rectal examination to detect tenderness, masses, and occult blood; in men, the position and condition of the prostate are noted. All patients should undergo assessments of the heart, lungs, and external genitalia since these organs can give rise to abdominal pain.

Nausea, vomiting, and diarrhea can result in significant hypovolemia if they persist, especially in very young, chronically ill, or elderly patients. Orthostatic vital signs (VS) are useful in detecting significant fluid depletion. Antinauseants, antiemetics, and antidiarrheal drugs may be used in conjunction with aggressive fluid replacement. Meanwhile, emergency physicians must take steps to determine the cause of the symptoms, which may include viral and bacterial infections, food poisoning, toxic ingestions, side effects of medications, and emotional disorders.

■ EMERGENCY MANAGEMENT OF GASTROINTESTINAL BLEEDING

If the patient presents to the ED with upper or lower GI bleeding or has a change in VS that suggests blood loss and developing shock, immediate steps to be taken include ensuring intravenous access and administering of normal saline (NS) or Ringer's lactate. Since there is a possibility that emergency surgery might be required, the patient is placed on NPO (nothing by mouth) status. A nasogastric (NG) tube should be inserted; suction may be indicated to control vomiting and to remove accumulation of gastric contents.

If the patient has been bleeding or there is evidence of blood loss reflected in the VS, supplemental oxygen should be given (15 L by mask or 6 L by nasal cannula), and continuous electrocardiographic (EKG), blood pressure (BP), and oximetric monitoring should be initiated at once.

With suspected hypovolemia, blood is drawn for type and cross-match as well as for coagulation studies. Other tests pertinent to diagnosis include electrolytes, blood urea nitrogen (BUN), complete blood cell (CBC) count, and serum amylase; liver function studies may be ordered for select patients. Urinalysis must be accomplished for all individuals who present to the ED with abdominal or GI complaints. Pregnancy testing may also be ordered at the discretion of the examiner.

The use of intravenous antiemetics is imperative to control vomiting, but analgesic and sedative administration is controversial because it is commonly thought that they mask important signs and symptoms that could be useful in localizing the problem. Antibiotics are given promptly in the ED if there is suspected or confirmed perforation and peritonitis.

There are many adjunctive studies, including abdominal radiographs, ultrasound, intravenous pyelogram (IVP) barium enema, angiography, computed tomography (CT), endoscopy, and magnetic resonance imaging (MRI), pertinent to the diagnosis of abdominal and GI complaints. No patients should undergo such studies, however, until their oxygenation and cardiovascular status are well stabilized.

GASTRIC LAVAGE

Bleeding in the upper and lower GI tracts stops spontaneously in four of five cases, and so there is adequate time to clinically stabilize the patient prior to diagnostic testing.[1]

Intravenous fluids (i.e., crystalloids) and in some severe cases the addition of blood or blood products may be the most vital element of ED management of the patient with significant hemorrhage. Other therapies such as antacid administration and the use of histamine H_2-blockers are ordinarily reserved for patients with known ulcer disease. If histamine H_2-blocking drugs are given, the EN should monitor for bradycardia, which often accompanies use of this agent, especially in the elderly.

Lavage may be done after there is radiographic evidence ruling out the presence of a ruptured viscus or pneumoperitoneum. The primary objective in the use of this procedure is not to arrest bleeding but to monitor blood loss and to prepare the patient for endoscopy. Either water or NS may be used; the solution does not have to be sterile. Ice water is no longer recommended.[1] With the patient in Trendelenburg and left-lateral decubitus position, a large-bore Ewald tube should be inserted orally. (Before insertion, some physicians choose to cut additional holes in the distal portion to facilitate removal of clots.) Emergency personnel should not use small-bore NG tubes for lavage since they do not permit removal of clots and the return of pink fluid may give a false sense of security that bleeding is not occurring. The irrigant should be introduced and removed in 200- to 300-mL increments. A Y-connector setup will facilitate easy introduction and gravity siphonage. Ordinarily, the lavage should be continued until the return is clear.

ENDOSCOPY

Endoscopy is the most important tool in detecting the source of GI bleeding and facilitating direct control of hemorrhage site. Thermal coagulation or thrombosing of the underlying artery can be accomplished with the aid of this device. Sclerotherapy (i.e. injecting epinephrine, polidocanol, or alcohol into the bleeding site) can also be used to stop acute hemorrhage from esophageal varices or ulcers. Conscious sedation may be required to accomplish the procedure in the ED (see Chapter 7). If bleeding is not controlled by procedures such as these, surgical intervention is indicated.

PROCTOSIGMOIDOSCOPY

Proctosigmoidoscopy is helpful in some cases of lower GI bleeding to pinpoint the exact source of hemorrhage. The EN must be prepared to assist with suctioning and swabbing because ongoing bleeding may interfere with visualization. Estimates of the amount of recovered blood may be useful to determine the extent of the hemorrhage and to guide resuscitative therapy. It is appropriate to use conscious sedation for anxious patients undergoing diagnostic proctosigmoidoscopy in the ED. VS and the EKG should be closely monitored because intense vagal stimulation associated with the procedure may slow the heart or induce dysrhythmias.

ACUTE PANCREATITIS

Acute pancreatitis is seen in varying degrees of severity and is usually associated with biliary tract disease, alcoholism, or both. Alcohol is thought to have a stimulating effect on the production of pancreatic enzymes in an indirect way. Pancreatitis may also be associated with other conditions, including bacterial disease, the use of certain medications (e.g., antimetabolites, antibiotics, diuretics, anticonvulsants), pregnancy, and hyperlipidemia. It may also occur after trauma or surgery.

Acute pancreatitis is caused by a change in pancreatic enzyme production and transformation. Ordinarily, the enzymes are secreted in an inactive form and are activated in the duodenum by enterokinase and trypsin. However, in pancreatitis, the inactive enzymes are prematurely transformed within the pancreas into active enzymes. The pancreas will begin digesting itself in the face of stimulation of secretions and duct obstruction, producing midepigastric or periumbical pain, right or left upper quadrant pain, and occasionally referred pain to subscapular areas if there is diaphragmatic irritation. Pain results from autodigestion and the outpouring of fluid into the retroperitoneal and peritoneal cavities. If large enough volumes are lost into these spaces, hypovolemia and shock may occur. In addition to pain and other peritoneal signs, the patient may also have nausea and vomiting, necessitating insertion of a NG tube. Meperidine (Demerol) must be used for pain control because morphine is known to produce spasms of the sphincter of Oddi.

Blood specimens should be obtained for serum amylase, serum lipase, and possibly urinary amylase levels. Although the serum amylase level may be characteristically high in pancreatitis, this is not a specific test. The flat plate of the abdomen may be useful in detecting pancreatitis, showing a dilated jejunal loop adjacent to the pancreas, an air-filled transverse colon, and an indistinct outline of the kidneys, psoas muscles, and ascites. A chest film may reveal an elevation of the hemidiaphragms, pleural effusion on the left side, pericardial effusion, atelectasis, and pulmonary edema. Ultrasound is sometimes helpful, but computed tomography (CT) is preferred because it provides better visualization of the organ itself and accurately depicts the various complications associated with the pancreatitis, such as fluid collections or necrosis.[2]

PERFORATED PEPTIC ULCER

Most perforations of peptic ulcers (gastric or duodenal) occur in the anterior wall and permit leakage of gastric contents into the peritoneal cavity, causing a chemical peritonitis. This results in copious secretion from the peritoneum, which rapidly develops into a purulent peritonitis. Without prompt intervention, mortality can be high from this type of bleeding. If bleeding has been prolonged, hypovolemic shock may be evident when the patient presents to the ED. Rapid fluid resuscitation must take place to prevent cardiovascular collapse.

ESOPHAGEAL VARICES

Liver disease and sometimes cardiovascular conditions result in portal hypertension. As portal pressure climbs, the communications between portal and systemic circulations open at the gastroesophageal junction, the anorectum, the retroperitoneum, and sometimes other areas in the region of the splenic and left renal veins, creating significant hemorrhage from erosion or high-pressure injury.

When the patient presents to the ED, bleeding may be profuse from the upper gastrointestinal tract or the rectum. Shock may be apparent, so prompt fluid resuscitation using Ringer's lactate is imperative; however, care should be taken not to infuse excessive fluids because doing so might actually overexpand the circulating volume and ag-

gravate blood loss. Saline solutions, either given intravenously or used for gastric lavage, must be employed sparingly, if at all, because they tend to contribute to the accumulation of edema and ascitic fluid. The patient should be promptly placed on a cardiac monitor and given supplemental oxygen. Although central venous pressure (CVP) may be monitored, it may be a poor reflection of the patient's status because these patients typically have increased cardiac output and decreased peripheral resistance.[2] Endotracheal (ET) intubation may be required prior to endoscopy or use of a balloon tamponade (Fig. 26–2) for those cases in which the risk of aspiration is high, the bleeding is brisk, or encephalopathy is already apparent.

Arginine vasopressin, a nonapeptide secreted by the posterior pituitary, has potent vasoconstric-

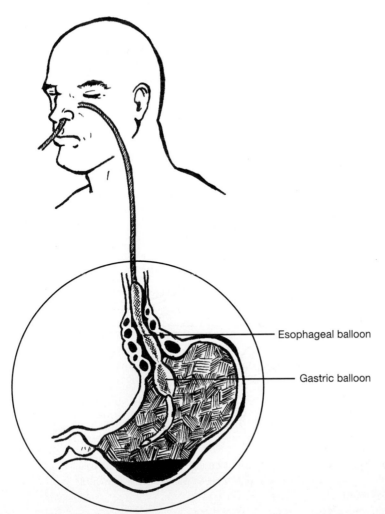

Esophageal balloon

Gastric balloon

Figure 26–2. Balloon tamponade achieves primary and temporary hemostasis in cases of bleeding esophageal varices. Esophageal balloon is inflated to compress bleeding varices. Gastric balloon anchors tube in stomach to accommodate suctioning.

tor effects on splanchnic arterioles and venules. It may be administered for patients with massive hemorrhage to decrease portal pressure and venous blood flow. It is given with transdermal, intravenous, or sublingual nitroglycerin, which tends to alleviate oppressive cardiovascular side effects. An added benefit is that when vasodilation occurs in response to nitroglycerin therapy, there is a concurrent reflex splanchnic vasoconstriction and reduction in portal pressure. Somatostatin, an octopeptide that reduces splanchnic blood flow and reduces portal pressure, is an alternative agent. Cessation of bleeding with either drug occurs in only about half of all cases.

The Sengstaken–Blakemore, Minnesota, or Linton–Nachlas tubes (Fig. 26–3) may be useful devices to tamponade control of upper GI bleeding due to esophageal varices. However, the source of bleeding should be detected first with the aid of endoscopy before insertion of these tubes. Vasopressin and nitroglycerin therapy should be used concomitantly with balloon tamponade.

The Sengstaken–Blakemore tube consists of three lumens: a gastric balloon that is inflated with 100–200 mL of air, an esophageal balloon that is inflated to 40 mm Hg (using a sphygmomanometer), and a third lumen to permit the aspiration of gastric contents. The Minnesota tube has an additional lumen and ports to permit the suctioning of pharyngeal secretions. The Linton–Nachlas tube consists of only a gastric balloon that is inflated with 500–600 mL of air. There are many openings in both the esophageal and gastric portions to permit the aspiration of secretions and blood. There are potential complications with these tubes, and their use is not favored as first-line therapy during the emergency treatment phase unless other measures fail to control the hemorrhage.

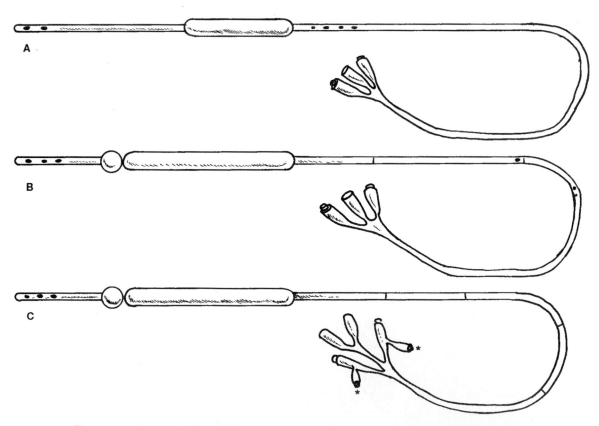

Figure 26–3. Variations of esophageal tubes. **A.** Linton–Nachlas tube (triple lumen, single balloon). **B.** Sengstaken–Blakemore tube (triple lumen, double balloon). **C.** Minnesota tube (four lumens, two balloons with ports (*) for pressure monitoring.

Endoscopic sclerotherapy and variceal ligation, accomplished in the operating room (OR), is considered the optimum treatment.[3]

The role of the EN in this situation includes assisting with tube insertion and clearing secretions and blood using suctioning. Like other patients in shock, the patient with esophageal varices requires supplemental oxygenation, close observation of VS, and cardiovascular monitoring. Care should be taken to prevent unnecessary heat loss; rewarming should be accomplished as indicated (see pages 519–521). The patient should be transported as promptly as possible to the OR or the intensive care unit (ICU) for further stabilization and treatment.

ACUTE APPENDICITIS

Appendicitis is the most common cause of the acute abdomen and usually results from an obstructive process in the appendix. Anatomically, the appendix may lie in many varying positions, and inflammation of the appendix mimics many other acute abdominal conditions. The common denominator is always pain, usually periumbilical, which localizes eventually to the right lower quadrant. As the pain progresses, it tends to become increasingly sharper, with anorexia, nausea, and vomiting as cofactors. The pain is usually constant and may radiate to the flank area. It is typically aggravated by walking, straining, or coughing. Some patients report a persistent, strong urge to defecate. Patients with suspected acute appendicitis should have a CBC count, which may reveal leukocytosis, suggestive of inflammation. If perforation is impending or is apparent from acute peritoneal signs, surgical intervention is imperative.

ABDOMINAL ANEURYSMS

Aneurysms of the abdominal aorta may cause abdominal pain. Since these are indeed life-threatening, ENs should quickly recognize their characteristic signs and symptoms (see pages 383–385).

CHOLECYSTITIS

The pain of cholecystitis is usually localized and is dominant in the right upper quadrant (see Fig. 26–1). The pain may first be coliclike and later become constant. The pain characteristically radiates to the right scapular tip. The patient may experience tenderness in the right upper quadrant or the epigastrium and demonstrate both guarding and rebound phenomena. A positive Murphy sign (see page 416) is suggestive of inflammation of the gallbladder. Nausea, vomiting, and fever are typical findings in these patients. Ultrasound is the most important diagnostic test in the ED setting.

HERNIAS AND BOWEL OBSTRUCTIONS

The patient who presents to the ED with constipation, obstipation, or bowel sound indices of an obstruction should be carefully evaluated to rule out conditions that could lead to perforation of the bowel or strangulation of the bowel with subsequent necrosis. These patients frequently will have the characteristic complaints of nausea, vomiting, and abdominal pain. Sepsis may be associated with certain bowel obstructions requiring immediate attention to the administration of antibiotics and surgical intervention.

FOREIGN BODIES IN THE GASTROINTESTINAL TRACT

There is a wide array of possible upper and lower GI foreign bodies that can create both obstruction and perforation of the bowel. History and x-ray are the best tools for identifying suspected foreign bodies, which may include coins, sexual stimulation aids, and other devices that are either accidentally or purposefully introduced via the mouth or rectum. Some may pose little or no threat (e.g., small coins) and pass normally with bowel evacuation. Others pose a threat for creating a major obstruction with associated perforation and peritonitis. These objects may be removed via endoscopy, rectosigmoidoscopy, or surgery. Conscious sedation and local anesthesia are often required for extraction procedures involving the esophagus or rectum.

The procedure for removing foreign bodies may be simple or complex, depending on the size, shape, and depth of the object. Tools that might prove useful include an anal speculum, anoscope, vaginal speculum, retractors, tenaculum forceps, ring forceps, tonsil snares, and suction darts. Occasionally, a ballooned tube (e.g., Foley catheter) can be passed beyond the foreign body and the bag can then be inflated to remove the object with gentle traction. In some instances, surgery may be required. Follow-up bowel studies are often indicated to ensure that there is no loss of integrity to the structures.

CROHN'S DISEASE

Crohn's disease is a chronic inflammation of the bowel that extends through all layers and involves the mesenteric and regional lymph nodes. Although rectal findings are not typical, fistulas and abscesses are often noted to coexist with the inflammatory process. The patient may visit the ED for persistent diarrhea (often bloody), abdominal cramps, fever, anorexia, and weight loss. A thorough diagnostic workup, usually on an outpatient basis, is required to evaluate the condition fully and to rule out any serious infections that could give rise to a similar aggregate of complaints.

ENTERAL FEEDING TUBE COMPLICATIONS

There are several types of enteral feeding tubes that are used for long-term patients in the home-care setting. Such tubes may become obstructed, dislodged, or malpositioned or may create problems at or near the site of insertion. The EN should be aware of common complications of enteral feeding tubes because patients often present to the ED for resolution of their predicaments (Fig. 26–4).

Nasogastric tubes may be properly positioned in the stomach or duodenum. However, at times, these devices become misplaced into the pulmonary spaces by perforation through the pharynx, esophagus, trachea, or bronchus. Feedings intended for the GI tract may instead be destined for the lungs, creating life-threatening ventilatory compromise. Pressure erosion can occur in the nostrils, pharynx, esophagus, stomach, and duodenum, too, resulting in either aspiration pneumonitis or peritonitis. Tracheoesophageal fistulas, although rare, have been noted. Gastrostomy tubes may also become dislodged or may leak, creating skin erosions and perhaps a nonhealing fistula. Complications common to jejunostomy tubes or catheters are dislodgement of the tube tip into the peritoneal cavity, an intestinal obstruction due to adhesion bands, or volvulus of the jejunum affixed to the abdominal wall.[4] Any tube, of course, can migrate forward or regress outward. Tube placement may be verified by radiographs. A chest x-ray may be required to detect pulmonary problems associated with enteral feeding tubes because regurgitation and aspiration commonly occur.

Any enteral tube can become clogged with feeding, crushed pills, or regurgitated GI contents. Saline flushing may be all that is required to clear the device. Cola, which is both acidic and effervescent, may also be used to resolve clogs. Use of rigid stylets is not recommended for removal of obstructions.

After prolonged placement, microorganisms may gain access to the lumen of the tube from the oral cavity, upper airway, or via retrograde migration from the bowel. Proliferation of the organisms is supported by the warm, moist, nutritive environment of the tube's lumen. Yeasts can grow quite rapidly and can completely obstruct the tube. Of course, the presence of the microbes can also contribute to gastroenteritis, pneumonia, and sepsis.

The EN should assess the placement of all feeding tubes when patients present with nausea, vomiting, abdominal distension, pain, or a feeling of unusual fullness. The port of entry should be scrutinized for indices of pressure, erosion, or necrosis. It is important to discern the feeding techniques used. How is the feeding introduced? Is the tube flushed routinely? If it is clamped, is it first flushed and filled with water to discourage microbe proliferation? Does the patient receive adequate fluids along with the feeding to prevent dehydration and electrolyte imbalances? Is the head of the bed elevated to at least 35 degrees after feeding to discourage regurgitation and aspiration?

ENs must ensure that the patient and the family understand the management of enteral feeding tubes. Referrals for follow-up care should be initiated as indicated.

■ NURSING DIAGNOSES

Appropriate nursing diagnoses for abdominal or GI emergencies include the following:

- Ineffective breathing pattern related to pain and abdominal distension
- Alteration in comfort due to pain

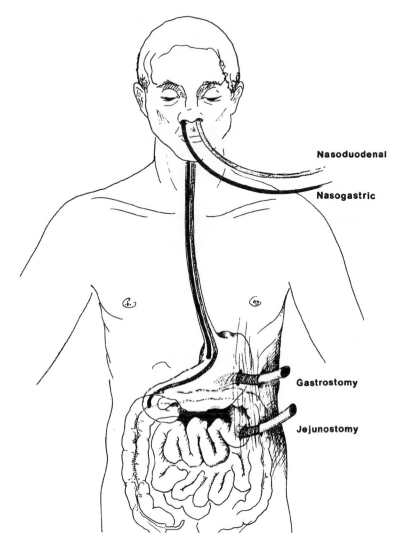

Figure 26–4. Proper positioning of enteral feeding tubes.

- Ineffective bowel elimination due to inflammation, obstruction, or ileus
- Decreased cardiac output related to hemorrhage and decreased venous return
- Ineffective airway clearance due to upper GI hemorrhage and excessive secretions
- Fluid-volume deficit, actual or potential, related to acute blood loss and gastric drainage
- Impaired gas exchange: ventilation–perfusion imbalance related to reduced circulating volume and compromised hemodynamics
- Anxiety related to bleeding, procedures, and pain

- Inadequate nutrition due to malpositioned, clogged, or mismanaged enteral feeding tube
- Potential for infection due to pulmonary aspiration of enteral feedings

■ REFERENCES

1. Rosen P, Barkin RM, eds. *Emergency Medicine: Concepts and Clinical Practice.* 3rd ed. St. Louis, Mo: Mosby-Year Book, 1992:1515–1532.
2. Railey D, Barkin JS. Pancreatitis. In: Carlson RW, Geheb MA. *Principles and Practices of Intensive Care.* Philadelphia, Pa: WB Saunders; 1993:1499–1506.

3. Korula J. Portal hypertension and variceal hemorrhage. In: Carlson RW, Geheb MA. *Principles and Practices of Intensive Care.* Philadelphia, Pa: WB Saunders; 1993:1445–1457.
4. Ayres SM, Grenvik A, Holbrook PR, Shoemaker WC. *Textbook of Critical Care.* 3rd ed. Philadelphia, Pa: WB Saunders; 1995.

■ BIBLIOGRAPHY

Barie PS, Shires GT. *Surgical Intensive Care.* Boston, Mass: Little, Brown; 1993.

Bongard FS, Sue DY. *Current Critical Care Diagnosis and Treatment.* E. Norwalk, Conn: Appleton & Lange; 1994.

Cardona VD, Hurn PD, Bastnagel Mason PJ, et al. *Trauma Nursing.* 2nd ed. Philadelphia, Pa: WB Saunders; 1994.

Chernow B, ed. *The Pharmacologic Approach to the Critically Ill Patient.* 3rd ed. Baltimore, Md: Williams & Wilkins; 1994.

Clochesy JM, Breu C, Cardin S, et al. *Critical Care Nursing.* Philadelphia, Pa: WB Saunders; 1993.

Grenvik A, Ayres SM, Holbrook PR, Shoemaker WB. *Pocket Companion to Textbook of Critical Care.* Philadelphia, Pa: WB Saunders; 1996.

Levine RL, Fromm RE Jr. *Critical Care Monitoring from Pre-Hospital to the ICU.* St. Louis, Mo: Mosby-Year Book; 1995.

Maull KI, Rodriguez A, Wiles CE. *Complications in Trauma and Critical Care.* Philadelphia, Pa: WB Saunders; 1996.

Moreau D, ed. *Nursing 96 Drug Handbook.* Springhouse, Pa: Springhouse Corporation; 1996.

Phippen ML, Wells MP. *Perioperative Nursing Practice.* Philadelphia, Pa: WB Saunders; 1994.

Physicians' Desk Reference. 50th ed. Montvale, NJ: Medical Economics; 1996.

Ruppert SD, Kernicki JG, and Dolan JT. *Dolan's Critical Care Nursing.* 2nd ed. Philadelphia, Pa: FA Davis; 1996.

Urden LD, Davie JK, Thelan LA. *Essentials of Critical Care Nursing.* St. Louis, Mo: Mosby-Year Book; 1992.

Weist PW, Roth PB. *Fundamentals of Emergency Radiology.* Philadelphia, Pa: WB Saunders; 1996.

■ REVIEW: ABDOMINAL AND GASTROINTESTINAL EMERGENCIES

1. Differentiate between the characteristics of visceral pain, somatic pain, and referred pain associated with abdominal assessment.

2. List the blood tests that should be obtained for a patient with gastrointestinal (GI) bleeding.

3. Outline the procedure for gastric lavage and identify the conditions that must be ruled out prior to initiating the procedure.

4. Explain the basis for the pain, nausea and vomiting, and hypovolemia that are associated with acute pancreatitis.

5. Describe the procedure for using balloon tamponade in controlling the bleeding associated with esophageal varices. Compare variations in design and usage of the:
   a. Sengstaken–Blakemore tube
   b. Minnesota tube
   c. Linton–Nachlas tube

6. Identify three methods for removing a foreign body from the GI tract.

7. Describe the characteristic presentation of Crohn's disease in the emergency department (ED).

8. Cite three complications associated with enteral feeding tubes that may be encountered by the emergency nurse (EN) and describe how each is assessed and managed.

Genitourinary Emergencies and Sexually Transmitted Diseases

27

Both trauma and infection of the genitourinary (GU) system account for significant numbers of problems seen in emergency departments (ED) and primary-care clinics. These problems are often less life-threatening than other clinical emergencies; when undetected, however, they contribute to high morbidity and mortality. Emergency nurses (ENs) are frequently the first to receive and assess patients with GU complaints; obtaining a detailed history and conducting a thoughtful assessment can have many positive outcomes. Further damage and future problems may be avoided when patients are educated about better methods of self-care with GU problems. GU trauma is discussed in Chapter 15; this chapter presents a brief review of the most frequently encountered GU tract infections and minor trauma difficulties, together with an overview of sexually transmitted diseases (STDs) and some guidelines for their assessment.

■ GENITOURINARY PROBLEMS

INITIAL ASSESSMENT

The ability to understand and evaluate bleeding sources, quite apart from multisystems trauma, is an important asset when dealing with medical-surgical GU emergencies. The patient experiencing bleeding or pain on urination or with the genital functions is usually quite anxious about the problem and needs reassurance.

If bleeding occurs in the urethra, blood will be evident at the meatus, but if blood is passed in the urine, look for a problem in the bladder or higher up the GU tract, in the ureters and kidneys. If hematuria is a complaint, be certain to ask the patient *where* in the stream the blood occurs. If blood is present throughout the stream, it is mixed in the bladder. If, however, blood is present at the beginning of the stream, there is a bleeding point somewhere down the urethra.

MINOR GENITAL PROBLEMS

Emergencies involving the external male genitalia are common and must be managed carefully and rapidly to avoid damaging consequences. Some of the rather commonly seen problems, with some very general guidelines for emergency intervention (as recommended by many urologists), are as follows:

- *Phimosis (constricted foreskin) with or without balanitis:* Treatment is a dorsal slit of the foreskin.
- *Adherent foreskin:* Treatment is morphine sulfate or meperidine for the severe pain, local anesthesia, and retraction of the foreskin.
- *Paraphimosis with strangulation:* Treatment is forceful drawing down of the foreskin, with a dorsal slit done if necessary to overcome the swelling. Hyaluronidase (Wydase), 1 mL, is sometimes injected locally to reduce swelling.

425

- *Ring constriction:* Occasionally seen in children, but more frequently seen in adults as a result of ring use to sustain penile erection. *Severe* tissue changes may result after 6 to 10 hours of the "tourniquet syndrome"; treatment is removal with a ring cutter or, if necessary, removal under general anethesia.
- *Zipper injuries:* Treatment is as follows:
  1. Sedate the patient as necessary to obtain cooperation.
  2. Cut the zipper fabric from the clothing with scissors if necessary, but *do not bend or cut* the zipper with wire cutters, because this may lock the teeth so that the slide cannot be pulled back.
  3. Holding the zipper firmly by both ends, close it a very short distance further and then gently disengage the entangled skin.
  4. Administration of a short inhalation anesthetic agent may be necessary, but most often a 2 percent lidocaine (Xylocaine) jelly or 4 percent topical lidocaine solution can be applied gently on the skin for some degree of local anesthesia.
  5. After removal of the tissue from the zipper teeth, an antiseptic ointment and dressing are applied, followed by application of cold compresses for 12 hours. Men should use a suspensory until healed, to reduce edema and to speed the healing process. Local anesthetic agents should *not* be injected, because this will add to the problem of local edema, making zipper removal more difficult, and because acute toxic reactions may occur owing to the extreme vascularity of the tissues, which causes rapid absorption of medications. The skin should *never* be cut free of the zipper teeth; doing so will produce a laceration requiring surgical closure, which may result in scar tissue, with contraction and permanent deformity.

SCROTAL EMERGENCIES

Specific emergencies involving the scrotum and its contents include the following.

Surgical Emergencies

Indirect hernia or communication hydrocele, with a palpable mass in the scrotum, scrotal pain, and vomiting, is a surgical emergency. This requires ruling out an incarcerated hernia.

Testicular torsion, a twisting of the supporting cord of the testis with pain (unrelieved by scrotal elevation), swelling, and tenderness, is another emergency. The majority of these males (65 percent) are between the ages of 12 and 18 years, and 85 percent of them experience an abrupt onset of testicular pain and testicular tenderness, with about half of them having had previous episodes. There may be scrotal edema, fever, and abdominal pain. The testicular survival rate has been shown to be approximately 47 percent in these cases. The major causes of the low salvage rate are a delay in surgery or misdiagnosis. Generally speaking, there is surprisingly little morbidity of the testis up to 6 hours after torsion onset; up to 10 hours, there is a 70 percent salvage rate. At more than 16 hours, the rate of testicular salvage is extremely low. Rapid evaluation and surgical intervention are required; *both* testes must be surgically fixed in place, or "pexed," within 6 to 12 hours to achieve a high probability of salvage.[1]

Cryptorchidism (usually with testicular torsion) can be confused with appendicitis. *Always* check for the presence of a testis in the scrotum on the right side.

Nonsurgical Emergencies

Epididymitis is a most frequently seen scrotal pathology in the ED, and it is essential to rule out (1) torsion in a young patient with resulting gangrene, (2) bleeding into a tumor, and (3) kidney stones, mimicked because the kidney, ureter, and testes basically have the same innervation (T-1, L-1). Epididymitis is an infection that is almost always secondary to prostatitis, is common in men over the age of 20, has a slow onset, and often follows clear-cut GU infection or instrumentation. Severe flank pain can be secondary to acute epididymitis. The treatment is bed rest, hot packs, and a scrotal "bridge." Relief of pain in epididymitis when the scrotum is elevated by a supporting "bridge" is known as Prehn sign.

Nursing Interventions

Nursing interventions for scrotal emergencies include:

- Bed rest
- Hot packs as ordered
- Application of a scrotal bridge

Nursing Diagnoses

Nursing diagnoses for scrotal emergencies would include:

- Pain
- Anxiety
- Body image disturbance
- Knowledge deficit regarding the therapeutic regimen

URETERAL STONES (URINARY CALCULI)

Probably all stones found in the ureter come from the kidney. The majority pass down to the bladder after one or several attacks of colic, although a smaller number are arrested in their passage because of their size or irregular shape. It is rare for the stone to pass through the ureter without pain, usually starting in the loin, passing through to the front, reaching the scrotum in the male and the vulva in the female. The pain is extremely severe, causing the patient to double up and writhe about in bed, sweating and groaning. There may be anuria, occurring when a stone blocks each of the ureters or only the functioning side. Hematuria may be present or absent, depending upon the degree of blockage. If there is a partial obstruction of the ureters, red blood cells (RBCs) will be found in the urinalysis. A total obstruction will usually reveal *no* RBCs.

Nursing Interventions

Immediate treatment includes generous medication for the severe pain, filtering all urine for stones, urinalysis, and culture and sensitivity (C&S) in case of an obstruction with infection, as well as continued close observation. Diagnosis is confirmed by an intravenous pyelogram (IVP), KUB (kidneys, ureters, and bladder) film, or both. The indications for intervention with renal or ureteral calculi are infection, obstruction, and intractable pain.

Nursing Diagnoses

Nursing diagnoses for ureteral stones would include:

- Pain related to obstruction or stone movement
- Altered urinary elimination related to obstruction
- Anxiety
- Knowledge deficit: therapeutic regimen
- Potential for infection due to obstruction and urinary blockage

URINARY RETENTION

There are many causes of urinary retention in the male patient, the most common being prostatic hypertrophy, followed by obstruction from various causes that may include strictures of the urethral meatus, the presence of foreign bodies, retention associated with trauma, gonococcal infections, and treatment with various drugs, including the belladonna alkaloids, amitriptyline HCl (Elavil), desipramine HCl (Pertofrane), and imipramine HCl (Tofranil).

Guidelines for Bladder Decompression

Decompression of the severely distended bladder requires great caution and careful observation when dealing with a patient who has *cardiovascular* complications; a severe hypotensive episode may be precipitated if the bladder is decompressed too rapidly. The guidelines for safe decompression are as follows. The maximum amount of urine to be removed at any time should be 500 mL. Clamp the catheter. Wait 1 hour and remove another 100 mL. Remove 100 mL/h until the bladder is empty, and then remove 200 mL/h as the bladder regains normal function and capacity.

Catheterization

Catheterization of the urinary bladder in most instances is a nursing procedure; it is one that requires great attention to technique and accountability. The patient suffering from trauma, debilitation, or illness may easily be compromised and subjected to extensive and potentially devastating complications if scrupulous aseptic technique is not exercised during the procedure. Too often, details of sterile technique are lost or neglected in the frequently harried efforts to "get all the tubes going" for a critically ill or injured patient; the available array of antibiotics is then relied upon to make up for all of the "violations." It *still* remains the primary nursing responsibility, however, to safeguard the patient's well-being by following every careful step of the procedure, as well as the following ones:

1. Discard contaminated catheters or gloves if technique is broken.
2. Prepare the meatus properly.
3. Introduce the catheter with strict aseptic technique and minimal trauma.
4. Immediately attach a sterile, one-way drainage unit, irrigant, or sterile plug if the catheter is to remain indwelling.
5. Tape the catheter carefully to the inner thigh or abdomen (of male patients) with a chevron tape to prevent pulling or undue pressure on the retention bulb.

Only sterile, *disposable* catheters should be used in the ED; most are now either silicone or silicone-treated to minimize traumatic irritation to the meatus. The Tieman Foley catheter is recommended by many urologists for male catheterizations because the configuration of the tip reduces trauma to the prostatic urethra and facilitates passage of the catheter.

Nursing Diagnoses

Nursing diagnoses appropriate for urinary retention would include:

- Pain related to distension
- Anxiety
- Altered urinary elimination
- High risk of infection
- Knowledge deficit regarding therapeutic regimen

INFECTIONS OF THE GENITOURINARY TRACT

Apart from the distal centimeter or so of the anterior urethra, the urinary tract is normally sterile, and it is abnormal for organisms to be present in the bladder. Infections do occur, however, in the kidneys, ureters, bladder, and the urethra—some together and some separately. In the male, any part of the genital system, the prostate, vesicle, vas def-

erens, epididymis, and testes may also be affected. The treatment for acute infection of the urinary tract requires accurate diagnosis of the infection, and before any definitive treatment is started, a *clean catch* or *midstream* specimen must be obtained in a sterile container for laboratory analysis and culture. Any urine specimen going to the lab should be marked—for safety's sake—"hold for C&S" until the physician decides whether C&S tests are needed.

The bacteria commonly responsible for infections of the urinary tract are *Escherichia coli;* one or more species of *Klebsiella, Enterobacter, Proteus,* or *Pseudomonas;* and various *Streptococcus faecalis* organisms, all normal constituents of the bowel flora. *E. coli* is the organism present in the great majority of acute infections of the bladder and kidneys in patients who have not been subjected to instrumentation and in whom no obstruction exists. Patients who have been treated with antimicrobial drugs and those who have been subjected to urologic procedures are more likely to have *Proteus, Pseudomonas,* or *S. faecalis* as the invading organisms.

Pathways of Infection

Pathogenic organisms invade the urinary tract by four pathways: (1) the ascending route, (2) urethrovesical reflux, (3) instrumentation, and (4) blood and lymph channels.

Invasion of pathogenic bacteria within the urethra represents the most common pathway of infection of the urinary tract. In the male, the length of the urethra and the antibacterial properties of prostatic secretion are thought to be effective barriers against invasion by this route, explaining why males have a much lower incidence of urinary tract infections (UTIs) than females. The high incidence of UTIs at the time of marriage, in association with sexual activity, clearly implicates the ascending urethral pathway in urinary tract pathology in females. Probably the major way in which most bacteria are introduced into the urinary tract, however, both in children and in adults, is by fecal soiling of the urethral meatus; the most frequent causative organism is *E. coli.*

Urethrovesical reflux occurs when intrabladder pressure increases suddenly in normal women, as during coughing, resulting in urine's being squeezed out of the bladder into the urethra. The urine may then flow back into the bladder when pressure returns to normal, and in this way bacteria is washed from the anterior portions of the urethra into the bladder.

The spreading of potentially pathogenic bacteria by instruments is an important cause of infection because it is commonly done, and it is usually preventable. Typical acute UTI and pyelonephritis *often* follow the use of a catheter or a cystoscope.

Infection of the kidney by the bloodstream is unusual but is to be strongly suspected in cases of *Staphylococcus* urinary infections (kidney infection is likely to be secondary to an infection elsewhere in the body), as well as in invasions of *E. coli* subsequent to severe gastrointestinal (GI) disturbances.

NONSPECIFIC INFECTIONS OF THE KIDNEY AND URETER

Pyelonephritis

Pyelonephritis is a fairly common disease that is a frequent cause of chronic renal failure and hypertension. *E. coli* is the most frequently identified pathogen; pregnant women, those with recurrent UTIs, immunosuppressed individuals, and those who have had instrumentation of the upper urinary tract are particularly susceptible. Prompt diagnosis and careful antimicrobial treatment are essential to prevent serious and permanent kidney damage.

In acute pyelonephritis, multiple inflammatory foci are scattered through the parenchyma of the kidney, with sudden onset of a general feeling of malaise, flank pain and tenderness, backache, shivering, fever, and an aching in one or both loins. Within 24 hours of onset, there is some disturbance of urination, usually with increasing frequency, burning, and occasionally frank hematuria. The temperature may go as high as or even over 105°F; examination of the urine will show pus and organisms with a few RBCs, and the organisms will grow on culture. This is probably the most common of all kidney diseases; it may occur in association with renal stones, although more frequently, no actual cause for the infection is found. When pathogens are identified, patients should be advised that they will need to have a follow-up examination and a test-of-cure culture (TCC) performed 1 to 4 weeks after completion of any antibiotic therapy.[2]

Nursing Interventions. Management includes hydration, accurate recording of input and output (I and O), analgesia as ordered, and careful technique for invasive procedures.

Nursing Diagnoses. Appropriate nursing diagnoses for pyelonephritis would include:

- Fluid volume deficit
- Pain related to inflammatory process
- Anxiety related to undiagnosed nature of illness
- Potential for repeat infection
- Knowledge deficit regarding therapeutic regimen and prevention of recurrence

Cystitis

A common occurrence, cystitis affects people of all ages, is especially prevalent in the female—in childhood, in pregnancy, and after menopause—and is frequently recurrent. The most common cause is a bacterial infection, and again, the most common affecting organism in the initial attack is *E. coli*. Acute inflammation usually starts quite suddenly with a little irritation in the bladder region and a desire to pass urine. Severity of the symptoms rapidly increases until there is an almost constant desire to urinate, and scant amounts are passed that burn and cause pain, especially severe at the end of micturition. The patient may appear flushed, have a dry tongue, and exhibit tenderness in the suprapubic region. Urinalysis (UA) will show an acid state, hazy appearance, and the presence of pus, bacilli, and a few RBCs. Again, culture will show the most common organism to be *E. coli*. If cystitis is treated promptly and adequately, the symptoms rapidly subside. However, if therapy is insufficient, the situation may quickly relapse or recur in a short period of time.

Nursing Interventions. Management includes hydration, accurate I and O, analgesia as ordered, and careful technique for invasive procedures.

Nursing Diagnoses. Appropriate nursing diagnoses for cystitis would include:

- Pain related to inflammation
- Risk of further infection

- Anxiety related to undiagnosed nature of illness
- Knowledge deficit regarding therapeutic regimen and prevention

Acute Urethritis

Acute inflammation of the urethra will occur within a few hours of exposure when the organisms have gained a firm foothold on the first part of the urethra. In the course of several days, pus forms and is discharged from the urethra. The symptoms, which may develop within 24 hours of exposure, at first consist of an itching, tickling, or burning sensation at the external meatus, which soon becomes red, feels hot, and burns on passing urine. There is increased frequency of urination, and a discharge soon appears, which may be watery or frankly purulent. There may also be hematuria. Acute urethritis is often associated with coitus.

Nursing Interventions. For acute urethritis, appropriate nursing interventions include:

- Forcing fluids as ordered
- Administering medications as ordered
- Monitoring output

Nursing Diagnoses. For acute urethritis, appropriate nursing diagnoses would include:

- Pain related to inflammation
- Risk of further infection
- Anxiety related to undiagnosed nature of illness
- Knowledge deficit regarding therapeutic regimen and prevention

Septic Shock

Septic shock, with profound vascular collapse and perfusion failure, is a systemic response to the release of bacterial endotoxins into the bloodstream, and it frequently follows procedures such as septic abortion, invasive instrumentation of the GU tract, and presence of long-term invasive devices such as indwelling urinary bladder catheters. Chronic debilitating illnesses and immunosuppression are also seen as predisposing factors.

Perhaps the major difference between the course of the hypovolemic shock and that of septic shock is *time*. In hypovolemic shock, the progress from hypotension to ischemia to anoxia usually takes several hours, time enough to stop the bleeding and institute treatment in most patients. In septic shock, stagnant anoxia (i.e., the hypodynamic phase) may develop in a very short period of time, depending on the amount of endotoxin released by the causative organisms, usually gram-negative bacteria, and the susceptibility of the patient. The overall prognosis (mortality between 70 and 90 percent) can be improved, and often the patient's condition, before shock develops, is the key to the possibility of survival. With the possibility of survival being so low, prevention of shock is far superior to the best treatment. Susceptible patients must be identified on initial assessment: newborns, patients over 60 years old, all debilitated patients, diabetics, cancer patients who have undergone tumor chemotherapy or whole-body radiotherapy, patients with open wounds or abscesses, surgery patients, patients on immunosuppressive medications, and catheterized patients.

Nursing Interventions. Once susceptible patients are identified, the EN must watch for subtle changes that may indicate sepsis. A patient may have normal skin temperature, pulse, and urine output and still go into shock. If a susceptible patient develops headache, fever, or a subnormal temperature; if breathing becomes rapid and shallow; if a *change* is noted in the patient's mental state; or if the urine output decreases slightly but steadily; begin intervention:

1. Support respirations. More septic shock patients die because of respiratory problems than because of perfusion failure. If an airway is needed, put it in early and supply enough high-flow oxygen to augment hemoglobin (Hgb) levels and reduce tissue hypoxia. Shunting is common in septic shock and should be suspected if the patient's extremities continue to be cold and pale and obliguria continues despite oxygen and fluid replacement.
2. Establish an intravenous line and provide adequate circulating volume. As endotoxin is released in the bloodstream, it causes intense vasospasms in small vessels, particularly in the kidneys, liver, and lungs; blood pools in the affected capillaries, fluid flows into the interstitial space,

and circulating blood volume is further reduced. Compensating for this loss of circulating blood volume calls for vigorous fluid replacement. The amount must be titrated on the basis of the patient's response (central venous pressure [CVP], blood pressure [BP], urine output, pulse, and sensorium). Several liters of crytalloid or colloid may be required over the first 2 to 6 hours, but hypotension may persist despite fluid replacement due to low systemic vascular resistance and decreased myocardial contractility. Continuous hemodynamic monitoring is required, since pulmonary failure poses a considerable risk.

3. Insert a urinary catheter with a urimeter to monitor hourly output.
4. Administer pharmacological support as ordered (i.e., antibiotics, steroids, cardiotonic agents, vasopressors, vasodilators, and antipyretics).
5. Continue ongoing assessment and monitoring vital signs (VS).

Nursing Diagnoses. For septic shock, appropriate nursing diagnoses would include:

- Impaired gas exchange related to decreased tissue perfusion
- Decreased cardiac output
- Altered tissue perfusion
- Anxiety related to shock state
- High risk of impaired skin integrity

■ SEXUALLY TRANSMITTED DISEASES

The term *sexually transmitted disease,* adopted in the 1970s by the World Health Organization (WHO), has replaced the old term *venereal disease.* The ever-broadening spectrum of disease entities transmitted by sexual contact has grown steadily in recent years, precipitating worldwide efforts at control and containment. The upswing in prevalence of STDs has been attributed not only to the "sexual revolution" that began in the 1960s but also to the fact that the general improvement in the socioeconomic status of most industrialized nations has produced environments that prevent development of immunity to many of the offending organisms; the general population of the United States is set up for recurrence of STDs. Additionally, the speed and ease of international travel permits those infected on one continent to spread disease on another continent before any signs of infection have made themselves known.

As renewed awareness and concerns about the STD problem have developed nationally and internationally, there has been a new determination by health-care providers to identify and manage STDs appropriately. Some of those STDs seen most frequently in EDs, and their cardinal differentiating signs and symptoms, are shown in Table 27–1 to assist ENs in their early recognition.

CONSIDERATIONS IN HISTORY TAKING

When gathering database information on patients who have GU complaints, ENs should be aware of the prevailing coexistence of multiple infections in many people. A number of factors have a direct influence on the proliferation, types, and increasing incidence of STDs; health-care providers must take all these factors into account when assessing presenting complaints. Histories should *always* include information relevant to the following areas:

- *Age:* The most sexually active age group consists of people aged 15 years and older (those between 15 and 29 years old are most active). In gay communities, the median age is 29.
- *Number of partners:* The more partners involved, the more encounters experienced, the greater the risk of infection. Persons involved sexually with multiple partners are most apt to have several STDs in concert—for example, the patient who has syphilis,

TABLE 27–1. GENITAL ULCERATIONS

Disease	Ulcer	Pain	Bubo
Syphilis	3 +	0	2 +
Chancroid	4 +	3 +	3 +
Herpes simplex virus 2	2 +	4 +	0
Granuloma inguinale	3 +	1 +	0
Lymphogranuloma venereum	2 +	1 +	0
Chlamydia (nongonococcal urethritis/nonspecific urethritis)	0	1 +	0

gonorrhea, and herpes progenitalis. Another example frequently seen in the gay community is gonorrhea, herpes, hepatitis B, *and* an acute enteric disease (referred to as "gay bowel syndrome") simultaneously. Multiplicity of participants (frequently anonymous) makes identification and treatment of partners extremely difficult and obviously facilitates the rapid and irresponsible spread of whatever diseases are present and transmissible.

- *Use (or lack of use) of methods of prevention:* The regular use of condoms is recognized as an effective disease barrier with a direct effect on the reduction of transmission. The contraceptive foams currently being marketed for heterosexual use are also antiviral and are somewhat effective against *Herpesvirus* and cytomegalovirus (CMV).
- *Homosexuality:* The growing number of practicing homosexual men in the United States (estimated at about 10 percent of adult men) contributes to increases in STDs through (1) aberrant sexual practices, (2) anonymous group sex with all its inherent risks, and (3) carrier states during which transmission continues without signs and symptoms.
- *Sexual practices:* Sexual practices—especially oral–anal and genital–rectal—are responsible for transmission of *most* severe problems that require treatment and surveillance.
- *Geographic distribution and prevalence:* There does seem to be a distributive pattern. Penicillinase-producing *Neisseria gonorrhoeae* (PPNG) seems to occur most often in crossroad cities of the world; herpes progenitalis and genital warts, in the Pacific Northwest; and so forth.
- *Socioeconomic status:* Differences in socioeconomic status may account for a higher incidence of reported treatment among more affluent groups, implying higher rates of transmission.

Transmission of many of the causative organisms of concern is accomplished by the exchange of secretions. Two situations that provide the setting for that exchange are early childhood, with mother-to-infant and child-to-child contact, and sexual activity.

ETIOLOGIC CLASSIFICATION

The most frequently treated STDs fall into two etiologic classifications: bacterial and viral. The bacterial group includes *Neisseria gonorrhoeae,* PPNG, and chromosomally mediated resistant *N. gonorrhoeae* (CMRNG); *Chlamydia trachomatis* (chlamydia); *Treponema pallidum* (syphilis); and *Haemophilus ducreyi* (chancroid). The viral group includes Herpes simplex virus 2 (HSV-2 or herpes progenitalis), CMV, and condyloma acuminatum (venereal warts).

THE BACTERIAL GROUP

Gonorrhea

Surprisingly, gonorrhea is still the most common infectious disease throughout the Western world. The causative organism is *N. gonorrhoeae,* commonly called gonococcus. It is a gram-negative diplococcus and does not possess spores, true capsules, or flagella; it is aerobic but grows best under stimulation of carbon dioxide. The organism has fastidious growth and survival requirements; it needs a medium on the alkaline side and dies on exposure to the weakest acid, requires a temperature of 35° to 36°C (95° to 98.6°F), and dies if the temperature is raised or lowered by 3 degrees. It must have moisture and dies immediately on drying.

Symptoms may occur as early as 1 day or as late as 2 weeks after contact. The average incubation period for males is 3 to 5 days; in the female, it is difficult if not impossible to know when symptoms first begin. There is a history of sexual exposure within the prior 2 weeks, and the early symptoms include uncomfortable sensations along the course of the urethra (a tickling sensation), followed by frequency of urination. In the male, this is commonly followed in a matter of hours by a purulent urethral discharge, dirty yellow in color. Infection is localized to the anterior urethra for the first 2 weeks or so and then spreads backward to the posterior urethra, involving the prostate and often the seminal vessels; from there, the infection follows the vas deferens to the epididymis, resulting in a painful, usually unilateral epididymitis.

In a female, acute gonorrhea usually involves the urethra, Skene's glands, Bartholin's glands, and the cervix. The vagina is never affected after the age of puberty. Pelvic inflammatory disease (PID) may immediately follow an acute ascending infection or may be delayed for several months, and it usually strikes during the childbearing years. When it occurs, both Fallopian tubes are frequently affected; resulting scar tissue may block the lumen or trap purulent discharge to form a pyosalpinx, which may in turn provoke peritonitis. Proctitis, when it occurs in males, is almost always a result of homosexual contact. In women, it may be caused by direct spread from vaginal discharges as well as genital–rectal exposures. A 50 percent failure rate in the treatment of pharyngeal gonococcal infections has been documented, as has an increased percentage of pregnant women with pharyngeal gonococcal infections. It has been recommended, therefore, that cultures of the cervix and the pharynx both be done in pregnant women with gonococcal infections.

Diagnosis in Females. Culture specimens should be obtained from the endocervical and anal canals and inoculated on separate Thayer–Martin culture plates or in separate Trans-grow bottles. Gram-stain smears are *not* adequately sensitive to rule out the presence of gonorrhea, according to the criteria and techniques for diagnosis of gonorrhea formulated by the Centers for Disease Control and Prevention (CDC).

Diagnosis in Males. Microscopic demonstration of typical gram-negative, intracellular diplococci on smear of a urethral exudate *does* constitute sufficient basis for a diagnosis of gonorrhea. When gram-negative diplococci cannot be identified under a smear of a urethral exudate or when urethral exudate is absent, a culture specimen should be obtained from the anterior urethra and inoculated on a Thayer–Martin or Trans-grow medium. In homosexual males, additional culture specimens should be obtained from the anal canal and the oral pharynx and inoculated on a Thayer–Martin or Trans-grow medium.

Nursing Interventions. Appropriate nursing interventions for gonorrhea are as follows:

- Instruct the patient carefully regarding follow-up treatment by the local health department.
- In uncomplicated gonoccoccal infection in both men and women, administer a single dose of ceftriaxone, cefixime, ciprofloxacin, or ofloxacin as ordered; no test of cure culture (TCC) is required.

Gonorrhea's Resistant Strains. One of the primary factors limiting the effective control of gonorrhea within the United States is the epidemic of organisms that are resistant to standard therapies.

PPNG, caused by a mutant gonococcus, suddenly appeared in many parts of the world in early 1976 and rapidly became endemic in all parts of the Far East. For a long time, it continued to spread and flourish in the crossroad cities of the world and among highly mobile members of the gay community, until the advent of newer drugs replaced penicillin as the drug of choice. If left untreated, PPNG progresses into disseminated gonococcal infection (DGI), known to have accounted for more than 50 percent of the cases of arthritis seen in patients between 15 and 30 years of age, as well as a high pelvic inflammatory rate in infected females.[3] Patients with proven PPNG infection or those who are likely to have acquired gonorrhea in areas of high PPNG prevalence *and* their sex partners require treatment beyond that of simple alternatives to penicillin, which is still given for gonorrheal infection in many parts of the world. Single-dose ciprofloxacin has become the treatment of choice.

CMRNG is seen in patients for whom standard treatment for gonorrhea fails or in those who are infected with penicillin-resistant strains that do not produce β-lactamase. Treatment of choice is with spectinomycin, ceftriaxone, and parenteral cephalosporins.[4]

Guidelines for gonococcal infection currently published by the CDC take into account several observations: the high frequency of coexisting chlamydial and gonococcal "ascending" infections; increased recognition of the serious complications of coexisting chlamydial and gonococcal infections; and the difficulty in diagnosing chlamydial infection.

Follow-up Treatment. Although initial recognition and culturing of gonorrheal infections may take place in the ED, the patient *should* be referred to the local health department for definitive treatment and follow-up evaluation of both patient *and* partner(s).

Chlamydia trachomatis

The most prevalent sexually transmitted bacterial pathogen in the United States today is *C. trachomatis.* There is a high frequency of coexisting chlamydial and gonococcal infections, and the importance of serious complications of chlamydial infections has been established. Frequently the cause of nongonococcal urethritis (NGU) or nonspecific urethritis (NSU), chlamydial infection often occurs as a bacterial overgrowth in males following penicillin administration.

Formerly classified as *Bedsonia* (a large virus), chlamydia is an obligatory intracellular bacterial pathogen, currently diagnosable by culture or the new fluorescent antibody test, and is easy to treat, once diagnosed.[2] Although the incidence of chlamydial infection is over twice that of gonorrhea, it is *not* considered a reportable disease. Its symptoms, less "florid" than those of gonorrhea, are frequently mistaken for it and treated as such until negative cultures are returned. For years, chlamydial infections went unrecognized and untreated; patients with subacute GU infections just "struggled along" without recognition of the problem and without effective treatment. Now it is recognized that tissues devitalized by chlamydia predispose to PID in females and cause other long-term problems (e.g., proctitis, perianal fistula) in areas drained by the common lymph system of the lower pelvis, especially in homosexual men.

Chlamydia is occasionally referred to as a TRIC agent, a term that has long been used as slang. TRIC stands for trachoma-inclusion conjunctivitis, an ocular infection that is widespread in Middle East and African countries. Spread by flies, foamites, and nonsexual contact, it causes blindness. *C. trachomatis* is also confused with trichomoniasis, another source of vaginitis and, occasionally, of male urethritis. *Trichomonas vaginalis,* a flagellated protozoan, is treated with metronidazole (Flagyl); again, *all* partners are treated. Patients receiving Flagyl must be warned to restrict alcohol intake for 48 to 72 hours; Flagyl is chemically related to disulfiram (Antabuse) and may cause a violent reaction if taken simultaneously with alcohol.

Treatment. Since about 75 percent of female partners tested have been found to have chlamydia present in the endocervix, it is recommended that both partners be treated simultaneously so that one will not reinfect the other. When taken as directed, azithromycin, tetracycline, and doxycycline have demonstrated cure rates of over 95 percent; TCC is not considered essential unless symptoms persist after treatment.

Syphilis

Once thought to have been conquered with the advent of penicillin, the ancient disease of syphilis remains an important public health problem, with the largest increases reported in California, Florida, and New York City, predominantly among black heterosexual males. *Treponema pallidum,* the causative organism, is a delicate spirochete found in lesions and in the bloodstream. The warmth and moisture of the body are necessary for survival; the organism is therefore transmitted by direct contact with infectious lesions of early syphilis.

Primary Stage. Following an incubation period of approximately 10 to 90 days (the average is 21 days), the lesion of primary syphilis begins as an indurated papule that breaks down rapidly to form a single, relatively painless, clean-based indurated ulcer, called a chancre. This chancre forms at the site of treponemal penetration, commonly the genitalia, rectum, mouth, and lips, although the chancre may occur anywhere on the body. A primary rectal chancre can easily be overlooked because its symptoms vary; internally, a chancre may cause significant pain, and one that has become secondarily infected may even be mistakenly diagnosed as rectal carcinoma.

Secondary Stage. Approximately 6 weeks to 6 months (the average is 6 to 8 weeks) following the onset of syphilis, the disease enters the secondary stage. This is marked by a great variety of dermatologic manifestations, which either are present as a generalized eruption or occur on only a small area of the skin. Macular lesions are a raw ham color and blanch on palpation. Papular lesions are usually reddish infiltrated lesions, approximately 0.5 cm in diameter, and are the most common lesions seen, occurring on flexor surfaces of the palms and soles. Mucous patches found in the mouth, rectum, and vagina are highly contagious. Lymphadenopathy is generalized, and the character of the enlarged lymph nodes is the same as is found in primary syphilis: firm, freely movable, nontender, round, and rubbery, without erythema of the overlying skin. In addition to having dermatologic manifestations, secondary syphilis is a systemic disease; that is, possible subacute meningitis and a mild, transient asymptomatic proteinuria may develop.

Latent Stage. In the absence of treatment, the lesions of secondary syphilis heal in approximately 4 to 12 weeks, and the disease enters the latent stage. Latent syphilis is defined as the absence of clinical lesions. Early latent syphilis (< 4 years' duration) is considered potentially infectious following relapse to the secondary stage. Late latent syphilis (≥ 4 years' duration) is considered noninfectious, although it is transmitted congenitally. Adequate treatment of the mother during the first 18 weeks of gestation prevents infection of the baby; adequate treatment after the eighteenth week cures the baby *in utero.*

Treatment. Primary and secondary syphilis share the same treatment protocol; latent and neurosyphilitic cases must be treated twice as long with twice as much medication. Follow-up evaluation and treatment are essential to controlling the spread of syphilis. It is desirable that follow-up urethral cultures be obtained from males 7 days after completion of therapy. Cervical and rectal cultures should be obtained from females 7 to 14 days after completion, and it is also recommended that gonorrhea patients have a serological test for syphilis at the time of diagnosis. Patients receiving recommended parenteral penicillin need not have follow-up serological tests. However, patients treated with spectinomycin or tetracycline should have a follow-up serological test for syphilis each month for 4 months to detect syphilis that may have been masked by treatment for gonorrhea. Patients with gonorrhea who also have syphilis should be given additional treatment appropriate to the stage of syphilis. Although long-acting forms of penicillin are effective for treatment of syphilis, they have no place in the treatment of gonorrhea. Alternative drugs are employed when penicillin allergy presents a problem.

Chancroid or Soft Chancre

A less frequently seen disease, chancroid is a highly infectious nonsyphilitic venereal ulcer caused by the gram-negative *H. ducreyi,* or Duprey's bacillus. The ulcer is usually situated on the external genitals but may occasionally be intrameatal in position, causing considerable pain on voiding. The incubation period varies between 1 and 3 days, and the ulcer first appears as a small reddish papule that soon becomes pustular and breaks down to form a painful, nonindurated ulcer with undetermined edges. The base is dirty gray or yellow in color; the lesions are invariably multiple fresh areas, often with a linear distribution, developing by autoinoculation. Papules, pustules, and ulcers are often seen on the same day, which is a helpful diagnostic point, and pain is a marked feature. The inguinal glands become enlarged and tender, and the lymphatics leading to the groin may stand out as red, painful threads. Treatment of choice is azithromycin or ceftriaxone.

THE VIRAL GROUP

The viral group of STDs include hepatitis B virus (HBV), three of the five *Herpesvirus hominis,* and human papillomavirus (HPV) infection. Among the five herpesviruses that affect humans, (*H. hominis,*) the three transmitted sexually are herpes simplex virus 1 (HSV-1), HSV-2 or herpes progenitalis, and CMV.

Hepatitis B Virus

HBV is a common STD; sexual transmission accounts for an estimated one third to two thirds of the estimated 200,000 to 300,000 new HBV infections that occurred annually in the United States from 1983 to 1993.[6]

The population most at risk for HBV infection include homosexuals, parenteral drug abusers, health-care workers in contact with blood or blood products, people with increasing numbers of recent and lifetime sexual partners, and those with a history of multiple episodes of STDs. HBV usually presents with jaundice, loss of appetite, and abdominal pain and usually together with signs and symptoms of one or several other STDs.

HBV leads to an estimated 5000 deaths annually in the United States from cirrhosis of the liver and hepatocellular carcinoma; a safe vaccine now exists to prevent infection, both in adults and neonates, to whom it can be transmitted if the mother is HBV-infected.

Hepatitis C (non-A, non-B HV, HCV) is becoming prevalent in the US, with 170,000 cases reported each year. The risk groups and modes of transmission are the same as for HBV. Unfortunately HCV is asymptomatic, is difficult to diagnose and treat, and is spread primarily through contact with contaminated blood and blood products or via organ and tissue transplantation. Universal precautions and body substance precautions are essential to prevent transmission since the condition has a very high probability of becoming chronic (50 to 80 percent) and creating devastating liver pathology including obstruction, scarring, and necrosis.

Herpes Simplex Virus 1 and Herpes Simplex Virus 2

Genital herpes has become the fastest spreading STD of modern times, causing significant concern and suffering among those who contract it. Herpes has no known cure; once inside the cell, the herpesvirus takes over the protein-producing apparatus of the host cell and begins replicating itself, recurring in cycles. Although both HSV-1 (causes cold sores on the lips) and HSV-2 have been identified as causative agents, HSV-2 causes most cases. On the basis of serological studies, approximately 30 million people in the United States may have genital HSV infection.[6]

The female patient may present with multiple small vesicular ulcerations of the skin and mucous membranes in the vulvovaginal area, which are extremely painful, and there may even be an enlargement of the inguinal lymph nodes. The primary episode may last from 14 to 21 days, and as the primary lesions heal, the virus travels up to the presacral ganglia, where it lies dormant between

recurrences, which will flare about every 2 months in approximately half the patients. Diagnosis is made by a papanicolaou (Pap) smear showing multinucleated giant cells recovered from the endocervix; male partners will have a high virus titer in their semen.

Primary HSV-2 infection in men frequently involves the entire penis, with extremely painful vesicular lesions and systemic symptoms similar to those of the female. Frequently, homosexual men present with extensive herpetic lesions of the penis, perianal area, and rectum. Patients in the primary phase of HSV-2 are desperately ill when they seek help. Congenital malformations as well as neurological defects can develop during the first month of life in 30 percent of newborns exposed to the herpesvirus, which is either swallowed in the birth canal or acquired from the mother's milk. There is also thought to be a possible relationship to hearing defects and, indirectly, to hampered intellectual development. There has been enough concern expressed to generate the medical judgment among many practitioners that the presence of herpetic lesions on the labia, at the time of delivery, is an indication for cesarean section. Neonatal herpes can result in aseptic meningitis, or blindness may result from keratitis; there is a 70 percent mortality rate.[7]

Treatment. Although most treatment measures are palliative (such as frequent sitz baths, soothing ointments, and analgesics), acyclovir has shown itself to shorten the median duration of first-episode eruptions by 3 to 5 days and may reduce systemic symptoms in primary episodes. Occasionally, patients with severe systemic complications may have to be admitted to the hospital for intensive acyclovir intravenous therapy.

Cytomegalovirus

Of the five forms of *H. hominis,* CMV is thought to be closely associated with immunodeficiencies, and while there are no presenting signs or symptoms of CMV infection, it is thought to be sexually transmissible. A study involving adolescent girls and women (and their partners) between ages 15 and 35 who sought care from STD clinics in a major western U.S. city demonstrated that CMV is commonly seen in semen and cervical secretions, that its presence is directly related to numbers of sex partners and histories of previous STDs, and that the incidence of CMV infection among the women studied was ten times higher than the incidence in the general population.[8,9]

CMV has a recognized relationship to congenital malformation and mental retardation following *in utero* infection; many physicians routinely test for CMV in all neonates with birth defects. With rubella largely controlled through vaccination, CMV is now one of the most common infectious causes of these syndromes.[9]

There is a markedly high prevalence of CMV infection in homosexual men; it is now recognized that these men, who shed CMV in their saliva and semen, probably have a higher than average risk of developing Kaposi's sarcoma, which has been linked to CMV infection and to immunosuppressions through seroepidemiological studies.[9]

CMV, then, often may exist in patients presenting to the ED with STDs. Remember that CMV is transmitted by direct contact with infected urine and saliva as well as with other bodily secretions. ENs should use precautions in dealing with body fluids; pregnant ENs should avoid any such exposure.[10]

Human Papillomavirus Infection (Genital Warts)

The genital wart is viral in origin, painless, has an incubation period of up to 6 months, and may flourish during pregnancy. The warts are found in the anal area, foreskin, and vaginovulvar region and have been associated with high rates of human immunodeficiency virus (HIV) infection. Genital warts have been treated with cryotherapy and topical application of a 10 percent solution of podophyllin in compound tincture of benzoin. The podophyllin solution is liberally applied to the warts *only,* because it may be toxic to normal skin, and is allowed to remain for 4 hours; it should then be washed off. The patient should return in 1 week for a retreatment. Podophyllin is known to be keratogenic, is capable of causing congenital abnormality, and should not be used on pregnant women.

ECTOPARASITIC INFECTIONS

Involving a parasite that lives outside the body, sexually transmitted ectoparasitic infections in adults include pediculosis pubis (pubic lice, or "crabs" as

they are called by the general public) and scabies, caused by an arachnid, *Sarcoptes scabiei,* the itch mite. Fleas, lice, and ticks are also ectoparasites but not considered to be sexually transmitted.

The lice are found in the pubic hair areas—although other hairy areas should be inspected as well for nits (eggs)—and have a 7-day egg cycle, during which time the larvae hatch, grow to maturity, and lay their eggs. Scabies mites are found in intensely itching papules and burrows that appear as slightly discolored or reddened lines that are between 2 to 3 mm and 2 to 3 cm in length.

Patients with pediculosis pubis and/or scabies usually seek treatment because of intense pruritis and are treated primarily with gamma benzene hexachloride (Kwell) or Lindane 1 percent cream or lotion. Lindane should not be left on the skin for extended periods; should not be applied following a bath or with extensive dermatitis, when pregnant or lactating, or on children under 2 years of age; and should be washed off thoroughly after 8 hours. Treatment must be repeated every 7 days for several weeks in order to be effective.

Both infestations require that bedding and clothing be machine-washed and dried using a high-heat cycle, or removed from body contact for 72 hours; fumigation of living areas is not necessary (see pages 532–533).

NURSING DIAGNOSES

Appropriate nursing diagnoses for STDs would include:

- Pain related to lesions, dysuria, pruritis
- Anxiety related to discussion of intimate information, diagnosis, and concerns for partner
- Body image disturbance related to lifestyle changes necessitated by STD treatment
- Knowledge deficit regarding disease, treatment, complications, recurrence, and communicability
- Potential for infection related to continuation of unsafe sexual practices

ACQUIRED IMMUNODEFICIENCY SYNDROME

No review of STDs would be complete without a review of the problems generated by acquired immunodeficiency syndrome (AIDS), although this section is meant to be simply an updated overview of current modalities in recognition and management of STDs. AIDS continues to present enormous problems and promises to present even greater ones as time goes on. On a day-to-day basis, however, health-care providers must educate themselves about protective practices in order to minimize *their* exposure to the AIDS virus.

Etiology

HIV and AIDS continue to spread globally. The incidence of these diseases has begun to slow in the United States, but they are spreading rapidly in Asia and Africa; cultural, social, and governmental practices of most of the countries on those continents do not permit examination of the problem in a solution-oriented manner.

Neither a vaccine to prevent HIV nor a cure for AIDS has been developed; both disease states are shrouded with uncertainties. The few known facts that *are* available to us as health-care providers are important ones:

- There are specific populations that are and have been at high risk of developing AIDS (male homosexuals, bisexual males and their female partners, intravenous drug abusers and their sexual partners, hemophiliacs, and neonates with mothers who have HIV).
- AIDS is probably infectious and transmissible through blood and body secretions (the distribution of AIDS cases parallels that of HBV infection, which is transmitted sexually and parenterally).
- All information to date argues against person-to-person transmission by ordinary household contact.
- Victims suffer from deficient immune systems that have been rendered *permanently* nonfunctional as a result of the viral attack.

Certain sexual practices (such as unprotected vaginal, anal, or oral intercourse) have been shown to potentiate the risk of transmission. However, since HIV *has* been demonstrated to be present in semen, saliva, tears, and blood of infected persons, *no* sexual practices between individuals that pass these fluids can be excluded as potential means of transmission.

Although HIV transmission through saliva or tears during casual contact has not been demonstrated, there have been several AIDS cases among health-care professionals who were contaminated with infected blood during procedures. Small protection is afforded ED personnel who are exposed many times unknowingly to infected blood and body fluids in the course of patient care; it would seem wise to follow certain precautionary guidelines, as outlined by the CDC, for *every* patient (i.e., universal precautions).

Precautionary Guidelines for Protection Against Acquired Immunodeficiency Syndrome

CDC's recommendations for prevention of HIV transmission in health-care settings in the workplace again outlines universal blood and body-fluid precautions that should be used in the care of *all* patients, especially those in emergency-care settings, in which the risk of exposure is increased and the infection status of the patient is usually unknown, as follows[11]:

1. All health-care workers (HCWs) should routinely use appropriate barrier precautions to prevent skin and mucous-membrane exposure when contact with blood or other body fluids of any patient is anticipated. Gloves should be worn for touching blood and body fluids, mucous membranes, or nonintact skin of all patients; for handling items or surfaces soiled with blood or body fluids; and for performing venipuncture and other vascular access procedures. Gloves should be changed after contact with each patient. Masks and protective eyewear or face shields should be worn during procedures that are likely to generate droplets of blood or other body fluids to prevent exposure to mucous membranes of the mouth, nose, and eyes. Gowns or aprons should be worn during procedures that are likely to generate splashes of blood or other body fluids.

2. Hands and other skin surfaces should be washed immediately and thoroughly if contaminated with blood or other body fluids. Hands should be washed immediately after gloves are removed.

3. All HCWs should take precautions to prevent injuries caused by needles,

scalpels, and other sharp instruments or devices during procedures; when cleaning used instruments; during disposal of used needles; and when handling sharp instruments after procedures. To prevent needle-stick injuries, needles should *not* be recapped, purposely bent or broken by hand, removed from disposable syringes, or otherwise manipulated by hand. After they are used, disposable syringes and needles, scalpel blades, and other sharp items should be placed in puncture-resistant containers for disposal; the puncture-resistant containers should be located as close as practical to the use area. Large-bore reusable needles should be placed in puncture-resistant containers for transportation to the reprocessing area.

4. Although saliva has not been implicated in HIV transmission, to minimize the need for emergency mouth-to-mouth resuscitation, mouthpieces, resuscitation bags, or other ventilation devices should be available for use in areas in which the need for resuscitation is predictable.

5. HCWs who have exudative lesions or weeping dermatitis should refrain from all direct patient care and from handling patient-care equipment until the condition resolves.

6. Pregnant HCWs are not known to be at greater risk of contracting HIV infection than HCWs who are not pregnant; however, if a HCW develops HIV infection during pregnancy, the infant is at risk of infection resulting from perinatal transmission. Because of this risk, pregnant HCWs should be especially familiar with and strictly adhere to precautions to minimize the risk of HIV transmission.

Otherwise, the same old common-sense guidelines apply: use of careful and thorough handwashing technique, careful labeling of blood specimens with "Blood Precautions" (when appropriate to do so), *immediate* cleaning and disinfecting after blood spills, and handling of soiled articles with isolation techniques when they belong to a patient known *or* suspected to have AIDS.

■ SUMMARY

Among certain high-risk groups, two or perhaps three STDs are frequently found occurring in concert; maintain an index of suspicion and look for more than one disease entity in a sexually active person with symptoms of STD. With behavioral changes taking place in the homosexual community, it is hoped that diseases spread by promiscuity and multiple anonymous partners will, in time, decline significantly. When STD problems *are* identified as part of the GU problem presenting in the ED, the patient perhaps may not receive primary treatment in the ED but will be referred to the local public health agency or perhaps a private physician for treatment. ENs have the opportunity to facilitate appropriate treatment referrals to community health agencies and to ensure adequate follow-up care.

■ REFERENCES

1. Jenkins JJ, Loscalzo J. *Manual of Emergency Medicine: Diagnosis and Treatment,* 2nd ed. Boston: Little, Brown; 1990:250.

2. Johnson JR. Recognizing and treating acute pyelonephritis. *Emerg Med.* February 1992; 33.

3. Lanros NE. Sexually transmitted diseases. In: Fincke MK, Lanros NE, eds. *Emergency Nursing: A Comprehensive Review.* Rockville, Md: Aspen, Publishers; 1986:395–415.

4. Cunha BA. Penicillinase-producing *Neisseria gonorrhoeae. Emerg Med.* February 1990; 97–98.

5. Jenkins JJ, Loscalzo J. *Manual of Emergency Medicine: Diagnosis and Treatment,* 2nd ed. Boston: Little, Brown; 1990:225–231.

6. Centers for Disease Control and Prevention. 1993 Sexually transmitted disease treatment guidelines. *MMWR.* 1993;42(RR-14):91–92.

7. Macek C. IV and oral acyclovir surpass topical use. *JAMA.* 1982;248:2942–2943, 2948.

8. Palella FJ, Murphy RL. Sexually transmitted diseases. In: Shulman ST, Phair JP, Peterson LR, Warren JR. *The Biologic and Clinical Basis of Infectious Disease,* 5th ed. Philadelphia, Pa.: WB Saunders: 1997:209.

9. Tan TQ, Warren JR. Infections at the extremes of life. In:Shulman ST, Phair JP, Peterson LR, Warren JR. *The Biologic and Clinical Basis of Infectious Disease,* 5th ed. Philadelphia, Pa.: WB Saunders: 1997:378.

10. Dworsky M, et al. Occupational risk for primary CMV infection among pediatric health-care workers. *N Engl J Med.* October 20, 1983;950.

11. Centers for Disease Control. Recommendations for preventing transmission of infection with HIV in the workplace. *MMWR CDC Surveill Summ.* 1985;34:681–686, 691–695.

■ BIBLIOGRAPHY

Carmichael CG, Carmichael JK, Fische M. *HIV/AIDS Primary Care Handbook.* 2nd ed. Stamford, Conn: Appleton & Lange; 1996.

Centers for Disease Control and Prevention. Recommendations and reports: 1993 sexually transmitted diseases treatment guidelines. Atlanta, Ga: USDHHS; 1993.

Centers for Disease Control. Update: universal precautions for prevention of transmission of human immunodeficiency virus, hepatitis B virus, and other bloodborne pathogens in health-care settings. *MMWR CDC Surveill Summ.* 1988;37:377–388.

Elam AL. The aftermath of love. *Emerg Med.* 1987;19(1):24–41.

Emergency Nurses Association. *Emergency Nursing Core Curriculum.* 4th ed. Chicago, Ill: ENA; 1994.

Faro S. UTI in adults: today's treatment strategies. *Emerg Med.* April 1992;145–158.

Freeman PB. Gonorrhea. *J Emerg Nurs.* 1980;6:17–22.

Handsfield HH. Sexually transmitted diseases. *Hosp Pract* (Off Ed). Jan. 1982;100–101.

Howes DS. UTI: advances and controversies. *Emerg Med.* Aug. 1992;218–227.

Iravani A. UTI in young women: breaking the cycle of recurrence. *Emerg Med.* Feb. 1992;33–49.

Lanros NE. Genitourinary emergencies. In: Fincke MK, Lanros NE, eds. *Emergency Nursing: A Comprehensive Review.* Rockville, Md: Aspen Publishers; 1986:382–394.

Lanros NE. Sexually transmitted diseases. In: Fincke MK, Lanros NE, eds. *Emergency Nursing: A Comprehensive Review.* Rockville, Md: Aspen Publishers; 1986:395–414.

Miles PA. Sexually transmissible diseases. *J Emerg Nurs.* 1980;6:6–12.

Moldwin RM, Mulholland SG. Three treatment choices for recurrent cystitis. *Emerg Med.* Mar 1992;30–46.

Muma RD, Lyons BA, Pollard RB, Borucki MJ. *HIV Manual for Health Care Professionals.* E. Norwalk, Conn: Appleton & Lange; 1994.

Roberts SL. *Critical Care Nursing: Assessment and Intervention.* Stamford, Conn: Appleton & Lange; 1995.

Rosen P, et al., eds. *Emergency Medicine: Concepts and Clinical Practice.* 2nd ed. St. Louis, Mo: CV Mosby; 1987.

Tintinalli JE, et al. Male genital problems. In: *Emergency Medicine: A Comprehensive Study Guide.* New York, NY: McGraw-Hill; 1992:385.

Walsh PC, et al., eds. *Campbell's Urology.* 5th ed. Philadelphia, Pa: WB Saunders; 1986.

Weems J. *Quick Reference to Renal Critical Care Nursing.* Frederick, Md: Aspen Publishers; 1991.

Willis D. Overgrown prostate. *AJN.* Feb 1992;34–40.

York JL. What to do about acute urinary retention. *Emerg Med.* May 1991;88–96.

Zahn AL, Craven RA. The acute scrotum: consider eight possibilities. *Emerg Med.* Jan 1994;47–51.

■ REVIEW: GENITOURINARY EMERGENCIES AND SEXUALLY TRANSMITTED DISEASES

1. Describe the rationale for determining where in the genitourinary (GU) tract bleeding is occurring when the patient complains of hematuria or blood appears at the meatus.

2. Outline some of the more commonly seen forms of genital trauma and describe the appropriate nursing interventions.

3. Identify two of the most commonly seen forms of nonsurgical GU emergencies and outline the appropriate nursing interventions.

4. Describe the guidelines for decompressing a severely distended bladder in a patient with cardiovascular complications, and explain the rationale for caution.

5. Identify the most commonly seen bacteria in urinary tract infections (UTIs) and describe the usual pathways of infection.

6. Describe the signs and symptoms of acute pyelonephritis, cystitis, and urethritis, and list the appropriate nursing diagnoses.

7. Explain the etiology of septic shock, compare/contrast septic shock to hypovolemic shock, and identify the most susceptible patient populations.

8. List four signs of incipient septic shock in the susceptible patient and outline the immediate nursing interventions.

9. Identify at least six areas of information to be covered when taking histories for patients with sexually transmitted diseases (STDs).

10. Identify the two etiologic classifications of STDs and list the specific diseases that fall into each.

11. Outline management protocols for emergency department (ED) treatment of STDs, including the gonorrheas *(Neisseria gonorrhoeae,* penicillinase-producing *N. gonorrhoeae* [PPNG], and chromosomally mediated resistant *N. gonorrhoeae* [CMRNG]), *Chlamydia trachomatis,* syphilis, hepatitis B (HBV), herpes simplex virus 1 (HSV-1), herpes simplex virus 2 (HSV-2), cytomegalovirus (CMV), human papillomavirus (HPV) or genital warts, ectoparasitic infections (pediculosis pubis and/or scabies), and acquired immunodeficiency syndrome (AIDS).

12. Explain the concept for use of universal precautions in the ED and outline the current Centers for Disease Control and Prevention (CDC) guidelines for preventing transmission of STDs and AIDS.

Obstetric and Gynecologic Emergencies

28

■ GYNECOLOGIC PROBLEMS AND EMERGENCIES

VAGINAL BLEEDING

When a female patient presents with a complaint of "vaginal bleeding," it is always a sound concept to assume that she is pregnant until proved otherwise. Menstrual cycles vary widely, as do amounts of menstrual flow. There are several normal variables influenced by oral contraceptives (OCs), the intrauterine device (IUD), hormone replacement and the perimenopausal years. Vaginal bleeding is considered a serious problem when associated with hemodynamic compromise or pregnancy.

The patient may complain of vaginal bleeding with or without pain and should be closely observed for the amount of bleeding and for evidence of impending shock. The emergency nurse (EN) should place a clean perineal pad in order to evaluate the amount of blood loss. The nursing history should include an evaluation of the vital signs (VS), the date of last menstrual period (LMP), number of pregnancies, number of living children, use of contraceptive devices or medications, any trauma (e.g., straddle injury, abdominal trauma, sexual abuse), and a description of typical menses as well as a full account of the present bleeding episode (onset, number of pads or tampons used, presence of clots, cramping abdominal pain, or other associated symptoms).

Determine if the individual is pregnant using a rapid-results pregnancy test. Obtain blood for a complete blood cell (CBC) count, including hemo-globin (Hgb) and hematocrit (Hct). A specimen for "type and hold" may be ordered in severe cases of vaginal bleeding. An intravenous line should be initiated if there are indices of orthostatic hypotension or shock. The patient should be prepared for a pelvic examination to determine the source of bleeding.

Bleeding during pregnancy can be especially problematic. In the first and through the middle of the second trimester, ectopic pregnancy and spontaneous abortion are probable. In the third trimester of pregnancy, placenta previa or abruptio placenta must be considered (see pages 448–449). If the patient has painless, bright-red bleeding suggesting placenta previa, pelvic and rectal examinations should be deferred.[1]

PELVIC INFLAMMATORY DISEASE

Pelvic inflammatory disease (PID) is a syndrome resulting from infection of the reproductive organs and their supporting structures. Organisms responsible for the condition include *Neisseria gonorrhoeae, Chlamydia trachomatis,* streptococci, and a variety of anaerobes.

The patient presents with lower quadrant cramping or a nonradiating aching pain, fever, and a characteristic vaginal discharge, with or without associated bleeding. The EN may note that the individual with PID tends to shuffle while walking, bent over, toward the treatment room. This is because the patient cannot endure the impact of a normal walking gait or standing upright, owing to the inflamed pelvic organs. The patient with PID has marked adnexal tenderness and experiences great pain as the cervix is deviated laterally during the examination. Since the patient may "hit the ceiling" because of the intense pain when the cervix is mobilized, this reaction is sometimes called the chandelier sign.

A CBC and sedimentation rate should be done and will usually show a very high white blood cell (WBC) count (20,000 to 30,000/mm^3) and an elevated sedimentation rate. A Gram stain may be positive, and a culture will demonstrate the suspect pathogen, often gonococci.

Individuals with high fever, chills, and peritoneal signs require prompt hospitalization for intravenous antibiotic therapy. The choice of agent will be based upon the dominant organism and its sensitivity. Some patients may require a culdocentesis for abscess drainage. If a pelvic abscess ruptures, prompt hysterectomy and bilateral salpingo-oophorectomy may be required. Nonpregnant patients with milder presentations may be managed on an outpatient basis. Sexual partners will also require treatment and follow-up evaluation to prevent recurrence of the infection.

TOXIC SHOCK SYNDROME

Toxic shock syndrome (TSS) is an acute, febrile illness that is due to actions of exotoxins, enterotoxins, and endogenous mediators liberated during infections, especially in menstruating women. Signs and symptoms include:

- High fever
- Myalgias
- Vomiting and watery diarrhea
- Headache
- Pharyngitis
- Hypotension
- Mucocutaneous findings (i.e., diffuse, blanching erythema on trunk and in axillary and inguinal folds; desquamation of palms and soles in late-stage cases; nonpitting edema; hyperemia of vaginal and other mucosal surfaces)
- Multisystem organ failure (MSOF)

The Centers for Disease Control and Prevention (CDC) bases definition of TSS on these six criteria: high fever, rash, desquamation, hypotension, and involvement of three or more organ systems, once other causes for these findings are excluded.[2]

Women at high risk for TSS are those who use a diaphragm or contraceptive sponge or who use high-absorbency tampons. Staphylococcal and streptococcal organisms tend to colonize in association with these devices and give rise to the infection. Cases have also been associated with influenza, childbirth, operative procedures, abortion, and the use of nasal packings. When the syndrome begins, there is a rapid onset of fever, vomiting, watery diarrhea, sore throat, and profound myalgias. Hypotension tends to be prominent within 48 to 72 hours, and organ failure follows. There may be renal failure, adult respiratory distress syndrome (ARDS), and pulmonary edema, refractory shock, ventricular arrhythmias, and disseminated intravascular coagulation[2] (see Chapter 24). Although the mucocutanous findings are common, they are not considered essential for the diagnosis.

The laboratory findings include leukocytosis with a shift to the left and thrombocytopenia. Coagulation study results may be abnormal if the patient has disseminating intravascular coagulation. Liver, renal, pulmonary, and cardiac function test results may reveal significant abnormalities. Infiltrates and pulmonary edema may be evident on the chest x-ray. ENs must be aware that the diagnosis of TSS is based on an aggregate of clinical findings, not the results of a specific test or group of tests. If TSS is suspected, tampons and any contraceptive devices or surgical packings must be promptly removed. Abscesses, empyema, or obvious infection sources should be surgically drained and irrigated. Intravenous antibiotics must be administered at once. Prompt admission to the intensive care unit (ICU) is essential for close invasive monitoring because MSOF is a common complication as sequelae of the shock syndrome (see Chapter 19).

ADNEXAL PATHOLOGY

Adnexal pathology includes torsion of the adnexa, ruptured ovarian cyst, and intra-abdominal bleeding associated with ovulation. Torsion of the adnexa is most common in ovaries with cystic or solid tumors and is related to unusual mobility. There is a sudden onset of severe lower abdominal pain, usually unilateral. Tachycardia, signs of pelvic peritonitis, and a slightly elevated temperature will be observed. Examination will show an exquisitely tender pelvic mass. The CBC count and temperature, which may be normal during the first 12 to 24 hours, will elevate as the ovary becomes gangrenous. Intervention requires immediate laparotomy and excision of the involved adnexa.

MITTELSCHMERZ

Mittelschmerz is one of the most common causes of abdominal pain in young women and occurs midcycle (as the term implies), during ovulation as the ovum is released. It is localized to one adnexa (often confused with appendicitis when the right ovary is involved) and is self-limiting. Mild to severe pain and rebound tenderness may be present, and the WBC count may be slightly elevated. The treatment is palliative. The important clue is the anticipated date of the next menstrual period.

INTRAUTERINE DEVICES

IUDs can cause many complications; in the past, for every 100 women who had one inserted, about 11 were expelled in the first year and about 12 required removal because of difficulties (although problems seemed to decline with parity). Fear of litigation has caused many manufacturers to withdraw most IUDs from general availability; many family planning agencies now provide a progestin-impregnated plastic device, which must be replaced annually.

IUDs may be still in use, however, and must be considered when a woman presents with (1) pain and bleeding, (2) PID (occurring in about 2 percent of cases, and (3) uterine perforation (occurring in about 0.4 percent of cases at time of insertion or later working through the uterine wall). Hospital admission and further evaluation is mandatory if any signs of possible IUD complications are present.

SEXUALLY TRANSMITTED DISEASES

There are many sexually transmitted diseases (STDs) that present to the ED as a primary problem. They may also be identified during treatment for other conditions. Because resistant organisms are associated with some of these, antibiotic therapy changes frequently. The ED physician must consider both the current Centers for Communicable Diseases recommendations and local antibiotic sensitivity data in formulating therapy regimens.

Gonorrhea

The symptoms of urethritis and vaginal discharge (creamy gray or white) frequently accompany acute gonococcal infections within 2 to 5 days of exposure. Women with gonorrhea may have severe lower abdominal pain. Although a Gram stain may be used for a presumptive diagnosis in the ED, Thayer–Martin cultures are required for definitive identification of the gonococcal organism. The EN must obtain calcium alginate swabs for these because ordinary cotton and rayon swabs inhibit growth of the organism. Pharyngeal and rectal cultures, as well as urethral and cervical ones, may be indicated. The antibiotics used to treat gonorrhea depend on whether the organism is susceptible to penicillin. Ceftriaxone (Rocephin), 250 mg IM, followed by doxycycline (Vibramycin), 100 mg PO every 12 hours for 7 days, is the treatment currently recommended by the U.S. Public Health Service.[3] The EN should inject the Rocephin deep into a large muscle mass, such as the gluteus maximus or the lateral aspect of the thigh. Because patients who have penicillin allergies also may be allergic to cephalosporins, the patient must be carefully observed before discharge for untoward reactions, including anaphylaxis.

Trichomonas

Trichomonas presents as a frothy, yellowish green discharge with pruritus and punctate hemorrhages of the vagina. Diagnosis is made by a saline or wet preparation of the discharge. A drop of the discharge is mixed with a drop of saline, placed on a slide with a coverslip, and viewed at a magnification of 100 to 400 to identify the motile organisms. Metronidazole (Flagyl) is the treatment of choice; all sexual partners must also be treated to prevent reinfection. When metronidazole is prescribed, the patient must be carefully instructed on the many significant precautions to be observed, including avoidance of alcohol to prevent precipitation of an "Antabuse" or disulfiram reaction. Nystatin-neomycin sulfate-gramicidin-triamcinolone acetate (Mycolog cream) is sometimes helpful in soothing the irritated vulvovaginal areas.

Gardnerella Vaginalis

Gardnerella vaginalis (Haemophilus vaginalis) produces a thin, watery vaginal discharge and the patient may present with dysuria. Treatment is similar to that for *Trichomonas*.

Genital Herpes

Genital herpes is caused by the herpes simplex virus, type II. In the initial presentation, which occurs 3 to 12 days after exposure, the patient will have tender inguinal adenopathy, fever, and often difficulty in urination. The herpetic lesions usually begin as clear vesicles, which ulcerate before healing in 7 to 10 days. Lesions may appear on vaginal tissue or anywhere on the perirectal areas. Following the primary infection, the herpesvirus remains latent in the sensory ganglia and recurs along with emotional stress, menses, or systemic infection. These recurrences, however, are typically less severe. However, the patient may report a prodrome of paresthesias that precede outbreaks of the secondary lesions. The infection is diagnosed by analysis of scrapings from the base of the lesions that reveal multinucleated giant cells and acidophilic inclusion bodies. Acyclovir may be selectively used to treat patients with genital herpes. The agent is available in intravenous, oral, and topic forms.

Syphilis

Syphilis is caused by the spirochete *Treponema pallidum.* Although the organism may infect many body systems, the usual ED presentation is genital. The lesion of syphilis is a painless chancre that occurs about 3 weeks after exposure; inguinal adenopathy may also be present. Secondary lesions, which occur 6 to 12 weeks later, are associated with fatigue, malaise, fever, and lymphadenopathy. Skin lesions (pink to tan macules) may be noted on the chest and abdomen. Moist papules on the perianal and vulvar areas as well as on other mucosal surfaces are frequently seen, and because they contain an abundance of spirochetes, great caution should be exercised by all health-care workers coming into direct contact with patients who have syphilis. The diagnosis of syphilis can be made by a dark-field microscopic examination of chancre scrapings but is usually made by the VDRL (Venereal Disease Research Laboratory) test, which shows positive results within a week or more after chancres appear. A long-acting penicillin is the drug of choice for treating syphilis; doxycycline (Vibramycin) and tetracycline (Achromycin) are alternatives for patients allergic to penicillin.[3]

OTHER INFECTIONS

Moniliasis, or candidiasis, is prevalent in patients with diabetes (high sugar in the vaginal flora), those on oral contraceptives, pregnant women, immunocompromised individuals, and in patients who are on an extensive antibiotic regimen. Symptoms are local edema, a cheesy discharge, and pruritis. Use of 10 percent potassium hydroxide (KOH) preparation demonstrates the organisms. Treatment includes use of an antifungal agent such as nystatin (Mycostatin), which is available as a cream or vaginal tablets.

■ EMERGENCIES OF PREGNANCY AND CHILDBIRTH

ECTOPIC PREGNANCY

Ectopic pregnancy should be suspected in any woman in the reproductive age group with acute abdominal pain of sudden onset. Abdominal pain and intermittent slight brownish spotting are frequent occurrences after a missed menstrual period. Profuse bleeding is seen in only about 5 percent of patients. Unilateral pain and cramping that is mild or sharp and excruciating is seen in over 90 percent of these patients. Occasionally, there is lateral lower abdominal pain with reflex shoulder pain from subdiaphragmatic irritation resulting from the massive intraperitoneal hemorrhage. In some, the sudden onset of pain is associated with syncope. In 40 to 60 percent of patients, a palpable pelvic mass is present, but repeated examinations can lead to rupture of the mass, with resulting intraperitoneal hemorrhage and shock. In 20 to 30 percent, there is no history of amenorrhea, but most do have a history of one or more periods missed. These women appear acutely ill and usually have a marked pallor and a distinctly "shocky" look about them. If there is rupture of the tube and its contents, signs of peritonitis will be evident.

A persistent corpus luteum associated with early pregnancy may be easily confused with ectopic pregnancy unless earlier tests have confirmed an intrauterine pregnancy. Examination will reveal asymmetry of the cul-de-sac or a palpable adnexal mass that is tender.[1]

Immediate establishment of intravenous access should be a priority, and either Ringer's lactate or normal saline (NS) should be used for volume replacement. Blood should be obtained for a CBC count, including Hct and Hgb and type and cross-match. If the patient is stable, pelvic ultrasound may be done to determine if emergency surgery is required. Cul-de-sac aspiration, using a 10-mL Luer-lock syringe and an 18-gauge spinal needle, is sometimes done; the return of fresh, nonclotting blood indicates intra-abdominal bleeding. Prompt surgical intervention is imperative in order to control the source of bleeding.

SPONTANEOUS ABORTIONS

Threatened abortion is associated with mild to moderate lower pelvic cramping that seems to be unassociated with the passing of fetal tissue.[1] Upon pelvic examination, the cervical os is closed; no cervical or adnexal tenderness is noted. Treatment involves bed rest, abstinence from intercourse, and reassurance. The patient is, of course, referred for follow-up treatment. In an inevitable abortion, the cervix may be dilated or effaced and fetal membranes may be detected at the os. Surgical closure of the os may be beneficial in some patients.

If the patient presents to the emergency department (ED) after passing fetal tissue or if there is evidence of displaced uterine contents in the os or the vagina, the patient is sent to the operating room (OR) for dilation and curettage. In complete abortions, all fetal tissue has been passed and bleeding is minimal. This patient is also referred to the gynecologic service for follow-up treatment, which may include a dilation and curettage.

In unrecognized fetal death, the uterus may not expel the fetus for several months, and the patient may be unaware of any problem until spotting or bleeding becomes apparent. In these cases of missed abortion, the cervix is closed and the uterus may seem small for the calculated gestation age. Disseminated intravascular coagulation may accompany the missed abortion. Surgery is indicated in these cases to remove intrauterine contents. Pregnancy test results may not be positive in these cases. A pelvic ultrasound is a standard for diagnosing this complication.

POSTABORTAL INFECTION

The symptoms of postabortal infection are chills, fever, and severe lower abdominal pain with foul vaginal discharge and dark, scant urine. Observations will reveal abdominal distension, hypoactive bowel sounds, and lower abdominal rebound tenderness. The vaginal discharge is extremely offensive, the entire pelvic area is extremely sensitive, and the cervix is dilated. Assessment of these patients would include a culture and sensitivity check of the endocervix for both aerobic and anaerobic organisms, Gram-stained smears, CBC, blood urea nitrogen (BUN) and creatinine for baseline of renal function, serum fibrinogen and clotting time for assessment of clotting ability, and blood type and screen for potential transfusion. An abdominal x-ray series or computed tomography (CT) may be used to identify specific indications of uterine perforation such as the presence of free air under the diaphragm. The patient must be admitted for massive antibiotic therapy and surgical evaluation of the uterine contents and adnexa. Nursing responsibilities include hemodynamic monitoring, antibiotic administration, and observation for organ dysfunction, peritonitis, and sepsis.

PREGNANCY-INDUCED HYPERTENSION

Pregnancy-induced hypertension (PIH), formerly referred to as toxemia of pregnancy, is a multisystem disease, possibly caused by renin-angiotensin-aldosterone changes associated with pregnancy.[4] It is thought that it begins early in pregnancy as a disease of elevated cardiac output and with continuing hemodynamic changes, eventually leads to pregnancy-induced hypertension later in pregnancy, characterized by low cardiac output and high systemic vascular resistence. A syndrome of problems associated include hypertension, proteinuria, oliguria, epigastric pain, pulmonary edema, seizures and encephalopathies, and cyanosis. These manifestations may occur singly or in combination. The patient may present to the ED with severe headache, seizures, or acute pulmonary dysfunction. Abdominal pain, nausea and vomiting, and edema are evident in many cases. Invariably, elevated blood pressure (BP) and albuminuria are present. A few will have severe multiorgan involvement (e.g., kidneys, liver, lungs, heart, central nervous system [CNS]) and will have disseminated intravascular coagulation as a secondary response (see Chapter 24).

Management Guidelines

Fluid therapy should include a crystalloid, given at a rate of 75–125 mL/h; adjustments may be made as laboratory test results and clinical assessment findings reveal the exact extent of hemoconcentration. In patients with untreated, prolonged hypertension, considerably more fluid may be required to prevent maternal hypotension and/or fetal distress, which might be precipitated by the use of vasodilator therapy.

Magnesium sulfate is used to prevent or control seizures associated with PIH. It is thought to act primarily as an agent to decrease small-vessel resistance and improve peripheral brain perfusion, although it has several other actions, including neuromuscular blockade and some central actions.[5] Hydralazine (Apresoline) is the agent normally selected for managing hypertension. The initial intravenous dose of 5 mg is followed by additional 5 to 10-mg doses at 20-minute intervals (up to a total of 40 mg) to achieve BP control. Other agents that may be used include nifedipine, verapamil, labetalol, and angiotensin-converting enzyme (ACE)–inhibitors.

The patient must be promptly transported to the ICU for hemodynamic monitoring and emergency interventions, including prompt termination of the pregnancy via fetal delivery, because this is the only known effective treatment.

HELLP Syndrome

HELLP syndrome (hemolysis, elevated liver enzymes, low platelet count) may be an alternative presentation of PIH. The patient with HELLP is characteristically a pregnant primigravida whose pregnancy is not near term and who has hypertension and proteinuria.[5] Epigastric pain and right upper quadrant pain are the keys to identification. The condition may be easily confused with cholelithiasis, hepatitis, pyelonephritis, viral illnesses, or other disorders, especially if the hypertension is not obvious.

Hemolysis and anemia will be noted in the CBC count in all cases because red blood cells (RBCs) are damaged passing through constricted blood vessels. Peripheral smears will reveal characteristic burr cells and color variations indicative of the anemia. Liver enzymes will also be elevated and the platelet count may be low.

Delivery is the only effective treatment for HELLP syndrome. Transfusion is usually required to boost the platelet count, even when there is no obvious clinical bleeding. Plasma exchange transfusion may be required for persistent postpartum thrombocytopenia.[5]

ENs and physicians should be alert for this somewhat unusual complication of pregnancy that can mimic other conditions. Obstetric consultation must be promptly obtained when the patient presents to the department, because complications include ruptured liver hematomas, renal failure, abruptio placentae, and intravascular coagulopathy, leading to maternal death in 1 out of 3 cases.[5]

EMERGENCY DELIVERY SITUATIONS

Placenta Previa

If the placenta is implanted close to the cervial os, the placenta may become dislodged from the uterine wall as the contour of the uterus changes later in pregnancy (after 28 weeks' gestation), causing brisk bleeding that is virtually painless. A few patients may experience contractions at this time. If this condition is suspected, the ED staff must defer pelvic, vaginal, or rectal examinations. If the patient is in labor and the infant is distressed, immediate oxygen support and fluid resuscitation must be provided while the patient is prepared for emergency obstetric intervention, which will be determined by the mother's condition and the gestational age of the infant. If the patient is stable, an ultrasound may be done to assist in evaluation of the problem.

Prolapsed Cord

Occasionally, the umbilical cord will push down through the cervix and vagina ahead of the baby, and will be visible at the vaginal opening. The baby's heart rate will indicate fetal distress. The cervix will compress the cord during contractions, preventing circulatory exchange between the mother and infant. In the event of a prolapsed cord, place the woman on her left side and elevate her hips. Give high-flow supplemental oxygen. Manual manipulation may be used to relieve cord compression by pushing the baby's head upward, thus allowing blood flow through the compressed cord. The EN may be required to continue this maneuver until the physician arrives. No attempt should be made to push the cord back through the cervical os at any time.

Premature Placental Separation or Abruptio Placenta

A premature separation of the normally implanted placenta, or abruptio placenta, presents with vaginal bleeding and uterine pains of varying degrees. Bleeding may be occult and should be suspected if there are signs of impending shock or if there is a rapid increase in the height of the fundus or excessive uterine irritability. This is a catastrophic situation with two lives at stake. The premature separation of the placenta may be classified as mild, moderate, or severe, depending on the stage of labor, the parity of the mother, and the amount of blood lost.

Supplemental oxygen and intravenous crystalloids must be administered at once. Blood should be drawn for a CBC count, Hgb and Hct, and type and cross-matched for blood transfusion. Frequent monitoring of VS and the fetal heart are imperative, marking the height of the fundus to determine whether the uterus is enlarging with hemorrhage. If the fetus is at term, emergency cesarean section is required.

Emergency Childbirth

Precipitous labor or emergency childbirth is a situation requiring quick thinking and a fast evaluation on the part of the EN as to the time allowable prior to actual delivery of the child. There are several questions for which the answers will help in making the correct decisions, and if at all possible, the patient should be transported rapidly to the delivery suite, where the child can be managed in a relatively protected and adequately equipped environment.

Nursing assessment: Initial points to evaluate systematically are the following:

1. Is the woman a primipara or multipara? This generally determines the length of the stages of labor unless the fetus is posterior, transverse, or breech.
2. Are the membranes intact? If so, time is on your side.
3. Is there any bright red "show"? This indicates active cervical dilation and generally is seen in the last stages of dilation.
4. Does the woman feel as though she has to "push" or "bear down"? This indicates delivery is imminent. Instruct the patient to pant with short, fast respirations and to *not* bear down or push. A forceful expulsion without control of the baby's presenting part can result in extensive lacerations to the mother and perhaps intracranial hemorrhage for the infant.
5. Is there "crowning"? This is the presenting part of the baby as it begins to bulge through the vaginal orifice. In a primipara, this may still leave enough time to get the patient to the delivery room if the contractions are not too intense.
6. How long do the contractions last? An effective labor contraction must last at least 45 to 60 seconds and be 1 to 2 minutes apart; shorter contractions usually do not indicate imminent delivery.

Nursing intervention: If you find yourself in the position of having to manage a precipitous birth, follow these simple guidelines. Allow the woman to lie down with her knees bent. Place a folded towel or sheet under her buttocks to elevate the perineum off the gurney or bed. With a gloved hand, place gentle pressure on the infant's emerging head to avoid a precipitous, "explosive" delivery that could be harmful to both the mother and infant. When the head is fully delivered, support it with your hands as natural rotation occurs, facilitating delivery of the shoulders. Make sure the cord is not around the infant's neck. If it is, remove it by slipping it over the head. Do not pull on it, because tearing could result in life-threatening hemorrhage for both the mother and infant. If it is too tight for removal, clamp it in two places, and cut between the clamps. If there are membranes covering the infant's face, snip them with sterile scissors at the nape of the neck and pull them from the nose and mouth. As soon as the head is delivered, the mouth and nose should be suctioned. Although infants are "nose breathers," the mouth and throat should be cleared first, with the head being held in an extended position. Oral and pharyngeal aspiration should always precede nasal aspiration, because the latter often causes reflex inhalation, which could result in secretions being aspirated into the respiratory passages. Delivery of the shoulders may be facilitated by guiding the head downward to deliver the anterior shoulder and then upward for the posterior shoulder. As the shoulders emerge, carefully hold and support the head while the remainder of the infant is delivered. Place the baby on its side, with the head in a dependent position, at the approximate level of the perineum. Aspirate any remaining fluid or mucus from the airways and keep the mother and infant warm. In the unlikely event that spontaneous breathing does not occur, stimulating the infant by brisk rubbing may encourage respiratory activity; if not, begin cardiopulmonary resuscitation. It is also essential to *cover the baby immediately* with warm blankets to offset a rapid heat loss, which can lead to hypoxia and hypoglycemia. It is desirable to place the infant on the mother's abdomen to conserve the infant's body heat. The cord should be kept at the level of the baby until all pulsations cease; it may be clamped in two places after it is pulseless (3 to 5 minutes after delivery). One clamp should be placed 6 to 8 inches from the infant and the other, 2 inches distally (close to the placenta). Cord cutting may be delayed until the infant reaches the delivery room suite.

Delivery of the placenta: During the final stage of labor, the placenta will be delivered along with a gush of blood. The placenta usually separates from the wall of the uterus in a few minutes after delivery of the child, but it may take as long as 15 to 30 minutes. As the cord advances farther out of the vagina, the uterus becomes round and rises noticeably upward in the abdomen. The woman may then bear down to expel the placenta. No force should be used to assist in the expulsion of the placenta because a torn placenta could result in a fatal maternal hemorrhage. The placenta should be placed in a basin and transported to the delivery suite along with the mother and infant. After delivery of the placenta, oxytocin (Pitocin) or methylergonovine maleate (Methergine) may be ordered to assist in involution of the uterus and to prevent postpartum hemorrhage. The uterus should be massaged to prevent excessive bleeding after the placenta has been delivered. The EN should

place one hand above the pubic bone to prevent downward displacement and the other should be cupped around the uterus and gently rotated until the organ is firm. Record the baby's time of birth and the Apgar score (Table 28–1). Sixty seconds after the *complete* birth of the infant (disregarding the cord and placenta), the five objective signs are evaluated and each given a score of 0, 1, or 2. A score of 10 indicates an infant in the best possible condition. Infants with scores of 5 to 10 usually need no treatment. A score of 4 or below indicates the need for prompt diagnosis and treatment. Approximately 90 percent of normal infants should score 7 or more 1 minute after birth.

Breech Delivery

In a breech presentation, the baby presents by the buttocks or feet rather than the head. Fetal distress from cord compression can occur, raising the possibility of fetal hypoxia and meconium aspiration. Intracranial trauma can also occur from the head's rapid descent through the pelvis.

In a buttocks presentation, instruct the woman to push with contractions to deliver the buttocks. The legs will follow. Traction must not be used to "pull the baby out"; rather, contractions should propel the infant. The head should be delivered by placing a finger in the mouth to flex the head as it appears over the perineum. At this point, the mouth and nose should be suctioned. If a second caregiver is present, instruct him or her to apply pressure over the pubic bone to complete the delivery. During a breech delivery, the infant must be provided oxygen if the umbilical cord is compressed by the head in the birth canal. An airway can be created by putting the middle and index fingers of a gloved hand along the face of the infant with the palm toward the face. The hand should be

TABLE 28–1. APGAR SCORE

Sign	0	1	2
Heart rate	Absent	< 100 beats per minute	> 100 beats per minute
Respiratory rate	Absent	Slow, irregular	Good
Muscle tone	Limp	Some flexion of extremities	Active motion
Reflex irritability (response to catheter in nostril)	No response	Grimace, cough, sneeze, or cry	
Color	Blue, pale	Body pink, extremities blue	Completely pink

extended into the vagina until the fingers reach the area of the infant's nose, thus forming an airway by pushing the vagina away from the baby's face.

If both feet present, the delivery can be accomplished with ease. However, if a single arm or foot presents, no attempt should be made to deliver the infant until expert medical help is at hand.

Baptism

If there is a "stillborn" infant or imminent death of the infant following birth, emergency personnel of any religion may baptize the newborn child of Christian parents, upon their request. The procedure is to put a drop or two of water on the bare head of the baby while saying, "I baptize thee in the name of the Father, and the Son, and the Holy Spirit." This exact wording should be followed. If resuscitation procedures are in progress, these should not be stopped for baptism. This religious rite should be performed only with expressed consent of the parent(s) of the infant.

TRAUMA DURING PREGNANCY

Trauma during pregnancy can be blunt or penetrating, but blunt trauma accounts for the majority of serious sequelae. Both direct and indirect harm can result to the fetus. Mechanisms include:

- Jarring, which can induce placental separation.
- Direct impact to the abdominal wall, which may injure the fetus, rupture the uterus, or cause the onset of premature labor
- Maternal skeletal fractures or dislocations that lacerate or contuse the uterus and its contents or create significant hemorrhage that threatens the unborn's life
- Penetrating trauma that perforates the uterus and creates hemorrhage and fetal anoxia
- Maternal hemorrhage/anoxia from any cause

Uterine trauma may not be noticed in the assessment of the patient in early pregnancy when abdominal girth is not markedly increased or a history of pregnancy is not known. However, the potential for pregnancy should always be considered.

Signs and symptoms of trauma in advanced pregnancy include vaginal bleeding; abdominal lacerations, contusions, abrasions; hematomas over the back or abdomen; acute abdominal pain; ma-

TABLE 28–2. PHYSIOLOGICAL CHANGES IN PREGNANCY: RELATIONSHIP TO TRAUMA

System Change	Significance
Increased circulating volume	No signs of shock until 30% loss of circulating volume
Increased heart rate	
Increased cardiac output	
Decreased vascular resistance	
Decreased arterial blood pressure	Uteroplacental perfusion decreased with supine position
Increased tidal volume	Chronic compensatory alkalosis
Increased oxygen consumption	
Decreased functional residual capacity	Decreased blood buffering capacity
Decreased arterial carbon dioxide pressure	
Decreased serum bicarbonate	Risk of acidosis if nonpregnant arterial blood gas values are used to guide ventilation
Decreased gastric motility	Less audible bowel sounds
Decreased gastroesophageal sphincter competency	Delayed gastric emptying time; increased aspiration risk
Increased renal blood flow	
Dilation of ureters/urethra	Increased stasis; infection risk
Bladder displaced	Increased injury vulnerability
Abdominal viscera displacement	Altered injury probability; altered pain referral patterns
Pelvic venous congestion	Increased risk of hemorrhage after injury
Uterine enlargement	Increased vulnerability to injury
Increased pelvic vascularity	Potential for great blood loss with uterine injury

ternal shock; muffled or absent fetal heart tones; uterine tenderness or onset of labor; and expanding fundal height. It is important to consider the relationship of the developing fetus to the mother's internal organs.

Assessment of the injured pregnant patient is complicated by displacement of abdominal viscera; referred pain is misleading, the stretched abdominal wall does not permit the usual responses to peritoneal irritation, and cardiorespiratory indicators of distress are obscured by the changes in fluid volume, expanded circulating volume, an elevated diaphragm and increased sensitivity of the respiratory center to small increments of carbon dioxide. Laboratory values are altered significantly, too (e.g., clotting factors, plasma protein levels, RBCs, Hct, and WBC count (Table 28–2). The initial history should include details of the ac-

cident and facts about the pregnancy. The gestational age of the baby can be estimated from abdominal measurements of the fundal height (Fig. 28–1).

Initial Management

Upon presentation, the patient may have a compromised BP. To eliminate hypotension induced by vena cava compression, the patient should be positioned with right buttock elevated and the uterus displaced to the left. Fetal monitoring should be initiated to detect distress that stems from either maternal hemorrhage or placental separation. A rectal and vaginal examination should be done to check for bleeding. Previous cesarian scars should be noted and the uterus should be palpated for irritability, tenderness, and the presence of contractions. A nasogastric (NG) tube and

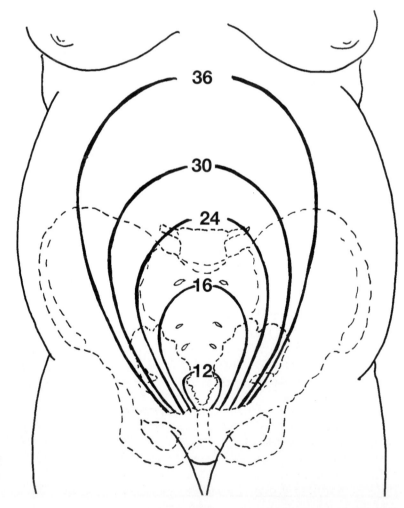

Figure 28–1. Pregnant uterus level at various gestational weeks provides a guide for estimation of fetal age.

Foley catheter should be inserted to decompress the stomach and bladder, respectively. In order to determine whether there is fetal blood in the maternal circulation from the trauma, a Kleihauer–Betke or acid-elution stain test may be done. The usual x-rays for trauma are indicated, with abdominal shielding when possible. Peritoneal lavage may be performed using a direct, open supraumbilical surgical approach to avoid intestinal injury.

If there are any penetrating injuries, foreign materials may have been introduced into the uterus or the baby's body. These may be visualized on radiological films.

The greatest risk to the mother and baby is often from undetected retroperitoneal bleeding, because 4 L of blood can be lost here from the highly vascular uterus and the engorged vessels of the broad ligament. A uterine rupture is likely in a patient with a previous cesarian section via a vertical incision. Upper uterine ruptures will cause a rapid maternal collapse and fetal death; lower ruptures create aching, labor, and fetal distress signs. Evidence of disseminated intravascular coagulation (DIC) should be noted because this condition can be induced by placental injury, which releases large amounts of thromboplastin. Vasopressors are not used, however, because they increase maternal BP and decrease uteroplacental blood flow.

Resuscitation Guidelines

The resuscitation of the pregnant traumatized patient is based upon the physical and physiological changes that accompany various stages of pregnancy. Since nasal mucosa become dramatically engorged in pregnancy, use of nasal airways should be avoided. If an endotracheal (ET) tube is required, a smaller than normal size should be selected for the patient in order to minimize tissue trauma and bleeding. Pregnant women have a high risk of aspiration, owing to the incompetence of the cardiac sphincter induced by the prolonged intra-abdominal pressure. Supplemental oxygen should be given promptly along with a generous fluid challenge. The pregnant woman has inefficient ventilation due to diaphragmatic displacement, and the expanded blood volume makes it possible to incur major hemorrhage before signs and symptoms suggest a hypovolemic state. The patient should be placed on her side, displacing the uterus to the left to ensure that it does not compress the vena cava, which would, of course, lead to further diminishment of the circulating blood volume. Monitoring should include constant vigilance for fetal distress. The resuscitation team should be prepared for operative intervention or an emergency delivery at all times.

■ REFERENCES

1. Jenkins JL, Loscalzo J. *Manual of Emergency Medicine.* Boston, Ma: Little, Brown; 1990:253–256.
2. Bongard FS, Sue DY. *Current Critical Care Diagnosis and Treatment.* E. Norwalk, Conn: Appleton & Lange; 1994:656.
3. Mahon CR, Manuselis G Jr. *Textbook of Diagnostic Microbiology.* Philadelphia, Pa: WB Saunders; 1995:404.
4. Harvey CJ. *Critical Care Obstetrical Nursing.* Gaithersburg, Md: Aspen Publishers; 1991: 49–69.
5. Carlson RW, Gehab MA. *Principles and Practices of Medical Intensive Care.* Philadelphia, Pa: WB Saunders; 1993:1593–1612.
6. Feliciano DV, Moore EE, Mattox KL. *Trauma,* 3rd ed. Stamford, Conn: Appleton & Lange;1996:700.

■ BIBLIOGRAPHY

Barber JM. *Controversies and Special Problems in Trauma Management.* Lewisville, Tex: Barbara Clark Mims Associates; 1994.

Cardona VD, Hurn PD, Bastnagel Mason PJ, et al. *Trauma Nursing.* 2nd ed. Philadelphia, Pa: WB Saunders; 1994.

Chernow B, ed. *The Pharmacologic Approach to the Critically Ill Patient.* 3rd ed. Baltimore, Md: Williams & Wilkins; 1994.

Genell L. *Flight Nursing: Principles and Practice.* St. Louis; Mo: Mosby-Year Book; 1991.

Levine RL, Fromm RE Jr. *Critical Care Monitoring from Pre-Hospital to the ICU.* St. Louis, Mo: Mosby-Year Book; 1995.

Maull KI, Rodriguez A, Wiles CE. *Complications in Trauma and Critical Care.* Philadelphia, Pa: WB Saunders; 1996.

Moreau D, ed. *Nursing 96 Drug Handbook.* Springhouse, Pa: Springhouse Corporation; 1996.

Phippen ML, Wells MP. *Perioperative Nursing Practice.* Philadelphia, Pa: WB Saunders; 1994.

Physicians' Desk Reference. 50th ed. Montvale, NJ: Medical Economics; 1996.

Weist PW, Roth PB. *Fundamentals of Emergency Radiology.* Philadelphia, Pa: WB Saunders; 1996.

■ REVIEW: OBSTETRIC AND GYNECOLOGIC EMERGENCIES

1. Identify the initial laboratory test indicated for patients who present to the emergency department (ED) with vaginal bleeding.

2. Describe the characteristics of the pain associated with pelvic inflammatory disease (PID) and the specific objective findings on abdominal examination.

3. Define *toxic shock syndrome* and list six signs and symptoms that might be detected by the triage nurse.

4. Outline the medical and surgical interventions for patients with toxic shock syndrome.

5. Describe the proper technique for administration of intramuscular ceftriaxone used in treating gonorrhea.

6. Identify the pelvic infection associated with paresthesias and lymphadenopathy and name the drug of choice for managing the symptoms.

7. Explain the variations in symptoms associated with ectopic pregnancy and cite the test and procedures indicated.

8. Differentiate among threatened, inevitable, and missed abortions in terms of history and presenting signs and symptoms.

9. List the major defects of the HELLP syndrome and identify the only definitive treatment for this life-threatening condition.

10. Describe nursing guidelines for the following emergency delivery situations:
    a. Placenta previa
    b. Prolapsed cord
    c. Abruptio placenta

11. List the six assessments to be systematically accomplished when a patient presents in labor.

12. Identify the part of an infant's airway that must be suctioned first after delivery of the head; explain the rationale.

13. Explain the nurse's role in assisting with delivery of the placenta and the observations that must be made and documented.

14. Describe the signs that rate an Apgar score of 10 and those that rate a score of less than 4.

15. Cite the five mechanisms of trauma that contribute to placing both mother and fetus in jeopardy.

16. Describe the signs and symptoms suggesting serious maternal or fetal risk after trauma.

17. Describe the way in which gestational age can be estimated when it is unknown (e.g., unconscious patient who cannot provide a history).

18. Identify the specific information that is derived from the Kleihauer–Betke or acid-elution stain test.

19. Describe modifications in the clinical management of shock states in advanced pregnancy.

20. Describe the way a pregnant patient should be positioned during shock resuscitation and explain the rationale.

Medical Emergencies of Childhood 29

■ NONACUTE PROBLEMS

When triaging, give immediate attention to any child with evidence of airway, ventilatory, or circulatory problems. An obstructed airway, inadequate ventilation, or compromised circulation from dehydration or blood loss must be addressed promptly. Other conditions meriting immediate attention include unconscious state; seizures; a history of high-impact trauma; toxic ingestions; fever with signs of sepsis or meningeal irritation; potential anaphylaxis, such as from multiple fire ant bites or wasp stings; and obvious evidence of child abuse, including sexual assault.

The emergency nurse (EN) who becomes skilled at triage develops a "sixth sense" for identifying the "really sick" infant or child. Lethargy, poor skin color, dull eyes, shallow respirations, and flaccidity are signs and symptoms that are red flags. The child who is generally weak and limp or unresponsive should always be seen promptly by the physician.

TRIAGE IN THE EMERGENCY DEPARTMENT

When triaging the pediatric patient, the EN must rely strongly on the initial impression and whether the child appears in real distress. The clinical criteria for children requiring immediate attention include:

- Airway difficulty of any degree
- Dehydration
- Coma
- Convulsions
- Possible meningitis
- Anaphylaxis
- Ingestion of toxic substances
- Rectal temperature of over 103°F in a child under 1 year of age

As the child is being undressed and quickly evaluated for vital signs, the parent should be asked simple questions, the answers to which provide an indication of the duration and severity of the child's illness (e.g., questions regarding fever, fluid intake and output, respiratory distress, changes in activity). For children under the age of 2 or 3 years, it is appropriate to obtain general background information relating to birth weight; health status during infancy; allergies; and any family history of diabetes, seizure states, or cardiac problems; along with any other pertinent data that might contribute to understanding the child's current problem.

During the course of physical inspection, it is important to make every effort to protect the child's modesty by providing a light blanket or drape; preservation and maintenance of body heat is an additional and very important consideration. Loss of body heat can contribute to deterioration of condition of the very sick child. If an examination is to be accurate and thorough, the child must be completely undressed to accommodate assessments of respiratory pattern, peripheral perfusion, skin color and condition, neuromuscular status, and general responses to the environment. A critically ill child will appear apathetic and pale or gray, have lackluster eyes, and reveal indices of compromised respirations and peripheral perfusion.

A quick triage history can be obtained while doing a head-to-toe assessment and checking the vital signs (VS). A natal history, including birth weight and chronic health problems, should be elicited. Any infant or child who has a history of neonatal health problems should receive care promptly. Other children requiring close scrutiny include the severely handicapped or mentally retarded; those with liver, renal, endocrine, or gastrointestinal (GI) pathology; and those who are immunosuppressed for any reason. As with any triage situation, when in doubt, decide in favor of immediate care.

TELEPHONE TRIAGE

The EN is frequently called upon to evaluate a child who is not acutely ill, as well as to answer all manner of inquiries over the telephone at any hour of the day or night. A card file or computer database, indexed according to symptoms, should be used for emergency department (ED) telephone inquiries. In addition to treatment algorithms, opportunities for input from emergency physicians and staff pediatricians should be inherent in the system. The reference material should be very explicit in covering abdominal pains, colds and coughs, diarrhea, earache, fever, rashes, sore throat, and vomiting. Conditions for which the child should be seen by a physician should be stated, home treatment should be outlined, and follow-up guidelines should be clearly spelled out. All telephone triage should be documented for reference and follow-up calls as needed. A telephone recording system that indexes all incoming calls is highly desirable.

The practice of providing telephone advice is laced with many pitfalls. In an excited or distressed state, the calling party may fail to provide an accurate or complete database for the EN. Because it is impossible to evaluate the child "through the telephone," be certain to convey this and encourage the parent or other caller to bring the child to the hospital for assessment. If it seems inappropriate or is unfeasible for the caller to transport the sick or injured child, provide information for accessing emergency medical services (EMS). It is important to remember that in many states and localities, the liability for paying for the ambulance is the responsibility of the individual requesting dispatch, so know your local policies and procedures before offering to call EMS as a favor to the caller.

Whenever parents seek emergency care for a child, they are seeking help in a situation they do not know how to manage. A crying child in the middle of the night who cannot be consoled may be reason enough for a mother to want professional intervention. A child who is not sick, or one who has no obvious illness, may actually pose a greater challenge for the EN than one who is obviously ill, with vomiting, a high fever, and dehydration. Why did the parents or baby-sitter bring the child to the hospital? What help are they seeking? Are they overwhelmed by responsibility or a serious stressor that makes them unable to cope with the child? Remember that in such instances, there are known risks of child abuse (see pages 458–460). In these cases, the children must be carefully evaluated so that serious problems in the family are not overlooked.

Any telephone advice must be well reinforced with instructions to the parent to bring the child in to be checked by a physician should any untoward symptoms develop. There are some good general guidelines to follow and some specific questions to ask (see below) about the various problems that will serve as aids to assessment and management of the situation. Always use simple direct questions, then paraphrase the response to be certain you understand what the parent or guardian (who is frequently excited) is trying to communicate.

When recording the chief complaint, use the words of the parent or caregiver. Remember that symptoms are relative and they may change quickly in the infant or young child. The following types of questions may be useful:

- When did play activities, eating, and/or behavior become abnormal?
- Does the child have any known physical defects or problems associated with congenital or chronic illness?
- Are there any ill family members or playmates?
- What has been done so far (e.g., giving medications or a tepid sponge bath, offering fluids)?
- What is the parent or other caregiver most concerned about now?

GUIDELINES FOR ASSESSMENT

If the child is over 6 months of age, perform the examination on the table; if the child is under 6 months, leave the child on the parent's or caregiver's lap, if feasible. A child over 3 years of age should be able to stand or sit without support. Casually observe the relationship between the adults and the child during the examination and note any evidence of anxiety or overreactions. Perform the examination as quickly as possible with the least amount of trauma and circumstances that could evoke crying. With practice, a head-to-toe checkup should take 1 to 8 minutes—without interruptions.

PHYSICAL EXAMINATION

Describe the child's appearance and behavior using terms such as *alert, active, well-developed, well-nourished, fretful, crying, lethargic,* or *playful.* It is usually not feasible to examine babies using the same routine as for adults—beginning at the head and going downward—because certain procedures, such as examination of the eyes, ears, nose, and throat, will frighten or annoy most children and initiate crying. An initial approach on a friendly basis will allow observation and general inspection, followed then by examination of abdomen, lungs, and heart. The frightening or painful parts of the examination are left to the end; however, the findings should be recorded in the following format:

1. Record weight, temperature, and pulse. If a temperature reading is questionable when an ear probe is used, make sure that tympanic membrane can be easily visualized and that the ear canal is free of cerumen before retaking the temperature. Impacted cerumen can interfere with the infrared sensor's perception of the tympanic membrane, resulting in a low reading. If taking a rectal temperature, take care to place the thermometer so that it is in contact with rectal mucosa and not imbedded in stool. Blood pressure (BP) should be checked in both arms and both legs if a heart condition is suspected. An electrocardiogram (ECG) may be indicated in rare cases of known or suspected cardiac disease. Measurements of head circumference should be taken if the child has an intracranial shunt. Errors in measuring VS can contribute to incorrect triage and care delays. (See pages 291–294 for tips on assessing pediatric VS.)

2. General appearance should be noted, along with a description of development and nutritional and mental status. Note any pertinent findings, such as pain, restlessness, abnormal posture, paralysis, abnormal respiratory pattern, adenopathy, or muscle flaccidity. Observe and record turgor, color, and texture of the skin and mucous membranes. Note the general condition of the skin, hair, and nails, which can denote poor nutrition, hygiene breaches, or signs of abuse.

3. The head and neck should be checked for skull conformation, size, and status of fontanels. Note if they are sunken, bulging, or closed. (The anterior fontanel normally closes at 6 to 18 months of age; the posterior closes at 2 months).

4. The eyes, ears, nose, and throat check should include the nasal and buccal mucosa, teeth, tongue, tonsils, and adenoids. Note and record the presence of any postnasal discharge, purulent exudate in the posterior pharynx, or redness and swelling of the structures.

5. The chest is examined for general conformation, symmetry, depth, and regularity of the respiratory pattern, noting any retraction of intercostals, paradoxical motion of the chest wall, or respiratory excursions that are atypical for the child's age range. Assess the heart rate and rhythm, noting any irregularities or murmurs. Breath sounds should be auscultated, with special attention given to any areas of decreased air flow or adventitious sounds.

6. When inspecting the abdomen, document the presence of herniations, scars, visible peristalsis, or abnormalities of the abdominal wall. Note generalized or point tenderness and percuss for tympany or dullness. Although bowel sounds may be difficult to assess and findings are frequently misleading, note the presence or absence of sounds. Note any abnormalities in the perineal and rectal areas. Carefully inspect the vulva in girls, noting any redness, edema, ecchymosis, or vaginal discharge. Boys' penises and testicles also

deserve scrutiny. Note any signs of trauma, irritation or infection. Positive perineal or rectal findings in a young child can suggest sexual abuse.

7. Inspect the back and extremities, too. Assess the length and general conformation of extremities, and note the presence of edema, clubbing of fingers, ridging of nails, or scars. Document evidence of trauma. Gross abnormalities of the axial skeleton, swelling or joint tenderness, curvatures of the spine, and muscle spasticity deserve follow-up evaluation and treatment.

8. Neurologically, the child should be encouraged to demonstrate status of the cranial nerves by performing such tasks as "making faces," looking from side to side and then up and down, wrinkling the forehead, and sticking the tongue out. Sensory and motor status can be evaluated by testing levels of response, coordination, strength, or weakness of muscle groups and noting gait, general posture, dystonia, or involuntary jerky movements.

9. Developmental evaluation will include what you objectively observe, as well as your opinion of the child and whether he or she falls within normal limits, taking into account the physical stature of the parent(s). In children under 6 months of age, estimate the relative maturity, the ability to hold the head up and follow objects with the eyes, grasp capability, hearing response, musculoskeletal tone, and whether the child generally impresses you as a "well baby," developing within normal limits.

■ CHILD ABUSE

The EN is usually the first member of the ED staff to receive the child and to evaluate the situation before the child and parent(s) have had significant time to react to the sights, smells, sounds, and inquiring glances of hospital personnel. This is an important time to gather preliminary data and observe the interaction between the child and parent(s) with an awareness of the statistics involving injuries in small children as well as "failure to thrive" states. When dealing with the possibility of child abuse, the EN must complete an accurate assessment, differentiating willfully inflicted injury from authentic, accidental injury, and if indicated, to proceed with an appropriate reporting to provide protection for the child and bring the abusive parent into contact with needed help. This will certainly require some astute observations and interpretations.

Child abuse includes any problem resulting from the lack of reasonable care and protection that ought to be provided by parents, guardians, or other caretakers. It may involve physical injury, emotional or mental abuse, neglect, or sexual assault or abuse. Recent definitions include injuries to the unborn resulting from drug and alcohol abuse. The EN should look especially closely for telltale findings in infants and children who are at high risk of abuse: those between 6 months and 3 years of age, premature infants, stepchildren, handicapped children, and those who pose special care problems. Since abuse tends to recur within the home, it is imperative that the problem of child abuse be recognized and managed promptly: returning a child to an abusive environment will surely lead to more abuse or even the child's death.

SIGNS OF ABUSE

The most frequently seen manifestations of physical abuse are bruises and welts, burns (e.g., "punched-out" appearance from cigarettes, burns of the perineum, buttocks, and hands and feet from being dunked into scalding water), abrasions, bizarre-shaped lesions, subdural hematomas and other head injuries manifesting in convulsions and coma, soft-tissue swelling, dislocations and fractures, lacerations and contusions around mouth from forceful feeding, and limited motion of extremities with loss of function and tender, painful areas.

Below are some valid criteria for identifying a case of suspected abuse.

- *Multiple injuries, clustered and on different body surfaces:* Look for multiple injuries, such as soft-tissue swelling on one shoulder with several bruises on the opposite anterior chest wall. Document the location, size, shape, and color of bruises.

- *Multiple lesions in various stages of healing:* Look for multiple lesions in various stages of healing, such as two fresh and weeping lesions, two crusty and pustular lesions, and one dry with pink edges and dark center, which could represent cigarette burns.
- *Injuries that reflect the outline of an object or mode of infliction:* Look for injuries that were possibly inflicted by belt buckles or looped electric cords or are in the patterns of heater grids or radiator grills.
- *Explanation of injury cause that is implausible or not fitting for the child's age:* Listen for implausible explanations of injuries, such as a 9-month-old child who is said to have climbed into a bathtub of hot water and who has clearly outlined burns 1 in. above both ankles.

Less obvious injuries will require more astute observation. Data must be gathered that will be as significant as the overt physical signs and should include an assessment of the history, behavior of the caregiver, and behavior of the child in response. The general pattern seems to be delay in seeking treatment until the morning after or several days later. The parents or caregivers are then likely to exhibit indifference to treatment, prognosis, and the child in general. If your suspicions are raised for any reason, make detailed assessments and document your findings both in the medical record and with photographic evidence. Common injuries are discussed below.

Skull Fractures

Look for skull fractures, 80 percent of which are linear, with the rest being depressed (ping-pong type). In addition to the usual signs of skull fracture, there may be tympanic membrane discoloration, otorrhea, and rhinorrhea.

Intracranial Hemorrhage

Look for intracranial hemorrhage:

- *Epidural hematoma:* From injury to the temporal area, with laceration of the middle meningeal artery developing within 12 hours. This injury is associated with a high mortality.
- *Subdural hematomas:* Most commonly seen on postmortem examination, often in a child who does not appear injured. They are usually bilateral, causing increased intracranial pressure (ICP) with ultimate brainstem depression and death. Seizures, lethargy, coma, and vomiting are easily attributed to other causes.
- *Chronic subdural bleeding:* Slow in developing, causing an enlarging head, bulging fontanel, hyperirritability, retinal hemorrhages, lethargy, coma, and occasionally occult bruises.
- *Subdural bleeds:* Occur with associated fractures.

Shaken Baby Syndrome

Shaken baby syndrome is often compared to a whiplash "deceleration traction" (acceleration or deceleration) injury. It occurs when violent shaking of a child's head induces subdural hemorrhage without any further extraneous trauma. This is now thought to be a major but often undetected cause of intracranial hemorrhage that can lead to permanent brain dysfunction or death.

Professionals who have worked with abused children agree that it is axiomatic that when one form of abuse exists, other forms usually coexist, such as nutritional neglect (sometimes to the point of frank starvation), drug abuse (e.g., chronic sedation), medical care neglect, sexual abuse, and safety neglect. Once abused, children are at high risk of being repeatedly abused and suffering the consequences, which include permanent disability, brain damage, developmental lags, personality disorders, and death.

CONTRIBUTING FACTORS

As difficult as it may be to imagine caregivers willfully harming a child, it should be remembered that many factors contribute to this tragic event. Those who care for children are human beings faced with conflicts of temperaments, daily pressures, and unexpected crises. They were possibly abused themselves as children. Many believe in physical punishment and lack the knowledge of child development that is necessary for understanding children's behavior and capabilities. Remember, too, that there may be limited options for the poor and economically deprived parents. Babysitters and weekend escapes without the children may not be feasible for the poor, and pressures escalate, eventually placing the child in danger of being the target of misdirected aggression.

NURSING ASSESSMENTS

The abused child will often manifest rather typical behavior readily correlating with physical signs of abuse; therefore, all behavior should be carefully observed and evaluated. There is usually no protest when the caregiver(s) leaves the room, and the child just lies there looking rather like a discarded object. Children under 6 years of age tend to be excessively passive, whereas those over 6 years old are apt to be excessively aggressive; children in both age groups appear to be constantly on the alert for danger, drawing back from physical contact.

Examination of victims of possible abuse requires complete examination of all body surfaces and parts, including genitals. This must be done gently to prevent further pain, fear, and distrust of adults. Simultaneously assess the child's behavior, including reactions to examination. It is considered good practice to conduct the examination and assessment with another EN or physician, sharing observations and thoughts. This also lends credence and validity to the assessment and provides support to the person doing the examination, who may find viewing signs of abuse to be emotionally taxing. Recordings must be objective and thorough; do not record subjective opinions that would not be appropriate for use in a court of law.

National Reporting Laws

All states now have laws making it mandatory to report child abuse, and although the details vary, the laws all contain two basic principles:

- There is a mandate to report any injury suspected of being caused by neglect or being willfully inflicted by the caretaker.
- There is exemption from liability for any professional person reporting suspected child abuse.

It is suggested that every EN become familiar with the reporting laws of the specific state, as well as with hospital policy for management of the suspected child-abuse cases.

Interviewing the Parents or Caregivers

When interviewing parents or guardians, ask them to explain the child's condition or injury in their own words. Note any inconsistencies in history and inappropriate explanations regarding the cause. Be careful to maintain a tolerant, nonjudgmental attitude throughout the interview: remember that your own emotions can interfere with your ability to collect and document objective findings. Demonstrate an attitude of caring, concern, and understanding. When there is a question of child abuse, action should always be taken in favor of the child: the child should be admitted or detained for observation. If the child is not admitted, ensure that a social services follow-up evaluation is scheduled.

■ MEDICAL EMERGENCIES

FEVER

Fever is among the most common problems that prompt visits to the ED, especially if it is accompanied by listlessness, "fussy behavior," and lack of interest in eating. Although health-care personnel realize that fever is not detrimental to the central nervous system (CNS) until it exceeds 106°F, parents are often alarmed by a temperature of even a degree or two above normal. In a febrile child who is seizing, initial therapy should be directed toward controlling the seizure, not the fever.

The cause of most febrile states is readily apparent after the initial assessment when baseline laboratory results are correlated. Most problems are viral in origin, and symptomatic treatment is instituted. Common etiologies are gastroenteritis, pneumonitis, upper respiratory tract infections (URTIs), viral exanthems, and otitis media. Because bacterial meningitis, urinary tract infections (UTIs), and bacteremia/sepsis are possible, however, a systematic approach to all febrile children is imperative.

Fever in neonates is always an emergency because their bodies localize infection poorly; thus, sepsis can progress rapidly. A complete sepsis workup is in order for such cases, including a complete blood cell (CBC) count with differential, blood cultures, urinalysis and culture, chest x-ray, and lumbar puncture. Hypothermia may also indicate sepsis, so any seriously ill neonate should receive a comprehensive evaluation.

Management

Fever alone does not usually require treatment unless it exceeds 103°F. Antipyretics may be indicated to control high fever. Although there are several suitable antipyretics, acetaminophen is considered the agent of choice for most cases. It has a half-life of about 3 hours and is available as elixir, drops, tablets, and suppositories. Aspirin is seldom used for pediatric patients because there is an established association between aspirin use in viral illness and the onset of Reye syndrome. The usual dose of acetaminophen is 1 grain (65 mg) per year of the child's age orally (PO) or rectally (p.r.) every 3 to 4 hours. For most noncomplicated viral illness, relief may be apparent in 20 to 30 minutes.

Tepid sponge baths are of questionable value. They cause peripheral vasoconstriction and shunt blood to the body core. When resultant shivering occurs, metabolism actually increases and raises the body's core temperature. Furthermore, most children become agitated in the process of sponging, and their increased body activity also increases metabolic demands and thus the production of heat. If a sponge bath is requested by the physician, use water of room temperature and permit ample skin exposure to facilitate the evaporation that is essential to promote heat loss. If shivering occurs, cover the child loosely to control the symptoms. In rare cases of prolonged fever, when shivering results from sponging, chlorpromazine may be ordered to control it, since shivering actually increases heat production. Ice-water enemas and bathing with alcohol and ice (which can result in isopropyl poisoning) are not appropriate.

Parent Education

The EN can use the time spent in managing the fever to provide valuable instruction for the parent(s) of the febrile child. It is important to explain that a fever is "nature's way" of telling us that something is wrong and that elevated temperatures are actually therapeutic in fighting infection. Furthermore, the presence of a fever quiets the child's activity and lessens demands for further metabolism and resultant heat production. It is crucial to reinforce the fact that mild fever is not cause for alarm but may actually be beneficial to the body's immune system. The child should be hydrated, fed, and kept comfortable within the ambient temperatures of the home. Always check to see if the parent(s) has a thermometer at home and knows how to use it. Take-home instruction sheets, with such titles as "How to Use a Thermometer" and "Fever," are useful for reinforcement and later reference. These tools prevent many calls from anxious parents who need advice about a mildly ill child.

Every encounter with a febrile child is an ideal opportunity to emphasize to the parent(s) that both aspirin and acetaminophen have serious toxicological potential if ingested in large quantities. These agents should be kept out of the child's reach and never given for minor, nondocumented complaints, because a youngster may use these to obtain good-tasting medicine.

Encouraging fluid intake to prevent dehydration is also an important element of instruction. A febrile child loses body water at a rapid rate and may promptly become hypovolemic, especially with the vomiting that may accompany some conditions. Maintaining hydration helps moderate core temperature and enhances the distribution and biotransformation of antipyretics. It also helps ensure that detoxification and elimination of the agents are not hampered by decreased fluid volume.

Many parents have been led to believe that fevers result from infections and therefore deserve antibiotic therapy. Only a few high-risk patients (e.g., neonates, asplenic children, and those with nephrotic syndrome, malignancy, immunosuppression, sickle cell disease or neutropenia, or a known structural defect) are candidates for antibiotics or hospitalization for treatment of a febrile condition. Even in these cases, cultures must be obtained prior to initiating therapy. Parents should be instructed that antibiotics may mask a serious infection, promote the growth of resistant flora, and create unnecessary antibiotic side effects.

INFECTIONS

Finding the cause of fever creates the necessity for a "workup" that includes a history, physical examination, and laboratory adjuncts.

The history should include data on other family members who are ill, as well as recent illnesses or incidents in the patient's life. A vacation that involved camping, unusual foods, or unusual environmental exposures may yield important clues to the cause of fever or other signs and symptoms. Dental work or other invasive procedures in the recent past may also be linked to current problems. Of course, a history should include the usual information about chronic illness, allergies, and other health-care problems.

The physical examination should include scrutiny regarding ears, nose, and throat, since otitis media and upper respiratory conditions rank among the chief causes of febrile illness in young children. Rashes, petechiae, nuchal rigidity, bone and joint swelling or tenderness, and chest congestion must be explored.

A CBC count with differential, blood cultures, and urinalysis with cultures are musts. A chest x-ray and lumbar puncture may also be indicated on the basis of symptoms. A white blood cell (WBC) count with a differential generally distinguishes viral infections from bacterial ones. If the total-segmental neutrophil count is greater than 10,000 mm^3 or total band count is greater than 500 mm^3, an 80 percent chance of bacterial infection exists. A WBC count that reveals a total count of 15,000 mm^3 with a left shift (i.e., an excess of segmented and nonsegmented neutrophils) points to bacterial infections, certain viral conditions, or even stress. It should be noted, though, that even using these criteria, the clinician still misses up to a third of cases involving children with septicemia or pneumonia. Since infants and young children with meningitis may lack classic signs, evidence of neutropenia or thrombocytopenia should be viewed with great suspicion.

RASHES

The EN is often confronted with a child with a rash who has vague symptoms that must be deciphered, such as fussy behavior, irritability, low-grade fever, or a runny nose. Sometimes the child has only a rash and essentially is playful and well. It is important to have a working knowledge of the most common rashes that present in the ED and whether they pose a hazard for the child or others in the environment because of their communicability.

The initial history and assessment should include questions about the child's general health for the past few days. Were there any signs or symptoms of a developing URTI? Were there changes in the child's behavior? Were any other members of the household or close associates ill with any condition that might be communicable? Has the child been immunized against common childhood illnesses? If so, recently? Has the child taken any new foods or medications that could have induced an allergic response? Remember that many rashes do not have an infectious etiology. Table 29–1 outlines common childhood illnesses that are associated with a rash and provides information for their differential diagnosis and disposition in the emergency department setting.

RESPIRATORY DISTRESS

The dyspneic child is apprehensive and restless and has expiratory stridor with wheezing and retractions, both intercostally and sternally. Airway obstruction results from myriad causes in children, including congenital anomalies, peritonsillar abscess, laryngeal obstruction, elevated diaphragm, cardiac failure, cystic fibrosis, drug intoxication, and pneumothorax. Sudden onset usually is indicative of obstruction by a foreign body or spasms somewhere along the respiratory tract. Gradual onset indicates pulmonary or cardiac insufficiency, with coughing and perhaps hemoptysis. Allergies and exposures to disease processes must be ruled out. When the child is mouth-breathing, has heavy nasal secretions, or both, consider adenoidal infections or infections caused by foreign bodies. Pharyngeal infection will produce dysphagia.

Nursing Intervention

With any respiratory distress, whether upper or lower airway, the child should be given comforting reassurance, a patent and protected airway should be established and ensured immediately in the most expedient and appropriate manner, high-flow humidified oxygen should be administered (with the exception of low-flow oxygen administration in asthma), and oximetry should be initiated to provide data for further treatment. Initial workups should include a CBC count, blood culture, culture and sensitivity tests on tracheal aspirate and throat swabs, and x-rays of the chest and lateral neck.

TABLE 29–1. RASHES

Disease	Incubation	Rash Characteristics/Comments
Varicella, chickenpox	14–16 days	Appears in crops over trunk first; rapidly spreads to face, scalp, and extremities over 3 days. Progresses rapidly: macule to papule, vesicle, ruptured vesicle, and crusts (8 hours per stage). Areas will have lesions in various stages. Other signs/symptoms include white ulcers on palate and genitalia, fever, headache, malaise. Prevent or minimize exposures to other children while in department.
Measles (rubella) 3-day measles	14–21 days	Onset is noted by sore throat and cervical lymphadenopathy. Reddish spots noted on soft palate (may follow URI symptoms). Discrete maculopapular rash first seen on face; spreads over entire body. On day 2 temperature subsides, and rash starts to fade from face but becomes a diffuse erythematous blush over trunk. Rash begins to disappear on day 3 without any desquamation. Nodes may continue to be tender. Keep patient away from possible or known pregnant patients or personnel.
Rubeola measles	10–12 days	After day or two of fever, malaise, brassy cough, and nasal congestion, Koplik spots appear on buccal mucosa (irregular red spots with white centers). Rash revealed on day 3 or 4, first at hairline of neck and forehead, then spreads down body (erythematous, maculopapular rash). Symptoms begin to subside on day 5 or 6. Immunization not valuable postexposure. Highly contagious; protect personnel and patients.
Scarlet fever	2–4 days	Begins with fever, headache, vomiting, and chills. Tonsils are highly exudative; the pharynx is beefy red. The tongue is strawberry-ish-white and remains exudative for a day or two. White exudative membrane peels off; tongue looks like ripe strawberry by day 4 or 5. Exanthem appears from 12 to 72 hours and is diffuse, erythematous, and papular. Starts at back of neck and proceeds to axillae, groin, and trunk. Circumoral pallor present. Lesions blanch on pressure with exception of flexor surface of elbow. Rash disappears in week. Isolate child and terminally clean unit. Give antibiotics to prevent complications.
Fifth's disease	5–14 days	Erythematous, maculopapular rash begins on cheeks. Areas are raised, warm; "slapped cheek" appearance. Circumoral pallor. Second stage appears next day, with maculopapular rash spreading distally. On day 6 to 10, it fades and leaves "lacelike" pattern. Rash may reappear periodically with stressors. No fever or lymphadenopathy; only pruritus.

Croup and Epiglottitis (Supraglottitis)

Croup and epiglottitis are both seen in the ED, and the EN must understand their similarities and differences to ensure appropriate management in each case.

Croup (laryngotracheobronchitis). Croup generally affects children between 6 months and 4 years of age and is considered to be slow-developing. Several days may elapse between the onset of the viral illness and the appearance of the barking "croupy" cough associated with the condition. It occurs primarily in winter or during heavy smog days in temperate zones. Usually these children are stricken between 11 P.M. and 2 A.M., exhibiting anxiety, restlessness, cough, and dyspnea, with the cough's severity decreasing and loosening after several hours. They may run a low-grade temperature, and these bouts may recur 2 or 3 nights in succession.

Croup develops as intracellular viral agents extend into tissue and increase the production of mucus. Eventually, there is a loss of ciliary action, and nasopharyngeal obstruction follows. Since the natural humidification mechanisms are bypassed, water must be extracted from the lower respiratory tract to saturate incoming air. Obviously, the patient who is febrile or dehydrated or who possesses thick, tenacious secretions may be unable to "cough up" anything. An increased heart rate and depressed respiratory rate are danger signals.

The edema creates smaller air lumens, especially at the level of the cricoid, the only complete, nonexpansible tracheal cartilage. A near 50 percent obstruction occurs easily, creating inspiratory stridor. Other signs and symptoms include hoarseness due to vocal cord edema, retractions, nasal flaring, and low-grade fever. Hypermetabolism promptly results from these variations, increasing both oxygen consumption and cardiac workload.

Atelectasis and alveolar infiltrates create carbon dioxide retention, hypoxemia, and pulmonary edema, leading to respiratory arrest if therapy is not instituted to improve ventilation. If croup has progressed to the point of near respiratory failure, racemic epinephrine by intermittent positive-pressure breathing (IPPB) and admission to the hospital are in order. Steroids are advocated by some authorities, too, but antibiotics are reserved for those children with an associated complication, such as pneumonia, which may have a bacterial origin.

Conservative treatment consists of administering cool, moist air to decrease subglottic swelling. Walking in the cool night air or sitting in a closed bathroom with cold water running provides a soothing, cool mist that reduces the obstructive symptoms; both procedures have long been used as at-home remedies. Hospital personnel, however, may use a number of other delivery modes to achieve cool-mist inhalations.

Epiglottitis. Epiglottitis is a life-threatening problem that is generally confined to children aged 3 through 7 years. It is not seasonal. The responsibility for the initial detection of epiglottitis frequently falls on the EN, who must expedite intervention by a physician.

The child with epiglottitis typically presents in an anxious state, with respiratory distress, frequently drooling because of difficulty in swallowing and breathing, sitting forward with neck extended, and usually appearing flushed and toxic. There is typically a history of high fever for 6 to 10 hours (above 102°F), sore throat, malaise, dysphagia, dyspnea, and drooling. The latter three symptoms, known as the three D's, are considered the classic signs and symptoms. The child's voice may be muffled, but it is not hoarse. The skin usually appears pale and mottled or ashen gray, and there may be audible respiratory sounds. Inspiratory stridor and retractions are typical. Characteristically, the child prefers to sit upright with the chin forward ("turtlelike") and the mouth open, drooling saliva because of painful swallowing. In a few children, the presentation may not be so obvious, and long observation is required before ruling out epiglottitis.

With this situation, as with all others involving respiratory compromise, do not wait too long before intervening; slow deterioration into severe hypoxia is possible. About 50 percent of children with acute epiglottitis require intubation, cricothyroidotomy, or tracheostomy, so it is mandatory to have ready the necessary equipment before any examination is done. Many clinicians advocate using aggressive approaches to the airway before addressing any other aspects of diagnosis or therapy, such as starting intravenous access or obtaining an x-ray.

The child should not be forced to lie down, since recumbency tends to favor abrupt airway obstruction. Rather, the child should be permitted to sit up and remain with the parents and should not be provoked. Avoid the temptation to examine the throat or to look at the cherrylike epiglottis, since such maneuvers invite increased secretions and even laryngospasm. Before the physician specialist is ready to intubate, the tube size should be determined. Ideally, it should be 1 to 2 mm smaller than usual. A 14-gauge angiocatheter should be at hand for cricothyroidotomy in case intubation cannot be achieved. If airway support is required before endotracheal (ET) intubation is accomplished, use a bag-valve mask with 100 percent oxygen. This may frighten the child initially, but the fear will be fleeting because breathing efforts will promptly be eased and the child will relax. Remember, the youngster is exhausted from the effort expended in breathing.

After ET intubation, intravenous access can be started and portable lateral neck films obtained using soft-tissue technique or serograms. It is dangerous to transport affected children to the radiology department without a secured airway, so all radiographic procedures should be done in the ED, which is ready to handle a full-scale resuscitation. Ordinarily, children are placed in a recumbent position for such neck films. In cases of suspected epiglottitis, however, they should be permitted to sit upright. The clinician can identify the thumblike outline of the swollen epiglottis, a diagnostic hallmark.

Blood cultures, not pharyngeal ones, should be obtained to determine the responsible pathogen. *Haemophilus influenzae,* type *b,* is the culprit organism in most cases. In the meantime, since much *H. influenzae* is ampicillin-resistant, combination therapy using chloramphenicol (Chloromycetin) or another alternative agent is begun, along with hydration and fever-control measures. Steroids are used by most clinicians as the aggressive protocol to alleviate symptoms.

If pulmonary edema is a complicating factor, it should be managed with mechanical ventilation, positive-end expiratory pressure (PEEP), and high fraction of inspired oxygen (FIO_2) as early as is feasible. Pulmonary edema occurs only once in every 400 cases of croup but can easily result in death if not managed judiciously. The time course of this acute condition is dreadfully rapid; obstruction and arrest can occur precipitously. Pulmonary edema can result from poor capillary–alveolar gaseous exchange. (A rising negative intrapleural pressure and increasing afterload net a decrease in left ventricular output.) Any child who presents with the three D's who appears truly ill should be considered a candidate for the emergency protocol for epiglottitis.

Initial laboratory work should include a CBC count, blood culture, and culture and sensitivity tests on tracheal aspirate and throat swabs, and x-ray films of the chest and lateral neck should be taken.

Retropharyngeal Abscess

Retropharyngeal abscess is most common in children between 6 months and 4 years of age and typically follows an URTI. In addition to fever, there may be torticollis, cervical adenitis, and nuchal rigidity. Like the child with epiglottitis, the youngster with a retropharyngeal abscess appears toxic, with respiratory distress, inspiratory stridor, and dysphagia. Physical examination reveals a bulging posterior pharyngeal wall. Lateral neck films will reveal an increase in the width of the prevertebral soft tissue. Hospitalization is required so as to provide treatment with high-dose antibiotics and surgical drainage.

Foreign Body Aspiration

The aspiration of small objects, such as parts of toys, beans, peanuts, and buttons, causes choking, gasping, and dyspnea alternating with silent periods and episodes of coughing. An upper airway obstruction is usually worse on inspiration, causing inspiratory stridor. There is, of course, concern, but complete airway obstruction is unlikely, and the item can be removed by laryngoscopy or bronchoscopy. X-ray films almost always are diagnostic and show the location of the foreign body, and demonstrate any tissue destruction or impingements.

Asthma

Asthma is discussed in Chapter 22, but asthma in the very small child requires even more delicate evaluation and management than described there. Large- and small-airway obstruction with wheezing, dyspnea, and coughing results from increased production of thick mucus with edema of the respiratory tract and bronchospasm. Asthma in the very small child is thought to be an allergic reaction aggravated by emotional and psychological factors. Toddlers with allergies to milk, wheat, fruit juices, peanut butter, and the like frequently exhibit a "failure to thrive," bouts of vomiting, excessive mucus secretion, frequent URTIs, and tendency to have bronchitis, skin rashes, and infantile eczema.

Treatment of these children consists of low-flow-rate humidified oxygen, administration of epinephrine (Adrenalin), 1:1000, 0.01 mL/kg of body weight, or epinephrine, 1:10,000, 0.1 mL/kg of body weight; bronchodilators; and antibiotics; with cautious use of sedation. Suppositories should never be used because of the uncertainty of uptake, and antibiotics are indicated only if there is (1) pneumonitis, (2) persistent attack over 24 hours' duration, and (3) a WBC count of over 15,000 mm^3. If sedation is necessary, chloral hydrate should be used with a respirator on standby; opiates may be used sparingly *if the child is on a respirator.* Acidosis must be corrected, and if the child is febrile, antipyretic therapy may be indicated.

Status asthmaticus in children mandates hospital admission and requires monitoring of arterial blood gases (ABGs) every 4 to 8 hours, electrolytes, a CBC count, throat culture, upper airway care, and x-ray films of the chest and lateral neck for soft tissue swelling.

Respiratory failure is manifested by:

- Increased partial pressure of carbon dioxide in the blood (PCO_2) (55 to 65 mm Hg)
- Decreased partial pressure of oxygen in the blood (PO_2) (40 to 60 mm Hg)
- Low pH (7.2 or less)
- Onset of cyanosis in 50 percent oxygen
- Increased dyspnea or distress
- Severe retraction and use of accessory muscles of respiration
- Decreased breath sounds
- Decreased level of consciousness (LOC)
- Decreased response to pain

Treatment must be immediate intubation and ventilatory support. Curare or succinylcholine (Anectine) is usually administered to the awake child prior to intubation. Use a team approach with respiratory therapy and anesthesia personnel.

Some further complications of asthma can be pneumonia, convulsions from a rapidly decreasing partial pressure of arterial oxygen pressure (PaO_2), aspiration of stomach contents, GI bleeding, stress ulcers, and pneumothorax.

Pneumonia

Both viral and staphylococcal pneumonia are common problems in infants and children; 75 percent of pediatric cases occur in the first year of life, with more than 50 percent in the first months. Peak incidence is in winter and spring.

Pneumonia is a prime example of lower respiratory tract infection leading to obstruction following a history of URTI, a gradually developing anorexia, irritability with lethargy, vomiting and diarrhea (a common symptom), tachypnea at rest with over 50 to 60 breaths per minute and with grunting and nasal flaring, temperature over 101°F rectally or subnormal (less than 97°F rectally in infants), peripheral cyanosis, impaired breath sounds, dullness to percussion, and rales. The "pneumonia triad" to look for is fever, tachypnea at rest, and a significant cough.

Diagnosis is made by CBC count and differential count, a blood culture, nasal aspirate culture, and a chest x-ray film. A child with pneumonia can deteriorate rapidly, making hospitalization mandatory.

Intravenous therapy is instituted with an appropriate antibiotic based on the suspected or confirmed microorganisms. Respiratory therapy may include aerosolized mists, percussion, drainage, and suctioning. Hydration and nutritional support must be maintained throughout therapy.

OTHER INFECTIONS

Bacteremia

Febrile children without localizing signs of an infection may have bacteremia. Those at risk are under 2 years of age, have a fever above 102°F, or have a WBC count of over 15,000/mm^3. Gum abscesses in infants add even more risk. Blood cultures should be drawn and antibiotics, such as ampicillin, amoxicillin, or penicillin, should be initiated. Hospitalization is required.

Otitis Media

Children are prone to otitis media because their eustachian tubes are shorter, more horizontal, and more collapsible than those of an adult; thus, they are easily blocked by increasing secretions that result from allergies or URTIs.

Antibiotic initiation and ear, nose, and throat (ENT) care referral are the only management requirements for emergency personnel to consider in uncomplicated cases.

Bacterial Meningitis

Purulent meningitis has a rapid onset, usually after an upper respiratory condition. Fever, lethargy, poor feeding, and irritability are the primary signs in infants and young children. Nuchal rigidity may be delayed or absent in infants, and some older children may resist examination, thus masking a stiff neck. Alternate assessments include inspecting the anterior fontanel for signs of elevated (ICP); testing for Kernig, Brudzinski, and tripod signs; and looking for head lag as the child is pulled up to a sitting position. Allowing the head to extend over the edge of the table relaxes the neck muscles and thus may facilitate examination for nuchal rigidity. Older children usually have a severe headache and nuchal rigidity. Altered sensorium and seizures accompany the worst cases.

Blood should be drawn for glucose, electrolytes, CBC count, and blood cultures, and a lumbar puncture should be done. The cerebrospinal fluid (CSF) will probably, although not always, be turbid or cloudy in purulent meningitis. Classically, cell counts are greater than 500/mm^3, the glucose level is 50 percent less than the serum level, and the protein level is high. Gram stains reveal pathogens in 80 percent of cases; CSF culture results, however, may be negative for one of five patients with purulent meningitis.

Aseptic Meningitis and Encephalitis

Aseptic meningitis and encephalitis are usually sequelae to viral illness and present with fever, headache, hyperesthesia, nausea, vomiting, and irritability. Viral exanthems may occur, especially with ECHO (Enteric Cytopathic Human Orphan) virus association.

Symptoms of encephalitis include bizarre behavior, diplopia, ataxia, paralysis, drowsiness or coma, and seizures.

Results of lumbar puncture distinguish these conditions from septic meningitis and Reye syndrome. The CSF has several thousand cells, the glucose is normal, and the protein is normal or barely elevated. No organisms are seen on Gram stain.

Etiologies and prognoses are varied, so affected children are usually admitted for supportive therapy.

Meningococcemia

A sudden onset of fever with purpura or petechial rash is a true emergency; such indicators may mean that the body's defenses are overwhelmed, and disseminated intravascular coagulopathy (DIC) and cardiovascular collapse from adrenal hemorrhage or septic shock will rapidly follow. Meningitis may or may not be present.

Laboratory tests (CBC count, platelet count, prothrombin time [PT], partial thromboplastin time [PTT], and erythrocyte sedimentation rate [ESR]) are done and a lumbar puncture is accomplished for cell count, culture, and Gram stain. A Gram stain is also done on petechial scrapings. The CSF fluid culture results may be positive but without cell or chemical abnormalities.

Circulatory support includes volume expanders and the establishment of central venous pressure (CVP) monitoring and renal monitoring. Antibiotics are given without delay, using a slow intravenous push followed by periodic infusion of later doses. If shock occurs, dopamine is the vasopressor choice because it supports renal blood flow. DIC is treated as usual with platelets, fresh-frozen plasma, and steroids.

All those having intimate contact with the child should have prophylaxis with rifampin, minocycline, or sulfadiazine. Any symptomatic contacts should, of course, be hospitalized and treated aggressively. Emergency personnel, unless they have provided mouth-to-mouth resuscitation, do not require prophylaxis, according to authorities.

Reye Syndrome

Reye syndrome presents as a viral illness that is improving, then suddenly worsens, with vomiting, delirium, lethargy, coma, and even seizures. There is usually progressive brainstem dysfunction and liver failure with hyperammonemia and hypoglycemia. The etiology of Reye syndrome is not clear, so all therapy is directed toward protecting the brain and vital functions while compensating for problems created by the failing liver.

Little can be done in the ED except to suspect the problem and do a quick test for hypoglycemia using a Dextrostix. An arterial blood sample should be obtained to test for ammonia levels. Other desired blood tests include CBC count, serum glutamic oxaloacetic transaminase (SGOT), PT, cholesterol, and triglycerides. A lumbar puncture is done to ascertain whether the child has meningitis.

Intravenous access must be initiated and D/25 (Dextrose 25 percent) pushed if necessary, followed by D/10; maintenance fluids with supplemental potassium should be the next consideration.

Definitive therapy to prevent cerebral edema and brainstem herniation is directed by a neurosurgical specialist and may include controlled hyperventilation, osmotic diuretics, and intraventricular monitoring. A nasogastric (NG) tube should be placed to prevent vomiting and to serve as a route for administering the neomycin used to treat elevated ammonia levels by reducing ammonia-producing bacteria in the intestinal tract.

When the child is in a critical care setting, an arterial line and a Swan–Ganz catheter, as well as a Foley catheter, should be placed for monitoring. Cerebral resuscitation, using steroids and barbiturates, antibiotics, and sedatives may be initiated in the ED if transportation to a pediatric intensive care unit (ICU) is delayed.

Urinary Tract Infections

UTIs account for the second highest number of pediatric infections; they are surpassed only by URTIs. These usually present obscurely in the ED as a fever of unknown origin (FUO). Every child with an elevated temperature should have a clean-voided urine sample collected; thus, if an obvious cause of fever (e.g., otitis media) is not discovered on physical examination, the urine sample will be ready for evaluation.

The technique for collecting the sample is critical to ensuring meaningful results. The sample may be caught in an infant's collection receptacle or it may be a midstream sample. Regardless of the method used to obtain the urine, foreskins must be retracted or labia major spread to accomplish proper precollection cleansing. Parents and older children must be instructed explicitly to ensure compliance. Sterile containers for the sample must be used and any culture plating completed within 30 to 45 minutes unless the sample is refrigerated. A suprapubic bladder tap is another method suitable for collecting some samples from pediatric patients.

If a UTI is discovered, parents should be given appropriate take-home instructions regarding fluid intake, drug therapy, and follow-up care.

ALTERED LEVEL OF CONSCIOUSNESS

Management

When a child arrives at the ED in an altered state of consciousness, the ABCs (airway, breathing, circulation, and cervical spine) should be promptly assessed and supported. Because trauma may be involved in the etiology, cervical spine immobilization should be a consideration in airway establishment and maintenance. If vital signs (VS) indicate hypotension or cardiac or respiratory problems as the basis for the change in LOC, initiate appropriate supportive care in accordance with advanced cardiac life support (ACLS) guidelines. If the initial pulse, respirations, and BP are satisfactory, initiate oxygen therapy (6 L/min by prongs or 10 L/min by mask). A wide variety of problems, ranging from trauma to congenital defects, meningitis, metabolic conditions, seizures, and poisonings, may exist.

An intravenous drip of normal saline (NS) should be established early and maintained at a "keep open" rate. Blood should be drawn for chemistries and blood counts. D_5W may be administered to compensate for the hypoglycemia that accompanies stress states in the young child. The usual dose is 125 mg for children less than 2 years of age and 250 mg for older ones. Naloxone (0.4 mg IV) may also be ordered. A series of examinations and procedures may be required to determine the cause of the altered LOC. During this time, ensure that the child is closely monitored and protected from thermal stress.

The history, of course, is essential. Has there been any recent trauma? Previous seizures? Febrile episodes? Ingestion of potentially toxic substances or medications, including alcohol or to-bacco? Environmental exposure to carbon monoxide, insecticide, or lead? Any recent infection that was treated with antibiotics? Did the parents note weakness, paralysis, or changes in the child's activity? Is there any family history of this or a similar problem?

Laboratory Indications

Diagnostic procedures should involve all routine laboratory workups, including a type and cross-match if bleeding is suspected and a toxicology screen for barbiturates, alcohol, and salicylates, along with x-rays of the skull and chest. Lumbar puncture may be done if there is no evidence of papilledema or increased ICP.

The child will be admitted for further study even if the condition improves remarkably in the ED. Serious underlying medical conditions, intracranial bleeding, toxic ingestions, and child abuse rank among the chief reasons for alterations in consciousness, and any of these, of course, may be life-threatening.

SEIZURES

Parents are usually alarmed when their child has a seizure. They rush the youngster to the ED to report the event, but often the cause of the seizure is a puzzle unless the seizure is clearly of febrile origin or the result of noncompliance with anticonvulsant therapy. Causes for seizures include a wide variety of metabolic conditions, infections, and CNS anomalies. Hyperventilation is a frequent cause among teenagers who experiment with smoking and drugs and then become frightened. Anoxia from any cause can also create seizure activity. It should be mentioned that more and more youngsters today are truly alcoholic, so if this condition exists, seizure may be linked to withdrawal syndrome. The ingestion of tobacco products can contribute to multiple signs and symptoms, including apnea and major motor seizures.

Neonatal

Neonatal seizure activity is atypical because it represents responses of an immature CNS. Undetected anomalies, metabolic derangements, and infections are likely etiologies. The EN needs to remember that the neonatal seizure is unique in its presentation. There is usually a transient abnormal posturing or rigidity, followed by repetitive flexion movements of the trunk, tremors, spasmodic crying, facial twitching, chewing movement, paroxysmal blinking or nystagmus, and hyperactivity unusual for the child's age. Some infants have apneic episodes and a sudden loss of muscle tone, during which they become limp. Such strange phenomena may not be judged as seizure activity by the novice practitioner. Remember, too, that seizures in the neonate may be linked to heroin withdrawal if the mother was addicted. This possibility, along with many others, including hypocalcemia, hypomagnesemia, meningitis, and pyridoxine (vitamin B_6) deficiency, must be considered.

An intravenous line should be established quickly because the treatment of neonatal seizures is begun with the prompt administration of D_5W (1 to 2 mL/kg); 10 percent calcium chloride (0.1 mL/kg) *or* 10 percent calcium gluconate (0.3 mL/kg), pyridoxine (50 mg) and 3 percent magnesium sulfate (up to 5 mL) given over several minutes.[1] These emergency interventions are followed with the usual endeavor to find the seizure's etiology while protecting the infant from the devastating metabolic problems associated with status epilepticus seizures.

Febrile

Febrile seizures, common between the ages of 6 months and 4 or 5 years, account for the greatest number of pediatric seizures. The seizure usually starts within 2 to 6 hours of fever onset accompanying respiratory infections, otitis media, *Shigella* gastroenteritis, or roseola infantum. Most often they are generalized and subside within 10 to 15 minutes. There is a significant incidence of recurrent febrile seizures and the onset of idiopathic epilepsy once such a disorder occurs. Febrile seizures cannot be dismissed without consideration of a wide array of contributory problems, including toxic ingestions and life-threatening infections. After the initial febrile seizure, a lumbar puncture is ordinarily done and the child is admitted for observation because meningitis is a likely cause. If the child recovers promptly and has little lethargy or confusion, serious etiology is unlikely. If the youngster is obtunded or comatose, however, assessments must be aggressively pursued.

In instances where glomerulonephritis or hypoglycemia is in question, the urine should be tested for occult blood and the blood for dextrose level. Intravenous glucose (25 to 50 percent) should be given at once for severe hypoglycemia and followed with an infusion of D_5W. Skull films are not generally justified, but computed tomography (CT) or magnetic resonance imaging (MRI) is often ordered to detect any underlying cranial anomaly.

Treatment of pediatric seizures involves the administration of undiluted diazepam (Valium), 0.1 to 0.3 mg/kg IV, not to exceed 10 mg, at 1 mg/min. Other benzodiazepines, such as lorazepam (Ativan), are suitable alternatives. Doses may need to be repeated because these drugs have relatively short half-lives. Phenobarbital, 5 to 10 mg/kg IV, given over 10 minutes, may be requested as adjunctive therapy. Paraldehyde, pancuronium, and general anesthesia are usually reserved for status epilepticus not controlled by benzodiazepines and barbiturates. Remember that during aggressive anticonvulsive therapy, respirations may be supported with supplemental oxygen because hypoxia lowers the seizure threshold, increasing the chance of another seizure onset. Supplemental oxygen is imperative, and some children may require assisted ventilations during the postictal period to correct hypoxia and limit acidosis progression. Repeat administrations of D_5W and additional benzodiazepines may also be ordered during this time.

The occurrence of a single seizure does not constitute epilepsy, either. The EN needs to take time to help anxious parents understand the possible causes and significance of seizures and to emphasize that seizures are "symptoms," not a disease.

Children requiring admission are those younger than 6 months of age, those who have had more than one seizure in a 24-hour period, or those with a focal seizure or one that lasted more than 15 minutes. One last criterion for admission is temporary inability by the child's parents to cope; institutional support may be necessary until they feel able to manage the child at home. It is often the EN who must assess the family resources and make appropriate recommendations for aftercare or specific follow-up treatment.

SUDDEN INFANT DEATH SYNDROME

The greatest cause of death in the first year of life after the neonatal period is sudden infant death syndrome (SIDS). Over 15,000 deaths per year are caused by this disorder. Most cases occur in children between 5 weeks and 5 months of age and in late autumn, winter, and spring, especially among nonwhite families from lower socioeconomic groups. There is a distinct increase in the risk to infants of low birth weight.

SIDS deaths come during sleep to children who have been essentially healthy except for a minor URTI in the previous 1 or 2 weeks.

Grief-stricken parents may call an ambulance or rush the dead child to the ED despite the fact that there is no hope of resuscitation. They find it unbelievable that their child is dead, and most feel guilty that they did not discover the problem before it was too late to change the course of events. These parents need much support, and referrals for follow-up psychological care are vital to ensure satisfactory adjustments. Meeting with community groups of parents who have experienced similar losses is beneficial to many parents. The EN must ensure that the parents are not dismissed to seek answers alone.

VOMITING, DIARRHEA, AND DEHYDRATION

There are both infectious and noninfectious causes for vomiting and diarrhea, but a viral etiology is probably most common. Pyloric stenosis, milk allergies, appendicitis, volvulus, brain tumor, toxic ingestions, and intussusception are among noncontagious causes.

Despite etiology, the state of hydration is the most important factor that must be evaluated. Do diapers remain dry for extended period of time? Are eyes and fontanel sunken? Are the mucous membranes dry? Is the skin turgor decreased? Is there measurable weight loss? Infants and young children are prone to significant fluid and electrolyte problems because their bodies are characteristically unable to concentrate urine or to reabsorb electrolytes selectively in an efficient manner. Hormonal adaptations are also somewhat unreliable.

A child with significant fluid loss should have intravenous fluids started at once, and baseline electrolyte studies ought to be performed. Table 29–2 illustrates one method of calculating fluid therapy for infants and young children. This table is a starting point for fluid therapy, but continuous adjustments must be made after admission, depending on the child's response.[2] The fluid of

TABLE 29–2. CALCULATING PEDIATRIC FLUID THERAPY FOR DEHYDRATION

1. Estimate the degree of dehydration(slight 3%–5%, moderate 6%–8%, and severe 10%).
2. Obtain the child's weight in kilograms.
3. Calculate fluid loss to produce the estimated % deficit.
4. Add maintenance fluid requirements.
   100 cc/kg—over 2 years
   120 cc/kg-–5–24 months
   150 cc/kg—small infants up to 6 months
5. Estimate continuing loss from diarrhea or vomiting (50–100 cc is average).
6. Total estimated fluid requirements for 24 hours.
7. Give half of the total in the first 8 hours and the remaining over the next 16 hours.

choice in most cases is half NS or its equivalent. If electrolytes are found to be imbalanced, later adjustments can be made accordingly. Volume replenishment is the first priority. Supplemental potassium (20 to 40 mEq/L) is also indicated despite normal serum potassium levels resulting from hemoconcentration and acidosis. The potassium will help counteract the long-term effects of vomiting and diarrhea-related fluid losses.[2]

The infant or child should undergo a careful abdominal examination for etiologic clues, such as enlarged organs or masses that could indicate tumors (e.g., Wilms tumor), hydronephrosis, or leukemia. Sepsis and meningitis must be ruled out through lumbar puncture if the child is febrile. The examiner should look for Kernig and Brudzinski signs and test for head lag, searching for meningeal origins. Many childhood illnesses present with vomiting, diarrhea and dehydration, so in addition to correcting fluid and electrolyte imbalances, the health-care practitioner must conduct a thorough enough physical examination to ensure that obvious problems are not overlooked.

Children with dehydration are usually admitted for treatment. Before case disposition, however, the EN should take time to help parents distinguish minor fluid loss episodes from major ones, which quickly compromise the young child, who has little reserve. Take-home instructional material should be available on ways to ensure at-home hydration when the child is vomiting and has diarrhea. Guidelines for when to seek emergency care for dehydration should also be emphasized in case simple measures fail to bring the problem under control.

BLEEDING DISORDERS

Besides the classic blood dyscrasias, such as aplastic anemia and leukemia, there are a number of problems that can result in bleeding. Parents must not delay bringing the child to the ED whenever there is any evidence of bleeding. Causes are multiple and include hemorrhage after tonsillectomy and adenoidectomy, esophageal varices, ulcers, volvulus, intussusception, tumors, ingested foreign bodies, and sexual abuse (rectal or vaginal).

If hemorrhage is severe, initial attention should of course be given to its control and to replacing cardiovascular volume. The clinician then gives attention to a detailed history, examination, laboratory, and radiological studies to discover the origin of the bleeding if it is not immediately obvious. Admission and follow-up treatment are dependent on the results of early findings and the apparent severity of the problem.

CARDIOVASCULAR EMERGENCIES

Management

The experienced EN is indeed familiar with the standards for both infant and child cardiopulmonary resuscitation as defined by the American Heart Association (AHA) or the American National Red Cross. It is useful, however, to consider the overall management of pediatric ACLS carried out in the hospital ED. Although cardiac and respiratory arrest are relatively uncommon crises, all ENs must be capable of participation in a pediatric resuscitation. ENs must periodically review the cardiopulmonary resuscitation (CPR) techniques to be used with infants and children. In children, cardiac arrest is generally secondary to respiratory arrest. When resuscitating, be careful not to hyperextend the head and neck, or the airway will be partially obstructed; always listen for bilateral breath sounds and watch for symmetrical chest expansion, remembering that sounds from one hemithorax dissipate readily into the other (see Chapter 18).

If a child is in cardiopulmonary arrest and CPR is in progress, the bag-valve device should have neither a pop-off valve nor one that is easily occluded, because pressures required to overcome resistance of small airways may exceed the pop-off limit. If an ET tube is placed, check its position with an x-ray film, looking also for any atelectasis or the presence of a pneumothorax.[3]

If dysrhythmias do occur and countershock is required, pediatric (4-cm-diameter) or adult paddles (8-cm-diameter) are recommended, depending on the size of child, with a setting of: 2 j/kg of body weight. If unsuccessful, use 4 j/kg of body weight; repeat twice if necessary. If ventricular fibrillation persists, the adequacy of ventilation and oxygenation should be assessed and acidosis or hypothermia should be corrected prior to more attempts.[3]

ENs should have a calculator at hand during resuscitation to aid in ensuring accuracy in drug dosages. It is helpful to have precalculated ACLS drug dosages (based on a child's weight in kilograms) posted on the code cart for prompt reference.

Special Cardiac Problems

Severe congenital anomalies such as the "four terrible T's" (transposition of the great vessels, tetralogy of Fallot, truncus arteriosis, and tricuspid atresia) are not dealt with here except to review the fact that they all produce cyanosis with a low pulmonary blood flow and right-to-left shunting with decreased $PaCO_2$ and increased PCO_2, which can rapidly result, during severe bouts of crying or stress, in a deterioration leading to convulsions, brain damage, and death. These children must be carefully handled, pacified, and carefully medicated to avoid disastrous developments.

Dysrhythmias are rare and usually not that severe in children, although ventricular fibrillation is occasionally seen after surgery or as a terminal manifestation.

Digitalis intoxication elicits a prolonged P-R interval greater than 0.2 seconds, vomiting, and diarrhea, which increases with the severity of the intoxication. Treatment is to stop the drug and if it has been ingested, lavage the stomach immediately. Give potassium chloride orally or intravenously, monitor with ECG, and have a pacemaker on hand if the intoxication is severe.

SHOCK STATES

Shock may present itself in the pediatric patient as a result of blood and other fluid loss (i.e., hypovolemia), sepsis, or anaphylaxis. It is seldom a result of cardiogenic factors. Determination of BP in a shock state is extremely difficult in infants and very small children. The "flush" method is sometimes employed, where a hand or foot is elevated and squeezed firmly and steadily to cause blanching; an appropriately sized cuff is inflated proximally without releasing the hand pressure until inflation is above the anticipated systolic pressure. As the cuff pressure is slowly released, the hand or foot will flush with arterial blood flow at a point corresponding to the systolic BP. Arterial palpation is an alternative if the pulse is palpable.

Normal limits of vital signs in children may be found on pages 291–294. Urine output must be monitored in the shock patient. Dry mucous membranes in cheeks and poor skin turgor indicate dehydration.

Dehydration as a Contributing Factor to Hypovolemia

Severe fluid deficits frequently contribute to shock. Gastroenteritis is common in infants and children and can be very serious because of the loss of fluid and electrolytes in stools (third-space loss), leading to severe dehydration, metabolic acidosis, shock, and death. Fever, vomiting, diarrhea, and decreased intake can all rapidly precipitate a state of dehydration for the small child.

At 2 weeks of age, an infant requires more than 150 mL/kg per 24 hours for adequate hydration; a baby should have a normal weight gain of 2 lb/mo. An infant or small child presenting with gastroenteritis or signs of dehydration must be weighed, and on the basis of the child's weight on its last examination, the percentage of weight loss is computed. Dehydration can be classified by percentage as follows:

- 2 to 4 percent weight loss = mild dehydration
- 5 to 9 percent weight loss = moderate dehydration (child should be hospitalized)
- 10 percent or more weight loss = severe dehydration, carrying a significant mortality in infants

See page 470 for emergency management guidelines.

Septic Shock

Septic shock fulminates rapidly, and death can occur in 24 hours without timely and effective intervention. Blood cultures, urinalysis, tracheal smears and culture, and a lumbar puncture are indicated diagnostically; airway support, oxygen administration, and volume replacement are the keys to initial therapy (see Chapter 11).

Anaphylactic Shock

Anaphylactic shock is, unfortunately, an all-too-frequent occurrence following injections of penicillin, allergy preparations, and various "boosters," as well as insect stings. There is a mass outpouring of histamine and a hormone-type substance called the slow-reacting substance in anaphylaxis (SRSA), which together cause vasodilation, local edema, hives because of increased capillary permeability, and bronchial constriction, which rapidly deteriorates into a shock state that is followed by collapse and sudden death. See Chapter 25 for a complete discussion of anaphylaxis.

CONGENITAL ANOMALIES OF THE GASTROINTESTINAL TRACT

Diaphragmatic hernia presents with symptoms of dyspnea, cyanosis, vomiting, absent breath sounds unilaterally, a scaphoid abdomen, and loops of bowel visualized in the thorax on x-ray films. The prognosis is good if there is no respiratory distress; treatment is immediate surgery.

Tracheoesophageal fistulas in newborns are recognized by excessive salivation, choking on feedings, cyanosis, and dyspnea. The treatment is immediate surgery.

Pyloric stenosis is generally seen in first-born boys. Symptoms are onset of projectile vomiting at between 2 to 3 weeks and 2 months of age, constant hunger despite vomiting, peristalsis that can be seen from left to right, and a palpable, smooth, olive-shaped epigastric mass. Treatment is a medical regimen of thick formula with phenobarbital added, followed up with early surgery.

Intestinal obstruction presents with symptoms of green, scant vomitus and sometimes an absence of stools. An upright x-ray film shows dilated loops of bowel. The treatment is to watch for peritonitis and fluid levels in the abdomen. Gastric suction and fluid replacement (milliliter for milliliter) with 0.5 percent NS/dextrose is the regimen until the decision for surgery is made.

Intussusception is a telescoping of one section of bowel into another; it may be small bowel into small bowel, small bowel into colon, or colon into colon. Most frequently, the small bowel inserts into the colon (ileocal intussusception). When this occurs, it is usually in the very young in the first year of life, but it may be seen in the older child. The contributing factors are thought to be diarrhea, constipation, cathartics, URTIs, or allergies. It is believed that, after age 3, other factors may be responsible. An occasional polyp, tumor, or Meckel's diverticulum may form the starting point for the process. The symptoms are classic and include the following:

- Severe spasmodic pain, explosive in onset
- Vomiting present in a previously healthy infant
- A characteristically "startled" look
- Knees flexed and relaxing as the pain eases
- "Currant jelly" stools usually 12 hours after the initial pain
- A tender, sausage-shaped mass that can usually be palpated in the ascending colon or transverse colon
- The right lower quadrant may feel empty
- Blood found by the examining finger

Surgical intervention is usually indicated; the intussusception is manually reduced and the bowel examined for compromise of the blood supply. Recurrence is unusual.

Volvulus is a twisting of the bowel upon itself that causes an obstruction, and it constitutes a surgical emergency. The symptoms are abdominal distension, occasional blood in the stool, vomiting of all feedings, and subnormal temperature (frequently). X-ray films show a "ground glass" appearance because the bowel loops are edematous and filled with fluid.

Inguinal hernia, commonly seen in boys in the first year of life, may be either unilateral or bilateral, with swelling in the inguinal canal. The swelling is usually reducible by applying steady, gentle pressure and elevating the legs. Sedation may be required, with cold packs to the swelling. Remember, however, that an incarcerated hernia is irreducible and is a surgical emergency!

It must be concluded that seeing these children early and carefully evaluating them may lead to early successful treatment; much of this initial assessment will fall to the alert and highly skilled EN.

Nursing Diagnoses

Appropriate nursing diagnoses related to congenital anomalies of the GI tract include:

- Alteration in comfort because of pain
- Ineffective breathing pattern related to altered ventilatory mechanics
- Ineffective airway clearance related to inability to handle secretions
- Impaired communication related to seizure activity and altered state of consciousness
- Altered cardiac output due to decreased venous return
- Altered tissue perfusion related to reduced circulating volume and myocardial depression
- Fluid volume deficit related to hemorrhage, fluid shifts, and vasodilation
- Potential for impaired gas exchange related to hypovolemia, altered alveolar/capillary membrane permeability, and compensatory tachypnea or hyperventilation
- Risk of infection due to interruption in integrity of skin barrier
- Potential disturbance in self-concept due to abuse from caregiver

■ REFERENCES

1. Jenkins, JL, Loscalzo J. *Manual of Emergency Medicine.* Boston, Ma: Little, Brown; 1990:64–68.
2. Barber JM. Pediatric emergencies. In: Fincke MK, Lanros NE, eds. *Emergency Nursing: A Comprehensive Review.* Rockville, Md: Aspen Publishers; 1986:305–331.
3. Standards for CPR and ECC. Part V: pediatric ALS. *JAMA* 1986:255.
4. Lynch VA. Forensic nursing in the emergency department: A new role for the 1990s. *Crit Care Nursing Quarterly.* 1991;14:69–86.

■ BIBLIOGRAPHY

Barber JM. *Trauma Update: Pediatric Trauma.* Lewisville, Tex: Barbara Clark Mims Associates; 1994.

Cahill SB, Balskus M. *Intervention in Emergency Nursing: The First 60 Minutes.* Rockville, Md: Aspen Publishers, 1986.

Campbell, LS, Campell JD. Musculoskeletal trauma in children, *Crit Care Clin North Am.* 1991;3:445–456.

Cardona VD, Hurn PD, Bastnagel Mason PJ., et al. *Trauma Nursing: From Resuscitation Through Rehabilitation.* 2nd ed. Philadelphia, Pa: WB Saunders; 1994.

Chernow B, ed. *The Pharmacologic Approach to the Critically Ill Patient.* 3rd ed. Baltimore, Md: Williams & Wilkins; 1994.

Dandrinos-Smith S. The epidemiology of pediatric trauma. *Crit Care Clin North Am.* 1991;387–390.

Day S, McCloskey K, Orr R, et al. Pediatric interhospital critical care transport: consensus of a national leadership conference. *Pediatrics.* 1991;88:696–704.

Fincke MK, Lanros NE. *Emergency Nursing: A Comprehensive Review.* Rockville, Md: Aspen Publishers; 1986.

Kelley SJ. *Pediatric Emergency Nursing.* E. Norwalk, Conn: Appleton & Lange; 1988.

Knezevich BA. *Trauma Nursing: Principles and Practice.* E. Norwalk, Conn: Appleton-Century-Crofts; 1986.

Lebet RM. Abdominal and genitourinary trauma in children. *Crit Care Clin North Am.* 1991;3:433–444.

Moloney-Harmon, PA. Initial assessment and stabilization of the critically injured child. *Crit Care Clin North Am.* 1991;3:399–410.

Nemes J. Epiglottitis: ED nursing management. *J Emerg Nurs.* 1988;14:70–75.

O'Boyle CM, Davis DK, Russo BA, et al. *Emergency Care: The First 24 Hours.* E. Norwalk, Conn: Appleton-Century-Crofts, 1985.

O'Brien R. Starting intravenous lines in children. *J Emerg Nurs.* 1991;17:225–230.

Smith MF. Renal trauma, adult and pediatric considerations. *Crit Care Clin North Am.* 1990;2:67–77.

Tecklenburg, FW. Minor head trauma in the pediatric patient. *Pediatr Emerg Care.* 1991;7:40–47.

Thompson, SW. *Emergency Care of Children.* Boston, Ma: Jones and Bartlett; 1990.

Wayland BW, Rowland MC. Pediatric immediate care. *J Emerg Nurs.* 1988;14:91–93.

■ REVIEW: MEDICAL EMERGENCIES OF CHILDHOOD

1. Name six pediatric problems that should be triaged for immediate attention from emergency personnel.

2. Explain five clinical presentations that should alert the emergency nurse (EN) to suspect child abuse.

3. Describe the pathophysiology of the "shaken baby syndrome."

4. Compare and contrast the presenting signs and symptoms of croup and epiglottitis and describe the difference in their emergency management.

5. Identify the life-threatening pediatric emergency that is characterized by a sudden onset of fever and purpura or a petechial rash.

6. Describe how neonatal seizures differ from other childhood seizures in terms of pathophysiology and presentation.

7. Outline four clinical assessments that are pertinent to the evaluation of pediatric seizures.

8. Explain the rationale for using one half normal saline solution (NSS) as the intravenous fluid of choice for volume restoration in the severely dehydrated child.

9. State the algorithmic sequence of defibrillation energy for a 6-year-old child.

10. Define *intussusception* and identify the history or assessment data that would suggest or confirm the presence of this condition.

11. Identify the type of pediatric hernia that could require immediate surgical intervention and explain why.

12. Cite three clinical scenarios that would mandate patient admission to a pediatric unit for further observation and management.

Metabolic Emergencies 30

■ DIABETES-RELATED EMERGENCIES

Diabetes mellitus is associated with three major emergencies; hypoglycemia, diabetic ketoacidosis (DKA), and hyperglycemic hyperosmolar non-ketotic coma or (HHNK).

HYPOGLYCEMIA

Hypoglycemia is defined as a low blood glucose level (usually < 40 mg/dL) that produces symptoms associated with impaired autonomic and central nervous system (CNS) functioning. Symptoms may be mild, such as tachycardia, cold clammy skin, and anxiety or lethargy. In severe cases, coma may occur. Other signs and symptoms that may accompany hypoglycemia include hyperactive or aggressive behavior, seizures, focal neurological deficits, and mild hypothermia. In severe and life-threatening cases, the patient may exhibit decerebrate posturing (see Chapter 6). Most patients will have a normal or near normal blood pressure (BP), and respiratory changes are usually not impressive. The rate of developing hypoglycemia tends to be an important factor in the type of symptoms that are manifested.

Emergency Management

In suspected hypoglycemia, blood should be promptly drawn for serum glucose level when possible, but a finger stick can be used alone in urgent cases. If the patient is in shock or has poor peripheral perfusion, finger-stick glucose results may be misleading and should not be used.[1] However, definitive treatment should not be delayed while awaiting laboratory results from a blood glucose test. The CNS is obliged to use glucose to meet its energy requirements. The brain is dependent on a constant perfusion of glucose, and oxygen extraction across the brain begins to fall when the blood sugar levels perfusing the brain are approximately 35 mg/dL. There is a striking resemblance between the effects of hypoglycemia and hypoxia on the brain tissue, and resultant symptoms may be similar. If prompt action is not taken, actual CNS cell death can occur. The body attempts to oppose the effects of hypoglycemia through the release of counterregulatory hormones (growth hormone, cortisol, glucagon, and catecholamines), further disturbing metabolic control for a period of time following the episode. Older patients in particular require several days to completely recover. Other patients may be discharged to home after stabilization and interim instructions for follow-up management have been given. If the hypoglycemic episode has been determined to result from an overdose of chlorpropamide (Diabinese) or other hypoglycemic agents, observation for at least 24 hours is considered judicious.[2]

Although hypoglycemia may occur in all patients with diabetes, those insulin-dependent diabetics whose disease is not well controlled are more apt to have wide swings in their blood sugar levels, with significant hypoglycemia. At times, oral hypoglycemic agents, particularly chlorpropamide, may cause profound and prolonged hypoglycemia, particularly in the elderly and in those with inadequate food intake.

Alcohol ingestion can also provoke hypoglycemia in a diabetic or nondiabetic patient who has been fasting. The consumption and metabolism of large amounts of alcohol causes a defect in the normal hepatic process of gluconeogenesis. It evolves gradually and often is not recognized by the person who is experiencing it.

Hypoglycemic coma should be suspected in all comatose or obtunded patients; remember that focal neurological deficits are not uncommon. Those patients who are not in coma may appear confused and combative and have sympathetic responses.

If a history is available, it is usually easy for the emergency nurse (EN) to determine what agent provoked the hypoglycemic attack. The EN should try to determine the patient's prior blood sugar history. If the patient has had repeated attacks of hypoglycemia, it is not uncommon for his or her body to dissipate the alarm reaction that accompanies a rapidly falling blood sugar. This depletion of catecholamine stores removes the primary mechanism by which the patient is alerted to a falling blood sugar. A further drug history is also important, for many patients take a variety of drugs that deplete or block the secretion of catecholamines, such as β-blockers and/or α-adrenergic antagonists.

The Somogyi phenomenon is one cause of hypoglycemia; it is triggered by excessive insulin dosage. Typically, the blood sugar falls in the early morning hours while the patient is sleeping. Consequently, the body triggers its emergency response system and a rebound hyperglycemic response ensues. Since high blood sugar may be noted the following morning, it may seem to warrant an increase in insulin dose, which, of course, would only make matters worse.[2]

Any treatment attempted by family or friends prior to the patient's arrival in the emergency department (ED) should be determined. Often juices or other oral agents are given to the patients while they are obtunded or comatose and without normal gag reflex. Aspiration pneumonia is always a possibility in such patients and must be considered after the acute emergency is treated.

In mild hypoglycemia, when the patient is responsive and has an intact gag reflex, sugar-containing substances may be given orally. There are several commercially available high-sugar drinks, but orange juice with added sugar or colas may be used. In individuals who are lethargic or unable to drink, a glucose-containing paste or gel substance can be placed in the buccal lining of the mouth for prompt absorption. Nasal glucose sprays are also available for home and prehospital use.

The clinical indications of hypoglycemia can be highly variable; therefore, it is most important to always be on the alert for this condition. The first priority is to protect the airway in all unresponsive patients. Then administer 50g of 50 percent glucose as an IV bolus after drawing blood for a blood glucose level and other appropriate laboratory work. (In infants and children, $D_{10}W$ or $D_{25}W$ should be used.) If an intravenous drip cannot be started, glucagon (1 mg IM or IV) can be used as an alternative. Intranasal glucagon is also available for in-home or prehospital use. ENs should be certain to inquire whether such a preparation was employed prior to the hospital admission. The response to glucagon is variable; it may take as long as 10 to 20 minutes for a patient to show an initial response. Peak responses take up to 1 hour. A dose of 1 mg of glucagon will elicit about the same results as an ample of D_5W.[2] Hypoglycemic patients will respond dramatically. (Ethanol-induced hypoglycemia does not respond to glucagon because hepatic glycogen stores have been depleted.) In the chronically malnourished patient (i.e., the alcoholic), 100 mg of thiamine should be given IV or IM prior to injecting glucose to prevent Wernicke's encephalopathy (see Chapter 20). Glucose administration should be continued at a rate of at least 10 g/h. In those patients able to take oral fluids, some form of oral glucose may be used. Frequent monitoring of the patient's status is mandatory; status is determined by the plasma glucose levels and the patient's response to therapy.

Those patients who became hypoglycemic after taking oral hypoglycemic agents must be hospitalized. It is not uncommon for the metabolism and excretion of oral hypoglycemic agents to take up to 72 hours. Patients discharged soon after supposedly successful treatment often encounter "rebound," a recurrence of their hypoglycemic state.

Once a patient is out of danger and the blood sugar has stabilized, it is important for the EN to give instructions prior to discharge. All patients should be encouraged to wear a medical alert bracelet or to carry other emergency identification. Both patients and their families should be instructed on the early symptoms of hypoglycemia: hunger, nausea, faintness, sweating, apprehension, rapid heart rate, and difficulty concentrating. The importance of not skipping meals and the need for extra food after unusual physical exertion should be stressed. Those patients who experience symptoms of hypoglycemia should be instructed to carry some form of concentrated simple sugar at all times. These patients should be reexamined by their own physicians at a later date for evaluation of their insulin dosages.

DIABETIC KETOACIDOSIS

DKA is a potential threat for all patients with diabetes. It occurs chiefly in the insulin-dependent diabetic and can cause great mortality and morbidity, especially in children. It can often be the first indication of a concurrent illness. The serum glucose ranges from 500 to 800 mg/dL in most cases, but in severe ones, it may rise well above 1000 mg/dL. However, ENs should understand that life-threatening DKA can occur without a dramatic elevation in blood glucose.

DKA is an absolute or relative deficiency of insulin. Consequently, hyperglycemia and the accumulation of ketone bodies occur and result in a metabolic acidosis of the anion gap type. If the appropriate treatment is delivered, most patients recover promptly.

Most cases of DKA are caused by the diabetic's failure to properly balance diet and insulin. Insulin converts glucose to glycogen, which is stored in the liver and muscles. It promotes the production of triglycerides from free fatty acids and glycerol, and it facilitates the passage of amino acids into muscle, where protein is manufactured. Insulin also inhibits the degradation of these proteins and the breakdown of fats (lipolysis). When the body is deprived of insulin, glucose cannot be transported into the cells and the body begins to starve at the cellular level. The body attempts to counteract this phenomenon by secreting counterregulatory hormones: glucagon, growth hormone, cortisol, and catecholamines. These hormones raise the blood glucose level by promoting hepatic and muscle glycogenolysis and gluconeogenesis from protein within muscle and glycerol in the fat deposits. The effects of the counterregulatory measures are hyperglycemia and ketosis.

When insufficient insulin is present in the body, the energy source changes from glucose to free fatty acids. Free fatty acids are metabolized in the liver with the production of ketone bodies; acetoacetic acid, B-hydroxybutyric acid, and acetone. Hepatic overproduction of ketone bodies is primarily responsible for the acidosis. These fatty acids are strong organic acids that completely dissociate at body pH, providing 1 mEq/L of hydrogen ion (H^+), which reacts with serum bicarbonate (NCO_3^-) to produce carbonic acid ($H_2CO_3^-$). The acid quickly dissociates into water and carbon dioxide (CO_2). The carbon dioxide is blown off by the lungs. Acidosis develops when the body buffer base (HCO_3^-) is reduced and inadequate respiratory compensation cannot maintain a normal pH. In uncomplicated DKA, the fall in bicarbonate (HCO_3^-) is equal to the rise in ketone bodies. This results in the exacerbation of electrolyte losses from ketone excretion in the urine as sodium and potassium salts. The hyperglycemia, which is the hallmark of insulin deficiency, results in glucosuria with a profound osmotic diuresis. Electrolyte losses accompany the water loss, and if the patient's body is unable to keep pace with the water loss through intake, hyperosmolality soon occurs.

Under the laws of physiology, the intracellular fluid osmolality must equal the extracellular fluid osmolality. Hyperosmolality causes a fluid shift from the intracellular fluid compartment to the extracellular fluid compartment in an attempt to equalize the osmolality between the two compartments. Unfortunately, the extracellular fluid is lost during osmotic diuresis, and the patient experiences both intracellular and extracellular dehydration. This condition can be compounded if the patient has nausea, vomiting, anorexia, and/or diarrhea.

DKA may develop over several weeks or in just a few hours in a diabetic patient whose disease is poorly controlled. Typically, however, the onset of polyuria, polydipsia, weakness, fatigue, muscle cramps, and weight loss occur over several days. Vomiting, anorexia, and abdominal pain may also be associated. Intercurrent infections, trauma, pregnancy, emotional stress, drugs (e.g., steroids, phenytoin, thiazides), and other diseases can increase the need for insulin in the unsuspecting patient. Although the incidence of DKA in non–insulin-dependent diabetes mellitus is low, the condition does occur.

Signs and Symptoms

Polydipsia, polyuria, and polyphagia are often the first manifestations of worsening insulin deficiency or a clue to newly acquired, undiagnosed diabetes. Despite the fact that the patient has signs of dehydration (poor skin turgor, hypotension, tachycardia, sunken eyeballs), urinary output remains high until profound volume depletion with shock ensues. The patient may report the continuing feeling of hunger with accompanying weight loss.

Severe abdominal pain often accompanies DKA, simulating appendicitis, cholecystitis, or pancreatitis. The hypothesis is that the liver swells secondary to hyperlipidemia, stretching the liver capsule and causing pain. The patient attempts to compensate for the acidotic condition with deep, labored respirations (Kussmaul respirations) that often have a fruitlike odor, indicating the respiratory elmination of acetone.

Coma is not a criterion of DKA. True coma is present in only a small portion of affected patients. Most present with only a clouded sensorium; in others, there is no mental change. The level of coma appears related to serum osmolality, not to the pH or serum glucose level.

Additional signs and symptoms of DKA include acidosis with a pH of usually less than 7.3, plasma glucose over 300 g/dL, positive serum ketones, urine glycosuria and ketonuria, increased specific gravity, serum HCO_3^- usually less than 12 mEq/L, hyponatremia, hyperkalemia, and an anion gap of over 10 to 15 mEq/L.

Laboratory and Clinical Assessment

The diagnosis of DKA depends on the presence of three major conditions: hyperglycemia, metabolic acidosis, and ketonemia. Major pitfalls may occur when interpreting laboratory results. For example, finding ketones in the urine is not a specific indicator of DKA. Urine test results that are positive for ketones are commonly found in starvation and vomiting, but a negative urine test result for ketones virtually rules out the possibility of DKA.

In addition to monitoring for hyperglycemia and ketonemia, an arterial blood gas (ABG) analysis is essential to determine the patient's degree of metabolic acidosis and serum bicarbonate level. The blood urea nitrogen (BUN) is usually elevated secondary to dehydration, but the EN should remember that diabetics are prone to diabetic nephropathy.

Despite the measured serum sodium, the total body sodium remains low. Factors that determine serum sodium are the degree of hyperglycemia, which causes dilutional hyponatremia with the movement of free water from the intracellular space to the extracellular space, and the state of hydration. Extreme dehydration causes hypernatremia.

In DKA, there is usually a marked deficit in total body potassium. Despite the magnitude of the deficit, the serum potassium levels are often normal or elevated because of the contracted intravascular volume and the metabolic acidosis, which causes potassium to shift to the extracellular compartment as hydrogen ions shift intracellularly to be buffered. Serum potassium levels begin to fall dramatically once treatment is instituted, however, and can reach an extremely low point 1 to 4 hours after treatment is begun. The drop in potassium levels occurs for two reasons: first, as insulin drives glucose into the cell, it carries potassium with it; second, once the acidosis is corrected, hydrogen ions shift back into the extracellular compartment and potassium reenters the intracellular compartment. Since phosphorus is mostly intracellular, it reacts in a way similar to the way potassium does.

Other necessary laboratory tests include a complete blood cell (CBC) count, urinalysis, electrocardiogram (ECG), an amylase, and perhaps a blood culture if infection is suspected.

The most common cause of DKA is infection, especially urinary tract infections (UTIs), pneumonia, and intra-abdominal sepsis. Because infection is so common in DKA patients, it is important to realize that these patients are often hypothermic, supposedly from irregularities in the thermoregulatory mechanisms in the hypothalamus; they may also have increased white blood cell (WBC) counts from stress. So the two common hallmarks of infection—fever and leukocytosis—may not be reliable indicators of infection.

Emergency Management

The major management problems in DKA are dehydration and acidosis. Once an adequate airway and oxygenation have been ensured, fluid therapy is the next priority, so the initial consideration is to establish an intravenous line. The insertion of a Foley catheter is often necessary for close monitoring of output, but it should be removed as soon as possible to prevent iatrogenic infection.

Acute gastric dilation is a common complication of DKA because of the gastric atony that accompanies the condition. This predisposes the patient to aspiration of gastric contents. The passage of a nasogastric (NG) tube can eliminate this complication and make the patient more comfortable.

Fluid Resuscitation

Normal saline (NS) is the fluid of choice for initial resuscitation of the DKA patient; 1L may be administered in the first hour, followed by another liter over the next 2 hours. Fluid replacement is important for reduction of both hyperglycemia and the associated acidosis. As circulatory flow improves, the kidneys will be able to clear more glucose and hydrogen ions from the bloodstream, owing to enhanced renal perfusion. Furthermore, this improved circulation will correct the tissue hypoxia and diminish further lactate production. Bicarbonate is seldom indicated as a means of correcting acidosis, because it impairs oxygen dissociation; makes the blood–brain barrier more permeable to carbon dioxide, creating cerebral acidosis; escalates the requirement for potassium administration; and triggers dysrhythmias, owing to electrolyte disturbances.[2]

Insulin

The use of intravenous low-dose regular insulin (5 to 10 units/h IV) has been investigated and its efficacy has been confirmed.[2] Because the half-life of insulin in plasma is short (i.e., 3 to 10 minutes), administration should be by infusion, not bolus. Insulin adheres to intravenous tubing and may affect the dose delivered into the bloodstream; therefore, the EN should flush the tubing with about 50 mL of the insulin solution initially, so hourly therapy doses will not be affected later.

The advantage of this new low-dose insulin method of treating DKA is that it significantly lowers the risk of hypoglycemia, hypokalemia, and possible cerebral edema. Some physicians use intramuscular injections of insulin (10 to 20 units/h) if the patient is well perfused, but if there is circulatory compromise or severe dehydration, it may accumulate in the tissues, resulting in hypoglycemia later in the patient's course of therapy. When the blood sugar is 300 mg/dL, dextrose should be added to the intravenous fluids to prevent iatrogenic hypoglycemia and cerebral edema.[2]

Potassium Replacement

Deficits for potassium may range from 300 to 1000 mEq/L, owing to intracellular-to-extracellular fluid shifts and renal losses caused by osmotic diuresis. Potassium replacement is begun only after volume restoration is well underway and after initial insulin therapy has taken place. Serial insulin infusions without potassium replacement, however, will further exacerbate the hypokalemia. Even if the initial laboratory values suggest a normokalemic serum, it will fall dramatically in the presence of fluid replacement and correction of acidosis. Potassium phosphate, alternating with potassium chloride, is recommended by some authorities.[3] During potassium-replacement therapy, the EN should carefully monitor the ECG for dysrhythmias.

The role of the ED is to diagnose and begin treatment for DKA. Admission is imperative to complete stabilization of the patient's metabolic derangement, which may require several days. Intensive monitoring of laboratory values and clinical status are usually accomplished within an intensive care unit (ICU), where invasive monitoring and ventilatory support can be easily instituted if necessary.

HYPEROSMOLAR HYPERGLYCEMIC NONKETOTIC COMA

HHNK is likely to be associated with the elderly, confused, and fragile patient who may not be able to recognize or respond to changing metabolic circumstances. For example, likely candidates for HHNK are individuals on high-protein tube feedings who are not receiving adequate fluid and diabetic patients with some degree of renal failure who are receiving multiple drugs. Impaired individuals (physically or mentally) who cannot perceive thirst or who cannot take fluids independently are likely victims, too.

The classic presentation of HHNK includes a high serum glucose, usually above 600 mg/dL and perhaps up to 1000 mg/dL; serum osmolalities of 320 mOsm or greater, accompanying the profound dehydration; and no ketosis, because there is sufficient insulin to prevent lipolysis. The patient's mental status may be confusion or obtundation. Aphasia, hemiparesis, seizures, and other neurological deficits may be present. Owing to the severe dehydration, hyperviscosity occurs and thrombi may obstruct both arterial and venous circulation. These thrombi and cerebral edema are considered the two potentially fatal complications of HHNK. The EN should be vigilant for arterial occlusions of the extremities, cerebral thrombosis, and mesenteric thrombosis, which is manifested by abdominal pain, vomiting, diarrhea, and/or constipation.

A multifaceted array of electrolyte and acid–base disturbances are common. Many patients have a high serum sodium (e.g., 160 mEq/L) in response to the severe volume deficit. Potassium deficits are certain at the cellular level, so potassium repletion is imperative, even when serum levels may not reflect significant hypokalemia. The ECG must be closely monitored for prompt detection of life-threatening dysrhythmias that can result from electrolyte imbalances.

The management of HHNK must be accomplished within the ICU, where invasive monitoring can be used along with other advanced therapies.

■ THYROID STORM OR THYROTOXIC CRISIS

Thyroid storm results from long-standing, poorly controlled hyperthyroidism. The body's thermoregulatory mechanisms fail, resulting in hyperpyrexia, altered mental status, and generalized body wasting from the hyperactivity of the thyroid gland. There are no particular laboratory markers of this life-threatening condition. Catecholamine excess has been thought to be related to the condition, but in most cases, circulating levels of epinephrine and norepinephrine tend to be normal.

The increases in adrenergic activity may be due to a heightened responsiveness to catecholamines and not to an actual overproduction of these substances. The result of the pathology, however, is increased metabolic rate and increased heat production, with an eventual wasting of muscle. Tachycardia and increased myocardial contractility occur in response to the thyroid's cardiostimulatory effects. Vasodilation can be remarkable; it is due to the compensatory cutaneous response to excessive heat production. Mental status changes include confusion, psychosis, extreme agitation, and even coma.

Treatment is directed toward two major goals: reduction of the thyroid hormone production or action and supportive measures to control symptoms. Propylthiouracil is given to control the synthesis of thyroid hormone. Ipodate sodium is given to lower serum triiodothyronine (T_3) and thyroxine (T_4) levels. Propranolol has several uses in the treatment plan, but it is primarily given to reverse the thyroid-induced accelerations of heart rate and cardiac output and to control the associated muscle tremors. Glucocorticoids may also be used to lower serum T_3 and T_4 levels, which are significant during thyroid storm. In immediately life-threatening circumstances, extracorporeal therapy (i.e., exchange transfusions) may be employed to assist in removal of excessive thyroid hormones from circulation.

Nursing management includes monitoring of fluid and electrolyte status and cardiac status, and institution of measures to control hyperpyrexia. Cooling blankets are a mainstay of thermoregulation. Antipyretic agents should not be used, because they increase levels of free-circulating T_3 and T_4, owing to their adverse effects on protein binding.

Patients with thyroid storm must be managed in the ICU, where continuous hemodynamic and cardiac monitoring can be ensured. Cardiac dysrhythmias and congestive heart failure are associated with uncontrolled hyperthyroidism.[3]

■ MYXEDEMA COMA

Myxedema coma is a feature of severe, long-standing hypothyroidism or can be a side effect of amiodarone (Cordarone), an antidysrhythmic agent.

It tends to occur most often in elderly women. The patient presents with a puffy, expressionless face; dry, rough, cold skin; nonpitting edema; loss of eyebrows and scalp hair; and an enlarged tongue. Patients frequently complain of feeling confused and somnolent. Hypothermia is an important finding in myxedema coma. Blood pressure may vary, but the heart rate and respirations are slow. Mental status may vary from confusion to somnolence or coma.

Thyroid function tests will reveal low T_4 and T_3 uptake. However, in the ED, the diagnosis is usually made based solely on history and the presenting signs and symptoms.

Adrenal insufficiency may accompany hypothyroidism. Treatment consists of thyroid hormone replacement, glucocorticoids, and supportive mechanical ventilatory support. Body temperature maintenance will necessitate the use of a warming blanket. The EN must ensure that the core temperature is gradually raised and that hypotension is prevented as vessels dilate in response to the thermal increases. Because thyroid replacement therapy is commonly associated with dysrhythmias, cardiac monitoring is essential.

ACUTE ADRENAL INSUFFICIENCY

Acute adrenal insufficiency is the result of inadequate cortisol production and the associated fluid and electrolyte imbalances that can lead to cardiovascular collapse. Abrupt cessation of steroid therapy may precipitate the problem, and it is likely when individuals with chronic adrenal insufficiency have an interposing illness. Presenting signs and symptoms include hypotension, dehydration, hypovolemic shock, hyperkalemia, hyponatremia, weakness, abdominal pain, nausea, vomiting, fever, and perhaps an associated infection. The term *acute adrenal crisis* is used when cardiovascular collapse and shock syndromes are apparent.

Treatment of acute adrenal crisis may be begun in the ED prior to the completion of definitive laboratory testing required to confirm the diagnosis. Dexamethasone is the initial drug choice because it does not interfere with later adrenocorticotropic hormone (ACTH) stimulation testing. Hydrocortisone hemisuccinate (75 to 100 mg IV)

should follow; NS is given along with suitable electrolyte replacements. Glucose administration may be required for some patients. Prompt admission to the ICU is indicated to ensure continuous cardiovascular monitoring during therapy.

DIABETES INSIPIDUS

Diabetes insipidus occurs in response to a lack of renal water conservation. It may stem from a defect in the release or synthesis of antidiuretic hormone (ADH) secreted by the posterior pituitary or may be caused by defects in renal tubular response to ADH. The patient will exhibit extreme thirst and a history of polyuria. In addition to marked weight loss, dehydration, headache, irritability, fatigue, and muscular pain, the patient may be hypothermic and have cardiac responses ranging from tachycardia to shock.

Pitressin is used for hormone replacement and may be given intravenously, orally, or, as is often the case, by inhalation. The forms often used in the ED are desmopressin acetate (DDAVP) nasal solution and vasopressin (ADH) tannate suspension in oil which is given intramuscularly. Since administration of pitressin can cause life-threatening dysrhythmias, the patient needs to be placed on continuous ECG monitoring in the ED and observed for CNS responses, which may include headache, dizziness, and tremors.

SYNDROME OF INAPPROPRIATE SECRETION OF ANTIDIURETIC HORMONE

The syndrome of inappropriate secretion of antidiuretic hormone (SIADH) is a condition in which the patient has excessive water retention, inappropriately high urine osmolality and sodium levels, along with low serum osmolality. Although the condition ordinarily presents during an ICU confinement, it may present on occasion in the ED as a result of advanced malignant disease and as a response to some chronic illnesses and medications. The individual has water intoxication with hyponatremia, lethargy, anorexia, nausea and vomiting, changes in mental status, and, in rare cases, seizures. If SIADH is suspected, the patient should be promptly transferred to the ICU for diuresis and management of the complicated fluid and electrolyte imbalances.

■ HYPERKALEMIA

Hyperkalemia (serum potassium > 5 mEq/L) can result from many causes including renal failure and tumor lysis syndrome, or as a side effect of some medications (e.g., potassium-sparing diuretics, digitalis, β-adrenergic blocking agents, angiotensin-converting enzyme [ACE] inhibitors). Occasionally, ENs encounter patients with hyperkalemia who have used excessive amounts of potassium chloride salt substitutes as a regimen in their sodium-restricted diets. Cardiac rhythm disturbances are among the most serious effects of hyperkalemia. The ECG is characterized by high, peaked T waves, a prolonged QRS complex, and a flattened or nonexistent P wave. Ventricular fibrillation and asystole can soon follow.

Therapy includes calcium to counter the effects of hyperkalemia on the heart and to redistribute potassium into the cells. Calcium will not directly affect serum potassium levels, however. Insulin is administered to assist the return of potassium into the intracellular spaces. If there is good renal function, furosemide may be used to promote potassium excretion. Exchange resins may be given orally or rectally to bind potassium in exchange for sodium if the gastrointestinal (GI) tract is functional. A dose (15 to 60 g) of polystyrene sulfonate (Kayexalate) is mixed with water or sorbitol solution. It can be instilled via a NG tube or given as a retention enema. Dialysis is used in life-threatening situations involving hyperkalemia.

The patient with hyperkalemia should be transferred to the ICU as quickly as possible for continuous ECG monitoring, which is imperative during therapy.

■ HYPOKALEMIA

Hypokalemia, a deficiency of potassium (serum level < 3.5 mEq/L), can occur from many causes, but it is seen most often in critically ill individuals. Low levels of potassium impair neuromuscular activity and the electrical activity of the heart, result-

ing in serious rhythm disturbances, including ventricular tachycardia and asystole. Orthostatic hypotension may be among presenting signs and symptoms in the ED.

Patients vulnerable to hypokalemia include those on diuretic therapy (loop, thiazides, osmotics), β-adrenergic bronchodilators, theophylline, corticosteroids, insulin, total parenteral nutrition, aminoglycosides, carbenicillin, and amphotericin B.[3]

Oral potassium replacement therapy is preferred. For those individuals who cannot tolerate oral replacement, intravenous therapy is used. Close cardiac monitoring is essential during any intravenous potassium administration.

■ OTHER ELECTROLYTE ABNORMALITIES

There are many other electrolyte abnormalities that can occur as a primary condition, but usually they occur in the presence of other serious illnesses. Excesses or deficits of sodium, magnesium, and phosphorus are encountered in laboratory results obtained in the course of emergency care. Therapy is directed at correcting the imbalance and providing supportive care and monitoring while searching for the cause of the imbalance.

■ TOXIC METABOLIC ENCEPHALOPATHIES

Toxic metabolic encephalopathy (TME) affects global cortical function by altering the biochemical function of the brain. Rather than a focal or localized CNS problem, this represents the neurological sequelae of a systemic metabolic disorder.[4] When a complicated patient presents to the ED, the physician must exclude the possibility of a primary CNS problem as the cause for change in mental status and then address metabolic disorders that may be life-threatening or create permanent brain damage if not corrected promptly. Problems that may mimic TME include brain tumor, closed head injury, a cerebrovascular accident, encephalitis or meningitis, and seizure disorders. Possible causes of metabolic encephalopathies include an array of endocrine disorders as well as organ failures of the liver, lungs, or kidneys. Advanced age, chronic illness, infection, nutritional deficiencies, and thermal dysregulation are considered important risk factors. There are also a significant number of medications that have been linked to the genesis of TME.

The role of the ED in managing TME is to suspect it and to obtain baseline laboratory values, including a CBC count, blood chemistries, renal and liver function, blood ammonia levels, ABGs, a toxicology screen, and blood and urine osmolalities. A brain imaging study and an electroencephalogram (EEG) may also be done soon after the patient's admission. (See Chapter 20 for emergency management of encephalopathies.)

■ NURSING DIAGNOSES

Appropriate nursing diagnoses in metabolic emergencies include:

- Alteration in acid–base balance related to ketoacidosis
- Ineffective breathing pattern related to hyperventilation
- Potential for physiological injury related to hypoglycemia resulting from ineffective dietary and insulin regimen
- Alteration in cerebral function related to hypoglycemia
- Potential for injury and organ failure related to altered neuronal cellular metabolism
- Fluid volume deficit related to osmotic diuresis from endocrine imbalances
- Electrolyte imbalance related to osmotic diuresis and endocrine organ dysfunction
- Potential for cardiovascular problems (dysrhythmias) related to endocrine and electrolyte imbalances

- Alteration in thermoregulatory control secondary to metabolic abnormalities related to endocrine dysfunction

■ REFERENCES

1. Winslow EH. Research for practice. *AJN.* 1995;65:60.
2. Rosen P, Barkin R, et al. *Emergency Medicine: Concepts and Clinical Practice.* 3rd ed. St. Louis, Mo: Mosby-Year Book; 1992:2176–2206.
3. Bongard FS, Sue DY. *Current Critical Care: Diagnosis and Treatment.* E. Norwalk, Conn: Appleton & Lange; 1994:603–617.
4. Thomas EA. Toxic metabolic encephalopathies (unpublished paper). University of Pittsburgh Medical Center, Department of Anesthesiology and Critical Care Medicine, 1995.

■ BIBLIOGRAPHY

Ayres SM, Grenvik A, Holbrook PR, Shoemaker WC. *Textbook of Critical Care.* 3rd ed. Philadelphia, Pa: WB Saunders, 1995.

Chernow B, ed. *The Pharmacologic Approach to the Critically Ill Patient.* 3rd ed. Baltimore, Md: Williams & Wilkins; 1994.

Grenvik A, Ayres SM, Holbrook PR, Shoemaker WB. *Pocket Companion to Textbook of Critical Care.* Philadelphia, Pa: WB Saunders; 1996.

Mahon CR, Manuselis G Jr. *Textbook of Diagnostic Microbiology.* Philadelphia, Pa: WB Saunders; 1995.

Maull KI, Rodriguez A, Wiles CE. *Complications in Trauma and Critical Care.* Philadelphia, Pa: WB Saunders; 1996.

Moreau D, ed. *Nursing 96 Drug Handbook.* Springhouse, Pa: Springhouse Corporation; 1996.

Physicians' Desk Reference. Montvale, NJ: Medical Economics; 1996.

■ REVIEW: METABOLIC EMERGENCIES

1. Describe the clinical glucose levels consistent with hypoglycemia and hyperglycemia.

2. Explain the common problems that are associated with precipitation of hypoglycemia.

3. Describe the Somogyi phenomenon and explain what it indicates.

4. Explain the rationale for administration of 100 mg of thiamine given prior to the intravenous administration of glucose for a patient who presents in an unresponsive state.

5. Compare and contrast diabetic ketoacidosis and hyperglycemic hyperosmolar nonketotic coma (HHNK) in terms of pathophysiology, presenting signs and symptoms, and clinical laboratory assessments.

6. Identify the three vital factors for treating diabetic ketoacidosis (DKA).

7. Name three types of patients who are prone to development of HHNK.

8. Identify two treatment goals for the patient with thyroid storm.

9. Name three important nursing responsibilities for monitoring the patient with a thyrotoxic crisis.

10. Identify the distinguishing electrocardiogram (ECG) characteristics of hypokalemia and hyperkalemia.

11. Describe the three major treatment regimens used to manage high serum potassium levels.

12. Define *toxic metabolic encephalopathy* and identify the conditions that mimic it.

Substance Abuse and Toxicology $\qquad$ 31

■ SUBSTANCE ABUSE

All drugs are potential poisons. When taken in medically prescribed amounts, drugs are therapeutic; any drug(s) taken in excess, from aspirin to alcohol to opiates, can kill. Rather than *drug abuse, substance abuse* is currently the term broadly applied to the abuse of both "street" and legal drugs, including alcohol. Abuse patterns involve many substances, chief among which are alcohol, cocaine, prescription drugs, the so-called street drugs and designer drugs made and distributed illicitly, marijuana and the various hallucinogenic plants (*Psilocybe* mushrooms, peyote, mescaline, jimsonweed seeds), and easily obtainable volatile solvents.

Substance abuse may account for between 5 and 10 percent of hospital admissions, depending on the catchment area of the hospital involved and the popular recreational drugs currently in use. The challenge presented to emergency departments (EDs) with these patients is one of complexity, because a variety of factors usually contribute to effective management, including the necessity for life support. Increasingly, substance abuse in this country is carried out against a backdrop of steady alcohol and marijuana abuse. Now, the new street/designer drugs being manufactured are used in addition to the old drugs of abuse, resulting in polypharmacy that is difficult to identify and many times has unpredictable outcomes.

GEOGRAPHIC PATTERNS

Although slang names and preferential usage vary from city to city, there have always been some distinctive regional differences and trends; there are also some consistencies of which the emergency nurse (EN) should be aware. Your regional poison control center is an excellent resource for current information on which drugs are most popular in your area, as well as for the latest research and recommended treatments.

In the larger U.S. cities along both coasts, the more expensive designer drugs, new variations of narcotics, and various amphetamines are being made by enterprising chemists; many fatalities have resulted because of the tremendously greater potencies of these drugs. Fentanyl derivatives, meperidine analogs, and MDMA (methyline dioxymethamphetamine or Ecstasy) have taken quite a toll among their users, since some of the narcotic analogs are up to 2000 times more potent than morphine. These are the users found dead with the needles still in their arms, moments after injection.

Coastal and border towns have the highest steady use of heroin and morphine; inland areas have tended to see higher uses of sedative and hypnotic drugs and alcohol among adolescents and young adults. LSD (lysergic acid diethylamide) is used sporadically across the country; inhalants of all varieties are employed as hallucinogenics (gasoline, Freon 12, cleaning fluids, paints, lighter fluids, glue, and even typewriter correction fluid); and PCP (phencyclidine) still enjoys steady popularity almost everywhere. With increased availability in a variety of forms, and resulting lower prices, cocaine has become *the* recreational drug of choice in much of this country.

ED management of substance abusers presents a full challenge to individual knowledge levels, clinical skills, and judgment. Manner of presentation is unpredictable; many of these patients will require life support, whereas many others will require only reassurance and "talking down." State-of-the-art polypharmacy being what it is, the challenge continues to grow; this chapter is designed to provide a general update of information on abuse substances and to reinforce the general management guidelines in order that the EN may be able to deal effectively with that challenge.

TERMINOLOGY OF CONTROLLED SUBSTANCES

The general terms that have been applied to the abuse of drugs are *habituation* (low-dose habit), *addiction* (physical dependence), *psychological dependence,* and *drug dependence. Drug dependence* is the term now used by the American Psychiatric Association (APA) to cover all of the other outdated terms.

Controlled drugs and other substances are regulated under federal law in the Controlled Substances Act (CSA) of 1970. The CSA places all substances that were in some manner regulated under existing federal law into one of five schedules, based on the substance's medical use, potential for abuse, and harm or dependence liability. The five schedules are important classifications and should be part of every EN's working knowledge base. They are as follows[1]:

- *Schedule I:* The drug or other substance has a high potential for abuse, it has no currently accepted medical use in treatment in the United States, and there is a lack of accepted safety for its use under medical supervision (e.g., heroin, methaqualone, LSD, mescaline, peyote, marijuana, hashish).
- *Schedule II:* The drug or other substance has a high potential for abuse, it has a currently accepted medical use in treatment in the United States or a currently accepted medical use with severe restrictions, and abuse may lead to severe psychological or physical dependence (e.g., opium, morphine, codeine, hydromorphone, meperidine, methadone, some barbiturates, cocaine, amphetamines, methylphenidate).
- *Schedule III:* The drug or other substance has a potential for abuse less than the drugs or other substances in schedules I and II,

has a currently accepted medical use in treatment in the United States, and may lead to moderate or low physical dependence or high psychological dependence (e.g., some barbiturates, glutethimide, tranquilizers).

- *Schedule IV:* The drug or other substance has a low potential for abuse relative to the drugs or other substances in schedule III, has a currently accepted medical use in treatment in the United States, and may lead to limited physical dependence or psychological dependence relative to the drugs or other substances in schedule III. (e.g., chloral hydrate, the benzodiazepines, some tranquilizers, some stimulants).
- *Schedule V:* The drug or other substance has a low potential for abuse relative to the drugs or other substances in schedule IV, has a currently accepted medical use in treatment in the United States, and may lead to limited physical dependence or psychological dependence relative to the drugs or other substances in schedule IV (e.g., some antidiarrheal and antitussive compounds containing opium derivatives).

CATGORIES OF ABUSED DRUGS

Drugs that fall into abuse "schedules" may be further categorized as follows:

- *Schedule I opiates:* Heroin, morphine, meperidine (Demerol), fentanyl, hydromorphone (Dilaudid), pentazocine (Talwin), oxycodone HCl (Darvon), codeine, and methaqualone (Quaalude)
- *Schedule II stimulants:* Cocaine, dextroamphetamine (Dexadrine), methylphenidate (Ritalin), methamphetamines (Desoxyn, Fetamin, Phelantin Kapseals), PCP, MDMA
- *Schedule III depressants:* Alcohol/barbiturates—same type of addiction as that of all psychotherapeutic drugs
- *Schedule IV hallucinogens:* LSD, mescaline, *Psilocybe* mushrooms, jimsonweed, inhalants
- *Schedule V marijuana (cannabis):* Buds, sinsemilla, hashish, hash oil

Physical dependence, psychological dependence, and tolerance of these categorized drugs can be broken down further to reveal the patterns that develop as a result of prolonged use (Table 31–1).

SCHEDULE I AND II DRUGS

Opiates (Schedule II), Heroin, and Methaqualone (Schedule I)

Opiate overdose is a severe problem; illicit opiates on the market (particularly in unskilled hands) will often overdose the victim when taken even in small amounts because of unexpected potency. Commonly abused agents in these situations include heroin, fentanyl, morphine, oxycodone HCl (Percodan), morphine suppositories, high doses of codeine, Darvon, and methaqualone (Quaalude). These highly addictive agents are the greatest cause for concern when overdose (OD) situations occur, but the abstinence syndrome that so frequently presents at EDs in patients looking for "help" is *not* lethal and, although serious in appearance, is not a medical emergency.

Effects of Overdose. The signs and symptoms of opiate OD are classic:

- Pinpoint pupils (not every narcotic will produce pinpoint pupils, however)
- Severe respiratory depression
- Depressed level of consciousness (LOC)
- Needle tracks—may be found, although the trend is away from needle sharing, in the face of the acquired immunodeficiency syndrome (AIDS) threat; the true addict may not have *any* needle tracks.

Nursing Interventions. The immediate interventions and treatments indicated with an opiate OD are establishment of an airway and of support ventilation and reversal of the opiate effects. For drug effect reversal, naloxone (Narcan) is the drug of choice for the following reasons:

- It reverses the opiate effects, including all degrees of opiate-induced respiratory depression.
- It will reverse the narcotic-like effects of other antagonists.
- Administration of naloxone can be diagnostic as well as therapeutic; failure to obtain significant respiratory improvement after repeated intravenous doses given at 2- to 3-minute intervals suggests a nonopiate cause for the crisis. If typical opiate symptoms are present but not reversed by the usual dose of Narcan, you may be dealing with a superpotency fentanyl-derivative designer drug. Higher doses of naloxone may be required for reversal of symptoms.
- The onset of action is generally apparent within 2 minutes of intravenous administration.
- It may be repeated at 2- to 3-minute intervals (usual dose, 0.4 mg to 1 mL) for two or three doses.
- It has no narcotic-like properties of its own.
- It exhibits virtually no pharmacological activity in the *absence* of narcotics.

Naloxone does not interfere with resuscitative procedures, such as the maintenance of the airway, artificial ventilation, cardiac massage, or vasopressor agents. It should be administered cautiously in cases of known or suspected narcotic dependence because abrupt and complete reversal of narcotic effects may precipitate acute withdrawal symptoms. The patient should be kept under continued close surveillance in the ED and given repeat doses if necessary; the duration of action of

TABLE 31–1. DRUG DEPENDENCE PATTERNS FROM PROLONGED USE

Category	Physical Dependence	Psychological Dependence	Tolerance
Opiates	+ + + +	+ + + +	+ + + +
Alcohol and barbiturates	+ to + + + +	+ to + + + +	+ +
Amphetamines	0	+ + to + + + +	+ + + +
Cocaine	0	+ + + +	0
Hallucinogens	0	+	+
Marijuana	0	+	0

some narcotics may exceed that of naloxone, glutethimide (Doriden) and methadone (Dolophine) being prime examples. Heroin stabilizes faster than many of the other opiates, but the degree of OD, or how much is "on board," must be determined. Remember that the patient may have ingested combinations of other medications as well, so obtain barbiturate, salicylate, and routine laboratory levels provided in the toxicology screen.

Opiate Withdrawal. The opiate addict believes he or she will die in withdrawal and makes urgent demands in the ED, in contrast to the barbiturate abuser, who underestimates his or her load. The opiate addict exaggerates the situation and need for medication. Do not respond to the addict's emotional escalation and be alert for one who is feigning other illnesses and begging for medication. The addict in true withdrawal will be yawning, perspiring, lacrimating, and will exhibit mydriasis, tremors, and piloerection (gooseflesh). Remember that all of these manifestations can be faked one way or the other—all that is, except piloerection. The patient who *is* suffering withdrawal should be referred to the closest alcohol and drug center for screening and treatment.

Nursing Diagnoses. Appropriate nursing diagnoses for opiate overdose would include:

- Ineffective airway clearance
- Ineffective breathing pattern
- Altered tissue perfusion related to depressed respirations
- Knowledge deficit related to opiate toxicity

Methaqualone (Quaalude)

Methaqualone, a sedative-hypnotic drug, is chemically unrelated to opiates and heroin. Known on the street as "soper" (for *soporific*), methaqualone has euphoric and mood-lightening qualities and an action equal to or greater than heroin. It rapidly became highly popular as a drug of abuse, was taken off the market entirely, and is now supplied illegally to street users as Mandrax, coming into the United States from Mexico, which is thought to be its main illicit source.

Users with overdoses of methaqualone may present with delirium, coma, convulsions, sponta-neous vomiting with the danger of aspiration, pulmonary edema, shock, and respiratory arrest. Most of the fatalities linked to methaqualone have occurred when the overdose was potentiated by alcohol ingestion. Narcan will reverse methaqualone's action.

Nursing Interventions. Nursing intervention includes establishing the airway and administering high-flow oxygen with large-bore suction on standby, initiating an intravenous line to support circulating volume, closely observing for pulmonary edema or respiratory arrest, and immediately administering Narcan intravenously.

Nursing Diagnoses. Appropriate nursing diagnoses for methaqualone overdose would include:

- Ineffective breathing pattern
- Impaired gas exchange
- Actual/potential fluid volume deficit
- Alteration in thought processes: delirium, coma
- Knowledge deficit related to sedative-hypnotic toxicity

MAJOR STIMULANTS: COCAINE, AMPHETAMINES, METHYLPHENIDATE (SCHEDULE II)

Cocaine

It is estimated that cocaine sales in this country exceed $30 billion a year, and that cocaine-related deaths and ED visits have increased 200 percent over the past 10 years, with admissions to government treatment programs increasing 500 percent during the same period.[2]

Cocaine, although officially designated as a narcotic under the CSA, engenders a reaction similar to that of the rest of the amphetamines, making it difficult to differentiate the cocaine reaction from that caused by other drugs, especially PCP. The best approach is to observe responses over 20 to 30 minutes; most cocaine reactions are short-lived and subside, whereas reactions to PCP and the other amphetamines tend to be of longer duration.[3] Many "experienced" cocaine users couple their cocaine use with alcohol or heroin to "smooth" the high; unfortunately, alcohol combines with cocaine to form cocaethylene. This drug provides the same pleasurable effects as cocaine and is more lethal than either parent drug. Users of cocaine and alcohol have 21.5 times the risk of sudden death than users of cocaine alone.[4]

The widespread usage of cocaine as a recreational drug has taken on a new profile with the practice of freebasing. Freebase, or crack cocaine, is processed cocaine alkaloids that have been treated with solvent and heated to crystallize the pure alkaloids. Freebase smokers are thought to be at greatest risk of toxic and overdose reactions because freebasing is the fastest way of getting the drug into the bloodstream and to the brain; it enhances the absorption of cocaine tenfold over snorting and has as rapid and as potent an effect as injection without the risk of needle contamination. Freebase cocaine, or crack, has demonstrated an incredibly high addiction potential from a very small amount of the drug because of its intense reaction.

Some Poison Control Centers in large cities are even reporting topical administration of the drug to various parts of the body, including insertion into the vagina and rectum. It is clear that cocaine can be absorbed from the gastrointestinal (GI) tract; smugglers ("body packers") who sometimes swallow prepackaged cocaine packets are at high risk of fatal overdose if the packaging ruptures internally in transit. Body packing should be suspected when a person—usually young—returns from a trip abroad and presents to the ED with signs and symptoms of bowel obstruction and adrenergic overdrive. Rectal examination or a KUB (kidneys, ureters, and bladder) film may produce a life-saving diagnosis.[2]

Nursing Interventions. There is no antidote for cocaine poisoning; ED treatment is symptomatic. Mild intoxication is treated with support, sedation if needed, and reassurance. If cardiorespiratory collapse occurs from extreme intoxication, intervention would include maintenance of the airway, high-flow oxygen, and circulation; prevention of injury in seizures; and close observation.

Amphetamines (Schedule II Drugs)

Amphetamines are very commonly abused drugs and include methylphenidate (Ritalin), dextroamphetamine (Dexedrine), and methamphetamine ("speed"). Although they are not considered addicting, there is a tremendous psychological drug

dependence developed by the user. These drugs are predominantly used on the street and are available as "cross-tops," "bennies," and so on, taken every 3 to 4 hours to get a high. Once the high has been achieved, the person experiences a letdown and then a rebound. Complete exhaustion, irritability, sleep, extreme depression, and fatigue result; this can become cyclic, with highs and "crashes."

Methylphenidate (Ritalin) is a popular amphetamine on the street, although it is a controlled drug (schedule II) and theoretically difficult to obtain. The drug is used effectively as an antidepressant in senile patients and does not have the long-term effect of the tricyclics. The blood pressure (BP) and all body processes elevate with methylphenidate ingestion, and heroin is frequently combined to "mellow out" the high effects. The injection of crushed tablets of methylphenidate mixed with talc causes microabscesses in the lungs, deposits in the eyes, and skin abscesses at injection sites; patients with emphysema and asthma are especially prone to respiratory arrest with the abuse of methylphenidate. Chronic abuse leads to acute psychotic episodes, often characterized by paranoia resembling paranoid schizophrenia *with* awareness of and insight into the problem. Abrupt withdrawal after chronic abuse may lead to cardiovascular collapse. There is no laboratory test that will define the presence of methylphenidate in serum, but a specialized procedure can be done to quantify its presence in the urine.

Nursing Interventions. Treatment of patients with amphetamine abuse involves the use of the benzodiazepams to decrease anxiety and bring the user "down"; beyond that, treatment is supportive. These patients may have to be hospitalized for observation in a quiet environment, with psychiatric counseling available.

Nursing Diagnoses. Appropriate nursing diagnoses for amphetamine intoxication would include:

- Potential for violence—self-directed or directed at others
- Potential for poisoning related to amphetamine toxicity
- Knowledge deficit related to amphetamine toxicity

DEPRESSANTS: ALCOHOL, BARBITURATES (SCHEDULE II AND III), AND PSYCHOTHERAPEUTICALS (SCHEDULE III AND IV)

Alcohol

Alcohol, a legal and openly available commodity, represents the number-one legal drug problem in the country, closely followed by the overuse of prescription tranquilizers. Many EDs treating older patient populations encounter a high percentage of patients with medical problems directly or indirectly related to alcohol. In assessing these patients for drugs, a fairly reliable use pattern is that older alcoholics rarely use drugs, whereas most drug abusers freely use alcohol in combination with their other drugs.

Abuse Patterns. Three different presentations of alcohol abuse are seen in the ED: intoxication, overdose, and withdrawal. Intoxication is defined variously by local statutes according to the blood level of alcohol found in laboratory determinations, and is discussed fully on pages 496 to 497. Alcohol is addictive and has a "developing" tolerance; the alcoholic can be walking and talking despite blood alcohol levels from 0.25 percent all the way to a rare documented 1 percent (1000 mg/100 mL). Overdose level is achieved at 0.5 percent (500 mg/100 mL) as a general rule, and is usually fatal beyond that point unless the alcoholic has developed an enormous tolerance level. Withdrawal from alcohol after long-term use manifests in four stages when abstinence occurs; these patients are medical emergencies and *must* be carefully monitored and managed to prevent stage 4 and a fatal outcome.

- *Stage 1:* Acute withdrawal begins within 6 to 12 hours or even 12 to 24 hours, with agitation, called "the shakes." Mild hypertension and tachycardia are seen, and there may be lateral nystagmus.
- *Stage 2:* May or may not be bypassed. There are early hallucinations (auditory, visual, and tactile), and a searching, "picking" behavior. Agitation is prominent, but the sensorium is gradually blunted.
- *Stage 3:* Disorientation; delusions and an altered sense of time, increased agitation, progressive paralysis, evidence of malnutrition, and serious electrolyte imbalances. (This patient often arrives by ambulance.)
- *Stage 4:* Seizures, generally the grand mal type, status epilepticus, and death. Acute abstinence can kill just as effectively as acute poisoning.

Nursing Interventions for Alcohol Withdrawal. Immediate steps are taken to assure the airway and an adequate circulating volume. Further treatment of the patient in acute withdrawal or delirium tremens (DTs) (stages 2 and 3) requires admission after initial management as follows:

1. Draw a blood sugar sample and start an intravenous drip with D_5W/NSS (normal saline solution).
2. Give 50 mL 50 percent glucose IV, because hypoglycemia secondary to the alcoholic state may contribute to the problem.
3. Give thiamine, 100 mg/L of IV fluid, to replace the deficiency, which is usually a contributory factor to DTs.
4. Administer high-flow oxygen.
5. Manage agitation and seizure activity with one of the following drugs:

   Hydroxyzine (Vistaril), 100 mg IM every hour, is the first choice for agitation.

   Magnesium sulfate, 50 percent 2 mL IM, is often given for motor agitation.

   Paraldehyde, an old standby, is effective with the "shakes," but it is *hepatotoxic* and should be avoided when possible.

   Diphenylhydantoin (Dilantin), 200 mg IM, works well in alcoholic seizure states when it is combined with other management techniques.

   Chlorpromazine (Thorazine) and droperidol (Inapsine) are less effective with alcoholics. They lower the seizure threshold and may produce a marked drop in BP.

Remember that mortality is as high as 15 percent when this condition is untreated; these patients must be hospitalized and evaluated further.

Nursing Diagnoses for Alcohol Withdrawal.

Appropriate nursing diagnoses for alcohol withdrawal, or abstinence, would include:

- Ineffective airway clearance
- Impaired gas exchange
- Decreased cardiac output
- Potential for injury related to seizures
- Potential for violence—self-directed or directed at others
- Sensory-perceptual alteration—visual, auditory, kinesthetic
- Disturbance in self-concept related to self-esteem
- Noncompliance with a detoxification program
- Knowledge deficit related to discharge instructions

Community Resource Referral.

Once the alcoholic's crisis is under control in the ED, an essential point of management is a "locked-in" and confirmed referral to the nearest community resource for alcohol treatment. Although getting the alcoholic patient to face the problem and follow through on treatment is frequently difficult at best, the responsibility for referral does lie with the ED and must be taken care of before the patient is discharged; referral acceptance and confirmation should be finalized with both patient and family.

Glutethimide (Doriden)

Although not a narcotic, glutethimide is a fast-acting nonbarbiturate hypnotic, effective with elderly patients and the chronically ill, and a controlled substance (schedule III). While not widely used now, it has been the source of many severe OD management problems. The patient with a glutethimide overdose will present with central nervous system (CNS) depression, including coma,

respiratory depression, dilated pupils fixed at midpoint, cyanosis, and a tendency to apnea following the manipulation of gastric lavage or endotracheal (ET) intubation.

Nursing Interventions.

The immediate nursing management requires stabilization of the airway with effective ventilation and supportive measures as indicated, including administration of naloxone. The patient will have recurrent episodes of drifting in and out of coma (sometimes for several days, even after lavage), because the low degree of water solubility of the drug and the high degree of fat solubility contributes to a redistribution phenomenon (recirculation through the biliary tract). Severe management problems result. Some investigative studies have indicated that lavage with a 1:1 mixture of castor oil and water is possibly capable of removing larger amounts from the stomach than a plain water or saline lavage. Lavage must be done as soon as possible but *not until* a cuffed ET tube is in place and the patient is being adequately ventilated. Following lavage, an activated charcoal "slurry" should be instilled into the stomach because the charcoal has a propensity to absorb large amounts of the drug and assist in its continued elimination.

Barbiturates

Barbiturates and the psychotherapeutic drugs are another group causing concern, with or without the additional potentiating effects of alcohol. Barbiturates are classified according to their duration of action, as presented in Table 31–2.

Nursing Assessment.

Symptoms of barbiturate overdose are nystagmus, ataxia, and slurred speech, followed by coma if intervention is not initiated rapidly. The following points are helpful to

TABLE 31–2. BARBITURATES CLASSIFIED BY DURATION OF ACTION

Type of Action	Drug	Duration of Action	Comatose Levels (mg/100mL)	Lethal Levels (mg/100mL)
Ultrashort	Thiopental (anesthesia)	Minutes	—	—
Short (put to sleep)	Pentobarbital (Nembutal)	2–4 h	> 0.5	> 1
	Secobarbital (Seconal)	2–4 h	> 0.5	> 1
Intermediate	Amobarbital (Amytal)	4–6 h	> 1	> 2
Long (keep asleep)	Phenobarbital	6 h	> 5	> 10

keep in mind, however, when dealing with a possible barbiturate abuse:

- Intoxication in a nonaddicted person can be caused by a very small dose.
- Tolerance to barbiturates develops to *very high levels.*
- The alcohol or barbiturate abuser will always *underestimate* intake to offset increasing tolerance.
- If barbiturate overdose is suspected, investigate *all* medications the patient may be taking for barbiturate ingredients (Belap, Fiorinal, and so on).
- Always suspect mixtures of medications and alcohol.

Nursing Interventions. The findings in a study done in Denmark in the 1970s showed that a mortality of 12 to 15 percent in barbiturate overdoses was reduced to 1 percent by simply supporting the patient's cardiorespiratory status on a respirator while the liver and kidneys metabolized and excreted the drug. The following protocol was observed:

1. Intubation with continuous close observation and respiratory support with a volume ventilator
2. Prevention or treatment of shock with intravenous fluid maintenance
3. Careful screening for blood levels of alcohol, other barbiturates, and salicylates
4. Maintenance of renal function, increasing rate of excretion and alkalinization of the urine by administering intravenous sodium bicarbonate
5. Penicillin prophylaxis against hypostatic pneumonia
6. Intensive nursing care with continual turning and suctioning of mucus
7. Restriction on use of stimulants
8. No lavage. (The average amount of drug recovered with lavage was about one therapeutic dose (100 mg), and it was not thought to be worth the medicolegal risk because questionable electrocardiogram [ECG] disturbances were associated with the procedure.)

Withdrawal Procedure. The barbiturate abuser who has developed an enormous tolerance for the drug cannot be withdrawn "cold turkey" without precipitation of a crisis. Improper management may result in the patient's having seizures and even a full-blown psychosis. For this reason, barbiturate abstinence must be treated as a serious withdrawal problem; these patients must be "re-addicted," which involves a rather complicated in-hospital procedure. Treatment consists of challenging the body with 200 mg of pentobarbital (Nembutal) every 6 hours until there is slurred speech, ataxia, and nystagmus. For example, a patient may require a total ingestion of 900 mg/d before the signs of intoxication develop, at which time the dosage is gradually decreased 100 mg/d until the patient is completely withdrawn. This regimen requires *close* medical management by a psychiatrist and qualified nursing personnel.

Nursing Diagnoses. Appropriate nursing diagnoses for barbiturate overdose would include:

- Potential for barbiturate toxicity
- Ineffective breathing pattern
- Alteration in renal tissue perfusion
- Knowledge deficit related to barbiturate poisoning

Caveat on Missing Drugs. In the hospital, watch where the "barbs" (*all* barbiturate-containing medications) go. Hospital personnel are known to take significant amounts of medications from their hospitals regularly; barbiturates are popular, and abuse is widespread among staff who have access without total accountability.

Psychotherapeutic Drugs
The wide group of psychotherapeutic drugs that are frequently abused includes the minor and major tranquilizers and tricyclic antidepressants.

Minor Tranquilizers. The benzodiazepines (such as Valium, Librium, and Serax) cause little concern alone, even though they are the most widely used. The problem develops when they act in concert with other drugs that may exert a CNS depressant effect, most frequently alcohol.

Major Tranquilizers. The phenothiazines, such as prochlorperazine (Compazine), chlorpromazine (Thorazine), fluphenazine (Prolixin), trifluoperazine (Stelazine), promazine (Sparine), promethazine (Phenergan), and thioridizide (Mellaril), when taken in excess, tend to have a cumulative effect, which produces a state of hypotension, possible ECG changes and arrhythmias, and extrapyramidal effects, resembling parkinsonian syndrome, (e.g., the neck is arched, the eyes are rolled back, and the patient is staring and drooling). The immediate first steps in management are to ensure airway patency, ventilate effectively, and administer diphenhydramine (Benadryl), 25 to 50 milligrams IV, by slow push to reverse the symptoms.

Tricyclic Antidepressants. When given in therapeutic dosages, tricyclic antidepressants are non-addictive, but they are often taken in combination with other minor tranquilizers or alcohol, again resulting in an OD. The most frequently abused in this group are amitriptyline (Elavil) and imipramine (Tofranil); others are doxepin (Sinequan), perphenazine (Etrafon), and desipramine (Norpramin). These patients may present in delirium or coma, with significant arrhythmias noted on the ECG.

Nursing Interventions. The specific treatment for an amitriptyline OD is administration (slow push) of 1 to 3 mg IV (1 mg/mL) of physostigmine (Antilirium) for rapid reversal of symptoms. It may be helpful to remember that physostigmine will also reverse the toxic effects of the belladonna alkaloids. The dose may be repeated in 20 minutes and every 30 to 60 minutes as needed (PRN). Diphenylhydantoin (Dilantin) is also effective with these patients in treatment of arrhythmias and CNS disturbances.

Nursing Diagnoses. Appropriate nursing diagnoses for tricyclic antidepressant toxicity would include:

- Decreased cardiac output
- Alteration in thought processes, especially perception
- Anxiety
- Knowledge deficit related to tricyclic antidepressant toxicity

HALLUCINOGENS: LSD, PCP, MDMA

Lysergic Acid Diethylamide

LSD has been the most widely used of the hallucinogens; it has both sympathomimetic and hallucinogenic effects. The LSD user on a "bad trip" usually presents with acute psychosis, often with bizarre hallucinations, and unless carefully managed can progress to a highly agitated state with acute panic reactions and paranoia; ataxia and seizures may occur. "Blotter acid," which is LSD sprinkled on blotter paper and cut into small squares for sale on the street, can account for a wide variety of idiosyncratic responses. Because blotter acid is highly impure with no quality control, there can be a variance of 1 to 250 times in potency.

Nursing Interventions. There are several approaches to management of this situation, but it should always be treated as an acute psychosis; 4 mL IV droperidol (Inapsine) is effective, but occasionally, an LSD "tripper" can be "talked down" successfully without use of adjunctive drug administration; a quiet environment is essential. Another backup method that has demonstrated effective results is administration of Thorazine, 50 mg IM, followed by diazepam (Valium), 10 to 20 mg IV.

Phencyclidine

PCP, originally marketed as a surgical anesthesia and subsequently discontinued for human beings because of severe adverse side effects, has become a widely abused hallucinogenic and sympathomimetic drug with many serious ramifications. PCP is ingested, injected, inhaled as smoke, and "snorted." According to law enforcement agencies, it is said to actually "breed violence," that "users end up playing hallucinogenic Russian roulette," and that "a physical encounter with a suspect under the influence of PCP is as potentially dangerous as confronting an armed suspect." PCP abuse manifestations are dose related. Low-dose abuse results in communication difficulty, blank stare, time and place disorientation apprehension, and aggressive or self-destructive behavior. Moderate-dose abuse results in a comatose or stuporous condition with the eyes open, response only to deep pain stimuli, and period amnesia. High-dose abuse produces a patient who is comatose, responds only to noxious stimuli, and has a long recovery period of alternating sleep and waking illusions and hallucinations with amnesia. Vital signs (VS) are accelerated, motor function varies from catatonia to seizures, and nystagmus is present in all directions.

Nursing Interventions. Nursing management is difficult and dangerous; ED personnel should exercise all caution. The best approach is to reduce *all* verbal, tactile, and visual stimulation; sensory isolation is key, with close physical observation and readiness to administer Valium or Ativan for seizure control; high-flow oxygen; and possibly naloxone HCl (Narcan), 0.4 mg IV, to reverse effects of a possible narcotic mixture.

Nursing Diagnoses. Appropriate nursing diagnoses for PCP toxicity would include:

- Potential for poisoning due to PCP toxicity
- Potential for violence—self-directed or directed at others
- Visual and auditory sensory-perceptual alteration
- Knowledge deficit related to PCP poisoning

Methylene Dioxymethamphetamine

MDMA, also known as Ecstacy or Adam, is an unregistered designer drug used in the past to facilitate psychotherapy; it is now out on the street as a drug of abuse. After an episode of discomfort, it is supposed to produce a mellow feeling. Users say it heightens one's insight into self and enhances communication; observers note that the drug markedly relaxes inhibitions. MDMA received considerable press in the late 1980s and subsequently developed widespread popularity on the street. Overdoses produce classic amphetamine reactions of hypertension and tachycardia, with a marked loss of touch with reality; severe medical emergencies resulting from its use are not known.

Mescaline

Mescaline and peyote are variants of the hallucinogens and may account for LSD-like behavior, but regardless of what the patient has ingested or what bizarre behaviors are manifested, the first respon-

sibility is protection of the patient with as quiet surroundings as possible and documentation of cogent, objective observations for the physician.

Nursing Diagnoses for MDMA or Mescaline

Appropriate nursing diagnoses for the hallucinogenic toxicities would include:

- Potential for poisoning from hallucinogen
- Alteration in thought processes
- Anxiety related to loss of self-control
- Potential for violence—self-directed or directed at others
- Knowledge deficit related to potential for poisoning

MARIJUANA (CANNABIS)

In 1985, the Centers for Disease Control and Prevention (CDC) reported that marijuana is the most widely used illicit drug in the United States; an estimated 50 million people in this country have used it at least once. The psychoactive ingredient in marijuana is δ-9-tetrahydrocannabinol, commonly referred to as THC, contained in the plant resins. THC content has been increased in recent years in the ongoing search for superpotency; one claim for Kentucky cannabis was 8 percent THC content, and Wisconsin followed closely with 6 percent. California sinsemilla currently averages about 5 percent; the U.S. average is about 3.7 percent. These levels are all considerably higher than levels found 20 years ago and are reflected in problems now being seen clinically.[5]

For years, cannabis was thought generally to be harmless and nonaddictive, but syndromes have developed over the years with chronic use of the stronger weed (grass, pot, hash, Mary Jane). The drug is *not* totally benign; it does alter perception of the environment and amplify sensory perception. Heavy users can develop chronic apathy, withdrawal, inattentiveness, and the inability to "get started." These characteristics may tend to be irreversible in some people, and there may be an atypical psychosis, paranoia, or "bad trip." There is no known associated CNS, cardiac, or respiratory depression associated with use, although it is recognized that the resins are strongly carcinogenic in the lungs. ST-segment and T-wave changes occur following ingestion.

Nursing Diagnoses

Appropriate nursing diagnoses for marijuana intoxication would include:

- Alteration in visual and kinesthetic perception
- Knowledge deficit regarding long-term harmful effects, including to the lungs

SUMMARY

Polydrug abuse, or polypharmacy on the street, is almost the rule in the many major cities, where overdosing on only one drug is rare. On the average, three drugs are involved in every two nonfatal emergencies, while five are found in every two overdose deaths.[6] Mixed-drug ingestions seriously potentiate the deleterious effects of the individual drugs, cloud the clinician's abilities to readily recognize and identify signs of the drugs involved, and significantly complicate emergency interventions. ENs must be aware that the drug scene is constantly changing (e.g., drugs' street names, routes of drug administration, drug availability, and appropriate emergency interventions). Street drugs are rarely pure; there is no quality control. Designer drugs may become contaminated in their formulation, and frequently the "adulterants" used to cut drugs may have their own harmful effects. Regardless of all else, response begins with support of the vital functions and monitoring of VS while the search is underway for the offending drug(s) and definitive interventions.

◼ TOXICOLOGY

Toxicology is the study of poisons. A poison is defined as a chemical agent that produces an adverse effect on living organisms; the effect can be relatively minor or it may be fatal. An adverse effect is a state of toxicity produced by too much of anything. It is estimated that there are more than 1 million compounds in the world that will kill you if you take enough of them, and this presents problems in trying to define specific agents responsible for toxicity. Fortunately, the offending compounds tend to group into a "frequency" pattern and can generally be identified.

It is recommended that every ED have reference materials to aid identification of toxic substances; two such volumes are suggested here:

- Rall TW, Nies AS, Taylor P, Gilman AD, eds. Goodman LS, Gilman A. *The Pharmacological Basis of Therapeutics.* 9th ed. New York, NY: McGraw-Hill–Pergamon Press; 1996
- Ellenhorn MJ. *Ellenhorn's Medical Toxicology: Diagnosis and Treatment of Human Poisoning.* Baltimore, Md: Williams & Wilkins; 1997

The latter text provides the following information: (1) an ingredient index with toxicity rating, including lethality; (2) an index of general formulations of most commercial compounds according to use; and (3) brand names with ingredients of each and indications of the degree of toxicity.

CLINICAL PATHOLOGY LABORATORIES

Clinical pathology laboratories provide analytic services in toxicology and are maintained in most states and the larger metropolitan areas. The services of these laboratories are made available, as a rule, for toxicology studies on samples submitted from EDs, monitoring of blood levels on samples submitted from outlying areas, medicolegal evaluations for law-enforcement agencies, and postmortem toxicology studies for the state medical examiner or coroner.

These laboratories employ a highly sophisticated methodology, based largely on gas chromatography and mass spectrometry techniques, to separate individual drug components from submitted samplings, identify them, and quantitate their presence. One of the chief services rendered is the computation of blood alcohol samples submitted as evidentiary material in drunk-driving cases.

POISON CONTROL CENTERS

Regional Poison Control Centers exist all across the United States, strategically located to serve massive population centers; generally they consist of several emergency medical service (EMS) regions, particularly in rural states, and may include one or more states. With 24-hour telephone access and staffing by nurses, pharmacists, and physicians trained in toxicology, these centers are the ultimate readily available resource for emergency management of drug ODs and toxic ingestions. Each center has a comprehensive information file, which includes access to the Micromedex POISINDEX, textbooks, the names of specialized consultants, and linkages to the vast array of agencies dealing with toxic substances. All are served by toll-free (800) numbers; be certain your area's Poison Control Center 800 number is posted in a *highly visible* place in your ED and on the poison treatment cart.

COMMONLY SEEN TOXIC INGESTIONS

The array of substances encountered in toxic ingestions is vast; this section briefly addresses some frequently—and less frequently—seen problem substances and their principal interventions, including alcohols, acetaminophen, salicylates, cyanide, iron, and organophosphates.

Alcohols: Classifications and Toxicities

To clarify the widely existing confusion about alcohols, there are three classifications: methanol, or wood alcohol (C-1), is used in the laboratory, chafing dish burners, and antifreeze; ethanol, or ethyl alcohol (C-2), is used for legal drinking; and isopropyl alcohol (C-3) is used for rubbing alcohol and sterilization in 70 percent and 90 percent dilutions. All three alcohol classifications present toxicity problems of varying degrees; methanol ingestion causes a profound metabolic acidosis, intoxication, and blindness; ethanol continues to be the most widely ingested toxic substance available; and isopropyl alcohol ingestion causes potent intoxication, CNS depression, and severe gastritis. Ethylene glycol, a component of antifreeze and windshield de-icers, has profound toxic effects when ingested; the first stage of CNS manifestations (including ataxia, nystagmus, and coma) and metabolic acidosis can progress to cardiopulmonary involvement with pulmonary edema or congestive heart failure. The final phase of toxicity, about 24 hours after ingestion, is oliguric renal failure that may be reversible if treated in time.

Ethyl alcohol (ethanol): The major effect of alcohol is an irregular, progressive, descending depression of the CNS. Low doses decrease attentiveness to the task at hand (an example is careless driving after two or three drinks) although chronic alcoholics may tolerate higher blood levels before their condition deteriorates. The first things affected are the higher centers of the brain, the most skilled task abilities, and the most recently learned tasks. As the blood level climbs higher, more of the brain's functions become depressed, and the effects become obvious. Alcohol does tend to be a self-limiting OD, with vomiting or coma limiting further intake, and for this reason lethality from alcohol alone is rare. Ethanol abusers, however, are predisposed to hypoglycemia, subdural hematoma (increased risk of falls and head injury), sepsis, and chronic liver disease.

Alcohol is a small molecule; 25 percent is absorbed directly into the bloodstream on ingestion, with the balance absorbed from the small intestine. Because alcohol follows water, it is widely distributed, and appears anywhere in the body where there is water. After alcohol ingestion, alcohol levels can be measured in chest and abdominal organs, muscle, brain, blood, urine, saliva, and perspiration. Once alcohol is absorbed into the bloodstream, 5 percent is eliminated through saliva, urine, and sweat; the other 95 percent is eliminated by means of oxidation in the liver.

Management of acute ethanol intoxication involves ensuring full support of the patient's airway, breathing, and circulation (ABCs); intravenous volume replacement if depleted; and intravenous administration of thiamine (50 to 100 mg), naloxone (2 mg), and glucose (25 mg), as discussed earlier in this chapter.

Legal Blood Alcohol Levels. Blood alcohol level is a complicated subject with an important medicolegal significance, frequently surrounded by confusion and misconception. The blood alcohol level is a "picture" of the extent to which the body's capacity to metabolize and get rid of alcohol has been exceeded. A single drink (1 oz.) is absorbed in about 20 minutes, and the drug remains in the body normally for approximately 1 hour, oxidizing at the rate of 15 mg/100 mL per hour. One ounce of 80-proof whiskey will register a blood alcohol level of approximately 20 mg/100 mL, proportionately, depending upon body weight. A 70-kg man (154 lb.), given 1 oz. of 80-proof whiskey, will show a blood alcohol level of 0.02 percent, or 20 mg/100 mL. A 12-oz. can of beer will produce a blood alcohol level of 25 mg/100 mL, and the rate of oxidation (or disappearance from the blood) will be about 15 mg/100 mL per hour, as with the 80-proof whiskey. Blood alcohol level can roughly be interpreted by these rules of thumb

- 20 to 50 mg/100 mL (0.02 to 0.05 percent)—within legal limit
- 50 to 80 mg/100 mL (0.05 to 0.08 percent)—nearing legal limit
- 450 to 500 mg/100 mL (0.45 to 0.50 percent)—toxic and lethal

In recent years, the trend has been to establish lower legal limits for blood alcohol levels. A level of 80 mg/100 mL (0.08 percent) has been adopted by England and Canada, and in mid-1996, Germany and Scandinavian countries were observing a legal limit of 50 mg/100 mL (0.05 percent).

Most states in the United States now have an implied-consent law, whereby, as a condition of accepting a driver's license, a person agrees to give a sample of blood or breath if a law officer has reasonable grounds to suspect the person has been drinking and driving a car irresponsibly. The option is either to submit a sample or to accept a 6-month suspension of the driver's license if cooperation is refused. Most states set the legal limit at around 100 mg/100 mL (0.1 percent), and if there has been a negligent homicide involving a motor vehicle accident (MVA), an alcohol blood level must be obtained to submit essential proof to a jury. It becomes necessary, therefore, to obtain a blood alcohol sampling in the ED if at all possible when a patient appears intoxicated; otherwise, there may not be any law-enforcement action available.

Guidelines for Obtaining Evidentiary Blood Alcohol Levels. Interpretation of the statutes relating to obtaining blood alcohol levels for evidentiary purposes varies from state to state, but some basic guidelines are given that can apply anywhere:

1. For the evidence to be admissible in court, the blood alcohol level determination must be done by a qualified laboratory duly authorized by the state jurisdiction.
2. Hospital policy should clearly articulate the procedure for obtaining blood alcohol samplings and the conditions of consent.
3. The consent of the patient is necessary, and it should be *informed* consent.
4. If blood is drawn, it should be drawn in the police officer's presence so that he or she can so testify, eliminating the need for other witnesses to appear and testify.
5. Blood drawn must be given to the officer requesting it, who then takes it to an authorized laboratory, preserving the chain of evidence.
6. A notation of blood drawn, by whom, and the time, must be documented in the ED record of the patient, and the blood must be so labeled before it is sealed with tape, cross-initialed across the cut end of the tape, and given to the officer.
7. If a blood alcohol determination is needed for medical purposes, draw separate samples.
8. The skin preparation for drawing blood alcohol sample should be done with aqueous benzalkonium (Aqueous Zephiran) and *never* with alcohol.
9. Draw 10 mL and label with the name, date, time drawn, and your initials. If the patient is accused of negligent homicide, record the exact time and draw *two* samples, 1 hour apart, to demonstrate the blood alcohol level curve as firm legal evidence. Either the blood alcohol level will have peaked and started down, or it will be higher, indicating that the subject took more alcohol immediately prior to the incident. It is estimated that the blood level will fall 15 to 20 mg/100 mL per hour, so if, for instance, blood is drawn 4 hours after an arrest and tests at a blood alcohol level of 0.18 percent (180 mg/100 mL), it can be legally assumed that the subject's blood level at the time of arrest was 0.26 percent, or 260 mg/100 mL.

Acetaminophen

Acetaminophen (Tylenol) ingestion has become a problem; severe liver toxicity, compounded by ingestion of other drugs such as the sedatives and hypnotics, frequently turns out to be the underlying cause of death. Toxicity is considered to be ingestion of any amount in excess of 7.5 to 10 g orally in 24 hours (24 to 30 325-mg tablets).

Nursing Interventions. Treatment of acetaminophen toxicity is (1) intravenous administration of the antidote N-acetylcysteine (NAC), or oral Mucomyst, according to protocols established by the regional Poison Control Centers, and (2) supportive care as appropriate. Mucomyst orally is unpleasant to take and may cause emesis; administration must be repeated, perhaps by way of a nasogastric (NG) tube to ensure delivery. The preferable intravenous NAC may be difficult to obtain in some regions; contact the Rocky Mountain Poison Control Center at (800) 525-6155 for availability. If the patient has received activated charcoal, wait 1 hour before giving NAC orally; charcoal will adsorb the antidote. The antidote should be aboard within 16 to 24 hours of reaching toxic levels of acetaminophen for most effective results.

Salicylate

Salicylate (acetylsalicylic acid [ASA]) ingestion is one of the most common forms of drug abuse and toxicity. Children seem to be more sensitive to its effect, consequently getting into disproportionate problems. Blood levels of salicylate should always be requisitioned in cases of questionable abuse: up to two tablets (10 grains) will give a blood level of 5 mg/100 mL; 10 tablets per day (50 grains) will produce a serum level of about 25 mg/100 mL; toxic serum level develops at about 50 mg/100 mL, or ingestion of 60 5-grain tablets; lethal serum level of salicylates is over 100 mg/100 mL.

Nursing Interventions. Excretion begins after 3 to 4 hours; treatment is symptomatic and supportive for nausea and vomiting, dehydration, tinnitus, acid–base imbalance, and metabolic acidosis. The patient should *always* be lavaged for stomach content, even up to 10 hours after ingestion. Alkalinization of urine will enhance excretion.

Cyanide

Cyanide is a cellular asphyxiant producing very rapid injury and, depending on concentration and duration of exposure, very rapid death. Cyanide's toxic effects are based on its attraction to ferric iron stored in hemoglobin (Hgb), shutting down the cytochrome oxidase system; profound metabolic acidosis, cellular asphyxiation, and organ

failure result. Symptoms of mild exposure are headache, nausea, dizziness, and tachycardia, just as in other hypoxic states; high concentrations of cyanide can cause rapid loss of consciousness, seizures, hypotension, bradycardia, and death.[7]

Since not everyone is able to detect the odor of bitter almonds that is characteristic of cyanide poisoning, the index of suspicion for cyanide intoxication may not be triggered unless the history points to cyanide exposure in the home or workplace.

Nursing Interventions. Immediate intervention means administration of the contents of the Lilly cyanide kit (Eli Lilly and Co, Indianapolis, Ind.): amyl nitrite, sodium nitrite, and sodium thiosulfate. Unless the intoxication has been too intense, there is an almost immediate return to consciousness in people who seem virtually dead.[7] ENs should familiarize themselves with the contents of the Lilly cyanide kit, with where it is kept for rapid access, and with the administration protocols (see Chapter 22).

Nursing Diagnoses. Appropriate nursing diagnoses for cyanide poisoning would include:

- Impaired gas exchange related to interference with cellular respiration
- Altered tissue perfusion related to interference with respiration

Iron

Normally, iron is a part of our diet; we ingest and absorb about 10 to 15 mg of elemental iron daily. Elemental iron is absorbed as the ferrous ion and converted into the ferric form in gastric or intestinal mucosa, then transported actively across the mucosal wall to the blood, where it combines with transferrin and eventually attaches to Hgb. Free iron, beyond that which can be absorbed and converted to use, is systemically toxic. An ingestion of more than 60 mg/kg of body weight of elemental iron can cause major toxicity, with hypotension and hypovolemia from leakage of blood and fluid. Ingestion of more than 150 mg/kg has been fatal.[8]

Iron toxicity manifests in stages: initial symptoms, within 30 minutes to 2 hours after ingestion, of GI irritation with hematemesis, lethargy, abdominal pain, and diarrhea; the latent phase of usually 6 to 24 hours, when symptoms subside;

and the third—and systemic—phase, with metabolic acidosis, onset of shock, cyanosis, and hepatic failure.

Nursing Interventions. Chelation (using a compound to enclose or grasp a toxic substance and make it nonactive) is accomplished in iron toxicity with intravenous administration of deferoxamine given at a rate of 15 mg/kg per hour mixed in Ringer's lactate, NSS, or D_5W. Chelated free iron will turn the urine pink to dark brown; return to normal color indicates that there is no free iron in the serum and chelation therapy may be discontinued. Competent supportive airway care and adequate fluid resuscitation, combined with chelation therapy, have markedly reduced mortality rates from iron poisoning to almost zero.

Organophosphates

Organophosphate and carbamate poisonings are seen in a wide range of toxicities; they are among the most toxic chemicals in use and are freely absorbed by *all routes* (i.e., skin, respiratory tract, GI tract). Excessive stimulation of neuroreceptors occurs when the organophosphate binds to acetylcholinesterase and causes an accumulation of acetylcholine at receptor sites; the result is a cholinergic crisis. The resulting syndrome is known as SLUD—salivation, lacrimation, urination, and defecation—sometimes accompanied by gastric upset and emesis. Organophosphate toxicity also causes bronchoconstriction, dyspnea, chest pain, headache, ataxia, bradycardia, seizures, muscle weakness, and coma.

Nursing Interventions. Interventions begin with supporting vital functions and providing immediate high-flow oxygen; respiratory failure is the most life-threatening feature of organophosphate toxicity. Gastric lavage, charcoal, and cathartics are administered if chemicals were ingested; decontamination of skin and clothing must be carried out immediately and with great care, using soap and water. All clothing, undergarments, and shoes must be removed and placed in plastic bags; ENs must protect themselves as well during decontamination.

Atropine is crucial and must be administered as soon as the diagnosis is considered; it must be given simultaneously with oxygen and in massive doses. Serious poisonings may require massive doses of atropine, both as initial intravenous bolus and every 15 minutes until signs of SLUD are reversed, and should be continued for at least 24 hours after initial contamination to ensure that the organophosphate is completely metabolized.

■ GENERAL MANAGEMENT OF OVERDOSES AND TOXICITIES

Effective ED interventions for OD and toxicity problems involve following proven steps of management, having necessary and appropriate equipment and drugs readily available at the bedside, and developing competency in teaching patients how to avoid future problems.

GUIDELINES

Treat the patient, not the poison or drug, as follows:

A. Establish the airway and maintain adequate ventilation as appropriate. Suction apparatus with a high-flow tonsil suction tip or large-bore tubing should be assembled, and held in readiness for airway protection.
B. Evaluate the state of coma:
   1. Response to verbal commands
   2. Response to painful stimulus
   3. Presence or absence of reflexes
   4. Cardiorespiratory status
C. Examine the patient carefully and obtain full VS. Although cardiorespiratory status is the primary concern, any patient with an altered mental status should have a temperature check. Both hyperthermia and hypothermia can mimic or complicate a drug overdose.
D. Initiate an intravenous line with large-bore needle.
E. Identify the poison or drug and obtain an accurate history if possible.
F. Get rid of the poison through one of the following:
   1. *Emesis:* No emesis should be elicited if (1) the patient is comatose, convulsive, or without the gag reflex; (2) the patient

has ingested a strong base or acid; or (3) the ingestion has been a petroleum distillate.

2. *Syrup of ipecac:* Induce emesis (test gag reflex first) with syrup of ipecac (30 mL for adults, or 15 mL for children). Do not store or use fluid extract of ipecac; it is a much stronger solution and can be dangerous. Follow ipecac with several glasses of warm water or 7-Up, ambulate the patient if possible, and if there are no results in 15 to 20 minutes, stimulate the pharynx while the patient is lying on the left side in a head-down position.

3. *Gastric lavage:* Lavage is used if the patient is comatose, except with petroleum products. A cuffed ET tube *must* be in place if a comatose patient is to be lavaged. Use a large Ewald tube (34 mm), again placing the patient on the left side, in a head-down position to prevent aspiration and promote better drainage, and lavage with saline. Use 300 mL per tidal wash for adults and 10 mL/kg of body weight per wash for children until the return is clear.[8,9] This procedure is effective after 4 to 6 hours and up to 12 hours with ASA, meprobamate (Equanil), and anticholinergic agents. Lavage samplings should be saved for possible laboratory analysis.

4. *Activated charcoal:* If syrup of ipecac has not been administered, activated charcoal should be given immediately. The finely powdered preparation is highly effective for adsorbing and binding many drugs and chemicals (e.g., propoxyphene hydrochloride, salicylates, phenobarbital and amphetamines). There are no known contraindications for its use, although it is ineffective with iron and lithium; maximum benefit occurs within 30 minutes after ingestion and onset of action is immediate. A "slurry" of activated charcoal is instilled via the lavage tube and will mark intestinal transit time as well as adsorb and bind ingested substances. The usual dose is between 25 and 100 g dissolved in water (30 to 60 g in children and 60 to 100 g in adults). Each 50 g takes about 250 mL water to dissolve it; the correct dose is about 5 to 10 times the amount of drug ingested, if known.[8] The finely powdered charcoal can make a considerable mess if not handled carefully; it can be easily mixed right in the disposable lavage bag. Sometimes magnesium sulfate (10 to 20 g) is instilled as a cathartic to hasten transit time.

G. Place a Foley bladder catheter with a closed drainage system and calibrated receptacle. Force diuresis for ASA, barbiturates, and isoniazid (antitubercular drug), and monitor output carefully.

H. Initiate hemodialysis or peritoneal dialysis if indicated.

I. Send urine to the laboratory for toxicology screening (analgesics [including saliclates], opiates, amphetamines, tricyclics, and phenothiazines).

J. Counteract the toxic effects of specific poisons as indicated (Table 31–3).

TABLE 31–3. AGENTS THAT COUNTERACT THE TOXIC EFFECTS OF SPECIFIC POISONS

Poison	Antidote
Acetaminophen	N-acetylcysteine (NAC)
Arsenic or mercury	British antilewisite (BAL)
Anticholinergics (tricyclics, phenothiazines)	Physostigmine (Antilirium)
Benzodiazepines	Mazicon
Calcium channel blocker	Calcium
Carbon monoxide	Oxygen
Coumarin	Vitamin K
Cyanide	Sodium nitrite (Lilly cyanide kit)
Digoxin	Digibind, or Digoxin immune FAB (ovine)
Ethylene glycol	Ethanol
Fluoride (hydrofluoric acid)	Calcium
Iron	Deferoxamine (Desferal mesylate)
Isoniazid	Pyridoxine
Methanol	Ethanol
Nitrites (methemoglobinemia)	Methylene blue
Opiates (including propoxyphene)	Naloxone (Narcan)
Organophosphates	Atropine and pralidoxime

ENs are responsible for remaining aware of the changing methods of management and for independently seeking current knowledge to be able to recognize and manage overdoses and toxic states. Be fully capable of airway management, including intubation and the use of ventilatory equipment, remembering that the best ventilator is the bag-mask unit. Document adequately before the patient leaves the ED for transportation to the intensive care unit (ICU) and see that the patient is always accompanied by respiratory support equipment, including oxygen. Have standing orders in your department for such procedures as administration of naloxone, intervention in respiratory arrest, arterial blood gases (ABGs), gastric lavage, and initiation of intravenous lines, and be alert to the hazards of management, such as aspiration, catheter contamination, overhydration, and further respirator problems.

THE POISON TREATMENT CART

A well-organized and logically equipped poison treatment cart can save untold, unnecessary mileage during the management of OD or toxic ingestion, because it can be taken directly to the patient's stretcher and worked much like a code cart.

The old standby antidotes of vinegar, olive oil, and salt have fallen into great disrepute; it is currently recommended that they be removed from the ED before damage is done, using the following rationale:

- If vinegar or citrus juice is given to counteract caustic material ingestion, it will generate chemical activity and burn the esophagus further. Ingested caustics should be diluted with copious amounts of water or milk.
- Instillation of olive oil or vegetable oil may lead to aspiration pneumonia and will certainly prevent effective endoscopy if that procedure is indicated.
- Saltwater ingestion (as an antidote) can cause severe hypernatremia and may rapidly result in death in children.

The small-wheeled cart with three drawers and a bottom compartment is recommended for use as a poison cart; the molded plastic type with rounded corners and large, quiet casters is preferred. The suggested poison treatment cart inventory is given in Table 31–4.

TABLE 31–4. RECOMMENDED CONTENTS OF THE POISON TREATMENT CART

Top drawer:
  60 mL Asepto syringes
  Y connectors
  Utillity tubing sections (standard size)
  Lubricant (water-soluble)
  Straws
  2 forceps for clamping tubing
  Alcohol wipes
  Medicine wipes
  Spoons
Second drawer:
  Assorted nasogastric tubes, including 32-mm red rubber
    Ewald tubes (or equivalent)
  Paper cups
  Disposable lavage bags (6)
Third drawer:
  Injectable medications:
    Mucomyst
    Physostigmine (Antilirium)

    Naloxone (Narcan)
    Diphenhydramine HCl (Benadryl)
    Epinephrine
    Atropine
    Methylene blue
    Lilly cyanide klt*
  Pitchers
  Activated charcoal (30-g doses)
  Ipecac (30-mL doses)
  Magnesium citrate
  Topical anesthetic spray
Bottom shelf:
  Supply of normal saline irrigant (1500-mL bottles)
  Cover gowns or aprons for personnel

---

*Eli Lilly and Co., Indianapolis, Ind.

PATIENT TEACHING

The ED is an excellent spot for teaching the public. Poison prevention is a critically important area, especially in light of studies showing that children who have ingested a toxin stand a 25 percent chance for a *repeat* ingestion in the next year, while their siblings have a 56 percent chance. Ask parents, while they are in the ED, where they keep the drain cleaners, insect sprays, rodent poisons, cleaning fluids, and medications of *all* kinds, and suggest special locked storage areas for all these hazardous materials—start people thinking.

■ SUMMARY

Several themes are central to recognition and effective management of the substance abuser or toxicologically affected patient. Recognition and effective management of these patients rests on understanding of the abuse substance categories and the basic abuse patterns: (1) most drug abuse is an overlay of one or more recreational drugs over baseline drug levels of alcohol and/or cannabis; (2) older alcoholic patients rarely use drugs; (3) younger alcoholics are multisubstance abusers and cross all the lines. Go with these concepts until proven otherwise. Some additional basic points to remember include the following:

- The rule foremost is to treat the patient, not the poison.
- The substance abuser typically discounts or denies the extent and chronicity of his or her abuse.
- The ED is the substance abuser's entry point to rehabilitation; its effectiveness as an entry point will depend on nursing efforts and persistence in providing referrals and setting up follow-up care.
- In order to be fully effective, ENs must be informed and in touch with contacts and entry procedures for both public and private treatment facilities.
- Regional Poison Control Centers and police agencies should be used as active resources for dealing effectively with substance abuse and toxic emergencies whenever the need arises.

■ REFRENCES

1. Fitzgerald PE, ed. *Drugs of Abuse.* Washington, D.C.: U.S. Department of Justice, Drug Enforcement Administration, U.S. Government Printing Office; 1989.
2. Kunkel DB. Cocaine then and now, part I. *Emerg Med.* 1986;18(11):125–138.
3. Lewin NA. Controlling the cocaine catastrophe. *Emerg Med.* 1984;16(16):80–81.
4. Randall T. Cocaine, alcohol mix in body to form even longer lasting, more lethal drug. *JAMA.* 1992; 267:1043–1044.
5. Kunkel DB. Marijuana: a few new thoughts on an old subject. *Emerg Med.* 1985;17(9):134–137.
6. Norman S. The drugs on the street where you live. *Emerg Med.* 1986;18(3):129–177.
7. Vance MV. Injury through inspiration. *Emerg Med.* 1985;17(19):20–48.
8. Stewart C. Overdose and poisonings. In: *Street Drugs, Decontamination, and Overdose Management.* Colorado Springs, Colo: Charles Steward and Associates; 1993.
9. Shannon BE. Poisonings and ingestions. In Jenkins JL, Loscalzo J. *Manual of Emergency Medicine.* Boston: Little, Brown; 1990:417–469.

■ BIBLIOGRAPHY

Bayer MJ. Reversing the effects of pesticide poisoning. *Emerg Med.* Feb 1992;61–68.

Becker CI. The role of cyanide in fires. *Vet Hum Toxicol.* 1985;27:487–490.

Cusak JR, Phillips JD, Malcolm R. Alcoholism: uncovering the hidden diagnosis. *Emerg Med.* May 1992; 71–76.

Dean BS. Substance abuse: drugs and alcohol. In: Fincke MK, Lanros NE, eds. *Emergency Nursing: A Comprehensive Review.* Rockville, Md; Aspen Publishers; 1986.

Dellinger RP. General management principles of poisoning and overdose. *Crit Care Med.* 1989;361–366.

Dellinger RP. Management of specific poisoning and overdose problems. *Crit Care Med.* 1989;367–374.

Derlet RW, Heischober B. Illicit methamphetamine: street drug on the rise? *Emerg Med.* June 1991; 39–41.

Doweiko H. Identifying street names of drugs. *J Emerg Nurs.* Nov/Dec 1979;41–47.

Drug Facts and Comparisons. Philadelphia, Pa: JB Lippincott; 1986.

Ellenhorn MJ, Barceloux DG. *Medical Toxicology, Diagnosis and Treatment and Human Poisoning.* New York, NY: Elsevier; 1987.

Elston PL. Management of methaqualone overdose. *J Emerg Nurs.* 1980;6(5):17–19.

Emergency Nurses Association. *Emergency Nursing Core Curriculum.* 4th ed. Chicago, Ill: ENA; 1994.

Farian K. Fentanyl analogs: deadly designer drugs. *Emerg Med.* June 1991; 75–80.

Fitzgerald PE, ed. *Drugs of Abuse.* Washington, D.C.: U.S. Department of Justice, Drug Enforcement Administration, U.S. Government Printing Office; 1989.

Goldfrank LR. Ask me about alcohol withdrawal. *Emerg Med.* 1992;1:169–175.

Goodman LS, Gilman A. *The Pharmacological Basis of Therapeutics.* 9th ed. New York, NY: McGraw-Hill, 1996.

Hall AH, Kulig KW, Rumack BH. Suspected cyanide poisoning in smoke inhalation: complications of sodium nitrite therapy. *J Toxicol Clin Exp.* 1989;9: 3–9.

Hall AH, Rumack BH. Hydroxocobalamin/sodium thiosulfate as a cyanide antidote. *J Emerg Med.* 1987;5:115–121.

Hall AH, Rumack BH. Clinical toxicology of cyanide. *Ann Emerg Med.* 1986;15:1067–1074.

Hart BG. Alcohol and trauma in the emergency department. *J Emerg Nurs.* 1996;21:426–427.

Holtman DJ. Acetaminophen overdose. *J Emerg Nurs.* 1978;4(3):50–52.

Ilo E. Charcoal: update on an old drug. *J Emerg Nurs.* 1980;6(4):45–48.

Jensen S. The initial management of acute poisoning. *J Emerg Nurs.* 1977;3(4):13–16.

Kulig KW, Ballantyne B, et al. Environmental medicine: cyanide toxicity. *Am Fam Physician.* 1993;107–113.

Kunkel DB. The divine plant of the Incas. *Emerg Med.* Aug 1992;77–94.

Levin SM. Coping with overdose/poisoning, part 2: alcohol, psychotropics, sedative-hypnotics. *J Crit Ill.* 1991;6:873–880.

Lowenstein S, Weissberg M. Alcohol intoxication injuries and dangerous behaviors and the revolving emergency department door. *J Trauma.* 1990;30: 1252–1258.

Marx JA, Jorden RC, eds. Alcohol related emergencies. *Top Emerg Med.* 1984;6(2):1–87.

McElroy C. Alcohol withdrawal syndromes. *J Emerg Nurs.* 1981;7:195–198.

Metz V, Hanenson I. Management of drug overdose in the adult. *J Emerg Nurs.* 1975;1:8–15.

Moreau D, ed. *Nursing 96 Drug Handbook.* Springhouse, Pa: Springhouse Corporation; 1996.

Morelli J. Pediatric poisonings: the 10 most toxic prescription drugs. *AJN.* July 1993;27–29.

National Institute on Alcohol Abuse and Alcoholism. Facts about alcohol and alcoholism. Washington, D.C., 1980. In: Witters PJ, Witters W, eds. *Drugs and Society.* Boston, Ma: Jones & Bartlett; 1986.

Norman S. The drugs on the street where you live. *Emerg Med.* 1986;18:129–177.

Physicians' Desk Reference. 50th ed. Montvale, NJ: Medical Economics; 1996.

Ross TM. Gamma hydroxybutyrate overdose: two cases illustrate the unique aspects of this dangerous recreational drug. *J Emerg Nurs.* 1996;21:374–376.

Scharman EJ, Lembersky R, Krenzelok EP. Whole bowel irrigation for foreign bodies. *Emerg Med.* Apr 1995;57.

Schneider SM. Mushroom poisoning: recognition and emergency management. *Emerg Med.* 1991;12(9): 81–88.

Segar DL, ed. Substances of abuse. *Top Emerg Med.* Oct 1985;7(3):75.

Sims D, Bivins B, Obeid F, et al. Urban trauma: a chronic recurrent disease. *J Trauma.* 1989;29:940–947.

Soderstrom C, Crowley R. A national alcohol and trauma center survey: missed opportunities, failures of responsibility. *Arch Surg.* 1987;122:1067–1071.

Soloway RAG. Street-smart advice on treating drug overdoses. *AJN.* 1993;65–71.

Spivey WH. Neurologic complications of cocaine abuse. *Emerg Med.* 1990;19:1422–1428.

Stewart CE. *Toxicology! Emergency Management of Overdoses and Poisonings.* Lewisville, Tex: Charles Stewart and Associates and Barbara Clark Mims Associates; 1993.

Stork CM, Hoffman RS. The toxic emergency: antifreeze. *Emerg Med.* Dec 1994;59–60.

Taylor RW. Management of the critically ill substance abuser. In: Taylor RW, Dellinger RP, eds. *Critical Care Medicine Review for Internal Medicine Based Intensivists.* Fullerton, Calif: Society of Critical Care Medicine; 1989.

Thomas DO. *Quick Reference to Pediatric Emergency Nursing.* Frederick, Md; Aspen Publishers; 1991.

Tintinalli JE, Krome RL, Ruiz E, eds. *Emergency Medicine—A Comprehensive Study Guide.* 2nd ed. New York, NY: McGraw-Hill; 1988.

Wrenn K, Rodewald L, Dockstader L. Ipecac: use it selectively. *Ann Emerg Med.* 1993;22:1408.

■ REVIEW: SUBSTANCE ABUSE AND TOXICOLOGY

1. Describe the five federally controlled schedules (or classifications) for drugs and their relative potential for abuse and cite at least four examples of each.

2. List five categories of drugs that are considered drugs of abuse.

3. Identify the classic symptoms and immediate steps of management with the opiate overdose.

4. Describe the presenting picture of an opiate addict in withdrawal and identify the one manifestation that cannot be faked.

5. List the advantages of naloxone administration and describe the reason it is the immediate drug of choice with unknown overdoses.

6. Identify the risk factor for sudden death incurred by ingesting cocaine and alcohol concurrently.

7. Describe the appropriate interventions for stimulant abuse.

8. Describe the three different presentations of alcohol abuse seen in the emergency department (ED) and outline the interventions for alcohol withdrawal.

9. Outline both the immediate and protracted management of glutethimide overdose.

10. List the principles of treatment and support in a barbiturate overdose and describe the management of the withdrawal procedure that should be followed.

11. Describe the dose-related manifestations of PCP (phencyclidine) abuse.

12. Identify the immediate nursing response to overdose of *any* drug while the definitive search is ongoing.

13. Describe the progressive effects of alcohol on the central nervous system (CNS) as they relate to performance.

14. Outline the guidelines for obtaining evidentiary blood alcohol specimens.

15. Enumerate the steps of ED interventions for general management of overdoses and toxicities, listing the most important step first.

16. List at least 12 antidotes that should be available on the ED poison treatment cart.

Burns and Environmental Emergencies

32

■ BURNS

This section is designed to provide a working knowledge of the pathophysiology of burns and an awareness of the essential considerations involved in nursing assessment and interventions in the emergency department (ED) setting. Appropriate nursing diagnoses and guidelines for initial management are presented, along with a review of preparations involved for the safe and orderly transport of the seriously burned patient to an organized burn unit.

A severe burn is one of the most physically and psychologically devastating injuries that can occur. A burn injury involving more than 20 percent of the total body area (TBA) of an adult and more than 12 percent of the TBA of a child is a pansystemic injury involving other organ systems that are essentially worked overtime to eliminate toxins and debris as well as to produce the means of fighting infection and stabilizing the fluid balance of the body.

The goals in care of the burn patient, then, are restoration of skin integrity, and preservation of life, function, and appearance. ED personnel have the opportunity to begin the establishment of these goals through a calm and organized system of care.

DETERMINING EXTENT AND SEVERITY

The skin, the largest organ in the body, has seven basic functions:

- Protecting against infection
- Preventing loss of body fluids
- Controlling body temperature
- Functioning as an excretory organ
- Functioning as a sensory organ
- Producing vitamin D
- Determining identity

There are two anatomic layers to the skin: the epidermis and the dermis. The epidermis consists of epithelial cells that form a barrier against the environment. The dermis consists of epithelial cells and connective tissue and contains blood vessels, hair follicles, nerve endings, and sweat and sebaceous glands, all of which contribute significantly to patient function and survival.

Depth

A first-degree burn is a superficial burn involving only the epidermis. It is red in color and somewhat painful, but it is not a serious burn and will heal within a few days without scarring.

There are two types of second-degree burns: superficial and deep. The superficial second-degree burn involves the epidermis and superficial dermis. It is reddened and has blisters that continue to increase in size; this is the most painful type of burn because the nerves have been damaged but not destroyed. This burn heals within 10 to 14 days and may leave some discoloration (which is probably temporary) or minor scarring. It does not require skin grafting.

The deep second-degree burn involves the epidermis down to the deep dermis and is very similar in appearance to the third-degree burn. This burn is usually whitish and may have a leathery feeling. It is somewhat anesthetic, and it often takes as long as 7 or 8 weeks to heal. A skin graft is not necessary to heal this wound, because even in deep dermis, there are epithelial cells around the hair follicles that will regenerate and form skin; because of the prolonged time involved, a skin graft is occasionally done to speed up the healing process. Heavy scarring may occur with the deep second-degree burn.

The third-degree burn involves the epidermis and all of the dermis, destroying all epithelial cells that can regenerate skin. This burn has a whitish or charred appearance, is anesthetic, and has a tough, leathery feeling. It does require a skin graft to heal unless it is a very small area that can heal in from the sides. The third-degree burn is the most serious of the burns.

The terminology now used more frequently to describe the depth of a burn is:

- Superficial partial-thickness: first-degree and superficial second-degree
- Deep partial-thickness: deep second-degree
- Full-thickness: third-degree

This method of classification is more accurate in describing the depth of a burn (Fig. 32–1).

Extent

The rule of nines is a fast, easy way to determine the amount of body surface burned (Fig. 32–2). The body is divided into multiples of 9, as allotted in Table 32–1. It should be remembered that the percentage of body surface for the head and legs of a newborn is *reversed* from that of an adult (the child's head is 18 percent and the legs are 14 percent). This ratio slowly changes until, at approximately 15 years, the percentages are the same as for an adult. The Lund and Browder Burn Chart (Fig. 32–3) is designed to account for changes in anatomic percentages due to growth. For small burns, a good rule of thumb is that the palmar surface of the patient's hand is approximately 1 percent of that patient's body.

Other Factors

Although the depth and extent of burn are two of the most important factors in determining the severity of the injury, there are other factors to consider. One of the most important to take into the evaluation is age. The very young and older patients do not tolerate even the minor or moderate burn, and the mortality for these age groups is high.

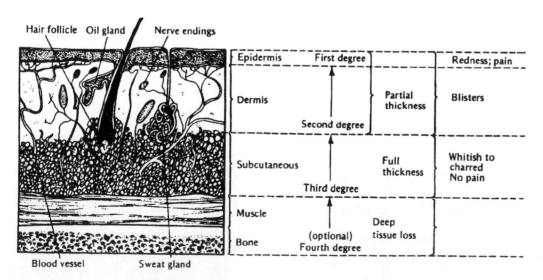

Figure 32–1. Classification of burns according to type and degree.

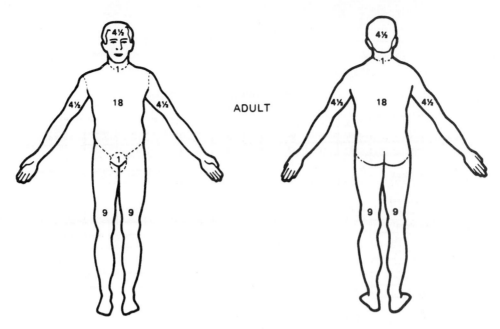

Figure 32–2. Rule of nines.

The patient with a history of other medical problems especially the patient with diabetes or with cardiac, renal, respiratory, gastrointestinal (GI) or cerebral problems can be significantly affected by a burn.

Injuries associated with the burn, and the area of the body burned are also factors to consider. Burns of the hands, face, feet, and perineum are serious in terms of (1) functional problems, (2) cosmetic problems, (3) inactivity problems, and (4) infection problems.

TABLE 32–1. RULE OF NINES IN BURNS

Body Part	Area (%)
Arms (shoulders to fingertips) each	9
Head (adult)	9
Each leg (adult)	18
Anterior trunk	18
Posterior trunk	18
Perineum or neck	1

Classification

Burns caused by exposing a small part of the body to a heat source (e.g., a finger, small part of the hand or arm, hot water splashing on a very limited area of the trunk) are considered nonserious burns and can often be treated at home with no complications. Burns are categorized by the American Burn Association by their severity as follows[1]:

- *Minor burn injury:*

    15 percent body surface area (BSA) or less in adults

    10 percent BSA in children or the elderly

    2 percent BSA full-thickness injury without cosmetic or functional risk to eyes, ears, face, hands, feet, or perineum
- *Moderate burn injury:*

    15 to 25 percent BSA mixed partial- and full-thickness injury in adults

    10 to 20 percent BSA mixed partial- and full-thickness injury in children under 10 years old and adults over 40 years old

    10 percent (or less) BSA full-thickness injuries that do not present a serious

BURN ESTIMATE AND DIAGRAM
AGE vs. AREA

Area	Birth 1 yr.	1-4 yr.	5-9 yr.	10-14 yr.	15 yr.	Adult	2°	3°	Total	Donor Areas
Head	19	17	13	11	9	7				
Neck	2	2	2	2	2	2				
Ant. Trunk	13	13	13	13	13	13				
Post. Trunk	13	13	13	13	13	13				
R. Buttock	2½	2½	2½	2½	2½	2½				
L. Buttock	2½	2½	2½	2½	2½	2½				
Genitalia	1	1	1	1	1	1				
R.U. Arm	4	4	4	4	4	4				
L.U. Arm	4	4	4	4	4	4				
R.L. Arm	3	3	3	3	3	3				
L.L. Arm	3	3	3	3	3	3				
R. Hand	2½	2½	2½	2½	2½	2½				
L. Hand	2½	2½	2½	2½	2½	2½				
R. Thigh	5½	6½	8	8½	9	9½				
L. Thigh	5½	6½	8	8½	9	9½				
R. Leg	5	5	5½	6	6½	7				
L. Leg	5	5	5½	6	6½	7				
R. Foot	3½	3½	3½	3½	3½	3½				
L. Foot	3½	3½	3½	3½	3½	3½				
						TOTAL				

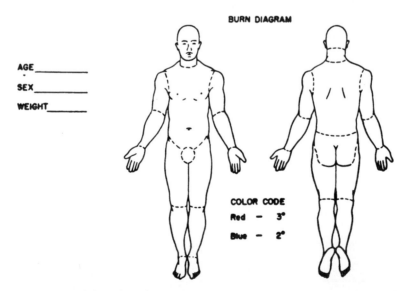

BURN DIAGRAM

AGE _____

SEX _____

WEIGHT _____

COLOR CODE

Red — 3°

Blue — 2°

Figure 32–3. Lund and Browder method for assessing extent of burn injury. The chart considers changes in BSA according to age.

threat of functional or cosmetic impairment of the eyes, ears, face, hands, feet, or perineum.

Major burn injury:

25 percent BSA in adults

20 percent BSA in children under 10 years old and adults over 40 years old

10 percent (or greater) BSA full-thickness injury

All burns of face, eyes, ears, hands, feet, or perineum likely to result in functional or cosmetic impairment

All high-voltage electrical burns

All burn injuries complicated by inhalation injury or major trauma

One common question asked by ED personnel is "What type of burn requires hospitalization?" Any burn of 10 percent TBA that is superficial partial thickness should be considered for admittance, and any burn of 3 percent TBA that is deep partial or full thickness should also be considered for admission. A patient with questionable problems (very old, very young, infirm, inhalation injury, other injuries) should also be evaluated for hospitalization. Those patients with a major burn belong in a designated burn center.

Pathiophysiology

Local Changes. Three major local changes occur with burn injury. These must be remembered when caring for the patient in the ED:

- Loss of the microbe barrier, which opens the way for massive infection
- Loss of the fluid barrier, so that exudate is allowed to seep from the wound (this is not the cause of the massive fluid shift that occurs following burn injury)
- Loss of temperature control, which can cause the patient to become hypothermic if exposed to subnormal temperatures

Renal Changes. Following the burn injury, the glomerular filtration rate is reduced as a result of hypovolemia and decreased renal plasma flow, which continues for 24 to 72 hours. The kidneys receive 20 to 25 percent of the cardiac output per minute normally, but after a burn, they may receive only 10 percent.

Tubular damage may also be caused by free hemoglobin (Hgb) from extensive red blood cell (RBC) damage that forms casts in the tubules. An inflammatory reaction develops around the casts, interstitial edema ensues, and there may be necrosis of the tubules.

Respiratory Changes. Frequently, the patient with a burn also sustains inhalation injury. The first problem that arises stems from the fact that the patient may have inhaled CO, which can rapidly displace O_2 on the Hgb and cause severe hypoxemia. The second problem is the formation of edema in the upper respiratory tract. This is due to chemical or heat injury and to the tremendous amount of fluids required to resuscitate the patient. Both contribute heavily to occlusion of the airway with edema. The third problem is that the lower respiratory tract may be injured from smoke or chemicals and foreign particles that may have been inhaled. Note that this injury is almost always chemical and not a thermal (heat) injury to the tract. The pharynx is very moist and will tend to cool down any flame or heat that has entered the mouth; at the same time, the glottis will rapidly close if heat advances that far. The last problem is eschar (burn tissue) restriction of the chest. With deep circumferential burns, the patient may have trouble expanding the lungs; the tight, leathery burn tissue around the chest will not allow normal inhalation.

Cardiovascular Changes. Very shortly after a major burn injury, there is a 30 to 50 percent decrease in the cardiac output, secondary to hypovolemic shock due to extensive capillary leakage, evaporative fluid losses, transudation, and sequestration of fluid in the burned area. An increase in circulating myocardial depressant factor (MDF) is also thought to contribute to the shock state. There may also be destruction of RBCs due to hemolysis, and the life span of other RBCs may be reduced owing to microangiopathic edema. Platelets and leukocyte levels are typically reduced after burns.

The major cause of burn shock, however, is capillary leak, which allows the plasma to leak out into the tissue. If the burn is less than 30 percent, the capillary leak is localized in the area of the burn. If the burn is over 30 percent, there is a generalized leak throughout the body. The patient with a major burn may lose up to 50 percent of the plasma volume within the first 3 hours after the burn.

NURSING DIAGNOSES

Appropriate nursing diagnoses for burn injury include:

- Potentially ineffective airway clearance
- Potentially ineffective breathing pattern
- Potentially impaired gas exchange
- Actual fluid volume deficit
- Decreased cardiac output
- Peripheral tissue perfusion
- Actual impairment of skin integrity
- Nursing problem: alteration in temperature
- Nursing problem: potential for infection
- Pain
- Anxiety
- Knowledge deficit regarding discharge instructions

NONSERIOUS BURN INJURY

Nursing Intervention

When a patient enters the ED with a small burn from a household injury or minor work injury, the wound should be cleaned with saline and a mild soap or antiseptic solution. If there is blistering, the intact blisters should be let alone, because they provide a comfortable, clean dressing for the wound. If the blisters are broken, *only* the very loose skin should be removed. Apply an antiseptic ointment or cream such as silver sulfadiazine (Silvadene) or an antiseptic gauze impregnated with 1 percent bismuth (Xeroform), and cover with a sterile, bulky dressing, which is to serve as a protective dressing. Have the patient return to the ED or doctor's office for a dressing change every 1 to 3 days until the wound is healed, and be certain that he or she understands that the wound and dressings must be kept clean and dry. Instruct the patient to watch for signs of infection, such as purulent drainage or a foul odor from the dressing, redness

around the edges of the wound, an increase in temperature, or a wound that will not heal. If these signs or symptoms occur, the wound should be cultured and treated with a topical agent specific to the causative organism.

SEVERE BURN INJURY

Nursing Intervention

When the ED is notified that a severe burn victim is on the way, a clean room that is as isolated as possible should be set up with gowns, masks, caps, gloves, and burn packs.

When the patient arrives in the ED, any smoldering clothing should be immediately removed. Once the heat source has been removed or cooled, the patient should be checked for respiratory involvement.

A history of where the burn occurred is important because any patient with a burn that involved the presence of smoke in an enclosed space has a significant chance of developing some respiratory complications. The nose and mouth should be examined for soot and singed hairs, and blood should be drawn to determine carboxyhemoglobin level and arterial blood gases (ABGs). It is also important to include a chest x-ray; findings on this initial chest film should be normal because the lower respiratory tract injury (which includes the lung infiltrates, pulmonary edema, and so on) often does not become evident for a few days. Thus, if the x-ray shows abnormality, there is a possibility that it is not related to the burn injury.

If any respiratory involvement is suspected, oxygen should be started at 2 to 4 L/min. Because major problems with smoke inhalation may not show up for 6 to 24 hours after injury, the patient should be under close hospital observation for 24 hours if there is any question of the severity of the smoke inhalation.

Signs of Severe Respiratory Involvement.
The most common signs of more severe respiratory involvement include singed nares and sooty mouth, a high carboxyhemoglobin level (normal is about 0 to 5), ABGs with a low partial pressure of oxygen in the blood (PO_2) and a high partial pressure of carbon dioxide in the blood (PCO_2), sooty sputum, increasing hoarseness, difficulty swallow-

ing, shortness of breath, and cyanosis (a rather late sign). These patients are probably developing an upper airway obstruction due to chemical (smoke) injury and edema. The treatment is endotracheal intubation with O_2 mist until the edema has subsided (probably 24 to 72 hours later). An upper airway obstruction could also be caused by a circumferential deep burn of the neck, and an escharotomy (incision into the eschar) may be needed. This is always done parallel to the circulatory path but a safe distance from major vessels. If suctioning is needed, it should be done with extreme caution, because the tissue has already been traumatized by the toxic gases and soot particles; careless suctioning could easily cause considerable further damage to an already compromised airway.

Lower Respiratory Complications. The complications that occur with a lower respiratory injury may not be seen in the ED because they usually occur 24 to 72 hours after the burn, but they are mentioned here because they frequently occur in patients who have had upper airway injury. As was mentioned before, the lower respiratory tract is never thermally injured. It can be chemically injured (even down to the alveoli) as a result of toxic gases. This will begin to manifest on chest x-ray films in a few days as possible atelectasis or infiltrates caused by the edema that forms. Patients with severe respiratory injury are candidates for respiratory distress syndrome, owing to the damaged alveoli and tremendous fluid loads. These patients are treated with an endotracheal tube, oxygen, a volume ventilator with positive end expiratory pressure (PEEP), and sometimes steroids for a very short time. Even as the patient's condition improves, vigorous pulmonary care is given to ensure movement of secretions and to prevent pneumonia.

The patient with a circumferential deep burn of the chest has trouble expanding the chest (as was mentioned earlier), and this tightness must usually be relieved with an escharotomy.

Fluid Replacement. Stabilizing circulation is extremely important in view of how much fluid the patient is losing. An intravenous line should be started on an adult patient with (minimally) a 20 percent superficial partial-thickness burn or a 10

percent deep burn, and on a child with a 10 percent burn of any depth, or if there is any nausea or vomiting. The formula that is most commonly accepted for fluid replacement is:

$$4 \text{ mL Ringer's lactate/kg body wt/\% of burn in first 24 hours}$$

Half the amount is to be given in the first 8 hours, and the balance in the next 16 hours. The formula is only a guideline, however, and the chief indicator of adequate fluid replacement is the urine output. Intravenous tubes are adjusted to keep the urine output at 30 to 50 mL/h for an adult and 1.5 mL/kg of body weight per hour for a child. If there is Hgb in the urine, the rate is increased until the urine clears, to prevent tubular necrosis.

Note that there is no dextrose in the Ringer's lactate. Dextrose given to the severely burned patient significantly increases the blood sugar and can cause an osmotic diuresis, thus giving an inaccurate picture of fluid replacement.

Colloids are not used to resuscitate the patient in the first 24 hours except in some small children or in patients with very large burns, because the albumin will leak out into the tissue and hold fluid in the tissue instead of in the circulatory system, where it is needed. After the vessels have sealed up again, plasma may be used to replace that which was lost initially. Although Ringer's lactate will also leak out into tissues, it is mobilized more easily and the resultant edema will subside faster.

Because of the amount of fluid needed to resuscitate the patient, it is important that the patient's body weight be obtained soon after admission, because these patients will gain a great deal of fluid weight in the first 24 to 48 hours. This can be done in the burn unit, but it *does* need to be done somehow—within the first 3 hours to be accurate.

Tubes. Foley catheters are inserted in all patients with burns of 30 percent TBA or more and in any other patient with less burn if there is a questionable renal or cardiac problem. Patients over 60 years of age especially should be evaluated for the need of an indwelling Foley catheter.

All patients should be kept NPO (nothing by mouth) while in the ED because a paralytic ileus can develop, owing to the stress of injury. Patients with burns over 30 percent or with deep facial burns (because of swelling) should have a NG tube connected to low intermittent suction for 12 to 24 hours. Any patient who is nauseous or vomiting should also have a NG tube.

Initial Evaluations. Initial laboratory studies should include the following:

- Complete blood cell (CBC) count
- Electrolytes
- BUN
- Creatinine
- Albumin and total protein
- ABGs and arterial carboxyhemoglobin levels
- Blood sugar
- Clotting studies
- Toxicology screen
- Urinalysis (should include a test for Hgb as well as myoglobin, which can help monitor for renal problems, and there may be an elevated glucose); dipstick test results that are positive for blood suggest myoglobinuria
- Electrocardiogram (ECG) should be done on patients with any question of cardiac problems and especially elderly patients; chest x-rays should be done on any questionable respiratory injury
- Photographs (should be taken as soon as possible in the ED to document initial involvement, as baseline information for later comparison)

Wound Care. After primary care has been given, ED personnel can turn their attention to the burn wound. All clothing articles should be removed to be sure that all burn areas have been accounted for, and the size of the burn should be reevaluated. It is helpful to estimate first the amount of burned area and then the amount of unburned area, which should add up to 100 percent. If it does not, you have over- or underestimated the size of the burn, and it should be reassessed. All gross debris should be cleaned away with sterile saline and a clean cloth, and any very loose hanging skin should be removed. *Do not,* however, debride intact blisters or peel off sheets of intact epidermis. Initial wound management should be

limited to cleaning, using bland soap, normal saline solution (NS), or an antiseptic soap as necessary. Commercial cleansers, available in automotive supply stores, will remove heavy grease and oils, whereas tar and asphalt deposits maybe removed with heavy applications of polymyxin B-bacitracin-neomycin ointment (Neosporin ointment) topped with saline compresses and applied every 4 hours, or less expensively with mineral oil applications.

As for application of topical agents to the wound, it is best to contact the facility to which the patient will be transferred to find out what the routine is. In some cases, if the transfer is to a close facility, it will be requested that the wound simply be covered with a clean or sterile sheet and no topical agent be applied. If it is to be a long transfer, the facility may have you apply the agent of its choice, and dress the wound prior to transfer. If antibacterial cream *is* to be applied in the ED, the wound should be washed first with a mild antiseptic soap and warm water. The purpose is to remove bacteria and debris from the wound. Covering areas other than those being cleansed helps keep the patient warm. The antibacterial preparation is then applied with a sterile tongue blade or the gloved hand and the part is covered with gauze dressing. When removing cream from the jar, avoid putting contaminated instruments or hands back into the jar; change gloves or instruments whenever necessary.[2]

In any case, the patient should be kept warm and dry. The only exceptions to this are a superficial partial-thickness burn that is less than 20 percent of TBA or a chemical burn. In those cases, the burn area may be kept moist for the patient's comfort.

Analgesia. Pain associated with burn injury can contribute to shock. All pain medication for a major burn must be given intravenously, owing to the erratic nature of intramuscular absorption after burn. It should also be remembered that the patient with deep or full-thickness burn will suffer less pain than will the patient with a superficial partial-thickness burn. Intravenous morphine is effective at controlling pain, but it should be used only after fluid resuscitation is well underway.

Continued close observation of the respiratory status and blood pressure (BP) should be maintained, because narcotics can depress cardiorespiratory function.

Tetanus Prophylaxis and Antibiotics.
Patients with burn injuries should have adequate prophylaxis for tetanus. If there is any doubt about the status of immunization protection, ensure that both active and passive protection are promptly provided.

Burn wounds seem to become infected from the patient's own organisms or from those that are inadvertently incorporated into the wound during the course of care. It does not appear that organisms find their way into the wound from the atmosphere around the patient as was previously thought.[3] Although gram-positive microorganisms of various types are at times implicated in burn wound infections, gram-negative bacterial contamination from GI and genital sources seems more likely. *Pseudomonas aeruginosa* is the most frequently encountered organism in burn wounds. Recently, there has been an increase in methicillin-resistant *Staphylococcus aureus* (MRSA) and vancomycin-resistant enterococcal (VRE) infections as nosocomial organisms and antibiotic resistance problems escalate within the hospital environment.

Prophylactic antibiotics are not usually favored in burn care; however, mafenide acetate (Sulfamylon) and silver sulfadiazine (Silvadene) are used for direct wound care applications in the form of ointments or pastes. Silver sulfadiazine is painless on the open wound and does not penetrate as far into deep tissue as mafenide acetate. The latter agent has also been associated with sensitivity reactions and increased chances of pulmonary infections.[3] For burn wounds that mandate transfer for specialized care, it is preferred that they are only cleaned, grossly debrided, and covered prior to transfer because any ointments or dressings would need to be removed upon arrival at the burn center to facilitate the burn team's assessment and definitive care of the wound.

NONTHERMAL BURNS

Chemical Burns
Acids (sulfuric or nitric acid) and alkalis (caustic soda and anhydrous ammonia) can cause extensive tissue damage. Generally, alkali burns are more serious because of the deeper penetration and difficulty of dilution. Degree of injury is related to (1) duration of contact, (2) amount of chemical, and (3) its concentration. Flushing with copious amounts of water is the immediate treatment; a hosing or showering for at least 10 to 15 minutes for acid burns is necessary. Alkali burns require longer irrigation; an alkali burn to the eye requires continuous irrigation for several hours. Periodically the pH should be checked and recorded. Prompt consultation with ophthamology is imperative.

Chemical burns must be treated by dilution and irrigation, not by efforts to neutralize them. It is important, however, to note that dry chemicals should be brushed away from the skin to remove much of the chemical reagent before adding water.

Electrical Burns
Surface appearance rarely indicates the extent of an electrical burn. Current passing through the tissues may result in vast amounts of cellular destruction with loss of fluid, acid–base imbalance, and liberation of myoglobin, which can cause acute renal failure.

The immediate threat is hypovolemia, acidosis, and precipitation of myoglobin in the renal tubules. Effective management strategies are crystalloid intravenous infusions, correction of acidosis with intravenous sodium bicarbonate, and administration of an osmotic diuretic (i.e., mannitol).[1]

TRANSFERRING THE PATIENT

The care of a burn patient is difficult and time-consuming. It involves a team of people, not just a physician and nurse. Because of the specialized care that a burn patient requires, patients with any major burn should be transferred to a designated burn center if one is not available within the local hospital.

Criteria for Transfer
The generally accepted criteria for transfer of the burn patient include:

- Third-degree burns of more than 10 percent of the TBA
- Partial-thickness burns of more than 20 percent of the TBA

- Any serious burns of the hands, feet, perianal area, or genitalia
- Burns associated with significant fractures or other major injury
- High-voltage electrical burns
- Inhalation injury, which may be indicated early on only by significant preexisting disease

If the decision is made to transfer, the burn center should be contacted so that transfer guidelines can be established. The following outline is a review of what has been previously covered but can serve as a standard guideline in preparing for the transfer:

A. Establish the airway; intubate if necessary.
B. Identify the source and circumstances of the burn and get medical history.
C. Cut away clothes and evaluate the entire patient for other trauma.
D. Keep as warm as possible while:
   1. Estimating extent and severity of burns
   2. Initiating a large-bore intravenous line above the waist with Ringer's lactate
   3. Drawing blood for laboratory analysis
   4. Placing an indwelling Foley catheter with a urimeter
   5. Placing a NG tube if indicated; (keep patient NPO).
E. Observe consistent, clean, protective technique.
F. Cleanse gross debris and debride loose hanging skin only, as time allows, and reevaluate burn.
G. Contact the burn center for specific instructions on burn care and transfer procedures.
H. Monitor vital signs (VS) and urine output.
I. Maintain fluid intake through an intravenous line.
J. Give intravenous analgesics as needed for pain and anxiety, and be certain tetanus prophylaxis has been addressed.
K. Send complete concise documentation with an appropriate transfer form.

SUMMARY

With the development of emergency medical services (EMS) systems across the United States, we have seen the emergence of well-equipped and expertly staffed burn centers that receive patients from a predetermined catchment area; critically injured patients are transported to them in vehicles that are fully equipped with life-support hardware and staffed by trained nurses and paramedical personnel. The chances for survival and return to a relatively normal lifestyle have increased greatly in recent years for the seriously burned patient but depend heavily on the integrity of care in each phase of management. Nursing care of the burned patient is a highly skilled, specialized, and demanding area—physically, emotionally, and professionally; this is all too obvious to those of us who receive burned patients initially and feel a total sense of loss on the patient's behalf. Emergency personnel are not necessarily expected to know all the fine points of advanced burn care but must certainly be expected to know the essential management philosophy and protocols while the patient is their responsibility.

■ OTHER THERMAL EMERGENCIES

HEAT-RELATED EMERGENCIES

Humans are homeothermal beings with a core temperature ranging from 97.5° to 99.5°F. Thermal regulation is controlled in the hypothalamus, which receives information from the temperature of the circulating blood and from skin sensors that relay data about environmental temperature. When the hypothalamus is stimulated, the respiratory rate increases to enhance heat loss via expired air; cardiac output is increased to facilitate cutaneous and muscular blood flow, which helps dissipate heat; and sweat glands help to sustain evaporative heat loss.

Normally, metabolic processes continuously produce heat that is dissipated to the outside environment, which is usually cooler. In certain instances, however, the body may gain heat. If there is increased metabolic production (600 to 900 kcal/h with maximal work), poor heat dissipation, uptake of heat from a hot environment, or any combination of these three, the hypothalamus is stimulated. Initially, shivering is inhibited and sweating occurs. (Nearly 600 kcal of heat is lost as 1 L of sweat is evaporated.) Vasodilation follows promptly, and the cardiac output increases in response. The enhanced blood flow to the skin surface assists in heat loss via radiation and convection. These regulatory mechanisms work together to continually balance the amount of heat produced and lost by the human body.

Acclimatization is the process that enables the body to cope with heat stress. The benefits of acclimatization are usually apparent, however, only when the individual has had daily exposure to heat stress for 3 to 6 weeks. During this time, the body gradually develops defenses against hyperthermia. Aerobic metabolism increases, thus ensuring that the body uses energy more efficiently and that heat production is lessened. The body also develops a new, lower point at which sweating begins, and even the rate of sweat production is increased. Fully acclimatized individuals nearly double their loss of heat by perspiring and therefore can dissipate heat more rapidly. The heart muscle responds by improving cardiac output and stroke volume. Cutaneous circulation improves, and again, heat dissipation is augmented. Finally, increased secretion of aldosterone aids in sodium conservation by the kidneys and sweat glands. Of course, the additional sodium enhances extracellular fluid volumes, which play a part in accelerated cutaneous blood flow and heat dissipation, too. Emergency nurses (ENs) working in hot climates need to remember that environmental heat stress can cause a loss of 1 to 3 L of fluid per hour, each liter containing 20 to 50 mEq of sodium chloride. Individuals who are not acclimatized can fall victim to heat-related syndromes rather rapidly.

Factors Predisposing to Heat Syndrome

Elderly individuals or those who have debilitating illness or alcohol-related problems have difficulty in thermoregulation. Any factor that results in increased heat production (rigorous activity, febrile state, agitation or tremors, hyperthyroidism, or the effects of certain drugs) can ultimately lead to a thermal emergency. The final category of predisposing factors is a wide range of problems that impair heat dissipation. Among these are lack of acclimatization, high ambient temperature or humidity, obesity, heavy clothing, certain drugs, sweat gland dysfunction, potassium depletion, age extremes, dehydration, and cardiovascular disease.

Types of Heat-Related Illness

Although various authorities categorize heat-related illness in unique ways, the EN must be familiar primarily with four such problems: heat cramps, heat syncope, heat exhaustion, and heat stroke.

Heat Cramps. Heat cramps is a rather common disorder; the painful cramps, or contractions, of skeletal muscle are due to the sodium depletion that typically accompanies profuse sweating. Oral replacement of water and sodium is usually all that is required to curb the annoying problem of heat cramps. Popular thirst quenchers for sports enthusiasts, such as Gatorade, are appropriate for this minor heat-related problem, both as a preventive and therapeutic measure.

Heat Syncope. Heat-related fainting episodes may occur through the interaction of several phenomena. Vasodilation and peripheral pooling of blood, volume deficit, and sluggish vasomotor tone may all contribute to this problem. Venous return does not support the required cardiac output, and syncope occurs. Treatment consists of water and sodium replacement, usually orally, and avoidance of prolonged standing, which encourages venous pooling.

Heat Exhaustion. Heat exhaustion is a more serious heat-related problem that tends to occur when the core body temperature reaches 39° to 40°C (103.5° to 104°F). It may encompass heat cramps and heat syncope, as previously described, but is also characterized by altered mental status, GI upsets (i.e., anorexia, nausea, vomiting), headache, dizziness, irritability, weakness, and marked volume depletion. Thirst, hypotension, tachycardia, and syncope may occur along with hyperventilation. Typically, the patient sweats profusely and body temperature is normal or mildly elevated. Treatment consists of oral water and sodium replacement and rest in a cool, quiet environment.

Heat Stroke. Heat stroke is the most serious of heat-related emergencies; it is a condition associated with high morbidity and mortality. Essentially, heat stroke results from the failure of the hypothalamus to regulate body temperature. The usually operant heat loss mechanisms are simply overwhelmed. The core body temperature ranges from 40° to 42°C (104° to 107°F). (The 42°C point is the temperature level normally established for the onset of heat stroke.) Temperature elevations above this lead to physiological disaster and collapse. Enzymes denature, membranes liquefy, mitochondria do not function, protein coding is disrupted, and most essential physiological processes cease normal functioning.

Assessment. Signs and symptoms of heat stroke are evident in several body systems. Although the CNS, the heart and lungs, and the GI tract provide considerable data, it is also important to explore other organs and their functioning especially the kidneys and liver.

CENTRAL NERVOUS SYSTEM. Irrational behavior, confusion, and sudden changes in the level of consciousness (LOC) often mark the onset of heat stroke. Seizures are common and may occur early or late in the course of this illness. Cerebral edema should be considered early and, if evident, should be managed with diuretics and steroids. If focal deficits are noted, early scanning should be undertaken to rule out intracerebral hemorrhage that could be surgically decompressed. If seizures occur, they should be treated with benzodiazepines and barbiturates in the usual dosages (see Chapter 20).

HEART AND LUNGS. Airway and breathing, as in all other emergencies, should be the primary considerations. Since pulmonary edema is likely, oxygen, intubation, and positive end-expiratory pressure (PEEP) ventilation should be provided. A central venous pressure (CVP) catheter or Swan–Ganz catheter is useful to differentiate the nature of the pulmonary edema and to guide the fluid management regimen because the volume deficit may be less than initially anticipated. Digitalis and isoproterenol may be ordered to improve cardiac functioning. A baseline 12-lead ECG and continuous rhythm monitoring are imperative because myocardial ischemia, infarction, and life-threatening dysrhythmias have been associated with heat stroke. Conduction disturbances and nonspecific ST-T wave changes are typically discovered. These problems may be due in part to actual cellular damage of the myocardium or to complications of intravascular coagulopathy, hypovolemia, pulmonary edema, or other conditions that accompany heat stroke.

GASTROINTESTINAL TRACT. The GI abnormalities stem from electrolyte imbalances, impaired perfusion, and intravascular coagulation. Ulceration and massive bleeding can occur with little or no warning. Hypokalemia, with resultant gastric atony, is also common with heat stroke, so early placement of a NG tube is imperative to prevent regurgitation of stomach contents and the accompanying hazard of pulmonary aspiration. Hematests should be done routinely on gastric aspirant because GI bleeding is often associated with heat stroke. Intravenous cimetidine (Tagamet) may be given to control any gastric hyperacidity.

OTHER FACTORS. The renal system is invariably involved in heat stroke, presumably as a sequela to hypovolemia and hypoperfusion. The vasomotor effects on the nephron may be pronounced, requiring dialysis. Some clinicians have described the urine of the heat stroke patient as resembling machine oil with a low specific gravity. RBCs and white blood cells (WBCs), casts, protein, and ketones are all common findings in the urine of patients with this condition. BUN and creatinine are also elevated. Mannitol or furosemide are the recommended agents to assist in reestablishing urine flow. If myoglobinuria is suspected, alkalinization of the urine, in addition to maintenance of accelerated urine flow, is indicated as a therapeutic adjunct to preserve renal functioning. The liver rarely escapes damage in heat stroke. Hepatocellular enzyme studies (e.g., SGOT, SGPT, LDH, GGT) reveal both hepatocyte death and membrane destruction. Clotting disorders are induced by impaired liver function as well as by other phenomena associated with diffuse intravascular coagulation.

Other Tests and Procedures. Hypotension, which is a life-threatening byproduct of both volume deficit and cardiovascular impairment, should be managed with intravenous fluids and electrolytes and careful CVP or Swan–Ganz monitoring, as suggested earlier. Fluids of choice are dextran, Hespan, and plasma. Up to 6 L may be required to restore volume. Complete blood counts, electrolyte levels, liver enzyme studies, urinalysis, and ABG determinations should be accomplished early in the course of management. Other recommended tests are prothrombin time (PT), partial thromboplastin time (PTT), platelet count, and fibrinogen levels to detect coagulopathy associated with heat stroke. Serum and urinary amylase, chest x-ray, stool for occult blood, and hematest of gastric contents complete the battery of recommended studies.

Body cooling is critical to the survival of the patient with heat stroke, and it must be initiated early. Sponge baths, cooling blankets, peritoneal dialysis, rectal lavage, cardiopulmonary bypass, gastric lavage, and administration of phenothiazines are techniques useful for lowering body temperature. Invasive procedures, such as peritoneal dialysis and cardiopulmonary bypass, however, are reserved for the most severe cases. Aspirin should not be used because it cannot correct the underlying problem and may aggravate associated coagulopathy. Alcohol sponges should not be used, either, since enough alcohol can be absorbed through a widely dilated periphery to induce deep coma from toxic blood levels of alcohol. Temperature should be reduced to 39°C as measured by rectal thermometer or thermistor probe in the bladder, rectum, or esophagus. An esophageal thermometric reading technique is considered highly desirable for obtaining accurate core temperatures. Once the temperature reaches the desired level, it must be monitored and maintained carefully because rebound hyperthermia can easily occur. If shivering develops, chlorpromazine is given intravenously to achieve control because shivering actually increases heat production and would aggravate the condition. When phenothiazines are used, however, care should be taken to monitor for side effects, including hypotension, arrhythmias, and seizures.

Prevention

Heat-related illness, with its devastating effects, can be avoided or at least reduced in severity through simple preventive measures. These include becoming acclimatized; avoiding alcohol during exposure in hot, humid areas; wearing protective, light-colored clothes and hats; ingesting adequate amounts of balanced liquids to maintain fluid and electrolyte homeostasis; and pacing personal activities through awareness of heat stress. The EN should ensure that patients with heat-related emergencies receive instruction and follow-up care, because these individuals tend to be repeat clients for the same problem, often with compounding and disastrous consequences.

COLD-RELATED EMERGENCIES

The human body loses heat in five ways: radiation, conduction, convection, evaporation, and respiration. Radiation loss occurs any time the body temperature exceeds that of the surrounding environment. Because the head and neck are especially vascular and often unprotected, heat loss from this area can occur readily. Conduction heat loss occurs when there is a direct transfer of heat from the body to another object. When any body part comes into contact with a cooler object, heat is conducted to the external object until its temperature is equal to that of the body. Thereafter, the object becomes an insulating device, actually preventing further heat loss. Much body heat is lost this way in cold environments. Convection heat loss requires that heat be conducted to the air and then carried away by convection currents. Windchill, which combines the forces of lower temperature and the velocity of air currents, can be a devastating form of heat loss from the human body. Charts are available to convert environmental temperature and wind velocity to a windchill index. Heat transfer in water is about 25 times faster than in air of the same temperature. It is obvious, then, that victims exposed to cold water in immersion accidents can succumb rapidly to hypothermia. Evaporative heat loss occurs when wind sweeps across the skin and vaporizes the water of perspiration. This type of heat loss is an aggravating circumstance when an individual is wearing perspiration-soaked clothing and being exposed to a very cold environment. The body also loses heat through the process of breathing. As cold air enters the respiratory tract, it is warmed by the body heat before exhalation. Prolonged breathing of cold air, therefore, contributes to a gradual loss of total body heat. In considering cold-related emergencies or hypothermic events, one must take these several factors into account; they usually occur in some combination to create a serious decline in body temperature. Injuries due to cold exposure may be local tissue injury only or they may be generalized (i.e., a reduction of the body core temperature or hypothermia.)

Local Tissue Injury

The pathophysiology of local, cold-related tissue injury occurs at the arteriole, capillary, and venule levels of the circulatory system. When the body is chilled, the arterioles constrict to conserve body heat. This is tolerated well for a brief period. After prolonged vasoconstriction and flow redirection, however, the microvasculature becomes occluded, and the capillary bed becomes inactive. Eventually, the associated cells become compromised as aerobic metabolism ceases. Furthermore, the shunted blood returning to the heart is chilled by the cold surrounding tissue, contributing to a gradual cooling of the core. The involved tissue is compromised in terms of its vital processes, and if the temperature is below freezing, ice crystals begin to form and expand extracellularly at the expense of adjacent tissue that may yet be functioning normally. Dehydration occurs promptly, and surrounding cells are adversely affected. Muscles, nerves, and blood vessels are initially insulted, followed later by the more resistant tissue, such as ligaments, tendons, and bones. It is important to note that critical tissue injury can occur in temperatures above the freezing point. Any prolonged exposure to cold that results in significant vasoconstriction and sluggish circulation can create injury to exposed areas of flesh.

Frostnip or Incipient Frostbite.

Frostnip occurs in cold weather and primarily affects exposed areas of the body farthest from the trunk, such as the nose, ears, cheeks, chin, hands, and feet. Initially, the nipped area blanches and the victim experiences a burning, tingling sensation that eventually evolves to numbness. The condition comes on gradually; very active people may be oblivious to its early warning signs.

Frostbite.

Frostnip, if not treated promptly, progresses to frostbite. In superficial frostbite, the skin and superficial tissue layers become solid from freezing, but the deeper tissues remain resilient. The skin has a waxy, white appearance and is numb. After rewarming, the area becomes mottled and purplish, but the numbness persists. Edema and burning and stinging sensations follow. The damaged tissue is often marked by blisters that dry up and become hard and black within 10 to 14 days. Resting the part encourages the early resolution of edema, but the throbbing and burning may last for weeks. Eventually, the skin peels away, and the underlying red, tender area retains its sensitivity to the cold and tends to perspire abnormally for an extended time.

Deep frostbite includes damage to the skin, subcutaneous tissue, muscle, and blood vessels. The area is hard and cannot be depressed when touched; its color is pale or gray. Tremendous swelling that may last for weeks occurs after rewarming. Blisters form within 3 days, and a blue-violet or blue-gray discoloration persists. A sharp, throbbing pain is typical and may be present for several weeks. The blisters dry, turn black, and slough, leaving a new, red layer of tender skin that is very sensitive to the cold and perspires and itches for up to 6 months. In rare instances in which rewarming has not been promptly executed, gangrene of the affected part may occur and amputation is ultimately required.

Treatment.

Frostnip can be treated rather simply, by merely applying warmth to the affected part. If the feet or hands are involved, remove socks or gloves, respectively, before rewarming. Never rub the affected parts, because friction increases tissue damage. For actual frostbite, a warm-water bath is useful for rewarming. The bath temperature should be 100° to 110°F (37.8° to 43.3°C) as measured by a thermometer, not an estimate. Parts should be suspended in the bath and not permitted to touch the bottom or sides of the container. The part should be completely surrounded by bath water. Measure the temperature of the water periodically and maintain it at the desired level. Of course, never add hot water without removing the body parts and stirring the water carefully afterward. Check the temperature with a bath thermometer before reimmersing the part. Remember that the victim does not perceive pain reliably. The affected part usually begins to thaw within 10 minutes, but up to 1 hour may be required for complete thawing. The victim does not experience pain at first, but as thawing nears completion, the area throbs, aches, and burns. Analgesics may be required. When rewarming is complete, the part should be patted (*not rubbed*) dry and covered lightly with dressings. Areas between fingers and toes should be packed with cotton or gauze to prevent tissue-to-tissue contact.

Deep frostbite requires hospitalization. In the hospital, the affected parts are elevated on sterile sheets and protected from the irritation of the linens by a bed cradle or similar device. Isolation may be necessary for large areas of involvement that are blistered or peeling. Tetanus prophylaxis is required, of course, but antibiotics are not usually indicated. Medical sympathectomy using intra-arterial reserpine (0.5 mg/d for 2 to 3 days) reduces pain and improves blood supply. Heparin is sometimes given to reduce venous thrombosis, but its value in the overall outcome is questioned. Low-molecular-weight dextran given daily to reduce blood viscosity and enhance microcirculation may be useful, however. In rare instances, large, edematous frostbitten areas may require fasciotomy to facilitate adequate circulation to the area. Although amputation is occasionally unavoidable, it is delayed until the damaged area can be thoroughly assessed for viability, a process that usually requires 2 or 3 weeks of observation. In the meantime, antiseptic whirlpool baths, range-of-motion (ROM) exercises, and other therapies may be used to enhance circulation. Treatments that involve wet dressings or petrolatum-impregnated gauze or ointments, however, are strictly contraindicated. Long-term effects of frostbite include excessive perspiration, sensitivity, and paresthesias over the involved tissue.

There are several important points to be included in discharge instructions for individuals with frostbite or prefrostbite damage to exposed skin:

- It is vital that to dress appropriately for the cold, wearing mittens rather than gloves so that fingers can benefit from the heat given off by adjacent digits. Cotton socks worn next to the skin should be supplemented by wool socks, and tight-fitting shoes or boots should be avoided because they tend to interfere with circulation. Layers of clothing are ideal because they trap air and form an insulating zone around body tissue. Hoods, hats, and scarves are always "in fashion" in cold weather.
- Alcohol should be avoided because it dilates peripheral circulation, thus adding to heat loss.
- Food ingested should be high in calories to generate heat.
- Activity is desirable because muscle work tends to produce heat and enhance the circulation.
- As with all cold-related problems, wet clothes and windchill should be avoided.

Systemic Hypothermia

Hypothermia is a life-threatening condition occurring when the core body temperature is less than 35°C (95°F). Most adverse physiological problems do not manifest themselves, however, until the body reaches 32.2°C (90°F). This is the point at which shivering stops and muscles become rigid. When the core temperature falls below 25.5°C (78°F), death usually occurs. ENs must bear in mind that hypothermia protects the brain and vital physiological processes that would ordinarily fall victim to anoxia associated with circulatory arrest. If a hypothermic victim is cold and stiff, resuscitation should still be attempted, because successful recoveries have been reported 2 or 3 hours after clinical death in such cases. Some authorities have advocated that no hypothermic patient be declared dead until rewarming has taken place and resuscitation been attempted with the "warm" body. Because the core body temperature is the key to most parameters in management, it is imperative that EDs have a "low-scale" rectal or esophageal thermometer to monitor resuscitation attempts in the hypothermic victim.

Emergency Management. When the hypothermic victim is received in the ED, the ABCs (airway, breathing, circulation, cervical spine) of basic life support should receive attention first. Peripheral pulses may not be palpable because of intense vasoconstriction. It should be recalled that pulse rate and respirations slow in relation to the degree of hypothermia, so the pulse may be only 40 to 50 beats per minute (bpm) and the respiration rate below 10 breaths per minute at core temperatures of 28° to 30°C. Oxygen should be given to restore the partial pressure of oxygen in the arteries (PaO_2) to normal without inducing hyperventilation. A sudden lowering of the partial pressure of carbon dioxide in the arteries ($PaCO_2$) and changes in pH increase the likelihood of ventricular fibrillation. All essential care must be provided with as little manipulation of the patient as possible, because *even routine handling* can precipitate ventricular fibrillation. Conservative approaches are in order because airway maneuvers, for example, can induce an arrest state. Obviously, however, if such measures are required for resuscitation, they should be promptly executed by a technically competent member of the team to minimize iatrogenic risks. In the meantime, all wet clothing should be removed, warm and dry linens should be provided, and two intravenous lines should be established. Venous blood samples should be drawn for CBC, BUN, serum amylase, electrolytes, blood sugar, and coagulation studies. ABG samples are also very desirable; pH levels should be corrected to the patient's temperature by adding 0.015 pH units for each 1°C drop in body temperature below normal. The victim should promptly be placed on a cardiac monitor to observe for conduction disturbances. Below 30°C, sinus bradycardia, atrial fibrillation, and nodal rhythms are most common. These rhythms do not require any treatment except rewarming. Asystole will probably have occurred if the core temperature has fallen below 21.1° to 23.8°C (70° to 75°F). Prolonged P-R, Q-T, and QRS intervals, along with T wave inversion, are also commonly associated with hypothermia. The most classically described ECG patterns, however, involve the appearance of peculiar J waves (or Osborne waves) that are characterized by a positive deflection of the terminal 0.04-second period of the QRS complex[4] (Fig. 32–4). When the core temperature approximates 26.5° to 27.1°C (88° to 90°F), ventricular fibrillation is common. Great care should be taken in attempts to defibrillate, because rewarming usually involves multiple basins of warm water. Rubber boots and a battery-powered defibrillator are ideal adjuncts in these circumstances.

Active rewarming through both core and external approaches must be attempted as soon as the patient's basic life support has been assured. Rewarming must be judiciously managed to ensure that the core temperature increases along with the external temperature to avoid ventricular fibrillation complications. If the periphery is rewarmed rapidly, the demand for oxygen will be initially high and the hypothermic heart will be unable to keep pace with the high demands by merely increasing cardiac output. Myocardial hypoxia and acidosis can quickly compromise resuscitation in this instance. Recommendations for rewarming include a variety of traditional and novel measures. A thermal blanket or a radiant warming hood may be used initially to increase the body temperature on a gradual basis by 1 or 2 degrees hourly. The desired setting is 29.5° to 30.1°C (98° to 100°F). Immersion baths of 31.3°C (104°F) are also useful if vital processes are relatively stable and if the effects of vasodilation (i.e., reduction in central circulatory volume) will not compromise the patient. Core rewarming techniques may include warmed intravenous fluids, warm lavages (e.g., peritoneal, thoracic, rectal, mediastinal), dialysis, cardiopulmonary bypass, and respiratory therapy with warm, humidified air.

Monitoring parameters should include laboratory values (ABGs, electrolytes, blood sugar, BUN, hematocrit [Hct] clotting studies), intake and output, CVP, neurological status, ECG, BP, and, of course, core temperature. (The risk of arrhythmia induction with the introduction of the Swan–Ganz catheter is thought to outweigh the potential benefits.) Pharmacological agents have limited value at this point in management and should be avoided because they do not seem to be

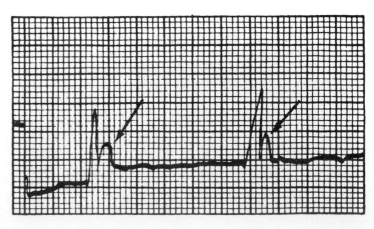

Figure 32–4. Characteristic J or Osborne wave of hypothermia.

effective. It is thought that detoxification and conjugation functions of the liver are depressed; thus, drugs merely accumulate until the body is sufficiently rewarmed and these processes recur normally. Pressor agents, antibiotics, and steroids are not recommended by most authorities during this initial treatment period, and fluid resuscitation must be judiciously but aggressively pursued to compensate for extravascular losses and the effects of peripheral vasodilation.[4] (Table 32–2).

The objective of gradual rewarming must constantly be in front of the therapeutic team in order to prevent overly aggressive, rapid external rewarming that exceeds core rewarming, thus predisposing the patient to ventricular fibrillation and cardiac arrest. Restraint during rewarming must be every team member's responsibility because haste in this critical period can result in the death of a potentially salvageable patient.

■ DECOMPRESSION SICKNESS AND DIVING-RELATED EMERGENCIES

Several emergencies are related to environmental influences of altitude and pressure, encountered primarily by divers. Among the physiological problems that occur when an individual descends under water (increasing pressure on the body) is that the gas volume in the lungs decreases. On ascent, however, the volume increases. This physical occurrence reflects Boyle's law: at a constant temperature, the volume of a gas is inversely proportional to the pressure. Obviously, diving problems are related to descent and ascent in water. On descent, the body is exposed to a greater atmospheric pressure than normal, and air cavities in the body (sinuses, the middle ear, and lungs) cannot adapt to that increasing pressure, particularly if any air passages are blocked. Experienced divers learn to avert serious problems, such as a ruptured tympanic membrane, by systematically descending and allowing air cavity pressures to equilibrate with the surrounding pressures gradually. The Valsalva maneuver is used to help equalize pressures. On ascent, the volume of gas in the lungs increases and additional hazards are created. Serious diving problems relate to failures of physiological adaptation and include decompression sickness, nitrogen narcosis, and air embolism.

DECOMPRESSION SICKNESS

When a diver has been at a particular depth long enough for nitrogen to be dissolved in the blood, a condition called dysbarism (or merely decompression sickness) develops. Nitrogen cannot be absorbed quickly enough when ascent occurs, and it

TABLE 32–2. SIGNS AND SYMPTOMS OF HYPOTHERMIA

Stage	Core Temperature	Signs/Symptoms
Mild	37°–35°C (98.6°–95°F)	Initial pulse and respiration; increase in BP, fatigue, sensation of coldness; shivering (may be delayed or absent)
Moderate	35°–32°C (95°–90°F)	Decrease in BP, pulse and respirations; difficult speech, loss of hand control; memory lapse, mood changes, combative; may have violent shivering
Marked (harsh movement of the patient at this stage may cause ventricular fibrillation)	32°–28°C (90°–82°F)	BP and pulse may be imperceptible, respirations hard to detect; pupils dilated, amnesia, shivering decreased to constant muscle tension or rigidity; heart irregularities, tachycardia, or bradycardia may exist; acetone odor to breath; characteristic J or Osborne wave of hypothermia starts to appear on ECG (see Fig. 32–4)
Severe	28°–25°C (82°–77°F)	Irrationality proceeding to unconsciousness; muscle rigidity similar to rigor mortis; skin may be edematous and cyanotic; loss of reflexes; pulmonary edema may develop; J or Osborne wave becomes more prominent; bradycardia leading to ventricular fibrillation likely
Profound	25°C (77°F) or below	Cardiopulmonary arrest; death

BP, blood pressure; ECG, electrocardiogram.

accumulates in small blood vessels, producing obstruction. Experienced divers follow a planned, gradual ascent pattern in which they pause at certain levels to permit the reabsorption of nitrogen. Diving tables are available that describe the rate of ascent and the number and length of pauses at various levels, based on the time spent at a given depth. Following these guidelines, divers seldom experience problems.

Signs and symptoms of decompression sickness may not occur until several hours after the dive. They include rash, pain in the joints, generalized weakness or fatigue, visual disturbances, shortness of breath, and dizziness. In several cases, paralysis, seizures, and unconsciousness have been noted.[4]

The treatment for victims of decompression sickness is recompression; hyperbaric chambers are used to create an external high pressure that simulates underwater pressure at depth. Nitrogen bubbles are reduced, forcing them back into body tissue. In the interval prior to hyperbaric intervention, ENs should place the victim in the left lateral Trendelenburg position to minimize the threat of air embolism and administer oxygen at 10L/min per mask.

NITROGEN NARCOSIS

Air contains oxygen, nitrogen, and carbon dioxide. About 80 percent of the air normally inhaled is nitrogen. In people remaining at depths, the increased external pressure dissolves the nitrogen gas in the nervous tissue and thus decreases tissue excitability. The effect produced is similar to alcohol intoxication and has been called the "rapture of the depths." Characteristically, exposure is required for 1 hour or more before dissolving nitrogen gas causes nitrogen narcosis. The treatment for nitrogen narcosis is performed on the scene in most cases: the victim merely ascends to shallow water.

AIR EMBOLISM

Air embolism can occur on ascent because of the expansion of air in the lungs. A spontaneous pneumothorax or pneumomediastinum can ensue. The expanding pressure in the alveoli forces air from the alveoli into the capillaries, thus permitting an embolus to travel to the heart, brain, or spinal cord or to block circulating blood to those areas. In some severe cases, air bubbles may accumulate in the heart, creating fatal dysrhythmias.

The prevention of air embolism requires that divers exhale during ascent to equalize and decrease the intrapulmonic pressure. Breath-holding during ascent is theorized to be the cause of fatal air embolism among divers. Any rapid ascent due to panic, disorientation, lack of air, or malfunction of support equipment, however, can contribute to this catastrophe. If an individual presents to the ED after a diving incident with any of the following signs and symptoms, air embolism should be suspected: chest pain or tightness in the chest with shortness of breath, blotching or itching of the skin, frothy pink sputum, nausea and vomiting, dizziness, seizures, speaking disorders, paralysis, and unconsciousness. This condition necessitates immediate recompression in a hyperbaric pressure chamber. Prior to chamber therapy, the victim should be maintained at rest in a left lateral Trendelenburg position, with 100 percent oxygen being administered. The cardiac status should be monitored and a chest x-ray should be obtained. Preparation for major resuscitation should be done proactively in all diving-related emergencies, and ENs should be ready to cope with catastrophe until the individual is fully stabilized postrecompression.

■ ALTITUDE-RELATED ILLNESS

The problem of altitude-related illness becomes apparent when nonacclimated persons are exposed to attitudes of 2,000 m (7,200 ft) or more. At this level, physiological adaptation is required by several body systems, a process that usually takes up to 2 or 3 days. In the meantime, because of the reduced P_{O_2}, hypoxemia and alkalosis occur.

During the initial physiological stress at high altitudes in a nonacclimated individual, the heart rate increases but the cardiac output remains unchanged. The net result, of course, is a decreased ability by the body's muscles to perform work. (It is estimated that people have only about 75 percent efficiency at such altitudes.) Respirations increase because of chemoreceptors in normal individuals, but such compensatory responses are not possible in patients with chronic obstructive pulmonary disease (COPD) who have already maximized their adaptation; thus, they experience an even more severe oxygen deprivation. The RBC mass increases gradually to increase its oxygen-carrying power, and this phenomenon, coupled with increased breathing, facilitates satisfactory adjustment to the reduced PO_2. However, because of the fact that a respiratory alkalemia and a reduced stroke volume occur as well, illness may result before the body experiences the spontaneous bicarbonate diuresis that occurs 24 to 36 hours after altitude stress has been realized.

Signs and symptoms of altitude illness include lethargy, headache, nausea, and difficulty sleeping. Although insomnia can be annoying, sedatives should never be taken during altitude stress, because they can induce catastrophic respiratory depression and life-threatening hypoxemia. Acetazolamide (Diamox) is useful, however, because it increases the excretion of bicarbonate by the kidneys. It must be used with caution because it can lead to systemic dehydration when other stressors, such as overexercise or heat, are present.

Acute "mountain sickness" can produce serious problems for some individuals who fail to adapt. The onset of retinal hemorrhages, cerebral edema, or coma signal that the individual requires immediate emergency care at a lower altitude. Oxygen should be given as soon as it is available and electrolyte imbalances corrected as indicated by blood gas studies and other clinical observations.

HIGH-ALTITUDE PULMONARY EDEMA

High-altitude pulmonary edema (HAPE) is a serious altitude related problem that presents in a manner similar to that of other cases of pulmonary edema. The signs and symptoms include increased respirations and shortness of breath; a cough producing pink, frothy sputum; lethargy; nausea and vomiting; cyanosis; and rales. A slight temperature elevation may be present that may confuse the presentation with that of a minor infection. HAPE is a noncardiogenic form of pulmonary edema that occurs in otherwise healthy individuals who rapidly ascend to altitudes above 10,000 ft without acclimatization. It is aggravated, of course, by concurrent strenuous activity, such as skiing. Individuals who live at high altitude, descend, and stay for a while may incur HAPE on reascent. It is also

known that recurrence is common in susceptible persons. Most victims who develop HAPE do so within 2 to 3 days after rapid ascent.[5] The condition must be promptly recognized and treated aggressively.

Early symptoms include a nonproductive cough, limitation of physical activity, dyspnea, and fatigue. As the edema progresses, ataxia, confusion, lethargy, and extreme air hunger are prominent indices. Cyanosis and confusion rapidly ensue. The pulmonic component of the second heart sound may be accentuated as a result of the elevated pulmonary artery pressure. The chest x-ray film reveals fluffy patches of infiltrates throughout the lung fields.

The pathophysiology of the condition is complex. In some individuals, hypoxia provokes a hyperreactive pulmonary vascular response (vasoconstriction) with associated pulmonary hypertension. The response is not uniform throughout the lung fields, so some regions of the lung are hypoperfused and others are hyperperfused. Blood flow velocity increases the shear stress on the endothelial lining of the hyperperfused regions of the lung, inducing endothelial injury and increased permeability. Excessive demands for cardiac output for increased workloads (i.e., exercise), of course, adds the final insult. An atrial natriuretic factor (ANF) may also be associated with the development of HAPE.[5]

Emergency care should include oxygen administration and immediate evacuation to a low altitude. A chest x-ray is indicated, too, to ensure that the presumptive diagnosis is correct. Bed rest alone may be therapy enough for high-altitude natives who are returning to their domiciles or adapting to sea-level environments. Morphine and other drugs commonly associated with pulmonary edema are not indicated, because they would adversely affect respiratory activity and interfere with physiological readaptation.

HIGH-ALTITUDE CEREBRAL EDEMA

The encephalopathy of high-altitude cerebral edema (HACE) is precipitated by factors similar to those causing HAPE. Higher mental functions are impaired and the individual has an unsteady gait and posture. Collapse and coma may occur in the most severe cases. Most patients, however, have constant, severe headaches that require narcotics for relief. Hallucinations, confusion, and psychotic behavior may accompany this state. If the patient is not evacuated to a lower altitude promptly, symptoms progress into unconsciousness and death. Clues to the condition are provided by the medical history; papilledema and retinal hemorrhages may be found on examination.[6] HAPE may coexist and should be suspected if there is tachycardia, tachypnea, and central cyanosis. The treatment is similar to that for HAPE: evacuation to a lower altitude administration of high-flow oxygen, and conservative use of steroids and other drugs.

■ LIGHTNING INJURIES

Lightning-related injuries often induce unresponsiveness and cardiac arrest. Cardiopulmonary resuscitation (CPR) should be started immediately when such victims are discovered, of course, regardless of the time that has elapsed since the injury. Successful resuscitations have occurred when CPR has been delayed far longer than the 4- to 6-minute "brain death" period, perhaps because of the fact that when an electrical force passes through the body, all cell metabolism is halted. A longer period of time than usual is required for cell degradation to occur in these injuries.

The individual struck by lightning usually becomes unconscious or has an altered state of consciousness that ranges from being "stunned," with retrograde amnesia, to coma. Motor paralysis and hyporeflexia that correspond to spinal cord levels often accompany the accident. Paralysis of the respiratory center is thought to be the cause of death in many cases, perhaps closely linked to the phenomenon of ventricular fibrillation. For individuals who are somewhat responsive after a lightning strike, deafness and loss of speech are common. The cardiovascular system is compromised by massive vasomotor spasm that causes loss of peripheral pulses, loss of sensation and color in the extremities, and the sequelae of peripheral arterial thrombosis, which may require fasciotomy or even amputation.

Other signs and symptoms related to lightning injury include hysteria and personality changes, deafness, cataracts, optic atrophy, retinal detachment, hyphema, vitreous hemorrhage, and other eye injuries. In addition to the usual resusci-

tation efforts, assessment for electrical burns, which often accompany lightning injuries, is important. The featherlike lightning imprint may be the real key to recognizing the lightning injury in the comatose patient. This imprinting is a linear, spidery, arborescent, and erythematous skin discoloration that relates to the pathways of decreased skin resistance. Pay careful attention to obscure areas for exit wounds, such as the bottom of the feet and the anus.

Emergency care should encompass the following considerations: providing a patent airway (intubation if the patient is apneic) and ensuring that oxygen is administered at 4 to 6 L/min, monitoring for ventricular fibrillation (one of the most common complications), and attaining an intravenous access route for drugs. Other care, of course, involves management of the electrical burn wound that characteristically is associated with lightning injuries.

Myoglobinuria often occurs after lightning injuries, so renal perfusion must be closely scrutinized. Urinary output must be assessed with great care, and vigorous fluid resuscitation should be undertaken to ensure a satisfactory urinary output of at least 50 mL/h. Osmotic diuretics, such as mannitol, may be useful to accelerate renal blood flow. A CVP or pulmonary artery catheter is advisable as an adjunct to monitor circulatory status. α- and β-adrenergic drugs may be indicated to support adequate renal perfusion. Because lightning injury causes cerebral edema, the usual approaches for managing this condition are indicated.

Tetanus toxoid, 0.5 mL, and hypertetanus immune globulin, 250 units, should be administered to lightning victims, but steroids and antibiotics should not be given without specific indications.

Other aspects of caring for the victim of lightning injury follow the usual protocols for resuscitation of the accident victim. Unlike patients with high-voltage injuries, those injured by lightning do not require fluid loading unless shock due to other injuries exists.

■ BOTANICAL POISONINGS

Quite a few plants, trees, and shrubs can cause skin irritations and multifaceted systemic poisoning. Among common ones are the philodendron, jade plant, Swedish ivy, poinsettia, African violet, yew, nightshade, pokeweed, spider plant, schefflera, wandering Jew, and rubber tree. Symptomatic plant ingestions arise from chickory, jimsonweed, dieffenbachia, many kinds of wild berries, chili peppers, caladium, and many types of leaves or stems. More than half of all plant ingestions involve the above-mentioned items. Fewer than 3 percent of the plant ingestions cause symptoms, and in over 1500 cases studied, only 1 child required admission.[6]

Although the problem of botanical poisoning seems insignificant, it poses several problems in the ED, especially if the plant, tree, or shrub involved is unknown. Use of the *Poisindex* or other suitable reference is essential, as is contacting a Poison Control Center for information and treatment directives (see pages 495–496). One important role of the EN is reassuring frightened parents of children who have ingested poisonous plants while sufficient data is being gathered to guide management decisions.

■ BITES, STINGS, AND IRRITATIONS FROM ARTHROPODS

There is no place in North America where human beings are totally free from the toxic or irritating effects of arthropods (invertebrate animals such as insects, spiders, and crustaceans). Although rare, some arthropods pose a serious threat to life, mainly because of the allergic response caused by their venom or saliva. Other arthropods have irritating or annoying effects on people but do not present a great medical concern (Table 32–3). Most arthropods are active from May through October; therefore, more bites and stings are expected in these months. However, some arthropods are active year-round. As a general rule, most venomous and irritating arthropods are prevalent in the southern half of the United States. This is because of the more mild environmental conditions and benign winters. Arthropods that harm or irritate humans do so by either biting or stinging, or both. Generally, a bite is an offensive maneuver used to obtain food: the bite is intended to kill or anesthetize a victim intended to be meal. A sting is used by certain arthropods as a defensive maneu-

ver and is not intended to kill its victim. Therefore, the lethal mixture of venom in certain snakes and spiders contributes to the more severe medical problems encountered because of bites from these creatures. Although the stings of such creatures as bees, wasps, and hornets contain less potent venom, they still represent a potential medical concern because of allergic reactions to the protein fraction of the venom that can occur. Signs, symptoms, and treatment of arthropod injuries are found in Table 32–3.

STINGS

The Hymenoptera: Bees, Wasps, Yellow Jackets, Hornets, and Ants

Stings from insects of the order Hymenoptera cause twice as many deaths as do rattlesnake bites. This is primarily due to the allergic response the victim has to the injected venom. These insects sting their victims as a defensive maneuver. A sting is caused by the anatomic injection of a stinger into the flesh of a victim; stingers differ in form and location from one insect species to another. Bees, wasps, yellow jackets, hornets, and fire ants have stingers that connect with a venom gland, located in the terminal portion of their abdomen. Stings can be given only by the female of each species; the stinger is a modification of the egg-depositing organ.

About 50 percent of the deaths that occur from stings by members of this group of insects are attributed to the honey bee. Most of these deaths occur within the first hour after the sting. The honey bee's stinger, unlike that of other stinging insects in this group, is barbed, so once it is injected into the flesh of its victim, it becomes anchored. Therefore, if an attempt is made by the insect to fly or crawl away or if it is brushed off, it loses a portion of the posterior abdominal contents, including the venom sac that connects it to the stinger. Because of this trauma, the bee subsequently dies. If the patient has a honey-bee stinger still attached, it should be scraped, rather than extracted, from the victim. Grasping the stinger with a forceps or other extraction device will force more venom into the wound of the patient.

The remaining groups of insects (wasps, yellow jackets, hornets, and ants) do not have barbed stingers; therefore, they have the ability to sting

TABLE 32–3. SIGNS, SYMPTOMS AND TREATMENT OF ARTHROPOD INJURY

Mechanism of Injury	Arthropod	Signs/Symptoms	Treatment	Complications
Stings	Honeybee Bumblebee Wasps Hornets Yellow jackets Ants	Local reaction Pain at sting site, Redness, swelling, itching. General reaction Hives, abdominal pain, nausea, vomiting, anxiety. Constriction feeling in chest, wheezing. Shock Reaction Any of the above, plus cyanosis; hypotension; incontinence; asthma; bloody, frothy sputum; glottal or laryngeal edema; unconsciousness.	Stinger of honeybee should be scraped away. DO NOT PULL OFF. Apply antiseptic solution to sting site. Apply coolant (ice bag or chemical cold pack) to sting site. Elevate part. Keep patient warm. Put patient in shock position if necessary.	The more rapid the onset of symptoms, the more severe the reaction is likely to be. Stings of the head, face, and neck tend to cause more serious effects. Anaphylaxis. Secondary infection.
Stings	Scorpions	Initial pain at sting site, followed by numbness. Muscle spasms, nausea, vomiting, incontinence, hypersalivation. Respiratory and circulatory depression. Scorpion stings produce little or no swelling or discoloration of local tissue.	Apply lymphatic/venous tourniquet above the sting site. Apply local coolant. Keep patient warm. Put patient in shock position if necessary. A specific antivenin exists for scorpion envenomation.	Secondary infection.
Bite	Black widow spider	Pinprick feeling at bite site, followed by numbing. Pain within fifteen minutes. A bite on the lower extremity can produce severe abdominal muscle cramping becoming rigid and tender. A bite on the hand or arm produces intense back, chest and shoulder pain, and pain on inspiration. Systemic symptoms may include: hypersalivation, nausea, vomiting, weakness, increased blood pressure.	Apply antiseptic solution to bite area. Apply ice locally A specific antivenin exists for the black widow.	Death may occur in children and elderly patients. Secondary infection.
Bite	Brown recluse spider	Bite may or may not be felt. 1–3 hours: Bitten area becomes painful and swollen. Blisters form around bite site. 18–24 hours: Bite site turns cyanotic and purple.	Apply antiseptic solution to bite area. DO NOT USE ICE on bite area since the cold will constrict the already compromised blood vessels and increase the tissue necrosis.	Nonhealing wound. Secondary infection.

TABLE 32–3. SIGNS, SYMPTOMS AND TREATMENT OF ARTHROPOD INJURY (Continued)

Mechanism of Injury	Arthropod	Signs/Symptoms	Treatment	Complications
		2–7 days: Tissue cells die and skin area turns black. 2–4 weeks: Blackened dead cells fall off leaving an ulcerated pit in the skin. Ulcerated pit fills with scar tissue.	The spider should be salvaged for positive identification. Ulceration may be avoided by surgical tissue excision at the hospital if done within four hours after bite.	
Bite	Centipede	Intense pain at bite site. Two red puncture wounds from bite. Redness, some swelling. Burning ache for four to five hours.	Wash area with soap and water or antiseptic solution. Apply ammonia in 10 percent solution. Apply cool wet dressing for pain.	Secondary infection. Allergic response to toxin.
Biting/ sucking	Conenose bug	Mild to no pain at bite sites. There are several reactions, depending on sensitivity: 1. Papule with a central redspot. 2. Small vesicles grouped around bite site with swelling and little redness. 3. Urticaric lesions with central redspots and edema. 4. Hemorrhagic nodules to blistering lesions on hands and feet.	Wash area with soap and water or antiseptic solution.	Anaphylatic shock. Secondary infection.
Biting/ sucking	Wheel bug	Intense pain at bite site, subsides within three to six hours.	Wash area with soap and water or antiseptic solution.	Anaphylactic shock. Secondary infection.
Biting/ sucking	Black flies Sand flies Deer flies Buffalo gnats Biting midges	Except for the black fly, there is intense pain at the bite site. It is thought that the black fly uses an anesthetic during the bite. Since it is not felt, the first thing noticed is a drop of blood on the skin. Within one hour, intense pain, itching and local swelling.	Wash area with soap and water or antiseptic solution. Oral antihistamines may be indicated. The use of active insect repellent such as "Deet" (Diethyltoluamide) keeps the insects at a distance.	Death has been reported from anaphylaxis. Secondary infection.
Blistering	Blister beetle	Pain at site where insect released clear amber fluid (Cantharidin). Blistering of skin.	Wash area with soap and water or antiseptic. Do not rupture blisters. Self-limiting.	Secondary infection.
Nettling	Caterpillars Puss Saddle back Io	Burning pain at nettling site, may be followed by numbing sensation. A double row of spine tracks may be seen with the saddle back or Io. Systemic reaction may include: nausea, vomiting, fever, and headache.	With cellophane or adhesive tape, strip away the spines on the skin surface. Keep affected limb away from the eyes. Apply ice packs to the area.	Anaphylaxis has been reported. Irritation of the eyes from spines.

their victims repeatedly, injecting more venom into the wound. These insects tend to swarm their victims, especially when their nesting quarters are disturbed. Some species are quite aggressive. Each species has its own distinct toxin, although there are some similarities. The venom of Hymenoptera contains a complex mixture of enzymes and nonenzymatic proteins that interact with human body tissues, causing local to severe reactions. Certain body chemicals (e.g., histamine, kinin) are released in response to the foreign protein in venom, and if the victim is hypersensitive to the venom, an anaphylactic reaction could occur (see Chapter 25).

Female ants have a stinger at the posterior tip of the abdomen. Species that can be quite dangerous in the United States include the fire ants *(Solenopsis)* and harvester ants *(Pogonomyrmex).* Both species can be easily identified by the mounds they build. Fire ants build their mound high (3 to 36 in.), leaving vegetation undisturbed around their home. Harvester ants build rather flat or slightly elevated mounds and usually destroy all vegetation in the vicinity of their homes (2 to 10 feet in diameter). Harvester ants, two to three times larger than fire ants, are predominately found in the southern half of the United States. They attack in mass when their mounds are disturbed. These insects can sting repeatedly and can bite as well. Thousands of these ants can attack within minutes. Infants and small children are especially vulnerable to envenomation from fire ants. Sometimes small infants are placed on a blanket in grass where mounds may be unnoticed and they are stung repeatedly by hundreds of ants. Children who are playing on sand or on the lawn may also unwittingly disturb a fire-ant mound and may be stung repeatedly by the ants, which readily cling to clothing and skin.

Scorpion Stings

Scorpions are relatives of spiders and all are poisonous, some species more so than others. There are approximately 40 species of scorpions in the United States. Of these, only one is known to possess lethal venom—the sculptured scorpion *(Centruroides sculpturatus).* This deadly species is localized in Arizona and its neighboring states. Stings from scorpions are a problem of considerable medical importance in Arizona because scorpions kill more people than do poisonous snakes. In scorpions, the stinger, or telson, is located at the terminal portion of the tail. Scorpions are nocturnal creatures and hide by day under rocks, leaves, lumber, and other similar places when outdoors. Favorite haunts when indoors include closets, shoes, stored newspapers, and cluttered areas. Children are stung more often than adults, which probably accounts for the high mortality rate. Most stings occur on the hands or feet of the victim.

The venom of the sculptured scorpion is principally neurotoxic, meaning there is minimal local tissue reaction when stung. Death may occur because of respiratory and circulatory collapse.

BITES

A bite from an arthropod is caused by viselike jaws (as in the species *Chelicera*) or a beak that pierces the flesh of a victim. Bites from different species of arthropods affect each person differently, and the signs and symptoms caused by different species' toxins or saliva varies considerably, based on the location of the bite, the immune response of the victim, the toxic chemical composition in the injected saliva, and any associated bacterial infection induced by retention of the bits and pieces of the animals' mouth parts in the wound. Arthropods in this category that bite or pierce the skin of their victims include ticks, spiders, centipedes, true bugs, mites, and flies.

Ticks

Ticks are eight-legged creatures that can be found almost anywhere on earth, primarily along pathways in the woods and on uncleared land. They feed entirely on blood, usually of animals but sometimes of humans. Once on the body (usually the head, neck, or groin) they attach by burrowing their heads into the skin of the victim (host) to feed on blood. With their barbed piercing organs, they take a firm grip on the skin and extract blood for up to several days before they are satiated. Ticks are quite flat when not engorged with blood, and they may be unnoticed when they crawl onto the skin to embed themselves, usually on hairy areas or within skin folds. While most tick bites are not painful and the victim may not even be aware of the presence of ticks, the wounds caused by the bites of some species are severe. The wood tick

(Dermacentor andersoni) is responsible for tick paralysis, which is due to the neurotoxin introduced into the victim while the tick is feeding. The victim of tick paralysis becomes very irritable, does not eat, and generally feels sick. Intermittent bouts of pain begin in the lower extremities, followed by ascending flaccid paralysis. If the paralysis extends into the respiratory system, the patient may die from respiratory failure. If the offending tick is found and removed, the symptoms will disappear.

Ticks also carry spotted fever, tularemia, relapsing fever, and Lyme disease. In areas infested with ticks, it is unwise to sleep or sit on the ground; clothing should be examined carefully at least once a day and ticks should be destroyed. When children play outdoors in wooded places, they should be inspected twice a day, and any ticks that have attached themselves should be removed carefully. If the tick is swollen from feeding, special care should be taken not to crush it so that the skin is not smeared. A slow, steady pull with tweezers will usually make the tick release his grip. Because the tick has breathing apparatus on both sides of its body, a dab of petroleum jelly or fingernail polish will cause it to withdraw the mouth parts in a few minutes; removal is easily accomplished within about 10 minutes. After the tick is removed, the offender may be placed in a container for identification by an entomologist. The wound should be thoroughly cleaned with an antiseptic solution.

Tick-Borne Diseases

Rocky Mountain Spotted Fever.
Rocky Mountain spotted fever is caused by *Rickettsia rickettsii,* an intracellular parasite of ticks, rodents, and perhaps some mammals. It is the most common form of tick-borne illness. The onset of the illness occurs from 5 to 7 days after infection. Fever, edema, and rash are the three common indices of this condition. The rash begins on the hands, palms, ankles, and soles of the feet. At first, it has a fine macular appearance, but later it deepens in color and becomes maculopapular, creating petechiae as the rickettsia multiply. Purpura and vascular collapse occur when the endothelium of vessels is sufficiently destroyed.[6] Most patients present with headache, lethargy, myalgias, a stiff neck, photophobia, and arthralgias that mimic meningitis. The edema may be the most useful sign to suggest Rocky Mountain spotted fever and to differentiate it from other conditions. Organ failure (renal, pulmonary, and GI) may be seen in rare cases. Laboratory serological tests do not provide meaningful data for 2 to 3 weeks, so the diagnosis is usually based on the patient's history and the triad of fever, edema, and rash. The antibiotic therapy is tetracyclines, including doxycycline, or chloramphenicol.

Lyme Disease.
Lyme disease is a tick-borne disease carried by such vectors as field mice and deer. Typically, the victim does not recall the tick bite, but several days to several weeks later, symptoms of spirochetemia, with lymphadenopathy and annular lesions, develop. The exact roles of the spirochete, its antigens, and the host immune responses are unknown, although it is thought that persistent live spirochetes are responsible for the many later manifestations of the disease. There is a variable response to antibiotics at each stage of the illness and an expansion of the antibody response to additional spirochetal antigens over subsequent months or years. This supports the belief that live spirochetes persist indefinitely within body fluid and tissues (liver, spleen, brain, eye, synovium, and myocardium).[3] Lyme disease shares features of syphilis, yaws, leptospirosis, and relapsing fever in that subsequent stages of the infection may become manifest after extended periods of latency. The incubation period may be days or weeks.

The initial signs and symptoms include erythema chronicum migrans (ECM), a rash that starts as a small bump and later develops into an area of redness with a bright red outer border resembling a bull's-eye, expanding to a diameter of 6 to 52 cm. During this spreading, the central area of the lesion clears, but the border remains bright red. ECM lasts up to 3 weeks.[3] In a few cases, the early lesions may become indurated or vesicular and necrotic. The rash results from the spirochetes' migration outward in the skin. At this point, lymphadenopathy is also noted, along with secondary organ involvement; the victim may complain of lethargy, malaise, and fatigue. Stiff neck, arthralgia, myalgias, backache, anorexia, sore throat, nausea, vomiting, and headache are among other symptoms. The organisms may be recovered from blood, cerebrospinal fluid (CSF), synovial fluid, and skin lesions early and for many years after the initial infection. A symptom-free period is typical between stages 1 and 2. Between 4 and 10 weeks after the EMC, neurological, cardiac, and ophthalmic involvement may also occur.

Lyme disease is a multisystem infection which evolves in three distinct stages. In stage 1, the rash is dominant. In stage 2, the most common neurological manifestation of Lyme disease is a fluctuating meningoencephalitis with superimposed symptoms of cranial neuropathy, peripheral neuropathy, or radiculopathy. Concurrent meningitis, cranial neuropathies (usually Bell's palsy), and radiculopathy have been described, but each may occur alone. Headache of varying intensity is present. Cardiac abnormalities in stage 2 range from 4 to 8 percent. The average time from onset of the initial illness to the onset of carditis is 5 weeks. Palpitations, lightheadedness, dyspnea, chest pain, and syncope occur as the presenting signs. Atrioventricular block, left ventricular dysfunction, and myopericarditis are common, with complete or high-grade block occurring in many cases. The inflammatory resolution is similar to an inferior-wall myocardial infarction (MI). Murmurs of mild mitral regurgitation, pericardial friction rub, or congestive heart failure (CHF) may be evident. ECG and radionuclide studies are used in diagnosis. Myocardial biopsies may also be required. Acute conjunctivitis, keratitis, choroiditis, retinal detachment, optic neuritis, and blindness may be noted either in stage 2 or 3. In the chronic stage of Lyme disease, arthritic and neurological manifestations prevail. Fatigue syndromes are common.

Antibiotic therapy is essential from the onset of Lyme disease. Doxycycline, 100 mg twice daily (or tetracycline, 25 to 50 mg/kg per day in four divided doses) for 10 days is the treatment of choice. Alternative therapies include amoxicillin and probenecid, erythromycin, and ceftriaxone (Rocephin).

Spiders

Almost all spiders are poisonous, but most are too small to harm man. Spiders have fangs associated with a gland, connected to their jaws. Like most biting arthropods, spiders use their fangs to inject venom into their prey in an attempt to anesthetize it so they can easily feed upon the body. In the United States, only two species of spiders are of considerable medical importance: the black widow (*Lactrodectus mactans*) and the brown recluse (*Loxosceles recluse*). These spiders are venomous and can cause serious bite wounds and envenomation. These spiders are found in every state except Alaska: they are more prevalent, however, in the southeastern portion of the United States. With the black widow spider, as with most venomous arthropods, it is the females that create the greatest medical concern. Although the males have lethal venom, they are one fifth to one third the size of the females and their bite cannot penetrate the thickness of skin. The shiny black female spider is approximately one half in. long and has a characteristic reddish orange hourglass on the underside of her round abdomen. This characteristic marking does have some variations: there could be only a red button or two red dots. The black widow spins her irregularly shaped web near the ground as a general rule. Other times, however, webs can be found in wood piles, loose bark, seldom-used storage areas, barns, water faucets, and outdoor toilets. It is a good practice to clear webs with a stick or with gloved hands whenever they are noticed. The black widow can live as long as 2 years. Humans are often bitten and envenomized when they unknowingly disturb a web or when the spider is trapped against a body part.

The venom of the black widow is neurotoxic; therefore, local tissue reaction will be minimal. If untreated, envenomation will produce muscle spasms, increased BP, nervousness, and possibly cardiopulmonary arrest. Healthy adults usually survive envenomation from the black widow without serious medical complications. However, bites from this spider incurred by children pose a great medical concern because of their size in relation to the amount of injected venom. Elderly patients and patients with underlying cardiac or respiratory illnesses also pose a serious medical concern if bitten by a black widow spider. The patient's past medical history is pertinent, especially if the patient has heart, respiratory, or high BP problems. Fortunately, a specific antivenin for the black widow spider bite is available.

Brown Recluse Spider (Brown Spider, Violin Spider). The brown recluse is most commonly found in Arkansas, Kansas, Missouri, and Oklahoma. Its range, however, extends into several states, including Alabama, Georgia, Illinois, Indiana, Iowa, Kentucky, Louisiana, Ohio, Mississippi, Tennessee, and Texas. Several localized populations of the brown recluse, probably imported from the south central states, have been reported from Arizona, California, Wyoming, Pennsylvania, New Jersey, North Carolina, Florida, and Washington, DC.

The brown recluse is about 1 in. long, including leg span, its color varies from yellow-tan to dark brown. Characteristics that make this spider easy to identify are its three pairs of eyes (most spiders have eight eyes) and a violin-shaped marking that extends from the area of the eyes to the abdomen. Both the male and female are dangerous. This spider is mostly nocturnal and seeks its prey in darkness. It can be found indoors, where it rests by day in closets, boxes, littered areas, and other dry, undisturbed places. Outdoors, it can be found under rocks, loose bark, and other undisturbed protected areas (hence the name *recluse*). This harmless-looking spider is nonaggressive and will seek shelter when disturbed. The victim is usually bitten in one of several ways: putting on clothing in which the spider is hiding, stepping on the wandering spider at night, rolling over in bed onto the spider, or encountering it while cleaning closets or other storage areas where the spider has its web.

The venom of the brown recluse is cytotoxic and, in some patients, hemotoxic, causing hemolysis of RBCs. This serious complication of envenomation is indicated by the appearance of myoglobin in the urine (see Chapter 19). Although people are rarely bitten by brown recluse spiders, such bites can produce large areas of tissue scarring and even death. Unfortunately, there is no specific antivenin for the brown recluse spider's bite.

Centipedes. Centipedes are multisegmented arthropods ranging in size from 1 to 10 in. or more. There is one pair of legs on each segment; different species have between 15 and 100 or more pairs of legs. Although centipedes are located throughout the United States, they are most numerous in the southern states. All centipedes are poisonous, but most are too small to harm humans. However, if even the smallest centipede succeeds in biting, it can cause intense pain. Centipedes inject their venom through two powerful jaws lo-

cated behind their head. A centipede very common in Arizona, *Scolopendra heros,* is very large and can inflict an extremely painful bite. Most centipedes cannot inject venom through their segmented legs. Most centipede bites occur when the creatures are picked up, stepped on, rolled over on, or otherwise trapped against the body.

True Bugs

Almost anything that crawls or flies is considered a bug by most people. As a general rule, insects have six legs, three body segments, a head, thorax and abdomen, and one pair of compound eyes. By contrast, spiders and their relatives have eight legs, eight simple eyes, a cephalothorax (combined head and thorax), and abdomen. Bugs are insects. Ones that cause medical concern include the conenose bug *(Triatoma sanguisuga)* and wheel bug *(Arilus cristatus).* Both insects can produce local tissue reactions or anaphylactic responses in their bitten victims.

Conenose bug (Kissing bug). The conenose bug is generally located in the southern half of the United states. Its size ranges from 0.5 to 1.5 in., and it has orange and black color markings, most noticeable on its abdominal periphery. This family of insects (Reduvudae) has a characteristic cone-shaped head, which helps to identify it, giving it the name *conenose.* This insect has a very flat back, which allows it to hide in small cracks and crevices. It is a nocturnal insect that feeds on blood when seeking its prey at night. Although it usually feeds on small animals, it readily feeds on humans in the absence of smaller prey. It is commonly referred to as a "kissing bug" because it occasionally takes a blood meal from around the lip area of humans. Other common sites of attack include the hands, arms, feet, head, and trunk. It is not known to bite through clothing.

Wheel Bug. The wheel bug occurs in the southern two thirds of the United States. This light-gray insect is about 1 to 2 in. long and has a head similar to that of the conenose bug. The identifying characteristic of this insect is a cogwheel-like crest located on its thorax—hence its name. Wheel bugs feed by day on soft-bodied insects that are found on vegetation and debris. Victims are usually bitten when they either pick up the insect or make accidental contact when working around vegetation. The insect penetrates the skin by using its long beak, or proboscis, and injects its salivary fluid, which is normally used in killing its prey. Its bite can be avoided by keeping a distance from the bug. Wearing gloves when handling vegetation and debris can also reduce the risk of being bitten by this unusual insect.

Biting Flies

Flies can be both a nuisance and a source of bites. The two groups that affect man most in producing extremely irritating bites include the black fly *(Simulium enustum)* and the sand fly *(Psychodidae)*.

Black Flies. Of approximately 80 or more different species known to occur in the United States, black flies that inhabit the northern United States, Canada, and Alaska are far more famous because of their numbers. The term *black fly* is somewhat misleading because color patterns of this insect are gray to tannish yellow. Generally, the females are the blood suckers. The males have piercing mouth parts to suck blood, but these are usually too small to penetrate the skin. Black flies are small, ranging in size from 1 to 5 mm. They have a characteristic humped back with a tiny head that droops. Black flies are outdoor daytime biters and tend to settle down about dusk. They are rarely found indoors. What makes black flies extremely annoying and unbearable is that they occur in enormous swarms. For breeding and development, they are found in areas where there is swift-flowing, well-aerated water. Some species breed continually from early spring to late autumn. Because of the vast number of rivers in Canada, the country is notorious for "black fly seasons." In season, the blackfly is just about inescapable. Their size enables them to maneuver through tent netting and loose clothing. People planning trips where the black fly exists should take head netting that is tightly woven and wear insect repellent on all exposed skin surfaces.

Sand Flies. The sand fly is particularly a nuisance in southwestern United States. As with the black fly, it is the female that is the blood sucker. Unlike black flies, the sand fly usually bites only at night and is active only when there is little or no wind. During the day, they hide in dark cracks and crevices of buildings, in vegetation, and hollows of trees. Characteristically, they fly in slow, weak, noiseless hops that one can follow. Although most species feed on cold-blooded animals, some will take a blood meal from humans. Unlike black flies, they are not aquatic, and they breed in places where there is darkness, humidity, and organic matter, which serves as food for the larvae. The sand fly is a carrier of disease and can cause medical concern when it occurs in overwhelming numbers. Its bite is extremely painful. Prevention rests with proper protection by clothing and application of insect repellent on exposed skin surfaces.

Similar biting flies that cause painful bites include the buffalo gnat and biting midges (popularly called "punkies" and "no-see-ums"). Protection against these small insects is the same as for black and sand flies.

Lice. Lice are not generally thought of as a medical concern because most people have never had association with them. However, they can create problems in the ED. It is important that the EN be able to recognize lice and take precautions against their spread by informing peers and properly cleaning the environment where the lice-infested patient has been.

There are three species of lice that one may encounter when examining a patient:

- Crab louse *(Phthirus pubis)*
- Head louse *(Pediculus humanus capitis)*
- Body louse *(P. humanus* [corporis]*)*

Pediculosis is the medical term used when there is lice present on any part of the body. All three species of lice suck blood and cannot exist away from their host for very long periods of time.

Crab Louse. The crab louse is also called the pubic louse, and to have them is popularly known as having the "crabs." This creature gets its name from its appearance—it looks like a crab. Crab lice are very stationary in habit and stay attached at a point on the skin for days. They particularly infest the pubic region of adults but may also infest armpits, eyelashes, beards, and mustaches. Crab lice are often transmitted by sexual contact and can be considered, in a sense, a venereal disease. The lice may also be transmitted by contacting clothing used by the infested person. Crab lice generally infest human adults and not prepubertal individuals. The bites of crab lice cause extreme itching and the human skin usually discolors with long infestation. The louse attaches its eggs on the coarse hair of the body.

Head Louse. The head louse is about 2 to 3 mm long and occurs especially on the human head. It is easily transmitted by physical contact. The louse attaches its eggs onto the hair of the body.

Body Louse. The body louse can be found anywhere on the body but tends to be common where clothing comes in contact with the body for continual periods of time, such as the underwear, waistline, and armpit. This louse usually stays on clothing, where it lays its eggs. It usually moves to the skin only when feeding. It may be transmitted by physical contact or by contact with objects (usually clothing) used by the infested person.

Treatment for Lice. All lice irritate the skin and cause extreme itching. Their saliva causes the formation of small red pimples after a bite. Scratching the area, which is tempting for the victim, can lead to infection. Severe infestation can lead to fatigue, irritability, depression and a generalized body rash. People who are continually infested with lice can develop pigmented and hardened skin, a condition known as "vagabond's disease."

All lice are generally treated in the same fashion. Those who have been infested should steam-clean, burn, or fumigate clothing. Antilice lotions, such as Kwell, may be used to clean the body; the hair should be shampooed with γ-benzene hexachloride (lindane or Kwell) shampoo. The shampoo should be worked into a lather and left on for 4 minutes before washing it off. It must be used with caution in infants and children, owing to the potential for CNS toxicity from systemic absorption. After the shampooing is complete, the hair should be combed with a fine-toothed comb to remove the lice and nits. An antilice cream or lotion (γ-benzene hexachloride) may be left on for 8 to 12 hours and then washed off, with a second treatment following in 1 week. Body lice are managed only with a bath and clean clothes. Body lice tend to live in clothing and bed linens, so these must be thoroughly laundered and then steam-pressed with a hot iron to kill remaining nits.

All clothing should be changed and washed in hot water. The hospital's housekeeping department should be notified of the problem to ensure proper clean-up of any rooms where patients with lice infestations have been treated.

Scabies

The scabies mite is probably the most common infestation of the human body. The female of the species burrows into the epidermis and deposits eggs over a period of 1 or 2 months. After hatching, larvae mature within 2 weeks, and the cycle continues. Lesions cause intense itching on the genitalia, in the axillae, and over the wrists. Nipple lesions are common in affected women. Scabies can be identified by skin scrapings treated with potassium hydroxide solution. Burrows may be highlighted by use of ink or another staining agent on the skin. Using an alcohol wipe to remove the dye, small dark thread-like burrows can be detected. Scabies infestations can occur in animal handlers and in ENs who do not use universal precautions when dealing with infestations.

Treatment involves application of 1 percent γ-benzene hexachloride cream over the entire skin surface and permitting it to remain in place for 8 to 12 hours. (Shorter-term therapy should be used for infants and young children.) Two applications, 24 hours apart, complete the therapy. Retreatment to rid the skin of eggs may be required within 1 week. Clothing and bedding should be handled as for pediculosis.

Vesicating and Urticating Arthropods

Arthropods that cause vesication include certain species of beetles and caterpillars.

Blister Beetle. The soft-bodied blister beetle ranges in size from 0.5 to 1 in. long and is considerably colorful, with patterns of iridescent black, purple, and brown. Blister beetles are found generally in the western half of the United States; they feed on other insects and are found on vegetation. They are readily attracted to bright light. Many human exposures occur when the insects land on a person. Adult blister beetles contain a clear, amber-colored fluid. When the beetle lands on the skin and is brushed away, the pressure of touching the insect causes the fluid to be released from its leg joints and other segmented areas of the body. It is this fluid that causes blistering. The beetle is most active during the months of summer; therefore, most cases of exposure occur in July, August, and September.

Prevention lies in identifying but not handling the insect. If the insect lands on the skin, it should be blown off, rather than brushed or picked off, to avoid release of the insect's vesicating fluid.

Caterpillars. Caterpillars are the larvae of moths and butterflies. Certain species contain protective hairs that connect with a poison gland; when disturbed, the hairs break off or become attached to the intruder, allowing venom to enter the skin. These netting hairs cause an intense burning and itching sensation when contact is made with the skin. This is especially true if the netting hairs enter the eye. There are several species of caterpillars that can cause irritating effects in humans. Three very common caterpillars reported, more so than others, as causing irritation include:

- The Io moth caterpillar *(Automeris Io)*
- The puss caterpillar *(Megalopyge opercularis)*
- The saddleback caterpillar *(Sibine stimulea)*

These caterpillars are found in the central and southeastern portion of the United States. Prevention lies in identifying but not touching the caterpillar.

■ INJURIES CAUSED BY VENOMOUS MARINE ANIMALS

In coastal areas of the United States, ENs should be familiar with the more venomous marine life that inhabits local waters. Most injuries due to venomous marine life occur to those who step on them, pick them up, or swim into them, especially scuba and snorkling enthusiasts. They should also be familiar with local treatments and specific antivenins. It is best to seek the most current treatment regimen from the local emergency medical service advisor. Certain medical supplies should be added to the medical supply kit for marine injuries, including agents that neutralize marine animal venom such as isopropyl alcohol, meat tenderizer, flour, ammonia, lemon juice, and equipment

used to heat fresh water when the injured parts need to be immersed. All persons stung or bitten by venomous marine life should have follow-up care by a physician. Although there are many species of venomous marine life, Table 32–4 lists only those that can produce a bite or sting that is cause for medical concern and offers tips for prehospital management.

■ SNAKEBITES

Depending on geographic location, the EN may have occasion to treat a victim from the bite of a venomous snake. Proper treatment in the prehospital setting will reduce the chance of permanent limb disability and perhaps death. There are about 120 species of snakes in the United States, of which approximately 30 are poisonous. Only Maine, Alaska, and Hawaii are currently free of poisonous snakes. Snakes that are dangerous to man in the United States, and therefore of concern here, are divided into two families and four major species:

- Family Viperidae—pit vipers:
     Species: rattlesnakes (Crotalus), moccasins, or cottonmouths *(Agkistrodon piscivorus),* copperheads *(Agkistrodon contortrix)*
- Family Elapidae—coral snakes:
     Species: eastern coral *(Micrurus fulvius),* Texas coral *(Micrurus tenere),* Arizona coral *(Micrurus euryxanthus)*

There are about 45,000 snakebites reported in the United States every year. Of this number, about 8000 are inflicted by venomous snakes. Fewer than 15 deaths per year, however, have occurred from snakebites during the last 8 years. Of these deaths, most occur in Texas, Georgia, Florida, Alabama, and South Carolina.

EXTREMELY DANGEROUS SNAKES

Extremely dangerous snakes include the eastern and western diamondback rattlesnake, coral snake, and the Mojave rattlesnake. The eastern and western diamondback rattlesnakes account for 95 percent of all deaths from snake venom in the United States. However, they account for only 10 percent of all snakebites. Their aggressiveness and size re-

TABLE 32–4. SIGNS, SYMPTOMS, AND FIELD TREATMENT OF INJURIES FROM VENOMOUS MARINE ANIMALS

Mechanism of Injury	Type of Marine Animal	Signs/Symptoms	Recommended First Aid	Complications
Traumatic lacerations	Shark, alligator gar, great barracuda	Tremendous soft tissue loss; possible amputations	Control bleeding; support airway; guard against shock	Shark attack has an 85% mortality rate; shock; secondary infection
Stings	Jellyfish, hydras, corals, sea anemones	Intense pain where stinging cells (nematocysts) have touched the skin; joint and muscle pain; respiratory difficulty; severe red rash; edema	Pull out the nematocysts that can be pulled out; pour alcohol over the wound (this fixes the nematocysts and prevents further stinging); sprinkle area with unseasoned meat tenderizer (this prevents further poisoning); dust area with flour or baking powder; scrape off with knife; wash with salt water (do not use fresh water); do not rub with sand	Secondary infection; respiratory arrest; shock; allergic reaction
Punctures	Coneshells, stingrays, sea urchins, sculpins	Intense pain; nausea; vomiting; weakness; syncope	Immerse injured part in hot water (110°–114°F) for 30–60 minutes to inactivate venom; elevate injured part; cover with a sterile dressing.	Shock; secondary infection; allergic reaction; tetanus
Bites	Sea snake, octopus	Two fang marks	Basic life support	Respiratory arrest; secondary infection

sult in the largest amount of venom deposited in victims of snakebite (the major reason for the high percentage of deaths incurred by this species). Their venom is more potent than any snake in the United States, except for the coral snake.

Coral snakes are a top contender, too, but they are scarce and their bite is usually not complete because their short mouth interferes with getting a firm grasp on their victim. Their short, erect fangs also make penetration of clothing difficult. Because of these physical deficiencies and their general lifestyle, they account for only 1 to 2 percent of the total deaths each year. Mojave rattlesnakes also have a deadly bite, but they are quite reclusive and attack very infrequently.

MODERATELY DANGEROUS SNAKES

Moderately dangerous snakes include the moccasin (cottonmouth, water moccasin) and most other rattlesnakes other than the ones mentioned above.

MINIMALLY DANGEROUS SNAKES

Minimally dangerous snakes include the copperhead, Massasauga, and pygmy rattlesnake. These snakes are not aggressive but will attack when provoked. These snakes also adapt well to the close proximity of humans, while other pit vipers seldom venture near people.

IDENTIFYING CHARACTERISTICS OF VENOMOUS SNAKES

Pit Vipers

Pit vipers are named for the facial pit located between their eyes and nostrils. This pit serves as a heat-sensing organ, allowing the reptile to locate warm-blooded prey. Also characteristic to pit vipers are a triangular head and movable, hollow upper-jaw fangs. The fangs of pit vipers are usually about 0.5 in. long but can be as long as 1 in. At rest, the fangs are folded back up against the roof of the mouth. Because of the fang curvature, the jaw must be opened about 180 degrees in order to provide a perpendicular angle to the striking surface to achieve effective penetration. These snakes have elliptical pupils (i.e., "cat's eyes"), but these are difficult to distinguish, even at close range. There is a single row of scales on the undersurface of the tail, and the pit viper has rattles. (Any snake that has rattles is poisonous; the moccasin and the copperhead do not have rattles.)

Coral Snakes

Coral snakes belong to the same family of snakes that include cobras, mambas, and kraits. There are three species found in the United States:

- Eastern coral *(Micrurus fulvius)*
- Texas coral *(Micrurus tenere)*
- Arizona coral *(Micrurus euryxanthus)*

Coral snakes have the following characteristics:

- Relatively short fangs. The fangs of coral snakes are not hinged and do not fold back up against the roof of their mouth as do pit vipers. Instead, they always stand erect toward the front of the mouth. They are not hollow but solid and sharply grooved where the venom slides down and into the puncture or scratch wound.
- A black snout with a yellow or yellowish white head ring and colored rings of red and yellow that touch. Coral snakes are quite colorful and vary considerably in color patterns. One should never rely on color markings alone to determine whether these snakes are poisonous.
- Round pupils

IDENTIFYING CHARACTERISTICS OF NONVENOMOUS SNAKES

Nonvenomous snakes have the following characteristics:

- Round pupils
- Lack of a facial pit
- Double row of scales on the undersurface of the tail

Because of a lack of knowledge about and general fear of snakes, many people believe all snakes are poisonous. Nonpoisonous snakes that are often mistaken for poisonous species include the hognose, scarlet, king, Mexican milk, and banded water snakes.

SIGNS AND SYMPTOMS OF ENVENOMATION

Signs and symptoms of envenomation and the rapidity with which they appear are dependent upon several factors:

- The size and species of the snake; as previously mentioned, the eastern and western diamondback rattlesnake, coral snake, and Mojave rattlesnake are extremely dangerous
- The location, depth, and number of bites; although rare, death can occur within several minutes of the injection of venom directly into a vein
- The amount of venom injected into the victim
- The age and weight of the victim; children and elderly victims are more prone to the lethal effects of venom
- General health of the victim; an individual with cardiovascular, respiratory, or CNS disease is more prone to the lethal effects from venom
- Individual sensitivity to venom
- Microorganisms (type and number) in the oral cavity of the snake that are injected with the bite

Envenomation by a poisonous snake may or may not have taken place in snakebite cases, so be skeptical and check quickly but thoroughly. Some 20 to 30 percent of all pit viper bites result in no significant venom injection. Another 25 to 30 percent of the victims bitten receive only small to moderate amounts of venom. Although it may seem logical to inspect for two fang marks, there may be only scratches, just one puncture wound, or more than two puncture wounds. The reasons for this vary. If the snake does not get a firm grasp on the victim, there may be only scratch wounds. The coral snake often has an incomplete bite, leaving scratch marks. One puncture wound may indicate that the other fang had been broken off in previous attack encounters. It is also possible that the snake may have more than two fangs. This is because several times a year, the snake sheds its skin, and when it does, it adds new fangs to replace old or broken ones. Therefore, the snake could be sporting one, two, or more fangs, depending on the given situation.

Early emergency assessment of any snakebite should be focused on the inflicted wound and condition of the patient. The immediate signs and symptoms of snakebites envenomation should be assessed before invasive management steps are taken. The bite from the pit viper may be minimal, moderate, or severe. A minimal bite may show a scratch or slight puncture wound. There may be some pain but minimal swelling after 30 to 60 minutes. A moderate bite may result in puncture wounds and swelling within 10 minutes. The patient will experience an intense, burning pain. A severe bite is characterized by puncture wounds from which capillary blood and fluid are oozing. The wound tends to be edematous and ecchymotic and is marked by either severe pain or numbness. Muscle fasciculations may be visible, and bleb formation may be present in wounds seen several hours after their occurrence. Some patients state that they have a tingling sensation around the mouth associated with a rubbery or metallic taste, and paresthesias may be present in fingers, toes, and scalp. Nausea, vomiting, and diaphoresis are noted in most patients because they are quite frightened. Some may be in shock from hypovolemia and third-spacing of fluids.

Coral snake bites produce minimal or no swelling at first. There may be paresthesia and discoloration, along with typical fasiculations around the wound. There may be little or no pain. Delayed responses include blurred vision, ptosis, slurred speech, dyspnea, hypersalivation, euphoria, paralysis, and respiratory failure. The EN must remember that with a coral snake bite, signs may be minimal and symptoms may be delayed for as long as 18 hours. The reason for this is that the main fraction of coral snake venom is neurotoxic and therefore has less effect on the envenomated tissues. On the other hand, the venom of pit vipers contains more hemotoxic properties that cause local tissue reactions; the exception is the venom of the Mojave rattlesnake, which is more neurotoxic. However, it is important to realize that the venom of all poisonous snakes is a complex mixture of enzymes and nonenzymatic proteins that include three main components that affect the human body's systems: neurotoxins, hemotoxins, and cardiotoxins. Because these poisonous components of venom are found in all poisonous snakes, it is incorrect to label certain snake species' venom as being just neurotoxic, hemotoxic, or cardiotoxic in nature.

EMERGENCY MANAGEMENT

Pit vipers have venom with proteolytic, hemotoxic, and neurotoxic properties. The venom contains enzymatic and digestive proteins that are responsible for the wound characteristics. The proteases cause tissue necrosis; the phospholipases break down cell walls and capillary membranes, creating edema; and the hyaluronidases assist in spreading the venom by breaking down cell–cell junctions. Both anticoagulant and hemorrhagic factors are contained in the venom, too, accounting for the coagulopathy associated with pit viper bites.[6]

When the patient arrives at the ED, the triage nurse should encourage the patient to stay calm while the ABCs are being assessed. The involved extremity should be splinted and elevated after all jewelry or constrictive clothing has been removed. Baseline neurovascular checks should be done at this time and repeated at least every 15 minutes during the early phase of emergency care. The limb circumference should be measured for a baseline and rechecked, along with the neurovascular status. Ice is not recommended for the wound since its use does not seem to improve outcome and may create a complicating frostbite injury. A lymphatic tourniquet may be useful in wounds in distal extremities by slowing absorption of the venom. Such tourniquets should not restrict either arterial or venous blood flow and should be loose enough for a finger to pass under the ligature.[6] The envenomation should be graded (Table 32–5) and

TABLE 32–5. GRADING OF ENVENOMATION

Degree of Envenomation	Signs and Symptoms
None	No local or systemic symptoms
Minimal	Local swelling only
Moderate	Edema progressing beyond the area of the bite; systemic reactions and laboratory abnormalities noted
Severe	Marked local reaction; severe signs and symptoms; multiple and significant laboratory abnormalities

an intravenous line should be established in an un-involved—preferably upper—extremity to deliver NS. Blood should be promptly drawn for CBC and platelet counts, electrolytes, coagulation screen, and for type and cross-match prior to using antivenin. Creatinine phosphokinase, a BUN, creatinine, and urinalysis are among other test samples obtained at this time. The patient should be placed on a cardiac monitor and closely observed for changes in ventilatory and cardiac statuses. A NG may be indicated to control nausea and vomiting; a Foley catheter may be useful in monitoring output and in detecting myoglobinuria in its earliest presentation.

The wound should be thoroughly cleansed with an antiseptic soap and water, and the patient's extremity should be assessed for developing compartment syndrome (see Chapter 19). In the most severe cases, invasive lines (CVP and Swan–Ganz catheter) may be justified, so the patient should be promptly transported to the ICU. The patient's tetanus prophylaxis status should be assessed and managed in accordance with established guidelines (see Chapter 17). Antibiotics must be given early, too, because there is high potential for infection of these wounds. If the patient presents in shock, fresh-frozen plasma or packed RBCs may be promptly required (Table 32–5).

Antivenin Therapy

Antivenin may be given in severe cases, but because it is made from horse serum, skin testing should be done prior to its administration when time permits. All resuscitation equipment should be immediately at hand, because reactions may be severe. Pain medication may be given as indicated via intravenous access.

The EN will need to procure several vials of the appropriate antivenin; at least six should be at hand. The antivenin is usually diluted with 50 to 100 mL of NS or Ringer's lactate and given intravenously. (A second line, of course, should be concurrently open in the event that resuscitation is required.) Although it has been a practice in the past to inject some antivenin directly into the wound, this is no longer recommended, because it further distends tissues and impairs local blood flow.[6] Intramuscular injections are not well absorbed, owing to alterations in perfusion, and are to be avoided. Some physicians use intravenous antihistamines and steroids to modulate adverse allergic reactions. The use of steroids is somewhat controversial because it may impair wound healing of the bite itself. It should be noted that some surgeons favor large doses of steroids and surgical decompression over the administration of antivenin, but considerable disfigurement may be associated with this alternate approach to snakebite treatment.

■ REFERENCES

1. Larson ML. Pathophysiology and management of burns. In Fincke MK, Lanros NE, eds. *Emergency Nursing: A Comprehensive Review*. Rockville, Md: Aspen; 1986:275.
2. Larson ML. Pathophysiology and management of burns. In Fincke MK, Lanros NE, eds. *Emergency Nursing: A Comprehensive Review*. Rockville, Md: Aspen; 1986:272.
3. Rosen P, Barkin R et al. *Emergency Medicine: Concepts and Clinical Practice*. 3rd ed. St. Louis, Mo: Mosby-Year Book; 1992:2348–2380.
4. Barber JM. *Emergency Nursing: A Comprehensive Review*. Rockville, Md: Aspen Publishers; 1986: 416–430.
5. Angerio AD, Kot PA. High-altitude pulmonary edema: a clinical crisis. *Crit Care Nurs Q*. 1996;19:70–76.
6. Stewart CE. *Environmental Emergencies*. Baltimore, Md: Williams & Wilkins; 1990:160–289.

■ BIBLIOGRAPHY

Ayres SM, Grenvik A, Holbrook PR, Shoemaker WC. *Textbook of Critical Care*. 3rd ed. Philadelphia, Pa: WB Saunders; 1995.

Barber JM, Dillman PA. *Emergency Patient Care for the EMT-A*. Reston, VA: Reston Publishing; 1981.

Barie PS, Shires GT. *Surgical Intensive Care*. Boston, Mass: Little, Brown; 1993.

Benumof J. *Airway Management: Principles and Practice*. St. Louis, Mo: CV Mosby; 1995.

Bongard FS, Sue DY. *Current Critical Care Diagnosis and Treatment*. E. Norwalk, Conn: Appleton & Lange; 1994.

Cardona VD, Hurn PD, Bastnagel Mason et al. *Trauma Nursing*. 2nd ed. Philadelphia, Pa: WB Saunders; 1994.

Chernow B, ed. *The Pharmacologic Approach to the Critically Ill Patient*. 3rd ed. Baltimore, Md: Williams & Wilkins; 1994.

Clochesy JM, Breu C, Cardin S, et al. *Critical Care Nursing.* Philadelphia, Pa: WB Saunders; 1993.

Levine RL, Fromm RE Jr. *Critical Care Monitoring from Pre-Hospital to the ICU.* St. Louis, Mo: Mosby-Year Book; 1995.

Maull KI, Rodriguez A, Wiles CE. *Complications in Trauma and Critical Care.* Philadelphia, Pa: WB Saunders; 1996.

Moreau D, ed. *Nursing 96 Drug Handbook.* Springhouse, Pa: Springhouse Corporation; 1996.

Physicians' Desk Reference. 50th ed. Montvale, NJ; Medical Economics; 1996.

Weist PW, Roth PB. *Fundamentals of Emergency Radiology.* Philadelphia, Pa: WB Saunders; 1996.

Wilkins RL, Dexter JR. *Respiratory Disease: Principles of Patient Care.* Philadelphia, Pa: FA Davis; 1993.

■ REVIEW: BURNS AND ENVIRONMENTAL EMERGENCIES

1. Identify the major advantage of using the Lund and Browder chart for estimating the percentage of burned body surface area (BSA).

2. Describe two methods of removing tar and asphalt from burned tissue.

3. Justify the current recommendations regarding the use of antibiotics for burn wound prophylaxis and infection management.

4. Differentiate among the various forms of heat-related illness:
   a. Heat cramps
   b. Heat syncope
   c. Heat exhaustion
   d. Heat stroke

5. Describe the effects of hyperthermia on the brain, heart and lungs, and the gastrointestinal (GI) tract.

6. Describe the recommended procedure for rewarming a frostbitten extremity.

7. Outline the emergency treatment of severe hypothermia, including essential cardiac monitoring.

8. Explain why rapid external rewarming can be life-threatening for a hypothermia victim.

9. Identify the physiological precursor to nitrogen narcosis.

10. List the signs and symptoms of high-altitude pulmonary edema (HAPE) and describe how it is treated.

11. Name two life-threatening events associated with electrical burns or lightning injuries.

12. Describe the characteristic neurologic, cardiac, and ophthalmic involvement of stage II Lyme disease.

13. Explain the proper procedure for using lindane products for the treatment of pediculosis infestations.

14. Outline the initial responsibilities of the emergency nurse (EN) when a patient presents with snakebite of an extremity.

15. Describe the recommended procedure for the preparation and administration of antivenin therapy.

Psychiatric and Behavioral Emergencies

33

■ PSYCHIATRIC EMERGENCIES

The emergency department (ED) has become the point of entry into mental health services for an increasing number of people, meaning that emergency nurses (ENs) can expect to deal with more psychiatric emergencies in the future. Deinstitutionalization, the cost-motivated early discharge of patients from hospitals, and the growing emphasis on community services rather than residential treatment all place the chronically mentally ill into the community served by the ED. An accelerating number of younger patients with emotional, behavioral, and alcohol- or drug-related problems adds significantly to the challenge. A psychiatric emergency arises when anyone comes into the ED for immediate relief from distress obviously of a psychiatric nature, or when anyone is brought in by family, friends, neighbors, or the police, who state that the patient was acting in a bizarre, dangerous, or ominous fashion.

PRINCIPLES OF MANAGEMENT

The general principles of management with all these patients involves careful assessment and observation, with an attempt to obtain pertinent information in five key areas:

- The chief complaint or reason for being brought to the ED
- The patient's general behavior as you observe it and the impression you have (e.g., frightened, angered, inappropriately responding, catatonic)
- The history—or as much as you can get from the patient or whoever accompanied the patient
- The physical examination with full vital signs (VS), if possible, as part of an effort to develop an accurate database
- An observation period, during which time the situation can be objectively evaluated, with an awareness that these patients are usually time-consuming

COMPONENTS OF AN EFFECTIVE APPROACH

There are several components to an effective approach with a psychiatrically disturbed patient, and it is important to realize that if you can exhibit a calm and confident manner at the outset, you may be able immediately to reduce the patient's anxiety level:

- Let the patient know you are interested and care about helping as well as offering hope for a reasonable short-term solution. To the shocked, confused, panicked, and despairing victim, you bring order, organization, calm, and hope; identify yourself and take charge of the situation. Let your voice be firm and strong, sympathetic yet businesslike. Give clear, simple directions; repeat them as necessary. The disoriented person needs to be reoriented with regard to time, place, person, and situation with simple, concrete information.
- Try to draw the patient out by sometimes sharing your observations, and elicit

enough information that you can prepare the physician for the general problem. Allow people to have and express their emotions. Telling them how they should or should not feel only adds to their confusion and guilt and may render them less cooperative. Give angry people permission to vent feelings, as long as they are not harming themselves or others; many times verbalization of rage will de-escalate a smoldering crisis.

In spite of the way we would *like* to be able to respond to behavioral crises, the reality is that enough time is rarely available nor are all personnel always qualified and ready to handle the mentally or emotionally disturbed patient calmly and patiently. Although many large hospitals have resident staff and psychiatrists on call to the ED, more often than not, the psychiatric emergency or crisis is accorded less priority than physical crises elsewhere in the hospital. ENs find themselves facing the patient alone, struggling to make an initial evaluation or analysis, and realizing their own anxiety levels and occasional shortage of coping skills. The highest professional standard demands no more than doing the best you can under the circumstances, so take a deep breath and do your best with these challenging patients.

MENTAL STATUS EXAMINATION

Components of the mental status examination can be grouped into four areas of content (e.g., appearance, emotions, thought processes and content, and cognition. Tables 33–1 and 33–2 address these areas in more detail. One key area of observation, however, that is frequently of great value in assessing the patient's thought processes is eye movements; they offer important clues to the patient's attitudes (e.g., evasive, darting, suspicious, or engaging).[1]

Remember, too, when conducting the mental status examination, that mood and affect must be differentiated; mood is the patient's own subjective description of his feeling over time. Affect is the immediate emotional state observed by the examiner (i.e., his or her objective view of how the patient appears to him or her).[1]

TABLE 33–1. MENTAL STATUS EXAMINATION

Facet	Details
1. Appearance	Neat or dirty, unkempt? Appropriate or bizarre attire? Extraoccular movements?
2. Behavior	Strange? Threatening or violent? Grimacing or tremors? Impaired gait? Agitation?
3. Speech	Rate, tone, quantity?
4. Thought, content and flow	Thought: content Suicidal? Delusional? Body preoccupation? Religious preoccupation? Thought: flow Random? Logical? Word salad?
5. Mood and affect	Sad? High? Angry? Fearful? Grieving?
6. Perception	Reality-based? Illusions? Hallucinations?
7. Cognitive capacity	Orientation? Attention span? Memory? Intellectual functioning? Insight and judgment?

Adapted from Bassuck and Birk.[4]

MANAGING THE VIOLENT PATIENT

In the event that a patient erupts into violence, the first consideration must be the safety of both patient and staff and appropriate de-escalation of the situation as soon as possible.

Use of Physical Restraints and Their Legal Implications

Whatever steps are taken, emergency staff need to be aware of the legal ramifications of their actions. Unnecessary restraint of patients against their will carries the potential for charges and legal action: assault (threatening to do bodily harm), battery (committing bodily harm), and physical damage.

TABLE 33–2. MENTAL STATUS EXAMINATION QUESTIONS[a] FOR COGNITIVE FUNCTIONING

Question	Function Tested
1. "Where are we now?"	Orientation to place
2. "What is the name of this place and where is it located?"	
3. "What is the day of the week and the date today?"	Orientation to time
4. "Who is . . . ?" Point to a familiar person, or ask for that person's name and relationship to the patient.	Orientation to person
5. "Please repeat this sentence after me; try to remember it, and I will ask you to repeat it later: 'The purple fox runs . . .'"	Immediate recall and short-term memory
or	
"Please repeat these items after me, and then I'd like you to remember them. I will ask you to repeat them later." (Then name three items/objects.)	Immediate recall and short-term memory
6. At 3- and 5-minute intervals, ask the patient to repeat the items of question 5.	Immediate recall and short-term memory
7. "Take this pencil and paper and draw a clock; make it read the time that you think it is now."	Construction, comprehension, copying, memory
8. "Please copy this cube."	
9. "Please write the sentence (or three items) I asked you to remember."	
10. To test the patient's fund of general information, ask about the names of the present and previous presidents, well-known historical events, or current affairs.	General information fund
11. "Please explain this proverb: 'A rolling stone gathers no moss' or 'People in glass houses shouldn't throw stones.'"	Proverbs (concrete versus abstract thought)
12. "Subtract 7 from 100 and continue down numerically by 7s."	Measure attentiveness
13. Give string of digits and have patient repeat forward order; repeat numbers and have patient repeat numbers backward.	

[a] Since history-taking and conversation will provide much of the information sought for mental status evaluation, it is suggested that the "examination" questions be used as sparingly as possible to prevent intimidation.
(Adapted from Bassuck and Birk.[4])

Comprehensive guidelines and restraint procedures must be in place; less restrictive alternatives should always be employed whenever possible, such as reduction of stimuli and use of quiet, limit-setting interventions early in the escalation process. Application of physical restraints must be the last resort, and only the minimum amount of control necessary should be used. Once restraints are employed, however, the following information must be clearly documented in the patient's record:

- Time restraints were applied
- Type and number of restraints applied
- Patient's condition at time of restraint application
- Clinical rationale for application
- Ongoing, frequent, and careful circulatory checks on the restrained extremities

An important component of every ED's orientation should be staff training and demonstrated competencies in (1) using physical control holds for violent patients and (2) locating and applying the appropriate restraint devices. Restraints should be located in a designated place and packaged in a complete four-point set for rapid access, transportation, and application when the need arises and time is critical. Restraint vests should also be available. Know your hospital's policy and legal restrictions for using restraints.

Chemical Restraints

When interpersonal interventions are inadequate and physical restraint represents too harsh an alternative, medications have a role in management of patients who are agitated, aggressive, or violent. Two classes of drugs are most commonly used to calm and provide what is alluded to as chemical restraint—the minor tranquilizer benzodiazepines and the antipsychotic butyrophenones. Barbiturates are seldom used because of unwanted sedative and hemodynamic effects.

The tranquilizing benzodiazepines, such as lorazepam (Ativan) and diazepam (Valium) are the treatment of choice in agitation due to sedative-hypnotic withdrawal states (including alcohol), panic attacks, and as an adjunct to antipsychotic medication for schizophrenia or affective disorder. They should *not* be used, however, in patients with acute alcohol intoxication because of the potential for respiratory arrest.

The antipsychotic group of butyrophenones include haloperidol (Haldol) and droperidol (Inapsine); their potent neuroleptic activity is indicated in psychiatric emergencies as a general aid in producing tranquillity and decreasing anxiety and pain. Other central nervous system (CNS) depressant drugs (barbiturates, major tranquilizers, narcotics, and general anesthetic agents) will have additive or potentiating effects with droperidol; therefore, the administration of any other CNS depressants after droperidol should be carefully monitored to avoid excessive CNS depression. Caution should be also exercised in administration to patients with known Parkinson's disease.

Current Psychotherapeutic Drug History

A current history of psychotherapeutic drugs the patient is taking may have a bearing on the clinical presentation. Phenothiazine tranquilizers (Thorazine, Mellaril, Stelazine), antidepressants (the tricyclics—Elavil, Norpramine, Tofranil, Aventyl), and monoamine oxidase inhibitors (MAOs) (Marplan, Eutonyl, Parnate, Nardil) can all have side effects from prolonged use. Some side effects generally seen from prolonged use of the tranquilizing drugs are hypotension (especially with chlorpromazine [Thorazine] and thioridizine [Mellaril]), blood dyscrasias and leukopenia. (White blood cell [WBC] count and differential should be done every month.) Other side effects may include obstructive jaundice, photosensitivity, retinopathy, a lowered seizure threshold, potentiation of analgesias, depression, akathisia (the inability to sit down from nervous fear) and tardive dyskinesia. Diphenhydramine (Benadryl) is effective in treating both of the latter.

Ingestion of the minor tranquilizers (alcohol, chlordiazepoxide [Librium]), and diazepam [Valium], has essentially the same effect as "a shot of booze" for most patients, and they may present with ataxia, drowsiness, and hypotension. Depression frequently follows the long-term use of diazepam (Valium).

■ CATEGORIES OF PSYCHIATRIC AND BEHAVIORAL EMERGENCIES

Psychiatric and behavioral emergencies can be placed into general categories of the forms in which they are most commonly encountered in prehospital and ED care:

- Depressive episodes
- Suicidal states
- Anxiety disorders
- Manic episodes
- Schizophrenic disorders
- Paranoid disorders
- Acute confusional states in the elderly
- Alcohol and substance abuse or dependence

DEPRESSIVE EPISODES

Depression affects 20 percent of the U.S. population and accounts for 70 to 80 percent of all psychiatric referrals. It is highly correlated with the risk of self-neglect, self-destructive acts, and suicide. Major indicators of depression frequently are manifest but go unrecognized much of the time. The dominant indicator of depression is a mood disorder—the helpless and hopeless mood. Loss of interest or pleasure in usual activities, insomnia, appetite changes, low energy levels, feelings of worthlessness, self-reproach, increased indecisiveness, inability to concentrate, and recurrent thoughts of death or a wish to die are all additional indicators. Three or more of these overlaying the basic mood disorder are the sign of a major depressive episode.

Depression in adolescents may present as detachment and a cynical, lonely attitude and is frequently a cause of reckless driving, drug abuse, and delinquency problems. The depressed adult typically exhibits careless dress; a slow gait; slumping posture; a monotonous, whiny voice, ruminating thought processes, loss of social interest, and decreased sexual activity. Physical complaints can be backache, headache, gastrointestinal (GI) upset, chest pains, and vertigo. A good way to spot the truly depressed patient is to remember that depression begets depression. Ask yourself: Does this patient make you feel depressed?

Nursing Interventions

These patients have a need to "ventilate"; talking with someone who is interested, empathetic, and warm can be both diagnostic and therapeutic for that patient. Depression may be symptomatic of organic illness, as with a brain tumor (organic brain syndrome), hypothyroidism, or a manifestation of long-term cortisone therapy; of a major psychosis; or of a toxic affective disorder from substance abuse or withdrawal.

A decision must be made about safe and effective case disposition. A severe depressive episode requires psychiatric consultation and hospitalization if signs of suicidal intent, self-neglect, or self-abuse are dominant. If the patient is to be sent home, it must be to or with a responsible person who can administer well-labeled medication. Because tricyclics take 2 weeks to achieve effect and sedatives are unsafe to send out with an already depressed patient, diphenhydramine (Benadryl), 50 mg PO, is frequently considered a safe measure. There must be clearly arranged plans for patient referral and outpatient follow-up care after discharge from the ED.

Nursing Diagnoses

Appropriate diagnoses for depressive episodes would include:

- Altered thought process related to depression
- Impaired verbal communication
- Ineffective individual coping
- Alteration in health maintenance
- Potential for injury related to hopelessness
- Alteration in nutrition: less than body requirements
- Self-care deficit in feeding, and grooming
- Disturbance in self-concept of body image and personal identity
- Sleep pattern disturbance
- Social isolation related to depression

SUICIDAL STATES

Each year, U.S. statistics from the Centers for Disease Control and Prevention (CDC) reflect that suicide is fourth of all causes of mortality in terms of years of potential life lost.[2] Suicide is the ninth cause of death overall and is responsible for approximately 30,000 deaths a year; at least ten times that number of people *attempt* self-destruction each year. Over the past 40 years, the rate of suicide among young Americans between the ages of 15 and 24 years has *tripled*.[3] After age 24, suicide rates generally decline until age 40, at which time they begin to rise and continue rising into the 70s. Men account for 70 percent of suicides; however, this is changing: professional women are showing increased rates of alcoholism, coronary heart disease, and suicide.[2] Suicide in males tends to be more violent and more successful; there are fewer suicide gestures with men, and they employ highly lethal means of accomplishing their end.

Red Flags

In assessing suicide potential of the patient who has threatened to take his or her life, attempted a suicide, revealed self-destructive thoughts, or manifested a severe depression, there are significant risk factors and clear signals to which ENs should be alert. Do not fear erring or exaggerating the patient's potential for suicide; patient safety is the first concern. Observe carefully and listen closely for key signals of extreme risk:

- Previous attempts (80 percent of successful suicide cases involve patients who made a previous attempt)
- Depression (suicide is 500 times more common among the severely depressed)
- Self-mutilation by young males (not common, but when it *does* occur, it is a desperate indicator)
- Age (15 to 24 years, high risk; above 45 years, rate begins to increase again)
- Alcohol or drug abuse (or withdrawal from)
- Marital status: divorced or widowed (the suicide rate for these groups is five times higher than for married people)
- Giving away of cherished personal property
- Living alone
- Psychotic with depression, suicidal, or destructive thoughts, or hallucinations about killing or death

- Homosexuality (depressed, aging, alcoholic, or with acquired immunodeficiency syndrome [AIDS])
- Major separation traumas (mate, loved one, job, money)
- Major physical stresses (particularly recent surgery, childbirth or postpartum psychosis, and severe insomnia)
- Loss of independence (disabling or catastrophic illness)
- Lack of plans for the future
- Suicide of same-sex parent

If you sense suicide potential in a deeply troubled patient, do not hesitate to discuss concerns in a straightforward manner. Ask focused questions, such as:

1. "How is life treating you?"
2. "How do you feel about life?"
3. "Do you feel like harming (killing) yourself?" (If there is a plan, ask how, when, and whether it has been rehearsed and practiced.)
4. "Have you tried before?"
5. "Has anyone else in your family attempted suicide?
6. "Have you had any recent losses?"

Again, go with your own feelings, remembering the importance of how the patient makes you feel.

Nursing Interventions

Remember, when intervening in suicide cases, to go with your "sense" of the situation and err on the side of patient safety. The first priority is to protect the patient from self-harm. While the patient remains in the ED, a safe environment must be provided; if the patient is admitted to the hospital for psychiatric care, that safe environment is the first and foremost consideration. If evaluation indicates the patient is dangerous to himself or herself, 24-hour protection is the minimum indicated, even if this requires involuntary admission.

The acutely suicidal patient should not be left alone at any time, even for a few minutes. The room should be suicide-proofed (equipped with impenetrable screens and wire-mesh shatterproof glass and stripped of all potentially harmful objects and hanging devices). Use physical restraints as necessary, although some patients may only require chemical restraints. Haloperidol (Haldol), intramuscular or intravenous, is considered by most to be the drug of choice and is a standard for psychotropic management in this clinically threatening situation.

With the relatively low-risk suicide patient, outpatient referrals are considered, with assurance of a supportive environment in the interim. Social services support should be enlisted if the patient is to be discharged. Following psychiatric evaluation in the ED, develop a contingency plan to be implemented if the patient feels like attempting suicide again. One study shows that of a group referred for outpatient care, only 3 percent completed the outpatient care; these are the patients who "fall through the cracks" of the system. Low-risk suicidal patients just do not follow through on treatment; social services, family, or friends need to be involved to ensure compliance.

Nursing Diagnoses

Appropriate nursing diagnoses for suicidal patients would include:

- Ineffective coping related to inability to manage situational crisis
- Hopelessness manifested by suicidal ideation
- Disturbance in self-concept: body image, self-esteem, and role performance
- Social isolation related to depression and feelings of hopelessness
- Spiritual distress related to suicidal ideation
- Alteration in thought processes related to self-harm
- Potential for self-directed violence

ANXIETY DISORDERS

Although anxiety is a normal response to stress, we frequently see patients in the ED who are overwhelmed by their anxieties; their anxiety levels have become so intense that they begin to feel helpless and experience impairment in their ability to function along normal lines. This is known also as panic disorder, panic attack, or anxiety attack, and typically, there is a sudden onset of intense terror accompanied by a sense of impending doom. As this continues, the patient begins to anticipate total loss of control.

Typical manifestations of such a panic disorder include:

- Fear of going crazy, dying, or losing control
- Hyperventilating
- Physical complaints of chest discomfort or pain, palpitations, dyspnea, choking or smothering, faintness, syncope, and vertigo
- Feelings of unreality
- Trembling and sweating
- Urinary frequency and diarrhea

Nursing Interventions

Give these patients time to unwind by talking with them; this is best done when the family is *not* present. The patient may need a minor tranquilizer such as 50 mg diazepam (Valium) or chlordiazepoxide (Librium) or one of the other antidepressants (such as desipramine or nortriptyline). Often, the problem can be talked out and the patient calmed, reassured, and sent home with a follow-up appointment with the local mental health clinic or a psychiatrist.

Nursing Diagnoses

Appropriate nursing diagnoses for anxiety disorders would include:

- Anxiety related to situational crisis
- Impaired gas exchange related to hyperventilation
- Ineffective individual or family coping skills
- Fear related to perceived inability to control situation
- Disturbance in self-concept related to loss of control
- Sensory-perceptual alteration regarding self and situation
- Disturbance in sleep pattern related to manifestations of anxiety
- Altered thought processes related to anxiety

MANIC EPISODES

The manic patient represents the extreme opposite of the severely depressed patient. Manic episodes frequently occur within a bipolar disorder and alternate with episodes of severe depression. During the manic episode, the mood is expansive and exuberant. The patient exhibits grandiose flights of ideas and inflated self-esteem. Normal cautions, social barriers, and concerns about consequences are overridden. Frequently, they are euphoric with omnidirectional enthusiasm and not always appropriate; irritability, however, lies just beneath the surface and can easily erupt in violent outbursts.

Red Flags

The following are prime indicators of a manic episode:

- Predominantly expansive, elevated, or irritable mood
- Hyperactivity and garrulous speech
- Flights of ideas
- Involvement in high-risk activities, such as expensive purchases, sexual promiscuity, reckless driving, and wild business ventures
- Function without normal sleep

Patients in the midst of extremely severe manic episodes exhibit delusions or hallucinations, usually concerning their special powers and knowledge.

Nursing Interventions

With excited, agitated, and aroused patients, be careful not to be intrusive. If you can determine the person is not assaultive, sit down at eye level to talk, this is perceived as nonthreatening. Firmly and matter-of-factly talk to the patient, remembering you are the professional, and avoid discussing the delusional symptoms. Leave the door open during your interview; do not place your chair between the patient and the door. When interviewing for history, ask the patient:

- Are you on medication, and have you been following the medication regimen?
- Are there any recent losses or dramatic changes in your life that may have triggered this episode?

Family members will need real support and guidance to deal with this patient, with emphasis on limit-setting and restriction of activities. The manic patient may need major tranquilizers, hospitalization, or at a minimum, referral and follow-up care. If the patient is assaultive, sedate him or her immediately. The psychotic patient who may erupt should be restrained either physically or chemically with medication like droperidol (Inapsine), 2 to 4 mL IM.

The true manic is not usually a threat in the ED, but the main problem is that the patient will exhaust himself or herself and indeed may finally die of exhaustion. A manic patient must be hospitalized and placed on medication. Starting lithium in the ED is a very controversial practice, and a patient who has never received lithium needs a complete medical workup before being placed on the medication, as well as close monitoring for lithium blood levels on a follow-up basis.

SCHIZOPHRENIC DISORDERS

Schizophrenia is most likely a group of disorders with certain characteristic symptoms. The schizophrenic process always involves deterioration from a previous level of functioning; people close to the patient say he or she "is not the same." A typical schizophrenic episode in a young adult may well provide an opportunity in the ED for initial recognition and treatment.

An undiagnosed family history is believed to exist with schizophrenia. Onset is usually during late adolescence or early adulthood. The more florid symptoms are usually preceded by an initial phase of social withdrawal, impaired hygiene, blunted affect, and disturbed communication. The schizophrenic is more likely to be seen in the ED during the active phase, which is often associated with specific stress. Mental status must be carefully assessed (see Tables 33–1 and 33–2).

Red Flags

Full-blown psychotic symptoms typically include the following red flags:

- Bizarre delusions, often with religious, persecutory, or jealous content
- Auditory hallucinations: ask if voices are male or female. Do they whisper or scream? Do they command, inform, or demand? A paranoid schizophrenic patient who is receiving commanding auditory hallucinations ordering him or her to do harm is a serious risk.[1]
- Incoherence and illogical thinking
- Inappropriate affect
- Marked disorganization of behavior

Nursing Diagnoses

Appropriate nursing diagnoses for schizophrenic disorders would include:

- Impaired verbal communication
- Ineffective individual coping
- Alteration in physical health maintenance
- Impaired home maintenance management
- Alteration in thought processes related to hallucinatory processes
- Visual, auditory, olfactory sensory alteration related to hallucinatory processes
- Potential for self-directed violence or violence to others

PARANOID DISORDERS

The boundaries of paranoid disorder are not clearly differentiated from schizophrenia; however, their essential features are persistent, organized, persecutory delusions, or jealousy delusions that may be directed against the mate. Anger, suspiciousness, and complaints about unjust treatment are common. Paranoid patients rarely seek treatment themselves, but they are often brought in by relatives or social agency representatives. Onset is typically in middle years, later than in schizophrenia.

Red Flags

The following are indicators of paranoid disorders:

- Persistent persecutory delusions or delusional jealousy
- Clear and organized thought patterns, in contrast to the incoherence or loose association seen in schizophrenic patients
- Possible presence of threatening or grandiose auditory hallucinations
- Suspiciousness and persecution ideation that may lead to violence; the veneer is often quite thin and requires careful handling.

Nursing Interventions for Schizophrenic and Paranoid Disorders

Management of both schizophrenic and paranoid disordered patients is similar in many ways. These truly "psychotic" patients need to be treated gently but firmly with simple, straight communication. They do not need to be encouraged to ventilate feelings; do not enter into their delusions, judge, or interpret them. Explain to these patients that they are now in a safe and secure place and give clear, matter-of-fact explanations of how they will be handled. Particular attention must be paid to the mental status examination, with reality-oriented questioning used in order to evaluate affect, mood, thought content, and judgment (see Tables 33–1 and 33–2).

One of the major goals in the initial assessment is determination of potential for homicidal or suicidal action. Quiet, firm management with chemical support (haloperidol) may produce substantial improvement within hours. These patients require psychiatric consultation immediately, before any decisions or case disposition can be made. If the patient appears extremely paranoid, he or she may well be dangerous, and the danger should be taken seriously. Management should include:

- Eye-level communication, maintaining a reasonable distance, respecting the patient's "space," and avoiding any touching
- Leaving the door open and letting the patient sit where he or she chooses
- Hearing the patient out, but not adding to the ideation of persecution
- Minimizing external stimuli (e.g., paging systems or radios)
- Maintaining a "hazard-free" environment, (i.e., removing anything that the patient could use as a weapon against self or others)
- Realizing that you may need powerful physical assistance if the patient resists medication

Nursing Diagnoses

Appropriate nursing diagnoses in paranoid disorders would include:

- Ineffective individual coping related to disease process
- Alteration in family dynamics related to self-isolation and delusional process
- Potential for self-injury by trauma
- Social isolation related to delusional process
- Alteration in thought processes related to hallucinatory activities
- Potential for violence directed at others

ACUTE CONFUSIONAL STATES IN THE ELDERLY

The syndromes of delirium (clouded state of consciousness) and dementia (loss of intellectual abilities) occur most frequently in the elderly and are difficult to distinguish from each other. Delirium is potentially reversible if the underlying problem is treated; without treatment, there well may be a progression to dementia and death.[5] Dementia itself may be progressive or may be remitting. Its reversibility depends on underlying pathology and timely treatment.

Signs of agitated depression are often seen in older people who are brought in by relatives. A "clouded state of consciousness" (reduction in clear awareness of the environment) is often self-evident. Relatives frequently report that lucid states interspersed with confusion are fluctuating and becoming less frequent. Restless pacing, hand wringing, and ruminative thought processes are often observed. Memory impairment is usually the prominent symptom of dementia, starting with simple forgetfulness and extending to forgetting the names of close relatives, addresses, and so on (see table 33–2). Hospital admission should be avoided if possible; be wary of families trying to "dump" a confused elderly relative in the ED. An unwarranted hospital admission may break the routine of daily life for an elderly person and cause him or her to lose contact with reality. Immediate referral to community services is a necessity, with family counseling encouraged. Maintaining a familiar environment for the aged is critical to their remaining quality of life.

ALCOHOL AND SUBSTANCE ABUSE OR DEPENDENCE

This is a real problem and a complex one that takes up a great deal of time in the ED. The greatest problem is that there is no really effective way of dealing with an alcoholic (or other substance abuser) in the ED. If the alcoholic can be motivated adequately, referral to Alcoholics Anonymous may be a path to pursue. If not, the patient should be directed to the closest referral agency in the community for further care. The alcoholic who presents complaining of "the jitters" and asking for medication may be a candidate for delirium tremens (DTs) within 24 hours. This patient should be sedated at once and admitted; if he or she refuses, you must obtain an AMA (against medical advice) release and make every effort to notify family or friends of the patient's dangerous situation. Chapter 31 discusses substance abuse management more fully.

SOME KEY POINTS FOR NURSING ASSESSMENT

In psychiatric emergencies, the following points are part of good nursing assessment:

A. Always record VS in psychiatric emergencies, if at all possible. Problems that produce psychological changes but are organic in nature can often be picked up by reviewing complete VSs. Examples are cerebral vascular accident (CVA) (such as aphasia), diabetes, cerebral arteriosclerosis, azotemia (blood urea nitrogen [BUN] elevated in renal failure), postictal states, systemic or CNS infections, decompensated hepatic disorders (cirrhosis), brain tumors, barbiturate withdrawal, clavus hystericus (the sensation as if a nail were being driven into the head), and toxic conditions.

B. When talking with a psychiatric patient:
   1. Listen to the patient.
   2. Try to remember that at any given time a person is doing the best he or she can at *that* time and under *those* circumstances.
   3. Relate to the *here and now* with the patient.
   4. Paraphrase during the interview and when necessary, briefly intercede with the rambling patient.
   5. In nonverbal behaviors, label the patient's reactions ("You seem to be . . .").
   6. Evaluate how the patient makes *you* feel.
   7. Ask for help from the patient in interpreting his or her words.
   8. Trust your own initial feelings toward the patient.

Remember that in schizophrenic patients, a fantasy world has become a dominant part of their lives, and auditory hallucinations are a manifestation of a schizophrenic psychosis. Visual hallucinations should always suggest organic problems such as toxic reactions, LSD use, encephalitis, overdose, or DTs.

■ SEXUAL ASSAULT

Victims of sexual assault (rape), either female or male, present to the ED by their own volition or are brought by law-enforcement officers to undergo a sexual assault examination. In addition to rendering any required emergency care for trauma associated with forced sexual contact, forensic evidence may be collected that will be used in later judicial proceedings, and follow-up care for the victim will be arranged.

TRIAGE, REGISTRATION, AND CONSENTS

The individual presenting for a sexual assault examination should be triaged immediately to a private area, and either a nurse or victim advocate from a local "rape crisis" team will be assigned to remain with the individual throughout their emergency department stay. The roles of such support personnel include counseling, human support, assistance with clothing changes, and serving as a liaison with follow-up care. Some victims may choose another support person, or desire to be alone throughout the examination and treatment period.

When registration forms are filled out, the ED staff *should not* use words such as "alleged rape," or "alleged sexual assault" since these tend to be prejudicial within the legal system. Use "sexual assault examination" or a similar neutral annotation, instead.

Before proceeding with the sexual assault examination, appropriate consents must be obtained for medical examination and treatment only, or for examination, treatment *and* the collection of forensic evidence. If law enforcement has not been notified, emergency personnel must initiate the contacts with local authorities since there may be criminal penalties for failure to report sexual assault cases to police. (Remember that *reporting* sexual assault cases is not the same as *filing charges,* a prerogative of the victim.) In most jurisdictions, a law enforcement officer must authorize the forensic aspects of the examination in which evidence is collected. In the event the patient cannot decide whether or not to pursue the perpetrator, provisions exist that permit the collection and holding of forensic evidence until the victim decides whether or not to move forward with legal proceedings. A separate, written consent is ordinarily required for photographs of injuries, especially any of the genital areas. Although hospitals are not required by law to perform examinations of the suspect, they may be requested to do so by the police. If the suspect has already been arrested, he or she cannot decline a sexual assault examination.

INITIAL ASPECTS OF HISTORY AND EXAMINATION

The medical management includes a detailed history of the assault, a survey of any injuries on the body, and treatment of associated trauma.

The patient's vital signs, along with the height and weight should be recorded initially. If there is any suggestion of hemodynamic instability or life-threatening trauma, the sexual assault examination should be delayed until these have been fully addressed and stabilized if necessary.

FORENSIC EVIDENCE COLLECTION

To ensure the successful pursuit of perpetrators of sexual assault, or to protect innocent individuals who may be falsely accused, it is imperative that forensic evidence be collected and preserved, while maintaining a flawless chain of custody. Although local or state jurisdictions may each have unique requirements for the sexual assault examination, the basic principles and techniques are quite similar. Equipment required for the examination must be assembled and organized in advance and typically includes a vaginal speculum, anal speculum, colposcope with 35 mm camera, Wood's lamp, microscope, swab dryer, and the local sexual assault evidence collection kit.

A chain of custody must be maintained during all aspects of the examination so that evidence is fully accounted for, thus preventing loss, adulteration, contamination, or tampering. Each individual who has custody of evidence at any time must annotate the forms with signature, date, and time prior to any transfers to others. Evidence must never be left unattended unless locked, and the patient should not be left in the room alone with evidentiary specimens.

The forensic examiner may be a sexual assault nurse examiner (SANE) or a physician. This individual must exhibit respect and concern for the victim, and remain nonjudgmental. Careful technique must be used to ensure that the details of the assault are elicited in a nonthreatening manner, and that precise scenario of the attack is recorded objectively and accurately, preferably in the patient's own words. All sexual acts must be documented since each results in a separate criminal charge within the judicial system. Since several areas of the body may have been assaulted and injured, a head to toe inspection is imperative, searching for bruises, bitemarks, ligature marks, abrasions, contusions, lacerations, or other evidence of trauma. Photographs are used to document such findings.

The victim should be instructed to stand on paper while undressing to ensure that any hair, fibers, or debris (i.e., trace evidence) can be preserved. All items of clothing should be saved, each in its own paper (not plastic) bag. (Plastic is not used because it preserves moisture and hastens the deterioration of certain elements of evidence.) Any evidence, such as the undressing paper, should be carefully folded into a bundle and sealed within an evidence envelope with tamper-proof tape marked with the examiner's initials or signature and the date of collection. This paper is submitted to the crime laboratory, along with the victim's clothing.

Both identification photographs and evidentiary photographs may be obtained for documentation. A body diagram should be used to annotate bruises, bitemarks, or other indices of trauma. All injuries should be swabbed with a synthetic (not cotton) applicator. Saline- or distilled water-moistened applicators should be used for collecting evidence from dry lesions; dry applicators are used to obtain evidence from moist areas. Both reference and control swabs are taken and carefully catalogued and air-dried prior to packaging to prevent deterioration of evidence and to preserve certain genetic marker enzymes which are useful to identify suspects. Heat should never be used to speed swab drying.

A Wood's lamp is used to identify semen and saliva that may be left on the victim's body; these substances fluoresce in the long-wave ultra-violet light source. Hair samples may be plucked or cut (very close to the scalp or skin) from the victim's head and pubic area. Some victim's may prefer to pluck their own hair exemplars and this, of course, is permissible. Although plucking from several sites may be painful, some authorities believe this is the best technique since DNA can be best detected on the hair root. Each sexual assault protocol will define exactly how this procedure is done. Other evidence that is collected may include fingernail scrapings, vaginal secretions, saliva and hair obtained from combing the genital regions.

Many sexual assault examinations include a colposcopic examination, which permits magnification and photo-documentation of occult injuries and well as obvious ones. A normal saline-lubricated speculum is used to inspect the vaginal vault and cervix; anal speculums are employed to search for evidence of rectal tears or other injuries. Toluidine dye, a substance that will stain denuded areas, is sometimes employed to assist in visualizing less obvious injuries. Some sexual assault protocols use a wet mount slide to detect motile sperm, but this is not considered essential for confirming sexual assault.

Depending upon local policies and procedures, laboratory studies may be done to obtain baseline information for sexually transmitted diseases or pregnancy, and specific prophylaxis may be offered. In some jurisdictions, HIV testing may also be done. Blood is usually obtained for DNA and ABO studies and toxicology screens, and urine as well, may be collected for pregnancy and toxicological tests.

After the examination has been completed, the patient is assisted with bathing and dressing activities by their advocate while the examiner completes details of documentation and preservation of evidence. The evidence may be secured within the emergency department in a locked, refrigerated unit, awaiting police pick-up, or may be directly transferred via chain of custody to an awaiting officer.

PEDIATRIC SEXUAL ASSAULT VICTIMS

Although there are some modifications required in examining the pediatric victim of sexual assault, the principles remain the same. Only individuals specifically trained in pediatric sexual assault should ac-

complish the pediatric examination, as there are some critical variations in the legal aspects of consents and the conduct of the examination.

AFTER-CARE INSTRUCTIONS

All sexual assault victims should be given written instructions prior to their leaving the emergency department with information such as the telephone numbers for the rape crisis counseling center, the victim assistance programs and any other resources that might be appropriate. Emergency personnel should also ensure that transportation is provided for the victim to home or another safe haven when they leave the department. The ED should elicit where the individual will be staying and contact them within 24 hours post-examination to ensure their well-being and to review follow-up plans for post-sexual assault care and counseling.

GOVERNMENTAL RESPONSIBILITY FOR SEXUAL ASSAULT EXAMINATION SERVICES

In most cities, there are designated centers that perform these examinations, and arrangements for assuming any incurred expenses vary. However, the victim may not assume any responsibility for charges associated with evidence collection for the prosecution of the perpetrator. Although the victim is ordinarily liable for any medical expenses and trauma treatment, they are usually reimbursable in most states under the Crime Victim Compensation or Victim Assistance Programs.

Philosophy

When medical evidence is offered in court for cases of alleged rape, it is essential that the district attorney be able to demonstrate that he or she is using the same evidence that was collected during the medical examination of the victim/plaintiff. He or she must, therefore, be able to identify all those who handled the evidence and account for each step in the process of collection, storage, transportation, and delivery. In order that this "chain of evidence" be completely traceable, it is essential that as few people as possible actually touch the evidence.

For hospital procedures, then, it seems most reasonable to have the person collecting the evidence hand it directly to the EN, who, after fully identifying and sealing the envelope, deposits it with "security" (either the police or the refrigerator). Proper chain of evidence sealing consists of placing all evidence in the provided container and sealing it with tape: the date, time, and name of the person sealing the container should be affixed in such a manner that the information covers both the container itself and the sealing tape. This should then be refrigerated and remain as is until handed over to the proper authority, who signs for it.

■ DEATH, DYING, AND GRIEF

In the past few years, a great deal of controversy has arisen regarding the definition of *death*. Death is not the clear-cut final stage of life that it once was; it has become a more prolonged process, creating an atmosphere of both hope and despair. To cope with this recent phenomenon, ENs must:

- Learn to accept death according to their own individual beliefs;
- Accept the cultural, ethnic, or religious beliefs relating to death of the people for whom they are caring;
- Recognize that everyone deals with death in his or her own unique way—surviving family or friends must be allowed the right to express their grief in any way that is not harmful to others or themselves.

The type of death most often encountered in the ED is sudden and unexpected, usually resulting from trauma or heart attack. Because of this, the survivors are faced with the sudden onset of a process they neither understand nor wish to accept—the process of grief. It is encountered by peoples of all cultures and has several recognizable stages. These stages, as outlined by Elisabeth Kübler-Ross, M.D., are apparent in the dying patient, in the dying patient's survivors, and in the survivors of the person who has died a sudden death. To help both patients and survivors, it is important to understand and recognize these stages: denial, anger, bargaining, depression, and acceptance.[6] To prevent the inappropriate support of any of these stages, ENs must also recognize these same stages within themselves. It is easy and dangerous for an EN to promote any or all of these

stages; this can undoubtedly lead to unnecessary feelings of guilt on the part of both the survivors and the EN who has helped this process along. Most importantly, it can leave the dying patient without the critical support of the family at a time it is most needed. Every effort should be made to contact the family of someone who is dying from an unexpected cause. If this cannot be done, the EN must provide as much support as possible to the dying person. It is generally not necessary to confirm or deny that one is dying. Instances in which the patient is conscious of the efforts to save his or her life may also afford the patient the awareness that he or she is dying. Even though the activities are hectic and often impersonal, it is imperative that the person be made to feel that he or she *is* still alive. The EN has the best opportunity to accomplish this, since it is the EN who spends more continuous time with the patient and can reassure the patient that he or she will not be left alone; and indeed, this should be the case.

Since dealing with death seems to be so difficult for everyone, there is a tendency to avoid allowing the family to be with the loved one who has just died and to send the family home with condolences and sedatives; however, this simply delays the grief process and in some cases seriously inhibits it. If the family wishes to see the deceased person, they should be allowed—even encouraged—to do so, and in fact should be asked if they would prefer to be alone with the person for a short period of time. If they decline, they are providing an indication of their method of and capacity for dealing with the death. ENs should never let their own feelings interfere with the normal bereavement process of the family.

Events surrounding death in the ED happen so quickly that ENs have very limited time to initiate the healthy first stages of grief. The more understanding an EN has of death, dying, and grieving, the better able he or she is to provide appropriate support and assistance. However, not all the questions related to these issues can be answered in a matter-of-fact manner. With a greater realization of their involvement with death, ENs frequently have the singular opportunity of providing understanding, comfort, and support in a meaningful fashion. ENs must realize that they are not impervious to the same feelings shared by the patient and the family and that they may be able to offer the only rational focal point from which others can gain perspective and stability.

■ COMMUNICATION WITH PATIENTS AND FAMILIES

The quality of the communication that ENs establish and maintain with patients and their families is a crucial factor in dealing with all psychiatric and emotional crises. The importance of communication with the trauma victim is often unrecognized, yet the trauma patient and family are frequently in an incapacitating emotional state not unlike the psychiatric crisis that brought them to the ED.

The EN must first of all be constantly aware of the depth of patient anguish and of the fact that these anguished emotions are "normal" human responses to severe crises. Emotional responses to traumatic events often follow a sequence similar to that concerning death and dying. A typical pattern is numbing; anger—in particular, outbursts of anger at the caregiver; disbelief and denial; guilt; searching and yearning for restitution; disorganization and despair; and depression and loneliness. These are all normal, rather than pathological, responses of humans in physical or emotional trauma states. ENs must anticipate this "venting" process verbally as well as nonverbally and be prepared to interact professionally and supportively. Although one can enumerate a bewildering variety of emotional and psychiatric entities, there are some common communication strategies that are appropriate across the entire spectrum of emotionally charged situations:

- Be aware of the intense emotions, and their probable sequence, that are engulfing your patient.
- Introduce yourself as early and as warmly as you can, both by name and as a professional.
- Recognize and treat the patient as a person, not as a clinical entity. Address this person by name and start supportive communication immediately, with reassurance, personal warmth, and professional confidence.
- Be aware that patients hear and sense what is said and felt by staff. They are particularly sensitive to emotional implications.
- Ensure the preservation of your patient's dignity and privacy.
- Listen, actively and responsively, but as a professional and not as a fellow victim.
- Monitor your own reactions and comments; know your own emotional biases or hang-ups and your early warning signs.
- Present and maintain an organized, confident, and assertive but caring manner, to provide the setting for a therapeutic climate.
- Allow and encourage the patient and family to express feelings. You can help them start working through the involved patterns of response to crisis and irretrievable loss.
- Plan for and allow time and space to explain and reexplain procedures, what to expect next, and options and resources available. People in distress need more explanation than may seem logically sufficient. Repeated efforts at explanation are an important part of the EN's therapeutic intervention.
- Remember always that the EN is the only constant in the patient's crisis environment and bears the responsibility of being the patient's advocate, an especially important role.

■ REFERENCES

1. Cusack JR, Malaney KR. The diagnostic psychiatric interview. *Emerg Med.* August 15, 1989; 27–36.
2. Centers for Disease Control. Premature Mortality in the United States. *MMWR CDC Surveill Summ.* 1986;35(2S):1S–11S.
3. Trautman PD, Harris HJ, Pferrer CR, et al: Spotting the suicidal adolescent. *Emerg Med.* September 1992: 155–169.
4. Slaby AE, Lieb J, Tancredi LR. *Handbook of Psychiatric Emergencies.* 2nd ed. New York, NY: Medical Examination Publishing; 1981:239.
5. Bassuck EL, Birk AW, eds. *Emergency Psychiatry: Concepts, Methods, and Practices.* New York, NY: Plenum; 1984:358.
6. Kübler-Ross E. *On Death and Dying.* New York, NY: Macmillan; 1969.

■ BIBLIOGRAPHY

Aiken F, Tarbuck P. Practical ethical and legal aspects of caring for the assaultive client. In: Kidd B, Start C, eds. *Management of Violence and Aggression in Health Care*. London, England: Gaskell; 1995.

Aiken MM, Speck PM. Sexual assault and multiple trauma: a sexual assault nurse examiner (SANE) challenge. *J Emerg Nurs*. 1995;21:466–468.

Andrews J. Sexual assault aftercare instructions. *J Emerg Nurs*. 1992;18:152–156.

Barber JM, Dillman PA. *Emergency Patient Care for the EMT-A;* Reston, Va: Reston Publishing; 1981: 425–446.

Beckmann CRB, Groetzinger LL. Treating sexual assault victims: a protocol for health professionals. *Phys Asst*. Feb 1990;123–130.

Blouin AM. Munchausen syndrome: a test of clinical reasoning. *J Emerg Nurs*. 1993;19:513–515.

Bradley V, Shawler C. One emergency department's guidelines for the care of suicidal patients. *J Emerg Nurs*. 1993;19:393–395.

Curry JL. The care of psychiatric patients in the emergency department. *J Emerg Nurs*. 1993;19:396–407.

Cusack JR, Malaney KR. The diagnostic psychiatric interview. *Emerg Med*. Aug 15, 1989; 27–36.

Dealing with Death and Dying: Nursing Skillbook. Jenkintown, Pa: Nursing 77 Books; 1977.

Foley JJ. Considerations in the use of benzodiazepines and antipsychotics in the emergency department. *J Emerg Nurs*. 1993;19:448–450.

Fulton R, Bendiksen R. *Death and Identity*. Bowie, Md: Charles Press; 1976.

Glasson L. The care of psychiatric patients in the emergency department: preparation, staff awareness, preventive practices, and the psychiatric patient. *J Emerg Nurs*. 1993;19:385–391.

Goldman B. Facing up to violent patients; part 2. *Emerg Med*. June 1994;121–126.

Goldman B. Facing up to violent patients; part 1. *Emerg Med*. May 1994; 19–34.

Grunfeld AF, Hotch D. Detecting domestic violence against women in the emergency department: a nursing triage model. *J Emerg Nurs*. Aug 1994;20(4):271–274.

Hampton HL. Care of the woman who has been raped. *N Engl J Med*. 1995;133:234–237.

Irons TG. Documenting sexual abuse of a child. *Emerg Med*. Apr 1993; 57–75.

Jezierski M. Profile of depression. *J Emerg Nurs*. 1994;20:80–81.

Jones WH, Buttery M. Sudden death: survivor's perceptions of their emergency department experience. *J Emerg Nurs*. 1981;7(1):14–17.

Kaplan HI, Sudock BJ, eds. *Comprehensive Textbook of Psychiatry*. 4th ed. Baltimore, Md: Williams & Wilkins; 1985.

Keep N, Gilbert P. California Emergency Nurses Association's informal survey of violence in California emergency departments. *J Emerg Nurs*. 1992;18: 433–442.

Ledray LE. Sexual assault evidentiary exam and treatment protocol. *J Emerg Nurs*. 1995;21:355–359.

Ledray LE. The sexual assault nurse clinician: a fifteen-year experience in Minneapolis. *J Emerg Nurs*. 1992;18:217–222.

Ledray LE. The sexual assault examination: overview and lessons learned in one program. *J Emerg Nurs*. 1992;18(3):223–232.

Levitt MA, Derrick GR. An evaluation of physiological parameters of stress in the emergency department. *Am J Emerg Med*. 1991;8:217–219.

Lynch VA. *Sexual Violence*. Lewisville, Tex: Bear Hawk Consulting Group and Barbara Clark Mims Associates; 1992.

MacKinnon RA, Michels R. *The Psychiatric Interview in Clinical Practice*. Philadelphia, Pa: WB Saunders; 1971.

Marshall JR, ed. Behavioral emergencies. *Emerg Care Q*. April 1991;7(1).

McFarlane J, Greenberg L, Weltge A, Watson M. Identification of abuse in emergency departments: effectiveness of a two-question screening tool. *J Emerg Nurs*. 1995;21:391–394.

Meade DM, Riccio JC. Violence in the emergency department. *Top Emerg Med*. 1994;16(3).

Mitchell JT. *Emergency Services Stress: Guidelines for Preserving the Health and Careers of Emergency Services Personnel*. Englewood Cliffs, NJ: Prentice-Hall; 1990.

Mizsur GL. Depression and paranoia: is your patient at risk? *Nursing 95*. Feb 1995; 67.

O'Carroll PW, Potter LB. Programs for the prevention of suicide among adolescents and young adults. *MMWR CDC Surveill Summ*. 1994;43:RR-6.

Open letter to emergency nurses from an overdose patient. *J Emerg Nurs*. 1992;18:244–247.

Piacentini J. Evaluating adolescent suicide attempters: what emergency nurses need to know. *J Emerg Nurs*. 1993;19:465–466.

Rosen P, Barkin RM, Fraen GR, et al. *Emergency Medicine Concepts and Clinical Practice*. 3rd ed. St. Louis, Mo: Mosby-Year Book; 1992.

Schultz CA. The dynamics of grief. *J Emerg Nurs* 1979;5(5):26–30.

Schultz CA. The dying person. *J Emerg Nurs*. 1979;5(3):12–16.

Schultz CA. Cultural aspects of death and dying. *J Emerg Nurs.* 1979;5(1):24–27.

Shybut J, Carter R. An ounce of intervention: developing a standard training program for behavioral emergencies. *J Emerg Med Serv* July 1983;41–45.

Sinkinson CA. Panic attacks: what most physicians don't know. *Emerg Med Rep.* 1990;11:201–209.

Solomon J. Decoding signals from the suicidal patient. *Emerg Med.* Feb 1992;201–205.

Solomon J. The suicide scenario: rewriting the final act. *Emerg Med.* Feb 1989;75–80.

Strawser DS. Management plan for a habitually combative patient. *J Emerg Nurs.* 1994;20:204–206.

Tardiff K. The current state of psychiatry in the treatment of violent patients. *Arch Gen Psychiatry.* 1992;49:493.

Thomas H, Schwartz E, Petrilli R. Droperidol versus haloperidol for chemical restraint of agitated and combative patients. *Ann Emerg Med.* 1992;21:407–413.

Trautman PD, Harris HJ, Pferrer CR, et al: Spotting the suicidal adolescent. *Emerg Med.* Sept 1992;155–169.

■ REVIEW: PSYCHIATRIC AND BEHAVIORAL EMERGENCIES

1. List the five key areas of pertinent information that are important in the assessment and observation of the patient with a behavioral emergency.

2. Describe the four content areas of a mental status examination.

3. Describe the procedures and safeguards for using physical or chemical restraints in behavioral emergencies.

4. List the general categories of psychiatric and behavioral emergencies that are generally seen in the emergency department (ED).

5. List at least six appropriate nursing diagnoses for the depressed patient.

6. Enumerate at least 10 "red flags" for suicidal risk in the depressed patient who comes alone or is brought to the ED, and describe the support systems that need to be developed and in place.

7. Describe the presentation of a patient having a manic episode and list at least four red flags for potential violence.

8. Outline the management plan for a truly paranoid episode and the underlying rules for communication.

9. Describe the significance of auditory hallucinations as opposed to visual hallucinations.

10. Describe the three cardinal goals in the management of a rape victim and outline the techniques that should be employed in the patient interview.

11. Explain the purpose and importance of the chain-of-evidence (COE) examination and describe the correct procedure for handling evidentiary clothing.

12. Identify three areas in which the sexual assault victim must have follow-up care.

Emergency Department Management and Professional Issues

Legal and Forensic Considerations

34

Legal implications of delivering emergency health care become increasingly more significant every day. State-of-the-art care grows in sophistication, and emergency department (EDs) meet greater patient demands and more complex challenges. Emergency nurses (ENs) are held accountable for quality care, through competent assessments, interventions, and careful documentation of those events. Both competency and documentation carry significant weight in medicolegal outcomes when those outcomes are challenged with lawsuits; ENs must be aware of risks involved with patient care and prepared to deal with them. Until recently, nursing education concerning legal matters was paid little attention. Today, however, there is much written, taught, and available to learn on the subject. As ENs adhere to the tenet *primum non nocere* (first do no harm) in protecting patient welfare, they must also protect themselves. That protection requires a working knowledge of legal responsibilities and risk areas in nursing practice; this chapter addresses many of those areas of concern.

■ TYPES OF LAW

American law is based on elements of English common law in an extremely abbreviated way. There are a number of types of law that relate to medical and nursing practice and guarantee a means by which the patient is treated safely and within his or her rights as a free citizen.

Statutory law is the result of a bill passed by a state legislature, with administrative rules and regulations promulgated pursuant to that law that has the force and effect of law but are more easily changed than a statute. Licensing laws fall into this category.

Case law is an interpretation by the courts of statutes, administrative rules, and the underlying common law.

Constitutional law determines the validity of both statutory decisions and case law in the context of the provisions of the Fourth Amendment (the right of the individual to be protected from illegal search and seizure), the Fifth Amendment (the right of the individual to be protected from self incrimination), and the Fourteenth Amendment, which provides the right to due process of law.

■ STANDARD OF CARE

Standard of care is an important term to ENs. In the past, each community had its own level of care, which followed local custom. Courts across the country have abandoned that concept, and it is now being held that a similarly trained person anywhere should provide the same level or standard of care as a person operating in the same capacity elsewhere. The amount of training or expertise one has does have implications in establishing the standard of care, and many times this is the factor that prolongs a court case.

Generally, you will be held to the ORPP standard of care—the standard of care provided by an ordinary, reasonable, prudent person with like or similar training in like or similar circumstances. It is each EN's responsibility to stay current educationally and in clinical practice and to know what the accepted standards of nursing practice are, as well to adopt improved standards as they develop.

■ NEGLIGENCE AND MALPRACTICE

There seems to be a general feeling among hospital personnel that any kind of incident that occurs in a hospital may result in a lawsuit. This may be true in broad terms; however, most incidents do not lead to lawsuits. Even if you were named as a party to a court action for malpractice or negligence, there are certain things that must be proved to the jury and to the court before you will be held liable. There are many occurrences in hospitals where blame cannot be attributed to any one person, and certainly not every instance of mishap is a malpractice situation.

■ LEGAL ASPECTS OF EMERGENCY HEALTH CARE

RESPONSIBILITIES OF HOSPITALS

Most hospitals today provide some degree of emergency service to the public, although there is no law requiring *every* hospital maintain an emergency facility. State laws and regulations demand that certain requirements be met by hospitals, and those wishing to participate in health insurance programs for the aged (Medicare) and to realize fiscal solvency must comply with the federal "conditions of participation," which are administered at the state level. The standards of the Joint Commission on Accreditation of Healthcare Organizations (JCAHO) are not statutory but may be compulsory if the particular state requires it within its licensing regulations. Noncompliance on the part of a hospital may well result in liability for negligence and may even disqualify it for governmental reimbursement and relicensure.

Essentially, if a hospital holds itself out as capable of providing emergency service, it must provide that service according to the standards set forth by the state, Medicare, JCAHO, or all three. These standards and their implications are discussed in Chapter 36.

Doctrine of Corporate Negligence

Corporate negligence means that the hospital or health-care agency, as a corporate entity, can be held liable if it fails to meet established standards of conduct and patient care to which it has sub-scribed. Negligence on the part of the hospital can be found in any one of four areas:

- Defective or improper equipment
- Physical condition of the premises
- Negligent drug handling
- Careless medical treatment

The governing body of the hospital or health center is the board of trustees; case law, statutes, and standards of accreditation all recognize the ultimate, nondelegable corporate and legal responsibility of the board to ensure that quality care is provided.[1]

Definitions

Negligence and *malpractice* are terms often used interchangeably, but there is a difference. *Negligence* is the omission of an act that should have been performed—or the commission of one that should not have been performed—coupled with unreasonableness or imprudence or both on the part of the doer. This is a general definition that can apply to any sector of the public, be it parents in the home or the professional nurse on duty.

Malpractice, on the other hand, is negligence on the part of a professional who is licensed to practice in a specific field; it is a term that is applied to that professional when his or her misconduct, lack of skill, omission, or misjudgment in the commission of duty causes harm to the person or property of the recipient of the services.

A *tort* is an unintentional negligent act upon the person of another that results in injury to that person.

Elements of Negligence

In a lawsuit, there are four basic elements of negligence that must all be alleged and proved. They are duty, breach of duty, proximate causation, and damages or injury. *Duty* means to perform in such a manner that your patient receives skilled care used by other nurses in like circumstances. *Breach of duty* is the failure to carry out that which is implied in the definition of *duty.*

Damage must be proved before an award is made, even though there may have been gross negligence. Proximate causation is more difficult to prove, and it must be shown that there was a causal relationship between a breach of duty and the resulting damages. A break in the chain of causation makes it difficult for the plaintiff to prevail. There are several defenses in negligence actions that are, by and large, statutory. One is assumption of risk, which is injury caused when instructions are ignored. Another is contributory negligence, wherein the injured person has contributed to the injury. Information of this sort should be carefully documented and made available for use to the defense lawyer. Comparative negligence determines whether there was negligence on the part of the defendant or the plaintiff, and if there was on both parts, to what percent or extent. It must be proved that the defendant was at least 51 percent negligent for an award to be made, and the award is made according to percentage. Several states now have this statute.

Remember, however, that the jury finds the facts, and the court (judge) determines the law.

CONSENTS

Assault and Battery

Consent for treatment is a necessity because the law protects individuals from unpermitted and unprivileged contact to their person.[2] Threatening to or attempting to carry out a threat to touch another person against his or her will is assault; battery is the assault carried out or completed.[1] Since battery, then, is the unlawful touching of another person without consent, any treatment given a patient without consent can be construed as technical battery, unless the treatment was required to save the patient's life, in which case the consent is implied.

Informed Consent

There is no law requiring written consent from a patient before treatment, and when a patient voluntarily presents for treatment, the consent is generally considered to be implied. It is considered essential practice, however, to document the consent for the protection of everyone involved, and this written consent should be an informed consent, with the patient participating, if at all possible. Many hospital attorneys feel that the patient should be required to write out the consent in his or her own words and sign it with a date, time, and witness. The patient must be advised of the contemplated course of action, the alternatives, if any, and the degree and kind of risk involved with the proposed treatment. In the ED, where time constraints are often a concern, it

may be helpful to explain the procedure or plan of treatment to the patient in the same way you would want it explained to you and in simple layperson's terms to avoid confusion and misunderstanding of what was said.

Specific Consent

When a patient has expressed consent directly, either orally or in writing, and has been informed fully about the procedure, alternatives, risks, and so forth, the patient has given general consent to subsequent treatment and has established the voluntary physician–patient relationship. This is generally adequate for the usual procedures involving physician examination, x-rays, injections, laboratory samplings, and so forth. There are medicolegal experts, however, who advocate a more specific additional consent form for further specific diagnosis procedures, such as lumbar punctures, intravenous pyelograms (IVPs) and others that carry a higher risk factor.

Emergency Doctrine of Consent

When intervention is instituted to sustain life and prevent further damage, consent is secured after the fact, if necessary, from the patient or from the family. Under these circumstances, emergency doctrine prevails, and consent is implied. Remember, however, that a patient can always withdraw consent at any time and that intoxication can invalidate a signed consent form. Generally, it is thought that if an intoxicated person cooperates with the procedure, the consent is implied.

Blood Alcohol Level Consent

When the EN is involved with obtaining blood alcohol level specimens, there are many caveats—the EN is frequently caught in a dilemma. Although consent requirements vary widely from state to state, good rules of thumb are as follows:

1. Draw blood only if the patient expressly consents. If an intoxicated person voluntarily holds out the arm for blood to be drawn, this consent is adequate.
2. When police have a search-and-seizure warrant, draw blood without the patient's consent, but use *no* physical force.
3. If there is no warrant and the patient refuses, *do not* draw blood.

Minors and Consent

Valid consents can be given only by competent adults; the age of majority varies from state to state. Most states now observe 18 years as the age of majority, although some states allow persons as young as 14 and 15 to consent to their own treatment. Some special situations require their own consent procedures and are as follows:

- Never accept a consent form for an abortion from parents unless the girl also signs an informed consent.
- A consultation should be requested for emergency treatment of a child if parents are absent and the next-of-kin cannot be reached.
- In the case of Jehovah's Witnesses, if a child needs blood replacement and the parents refuse on religious grounds, a court order can be obtained to allow administration; this does *not* apply to adults.

If and when a life-and-death situation or a possibility of serious harm without treatment present itself and the patient refuses consent, the administration should be involved as soon as possible so that every available legal avenue can be explored.

DOCTRINE OF *RESPONDEAT SUPERIOR*

The various functions of the EN are governed not only by state law, as it affects both professional practice (Nurse Practice Act) and hospital licensure, but by hospital policy as it specifically relates to that which the EN may and may not perform within that particular hospital. How binding is hospital policy on the EN? This is a problem that frequently surfaces.

The doctrine of *respondeat superior* (let the master answer) holds that the employer is vicariously (or secondarily) liable for acts of its employees and has a shared legal responsibility for negligent acts. The EN, as a licensed professional, has a duty to respond to hospital policy as well as to the patient. Any decision must be carefully weighed before hospital or physician judgment is overridden, with the realization that *respondeat superior* requires that the employer be responsible for the acts of a professional employee. Ordinarily, decisions of such weight are not within the EN's province.

LIABILITY AND MALPRACTICE INSURANCE

There is also a doctrine of law known as the borrowed servant. The classic example is the nurse who is employed by the hospital but is under the exclusive control of a surgeon at the operating-room (OR) table. That person is deemed to have been "borrowed" by the surgeon and technically becomes the employee of the physician while at the OR table. The hospital will not be secondarily liable for the negligent acts of that employee. The circulating nurse in the OR is *not* deemed to be a borrowed servant, but rather is doing clerical or administrative work in the OR that is ordinarily embraced within the scope of his or her employment. This nurse remains the employee of the hospital even though he or she also responds to the surgeon's needs.

Many hospitals carry insurance for "all named employees," which is the same as *all* employees. If the hospital policy so states, the EN is covered by the hospital's insurance, so there is not necessarily a need for the EN to carry personal malpractice insurance. However, unless the hospital insurance policy is so written, it may not insure him or her, and the EN named as a defendant would then be obliged to retain and pay his or her own defense counsel. ENs should determine their coverage as "named employees"; if not covered, they should arrange coverage under the hospital policy or obtain personal liability insurance coverage.

Generally, the hospital liability coverage will protect the employee only while he or she is acting within the scope of employment. If an EN is performing nursing acts outside of hospital employment, personal liability insurance should definitely be carried. The prevalent belief among nursing personnel to the effect that having no significant assets makes them "suit-proof" is highly erroneous. They are foolhardy in overlooking the unhappy fact that if they are married, commonly held assets are in jeopardy, because a judgment can be collected many years later when the couple's joint assets are sufficient to satisfy the claim. Essentially, most who are in a position to counsel professional personnel warn them that as professional persons, they are responsible for their own acts of wrongdoing or acts of nursing negligence, whether shared with other parties (hospital, physician, or both) or not.

AREAS OF SPECIAL CONCERN

Medications and the Law

Medications are not only administered in most EDs, they also may be dispensed. Dispensing (identifying, counting, packaging, labeling, and so on) is the responsibility of the pharmacist, but many state laws are conflicting in this area. Most state laws provide for licensed nursing personnel to administer drugs and to withdraw any drug from the drug room, if the pharmacist is not on the premises, in the amount needed to treat a patient with a "starter" or "carryover" dosage, but *not* to dispense medications.

Take-home Medications. The ED presents

unique problems and situations with providing take-home medications, problems that do not exist in the inpatient hospital setting. In order to be in compliance with the laws in many states, there should be a tray or cabinet in the ED containing pharmacy-prepared, precounted, prepackaged, pre-labeled medications of the types most likely to be given out to patients. Most state laws also provide that a physician may dispense in an emergency situation and may go to the hospital pharmacy for any medication needed to send with the patient.

In reality, the EN, for the most part, is the one who performs this function for the physician; great care must be taken to carefully verify the medication with the physician to be very certain that the medication(s) is (are) properly identified with the date, name of the patient, doctor, and instructions for taking the medication before it is given to the patient. Most state hospital associations now make available a publication on "guidelines for hospital pharmacy," which contains an ED section with suggestions for the handling of packaged and labeled drugs most likely to be given out to patients. These guidelines are approved by most state boards of pharmacy and would be extremely supportive, should a case on "dispensing" drugs from the ED go to court. Guidelines should be carefully followed on labeling; these are included in the publications of State Hospital Associations.

Privileged Communication

Ethically and legally, the EN has an obligation to hold confidential anything communicated by the patient. This is known as the nurse–patient relationship of privileged communication. You cannot be required to testify in court about a confidential communication between the patient and you, but this is the *patient's* right, not yours. Therefore, if the patient files suit and brings out the confidential matter, it is deemed to be a waiver on the patient's part to the right of confidentiality, and you then can testify. In most states, this statute applies to physicians and nurses in civil cases only. The lawyer–client relationship applies to both civil and criminal cases, as does the clergy–parishioner relationship.

Intentional Torts

Intentional torts are legal wrongs intentionally perpetrated. Defamation of character is an intentional tort and includes both slander (the spoken word) and libel (the written word) generally, although this is not always true. Defamation of character is a defamatory remark made by one person about another person *in the presence of a third party*. The theory is that the defamatory remark has damaged that person's reputation in the community, and there are certain things for which punitive damages can be awarded if the plaintiff prevails:

- Damaging a person's business reputation
- The implication of the presence of a "dread" disease, such as a sexually transmitted disease (STD), acquired immunodeficiency syndrome (AIDS) or AIDS-related complex (ARC), or Hansen's disease (leprosy)
- Derogatory remarks about a woman's chastity or lack thereof

The only defense available to a defendant is to be able to prove that everything said to the third party is truth, but the burden of proof is on the defendant. There is no requirement for the plaintiff to prove that any damage actually occurred.

Right to Privacy

The patient has the right to withhold himself or herself from public scrutiny, with a few exceptions (as, for instance a holder of public office). The EN's responsibility is to the patient and to prevent, if possible, the invasion of the patient's right to privacy.

Photographs. The most frequent problem in preserving the right to privacy is that of photographing patients. Everyone has the right to withhold himself or herself from public scrutiny, and this must be upheld. If a patient is to be photographed, a consent form should be obtained, and the use to which the photograph will be put must be clearly explained. If the patient's knee is to be photographed, without any patient identification, you probably do not need a consent. If, however, you are going to photograph a patient's face for a scientific reason and identify the pictures only by number as "before" and "after" photographs, the patient should be informed of the reason and be asked to consent to *both* "before" and "after" photographs. The patient then has the right to withdraw his or her consent for either or both of the pictures if he or she wishes to do so, at any time up to the time the picture(s) will be used or published. In short, written permission is needed for any photograph in which there is a possibility that the patient may be identified.

The press: The press has a right to photograph a patient in the public areas of the hospital (parking lot, corridors, lobby) without consent. Once inside the ED, however, the press *does not* have the right to photograph without consent or even to be in the department. News personnel *do not have access to patient areas without permission.* Police officers *do* have the right to photograph in the ED, *in pursuit of duty only,* and the EN has an obligation to assist the officer in doing so.

Required Reporting

Certain cases and situations are required by law in most states to be reported to the proper authorities (although requirements may vary widely). Such reporting is required even though it might be deemed to be a breach of the confidential relationship. These cases are as follows:

- Gunshot wounds (GSWs), self-inflicted or otherwise
- Stab wounds, self-inflicted or otherwise
- Anything that appears to have been the result of violence, including motor vehicle accidents (MVAs) and sexual assaults
- Communicable diseases
- Child or elder abuse (now mandatory in most states for physicians and nurses to report)

- Any death occurring in-hospital within 48 hours of admission (including persons dead on arrival [DOAs]) when involving patients not previously treated by a physician
- Drug abuse
- Poisonings
- Seizures
- Fetal deaths

Incident Reports

Incident reports must be made out by the one who observes the incident, should *never* become part of the medical record, and must be kept confidential. ENs have the obligation to know the specific requirements of the insurance carrier for the hospital in which they work. The form should be dispatched to the administrator (or designee), who should review the incident report and send it directly to the hospital attorney or risk manager. This then becomes confidential information because the chain of confidentiality has been maintained (and is more credible if a case develops and is taken to court), and becomes inadmissible (privileged) evidence. The EN should put what is *medically* relevant to the incident into the patient's chart and what is *legally* relevant into the incident report.

Statute of Limitations

In a medical malpractice situation, the statute of limitation in most states is 2 years, unless a foreign body has been left in the patient or unless the patient had no reason to know or could not have known that the untoward incident occurred. In these cases, the term would run from 2 years from the discovery up to 5 years, and if fraud is involved, the statutes usually provide that the time may be extended further.

Self-Defense in the Emergency Department

In any ED situation, the EN has the right of self-defense, but only to the extent of avoiding or escaping grave bodily harm. There is no right to reprisal, except as a defensive maneuver.

Presence of Foreign Bodies

As an all-around protection against the loss of foreign bodies in patient's tissues (needles, catheters, gauze sponges), the EN and physician should be absolutely certain to check that no item is put into a patient's body or through the tissues that is not radiopaque. (This should include materials like infant feeding tubes, frequently used for cutdowns.)

Record Accuracy and Completeness

Accurate times and dates are essential on ED records. In a court of law, a medical record can be very damaging if it is incomplete and does not accurately reflect the treatment given a patient. Medical records must be concise, complete, and properly signed. To all legal intents and purposes, *if it was not documented, it was not done.* The statute of limitations can be affected in litigation without accurate date and time, and estate questions can be complicated should one spouse predecease the other by a matter of moments in the ED; the order of death will be settled by the time recorded.

Witnessing Wills

Two witnesses are required for attesting to the signature on a last will and testament. If called upon to sign as a witness to the person's signature, do so with blue ink; this will confirm the signature as being part of an original document rather than a possible photocopy.

Living Wills

The Patient Self-Determination Act of 1990 was upheld by the U.S. Supreme Court, allowing living wills and other advance directives to be executed by individuals, basically stating that "if at such a time the situation should arise where there is no reasonable expectation of my recovery from extreme physical or mental disability, I direct that I be allowed to die and not be kept alive by medications, artificial means, or "heroic measures." I do, however, ask that medication be mercifully administered to me to alleviate suffering, even though this may shorten my remaining life." The signator must have two witnesses, neither of which may be the person's health-care agent, and at least one witness must not have a financial interest in the person's death. The name of the person's physician should be written at the bottom of the page and copies should be in possession of the physician, family members, and any others likely to be concerned for the individual's well-being. Living wills are tantamount to "do not resuscitate" (DNR) orders and are accorded respect and legal standing as the "law of the land." As patient advocates, ENs may be called upon to make their patients' wishes

known in given situations, although patients facing serious emergencies are unlikely to be prepared with the document in possession on admission. If, however, your patient shares his or her wishes with you, it is your obligation to inform the physician and seek the advice and support of both physician and family, if possible.

Leaving Against Medical Advice

Treatment cannot be instituted against a patient's will, and generally speaking, a conscious adult or emancipated minor has the right to refuse medical treatment. When such a situation arises, it is essential that the refusal of treatment be documented and that the patient sign the hospital's form for leaving "against medical advice" (AMA). If the patient is a child and the parent, guardian, or next-of-kin refuses treatment for that child, a child's AMA form should be signed by the responsible adult. These situations demand cool thinking and as much common sense as can be mustered. Generally, it is believed that the safest guidelines are to err on the side of patient safety and to do everything possible to convince the patient to remain for treatment, arguing gently and cajoling all the way. If a patient leaves the hospital premises without signing the AMA form, the incident should be *carefully* documented and signed by all personnel involved. Again, when a life-and-death situation presents itself and the patient refuses consent, it is wise to involve the hospital administration as rapidly as possible.

SPECIFIC AREAS OF MEDICOLEGAL VULNERABILITY

Medical and legal communities alike agree that we live in a litigious society. ENs must realize and fully understand that they are practicing in a high-risk arena; fertile ground exists for error, augmented by high anxiety levels, widely fluctuating patient expectations, frequent staffing problems, and constant pressure for rapid decision making and response.

A profile of vulnerable areas has emerged through the years of ED growth and development that now provides valuable guidelines for minimizing legal liability in the routine of daily practice (if indeed it can be called routine). The following list identifies those areas that are often the vulnerable, central issues in legal actions—all of which can be avoided by careful nursing practice:

- Lack of, or incomplete, documentation (not documented is not done):
    Flow sheets, vital signs (VS), level of consciousness (LOC): baseline observations with ongoing, timed monitoring
    Medications given, and their route, site, time, and response
    Incident reports or anecdotals
    Interhospital transfer documents (American College of Surgeons [ACS] guidelines)
- Failure to maintain cervical-spine immobilization until injury is ruled out
- Medication errors:
    Medicating wrong patient—check identification
    Missed or ignored allergies to medication
    Verbal orders—*always back up* with written orders
    Preloads and look-alikes in packaging
    Dispensing take-home medications without prepackaging
- Use of nonradiopaque invasive materials:
    Intravenous catheters
    Infant feeding tubes used in cutdowns
- Negligence (rebuttable if reasonable):
    Side rails left down
    Seizure in unobserved comatose patient causing injury
    Restrained person left unattended causing injury
- Patient misidentification:
    Wrong medications
    Wrong treatments
    Wrong surgical procedure
- Right to privacy, confidentiality:
    Privileged communication between physician and EN in civil cases
    Patient may disclose
    No photographs in patient-care areas without permission
    No press in patient-care areas
- Blood alcohol levels—observe parameters to avoid battery suit
- Recognition of high-risk patients:
    Acute psychotic—suicidal, violent, substance-dependent
    Unconscious patient
    Geriatric or pediatric patient
    No comprehension, no response
- Restraints:
    Use only if and when appropriate to protect the patient from harm
    Never leave restrained patient unattended and document carefully
    Always err on the side of patient safety
- Change of shift: maintain ongoing awareness that significant numbers of mistakes and incidents occur during shift changes

THE EMERGENCY NURSE AS WITNESS

Although ENs certainly hope never to be involved in legal action resulting from injury (either real or perceived) as a result of ED care, they would be well advised to prepare themselves for that occasion should it ever present itself. Here are some helpful guidelines for conduct in the course of giving a deposition or appearing on the witness stand in a court of law:

- Do not allow yourself to be queried by an unknown attorney, especially on the telephone; know with whom you are speaking and keep written notes of the date, time, and content of your conversation.
- Always tell the truth—do not guess or exaggerate. If you guess wrong, you may be falling into a trap. Answer honestly and frankly; any display of embarrassment or reluctance to answer will tend to discredit your testimony.[3]
- Always understand the question before answering; take your time.
- Answer the question and then stop. Talk loudly and distinctly enough; speak to the jury (do not look at your lawyer), maintaining eye contact while doing so.
- Do not allow yourself to be forced into a flat yes or no answer if a qualified answer is required. You have a right to explain or qualify if that is necessary for a truthful answer.[3]
- Use plain language—do not be pompous.
- Do not fence or argue with the cross-examination lawyer.
- Do not lose your temper.
- Be courteous no matter what the provocation; do not joke or wisecrack.

- At the blackboard, face the jury and attempt to draw in proportion.
- Be pleasant—be yourself—and remember you are a professional EN.

AVOIDING LITIGATION

When ENs are familiar with, understand, and follow the written policies and procedures of their department, and practice conscientiously, they will rarely be involved in litigation. A great number of nurse-attorneys and physician-attorneys, speaking to EN groups, generally agree that there are several points central to safe and litigation-free nursing practice:

- Caring personnel, who involve themselves with supportive care for both patient and family and strive to maintain close communication, are not apt to be blamed or named in suits by themselves.
- Anyone can sue anyone else for anything, but damage must be proven in order to win a case; accountable nursing practice, therefore, will protect the health care practitioner.
- ENs who are responsible—who double-check their actions closely, document concisely and accurately, and ensure full accountability for their actions—will have minimal worries about litigation.
- ENs will not be sued so long as they err on the side of patient safety and do no harm.

■ ROLE OF THE MEDICAL EXAMINER

The medical examiner system has evolved from the days of the Roman legions, when a physician was assigned to determine death and the causes of death among members of the legions. The first medical examiner system was established in the United States in the 1890s; many states now have a medical examiner system that functions within the framework of that state's statutory provisions. There are still other states, however, that operate under a coroner system, in which the office is elective, with no prerequisite medical background, as opposed to the medical examiner system, which requires that the medical examiner be a licensed physician in that state. The term *coroner* dates back into early times in England, when the king

sent a man to claim the estates and holdings of slain knights. The term *Crown's man* was applied, later becoming *crowner* and then as *coroner*. Whether your state or county functions under the jurisdiction of a medical examiner or a coroner, there are responsibilities that fall to ED personnel that should generally be handled along well-established lines of policy, employing common sense and judgment at the same time.

REPORTABLE DEATHS

Particular types of deaths are of such general importance to society that for centuries a government agency (the medical examiner or coroner) has assumed jurisdiction of these deaths:

- Deaths involving criminal activity (homicides or suspicious deaths), which may include unlawful use of dangerous or narcotic drugs or the use or abuse of chemicals or toxic agents
- Cases of self-destruction
- Traumatic deaths, including those that are apparently accidental or that follow an injury
- Persons dying without medical attention during the period immediately prior to death or not under the care of a physician during the period immediately prior to death

The term *immediately prior to death* is intentionally vague. A person seen by a physician in a small, remote town within a week of death may well be under closer care than a person seen in a clinic setting in a large metropolitan area the day of demise. The time period defining an "unattended death" is left to the individual physician's good judgment.

Many jurisdictions require that all deaths of persons admitted to a hospital or institution for less than 24 hours be immediately reported to the medical examiner but stipulate that they need not always be investigated and certified by the medical examiner or coroner. Reportable deaths should be made known to the medical examiner, his or her deputy, or the coroner immediately. If this becomes difficult and time-consuming in the ED, the problem should be conveyed to the supervisor or administrator on duty. Your county medical examiner or coroner should provide your ED with names and telephone numbers of the on-call personnel for their offices at all times.

Determination of Death

Deciding or determining death means merely that one is able to ascertain that death has occurred by the absence of VS. *Pronouncing* death, a term frequently used, means little or nothing, since death must first be determined and then must be certified. The determination of death can be made by any person under appropriate circumstances, but the certification of a death must be done by a licensed physician attending the death or by the medical examiner or coroner in that particular jurisdiction. The death certificate is documentation of the date, time, cause of death, contributing cause of death (if indicated), manner of death, and disposition. This certificate is a document that will be filed with the state bureau of vital statistics.

Management of the Person Dead on Arrival

The person DOA from natural causes, under the care of a private physician who is in attendance, is reportable but will generally not be a medical examiner case. Once this natural death is reported to the medical examiner by phone, the latter generally will "release" the body, which simply means that there is no further need for a governmental agency to be involved, since the private physician will complete the death certificate. This body then can be removed to the funeral establishment.

The person who is brought to the ED by car or ambulance DOA may present a problem of jurisdictional responsibility. ENs must be aware of the local lines of authority, realizing that two possibilities exist. The person DOA becomes the responsibility of either the county in which the death was discovered or the county from which the body has been transported; the exact time and place of death may be uncertain during transportation and difficult to confirm, but the county in which the death occurred is key. This area must be clarified for proper reporting and subsequent release of the body.

Confirmation of Death on Arrival

When DOAs arrive at the ED or patients die while in the ED, a careful examination must be made to determine death and the absolute cessation of VS. The following are guidelines that must be observed to avoid extremely embarrassing errors in judgment:

- Do *not* allow the examination to be conducted in the ambulance or other vehicle.
- *Always* remove the body to an area with adequate space and adequate light for a thorough, complete examination.
- Remove or open enough clothing to clearly expose the precordium, neck, and head for the physician to examine.
- Expect the ED physician to do a thorough and careful examination to determine death. If there is any doubt, record findings from a single electrocardiogram (ECG) lead.

SUDDEN INFANT DEATH SYNDROME

The disease known as sudden infant death syndrome (SIDS), or crib death, is a condition causing the sudden death of a normal, generally healthy infant during sleep, with no apparent cause. SIDS is the most common cause of infant death after the first month of life. The majority of SIDS infants are between 1 and 6 months of age, 90 percent are under 25 weeks at death, with the majority being between 2 and 4 months of age, and most studies show that 60 percent of SIDS babies are male. Though estimates vary for the number of infant deaths from SIDS in the U.S., the incidence nationwide is about 2 to 3 per 1000 live births.[4]

Some further studies reveal that SIDS occurs less commonly in summer months and occurs in cluster patterns during the winter among populations with "colds." The incidence among premature infants is higher than that among infants with a normal birth weight. SIDS is generally more commonly seen in the lower socioeconomic groups but is also routinely seen in more affluent population groups; almost all of these babies die while asleep, a fact suggesting that sleep has something to do with the cause of this obscure syndrome.[5]

Three common theories regarding SIDS have been unequivocally disproved in recent years. It is now well known that:

- The victims *absolutely do not* smother or suffocate in their pillows or bedclothing;

- The victims *do not die* from vomiting or choking on their milk;
- The victims *are not* battered children.

Many untrained investigators too often consider the death "suspicious" and react accordingly. A pathologist can easily and rapidly differentiate a case of child abuse from a crib death at autopsy, and before any serious consideration of parental interrogation occurs, an autopsy should be requisitioned immediately.

SIDS is a common and complex medical problem but is also a tragic situation for the parents, who frequently blame themselves until someone with knowledge of the syndrome explains the disease. Frequently, too, older children are psychologically devastated by the loss of the sibling, and all too often other family members (in-laws, grandparents, and even neighbors) may become suspicious and accusative. Everything possible should be done in the ED to support and comfort the parents of the SIDS victim and to provide counseling through a public health nurse or someone equally knowledgeable on the subject.

Procedures for Fatalities

A written policy on notification of the medical examiner or coroner should be readily available in the ED. The details of the notification procedure will vary with the local situation, but definite written policies should exist to ensure that a medical examiner's or coroner's representative knows of the death as soon as possible. Whether or not a statutory requirement exists, notification should be made immediately and directly. Do not depend on police agencies unless the officer with whom you talk is a deputy medical examiner or deputy coroner. Your county examiner may prefer to work through a deputy, so make an effort to know the county policy and determine who will respond to your call.

The Family

If the family has accompanied the body, notification of family depends on the particular circumstances of the death and may be handled by the physician who has made the determination or by the medical examiner, coroner, or deputy. If telephone notification is unavoidable, care must be taken to choose words carefully and to ensure that family members are prepared for the news. The physician may not always be the ideal person to make a death notification, and many hospitals use a social worker, chaplain, or bereavement nurse for this call. Words must be carefully selected and great care should be taken to ensure that the one called is ready and willing to accept news of a death, and that the caller has ample time to discuss any concerns he or she may have. In making telephone notifications, one must remember the right of the hearer to refuse the news.[6]

When relatives and friends do accompany the body of a DOA, make every effort to provide them with a private area, and ask that they remain at the ED until the medical examiner is contacted. Ask the medical examiner or coroner for his or her expected time of arrival and ask if he or she wishes the family detained. If an unreasonably long time ensues or if the family has insisted on leaving, always find out the address or telephone number where they can be reached. Families frequently do not return home and may be unavailable when it is vitally important to reach them. The information obtained from these people is often the most important part of the death investigation. If they are gone and cannot be reached for interview, significant problems and delays may arise.

The Postmortem Database

The EN can participate in valuable database collection by obtaining and recording as much information as possible from the ambulance or fire attendants, including their names and a telephone number where they may be reached. Their story is often crucial in arriving at judgments concerning disposition of the case. Any information that can be obtained from family or friends that may have a bearing on the medical history of the deceased person should be recorded objectively and accurately; the medical examiner will be appreciative.

In some states, the person investigating the death has a right to review the hospital chart, and it is extremely helpful to have this readily available to expedite the proceedings. If a deputy medical examiner or deputy coroner responds, explain the examining physician's observations, treatment, and diagnoses. Better yet, if the ED physician is available, have the physician talk directly with the deputy.

SPECIAL SITUATIONS

The following are guidelines for management of some of the special situations that may arise in the ED, all of which should be applied with common sense and judgment.

Autopsies

Generally speaking, the medical examiner, coroner, district attorney, or their designees have the authority to order a forensic autopsy. The family need not give permission, and in fact, if the autopsy is clearly indicated, they will not be asked. This is the medical examiner's, coroner's, or district attorney's decision alone. Clinical autopsies may be requested by either the family or members of the medical staff.

Handling Evidence

A general rule for handling any evidence in a criminal case or a reportable fatality is the less handling of evidence, the better. A chain of evidence (COE) must be established and that evidence must be handled properly and as carefully as possible if it is to serve its rightful purpose. Improper or excessive handling may destroy fragile bits of trace evidence. Every ED should provide and have in readiness evidence collection or forensic "kits" made up of brown paper bags, large and small, and plain envelopes for depositing and identifying clothing, weapons, and bits of evidence.[7]

Protecting Hands and Feet. Paper bags should be placed on victim's hands, feet, or head as appropriate to ensure that no trace evidence is lost.[8]

Identification of Treatment Sites. If venipunctures, cutdowns, chest tube insertions, or any other incisional procedures were done, be certain this is explained to the deputy so that these are not misinterpreted as wounds. If a preexisting wound was incorporated into a surgical incision, this also needs to be indicated by ink markings, sutures, or documentation.[9]

Clothing Removal and Handling. Do not cut the victim's clothing unless absolutely necessary. If an immediate examination of the wound is necessary, try to either unbutton or pull up the clothing. If cutting or ripping the clothing is not a life-saving necessity, spend a few seconds and try to avoid tearing or cutting through either a bullet wound defect or a knife slash in the clothing; cut along seam lines if necessary to cut. Always remember that some other persons (hours, days, or weeks later) must carefully reconstruct this clothing, matching knife wounds and bullet holes. Do not make their task more difficult; always save clothing for the investigators and never discard any articles that accompany the victim, since this is often important evidentiary material.

If clothing is wet (blood, water) hang it to air-dry for as much time as possible (in a secured area), carefully fold and bag each piece of clothing in its own brown paper bag, which "breathes"; identify with name, date, time, and your initials before it is turned over to the death investigator or crime scene officer. Never cram wet, soiled clothing for potential medical investigation into a bag to sit at room temperature and "vegetate"; fungal and bacterial growth are enhanced, and again, important trace evidence may be altered. Blood-soaked clothing that must be transported wet should be placed and sealed in brown paper bags and then put into large plastic biohazard sacks, left open to the air.

Caring for Valuables. Valuables accompanying the deceased person are a source of never-ending grief to everyone involved unless very carefully handled. The best policy is to entrust rings, watches, wallets, money, credit cards, and other valuable items to safekeeping in the hospital vault, following hospital policy. The rightful survivors may claim the belongings, subsequent to establishing their identity, and this will avoid untold problems for the hospital, ENs, medical investigation personnel, morticians, and the survivors themselves.

Evidentiary Materials. If bullets or fragments of any significance (e.g., hairs, fibers, soil, vegetable matter, paint chips, fingernails, glass fragments) are found in, around, or beside the body, save them for the investigators along with the clothing and assign them the same careful identification procedure. Each should be placed in separate paper envelopes.

Drawing Postmortem Blood Samples

Generally, the medical examiner's authority applies only to bodies of deceased persons. There is nothing in the statutes, by and large, that relates to living patients or living suspects insofar as the medical examiner or coroner is involved; for example, an injured but living driver who may be charged with causing a death as a result of negligent homicide is not the coroner's concern. The medical examiner or coroner has the authority to draw postmortem blood or urine samples without an autopsy order. The deceased individual no longer has any rights of protection under the Fourth Amendment of the U.S. Constitution.

Multiple Homicidal Gunshot Injuries

X-ray films, both anteroposterior (AP) and lateral, of a body shot several times are generally of great help to the pathologist. If films of this sort can be obtained before the body is removed, you may be able to help expedite the death investigation and will earn the pathologist's gratitude.

Releasing the Body

The body should be released to a funeral home *only* after the medical examiner or his or her representative has specifically authorized that it be released. If the family elects cremation, some jurisdictions require a special permit that authorizes the disposal of the physical remains, even in nonforensic cases. If the body is donated for scientific purposes, other procedures may be involved.

◼ ORGAN PROCUREMENT

Medicine entered the era of organ transplantation in 1951 with the first successful transfer of a kidney from a healthy donor to an identical twin. Since that first dramatic step, organ and tissue transplantation has become an almost routine fact of life, with multiple solid organ transplantations successfully carried out in centers all over the United States and various other tissues procured, banked, and transplanted on a regular basis in many smaller hospitals.

Organ procurement has developed into a unique medical speciality in response to the critical need for transplantable organs, and programs have been developed across the United States to promote the procurement, preservation, and distribution of organs and tissues to meet that need. Presently, there are two types of procurement programs: hospital-based organ procurement agencies (OPAs) serving their own transplantation center, and independent organ procurement agencies (IOPAs), which are freestanding, nonprofit organizations, serving one transplantation center or several centers within a specific geographic area.[10] Any organ procurement agency in the country can belong to the United Network for Organ Sharing (UNOS) and use their computerized placement system. If you are unfamiliar with the organ sharing agency nearest you, call the nearest medical school or UNOS at their computerized 24-hour-alert telephone system's toll-free number.[10] The waiting lists are growing at every center as kidneys, livers, hearts, heart-lung units, and even the pancreas are being successfully transplanted into desperately ill recipients; one of the greatest problems faced is identifying and obtaining enough organs to meet those needs. Bone, ligament, skin, and other tissues are also in high demand for surgical implantation and research.

ROLE OF THE EMERGENCY DEPARTMENT

ENs and ED physicians are routinely presented with opportunities to assist in obtaining needed organs and tissues by identifying donors and, when appropriate, preserving donor tissue. It is recognized, of course, that most patients who die in the ED are generally in an unstable condition and some organs may not be suitable for transplantation; many donors are identified in the intensive care unit (ICU) while on life support, but the initial potential may be recognized as stabilization is underway in the ED, and the process may be tentatively begun. Although vascularized solid organs are most sought after, a number of other tissues and organs may be donated, such as skin, bone, eyes, and corneas; many larger hospitals maintain tissue banks for their storage. When solid organs as a whole cannot be used, specific parts can be used. For example, it may be possible to retrieve and transplant heart valves, or extract pancreatic islet cells for research use.

THE UNIFORM ANATOMICAL GIFT ACT

The Uniform Anatomical Gift Act of 1968 has been passed in all 50 states and provides that an individual of 18 years or older can give prior consent for removal of any or all organs after death and can carry a signed, witnessed card to that effect. Most states support this and indicate the permission on the individual's driver's license. Even with the signed donor consent, family permission must be obtained; only the most available ranking next of kin need sign a consent for removal of organs from a dead relative.

OBTAINING PERMISSION FOR ORGAN DONATION

When obtaining permission from next of kin for organ or tissue donation, a surgical permit is used. The procedure to be written in is "removal of (specify organs or tissues) after death for transplantation purposes." Many eye banks and kidney donor programs require written permission from the next of kin if at all possible but waive that requirement if a donor card giving the individual's consent (if over 18 years of age) has two witnesses' signatures; this represents complete legal consent and can be used even when relatives cannot be contacted. It is best, however, to wait for relatives' consent.

When a suitable donor is recognized in the ED, it is understandably difficult for the family to make that very final decision quickly; the request must be carefully handled, preferably with the family physician and clergy present. If appropriate to the situation, instead of requesting donation, explain to the patient's family that it is an option; plant the seed but do not coerce them. Perhaps the knowledge that some part of their loved one will live on in another human being will allow the family to be at peace with the donor decision.

Deaths resulting from trauma, violence, and questionable causes fall into the jurisdiction of the medical examiner; any organ removal requires release from the medical examiner's office as well as next of kin permission or witnessed signed donor consent, prior to donation.

FINANCIAL ASPECTS OF ORGAN DONATION

No payment is made to the family for the organ donation and no charges are billed to them for the procedures involved. Those are passed to the transplantation center, which in turn bills the recipient, recipient's insurer, or Medicare if it covers the particular transplant.[11]

DONOR RECOGNITION

Ideal organ donors are previously healthy individuals who have suffered an irreversible catastrophic brain injury from any cause. The criteria for age varies from center to center and should be confirmed directly if a potential donor presents; age limits may stretch from birth to about 60 years. Other variances exist as well: in order to become a candidate for kidney donation, the patient must not lose circulation for longer than 10 minutes, while corneas are salvageable for 6 hours after clinical death and skin may be procured up to 12 hours after clinical death. Corneal transplantation has restored sight to countless numbers of people and is now the most successful type of organ transplantation, with over 3000 procedures performed annually in the United States. Corneal procurement is done by local eye bank technicians or trained mortician-embalmers, who then send tissues to local eye banks; immediate preservation of the cornea after death is best obtained by closing the eyelids.

Potential organ donors ideally must also be free of any infectious disease processes such as sepsis or viruses such as human immunodeficiency virus (HIV). Tissue donors (bone, skin, ligaments) have less stringent criteria and are desperately needed to meet the large demand for surgical implants.

DETERMINATION OF DEATH FOR ORGAN DONATION

Probably the most difficult dilemma facing physicians in EDs and neurosurgical services is the final determination of brain death in a young person whose circulatory and respiratory functions have remained intact. The physician who makes the final determination *cannot* be affiliated with the transplantation team and must follow specific criteria in arriving at the determination of brain death.

Brain Death Criteria

In 1968, criteria were established by the ad-hoc committee of the Harvard Medical School by which to determine brain death. These criteria have since been modified as new diagnostic modalities have become available; the following criteria for establishing the diagnosis of brain death must now be met[11]:

- *Unresponsiveness to extra stimuli:* The most intense painful stimuli evoke no vocal or purposeful responses.
- *Apnea:* No obvious spontaneous respiration after removal from a mechanical ventilator. The patient is provided with 100 percent inspired oxygen at normal tidal volumes for

10 minutes; ventilation is then discontinued and a catheter is placed in the endotracheal (ET) tube to deliver 100 percent oxygen passively. Arterial blood gases (ABGs) are drawn after 3 to 5 minutes; if the carbon dioxide level reaches 60 mm Hg and there is no spontaneous respiration, test results are conclusive. Careful hemodynamic monitoring during the apnea test is essential to ensure that organ perfusion is not compromised.

- *No reflexes:* Physical examination demonstrates that there are no cranial or brainstem reflexes. Ice-water calorics are absent; postural activity is absent; swallowing, yawning, and vocalization are absent; pupils are fixed and do not respond to light; deep tendon reflexes are absent; spinal cord reflexes may remain intact.

Diagnosis of brain death also depends upon the exclusion of two extenuating circumstances:

- *Hypothermia:* The patient must be normothermic.
- *Central nervous system (CNS) depression:* The CNS must not be depressed by drugs such as barbiturates.

Confirmatory tests for brain death include electroencephalograms (EEGs) and cerebral blood flow studies. Overall, brain death is a clinical diagnosis.

An extended period of observation may be required in infants and young children, and in patients who have had anoxic or ischemic etiologies for brain death. State laws and hospital policies regarding documentation must be observed.

SUPPORT OF POTENTIAL ORGAN DONORS

Once death is pronounced, emphasis shifts to supporting the viability of the organs being donated. During the interim period, with the body kept on a respirator, four main goals are involved:

- Adequate hydration of the donor
- Maintenance of normal blood pressure (BP)
- Establishment of diuresis
- Maintenance of adequate oxygenation

Although the donor body will probably be stabilized and transferred out of the ED to a holding area, ENs will initiate the support activities and need to be aware of general management guidelines. Adequate kidney function is achieved with intravenous normal saline solution (NSS) or Ringer's lactate in quantities necessary to maintain a central venous pressure (CVP) of at least 10 cm H_2O and urine output of at least 50 mL/h.[11] Vasopressors are to be avoided in maintaining BP and perfusion; if necessary to employ them, the preferred order of use is (1) dopamine, (2) isoproterenol (Isuprel), (3) metaraminol (Aramine), and (4) levarterenol (Levophed).

Once death is pronounced, the OPA will become directly involved in donor management, making futher evaluations and managing the donor to get the organ into optimal condition. Tissue typing to determine histocompatibility (human leukocyte antigen [HLA] typing) between donor and recipient and cross-match testing are usually initiated after death is pronounced; in some cases, lymph nodes as well as blood will be needed for tissue typing.

OUTCOMES OF ORGAN AND TISSUE DONATION

A decade ago, of the major organs transplanted, the one-year survival rate among heart recipients was 80 percent; kidney recipients, 91 percent and liver recipients, 65 to 70 percent; today, the success rates are significantly higher. The limiting factor in the provision of this successful mode of therapy remains donor availability.[13] ENs are undeniably in a position to identify likely candidates for organ and tissue donation if they are alert to the need. So many times, viable organ recovery is possible in young and otherwise healthy adults who are victims of trauma; if the possibility is recognized in time and handled properly with families, an opportunity is provided to give others a chance for life and health, and for loved ones to salvage meaning from an otherwise needless and tragic loss.

■ REFERENCES

1. In: Hemett MD, Mackert ME. *Dynamics of Law in Nursing and Health Care.* Reston, Va: Reston Publishing; 1978:3–43.
2. George JE. Consent in the ED. *Emerg Nurs Legal Bull.* 1975;1(4).

3. Lynch V. Expert witness testimony. In: *Sexual Violence.* Valdosta, Ga: Bearhawk Consulting Group, and Barbara Clark Mims Associates; 1992:ix-4–ix-5.

4. Lewman LV. Crib death. In: *Oregon State Medical Examiner's Case of the Month.* Portland, Ore: Oregon State Health Division; May 1986.

5. Brady WJ. *Medical Investigation of Deaths in Oregon.* 3rd ed. Salem, Ore: Oregon State Health Division: 1982.

6. Maroni Leash R. Health notification: Practical guidelines for health care professionals. *Crit Care Nurs Q.* 1996;19:21–34.

7. Easter CR, Muro Ga: An ED forensic kit. *J Emerg Nurs.* 1995;21:440–444.

8. Symposium on forensic pathology. *Clin Lab Med.* 1983;3:356–368.

9. Besant-Matthews P. *Gunshot and Stab Wounds: A Medical Examiner's View* (syllabus). Dallas, Tex.: Barbara Clark Mims Associates; 1992.

10. Davis FD: Organ procurement in the 1980s. *Point of View.* 1987;24:20–21.

11. Organ procurement: new organs for old. *Emerg Med.* 1987;19(11):24–40.

12. In: Knezevich BA. *Trauma Nursing Principles and Practice.* E. Norwalk, Conn: Appleton-Century-Crofts; 1986:445–455.

13. Organ transplantation (Publication no. HRS-A-OC 86-1). Washington, D.C.: U.S. DHHS; 1985.

■ BIBLIOGRAPHY

ABC's of charting. *Advantage.* 1995;1:4–6.

Besant-Matthews, PE. *Gunshot and Stab Wounds: A Medical Examiner's View.* Dallas, Tex: Barbara Clark Mims Associates; 1992.

Brady, WJ. *Medical Investigation of Deaths in Oregon.* 3rd ed. Salem, Ore: Oregon State Health Division; 1982.

Cahill J, ed. *Nurse's Handbook of Law & Ethics.* Springhouse, Pa: Springhouse Corporation; 1992.

Creighton H. *Law Every Nurse Should Know.* 5th ed. Philadelphia, Pa: WB Saunders; 1986.

Davis AJ, Aroskar MA: *Ethical Dilemmas and Nursing Practice.* E. Norwalk, Conn. Appleton & Lange; 1991.

Downey VW, Wessman PT. Liability insurance for nurses: a professional necessity.

George JE, Quattrone MS. A matter of credibility. *J Emerg Nurs.* 1994;20:69–70.

George JE, Quattrone MS. Erroneous reporting of sexually transmitted diseases. *J Emerg Nurs.* 1994;20: 148–149.

George JE, Quattrone MS. The reemergence of tuberculosis as an emergency department concern. *J Emerg Nurs.* 1994;20:323–324.

George JE, Quattrone MS. Restraining patients: can you be sued? Part II. *J Emerg Nurs.* 1993;19:57.

George JE, Quattrone MS. The "discovery doctrine" in nursing malpractice. *J Emerg Nurs.* 1993;19:346–347.

George JE, Quattrone MS. Professional malpractice or simple negligence? *J Emerg Nurs.* 1993;19:532–533.

George JE, Quattrone MS. Emergency department overload: How to "CYA." *J Emerg Nurs.* 1992;18: 157–158.

George JE, Quattrone MS. Patient advance directives and the emergency nurse. *J Emerg Nurs.* 1992;18: 415–416.

George JE, Quattrone MS. Restraining patients: can you be sued? Part I. *J Emerg Nurs.* 1992;18:536–537.

George JE, Quattrone MS, Goldstone M. Phone consultations with the ED physician: is there nursing liability? *J Emerg Nurs.* 1995;21:163–164.

George JE, Quattrone MS, Goldstone M. A pediatric right to die? *J Emerg Nurs.* 1995;21:341–342.

George JE, Quattrone MS, Goldstone M. Emergency department telephone advice. *J Emerg Nurs.* 1995;21: 450–451.

Goldman B, (ed). Curbing the threat of litigation in the emergency department: a risk management approach. *Emerg Med Rep.* Jan 15, 1990;13–14.

Guido GW. *Legal Issues in Nursing: A Source Book for Practice.* E. Norwalk, Conn: Appleton & Lange; 1988.

Hogue EE. Liability for premature discharge. *Pediatr Nurs.* 1991;17:76–78.

Informed consent. *Advantage.* 1995;1:6–9.

Irons TG. Documenting sexual abuse of a child. *Emerg Med.* April 30, 1993;75.

Jehovah's Witnesses in the emergency department: a clinicolegal challenge. *Emerg Phys Legal Bull.* 1991; 2:1–8.

Kirksey KM, Holt-Ashley M, Williamson KL, Garza RO. Autoerotic asphyxia in adolescents. *J Emerg Nurs.* 1995;21:81–83.

Lynch VA. Expert witness testimony. In: *Sexual Violence.* Valdosta, Ga.: Bearhawk Consulting Group and Barbara Clark Mims Associates; 1992:ix–1.

McLaughlin W. Allowing a patient to make the "wrong" choices. *Etcetera.* 1993;1:7.

Mason R, Chave W, Walleck CA. Legal concerns in trauma nursing. In: Cardona VD, Hurn PD, Bastnagel Mason PJ, et al., ed. *Trauma Nursing: From Resuscitation through Rehabilitation.* 2nd ed. Philadelphia, Pa: WB Saunders; 1994:51–62.

Mental status and the patient's rights. *Emerg Med.* Aug 14, 1992;208–213.

O'Mara RJ: Ethical dilemmas with advanced directives, living wills, and do not resuscitate orders. *Crit Care Q.* 1987;10:17–28.

Reeves K. Avoid the hopeless horror: the green armband solution to unwanted resuscitation in the pre-hospital setting. *Etcetera.* Sept 1993.

Salvatore NG. Restraints: a sampling of current practice. *J Emerg Nurs.* 1993;19:417–421.

Siebelt B. Are living wills really alive? *Etcetera.* Nov/Dec 1993;4.

Snyder JA. Documentation of nursing care for patients who have been restrained. *J Emerg Nurs.,* 1993;19: 461–464.

Spitz W, Fisher R. *Medico-Legal Investigation of Deaths.* Springfield, Ill: Charles C Thomas; 1973.

Tarbuck P. Use and abuse of control and restraint. *Nurs Stand.* 1992;6:30–32.

Warden VD. Blood and breath alcohol testing. *J Emerg Nurs.* 1992;18:278–282.

Weber P. The human connection: the role of the nurse in organ donation. *J Neurosurg Nurs.* 1985;17:118–122.

■ REVIEW: LEGAL AND FORENSIC CONSIDERATIONS

1. Identify the three types of American law.

2. Define the ordinary, reasonable, prudent person (ORPP) standard of care.

3. Define *malpractice, negligence,* and *tort* and identify the four basic elements of negligence that must all be alleged and proven in a court case.

4. Identify and define three types of consent and explain the implications of technical battery.

5. Cite three rules of thumb dealing with consent when obtaining blood in the emergency department (ED) for blood alcohol level determinations.

6. Cite the consent precautions that should be observed when caring for minors in the ED.

7. Define the "borrowed servant" doctrine and "named employee" coverage; explain the rationale for nurses' having their own liability insurance.

8. Explain the role of the nurse as opposed to the role of the pharmacist in "dispensing" take-home medications and the legal implications involved.

9. List the 10 situations that the ED is required by law to report.

10. Explain the importance and legal implications of recording accurate times and dates on ED documents and identify at least 10 areas of medicolegal vulnerability for emergency nurses (ENs).

11. Describe the procedure for witnessing a will in the ED to make the will legally valid.

12. Outline the way in which nurses should conduct themselves when required to be a witness in court.

13. Describe the role of the medical examiner and the postmortem database that is of value in death investigations.

14. Describe the ways in which evidence can be preserved on the deceased body and how garments and belongings of the deceased should be managed.

15. List the ways in which ENs can support and participate in organ and tissue donation; list the guidelines for donor selection.

16. Describe the currently accepted criteria that must be met for establishing the diagnosis of brain death and outline the ED support of the potential donor.

Communication and Disaster Management

35

■ COMMUNICATION SKILLS

Interpersonal communication skills are basic both to a meaningful quality of life and effective professional performance. The importance of skilled communication merits more than merely a passing mention in this chapter; readers are urged to reflect seriously upon their own proficiencies and limitations, determining where they can expand and refine their skills. Emergency nursing requires the ability to transfer complex bodies of information accurately and comprehensively, as well as to perceive and to respond with warmth, empathy, and accuracy.

CONTEMPORARY THEORIES OF COMMUNICATION

Three distinct approaches to communication have evolved in recent decades. Although they have some similarities, each approach offers differing insights into interpersonal communication.

Informational Approach
The informational approach deals with the transmission of factual messages between senders and receivers, stressing information processing in a linear sequence. Major factors include encoding, transmission channels, decoding, noise, filters, and redundancy; radio communication is often patterned after this approach.

Interaction Approach
The interaction approach asserts that communication takes place as long as individuals perceive one another, irrespective of their wishes or intentions. In other words, communication cannot be avoided: one cannot *not* communicate. Each person learns complex programs—cultural, context-specific, and not altogether conscious—that are used to coordinate and modify interpersonal communication. The implication of this approach is the absolute impossibility of not communicating while in another's presence or line of sight. Silence communicates, as does withdrawal, immobility, body language, preoccupation, and ignoring the presence of others. Withholding interest in or acknowledgment of another person communicates. A multitude of demonstrations of this concept are readily observable in our daily interaction with co-workers, patients, and supervisors.

Relational Approach
The relational approach uses communication to designate the system of relationships among people; that is, we don't engage in communication but are immersed in it, willy-nilly, from cradle to grave. Changes in the system are called information. The relational approach has generated two conceptual models that have relevance to communication in the emergency department (ED):

- *The double bind model:* Two important, contradictory messages have been delivered, both of which must be carried out. Both cannot be, however, resulting in an inescapable no-win situation.
- *The family system model:* This is an equilibrium-maintaining system applicable to families and to other working units such as

577

an ED. As group members interact, each change that tends to upset the balance triggers a group system response to restore the original status. This model predicts the extreme difficulty in effecting any fundamental change in a family or a working unit; at best, a temporary facelift is accomplished. Change always threatens the old balance.

FACTORS IN COMMUNICATION

Communication involves two factors: the ability of a person to make his or her thoughts, feelings, and needs known to others and the ability to be receptive to the attempts of others to impart similar information in return. Simply stated, communication is a two-way process: the sending and receiving of a message. However, in every transaction between two people, several levels of communication take place at the same time. A portion of the communication is the words that are used, another is the tone of voice, and another is nonverbal—the actions of the people while the words are being exchanged. Once one realizes that different levels of communication exist, one is more able to control the communication process.

COMPLICATIONS OF COMMUNICATION

In the verbal portion of the communication process alone (or the words spoken), there are six ways in which miscommunication develops. For example, consider that I am the sender and you are the receiver of a message. In sending a message, three important things can differ:

- What I say
- What I meant to say
- What you heard me say

The process is parallel in receiving the reply. Three *more* possible meanings exist:

- What you say
- What you meant to say
- What I heard you say

Only when all interpretations are the same is the communication totally successful. Verbal communication becomes more complex with the addition of more people to the transaction. Three people in a transaction increases the number of possible meanings to 18, thereby tripling the possibility of misunderstanding.

LEVELS OF COMMUNICATION

Communication can be viewed from two distinct vantage points: the content level and the feeling level. The content level is the surface communication—the who, what, when, and where of the message. Content level communication is important, but frequently, it is not as powerful or meaningful as the feeling level of the message. The tone of voice one uses is part of the feeling level of communication. The tone of voice may confirm, deny, or confuse the meaning of the words that are used. For example, a person who uses a cold, remote tone of voice while saying "Well, you did the best you could" conveys a message that changes the meaning of the words.

Nonverbal communication takes place at the feeling level. What is not said can be more powerful than what is said. Hunches often are built on the feelings aroused in astute individuals. Communication or understanding breaks down more frequently at the feeling level than at the content level. For example, management and union representatives may discuss a contract and not hear a word that is said until the feeling level of communication is heard. Once negotiators develop a feeling of trust between the people on both sides, the words begin to have meaning. People who have trouble understanding each other probably communicate at the feeling level, and the nonverbal communication blocks the understanding of the verbal communication.

BREAKDOWNS AND BLOCKS

Preoccupation blocks communication. A person who is occupied with other matters will not be able to listen at the feeling level of the transaction. The words will be heard and a decision might be made, but the person attempting to communicate will leave with the feeling that the other person was not listening.

Hostility creates misunderstanding. When one has hostile feelings, whether they are directed toward the person speaking or caused by some recent experience, one is too preoccupied with those feelings to listen to the feelings of another. For example, if a charge nurse has hostile feelings, whatever that charge nurse hears or says will be distorted; therefore, a charge nurse must be on guard when experiencing hostile feelings, for if he or she radiates the hostility, a staff nurse then will only hear the hostile feelings and not the intended message. The staff nurse will leave the conversation wondering why the charge nurse was so upset.

Stereotyping because of past experience creates a block to effective communication. Once a person's expectations are set, the other person will often live up to them. This is called the fulfillment prophecy. When a person expects above-standard performance and reliable information from a co-worker, it usually will be forthcoming. However, if a person expects below-standard performance and false information, this also will be provided.

Other factors that are likely to be major obstacles to good communication are an uncomfortable physical environment, fatigue (instructions given a few minutes before quitting time frequently have to be repeated the following day), insecurity, and status (which may bring out feelings of hostility, envy, power worshipping, or stereotyping).

Finally, as in the parlor game of telephone when one person tells a story that must be passed from person to person, the last story is usually quite different from the original. Communication from a staff person to a head nurse or supervisor, then to an administrator, and then to the board of directors can become quite distorted. As each person hears the words, past experience and feelings condition that person to interpret those words in his or her own manner.

FACTORS AND FEEDBACK

Communications in the ED on a verbal plane involve a sender (mouth) and a receiver (ear), and many factors affect the message sent and the message heard. In addition to the factors discussed previously, general environment, background, education, experience, mood, facial expression, purpose, and vocabulary level may also hinder good communication. The receiver must understand the sender's symbols; written messages must be clear and phrased in commonly understood terms.

A breakdown in communication occurs when the perceptions of the receiver do not match the perceptions of the sender; the communication process is not complete until the message from the sender is fed back. Communication is always most effective on a one-to-one basis when the message is paraphrased and, again, fed back.

■ COMMUNICATING WITH PATIENTS

The quality of nursing communication with patients and their families in the ED can be a potent factor for initiating compliance with treatment, augmenting recovery, and increasing patient and family satisfaction with emergency services and care. A high proportion of legal actions taken by patients against health-care professionals and hospitals is because of poor communication. Research indicates that patients' judgment of the competence of health-care professionals depends, to a large degree, on the interest shown in their problem and the concern and the respect demonstrated.

Effective communication with patients is well defined. In the ED, the relative briefness of patient stay places an even greater emphasis on the initial facilitating dimensions of this communication:

- Listening and responding to the patient's questions and feelings
- Respecting the patient as a person and respecting his or her concerns and needs
- Showing empathy or understanding the patient's perception
- Demonstrating warmth through attention to and care about the patient

No one has mastered flawless communication, even the most adept professionals flag and wilt under difficult circumstances. However, all nurses can enhance their patient communication skills through self-awareness, monitoring their responses, and committing to a consistent effort toward improvement. Communication training, focused on these dimensions, is available through texts, (see References and Bibliography at the end of the chapter), professional seminars, and workshops.

■ FORMS OF EMERGENCY DEPARTMENT COMMUNICATION

The ED is a critical-care area, and when primary care is given in a critical-care setting, there is an absolute need for highly skilled personnel who are capable of effective communication on a continual basis. The department employs many systems in communicating with staff, patients, other departments, the consumer public, and the media. A full awareness and working knowledge of all these areas is the responsibility of the emergency nurse (EN). Some examples of everyday lines of communication are the hospital policy book, ED policy and procedure book, orientation procedure within the department (with skill validation or proficiency list), department "communication book" with all pertinent information recorded from shift to shift, call list within the department for the on-call physicians' roster, accounting log for long-distance telephone calls, and the phone message book.

BULLETIN BOARDS

Bulletin boards can be used for posting schedules, meetings, jobs, social functions, Emergency Nurses Association (ENA) notices, staff development functions, hospital memos, and new procedures. Bulletin board contents should remain current and should be divided into official and unofficial communications. All officially posted materials should be dated and remain posted for a specified period of time. Official bulletins should be initialed by all staff members as documentation that the message has been acknowledged. Certain communications and some intradepartmental communications should be filed for future reference; often they are incorporated into new policies and procedures for the ED. All required official regulatory guidance or directives (e.g., Consolidated Omnibus Reconciliation Act [COBRA], human abuse reporting, adverse drug reactions [from the Food and Drug Administration]) should remain posted in a designated location within the public area of the ED.

CHANGE-OF-SHIFT REPORT

The change of a shift is the most vulnerable part of the day in the ED and is when most mistakes are made. All members of the oncoming shift and the charge nurse of the offgoing shift should review a written shift report. The status of all patients, including those in the waiting room and those waiting for x-rays to be taken, should be reported; walking rounds are imperative to ensure continuity of care. The staffing pattern and assignments and the status of all emergency supplies and equipment should be reviewed; narcotic inventory should be validated. The operating room (OR) availability, critical bed status, emergency medical services (EMS) diversions, and any other conditions that might affect the ED (e.g., power outages, com-

puter down-time) should be reviewed. The hospital-to-ambulance radio network system should be checked for proper operation and its status documented per departmental policy.

EMERGENCY MEDICAL SERVICES CYCLE

Prehospital communication requirements for emergency medical care are similar whether there is a single case of sudden illness or injury or a disaster involving large numbers of victims. The normal EMS cycle consists of the following stages and functions:

- *Incident:* The occurrence that generates the need for emergency services—patient(s) with acute illness or injury
- *Detection:* The action that determines that the incident took place
- *Notification:* The action that informs the emergency resource control agency where and when the incident took place and the nature of the incident
- *Dispatch:* The act that orders emergency resources to the scene of the incident
- *Closure:* The process that transports emergency resources to the scene of the incident
- *Action:* The necessary acts that correct or alleviate conditions generated by the incident, including both immediate care and transportation to a medical facility
- *Return to station:* The return of all emergency resources to a state of readiness for a new cycle

Once the incident is detected, communications are necessary complements to each successive stage of the EMS cycle, from initial detection and notification of the incident to the return to station, so that the dispatching center knows immediately when an ambulance is ready to begin a new cycle.

Radio Communication

The use of two-way radio equipment is by no means limited to the dispatching center and the ambulance–ED relationship. Other uses of the two-way radio system are:

- Having an operable communication system when the local telephone network is severely damaged or overloaded during a major disaster

- Having the fastest mechanism for coordinating emergency medical activities with other disaster services in the community
- Providing rapid intercommunication among hospitals about distribution of casualty loads
- Effectively alerting enough medical personnel to report to meet emergency needs

The 911 System

In January 1968, the American Telephone and Telegraph Company (AT&T) announced the establishment of 911 as the single emergency telephone number for use in the United States. The single emergency number concept was not new; it had been used in England for a number of years. It was developed to provide the general public with easy, immediate, direct access to emergency service resources. The system eliminates the need for callers under stress to make decisions for which they may be ill prepared, particularly when outside their home community. There are 911 systems in existence today in jurisdictions that range in population from several thousand to several million. For the system to be efficient, there are some size limitations on service areas, but a particular area does not have to conform to any geographic or other jurisdictional boundaries (although it normally does coincide with those boundaries). The public has a major role in the successful operation of the 911 system. The term *emergency* is highly subjective; it defies precise definition. The public must be educated to use the 911 system correctly—for emergencies—and intelligently; the number must not be used as an information service or as a means of airing grievances. Properly used, the 911 system is effective for the young, the old, the handicapped, the illiterate, and those with limited knowledge of English to report an emergency, allowing almost every citizen quick access to EMS agencies to receive fast emergency care.

Ambulance-to-Hospital Radio

Two-way radio communication between ambulance and hospital is necessary during the action stage of the EMS cycle if optimum emergency medical care is to be provided. The voice channel to the ED from the scene of the incident enables the emergency medical technician (EMT) to request advice for managing the condition of the ca-

sualty prior to transportation. It also permits the EMT to advise the treatment facility of the patient's condition, allowing time to prepare for provision of any special care once the patient has reached the facility, the estimated time of arrival (ETA) and other pertinent information. Radio is the vital link necessary to provide continuity of care.

Radio Regulations. The radio frequency spectrum is a national and international resource in the public domain. Since 1906, international administrative radio conferences have controlled the orderly development of this vital resource through carefully planned frequency allocations to various radio services. The Federal Communications Commission (FCC), established by act of Congress in 1934, controls U.S. frequency allocations to various nongovernment radio services and licenses individuals. The FCC has set aside specific radio band assignments for very high frequencies (VHF) that are available to the Special Emergency Radio Service, which includes hospitals, ambulances, and rescue organizations. All of these frequencies are subject to FCC regulations, some are:

- Hospital radios, except for test transmissions, may be used only for the transmission of messages necessary for the rendition of an efficient hospital service.
- Ambulance operators and rescue organizations, except for test transmissions, may use these frequencies only for the transmission of messages pertaining to the safety of life or property and urgent messages necessary for the rendition of an efficient ambulance or emergency rescue service.
- Test transmissions may be conducted by any licensed station as required for proper station and system maintenance, but such tests shall be kept to a minimum, and precautions shall be taken to avoid interference with other stations.

Radio Guidelines. Most EDs across the country now have or will soon have an emergency radio base station with hospital-to-ambulance radio capability. There are several console models in use; the operating particulars vary slightly from manufacturer to manufacturer. However, the basic general guidelines to follow when using the radio do not vary. Some key points are discussed below.

Time. Time is a very important factor in two-way radio communication because only one person can talk on a frequency at any given time. When a message is interrupted, the receiving station will not be able to receive the transmission, and this prolongs air time needed for clarification, creates confusion, and increases the chances for errors. Therefore, always be certain the air is clear before initiating a message, and always listen first to be certain no one else is talking.

Keep your message as brief as possible and pronounce words slowly and distinctly. Numbers should be transmitted first as individual numbers and then repeated reading the number as a whole; reading numbers in this fashion minimizes the possibility of error. Messages longer than 30 seconds should be broken at 30-second intervals, waiting for 2 to 3 seconds before resuming transmission in order to allow another station that might have a more pressing emergency message to go ahead.

Receiving Calls. When receiving a call, wait until the signal tone has stopped, press the transmit bar or button, and say, "This is [name of hospital] Emergency. Go ahead." Release the transmit bar and listen to the message.

Recording Messages. Keep a permanent log near the radio to record the time of transmission, ambulance identification by company or number, message contents (patient age, gender, chief complaint, vital signs [VS], ETA, transmission time, and initials of person receiving the call). Although the FCC does not require that such a log be kept, it is a vital document for retrospective assessment of the EMS response and its interfaces with the ED.

Transmitting. When transmitting, relax and speak in a normal, clear manner with your mouth close to the microphone or handset. There is no need to shout, because the radio takes care of amplification, and speaking too loudly may distort the voice and make the message unintelligible. Emotion will also lend to distortion, so attempt to speak as emotionlessly as possible. Courtesy is understood, so there is no need to say "please" or "thank you"— time is of the essence on the air. Be impersonal and do not use the name of the person to whom you are speaking or the word I, because stations

in Emergency Radio Service are not licensed for person-to-person communications. A phonetic alphabet (e.g., A = alpha, B = bravo, C = Charlie) may also be used in your facility to assist in spelling and understanding unusual words. When using a phonetic spelling, proceed slowly, pausing slightly after each letter.

Checking. When the message is completed, be certain you have understood the content. Do not guess at transmissions. Verify any doubtful portions with the sending operator; do not acknowledge a message until you are certain you have received it accurately. If the message is clear and you have no questions, simply acknowledge receipt of the message by pressing the transmit bar, saying "Roger" or "10-4" (commonly understood radio terms) and then identifying yourself with your call number and time of day, and releasing the transmit bar. For example, say, "10-4, this is Base Station 621, clear at 0715." Since the use of numeral codes (the "10 code" and the "12 code") varies in meaning from locale to locale, the EN should be familiar with the codes used in his or her place of employment.

■ DISASTER MANAGEMENT

This section of the chapter has been designed to provide an overview of some general aspects and problems that might be encountered in a disaster situation. Every ED should be prepared well in advance with supplies, personnel, and a carefully constructed disaster plan. This section also reemphasizes some basic guidelines for readiness.

A disaster is an unpredictable unknown. No one knows where it may hit, how it will occur, or the extent of damage it may cause. We do know that disaster usually brings the tragedy of death and injury, destruction of homes, and disruption of family life and the established patterns of community organization. We also know that in every disaster, there is a need for someone to help care for the victims.

It is realistic for ENs to recognize that they will be expected to assume leadership roles in disaster situations; thus, it is important to visualize the conditions under which they will be expected to function.

WHAT IS A DISASTER?

Disaster has been defined by some as a sudden, massive disproportion between hostile elements of any kind and the survival resources that can be brought into action in the shortest possible time. Disaster does not necessarily mean that the situation is of mammoth disruptive proportions, involving numerous dead and injured. In a small community, disaster may consist of a two-car accident involving five seriously injured people. Each community and its medical facilities must define what constitutes a disaster for it. Most disasters involve victims who have need for food, clothing, shelter, medical and nursing care, and other necessities of life. There are many types of disasters, all which have a unique impact. Disasters are usually divided into two categories:

- Natural (violence of nature), such as tornadoes, hurricanes, earthquakes, blizzards, epidemics, and conflagrations (i.e., large, destructive fires)
- Man-made (human error), such as fires, explosions, transportation accidents, civil disorder, and nuclear incidents

These vary in degree of suddenness of onset, the degree of preparation possible immediately before disaster strikes, and the problems created that require EMS response. Persons providing medical and nursing service must be prepared to serve in a variety of capacities and should realize that each disaster situation will pose its own complex problems.

Tornadoes, fires, explosions, major or even minor transportation mishaps, and other disasters all tend to produce more illnesses and health problems. Communicable disease is usually a lurking public health threat, and there is a sudden demand for short-term provision of special care for the aged, the chronically ill, infants, young children, and expectant mothers.

DISASTER EMERGENCY CARE

Disaster emergency care is practiced when the number of casualties overwhelms the human and physical resources of the treatment facility, precluding use of the typical administrative and treatment regimens. The basic principles of medical care administered during disaster situations are no different from those used in ordinary circumstances, but their application requires special organization in order to be effective. In disaster conditions, with large numbers of casualties, additional physicians must immediately be summoned, as must nursing staff, medical assistants, and hospital volunteers. These personnel must be thoroughly indoctrinated in their roles for participating in a disaster scenario and ready to improvise when necessary, following a carefully engineered master plan for the hospital and community, known as the disaster plan.

FACTORS IN EFFECTIVE MANAGEMENT

One major key to success in meeting disaster situations is training not only of physicians and nurses but of all the paramedical and ancillary personnel who will be involved in the situation. This training must be followed up by refresher courses and exercises on a regular basis in order to maintain levels of proficiency and to identify the needs to revise and update the master plan. During disaster drills, both human and physical resources must be realistically tested to ensure their readiness for an actual event.

Another key factor is organization, which can never be stressed too much. Each disaster situation is different in some respects from every other, and by nature disasters are chaotic. If disaster management is to be effective to any degree, order must be developed out of chaos. In many instances, this responsibility will be largely assumed by ENs because they are the primary resources in the ED.

Compounding problems in a disaster include disruptions of transportation, communications, and electrical power; destruction of or damage to other utility services, such as water and sanitary sewers; disruption or overburdening of public services, such as fire, police, EMs, and the American National Red Cross; and inability of emergency personnel to respond because of weather conditions, family or neighborhood casualties, and roadways blocked by accumulations of debris. In a disaster, emergency personnel must be able to cope with the many facets of the event and be ready to effect efficient traffic control, triage, and emergency interventions for the wounded and distressed and to manage hospital resources to benefit the most casualties.

SPECIFIC DISASTER-ASSOCIATED PROBLEMS

Diseases can occur during large-scale disasters because of disruption of safe water supplies and disabling of sewer systems and normal food handling capabilities (e.g., storage, refrigeration, and heating). Flooding produces risks for typhoid and other water-borne communicable diseases. Public health officials are normally involved in large-scale scenarios to assess and manage any risks for outbreaks by such means as issuing public directives (e.g., to boil all water or drink only bottled water), to assist in establishing suitable shelters and public toilet facilities, and to operate mass immunization clinics in certain instances if disease risks are high.

Blood Supplies

Another problem that arises in some disasters is the shortage of whole blood, blood expanders, and plasma when large quantities are needed for many wounded patients requiring surgery. Each hospital and community is linked to local or regional blood banks to supplement in-house supplies for blood and blood products, but donors are often requested to report for blood donations. Volunteers from the American National Red Cross often assist with coordinating blood drives for victims of disasters.

Disaster Supplies and Resources

Extra supplies should be readily available to the ED and critical care unit (CCU) from sources both within and outside the hospital. Emergency and key hospital personnel should be well informed of the location of such resources and must know how to access them readily when needed. Emergency personnel usually have prepositioned disaster boxes for triage, decontamination, wound care, record-keeping, and other subfunctions.

Shelters

Space in which to locate patients will be at a premium. Any area can be used for this purpose that is not already dedicated to patient care, such as waiting rooms, hallways, and even parking areas adjacent to the ED entrance. These areas can be cleared of all people not needing medical attention and can be declared patient areas and kept off limits to the press and bystanders. Families can be referred to the American National Red Cross or other shelter facilities to wait for word on the injured. A well-coordinated communications system should be established and maintained between the medical facilities and these shelters.

Press

One person, usually the hospital administrator or a designee, should be responsible for serving as a liaison with the press. A specific location for press personnel should be established outside the ED. Access of these personnel to the ED should be tightly restricted during a disaster, and at no time should they be permitted to invade patient treatment areas. In situations involving hazardous substances or environmental contamination, traffic control is a high priority in order to ensure the safety of the public, who may not understand the gravity of the situation.

Volunteer personnel can be effectively used to carry messages from the patient-care areas to waiting family members or to other areas of the hospital, thus allowing more qualified personnel to focus on providing direct patient care.

Evacuation

In disaster situations, many people will not leave their homes to seek medical attention; therefore, medical personnel or Red Cross workers are permitted access to disaster areas to render medical assistance when it is feasible. There may be times when, for their own safety, people must be forcibly removed from their property by the appropriate authorities; if this occurs, there will frequently be anger and hostility exhibited toward anyone attempting to render assistance. ENs must be prepared to cope with these reactions, understanding their cause.

Missing Persons

Usually, American National Red Cross personnel attempt to help people locate missing friends or relatives. They are well trained to assume this responsibility, thereby removing another time-consuming burden from medical personnel. If people inundate the hospital looking for missing persons, they should be referred to the appropriate agencies.

DISASTER READINESS

The Joint Commission on Accreditation of Healthcare Organizations (JCAHO) has specific standards for emergency preparedness that encompass disasters and equipment failures or disruptions, as well as incidents involving hazardous materials and spills. Hospitals are required to have a documented management plan, with orientation and educational programs designed to acquaint personnel with their roles and responsibilities in such emergency situations. This includes a requirement for performance standards to measure the effectiveness of these plans and programs (e.g., disaster drills, inspections, and testing of emergency resources such as back-up utility and communication systems on a regular basis).[2] Therefore, all employees, especially those in the ED, should be well versed in their specific duties in a disaster.

Federal Emergency Management Agency

The Federal Emergency Management Agency (FEMA) coordinates a wide range of emergency management functions during disasters and ensures that there is prompt mobilization of resources when there is concern for national security during any incidents. FEMA also supports local and state agencies in planning to meet contingencies. When the president declares a disaster within a given area of the country, FEMA is responsible for ensuring that federal aid is administered in a timely manner. This agency also assists in providing education and training programs for key personnel who manage disaster programming at local, state, and federal levels. Developing community awareness programs for both home safety and weather-related disasters is also among FEMA's responsibilities (Fig. 35–1).

A recent FEMA initiative is CABIN (Chemical and Biological Information Network). This is a terrorism preparedness database that contains information on chemical and biologic threats, along with detailed information on the specific agents. Medical information, precursors, countermeasures, and information on scenarios is provided in a software package in order to assist the user in determining the identity of an unknown substance.

The hospital and local community should become very familiar with FEMA because this fed-eral agency can provide much valuable assistance in planning for disasters and in meeting the needs of victims after a disaster has occurred. Local and state FEMA contacts should be listed in the hospital's disaster plan resources.

National Disaster Medical System

The National Disaster Medical System (NDMS) has been designed to supply a capable and immediate response, often from a remote area of the country, when local resources have been disabled or are inadequate to meet the needs of the victims. Organized disaster medical assistance teams (DMATs), made up of volunteers, provide the major manpower for the NDMS and may include nurses, physicians, search-and-rescue personnel, and others who have received special education and training in disasters. They may work with other agencies such as the American National Red Cross in providing specific disaster services.

The Disaster Plan

Even with pictures, charts, and discussions, it is hard to visualize the overwhelming stress that disaster brings to a community. Until one has actually witnessed a disaster, it is also hard to imagine that "it can happen here." However, real-life disasters prove that no community or segment of our society is immune; they also prove that the public expects the EN to function efficiently in the emergency. ENs should be alert to this expectation but still recognize their own right to react with the same anxieties and feelings of inadequacy as others do.

In a disaster, the demands may be greater and the circumstances unusual, but the nursing fundamentals practiced in lesser crises will be applicable. Disaster nursing requires the adaptation of professional skills in recognizing and meeting the medical and nursing needs evolving from a disaster situation. To respond in a rational manner to the demands of a disaster situation, it is essential that every hospital have a disaster plan in writing and available to every department. This plan must:

- Provide for admission, disposition, discharge, and transfer of patients into and out of the hospital
- Include provisions for notifying clinical personnel and key administrative resources

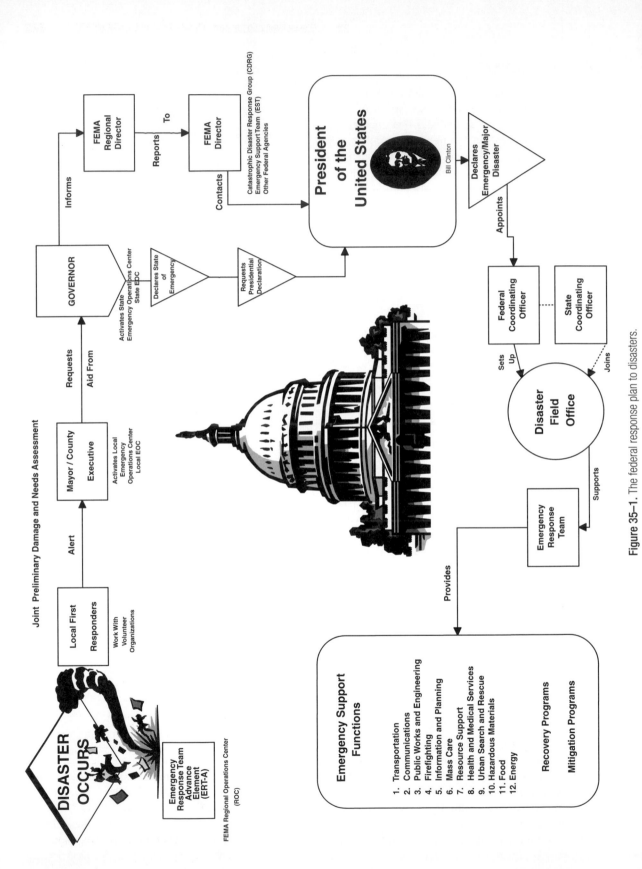

Joint Preliminary Damage and Needs Assessment

DISASTER OCCURS

Emergency Response Team Advance Element (ERT-A)

FEMA Regional Operations Center (ROC)

Local First Responders

Work With Volunteer Organizations

Alert

Mayor / County Executive

Activates Local Emergency Operations Center Local EOC

Requests Aid From

GOVERNOR

Activates State Emergency Operations Center State EOC

Informs

FEMA Regional Director

Reports To

FEMA Director

Contacts

Catastrophic Disaster Response Group (CDRG) Emergency Support Team (EST) Other Federal Agencies

Declares State of Emergency

Requests Presidential Declaration

President of the United States

Bill Clinton

Declares Emergency/Major Disaster

Appoints

Federal Coordinating Officer

State Coordinating Officer

Sets Up

Joins

Disaster Field Office

Supports

Emergency Response Team

Provides

Emergency Support Functions

1. Transportation
2. Communications
3. Public Works and Engineering
4. Firefighting
5. Information and Planning
6. Mass Care
7. Resource Support
8. Health and Medical Services
9. Urban Search and Rescue
10. Hazardous Materials
11. Food
12. Energy

Recovery Programs

Mitigation Programs

Figure 35–1. The federal response plan to disasters.

- Include a means of securing disaster supplies and services from other areas and a list of suppliers, addresses, and telephone numbers
- Designate the specific physical spaces for functions such as patient triage operations, decontamination, minor surgery, or resuscitation; a temporary morgue may also be prepositioned
- Outline roles of health-care personnel, various departments, administrators, volunteers, and others
- Provide a plan for regular, periodic drills to ensure that all staff are familiar with their roles and responsibilities

Disaster Tags

Disaster tags are an essential adjunct to disaster management in the ED. An adequate supply of tags, along with numbered bags for victim's clothing, should be available in the department and ready to use if needed. There are several types of disaster tags available, but whatever is used should contain at least the following:

- Patient name or other identification information and a color-coded or numerical triage classification
- Allergies, current medications, or medical conditions
- Care rendered by prehospital personnel; including recording of VS, medications and treatments given, and x-ray films taken
- Disposition of patient

Personnel Identification

Identification should be provided to emergency personnel so that they can gain admission through police lines and past hospital security during disasters and large-scale emergencies. If your hospital does not provide employee identification for disasters, your hospital identification card or name badge may suffice. In some communities, your parking sticker may be used to indicate your official role during a disaster. Provisions should be made with the appropriate local authorities for acceptance of these employee designations during a disaster to prevent delays and to ensure immediate access to the facility where they are assigned.

COMMON PROBLEMS

An analysis of disaster responses within the United States since 1900 to events involving 100 or more deaths suggests common problems:

- Recklessness or excessive speeds cause additional injury to many transported victims; sightseers and volunteer vehicles invariably converged in the disaster zone and clogged the roads.
- In spite of efforts at traffic control, the general pattern was that the nearest hospital was overwhelmed and the more remote hospitals received fewer than their reasonable share of victims.
- Where no previous plans for control of traffic were developed, an uncontrolled flood of traffic seriously handicapped operations and overloaded access roads and parking areas of the hospitals.
- The vast majority of injured received medical care at hospitals and not in homes or physicians' offices.
- Hospitals with more highly developed disaster planning and longer periods of warning have been successful in establishing medical control over admission of the injured.
- Triage was possible only when certain key posts were manned, facilitating the flow of the injured. This success appeared to depend absolutely upon arrangements made before the disaster occurred. Records can be started by a system of tagging at this point, although no hospital successfully improvised a spur-of-the-moment record or tagging system.
- Misuse of personnel occurred frequently in the absence of planning. Too many personnel or volunteers without specific directions or assignments were common.
- There was a sufficient supply of blood in most disasters because there seemed to be a tendency to use less blood, blood products, and plasma volume expanders in mass-casualty situations.
- Communications between hospitals and other agencies presented serious problems, with poor central control of telephone traffic, resulting in heavily overloaded switch-

boards that eventually became jammed. This indicates the necessity to closely monitor the use of radio transmission because the volume of traffic that can be accommodated is extremely limited.

- Notification of responsible officials and call-in staff was seriously hampered because of haphazard preparation for the event, such as unlisted numbers for emergency personnel, messages lost on an answering machine, and listings of phone numbers that were not current. All employees should review the recall roster and be required by hospital policy to make updates as necessary. A calling chain may be useful to reduce the burden on hospital personnel already in-house.

- Adequate record-keeping can be accomplished only when a high degree of pre-planning and organization has been accomplished at the hospital. An effective system is to start the record by prearranged tagging at the triage point, with specific designation made to continue maintenance of the record after the patient has left the triage point.

HAZARDOUS MATERIALS IN DISASTERS

In recent years, there has been an increase in the number and types of hazardous materials that can pose threats for hospital personnel who are not adequately equipped to handle and care for the contaminated victim. Although prehospital personnel (e.g., fire, HAZMAT [hazardous materials], and EMS) may had accomplished field decontamination procedures, victims still require special handling when they arrive at the emergency facility.

There are federal regulations that mandate use of personal protective clothing and equipment (PPE) to shield or isolate individuals from the chemical, physical, and biologic hazards that may be encountered at a hazardous waste site or at an incident involving hazardous materials. OSHA (Occupational Safety and Health Administration) standards outline training requirements (40 hours of initial training and at least 3 days of initial field experience) for employees at uncontrolled hazardous waste operations. All hazardous-waste site operators must develop a safety and health program and provide for emergency responses. These standards are also designed to provide additional protection for those who respond to hazardous materials incidents, such as firefighters, police officers, and EMS personnel. OSHA's directive, as it applies to emergency medical personnel, states that training shall be based on the duties and functions to be performed by each responder of an emergency response organization.[1] This, of course, includes ED personnel who continue the care of a victim of a HAZMAT exposure.

No combination of PPE is capable of protecting an individual against all hazards. There are specific types of protection that are recommended when dealing with different known and unknown substances. Personnel must receive in-depth training in regard to using any PPE.

Respiratory Protection

There are two types of respirators used for hazardous materials: air-purifying respirators (APRs) and air-supplying respirators (ASRs), which include self-contained breathing apparatuses (SCBAs) and supplied-air respirators (SARs).

Air-Purifying Respirators. An APR depends on ambient air purified through a filtering device before inhalation. The three types of APRs used by emergency personnel are chemical cartridges or canisters, disposables, and powered-air units. One advantage of the APR system is that it permits the wearer considerable mobility. Since APRs filter only the air, the ambient concentration of oxygen must be sufficient (> 19.5 percent) for the user. The most commonly used APR is the cartridge or canister unit, which purifies inspired air by a chemical reaction, filtration adsorption or absorption. Disposable APRs are used for particulates, such as asbestos. Some may be used with other contaminants. These respirators often are half-masks that cover the face from nose to chin but do not provide any eye protection. This type of APR depends on a filter to trap particulates. Filters may also be used in combination with cartridges and canisters to provide increased protection from particulates.

Air-Supplying Respirators. ASRs are available in two basic designs: the SCBA, which has its own air supply, and the SAR, which depends on an air supply from a distant source. The SCBA has a face mask connected to a source of compressed air for breathing; exhalation is into the atmosphere. There are also closed units that rely on a "rebreather" mask. The most popular SCBA is an open-circuit, positive-pressure unit in which air is supplied from a positive-pressure cylinder. In contrast to the negative-pressure unit, there is a higher air pressure maintained within the mask that affords maximum protection against airborne contaminants: any leakage forces the contaminant out. With a negative-pressure apparatus, contaminants may enter a poorly sealed face mask.) SARs are connected to an air source outside the contaminated area. These are used only at hazardous waste sites where an individual may need to work for a long period of time around a potentially dangerous substance.

Personnel must be fit-tested for use of all respirators. A fit-test is usually conducted on a yearly basis, and is performed using a substance such as amyl acetate (banana oil) and irritating fumes to test the adequacy of the seal of the wearer's APR device.

Chemical Protective Clothing

The intent of chemical protective clothing (CPC) is to prevent the individual from coming into direct contact with a chemical contaminant. No CPC will provide protection against all substances, so ENs must know the capabilities and limitations of the garments provided for their use. Furthermore, they must receive specific information on how to don and remove the various items, such as suit, gloves, mask, shoe covers, or head gear, to ensure that accidental contamination does not occur during these maneuvers.

The level of protection required to shield an individual against contact with known or anticipated toxic chemicals has been divided into four categories:

- *Level A:* Highest level of respiratory, skin, and eye protection is needed
- *Level B:* Highest level of respiratory protection is needed, but a lesser level of skin protection is required
- *Level C:* Used when air-purifying is required
- *Level D:* Not used for situations in which there is any risk to respiratory tract or skin; provides minimal protection against skin

hazards and no protection against respiratory hazards

The level of protection required is determined by the type of hazardous substance, its toxicity, and the concentration of the substance in the ambient air. Another factor involves the potential for exposure to this substance from the air, splashes of liquids, or other direct contact with materials that may occur during work. ENs must often use CPC gear that is typical for Level D protection but occasionally use certain items associated with Level C protection.

PATIENT DECONTAMINATION

The goals of decontamination in the field are to reduce risks for the victim and to minimize any potential contamination for the environment or for health-care providers involved in subsequent treatment of the victim.

Notification

When a hospital is notified about a potential HAZMAT incident, it is vital to obtain as much information as possible. Information that will aid in initiating appropriate actions includes the following[3]:

- Type and nature of incident
- Caller's telephone number
- Number of patients
- Signs/symptoms being experienced by the patient(s)
- Nature of injuries
- Name of chemical(s) involved
- The preliminary treatment given
- Extent of patient decontamination conducted in the field
- ETA

After the above information is received, a resource center (see Information Sources on Disasters and Hazardous Materials, pages 593–597) should be contacted for further directives. When calling a resource center, be able to provide the name of the chemical substance and its physical state (i.e., gas, liquid or solid), the type and length of exposure, the decontamination procedures or other interventions (e.g., antidotes) already used, and current status of the victims. The resource center will provide further information regarding the substance and supply guidelines for additional decontamination along with PPE requirements.

Emergency medical personnel should be notified of any special approach or entrance and be advised not to bring the patient into the ED until the contamination of the patient has been assessed and accepted by the ED staff. ENs should remember that victims contaminated by hazardous materials may arrive by other than regular EMS channels and may not have undergone any field decontamination. These individuals must be confined and not be permitted to enter until a determination of risk has been made by qualified HAZMAT personnel or the emergency physician after consultation regarding the type and amount of contamination. In incidents of an unknown nature, full protective gear should be used until the risks to personnel and the department can be ascertained. The HAZMAT guidelines for emergency department preparation appear in Tables 35–1 and 35–2.

Decontamination Team Preparation

Those individuals participating in the decontamination team must be properly protected using the level of protection recommended for the substance(s) involved. This is usually determined by

consulting with one of the reference resources (see page 593). Wide (2-in.) tape should be placed on the back of the workers' protective suit for easy identification and to assist in communication.[3]

Patient Arrival

ENs should assume that all casualties from HAZMAT incidents will need decontamination. All clothing should be removed from the victim (if it was not previously removed at the scene), because getting rid of clothing will substantially reduce the risk of contamination to the patient, healthcare personnel and the environment. Contaminated clothing must be double bagged in impermeable receptacles, sealed and labeled with all pertinent identification information. Members of the decontamination team should retrieve the patients and remove them directly to the decontamination area using a predesignated route as prescribed in the facility's disaster plan. As in all emergencies, priority should be given to basic life support and simultaneous reduction of contamination. When these basics have been addressed, attention may be given to other assessments and interventions (see Table 35–2).

TABLE 35–1. DECONTAMINATION AREA PREPARATION

Ideally, the decontamination area should have a separate entrance. The route from the emergency entrance to the decontamination area should be protected with plastic or paper sheeting. This barrier should be taped securely to the floor.

Security personnel should restrict accessibility to the decontamination area. The decontamination area should be large enough to facilitate decontamination of more than one patient and accommodate the necessary personnel involved in patient treatment and decontamination.

The ventilation system should be either separate from the rest of the hospital or shut off in order to prevent spread of airborne contaminants throughout the facility. Adequate ventilation should be a priority for both the patient and emergency department personnel. An exterior or portable decontamination system is a viable substitute in preventing spread of contamination.

All nonessential personnel and nondisposable equipment should be removed from the decontamination area prior to patient entry. All doorknobs, cabinet handles, light switches, and other areas that have contact with hands should be taped.

The floors should be covered with plastic or paper sheeting to prevent contamination. The floor coverings should be securely taped to prevent slippage, and the entrance to the room should be marked with a wide strip of colored tape to indicate a contaminated area. Personnel should not enter the area unless properly protected, and no personnel or equipment should leave the area until properly decontaminated.

A "clean" member of the staff should stand on the clean side of the entrance to hand in supplies and receive medical specimens.

The essential requirements for any decontamination task are:

   Adequate protection for personnel handling the patient

   A safe area to place a patient undergoing decontamination

   A method for washing contaminants off a patient and containing the rinsate

   Disposable or cleanable medical equipment to treat the patient

---

From Hospital Emergency Room Hazmat Decontamination Course.[3]

TABLE 35–2. DECONTAMINATION OF PATIENT

The basic purposes of decontamination are:
  To reduce external contamination
  To contain the contamination present
  To prevent the further spread of potentially dangerous substances
Decontamination should begin at the patient's head and proceed downward, with initial attention to contaminated eyes and open
  wounds. Facial area and wounds can be decontaminated simultaneously.

Skin
Contaminated areas should be gently washed under a spray of water, using a sponge and a mild soap to prevent damage to the epidermal layer. Hot water, stiff brushes, or vigorous scrubbing should never be used because they cause vasodilation and abrasion, increasing the chances for absorption of hazardous materials through the skin. Care should be taken so that contaminants are not introduced into open wounds, using such methods as covering wounds with a waterproof dressing. All runoff from decontamination procedures should be collected for proper disposal.

Wounds
The first priority in the process of decontamination should be contaminated open wounds. These areas allow for rapid absorption of hazardous materials. Wounds should be irrigated with copious amounts of normal saline (NS), and deep debridement and excision should be performed only when particles or pieces of material have been embedded in the tissues. Once wounds have been cleaned, care should be exercised so that the wounds are not cross-contaminated.

Eyes
Decontamination of the eyes should also have high priority. Gentle irrigation of the eyes should be performed with the stream of NS diverted away from the medial canthus so that it does not force material into the lacrimal duct.

Nose and Ears
Contaminated nares and ear canals should also be gently irrigated, using frequent suction to prevent forcing any material deeper into those cavities. Washing with soap and tepid water is usually all that is needed to remove contamination. Effective decontamination consists of making the patient as clean as possible. This means that the contamination has been reduced to a level that is no longer a threat to the patient or the hospital personnel. The recorder should note (on a diagram of the body) the areas found by the physician to be contaminated. Basically, a contaminated patient is like any other and may be treated as such except that staff must protect themselves and others from potential exposures to contamination.

Removal of Patient from Decontamination Room
Place a clean piece of plastic on the floor for the patient and staff to use when exiting the area. If the patient is not ambulatory, a clean stretcher or wheelchair should be brought to the doorway by a protected individual.
Once the patient has been removed from the decontamination room, staff should proceed to remove all protective clothing and equipment. These should be placed in a proper waste container. The undressing sequence is as follows:
  Remove outer gloves
  Remove protective shoe coverings
  Remove coverall; be sure to roll it downward from inside out
  Remove mask
  Remove inner gloves last
After the patient is transferred to the clean area, the physician can perform the physical examination and initiate routine patient management.
Note: The attending staff must remember that since exposure to some substances can result in serious delayed effects, sustained observation and monitoring are required.

From *Hospital Emergency Room Hazmat Decontamination Course.*[3]

■ REFERENCES

1. OSHA. *Occupational Safety and Health Guidance Manual for Hazardous Waste Site Activities.* Washington, D.C.: U.S. Government Printing Office, 1995.
2. *Accreditation Manual for Hospitals.* Vol. 1. *Standards.* Oakbrook Terrace, Ill: Joint Commission on Accreditation of Healthcare Organizations; 1996.
3. Hospital Emergency Room Hazmat Decontamination Course. U.S. Environmental Protection Agency, Region III, and U.S. EPA Region III Site Assessment Technical Assistance Team, 1996.

■ BIBLIOGRAPHY

Benumof J. *Airway Management: Principles and Practice.* St. Louis, Mo: CV Mosby; 1995.

Cardona VD, Hurn PD, Bastnagel Mason PJ, et al. *Trauma Nursing.* 2nd ed. Philadelphia, Pa: WB Saunders; 1994.

The Director of Central Intelligence, Interagency Intelligence Committee on Terrorism. *Chemical Biological Incident Handbook.* 1995.

Hazardous Materials Operational Level Course. Hazardous Materials International Emergency Response. May 1995.

Lee G. *Flight Nursing: Principles and Practice.* St. Louis, Mo: Mosby-Year Book; 1991.

Levine RL, Fromm RE Jr. *Critical Care Monitoring from Pre-Hospital to the ICU.* St. Louis, Mo: Mosby-Year Book; 1995.

Maull KI, Rodriguez A, Wiles CE. *Complications in Trauma and Critical Care.* Philadelphia, Pa: WB Saunders; 1996.

Weist PW, Roth PB. *Fundamental of Emergency Radiology.* Philadelphia, Pa: WB Saunders; 1996.

Wilkins RL, Dexter Jr. *Respiratory Disease: Principles of Patient Care.* Philadelphia, Pa: FA Davis; 1993.

■ REVIEW: COMMUNICATION AND DISASTER MANAGEMENT

1. Describe the protocol for receiving and acknowledging a radio transmission from a pre-hospital unit.

2. List six major problems that are commonly associated with a disaster.

3. List the types of information that can be obtained via the CABIN program (Chemical and Biological Information Network) of the Federal Emergency Management Agency (FEMA).

4. Differentiate between the two types of respiratory protection units employed for managing patients in a hazardous materials environment.

5. Outline eight items of essential information that should be obtained about patients who are being transported by emergency medical services (EMS) to your emergency department (ED) for treatment.

6. Describe three clinical scenarios mandating that ED personnel don chemical protective clothing (CPC).

7. Cite four essential requirements for any decontamination.

8. Outline essential steps for preparing a decontamination area for the receipt of casualties from a hazardous materials accident.

9. Identify the single step in the decontamination procedure that eliminates the greatest amount of potentially hazardous residue.

10. Describe the proper sequence for removing items of personal protective clothing and equipment (PPE).

Information Sources on Disasters and Hazardous Materials

■ EMERGENCIES

- National Response Center: 24 hours, (800) 424-8802
- CANUTEC (Canadian Transport Emergency Center): 24 hours, (613) 996-6666
- CHEMTREC (Chemical Transportation Emergency Center): 24 hours, (800) 424-9300
- Bureau of Explosives (Association of American Railroads): limited hours, (202) 639-2222

■ REGULATORY/TECHNICAL

- EPA Superfund and RCRA Hotline: limited hours, (800) 424-9346
- EPA Toxic Substances Control Act Hotline: limited hours, (202) 554-1404
- EPA Safe Drinking Water Act Hotline: limited hours, (800) 426-4791
- EPA Chemical Emergency Preparedness: limited hours, (800) 535-0202
- Program/Community Right-to-Know Hotline, EPA Asbestos Technical Information Center: closes at 5 P.M., (800) 334-8571, extension 6741
- EPA Radon Technical Information Center: closes at 5 P.M., (800) 334-8571
- Agency for Toxic Substance and Disease Registry: 24 hours, (404) 639-0615
- OSHA Technical Data Center: closes at 4:45 P.M., (202) 219-7500

- Centers for Disease Control: 24 hours, (404) 633-5313
- FEMA/DOT Hazardous Materials Information Clearinghouse: closes at 5 P.M., (202) 366-4900
- U.S. Department of Commerce, Weather Division: closes at 5 P.M., (704) 259-0682
- American Petroleum Institute: closes at 5 P.M., (202) 682-8000
- Chemical Manufacturers Association: closes at 5 P.M., (202) 887-1100
- Chemical Manufacturers Association: closes at 5 P.M., (800) CMA-8200
- Chemical Reference Center, Spill Control Association of America: closes at 5 P.M., (313) 552-0500

■ COMPUTERIZED DATABASES

There are a number of computerized databases that can be effectively used in preparing for sampling investigations, preliminary field assessments, or emergency response situations.

CHEMICAL INFORMATION SYSTEM

The Chemical Information System (CIS)—(800) 247-8787—is a collection of scientific and regulatory databases as well as data analysis computer programs. It contains numerical data (as opposed to bibliographic information) in the areas of toxicology, environment, regulations, spectroscopy, chemical and physical properties, and nucleotide sequencing. It allows for structure, substructure, and full or partial name searching on over 225,000 unique chemical substances. CIS also has an electronic mail (e-mail) system for communication between users.

OCCUPATIONAL HEALTH SERVICES HAZARDLINE

The Occupational Services (OHS) Hazardline—(800) 638-6660 or (800) 223-8978—is a useful database that provides specific information on more than 3000 chemicals. Most of the data is in an easily accessible format that is especially useful in workplace emergency situations. Categories include such topics as first-aid procedures, symptoms, use of respirators, PPE, organs affected, and leak and spill mitigation procedures.

OCCUPATIONAL HEALTH SERVICES ENVIRONMENTAL HEALTH NEWS

OHS Environmental Health News is a headline and updating service that provides news of breaking developments in the environmental and occupational health fields. It can be searched by key word to show the latest developments on a particular topic.

TOXICOLOGY DATA BANK

The Toxicology Data Bank—(301) 496-6531—includes information on approximately 15,000 chemicals and is available through the National Library of Medicine. Data include such topics as fire potential, explosive limits, radiation limits, occupational exposure, antidote and treatment, warnings and cautions, shipment and disposal methods, and manufacturing information.

TOXLINE

Toxline—(301) 496-6531—is a bibliographic database that includes information on the physiological and toxicologic effects of drugs and chemicals. It is produced by the National Library of Medicine and is a useful source for additional information on particular substances.

REGISTRY OF TOXIC EFFECTS OF CHEMICAL SUBSTANCES

The Registry of Toxic Effects of Chemical Substances (RTECS)—(301) 496-6531—is a database that provides acute and chronic toxicity information for thousands of potentially toxic chemicals, including exposure standards and status under various federal regulations.

OTHERS

There are several systems available that deal with regulatory updates on both the state and federal levels. Examples of these systems would include CLDS (produced by the Army Corps of Engineers), Public Affairs Information Service, and Federal Register Abstracts. These systems are useful for a more detailed understanding of the regulatory status of particular chemicals. There are also databases that can produce material safety data sheets (MSDSs) on demand.

■ GENERAL REFERENCES FOR HAZMAT OPERATIONS

Merck Index
Merck and Co
Rahway, NJ 07065
(201) 594-4000

Covers:
- Chemicals, drugs, and biologicals
- Physical properties
- Chemical structure
- Some reactivity information
- LD_{50} (median lethal dose) values

Condensed Chemical Dictionary
Gessner G. Hawley, revised by N. Irving Sax and Richard J. Lewis Sr.
Van Nostrand Reinhold
135 W. 50th Street
New York, NY 10020

Covers:
- Industrial chemicals currently in production
- Trademark products
- CAS registry number
- Formula

- Physical properties
- Source of incident
- Use
- Some hazard information

Registry of Toxic Effects of Chemical Substances
U.S. Government Printing Office
Washington, D.C. 20402

Self-described as dealing with "all mined, manufactured, processed, synthesized, and naturally occurring inorganic and organic compounds." Includes information on drugs, food additives, preservatives, ores, pesticides, dyes, detergents, lubricants, soaps, plastics, extracts from plants, microorganisms and animals; plants and animals that are toxic upon contact or consumption, pyrolysis products, and industrial intermediates and waste products from production processes. Commercial product trade names are included only if they represent a single active chemical entity or well-defined mixture of relatively constant composition.

Covers:

- Prime name
- Date entry last revised
- CAS number
- Molecular weight and formula
- Synonyms, common names, trade names
- Data on skin and eye irritation
- Mutation data
- Reproductive effects data
- Data on tumorigenicity
- Toxicity data
- Review of substance regarding:
    Standards and regulations promulgated by federal agencies
    Recommended exposure level published by National Institute for Occupational Safety and Health (NIOSH)
    Department of Transportation, NIOSH, and EPA status information

Dangerous Properties of Industrial Materials
Edited by N. Irving Sax
Van Nostrand Reinhold
135 W. 50th Street
New York, NY 10020

Covers:

- Inclusions similar to those of RTECS
- NIOSH and CAS numbers
- Synonyms
- Clinical toxicologic data similar to that of RTECS
- Incompatibles
- Fire and explosion hazards
- Disaster hazards
- Also: general toxicology, detailed ventilation procedures, industrial and environmental risks from carcinogens, biohazards in the laboratory, nuclear medicine applications

Clinical Toxicology of Commercial Products
by R. Gosselin, H. Hodge, R. Smith, M. Gleason
Williams & Wilkins
Baltimore, Md

Covers:

- Commercial products used in and around home and farm
- First aid and general emergency treatment
- Ingredients
- Therapeutics (grouped by related substances)
- Supportive treatment
- Trade names
- General formulations
- Manufacturers

Handbook of Toxic and Hazardous Chemicals and Carcinogens

Covers:

- Substances in 1983–84 American Conference of Governmental Industrial Hygienists (ACGIH) threshold limit values (TLVs)
- Substances in 1981 NIOSH Standards Completion Program
- Priority toxic water pollutants defined by EPA in 1980
- Hazardous wastes defined by Resource Conservation and Recovery Act (RCRA) in April 1980
- Hazardous substances defined by Clean Water Act (1972)
- Carcinogens identified by the National Toxicology Program
- Description

- Department of Transportation (DOT) designation
- Synonyms
- Potential exposure
- Incompatibilities
- Permissible exposure limits in air
- Permissible concentration in water
- Determination of levels in water
- Routes of entry
- Harmful effects and symptoms
- Points of attack (target organs and systems)
- Medical surveillance
- First aid
- PPE
- Respirator selection
- Suggested disposal methods
- References

Threshold Limit Values and Biological Exposure Indices

Covers:
- Chemical substances (623), 1987–88
- TLV-TWA (time-weighted average)
- TLV-STEL (short-term exposure limit)
- TLV-C (ceiling)
- BEI (biological exposure indices)
- Physical agents: heat stress, cold stress, hand/arm vibration, ionizing radiation, lasers, noise, radiofrequency/microwave radiation, notice of intended changes

NIOSH Pocket Guide to Chemical Hazards
Publication Dissemination DSD11
National Institute for Occupational Safety and Health
4676 Columbia Parkway
Cincinnati, OH 45226
(513) 533-8287

Covers:
- Chemical substances (397)
- Chemical name and formula
- Synonyms
- Exposure limits: OSHA PEL (personal exposure limit); NIOSH REL (recommended exposure limit)
- IDLH level (immediately dangerous to life and health)
- Physical description
- Chemical and physical properties (some IPs)
- Incompatibilities

- Measurement method
- PPE and sanitation
- Respirator selection
- Route of health hazard
- Symptoms
- First aid
- Target organs

Farm Chemicals Handbook
Meister Publishing
37841 Euclid Avenue
Willoughby, OH 44094

Covers:
- Fertilizer and agriculture chemicals
- Synonyms and trade names
- Structural formulation
- Action
- Application/use
- Signal work
- Toxicity class and LD_{50} information
- Chemical properties
- Solubility
- Handling and storage cautions
- PPE

NFPA Fire Protection Guide on Hazardous Materials
National Fire Protection Association (NFPA)
Battery March Park
Quincy, MA 02269

Covers:
- Fire hazard properties of flammable liquids, gases, and volatile solids (over 1300 flammable substances)
- Hazardous chemical data on 416 chemicals regarding fire, explosion, and toxicity
- Hazardous chemical reactions data on 3550 mixtures of two or more chemicals reported to be potentially dangerous in that they may cause fires, explosions, or detonations at ordinary or moderately elevated temperatures
- National Fire Protection Agency (NFPA) fire hazard identification system on 704 chemicals

Chemical Hazard Response Information System
Hazardous Chemicals Data Book
U.S. Government Printing Office
Washington, D.C. 20402
GPO Stock Number 050-012-00147-2

Covers:
- Chemical substances (1015)
- Physical and chemical properties
- Hazard classifications
- Labeling
- Shipping information
- Fire, exposure, and water pollution effects and methods of handling
- Health hazards and toxicity
- Protective equipment
- Guide to compatibility of chemicals

Occupational Health Guidelines for Chemical Hazards (NIOSH/OSHA)
Publication No. PB83-154609, 3 parts
National Technical Information Service
Springfield, VA 22161

Covers:
- Technical information under the Standards Completion Project, involving OSHA, NIOSH, and several contractors
- Name, formula, synonyms, appearance, and odor
- Permissible exposure limit
- Effects of overexposure
- Recommended medical surveillance
- Summary of toxicology
- Physical data

- Reactivity
- Flammability
- Warning properties
- Monitoring and measurement procedures
- PPE
- Sanitation
- Common operations and controls
- Emergency first-aid procedures
- Spill, leak, and disposal procedures
- References
- Respiratory protection guidelines

DOT Emergency Response Guidebook
Department of Transportation
Washington, DC 20407

Covers:
- United Nations Classification System
- United Nations/North American number index to material name and response guide
- Material name index to United Nations/North American number and response guide
- Response guides (76) regarding fire or explosion and health hazards
- Emergency action: fire, spill or leak, first aid
- Also provides initial isolation/evacuation tables for selected hazardous materials

Emergency Department Management

36

Emergency department (ED) management has always been challenging in the face of federal regulations, standards of care set by the Joint Commission on Accreditation of Healthcare Organizations (JCAHO), hospital policies, staffing problems, financial constraints, quality-of-care issues, requirements for continuing staff development, equipment shortages, communications, disaster drills, stress, and the never-ending flow of patients needing immediate intervention (or perceiving that they need immediate intervention). Now ED managers must meet additional challenges presented by managed health-care systems as they begin to superimpose their gatekeeping policies on the accepted standards of practice for delivery of emergency health care to the American public. This chapter addresses many of these areas of concern.

■ MANAGED CARE AND THE EMERGENCY DEPARTMENT

Health-care reform in the United States is bringing change to EDs and the professionals who staff them. Along with the hope for delivery of cost-effective, high-quality care comes several very real concerns about meeting required standards of care, maintaining adequate staffing numbers, and ensuring patient safety and optimum case outcomes. With managed care funneled through health maintenance organizations (HMOs) and large insurance companies, emergency care will find itself defined and controlled by an array of gatekeepers deciding who qualifies for care and who does not. Obtaining timely authorization from gatekeepers when patients are in need of emergency or urgent care may present major problems for the ill and injured, for those who provide the care, and for those who bill for reimbursement. Timely and appropriate consultations within specific health-care plans may become difficult, and demands to transfer unstable patients to specific participating facilities may create violations of federal Consolidated Omnibus Reconciliation Act (COBRA) regulations. Retrospectively, managed-care groups may determine services were not of an emergency nature or not medically necessary and deny payment to providers. How will these losses be absorbed? While our emergency-care delivery system must ensure that no preauthorization rules deny or delay needed care, making that concern a reality will often prove difficult to emergency-care professionals.

CONTINUOUS QUALITY IMPROVEMENT

Delivery of cost-conscious quality care, then, becomes even more of a concern than in the past. One important development in the attempt to provide such care has been implementation of continuous quality improvement (CQI) programs, supplanting quality assurance (QA) efforts. CQI differs from QA but does not replace it; it complements and enhances existing efforts to maintain and improve quality.

Six key elements distinguish CQI from traditional QA programs[1]:

- A focus on process, not on people
- Defining *quality* as meeting the needs of the customer
- Improving quality to reduce costs

- Building quality into the process
- Using a scientific approach to problem solving
- Approaching quality as a management strategy

Quality not only is the "name of the game" but additionally has been shown to translate into lower operational costs as well as savings to the consumer, significant concerns in these cost-conscious times. Costs are increased when treating patients with nosocomial infections or complications and when tests and x-rays must be repeated because the first one was lost or unreadable. ED nurse managers, facing increasing pressure to reduce waste, eliminate errors, minimize staffing, and continue cutting costs wherever possible, will find that the value of CQI policies and procedures increases as standards of care are reviewed and evaluated.

■ STANDARDS OF CARE

Nurses who work or expect to work in an ED have the obligation to be familiar with federal and state regulations governing their hospitals and nursing practice, as well as practice standards defined in the *Accreditation Manual for Hospitals* prepared and administered by the JCAHO. Federal regulations revolve specifically around COBRA policies and/or interfacility transfers and apply to all Medicare-participating hospitals expecting reimbursement; each state's regulations govern that state's nurse practice act, as well as the practice of other licensed and certified professionals working in hospital and prehospital settings.

JOINT COMMISSION ON ACCREDITATION OF HEALTHCARE ORGANIZATIONS

The JCAHO evolved originally from the Hospital Standardization Program, which had been established by the American College of Surgeons (ACS) in 1918 to encourage the adoption of a uniform medical record format that would facilitate accurate recording of a patient's clinical course. The founding sponsors were the ACS, the American College of Physicians (ACP), the American Hospital Association (AHA), the American Med-

ical Association (AMA), and the Canadian Medical Association (CMA), which participated until 1959, when the Canadian Council on Hospital Accreditation was established.

Through the years, the standards have been revised and updated to meet the rapid pace of change that has occurred, and the JCAHO has developed its own full-time field staff, which now surveys well over 2000 hospitals a year. A survey fee was established in 1964 to make the field program self-supporting. Although the standards were aimed initially at minimal achievement in terms of the elements necessary to support life, voluntary accreditation was offered as a yardstick to progressive institutions that wished to attain a level of care set by a professional and nationally recognized group. In the absence of legal and other regulatory requirements, the accreditation program was the only benchmark by which to identify those hospitals.

MEDICARE CONDITIONS OF PARTICIPATION

In 1965, Medicare was established, and written into the medicare act was the provision that the hospitals participating in that program were to maintain the level of patient care that had come to be recognized as the norm. The standards of JCAHO at that time were cited in the law as reflecting that norm and were incorporated into the law by reference. The "Conditions of Participation for Hospitals," subsequently promulgated and published by the Social Security Administration, reflected the 1965 standards of the JCAHO. These conditions of participation, updated periodically, are administered at the state level through the licensing and certification divisions of most state governments to ensure safety and quality care in all hospitals that are not accredited by JCAHO.

EMERGENCY SERVICES STANDARDS

Most nurses, ENs included, know very little about official care standards. They know only that "before JCAHO comes around," all the policy and procedure books disappear from the department and are nowhere to be found for several weeks, only to reappear again, "shining and golden," newly updated and jacketed the very day before the JCAHO surveyors arrive. Section 4 of the standards (*Emergency Services*) should in reality be a working tool for ENs, because it clearly spells out the components that must be present to maintain an effectively operating department, provide safe surroundings, and promote high-quality care to ensure optimum patient benefit. The standards deserve your attention; they are on your side and should be your tools.

The standards, from those that focus on capability to those that focus on outcome and performance, have been revised and rewritten. The new standards address the same areas as the preceding standards, guided by the broad vision that ensures effective, accessible, and affordable patient care; outcomes management, CQI, and service to the patient remain the primary objectives. The 1994–1995 revised standards are grouped into four sections: care of the patient, organizational functions, structures with important functions (governing body, administration and management, medical staff, and nursing), and other department/service-specific requirements.[1,2]

Sections 1 and 4 of the revised standards directly concern ENs, as JCAHO surveyors are currently looking more closely at nurses' current competencies and their role as teachers, as well as at efforts to implement CQI.

The new section 1 focuses on the functions and processes directly related to patient care, and contains seven new sets of performance focused standards:

- Assessment of patients
- Treatment of patients
- Operative and other invasive procedures
- Education of patients and family
- Entry to setting or service
- Nutritional care
- Coordination of care

Section 4 of the new standards addresses ED organization, staffing, ancillary services, design, and equipment.

Obtain a copy and familiarize yourself with the JCAHO mission as it is defined. It is strongly suggested that if you do not have access to the full standards in your department, send for a copy of your own with the full interpretations. The standards can be obtained from the JCAHO, One Renaissance Boulevard, Oakbrook Terrace, Ill. 60181.

■ EMERGENCY DEPARTMENT POLICIES AND PROCEDURES

An updated and workable policies and procedures book is essential to a smooth-running department, providing answers to questions when personnel are in doubt as to specific management approaches, preventing errors in judgment when a situation arises that the person may never have had to cope with, and contributing to the CQI in patient care. Policies are guidelines by which to function, and policies that have been established and approved by administration, the medical staff, and the nursing staff have the full weight of authority when quoted. Emergency personnel should pay close heed to what their policy books state.

One of the most helpful policies is that which distinctly defines authorized procedures and unauthorized procedures for the ED, thereby eliminating tie-up of the department for minor surgery, general anesthesia, contaminated (dirty) cases, and elective sigmoidoscopy and endoscopy when time, space, and personnel are unavailable to cope with these procedures. Enemas and removal of fecal impactions likewise have no place in the ED, which is primarily an acute-care area and usually has neither staff nor space for these procedures. Some of the other important policy areas, most of which the JCAHO standards address, involve the following situations and should have well-defined, written interpretation in your ED's policy books:

- Child abuse
- Treatment of a minor child both with and without that child's consent
- Elder abuse
- Intravenous conscious sedation
- Use of restraints
- Consent in absentia for minors
- Management of the press
- Procedures for obtaining blood alcohol levels
- Procedure for DOA (dead on arrival) patients
- Interfacility transfers and COBRA guidelines
- Release from responsibility for transfer
- Release from responsibility for leaving against medical advice (AMA)
- Handling pathology specimens

- Helicopter landings
- Decontamination after exposure to hazardous substances
- Handling hazardous materials
- Management of sexual assault victims
- Expiration times on sterile supplies
- Reporting of contagious disease, acts of violence, overdoses, and so on
- Management of psychiatric patients
- Management of patients under the influence of drugs or alcohol
- Activation of the disaster plan
- Housekeeping and linen guidelines
- Infection control and management of communicable diseases
- Scope and limitations of duties of various ED personnel

■ PERSONNEL

STAFFING

Emergency Nurses

Work Schedules. To arrive at the number of nurses needed to staff an ED and to schedule them in the most appropriate time slots, EDs should carefully analyze their patient loads during weekday and weekend hours. There is no hard-and-fast rule requiring staffing schedules in the ED to correspond to staffing schedules elsewhere in the hospital, nor is it necessary for all members of a shift to change at one time. It may well be that one nurse would be most valuable spanning two shifts (e.g., 11 A.M. to 7 P.M., or 2 P.M. to 10 P.M.), providing not only continuity between shifts but augmenting the staff capability during the usually heavier patient-load hours. Staffing will be determined by the mission of the ED, the mix of professional and nonprofessional personnel, and whether or not the ED is expected to serve also as a primary care facility. Some EDs may require additional personnel on weekends to accommodate their patient loads.

Because of the unique demands of emergency nursing, many departments are testing various staffing patterns, and one hears frequently of such arrangements as:

- The "7–70" (7 shifts in a row for 10 hours a day, with the next 7 days off), which requires two crews to alternate

- Regular 10-hour shifts (4 shifts in a row with 3 days off)
- 10-hour shifts with a 2-week cyclic pattern (OO-SSM-O-WT-OOO-MTW), which gives 3 days off every other weekend
- 12-hour shifts in various patterns

The distinct advantage of all these extended shifts (aside from more scheduled time off) is the shift overlap of coverage, which provides a greater continuity of care in the department.

Many departments have realized that expensive staff turnover rates can be reduced by implementation of self-scheduling, as nursing personnel enjoy a perceived autonomy when allowed to create their own schedules. Participating staff are asked to sign up for four "requested" days off, which will not be altered unless absolutely necessary; diversity of shifts are offered (e.g., 8-hour; 12-hour; 8–12-hour; straight day, evening, or night shifts; and combinations of the above), as are cyclical schedules. This approach allows nursing personnel both control and flexibility.[3]

Expediting Patient Flow. The triage nurse is generally the person who carries the responsibility for management of patient flow, using the most appropriate area at the time for the care of specific patients. The triage nurse expedites patient care, assigns patients to specific areas, keeps the staff advised of the status of patients in the waiting room, and even, at times, participates in EMS traffic control activities. To shorten the elapsed time in the department for patients, it is good practice to ready them for discharge as soon as the physician has finished evaluation and treatment, helping them dress and then allowing them to wait for instructions, medications, or transportation in a non-treatment area of the department. This allows preparation of the patient area for the next admission and significantly accelerates the patient flow, increasing the number of patients who can be treated in a given period of time.

Departments that are fortunate enough to have "holding" or observation beds are able to use this means of freeing up acute-care areas for incoming patients. Unless your department has facilities for providing adequate extended observation when necessary, the patient should either be admitted or transferred to an institution that can provide the necessary observation.

Emergency Medical Technicians and Paramedics

Initiated in 1970, the emergency medical technician (EMT) training program was the direct result of studies, done in 1968 by the National Academy of Sciences and the U.S. Department of Transportation (DOT), pointing up the dire need for a standardized training program for prehospital ambulance and rescue personnel. In most communities, a cadre of EMTs serves as the most valuable lay member of the medical care team outside the hospital. Standards for the training of EMTs have varied widely from state to state and in some states, from county to county, although most jurisdictions have recognized the 110-hour basic DOT curriculum as the standard. Certification as a basic EMT (EMT-B) is achieved by a program of either state or national testing (by the National Registry of EMTs), which includes a practical skills component in addition to a comprehensive written examination. EMT intermediate credentials (EMT-I) may be earned with an added course, which includes 150 to 200 hours of content in more advanced shock management, trauma care, and special resuscitation techniques. The paramedic (EMT-P) has extensive education and training in advanced procedures and the use of mechanical and pharmacological adjuncts required for all phases of prehospital cardiac life support.

In the day-to-day operation of the Emergency Medical Services (EMS) system, it is the EN to whom EMTs and paramedics most directly relate. It is, therefore, vital that a close working relationship exist between ENs and EMTs/paramedics. This EMT–nurse relationship is vital to the continuity of care of each patient involved. It is critical to the patient's well-being that ENs pay close attention to the information the EMTs convey concerning the prehospital condition of the patient and the care administered. A written record of each patient's prehospital condition and emergency care rendered should be prepared by the EMT and a copy should be made part of the patient's permanent hospital record.

This interaction has other benefits as well. It provides a sort of "checks and balances" system whereby the emergency healthcare providers involved can constructively criticize or question each other's actions, thereby reducing the likelihood of repeated inappropriate action. Also, such interactions frequently result in learning experiences from the advice or explanations that ENs can offer EMTs on patient care, anatomy, and physiology or pathophysiology and that EMTs can offer ENs on prehospital care techniques and actions. When possible, joint emergency-care training programs should be held on topics and skills common to both groups. Ideally, systems for joint case audits should be established and every opportunity should be used to foster professional growth and working relationships. The Emergency Nurses Association (ENA) recognizes that in some parts of the country, ENs may be called upon to take a more direct role in emergency ambulance services by actually delivering or assisting in the delivery of sophisticated prehospital emergency care. In such cases, ENA urges these nurses to complete such specialized training programs as needed before assuming these duties.

The professional interaction between EMT/paramedics and ENs includes but is certainly not limited to the following premises:

- The EMT provides valuable and accurate baseline data (e.g., vital signs [VS], history of accident or illness, emotional status of patient, evidence of ingestion such as pill bottles)
- The EMT can give valuable assistance in the ED with patient management problems.
- The EMT is capable of providing life support on the way to the ED and can communicate information about patient status prior to arrival. Conversations on the emergency radio must be kept to a minimum, so only pertinent information should be given or requested, but it should include running code (1, 2, or 3), number of patients aboard, sex and age of each and whether "up" (sitting) or "down" (stretcher), possible diagnosis or chief complaint, VS, level of consciousness (LOC), and ETA (estimated time of arrival).

A close rapport and team spirit between ENs and EMTs will ensure continued learning experiences and optimal continuity of care for the patient and will provide the EMT with opportunities to critique situations, benefit from experience, and become an increasingly capable and contributing member of the emergency medical care team.

Emergency Department Technicians

With the increasing number of qualified EMTs available and the many experienced people seeking employment in EDs, a need developed early on to define a job description for EDTs who can function in a productive role without assuming the registered nurse's (RN's) responsibilities and violating the nurse practice acts in most of the 50 states. "Turf battles" must and can be avoided if individual facilities define roles in written position descriptions, making use of input from appropriate participants (nurses *and* EMTs/paramedics). Such a suggested job description is given here in a basic format; it can easily be adapted to individual department needs.

Job Description. There is a need for skilled EDTs to assist the professional nursing and medical staff of the ED in providing the highest quality medical care possible to emergency patients, with every due consideration for the personhood, privacy, and safety of the patient. A formally structured educational program of sufficient depth with a minimum core curriculum of 15 hours is administered to define standards of performance as well as to ensure competence consistent with the responsibilities delegated to the EDT.

Basic Qualifications. Intelligence, the ability to relate to people and exhibit empathy for them, a capacity for calm and reasoned judgment in meeting emergencies, and an orientation toward service are essential attributes of the EDT. The candidate must be a high-school graduate with one or more of the following:

- Two years' prior experience in ED work
- Military training with designation as a specialist in the medical field
- Intensive on-the job training administered by an accredited hospital

Skill Areas. The EDT must demonstrate competence and current knowledge in the following areas:

- Airway management
- Oxygen administration
- Suctioning techniques
- Bag-and-mask techniques

- Cardiopulmonary resuscitation (must qualify for current state AHA certification)
- Obtaining and recording VS, including visual acuity
- Gross neurological examination, including pupil size, equality, and reaction to light and accommodation (PERL-A)
- 90-second trauma evaluation
- Documentation procedures
- Nasogastric (NG) intubation
- Orthopedic procedures as outlined
- Assisting with setups for lacerations, minor repairs, Crutchfield tongs, chest tubes, lumbar punctures, and orthopedic appliances
- Obtaining specimens
- Medicolegal aspects of the ED, including limitations on the job, as defined by state statutes

Duties and Responsibilities. The EDT is responsible for performing assigned duties within his or her capabilities and under the direct supervision of an RN. EDTs shall not assume any responsibility of the physician and shall not mislead patients or visitors as to their identity, shall not accept verbal orders for medications or administer medications, and all such matters shall be referred to the registered professional nurse on duty. Duties include the following:

1. Maintain and stock supplies in:
   Resuscitation rooms
   Holding, treatment, and monitoring rooms/areas
   Cast room and suture areas
   Utility rooms.
2. Maintain linen supply in all rooms.
3. Clean up after procedures, observing appropriate guidelines and precautions.
   Disinfect and prepare stretchers after discharges.
   Maintain the utility workroom in orderly fashion.
4. Dispose of trash and linen during and at end of each shift.
5. Practice clean technique at *all* times and have a working knowledge of formal precaution, isolation, and clean techniques, employing them as indicated.

Emergency Procedures. The EDT must be able to:

1. Establish an airway, inserting plastic oropharyngeal airway as necessary.
2. Ventilate patient with a bag or mask unit, if necessary.
3. Initiate and maintain cardiopulmonary resuscitation (CPR) until relieved.
4. Apply monitor electrodes for the cardiac monitor and the electroencephalogram (ECG) machine.
5. Suction patient as necessary:
   Oral
   Nasal
   Endotracheal (ET).
6. Apply direct pressure to control bleeding or employ arterial pressure points if necessary.
7. Immobilize injuries on multiple-trauma patients.

Assistance with Nursing Procedures. The EDT must be able to:

1. Assist in admitting and discharging patients (*all* trauma patients must be fully disrobed for examination).
2. Perform primary evaluation of the patient in the absence of a RN by obtaining VS on every patient, including temperature, pulse, respiration, and blood pressure (BP), and recording the information on the patient's chart.
3. Check neurological signs (if indicated) and record as necessary:
   LOC and degree of orientation
   Condition of PERL-A
   Postures or position.
4. Provide bedpans and urinals as needed.
5. Assist in obtaining specimens and transporting them to the lab as necessary:
   Urine
   Stool
   Sputum
   Blood
   Throat
6. Chart observations.
7. Perform Clinitest, Acetest, and guaiac test.
8. Apply heat or cold packs.

9. Position patients rapidly as indicated for coma, seizures, shock, dyspnea, and combativeness.
10. Restrain patients as necessary in the safest and most effective fashion, according to hospital policy.
11. Lift and move patients as necessary, being aware of and using precautions for possible injuries.
12. Transport patients:
    To the radiology department
    To and from automobiles
    To in-patient unit following admission
    To the morgue.
13. Lend general support to the nursing staff in whatever areas are indicated that fall within the scope of the technician's training and capabilities.

Assistance with Physicians' Procedures

EDTs must assist physicians as follows:

1. Employ sterile technique at all times when indicated.
2. Carry out sterile preparation and irrigation for minor surgeries as necessary.
3. Assist in minor surgeries as necessary and as directed.
4. Set up for sterile procedures:
   Chest tube insertions
   Laceration repairs
   Elective minor surgeries
   Lumbar punctures
   Chest and abdominal taps (thoracentesis and paracentesis)
   Bone-marrow taps
   Orthopedic pin insertions and Crutchfield tongs.
5. Apply Steri-strip skin closures.
6. Apply dressings:
   Surgical
   Compression, for control of bleeding
   Burn.
7. Set up traction as directed by a physician.
8. Assist in cast application.
9. Perform cast cutting:
   Removal of cast
   Windowing and bivalving of casts.
10. Apply Buck's extension traction as directed by a physician.

11. Apply forearm splints and finger cages, Ace bandages, Manchu compression dressings, and traction splints.
12. Fit patients for crutches and instruct them in crutch walking.
13. Insert urethral catheters in male patients as ordered.
14. Irrigate eyes for chemical injuries as directed.

Other Out-of-Department Responsibilities (Optional). The EDT may be on call to rest of house for male catheterizations and for lifting and moving patients.

Core Curriculum. A formal 15-hour education program following general orientation should consist of a minimum of the following:

- *Airway management (3 hours):* airway placement (nasopharyngeal, oropharyngeal), oxygen administration (mask, catheter, prongs, liter flow gauge), tank capacity and oxygen concentrations, bag-and-mask techniques and suctioning techniques
- *Cardiopulmonary resuscitation (3 hours):* standards I and II of basic life support
- *VS (3 hours):* temperature and pulse rate, BP and the sounds of Korotkoff, visual acuity, gross neurological assessment with PERL-A, LOC, orientation, pathological posturing
- *Tubes, specimens, and techniques (3 hours):* tubes (NG tubes, urinary catheters, chest tubes and the Pleurovac or three-bottle underwater seal, epistaxis setups), specimens (urine, stool, throat cultures, sputum), techniques (universal precautions, sterile, isolation)
- *Communication (3 hours):* interpersonal skills, interdepartmental skills, emergency radio (HEAR [hospital-emergency-ambulance-radio] system, Med-Net, and so on), telephone techniques

CERTIFICATION FOR EMERGENCY NURSES

Certification in the nurse's area of practice has become a valuable and highly sought-after qualification for employment. Nurse anesthetists became the first group to establish certain standards for practice in 1946, and since that time certification has grown to almost 60 practice groups. Critical care nurses, ENs, psychiatric and mental health nurses, and medical/surgical nurses are but a few.

Certification for ENs in the United States became a reality in 1980; international certification has now been extended to Canada, Australia, and New Zealand. With certification, ENs have a means by which to demonstrate their knowledge base and abilities to apply clinical judgments. Certification provides a mechanism to regularly measure the attainment and simulated application of a defined body of emergency nursing knowledge needed to function at the competent level; it assures the public, consumers, employers, and peers that the Certified Emergency Nurse (CEN) has attained the knowledge necessary to provide effective quality care. The Board of Certification for Emergency Nursing (BCEN) conducts two annual examinations across the United States in 95 metropolitan areas throughout 49 different states. Information can be obtained by calling their office in Illinois at (800) 243-8362.

ADVANCED NURSING PRACTICE IN THE EMERGENCY DEPARTMENT

Acceptance of nurse practitioners (NPs) has been a long time coming, but the new demands of managed care may well place NPs into a new position of regard they have quietly earned through the years. Full use of NPs has been strongly resisted by a large segment of the medical community in spite of the facts that many physicians use NPs in their practices and that many of the larger healthcare providers have developed NP-staffed fast-track programs.[4,5]

Emergency nurse practitioner (ENP) programs, first established in the 1970s and allowed to "fade away" after lack of acceptance, produced enough interest and awareness of potential that renewed efforts to develop supportive courses may well result in their increased numbers. It is hoped that as part of health-care reform, NPs will probably be recalled into emerging hospital-based managed-care clinics, enjoying greater autonomy in determining care protocols, selecting medication therapies, and choosing diagnostic studies than they did in the ED, as well as enjoying better working hours.[4]

Education about the role of ENPs, together with clearly written guidelines and policies, will contribute to their successful integration into the ED and further strengthen nursing's contribution to quality patient care.

■ MANAGING NURSE STRESS

More is being written all the time about stress factors in nursing. Consideration of the emotional aspects of emergency nursing and the resulting stress levels seems entirely appropriate here.

Every nurse entering the emergency nursing field should be totally aware of the emotional highs and lows that will be encountered in the course of daily assignments and challenges; a re-orientation to this reality each time a new employee joins the department staff would be an excellent idea.

Stress is an essential component of healthy function, but when demands on physical and emotional stamina exceed the individual's "buffering" capacity, stress becomes distress and manifests itself in what could be called the "overloaded circuit syndrome" that sooner or later (if not unloaded) blows fuses. One of the easiest places in the world to acquire the syndrome is a busy ED, where patients present for care and bring with them a host of personal complexities that must be dealt with, and where there are mounds of paperwork and documentation, jangling telephones and alarms, ambulance radio calls, attending physicians bustling in and out with requests, communication foul-ups, sudden and unexpected death, broken equipment, short staffing, interpersonal misunderstandings, back-to-back codes, and more patients than stretchers and wheelchairs.

It is the rare individual who has not stood in the midst of all this, fighting back frustration at the seeming futility of it all and trying desperately to clear the thought processes to determine priorities while struggling to maintain equilibrium and the ability to respond to the situation rather than blindly reacting. The demands of patient care may trigger so many feelings of inadequacy in the nurse (because one person can move only so fast and do just so many things correctly in a given period of time) that suddenly responses to patients and co-workers take on a different and very terse note. Realize that if you work in ED, you will be subject to stress, crises, and emotional peaks and valleys that occasionally take their toll in extreme physical as well as mental and emotional fatigue. For this reason, ENs must pay special attention to their own well-being in order to cope with demands on the job and should protect their physical and mental health by getting enough rest and maintaining a sound nutritional status to provide required energy levels.

All of us encounter potentially stressful events each day of our lives no matter what we do. These external situations are stressors. Our reaction to these constitutes the stress. Stress is our own response; Hans Selye, M.D., probably the leading authority on stress research, defines stress as "the nonspecific response of the body to demands made upon it."[6] Stress is not always harmful; some is helpful, energizing, and positive. In fact, complete absence of stress is impossible; only the dead are totally without stress. When stress is pleasantly exciting, the "roller coaster" effect, our response is often referred to as eustress. By contrast, the unpleasant pressure level response is called distress. The major misconception about stress is that it is all bad and that the effects are always destructive. This distorted view is reinforced by large-scale commercial enterprises promoting tranquilizers, alcoholic beverages, varied therapies, relaxation aids, and so on. By contrast, Selye has pointed out that stress is "the spice of life."[6] In the right amount, it enhances the flavor of life. Too low a level may be bland and boring. If the level is too high, it becomes unpalatable and upsetting. The key is not to eliminate stress (an impossible task) but to manage it and to find the appropriate level—your personal "just right" cruising range.

EVALUATING STRESS LEVELS

Almost all of us have experienced traumatic events—major changes, personal disasters, painful experiences—in our lives. Holmes and Rahe[7] developed a social readjustment scale that identifies the mean stress impact of each of 43 generally representative events, the top 10 of which are rated as follows:

Life Event	Mean Value
1. Death of spouse	100
2. Divorce	73
3. Marital separation	65
4. Jail term	63
5. Death of close family member	63
6. Personal injury	53
7. Marriage	50
8. Fired from job	47
9. Marital reconciliation	45
10. Retirement	45

Not everyone would consider *all* of these events negative. However, some people have difficulty coping with even "positive stressors." All of us probably carry scars from old or recent personal disasters, but most stress isn't caused by explosive dramatic catastrophies; it builds day to day from the relatively minor but chronic wear-and-tear pressures.

Some stress-producing events are episodic. Others are chronic, occurring continually. Working in an ED involves an abundance of both episodic and chronic stressors, some of which typically include:

- Episodic stress:
  Sudden changes in the pace of work
  Another reorganization in the department
  Transfer to a new shift or position against your will
  Frequent changes in policies and procedures
  Transfer, resignation, or termination of a valued co-worker
- Chronic stress:
  Co-workers seem unclear about what your job is
  Conflicting demands on your time
  Expectation that you will interrupt your current task for new priorities
  Receiving feedback only when something is wrong
  Decisions and changes affecting you are made without your knowledge

Sound familiar? These were not derived from EN surveys but came from a range of studies across business, professional, and industrial work areas.

A complete set of work and nonwork stress scales with comparable scores from a large sample is contained in the review by Adams.[8]

Stress management doesn't mean avoiding all stressors; it means identifying your stressors, attending to your own reactions to stressors, and finding better ways to cope. Most of us have favorite ways of coping with our stress and keep using them regardless of whether they work. There is probably no "one right way" of coping with all stressors. Most of us can profit significantly, however, from assessing our present coping styles and deciding where and when we need to try new strategies.

The point is to keep yourself healthy and be aware that (1) your emotions will be affected strongly by what goes on around you in a busy department, and conversely, that (2) your response will certainly have its own unique effect on both patients and co-workers. Whether the patient has a serious emergency or something that can be seen as a lesser priority should have no effect on the manner in which the EN responds to the request for help. The patient is entitled to a courteous and, it is hoped, concerned reception on entering the department (which will automatically help reduce the *patient's* stress level and anxiety). In actuality, the EN who manages the patient skillfully in this regard reaps a double bonus: the personal satisfaction goes a long way toward offsetting the personal stress load, making for a happier situation all the way around. The problem of stressful situations must be handled realistically. It may be helpful, when the going gets rough, to break the pace as soon as possible with a breath of fresh air, a cup of coffee, or perhaps just a quiet moment *alone* for a brief period of meditation to "get it all together." Most of us take ourselves too seriously too much of the time, but a wonderful way to offset this tendency is to look for the humor in a situation and develop the ability to laugh at yourself, smile at your patients and co-workers, and mean it. There is a lot of truth in the old saying, "Laugh just to keep from crying," and it is a fact that a warm smile can break a tense situation. So as you evaluate your own response to heavy stress, realize that stressful situations cannot always be prevented but *can* be reversed before the dominoes start falling—*if* healthy, aware attitudes prevail.

COPING STRATEGIES

Basically, there are four major clusters of coping strategies. Within each cluster, you can select and develop specific stress management skills. The basic approaches are as follows:

A. *Reorganize Yourself:* Manage the way you spend time and energy—take more control of your day. Coping skills in this cluster include:
   1. Managing time.
   2. Pacing—develop a tempo that is right and consistent for you.
   3. Value and goal setting—get in touch with what is really important and develop a daily program that invests more time for you.
B. *Change Your Relations With People:*
   1. Develop support groups—contact others and develop some sharing and accepting relationships.
   2. Listen—tune in and respond to the feelings of others.
   3. Learn to say no—express your own preferences and reduce the pressures of others' requests and expectations but in a considerate way.
   4. "Flee the scene"—find suitable ways to retreat, to take a legitimate time-out.
C. *Change Your Own Perceptions:*
   1. Relabel—discover other meanings in each experience; find out that every event has many possible meanings and learn to select those that are helpful.
   2. Imagine and laugh—creativity and humor allow you access to the most powerful "high" known.
   3. Speak gently to yourself—learn to give yourself the positive, considerate messages you often choose to give to others.
E. *Build up strength and resistance:*
   1. Exercise.
   2. Maintain a healthy diet.
   3. Use relaxation techniques.

Concerning the final point above, disciplined daily or regular deep-relaxation exercises have the maximum payoff for the time and energy invested. Any of a number of approaches work (e.g., the Benson system,[9] which uses progressive relaxation, controlled imagery, and meditation). The main point is to do the exercises frequently and as part of your daily routine. Fifteen to 20 minutes devoted daily to deep relaxation will have cumulative, positive results on your outlook, energy levels, and physical well-being. The cost-to-benefit ratio is fantastic! Each strategy is appropriate some of the time with some of the stressors in each individual's daily life. Often, however, we keep repeating one favorite technique, just like the little boy with the hammer looking for *anything* he can hit.

The destructive effects of too much stress are immense. Recent research attributes to stress an even larger role in arteriosclerotic heart disease, vascular lesions, cirrhosis, breast cancer, lung cancer, auto accidents, diabetes, and on and on. The unexamined ways in which we cope with daily stressors, multiplied thousands of times, become our lifestyle, often a terribly destructive one. Because we are each solely responsible for our actions and behaviors, we each have the opportunity to change and develop healthy coping patterns by identifying stressors, reorganizing or planning a personal stress-management approach, and putting it into daily action. Investing this personal thought and time can be one of the most productive activities, both short and long-term, for the EN, his or her family, patients, and last but not least, coworkers. Many good references and guidebooks are available; several of the better works are listed in the Bibliography for your enrichment.

■ SUMMARY

For many reasons, today's ED finds itself in the position of providing the general public access to the health-care delivery system of this nation, simultaneously functioning as the interface between the hospital and a sophisticated level of prehospital care. The ED is seen as the "face" of the hospital by the public; impressions made on patients and their families linger long after the fact. ENs find themselves in a pivotal role in the doorway, receiving patients, dealing with their families and friends, and contributing heavily to the lasting impressions made. The complexities of these responsibilities require a highly skilled and well-educated group of dedicated people who take pride in their abilities to effectively manage the patient loads and deliver quality care with total accountability; trends toward managed care will increase those complexities. Many existing factors, however, can be put to advantage in ED management, resulting in the efficient, economical, and consistent levels of performance that providers and consumers expect.

The JCAHO standards are to be used as working tools, ensuring the operation of a safe, well-staffed, and well-equipped department. Staffing patterns can be tailored to patient load demands, with shift overlaps scheduled appropriately for the busiest hours. An intelligent triage system can be formulated to meet department needs and use personnel and space in the most productive fashion. Ambulance personnel can be made a part of the emergency team and included in joint training programs with ongoing critiques and provision for feedback that will build morale and contribute significantly to improved performance and quality of care. EDTs can be recruited from the ranks of interested EMTs/paramedics and trained for use in numerous areas to release ENs for the primary nursing responsibilities of assessing, evaluating, intervening where necessary, and teaching patients.

Effective management of an efficient and patient-oriented ED will depend heavily on the quality and accountability of leadership, the philosophy of patient care that is established, proper use of personnel who are qualified for their responsibilities, and the continued pursuit of educational opportunities appropriate to the field of emergency medical care. All of these ultimately ensure the patient's access to competent emergency assessment and intervention by skilled, caring professionals. ED managers have their work cut out for them.

■ REFERENCES

1. Andrews AL. QA vs. QI: the changing role of quality in health care. *J Qual Assur.* January/February 1991;14–38.
2. Joint Commission on Accreditation of Healthcare Organizations. *1996 Accreditation Manual for Hospitals.* Oakbrook Terrace, Ill: JCAHO; 1996.
3. Hensinger B, Harkins B, Bruce T. Self-scheduling: two success stories. *AJN.* March 1993;66–68.
4. Covington C, Erwin T, Sellers F. Implementation of a nurse practitioner-staffed fast track. *J Emerg Nurs.* 1992;18:124–129.
5. Curry JL. Nurse practitioners in the emergency department; current issues. *J Emerg Nurs.* 1994;20:207–215.
6. Selye H. *The Stress of Life.* New York, NY: McGraw-Hill; 1976.
7. Holmes TH, Rahe RH. The social readjustment rating scale. *Psychosom Res.* 1967;11:213–218.
8. Adams J. *Understanding and Managing Stress: A Workbook in Changing Life Styles.* San Diego, Calif: University Associates; 1980.
9. Benson H, Zipper MZ. *The Relaxation Response.* New York, NY: Avon; 1975.

■ BIBLIOGRAPHY

Adams J. *Understanding and Managing Stress: A Workbook in Changing Life Styles.* San Diego, Calif: University Associates; 1980.

American Nurses Association. Questions and answers for RNs working with unlicensed assistive personnel. ANA, Nov 1991:1, 4.

Amundson ME, Hart CA, Holmes TA. *Manual for the Schedule of Recent Experience (SRE).* Seattle, Wash: University of Washington Press; 1986.

Andrews J. Emergency department patient follow-up. *J Emerg Nurs.* 1992;18:265–266.

Benson H. *Behavioral Medicine—Work, Stress, and Health.* Boston, Ma: Klawer; 1985.

Benson H, Zipper MZ. *The Relaxation Response.* New York, NY: Avon; 1975.

Brown BJ. *Nurse Staffing: A Practical Guide.* Frederick, Md: Aspen Publishers; 1980.

Cahill SB, Balskus M. *Intervention in Emergency Nursing: The First 60 Minutes.* Rockville, Md: Aspen Publishers; 1986.

Capozzoli J. Consolidating middle management. *Pediatr Nurs.* 1991;17:65–66.

Curry JL. Oil on troubled waters: unlicensed assistive personnel in the emergency department. *J Emerg Nurs.* 1992;18:428–431.

Douglass LM. *The Effective Nurse: Leader and Manager.* 4th ed. St. Louis, Mo: CV Mosby; 1994.

Dracup K. Putting clinical practice guidelines to work. *Nursing96.* Feb 1996;41–46.

Emergency Nurses Association. Position statement: the use of non-registered nurse (non-RN) caregivers in emergency departments. Chicago, Ill: ENA; 1990.

Emergency Nurses Association. *Standards of Emer-*

gency Nursing Practice. 2nd ed. St. Louis, Mo: Mosby-Year Book; 1991.

Fainter J. Quality assurance—quality improvement? *J Qual Assur.* Jan/Feb 1991;8–34.

Hannas RR. Staffing the emergency department. *Hospitals.* May 16, 1973;47.

Henderson DP. The Los Angeles pediatric emergency care system. *J Emerg Nurs.* 1988;14:96–100.

Hogue EE. Inadequate staffing situations: implications for nurses. *Pediatr Nurs.* 1991;17:183–185.

Holmes TH, Rahe RH. The social readjustment rating scale. *Psychosom Res.* 1967;11:213–218.

House J. *Work Stress and Social Support.* Menlo Park, Calif: Addison-Wesley; 1981.

In pursuit of "quality," JCAHO moves "to place the patient at the center." *AJN* Feb 1993;4.

Jacobsen E. *You Must Relax.* 5th ed. New York, NY: McGraw-Hill; 1976.

Jezierski M. Stresses and coping mechanisms: a report of interviews with eleven emergency department nurse managers. *J Emerg Nurs.* 1993;19:89–95.

Johnson RI, Herron HL. Regulation of prehospital nursing practice: a national survey. *J Emerg Nurs.* 1993;19:437–440.

Joint Commission on Accreditation of Healthcare Organizations. *1996 Accreditation Manual for Hospitals.* Oakbrook Terrace, Ill: JCAHO; 1996.

Juran JM. *Juran on Planning for Quality.* New York, NY: The Free Press; 1988.

Keep N. Under siege 3: will this be a sequel? *Etcetera.* 1996;20:2.

Key DD, Neely KA, eds. Prehospital care update. *Top Emerg Med.* April 1987;9(1).

Kidd P. Developing and evaluating an emergency nursing orientation pathway. *J Emerg Nurs.* 1995;21:521–530.

Kirz H. The greening of an emergency department nurse. *Point of View.* 1974;11:3–6.

Koch MW, Fairly TM. *Integrated Quality Management: The Key to Improving Nursing Care Quality.* St. Louis, Mo: CV Mosby, 1993.

Lazarus RS. *Stress Appraisal and Coping.* New York, NY: Springer Publishing; 1984.

Levy DB, Evans, TC: Medical informatics. *Top Emerg Med.* 1994;16:1–8.

Mallison MB. Editorial: the great white lie hits a nerve. *AJN.* March 1992;7.

Managed care and the morality of the marketplace. *New Engl J Med.* 1995;333:50–52.

Mitchell JT. *Emergency Services Stress: Guidelines for Preserving the Health and Careers of Emergency Services Personnel.* Englewood Cliffs, NJ: Prentice-Hall; 1990.

Nield-Anderson L, Doubrava J. Defusing verbal abuse: a program for emergency department triage nurses. *J Emerg Nurs.* 1993;19:441–445.

Payne T, Kranz JM, Eade GG. A survey of hospital emergency rooms in the state of Washington. *Bull Am Coll Surg.* 1973.

Rakowski J, Groskopf E, Walsh M, Brook S. An emergency department telephone follow-up service. *J Emerg Nurs.* 1994;20:199–203.

Sapolsky RM. *Why Zebras Don't Get Ulcers: A Guide to Stress, Stress-Related Diseases, and Coping.* New York, NY: WH Freeman; 1994.

Scherkenbach WW. *The Deming Route to Quality and Productivity.* Mercury Press; 1986.

Schroeder P. *Improving Quality and Performance: Concepts, Programs, and Techniques.* St. Louis, Mo: CV Mosby; 1994.

Selfridge J. A competency-based orientation program for the emergency department. *J Emerg Nurs.* 1984; 10:246–253.

Selye H. *The Stress of Life.* New York, NY: McGraw-Hill; 1976.

Tidwell K. Alabama Emergency Nurses Association takes a stand against proposed emergency department paramedics with broad emergency department functions. *J Emerg Nurs.* 1992;18:464–468.

Townsend PL. *Commit to Quality.* New York, NY: John Wiley & Sons; 1986.

Update your management style. *Nursing 96.* March 1996;70–72.

Weinstein R. Hospital case management: the path to empowering nurses. *Pediatr Nurs* 1991;17:289–293.

Whitehead DC, Thomas H Jr, Slapper DR. A rational approach to shift work in emergency medicine. *Ann Emerg Med.* 1992;21:1250–1258.

Yochem B. Counseling: a "how-to" for new nurse managers. *Pediatr Nurs* 1991;17;201–202.

Zimmerman PG. Use of unlicensed assistive personnel: anecdotes and antidotes. *J Emerg Nurs.* 1996;22: 42–48.

Zimmerman PG. "That will look good on a resume!": padding, fluffing, or maintaining our values? *J Emerg Nurs.* 1996;22:3.

Zimmerman PG. Replacement of nurses with unlicensed assistive personnel: the erosion of professional nursing and what we can do. *J Emerg Nurs.* June 1995;21:208–212.

Zimmerman PG. Increased use of unlicensed assistive personnel: pros and cons. *J Emerg Nurs.* 1995;21: 541–549.

■ REVIEW: EMERGENCY DEPARTMENT MANAGEMENT

1. Identify the primary purpose of continuous quality improvement (CQI) programs.

2. Outline six key elements of CQI that distinguish it from traditional quality assurance (QA) programs.

3. Name three administrative agencies that directly affect the practice of nursing.

4. Identify the three primary objectives of Joint Commission on Accreditation of Healthcare Organizations (JCAHO) standards for emergency services.

5. List at least 12 specific areas of patient care that should be reinforced with written policies and procedures in every emergency department (ED).

6. Describe some variations of staffing patterns that can be employed to advantage in ED scheduling.

7. Identify four ways in which the triage nurse is able to expedite patient flow through the department.

8. Describe some of the beneficial results of a professional interface between emergency medical technicians (EMTs) and emergency nurses (ENs).

9. List several examples of both episodic and chronic stressors that typically occur in the ED work setting.

10. Identify four major clusters of coping strategies for the harried EN.

appendices

Arterial Blood Gases

■ BASICS FOR INTERPRETATION OF ARTERIAL BLOOD GASES

pH: Acid–base level—an indication of acidosis or alkalosis in the body. Normal serum pH is 7.4; the body functions normally, as a rule, between 7.35 and 7.45. A pH of lower than 7.35 indicates acidosis; a pH of higher than 7.45 indicates alkalosis.

Pco_2: An indicator of the partial pressure of carbon dioxide (CO_2) in the arterial blood. A normal value for CO_2 is 40 mm Hg ± 5 mm. A high CO_2 partial pressure indicates hypoventilation of some type and is usually reflected by a lowering of the pH. A low CO_2 partial pressure usually reflects hyperventilation with an accompanying rise in the pH.

Pao_2: An indicator of the partial pressure of oxygen dissolved in arterial blood. Normal arterial oxygen pressure is 90 to 100 mm Hg in a healthy young adult at sea level, on room air. A higher Pao_2 is usually insignificant except when prolonged and the patient becomes oxygen-toxic. A high Pao_2 value in the presence of other clinical signs of respiratory problems may reflect laboratory error.

Sao_2: An indicator of oxygen saturation. Sao_2 represents the percentage of hemoglobin carrying oxygen, compared to the total amount of circulating hemoglobin. An Sao_2 of 95 percent or greater is normal. Optimal oxygen saturation is 100 percent; the pH, however, determines the availability of this oxygen to the tissues, as demonstrated by the oxyhemoglobin dissociation curve (Figure A–1).

Standard bicarbonate: An indication of the buffering capacity of the blood, with normal values of around 25 mEq/L (± 3 mEq/L).

Base excess: An indicator of treatment with extraneous bicarbonate. Normal value is 0 ± 2 or 3. Treatment of a minus base excess should be administration of specific milliequivalent of bicarbonate per kilogram of body weight, thereby minimizing the risk of iatrogenically induced alkalosis.

Respiratory versus metabolic imbalance: Effective patient management requires determining initially whether the acidosis or alkalosis imbalance is respiratory or metabolic in nature. The acid–base balance of the body is carefully maintained by the interaction of (1) the lung, which gets rid of the carbon dioxide produced in metabolism; (2) the kidney, which is primarily responsible for regulation of plasma carbonate; and (3) the buffers in the blood (e.g., hemoglobin and proteins). The determination of respiratory versus metabolic underlying causes and mechanisms requires asking the following:

1. Is the pH normal (7.40 ± .05), high (alkalosis), or low (acidosis)?
2. Is the main process respiratory (main abnormality is the Pco_2), or metabolic (main abnormality is in the bicarbonate [HCO_3] level)?
3. Is the process compensated (indicated by a normal pH), partially compensated, or uncompensated?
4. If the main abnormality is respiratory, is the process acute (no compensatory

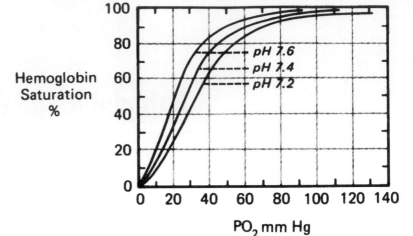

Figure A–1. Oxyhemoglobin dissociation curve. A small increase in PaO$_2$ in the 10 to 50 mm Hg range results in a large increase in the oxygen saturation of hemoglobin. Above a PaO$_2$ of 60 mm Hg, a large increase results in very little increase in the oxygen saturation of hemoglobin (*courtesy of the American Lung Association*).

change in the HCO$_3$), or chronic (the kidneys have had hours to days to regulate the bicarbonate)?

■ TWO SIMPLE METHODS OF EVALUATING ARTERIAL BLOOD GASES

THE THREE-STEP APPROACH TO ARTERIAL BLOOD GAS INTERPRETATION

A. Label the pH.
   1. If the pH is less than 7.35, there is acidosis.
   2. If the pH is greater than 7.45, there is alkalosis.
   3. A pH between 7.35 and 7.45 may fall within normal range; compensation may also have occurred.
B. Find the cause; evaluate the PaCO$_2$ and the HCO$_3$ in relation to the pH.
   1. pH less than 7.35 and PaCO$_2$ above 45 mm Hg—respiratory acidosis
   2. pH less than 7.35 and HCO$_3$ less than 22 mEq—metabolic acidosis
   3. pH above 7.45 and PaCO$_2$ less than 35 mm Hg—respiratory alkalosis
   4. pH above 7.45 and HCO$_3$ above 26 mEq—metabolic alkalosis
C. Check for compensation. The body tries to restore a normal pH by altering the buffer system component (PaCO$_2$ or HCO$_3$) that is not involved in the imbalance; this value

will move in the same direction as the other component.
   1. pH is normal (7.35 to 7.45)—compensated
   2. pH is under 7.35 or above 7.45—uncompensated

THE TWO-STEP APPROACH TO ARTERIAL BLOOD GAS INTERPRETATION

A. Look at the pH.
   1. Normal range indicates compensated
   2. Under 7.35 or over 7.45 indicates uncompensated
   3. Under 7.35 indicates acidosis
   4. Over 7.45 indicates alkalosis
B. Look at the cause and determine which is responsible for acidosis or alkalosis.
   1. Is the cause respiratory—low CO$_2$ or high CO$_2$?
   2. Is the cause metabolic—low HCO$_3$ or high HCO$_3$?

EXAMPLES

- A pH of 7.30 indicates an uncompensated acidosis.
  A PaCO$_2$ of 48 mm Hg and an HCO$_3$ of 28 would indicate a respiratory cause.
- A pH of 7.56 indicates an uncompensated alkalosis.
  A PaCO$_2$ of 36 mm Hg and an HCO$_3$ of 34 indicates a metabolic cause.

PRACTICE

Interpret the following arterial blood gas (ABG) values using either approach you prefer.*

pH	PaCO$_2$ (mm Hg)	HCO$_3$ (mEq/L)
7.01	62	20
7.52	40	32
7.20	32	16
7.12	26	12
7.37	50	28
7.38	38	26

The two simple methods for interpreting ABGs are simplified but appropriate much of the time. If the results of your interpretations do not seem to "compute" clinically, look further and suspect situations requiring more complex evaluation and intervention(s).

■ FURTHER READING

Mims BC. *Mechanical Ventilation: Process and Practice.* Lewisville, Tx: Barbara Clark Mims Associates; 1990.

Mims BC. Interpreting ABGs. *RN* 1991;42–47.

Shapiro BA. Arterial blood gases. *Cur Ther Crit Care.* 1987;14.

Whitten R. "Interpreting your, er . . . blood gases." *J Emerg Nurs.* 1992;18:273–274

---

*Answers to the ABG values given above: 1. uncompensated respiratory acidosis, 2. uncompensated metabolic alkalosis, 3. uncompensated metabolic acidosis, 4. uncompensated metabolic acidosis, 5. compensated respiratory acidosis, 6. normal blood gas.

Glossary of Abbreviations

A: alveolar.

a: arterial.

ABC: airway, breathing, circulation, cervical spine.

ABG: arterial blood gas.

ACE: angiotensin-converting enzyme.

ACEP: American College of Emergency Physicians.

ACLS: advanced cardiac life support.

ACS: American College of Surgeons.

ADH: antidiuretic hormone.

AEIOU: mnemonic for *alcohol, encephalitis, insulin, opiates, uremia.*

AIDS: acquired immunodeficiency syndrome.

ALVD: acute left ventricular decompensation.

AP: anteroposterior.

APPG: aqueous procaine penicillin G.

APR: air-purifying respirator.

ARC: AIDS-related complex.

ARDS: adult respiratory distress syndrome.

ATLS: advanced trauma life support.

ATLSN: advanced trauma life support for nurses.

ATM: atmospheres of pressure.

ATP: adenosine triphosphate.

AV: atrioventricular.

AVNRT: atrioventricular nodal reciprocating tachycardia.

AVRT: atrioventricular reentrant tachycardia.

BBB: bundle branch block.

BCLS: basic cardiac life support.

BE: base excess of bicarbonate.

BP: blood pressure.

bpm: beats per minute.

BSA: body surface area.

BUN: blood urea nitrogen.

BVM: bag-valve-mask (unit).

Ca^{2+}: calcium cation.

CABIN: Chemical and Biological Information Network.

CAD: coronary artery disease.

CBC Count: complete blood cell count.

CCU: coronary care unit.

CDC: Centers for Disease Control and Prevention.

CEN: certified emergency nurse.

CK–BB: creatinine kinase–brain bands.

CK–MB: creatinine kinase–myocardial bands.

CK–MM: creatinine kinase–muscle myosin.

Cl–: chloride anion.

CMRNG: chromosomally mediated resistant *Neisseria gonorrhoeae.*

CNS: central nervous system.

CO: carbon monoxide *or* cardiac output.

c/o: complains of (used in patient's chart).

COE examination: chain-of-evidence examination.

COHB: carboxyhemoglobin.

COLD: chronic obstructive lung disease.

COPD: chronic obstructive pulmonary disease.

CPAP: continuous positive airway pressure.

CPC: chemical protective clothing.

CPK: creatinine phospokinase.

CPP: cerebral perfusion pressure.

CPR: cardiopulmonary resuscitation.

C & S: culture and sensitivity [test].

CSA: Controlled Substances Act.

CSF: cerebrospinal fluid.

CT: computed tomography.

CVP: central venous pressure.

DEA: Drug Enforcement Agency.

DGI: disseminated gonococcal infection.

DIC: disseminated intravascular coagulopathy.

DKA: diabetic ketoacidosis.

DOA: dead on arrival.

D_5/W: 5 percent dextrose in water.

DO_2: dissolved oxygen (delivery transport)

ECC: emergency cardiac care.

ECG: electrocardiogram.

ECM: erythema chronicum migrans.

ED: emergency department.

EN: emergency nurse.

EDT: emergency department technician.

EEG: electroencephalogram.

EMS: emergency medical services.

EMT: emergency medical technician.

ENA: Emergency Nurses Association.

EOA: esophageal obturator airway.

EOM: extraocular eye movements.

ESR: erythrocyte sedimentation rate.

ET: endotracheal.

ETA: estimated time of arrival.

ETOH: ethyl alcohol.

FCC: Federal Communications Commission.

FEMA: Federal Emergency Management Agency.

FEV$_1$: forced expiratory volume in 1 second.

F$_{IO_2}$: fraction of inspired oxygen.

FRC: functional residual capacity.

FUO: fever of unknown origin.

GABA: γ-aminobutyric acid.

GCS: Glasgow Coma Scale.

GI: gastrointestinal.

GSW: gunshot wounds.

GU: genitourinary.

HACE: high-altitude cerebral edema.

HAPE: high-altitude pulmonary edema.

HAZMAT: hazardous materials.

HBV: hepatitis B virus

HCO$_3$: bicarbonate anion.

Hct: hematocrit.

HCW: health-care worker.

HDCV: human diploid cell vaccine.

HEAR: hospital–emergency–ambulance–radio.

HELLP: hemolysis, elevated liver enzymes, low platelets.

HES: hetastarch.

Hg: mercury.

Hgb: hemoglobin.

HHNK: hyperosmolar, hyperglycemic, non-ketonic [coma].

HIV: human immunodeficiency virus.

HLA: human lymphocyte antibody (histocompatibility tissue typing)

HR: heart rate.

ICP: intracranial pressure.

I and O: intake and output.

IPPB: intermittent positive pressure breathing.

ISS: Injury Severity Score.

IUD: intrauterine device.

IV: intravenous.

IVP: intravenous pyelogram.

JCAHO: Joint Commission on Accreditation of Healthcare Organizations.

JEN: Journal of Emergency Nursing.

K$^+$: potassium cation.

kg: kilogram.

KUB: kidneys, ureters, and bladder (x-ray series)

LDH: lactate dehydrogenase.

LLQ: left lower quadrant.

L/min: liters per minute

LMP: last menstrual period.

LOC: level of consciousness.

LSD: lysergic acid diethylamide.

LUQ: left upper quadrant.

MAO: monoamine oxidase.

MAP: mean arterial pressure

MCL: midclavicular line.

MCL$_1$: modified chest lead I.

MDMA: methylene dioxymethamphetamine.

mEq: milliequivalent.

MI: myocardial infarction.

mL: milliliter.

mm: millimeter.

mm Hg: millimeters of mercury.

MRI: magnetic resonance imaging.

MRSA: methicillin-resistant *Staphylococcus aureus.*

MSOF: multisystem organ failure.

MVA: motor vehicle accident.

Na$^+$: sodium cation.

NG: nasogastric.

NGU: nongonococcal urethritis.

NPO: nothing by mouth (*nil per os*).

NSS: normal saline solution.

NSU: nonspecific urethritis.

n&v: nausea and vomiting.

OC: oral contraceptive or over-the-counter.

OD: overdose *or* oculus dexter (right eye).

OR: operating room.

ORPP: ordinary, reasonable, prudent person.

OS: oculus sinister (left eye).

OSHA: Occupational Safety and Health Administration.

OU: oculus uterque (each eye).

PA: posteroanterior.

PaCO$_2$: arterial partial pressure of carbon dioxide.

PAF: platelet activating factor.

PAO$_2$: alveolar partial pressure of oxygen.

PaO$_2$: arterial partial pressure of oxygen.

PASG: pneumatic antishock garment.

PAT: paroxysmal atrial tachycardia *or* penetrating abdominal trauma.

PCO$_2$: partial pressure of carbon dioxide.

PCP: phencyclidine.

PCV: packed cell volume.

PEEP: positive end-expiratory pressure.

PERL: pupils equal, react to light.

PERLA: pupils equal, react to light, and accommodate.

pH: hydrogen ion concentration of a solution— acidity or alkalinity.

PID: pelvic inflammatory disease.

PIH: pregnancy-induced hypertension.

PMI: point of maximum impulse.

PMN: polymorphonuclear neutrophil.

PND: paroxysmal nocturnal dyspnea.

PO: by mouth (*per os*).

PO₂: partial pressure of oxygen.

PPE: personal protective clothing and equipment.

PPNG: penicillinase-producing *Neisseria gonorrohoeae.*

PRN: as needed.

psi: pounds per square inch.

PSVT: paroxysmal supraventricular tachycardia.

PT: prothrombin time.

PTCA: percutaneous transluminal coronary angioplasty

PTS: Pediatric Trauma Score.

PTT: partial thromboplastin time.

QRS: ventricular contraction wave complex.

RAS: reticular activating system.

RICE: mnemonic for *rest, ice, compression, elevation.*

RIG: rabies immunoglobulin.

RLL: right lower lobe.

RLQ: right lower quadrant.

RN: registered nurse.

R/O: rule out.

ROM: range of motion.

RR: respiratory rate.

RT: respiratory therapist.

rTPA: recombinant tissue plasminogen activator.

RUQ: right upper quadrant.

RV: residual volume.

SA: sickle cell trait.

SaO₂: oxygen saturation of hemoglobin.

SAR: search and rescue units *or* supplied-air respiration.

SC: subcutaneous.

SGOT: serum glutamic oxaloacetic transaminase.

SIADH: syndrome of inappropriate secretion of antidiuretic hormone.

SIDS: sudden infant death syndrome.

SOB: shortness of breath.

SS: sickle cell anemia.

ST: segment of electrocardiogram between the S wave and the T wave.

STD: sexually transmitted disease.

SV: stroke volume.

TBA: total body area.

TCC: test-of-cure culture.

THC: δ- tetrahydrocannabinol.

TIPS: mnemonic for *trauma, infection, psychosis, syncope.*

TME: toxic metabolic encephalopathy.

TNF: tumor necrosing factor.

TNS: transcutaneous nerve stimulator.

T-PA: tissue plasminogen activator.

TPR: temperature, pulse, respiration.

TS: Trauma Score.

UNOS: United Network for Organ Sharing.

URTI: upper respiratory tract infection.

UTI: urinary tract infection.

VA: visual acuity.

VC: vital capacity.

VHF: very high frequency [radio].

V/Q: ventilation–perfusion ratio.

VRE: vancomycin-resistant enterococcus.

VS: vital signs.

VT: ventricular tachycardia.

VT: tidal volume.

WBC count: white blood cell count.

WHO: World Health Organization.

WPW: Wolff-Parkinson-White (syndrome).

Organ and Tissue Donor Criteria*

■ MANAGEMENT OF THE POTENTIAL DONOR

When irreversible brain injury seems apparent, vigorous supportive measures to maintain cardiovascular function and organ perfusion in a potential donor must be continued. There are six basic principles for maintaining the potential donor of which emergency nurses (ENs) should be aware and for which they should be prepared:

A. *Resuscitation in the Event of Cardiac Arrest:* Fifteen minutes of external cardiac massage or prolonged hypotension is the maximum amount of time that can be tolerated for a patient to still be considered as a donor.
   1. Arrhythmias are common in the donor. Transient bradyarrhythmias may be seen as part of the Cushing reflex. Bradyarrhythmias are not treated if associated with hypotension; remember that they will not respond to atropine sulfate. Ventricular and supraventricular tachyarrhythmias may be seen later in brain herniation, presumably due to high endogenous catecholamine levels or as a sign of hypovolemia. Despite all efforts, all brain-dead patients will eventually have an arrhythmia resistant to therapy.
   2. After brain death has been declared, normalize $PaCO_2$ to maintain normal pH. Arterial blood gas (ABG) values for pH and PCO_2 should not be corrected for temperature. Maintain a slightly alkalemic pH.
   3. The PaO_2 should be maintained at 80 to 100 mm Hg by using the lowest FIO_2 possible without excessive positive end-expiratory pressure (PEEP). Neurogenic pulmonary edema may occur rapidly in the brain-dead patient. These patients should be monitored with a pulmonary artery catheter rather than simply a central venous line.
B. *Adequate Organ Perfusion as Indicated By:*
   1. Urine output above 80 mL/h.
   2. Systolic blood pressure (BP) above 100 mm Hg.
   3. Central venous pressure (CVP) of 10 to 15 cm H_2O.
   4. Adequate PaO_2 and oxygen saturation.

After declaration of brain death, organ functions of the suitable donor must be carefully maintained to protect the perfusable organs. The major treatment goal in the donor is adequate tissue perfusion. The relationship between donor BP and allograft (same-species tissue) has been best demonstrated in kidneys. The risk of acute tubular necrosis increases when the donor systolic BP has been less than 80 to 90 mm Hg. Experimental data also suggest that this level is critical for hepatic graft function.

---

*Adapted in part from Feliciano DV, Moore EE, Mattox KL. *Trauma*, 3rd ed. Stamford, Conn: Appleton & Lange; 1996:992–993.

C. *Vigorous Hydration:* Hydration is accomplished with crystalloid and colloid solutions to correct hypovolemia that may have resulted from fluid restriction in the management of head injury, prior use of diuretics, loss of the normal vasoregulatory mechanisms secondary to head injury, or diabetes insipidus.

1. Ringer's lactate or albumin solution should be rapidly infused to achieve a systolic BP of 100 mm Hg or higher.
2. Attempts should be made to wean the patient from all vasopressors by volume loading.
3. If a vasopressor is needed, dopamine is recommended. If dopamine is needed, attempt to keep the dosage at 10 g/kg or more per minute.
4. α-Adrenergics, such as Aramine or Levophed, should be avoided.
5. After adequate volume loading, infuse a sufficient quantity of crystalloid solution to match hourly urine output.

D. *Diuresis:* Maintain diuresis at above 0.5 to 1.0 mL/kg per hour; mannitol and furosemide may be used. If the patient develops diabetes insipidus, Pitressin may be required to control the diuresis. Electrolyte abnormalities occur commonly in the organ donor; hyperglycemia is also common in the brain-dead patient. Serum electrolytes should be frequently monitored, as these abnormalities interfere with cardiac stability and ultimate transplant viability.

E. *Avoidance of Infection:* Avoid infection during extended maintenance after death in the emergency department (ED):

1. Prophylactic antibiotics should be avoided.
2. Obtain a daily chest x-ray.
3. Obtain a daily sputum culture.
4. Obtain frequent urine cultures.
5. Draw two blood cultures 30 minutes before donor surgery.
6. The patient who has had a systemic infection may still be a candidate for organ donation if the infection has been eliminated prior to donor surgery.

F. *Maintenance of Normothermia:* The majority of organ donors require a warming blanket to maintain core temperatures above 35° C (95°F). The major risk with hypothermia is myocardial depression.

TABLE A–1. ORGAN AND TISSUE DONOR CRITERIA

Organ/ Tissue	Age Range	Exclusion for Donation	Benefit	Length of Viability (h)
Kidney	1–55 y	Metastatic cancer; infection at time of death; prolonged hypertension; existing renal disease	Patients with end-stage renal disease	48–72
Liver	6 mo to 45 y	Cancer or infection at time of death	End-stage liver disease with < 1 y life	4–6
Heart	Neonate to 40 y	Cancer or infection at time of death	End-stage cardiac disease with < 1 yr life	8–10
Heart-lung	12–20 y	Cancer or infection at time of death	End-stage heart disease with pulmonary complications and limited survival time	8–10
Pancreas	14–45 y	Cancer or infection at time of death	Long-term insulin-dependent diabetics suffering from complications	24
Bone/ tissue	15–65 y	Cancer or infection at time of death	Reconstructive orthopedic, neurosurgical, oral/maxillofacial surgery	24
Skin	~ 0–65 y (> 5 ft. and > 100 lb.)	Skin infection at time of death	Interim skin grafts	24
Eyes/ corneas	Neonate to 80 y	Infection at time of death	Corneal transplant (any age for research)	72

■ NURSING GUIDELINES FOR OBSERVATIONS AND DOCUMENTATION

- Main parameters:
    Diagnosis
    Admission date and time
    Brief review of patient's past medical history and prior surgery
    BP trends
    Hourly urine output
    Medications—vasopressors
    Blood urea nitrogen (BUN) and serum creatinine
    Blood typing
    Urinalysis

- Also helpful if available:
    Culture reports
    Hepatitis B surface antigen (HBSAg) test results
    Human immunodeficiency virus (HIV) status
    VDRL (Veneral Disease Research Laboratory) test results
    Electrolytes
    Temperature

- After patient's approval as a donor, the following may also be requested:
    Urine culture and sensitivity—*drawn from Foley catheter,* not bag
    Two blood cultures drawn from peripheral sticks

Recent chest x-rays
Six red-top tubes with 5 mL blood in each
Six green-top tubes with 5 mL blood in each (transplantation coordinator will take these for tissue typing)

- Additional studies for liver donations:
    Liver enzymes
    Total and direct bilirubin
    Prothrombin time (PT), partial thromboplastin time (PTT)

- Additional studies for heart donations:
    Cardiac enzymes
    Cardiology evaluation
    Twelve-lead electrocardiogram (ECG)
    Echocardiogram

■ OPERATING ROOM REQUIREMENTS FOR DONOR SURGERY

The cadaver organ donor has been pronounced dead prior to transfer to the operating room (OR). Adequate cardiopulmonary function and perfusion are maintained by the anesthesia team until the organs have been removed. This specifically means that BP is maintained above 100 mm Hg, the central venous pressure (CVP) is maintained at 10 to 15 cm H_2O, and the urine output is maintained at 0.5 to 1.0 mL/kg hour. General anesthesia is not required, but muscle relaxants are often necessary to minimize spinal reflexes.

Review Questions for Certification in Emergency Nursing

The following questions are multiple-choice. Answers may be found on pages 663–664.

1. Which of the following patients would not be suitable candidates for the use of conscious sedation?
   A. A 3-year-old with 15 percent body surface area (BSA) burns from hot-water immersion
   B. A 14-year-old with a penetrating globe injury incurred in a street fight
   C. A developmentally disabled person with a scalp wound incurred during a seizure
   D. All of the above

2. All of the following are recommended requirements for emergency nurses (ENs) who participate in administration of conscious sedation in the emergency department (ED) except:
   A. Certified emergency nurse (CEN) certification
   B. Advanced cardiac life support (ACLS) qualification
   C. Completion of ED skills/competency validation checklist
   D. Education regarding pharmacology of narcotics, benzodiazepines, and central nervous system (CNS) depressants

3. When administering Ativan for conscious sedation, the EN should:
   A. Prepare scopolomine to be given concurrently.

   B. Dilute the drug 1:1 with normal saline solution (NSS).
   C. Deliver the dosage within 5 minutes of beginning the procedure.
   D. All of the above

4. The reversal agent for benzodiazepines (e.g., lorazepam [Ativan], diazepam [Valium]) is:
   A. Scopolamine
   B. Naloxone (Narcan)
   C. Flumazenil (Romazicon)
   D. None of the above

5. Which of the following findings should contraindicate the discharge of a patient who has received conscious sedation in the ED?
   A. Vomiting
   B. Distended bladder
   C. Inability to walk without assistance
   D. All of the above

6. All of the following are appropriate measures to control elevated intracranial pressure (ICP) except:
   A. Maintain the head in alignment using sandbags.
   B. Administer oxygen at 10 to 12 L/min using positive-pressure ventilation.
   C. Administer furosemide or mannitol to promote diuresis.
   D. Give antihypertensives to lower blood pressure (BP).

7. Which of the following is a true statement about the use of sedation and analgesia in acute head injury?
   A. Sedation and analgesia should not be used, because they interfere with neurological assessments.
   B. Sedation and analgesia use should be reserved for patients with a Glascow Coma Scale (GCS) score greater than 12.
   C. Narcotics should not be used, because they alter pupillary size and depress respirations and heart rate (HR).
   D. Sedation may be used for intubated patients as a method to control ICP.

8. Which of the following events constitutes a valid reason to interrupt or discontinue cervical spine precautions?
   A. No evidence of cervical spine injury is evident on clinical examination.
   B. Cervical spine series reveals no evidence of fracture, subluxation, or dislocation.
   C. The historical account of the accident is inconsistent with the mechanism of injury that would produce cervical spine injury.
   D. None of the above

9. Which of the following would *not* be a guideline for management of the seriously traumatized patient?
   A. Do not let yourself think the worst first.
   B. Do not panic; use a systematic approach to assess and intervene.
   C. Look beyond the obvious.
   D. Be aggressive with your management and monitoring.

10. A cardinal rule of management with injuries involving a penetrating object is:
    A. Always remove the penetrating object and cleanse the wound.
    B. Never remove the penetrating object; this is the physician's (surgeon's) responsibility.
    C. Leave the penetrating object in place and stabilized until surgical removal.
    D. Both B and C

11. Packing for treating nasal fractures is left in place:
    A. One to 2 days
    B. Three to 5 days
    C. Seven to 14 days
    D. Until all bleeding has ceased

12. When a patient presents with a blowout fracture, the EN should:
    A. Apply bilateral eye patches.
    B. Perform a cranial nerve assessment.
    C. Perform a visual acuity (VA) test.
    D. All of the above

13. When a patient has epistaxis involving Little's area, the EN should:
    A. Arrange for posterior packing.
    B. Prepare equipment for nasal tamponade.
    C. Instruct the patient to sit upright, lean forward, pinch the nose, and hold direct pressure for 5 minutes.
    D. All of the above

14. The initial action recommended when a laryngeal fracture is identified is:
    A. Placement of an oropharyngeal airway, suctioning, and supplemental oxygenation via a bag-valve-mask (BVM) unit
    B. Preparation for tracheostomy
    C. Both A and B
    D. None of the above

15. The major rationale for using the Pediatric Trauma Score (PTS) is to:
    A. Determine severity of injury
    B. Predict outcome of multiple trauma
    C. Ensure that the child is triaged to an appropriate treatment facility
    D. Gather information for the trauma registry

16. Recommendations for modifying shock resuscitation protocols for pediatric patients include:
    A. Initial fluid bolus of 10 mL/kg
    B. Warming all fluids before infusing
    C. Using a 2:1 rule for crystalloid replacement
    D. All of the above

17. The best indicator that a 4-year-old boy has lost 20 percent of his circulating volume is:
    A. Decreased responsiveness to stimuli
    B. BP of 76/40
    C. Tachycardia
    D. Low urine output with highly concentrated urine

18. Which of the following can be safely infused by the intraosseous route?
    A. Whole blood
    B. Saline and glucose
    C. Dopamine
    D. All of the above

19. The EN is monitoring an infant who has incurred a head injury as an unrestrained front-seat passenger. Which observation suggests intracranial bleeding?
    A. Vomiting
    B. Ipsilateral cranial nerve III palsy, limb weakness, and decerebrate posturing
    C. Tachycardia and pale, cool extremities
    D. None of the above

20. Which assessment of a 9-year-old boy suggests that there is a genitourinary (GU) injury?
    A. Hematuria
    B. Blood at the urinary meatus and on the underclothing
    C. Patient expresses need to void even though the bladder is not distended
    D. All of the above

21. Two thirds of all significant childhood trauma involves:
    A. Head and neck
    B. Muscles, bones, and joints
    C. Abdominal organs
    D. Heart and lungs

22. Which of these musculoskeletal injuries should alert the EN to suspect child abuse?
    A. Limb fractures in a toddler
    B. Multiple shin bruises in a 5-year-old girl
    C. Femur fracture in an 8-year-old boy
    D. Type III Salter–Harris fracture in a 9-year-old girl

23. When pediatric orthopedic injuries result in damage to the epiphyseal plate, it is imperative that these children have long-term follow-up evaluation because such injuries are associated with:
    A. Asymmetry of the limbs
    B. Retarded bone growth
    C. Deformities
    D. All of the above

24. Which statement about geriatric trauma patients is false?
    A. All elderly trauma patients should be considered for an acute myocardial infarction (MI).
    B. Early placement of an endotracheal (ET) tube is indicated when the injury severity score is greater than 25.
    C. The urinary output is the most reliable indicator of hypovolemia
    D. Prompt fluid resuscitation is required to sustain preload in low perfusion states

25. Which statement is true regarding analgesia administration for geriatric trauma patients?
    A. Pain medication should not be used, because it depresses respirations and interferes with neurological assessments.
    B. Pain control is imperative for ensuring maximum respiratory effort without mechanical ventilation.
    C. With emotional support of patients by ENs, analgesia administration can usually be avoided in the ED.
    D. Analgesia and sedation are not indicated if the patient is unresponsive.

26. The "golden hour" in trauma response and resuscitation is:
    A. The hour immediately prior to impact
    B. The time at which the trauma surgeon arrives to take charge of the ED
    C. The post-trauma period when the patient regains consciousness and remembers
    D. The hour immediately following trauma when appropriate interventions can begin and optimum outcomes can be assured.

27. Which statement about angioedema is true?
    A. It is not associated with any visible swelling of the skin or mucous membranes.
    B. The condition, although anxiety-provoking and uncomfortable, is never life-threatening.
    C. It is often accompanied by gastrointestinal (GI) complaints such as nausea, cramping, and abdominal pain.
    D. There are no laboratory tests useful for evaluating this condition.

28. Skin manifestations of allergic reaction include all of the following except:
    A. Bullae
    B. Angioedema
    C. Urticaria
    D. Hives

29. The EN becomes aware that a child with severe vomiting has been recently discharged from the hospital following a bone marrow transplant. What nursing actions minimize risks for the child in the ED?
    A. Place the child in an isolation room and tag the chart "Special precautions: bone marrow recipient."
    B. Notify the nurse assigned to the patient and review special precautions regarding blood draws and other procedures.
    C. Place isolation masks for staff to use when coming in contact with the patient.
    D. All of the above

30. A worried mother calls the ED and says her 6-year-old daughter has head lice. What instructions should be provided?
    A. Obtain a prescription for Kwell or a similar lindane shampoo; leave the shampoo lather on the head for about 4 minutes before rinsing it off.
    B. Comb the child's hair with a fine-tooth comb to remove lice and nits.
    C. Wash clothes, bed linens, and towels in hot, soapy water.
    D. All of the above

31. When a person calls the ED to ask how a wasp stinger should be removed, he or she should be instructed to:
    A. Grasp the stinger securely with a tweezer and pull *up* sharply.
    B. *Scrape* away the exposed stinger, avoiding any tissue compression.
    C. Cleanse the site with an antiseptic solution and avoid any effort to extract the embedded stinger.
    D. All of the above except A.

32. When educating patients regarding environmental emergencies, it is important to stress:
    A. Acclimatization prior to vigorous activity at altitude
    B. Avoiding alcohol when physical stressors and thermal conditions are extreme
    C. Wearing protective clothing in both heat and cold extremes
    D. All of the above

33. The EN should ensure that the patient being discharged from the ED following treatment has been given instructions and understands their meaning. This is best accomplished by:
    A. A follow-up telephone call by the unit secretary 24 hours later
    B. Providing the patient with specific printed instructions and ascertaining whether he or she is able to read what is printed
    C. Having the patient paraphrase the instructions back to you in his or her own language
    D. B and C only

34. Which of the following signs, symptoms, and laboratory studies are consistent with ventilatory failure?
    A. Pulse rate at rest greater than 120 beats per minute (bpm)
    B. Irritability and confusion
    C. P_{CO_2} of 70
    D. All of the above

35. Epiglottitis is characterized by all of the following except:
    A. High fever
    B. "Seal bark" cough

C. Drooling

D. Muffled voice and stridorous breathing

36. What nursing actions would be inappropriate for the child with suspected epiglottitis?
    A. Forcing the child to lie down
    B. Separating the child from the mother
    C. Using a tongue blade to assess the throat for redness and edema
    D. All of the above

37. Select the statement that describes the correct method for using a metered-dose inhaler:
    A. Hold the mouthpiece tightly between the lips and discharge the drug while holding the breath
    B. Hold the unit between the lips and discharge the drug during inhalation
    C. Hold the cannister 1½ in. from the open mouth and inhale while discharging the agent
    D. None of the above

38. The characteristic dizziness, numbness and tingling, and carpopedal spasm associated with hyperventilation syndrome is due to:
    A. Alkalosis
    B. Fall in concentration of free ionized calcium
    C. Elevated P_{CO_2}
    D. All of the above except C

39. Which inhalation poisoning emergency mandates the use of chemical protective clothing (CPC) *and* respiratory protection?
    A. Unknown agricultural herbicide
    B. Hydrogen sulfide
    C. Cyanide
    D. All of the above

40. Which is a characteristic finding associated with cyanide poisoning?
    A. Pallor and cyanosis
    B. Odor of bitter almonds on the breath
    C. Metabolic alkalosis
    D. None of the above

41. The characteristic sputum of *pneumocystis carinii* pneumonia could be described as:
    A. Thick and green
    B. Yellow and tenacious
    C. White and foamy
    D. Watery and blood-tinged

42. The EN recognizes than an asthmatic attack is life-threatening when:
    A. The patient avoids talking
    B. The peak flow falls below 100 L/min
    C. Wheezing is absent
    D. All of the above

43. What treatment strategies are recommended for treating croup after the traditional home remedies have failed and symptoms progress?
    A. Warm, humidified mist treatments
    B. Racemic epinephrine by aerosol
    C. Antibiotics
    D. All of the above

44. What equipment adjuncts are useful for monitoring patients with carbon monoxide poisoning?
    A. Pulse oximetry
    B. Arterial blood gases (ABGs)
    C. Carboxyhemoglobin spectrophometry
    D. All of the above

45. Which patient with CO_2 poisoning would be a likely candidate for hyperbaric therapy?
    A. A firefighter with a 10 percent carboxyhemoglobin level
    B. A pregnant woman with a carboxyhemoglobin level of 45 percent
    C. An elderly woman with a carboxyhemoglobin level of 20 percent
    D. None of the above

46. Which nursing diagnosis is most specific for a patient with a pulmonary embolus?
    A. Alteration in oxygenation due to ventilation–perfusion mismatching
    B. Impaired gas exchange related to upper airway edema

C. Ineffective breathing pattern related to hyperventilation

D. Ineffective airway clearance related to mechanical obstruction

47. Which of the following agents used in treating anaphylaxis is specifically selected to reduce respiratory work?
   A. Aminophylline
   B. Racemic epinephrine
   C. Heliox
   D. Benadryl

48. In mouth-to-mask resuscitation efforts, the addition of supplemental oxygen is recommended because:
   A. Rescue breathing delivers only about 16 percent oxygen.
   B. Rescue breathing delivers only about 10 percent oxygen.
   C. Rescue breathing should be diluted with fresh air because of the impurities and bacterial contamination present in the breath of most rescuers.
   D. Both B and C

49. Aside from administration of oxygen, an essential item of equipment for preserving airway integrity once the airway is established is:
   A. An accurate flow meter
   B. Adequate suction in readiness
   C. An ET tube
   D. A laryngoscope

50. An ET tube inserted too far results in:
   A. Plugging and hyperinflation of the left lung
   B. Hyperinflation of the right lung with back pressure
   C. Passage into the right mainstem bronchus with nonexpansion of the left lung
   D. Passage into the left mainstem bronchus with hyperventilation of the lingula

51. The rate at which irreversible brain death occurs from hypoxia is dependent upon:
   A. Circulatory dynamics
   B. Core temperature of the victim

C. Metabolic demands of tissue
D. All of the above

52. The top priority in emergency nursing intervention must always be:
   A. Establishment and maintenance of a patent airway
   B. Cervical spine protection
   C. Intravenous access
   D. Use of supplemental oxygen

53. The greatest threat to airway management when mechanical airways are employed during resuscitation is:
   A. Undertreatment and airway blockage
   B. Tissue trauma from mechanical manipulation
   C. Triggering the gag reflex, vomiting, and aspiration
   D. Too much suctioning

54. While the American Heart Association (AHA) recommends head-tilt/chin-lift maneuver first, the next best maneuver, which reduces risk of further neck injury, is the:
   A. Triple airway maneuver
   B. Heimlich maneuver
   C. Jaw thrust
   D. Chest thrust

55. Although the Heimlich maneuver/abdominal thrust is recommended for obstructed airways, significant dangers are inherent in the application of the abdominal or chest thrust because of:
   A. Possible rupturing or laceration of viscera
   B. Fracture of ribs in the elderly
   C. Damage to pregnant women and their fetuses
   D. All of the above

56. The patient whose airway has been "managed" is always a candidate for aspiration. Immediate signs are:
   A. Dyspnea and bronchospasm
   B. Frothy sputum and white, fluffy lung fields on x-ray
   C. Hypotension and lungs filling with fluid
   D. All of the above

57. Normal gastric emptying time after a meal is probably:
    A. 3½ to 4 hours
    B. Less than 2 hours in a healthy adult who eats fast
    C. Slowed greatly by pain or emotional crisis
    D. Both A and C

58. The EN is caring for an 8-year-old child who has had a chest tube placed for hemothorax. Which observation would be cause for alarm within 30 minutes of tube placement?
    A. Bubbles in the drainage tubes
    B. Presence of 150 mL of blood in the collection chamber
    C. Persistent tachycardia at a rate of 130 bpm
    D. Dullness over the inferior chest wall on the affected side

59. Spinal shock is characterized by:
    A. Hypotension and tachycardia
    B. Poikilothermia
    C. Decline in cardiac output and altered blood flow at the site of injury
    D. All of the above

60. Which of the following is not recommended for treatment of spinal shock?
    A. Respiratory support
    B. Shock position
    C. Administration of atropine
    D. Use of benzodiazepines to control anxiety

61. When assessing a multiply traumatized patient, which observation would suggest a spinal cord injury?
    A. Flaccid and areflexic extremities
    B. Atonic rectal sphincter and priapism
    C. Diaphragmatic respirations
    D. All of the above

62. Shock may be best characterized as a condition in which there is:
    A. Inability of cells to obtain and use oxygen
    B. Low blood flow state
    C. Unevenly distributed blood flow
    D. Inadequate perfusion

63. What is the primary role of adrenocorticotropic hormone (ACTH) in the compensatory phase of shock?
    A. Sensitizing arteriolar smooth muscle to effects of catecholamines
    B. Mediates the release of angiotensin II
    C. Aids renal conservation of blood volume
    D. Increases mesenteric and renal blood flow

64. Which of the following is an appropriate nursing diagnosis for hypovolemic shock?
    A. Altered cardiac output due to decreased venous return
    B. Potential for impaired cellular perfusion due to fluid shifts
    C. Fluid volume deficit due to peripheral vasoconstriction
    D. Altered renal blood flow due to peripheral vasoconstriction

65. Orthostatic vital signs (VS) reflect a hypovolemic crisis by demonstrating the body's failing ability to:
    A. Maintain cardiac output
    B. Constrict capacitance vessels
    C. Dilate the cerebrovascular beds in response to hypoxemia
    D. Redistribute blood flow to vital organs

66. Select the set of orthostatic VS that reflect decompensated hypovolemia when the patient sits upright (the baseline supine values were BP, 120/80, and HR, 84)
    A. BP, 130/70; HR, 74
    B. BP, 120/90; HR, 80
    C. BP, 90/60; HR, 104
    D. BP, 86/78; HR, 168

67. Positive orthostatic VS suggest a blood loss of more than:
    A. 5 percent
    B. 10 to 20 percent
    C. 40 percent
    D. None of the above

68. Select the statement that describes the appropriate procedure for assessment of "upright" VS when hypovolemia is suspected. After taking BP and pulse in the supine position:

A. Assist the patient to sit up and immediately record another set of VS.
B. Allow the patient to relax for a few minutes before sitting up for reassessment of VS.
C. Assist the patient to a sitting position, wait 1 minute, and reassess the BP and HR.
D. Wait at least 5 to 10 minutes before assisting the patient to a sitting position; wait 3 to 5 minutes and reassess VS.

69. During advanced shock states, capillary refill will be:
A. Less than 2 seconds
B. Sluggish over all body regions
C. Absent in the periphery over large muscle masses
D. Affected *only* in the extremities

70. Which monitoring parameter during shock will provide the best index of the multiply traumatized patient's response to a volume challenge?
A. Level of consciousness (LOC)
B. Serial VS
C. Urine output
D. Serial central venous pressure (CVP) readings

71. Which of the following represents the best clinical judgment for intravenous line placement in a 36-year-old pregnant patient with chest and abdominal injuries (her BP is 126/80)?
A. A 16-gauge angiocatheter in the antecubital and a saphenous cutdown
B. Two 14-gauge angiocatheters in the upper extremities
C. Two saphenous cutdowns and a subclavian line for CVP monitoring
D. An 18-gauge butterfly in the upper extremity with fluids at keep-open rate

72. Although hypertonic saline may be useful in shock states, some risks are associated with this fluid, including:
A. Heart failure from increased volume load
B. Impaired cardiac contractility
C. Increased bleeding
D. None of the above

73. Which of the following represents the initial step in a crystalloid fluid challenge:
A. Administer a 100-mL bolus over 10 minutes and reassess BP and HR.
B. Administer a 400-mL bolus over 3 to 5 minutes and reassess BP and HR.
C. Administer a 20-mL/kg bolus until the CVP reading improves.
D. None of the above

74. What laboratory specimen should be obtained prior to starting an infusion of Dextran 40?
A. Venous blood for glucose
B. Venous blood for type and cross-match
C. Arterial blood for carbon dioxide saturation
D. Urine for sugar and ketones

75. If blood or blood products are urgently needed but results from a type and cross-match are pending, which of the following can be used to improve oxygen-carrying capacity of the blood?
A. Low-titer type O-negative red blood cells (RBCs)
B. Human plasma or artificial colloid
C. Hydroxyethyl starch (HES) or dextran
D. None of the above

76. All of these patients are suitable candidates for autotransfusion except:
A. Acquired immunodeficiency syndrome (AIDS) patient with penetrating chest trauma
B. Child whose parents are Jehovah's Witnesses who object to blood transfusion
C. Intravenous drug abuser with chest and abdominal trauma
D. Pregnant patient with gunshot wound (GSW) to the chest

77. Which of the following conditions meets the criteria for application of the pneumatic anti-shock garment (PASG)?
A. Massive blood loss involving the chest and upper extremities
B. Unstable injuries of the pelvis
C. GSW of the head with associated shock
D. Cardiogenic shock associated with acute MI

78. Which of the following statements is true regarding hypothermia during a trauma-induced shock state?
    A. Hypothermia minimizes adverse effects from depleted cellular oxygen and glucose levels.
    B. A low core temperature contributes to clotting abnormalities.
    C. Sustained hypothermia reduces the requirement for blood transfusion.
    D. A low core temperature favors hemodynamic compensatory activities.

79. In septic shock states, which of these interventions would least assist in improving the patient's condition?
    A. Fluid administration to improve preload and increase the FIO_2
    B. Antibiotic therapy
    C. Use of inotropic-vasodilator drugs to enhance cardiac functioning and control pulmonary hypertension
    D. Avoidance of thermal stressors

80. Rhabdomyolysis is a trauma-related complication characterized by:
    A. Reddish brown urine that is heme positive
    B. Elevated creatine kinase (CK)
    C. Compartment syndrome
    D. All of the above

81. Emergency personnel can minimize the risk for fat emboli by:
    A. Limiting movement and manipulation of fractures
    B. Using a filter for administration of all intravenous infusions
    C. Limiting fluid resuscitation in isolated, uncomplicated fractures
    D. Avoiding splints and other immobilization devices for open fractures

82. Compartment syndrome is recognized by:
    A. Severe pain upon passive stretching
    B. Obliteration of arterial pulses
    C. Normal two-point discrimination test
    D. All of the above

83. All of these factors have a negative impact on the immune system except:

    A. Cold stress
    B. Advanced age
    C. Shock
    D. Fever

84. Which nursing diagnosis is appropriate for rhabdomyolysis?
    A. Alteration in pulmonary and peripheral nutrition secondary to microcirculatory obstruction
    B. Impaired gas exchange due to altered pulmonary blood flow
    C. Alteration in fluid volume due to impaired renal functioning
    D. Potential for infection

85. Disseminated intravascular coagulopathy (DIC) is characterized by:
    A. Elevated platelet, fibrinogen, and thrombin levels
    B. Decrease in partial thromboplastin time (PTT)
    C. Both A and B
    D. Neither A nor B

86. Which of these actions assists in minimizing the risk for multisystem organ failure (MSOF)?
    A. Aggressive fluid resuscitation
    B. Early ventilatory support with high-flow oxygen
    C. Meticulous wound cleansing and debridement
    D. All of the above

87. Which of the following does not occur in relation to cold stress after trauma?
    A. Increased synthesis of adenosine triphosphate (ATP)
    B. Greater transfusion requirements
    C. Clotting abnormalities
    D. Capillary leak syndrome

88. Following deceleration trauma, one symptom of cardiac contusion is retrosternal pain that is:
    A. Anginal in character
    B. Refractory to nitroglycerin
    C. Frequently responsive to O_2
    D. All of the above

89. A patient who has suffered penetrating injury to the pericardium and heart muscle may suddenly go into shock and die if the volume of blood trapped in the pericardial sac reaches:
    A. 15 to 20 mL
    B. 50 to 75 mL
    C. 100 mL
    D. 150 to 200 mL

90. The most frequently occurring aortic rupture site following trauma occurs from shearing forces on deceleration at:
    A. The aortic arch
    B. The innominate branch at the arch
    C. The renal artery bifurcation
    D. The point distal to the left subclavian artery

91. Cardinal indications of aortic rupture following significant deceleration trauma include:
    A. Upper limb hypertension
    B. Unilateral bounding femoral pulse
    C. Reduction in urine output
    D. A and C

92. Aortic injuries require immediate aggressive management because the death rate within the first hour of trauma is:
    A. 30 percent
    B. 80 to 90 percent
    C. 50 to 60 percent
    D. 15 percent

93. The most common cause of myocardial contusion is recognized to be:
    A. Steering wheel injury on sudden vehicle deceleration
    B. Blow to the rib cage in a fist fight
    C. Left-sided impact of the vehicle "telegraphed" to the left ventricle
    D. Poorly executed chest compression during CPR

94. In order to assess circulatory compromises that may suggest aortic dissection, the EN should:
    A. Compare BPs in the arms and legs.
    B. Obtain orthostatic VS.

C. Requisition a computed tomography (CT) scan of the chest and abdomen.
D. Auscultate the neck, chest, and abdomen for bruits.

95. Which cardiac enzyme studies provide the most precise indication of damage to the myocardial tissue?
    A. CK and serum glutamic oxaloacetic transaminase (SGOT)
    B. Creatine kinase–muscle myosin (CK-MM) and lactate dehydrogenase (LDH)
    C. Creatine kinase–myocardial bands (CK-MB) and LDH isoenzymes
    D. SGOT and LDH

96. When monitoring a patient with supraventricular tachycardia of unknown origin, the EN should use:
    A. MCL_1
    B. Lead II
    C. Lead I
    D. ST segment monitoring

97. Right ventricular lead placement is recommended for:
    A. Detecting right ventricular pathology
    B. A pediatric electrocardiogram (ECG)
    C. Both of the above
    D. Neither of the above

98. The initial response to myocardial ischemia is:
    A. Appearance of a Q wave
    B. ST segment depression
    C. ST segment elevation
    D. None of the above

99. ST segment monitoring is indicated for all the following conditions except:
    A. Atrial dysrhythmias
    B. Chest pain of unknown origin
    C. Unstable angina in a patient with known cardiac ischemia
    D. After administration of a thrombolytic agent

100. What is the major goal of using intravenous nitroglycerin in the ED?
    A. Relieve chest pain

B. Lower systemic vascular resistance and increase venous capacitance

C. Both of the above

D. Neither A nor B

101. Which statement accurately reflects the accelerated dosing schedule for recombinant tissue plasminogen activator (rTPA)?

A. Infuse 100 mg over 30 minutes.

B. After an initial 15-mg bolus, 50 mg is infused over the next 30 minutes.

C. Three doses of 50 mg each are given over 90 minutes.

D. A 2-mg/kg bolus is infused over 30 minutes.

102. Which of these observations would suggest reperfusion after administration of a thrombolytic?

A. Resolution of chest pain

B. Disappearance of ST segment elevation

C. Development of sinus bradycardia or an accelerated ventricular rhythm

D. All of the above

103. When ventricular tachycardia occurs during thrombolytic therapy, the EN should:

A. Place the patient flat and give the patient a 200-mL fluid bolus

B. Annotate the event on the chart and continue to monitor

C. Immediately defibrillate

D. Prepare bretylium (Bretylol) for administration

104. What therapies are not appropriate for managing right ventricular infarctions?

A. Volume expansion with saline

B. External or transvenous pacing

C. Diuretics

D. Inotrope vasodilators (e.g., dobutamine)

105. When using the initial bolus of an angiotensin-converting enzyme (ACE)-inhibitor drug, the EN should anticipate:

A. Cardiac dysrhythmias

B. Profound hypotension

C. A brief period of apnea

D. Asystole

106. In which of the following conditions should the EN anticipate the onset of congestive heart failure (CHF)?

A. Acute MI

B. Complete heart block

C. Supraventricular tachycardia

D. All of the above

107. Which emergency nursing actions are consistent with the appropriate management of acute pulmonary edema?

A. Place the patient in shock position.

B. Withhold the administration of β_1- and β_2- agonists.

C. Administer diuretics

D. None of the above

108. Select the factors that distinguish hypertensive crisis from all other hypertensive emergencies.

A. The diastolic BP is over 150 mm Hg.

B. There is associated organ dysfunction.

C. The condition does not respond to ordinary antihypertensive agents such as β-blockers.

D. None of the above

109. The danger associated with a precipitous drop in BP during administration of intravenous antihypertensive therapy is:

A. Acute MI

B. Seizure

C. Stroke

D. Cardiogenic shock

110. Which of the following manifestations are associated with a dissecting aneurysm?

A. Intense and variable chest pain

B. Hoarseness

C. Oliguria, hematuria, anuria

D. All of the above

111. Complications associated with a dissecting aortic aneurysm include:

A. Arterial occlusion

B. Acute MI

C. Renal failure

D. All of the above

112. When the EN is obtaining the history from an elderly and somewhat confused cardiac patient, complaints of visual disturbances, fainting spells, nausea, and diarrhea are noted. The patient's current medications include Lasix, digitalis, insulin, amiodarone, Reglan, and Ativan. From this data, the EN should suspect:
    A. Adverse interactions of cardiac drugs
    B. Diabetic ketoacidosis (DKA)
    C. Hypokalemia
    D. Digitalis toxicity

113. The initial drug of choice for paroxysmal supraventricular tachycardia (PSVT) of unknown etiology is:
    A. Adenosine (Adenocard)
    B. Verapamil (Calan)
    C. Diltiazem (Cardizem)
    D. Esmolol (Brevibloc)

114. Antidromic tachycardia:
    A. Indicates atrioventricular (AV) retrograde conduction
    B. Is characterized by a narrow QRS complex
    C. Both of the above
    D. Neither A nor B

115. What is the danger of giving calcium channel–blocking or β-blocking drugs for initial management of a patient with PSVT?
    A. The accessory pathway may become the dominant pacer of the heart.
    B. Slowing AV conduction may precipitate ventricular tachycardia.
    C. Both of the above
    D. Neither A nor B

116. Which is the recommended method of giving adenosine (Adenocard)?
    A. Dilute 6 mg in 5 mL of NSS and push over 3 to 5 minutes.
    B. Place 6 mg in 50 mL of NSS and infuse over 5 to 10 minutes.
    C. Administer a 6-mg bolus over 1 to 2 seconds.
    D. None of the above

117. Which of the following ECG changes should be expected after the administration of adenosine for PSVT?
    A. AV conduction defects
    B. Asystole followed by rapid return to normal sinus rhythm
    C. Both of the above
    D. Neither A nor B

118. What procedure should be anticipated when a patient presents with PSVT, is severely hypotensive, and nonresponsive to vagal maneuvers?
    A. Defibrillation
    B. Synchronized cardioversion
    C. Pericardiocentesis
    D. External pacing

119. What is the recommended initial energy level for synchronized cardioversion?
    A. 25 J
    B. 50 J
    C. 100 J
    D. 200 J

120. The management of complete heart block includes:
    A. Dopamine and epinephrine
    B. Atropine and pacing
    C. Both of the above
    D. Neither A nor B

121. Doll's eye reflex indicates:
    A. Compression of cranial nerve III
    B. Brain death
    C. Brainstem dysfunction
    D. Herniation of the falx tentorium

122. A doll's eye reflex is considered to be present when the head is rotated horizontally and:
    A. A rapid nystagmus is produced.
    B. The eyes move in an opposite direction.
    C. The eyes remain in midline and then rest opposite the direction of the head turning.
    D. The eyes move in the same direction as the head is turned.

123. To evaluate vestibular function using a cold caloric test, the EN should:
    A. Place the patient in a 30-degree upright position.
    B. Ensure that the patient is alert and responsive before ice water is introduced into the ear canal.
    C. Wait 1 to 3 minutes before assisting a physician with irrigation of the opposite ear.
    D. All of the above except B

124. A positive Babinski reflex is associated with:
    A. Meningitis
    B. Cranial nerve IX dysfunction
    C. Organic lesion of a pyramidal tract
    D. Spinal cord transsection

125. Decerebrate posturing is characterized by:
    A. Rigid leg extension and plantar flexion
    B. Extended adducted and hyperpronated arms
    C. Opisthotonus
    D. All of the above

126. A GCS score of 13 to 15 indicates:
    A. Coma
    B. Mild head injury with an excellent prognosis
    C. Moderate head injury
    D. Optimum cerebral functioning

127. Which of the following nursing diagnoses are pertinent for a patient with an acute spinal cord transsection?
    A. Ineffective breathing pattern
    B. Potential for infection due to impaired skin integrity
    C. Decreased cardiac output
    D. All of the above

128. The "lucid interval" describes:
    A. The period between initial injury and a decline in consciousness
    B. The period of wakefulness that occurs between seizure episodes
    C. The time period that immediately follows a concussion in which the patient feels dazed and confused
    D. None of the above

129. Which statement is true regarding intracranial hemodynanics of patients with an acute head injury?
    A. Hypercarbia induces cerebral vasoconstriction
    B. A $PACO_2$ between 25 and 30 mmHg increases cerebral blood volume
    C. The $PACO_2$ should be maintained at less than 20 mmHg
    D. Vasoconstriction can cause ischemia and cerebral infarction

130. Which of these assessment findings suggest a basilar or frontal skull fracture?
    A. Otorrhea, rhinorrhea, and Battle sign
    B. Hemotympanum
    C. Salty taste in the mouth
    D. All of the above

131. What is the major crisis associated with a carotid–cavernous sinus fistula?
    A. Exsanguination
    B. Blindness
    C. Impaired cerebral blood flow (CBF)
    D. Increased ICP

132. The most common type of skull fracture is:
    A. Linear
    B. Depressed
    C. Basilar
    D. None of the above

133. Which of the following statements describes the distinction between cerebral concussion and cerebral contusion?
    A. Concussion is not associated with major structural changes in brain tissue.
    B. A contusion may occur without loss of consciousness.
    C. Concussions are limited to the cerebral cortex.
    D. Contusion does not involve permanent structural damage to the brain.

134. Threat of herniation is marked by:
    A. Rapid pulse and low BP
    B. Kussmaul respirations
    C. Spontaneously dilated and fixed pupil
    D. All of the above

135. Hemisection of the spinal cord that results from penetrating trauma produces:
    A. Brown–Sequard syndrome with ipsilateral paralysis
    B. Contralateral paralysis
    C. Paralysis of the limbs and trunk below the level of the lesion
    D. Posterior spinal cord syndrome with loss of vibration, proprioception, and touch below the level of the injury

136. Respiratory failure is associated with vertebral fractures above:
    A. T-4
    B. T-2
    C. C-7
    D. C-4

137. The EN should anticipate prompt surgical intervention for spinal cord injuries characterized by:
    A. Loss of deep tendon reflexes
    B. Central cervical spinal cord syndrome
    C. Axis fractures
    D. Progressive neurological deterioration

138. The mechanism of the "shaken baby" syndrome is:
    A. Acceleration/deceleration
    B. Rotational
    C. Compression
    D. None of the above

139. Which of the following statements regarding meningococcemia is true?
    A. Meningitis is the precursor to meningococcemia.
    B. Onset is sudden with fever, purpura, or petechial rash.
    C. Death may occur because of DIC, cardiovascular collapse, and septic shock.
    D. All except A

140. Reye syndrome may result in death because of:
    A. Brainstem dysfunction
    B. Liver failure
    C. Cerebral edema and herniation
    D. All of the above

141. When an unconscious child is received in the ED, what drug should be available for prompt administration after the airway has been ensured and intravenous access has been established?
    A. Naloxone
    B. Dextrose, 50 percent
    C. Calcium chloride
    D. All except C

142. What is the dread complication of infections that may be associated with a septal hematoma?
    A. Meningitis
    B. Cartilage erosion
    C. Tear duct disruption
    D. None of the above

143. Which additional facial structure is likely to be damaged in conjunction with a naso-orbital fracture?
    A. Teeth and gums
    B. Maxillary sinuses
    C. Zygomatic process
    D. Lacrimal duct

144. A blowout fracture is characterized by:
    A. Disruption of the lateral orbital wall
    B. Fracture of the floor of the body eye orbit and invasion of the adjacent maxillary sinus
    C. Entrapped inferior rectus muscle
    D. All of the above

145. Le Fort I fractures result from forces applied to the face:
    A. Directly below the nose
    B. At the zygomatic arch
    C. At or near the base of the skull
    D. Just superior to the temporomandibular joint

146. A Le Fort III fracture is characterized by:
    A. An open bite
    B. Flattened facial features
    C. Periorbital ecchymosis and cerebrospinal fluid (CSF) rhinorrhea
    D. All of the above

147. Surgical intervention for uncomplicated Le Fort and panfacial fractures is usually performed:
    A. Immediately after trauma
    B. Within 24 to 48 hours after trauma
    C. Within 3 to 7 days after injury
    D. When all other physical injuries are stabilized

148. The major purpose for obtaining anteroposterior (AP) and lateral skull films in penetrating facial injuries is to:
    A. Identify fractures
    B. Visualize free air within the sinuses
    C. Locate foreign bodies
    D. Assess alignment of facial structures

149. What is the life-threatening complication associated with oropharyngeal hematoma?
    A. Exsanguination
    B. Airway obstruction
    C. Brainstem compression
    D. Carotid compression

150. Which of these findings suggest laryngeal fracture?
    A. Hoarseness or aphonia
    B. Respiratory stridor
    C. Drooling
    D. All of the above

151. All of the following nursing diagnoses are pertinent to maxillofacial injuries except:
    A. Impaired gas exchange
    B. Risk for infection
    C. Fluid volume deficit related to hemorrhage
    D. Ineffective airway clearance

152. When examining the eyes, which of the following statements is not true in the assessment of pupil size and shape?
    A. Dilated pupils accompany barbiturate intoxication, as well as many functional disorders.
    B. Pinpoint pupils *always* indicate the use of narcotics.
    C. PERLA (pupils equal, react to light, accommodate) documentation indicates normal status of pupillary function.

D. Anisocoria is the congenital inequality of pupil diameter and has an important implication in assessment of head trauma.

153. All of the following statements are true except:
    A. Visual acuity (VA) should be checked with the patient's glasses removed.
    B. The Snellen eye chart should be used with the patient's glasses on.
    C. VA is recorded as OD (right eye) and OS (left eye).
    D. The small hand-held eye chart should be held 14 in. from the eyes.

154. The most common ocular injury seen in EDs is:
    A. Corneal burns
    B. Ultraviolet exposure
    C. Foreign bodies
    D. Hyphema

155. History of foreign-body eye penetration is important and patients with it should be referred to an ophthalmologist directly because:
    A. The tearing and blurred vision will continue otherwise.
    B. Foreign bodies are common injuries and are cumulated by medical records.
    C. Penetration by oxidizing metals (e.g., ferrous metals, copper, leaded glass) may cause development of late problems, scarring, and blindness.
    D. The injury is usually too complicated to be handled in the ED.

156. Eversion of the upper eyelid is accomplished by:
    A. Gently pulling both lower lids down while the patient looks up
    B. Grasping the eyelashes of the upper lid as the patient looks down, exerting downward/outward pull, and turning the lid back over an applicator stick
    C. Grasping the eyelashes of the upper lid as the patient looks up and then down quickly as the lid is "flipped"
    D. Any of the above

157. All of the following are considered ophthal-
mologic emergencies except:
A. The presence of hyphema
B. Foreign body penetration
C. Ruptured globe and retinal detachment
D. Corneal burn

158. Central retinal artery occlusion, generally
seen in the older population and considered a
true ocular emergency, is identified by:
A. Sudden and painless unilateral loss of vision
B. Sudden and painless bilateral loss of vision
C. Affected eyes are dilated, nonreactive,
and perceive light only
D. Both A and C

159. Which of the following nursing interventions
is not appropriate when managing eye emergencies?
A. Always check the eyes for injury after
any head or facial trauma has been sustained.
B. Leave contact lenses in place when instilling eye medications; they are easily
lost otherwise.
C. Gentle lid retraction and topical anesthesia are necessary when eyes require irrigation.
D. When administering any eye medication,
never put any steroid-containing medication into an inflamed eye.

160. Patching the eyes is frequently the responsibility of the EN; the correct procedure for
achieving desired results includes:
A. Patching so that just enough pressure is
exerted to allow the lid to move lightly
across the corneal surface for lubrication
B. Applying enough patches to exclude
light and keep the eye totally at rest
C. Firmly taping the patches down with 1-
in. highly adhesive tape, high across the
forehead and down across the cheek, anchoring well
D. B and C only

161. When assessing blunt abdominal trauma
(BAT), the three forces of injury that must
be kept in mind are:
A. Frontal, lateral, and rear
B. Compression, deceleration, and shearing
C. Constrictive, concussive, and retrospec-
tive
D. High speed, from heights, and atmos-
pheric

162. A motor vehicle accident (MVA) victim was
the right front-seat passenger at time of impact; in assessing this patient you would suspect:
A. Head injury with concomitant facial
trauma
B. Potential neck and cervical spine injury
C. Potential for serious head injury
D. All of the above

163. The most common cause of combativeness
in a severely traumatized patient with torso
injuries is:
A. High blood alcohol level
B. Anxiety about the extent of injury
C. Hypoxia
D. Impatience about invasive procedures

164. When trauma occurs with rapid deceleration
and lap belts in place, the EN should *always*
suspect:
A. Occult abdominal injury
B. Paradoxical respirations
C. Ruptured aorta
D. Neck injury

165. A 2-year-old child is brought to the ED with
vomiting; the mother reports that she thinks
the problem is constipation. The child is fretful and throughout your attempts to examine
the abdomen, the child flexes the knees and
cries, especially when you palpate the colon
loops. Which of these conditions should be
suspected?
A. Pyloric stenosis
B. Intussusception
C. Inguinal hernia
D. None of the above

166. A MVA victim was wearing a lap belt at time of impact; in assessing this patient you would suspect:
    A. Blunt chest trauma
    B. Soft-tissue trauma to lower abdomen
    C. Possible rupture of the urinary bladder
    D. Both B and C

167. A child thrown from the vehicle on impact should be suspected of having:
    A. Massive soft-tissue trauma
    B. Potential for extensive internal injury
    C. Potential for serious head injury
    D. All of the above

168. The most frequently injured solid abdominal organs are:
    A. The kidneys, followed by the pancreas
    B. The spleen, followed by the liver
    C. The pancreas, followed by the liver
    D. The liver, followed by the spleen

169. Urine output, as a major monitor of visceral blood flow, is known as:
    A. The window of the viscera
    B. The drain field of the viscera
    C. The osmolarity index
    D. The hourly report

170. A 19-year-old man is brought by ambulance from a MVA; the pickup truck he was driving struck a utility pole while traveling at an estimated speed of 85 mph. His gurgling respirations are labored, VS en route to the ED were unstable, and his pulse now is rapid and thready. The current order of intervention priorities is:
    A. Get his clothes off, inspect his injuries, start intravenous lines, and give O_2.
    B. Ensure airway patency by whatever means is appropriate, administer high-flow O_2, initiate large-bore intravenous lines, and cut his clothes off for inspection of injuries.
    C. Initiate intravenous lines, order hematocrit (Hct) and ABGs, start high-flow O_2, and remove his clothes for inspection of injuries.

    D. Notify nursing services, call for an intensive care unit (ICU) bed, start intravenous lines, and administer high-flow O_2 by face mask.

171. A critical concern with rupture of the diaphragm is that:
    A. Abdominal contents may be herniated into the chest cavity.
    B. Herniation of abdominal contents may cause severe lung and mediastinal compression.
    C. Decreased venous return will result from herniation of organs.
    D. All of the above

172. The most important step in the initial examination of the traumatized abdomen is:
    A. Visualization for minor scars
    B. Auscultation
    C. Visualization for abdominal breathing
    D. Palpation

173. Pain in the right lower quadrant (RLQ) that is aggravated by walking, straining, or coughing is characteristic of:
    A. Renal calculi
    B. Acute appendicitis
    C. Pancreatitis
    D. Ovarian cyst

174. When the EN is performing an abdominal assessment and elicits a positive Murphy sign, for which surgical condition is there a high level of suspicion?
    A. Cholecystitis
    B. Appendicitis
    C. Tubal pregnancy
    D. Strangulated hernia

175. An elderly patient is brought into the ED by a family member who says that "the gastric feeding tube is clogged." The EN should initially:
    A. Requisition a flat plate of the abdomen to confirm tube position.
    B. Aspirate and irrigate the tube with saline to test its patency.

C. Insert a stylet to dislodge the clot.

D. Use a carbonated cola to dissolve the clot.

176. Periumbilical pain reflects abnormal conditions of:
    A. Gallbladder and liver
    B. Appendix
    C. Small intestine
    D. All except A

177. The five P's characteristic of acute compartment syndrome resulting in vascular occlusion, which provide excellent guidelines for assessment of all closed fractures, are *pain, pallor, paresthesia, paralysis,* and:
    A. *Panic*
    B. *Pressure*
    C. *Prostration*
    D. *Pulselessness*

178. Severe prolonged tamponade of distal circulation may easily result in:
    A. Temporary restriction of movement
    B. Transient loss of sensation
    C. Hyperesthesia of proximal parts
    D. Amputation of the distal part(s)

179. Continuous evaluation of pulses distal to the injury site, with bilateral comparison and documentation, is an important nursing responsibility:
    A. Only at change of shift and when completing a patient report
    B. Immediately upon getting a patient report
    C. On an ongoing and frequent basis
    D. Both B and C

180. Appropriate nursing diagnoses for fractures would not include:
    A. Skin integrity and potential for impairment
    B. Alteration in tissue perfusion
    C. Impaired physical mobility
    D. Alteration in cardiac output: decreased

181. The three cardinal signs/symptoms of a bone/joint dislocation are severe pain, inability to move the joint, and:
    A. Shock
    B. Thready pulse

C. Obvious deformity

D. Both A and B

182. The most common type of dislocation seen is:
    A. Elbow
    B. Knee
    C. Hip
    D. Shoulder

183. The "kindest" way to manage a patient in severe pain with a dislocated shoulder is:
    A. Allow the patient to take a position of comfort
    B. Place the patient facedown on gurney
    C. Place the patient supine with arms lowered from gurney.
    D. Place the patient on his or her side with the affected arm elevated 90 degrees.

184. Two very simple nursing interventions that can reduce or minimize venous congestion in an injured part and promote patient comfort are:
    A. Warm blankets and active listening
    B. Moderate, passive ROM (range-of-motion) movement and reassurance
    C. Immobilization and elevation of part
    D. Massage and deep-heat packs

185. The consequences of failure to properly assess and intervene in a timely fashion in musculoskeletal injuries are:
    A. Occult blood loss leading to shock and/or acute compartment syndrome
    B. Risk of infection and chronic osteomyelitis
    C. Loss of distal parts due to vascular tamponade
    D. All of the above

186. If upon inspection an open fracture is suspected:
    A. Motor activity must be tested.
    B. The limb should be moved slowly but deliberately.
    C. Care must be taken to prevent further contamination of the fracture site.
    D. An air splint should be applied and inflated.

187. Successful replantation and revascularization of amputated parts depends on:
    A. The extent of crush injury to the circulatory base
    B. The length of the ischemic interval
    C. Neither of the above
    D. Both A and B

188. The fat embolus syndrome, or adult respiratory distress syndrome (ARDS), associated with long-bone fractures and crush injuries, is thought to be reduced by:
    A. Timed manipulation in the ED of the fracture site
    B. Administration of high-flow O_2 and mannitol immediately upon admission
    C. Early fixation of long-bone fractures to prevent further manipulation
    D. None of the above; it is unavoidable in long-bone fractures

189. Emergency management of a fractured clavicle includes:
    A. Stabilization by the sling and swath, or a "figure-eight" splint
    B. Careful monitoring of the quality of distal pulses
    C. Ongoing observation for possible compromise of pulmonary status
    D. All of the above

190. The stiff forearm and clawlike hand deformity known as Volkmann's ischemic contracture is:
    A. The result of constricted circulation distal to a dislocated elbow
    B. Preventable with early intervention and restoration of circulation distal to a fractured elbow
    C. Identifiable by an absent radial pulse in the presence of a supracondylar fracture
    D. Both B and C

191. The most anatomically complicated joint in the upper extremity is:
    A. The first metacarpal joint of the fifth finger
    B. The head of the humerus
    C. The elbow
    D. The radiocarpal interface

192. The most frequent site of dislocation is the shoulder; approximately:
    A. 95 percent are anterior.
    B. 95 percent are posterior.
    C. 65 percent are subcorocoid.
    D. 75 percent are anterior.

193. Any numbness or paralysis distal to an elbow dislocation requires immediate intervention because it is an indication of:
    A. Pressure on the capillary beds
    B. Pressure on the neural structures
    C. Pressure on the venous return
    D. All of the above

194. When orthopedic injuries are splinted, whether prehospital or in the emergency department, they should be splinted:
    A. In a way that will do no harm
    B. As if they were fractures until proven otherwise
    C. In unhurried fashion, unless open and bleeding massively
    D. All of the above

195. ENs should remain aware of and alert to the potential for serious occult blood loss in fractures of the pelvic girdle, which can account for bleeding of:
    A. Up to 3 U
    B. Up to 6 U
    C. Up to 3 L
    D. Both B and C

196. In management of surface trauma and wound repair, the goal is always:
    A. To restore function of the injured part
    B. To achieve the best cosmetic result
    C. To accomplish both A and B without doing further harm
    D. All of the above

197. Which one of the following statements regarding the skin is not true?
    A. Skin makes up about 5 percent of the body's dry weight.
    B. Skin serves as both the principal water and bacterial barrier between humans and the environment.

C. Skin is never static but constantly changes, renews, and adapts.

D. Skin provides a means of communication between humans and the environment.

198. Further definition of an open wound, involving a break in the skin surface or in the mucous membrane that lines external body orifices, would include:
  A. Partial versus almost partial thickness
  B. Skin flaps versus pedicles
  C. Full thickness versus dermal shavings
  D. Partial versus full thickness

199. Which of the following is not a factor in the rate of resolution and fading that contusions undergo as they heal?
  A. Age of the patient
  B. Size of the bruise
  C. Location of the bruise
  D. Efficiency of local circulation

200. Open wounds of soft tissues are classified as:
  A. Abrasions, hematomas, lacerations, or puncture wounds
  B. Abrasions, lacerations, avulsions/amputations, or puncture wounds
  C. Lacerations, avulsions, amputations, or puncture wounds
  D. Impact lacerations, surgical lacerations, amputations, or hematomas

201. With management of abrasions, particular care must be taken to remove *all* imbedded foreign material to prevent:
  A. Infection and permanent tattooing
  B. Bleeding and infection
  C. Permanent tattooing and lawsuits
  D. All of the above

202. The primary goal in management of lacerations is to:
  A. Avoid lawsuits because of poor cosmetic results
  B. Remove foreign objects and contamination
  C. Achieve satisfactory wound closure, preserving function and cosmetic integrity
  D. All of the above

203. Avulsed or amputated tissue requires special management if replantation is to be successful. Which of the following is not a recommended action in the interim management of tissues?
  A. Moisten the tissue with sterile NSS.
  B. Seal the tissue in a plastic bag and place the bag in iced NSS.
  C. Place the tissue in a bag of NSS, seal it, and place the bag on a bed of ice.
  D. Protect the tissue from drying and heat.

204. The two major concerns in management of puncture wounds are:
  A. Hemorrhage and infection
  B. Cosmetic integrity and tetanus
  C. Hemorrhage and tetanus
  D. Damage to underlying structures and infection

205. The standing rule for management of penetrating injury with deeply impaled foreign bodies is:
  A. Remove the object immediately and apply direct pressure over the wound.
  B. Never remove the object; cleanse the area around the wound and stabilize the impaling object until it can be removed by the physician.
  C. Remove the object gently with steady traction, then attach the object to the ED chart.
  D. Both A and C

206. The two essential prerequisites to ensure proper healing with minimal scarring are:
  A. Absolute hemostasis and precise approximation of wound edges
  B. Relative hemostasis and close approximation of wound edges
  C. Hemostasis with carefully monitored granulation
  D. Thorough cleansing and absolute hemostasis

207. Three key factors that affect the rate of wound healing are:
  A. Condition of patient, type of wound, and degree of contamination

B. Age of patient, type of wound, and skill of closure

C. General nutritional status, age of wound, and location of wound

D. Location of wound, degree of cleansing, and skill of closure

208. The key to proper wound cleansing is:
  A. Mechanical irrigation
  B. Irrigate, irrigate, irrigate
  C. Appropriate volume of cleansing solution
  D. All of the above

209. A young woman arrives at the ED with her hand tightly wrapped in a kitchen towel, having controlled a moderate bleed with pressure. She has a 2-in. laceration on the thenar eminence or palmar surface of her left hand from opening a tin can about 15 minutes earlier. Using the Kirz formula for wound irrigation, her wound will require a sterile NSS or sterile water irrigation with a minimum of:
  A. 100 mL
  B. 200 mL
  C. 300 mL
  D. 400 mL

210. Which type of burn does not require treatment at a burn center, according to advanced trauma life support (ATLS) criteria?
  A. Burns to the hand, feet, and genitalia
  B. High-voltage electrical burns
  C. Burns associated with inhalation of toxins or other systems trauma
  D. Burns of 15 to 25 percent BSA with mixed full- and partial-thickness burns

211. Which of these therapies is not indicated for routine burn treatment in the ED?
  A. Wound cleansing
  B. Debridement of devitalized tissue
  C. Prophylactic antibiotics
  D. Silvadene and Sulfamylon applications

212. Burn wounds become infected most often because of:
  A. Microrganisms on the hands of health-care personnel
  B. The environment

C. The patient's own organisms

D. Foreign materials introduced into the wound at the time the burn occurred

213. What is the major advantage of using the Lund and Browder chart for estimating the extent of BSA? The Lund & Browder chart:
  A. Takes into account the changing percentages of BSA from infancy to adulthood
  B. Can readily be used by individuals without mathematical skills
  C. Divides the body into more specifically delineated zones
  D. Permits comparison of burned and non-burned BSAs

214. Migraine headache is characterized by:
  A. Cerebral vasospasm and neurological deficits
  B. Vasodilation and congestion of cerebral vessels
  C. Photophobia
  D. All of the above

215. The agent used to reverse dystonias and akathisias induced by emetics used during migraine is:
  A. Sumatriptan (Imitrex)
  B. Ergotamine
  C. Diphenhydramine (Benadryl)
  D. Metoclopramide (Reglan)

216. What neonatal emergency is marked by tremors, loss of muscle tone, chewing motions, facial twitching, and spasmodic crying?
  A. Epiglottitis
  B. Hypothermia
  C. Hypoglycemia
  D. Seizures

217. Which nursing intervention is not recommended for protecting the patient who is experiencing a series of grand mal seizures?
  A. Placing a padded tongue blade in the patient's mouth
  B. Wedging a plastic bite stick between the patient's teeth

C. Administering oxygen after tonic/clonic activity has stopped, using a BVM device
D. Permitting the patient to remain postictal without stimulation

218. What are the physiological consequences of status epilepticus?
A. Hypoxia and acidosis
B. Hypertension and increased ICP
C. Hyperthermia
D. All of the above

219. Why is lorazepam (Ativan) the drug of choice for treating status epilepticus?
A. It has numerous active metabolites
B. It can be given by direct intravenous push, undiluted
C. It is short-acting and can be reversed with Narcan
D. None of the above

220. What is the strategy for preventing Wernicke's encephalopathy?
A. Administer propofol (Diprivan) to alcoholic patients who are agitated.
B. Administer thiamine before giving 50 percent dextrose.
C. Both of the above
D. Neither A nor B

221. If intravenous access cannot be achieved for an unconscious diabetic who is hypoglycemic, what alternative therapies may be used?
A. Glucose paste for buccal administration
B. Intranasal glucagon
C. Intramuscular glucagon
D. All of the above

222. When an EN administers glucagon for hypoglycemia, how much time must elapse before a peak response occurs?
A. 5 to 10 minutes
B. 10 to 20 minutes
C. 30 to 40 minutes
D. Approximately 1 hour

223. Why must patients be admitted and monitored when their hypoglycemia is the result of an oral hypoglycemic agent?
A. Dosage adjustment requires hourly blood sugar assessment.

B. Patients require behavioral modification to correct noncompliant behavior.
C. Rebound hyperglycemia is a common occurrence.
D. Most oral hypoglycemics require up to 72 hours for metabolism and excretion.

224. In the management of DKA, what is the priority that immediately follows airway and oxygen initiatives?
A. Insulin administration
B. Fluid therapy
C. Correction of acidosis
D. Treatment of hyperkalemia

225. Which action will assist the EN in delivering the optimum insulin dosage to the DKA patient with a blood sugar of 600?
A. Calculate the dose using the patient's sliding scale.
B. Administer half of the insulin dosage subcutaneously.
C. Flush the tube with insulin prior to starting an intravenous drip.
D. All of the above

226. Which of these statements describes how hyperglycemic hyperosmolar nonketotic (HHNK) coma differs from DKA?
A. In HHNK coma, there is sufficient insulin to prevent lipolysis.
B. In HHNK coma, the blood sugar is inordinately high.
C. In HHNK coma, hyperviscosity of the blood creates obstructive thrombi.
D. All of the above

227. Which of these nursing management problems occur with a thyrotoxic crisis?
A. Hypothermia
B. Confusion, agitation, and coma
C. Bradycardia
D. None of the above

228. What endocrine dysfunction is characterized by an expressionless face; dry, rough, cold skin; nonpitting edema; hair loss; and hypothermia?
A. Diabetes insipidus
B. Myxedema coma
C. Thyroid storm

D. SIADH (syndrome of inappropriate secretion of antidiuretic hormone)

229. What are the ECG characteristics of hyperkalemia?
    A. High, peaked T waves
    B. Short QRS complex
    C. Inverted P wave
    D. None of the above

230. What factor in the nursing history would suggest that a patient who presents with hypotension and fatigue may be hypokalemic?
    A. Recent use of antibiotics
    B. Ongoing diuretic therapy
    C. A regimen of theophylline and bronchodilators for asthma
    D. All of the above

231. The primary role of the EN in managing toxic metabolic encephalopathies (TME) is to suspect it and:
    A. Obtain blood samples for laboratory tests for baseline values.
    B. Prepare for immediate administration of antihypertensive drugs.
    C. Ready the patient for a stat CT scan.
    D. Isolate the patient in a single-bed room and place on continuous ECG monitoring.

232. The primary purpose(s) of gastric lavage in GI bleeding is (are) to:
    A. Arrest bleeding
    B. Monitor blood loss
    C. Prepare the patient for endoscopy
    D. All of the above except A

233. What adjunct is considered the most important tool for detecting and managing the source of upper GI bleeding?
    A. Sclerotherapy
    B. Balloon tamponade
    C. Gastric lavage
    D. Endoscopy

234. When assisting with a proctosigmoidoscopy to detect the source of bleeding, the EN notes bradycardia on the monitor. The most likely cause is:
    A. Anxiety and pain
    B. Hypovolemia

C. Reaction to the drugs used for conscious sedation
D. Vagal stimulation

235. Which of these medications would not be appropriate for pain of acute pancreatitis?
    A. Meperidine (Demerol)
    B. Morphine
    C. Ketorolac (Toradol)
    D. Acetaminophen (Tylenol)

236. Which of the following agents are useful when managing esophageal varices?
    A. Pitressin (Vasopressin)
    B. Sublingual nitroglycerin
    C. Somatostatin
    D. All of the above

237. A 26-year-old man with a history of factor VIII deficiency reports to the ED after dental surgery. He reports that he has experienced persistent bleeding for 2 days. The specific therapy that the EN should anticipate for his condition is administration of:
    A. Packed RBCs
    B. Salt-poor albumin
    C. Cryoprecipitate
    D. None of the above

238. DIC is treated with:
    A. Packed RBCs, whole blood, cryoprecipitate, or selected clotting factors
    B. Heparin
    C. Both A and B
    D. None of the above

239. Nursing diagnoses pertinent to hemoglobinopathies include:
    A. Altered perfusion of vital organs related to microcirculation obstruction
    B. Acute pain related to sickling and oxygen deprivation to tissues
    C. High risk for infection related to compromised tissues
    D. All of the above

240. All of these nursing interventions are appropriate for the patient in sickle cell crisis except:
    A. Oxygen therapy
    B. Fluid restriction

C. Analgesic administration

D. Transfusion of packed RBCs

241. The EN notes at the end of the shift that there are 2 U of whole blood in the major resuscitation room that remained behind when the patient was transferred to surgery. The appropriate action of the EN is to:

A. Call the blood bank and ask for guidance.

B. Send a technician to the operating room (OR) with the blood.

C. Put the blood into the medication refrigerator.

D. Discard the blood in the hazardous-waste container.

242. Any extravasation of blood within the pelvic floor will not be evident externally, owing to the barrier effect of:

A. The visualization technique employed

B. The loss of hemodynamic stability after trauma.

C. The GU (or urogenital) membrane

D. Bladder neck constriction due to irritation caused by free blood in the bladder

243. Pain and the inability to void, or a stuttering stream, following trauma to the male genital area would be an indication of:

A. Periurethral abscess

B. Pyelonephritis

C. Straddle injury

D. Torsion of the spermatic cord

244. Insertion of a Foley catheter is indicated in all severe multisystem injuries except:

A. Straddle injury

B. When blood is evident at the urethral meatus

C. Renal trauma

D. Both A and B

245. A cardinal rule to follow in caring for a traumatized male in whom there is blood at the urinary meatus is:

A. Call a urologist.

B. Do not insert a urinary catheter.

C. Insert a catheter only if the bladder is highly distended.

D. Both A and B

246. Torsion of the spermatic cord is surprisingly common in pubescent boys and may:

A. Present with abrupt onset of testicular pain, tenderness, and vomiting

B. Result in testicular gangrene if surgical intervention is delayed longer than 6 to 10 hours following onset

C. Subside spontaneously and is not a cause of alarm or intervention

D. Both A and B

247. When severe retroperitoneal bleeding continues and surgical intervention is being considered, visualization of *both* renal pelvises is required:

A. To verify presence of both kidneys because unilateral renal agenesis exists in 1 of every 500 people

B. To prevent litigation resulting from procedural complications

C. To meet the quality assurance (QA) standards

D. All of the above

248. Urine retention in the male patient may require decompression; cardiovascular complications can precipitate a severe hypotensive episode unless the bladder is decompressed safely as follows:

A. Remove no more than 50 mL of urine at any time.

B. Remove no more than 250 mL of urine at a time, clamp the catheter and wait 15 minutes, and remove the rest of the bladder content with slow flow.

C. Remove 200 to 300 mL of urine; clamp the catheter and wait 1 hour; repeat, removing 100 mL/h until the bladder is empty and then remove 200 mL/h as the bladder regains normal function.

D. None of the above

249. The most prevalent sexually transmitted bacterial pathogen in the United States today is:

A. Penicillinase-producing *Neisseria gonorrhoeae* (PPNG)

B. Ducrey's bacillus

C. *Chlamydia trachomatis* (chlamydia)

D. Primary syphilis

250. The group of viral diseases that are sexually transmitted includes:
    A. Hepatitis B (HBV) and *Herpesvirus hominis* (type I and II)
    B. Cytomegalovirus (CMV) and human papillomavirus (HPV), or genital warts
    C. Human immunodeficiency virus (HIV) or AIDS
    D. All of the above

251. Concerning the nursing history for patients with complaints or indications of sexually transmitted disease (STD), which of the following statements is not true?
    A. The more partners involved, the greater the risk of contracting infection.
    B. Persons participating sexually with multiple partners are most apt to have several STDs in concert.
    C. The number of partners is insignificant; one dose of cephalosporin will clear all infections.
    D. Syphilis, gonorrhea, herpes progenitalis, and chlamydia are the most commonly seen STDs in those who have had multiple partners.

252. The following statements regarding testicular torsion (a twisting of the supporting cord of the testis) are all true except:
    A. Sixty-five percent of these males are between the ages of 12 and 18 years and about half have had previous episodes.
    B. Pain, swelling, and tenderness are relieved by scrotal elevation.
    C. Testicular survival rate is approximately 47 percent, owing to misdiagnosis or delay in surgical repair; this is a surgical emergency.
    D. There may be scrotal edema, fever, and abdominal pain.

253. The following statements regarding epididymitis are all true except:
    A. It is the most frequently seen scrotal pathology in the ED.
    B. It is an infection that is almost always secondary to prostatitis and is common in men over the age of 20 years.

C. Treatment is exercise and cold packs to reduce the inflammation and congestion.
    D. Relief of pain when the scrotum is elevated by a supporting "bridge" is known as Prehn sign.

254. Toxic shock syndrome (TSS) is characterized by:
    A. Myalgias, fever, and hypotension
    B. Vomiting and diarrhea
    C. Pharyngitis
    D. All of the above

255. Which information should be elicited by the triage nurse when a 26-year-old woman presents with headache, vomiting, and high fever?
    A. Potential for pregnancy
    B. Method of contraception used
    C. Type of protection used during menses
    D. All of the above

256. What parenteral drug is recommended for use in the ED to treat acute manifestations of gonorrhea?
    A. Procaine penicillin G
    B. Ceftriaxone (Rocephin)
    C. Doxycycline (Vibramycin)
    D. None of the above

257. All of the following statements are true regarding trichomonas except:
    A. It presents as a frothy, yellowish green discharge with vaginal itching and burning.
    B. It is confirmed by viewing the organism on a slide prepared with 10 percent potassium hydroxide (KOH).
    C. The recommended treatment is metronidazole (Flagyl).
    D. Alcoholic beverages must be avoided during the course of treatment.

258. The acute evidence of initial infection with *Treponema pallidum* is:
    A. One or more painful blebs with associated paresthesias on genital or perianal areas
    B. Papules on perianal and/or vulvar tissues

C. Painless chancre and inguinal lymphade-nopathy

D. None of the above

259. Which type of organism is likely to cause vaginitis in diabetic women or in those on a prolonged course of antibiotics?
    A. Spirochete
    B. Enterococcus
    C. *Rickettsia*
    D. *Candida*

260. The signs and symptoms seen in over 90 percent of patients with an ectopic pregnancy are:
    A. Abdominal pain and intermittent slight brownish spotting
    B. Profuse bleeding.
    C. Pain and cramping that is unilateral
    D. Both A and B

261. Upon pelvic examination, the pregnant patient experiencing a threatened abortion will show:
    A. A closed cervical os; no cervical or adnexal tenderness will be noted
    B. A dilated or effaced cervical os; possibly fetal membranes will be in evidence
    C. Minimal bleeding evident at the cervical os
    D. None of the above

262. A female with pregnancy-induced hypertension (PIH), formerly referred to as "toxemia of pregnancy," comes to the ED complaining of a severe headache. The EN should be alerted to anticipate:
    A. The possibility of seizure activity
    B. Sparse urine output
    C. The possibility of respiratory distress
    D. All of the above

263. A primagravida in the first trimester of her pregnancy has been diagnosed by her obstetrician with the HELLP syndrome (hemolysis, elevated liver enzymes, low platelets). The EN should be alerted to monitor for complications that include:
    A. Ruptured liver hematomas
    B. Renal failure

C. Abruptio placentae

D. All of the above

264. Which of the following is not an appropriate intervention for prolapsed cord as labor is progressing?
    A. Immediately place the mother on her left side with her hips elevated.
    B. Administer high-flow O_2.
    C. Apply gentle, steady traction on the cord.
    D. Gently push the cord back through the cervical os between contractions.

265. At 2 A.M. a young woman is brought to the ED by her husband; she is in labor with her first pregnancy. She states that her bag of waters has not broken, there is no bleeding (show), and her contractions are long and hard at 4- to 5-minute intervals. The EN should immediately:
    A. Set up the emergency delivery pack.
    B. Take the woman directly to the delivery suite.
    C. Arrange for transportation to the delivery suite.
    D. Send the woman home until the pains are longer, harder, and closer together.

266. If the EN is alone at night in the ED and the same young woman as in question 265 arrives with her membranes ruptured, slight bloody show, and contractions long and hard at 4- to 5- minute intervals, the best action would be to:
    A. Set up the emergency delivery pack.
    B. Take the woman by wheelchair to the delivery suite without delay.
    C. Notify the switchboard to have the night supervisor stand by in the ED while the EN takes the patient to delivery.
    D. Both B and C

267. All of the following are correct regarding the baptism of a stillborn infant or the imminent death of an infant following birth except:
    A. Baptism can be performed at the request of Christian parents or because of personal religious convictions of the nurse attending.
    B. Any words are appropriate as long as the parents have requested the baptismal rite.

C. If resuscitation procedures are in progress, these should not be stopped for baptism.

D. The EN puts a drop or two of water on the bare head of the baby while saying, "I baptize thee in the name of the Father, and the Son, and the Holy Spirit."

268. What specific test reveals amniotic fluid in the maternal circulation?
A. Kleinhauer–Betke test
B. Thayer–Martin assay
C. Amniotic photospectrometry
D. None of the above

269. Which of the following modifications in trauma resuscitation are indicated for the patient with a third-trimester pregnancy?
A. If shock is present, the patient should be positioned on her right side.
B. Eliminate x-rays, scans, contrast-dye procedures, or peritoneal lavage.
C. Neither of the above
D. Both A and B

270. The following statements about the pregnant trauma patient are true except:
A. They have a high risk of vomiting and aspiration
B. Signs and symptoms of hypovolemia are delayed because of expanded blood volume
C. Undetected retroperitoneal bleeding is among major life threats facing the mother.
D. Rectal and pelvic exams should be deferred.

271. The dominant indicator of depression is:
A. Inability to concentrate
B. Careless dress
C. Thoughts of death
D. Helpless and hopeless mood

272. Which of the following is not a red flag for risk of suicide?
A. Previous attempt
B. Depression
C. Agitation and confused thoughts
D. Alcohol/substance abuse

273. Nursing interventions with the dangerously suicidal patient include all of the following except:
A. Preventing him or her from continuing to elaborate suicidal ideations
B. One-on-one nursing presence at all times; never leave this patient alone
C. Using restraints, chemical or physical, as indicated for patient safety
D. Providing a protective environment

274. Red flags for a manic episode include all of the following except:
A. Grandiose flights of ideas
B. Involvement in high-risk activities (e.g., expensive purchases, wild business ventures)
C. Rare irritability; too filled with good feelings toward life
D. Functioning without sleep

275. In managing a potentially dangerous patient, pursue all of the following guidelines except:
A. Leave the door open and let the patient sit where he or she chooses.
B. Maintain eye-level communication and reassure the patient by your close presence and touch.
C. Minimize external stimuli (e.g., paging systems, radios).
D. Realize the potential need for—and prepare for—ample assistance.

276. When application of physical restraints becomes the last resort with a violent or self-destructive patient, the following points of information must be documented:
A. Time applied, type and number of restraints
B. Storage bin from which they were obtained
C. Patient's condition at time of and clinical rationale for application
D. Both A and C

277. The two classes of drugs most commonly used to calm and provide what is alluded to as chemical restraint are:
A. Analgesics and benzodiazepines
B. Butyrophenones and benzodiazepines

C. Chlorpromazines and benzodiazepines
D. Sedatives and opiates

278. During primary assessment, a good way to identify a truly depressed patient is to remember that:
    A. Depressed patients have low energy levels and an inability to concentrate.
    B. A truly depressed person will make *you* feel depressed.
    C. Physical complaints may be vague and difficult to substantiate.
    D. All of the above

279. Statistics from the Centers for Disease Control and Prevention (CDC) reflect that in terms of years of potential life lost, suicide is:
    A. Fourth of all causes in the United States
    B. The ninth cause of death overall in the United States
    C. Responsible for approximately 30,000 deaths a year
    D. All of the above

280. Typical manifestations of an acute anxiety attack, or panic attack, include:
    A. Hyperventilation, trembling, and sweating
    B. Chest pain, palpitations, dyspnea, choking, syncope, and faintness
    C. High levels of euphoria and disorientation
    D. Both A and B

281. Full-blown schizophrenic psychosis usually is accompanied by auditory hallucinations; the EN should ascertain and document whether:
    A. The voices are male or female
    B. The voices whisper, scream, defame, or command
    C. The voices are recognizable
    D. Both A and B

282. When managing a truly schizophrenic or paranoid patient, which of the following is not an appropriate nursing approach?
    A. Explain that the patient is now in a safe and secure place.

B. Treat simply but gently with simple, straight communication.
C. Encourage the patient to ventilate feelings and enter into his or her delusions.
D. Quietly administer the mental status examination.

283. The goals of management for the victim of rape who is brought to the ED are:
    A. To provide privacy, notify authorities, and administer antibiotics
    B. To provide privacy, notify family, and call authorities
    C. To provide privacy, assist with collection of evidence, and refer to community agency for follow-up care
    D. To provide privacy and return control to the victim as you conduct the medical and chain-of-evidence (COE) examinations.

284. Emergency personnel must remember that application of physical restraints should be a last resort in managing the violent patient because unnecessary restraint of patients against their will carries the potential for legal suit on all but one of the following grounds:
    A. Assault (threatening to do bodily harm)
    B. Battery (committing bodily harm)
    C. Physical damage
    D. Libel (defamation of character)

285. Examples of Schedule II, or C-II, drugs controlled by the federal Controlled Substances Act (CSA) are:
    A. Heroin, methaqualone, marijuana, and hashish
    B. Opium, morphine, codeine, and amphetamines
    C. Benzodiazepines, chloral hydrate, some tranquilizers, and some stimulants
    D. None of the above

286. A patient brought by ambulance to the ED demonstrates the classic triad of narcotic overdose with:
    A. Severe respiratory depression, depressed LOC, and pinpoint pupils

B. Gasping respirations, obtunded consciousness, and dilated pupils
C. Severe respiratory depression, depressed LOC, and dilated pupils
D. Any of the above

287. With narcotic use/abuse, there may or may not be:
A. Pinpoint pupils
B. Respiratory distress
C. Needle tracks in the arms
D. All of the above

288. Naloxone (Narcan) is the drug of choice for immediate intervention with an opiate overdose because it will:
A. Reverse the opiate effects and all degrees of opiate-induced respiratory depression
B. Reverse narcotic-like effects of other antagonists
C. Provide diagnostic clues if significant reversal of overdose does not occur
D. All of the above

289. The difficulty of overdose management in the ED is compounded because of:
A. The practice of polypharmacy that occurs on the streets
B. The impurities and variables of available drugs of abuse
C. The harmful diluents that are added to street drugs for marketing
D. All of the above

290. Methaqualone (Quaalude), an illegal sedative-hypnotic drug that is now supplied from Mexico as Mandrax, has actions that are:
A. Equal to or greater than those of heroin
B. Short-acting and of no serious consequence
C. Effectively reversed by naloxone
D. Both A and C

291. The risk of sudden death for those who practice polypharmacy in their substance abuse is potentiated:
A. 21.5 times when cocaine and alcohol are combined
B. 10 times when cocaine and barbiturates are combined

C. Insignificantly when alcohol is the primary substance of abuse
D. None of the above

292. The primary nursing assessment of an unresponsive patient brought to the ED should begin with:
A. Status of the airway
B. Respiratory pattern
C. Size of pupils
D. Both A and B

293. A man with a history of long-term alcohol use is brought by ambulance to the ED disoriented and delusional and with increasing agitation after he has attempted to stop drinking. Immediate interventions include:
A. Giving him 30 mL of paraldehyde to drink
B. Administering 50 percent glucose IV and thiamine 100 mg IV in D_5W/NSS
C. Administering high-flow oxygen
D. Both B and C

294. Once an alcoholic crisis is under control in the ED, an essential point of management is follow-through with:
A. Continued clear nonalcoholic liquids to prevent dehydration
B. Confirmed referral to the nearest community resource for alcohol treatment
C. Constructive criticism of the demonstrated drinking habits
D. All of the above

295. A well-dressed woman walks unsteadily and with great difficulty to the triage desk; with slurred speech, she asks to see a doctor. The triage nurse notes the woman's rapid lateral eye movements and is immediately alerted to the possibility of:
A. Alcohol intoxication
B. Valium overdose
C. Barbiturate intoxication
D. Both A and B

296. A young woman brought in by ambulance is unresponsive but mumbling unintelligibly; the emergency medical technicians (EMTs) hand you an empty bottle labeled as Elavil.

After ensuring patency of her airway, the specific treatment for this overdose would be:

A. Naloxone (Narcan), 0.4 mg, IV push
B. Diphenhydramine (Benadryl), 50 mg, IV push
C. Nalorphan (Nalline), 100 mg, IV push
D. Physostigmine (Antilirium) 1 to 3 mg, slow IV push

297. Because phencyclidine (PCP) abuse manifestations are known to be dose-related, the high-dose PCP user would be expected to present with:

A. Communication difficulty, blank stare, and highly aggressive behavior
B. Stuporous condition with eyes open, response only to deep pain, and period amnesia
C. Coma, response only to noxious stimuli, and waking illusion alternating with hallucinations and amnesia
D. None of the above; PCP effects are not dose-related

298. Identify the true statement in the following list:

A. On the average in urban situations, three drugs are involved in every two nonfatal emergencies
B. On the average in urban situations, five drugs are found in every two overdose deaths.
C. Polypharmacy is the rule in most city settings of substance abuse.
D. All of the above

299. Ingestion of methanol, or wood alcohol, causes a profound:

A. Metabolic acidosis, intoxication, and blindness
B. Metabolic alkalosis, hyperirritability, and horizontal nystagmus
C. Respiratory acidosis, intoxication, and severe ataxia
D. Metabolic acidosis, delusions of grandeur, and paranoia

300. Appropriate nursing diagnoses for marijuana intoxication would not include which of the following?

A. Visual and kinesthetic alteration in sensory perception
B. Modified sensory perception
C. Knowledge deficit regarding long-term harmful effects on the lungs
D. Both A and C

301. Alcohol, widely distributed in the body, appears everywhere because it follows:

A. Blood and can be measured in all the organs
B. Lymph and can be measured in lymphatic exudate and saliva
C. Water and can be measured in blood and urine
D. Water and can be measured in blood, urine, saliva, and sweat

302. When gastric lavage is carried out, the stomach is lavaged with NSS until the return is clear; the formula for each tidal volume (VT) for adults and children, respectively, is:

A. 300 mL per tidal wash; 10 mL/kg body weight
B. 300 mL per tidal wash; 20 mL/kg body weight
C. 500 mL per tidal wash; 20 mL/kg body weight
D. Any of the above; the stomach tolerates distension well

303. The bottom line in effective general management of all overdoses and toxicities is:

A. Keep it cost effective
B. Treat the family, not the patient
C. Treat the poison, not the patient
D. Treat the patient, not the poison

304. When attempting to get rid of ingested toxic substances, no emesis should be stimulated if:

A. The patient is comatose, convulsive, or without the gag reflex.
B. The patient has ingested strong base or acid or petroleum distillate.
C. Both A and B
D. The family is present.

305. The life-threatening condition of heat stroke results from:
    A. Hypothalamus failure
    B. High ambient temperature
    C. Dehydration
    D. Tissue enzyme dysfunction

306. In the therapeutic plan for heat stroke, all of the following are recommended except:
    A. Cimetidine (Tagamet) for gastric hyperacidity
    B. Mannitol and furosemide to enhance renal flow
    C. Antipyretics to reduce the core body temperature
    D. Benzodiazines and barbiturates for seizures

307. If frostbite of the feet or hands occurs in an isolated environment, the individual should:
    A. Heat a bucket of water for rewarming the part.
    B. Resist the temptation to rub or massage the part.
    C. Place soft padding between fingers and toes after thawing.
    D. All of the above

308. Aggressive and poorly controlled oxygen administration to hypothermia patients can result in:
    A. Precipitant fall in the $PaCO_2$
    B. Hyperventilation
    C. Ventricular fibrillation
    D. All of the above

309. Why is core rewarming preferred over external rewarming for patients with severe hypothermia?
    A. External rewarming drains oxygen from the vital organs.
    B. During external rewarming, the cold heart will be unable to supply oxygenated blood to the vasodilated periphery.
    C. Core rewarming minimizes myocardial hypoxia and acidosis and enhances efficiency of redistributing blood supply.
    D. All of the above

310. Medications recommended during rewarming include:
    A. Steroids
    B. Vasopressor agents
    C. Antibiotics
    D. None of the above

311. The treatment for most nitrogen narcosis incidents is:
    A. Descent to deeper water
    B. Ascent to shallow water
    C. Hyperbaric therapy
    D. Decompression in a special chamber operated by the U.S. Navy

312. All of the following are useful in treating high-altitude pulmonary edema (HAPE) except:
    A. Oxygen
    B. Morphine
    C. Bed rest
    D. Descent

313. The life-threatening results from lightning injuries are:
    A. Ventricular fibrillation
    B. Myoglobinuria
    C. Sepsis
    D. All except C

314. Stage II Lyme disease may include manifestations of:
    A. Erythema chronicum migrans (ECM)
    B. Ophthalmologic problems, (e.g., keratitis, retinal detachment)
    C. Cardiac abnormalities, (e.g., myopericarditis, palpitation, AV block)
    D. Both B and C

315. Before the administration of antivenin, the EN should:
    A. Draw blood for complete blood cell (CBC) count, platelets, blood urea nitrogen (BUN), CK, coagulation screen, and type and cross-match and obtain a urine specimen.
    B. Place the patient on a cardiac monitor.
    C. Insert a nasogastric (NG) tube and Foley catheter.
    D. All of the above

316. Which is (are) not recommended for treating a snakebite?
    A. Venous tourniquet
    B. Ice
    C. Antibiotics
    D. Both A and B

317. What statements are true regarding administration of antivenin?
    A. It is diluted with NSS prior to administration.
    B. A portion of the calculated dose should be injected at the wound edges.
    C. Antihistamines should be available for immediate use during therapy.
    D. Both A and C

318. Which of the following is not required for an institution to be in compliance with the Joint Commission on Accreditation of Healthcare Organizations (JCAHO) standards for hospital disaster planning?
    A. The hospital must participate in an annual communitywide mass casualty exercise.
    B. The hospital plan must address the handling of victims from hazardous materials exposures.
    C. Provisions must be in place for failures of critical equipment and hospital utilities.
    D. Performance standards must exist to measure effective performance of the hospital disaster plan.

319. Which of these is not within the designated roles of the Federal Emergency Management Agency (FEMA)?
    A. Providing support to local and state disaster planning agencies
    B. Administering food, medical supplies, and support equipment to victims of a disaster
    C. Providing education and training of disaster-response personnel
    D. Managing an information database on chemical and biologic threats to the U.S. population

320. Which federal agency would be tasked with sending a medical team to care for the sick and wounded in a locale where a hurricane has destroyed the hospital?
    A. FEMA
    B. National Disaster Medical System (NDMS)
    C. American National Red Cross
    D. U.S. Department of Defense (DOD)

321. Select the true statement about chemical protective clothing (CPC):
    A. CPC is not worn within the hospital ED.
    B. The highest level of protection is used for unknown chemicals.
    C. Level D protection is used when rescue personnel report multiple deaths at the scene.
    D. None of the above

322. When assisting with decontamination, requirements are:
    A. Essential CPC for ED personnel
    B. A designated space within the ED to carry out the task
    C. A receptacle to collect water used in the decontamination processes
    D. Both A and C

323. What is the first item of CPC to be removed after chemical decontamination procedures are completed?
    A. Mask
    B. Coverall
    C. Outer gloves
    D. Shoe covers

324. Which of the following statements is true regarding decontamination procedures and associated wound care?
    A. Vigorous scrubbing with a brush is required to effectively remove wound contaminants.
    B. Hot water should be used for intact skin cleansing.
    C. When possible, the body should be showered or spray-washed.
    D. Considerable friction with a sponge or cloth should be used to remove contaminants.

325. Which of the following is not one of the four basic areas of negligence that must *all* be alleged and proved in a successful legal action?
    A. Duty
    B. Comparative negligence
    C. Proximate causation
    D. Damages/injury

326. An EN who gives an intravenous medication during a code procedure after receiving a shouted verbal order and who finds out later that the wrong drug was given the patient—who subsequently expired—could conceivably be named in a malpractice suit and charged with professional negligence for:
    A. Omission of an act that should have been performed
    B. Commission of an act that should have been performed
    C. Commission of an act that should not have been performed
    D. None of the above

327. In the emergency setting, when treatment is given because it was required to save the patient's life, consent becomes:
    A. Essential
    B. Reassuring
    C. Mandatory
    D. Implied

328. In the case of Jehovah's Witnesses, when blood transfusions (even autotransfusions) are required for life support but are refused, a court order can be obtained to:
    A. Give blood to both children and adults
    B. Give blood to adults but not to children
    C. Give blood to children but not to adults
    D. Give whatever is necessary to sustain life in a child or an adult

329. ENs are able to be of great value in assisting the medical examiner's office with death investigations and collection of evidence if they:
    A. Obtain autopsy permission before the family leaves the ED
    B. Develop and employ forensic kits for collection and preservation of evidence
    C. Identify invasive treatment sites (e.g., cutdowns, chest tube insertions)
    D. Both B and C

330. Potential organ donors, frequently identified in the ED, must meet certain criteria, including:
    A. Normally functioning organs with no preexisting hypertension
    B. Freedom from any infectious disease processes such as sepsis, retroviruses, or malignancies other than brain tumor
    C. A lifetime history of no tobacco or alcohol use
    D. Both A and B

331. When a situation arises in the ED that presents special problems in the decision-making process, one of the best resources for the EN is:
    A. A colleague
    B. The administrator's office
    C. The physician on duty
    D. The department policy manual

332. One of the truly important assets to maintaining effective patient flow and optimal use of personnel and equipment in the ED is:
    A. Maintaining a reserve of holding beds
    B. Diverting old repeat customers
    C. Using the triage nurse concept
    D. All of the above

333. A major function of the ED policies and procedures manual is to:
    A. Answer issues of management approach and reduce errors in judgment calls
    B. Define authorized and unauthorized procedures for the ED
    C. Contribute to consistency of performance and continuing quality improvement (CQI) in the department
    D. All of the above

334. Normal responses to loss of loved one(s) frequently encountered in the ED include:
    A. Disbelief, numbing, and inability to comprehend what has happened
    B. Outbursts of anger and blame directed toward EMTs and emergency staff

C. Outbursts of violence and assault with weapons

D. Both A and B

335. Of the numerous stress-management skills available to emergency personnel, one that has a maximum payoff for the time and energy invested is:
A. Goal setting
B. Deep relaxation exercises
C. Learning to say no and expressing your own preferences
D. Taking 1 week off each month

336. An effective strategy to help ensure a safe, well-staffed, and well-run ED would be to:
A. Tailor staffing patterns to patient load demands.
B. Schedule appropriate shift overlaps for the busiest hours.
C. Formulate an efficient and effective triage system to meet department needs and use personnel and space in the most productive fashion.
D. All of the above

337. You are tasked with assisting and loading a patient for air transportation; which of the following statements describes the recommended way to approach a rotor aircraft?
A. Crouch down and approach from the tail of the craft.
B. Approach from a 45-degree angle from the front of the craft.
C. After the blades have come to a complete stop, maintain a low silhouette and approach from the left side.
D. Approach from the right side of the aircraft, staying in view of the pilot at all times.

338. The discomfort associated with barotitis media that occurs on descent of aircraft is due to:
A. A discrepancy between air pressures in the external ear canal and the ambient air
B. A clogged eustachian tube or sinus congestion
C. A vacuum in the middle ear that places tension on the tympanic membrane
D. Air expansion within the middle ear

339. Which of the following trauma patients should not ordinarily be considered for a fixed-wing air transport at altitudes exceeding 18,000 ft?
A. A child with 45 percent BSA burns that include the face and head
B. A 14-year-old with an open head injury
C. A 65-year-old stroke patient with status epilepticus
D. A 34-year-old who is 8 months pregnant and bleeding

340. In order to be in compliance with the Consolidated Omnibus Budget Reconciliation Act (COBRA) when transferring a seriously injured trauma patient to a level 1 facility, the following statements are true except:
A. Appropriate equipment and personnel for transfer must be available.
B. Medical benefits outweigh the risk of transfer.
C. Family members cannot decline recommended transfer procedures.
D. Patients cannot be arbitrarily transferred to other facilities.

■ ANSWER KEY

1. D	48. A	95. C	142. B	189. A	236. D
2. A	49. B	96. A	143. D	190. D	237. C
3. B	50. C	97. C	144. D	191. D	238. C
4. C	51. D	98. B	145. A	192. A	239. D
5. D	52. A	99. A	146. D	193. B	240. B
6. D	53. C	100. C	147. C	194. D	241. A
7. D	54. C	101. B	148. C	195. D	242. C
8. B	55. A	102. D	149. B	196. D	243. C
9. A	56. A	103. B	150. D	197. A	244. D
10. D	57. D	104. C	151. C	198. D	245. D
11. B	58. B	105. B	152. B	199. C	246. D
12. D	59. B	106. D	153. A	200. B	247. D
13. C	60. C	107. C	154. C	201. D	248. D
14. B	61. D	108. B	155. C	202. D	249. C
15. C	62. A	109. C	156. B	203. C	250. D
16. B	63. A	110. D	157. D	204. D	251. C
17. A	64. A	111. D	158. A	205. B	252. B
18. D	65. B	112. D	159. B	206. A	253. C
19. C	66. C	113. A	160. D	207. A	254. D
20. D	67. B	114. A	161. B	208. B	255. D
21. B	68. C	115. C	162. D	209. A	256. B
22. A	69. B	116. C	163. C	210. D	257. B
23. D	70. D	117. C	164. A	211. C	258. C
24. C	71. B	118. B	165. B	212. C	259. D
25. B	72. D	119. C	166. D	213. A	260. C
26. D	73. B	120. B	167. D	214. D	261. A
27. C	74. B	121. C	168. B	215. C	262. A
28. A	75. A	122. D	169. A	216. D	263. D
29. D	76. B	123. D	170. B	217. A	264. C
30. D	77. B	124. C	171. D	218. D	265. C
31. D	78. B	125. D	172. B	219. D	266. D
32. D	79. A	126. B	173. B	220. B	267. B
33. D	80. D	127. D	174. A	221. D	268. A
34. D	81. A	128. A	175. B	222. D	269. C
35. B	82. A	129. D	176. D	223. D	270. D
36. D	83. D	130. D	177. D	224. B	271. D
37. C	84. C	131. B	178. D	225. C	272. C
38. D	85. D	132. A	179. D	226. D	273. A
39. D	86. D	133. A	180. D	227. B	274. C
40. B	87. A	134. C	181. C	228. B	275. B
41. C	88. B	135. A	182. D	229. A	276. D
42. D	89. D	136. D	183. A	230. D	277. B
43. B	90. D	137. D	184. C	231. A	278. D
44. C	91. D	138. A	185. D	232. D	279. D
45. B	92. B	139. D	186. C	233. D	280. C
46. A	93. A	140. D	187. D	234. D	281. D
47. C	94. A	141. D	188. C	235. B	282. C

283. D	293. D	303. D	313. D	323. C	333. D
284. D	294. B	304. C	314. D	324. C	334. D
285. B	295. C	305. D	315. D	325. B	335. B
286. A	296. D	306. C	316. D	326. C	336. D
287. C	297. C	307. D	317. D	327. D	337. B
288. D	298. D	308. D	318. A	328. C	338. C
289. D	299. A	309. D	319. B	329. D	339. B
290. D	300. B	310. D	320. B	330. D	340. C
291. A	301. D	311. B	321. B	331. D	
292. D	302. A	312. B	322. D	332. C	

Index

O

Other Related Nursing Titles
Published by Appleton & Lange